- *Leonard Herman has done it again. If you really want to be able to have access to a videogame history that is thoroughly researched, then his new book covering the vast videogame history scene is for you.*
  Ralph Baer – Inventor of the home videogame console

- Phoenix *is a must-read, must-study, must-own for anyone proclaiming a love for the gaming industry. Now that it's on its fourth edition, I can all but promise you it's 5,000 times more accurate than* Wikipedia.
  Dan "Shoe" Hsu, former editor-in-chief, *Gamesbeat* and *EGM*

- Phoenix *is one of the most impressive and comprehensive accounts of the history of video games. I refer to it often and I'm continually surprised by the sheer magnitude of content in each revision.*
  Mike Mika, Game Developer and Game Historian

- *Clearly written and thoroughly researched,* Phoenix *is the cornerstone upon which every serious videogame enthusiast should start building their own library.*
  Dr. Roberto Dillon, author of *The Golden Age of Video Games*

- *The video game industry has a true historian. His name is Leonard Herman. The video game industry has a history of record. Its title is* Phoenix.
  Steven Kent, author of *The Ultimate History of Video Games*

- *Anyone who loves video games and wants a fact-filled deep dive into its origins, evolution, and key players – as well as ancillary technologies like home computers and the Internet – should look no further than Leonard Herman's fourth edition of* Phoenix. *Easy to pick up but hard to put down, Herman's 800+-page tome is a fun and insightful read that chronologically covers the video game personalities, iconic games, platforms, and publications – from Atari to Zelda. While the previous third edition was ideal for retro gamers with nostalgic leaning towards the '70s, '80s and '90s, this ambitious new fourth edition version also covers current consoles, platforms, and services, up until 2015. Young or old, gamers will no doubt appreciate the effort poured into this massive book.*
  Marc Saltzman, syndicated columnist, author, speaker and TV/radio personality

- *An incredible treasure trove of information. Perfect for gamers, collectors or anyone looking to take a fascinating stroll down memory lane.*
  Blake J. Harris, author of *Console Wars: Sega, Nintendo, and the Battle that Defined a Generation*

- *People calling themselves 'game historians' today should be using* Phoenix *as their backup for fact-checking. Len isn't just this industry's first historian, he lived through and clearly enjoyed the history as it was being made.*
  Joe Santulli, Curator, National Videogame Museum

- *Leonard Herman is the original videogame historian, and* Phoenix *is where the serious study of the game industry began. I'm super excited to see the updates in the latest edition.*
  Chris Charla, Director, ID@Xbox at Microsoft

- *For the past decade, I have exclusively used* Phoenix *in my college classrooms. No other publication is as accurate, complete, wide-ranging, comprehensive, all-embracing, thorough and extensive as Leonard Herman's weighty tome. This is the book that experts, such as myself, respect and use as a resource.*
  Professor Michael Thomasson, Canisius College

- *Filled with incredible detail and eyewitness accounts of the industry from its roots in the late '60s to the boom of the 1990s,* Phoenix *(in any of its editions) is still the first place to start any study of gaming history.*
  ***Game Informer* magazine**

- Phoenix *is the most fascinating book to ever tackle the subject. The exceptional level of detail is rivaled only by Herman's obvious love and respect for the subject matter. An absolute must-read.*
  Kris Randazzo, Editor-in-Chief, *Geekade.com*, former writer, *examiner.com*

- Phoenix 4 *is an important book and no one is better suited to get the story right than Leonard Herman.* Phoenix 4 *(and all future updated editions) will remain the definitive text on this part of video game history.*
  Walter Day, Founder of Twin Galaxies

PHOENIX IV

The History of the Videogame Industry

LEONARD HERMAN

ROLENTA PRESS
SPRINGFIELD, NJ

PHOENIX IV: THE HISTORY OF THE VIDEOGAME INDUSTRY

This book was originally published under the titles:
Phoenix: The Fall & Rise of Home Videogames
&
Phoenix: The Fall & Rise of Videogames

Published by Rolenta Press
Springfield, NJ 07081

www.rolentapress.com

Fourth Edition Color • August 2017

Hardback Edition
ISBN-13: 978-0-964384-80-4

Cover Designed By
Michael Thomasson & Cory Golabek

This book is dedicated to my friend & mentor
Ralph H. Baer

CONTENTS

FOREWORD 1
By TED DABNEY

Phoenix, The Fall & Rise of Videogames documents the history of the Video Game Industry. This is a difficult task because it goes back a long way and involves so many concepts and personalities. The task becomes even harder when there is so much misinformation floating around. A book on history can be pretty dry reading but Mr. Herman's book will guide you through the maze and give you a sense of participation in the process.

For those of you that don't know the story, around the early part of 1970, Nolan Bushnell and I formed a partnership called "Syzygy Engineering". Our original plan was to use a computer to control the movement of objects on a TV screen and then time-share a game between several play stations. Once we got started, we realized that this approach would not, and could not be cost-effective. I designed a digital motion circuit that replaced the computer and we used it to create a video game named *Computer Space* for Nutting Associates.

We became Atari only because we couldn't incorporate using the name Syzygy. We subsequently landed a contract from Bally for a pinball machine and a video game. The video game became *Pong*.

Although there were several video games before Syzygy/Atari came along, none of them had real commercial value. The Video Game Industry was actually created by us when Bally rejected our Pong game. Bally was certainly in a prime spot to get all the credit for creating this industry. It could even have begun with Nutting if *Computer Space* hadn't been so complicated or if they had been willing to follow up by keeping Nolan and me on as participants.

It should be noted that, although *Computer Space* is over 40 years old and uses no modern electronics, it has become a "must-have" for many video game collectors. I have had the privilege of autographing some of these collected items.

The Video Game Industry has been evolving at a very rapid rate. Many video game enthusiasts would like to know just how all this stuff came together and what the current trends are. This edition of *Phoenix* will bring you up to date and dispel many of the distortions that have occurred over the years. It represents many years of dedicated research into every aspect of the development of video games over these many decades.

Ted Dabney is the co-founder of Atari Corporation. In 1971 he co-developed Spacewar, *the first commercially released arcade videogame.*

FOREWORD 1

FOREWORD 2
By CHRIS KOHLER

"Was there really a video game crash in 1983 for North America?"
-- Title of a post on the NeoGAF forums, December 31, 2011

Yes, you poor misguided child, there was. Just because the $20 billion U.S. videogame industry is much larger and healthier now, and just because you weren't around to see it, doesn't mean that the big crash of 1983 didn't happen. It doesn't mean people didn't lose their jobs, it doesn't mean that many game publishers didn't close their doors and it doesn't mean that there was not a feeling that home videogaming was a fad that had run its course.

On the publication of the first edition of *Phoenix* in 1994, gamers and the game industry were not that far removed from the big crash. In fact, if you were marking the beginning of the home game business as the release of the original Odyssey, more time had elapsed before the crash than after it. So the crash was at that point the singular, pivotal, central event in the history of electronic games. The most fascinating thing about the game industry was its phoenix-like rise from the ashes, hence the title of Leonard Herman's early attempt to document its history.

But much more time has passed now, on the occasion of the fourth edition of *Phoenix*. And if certain members of the younger generation are questioning whether or not the crash actually happened, it raises the question: Is the crash from which this book's title springs still relevant today? Or is it merely a historical footnote, something that happened long ago but has little to teach us about today's industry?

In Japan, there was no crash. This is in large part because there was no airplane to speak of. In this edition of *Phoenix*, Len has greatly expanded his coverage of early Japanese game machines. As you read these revised sections, you will quickly get a sense of just how confused the Japanese market was in those early days, how full of competing pieces of hardware.

And it was a small, expensive market that didn't reach an especially wide audience. When I moved to the city of Kanazawa in 2000, I spent the better part of a year scouring every store in the area for old videogames. I am not exaggerating in the slightest when I say that I did not find one single piece of evidence that the Atari 2800, Bandai Intellivision, et cetera ever actually existed. It was only on a trip to Tokyo later in the year that I saw a small handful of those early machines in specialty stores, selling for exorbitant prices. I once found a Japanese copy of *E.T. The Extra-Terrestrial* for the Atari 2800 for $200. Suffice it to say there was no landfill in Japan in which piles of them were buried.

In other words, there was a great big void begging to be filled with a low-cost consumer game machine that featured quality software, which Nintendo's Famicom certainly was. It was to Nintendo's great fortune that a similar void had opened up in the U.S. after the decline and fall of Atari. But whereas Japanese consumers had not yet fallen in love with a particular home gaming machine and were thus ready to embrace a product like Famicom with open arms, the American market was wary. They'd been burned by videogames before, and it was Nintendo's job not simply to introduce a solid new product but also to assuage their fears.

In taking steps to fix the broken American game biz, Nintendo laid down the foundations of the industry as they exist today. The major hardware makers still use the system of third-party licensing that Nintendo pioneered in response to the glut of unauthorized games on Atari platforms. It is still, for all intents and purposes, impossible to make a videogame that runs on the Xbox One or PlayStation 4 without Microsoft's or Sony's explicit approval.

That paradigm is only just now being challenged by companies like Google and Apple, whose game marketplaces welcome any and all game developers with arms wide open.

So yes, that crash of 1983 does still matter today, because what happened in its wake affects how games are made. And because it could happen again. Then and now, the only constant in the videogame industry has been catastrophic change.

San Francisco, California
October 20, 2014

Chris Kohler is a writer and editor who has covered gaming for over 20 years. He is the author of several books including Power-Up: How Japanese Video Games Gave the World an Extra Life. *He is currently Features Editor at* Kotaku.

INTRODUCTION
By LEONARD HERMAN

Welcome to the fourth edition of *Phoenix: The Fall & Rise of Videogames*... No, that's not correct.

Welcome to *Phoenix IV: The History of the Videogame Industry*.

Why the change?

When the first edition of this book, the first-ever comprehensive book on videogame history, was published in 1994, a mere 11 years had passed since the infamous American videogame industry crash of 1983, which was still very fresh in the minds of many gamers. The mythical Phoenix bird had died in a pile of ashes, and then was reborn even more powerful than the one before it. By 1984, the American videogame industry was practically dead, only to be revived a year later. By 1994, when the first edition of *Phoenix* was published, the videogame industry was bigger and more powerful than it had ever been, just like the Phoenix. And considering that the industry was 22 years old at the time of that book's publication,[1] half of the industry's history took place before the crash and the other half took place afterwards.

In 2016, when this fourth edition was published, 33 years had passed since the crash. Most of the industry's history, 73%, occurred post crash. The "fall & rise" is no longer the central core of the industry and therefore there is no reason for it to be included in the book's subtitle.

But by using that logic, even the word *Phoenix* in the title is no longer relevant either, since the subtitle merely emphasized the title. However, I had a hard time changing that since it is a well-known title. Changing it would have made this a completely new book altogether. So *Phoenix* stayed in the title followed by the Roman numeral IV to indicate that this is the fourth book in the series.

The new subtitle was a little more difficult to come up with. I needed something that conveyed what the book was about, since *Phoenix* by itself didn't give new readers any idea. I liked the "The Chronology of Videogames" but my advisors said that a chronology didn't necessary mean a history, which is primarily what the book is. So I ran a contest to see who could come up with the best subtitle. Some titles had to be tossed out right away. Anything that said 'definitive' or 'complete' couldn't be used because there will always be someone out there who will find something not mentioned in the text, which would therefore render it as incomplete. So we went with something simple: "The History of the Videogame Industry", which had been submitted by Chris Buckmister.

Other Changes

But as the section heading that precedes this paragraph implies, there are other changes to this edition besides the title. For one, the chapters are now

[1] It is generally agreed that the videogame industry began in 1972. However, there were videogames before that year.

broken into titled sub-sections. However, don't be fooled by these titles. In many cases a section may contain more topics than what is called out in the title.

When I originally began working on this fourth edition, my goal was to bring the book to the present by adding all of the years that had come and gone since the publication of the third edition in 2001. But I simply didn't want to just add all of the new years beginning with 2001. I also wanted to expand on the Japanese gaming scene from the little that had been included in *Phoenix 3*. So that brought me back to the beginning of the book from which point I basically rewrote most it. And instead of adding just the Japanese consoles, I also added a few that were from Europe.[2]

The footnote that appears at the end of preceding paragraph was used to highlight another new feature in this edition. I have added hundreds of footnotes throughout the text to expand upon the subject. The book was designed to be read from cover to cover, and since I'm a big fan of mystery novels, I didn't want to "give away" anything that would take place in later chapters. So whenever I wanted to reference something "from the future", I mentioned it in a footnote. I also used footnotes to expand upon some of the text or to include some statistics.[3]

Videogames VS Computer Games

While this book is indeed a history of the videogame industry, I need to point out that it does not include *computer* games, i.e. game software that gets loaded into computers. While many may not distinguish a difference between the two, I will simply state that in my mind, the computer doesn't care if it is game software or business software that is loaded into it. And, a PC game may not even play on all PCs depending upon different configurations including memory and sound and video cards. But all PS4 software will always play on all PS4 hardware.[4] My friend Patrick Wong best defined what is covered in this book: "It all comes down to the primary purpose a system is made for and a console or handheld's primary function is to play games. While a computer's primary function is not playing games." That definition also covers arcade games which are also mentioned in this book. On the other hand, smart phones are not covered either although Android-based videogame consoles are.

The Cover

I'm sure that the cover that graces this volume may seem familiar to some readers. It had also been used for the later printings of the third edition. I had designed the covers for the first three editions of *Phoenix*, and as anyone who saw these covers can attest, I am artistically challenged. Fortunately, my friend Michael Thomasson, a talented graphic designer, had come to my rescue by creating covers for other books I published, notably Ralph Baer's *Videogames:*

[2] And a few South Korean systems are mentioned as well.

[3] Actually these appear as endnotes, not footnotes. All of the endnotes can be found at the end of the book in a section called *Endnotes*.

[4] Some Nintendo 3DS software can only be played on the *New* Nintendo 3DS.

In the Beginning and Bill Kunkel's *Confession of the Game Doctor*.

As I began working on the fourth edition sometime in 2005, I got the idea of having the Phoenix bird rising from a pyre of old videogame systems. Since I wasn't capable of drawing one myself, I asked Michael if he could do such a cover, with the intention of using it for the eventual fourth edition. Michael collaborated with a colleague of his, Cory Golabek, and came up with a cover that was similar to the one on the front of this book. It showed the Phoenix rising from the pyre up towards the heavens where the Wii, PS3 and Xbox 360 awaited it. It was just the cover that I had imagined.

In 2010 I had signed a contract with a commercial publisher to print and distribute the book. Unfortunately, they were not interested in the cover that Michael and Cory had designed. When I broke the news to Michael that his cover wouldn't be used, he was disappointed and suggested that I use it the next time I reprinted the third edition. I thought that was a great idea and copies of *Phoenix 3* that were printed in late 2010 and beyond featured the new cover.

Unfortunately, the publisher and I disagreed on many issues concerning the direction of the book, and in early 2015 we mutually parted company. Although I had discussions with two other publishers following the breakup, in the end it made sense for my company, Rolenta Press, to publish the book once again. And since I was doing it, I was free to use the cover that had originally been designed for it. Of course some changes needed to be made. First of all, the cover has been updated so the newest consoles, the Wii U, PS4 and Xbox One are prevalent at the top where the Phoenix is rising towards. Also, the book's logo that contained its title and sub-title needed to be changed as well.

Dedication

Originally, this edition was supposed to be published in early 2015 and it was going to be dedicated to two extremely important people in my life who unfortunately passed away within two weeks of one another. The first was my mother, Rosalyn Herman, who entered a hospital on October 19, 2014 with a sore throat and passed away on November 24 from acute leukemia, which none of us knew she had. Although my mother was clueless when it came to videogames, she supported everything I did. While cleaning her house I came across a set of the three previous *Phoenix* editions, along with the 'prototype' edition, all in mint condition.

The other person who I mourned was the one who, in a way, was the one most responsible for this book. Ralph Baer passed away on December 7. But I didn't mourn him because of his contribution to videogame history; I mourned the man because he was a close friend.

I first met Ralph and his wife Dena in 1998 at their New Hampshire home. He had invited me to visit after I had sent him a copy of *Phoenix 2*. We hit it off right away and he invited me up several more times. Dena once referred to me as her 'surrogate' son, a title, which I proudly accepted. And since my own father had passed away in 1991, I looked at Ralph as a surrogate father.

Ralph had written the Foreword to *Phoenix 3*, and I asked him to write a blurb for the back cover of this edition. He finally sent me his blurb in November, 2014 and it was the last email I ever received from him.

My last visit with Ralph was in August, 2014, and he had been excited because people from the Smithsonian were taking his basement lab apart, and were recreating it in Washington, D.C. Ralph had donated his Brown `Box to the Smithsonian nearly a decade earlier and he had been dismayed that the famed museum had never displayed it. He was excited about the exhibit and he showed me the diagrams of how it would look. His fervent hope was that he would live long enough to actually see it when it opened in 2015.

Within a month his health steadily began to decline. When I spoke to him on the phone he said to me that he didn't think he'd live to see the museum exhibit. It was the first time I heard him utter something negative. Previously, even when he felt lousy, he still believed he'd get to Washington.

I talked to Ralph a few times on the phone after that and each time he'd ask me when I was going to go up to visit him. By that time, my mother was dying in the hospital and I knew I wouldn't be able to get to New Hampshire. Still, I couldn't tell him about her and I had to always lie and say I'd visit him soon. I remember one time I left her room to talk to him and I apologized for leaving her when I returned. She said she understood because she knew how important Ralph was to me. And I responded by saying, "Yes, but you're more important to me and I shouldn't have left you."

I last spoke to Ralph from my mother's room a few days before she passed away. He was weak and spoke very softly, but the last thing he asked me was when I would be up there to see him. It broke my heart when I said, "I'll try to be there soon."

My mother died on Monday, November 24, 2014. In Judaism we have a tradition called *Shivah* where we mourn for seven days and friends and family visit to console us. We sat *Shivah* through the following Sunday, November 30. And then Ralph's daughter, Nancy, called me seven days later to tell me that her father had passed away. I told my 'friends' on Facebook, and ultimately the world, and then I started mourning all over again.

The publication of this volume took much longer than I had planned and it was finally released nearly two years after the passing of my mother and Ralph Baer. Although my mother's memory will always be in my heart, I decided to remove her name from the dedication, and leave it solely to the father of the videogame console, who I still think about daily.

Acknowledgements

Even though only my name appears on the cover, this book is actually the product of many people. Some have made major contributions and others have performed such roles as simply answering a single question.

First, I want to thank Chris Federico, who edited the entire book. Even before I began writing the fourth edition, many people came to me offering editorial services. Since one of the major complaints about the first three editions was poor editing, I took one of them on their offer. This turned out to be Chris, who is a professional editor and writer, and who had contributed to a fanzine, *Orphaned Computers & Game Systems* in the late nineties, and which he still co-maintains online at http://www.orphanedgames.com. For the past ten years I've been sending him chapters after I completed them. And even though he was burdened with his own work, he always managed to return the chapters with the inevitable corrections, in a timely fashion. If you find any grammatical errors in this book, it's because I didn't agree with what Chris told me to fix.

I also want to thank Rob Faraldi, a videogame industry veteran and historian who continues to contribute via the independent game scene as well as producing and directing independent cinema and other projects, some of which are videogame-themed (www.bluespikefilms.com). He was heavily influenced by previous editions of *Phoenix* and jumped at the chance to fact-check the entire volume. He made additional contributions in terms of content suggestions and text. As with Chris' editing, if you think some fact is wrong, it's because I didn't follow Rob's advice.

As mentioned earlier, Michael Thomasson did the cover of the book. In addition to graphic design, Michael holds many hats including college professor, Mensa member and he was even recognized by the *Guinness Book of World Records* for owning the world's largest videogame software collection. Michael is also an online retailer who sells homebrews, i.e. new games for classic systems. You can visit his site at www.gooddealgames.com.

My thanks also go out to Ted Dabney, the co-founder of Atari, for agreeing to write a foreword to this edition. My association with Ted began around 2006 when he decided to tell his side of the Atari story for the first time, which ran contradictory to the stories that Nolan Bushnell had been saying for over thirty years. He allowed me to write his story, which was published as "The Untold Atari Story" in the April, 2009 issue of the British magazine, *Edge*. Unfortunately, Ted was modest with his newly-found fame and the foreword he wrote was very short. So I'm also indebted to Chris Kohler for writing the second foreword. I know Chris since he wrote and published the fanzine, *Video Zone*, during the early nineties. Currently, Chris writes for *WIRED.com*'s Game|Life channel, which he founded in 2005. Chris was my first choice to write a second foreword to this edition because new to *Phoenix IV* is a complete history of the Japanese videogame industry and Chris, who wrote *Power-Up: How Japanese Video Games Gave the World an Extra Life*, is one of the world's leading authorities on that subject. Thank you so much, Chris!

Others who have contributed whether they know it or not are (in no particular order): Ken Jong, Patrick Wong, Ryan Fahy, John Hardie, Joe Santulli, Sean Kelly, Jon-Paul Dyson, Gary Vincent, Patrick Scott Patterson, Chris Johnston, Curt Vendel, Marty Goldberg, Keith Feinstein, Chris Cavanaugh, Tommy Freeman, Chris Bieniek, Mike from Arcade Gear (http://jap-sai.com/Index.htm), Carlson Stevens from Mad Gear (http://www.mad-gear.com/), Damien McFerran from *NintendoLife* (http://www.nintendolife.com), Fayez Fawzi, Matt Reichert, Jim Levy, Frank Cifaldi, Bill Loguidice, Martin

Kristensen, Frankie Viturello, Tommy Tallarico, David Perry, Scott Stilphen, Mike Markowski, Joel Gallof, Steve Kent, Cassidy Nolen, David Winter, Brett Weiss, Jeff Ryan, Russ Perry, Jr., Andy Gaven, Bardin Levavy, Dan Kramer, Jerry Jessop, Brianna Blank, Kevin Ram, Lawrence Block, Paul Herman, Jason Glasgow, Cory Golabek, Tom Schissler, Larry Handeli, Howard Bloom and Katie Gallof. And a special thanks to Rawson Stovall who helped me with matters outside of the book. I'm sure there are many others who need to be included in this list, and please forgive me if you should have been and weren't.

Unfortunately, a book of this scope is not perfect, despite my best efforts to try and make it so. Shortly after the B&W edition was published, I received word of errors that had unfortunately crept into the book. I have done my best to clean them up for this color edition. Since the B&W edition cannot be fixed so easily, I have listed the corrections online at http://www.rolentapress.com/Products/Phoenix/Phoenix4/errata. I'd like to especially thank Alexander Smith, Kris Randazzo and Kevin Butler for providing me with this information, which no writer ever likes to admit.

Finally, I must thank my immediate family who had to live with this edition for the past eleven years. I am nothing without my wife, Tamar, and my sons, Ronnie and Greg. I love you all.

Photo Credits:
Page 85 - Atari Remote Control VCS Controller & Atari Remote Control VCS
Photos by Dan Kramer used with permission

Page 239 - NEC TurboDuo
Photo by Evan Amos

Page 252 – Fujitsu FM Towns Marty
Photo by Evan Amos

Page 254 - NEC PC Engine Duo-R
Photo by Evan Amos

Page 260 - JVC WonderMega M2
Photo by Evan Amos

Page 276 - Capcom CPS Changer & Capcom CPS Changer Cartridge
Photos by Lawrence Wright

Page 278 - NEC PC Engine Duo-RX
Photo by Rob Faraldi used with permission

Page 296 - New Leaf Genesis Cartridge
Photo by Rob Faraldi used with permission

Page 317 – Tiger R-Zone Headgear
Photo by Evan Amos

Page 347 – Tiger R-Zone Super Screen
Photo by Evan Amos

Page 363 – Tiger R-Zone XPG
Photo by Evan Amos

Page 560 - Ralph Baer & President George W. Bush
White House Photo by Eric Draper

CHAPTER ONE
1951-1970

On January 25, 1947, Thomas T. Goldsmith, Jr., and Estle Ray Mann, of DuMont Laboratories, filed a patent entitled "Cathode-Ray Tube Amusement Device." The patent described a method wherein targets were physically placed on a screen. Using controllers, players could move an electron beam around the screen to collide with one or more targets. The patent, # 2,455,992, was granted on December 14, 1948, and while this certainly appears to be the first indication of a videogame, there is no evidence that a prototype of the unit had actually been built.

The first computer that people could actually play games on made its debut on August 25, 1950 at the Canadian National Exhibition in Toronto. It had been built by Josef Kates, an engineer who had immigrated to Canada after escaping Austria and the Nazis in 1938 following the *Anschluss.*[1]

While part of a team to build *UTEC (University of Toronto Electronic Computer),* Canada's first working computer, Kates was troubled that the machine required dozens of vacuum tubes, which rendered it too large, clunky and expensive. With the assistance of friends from Rogers Majestic,[2] a leading manufacturer of vacuum tubes where Kates had worked upon arriving in Canada, he hit upon a solution by inventing the *Additron,* a tube that could perform binary addition and replace 10 ordinary tubes. Computer scientists quickly recognized the value of the Additron but Kates realized that he had to prove to the public that his invention would lead to a smaller, less expensive computer that could solve practical problems.

Kates decided to use the game *Tic-Tac-Toe,* which was a simple game that everyone knew how to play, as a practical example of what the Additron could do. He built *Bertie the Brain,* a smaller version of UTEC. The machine was put on display at the Rogers Majestic exhibit at the Canadian National Exhibition where people lined up to play against the machine. Humans played "O" and the computer played "X". Players inputted their selection by pressing buttons in a 3x3 grid. Light bulbs in the shape of an "O" or "X" would illuminate on the grid. A larger 3x3 grid was built into the front of the machine, which also utilized the "O" and "X" shaped bulbs. A panel to the right of the large grid displayed a large "X" and read ELECTRONIC BRAIN, and another to the right of it displayed a large "O" and read HUMAN BRAIN. The word WIN illuminated on the panel of the winner, usually the computer. However, to appease the visitors, Kates was able to adjust the level of the computer's intelligence and he often lowered it so guests, especially children, could "beat" the computer.

Bertie the Brain proved that the Additron could be used to build small, reliable and inexpensive computers. Following the end of the Canadian National Exhibition in September, 1950, Kates dismantled the computer. Due to patent issues, the Additron tubes were never used again.

In February 1951, Ferranti, a British electrical engineering company, delivered the *Mark I,* the world's first commercially available computer. Two months later, Ferranti, a British electrical engineering firm, displayed the *Nimrod Digital Computer* at the Festival of Britain's *Exhibition of Science.* Like Bertie the Brain, the Nimrod was designed to do only one thing – play a game. In this case the game was *Nim,* an ancient game where players took turns removing 12 objects from three heaps, each consisting of between three and five objects. Players alternate removing one or more objects from the heaps, and the winner is the one who removes, or doesn't remove (the rules are agreed to in advance), the remaining object. On the Nimrod, players removed objects by pressing buttons on a control panel and the results were displayed by a series of light bulbs. When the Festival of Britain ended in November 1951, the Nimrod was moved to Germany, where it was displayed at the Berlin Industrial Show.

Bertie the Brain and the Nimrod both utilized light bulbs to display their output. The first use of a screen for such a purpose occurred in 1952 when a Ph.D. candidate at the University of Cambridge named A.S. Douglas programmed a game called *Noughts and Crosses* (Tic-Tac-Toe) on an early British mainframe computer called EDSAC[3] to illustrate his thesis on human-computer interaction. He entered commands into EDSAC via a telephone-like dial, with output displayed on the computer's 35×16-pixel screen as a *Noughts and Crosses* board.

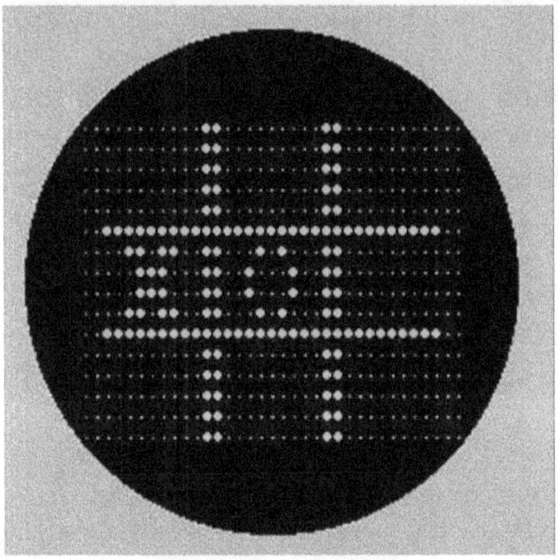

Noughts and Crosses

Higinbotham's Tennis Game

In the 1950s, the U.S. Government's Brookhaven National Laboratory for nuclear research was in the habit of holding public open houses to introduce people to its research. But the exhibits were a bit dull, and in 1958, one Brookhaven physicist, Willy Higinbotham, wanted to create something a bit more interactive and exciting. He was intrigued by the idea of graphing the paths of bouncing balls on an oscilloscope screen, which was normally used to display varying signal voltages. After spending a few hours studying the instruction manual for the laboratory's computer, he learned how to plot trajectories, which he later used to create a game of tennis that the laboratory's visitors could play on the computer.

Unsurprisingly, his game was quite primitive. The oscilloscope displayed a horizontal line along the bottom and a small vertical line in the center, to represent the side-view of a net. A spot (the "ball") moved across the screen and bounced whenever it hit the horizontal line. Two small boxes attached to the oscilloscope each had a button and a knob. These were the rudimentary controllers for two "players." A player pressed the button when the ball was on his side of the net to return the ball to the opposite side. The knob controlled the angle of the return.

Higinbotham's game, which he called *Tennis for Two,* couldn't keep score, and players could compete as long as they wanted. Visitors to the lab loved it, and Higinbotham improved the game the following year by displaying it on a 15-inch screen.

Higinbotham had no plans to market his tennis simulation, and it never left the Brookhaven Labs. He never even bothered to patent his game, because he never felt like he had invented anything. Of course, if had he foreseen the game's commercial possibilities, the history of videogames might have taken a different path altogether. However, even if he had applied for a patent, the owner of that patent would have been his employer, the United States Government.

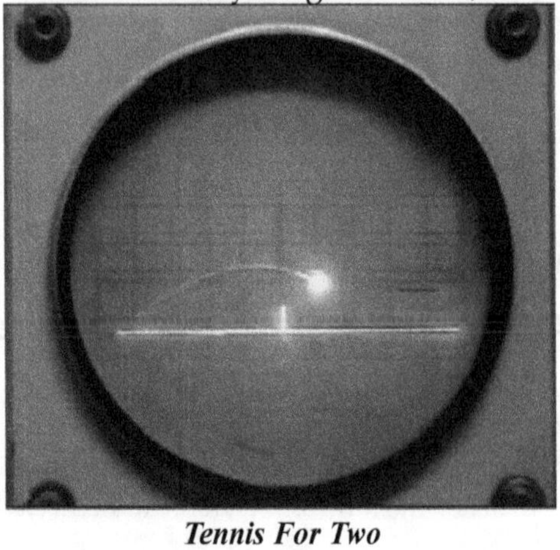

Tennis For Two

Spacewar

In 1962, Steve Russell, a member of the Tech Model Railroad Club at the Massachusetts Institute of Technology (MIT), thought that it would be fun to write a game on the school's PDP-1 mainframe computer. He chose a science-fiction theme because, in those days, most people considered computers to be pure science fiction. His game, *Spacewar*, was a basic shoot-out in which two players controlled spaceships that fired missiles at each other. To make things difficult, Russell included a sun that pulled the spaceships toward the center of the display with its heavy gravity. Not only did the player have to avoid his opponent's shots, but he also had to navigate around the sun to avoid hitting it.

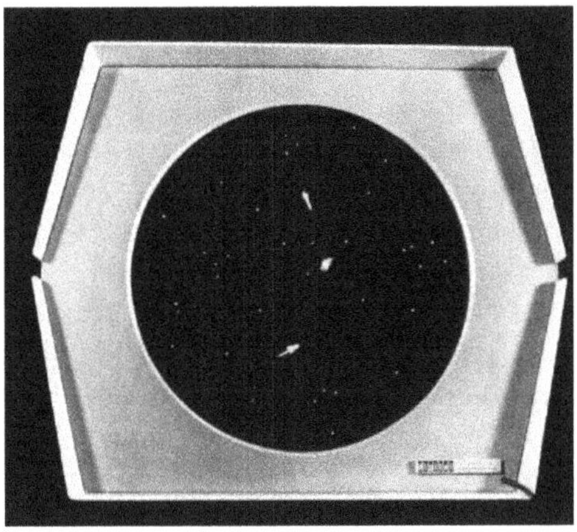

Spacewar

Spacewar was an underground hit. Other students not only played the game, but also tinkered with its code. One student added stars that represented actual constellations; another added the option to instantly transport a ship from one part of the screen to a random spot somewhere else on the screen, at the touch of a button. Before long, *Spacewar* began appearing on mainframe computers around the country.

The University of Utah was one of the schools hosting *Spacewar* on its computer, and by 1965, many of its students were spending their evenings endlessly playing the game. One of these students was a 22-year-old engineering major named Nolan Bushnell.

Like thousands of other students around the country playing *Spacewar*, Bushnell didn't think about commercial possibilities for the game. This changed, however, when he found himself working summers as the arcade manager at Lagoon Amusement Park in Salt Lake City. It occurred to him that people strolling along the midway, where the amusement rides were concentrated, might pay to play computer games like *Spacewar*. Unfortunately, since computers were still too large and expensive to make such an idea plausible, Bushnell put the thought on the back burner.

Developing the First Videogame Console

While Bushnell was toying with the idea of coin-operated videogames, Ralph Baer, manager of the Equipment Design Division at Sanders Associates (a military contractor), was already developing videogames for the home. In September 1966, Baer was brainstorming about ways to use a television beyond merely turning it on and watching it. These ideas were focused, of course, around methods of using its screen to play games. Baer told the director of Sanders' Research & Development about his idea, and he was given the go-ahead and $2,000 in corporate backing (enough to get started in those days). Baer assigned engineers Bill Harrison and Bill Rusch to the project, and the three worked part-time in a room that was off-limits to the rest of the company.

By December 1966, Baer and his team had succeeded in getting spots to move around a TV screen. By May 7, 1967, they had completed basic ball-and-paddle games. They

FOCUS ON SANDERS ASSOCIATES

The importance of Sanders Associates' role in the development of videogames is certain. The real question is: Why did they get involved in the first place? The company had no experience in developing consumer-based products, and even after they gave Ralph Baer the green light to develop his videogame, they had no idea what they were going to do with it. In 1986, Sanders was purchased by the Lockheed Martin Corporation, and became part of the company's Lockheed Martin Aerospace Electronic Systems.

In 1996, Lockheed Martin Aerospace Electronic Systems purchased Loral Corporation, the company that Ralph Baer had worked for before he went to Sanders.

In late 2000, BAE Systems purchased Lockheed Martin Aerospace Electronic Systems for $1.67 billion finished video versions of tennis, handball and volleyball shortly afterwards. In June, they created a prototype light gun out of a toy rifle, and were able to "shoot" spots on the screen. In November of 1967, they demonstrated their video table-tennis game for the first time, and began to concentrate on marketing it. At this time, Baer faced one of his biggest obstacles yet: how to explain the need for such an invention. And if there was such a need, how would they market the device?

Sanders was a defense contractor and wasn't in a position to manufacture and distribute consumer products, so Baer went elsewhere. In January, 1968, after applying for a patent, he demonstrated his game to the management of TelePrompter, then the largest cable operator in the United States. The general idea was to have the cable system provide colorful backgrounds for a home game system, which would superimpose things like ball-and-paddle symbols on these backgrounds. TelePrompter created colorful wall charts depicting scenes like a tennis court. These charts were then televised with a color video camera, and the video signal from the transmission was sent via cable to the game hardware, which merged the colorful backdrops with the electronic ball and paddle. The effect was that of a game with sophisticated, colorful graphics.

Unfortunately, this early effort came to a halt, due to struggles in the cable industry and a negative cash flow. As a result, in 1968, Baer decided that it made more sense to license the game to a consumer-electronics company that could manufacture and sell it under its own brand -- probably one that also manufactured television sets, since his prototype used the same components.

In November, 1968, the group built their seventh prototype unit. The finished device featured 16 switches on its front panel. By arranging the switches in varying positions, the unit was able to play a number of ball-and-paddle games with several background colors. The prototype unit was covered with brown wood-grain Contact paper, which prompted Baer to dub it the "Brown Box."

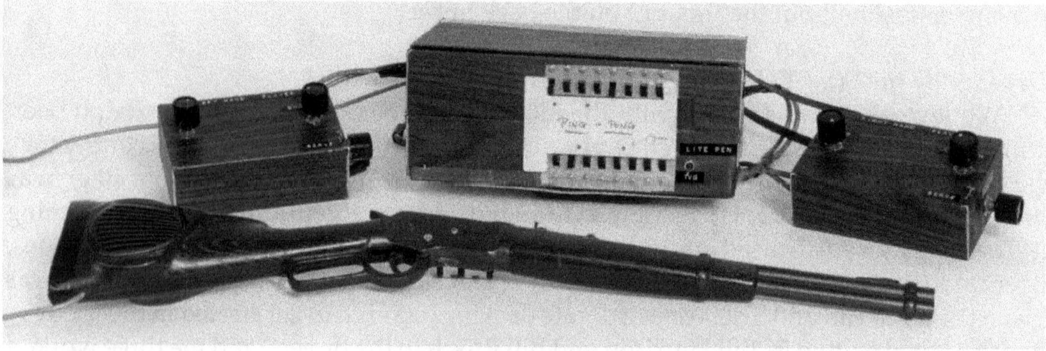

The Brown Box

The Brown Box had two smaller boxes, also encased in Contact paper, that were attached to the back of the main unit with cables. Each of these boxes had three dials and a reset button. Two of the dials controlled the horizontal and vertical movements of a spot of light on the screen, which the player used as a paddle. Each box controlled its own paddle. The third dial applied "English" to the third spot of light on the screen, which acted as a ball. After a player retracted the ball with his paddle, turning the English dial would cause the ball to move up or down in a manner unpredictable to the opponent. Baer felt that the English control was the game's secret weapon, by providing a level of skill and unpredictability to a game that might otherwise have been bland and repetitious.

In 1969, Baer demonstrated the Brown Box to several television manufacturers, including Sylvania, Philco, Admiral, General Electric and Zenith. All of them marveled at the concept, but were afraid to risk manufacturing such a revolutionary new product. RCA visited Sanders for a demonstration in March, 1969. As it turned out, RCA had also experimented with videogames, and in honor of the twenty-fifth anniversary of RCA

FOCUS ON RALPH BAER

In 1951, Ralph Baer began working for Loral Corporation, a defense contractor that developed RADAR and SONAR detection methods for the U.S. Navy. His first assignment was to build a television set. He wanted to build an interactive game into the set, but his boss, Sam Lackoff, wasn't interested. Baer never lost sight of his goal, though, and his TV game reappeared 17 years later to become the foundation for the Odyssey, the first home videogame console.

In addition to the Odyssey, Baer was involved with many early videogame systems from Coleco: *Telstar*, *Telstar Combat*, and *Telstar Arcade*. Although he was one of the first people in the world to receive a degree in television engineering, his inventions weren't limited to TV-based videogames. He produced several electronic games, including Amazatron, Maniac, and Computer Perfection. But his most famous invention was a round disc with four large, colorful buttons: what we all know as Simon.

Baer went on to invent the first talking greeting card for Hallmark, as well as talking doormats and talking bicycle speedometers. This list only cracks the surface of Baer's phenomenal output, though. In all, this modern-day Edison boasted over 150 patents.

Labs, engineers had created a video version of pool on a $90,000 computer. But despite the money and knowledge that RCA had invested, the game was pretty primitive, and RCA couldn't see any commercial applications for it. Following Baer's demonstration, RCA began seeing commercial possibilities with the Brown Box, and began a lengthy negotiation with Sanders that lasted several months. Ultimately, RCA insisted on terms that Sanders could not live with, and the negotiations ended.

By late 1969 the demonstrations came to a halt, as most of the television manufacturers had already seen one. Baer traveled to Chicago in January 1970 to demonstrate the Brown Box to Sears officials, but they weren't interested in it, either.

By July 1970, when the designers of the Brown Box had pretty much given up any hope of licensing the device, a change had occurred at RCA. Bill Enders, who had been one of the main RCA negotiators, left to join Magnavox as a vice-president for marketing. Enders had always been very impressed with Baer's invention, and one of the first things he did at Magnavox was to tell his management about the Brown Box. After a demonstration at Magnavox's Fort Wayne, Indiana headquarters, Magnavox's management agreed with Enders' assessment, and Sanders and Magnavox quickly entered a period of negotiations. This time, Sanders and Enders would be happy with the results.

FOCUS ON PATENTS

Ralph Baer applied for his first videogame patent on March 18, 1968. Titled "Recoding CRT Light Gun and Method," Patent #3,599,221, dated August 10, 1971, covered a process that displayed coded information on a television screen, and a device that decoded it. Baer used this process for quiz games that he designed. Players would receive preprinted questions, similar to those in *Trivial Pursuit*, and multiple answers would appear on the screen via overlays. Alongside each answer, invisible to the players themselves, was a code that could be read by a light pen, the forerunner of a light gun. Players chose from among the answers on the screen, and the gun would detect correct answers by reading the code.

But Baer's landmark patent was one that covered consoles connected to television sets. Patent #3,728,480, "Television Gaming and Training Apparatus," was issued on April 17, 1973. As far as the courts were concerned, this patent answered the question of who invented videogame consoles.

CHAPTER TWO
1971-1972

On March 3, 1971, Sanders and Magnavox completed their negotiations and signed a contract for Magnavox to begin manufacturing a production version of the Brown Box. Sanders immediately sent a package of engineering drawings and diagrams to Magnavox's headquarters in Fort Wayne, Indiana. Baer and Bill Harrison soon followed, and began working on the games that would be included in the final version.

For the next several months, Baer's life would be consumed by the project of turning the Brown Box into a commercial product. He was completely unaware that a similar project was taking place simultaneously on the opposite side of the country.

Computer Space: The First Video Arcade Game

Nolan Bushnell graduated from college in late 1968 and, soon afterwards, moved his wife and young daughters to California, where he began a new job as an electronic engineer at Ampex, the Sunnyvale company that had invented the modern videotape recorder. Although Bushnell's $12,000 salary was a decent amount at the time, he wanted more. His dream was to open his own business, a pizza parlor that had an arcade and animated Disneyland-like characters.

As computers became smaller and cheaper, Bushnell realized that it might be economically feasible to connect several monitors up to one minicomputer, which would serve as the brains for the monitors, displaying images on several screens at once: a kind of *time-sharing*. Bushnell discussed this concept with Ted Dabney, the fellow Ampex electronic engineer with whom Bushnell shared an office. Dabney liked the idea, and after months of discussion, they modified a TV so it could simulate address programming. This meant that they could turn on a spot of light at a certain location on the screen. They could then quickly turn off that spot and turn on the adjacent location. They would repeat this until the spot of light arrived at the side of the screen. Because it was done so rapidly, it looked like the spot of light moved across the screen.

Once they knew they were onto something, Dabney relocated his young daughter from her bedroom to the living room, so that he and Bushnell could use her room as a workshop. They then began to bombard Larry Bryan, an Ampex computer programmer, with questions about the type of programming that would be needed for their project. Once they were satisfied that their idea would work, the three men agreed that each would contribute $100 to start a venture. Bushnell and Dabney put in the money, but Bryan never did.

The team quickly realized that available computers were still too expensive and slow to make their time-sharing project feasible, so they abandoned it. But that didn't stop Dabney and Bushnell. They realized that they could build cost-effective videogames using ordinary of-the-shelf integrated circuits. Bushnell decided that *Spacewar*, the computer game he had played as a student, was the game that people would want to play with his new technology.

Bushnell quit Ampex in March 1971 to devote all of his time to cloning *Spacewar*, which he renamed *Computer Space*, and set up a new partnership with Dabney, this time without Bryan. Bushnell soon met Bill Nutting, owner of Nutting Associates, a manufacturer of mechanical coin-operated arcade games - including the popular *Computer Quiz*. Nutting liked the *Computer Space* concept and wanted to buy the rights to it outright, but Bushnell and Dabney chose to license a single-player version of the game to Nutting Associates instead. They would receive a royalty for each machine sold to arcades. The license also granted Nutting the right to manufacture a two-player version of *Computer Space*, which

Bushnell and Dabney could not actually claim any ownership to. Nutting contracted Bushnell to design the new machine.

Bill Nutting hired Bushnell as chief engineer in August 1971, along with Dabney so that they could refine *Computer Space* as it went into production. Nutting Associates built 1,500 *Computer Space* units, complete with futuristic-looking fiberglass cabinets that had been designed by Bushnell, and began selling them to arcade distributors in November, 1971.

The sales were disappointing. Although Bushnell's engineering friends found the game exciting and fun to play, the general public didn't. The game's controls were just too complicated for people who had been raised on pinball. Bushnell approached Nutting about releasing a simpler version of *Computer Space*, and Nutting was enthusiastic. But before Bushnell actually began working on the new game, he demanded that Nutting give him a bigger share of the profits, since he considered himself the brains behind the game. He wanted 33% of Nutting Associates. Bill

Nutting Computer Quiz

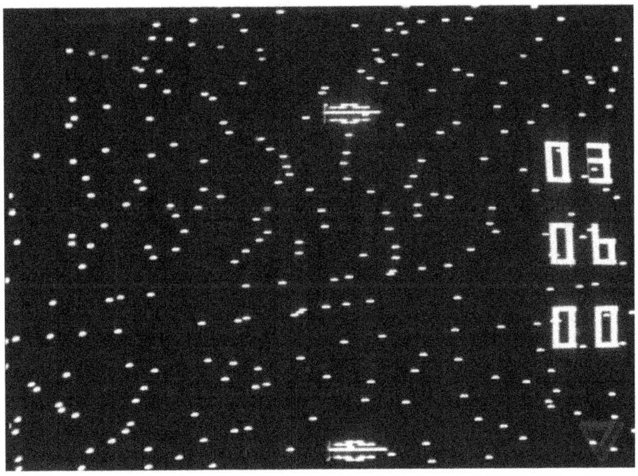

Nutting Computer Space

Nutting countered with 5%, provided that Bushnell agreed to remain with the company as an engineer. Bushnell didn't accept Nutting's counteroffer, but continued to work for Nutting Associates with the intention of offering his designs elsewhere.

Dabney and Bushnell began searching for new partners to sell and manufacture their as-yet nonexistent new games. In April 1972, with *Computer Space* under his belt, Bushnell went to Chicago and met with Bally, the leading manufacturer of pinball and slot machines. Bally had expressed interest in the idea, and told Bushnell that they would have a deal as long as he and Dabney were no longer employed by Nutting.

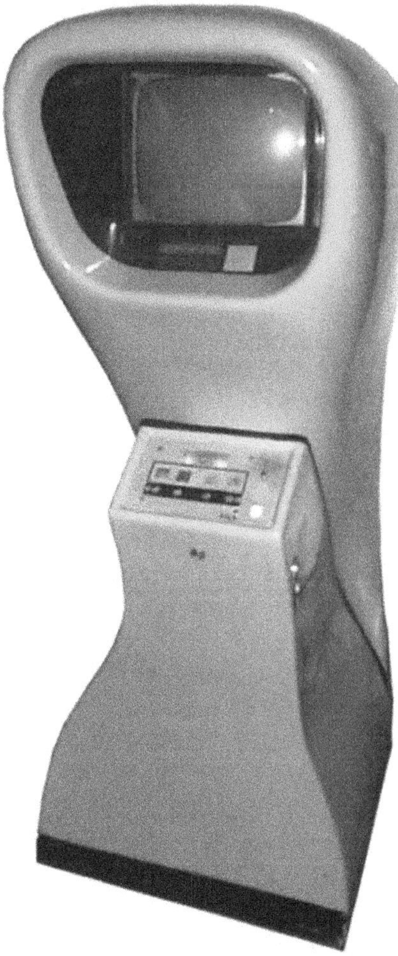

Nutting Computer Space

FOCUS ON: GALAXY GAME

In late 1970, Digital Equipment Corporation released the PDP-11, a minicomputer which, at $14,000, was much more affordable than previous models. Bill Pitts, who had recently graduated from Stanford University, saw this as an opportunity to bring *Spacewar* to the masses that hadn't had the opportunity to play the computer game. In June, 1971, Pitts and a high-school friend, Hugh Tuck, formed a company called Computer Recreations to build an arcade version of *Spacewar*.

The pair purchased a PDP-11, and Pitts programmed the game. Tuck designed and built a cabinet. After nearly four months, a prototype of the game was ready. To avoid anti-war sentiments, they renamed it *Galaxy Game*.

The prototype was placed in Tresidder Union of Stanford University in November 1971, approximately the same time as the debut of *Computer Space*. The game, which cost ten cents for one play, and 25 cents for three plays, was an instant hit. The only problem was that it couldn't make a return on its investment. Between the PDP-11 computer, a monitor, and a point-plotting display interface, the entire apparatus cost Pitts and Tuck around $20,000 ($108,000 today). Because of this, *Galaxy Game* never went beyond the prototype phase.

In 1972, Pitts and Tuck upgraded the display interface so the PDP-11 processor could control four to eight consoles at one time. However, the costs were still too prohibitive to release it commercially. This version of the game was placed in the Tresidder Union in June 1972, where it remained in constant operation until May 1979.

Since the two men were receiving royalties from *Computer Space*, they figured they could leave Nutting and start their own independent company to design games. Bushnell and Dabney each kicked in $250 from their royalties and started *Syzygy* - a name proposed by Larry Bryan that meant "the straight-line configuration of three celestial bodies," such as a solar or lunar eclipse. They leased an office in Santa Clara, California to create new games. They both resigned as employees of Nutting Associates in early May, but Bushnell immediately became an independent contractor for Nutting to produce the two-player version of *Computer Space*.

During that month, Bill Nutting received an invitation to attend a showcase of Magnavox's new products, which would include a device that would hook up to a television set and let people play games through the TV. The demonstration was to be held in Burlingame, California on May 24. Since Nutting had thought that *Computer Space* was the only device that allowed people to play games through a television screen, he decided to send three associates, one of them being Bushnell, to investigate.

From Prototype To Product

Magnavox had begun production of Ralph Baer's Brown Box on January 27, 1972. During May, Magnavox's marketing department went out on a promotional tour called the 1972 Magnavox Profit Caravan, in which the company's new product line was demonstrated to people in the industry, such as dealers. The highlight of the product line that year was Baer's invention, which had been named the *Odyssey* by Magnavox. This "electronic game simulator", as Magnavox described it, debuted in Phoenix, Arizona on May 3, 1972.

Internally, the Odyssey was Baer's Brown Box. But externally, the part that consumers would see was completely

Magnavox Odyssey

different. The white and black plastic console looked futuristic and simplistic at the same time, without any distracting buttons or switches.

Like its prototype, the Odyssey had several dedicated games built into it, including ping-pong, tennis, handball, volleyball and chase games. But since the switches from the Brown Box had been removed, Magnavox's engineers thought up an innovative way for players to select their desired games. The Odyssey would be packaged with six plug-in circuit boards, which, when inserted into a slot in the front of the console, would act like keys that would unlock the desired game. Magnavox also planned to release several additional circuit boards that would retail for $5.95 each, as well as a $25 shooting-gallery package that would come with four additional circuit boards and a light-sensitive rifle - the world's first videogame peripheral. The controllers that accompanied the Odyssey were also clothed in white and black colors, but they basically contained all of the functionality that Baer had originally incorporated into his design: horizontal, vertical, and English dials.

Magnavox Odyssey Light Rifle

To make the price of the unit affordable, Baer and his team had used only 40 transistors and diodes, which had given the Brown Box the ability to generate only the most minimal of on-screen affects, basically three spots of light. But Baer's prototype could generate color. Magnavox removed the color generator from the final product, so the Odyssey could only play in black and white, even on color TV sets. But to make the games appear complex and colorful, Magnavox planned to package the Odyssey with a variety of plastic graphical overlays that would be placed over the TV screen.

The Birth of Atari

When the *Magnavox Profit Caravan* stopped at the Airport Marina Hotel in Burlingame, California, on May 24, the three representatives that Bill Nutting had sent were in attendance. But Bushnell was less worried about how Magnavox's Odyssey would be a threat to Nutting Associates, and more concerned about its possible competition with Syzygy. After he signed the guest book,[1] Bushnell sampled the Odyssey's ping-pong and handball games for a half-hour. However, he had failed to learn about the Odyssey's challenging English dial that gave players complete control over the path of the ball after it left their paddles. He didn't find either game interesting or fun. But he did find the game simple to play, and with that thought, the wheels began turning in Bushnell's head.

FOCUS ON NOLAN BUSHNELL

Although he is best known as the "father of the videogame industry," Nolan Bushnell made a hobby out of starting up businesses the way others have collected stamps. Besides the companies, that are featured in this book, Atari, Pizza Time Theatre, Sente and Androbot, Bushnell founded over 20 technological and interactive companies including Catalyst Technologies, Etak, Axlon, Irata, AAPPS, ByVideo, uWink.com and Anti-AgingGames.com, a company that creates online memory, concentration and focus games designed to stimulate the brains of healthy people over 35. He has also served as a consultant for many major companies, including Commodore, IBM, Cisco Systems and U.S. Digital Communications.

Bushnell's latest venture is Brainbush, which uses games to make learning faster, fun and fullfilling.

On April 19, 2010 Bushnell came full-circle when he joined the Board of Directors of Atari, SA.

Bushnell continued to contract with Nutting on the two-player *Computer Space* throughout the summer. Despite this involvement with Nutting, he swore to Bally that he was no longer associated with his former employer, and secured a six-month contract that awarded him and Dabney $24,000 to design a new arcade videogame and a new pinball game. Bally would own the rights to whatever they produced. Unfortunately, aside from the basic idea of a simple videogame design, Bushnell wasn't sure what kind of videogame he would actually deliver to Bally.

When Bushnell and Dabney attempted to incorporate their company, they were informed that the Syzygy name was already in use. When the pair decided to come up with a new name for the arcade videogame business, they turned to *Go*, their favorite board game. Bushnell wrote down his three favorite Japanese terms from the game. *HANNE* meant that a player was about to lose a piece. *SENTE* was similar in meaning to the chess term "checkmate." Finally, there was *ATARI*, which was something akin to the term "check" in chess. He took his list to the office of California's Secretary of State, where someone liked the name ATARI the most.[2] So Atari it was.

Atari's First Game

Atari was officially incorporated on June 27, 1972. Once the company was established, Bushnell decided to build an easy-to-play arcade driving game. Although the game itself would be simple, he needed an engineer to put together the complicated circuitry. While at Ampex, Bushnell had been friendly with a young college student named Al Alcorn, who had been there under a work-study program. Bushnell contacted the fresh graduate and hired him as Atari's first engineer.

Because Alcorn was inexperienced, Bushnell felt that he wasn't ready to design the driving game. He started the new recruit with a simple video ping-pong game. Instead of telling Alcorn that it was merely a training exercise, Bushnell told him that it was needed to fill a contract that he had with General Electric.

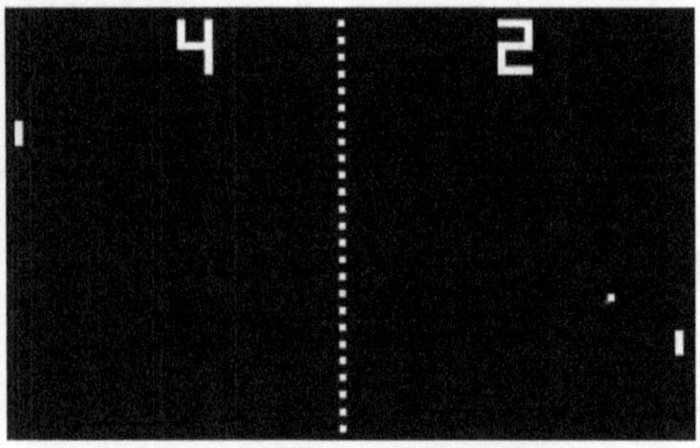

Atari Pong

Although Alcorn designed the game according to Bushnell's specifications, he added one extra feature. The game made a sound every time the ball bounced off a wall or paddle. Bushnell liked it so much that he named the game after the sound: *Pong*.

The sound was one feature that made *Pong* different from the video ping-pong that Bushnell had played on the Odyssey, which had no sound capabilities at all. The *Pong* paddles could only move vertically, and they were segmented, although not visibly. The segment of the paddle that the ball bounced against determined the angle of its rebound. This was *Pong*'s answer to the Odyssey's English control. Finally, and most notably, each player's score was visible at the top of the *Pong* playfield.

Bushnell wasn't prepared to manufacture the machines. He wanted Atari to strictly design and program videogames for other companies to license and manufacture. And since Atari already owed Bally a videogame as per their contract, Bushnell figured that they were already on the path that he envisioned. He offered *Pong* to Bally executives, and to his surprise, Bally wasn't interested in the game at all.

Dejected, Bushnell and Dabney decided to build a table-top *Pong* prototype unit themselves, which they installed in a Sunnyvale bar called Andy Capp's. That night, the regulars at the bar curiously looked at what appeared to be a coin-operated television. On the screen appeared a simple message that beckoned people to "**AVOID MISSING BALL FOR HIGH SCORE.**" One brave soul inserted a quarter and watched with confusion as a ball whisked across the screen, and an on-screen counter changed from zero to one. After the counter advanced several more times, someone realized that the knobs on the console controlled "paddles" that moved vertically along the sides of the screen. There was no stopping them after that. Everybody in the bar tried the game before the night was over.

Atari Pong Prototype

News of the game spread rapidly, and when Andy Capp's opened at ten the following morning, there was a long line outside filled with people waiting to get in and play *Pong*. Alcorn received a phone call from Bill Gattis, the bar's owner, two weeks later. Gattis informed Alcorn that the prototype machine had stopped working, and asked him to fix it, because the game had become very popular. Alcorn quickly drove to the bar and examined the machine. After he unlocked the front of the cabinet, he pressed a switch that allowed him to play without paying. The game performed flawlessly. When he was satisfied that there wasn't anything wrong with the circuitry, he further examined the machine. He smiled when he found the problem.

The machine had broken down was because the milk carton used to catch the player's quarters had filled up. The quarters had overflowed and jammed the machine!

Thanks to *Pong*'s enthusiastic reception, Bushnell, Dabney and Alcorn hand-built twelve upright *Pong* arcade units, and set up ten of them around Silicon Valley. Meanwhile, Bushnell again tried convincing the Bally executives to change their minds about *Pong*. He sent sales reports to them that were downplayed by a third of *Pong*'s actual earnings in bars, yet Bally believed that even those figures had been inflated. Bushnell finally sent Bally one of the remaining hand-built *Pong* units so the executives could try it out for themselves. But it didn't matter. They simply weren't interested in *Pong*, no matter what.

Bushnell, Dabney and Alcorn pondered how they should proceed. The ten hand-built machines were each averaging $400 a week, a substantial amount in 1972. With earnings like that, it only made sense for the three members of Atari to produce the machines themselves. The only problem was that Bally technically owned the game, since it had paid Atari $24,000 for a videogame. Dabney wrote a letter to Bally, telling them that if they didn't want *Pong*, they had to officially reject it in writing. They complied, and *Pong* belonged to Atari, free and clear.

Release of the First Videogame Console

While Bushnell and Dabney were wondering what they were going to do with their arcade ball-and-paddle game, Magnavox began promoting its home version with heavy print and television advertising. The console was released in September 1972 and retailed for $100. But the Odyssey didn't take off as rapidly as Magnavox had anticipated. As it turned out, the company did a poor job promoting the console. There is no actual recorded number that tells how many people shied away from the device because they simply didn't comprehend it. Somehow, potential customers misunderstood the advertising, and were under the impression that the Odyssey would only play on Magnavox television sets.

To make matters even worse, Magnavox only sold the game through its own network of stores, where some overly zealous salesmen probably supported the myth that the game was incompatible with other manufacturers' TV sets, just so they could sell Magnavox televisions along with the Odysseys. The additional circuit boards and the optional light rifle wound up beneath the retailers' counters, where they were eventually forgotten. Additionally, by limiting the game to its own stores, Magnavox lost all of the impulse buyers who were shopping elsewhere.

Releasing Pong

The Odyssey needed a catalyst to jumpstart its sales. Inadvertently, that catalytic event was triggered in California, where the founders of Atari decided to build 50 additional *Pong* units. Bushnell and Alcorn obtained the circuit boards and components, and Dabney purchased the TVs and cabinets. Dabney and Alcorn built the 50 machines by hand, and Bushnell's job was to sell them. With a list of arcade distributors in hand, he went off to try and sell the machines over the phone. His first three cold calls were successful The first distributor ordered 50 units, the second 100, and the third 150!

The three men knew that they were out of their league, as there was no way they could produce the additional 250 machines by themselves. Bushnell leased an old Santa Clara roller rink and converted it into Atari's first factory. In order to staff their facility, they visited unemployment offices and hired people off the streets to work the production line, unaware that many of the hired were criminals and hippies. Fortunately, the system worked well, and Atari shipped its first videogame on November 29, 1972.

The game was an immediate success. Just as they had with the prototypes, people lined up to play *Pong*, which was so different from the pinball machines that they were used to. And this popularity had an unexpected effect on the sales of the Odyssey. When people learned that the Odyssey's video ping-pong game was essentially a home version of *Pong*, they purchased the Magnavox console in droves. By the end of the year, Magnavox had sold over 69,000 units. Unfortunately this accounted to little more than half of the number of systems that had been actually manufactured.

At the end of 1972, Magnavox was the lone player in the home videogame market, and it would stay that way for several years, as most manufacturers viewed home videogames as a passing fad and didn't see any future in them. At the same time, Atari had the arcade videogame market all to itself. But that was about to change.

Atari Pong Cabinet

CHAPTER THREE
1973

Within six months after it began producing *Pong,* Atari had grossed over one million dollars. This quick success had a alienating effect on Bushnell. While constantly surrounding himself with people who worshipped him, he hired a PR firm to promote himself, not Atari. Dabney, who hadn't been overly impressed by all of the money the company had made, became disenchanted with Bushnell's behavior. Finally, Dabney decided that he didn't need to deal with it any longer, and he had Bushnell buy out his half of the company.

Pong was a major hit throughout 1973. Atari manufactured 10,000 units, an astounding number considering that pinball makers only churned out 3,000 of their popular machines. However, things weren't really very rosy for Atari. The company that had started the entire arcade videogame industry was in danger of disappearing, due to a variable that would plague it and nearly cause its extinction ten years later.

The name of the variable was clearly "competition." Even though Atari had applied for a patent and trademark for *Pong,* the company didn't receive it in time to stop the gush of copycat games that had been released on the wave of *Pong*'s success. By the end of 1973, more than twenty-five competing companies had released 90,000 cumulative units of their own versions of video tennis. Atari only claimed 10% of a market that it should have dominated.

But some companies released versions of *Pong* that were perfectly legal. One of them was Midway, a Chicago-based manufacturer of arcade machines that was owned by Bally. In March, Midway released its first arcade videogame, *Winner,* which was its version of *Pong*. The game was one of the few legal copies, as Midway had paid Atari $200,000 to actually license *Pong*. Ironically, Bally had turned down the rights to *Pong* when Bushnell had first offered it as per their contract.

Videogames in Japan

Meanwhile, Bushnell started Atari Japan to import Atari's products. But Bushnell knew little about Japan's business culture, which frowned upon American companies and reluctantly did business with them. Bushnell also had to compete with Japanese companies that were releasing their own videogames.

Among them was Sega, which had a long and complex pedigree. The company's earliest ancestor was a Honolulu-based company called *Service Games,* which had been started in 1945 by three men, Irving Bromberg, his son Martin Bromley and James Humbert, to provide coin-op games onto military bases.[1] At the time Bromley and Humbert were employed by the U.S. Navy and had the right contacts to ensure that they would be the sole distributor of these products to the bases.

In 1951, the U.S. Congress passed the *Gambling Devices Transportation Act of 1951,* a bill that made it a crime to transport gambling devices, such as slot machines, across state and territory lines, to any state or territory where gambling was illegal. Because Service Games had to take back all of its slot machines from the military bases, it had to find a new outlet for them. Fortunately, this law didn't apply to transporting the machines out of the country. In February, 1952, Bromley sent a Service Games salesman named Richard Stewart and a mechanic named Raymond Lemaire to Japan to sell their machines on the U.S. military installations in that country. However, since the two men didn't have a financial stake in Service Games, they formed their own company called *Lemaire and Stewart,* which also did business as *Service Games of Japan*.

In September, 1953, Stewart and Lemaire rejoined their former company as equal partners when a new business, *Service Games, Panama* was incorporated. This company became the controlling corporation that the original Service Games and Service Games of Japan were under.

The first use of the Sega name occurred as a trademark for a slot machine in April, 1954. The word was formed from the first two letters of **SE**rvice **GA**mes. Unfortunately, the various Service Games companies were under investigation for a battery of charges including, smuggling, fraud, bribery and tax evasion. In 1960, Service Games of Japan was abruptly shut down and replaced three days later by two new companies that acquired its assets: *Nihon Kikai Seizo,* which manufactured coin-op slot and amusement machines, and *Nihon Goraku Bussan,* which distributed them. Raymond Lemaire was in charge of the manufacturing company, and Richard Stewart ran the distribution company. Both companies did business as Sega, Inc. The Sega name was officially filed for trademark protection in April, 1962.

Nihon Goraku Bussan eventually absorbed *Nihon Kikai Seizo* in 1964. A year later it acquired *Rosen Enterprises* and a new company, *Sega Enterprises, Ltd.*, was formed.

Sega Pong-Tron

Rosen Enterprises had been founded in 1951 by an American named David Rosen, who had returned to Japan following World War II with plans to marry his Japanese girlfriend. Initially, Rosen Enterprises exported art. In 1954, Rosen began importing instant-photo booths from the United States, and these were very successful. Rosen then modified the imported booths and improved them. In 1957 Rosen began importing coin-op games.

Rosen was appointed CEO of the new Sega Enterprises, Ltd. The company began producing new arcade games for the Japanese market, which challenged the American imports. Their first major game was a mechanical submarine simulator called *Periscope,* which became a worldwide hit in 1966.[2] Three years later, Gulf & Western, the parent company of Paramount Pictures, purchased Sega. Rosen remained with the company as CEO. Sega continued to release mechanical arcade games, including pinball machines, for several years. In July 1973, the company entered a new realm when it introduced a *Pong* clone called *Pong-Tron.*

Although *Pong-Tron* was the first Japanese-built videogame to appear, it had been preceded by the release of a game called *Elepong,* from another Japanese company, Taito. The Taito Trading Company had been founded in 1953 by a Russian businessman named Michael Kogan. Initially, Kogan had successfully brewed and sold the first Japanese vodka. He also imported peanut-vending machines and sold them in Japan. In 1954, he began importing jukeboxes from the United States, and two years later, began manufacturing his own. The company then expanded into selling and leasing amusement equipment. In 1972, it officially changed its name to Taito Corporation.

Taito began purchasing used *Pong* machines from Atari. It then refurbished and distributed them under the *Elepong* name. However, this proved to be an expensive and tedious process, and Taito management realized that they could produce their own *Pong* clones inexpensively. Tomohiro Nishikado was the only Taito employee who had experience with electrical circuits, so he was assigned the task of creating the company's first games. He created two. *Soccer* was basically another *Pong* clone, with an added twist. To score, a player not only had to get the ball past his opponent's paddle, but into the narrow, centered goal behind it. The playing field was completely surrounded by a white border that the ball bounced off of when hit. Along both sides of the field were goals, openings in the border, which were the only places through which the ball could score. The screen was also green, instead of black, to simulate a soccer field. The second game, *Davis Cup*, was also a *Pong* clone, but it allowed four people to play at one time, and was the first videogame to do so.

Taito Elepong

More Games From Atari

Atari's second game, released in July, did not follow the ball-and-paddle theme that was being copied *en masse*. In *Space Race*, each player controlled a small spaceship that started at the bottom of the screen and had to make its way to the top, while avoiding obstacles that passed across the screen. The ships could only fly upwards, but players could control their speed in order to avoid the obstacles, which forced them back to the bottom of the screen if they collided. A point was awarded when a ship reached the top of the screen, which would then reappear at the bottom to try again. The player with the most points when time ran out was the winner.

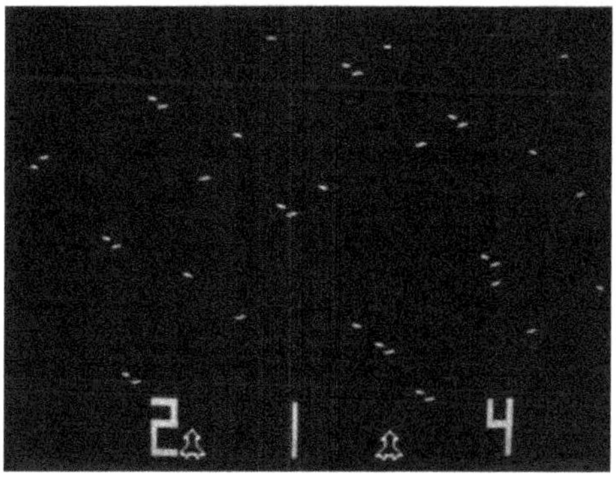

Atari Space Race

Since *Space Race* was not a ball-and-paddle game, it required a different controller than a dial. Atari opted to use a joystick controller. This was a rod that stuck out from the cabinet and could be pushed forward to make the ship go faster, or backward to slow it down.

Although Midway had paid to license *Pong* from Atari, Bally management realized that they had already paid Bushnell and Dabney to produce a videogame for them. Although they had turned down *Pong* when it was offered to them, Bally determined that Atari still owed them a videogame. Rather than fight, Bushnell offered *Space Race*, which Midway quickly released under the name *Asteroid*. Atari then stopped manufacturing *Space Race* and disposed the units that had already been made.

For its next game, Atari returned to the ball and paddle theme with *Pong Doubles*. This was a version of *Pong* that allowed up to four players to compete at one time. The screen displayed two sets of paddles and the cabinet featured two pairs of controllers, one for each paddle on the screen.

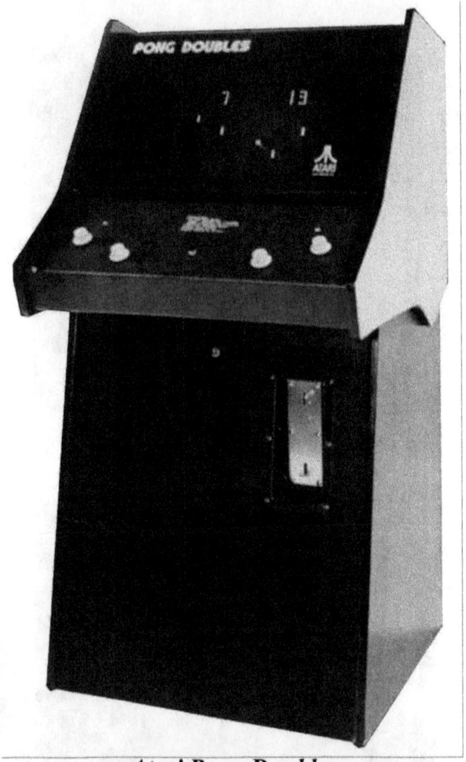

Atari Pong Doubles

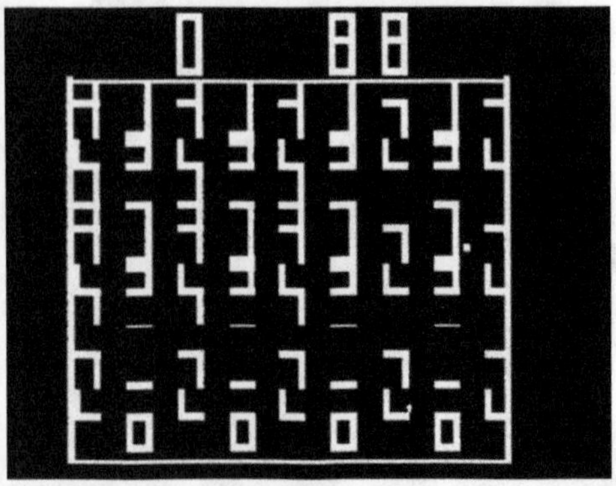

Atari Gotcha

Atari also released *Gotcha,* which was a chase game where one player (a square) pursued another player (a plus sign) through a maze. The game was controversial because of its controllers. Although joysticks were the logical choice for this game, some engineers commented that the joystick was a phallic symbol, and that they preferred to produce a "female game" instead. What they came up with were two large, round, pink orbs that protruded from the cabinet, and these orbs needed to be squeezed in order to make the square and plus sign move. After being bombarded with complaints, Atari manufactured all-new *Gotcha* machines with joysticks.

Nolan Bushnell realized that merely having good, innovative games wasn't enough if people didn't get to play them. So he was determined to get Atari's games into as many arcades and other public gathering places as possible. And Bushnell knew that the key to this strategy was to sign contracts with as many distributors as he could. Distributors usually covered particular territories, and in many cases, a territory only had one distributor representing it. However, a problem that Bushnell encountered was that large, populous territories could each have two distributors representing them. Because of exclusivity practices that had been in place since the pinball days, two distributors within the same geographical territory could not represent the same manufacturer.

In turn, the end customer, the arcade or bar owner who wanted to lease or purchase an arcade machine, only did business with one distributor. Therefore, if Bushnell had a contract with one distributor in a territory, the customers who did business with the other distributors wouldn't be able to obtain Atari machines for their locations. And even though *Pong* was a major hit, arcade operators would willingly lease a *Pong* clone if the original wasn't available. Bushnell found this practice abhorrent, and set out to do something about it.

Bushnell's reaction to the exclusivity problem was ridiculously simple. On October 1, 1973, he formed a new company, Kee Games, to take care of the distributors who couldn't buy from Atari. Kee Games was named after and headed by Joe Keenan, a close friend of Bushnell's. Atari and Kee Games were completely autonomous, to the point at which they had their own separate research departments.

A four-player *Pong* variant called *Elimination* was the first game released by Kee Games. Unlike in *Pong Doubles* where multiple players acted in concert, in *Elimination,* all players competed against each other. While *Pong* had "goals" on each side of the playfield, *Elimination*[3] also featured goals along the top and bottom of the playfield. The object of the game was for each player to use their paddle to block a ball from passing through the goal that they controlled. If a ball passed through a player's goal four times,

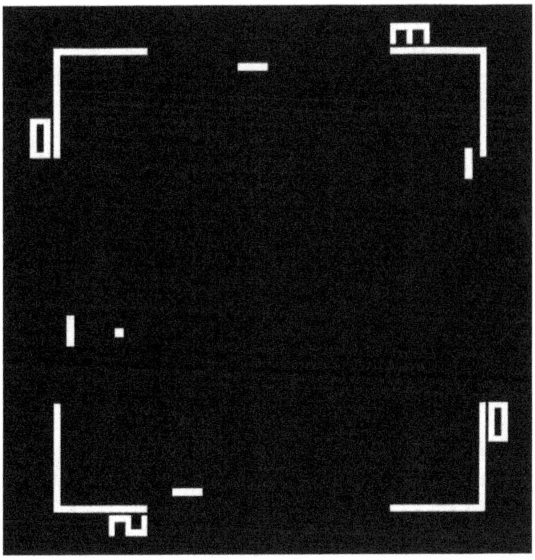

Kee Games Eliminator

the player would be eliminated and their paddle would disappear and their goal would close into a solid wall. The sole player remaining would be the winner.

Instead of being housed in a cabinet, *Elimination* was the first videogame housed in what appeared to be a table.[4] Players looked down at the screen at that formed the top of the table and paddle controllers were located at each corner of the table.

Despite Atari's problems, 1973 was a great year for coin-operated videogames, as the industry broke away from the ball-and-paddle theme with exciting, new games. The home videogame industry wasn't as thriving, and Magnavox remained the sole player in the field. After a healthy first year on the market, sales of the Odyssey had crumbled in 1973, mainly due to the mistakes made by Magnavox.

Because Magnavox didn't sell as many Odysseys as it had manufactured, the company halted all production and advertising. By the end of 1973, the company that had pioneered the home videogaming industry looked at it as a dead market. Fortunately, the company that had started the coin-operated videogame industry didn't agree.

CHAPTER FOUR
1974-1976

Although Magnavox had been aware of *Pong* and its similarities to the Odyssey's video ping-pong game, it did nothing to suppress the manufacture and sale of the arcade game. At first, the quantities of infringing machines being built by Atari and others were not sufficient enough to initiate an expensive lawsuit. But by 1974, the situation had changed, as large numbers of games that violated Ralph Baer's patents began appearing. Therefore, Magnavox and Sanders decided to sue several of these firms for patent infringement, a procedure that would become all too familiar in the years to follow. In Atari's case, Nolan Bushnell insisted that he hadn't copied *Pong* from the Odyssey, but a U.S. District Judge didn't see it that way.

District Judge John F. Grady stated that Bushnell couldn't persuade him that he had dreamed up the video-tennis idea before he witnessed the Odyssey demonstration. As far as the judge was concerned, the co-founder of Atari had plainly copied the Odyssey's patented game play, which involved the interaction and behavior of manually and machine-controlled objects. Rather than try to defend Atari in a lawsuit that Bushnell estimated would cost the company $1.5 million in fees that it couldn't afford, he finally decided to settle out of court. Atari paid Magnavox $800,000 in June 1976, to become Magnavox's first licensee. Atari had gotten off easy. Other companies that produced videogames, including Chicago Dynamic and Seeburg, elected to challenge Magnavox in court, where they eventually lost and were penalized large sums of money in restitution and fines.

Innovative Leisure

Atari was one of the few companies that invested in the development of new videogames. However, it soon ran into financial difficulties, because its games were eventually illegally copied by dozens of other companies that Atari then had to compete with. Many of Atari's games were so pioneering that a tag-line, "Innovative Leisure," was created to describe its business.[1]

In June 1974, Atari released a game that was a departure from the direction in which the company had been heading. *Touch-Me* was neither a videogame nor a pinball machine. The machine consisted of four giant buttons, each containing a light. The computer randomly flashed the lights, and the player had to recreate the sequence from memory by pressing the buttons in the same order in which the lights had flashed. *Touch-Me* was a failure, at least in the arcades.

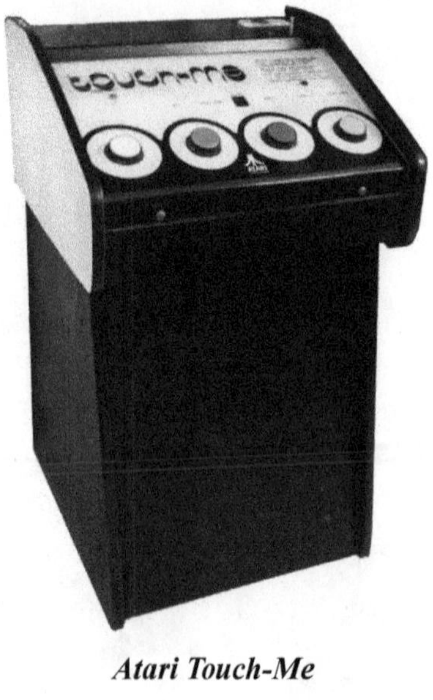

Atari Touch-Me

Fortunately, Atari continued to devise creative videogames as well. *Gran Trak 10* was the first driving game, and its controller was an actual steering wheel that was connected to the cabinet, which also featured a four-position gear shift, along with accelerator and brake pedals. But the game also featured advances in internal hardware. The sprites that formed the on-screen cars and time and score displays were stored, for the first time, in computer memory. Atari followed the one-player *Gran Trak 10* with *Gran Trak 20*, the first two-player racing game. Its oversized cabinet featured two

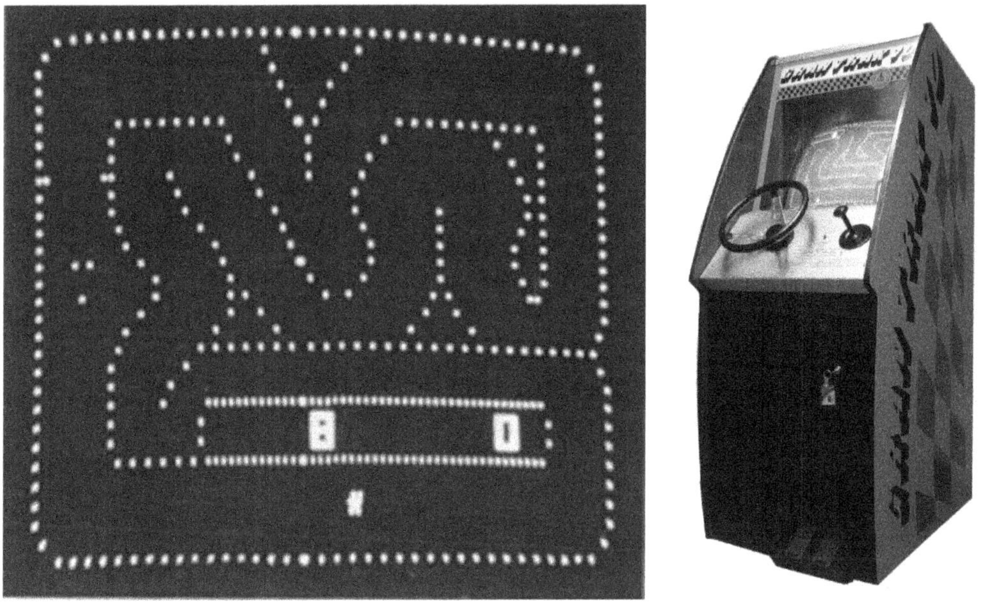

Atari Gran Trak 10

full-size steering wheels that allowed for head-to-head competition.

Taito

But Atari wasn't alone in revolutionizing videogames. Taito in Japan was also making pioneering strides. Tomohiro Nishikado's *Basketball* was similar to his previous *Soccer*, with some important, historic differences. As in *Soccer*, players controlled on-screen paddles.

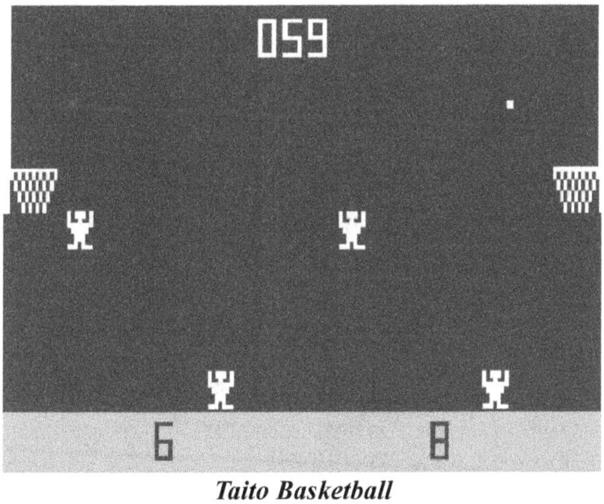

Taito Basketball

The rectangular "paddles" from the earlier game were replaced with sprites which, for the first time, actually resembled human figures. And some of the playing field's pixels were designed to look like baskets. Instead of the ball traveling in a horizontal direction and bouncing off paddles, it traveled in a vertical direction and bounced off the on-screen players. The object of the game was to bounce the ball off an on-screen character, and then have it rebound off the border at the top of the screen, and then finally fall into a basket.

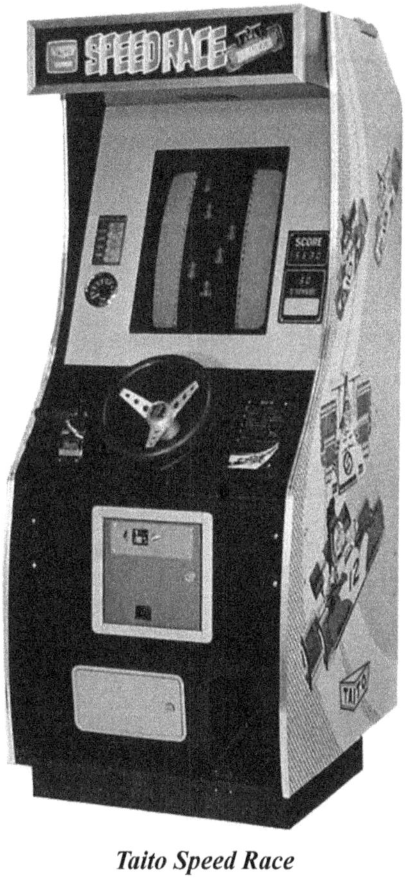

Taito Speed Race

Basketball also had the distinction of being the first Japanese game to be licensed by an American company. In February, 1975, Midway released the game in the United States, where it was called *TV Basketball*.

Nishikado's next game, *Speed Race*, borrowed elements from his earlier *Astro Race* and Atari's *Gran Trak 10*. Like the latter game, *Speed Race*'s controls consisted of a steering wheel, a shift and a foot pedal. The format of the game was the same as *Astro Race's*, where the player controlled an object, in this case an Indy racer, and had to avoid other cars on the roadway by steering to the left or right. But whereas the ship in *Astro Race* traveled to the top of the screen and reappeared at the bottom, the car in *Speed Race* remained at the bottom of the screen as the opposing cars traveled down from the top. This was the first use of a scrolling playfield as this gave the appearance that the player's car was travelling along a playfield that was not limited to inside the TV screen.

Nishikado's following game for Taito was also licensed by Midway. In *Western Gun*, the player controlled an on-screen cowboy who was caught in a gunfight against an opposing cowboy, who was controlled by the computer in one-player games or by a second player in two-player games. The playfield also featured obstacles, such as cactuses and rocks and the cowboys looked almost human, in a comical sort of way. Each player used two joysticks. One was an eight-directional stick that controlled the cowboy's movement. The other was in the shape of a pistol grip and could be pushed forward or backward to change the angle of the cowboy's aim. It also had a trigger that was used to fire the cowboy's gun. *Western Gun* was notable for being the first videogame to depict human-against-human combat, and the first game to display an on-screen gun.

Integrated Circuits

When Midway released *Western Gun* in the United States, they completely altered it.
4 The game's title was changed to *Gun Fight* and the graphics were completely transformed. The rocks were removed and replaced, in later levels, by stagecoaches. The cowboys' bodies became more proportional with real humans, although they became featureless silhouettes. But that wasn't all that was changed.

For more than a decade, discrete components,[2] which were used to build videogames, had gradually become smaller, faster and less expensive. They eventually reached the point at which they became small enough to be stamped onto small silicon chips called integrated circuits (ICs). These ICs had been in their infancy when Ralph Baer began working on his Brown Box, but at that time, they were too expensive to be effectively used in consumer products. *Pong*, on the other hand, had been designed with three ICs.

Despite whether the machine used discrete components or integrated circuits, game logic could only follow the paths that the circuitry led it down, and this couldn't be changed. These primitive game machines were not computers. They could neither store nor process new information. And the ability to design and build them was left to electrical engineers.

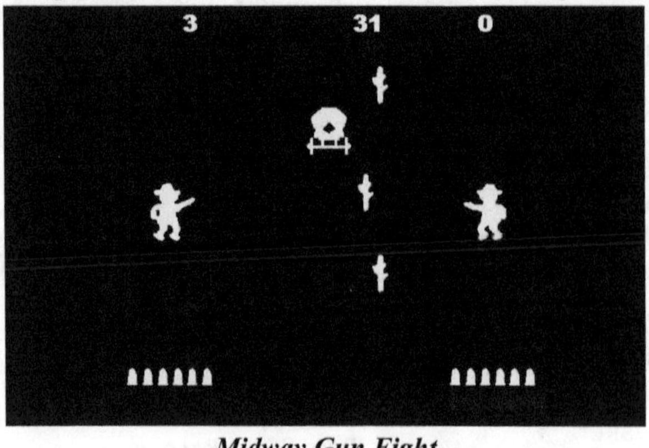

Midway Gun Fight

This changed in the late '60s, with the advent of microprocessors from Texas Instruments and Intel. Basically, a microprocessor is a very complex integrated circuit. Intel's first microprocessor, the 4004, which was released in late 1971, contained 2,300 transistors. But it also included a central processing unit (CPU), the actual brains of a computer. The CPU could perform arithmetic and logical operations, and extract and decode instructions from memory, which was stored on a separate chip.

Bally was interested in making the move from electromechanical pinball machines to solid state. In 1974 it had contracted with Dave Nutting Associates (DNA) to do the preliminary groundwork in creating solid state machines.[3]

Bally supplied a electromechanical pinball machine *Flicker*, which DNA replaced all of its wires and circuitry with integrated circuits that were controlled by an Intel 4004. Based on DNA's prototype *Flicker*, Bally established its own internal group to design solid state pinball machines. Once Bally and other manufacturers began releasing microprocessor-controlled machines, sales for existing mechanical pinball machines came to a halt.[45]

Midway, the videogame arm of Bally, next wanted to do the same thing with videogames. After it licensed *Western Gun* from Taito, DNA was asked by Midway to redesign it around a microprocessor. DNA successfully utilized an Intel 8080 processor, and the resulting *Gun Fight* became the first videogame to employ a microprocessor. Unlike the previous videogames that had been built from discrete logic chips that required engineers to put together, the microprocessor-based game needed computer programmers. Jay Fenton and Tom McHugh, two computer science students, were given that assignment.

Taito's Nishikado was impressed with the results. Although he believed that his *Western Gun* was more fun, he thought that the graphics and animation in *Gun Fight* were better. He decided to incorporate microprocessors in all games that he designed from then on.

Namco

As Japanese games were becoming available in the United States, Atari Japan was having a difficult time getting its games distributed in Japan, because few Japanese distributors wanted to deal with an American-based company. With Atari Japan nearly bankrupt, Bushnell decided to sell it and took bids. Several Japanese arcade companies showed an interest, but Sega's $50,000 bid was the highest, until it was outbid by Namco.

Nakamura Manufacturing began in 1955 by Masaya Nakamura, to operate a children's rocking-horse ride on the roof of a Yokohama department store. In 1958, after the company expanded into Tokyo, it reorganized and was renamed the Nakamura Manufacturing Company. In 1965 it released its first arcade game, a massive three-player mechanical coin-operated game called *Periscope*. In 1970, it produced *Racer*, an electromechanical game that was housed in an arcade-style cabinet. Two years later, the company began calling itself Namco, an abbreviation of **NA**kamura **M**anufacturing **CO**mpany.

Namco saw Atari Japan as its way to enter the new videogame industry, and submitted a bid of $800,000, scaring all other potential suitors out of the running. In the end, Namco acquired Atari Japan for $500,000, which gave it the exclusive Japanese rights to Atari's titles for ten years.

The half-million dollars that Atari received from the sale of Atari Japan helped its cash flow. But it still wasn't enough.

Kee Games' Success

During the first half of 1974, Kee Games released three new games that were all knockoffs of Atari games. Kee Games' *Spike* was Atari's *Rebound*. *Formula K* and its sequel *Twin Racer* were modeled after Atari's racing games, *Gran Trak 10* and *Gran Trak 20*. Kee Games introduced its first original game in November 1974. *Tank* featured two combat tanks that had to navigate through a

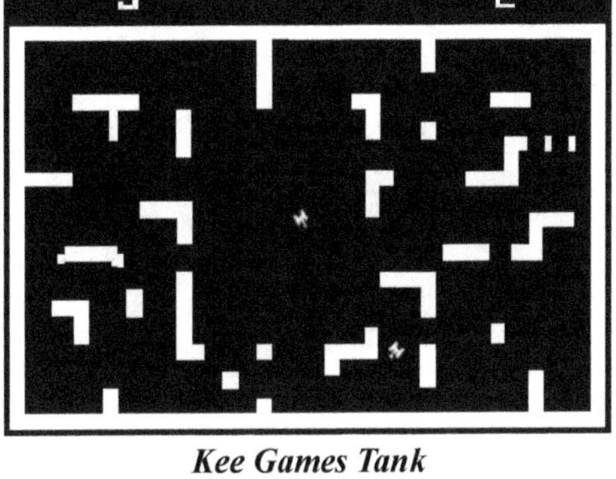

Kee Games Tank

maze while avoiding land mines, in an effort to shoot at each other and amass points. Each player utilized a pair of joysticks to control the movements of their tank. By pushing the pair of joysticks forward and back in different configurations, players could make their tanks move forward, stop or turn. Each player's right joystick also had a firing button at its top, which was used to fire shells. The graphics in *Tank* were more detailed than in prior games, because it utilized ROM chips to store the addresses of the graphics.

Tank was so successful that distributors who weren't doing business with Kee Games because of their exclusivity agreements, requested to purchase it. Atari desperately needed a hit in order to generate much-needed cash. The company could have released a similar tank game with its own title in order to raise the money it needed but Bushnell realized that such a game would have been perceived as a *Tank* knock-off. So instead of Atari distributing a *Tank* clone, Bushnell decided to have Atari release the real thing. In order to obtain the rights to *Tank*, Atari successfully "merged" with Kee Games, and Joe Keenan, who had been very successful at managing his company, became Atari's new president.

Following the merger, Kee Games officially became a subsidiary of Atari and continued to release games. On February 3, 1975, it released *Indy 800*, an 8-player update of its overhead-racing *Formula K* from the year before. Its 25-inch screen was mounted upwards in the center of a four-sided cabinet that measured 16 square feet. Each side of the cabinet could accommodate two players with their own steering wheels and gas and brake pedals. The game was very popular and even had a remote starter that allowed arcade operators to hold tournaments. Two large mirrors could be hung from the top, so spectators could watch the action.

On March 11, 1975, roughly one month after Kee Games released *Indy 800*, Atari introduced a different type of racing game. In the single-player *Hi-Way*, the player steered an on-screen car along a very curvy road. The object of the game was to travel as far as

Atari Indy 800

Kee Games Hi-Way

possible in the allotted time. Driving off of the road, or colliding with another car, slowed down the player's progress.

As in *Indy 800*, the screen displayed an overhead view of the road. The player's car remained at the bottom center of the screen, and the player could only steer to the left or right. The road, with many randomly generated curves, scrolled downwards. Pressing the accelerator pedal increased the speed of the scrolling.

Hi-Way was housed in a fiberglass cabinet, similar to *Computer Space's.* But the design was completely new, as it also included a seat that allowed the player to sit in front of the screen and access the steering wheel and accelerator, as if he were driving a real car. The idea of a *sit-down* cabinet was so original that Atari received a patent for it on October 20, 1975.

Controversy

Not all driving games were contests where players raced against others and had to avoid objects that got in their way. In 1975, Exidy released a 1 or 2 player game called *Destruction Derby*. In this game, each player controlled their own cars on the screen, which they could steer using their own steering wheel, move by pressing down on the accelerator pedal with their foot, and switch between forward and reverse by pressing a gear shift lever.

As the cars moved around the screen according to where the players propelled them, computer-controlled drone cars also travelled in unpredictable paths around the screen, and slightly faster than the human-controlled cars. The object of the game was to crash into the other cars and knock them out of commission. Although dead cars would then remain on the screen for the controlled cars to avoid, a new drone would take its place. The object of the game was to have to have the last remaining operable car. Of course this meant that even in two-player games, the computer could be the victor.

Destruction Derby was an immediate hit for Exidy. But Exidy ceased production of the game when it licensed it to Chicago Coin, who released the game as *Demolition Derby*. The problem here was that Chicago Coin was on the brink of bankruptcy, and could not pay Exidy the royalties that it owed. Exidy soon found itself in a quandary. It couldn't again produce *Destruction Derby* because of its contract with Chicago Coin, yet it couldn't collect any income on the game because of Chicago Coin's dire financial condition.

Exidy's solution was to devise a game that had similar play mechanics as *Destruction Derby*. However, Exidyreplaced the computer-controlled drone cars with humanoid-like creatures called gremlins. The object of the new game was to score as many points as possible by driving into these gremlins, which when hit, emitted an audible scream and was replaced by an unmovable tombstone. This new game, which was released in April, 1975, was called *Death Race.*[6]

Death Race became an instant hit just like *Destruction Derby*, and lines formed outside of arcades as people waited to play. One line at a Seattle shopping center was noticed by an Associated Press reporter who had been shopping at the mall. She followed the line into the arcade and made her way to the *Death Race* machine, which she watched in play. She was immediately horrified as she watched kids directing their on-screen car to run over what she thought were fleeing people. She quickly filed a story about how terrible the game was, and it was picked up by most newspapers in the country. Pretty soon everyone heard about this

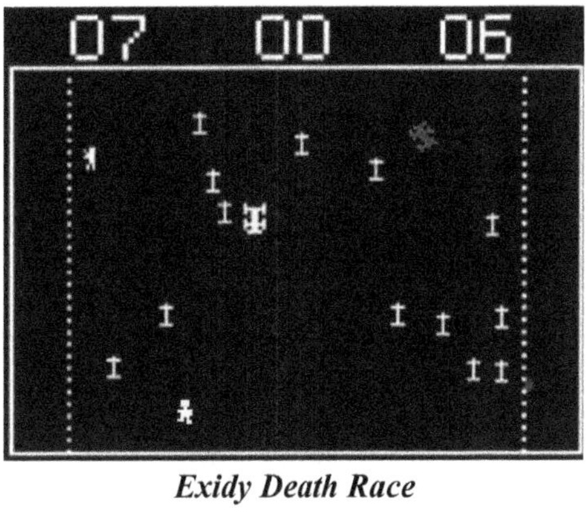

Exidy Death Race

violent game called *Death Race* and people began protesting this new form of sadistic entertainment that their children were being subject to.

Electra Pace Car Pro

Colorful Images

In 1974, Nutting Associates released the first commercial arcade game that used a color monitor.[7] *Wimbledon* was a *Pong*-clone that featured a green playfield surrounded by white borders. The paddles on the left were red and the ones on the right were blue and the colors of the numerical scores at the top of the screen matched the paddles that they represented. While it looked nice, the color didn't add to the game's playability. On December 10, 1974, Electra Industries released *Pace Car Pro*, an indy-racer type game that was similar to Kee Games' *Indy 800*, which would follow two months later. Up to four players each controlled their own car using joysticks that had knobs that were color coordinated with one of the on-screen cars. The center of the screen displayed the number of laps that each car completed, each numeral in the same color as the car it represented. Color was used in a similar way in *Indy 800*, where each player's score was displayed directly in front of where he stood, and the color of the numerals matched the corresponding car.

Since black & white monitors cost substantially less than color ones, videogame manufacturers continued to use them and employed color overlays whenever color was required.

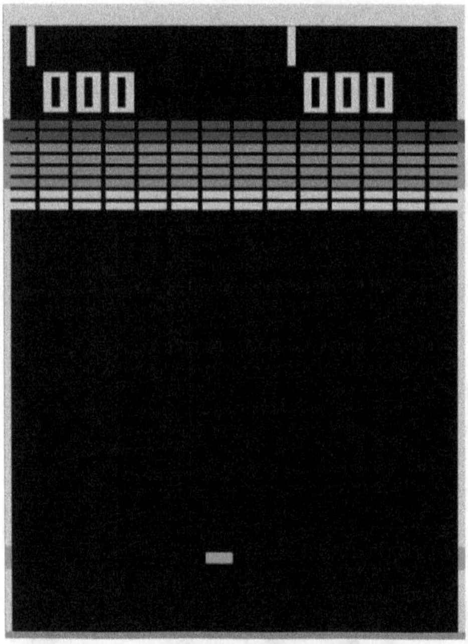

Atari Breakout

Breakout

Atari returned to its roots and released *Breakout* on April 20, 1976. This game was the culmination of the ball-and-paddle evolution that had originated with *Pong*. In this game, the player controlled a paddle that moved horizontally along the bottom of the screen. Near the top of the screen were four sets of two rows, each comprised of fourteen bricks. Each pair of rows was a different color.[8] As a ball descended towards the bottom of the screen, the player had to deflect it with the paddle or lose a turn. Three misses ended the game. But if the ball was hit back towards the bricks, then each brick that was struck was removed and scored points, which varied by the color of the row. The object of the game was to clear the screen of all the bricks. When this happened, the screen refreshed with a new set of 112 bricks. The game ended successfully for the player when the second screen was completely cleared.

Breakout turned out to be the hit that Atari so desperately needed. In fact, it was the most popular game that Atari had released up to that point.

Video Pinball

But in 1975, a year before *Breakout* was released, it was still unclear whether or not videogames would overtake pinball machines in sales. Gottlieb stayed clear away from videogames, and continued to strictly design and manufacture pinball machines. But many of the other long-time pinball companies weren't willing to take any chances, and waddled into the videogame waters. Williams released two *Pong* clones in 1973, the two-player *Paddle-Ball* and the four-player *Pro Tennis*, before retreating from the industry and returning strictly to pinball for several years. Also in 1973, Bally released a *Pong* clone called *Crazy Foot* only in Belgium. The company never released another videogame anywhere under its own name. However, in 1976, it turned Midway, which it had purchased in 1969, into its videogame division.

Chicago Coin, one of the world's oldest pinball manufacturers, also released two *Pong* clones in 1973. But the company also released two videogames that contained the company's pinball DNA. Its *TV Pin Game* was the first to incorporate pinball and video, although the former was simulated on the latter, as opposed to the incorporation of a physical pinball table. Although the game featured bumpers, pockets and moving targets, one of the main ingredients of pinball, flippers, were oddly missing. Instead, the player rebounded balls with a dial that controlled a paddle that moved along the bottom of the screen. Atari released *Pin Pong* a year later. It actually had flippers, which were controlled by buttons located on both sides of the cabinet, as on a real pinball machine. Chicago Coin came back

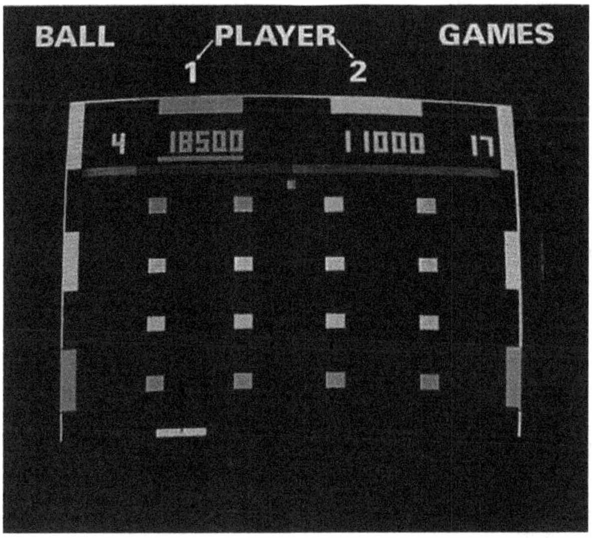

Chicago Coin TV Pin Game

Chicago Coin Super Flipper

in 1975 with *Super Flipper*, a full-sized pinball table that had a monitor that faced upward and replaced the familiar, physical pinball playfield. Pulling a plunger released a ball into play, and the score was displayed digitally on the back-glass. But again, Chicago Coin missed the mark with a video pinball game. While the table featured flipper buttons on each side, those buttons controlled horizontally moving paddles.

As most of the pinball companies were dabbling in videogames, the original videogame company delved into the pinball world. In 1975, Atari started a pinball division, with the goal of creating pinball machines that were as innovative as its videogames. Its first machine, *The Atarians*, was test-marketed in November 1976, and introduced the type of pinball machines that Atari would offer: wider tables, up to four players, and complete solid-state microprocessors that controlled the gameplay. But all these extras would not come cheap. At the time of its release, *The Atarians,* with a price tag of $1,295, was the most expensive pinball machine ever produced.

Additional Odysseys

Although approximately 300,000 Odyssey home consoles had been sold between 1972 and 1975, Magnavox concluded that it couldn't continue marketing the console. Because it had been built using discrete solid-state circuits and was packaged with literally hundreds of extra pieces, the Odyssey was too expensive to manufacture and sell. Ralph Baer had recognized this early in 1973, and began researching integrated circuits as a way to reduce its costs. In May 1974, Magnavox signed an agreement for Texas Instruments (TI) to design chips that would reproduce some of the Odyssey games. Two new consoles that utilized these chips were released in 1975.

The *Odyssey 100* was built around four TI chips that duplicated two simple games from the original Odyssey, tennis and hockey. The controllers, while built into the unit, were reminiscent of the original console's as they contained separate knobs for horizontal, vertical and "English" control. Since it was basically the original Odyssey on a few chips, it didn't feature on-screen scoring. However, the hardware featured two physical, sliding bars that allowed players to keep score manually.

The *Odyssey 200,* which was released later in 1975, contained two additional chips that included a third game called *Smash*. The 200 was the first home console that allowed

4

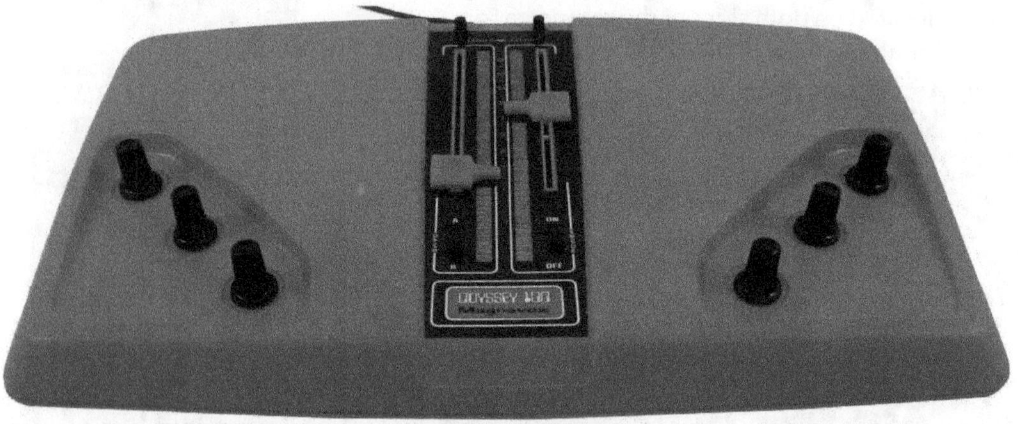

Magnavox Odyssey 100

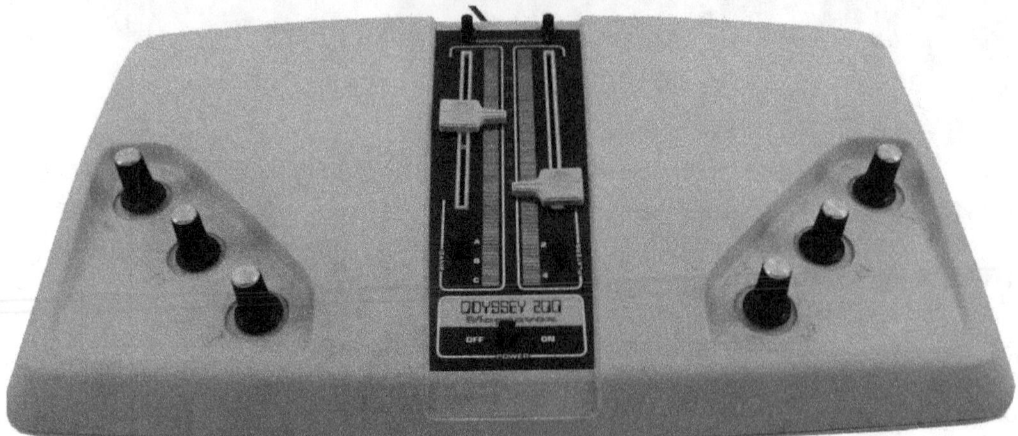

Magnavox Odyssey 200

up to four players to compete at once. It also included a rudimentary on-screen scoring system that consisted of a series of small rectangles that advanced across the top of the screen whenever someone scored.[9]

Although Baer wasn't satisfied with the technical innovation in these new consoles, he was at least encouraged that Magnavox wasn't abandoning home videogame consoles.

By Christmas 1975, Magnavox had sold all of the Odyssey 100 and 200 consoles that it had produced. Sadly, the company only manufactured 180,000 units combined, even though its own marketing department had recommended that they produce four times that number.

Home Pong

By the end of 1975, Magnavox wasn't the only company selling home videogame consoles. In early 1974, an Atari engineer named Harold Lee had proposed to build a home version of *Pong*. Initially, most of Atari's top management was against entering the consumer market. Their fears were understandable, because they felt that Atari's cash, which, thanks to *Tank*, was only starting to become manageable, would be tied up in inventory that would only sell primarily at Christmas. They also worried because Atari knew nothing at all about distributing consumer goods. But Nolan Bushnell thought that a home version of *Pong* was a good idea, and he gave Lee the go-ahead. *Pong's* original designer, Al Alcorn, and a third engineer, Bob Brown, were added to the project.

The goal of the three engineers was not to produce a console similar to the Odyssey with the *Pong* name on it, even though they believed that such a unit would sell. They decided to go one step further and take all of the electronic components that comprised the arcade *Pong*, and shrink them down onto one custom chip. By the fall of 1974, they achieved what they had set out to do. The game that the home *Pong* unit played was exactly the same as the arcade version, right down to the sounds and on-screen scoring, a feature that all of the Magnavox consoles lacked.

In January 1975, Bushnell and his team had tried selling the home version of *Pong* on their own, but were not successful. They believed that the product needed to be sold in toy stores, but they couldn't find any that were interested. They then decided to try major department stores, beginning with Sears. The toy buyer at Sears wasn't interested, so they next tried the sporting-goods department, with the belief that a computer version of tennis might sell alongside the real thing. The sporting-goods buyer, Tom Quinn, agreed with them.

Quinn offered to buy all the *Pongs* that Atari could put together. When he was told that they could only manufacture 75,000 units, he told Bushnell to double the production, and that Sears would finance it. In return, Sears wanted to exclusively sell the game throughout 1975. Although Atari wouldn't allow this, it did promise that all Sears orders would be fulfilled first. Sears ordered every unit that came off of the assembly line thus guaranteeing the exclusivity that it wanted.

Bushnell jumped at the offer. Since Sears promised to pay for all of the advertising and to assume complete control of distribution, Atari had little to risk.

Sears sold *Pong* under the Tele-Games label[10] in its 900 stores across the United States. Thanks to this deal, Atari sold $40 million worth of *Pongs* in 1975, netting the company $3 million. The Sears *Pongs* were the hottest toys during the 1975 Christmas season.

Boxed Atari Pong

Sears Tele-Games Pong

In 1976, Atari began selling *Pong* consoles under its own name in stores other than Sears, while Sears continued to sell them under the Tele-Games label in its stores. Atari improved on the product throughout the year, which resulted in the release of several additional consoles. *Pong Doubles* allowed four players to compete at one time. *Super Pong* was for two players and contained four different games. *Super Pong Ten* allowed four players to compete in ten different games.

4

Sears also sold these consoles in its stores under the Tele-Games label. In some cases, the names were changed from their Atari counterparts. Atari's *Pong Doubles*, for example, became Tele-Games' *Pong IV*. In other cases, there were some differences between the Atari consoles and their Tele-Games counterparts. Atari's *Super Pong* had built-in paddle controllers, while the Tele-Games model included detachable controllers. Sears also released an exclusive console that had been built by Atari but didn't have an official Atari counterpart. *Speedway IV* was basically a home version of Taito's *Speed Race,* in which players controlled on-screen cars that appeared to travel up the screen while avoiding obstacles.

But Atari also released an exclusive non-*Pong* console that was not available at Sears. In fact, Bob Brown's *Video Music* was not even a videogame. It was a component that sat between an audio system and a television. When music was filtered from the amplifier through the *Video Music* unit, it sent signals to the television, displaying a light show on

Atari Video Music

the screen that danced to the rhythm of the music. But *Video Music* did poorly in the retail arena, and Atari discontinued it after a year.

In 1975, home videogames began taking off in Japan. According to the Japanese business newspaper, *Nihon Keizai Shimbun*, the Magnavox Odyssey was imported into Japan on April 17, 1975, where it sold for ¥58,000 ($200).[11] But some companies weren't content with importing American consoles. One such toy company, Epoch, became the first Japanese company to develop its own home-grown videogame console when it released its *Electrotennis* console during the following September. The Electrotennis shared some limitations with the Odyssey, such as the inability to keep score, at least on the screen. Built into the Electrotennis console were numbered counters that players manually increased every time they scored a point. The ¥19,500 ($66) Electrotennis was only capable of playing video tennis, and as in the version that appeared on the Odyssey, players could move their paddles vertically and horizontally. However, Epoch's console also included a one-player version of video tennis. Another unique feature of the Electrotennis console was that it was completely wireless. The unit actually broadcasted its signal into the airwaves, where it was picked up by the TV's antenna.[12]

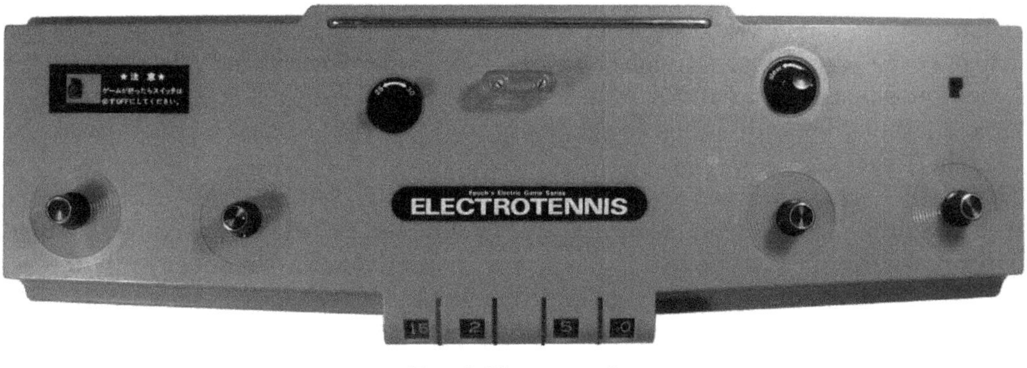

Epoch Electrotennis

Coleco

In March 1975, Ralph Baer was invited to General Instrument's Long Island factory, where he was given a preview of the chip manufacturer's new AY-3-8500 multi-game chip. Baer was immediately pleased with the chip and saw the potential in it. The Odyssey 100 had contained four TI chips, while the 200 contained six. The single General Instrument chip that Baer previewed had four paddle and two shooting games built into it, yet it only cost $5. Because he was becoming increasingly frustrated with the way Magnavox was handling the marketing of its videogames, Baer pitched the chip to an acquaintance named Arnold Greenberg, who happened to be the president of a Hartford, Connecticut company that marketed home pinball machines.

General Instrument AY-3-8500 Chip

The *Connecticut Leather Company* began in the early '30s as a distributor of leather products to shoemakers. By the early '50s, it marketed its own leather goods, and heavily used licensed properties like *Mickey Mouse* and *Howdy Doody*. In 1956, the company purchased a small vacuum-forming machine so it could produce plastic toys. The plastics line evolved into outdoor sporting equipment, including sandboxes and sleds. By 1961, when it shed most of its name in favor of an acronym, *Coleco* was the leading manufacturer of above-ground swimming pools.

Coleco Telstar

Coleco purchased Eagle Toys, a manufacturer of tabletop hockey games, in 1968. This led to the production of other home games, such as *Electric Football* and pinball machines. Home videogames were a natural progression. After seeing the AY-3-8500 chip, Greenberg placed a large order with General Instrument, and Coleco designed a system around it called the *Telstar*.

As 1975 came to a close, Coleco had approximately $30 million worth of Telstar inventory sitting in a warehouse awaiting assembly. But before Coleco could complete the final product, the console had to pass a stringent FCC Radio Frequency Interference (RFI) test. If the unit didn't pass, valuable time would be needed for Coleco's engineers to locate and fix the problem while the large inventory would continue to sit, causing a cash-flow problem for Coleco. Unfortunately, the FCC failed the system after it found too much radiation in the Channel 3/4 signals that the Telstar generated. Coleco was told to fix the problem and return for retesting by the end of that week, or else the FCC approval process would have to restart from the beginning, and potentially delay the final assembly by months.

Nobody at Coleco could figure out what was wrong, and time was running out. Greenberg decided to get assistance from Ralph Baer who, coincidentally, had controlled Sanders' RFI test lab, which happened to be the largest RFI testing facility in the Northeast. Baer quickly informed Greenberg that he would help out, but Coleco first had to sign a Licensing Agreement with Magnavox. Coleco complied and supplied Baer with a Telstar two days before the FCC's deadline. Baer and his crew spent all day trying to figure out the problem, but it came to no avail. Then, early in the morning before the deadline, Baer was in the lab alone when he realized that perhaps a small ferrite toroid (powdered iron ring) could catch the stray signals that the Telstar sent. After retrieving a ferrite toroid from a supply cabinet, Baer slipped it over the coaxial cable that connected the Telstar to a television. To his relief, he discovered that the ring had indeed solved the problem. The Telstar with a built-in ferrite toroid was then rushed back

Ferrite Toroid

to Maryland, where it passed the FCC tests.

Coleco released the Telstar in time for Father's Day, 1976. Like *Pong*, the Telstar could only play video tennis, but since it retailed for only $50, it appealed to budget-minded families. Coleco sold over 1 million units that year. One reason for the excellent sales can be traced to a severe chip shortage. Because of the onslaught of manufacturers who wanted to produce videogames, General Instrument underestimated the number of chips that it needed to fulfill the demand by 60%. Thanks to Ralph Baer, Coleco had been the first company to place an order with General Instrument, so it received its entire order. No other company received a complete order, with many only receiving 20% of what they had requested.

APF Electronics TV Fun

APF Electronics of New York City, a developer of calculators and other small electronics, was one of the companies that had received an incomplete order of AY-3-8500 chips from General Instrument. The result was the *TV Fun*, a dedicated console that featured four basic *Pong*-type games: two-player tennis, hockey and squash and the single-player handball.[13]

Magnavox was another company that received an incomplete order. The chips that it did receive were used in its next console, the *Odyssey 300*, which competed directly with Coleco's Telstar. It played the same three games as the earlier Odyssey 200, but each game now had three levels of difficulty.[14] Magnavox returned to the TI chip with

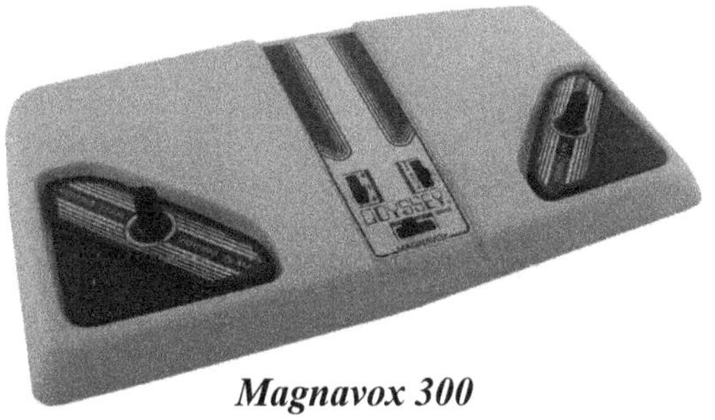

Magnavox 300

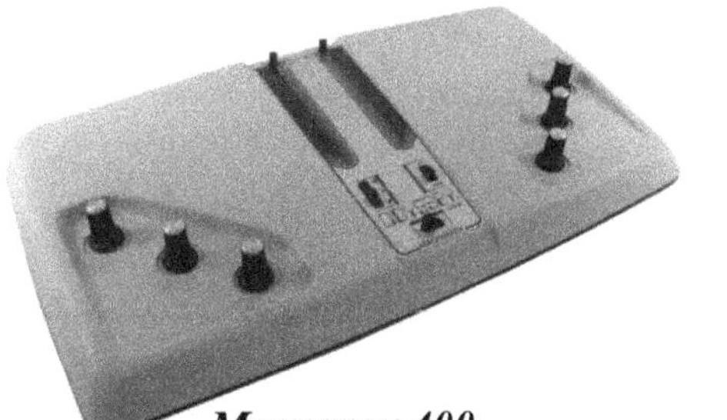

Magnavox 400

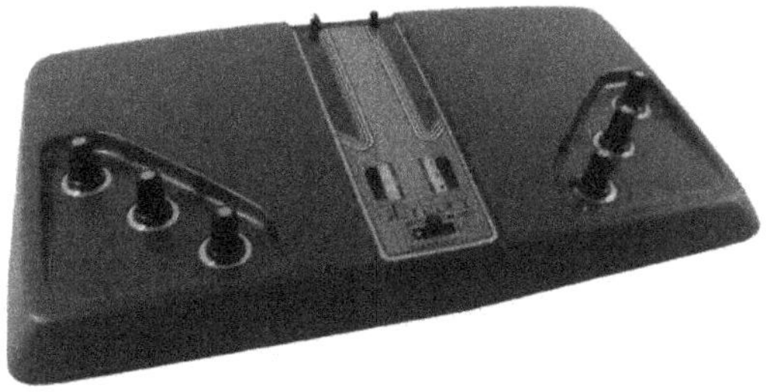

Magnavox 500

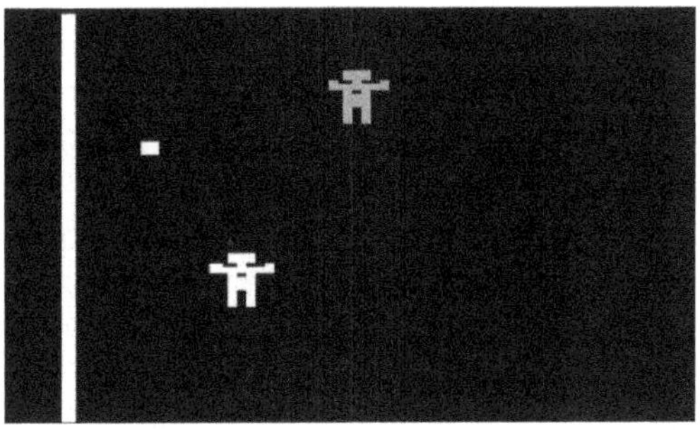

Single Character Graphics

the *Odyssey 400*, which was also basically the same as the 200, but used an additional chip that provided on-screen scoring. The 400 was followed by the *Odyssey 500*, which was the first Magnavox console to feature on-screen color. Its graphics also surpassed the graphics of any system that came before it. Instead of utilizing white squares for paddles, the 500 actually displayed crude graphics of human characters, marking the first time human characters appeared in a home videogame.

Handheld Electronic Games

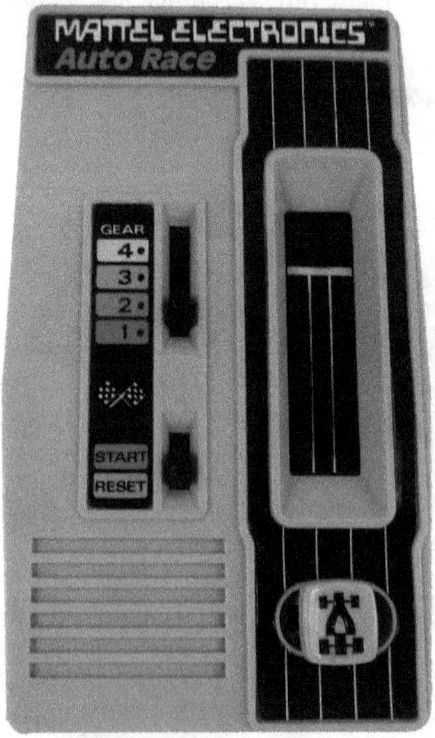

Mattel Electronics Auto Race

The graphics on the Odyssey 500 marked the first time human characters appeared in a home videogame. But as the graphics on the TV screen began to get more sophisticated, a new type of videogame pushed graphics back to something more primitive than even what the original Odyssey had to offer.

Mattel, the world's largest toy company, had created a new division called *Mattel Electronics*. Its first release was *Auto Race*, a self-contained console that was roughly the size of a paperback book. It played a game that was basically a handheld version of Taito's *Speed Race*, in which the object was to drive a car from the bottom of the screen to the top four times in the shortest time possible, while avoiding other "cars." As a videogame, *Auto Race* had the sparsest of graphics. The cars were merely tiny red blips created by light-emitting diodes (LEDs). But it marked the first time that an electronic game escaped from the dependency of a television.

Joysticks and Cartridges

As Magnavox and other manufacturers were building consoles around variants of General Instrument's AY-3-8500 chips, a European manufacturer came up with the idea that they could purchase individual chips from General Instrument and place them in a separate housing, which could then be inserted into one universal console, so that new games could be played without purchasing an entire new console. Thus was born the *PC-50x* family of consoles.

The PC-50x consoles were manufactured by dozens of companies in Europe, including Prinztronic, Hanimex and Radofin, and sold for approximately $90 apiece. Although the consoles may have had different names and varied in appearance depending upon the manufacturer, they all shared some basic similarities. For one, they all featured ten selection buttons. Secondly, they each included, for the first time, a pair of *joystick* controllers. Unlike the standard paddle controllers, which were knobs that rotated, the joystick controller was a metal or plastic stick that protruded from a base. The stick could be pressed in to any of eight positions, causing a different result on the screen.

This more precise form of input was required because the games for the PC-50x consoles went beyond the standard ball-and--paddle variants that were so prevalent. Additional games could be played through the console by inserting a plastic cartridge that contained its own General Instrument chip. Eight cartridges were available, each having its own stock number beginning with PC-501 and extending to PC-508, which is why this console was referred to as the PC-50x, in which the "x" indicated one of the eight

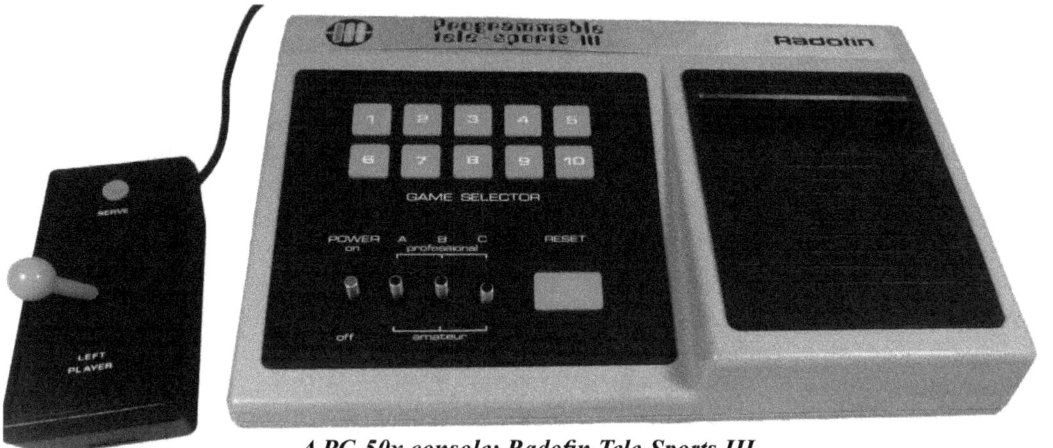

A PC-50x console: Radofin Tele-Sports III

available cartridges. Each cartridge included up to 10 games, which could be selected by pressing one of the console's selection buttons.

In many cases, the dozens of companies that produced the PC-50x consoles also manufactured their own cartridges, so the style of the cartridges varied from company to company. In some cases, cartridges from one company played on a competitor's console, while in other cases, they didn't. The only thing that was standard was the cartridge's stock number and the General Instrument chip inside of it. Even the names of the cartridges varied between manufacturers.

The Fairchild Video Entertainment System

None of the PC-50x systems were available in the United States, so consumers there had to continue buying new, dedicated consoles in order to play new games. But that changed in November, 1976 when Fairchild Semiconductor, a manufacturer of integrated chips, entered the videogame business with its *Video Entertainment System (VES).*

The system had been conceived in 1974 by Wallace Kirschner and Lawrence Haskel, two men who worked for a small Connecticut-based start-up company called Alpex Computer Corporation. Initially, the company, which consisted of only three employees, formed a joint venture with Pitney Bowes to create an electronic cash register, but fierce competition from the industry leaders IBM and NCR forced them out of that business. They immediately began searching for a new technology that they could jump on to, and Kirschner came up with the idea to create a videogame console.

Kirschner quickly designed his own version of video tennis and then expanded on it to create a hockey game with defined goals and goalies. Although the on-screen "players" were still represented as rectangles, Kirschner designed the paddles to be rotated, which varied the possible angles from which the "puck" ricocheted. He followed that game with *Tic-Tac-Toe, Shooting Gallery* and *Doodle,* which allowed the player to draw pictures on the screen. By this time, Kirschner determined that the console he wanted to create would have to be one where consumers purchased the expensive hardware once, and then supplemented it with additional, inexpensive software. The immediate problem was finding a method of external storage that an average, non-technical person would be able to use easily.

Fortunately, Kirschner had access to an Intel 8080 development kit. This allowed him to save programs that he wrote directly onto an EPROM (Erasable Programmable Read-Only Memory) chip. After each program was in a finished state, it could be stored onto a ROM (Read-Only Memory) chip. Once Kirschner realized that ROM chips were the way to go, he still needed to figure out how these fragile chips could be handled in such a way that the average consumer couldn't destroy them. Together with Haskel, he conceived of a way to mount the chip onto a circuit board that could be inserted and removed from the console indefinitely without wearing it out. And to prevent the user from manhandling the chip itself, they stored it inside a plastic case.

At this point, Kirschner presented his invention to Norman Alpert, the founder of Alpex. Alpert liked the idea but knew that his company didn't have the finances or the know-how to manufacture and release the console. So in a move reminiscent of Ralph Baer and Sanders Associates, the team began visiting television companies, with the intent of partnering with one of them to build the console. Unfortunately, as Baer had discovered, the TV companies didn't have the vision to market the console. Unperturbed, the team moved on to semiconductor manufacturers. Among them was Fairchild Semiconductor, a company that Alpex had dealt with for components while they were designing their electronic cash register. After seeing what Alpex had to offer, Fairchild was ready to partner with them under one condition: The console had to be redesigned to use Fairchild's microprocessors. Jerry Lawson, a Fairchild engineer, was assigned to work with the Alpex team to make this happen. He was the perfect choice, since he had once built his own arcade videogame.[15]

With Lawson's assistance, Haskel and Kirschner were able to get their system running using Fairchild's F8 microprocessor, which had been available since 1975. Once the processor was in place, a contract between Fairchild and Alpex was signed.

Lawson next designed a controller that would be able to incorporate all of the features of the hockey game that Kirschner had previously developed. The design he came up with allowed for the on-screen players to move up and down, left and right and diagonally, and even rotate.

4

Fairchild VES Hand Controller

Once the prototype was completed, Lawson took over the project to turn it into a marketable product. The final production model featured two hand controllers that were hard-wired into the console, and which were extremely different from any controller that had preceded them. They closely resembled Lawson's original conception. These controllers were free-standing sticks with triangular knobs that protruded from the top. In addition to rotating left or right like a standard paddle controller, the knob could be pressed in eight directions like the joystick controllers on the PC-50x systems. Finally, the knob could also be pressed down.

In addition to the innovative controller, the VES introduced other features that had never been offered in the established ball-and-paddle consoles. For the first time, gamers were given the ability to change the speed of an on-screen ball, or the duration of a timed game. Games could also be paused at the press of a button.

And the inclusion of the F1 chip that powered the VES made it the first console that employed a microprocessor, which made it the first *programmable* videogame system. All the consoles that had preceded it, were *dedicated*

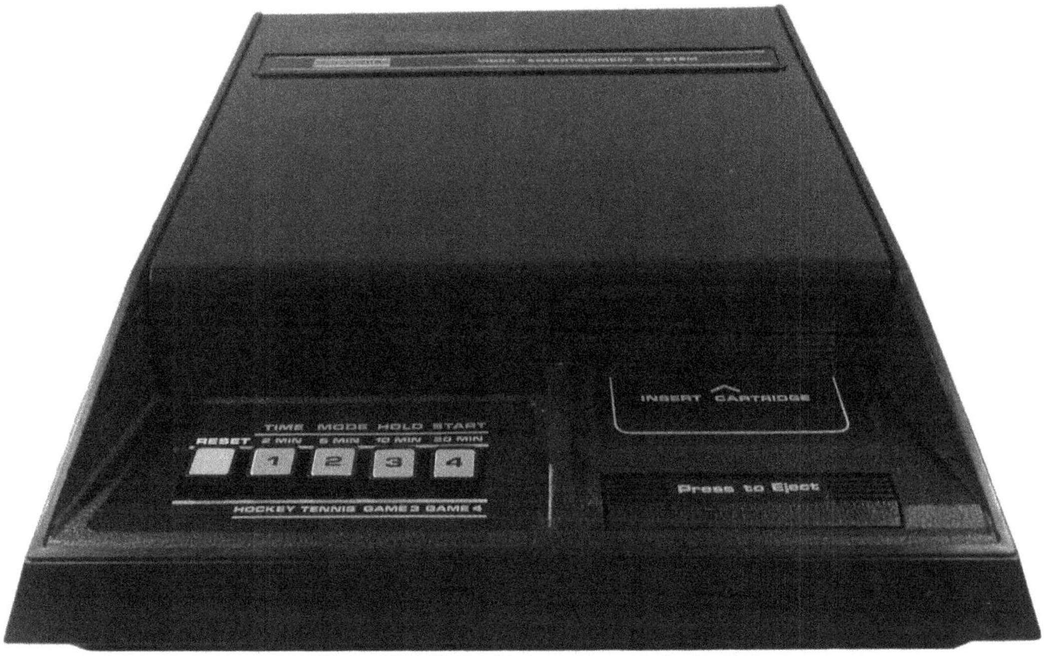

Fairchild Video Entertainment System

systems that could only play the games that were encoded on their chips that were either built-in to them, or inserted into them as was the case with the PC-50x family. With a programmable system, the brains of the console, the CPU,[16] resided in the console, and changes could be made to it by loading different programs into it from an external source. In the case of the VES, the external source was the ROM cartridge.

The ROM cartridge that Jerry Lawson and his team designed for the VES wasn't much different from the one that Haskel and Kirschner had invented for the prototype. An industrial designer named Nick Talesfore was assigned the task of conceiving the cartridge itself. He settled on a design that closely mimicked the look of an audio 8-track cartridge. He decided that the color of the cartridges, which were to be called *Videocarts*, would be bright yellow, so they would stand out from the console.

The $170 Fairchild Video Entertainment System was released in November 1976, along with three Videocarts. Each Videocart was numbered and contained up to four games. *Videocart-1* featured *Tic-Tac-Toe, Shooting Gallery* and *Doodle*, the same games that Kirschner had written when he first came up with the idea to create a videogame console.

Fairchild VES Videocart

The VES quickly made all of the dedicated consoles obsolete. Why would anybody buy a dedicated game console that he might tire of a month later, when he could get one console that could play every new game as it became available?

The manufacturers of the dedicated consoles quickly saw the writing on the wall. In order to compete, they had to market programmable consoles similar to the VES. RCA, which had wanted to enter the home videogame market ever since Ralph Baer first demonstrated his Brown Box, announced in September 1976 that it was developing its own programmable game system. Meanwhile, several Atari designers, Joe Decuir, Steve Mayer, Ron Milner and Jay Miner, had already built a prototype of a programmable machine that they called *Stella*. The release of Fairchild's programmable console caught them by surprise and they realized that they had to get their project to market before other companies released a programmable system. Unfortunately, Atari didn't have the money to perfect and manufacture it.

Bushnell knew that Atari couldn't remain a major force in the home videogaming field if it couldn't develop the new home system adequately. In order to do that, the company needed a sufficient supply of money, which it didn't have. After dwelling on the problem, Bushnell finally sought help from Don Valentine, a venture capitalist. Valentine suggested to Bushnell that he should find someone to buy the company. Bushnell really didn't want to go that route, but he felt it was absolutely necessary to save the company. He asked his top executives to make a list of ten companies that they thought they would be willing to merge with theirs. The company that would wind up buying Atari wasn't even on their list.

Warner Communications was a huge entertainment conglomerate that was already involved in movies, publishing and music. By the mid-seventies, the sales from Warner's most profitable division, its music division, began falling. Warner's executives concluded that the music business had reached its peak, and that the huge profits that they had been receiving weren't going to continue for long. They felt that Warner should branch into a hot, new field, and they hired Manny Gerard to find it. When Gerard heard that Atari was on the market, he became very interested. Atari and videogames seemed to be just what Warner was looking for.

In October 1976, Warner Communications bought Atari for $28 million, and a new era in home videogaming began.

CHAPTER FIVE
1977

At the end of January, Signetics[1] announced the MUGS-1, a new chip that featured racing and war games. Since Philips, the Dutch-based electronics company that owned Magnavox, had purchased Signetics in June 1975, it was only natural that Magnavox would be the first company to begin developing a new console around it.

However, while Magnavox planned its new game machine, the company did release several new, dedicated consoles throughout the year. They were all similar to the Magnavox consoles that had preceded them, and all of them used General Instrument's AY-3-8500 chip. The *Odyssey 2000*, which came out in May, was basically the same as the Odyssey 300, except that the rotary dials that were used as controllers were much larger and more consistent with Atari's paddle controllers. It also featured a one-player variation of *Squash* that had not been included on the 300.

The *Odyssey 3000*, which came out the following month, played the same games as the 2000, but the style of the console was much more contemporary. It was also the first Magnavox console since the original Odyssey that included detachable controllers. The final like-numbered Odyssey console to be released in the United States was the *Odyssey 4000*, which came out in September. This system featured eight variations of *Tennis*, *Hockey* and *Squash* and included detachable joystick controllers. In Europe, Philips released the Odyssey *2001*, which looked very similar to the Odyssey 4000, except that the Odyssey 2001 included detachable paddle controllers in place of the joysticks. Internally, the European console had a National Semiconductor MM-57105 chip, which played the same games as the 4000.[2] Another feature, which was not available on the American consoles, was that game sounds emitted from the TV itself, and not the console.

The new system that Magnavox was developing around the Signetics MUGS-1 chip, was to be called the *Odyssey 5000*. It was to be a four-player dedicated system that would feature 24 built-in games and would sell for under $100.

The style of the Odyssey 5000 would be different from the previous Magnavox consoles. While the 4000, 2001 and 2100 all featured slanted fronts, and controller storage

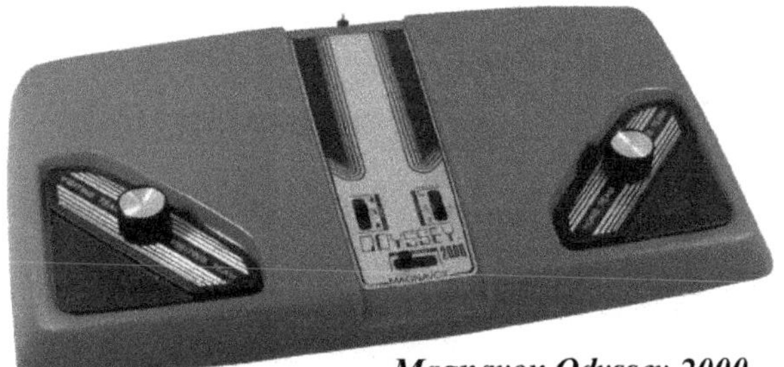

Magnavox Odyssey 2000

Magnavox Odyssey 3000

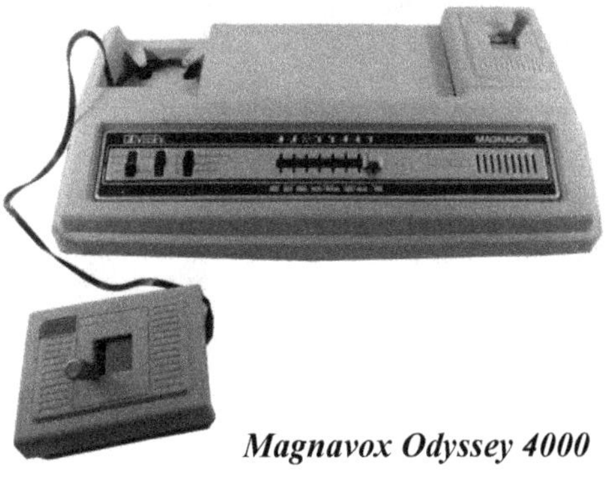

Magnavox Odyssey 4000

Philips Odyssey 2001

Magnavox Odyssey 5000

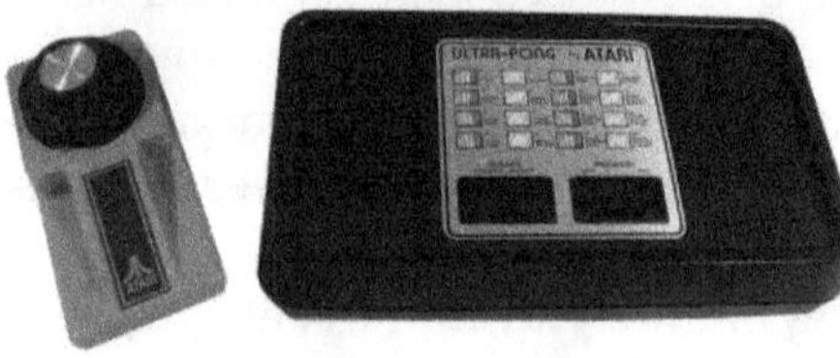

Atari Ultra Pong Doubles

areas at the top rear of the unit, advertising drawings from Magnavox showed the 5000 to have a flat top with a slanted area rising in the back. The flat top would house the four joystick controllers, which were very similar to the ones used by the 4000.

Magnavox wasn't alone in creating dedicated systems with multiple games. Atari, which used its own custom chips, continued to cash in on the *Pong* name with *Ultra Pong Doubles*, a dedicated console that featured 32 built-in games that could be played by up to four people.

Atari followed *Ultra Pong Doubles* with two dedicated machines in which the hardware was part of the games. The left and right sides of the *Video Pinball*[3] console featured buttons that had to be pressed to enable on-screen flippers, just as on a real pinball machine. And *Stunt Cycle,* which was based on a 1976 Atari arcade game of the same name, had controls that were shaped like motorcycle handlebars.[4] These controls were gripped and twisted to accelerate an on-screen motorcycle that had to soar over several buses. In a similar vein, Coleco marketed its *Telstar Combat* console, which featured tank controls similar to the ones that had appeared on Kee Games' *Tank* arcade game, on which this home version was based.

Japanese Consoles

In Japan, the status of home videogame consoles was roughly two years behind that of the United States. Although the original Odyssey had been imported into Japan in 1975, it wasn't until 1977 that Japanese companies manufactured and released their own consoles. One such company was Bandai, a toy company that released a series of home videogame consoles under the brand name *TV Jack.* These systems were similar to the various Odyssey and *Pong* consoles that Magnavox and Atari had released between 1975 and 1977. The *TV Jack 1000* featured four video tennis variations and employed two built-

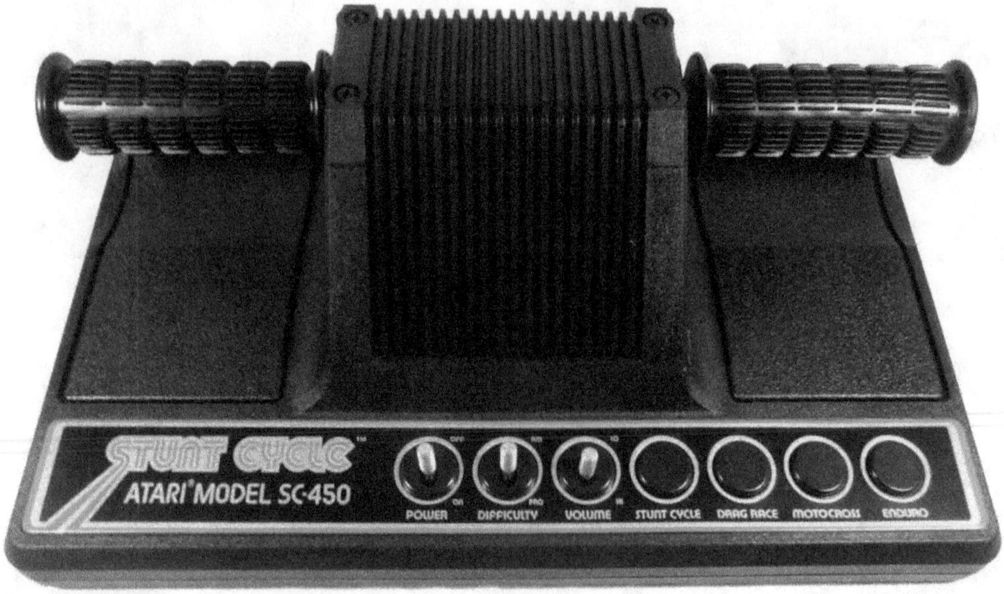

Atari Stunt Cycle

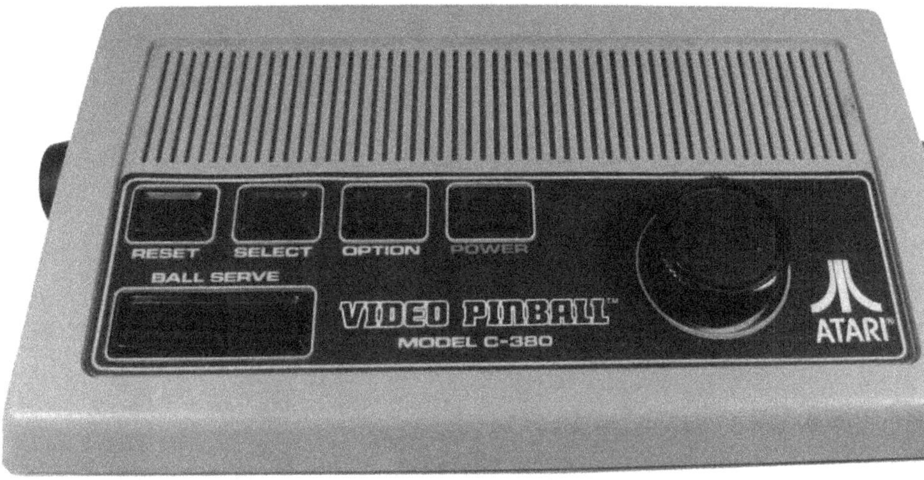

Atari Video Pinball

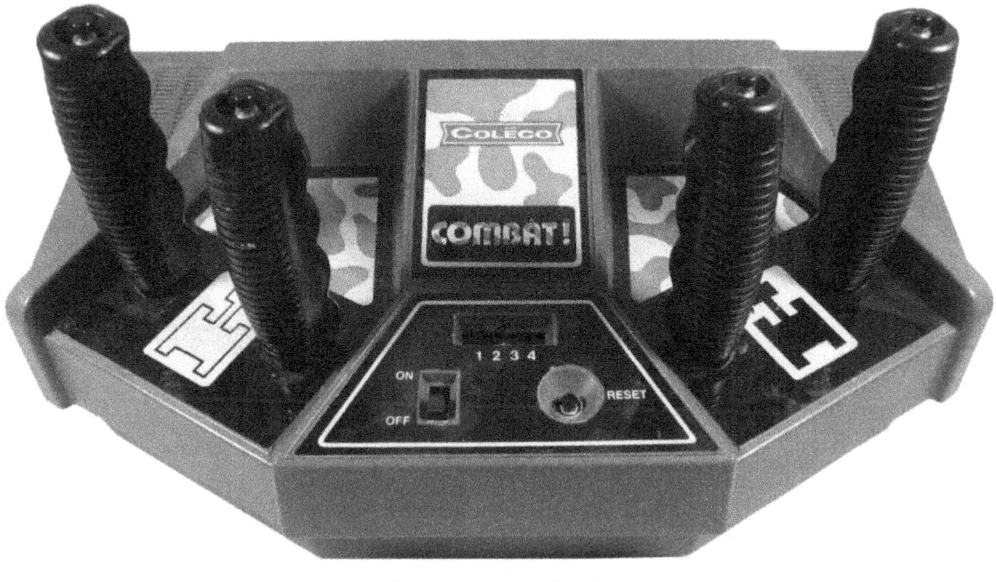

Coleco Telstar Combat

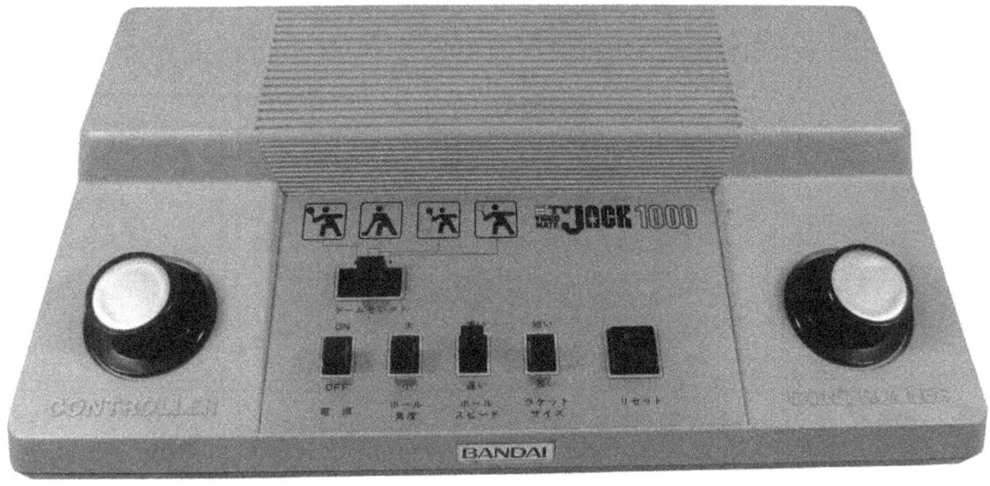

Bandai TV Jack 1000

in controller knobs. The *TV Jack 1200* was basically a four-player version of the 1000 and included two additional, detachable paddle controllers. The *TV Jack 1500* was a two-player console that featured eight built-in games and included detachable paddle controllers. The *TV Jack 2500* contained the same four games as the original *1000*, but each of the four games had five variations. In addition, the console itself was much smaller. Finally, the *TV Jack 3000* was a four-player system with ten built-in games.

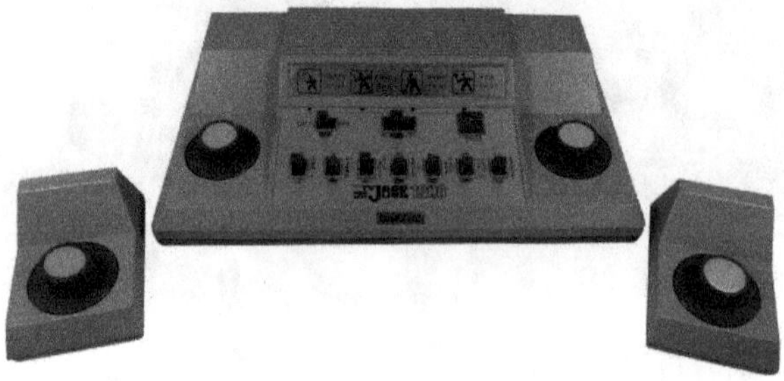

Bandai TV Jack 1200

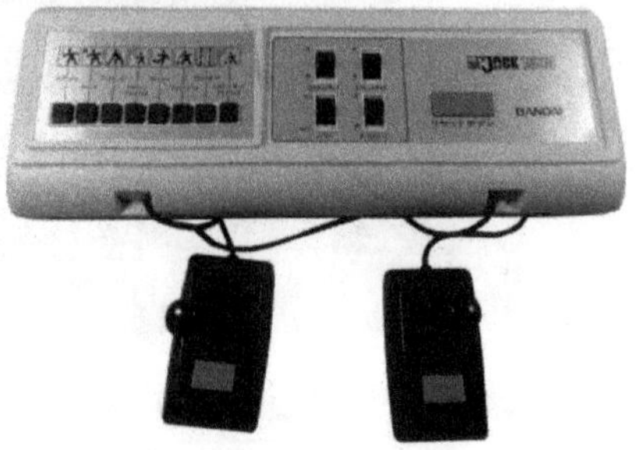

Bandai TV Jack 1500

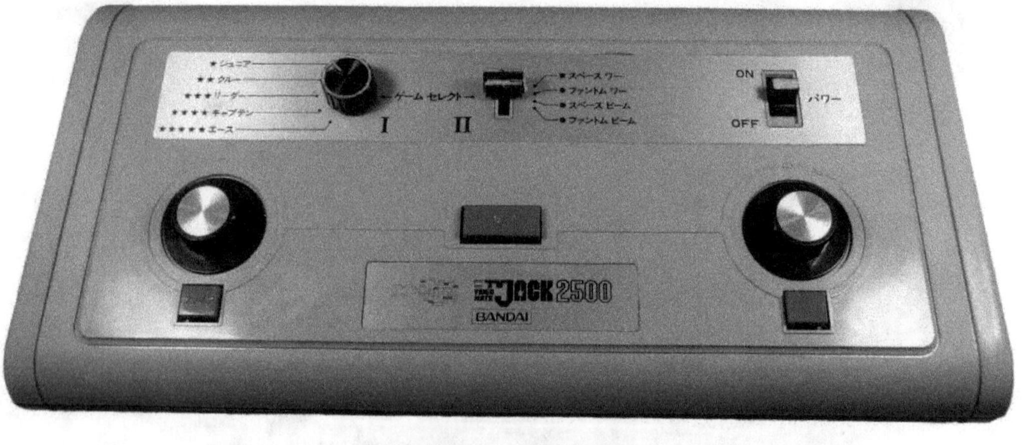

Bandai TV Jack 2500

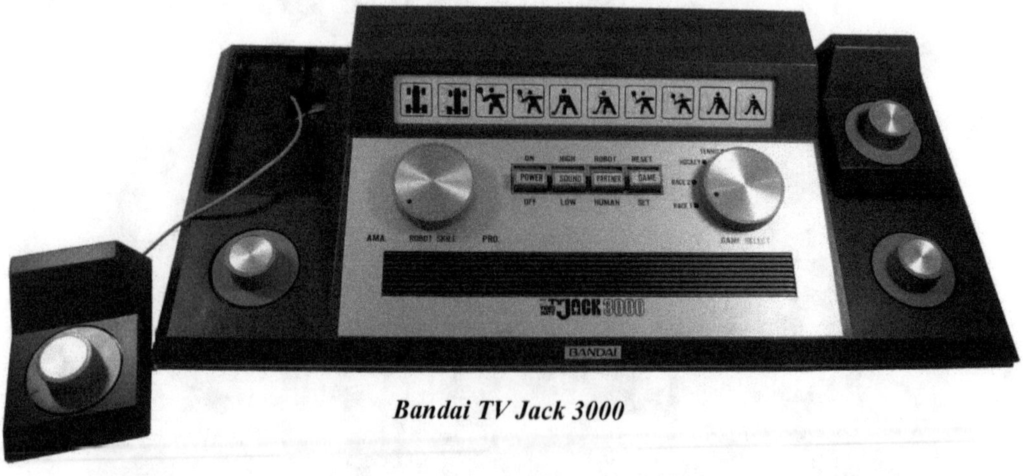

Bandai TV Jack 3000

Nintendo, the company that had imported the Odyssey into Japan, also went ahead to release its own home console. Unfortunately, the company didn't have engineers that were skilled in the design of home games, so they sought help from Mitsubishi Electric Corporation. Nintendo's management determined that they would have to sell a system at ¥12,000 ($44) in order to make it profitable. However, Nintendo's president, Hiroshi

Yamauchi, wanted to keep the retail price under ¥10,000 ($37). A decision was made to sell two consoles, one with less features for a lower price.

The two consoles were released in June. Both played ball-and-paddle games in color, at a time when most of the Japanese systems were still black and white. The lower-priced model, the *Color TV-Game 6*, was similar to Bandai's TV Jack 1000 and Magnavox's Odyssey 100. It played six games[5] and retailed for ¥9,800 ($36), which was roughly half the price of similar consoles. People purchased it in droves. At a time when any company was happy to sell 10,000 units, Nintendo sold 360,000.

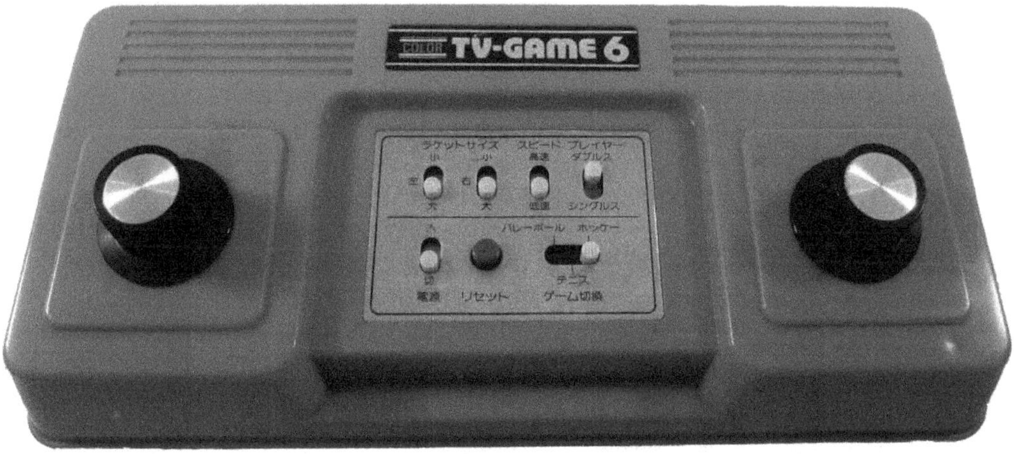

Nintendo Color TV 6

Nintendo's more expensive console, the ¥15,000 ($55) *Color TV-Game 15*, included all of the games from the Color TV-Game 6, as well as four additional one- and two-player ball-and-paddle variations.[6] The console also included two detachable paddle controllers.

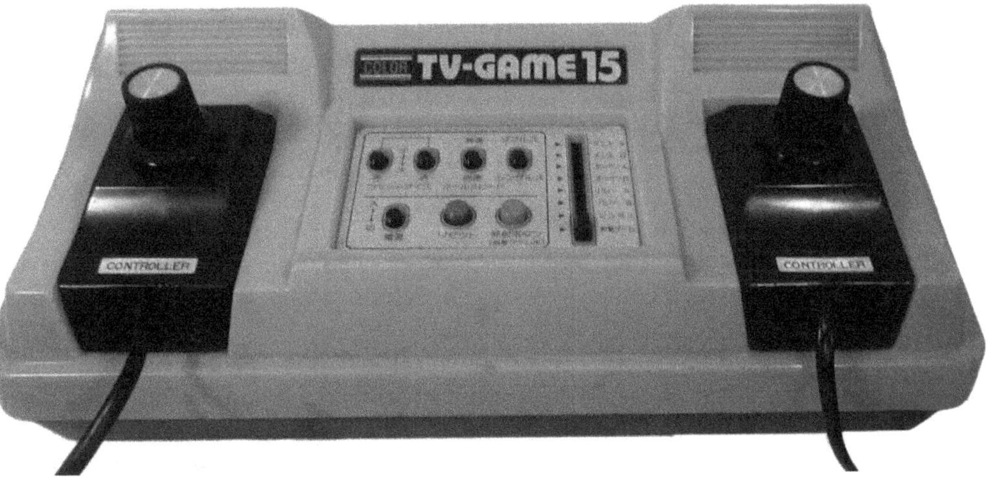

Nintendo Color TV 15

About Nintendo

Of all the companies that had released videogames throughout the world thus far, Nintendo was the oldest. The company had begun in 1889 as Nintendo Koppai, a manufacturer and distributor of *Hanafuda,* Japanese playing cards. The Japanese word *nintendo* roughly means "leave luck to heaven." Nintendo Koppai became the largest playing-card company in Japan and, in 1907, began producing the Western playing cards that were becoming popular throughout the country. In 1947, Nintendo Koppai established a distribution company called Marufuku to distribute new Western decks, such as pinochle and poker. The company changed its name to the Nintendo Playing Card Company in 1951, and twelve years later became Nintendo Company Limited.

In 1964, the company began developing toys and games. The first game it released was a marble racing game called *Rabbit Coaster*. In 1966, Hiroshi Yamauchi, Nintendo's president, visited a Hanafuda factory and spotted a maintenance engineer named Gunpei Yokoi working on a toy of his own design during his free time. Yamauchi purchased the rights to Yokoi's toy and then promoted him to a product-development position in the Games Division, where he could work on his toy in an official capacity that would enable Nintendo to release it in time for Christmas. The *Ultra Hand*, featuring an extendable plastic claw, became Nintendo's first hit game.

In 1970, Nintendo struck a deal with Sharp Corporation to use Sharp's light-sensor technology in its toys. Gunpei Yokoi collaborated with Sharp's Masayuki Uemura and created the *Kousenjuu* (Beam Gun) series of games. Each game came with a light-sensor gun and a target. In 1973, following the success of the *Kousenjuu*, Nintendo purchased several abandoned Japanese bowling alleys and converted them into arcades that used large-scale versions of the *Kousenjuu*. A year later, Nintendo combined the *Kousenjuu* technology with a 16mm film-projection system to produce very successful stand-alone, electro-mechanical coin-op games. One such game was *Wild Gunman*[7] where the player had to draw his mechanical pistol and outshoot the live-action gunslinger on the large screen. Several of these new coin-op machines, including *Wild Gunman*, were also exported to the United States, which provided Nintendo with a new market for its products.

Nintendo Wild Gunman

After the overwhelming success of Nintendo's two home videogame consoles, the company controlled 70% of the home console business. As many as 20 other companies competed for the other 30%.

More Programmable Videogames

But just as primitive, dedicated, ball-and-paddle consoles were being introduced into Japan the era of the dedicated console was quickly coming to an end in the United States, following the release of Fairchild's programmable VES in 1976. In January 1977, RCA released its long-awaited home videogame console, the *Studio II*. The console's name was somewhat confusing, since there had never been a "Studio I." It had actually been derived from RCA's famed Nashville studio, where many famous musicians had recorded hits. The Studio II name conveyed the idea that the console would represent a second studio for which artists could create products. This vague tie-in was unfortunately lost upon most consumers.

Like Fairchild's VES, the Studio II was programmable by inserting different game cartridges. Retailing for $150, $20 less than Fairchild's console, the Studio II also came with five built-in games. Regrettably, it wasn't the bargain that it had appeared to be, as it was technologically obsolete the moment it appeared on store shelves.

For one, to save costs the system only played games in black and white, even though the games themselves had been programmed to display in color. Magnavox had employed the same cost-cutting measures when it had released the Odyssey in 1972. But by early

RCA Studio II

1977, there were already affordable color systems on the market from Magnavox and Fairchild.

The Studio II's controllers were very different from what people were getting used to. Increasingly, consoles were being released with detachable controllers, so games could be played farther away from the television. But the Studio II's two controllers were built into the console. And they were completely unlike any other controller that came before them. Unlike the common dial used by Atari and Magnavox, or the relatively efficient multi-directional handle used by Fairchild, the Studio II's controls consisted of two ten-digit numeric keyboards, with most of the buttons used to guide on-screen objects in specific directions, requiring players to look down at the console to make sure they pressed the correct buttons.

Consumers weren't willing to purchase a system that was technologically backwards. RCA removed the Studio II from the market less than a year after it had been introduced, and never again delved into videogames.

Meanwhile, the VES undertook a major change. In March, the marketing department at Fairchild subtly renamed its VES console. Ads began appearing where the system was now called *Channel F*. The "F" in Channel F represented the console's F8 processor, which was manufactured by Fairchild. Oddly, this name change only occurred on paper, i.e. the box and advertisements. New boxes were printed with the Channel F logo but the console inside the box was the same one that was sold in the boxes labeled "Video Entertainment System". The only place the name of the console appeared on the console was in the center of the plastic dust cover, and it remained as "Video Entertainment System".

Vector Games

While home gamers were treated to the RCA Studio II, a system that was technologically a step backwards, arcade gamers got to play an archaic game that utilized new technology.

Larry Rosenthal had been a student at MIT during the late '60s. He saw *Spacewar* in operation but had never actually played it. And he never thought about it while attending the University of California - Berkley as a graduate student. That was until revisited MIT during a Christmas break and saw Nutting Associates' *Computer Space* in the student union. He thought the game was crude and was appalled that it was at MIT. After graduating from Berkley in 1973 with a master's degree in electrical engineering, Rosenthal was offered a job at MIT but wasn't exactly sure if he wanted to return to Massachusetts or stay in California. He decided to roam the Pacific Northwest during the summer after graduation to decide on what he wanted to do. He did a lot of thinking during this trip and finally made up his mind. He decided to right a wrong and build a superior, home version of *Spacewar* based upon his five-year old memories of the game he never played. So he remained in California and began his new task.

Rosenthal basically built a computer from scratch. But after working on the project for several weeks, he came to the conclusion that the technology didn't exist for him to create a home version of the game. So he decided to build an arcade one instead. One problem that Rosenthal encountered was that he couldn't get his spaceships to look correct within the 256 scan lines of an NTSC raster monitor.[8]

So Rosenthal next looked at *vector* displays. In this method, the electron gun moved to two coordinates on the screen and then lit up all the phosphors between the two points. Although the vector graphics contained less detail, what was displayed was sharper and clearer than what appeared on screens displaying raster graphics. Unfortunately the only vector displays at that time were commercial ones, which cost around $100,000. Rosenthal decided to figure out a way to get the cost of a vector display system down.

Rosenthal took apart a standard raster CTR and substituted a high voltage power supply. He cut some corners where accuracy didn't matter and eventually turned his standard black & white television into a low-cost vector monitor and with that he was able to successfully produce the game that he had been working on for months. He called the game *Space Wars,* after the original computer game that it had been based upon.

Rosenthal searched for a company to distribute his game. However, since he insisted that he receive 50% of the profits, most of the arcade companies that he went to turned down his offer. Meanwhile, Cinematronics was an arcade-game company that had been established in 1975 and had released only three games, all of which went relatively unknown. Cinematronics was desperate for a hit, so when Rosenthal offered them *Space Wars* with his outlandish royalty demand, they eagerly accepted.

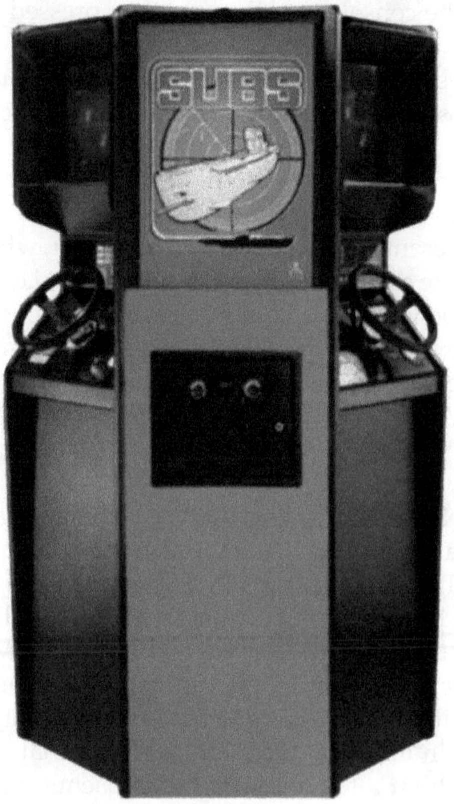

Atari Subs

Space Wars was a mild success, but because Cinematronics had not perfected the technology, *Vectorbeam* monitors went dead more often than not. Since a cabinet with a dead monitor couldn't generate revenue, arcade operators quickly became unwilling to put up with it, and most had the machine removed from their arcades.[9]

Atari, which had an infusion of nearly $100 million from its new parent, Warner Communications, also released a new arcade game. *Subs,* which was released in May, put the player in charge of a submarine, in which he searched for and tried to destroy an enemy sub. And although the game wasn't a commercial success, it paved the way with three pioneering features.

Subs was the first arcade game to feature two monitors, which allowed two players to compete simultaneously on their own screens. It was also the first game that had action occurring off-screen. This was accomplished with the incorporation of a "radar screen" that gave players an overview of the entire playfield, and not just the visible one. Finally, Atari included an *Add-a-Coin* feature. A game normally ended after a certain time limit expired. Add-a-Coin allowed players to continue a game by inserting additional coins. This proved to be a popular feature, which would eventually be employed by most arcade-game manufacturers.

Pizza Time Theatre

Atari also changed the collective face of arcades themselves.[10] On May 16, the company opened *Chuck E. Cheese's Pizza Time Theatre*, in San Jose, California. This was an idea that Nolan Bushnell had entertained since his Ampex days. He had noticed that after people ordered pies at pizza parlors, they had nothing to do for several minutes while the pie baked. He concluded that if arcade games were available, customers could be entertained until their orders were ready.

In 1977, arcades were considered unsavory places where parents didn't like their kids to gather. Bushnell envisioned a wholesome arcade that also sold pizza. In his mind, he saw an arcade that might attract kids who didn't normally go to arcades. And, of course, more people visiting arcades meant more people playing Atari videogames.

Pizza Time Theatre Logo

As Bushnell developed the concept, he felt that it would be a nice touch for the place to have Disneyland-like robotic animals that could perform music for the children as they ate. He asked his engineers at Atari to design these robots. One of the first that they thought up was a huge rat named Chuck E. Cheese.

Despite Bushnell's optimism about an entire chain, no one at Warner shared this excitement, and a second restaurant was never authorized.

Atari's VCS

Warner was more excited about Atari's consumer division. Even though it released several new dedicated consoles, once the Fairchild VES came out, Atari saw the writing on the wall and knew that the future was in programmable consoles that used ROM cartridges. The company was secretly designing its own but in the meantime it had a surplus of the custom chips that it used to drive its dedicated machines, and it needed to get rid of them. With the success of the PC-50x consoles in Europe, Atari figured it could release a new dedicated console that accepted cartridges that contained the chips from its earlier consoles. So the *Game Brain* was born. The console was basically a shell that had a paddle knob and four control buttons (and a reset button) on each side. The cartridges that were created for it contained the chips from several of Atari's earlier consoles, including *Ultra Pong, Stunt Cycle, Video Pinball* and even *Video Music.*

The Game Brain wasn't expected to sell in high numbers, but Atari figured it would cut down its inventory of the custom chips in a major way. However, shortly before the Game Brain went into production, the project was abandoned so the company could step up the work on its secret programmable system.

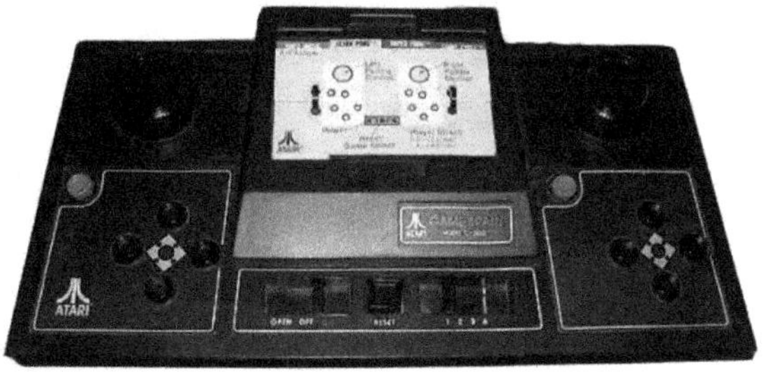

Atari Game Brain

That system, the *Video Computer*

System (VCS) was first shown at the *Consumer Electronics Show (CES)* in June. The CES was the largest trade show in the world, where people in the electronics trade came from all around the globe to display their latest products that would be available during the forthcoming year. Retailers attended the show to place orders for these new products. A product's appearance at CES was integral for its success. And the VCS almost missed it.

Atari want to make sure that it didn't carry any baggage so it decided to settle its lawsuit with Magnavox. Atari agreed to a non-exclusive license to Magnavox's patents in exchange for approximately $1.5 million paid out over several years. However, it also gave Magnavox the right to any technology that Atari developed between June 1, 1976 through June 1, 1977. Atari kept the VCS a secret until its official announcement at CES on June 4.

The *VCS*,[11] went on sale on October 9[12] and retailed for $200 - a steep price that nonetheless returned very little in the way of profit. However, the Warner executives knew that the secret to financial success was in the software that was sold separately. Every $30 cartridge that Atari sold cost less than $10 to manufacture.

The VCS was technologically superior to the Channel F. Games could display equally as well on both color and black-and-white TVs, thus guaranteeing the best picture quality from any videogame console. And the VCS had been designed so it wouldn't damage the TV, which had been a concern that had plagued many videogame owners since the Odyssey. If a videogame console and a television were both turned on for too long without being used, the image on the screen would eventually "burn" into the picture tube and always be visible - even after the console had been turned off. To avoid this problem, the VCS rotated through a series of colors if the console sat idle for several seconds. This series of random colors prevented any image from being "etched" into the picture tube.

Atari went all-out, in terms of variety, with the nine games that launched with the VCS. Several were based on Atari arcade titles that were already familiar to the public. *Combat,* which was packaged with the VCS, featured home versions of Kee Games' groundbreaking *Tank* and Atari's *Jet Fighter. Air-Sea Battle* was modeled after Atari's *Anti-Aircraft*. And in order for experienced players not to have an edge over novice ones, the system featured two *difficulty switches*. When the difficulty was engaged for a player, he might find that the range of his missiles would be shorter, or that his plane would fly slower, than those of his opponent who didn't apply the difficulty.

The VCS was packaged with a pair of *joystick* controllers, each consisting of a narrow stick that sat on a square plastic base and which could be pushed in any of eight directions.

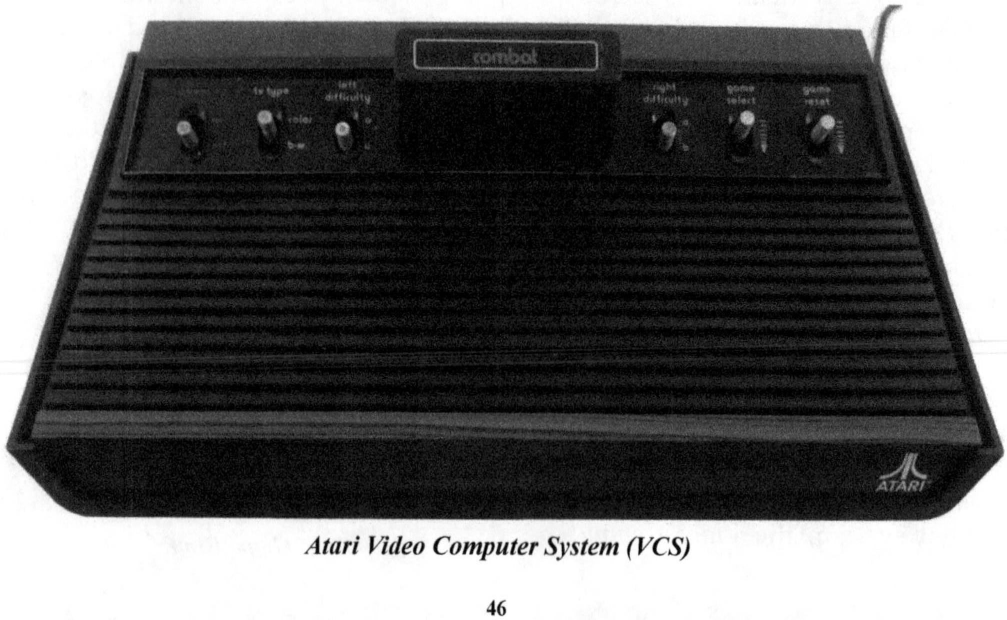

Atari Video Computer System (VCS)

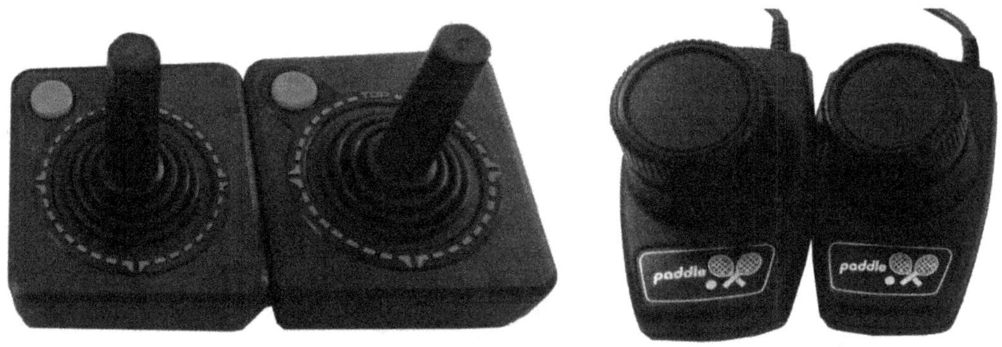

Atari VCS

Joystick Controllers ***Paddle Controllers***

The stick returned to its central, neutral position when released. A red firing button sat in the upper-left corner, on the base of the stick.

Five of the nine initial cartridges that Atari offered used the joystick controllers. Because three of the remaining cartridges featured driving and *Pong*-type games that the joystick wasn't practical for, Atari also included a pair of *paddle controllers,* which featured dials. And a pair of a third type of controller, *steering controllers,* were bundled with *Indy 500,* a racing game based on Atari's *Gran Trak 20.* All of the controllers plugged easily into either of the two ports at the back of the console. This was especially useful if a controller broke, because only the controller, and not the entire console, needed to be repaired or replaced. The VCS featured two controller ports, which allowed for one- or two-player games. But since the pair of paddle controllers was conjoined into one plug, some paddle games could accommodate up to four players.

Like the Channel F programs, the individual VCS games were each stored on a ROM (Read-Only Memory) chip housed in a plastic cartridge. The VCS used a MOS Technology 6507 CPU, an inexpensive chip that could only access 8k (8,192 bytes) of external memory. The VCS's designers didn't see this memory limitation as a barrier, since most games only used 2k (2,048 bytes) anyway, and they didn't see a need for any more than that. But after Atari was able to get a good price on 24-pin connectors for the console's cartridge socket, this lowered the amount of accessible memory to 4k.[13]

Bally's Home Console

Bally, the parent company of Midway, decided to enter the home videogame market and formed a consumer-products division in order to do so. With the help of Dave Nutting, they designed a programmable console that was to be called the *Bally Home Library Computer.* The word *computer* in the system's name reflected the fact that Bally intended for the system to be upgradable to a personal computer. A computer keyboard that included two cassette-tape ports, 16k of additional memory, a serial port for printers and modems, an expansion port for disk drives, and the BASIC programming language was planned to be released shortly following the console's launch.

The unit was scheduled to be available in September, but production problems caused it to be delayed. Although Bally accepted mail orders for the console, it wouldn't be able to deliver on them until January, 1978. This delay caused Bally to miss the crucial Christmas buying season altogether.

Coleco also jumped onto the programmable console bandwagon with a new system that did manage to get released in time for the Christmas rush. The *Telstar Arcade,* which had been designed by Ralph Baer, was a bizarre-looking, triangular unit that featured a different type of game on each of its three sides. One side featured a standard paddle controller for *Pong*-type games. A second side featured a pistol for target games. And the

Coleco Telstar Arcade

third side included, for the first time in a home console, a steering wheel and gear shift for driving games. Game cartridges that were also triangular in shape plugged into the center top of the unit. The four available cartridges were unlike the ROM cartridges that were available for the Atari VCS and Fairchild Channel F. Instead, they were similar to the European PC-50x line of consoles, where each cartridge contained customized chips. In this case, the chips were manufactured by MOS Technology. This was the only system ever released in the United States that had this type of setup.

Coleco Handhelds

Coleco also launched a line of handheld dedicated units after witnessing the success that Mattel Electronics was enjoying, especially after June, when the latter released its second handheld electronic game, *Football*. It was such a major success that Mattel Electronics was soon manufacturing 500,000 units a week, a number that had never been achieved by Mattel's flagship toy division. Mattel Electronics quickly followed up with other sports games, such as baseball and basketball.

Coleco saw the potential in handheld games and hired Michael Katz, the marketing director from Mattel Electronics who had been responsible for the handhelds. Under Katz's direction, Coleco released a series of electronic, handheld sports games under the generic brand name of *Head-to-Head*. This line of games differed from Mattel Electronics' offerings, as it allowed two players to compete with each other simultaneously. Although each was technically a "handheld" unit that could be played by one person, when two people competed, the unit was most comfortably played on a tabletop, because the controls for the two separate players were situated on both ends of the device, and the common screen was in the center.

As it turned out, Christmas was a poor one for the videogame industry, as the hot items that season were the inexpensive, electronic handheld games. Coleco had been unable to ship any of its various Telstar inventory into stores in time for Christmas, because of assembly-line problems and a dock strike. The company had to liquidate

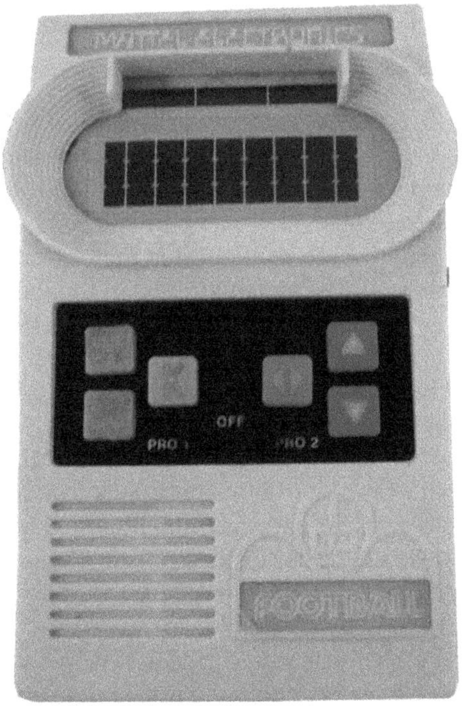

Mattel Electronics Football

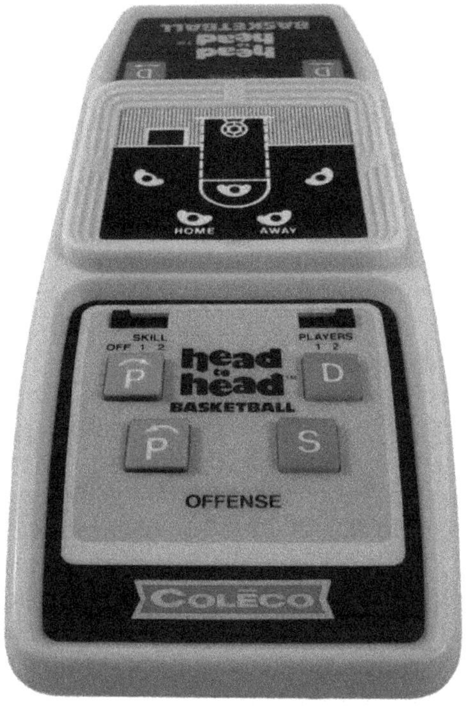

Coleco Head to Head Basketball

them at bargain prices when they finally arrived at stores in January 1978, which caused a devastating $27-million loss for the company. Fortunately, Coleco had been the only videogame manufacturer that had also ventured into the electronic handheld market, and the money it brought in from the handhelds saved the company from certain bankruptcy. Following this fiasco, Coleco made a hasty departure from the console videogame arena and concentrated on the handheld market.

As if the threat from the handheld industry weren't bad enough, the videogame companies were also menaced from within. Because of the influx of programmable machines, the manufacturers of dedicated units began dumping their merchandise at bargain prices, which were well below what it had cost to manufacture them. This glut of inexpensive, dedicated, TV-connected units then affected the sales of videogame consoles as a whole. People weren't willing to spend over $170 for a programmable console, and then additional money for individual game cartridges, when they could purchase several dedicated machines at once for less.

The sales slump caused many casualties. Although RCA's termination of its poorly received Studio II came as little surprise, Fairchild was also forced to discontinue its Channel F because of disappointing sales. Magnavox scrapped its plans for its 24-game Odyssey 5000.

Atari's VCS, fueled with cash by its powerful parent, Warner Communications, was the only videogame console that managed to survive the stormy holiday season of 1977. With little competition, Atari executives hoped for a change in their home videogame sales in 1978. Unbeknownst to anyone at the time, sales wouldn't be the only thing to change.

CHAPTER SIX
1978

By early 1978, Atari was in complete disarray with $40 million worth of inventory tied up because of poor Christmas sales. Manny Gerard, a Warner executive, was concerned about getting Atari back on target. Since he was the person who had recommended that Warner buy the videogame company, he had the most to lose if the company performed poorly. CEO Nolan Bushnell and President Joe Keenan, both millionaires many times over from the sale to Warner Communications, no longer had much interest in the day-to-day operations of the company. Gerard knew that he had to hire someone who could take charge of Atari.

In February, after careful consideration, Gerard hired Ray Kassar, a former marketing vice-president from Burlington Industries, a major textile corporation, to become president of Atari's consumer division. Kassar's personality clashed with Bushnell's immediately and caused much conflict within the company. Kassar had come from a business background, which dictated that hard work was the only way to achieve good results. Bushnell, on the other hand, believed that fun should also be included in the formula. While Kassar came to work early every morning dressed in a three-piece suit, Bushnell typically arrived whenever he felt like it wearing tennis shorts.

Bushnell disagreed with the direction in which Warner was steering Atari. The parent company wanted to add a home computer division, which Bushnell was totally against--he estimated that the company would lose $50 million just to set it up. Bushnell had also insisted that the VCS was already obsolete when it hit store shelves in 1977 and that Atari should discontinue it in favor of a more powerful console. Eventually every board meeting at Warner's New York home office turned into a shouting match between Bushnell and Gerard.

In November, during one of the many arguments between the two men, Bushnell's position as Chairman of the Board and CEO of Atari was terminated. Officially, Bushnell's contract called for him to remain with Atari as a creative and engineering consultant, but while he was never required to perform these duties, he was prohibited from working with any of Atari's competitors for a period of five years, until October 1, 1983. In effect, he was banned from participating in the industry that he created.

When Bushnell left Atari, he requested to buy the sole Pizza Time Theatre that Atari had opened in 1977. Warner, which had never been interested in the restaurant, happily complied and sold it to him for $500,000.

Following Bushnell's departure, Joe Keenan assumed the role of Chairman while Ray Kassar replaced him as President of the entire company where he quickly worked on a marketing strategy for Atari. First he axed the Microelectronics division by merging it with the Consumers division, and then he brought in salesmen and marketing people to develop a plan so Atari could reduce its inventory.

Other changes directly involved the employees. Flex-time was discontinued, and everyone had to report to work by 8:00. They also had to adhere to dress codes and punch timecards. The free spirit of Atari was gone. Warner Communications had transformed it into a cold and impersonal company. Eventually, all of the people who had been involved with Atari from the beginning were no longer with the company.

Another change in the company involved the intimacy that the managers had with their products. When Bushnell ran Atari, everybody had been involved in all aspects of the games, from designing to playing. This changed when Kassar took over. His major concern was the bottom line in the accounting ledger. As long as a product was profitable, it didn't matter to him what the product might be. Although Atari was a company that created videogames, Kassar and the other top Warner-instilled brass at Atari had never bothered to play them.

Bally Arcade Controller

Bally Home Console Computer

As Atari went through its growing pains, Bally also encountered difficulties with its new consumer division as it finally shipped its Bally Home Library Computer to stores in January. The system had two built-in games, including *Gunfight*, as well as a doodle program and a calculator, which was used with a 24-key keypad that was built into the unit. But unlike RCA's Studio II, the keypad was not used in lieu of actual hand controllers. Its controllers resembled the pistol-like controls that were on the *Gun Fight* arcade machine, with the addition of tiny dials on their tops. The grip had a built-in trigger that was used for shooting contests. Games for the console were housed in cartridges called *Videocades*, which looked very much like audio cassettes. And the Videocades could be stored atop the console itself, beneath a plastic cover, similar to the one that covered the storage area for the Channel F's controllers.

The Bally Home Library Computer utilized the Z-80, a microprocessor from Zilog that was compatible with Intel's 8080. The console outshone the VCS and the Channel F with its dazzling graphics and sound. But there was a price that went with these luxuries. The Bally Home Library Computer retailed for $299, which was $100 more than the VCS.

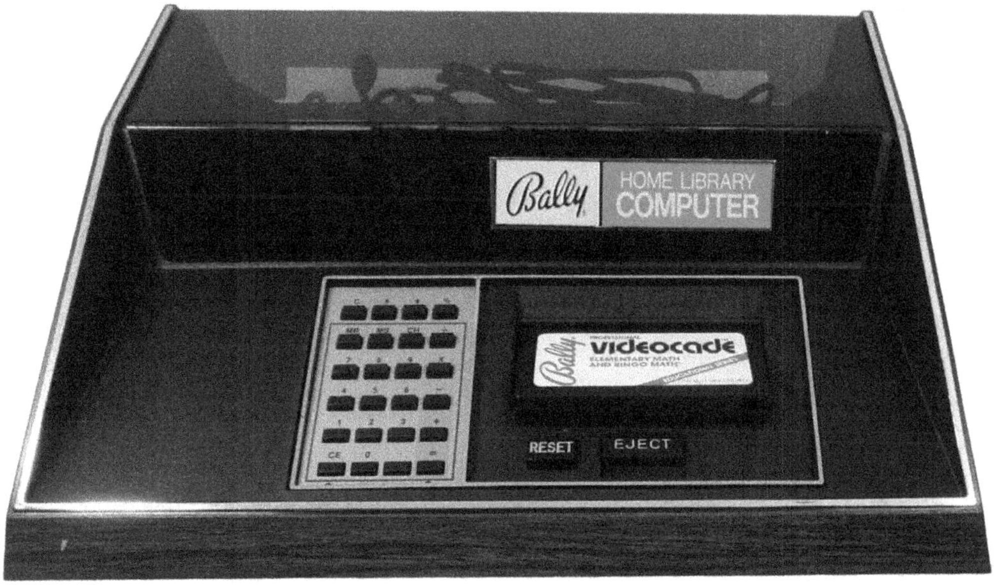

Bally Home Library Computer

Bally encountered problems when the majority of Bally Home Library Computers turned out defective and had to be returned. Following the production problems that it had with the unit, Bally decided to put the promised keyboard on hold indefinitely. To prevent consumers from remotely believing that the console was a computer, its name was changed to the *Bally Professional Arcade* after the first batch

Bally Arcade Label

1978

had gone out to retail outlets. However, not all aspects of the planned computer were disregarded. The BASIC programming language was released as a separate Videocade cassette, and all programming could be done through the console's keypad. An optional adapter that connected the Bally console to an audio cassette player was available, so homegrown programs could be saved on tape.

In April, Bally finally shipped consoles that they claimed were perfect, but many of them were still found to be defective. But manufacturing difficulties wasn't the only problem that Bally had to contend with. Since the company had never marketed a consumer product before, its staff knew little about marketing strategies. Inexperienced with retail distribution, they concentrated on computer stores instead of department and electronic stores, where the consoles would have received the most attention. Personnel in the stores that did carry it knew very little about its capabilities, so they displayed it alongside the VCS, which cost much less.

Space Invaders

However, while Bally's entry into the home was less than the company had hoped it would be, its arcade division, Midway, struck gold.

For ages, the arcade game of choice in Japan was Pachinko, which was sort of a cross between pinball and slot machines. Standard pinball machines, as well as mechanical coin-op machines didn't make much of an impact against the Pachinko phenomenon. Even videogames like *Pong*, which were imported from the United States, couldn't come between the Japanese and their Pachinko.

By 1978, Taito had 21 videogames in Japanese arcades but none of them came near the popularity enjoyed by Pachinko. Tomohiro Nishikado, Taito's most prolific developer, turned to Atari's *Breakout* and H.G. Wells' book, *The War of the Worlds*, and came up with a game that he wanted to call *Space Monsters*. Taito executives made him change that since Taito had already released an old electro-mechanical game called *Space Monster* in 1972. The name that Nishikado chose in place of *Space Monster* had no precedent.

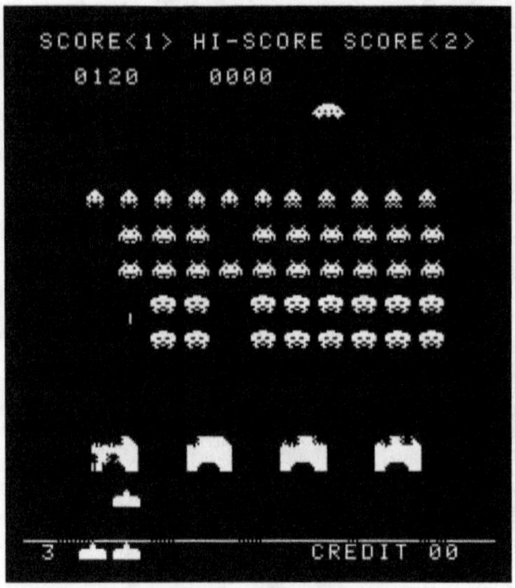

Taito *Space Invaders*

Space Invaders was a game where the player had to shoot down rows of descending space creatures before they could reach the bottom of the screen. The player controlled a laser cannon that could be moved horizontally along the bottom of the screen. When a button was pressed, the cannon would shoot missiles upwards, and if a creature was hit, it would disappear from the screen.

The creatures were arranged in five horizontal rows, each containing eleven monsters. All 55 creatures moved across the screen in unison and when they reached one side of the screen they all dropped one row and began "marching" towards the opposite side of the screen. The speed of their march increased as the number of invaders decreased. Along their way, several of the creatures in the bottommost row fired laser bullets downwards towards the player's cannon, and the player lost a life if his cannon was hit. The game ended when the player either lost all of his lives, or the bottom row of creatures hit the ground. The player could never win because once he wiped out all 55 invaders, a new set appeared beginning one row lower than they had in the prior wave, and marching at a slightly quicker pace, making each wave more challenging than the one that preceded it.[1]

Within six months of its introduction, *Space Invaders* overtook Pachinko in the Japanese arcades. It eventually became so popular that there was a shortage of the ¥100 coin needed to play the game.

One appeal of *Space Invaders* was the fact that the game could conceivably last forever. Prior to the release of *Space Invaders,* games ended when either time ran out or when a certain score was attained. In *Space Invaders,* as long as players could shoot down all of the invaders and prevent their final laser cannon from being hit by enemy fire, they could keep tallying points.[2] Nishikado also introduced the concept of the HIGH SCORE to the seemingly endless game. The highest score was displayed at all times, which gave players something to try and beat. Before long, players were trying to set the high score records and in doing so, were also breaking records with the amount of time they spent playing the game.

Naturally, something as huge as *Space Invaders* couldn't miss the attention of American manufacturers who were eager for a monster hit themselves. Rather than attempt to conceive a game that could be as popular as *Space Invaders,* Midway went straight to the source and licensed *Space Invaders* for release in the United States, where it took off just as it had in Japan. *Space Invaders* became the first Japanese arcade videogame to find success in the United States.

In October, around the same time that Midway introduced *Space Invaders* to American gamers, Atari also released an innovative arcade game. Although Atari's *Football* wasn't the first football videogame, it stood out from the prior ones because of its unique controllers, which were radically different from anything that preceded them. Instead of paddles, sticks, or buttons, a ball controlled the action. The *trackball* accelerated the action as gamers controlled the speed of their on-screen players by spinning it as quickly as possible. Speed was very important in this game, because 25¢ only bought 90 seconds of playtime. When this time ended, the players had the option to continue for another 90 seconds for an additional 25¢. At that rate, gamers could play a regulation one-hour game without overtime for ten dollars. Gamers didn't seem to mind, and *Football* was a mild success, earning as much as *Space Invaders* during its first three months.[3]

Atari Football

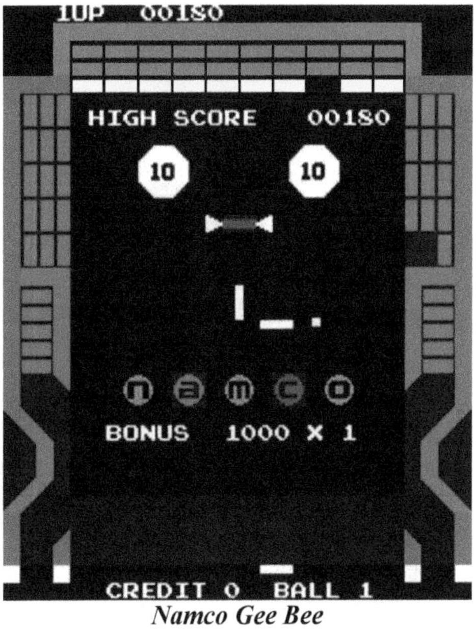

Namco Gee Bee

Elsewhere in Japan, Namco, the company that had purchased Atari's Japanese division, introduced its first original game into arcades. *Gee Bee,* which was designed by Tōru Iwatani, was a combination of *Breakout* and traditional pinball, where the goal was to keep the ball in play as long as possible while amassing points.

Namco opened a subsidiary in the United States and called it Namco America. The purpose of Namco America was to license Namco's

Japanese games for distribution in the United States. *Gee Bee* was licensed by a small company called Gremlin Industries, which had released a handful of arcade videogames since 1976.

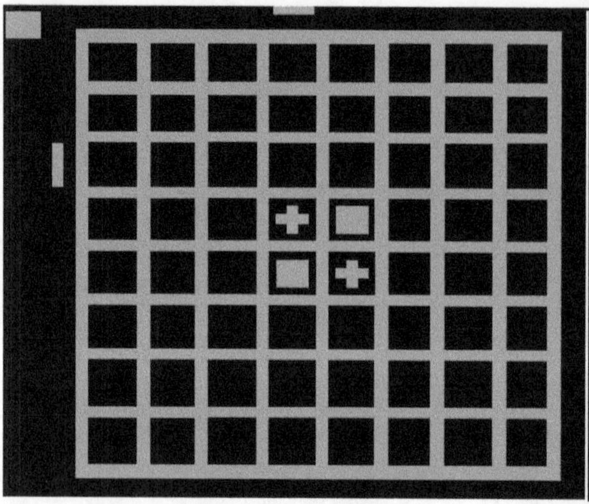

Nintendo Othello

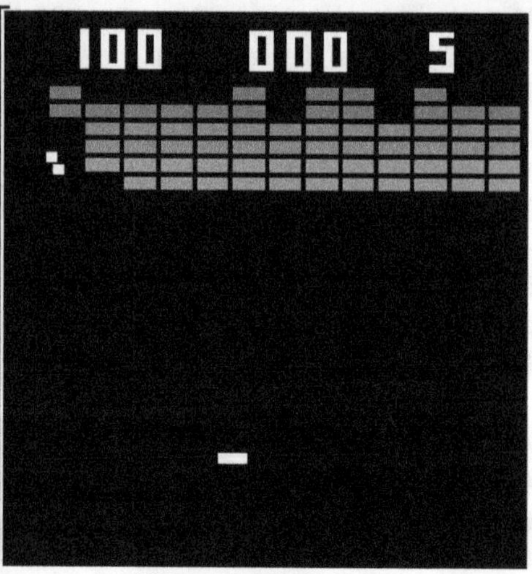

Nintendo Block Fever

Nintendo Enters Arcades

Nintendo, which had released mechanical amusement games, delivered its first arcade videogame, making it the first company to make a transition from home videogames to arcade videogames. Its first game, released in June, was *Computer Othello*, an electronic version of the board game. Nintendo followed it in November with *Block Fever*, which was a virtual clone of Atari's *Breakout*.

In June, Nintendo also released a new dedicated home console. The ¥12,500 ($58) *Color TV-Game Racing 112*, which was also designed by Mitsubishi, featured racing games similar to Taito's *Speed Race* where the player had to steer his car out of the path of other Indy racers. Like the Taito arcade game, the console featured a steering wheel and a built-in gear shift. In addition, so two players could compete evenly, two detachable paddle controllers, which were also used for steering, were included. Between the one

Nintendo Color TV Game Racing 112

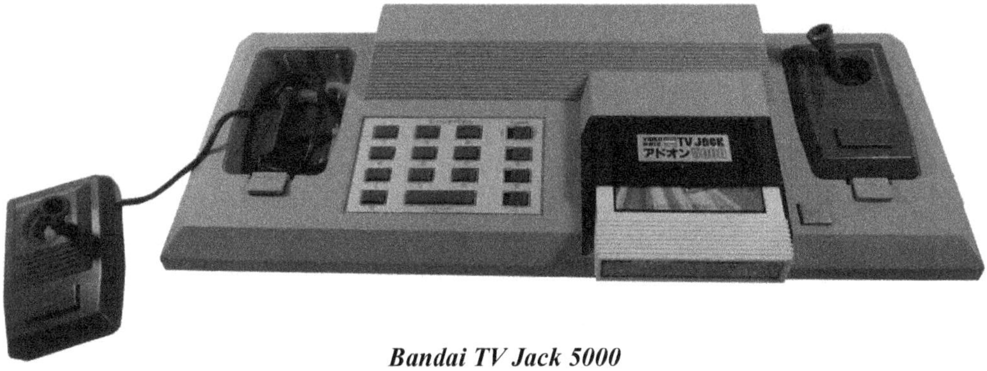

Bandai TV Jack 5000

and two-player games, the console featured 112 variations of the racing game.

If the Nintendo consoles were any indication, then the Japanese console scene was lagging behind the American one where programmable systems were the norm. But Japan took a step closer to catching up when Bandai released its *TV Jack 5000*, which accepted cartridges.

Bandai TV Jack 5000 Cartridge

The cartridges for the 5000 looked like they were cast from the same mold as the Fairchild Channel F's cartridge. They were the same bright yellow color and they were approximately the same size. But that was where the similarity ended. These were not ROM cartridges. Bandai simply used the cartridges to house chips that already had games stored on them, just like the PC-50x line of consoles. Two cartridges were included with the console, and two additional cartridges were available for sale separately.

In addition to the cartridges, the TV Jack 5000 was similar to the PC-50x consoles in another fashion. The system also came with a pair of joystick controllers, the first Japanese console to do so.

Analog Controllers

The joystick controllers that were used with the TV Jack 5000, as well as the Atari VCS, were digital controllers. Digital controllers operate on two simple states: on and off. If a

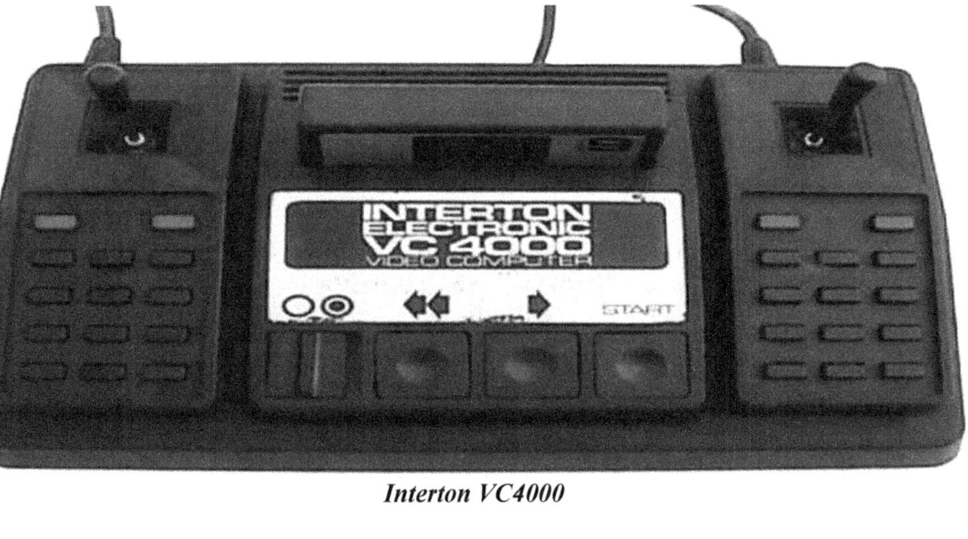

Interton VC4000

stick was pressed to the left, a certain circuit was turned on and told the computer what to do in response. The paddle controllers, on the other hand, were analog. They operated by having a continuous flow of electricity pass through a potentiometer.[4]

In 1978, a German company called Interton released a console that featured a new analog joystick controller, which combined the selections of the joystick with the fluidity of the paddle. The *VC4000* was a programmable console that was powered by Signetics' 2650A processor. It played games stored on ROM cartridges, which were basically patterned after games already available for the VCS. Interton compiled a list of 40 games that it wanted to produce, and then searched for someone who could program a particular game.[5]

The console itself somewhat resembled an audio cassette tape player with four buttons: a power button, a reset button, a game select button, and a game start button. Because the system had limited memory, the reset button had to be pressed after a cartridge was inserted, to let the console know that it had to access the cartridge. The cartridge slot itself was located behind the buttons, and the two controllers were stored on each side of the console.

The analog controllers from were substantially different from the joystick controllers that were available with other consoles. These controllers were rectangular-shaped, with a self-centering stick at the top end. "Self-center" meant that whatever direction the stick was pressed, it would automatically return to the center neutral position. Below the stick were two red action buttons, and below them were 12 black buttons. These buttons were used for various purposes. Some games were included with cardboard overlays that sat over the controller and informed the player what the button was used for. In "Soccer", for example, each button gave the gamer control of one of the eleven on-screen players.

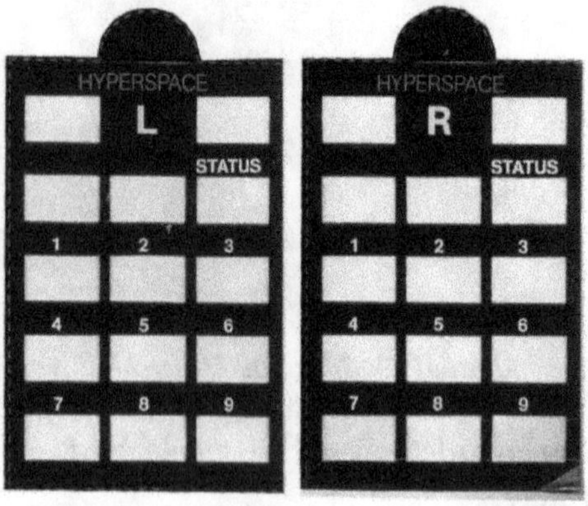

Interton VC4000 Controller Overlays

The VC4000 is celebrated for being the only console that was completely designed in Germany. Although it was released in 1978, Interton claimed that work on it actually began four years earlier. Interton licensed the console to other manufacturers who released it under their own labels, among them being the ITMC *MPT-05* and the Karvan *SOE 2000*. The Grundig *Super Play 4000* also fell under this category, but that console had actually been manufactured by Interton for Grundig. Interestingly, the Grundig Super Play 4000 could only play on Grundig television sets, by plugging it into a special adapter in the back of the TV.

Magnavox's Odyssey^2

While Philips was selling its Signetics chips to console manufacturers in Europe, it was purchasing Intel 8048 chips for its own new console. Its new programmable Magnavox *Odyssey^2* had been designed to compete directly against Atari's VCS.

The style of the *Odyssey^2* strongly resembled the artist conceptions of the abandoned Odyssey 5000. The raised area at the rear of the Odyssey 5000 was where the cartridge slot and power button were located on the Odyssey^2. But the top flat area of the console that would have been used to store controllers on the Odyssey 5000 was used for a different purpose on the Odyssey^2.

The Odyssey^2 was designed to capture the attention of computer-conscious consumers and included an actual 49-character alphanumeric keyboard that was built-into the top

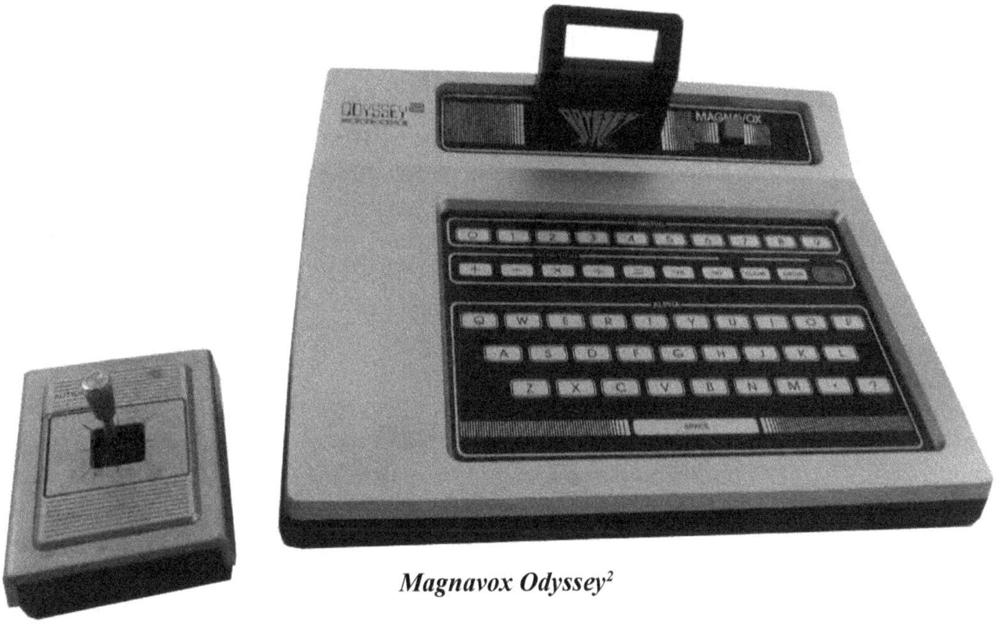

Magnavox Odyssey²

of the console. The "keys" were pressure-sensitive, which made the machine perfect for families with young children since there weren't any buttons on the unit that could break off. Although Magnavox never actually purported that the Odyssey² could be upgraded to a computer, the appearance of the keyboard gave many people the impression that it could. Magnavox even released *Computer Intro*, a program designed to actually teach Odyssey² users how to program a computer. An accompanying spiral-bound tutorial provided an overview of computer history, basic programming fundamentals and sample code so users could create simple games that they could run on the console. It also included decimal-binary-hexadecimal charts, instruction sets and a computer glossary. *Computer Intro* taught its users how to program in Assembler Language, a first-generation programming language that was close to the binary machine language that the console understood. The package turned the Odyssey² into a reasonable copy of a personal computer, which still wasn't a household object at the time. Unfortunately, the Odyssey² couldn't actually perform as a real computer due to its limited amount of memory and lack of a storage device.

But since the graphics and suggested retail price of the Odyssey² and VCS were similar, the keyboard appeared to give Magnavox an edge. Parents who wanted educational games for their kids saw the benefits of the keyboard. One of the initial releases for the VCS, *Basic Math*, displayed math problems on the screen. The child could only get the

Philips G7000

correct answer on the screen by cycling through all of the numbers via the joystick. In "Math-A-Matic", the Odyssey^2 version of the game, the child simply had to press the correct numerals on the keyboard.

Philips, the parent company of Magnavox, released the Odyssey^2 in Europe, where it was called the *Videopac G7000.*[6] Basically, the two units were virtually identical, although the Videopac G7000 didn't have a power switch.[7] And unlike the Atari VCS that wouldn't permit European PAL cartridges to play on North American NTSC systems and vice versa, most Videopac G7000 cartridges could easily play on American Odyssey^2 consoles. The Videopac G7000 was much more popular than the Odyssey^2 and many games that were never released in North America came out in Europe.

New VCS Games

Shortly following the debut of the Magnavox Odyssey^2 with its "*the keyboard is the key*" advertising campaign, Atari released its own "keyboard" for the VCS. The *Keyboard Controllers* were in fact a pair of two connectable keypads that plugged into the controller ports. Each controller featured twelve buttons, which were configured like a telephone keypad. While it appeared as if Atari had released the Keyboard Controllers as its answer to the Odyssey^2, Atari actually did it for legal reasons. Although the official name of the VCS was the 'Video Computer System', Atari was sued for misrepresentation because the unit clearly wasn't a computer--there wasn't any way for users to input data. Atari took the suit seriously and quickly designed and released the keyboard controller, thus eliminating the main contention of the lawsuit.

Atari VCS Keyboard Controllers

Atari released a trio of game cartridges to accompany the controllers. *Hunt & Score* was Atari's version of *Concentration*[8]. *Codebreaker* was *Mastermind.* The third cartridge consisted of a group of memory games and was simply called *Brain Games.*

One of the variations on the *Brain Games* cartridge, "Touch Me", was the videogame version of an arcade game that Atari had released in 1974. The arcade game, also called *Touch-Me,* consisted of large buttons that randomly flashed. The player had to press the buttons in the same order in which the machine flashed them to stay in the game. When a person lost, the machine made an annoying rasping noise. Although the game had been a flop, the marketing minds at Atari decided to include it on the *Brain Games* cartridge. They also designed a handheld version of the game. Coincidentally, Atari wasn't the only company that released a handheld version of *Touch-Me* in 1978.

Simon

In November 1976, Atari had displayed the arcade *Touch-Me* at the Amusement & Music Operators Association (AMOA) show. Attending the show was Ralph Baer, the inventor of home videogames. He noticed *Touch-Me* and played it. While he liked the idea of the game, he wasn't impressed with the way it was presented.

A few months later, Baer decided to build a handheld game based on the children's game *Simon Says.* Using the arcade *Touch-Me* as a model, Baer and his partner Howard Morrison discarded the things they didn't like about the arcade game such as its annoying sounds. They replaced the sounds with four pleasant-sounding bugle tones, and they made each of the four buttons a different color. The finished product was sold to Milton Bradley, who had no idea that Atari was releasing a similar game. Milton Bradley called the game *Simon* and released it in time for the 1978 holiday season.

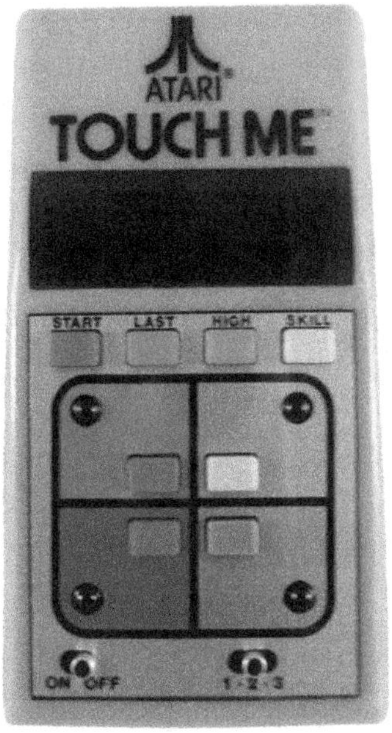

Atari Touch Me

Milton Bradley Simon

Atari's handheld system, *Touch Me*, which resembled a yellow calculator, came out first, but it failed to attract an audience. Milton Bradley's *Simon* was shaped like a disc and featured bugle notes and four large colored buttons that randomly lit up. The player then had to press the buttons in the correct sequence. *Simon* went on to become the top selling electronic game of all time.

1978

Video Chess

The lawsuit that had been filed against Atari because of the VCS' name wasn't the only frivolous suit from which Atari had to protect itself. When the VCS had first been released, Atari's marketing department had designed a box that had a picture of a chess piece on it. One man who had purchased the system sued the company for misrepresentation because a chess game was not available. The marketing people went directly to the

Atari VCS Box

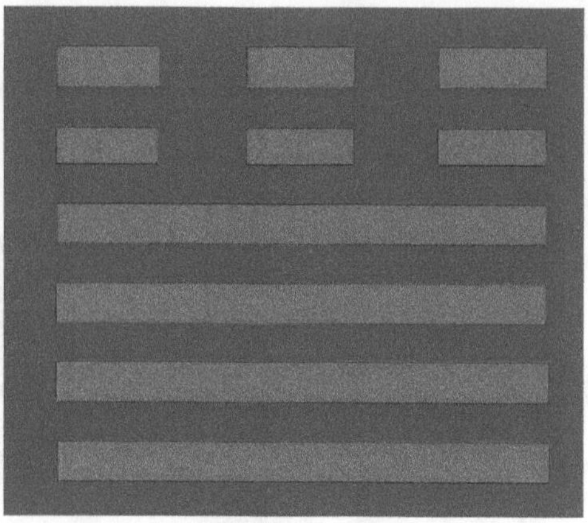

Atari VCS Video Chess Rook

programmers and asked them to create a chess game for the VCS, only to be informed that this would be impossible.[9] Larry Wagner, one of the original designers of the VCS, said that although he could write an algorithm to play chess, the VCS simply didn't have enough memory to portray an on-screen chessboard. Wagner was told to proceed anyway and then spent the next two years designing the algorithm with the help of a national chess champion. By that time, programmer Bob Whitehead solved the display problem with an innovative solution that he designed in two days.

In non-technical terms, the television screen builds a picture by painting dots that add up to form images on each of the TV's scan lines. Whitehead figured that each chess piece could fit within twelve scan lines. However, the VCS didn't have the capacity to display eight objects on a horizontal scan line, which was needed. Whitehead's solution, called *Venetian Blinds*, simply had each object built on every other scan line. Instead of each piece using twelve scan lines, they used six scan lines. Four pieces were drawn beginning at an even numbered scan line and four were drawn beginning at an odd numbered scan line. The resulting pieces were crude, each containing six blank gaps throughout them, but they were clear enough that the chess pieces could be recognized.

Video Chess, which was released in 1980, was not the first instance where Atari's programmers took an innovative approach to satisfy design problems. When Alan Miller wrote *Basketball* for the VCS, he was wary about designing a simple two-dimensional game like the Odyssey^2's *Basketball!*. After considerable thought Miller designed the court like a trapezoid, where it appeared to have depth as well as width. Although primitive, Atari's *Basketball* was the first example of a videogame with a 3D perspective.

Basketball wasn't the only sports game that Atari released for the VCS. Other titles included *Home Run,* a simple baseball game, and *Miniature Golf.* All in all, Atari doubled its lineup with titles that also included arcade hits. *Outlaw* was a blocky version of Midway's *Gunfight,* and *Breakout* was a true rendition of Atari's own famous brick-smashing game. In homage to the game that indirectly led to the birth of Atari, the company also released a VCS version of *Spacewar.*

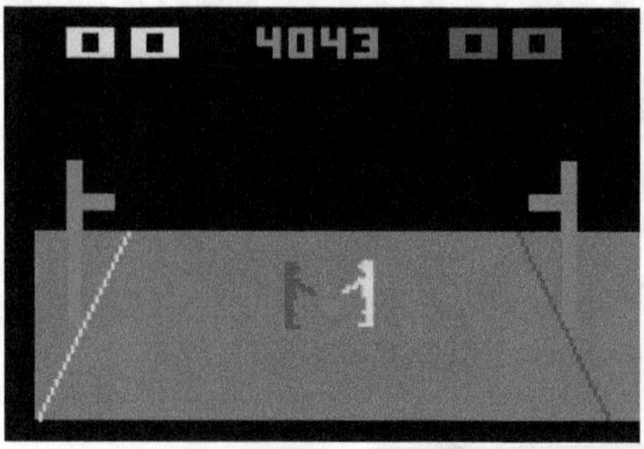

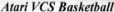

Atari VCS Basketball

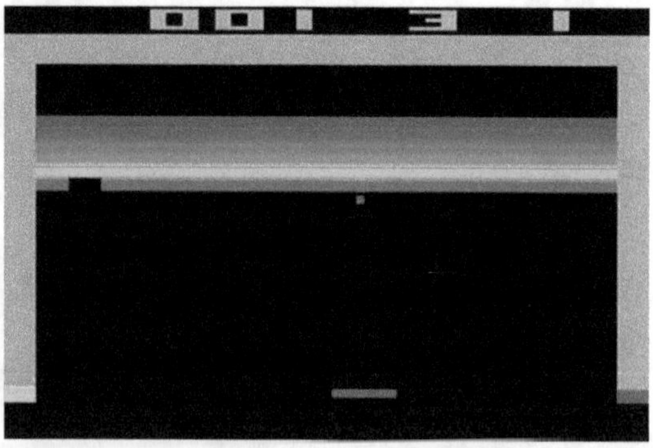

Atari VCS Breakout

Channel F System II

Meanwhile Fairchild was struggling for its groundbreaking Channel F to compete against the VCS, which was increasingly growing in popularity. The Channel F was redesigned to make it more attractive to prospective videogame buyers. Along with five

Fairchild Channel F System II

new games, the newly-redesigned system was released in December under the name *Channel F System II* and the retail price was reduced to $100. Unfortunately, the new features really didn't amount to much. The sound was channeled through the television set's speaker, rather than from the unit itself and the controller storage area was relocated to the rear of the unit. The controllers themselves became detachable from the console. A new optional 16-button keyboard controller, which looked amazingly like Atari's keyboard controllers, was featured in Fairchild's Channel F catalog that was packed with the unit and three new Videocarts were mentioned to be available for it.[10]

Fairchild Channel F Keyboard Controller

Thanks to the popularity of *Space Invaders,* the 1978 holiday season wound up being the best one so far for the home videogame companies. Demand for the Atari VCS was so high that the company had to ration the units out to retailers, and the 400,000 stockpiled consoles eventually were sold. The VCS sold so well that the Atari management began thinking that maybe their little seasonal product wasn't so seasonal after all.

CHAPTER SEVEN
1979

When Atari originally entered the consumer business with *Home Pong*, Nolan Bushnell believed that it was a product that would only sell during the holiday season. It was this belief that caused Bushnell to sell Atari in 1976, when all of the company's money was tied up in merchandise that would move at Christmas time.

Following Atari's sensational 1978 Christmas season, its management pondered whether the VCS could sell year round. After all, people played arcade games year round, so why not home games? With this in mind, Atari began promoting the VCS on national television at the end of January. Before long Atari was selling the VCS to people who had been exposed to it from the TV commercials. To capitalize on this major purchasing rush for the VCS, Atari began releasing cartridges for the unit en force. When the television blitz began, Atari introduced four new cartridges.

By the end of the year, Atari had released several more games and one of them demonstrated just how innovative Atari's designers were when it came to new and interesting games.

Superman had been produced as a tie-in to the *Superman* movie that Warner Bros. had released a year earlier. It was the first home videogame that was a movie tie-in as well as the first RPG (role-playing game) released for a home videogame console. In this game, the player assumed the role of the Man of Steel who had to explore Metropolis in the shortest time to find and retrieve three pieces of a bridge that that been blown up by Lex Luthor.

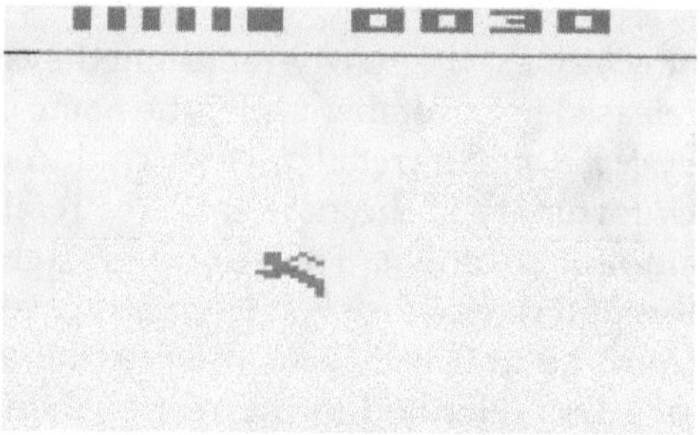

Atari VCS Superman

Europe Revisited

In Great Britain, Radofin Electronics released its *1292 Advanced Programmable Video System (APVS)*, which internally was very similar to Interton's VC4000. Both used the Signetics 2650A chip as their CPU and the Signetics 2636 chip for their video controller.[1] And both came with a pair of analog joysticks, which looked remarkably similar, although

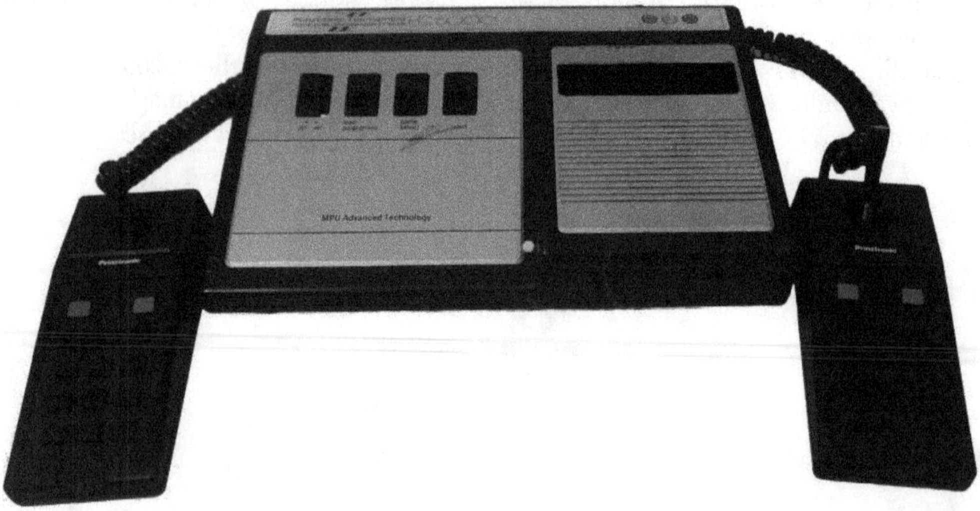

Prinztronic Tournament VC6000

the Radofin controllers were not self-centering. Externally, the 1292 APVS differed from the VC4000, as its cartridge slot was to the right of its four buttons and it didn't feature a storage area for its two controllers.

Like Interton, Radofin licensed its console out to other companies, who released similar systems under their own brand names. Among these systems were the Audiosonic *PP-1292* and the Prinztronic *Tournament VC 6000*. Although Interton and Radofin both released the same games for their respective systems, the cartridges were not interchangeable as the shapes of the cartridges were different. However, even among the 1292 APVS clones, it wasn't always guaranteed that a cartridge from one company would play on a console from another.

Radofin quickly followed the 1292 ACVS with the *1392 ACVS*, which was basically the same console except that its power pack was located inside the unit.

Videogame Consoles as Computers

As VCS owners hit pay dirt with new game releases, owners of the Bally Professional Arcade discovered that their major supply of games wound up being the ones they wrote themselves with *Bally BASIC*. Executives at Midway realized that they really didn't want to be in the home videogame business, which was a completely different world from the arcade enterprise they were accustomed to. At the same time they were spending most of their time trying to start up a new casino division. They simply didn't have any time or energy to spend on the Arcade.

With only a trickle of titles now being released Arcade owners began writing their own games in earnest. Eventually user groups formed and people began trading their home-grown games for those written by others. The first established group began printing a newsletter, *The Arcadian*, which included ads by people who wanted to trade or sell their games to others. The editors *of The Arcadian* even rated some of these games for the benefit of its readers. But even as the underground market for Arcade games boomed, Midway steadily decreased its number of new releases.

While Arcade owners used their consoles to write computer programs, Odyssey² owners used their console and its *Computer Intro* cartridge to learn about computers. Atari refused to be outdone and released its own programming cartridge for the VCS. *BASIC Programming* allowed VCS owners to write rudimentary programs via the keyboard controllers that simply weren't suitable for the task. Each button on the controller served three functions and several served four. The user had to keep pressing a shift button a number of times to make sure that the right button would yield the correct response.

While *Computer Intro* taught Odyssey² owners how to program in *Assembler*, Atari's *BASIC Programming*, despite the title, didn't even teach *BASIC*. The only thing that the instruction booklet did was describe which buttons to press in order to do certain things. It was a far cry from Magnavox's wonderful tutorial and only left its users utterly confused.

Despite its keyboard and excellent introduction to programming software, Magnavox didn't go out of its way to confuse consumers into believing that the Odyssey² was a computer. But Philips, its European counterpart, had other ideas. From the beginning, Philips had dubbed the Videopac G7000 console as the *Videopac Computer*. And instead of letting its customers know that its programming cartridge was merely an introduction into programming, it boldly called the software *Computer Programmer*. Philips even introduced a new Videopac model that completely resembled a home computer. The *Videopac G7200* had a built-in 9" black & white monitor nestled behind the keyboard.

Management at other videogame companies believed that personal computers were the way to go. Atari, the number one game company, even opened its own computer division a year earlier. Ironically, one major computer company seemed to think that it needed to have a stake in the videogame business.

Philips Videopac G7200

In the spring of 1979, Mike Markkula, the chairman of Apple Computers, called in Jef Raskin, who was then the manager of Apple's publications department. Markkula's intent was to have Raskin work on a project that had been code-named *Annie*. Markkula explained that he wanted the company to market a product that cost less than their popular Apple II, which retailed at $1,000. Annie would be a $500 videogame console.

Although Raskin told Markkula that Annie sounded like a fine product, it wasn't something that he was especially interested in working on. Instead, he wanted to design a computer that would be easy to use from a human perspective. Within a month the Annie project was dead before it even began and Raskin was deep into developing his plans for his "Person In The Street" computer.[2]

Epoch and Bandai

In April, Nintendo released its fourth inexpensive, dedicated Japanese console, the ¥12,500 ($58) *Color TV-Game Block Kuzushi*. This single-player system played several variations of Nintendo's arcade game, *Block Fever*, which itself was a *Breakout* clone. The unit was the first from Nintendo that hadn't been designed by Mitsubishi. As if to honor this achievement, the company displayed, for the first time, the "Nintendo" brand name on the front of the console, which had been designed by a young junior Nintendo employee named Shigeru Miyamoto.[3]

The Color TV-Game Block Kuzushi was not the only dedicated Japanese console that played *Breakout*-styled games. Epoch, a Japanese toy company, had been interested in entering the videogame business and licensed the Video Pinball console from Atari's consumer division, which had been interested in entering the Japanese market. Epoch gave the console a complete facelift and the result was the Epoch *TV Block*. With its rounded edges and red and white motif, the TV Block bore little resemblance to the Video Pinball console from which it had derived.

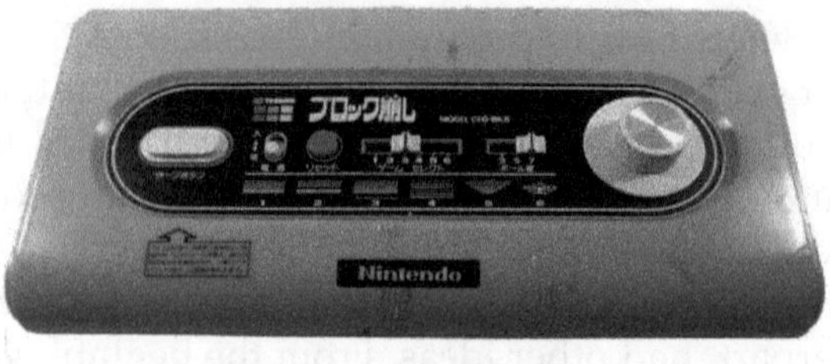

Nintendo Color TV-Game Block Kuzushi

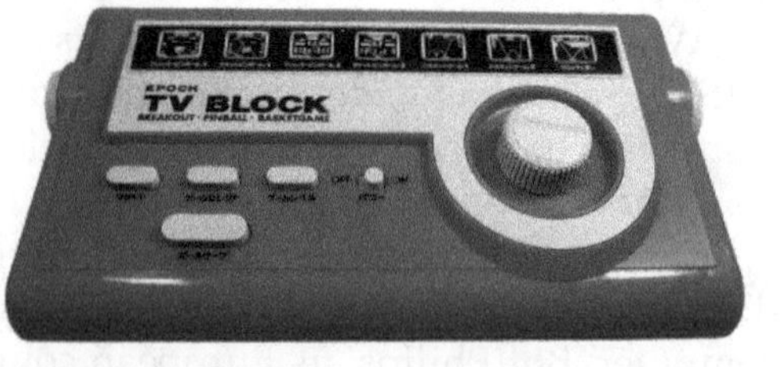

Epoch TV Block

Unfortunately, the TV Block couldn't compete against Nintendo's Color TV-Game Block Kuzushi, which had sold more than 400,000 units. When Epoch next licensed the VCS from Atari a decision had been made to sell the console under the "Atari" brand name, rather than "Epoch" name. When the console appeared on Japanese store shelves in its American packaging in October, only a small label on the box indicated that Epoch had anything to do with it.

For two months, Epoch's VCS was the only programmable system available in Japan. It faced competition in December when Bandai released its newest console in the TV Jack

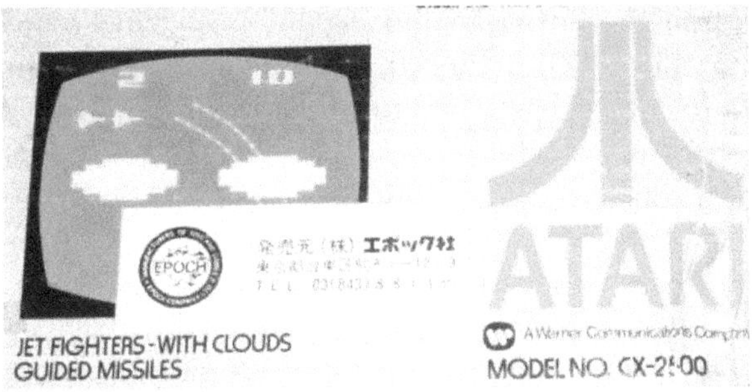

Japanese VCS with Epoch label

Bandai Super Vision 8000

series. The *TV Jack 8000,* which was also known as the *Super Vision 8000,* accepted cassettes[4] as did the TV Jack 5000 that preceded it. But unlike the TV Jack 5000 where the cartridges merely unlocked built-in games, the Super Vision 8000 was a true programmable console that used ROM cassettes, the first Japanese console to do so.

The ¥59,800 ($249) Super Vision 8000 was a powerful machine, much more powerful than anything already available in Japan, including the VCS. Its 8-bit NEC D780C processor ran twice as fast as the 6507 processor in the VCS and it had its own General Instrument sound chip that could support three sound channels.

The Super Vision 8000's controllers were revolutionary. Each rectangular-shaped controller featured a twelve-button telephone-style keypad, which was used for inputting game selections. Beneath this keypad was a disc, which was in place of a joystick and could be pressed in any of sixteen directions. Finally, along the side of each controller was a small firing button.

The console itself was sleek looking with a square design that sloped at a 15° angle from top to bottom. The cassette slot was located at the top center of the unit, with power and game selection buttons directly beneath it. The two controllers sat in recessed cradles on both sides of the cassette slot and buttons. The system was sold with *Missile Vader*, a *Space Invaders* clone, and six additional games were available separately.

The Mattel Intellivision

Mattel Intellivision

During December, the same month that the Super Vision 8000 debuted in Japan, Mattel Electronics began test marketing the Intellivision (***Intelli**gent Tele**vision***) in Fresno, California. The Intellivision was a rectangular-shaped unit. Across its center was a recessed compartment where the system's two-hardwired controllers sat end-to-end. The controllers were near exact copies of the ones were used with the Super Vision 8000. In fact, there were only two real differences between the two. The Intellivision controller featured four *action* buttons, two on side, instead of the Super Vision 8000 controller's one. And the keypad on the Intellivision controller was recessed, which allowed the player to insert a plastic overlay over the keypad. This overlay, which was different for every cartridge that it came with, allowed the player to easily know which buttons were used for a game.

Another similarity between the two consoles was that they both employed the General Instrument AY-3-8910. audio chip.[5] However, for processing, the Intellivision used General Instrument's CP1610, a 16-bit microprocessor, which at .9Mhz ran even slower than Atari's VCS. But the CPU ran in tandem with a Standard Television Interface Chip (STIC), a General Instrument AY-3-8900-1 chip that controlled the video display, which were truly outstanding, especially when compared to the VCS. One of the initial games, *Armor Battle,* was a tank game that was compared to Atari's *Combat,* where two players used tanks to shoot at one another and the player with the most points at the end of the timed competition won. In *Armor Battle,* each player was allotted fifty tanks, but only two appeared on the screen at a time. The playfield consisted of water, highways and woods and each had a different effect on how a tank could move. A tank was destroyed when it was hit three times by the opponent or when it ran into an invisible mine. When a player lost both tanks, a new battleground appeared (there were 240 different playfields altogether) along with two tanks from his remaining supply. The game continued until someone lost all fifty of his tanks. While *Combat* was simply a game of duck and shoot, *Armor Battle* involved strategy and patience.

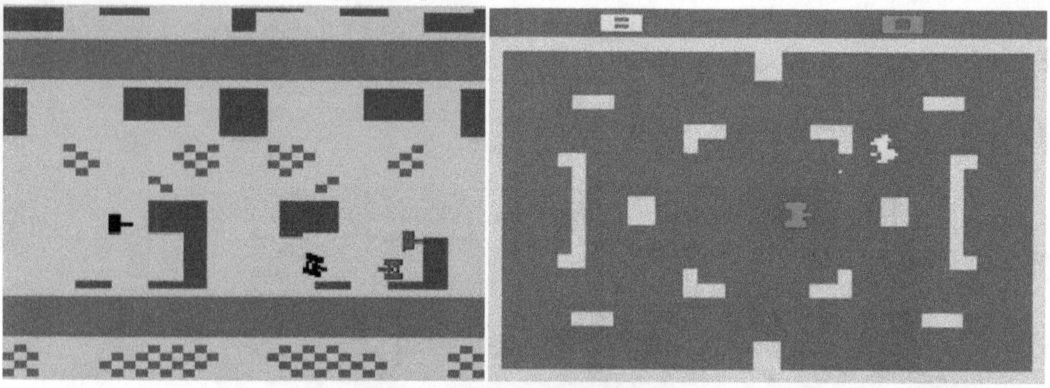

Mattel Intellivision Armor Battle vs. Atari VCS Combat

Initially, Mattel Electronics only test marketed the game-playing Master Component, but the company announced that a Computer Component that included a cassette tape deck for saving programs and full-sized typewriter-style keyboard would be available at a later date.

The APF MP-1000

Consumers already were able to purchase a system that was amazingly similar to what Mattel Electronics planned to offer. Early in the year, APF Electronics, which had released several dedicated ball & paddle consoles since 1976, released a $130 programmable console called the *MP-1000.* Although the console included a built-in game called *Rocket Patrol,* additional games stored on ROM cartridges were available for purchase. The games featured graphics that were large and colorful and were more comparable to those on

APF MP-1000

the Bally Professional Arcade than on the Atari VCS.

The controllers that came with the MP-1000 differed from those on the other available consoles. Like the Intellivision controllers, they featured twelve numeric buttons for data input. At the upper part of each controller was a short four-position joystick with a large handle. A fire button was mounted into the top edge of the controller behind the joystick.

The MP-1000 was one of the faster consoles available. It's Motorola 6800 chip processed at a speedy 3.579MHz. But the real power of the machine became apparent with the addition of the $499 *MPA-10* module, which had a built-in real typewriter-style keyboard and a data cassette recorder-reader. There was a large indentation in the module where the MP-1000 console could be placed, and together they became the *Imagination Machine*, a bona fide home computer that contained 14k of ROM and 9k of RAM. And additional peripherals such as a disk drive were also available. The MP-1000 console and the MPA-10 module could also be purchased together for $599, which made it one of the more inexpensive home computers on the market. As a computer, the Imagination Machine attracted first time computer buyers with its low price. And for fledgling programmers, BASIC and 6800 Assembly languages were to be had. In addition, several productivity programs and additional games were available on cassette tapes.

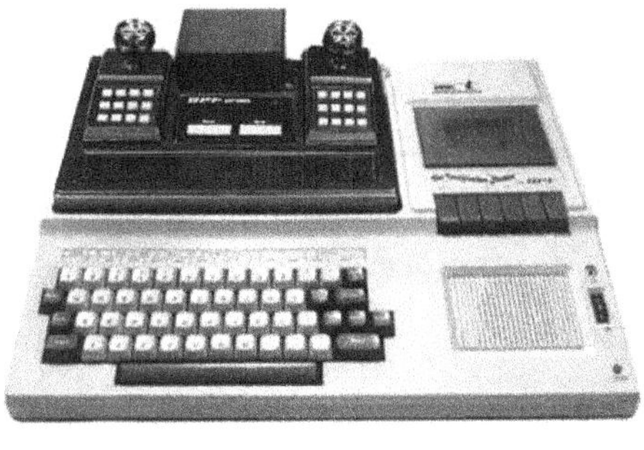

APF Imagination Machine

Meanwhile Bally, which had promised a computer keyboard for its Bally Professional Arcade, made it known that it wanted to sell off its Consumer Products Division if it could find a willing buyer. This was the result of the console's sluggish sales and the company's recent entrance into the casino gambling business.

Bally canceled the computer keyboard and ceased development of new games for the console. But three new titles, including the home console debut of *Space Invaders*, were released during the year. And although it was the first time *Space Invaders* was available at home, it was released with little fanfare.[6] Bally hadn't actually licensed a home version of the game from Taito.

Bally Professional Arcade
Space Invaders Videocade

Instead, it assumed that its license for the American arcade version automatically included a home version as well.

Zircon International

Bally wasn't the only company that wanted to get out of the home videogame business. With sales for its Channel F not where they would have liked them to be, and interest in the Channel F System II nearly non-existent, Fairchild began seeking a buyer for its Video Products Division. Zircon International, a four-year old company that manufactured digital watches, purchased the division and immediately began closing out excess stock from a warehouse in Campbell, California. Brand-new original consoles were sold for $50 and the System IIs went for $75. All 20 Videocarts were available for $20 each.[7]

Some items that were not available in the clearance were the keyboard controller and the games that were to be available for it. Once Zircon took over, these products were quietly cancelled without ever being released.

Zircon did not change the packaging or the markings on the consoles in any way. So even though Fairchild was no longer involved in the marketing of the system, its name still appeared everywhere.[8]

Programmable Handhelds

Unfortunately, the Channel F simply couldn't compete against the Atari VCS, despite it being the first console to use ROM cartridges. More and more consoles were using this technology so it was apparent that it was only a matter of time before handheld consoles began using them as well. But just as the programmable consoles had been preceded by the dedicated PC-50x consoles, which also employed cartridge, the handheld devices would have to follow a similar path.

Microvision, which would be the first handheld unit that used cartridges, was released in November by Milton Bradley. Designed by Jay Smith of Smith Engineering, the Microvision had a two-inch square LCD screen and a dial controller. The graphics were small and blocky but they allowed more movement than the light emitting screens that were on the dedicated handhelds from Mattel Electronics and Coleco. In a way, the graphics were similar to the early VCS graphics-crude, yet effective.

Milton Bradley released a series of cartridges for the Microvision that were challenging despite the small screen. With titles like *Bowling, Cosmic Hunter* and *Connect Four,* the compny proved that it could be diversified in the types of games that it developed. Unlike the programmable consoles that were on the market, the Microvision did not have its own CPU, the Central Processor that processed all data. Instead, each of the Microvision cartridges had their own 4-bit microprocessors that allowed the system to be easily upgradeable as new cartridges came along with more powerful CPUs.

Milton Bradley Microvision

When the Microvision was released, Atari was already working on its own handheld unit that would also use cartridges to change games. But Atari wasn't hoping to make an impact with a system that merely allowed the purchase of new games. *Cosmos,* its programmable handheld unit, came complete with its own holographic screen. When the Cosmos prototype was brought to a trade show, it impressed the crowd so much that enough advance orders were written to make the project profitable. Atari planned to release Cosmos in 1981.

Innovative Arcade Games

In the arcade world, several innovations were introduced. In April, Exidy released *Star Fire,* which had the look and feel as if it had been a licensed *Star Wars* game, from the opening title that spelt out the game's name, to the action that featured dog fights in space. Somehow it failed to garner the attention of George Lucas' attorneys.

In this first-person space game, players sat in front of the screen and pretended that they were in the cockpit of a ship. While this wasn't the first time a cabinet had a built-in seat that allowed the player to truly play from a first-person perspective, it was the first to offer a *cockpit* cabinet, one in which the seat was enclosed to simulate the interior of a ship's cockpit.

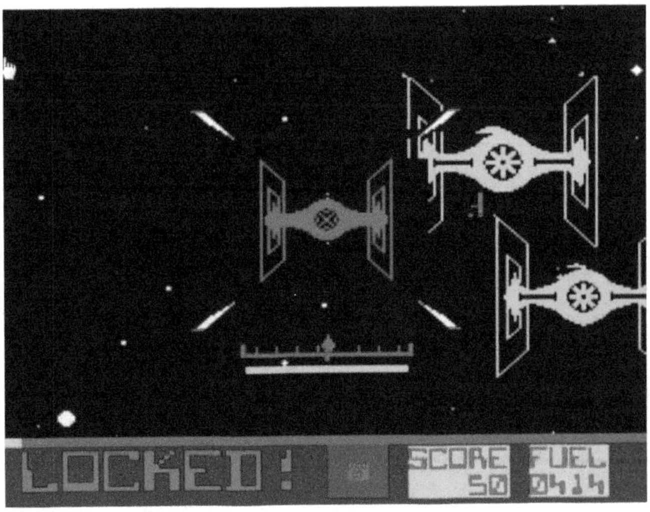

Exidy Star Fire

Star Fire was also the first game to credit players who achieved high scores. Unlike *Space Invaders*, which pioneered the HIGH SCORE concept by keeping the highest score on the screen at all times, *Star Fire* remembered the initials of the people who accomplished the twenty highest scores, and displayed them during the game's attract mode. People soon began playing the game like crazy so they could get their initials on the screen along with their high score.

Star Fire made ample use of color graphics, such as enemy ships that awarded points that varied with their color. However, like the handful of color arcade games that preceded it, each object was rendered in a single color. That changed in October when Namco introduced *Galaxian* in Japan.

At first glance, *Galaxian* appeared to be a *Space Invaders* rip-off. Players controlled a laser cannon that moved side to side at the bottom of the screen and had to shoot down rows of approaching creatures. But things got harder when individual creatures would fly out of formation and dive bomb towards the cannon. The player lost a turn if the creature hit the cannon. And the creatures could also fly off one side of the screen and

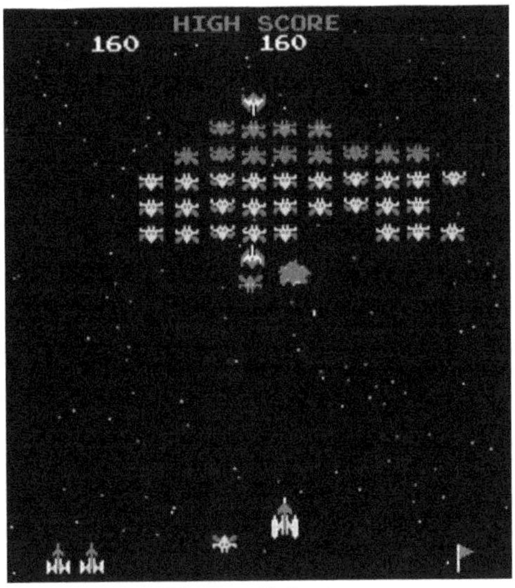

Namco Galaxian

reappear on the other.

But the most notable part of *Galaxian* was its use of color. All of the creatures in a row were the same color, which might be different from those in another row. But some of them were multi-colored as the individual sprites that made up the creature were of different colors. This had never been done before and set the standard of the games that followed.

Midway, the same company that had licensed *Space Invaders* from Taito, licensed *Galaxian* from Namco and released it in the United States in December. Midway had turned to Namco as a new source for Japanese games because Taito began distributing its own games in the United States through its new American subsidiary Taito America. As it turned out Midway would strike gold in less than a year through its Namco partnership.

In December, Nintendo released an arcade game that was very similar to *Galaxian*. In *Radar Scope*, the player had to use his laser cannon to destroy 48 enemy *Gamma Raiders* that dive bombed from the top of the screen. The point value of the raider increased as it came closer to the bottom of the screen. Another difference between *Galaxian* and *Radar Scope* was the three-dimensional perspective in the latter. As the raiders descended, they also became proportionally larger, which gave the impression that they were flying towards the player from a distance. The game had been partially designed by Shigeru Miyamoto, who had created the art work for Nintendo's early arcade game, *Sheriff*.

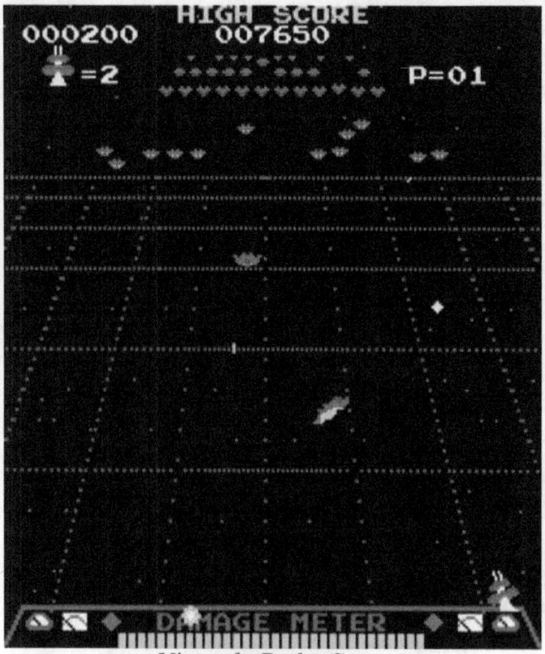

Nintendo Radar Scope

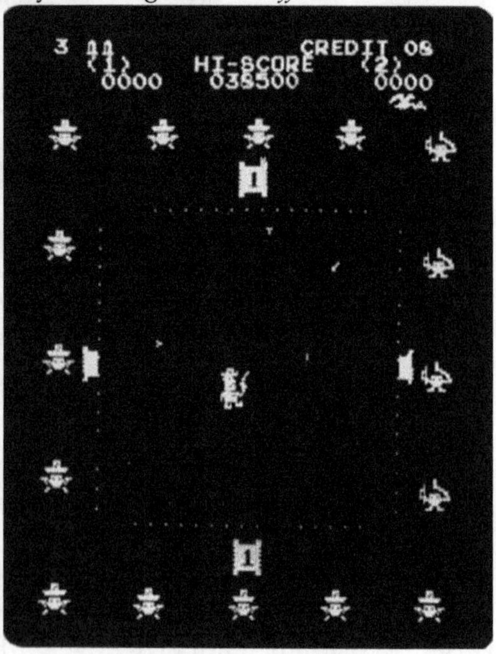

Nintendo Sheriff

Atari was also designing games that were set in outer space. In August, the company released *Lunar Lander*, a game where players had to land a space craft on the moon's surface while fighting gravity. Although the premise of the game had existed for years in text form on PDP and IBM mainframe computers, Atari's release was the first time it had graphics. The game also marked Atari's first use of vector graphics, the system that Cinematronics introduced a year earlier with its *Space Wars* arcade game.

Asteroids

Atari had built 5,000 units of *Lunar Lander* before ceasing production in November. This was done to make room for a new game that created such a sensation that the assembly line stopped just so the employees could play it. No other game had ever generated as much excitement and it had been rushed onto the market so fast that the first 200 units

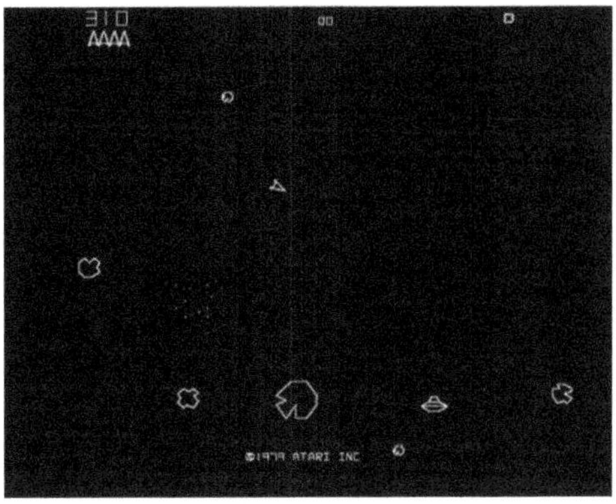

Atari Asteroids

were shipped in *Lunar Lander* cabinets.

Asteroids had been the brainchild of an Atari engineer named Lyle Rains. Although Rains had been with Atari's coin-op division since 1973, through much of 1978 he had been working on a two-player outer space dogfight game for Cosmos, Atari's holographic game system. The 3D screen for Rains' game displayed two moving spaceships and several planets and asteroids, which the players could destroy and had to avoid. Although the game was never produced, Rains was very fond of it and thought about it constantly. When *Space Invaders* caught on in the United States, Rains suddenly thought about what his game might be like if the asteroids moved. He mentioned this idea to an Atari programmer named Ed Logg and within two weeks Logg had a working prototype. The game was so much fun that Logg had to build a second prototype just so his friends could play.

In *Asteroids*, the player controlled a tiny spaceship that appeared in the center of the screen. After a few seconds, the ship got bombarded with big asteroids from all directions. The player could shoot at a big asteroid and earn points but this caused the asteroid to break apart into several smaller asteroids. These medium-sized asteroids could also be fired at and they too would split into smaller pieces when they were hit. When all of the asteroids were finally destroyed, a new barrage appeared on the screen.

Asteroids was proof on how a basic idea could be recycled and appear in many different forms. If the moving asteroids were removed and an opposing spaceship was added, the game would have been *Computer Space*, the very first arcade videogame.

Videogames had evolved and what had been complex to gamers in 1971 was something spectacular eight years later. By the time *Asteroids* came out, gamers had grown accustomed to several controllers and weren't scared off by the multiple buttons that it used for thrust, firing, hyperspace and several other options.

Like *Lunar Lander* that preceded it, *Asteroids* used vector graphics that allowed the outlines of the on-screen asteroids and spaceship to appear very detailed. *Asteroids* soon replaced *Space Invaders* as the king of the arcades and Atari wound up selling 70,000 *Asteroids* units at $2,700 each. For the first time in its history, the company was taking in serious money, which gave it financial independence from Warner. Because Atari earned so much money, it also had a lot of cash to spend. Atari once again dominated the arcades in the industry that it created.

The stellar success of *Asteroids* and *Space Invaders* finally meant that the videogame industry was a force to be reckoned with and the days of pinball ruling the arcades were numbered. It was amid this backdrop that Atari closed its pinball division. Although the company had released innovative machines like *Middle Earth*, which was the first pinball machine to use two playing fields and *Hercules*, which was

Atari Hercules

the largest pinball machine ever manufactured, the fact was that Atari had never been very skilled at manufacturing the machines efficiently. It took the company four months to build a machine that Bally could have produced in two weeks. *Superman* was the last pinball machine that Atari built and distributed.

Atari Computers

But as Atari closed one division, it opened another. Announced in December 1978, Atari officially entered the computer business in October when it began shipping its pair of home computers, the *400* and *800*.

The $550 *400* was a lower-priced unit that somewhat resembled the Odyssey² with a membrane keyboard. However, this keyboard was useless for any serious applications that required typing, such as word processing and programming. The $1,000 *800*, on the other hand, featured a real typewriter-style keyboard.

Atari 800

Atari 400

Atari released several peripherals with the computers, including a disk drive for the 800, a cassette drive for both machines and a dot-matrix printer. On the software side, the company released programming languages such as *BASIC,* word processing and accounting programs, and, of course, games. Most of the productivity software came on disks, which couldn't be used with the 400 because it didn't have enough internal memory to support the disk drive. But other programs, especially games, were available on cassette, and ROM cartridges. Many of the game titles were already familiar to VCS owners, but the graphics capabilities of the computers were far superior than what the VCS offered so the games looked better than anything displayed on the videogame console.

Basketball, for example, was an early game for the Atari computers. Like its VCS cousin, *Basketball* featured a trapezoid court that gave the 3D effect. However, where the VCS game only displayed two featureless players, the computer game displayed characters that actually looked like men.

Unfortunately, because of its poor keyboard, and its ability to basically only play games, the 400 was really just a very expensive game console. The 800, on the other hand, was a serious, versatile computer that could hold its own against the popular Apple II. But it was handicapped by the fact that it had the Atari name, a name that was forever linked with videogames.

With innovative products like Cosmos, Atari intended on controlling the industry that Magnavox had created. By the end of 1979 sales for the VCS and Odyssey² were just about running neck and neck. By using the money that it made from *Asteroids*, Atari intended to end the home videogaming race once and for all.

CHAPTER EIGHT
1980

Videogame popularity continued to grow as more and more people were introduced to them. *Video*, a magazine whose title revealed exactly what it was about, introduced videogames to its audience by featuring a monthly column called "Arcade Alley". The column had been written by two self-acclaimed veteran videogame addicts, Arnie Katz (writing under the pseudonym "Frank Laney, Jr.") and Bill Kunkel.

Battlezone

As public interest in videogames escalated, it was the Atari name that was most remembered. Atari became synonymous with videogames and the company continued to introduce new and exciting games. In November, Atari's arcade division released *Battlezone*, a first-person tank game. This game was so realistic that the U.S. Army ordered a modified version for real combat tank training. The publicity that this brought Atari didn't hurt the company one bit.

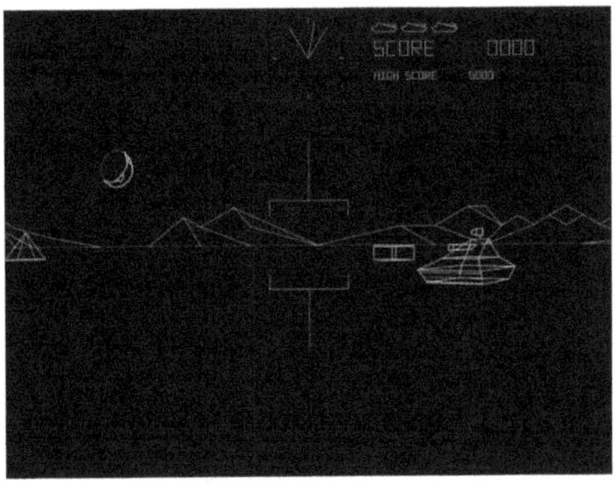

Atari Battlezone

Battlezone's screen depicted a view as seen through a tank's periscope. The player had to shoot down enemy tanks while avoiding the adversary's fire, which could come from any direction, even from behind. As they had to do in 1979's *Subs*, players again contended with action that took place off-screen. An on-screen radar displayed a simplified view of the entire playfield and showed players where enemies were located.

Even though *Subs* hadn't been a commercial success, game designers liked its idea of having the action take place anywhere in the game's "world," whether the player was nearby or not. At the Amusement & Music Operators Association's (AMOA) annual expo in October, *Battlezone* was one of three games shown that had this feature. The second was Midway's *Rally-X*, a Namco-designed game where the player steered a car through a gigantic maze. It was considered the hit of the show and predicted to be the top money earner. The analysts were wrong in their projections.

Defender

Defender, the third game at the AMOA with a playfield so expansive that a radar scanner was needed, marked pinball manufacturer Williams' return to videogames. In this horizontally scrolling game, the player had to save the planet's inhabitants from being abducted by enemies while avoiding and destroying them. In addition to the visual radar, sound effects alerted the player when a citizen was being abducted off-screen.

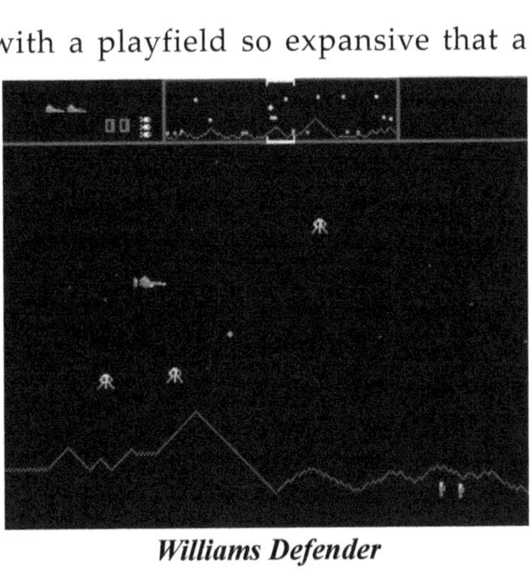
Williams Defender

Defender was a very difficult game, because of all of the action happening at the same time. Adding to this intricacy, *Defender* players had to contend with a record number of seven control buttons. Because of its complexity, *Defender* was practically ignored at the AMOA, where arcade owners preferred the much simpler *Rally-X*. They reasoned that an easy-to-learn game would earn more revenue than a difficult one. However, the arcade owners who did decide to display *Defender* received a surprise. Perhaps because of its complexity, the public became enamored of the game. *Defender* was an unexpected instant hit and put Williams onto the videogame map.

Pac-Man

Defender wasn't the only arcade game that was initially ignored at the 1980 AMOA. Another overlooked game was another Namco maze game that had been designed by Tōru Iwatani and licensed to Midway. In this simple, non-violent game a player navigated a round yellow object through a maze that was lined with dots. Players scored points each time the yellow object ran over a dot and "ate" it. When all the dots were eaten, the player was awarded with a new maze filled with more dots.

Naturally, the game wasn't quite that easy. Trying to thwart the player from eating all the dots were four monsters that caused the player to lose a turn if they caught the yellow object. However, when the yellow object ran over any of the four power pills that were scattered around the maze, the monsters momentarily turned blue and avoided the yellow object. During that time, the yellow object could run over the monsters and score bonus points.

In Japan, the game was called *PuckMan*, a derivative of paku-paku, a Japanese term used to describe the sound of eating. However, Namco feared that American vandals would change the "P" in *Puck Man* to an "F", so they wisely changed the name to *Pac-Man* when they licensed it to Midway.

Puck Man Logo

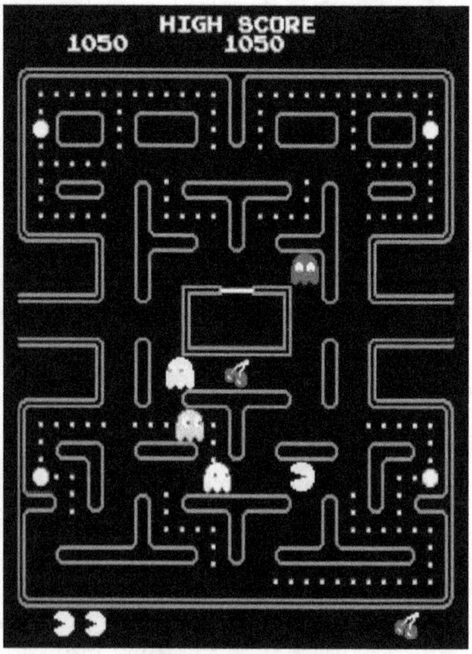

Namco Pac-Man

Primarily because of its non-violent theme, girls began playing *Pac-Man* and quickly discovered that they could be just as good as the boys. Before long, *Pac-Man* replaced *Asteroids* as the most popular arcade game, and eventually it would become one of the top-selling arcade games of all time.

Pac-Man became a national phenomenon. When it was discovered that the monsters (by this time commonly referred to as 'ghosts') moved in patterns, volumes of books were written about how to beat the game. Record-company executives complained about a significant drop in business because teenagers, who had comprised the largest group of record buyers, were spending most of their money in arcades, especially on *Pac-Man*. Many towns passed ordinances that prohibited minors from entering arcades during school hours. It didn't matter. The kids just went to the arcades after school and spent their lunch money then.

While *Pac-Man* was the number one game in Japan, Nintendo's *Radar Scope* was the second most popular. The company's executives believed that the game would find similar success in the United States. Instead of licensing the game to an American company as they had done previously, they decided to distribute the game themselves. Nintendo of

America was set up at 1107 Broadway in New York City, also known as the Toy Building. Most toy and game companies had sales offices there and it was also the site of the annual International Toy Fair that was held every February. Minoru Arakawa, the son-in-law of Nintendo's president, Hiroshi Yamauchi, was placed in charge of the new division.

After *Radar Scope* had a positive test run in Seattle, Arakawa ordered 3,000 units. It took four months to ship the cabinets from Japan to a warehouse in New Jersey, not far from Nintendo of America's offices. But by the time they arrived, the game's appeal had passed. Although Nintendo of America managed to sell 1,000 of them, the remaining 2,000 *Radar Scope* units sat idly in the warehouse.

Game & Watch

Early in the year, before Nintendo opened its American subsidiary, the company released its final dedicated console to Japanese consumers. The *Computer TV Game* was actually a home version of Nintendo's first arcade game, *Computer Othello*. Although it retailed at ¥48,000 ($202), approximately five times the cost of Nintendo's prior dedicated consoles, the Computer TV Game was actually a step backwards as it featured black and white graphics.

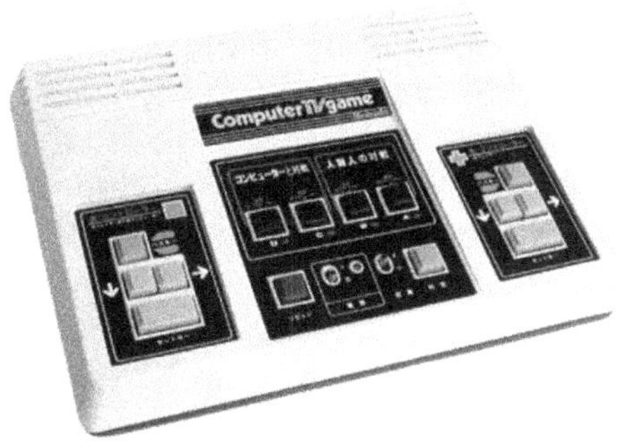

Nintendo Computer TV Game

Because of its high price and low value, few were interested in purchasing the Computer TV Game and Nintendo distributed it in very low quantities. But Nintendo had little interest in making the product more commercial because the company was moving away from dedicated consoles to something much smaller and lot less expensive.

Nintendo entered the handheld gaming market with the release of the *Game & Watch*, a series of credit-card sized units that fit in the palm of a player's hand. The device featured a large LCD screen and several buttons. If a "*game*" button was pressed, a game would begin and a score would appear on the screen. If the "*time*" button was pressed, the game action would disappear and the score would be replaced by the time of day, allowing the unit to act as a watch, complete with an alarm.

The series had been conceived by Gunpei Yokoi, a product developer for Nintendo. The idea had come to him in 1979 as he rode a bullet train, where he had observed a bored passenger playing with a pocket calculator by pressing its buttons. Yokoi thought that a calculator with a built-in game would be a great way for people to kill time while traveling.

Nintendo released its first Game & Watch on April 28. The object of the simply-named *Ball* was to move a juggler horizontally by pressing either a "left" or "right" button, and prevent him from dropping the balls. Retailing at only ¥5,800 ($23), *Ball* was extremely

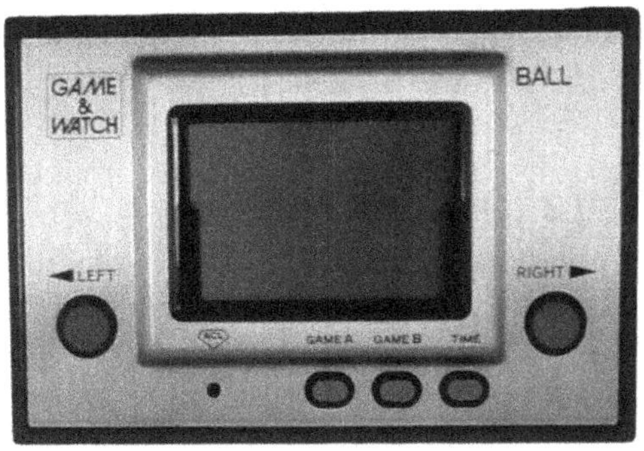

Nintendo Game & Watch

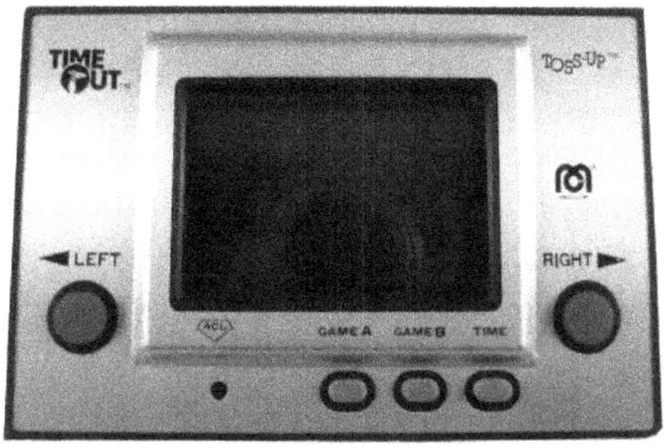

Mego Time Out

popular and Nintendo released four additional titles in the series before the end of the year.

Because Nintendo did not yet have a foreign distribution channel set up, it licensed the Game & Watch's distribution rights to various companies around the world. In the United States, the series was released by Mego, an American toy company that was well-known for its action figures. Mego had come to Nintendo's attention because of its excellent distribution network with toy stores. Mego released all five games in the series on the same days that Nintendo released them in Japan, but it changed the name of the series from Game & Watch to its own distinctive brand, *Time Out*, and the name of each individual game was altered as well. The first game, the one that featured the juggler, was called *Toss Up* in the United States.

Intellivision Nationwide

The LCD graphics on the Game & Watch series, while primitive, were still more advanced than the LED lights on the current handheld systems. Following its 1977 hit, *Football*, Mattel Electronics continued to release handheld units but none of them matched the gridiron game in sales. By late 1979, Mattel Electronics began focusing on its new videogame and computer system, the Intellivision.

Following its successful test marketing campaign in Fresno, Mattel Electronics released the Intellivision console nationwide in February. Even without the promised keyboard, the games on the Intellivision seemed to be worlds ahead of those played on the Atari VCS.

The on-screen characters actually looked like real people, instead of Atari's blocky, computer-generated characters. *Major League Baseball* displayed an entire diamond, and the gamer could individually control all nine on-screen players by pressing different buttons on the keypad.

Mattel Intellivision Major League Baseball

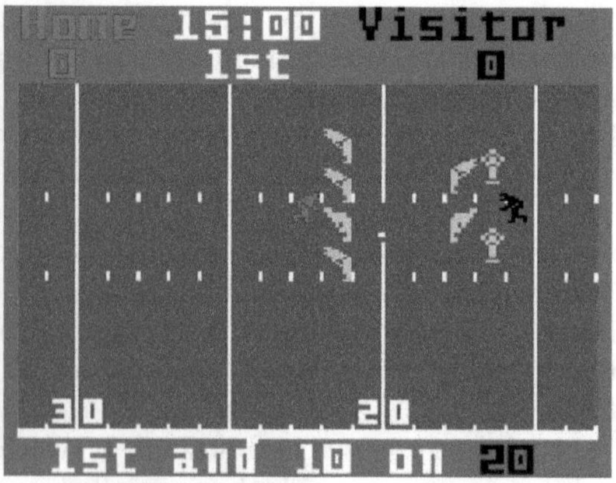

Mattel Intellivision NFL Football

Intellivision games weren't designed to be played quickly. The sports games could only be played by two gamers and took immense concentration on both parts. *NFL Football* allowed players to choose from 160 offensive and 10 defensive plays.

The Intellivision specialized in sports games, a genre that the VCS lacked, and Mattel even licensed the names of organizations that gave the impression that these games had been endorsed by the NFL, PBA, NBA and others. The sports games that debuted with the system included football, baseball, basketball, hockey and skiing. Although Mattel didn't offer an array of arcade games, consumers didn't seem to mind. The Intellivision quickly replaced the Odyssey² as the number two console, and it challenged the established VCS. The latter, thanks to its larger catalog, held an edge over Mattel's system but many of its games seemed visually trite when compared to similar games on the Intellivision.

Although only ten games launched with the Intellivision, Mattel assured consumers

Jerrold PlayCable Box

Mattel Intellivision Computer Component

that that number would double by the end of the year, followed by twenty new games annually. Some Intellivision owners were also offered an alternative method of getting games without buying any cartridges at all. In June, the company began test-marketing a service that it had developed in conjunction with Jerrold, a manufacturer of cable-television equipment. *PlayCable* actually delivered games into homes through cable TV, a distribution method that Ralph Baer had first envisioned ten years earlier. Cable subscribers who signed up to PlayCable had to purchase a $48 adapter, which plugged into the side of the Intellivision console through the cartridge slot. Then after paying a monthly subscription price of $6-$10, they had access to a limited number of titles 24 hours a day. Mattel declared that if the tests proved successful in the four U.S. test cities, PlayCable would go nationwide by the summer of 1981.

The Intellivision impressed the gaming public but it didn't come cheap. The Master Component retailed for $299, $100 more than the VCS. And even at that price, Mattel marketed the Intellivision as an entry-level videogame console for people who weren't ready for computers. The company was betting that after these people owned and sampled the machine for a few months, they would then be ready to spend another $700 to upgrade the console to a computer, which was planned to be released in 1981.

At this time, personal computers were growing in popularity but they were still too expensive for most people. And of those who could afford one, very few had any idea of what they needed a computer for. Bally's approach had been a sound one. By introducing a game console that could be upgraded to a computer, people could introduce a computer into their homes in stages. Unfortunately, because of poor distribution and a high price, the few people who even knew about the Bally Professional Arcade, bought the VCS.

In August, Bally found a buyer for its Consumer Products division, a company called Astrovision. The console was briefly renamed as the *Bally Computer System*, but Astrovision soon settled on *Astrocade*. Bally continued servicing the unit and offered Astrovision the home rights to several Midway arcade games. Astrovision promised that new games would be available, along with the long-awaited computer keyboard.

New VCS Games

Ironically, as Bally was shedding its consumers division, Atari began investing heavily into its own. With the VCS running neck and neck with the Odyssey² in sales, Atari used revenue from its coin-op division, particularly from *Asteroids*, to inject more life into the VCS.

Atari had released twelve new cartridges for the VCS in 1979. But Ray Kassar concluded that consumers wouldn't evaluate a system solely upon the number of games that were available. He figured that people would rush out and purchase a VCS if it could play particular games that they favored. One game that people definitely wanted was

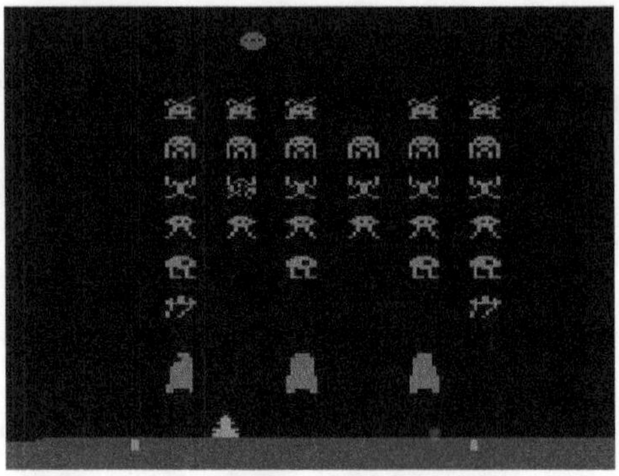

Atari VCS Space Invaders

Space Invaders so Atari went directly to Taito in Japan and licensed *Space Invaders* for home play, marking the first time that an arcade game was licensed for home use.[1] By that time it was the only home version of *Space Invaders*. Astrovision had renamed its version of *Space Invaders* for the Astrocade to *Astro Battle.*

Atari released the VCS version of *Space Invaders* in January and the result was just as Kassar had predicted, it was successful just like its arcade predecessor. People purchased VCS consoles just so they could play *Space Invaders* at home. Atari's 1980 gross income, $415 million, was twice as much as it had been in 1979. The company's operating income rocketed to $77 million, and accounted for 1/3 of Warner Communications' net income. This in turn caused the conglomerate's stock to rise 35 percent. Atari had become the fastest growing company in history.

Easter Eggs

Atari also released a new RPG called *Adventure*, a game that somewhat resembled *Superman* in play. *Adventure* had actually been written before *Superman* and parts of its code had been incorporated into the latter game. In *Adventure*, the player assumed the role of an on-screen character (displayed as a square cursor) who had to search for a magic chalice and return it safely to a gold castle. During the quest, the player had to find keys to enter locked castles and avoid three dangerous dragons. The player could also collect pieces that would aid in the quest, such as a sword that could slay the dragons and a magnet that could collect pieces from out-of-reach places on the screen. The only catch was that the player could only carry one piece at a time. Unlike *Superman*, which was a race against time, *Adventure* ended when the player either returned the chalice to the gold castle, or was eaten by a dragon.

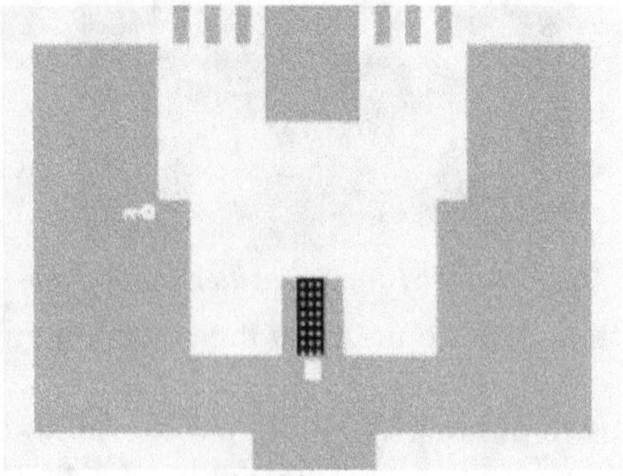

Atari VCS Adventure

While *Adventure* was a fun and innovative game in its own right, it gained notoriety because it revealed to the public the growing tension between Atari's programmers and its management.

Following the Warner buyout in 1976, Atari's programmers, who had previously been revered by the company, were suddenly treated like all other Atari employees. Management's attitude was that the programmers were expendable and could easily be replaced by any other programmer who needed work. The programmers were also getting increasingly unhappy with the fact that Atari made a lot of money from the games they designed, yet they didn't receive a bonus for writing a popular game. The games that they created were the property of Atari and they couldn't make any claims to them.

Like many other programmers, *Adventure's* designer, Warren Robinett, resented the fact that he didn't even receive credit for his games.

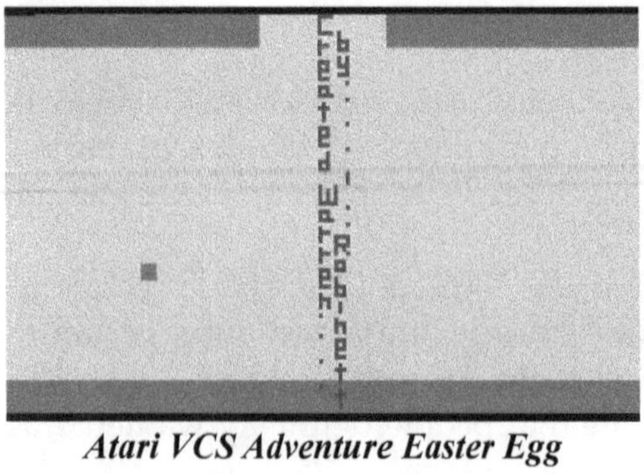

Atari VCS Adventure Easter Egg

FOCUS ON: WARREN ROBINETT

Although Warren Robinett wanted to write a sequel to his popular *Adventure* game, he had already left Atari by the time his Easter Egg was discovered. However, when he left he had the idea for another adventure game where the player had to combine objects in order to build machines to defeat monsters. This idea eventually turned into an educational game called *Rocky's Boots*, one of the initial games released by *The Learning Company*, an educational software company that Robinett co-founded in 1980. The program won Software of the Year awards from *Learning, Parent's Choice*, and *Infoworld* magazines, and received a Gold Award from the Software Publishers Association.

In the mid-1980's Robinett developed the first software for a virtual reality system at NASA's Ames Research Center.

During the early '90s, Robinett was a Research Associate Professor at the University of North Carolina in Chapel Hill where he continued to design interactive computer graphics software. While there he co-invented the *nanoManipulator*, a virtual reality interface to a scanning-probe microscope, which gave scientists the impression that they were actually on the surface of a microscopic sample within the microscope.

Currently, Robinett is part of a research group at Hewlett-Packard.

The Learning Company, which began with a $130,000 grant from the National Science Foundation, was sold to Softkey in 1995 for $660 million. Softkey retained The Learning Company name. In 1998, when The Learning Company was the second largest consumer software company in the world after Microsoft, the company was sold to Mattel for $4.3 billion. After under-performing to Mattel's expectations and causing Mattel's CEO to step down, The Learning Company was sold to Gores Technology Group in October 2000.

Inspired by artists who signed their paintings, Robinett decided to include a secret room in *Adventure* that displayed his name when it was entered. However, because he feared that he would lose his job if anyone ever found out about it, Robinett didn't tell anyone what he had done.

After Robinett eventually left Atari, a twelve-year old boy in Salt Lake City, Utah, discovered the secret room and Robinett's name. After *Electronic Games* mentioned the achievement, Atari executives wanted to remove Robinett's name from the game but they chose not to because it would have cost the company $10,000 to make a new ROM mask. However, they wanted to punish Robinett in some way but his manager, Steven Wright, wouldn't do so. His reasoning was that kids liked to find hidden items, just like they enjoyed finding Easter Eggs at Easter time. He soon encouraged other designers to hide "Easter Eggs" in their programs.[2]

Before becoming a manager over the designers, Wright, had been a game designer himself. Remarkably, he had taught himself 6502 programming only a year earlier when he joined Atari's consumer division. But despite being a novice, Wright managed to design a VCS game that stretched the limits of what the system had been designed to do. Wright's *Championship Soccer* was the first game that Atari shipped in a 4K cartridge. The game itself was revolutionary because it was the first VCS game that featured scrolling graphics. And it was the first game that offered the player a payoff for scoring. Every time a goal was made, the screen displayed a fireworks display accompanied by a cheering crowd.[3]

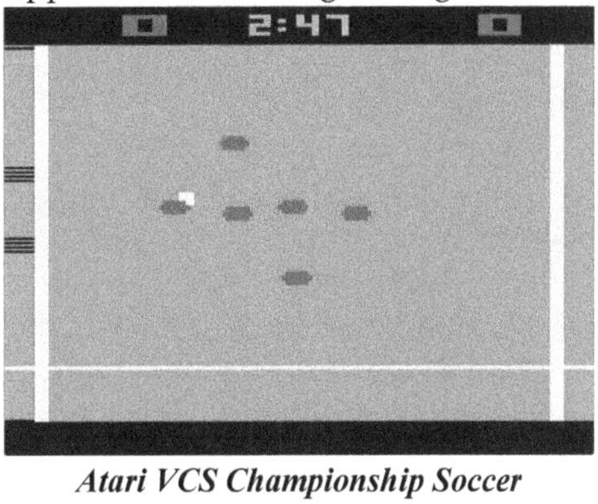

Atari VCS Championship Soccer

Activision

Despite the use of the fireworks whenever a goal was made, or the vertical scrolling playfield, the graphics of *Championship Soccer* were still pretty bland. Each team consisted of only three players, and they basically looked like rectangles. The bottom line was that games looked better on the Intellivision than on the VCS. Atari's executives weren't particularly concerned since the two million systems that it had sold were played in two thirds of all households that had videogame consoles. And since the majority of Atari's revenue derived from the sale of software, the company was sitting pretty since it was the sole supplier of games for those two million consoles.

That changed on April 25, 1980, and suddenly Atari had something to worry about.

It was on that date that news had been released announcing the formation of a new company called *Activision*. Unlike the previous companies that had entered the videogame market with a console, Activision intended to only sell software for the VCS.

Naturally, Atari's management wasn't happy with this new competition. However, it had been the working conditions at Atari that led to the birth of Activision. Like Warren Robinett, who had vented his anger by secretly programming his name in *Adventure*, other game programmers were just as peeved about not receiving the recognition that they thought they deserved. Four of them, David Crane, Alan Miller, Bob Whitehead and Larry Kaplan, decided to leave Atari and start their own company.

The "Gang of Four" actually began formulating their plans in the summer of 1979. They reviewed their ideas with an attorney who felt that the idea was sound, except for one hitch: none of them had the business experience needed to run a company. The lawyer contacted a friend named Jim Levy, a marketing professional who had worked for Hershey's, Time, Inc. and GRT Corp., a manufacturer of records and tapes. Although Levy didn't have any experience in the videogame industry, he quickly saw parallels between it and the recording industry.

During the 1950's, RCA had broken new ground when it introduced a new phonograph that could play new 33-RPM records, in addition to the standard 78-RPM records. These new records rotated at a slower speed than the 78s and contained more music. The 33s were successful, as was RCA's phonograph, which was the only one that could play the 33s. And since RCA was also the only company that manufactured the records, it enjoyed a success similar to the one that Atari would later have with the VCS. Eventually, other companies began manufacturing 33-RPM records, as well as the phonographs to play them on. Levy envisioned a similar system for videogames, where competing companies would produce software for popular gaming consoles.

Levy met with the four renegade programmers, and together they decided to start a company that they called Activision. Since the programmers were all skilled in programming the VCS, they decided to initially release software solely for that system. It didn't hurt that the VCS was in more homes than all the competing consoles combined. However, they planned to watch the Intellivision and Odyssey^2 closely, and if those machines began selling in considerable numbers, Activision planned to also produce software for them.

By the time the first four Activision cartridges were released in the fall of 1980, the Intellivision was enjoying a large following. Despite its heftier price, people became hooked on it after seeing the difference between its graphics and the VCS's. Even though the latter was ensconced in millions of households, the threat of the Intellivision surpassing it seemed more tangible every day.

Although Atari wouldn't admit it, the release of Activision's first four games couldn't have come at a better time to divert the enthusiasm away from the Intellivision. The games, *Dragster, Fishing Derby, Checkers* and *Boxing* were fun and challenging, and all featured crisp graphics that rivaled many of the games that Mattel produced.

Activision's designers were innovative beyond the graphics. *Dragster*, for instance, allowed players to start a new game by pressing the joystick button, a feature not previously available on any VCS game.

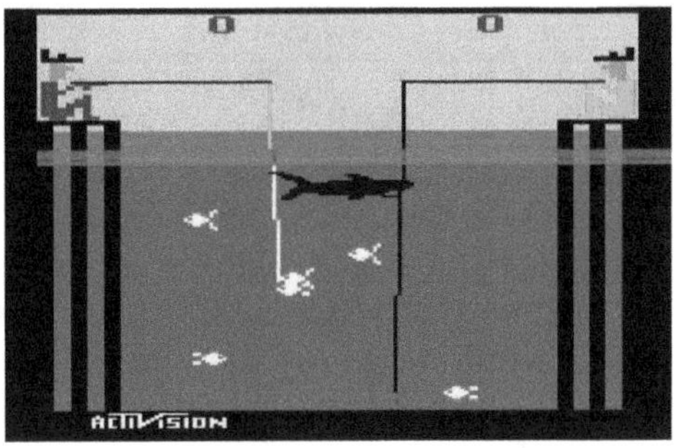

Activision Fishing Derby

Even before a cartridge was inserted into a VCS, one look at the instruction manuals showed players that the games were not from Atari. The Activision manuals included signed letters from the designers that offered hints and suggestions on how to play the games. The designers' photos accompanied the letters. The former Atari designers finally received the recognition that they had sought.

Even though the Activision games may have actually helped Atari sell VCS consoles, Atari executives naturally weren't happy about the new competition. Atari quickly sued Activision, citing that the four renegade designers had used company secrets to create their games. Atari also claimed that *Dragster* was really a home version of the arcade game *Drag Race,* which Atari had released during the summer of 1977. Atari sought an injunction to halt the sale of Activision cartridges, but the restriction was never granted, allowing Activision to continue selling what many consumers considered to be superior games. By the end of 1980, Activision grossed $65.9 million, which netted the young company $12.9 million. Since many VCS owners rationed their money and only bought a limited number of cartridges, it was easy to see that Activision did indeed take a big slice out of Atari's pie.

FOCUS ON: DAVID CRANE

After co-founding Activision, David Crane created some of the best and well-known games for the Atari VCS. Among them was *Pitfall!*, which was named 1982's videogame of the year. For its 1984 sequel, *Pitfall II: Lost Caverns*, Crane also designed the "DPC" chip, which allowed the game to include a four-part harmony music soundtrack throughout. He also created *Little Computer People*, which played on several computers. The premise of *Little Computer People* is a day in the life of animated characters that require little input from the player. The game is often considered a precursor to Will Wright's popular *Sims* series.

Crane left Activision in 1986 and co-founded Absolute Entertainment with several other Activision alumni. While Absolute released several Atari VCS titles late in that console's life, it also created games for the NES, SNES, Genesis and computers. The company was dissolved in 1995 and Crane's next company, Skyworks Interactive, was formed soon afterwards. Crane is still involved with Skyworks Interactive today, which now is one of the top producers of game apps for the iPhone. By the end of 2011, the company had 21 of the top 100 apps in the Apple App Store.

By year's end the VCS was ahead of the Intellivision in sales, but the gap was dramatically closing. The Odyssey^2 fell into third place and the Astrocade wasn't even a contender. As far as software was concerned, the companies still sold cartridges in numbers that were proportional to the amount of consoles in homes. Atari had a record year, but it would have been better if not for the presence of Activision.

And unfortunately for Atari, Activision was just the beginning.

CHAPTER NINE
1981

One way that Atari effectively marketed the VCS against its competitors was by taking advantage of its large catalog of well-known arcade titles and making them available for the home. The VCS catalog also boasted many non-arcade games that Atari assumed people would buy once they owned a VCS. Since it was a seller's market, Atari was able to release games like *3D Tic-Tac-Toe* and *Maze Craze* and be confident that they would sell.

The arrival of Activision brought an end to this. Suddenly, Atari had to deal with a competitor to vie for the gamer's dollars. Now the public had a choice about whether to buy what Atari released or not.

This new competition made Atari realize that it had to design games that people really wanted. In January 1981, the company released, without any advance fanfare, a home edition of *Missile Command*. Although the game played very well, considering the limitations of the VCS, arcade gamers were quick to point out that the home version wasn't as playable as the original arcade edition. For instance, the arcade version of *Missile Command* used the trackball for pinpoint movement. The VCS edition, on the other hand, utilized the joystick, which wasn't nearly as accurate as its arcade cousin.

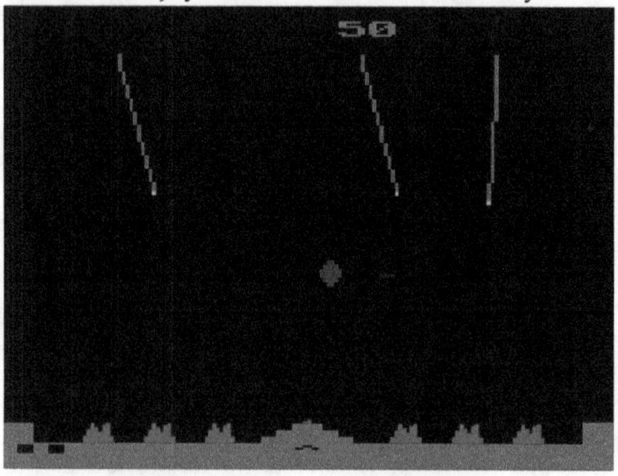

Atari VCS Missile Command

The VCS version of *Missile Command* featured 34 variations, including a special children's version. In this slower and easier rendition, young kids were able to adequately play a "grown-up" game that their older siblings or parents enjoyed. By offering games that appealed to all ages, Atari executives felt that consumers were getting a value when they bought Atari products. Although Activision didn't offer multiple variations, it was certain that the marketplace could sustain two companies. No one in either company ever imagined that there would be even more competition. However, the success of Activision and the dissension at Atari practically demanded it.

Additional Third-Party Vendors

In January, Bill Grubb resigned from his position as Vice-President of Marketing for Atari. Unlike the game designers, Grubb didn't leave because of his lack of recognition. Instead, he had grown tired of the corporate life and wanted to spend more time with his family. After leaving Atari, he learned that he could earn a good living as a manufacturer's representative, so he quickly formed a company called New West Marketing. One of his first clients was Activision.

Grubb thought that the young software company did an excellent job. The profits that they posted at the end of their first year proved that. He also believed that there was room in the marketplace for another company to come in and successfully do the same thing that Activision was doing.

Coincidentally, Grubb was not alone with these ideas. Dennis Koble had been with Atari for over five years, and was at the point where he constantly dreamed about quitting Atari and getting rich by forming his own company. Koble was an engineer who had been responsible for several coin-op games. One of them, 1976's *Sprint 2*, had been Atari's first mass-produced, microprocessor-based game. Another Koble game was *Avalanche*, which had been released in early 1978. The object of *Avalanche* was to catch falling snow and rocks with buckets that the player moved across the screen. The game wasn't a commercial success at all. Ironically, while Koble was dreaming about escaping Atari to form his own company, Larry Kaplan was secretly designing *Kaboom*! – a game that Activision would release later that year. The object of *Kaboom!* was to catch falling bombs with a bucket of water that the player moved across the screen. *Kaboom!* had been based on Koble's unpopular *Avalanche*, and it became one of the first best-sellers for the fledgling Activision.

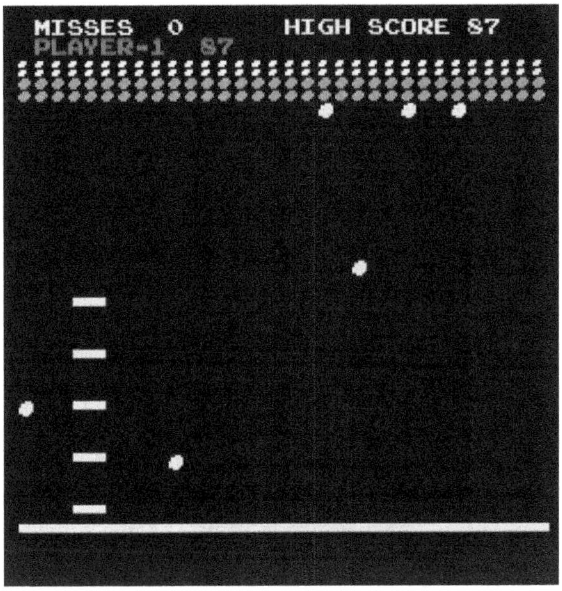

Atari Avalanche

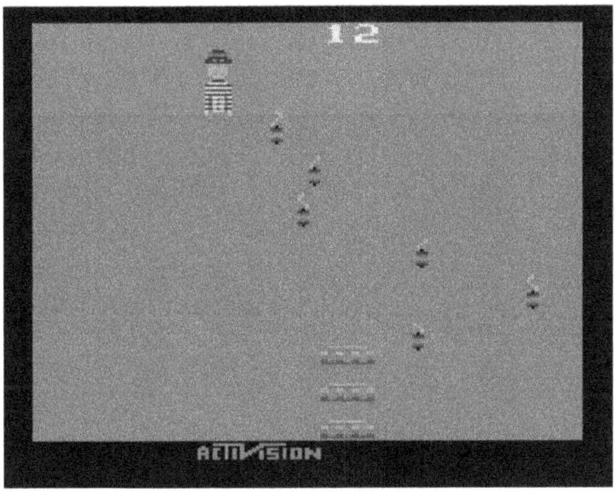

Activision Kaboom!

There was only one thing that prevented Koble from leaving Atari to form his own company: he was an engineer who didn't have any marketing experience. As he pondered this problem, he remembered Bill Grubb. Koble called the former VP of Marketing and discussed his ideas, and was surprised to learn that Grubb had been weighing the same ideas.

Koble and Grubb were not alone. Activision's success caused a lot of people to have the similar thoughts. Grubb met one of them a week after he spoke to Koble, when he was hired by Mattel. There he met an Intellivision designer named Jim Goldberger. Goldberger told Grubb that he and his roommate, a senior Intellivision engineer named Brian Dougherty, had dabbled with the idea of leaving Mattel and starting their own software company that would market Intellivision-compatible games.

Koble, Goldberger and Dougherty were all eager to join Grubb's new venture, so financial backing was quickly sought. After raising $2 million from several private investors, Grubb recruited two Atari game designers and three hardware experts. On July 17, 1981, *Imagic* was founded with its first nine employees. The name of the company was formed from the combination of the words *imagination* and *magic*, the two key components of every game that the company planned to release.

Like Activision, Imagic intended to strictly sell software. However, comprised of former Atari and Mattel personnel, Imagic planned to sell software for both the VCS and Intellivision, betting that the latter would eventually become a market leader.

Although Imagic was the second third-party software company to start up, it wouldn't deliver a cartridge until early 1982. Before then another company beat it to the marketplace. Games by Apollo formed in October 1981 and had its first game in stores by December.

Games by Apollo was different from the other software companies. First of all, it wasn't located within Silicon Valley. The company was headquartered in Richardson, Texas, just north of Dallas. Instead of a design team that consisted of renegades from Atari and Mattel, Games by Apollo team employed only one designer.

The company was the brainchild of Pat Roper, president of National Career Consultants (NCC), a producer of educational films for eleven years. On October 6, 1980, Roper was playing Intellivision's *NFL Football* when he thought about the profits that the videogame companies earned. He wondered if there was anything that could stop him from manufacturing games. When he discovered that there wasn't, he went ahead with his project to make Richardson the new videogame capital of the world.

Although Roper was basically ignorant about the videogame industry, he did know enough to realize that he couldn't sell anything if he didn't have a product. Since he himself didn't know how to design a game, he sought out a designer the only way he knew how: by placing an ad in the paper. The classified ad calling for a videogame programmer was published on October 17, 1981 in both the *Dallas Morning News* and the *San Francisco Chronicle*. A high-school student named Ed Salvo answered the ad and sent off a game that he had been working on at home.

The game was called *Skeet Shoot*. Unlike the games that were being released by Atari and Activision, *Skeet Shoot* consisted of very simple graphics that were very reminiscent of the games that had been originally released with the VCS in 1977. Under ordinary circumstances, a game like *Skeet Shoot* would never have been released, but Roper knew very well that VCS owners were so desperate for new titles that they bought anything that was available. Because of this, he bought the game and quickly hired Salvo as a full-time programmer. Roper released *Skeet Shoot* on December 6, 1981 in boxes that looked just like the boxes that the Atari and Activision cartridges came in. The game sold out and was a success. Most people bought the game sight-unseen and thought they'd bought a cartridge from a major company. The fact that most people were disappointed with *Skeet Shoot* didn't deter Roper in the slightest. He already had Salvo programming a second game for the VCS.

Spacechase was similar to *Space Invaders*, because the player again controlled a horizontally moving ship at the bottom of the screen. The computer controlled four ships that flew haphazardly in the upper center of the screen. The player had to shoot at the quick moving ships while avoiding their missiles. While the game itself was nothing to rave about, the graphics were spectacular. The ships appeared to be flying over the terrain of a planet, thanks to a scrolling background. Even though this didn't affect the game-play, it showed that Games by Apollo was capable of raising the graphics bar on the VCS.

Bank-Switching

When the VCS had first been conceived in 1977, it had been designed to access up to 4K of external ROM. It was never anticipated that any program would ever utilize even that much memory. Four years later, as competition among the third-party suppliers bloomed and programmers strove to design more complicated VCS games, they realized that the only way they could do this was by using the VCS's memory to the max. Atari's *Championship Soccer* had been the firest game to utilize 4K, but designers soon discovered that even 4K wasn't enough.

When Atari decided to convert its mega-hit *Asteroids* to the VCS, the designer who had been given the task, Brad Stewart, quickly tangled with the limits of the machine. *Asteroids* was an important title for Atari, especially since Activision had begun taking away some of its business. At the time, *Asteroids* was the top-selling arcade game ever and Atari hoped to match that feat with the VCS version. However the company wasn't willing to sacrifice any of the coin-op's action. This proved a problem for Stewart. The game simply couldn't be written within the VCS's limit of 4K.

Stewart decided to use a method called "bank-switching", which had been developed a few years earlier, but had never been used commercially. The technique involved dividing memory into disjointed sections or banks. Although all of the banks were available to the program, only one could be accessed at a time. In the case of the VCS, an instruction within the first 4K bank branched to an address in the second 4K bank, where processing continued. The branch to the second bank of 4K was transparent to the CPU. In effect, this allowed the VCS to process games that were larger than 4K. When it was completed, *Asteroids* utilized 8K of code.

Asteroids was one of the most highly anticipated games for the VCS, and many retailers sold out of them on the day they went on sale. The home version was very faithful to the arcade original, aside from a few differences, such as using the joystick (the arcade game used buttons) and using raster graphics (home televisions were incapable of vectors). Atari even included 66 variations.

Le Stick

It was only natural for third-party companies to begin marketing controllers for the VCS, as well as games. One of these companies was Datasoft, a company that was founded a year earlier that provided arcade titles for personal computers. Oddly enough, *Le Stick,* their revolutionary controller, was their only offering for a videogame console.

Le Stick replaced the standard Atari joystick controller. The unit consisted of a plastic shaft with finger grips and a cord that plugged into the console. A red controller button sat at the top of the shaft. The unit worked by holding the shaft and twisting the hand in any direction. Moving the shaft forward was the same as pushing a joystick forward. Incline switches inside the unit were filled with mercury, which sensed every movement Le Stick made.

Unfortunately, besides being expensive for a controller ($40), Le Stick was very difficult to use. The device simply had no point of reference. While a basic controller had a base that it sat on, and a self-centering joystick, Le Stick had neither. A gamer needed a steady hand to be able to use Le Stick accurately, but few did.

Datasoft released an improved version of Le Stick in 1982 but the improvements didn't surpass the flaws, and the controller quickly faded from the scene.

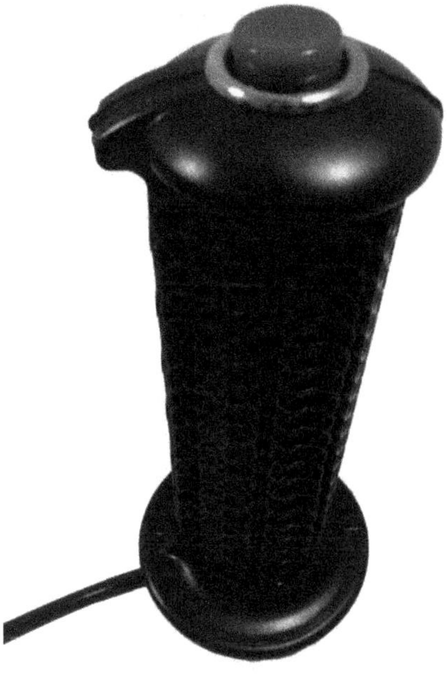

Datasoft Le Stick

Tabletop Games

The market for portable gaming devices dried up considerably since the 1980 Christmas season, so manufacturers sought new ways to revive the once rewarding market. Entex, a company that made handhelds, introduced the Select-a-Game Machine. Essentially, this unit played two-player versions of the games that Entex already had available in handheld models. The graphics consisted of a 7x16 array of red LEDs and a plastic overlay. The games were available on interchangeable cartridges that had self-contained processors, which plugged into the main unit. Among the available games were *Space Invader 2* (a *Space Invaders* clone), and *PacMan 2,* which was quickly removed from the market after

Entex Select-A-Game

Entex was sued by Coleco who owned the handheld rights to the game.

Coleco, which had abandoned console videogames because it felt that the portables were more lucrative, introduced new *tabletop* electronic games. *Pac-Man, Ms. Pac-Man, Frogger* and *Galaxian* all looked like miniature versions of their arcade counterparts, with authentic-looking cabinets that featured banners and decals that appeared to be copied directly from their larger arcade cousins. Unfortunately, the games themselves couldn't emulate the actual arcade experience. Each of the tabletop units had its own screen, but it only displayed LED graphics, which were similar to those found in the handheld games.

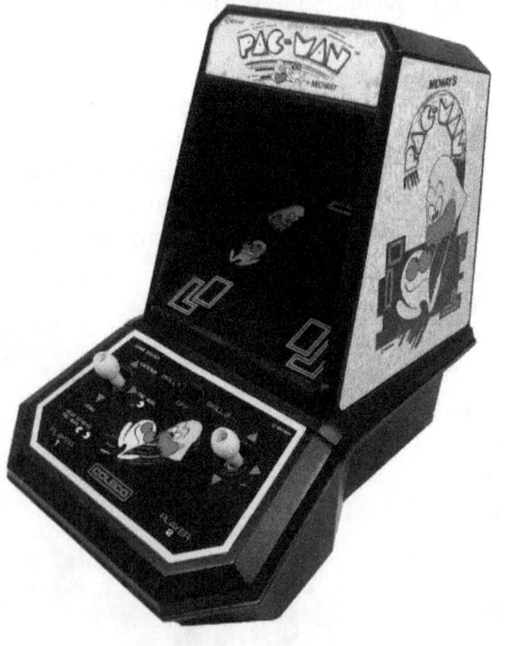

Coleco Pac-Man

Atari also planned to release a tabletop unit during 1981. The Cosmos was the holography game system that Lyle Rains had been working on when he came up with the idea for *Asteroids*. In May, Atari stated that the device was ready to be released, although a shipping date was never given. The retail price of the console was set at $100, and eight initial game cartridges, including the ever-popular *Asteroids* and *Space Invaders*, were to be sold for $10 each. Advance reviews of the unit complained that the holograms didn't enhance the game-play and were merely used as backdrops. Atari conceded that this was true, but defended it by saying that since Cosmos was the first of its kind, such trivialities could be overlooked.

Cosmos was indeed an important breakthrough for Atari. For several years, the

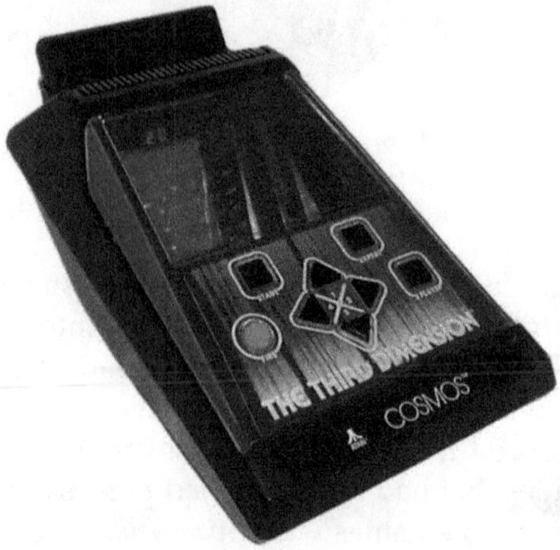

Atari Cosmos

Atari Cosmos Asteroids Hologram

company had been quietly buying every hologram-related patent it could find, without any idea of how they were even going to use them. By the end of 1979, Atari's engineers had learned how to mass-produce holograms. While it was only natural that Atari's first hologram product would be videogame-related, the hologram engineers were looking into other forms of entertainment in which holograms could be applied. Even as Cosmos was being readied for release, its inventors were exploring how to tie holograms into television and film.

Consumers anxiously awaited Cosmos, but they waited in vain. By year's end, Atari announced that it was redesigning the Cosmos holographic game system so that the holograms did more than just provide a nice background to the action. While it appeared that Atari was caving in to the critical complaints, it is possible that the sagging stand-alone market had much to do with Atari's withdrawal. Following that announcement, Cosmos, and the rest of Atari's holographic research, were never heard about again.

Vaporware

Although the Cosmos wasn't the first product that Atari announced that was never actually put into production or released, it was the first one that people were eagerly waiting for. The term *Vaporware* was soon used to label such products.

The Cosmos wasn't the only new console that Atari planned to release. In mid-1981, the company announced a replacement for its best-selling VCS. The new unit had a neat, slanted appearance, and all of the switches from the old console were replaced with pressure-sensitive buttons. At the rear of the console was a hinged door that covered a compartment where the controllers could be kept when they weren't being used.

It was the controllers that really set the new system apart from the original. While the old VCS came with two sets of controllers: paddles and joysticks, the new one featured a new all-in-one controller that combined an 8-direction digital joystick with a 270-degree paddle. This controller also had game-select and restart buttons built into them, so gamers didn't have to get up every time they wanted to play a new game or variation. This was a pretty handy feature, because the players didn't have to be near the console to play. Unlike any other console on the market, the controllers of the new *Remote Control VCS*[1] were wireless and operated via radio signals.

Atari displayed the *Remote Control VCS* at the Consumer Electronics Show (CES) in June. Unfortunately, Atari couldn't perfect the technology that it used. While the wireless controllers could be used in a radius up to 1000

Atari Remote Control VCS Controller

Atari Remote Control VCS

1981

feet, there was no way to pair the controller to a specific console. Atari feared that people would be able to take over a neighbor's game with their own controller, or even toy around in someone's garage since the technology was similar to that used by garage door openers. Even though Atari wrote up many orders for the Remote Control VCS at CES, the company decided to cancel the product before it could ship.

Atari wasn't the only company that announced vaporware. In April, Mattel proclaimed that the long-awaited Intellivision Keyboard Component was finally going to be available in May, at the originally quoted $700 price. May came and went and the keyboard never appeared. Mattel changed its tune in November, when it announced that the Keyboard Component would first be test-marketed in several cities, and could possibly be in the stores nationwide by July 1982.

Arcade Upgrades

Arcade gamers didn't have to worry about promises from the game producers that would never materialize. The only thing these gamers waited for from the coin-op companies was the next potential hit, and that could come from anywhere. Atari always used the latest technology when designing new games and distributors were aware of this. *Tempest*, which had originally been designed as a first-person *Space Invaders*-type game, was the first game to incorporate color vector graphics. The expectations for this game were so high that distributors preordered the game before it was even completed. Despite the fact that it was state-of-the-art and allowed up to 96 levels of fast, furious play, *Tempest* never became the hit game of 1981.

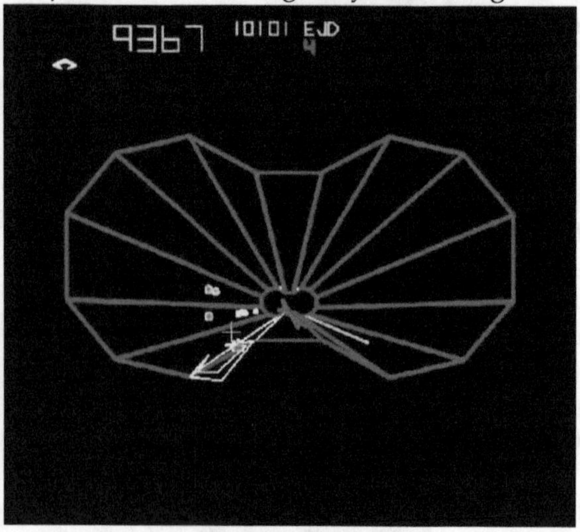

Atari Tempest

New arcade games came from unlikely places. A group of MIT students led by Kevin Curran, started a company called GCC (General Computer Corporation). GCC created *Super Missile Attack*, which they sold for $295. Rather than being a stand-alone game, *Super Missile Attack* was a board that was added to Atari's *Missile Command* coin-op that allowed arcade operators to modify the game by adding options, and changing difficultly levels.

Atari learned of the *Super Missile Attack* upgrade, and feared that gamers would believe that the modified *Missile Command* was an Atari product. The company filed a $15 million lawsuit against GCC. However, after Atari realized how talented GCC's engineers were at designing games, they dropped the lawsuit and settled out of court. Atari then employed GCC to design both arcade and home games for them.

Unfortunately, GCC didn't design for Atari the next blockbuster arcade hit that everybody was waiting for. They unwittingly designed it for another company.

After *Super Missile Attack* began selling steadily, the group at GCC began designing an upgrade for *Pac-Man*, which they called *Crazy Otto*. By the time they were ready to market it, they had already signed a contract to design new games exclusively for Atari. They approached Atari and asked if it was okay for them to still sell their new upgrade kits. Atari allowed them to as long as they had the permission of the manufacturer of the game that *Crazy Otto* was upgrading.

By this time, it was known in the industry that Atari settled its differences with GCC out of court. Curran called the president of Midway and told him that they were about to release *Crazy Otto*. He also added that they had already beat Atari in court and they were willing to do the same to Midway. However, if Midway was willing to permit GCC to release *Crazy Otto*, they would avoid litigation altogether. After Midway saw *Crazy Otto*, they signed a contract for GCC to provide a full-blown sequel to *Pac-Man*, rather than have it ship as a *Pac-Man* upgrade, where GCC would receive a royalty for each unit that was sold. Both Namco and Midway provided input into the new game. *Ms. Pac-Man* went on to become one of the most popular arcade games of all time.[2]

Donkey Kong

Minoru Arakawa started Nintendo of America in New York, but quickly realized that it took games too long to get to the East Coast from Japan. He calculated that he could shave months off of a delivery if he relocated his warehouse to the West Coast so he moved the company to Redmond, Washington, and then shipped the 2,000 idle *Radar Scope* machines by train to a new warehouse in Washington, owned by a man named Mario Segali.

Basically, all arcade machines were the same. They included a cabinet, a monitor and integrated chips. Arakawa was advised that if the cabinets were repainted and new chips were installed, the 2,000 *Radar Scope* cabinets could be salvaged as a new game. Arakawa liked that idea so he notified his father-in-law in Japan that he needed a new game that would appeal to Americans. Hiroshi Yamauchi agreed but all of his designers and engineers were busy on other projects that he couldn't afford to take them away from. So Yamauchi recruited a young designer who had contributed to some earlier arcade games, Shigeru Miyamoto, to design a new game under the auspices of Gunpei Yokoi, who had come up with the idea for the Game & Watch.

Miyamoto not only created a game, but he also produced an interactive version of the *Beauty and the Beast* fable. The game involved a carpenter simply called *Jumpman*, whose girlfriend Pauline had been snatched by an escaped gorilla. Jumpman had to climb scaffolds and avoid barrels tossed by the gorilla, in an effort to get to the top of the screen from where he could rescue the girl.

Miyamoto wanted to call the game *Gankona Gorira*, the Japanese equivalent of "Stubborn Gorilla". However, Yamauchi demanded that the game needed an English title for it to succeed in the United States. Since Miyamoto spoke little English, he consulted a Japanese-English dictionary to get the right words, and the ones he came up with were *donkey* for stubborn and *kong* for gorilla. The game became *Donkey Kong*.

After being assured that the game would be successful in the United States, Arakawa hired a local attorney named Howard Lincoln to trademark the game's title. He also gave the Jumpman character a real name. Arakawa felt that the character looked a little like the landlord of his warehouse, Mario Segali, so he renamed Jumpman to Mario in his honor.

As Yamauchi had predicted, *Donkey Kong* became Nintendo's first U.S. blockbuster.

Meanwhile, Nintendo released three more Game & Watch games between February and April. They differed in style

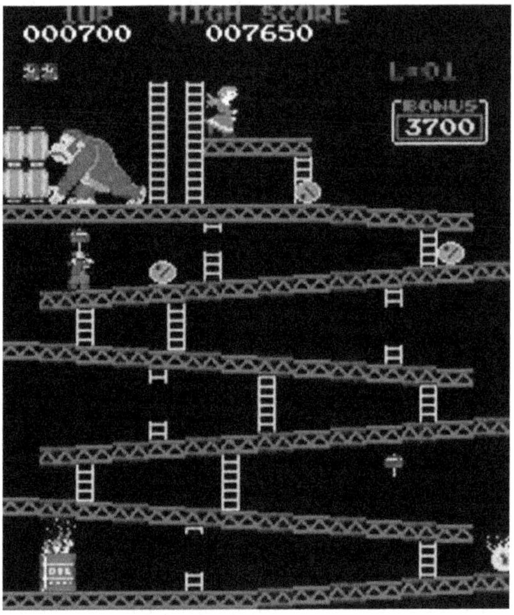

Nintendo Donkey Kong

from those released in 1980 by having a gold faceplate instead of a silver one. But a major difference was that they were released directly by Nintendo in the United States. The company next released an additional seven Game & Watch units between June and December that featured larger screens than the ones that had been on the previous units in the series.

Epoch Cassette Vision

As Nintendo was establishing its name in the United States in both the arcade and home markets, other Japanese companies were concentrating strictly on the home market in Japan. On July 30, Epoch, which had previously imported the Atari VCS, released its own programmable videogame console. Despite its name, the ¥13,500 ($56.45) *Cassette Vision* utilized standard videogame cartridges rather than tape cassettes. The games featured graphics that were less refined than those on the older Atari VCS. Even the external design of the console looked old as the four built-in controller dials brought flashbacks of the *Odyssey* console, where each player controlled two knobs, one for horizontal, and the other for vertical movement. Technically, the system was similar to Milton Bradley's Microvision as the individual cartridges each included their own CPU, memory and video processors. The console was only used as a pass-through and provided the built-in controllers and the power supply. The ¥13,500 ($91) retail price made the system much more attractive to potential customers than the much-too expensive Super Vision 8000.

Epoch Cassette Vision

Atari Vs. Mattel Electronics

Atari and Mattel's battle to dominate the videogame industry went public when Mattel aired a number of Intellivision television commercials, in which writer George Plimpton compared the Mattel's sports games to the comparable VCS games. The comparison didn't amount to much, since the Intellivision was known for its realistic sports games, an area that everyone knew Atari was weak in. Atari responded to Mattel's ad campaign with a commercial that showed a nerdy looking kid who wanted to compare VCS games like *Asteroids* and *Missile Command* with similar games from 'the other company'. When he discovered that the other company didn't offer similar games, the kid said "Nobody compares to Atari".

Mattel retaliated with a commercial that began where Atari's left off, displaying a similar nerdy kid who made the same comment that nobody compared with Atari. However after he made the remark, George Plimpton materialized in front of him to inform him that there were new Intellivision titles available that were better than the arcade titles that Atari offered. Atari complained about the ad to the networks and ABC and NBC yanked ads from both of the sponsors. CBS continued to air Intellivision's ad.

The ads did uncover some truth about the two competing systems. While Intellivision was indeed the dominant force when it came to sports, it couldn't compete at all against Atari's arcade games. The reason for this was the abundance of limitations in the Intellivision. The fact of the matter was that in order for the console to generate such great graphics, much memory had been sacrificed from elsewhere. The Intellivision gave up speed, an element not necessarily needed in sports games, but crucial in most arcade games.

Laserdisc Games

Regardless whether gamers chose the VCS, Intellivision or Odyssey², the technology behind the systems was basically the same. However, many video experts believed that new videodisc technology would change the way people played games.

Actually, the laserdisc had first appeared on store shelves in selected cities in 1979. Developed as a joint venture by MCA and Philips (by then, the parent company of Magnavox), the twelve-inch discs had been designed as alternatives to the expensive videotapes. Before videotape rental outlets flourished on every American street, the only way to view videotapes was by buying them at an average price of around $90 each. Laserdiscs were to sell for between $5 and $20 and offered a medium that could never wear out, since there wasn't any contact between the laser beam that "read" the information encoded onto the disc and the disc surface itself. Videodiscs also offered high resolution and featured special effects such as slow motion and instant access. Unfortunately for the marketers of this phenomenal device, most people still bought videotape recorders, just so they could record TV programs. Since the laserdisc couldn't record, it was impractical for most people. The fact that laserdisc players cost more than most video recorders didn't help their popularity too much either.

Despite low sales, the videodisc format had eked out an existence, supported mainly by video connoisseurs. In early 1981, RCA released its CED (Capacitance Electronic Disc) videodisc, which was considerably less expensive than the laser disc, but much more fragile. Like audio records, a diamond stylus read marks that were etched into the disc. Because they were very sensitive, the discs were sold in plastic caddies, where they remained until they were safely inside the player. Since the CED player cost less than most videotape recorders, RCA could sell it to people who normally weren't interested in buying inexpensive, pre-recorded video. RCA sold consumers on the idea that the videotape recorder's purpose was to allow the taping of programs, while the CED videodisc existed so they could watch their favorite movies that rarely appeared on television.

Since the laserdisc manufacturers couldn't compete against RCA in price, they issued advertising that compared the two videodisc technologies and explained why the laserdisc cost more and was better. Naturally, they mentioned that CED discs would begin wearing out after a few dozen plays, while laserdiscs would remain unscathed after thousands of plays. However, the main focus of their advertising campaign was the special effects that were available in the laser format.

Every frame on a laserdisc was digitally numbered, and the player could randomly access each frame almost instantly. The CED was incapable of this, because it used a needle that traveled within a confined groove. The companies that manufactured laserdisc players made these special features their major selling points. And to drive this home, they developed software that took full advantage of these capabilities.

MCA, Magnavox, and Pioneer set up a joint venture called Optical Programming Associates (OPA) to create these new interactive discs. The earliest, *The First National Kidisc*, provided two dozen activities for kids. Although the running time of the disc was only 27 minutes long, it could keep children entertained for nearly ten hours by utilizing the freeze-frame and frame-by-frame capabilities of the laserdisc player.

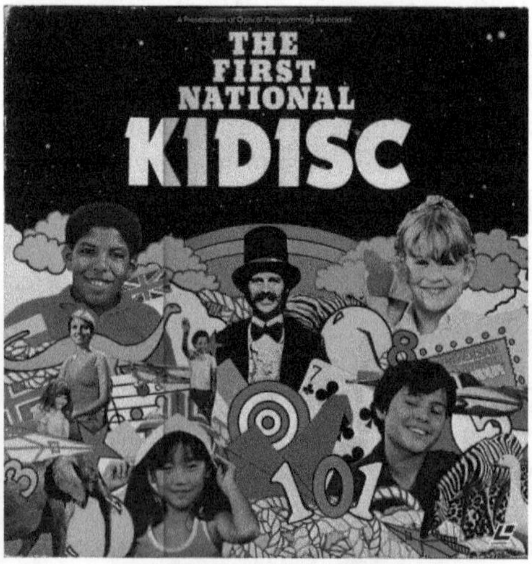

The First National Kidisc

Another disc that OPA released was *How To Watch Pro Football*. It featured a game called *Freeze When*, which showed a series of plays and asked the viewer whether a pass or a run would follow.

Although these new interactive discs couldn't be considered videogames in the conventional sense, they still allowed people to interact with their television sets. Even the Army used laserdiscs to train tank gunners. Although Magnavox marketed both a laserdisc player and the Odyssey², the company didn't reveal any plans to release laserdiscs under the Odyssey² name. Neither Atari nor Mattel expressed any interest in the new format, either.

Laserdisc games also debuted in arcades. Electro Sport, a manufacturer of video slot machines, released *Quarter Horse*, the first laserdisc arcade game. *Quarter Horse* was a horseracing simulator in which players reviewed the odds of racehorses on a 13-inch color screen, and then bet on the horse that they thought would win, using available credits that they'd received when the game had begun. They could then watch the actual race on a 19-inch screen, and if they bet correctly, additional credits would be added to their bank.

The races viewed were actual live-action horse races, using the random-access features of the laser disc. Part of the attraction of the game was that the players were made to feel like they were at an actual racetrack, watching a race, and hearing the track announcer and cheers of the crowd. The only problem with *Quarter Horse* was the same problem that haunted many of the gambling-related videogames. They simply weren't fun when the element of gambling was excluded. After a few plays, the appeal of betting imaginary money on virtual races simply dissipated.

Electro Sport Quarter Horse

As 1981 came to a close, so did the first decade of the home videogame industry. In those ten years, the industry had exploded beyond anyone's expectations, and gamers now wanted access to information about what was on the horizon. In November, that information emerged in the form of two magazines that was totally dedicated to electronic games.

The first was a British magazine called *Computer and Video Games* (C&VG). Despite its title, the magazine leaned heavily towards the computer gaming market and included reviews for computer games as well as lines of code for games that users could input themselves. Even the ads were geared for the computer market.

Two weeks later in the United States, *Electronic Games* debuted on a quarterly schedule. Edited by Arnie Katz and Bill Kunkel, the two men responsible for *Video*'s "Arcade Alley", the magazine focused on all aspects of electronic gaming, including arcade, handheld, and computer games. But the main focus of the magazine was on console videogames, which made it the first true videogame magazine ever published.

In no time at all *Electronic Games* became the *de facto* standard that all succeeding videogame magazines would try to imitate. And there would be plenty of magazines that would follow because there was just too much information and products coming out for one quarterly magazine to keep up with. Whether this was good in the long run was anybody's guess.

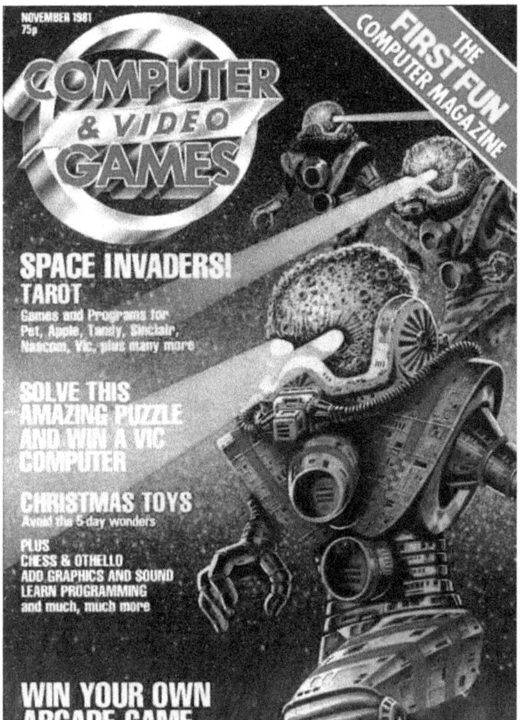

Computer & Video Games

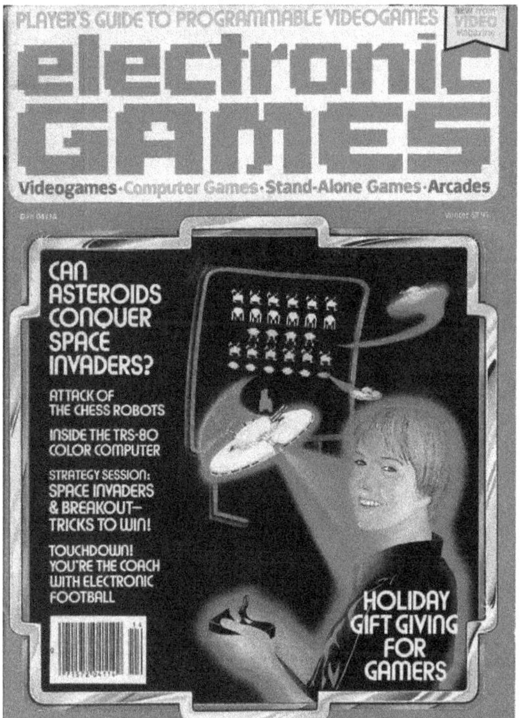

Electronic Games

CHAPTER TEN
1982

As 1982 began, the first issue of *Electronic Games* magazine proved to be more popular than anybody could have imagined. The schedule was quickly changed to bi-monthly with its second issue, and within a few months, that frequency was upgraded to monthly. Its success also spawned several more game magazines that year. *Video Games* and *Videogaming Illustrated* began in August, and the first issue of *Electronic Fun with Computers & Games* debuted in November. Besides reporting on the latest home videogames, all four magazines also included extensive coverage about computer, arcade, and portable games.

Coleco Returns

Much of the news that the magazines reported was about several new systems that were introduced throughout the year. Among them was Coleco's first console since its release of the Telstar Colortron in 1978. In the spring of 1982, the company announced that it would release a brand new videogame system, the *ColecoVision*, in July. Coleco promised that its system would have ten times the graphics RAM that the Intellivision had, providing arcade-style graphics that would display up to 48 objects moving simultaneously on the screen. Each game, which would be available on cartridges, could contain up to 32K of code. The controllers would feature a telephone style keypad and a joystick. Each controller would also have a special dial that would allow gamers to regulate the speed of the on-screen objects.

Coleco ColecoVision

Despite the hype that it built up for the new console, Coleco couldn't release the ColecoVision in July as it had originally planned. In order to make up some time, the company jumped the gun and shipped its first units to stores in August, prior to receiving the FCC's approval. Although Coleco was fined $2,000 by the FCC, the company felt that it was money well spent.

When it came out, the ColecoVision was nearly everything that Coleco had promised. The only thing missing was the speed roller in the controller, which test players discovered had made the controller more difficult to hold and use at the same time. The speed roller wasn't missed once players witnessed the astounding graphics that the new console had to offer. They surpassed the incredible graphics that Intellivision had built its reputation around, and the system didn't have to sacrifice memory elsewhere to achieve it. The ColecoVision contained 48K RAM, basically the same amount of memory that was available in most of the home computers at the time.

Coleco went out and licensed every arcade game that they could get from Nintendo and Sega, as well as some lesser-known companies. They produced faithful renditions of arcade games such as Nintendo's *Donkey Kong*. Sega's *Zaxxon,* which had just been introduced to arcades the same year, brought a new perspective to videogame graphics. In *Zaxxon,* the player piloted a spaceship over an isometric landscape that scrolled from the bottom left of the screen towards the top right. The player's objective was to destroy everything in sight, and ultimately facing off against a large 'boss' character. However, what made *Zaxxon* different from its predecessors was the fact that the player had to avoid objects by turning left, right, up, and down. For the first time, videogame images came very close to being three-dimensional,[1] and the ColecoVision version displayed them as elegantly as the arcade version.

ColecoVision Zaxxon

However, the designers at Coleco realized that great arcade-style graphics wouldn't be enough to woo consumers away from either the VCS or Intellivision, especially after they invested a lot of money in those systems to purchase software. Since Coleco couldn't hope to offer as many games for the ColecoVision that were available for the VCS, they did the next best thing - they developed an expansion module that allowed the ColecoVision to play VCS cartridges. The $60 "Expansion Module #1" plugged into a slot in the front of the ColecoVision that had been labeled "Expansion Module Interface". The module featured all of the switches found on the VCS and accepted all of the VCS' controllers. Coleco made it clear, however, that although the games would be played on the ColecoVision, they would be exactly the same as if they were played on a bonafide VCS. Coleco executives hoped that the "Expansion Module #1" would entice VCS owners to buy the new system because they could do so without having to sacrifice any of their existing cartridges. With this in mind, Coleco also announced a forthcoming module that would permit Intellivision games to be played on the ColecoVision.

In addition to the expansion modules that allowed games from competing systems to play through the ColecoVision, Coleco also offered expansion modules that enhanced the playing experience. "Expansion Module #2" was a driving module that featured a large steering wheel and allowed fans of racing games to feel as if they were really competing

ColecoVision Expansion Module 1

ColecoVision Expansion Module 2

in a race.[2] The unit was packaged with *Turbo*, a first-person driving game that Coleco licensed from Sega. And although no official statements were made, Coleco also hinted that a home computer interface would be available for the ColecoVision in 1983.

The ColecoVision was viewed as a winner. It played authentic looking arcade games, which made VCS owners envious and it had supreme graphics that Intellivision owners could only wish they had. For those gamers who weren't ready for the ColecoVision, Coleco also released VCS and Intellivision versions of many of the games that it released for the ColecoVision. Naturally, due to the limitations of the individual systems, these third-party titles couldn't offer the same incredible graphics as their ColecoVision counterparts. However, many speculated that Coleco intentionally produced inferior games for the VCS and Intellivision just so the ColecoVision would shine in comparison.

Atari 5200

The ColecoVision didn't deter Atari. The company had been developing a powerful new system, which they had code-named "Sylvia", to compete against the Intellivision. Plans called for the new system to be compatible with the VCS, which unfortunately limited its design. However, after Coleco revealed its plans for the ColecoVision, Atari realized that it had to get an even more powerful system on the market. Since they had to do this rather quickly so they could be ready when the ColecoVision was released, Atari's designers looked at their line of computers, which were able to play arcade quality games, and decided to take an Atari 400 computer, and strip away its keyboard. The result was a brand new console that was called the *5200* after its model number. Although games for the 5200 weren't compatible with the Atari computers, most of the titles that were available for both systems were virtually graphically identical. Since only a little work was needed to convert existing computer games to play on the 5200, Atari was able to offer an abundance of arcade titles during the console's initial months. In addition to licensed games such as *Space Invaders* and *Pac-Man*, Atari was also able to release its large catalog of arcade titles that were already available for the VCS.

Atari released the 5200 in October, only two months after the ColecoVision debuted. Most gamers who purchased the system upon its release basically loved the 5200, although many found minor things to gripe about. For one thing, the 5200 was incompatible with the VCS. Atari couldn't rectify this right away and promised that a VCS adapter would be available in 1983.

One complaint that was not rectified immediately concerned the controllers. The controllers strongly resembled the controllers that were packed with the European Interton

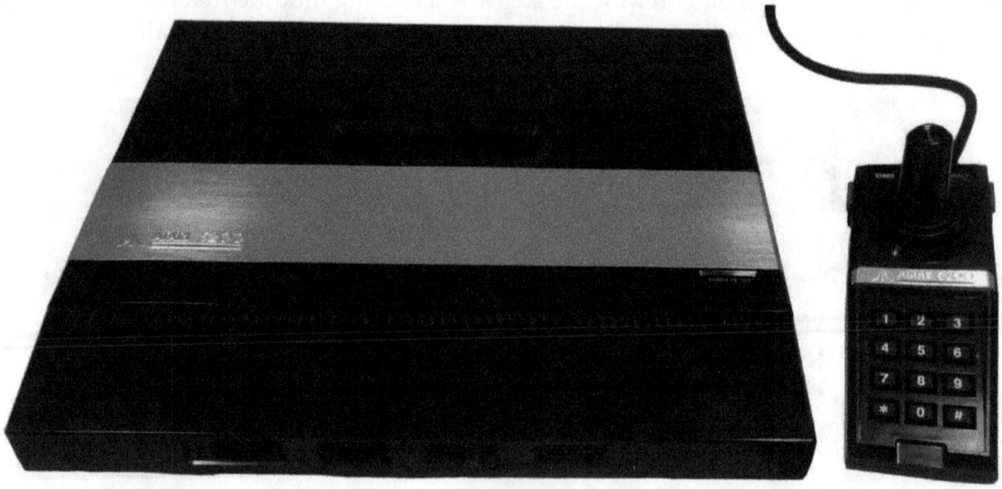

Atari 5200

VC4000 and Radofin 1292 APVS systems. The controllers were oblong with the stick at the top and a 12-rubber-button keypad beneath it, which could incorporate the use of overlays. The controller also included a pause button so players could stop the gaming action at any time and take a break. Unfortunately, the materials that Atari used to make the stick self-centering, was poorly constructed and usually failed to return the stick to the center position. This meant that if it was pressed in any direction and then let go, the stick would remain in the pressed position. Most players found this very awkward and difficult to adapt to.

In addition to the pause button, Atari borrowed another feature from the Channel F and this was a controller storage area at the rear of the console, covered by a plastic lid.

But Atari also made innovative strives with the 5200. While all other systems that used joysticks up to that point featured two controller ports, the 5200 had four. And its TV/Game switch, which controlled the signal to the TV, also differed from its predecessors. All prior consoles had been sold with separate TV/Game switches that attached to the back of a TV set. When someone wanted to watch TV, the switch was positioned at the TV setting. Likewise, if someone wanted to play a game, then the setting had to be manually switched to 'game'. The 5200 abandoned this practice by having its TV/game switch built directly inside the console. This automatically allowed broadcast signals to pass through if the console was turned off and sent game signals to the TV when the unit was on. Atari also merged the power and video cables into one, so the 5200 wouldn't be cluttered with wires.[3]

The VCS Becomes the 2600

Although there was the promise of a forthcoming VCS adapter for the 5200, owners of the older console feared that Atari would concentrate on the new console and push the VCS into obsolescence. Atari had other plans for the unit and the marketing department formally changed the name of the system in order to keep its product lines uniform. Following the lead of the new console, the name of the VCS was officially changed to the *2600* after its model number: CX2600.

Atari also lowered the price of the 2600 to under $100, which naturally made the unit more inviting for people who were shopping for a game console. Of course, these people had a tougher time deciding which system to choose between, since the 2600 was competing against the Odyssey^2, Astrocade, Channel F System II, Intellivision, 5200, and ColecoVision for the same customers.

The 2600 was a hit among gamers who wanted to purchase an inexpensive system. However, its graphics were inferior to those depicted on the newer and more expensive consoles like the 5200 or ColecoVision, despite the spectacular works that came from third-party companies such as Activision and Imagic. It was thought that these companies had taken the 2600 as far as it could possibly go.

The reason the 2600 couldn't produce breathtaking graphics was that it only contained 128 bytes of screen RAM, less than 2% of the 7K of screen RAM in the Intellivision. While an NTSC (the broadcast standard in North American and Japan) television display is made up of 263 horizontal lines, the 2600 could only scan half of them to draw pictures. Bob Brown, a former Director of Research at Atari, and Al Alcorn, one of the men responsible for bringing *Pong* into the home, figured out a way to add an additional 6K of screen RAM to the 2600 and allow it to scan every line on the TV screen, resulting in high-resolution graphics.

Brown co-founded a company called Arcadia to market the *Supercharger*, a device he had designed to contain the additional screen RAM, as well as 2K of ROM. The $70 Supercharger, which looked like an extra-long cartridge, plugged into the cartridge slot of the 2600. Software for the Supercharger came on cassette tapes that retailed for $15 apiece,

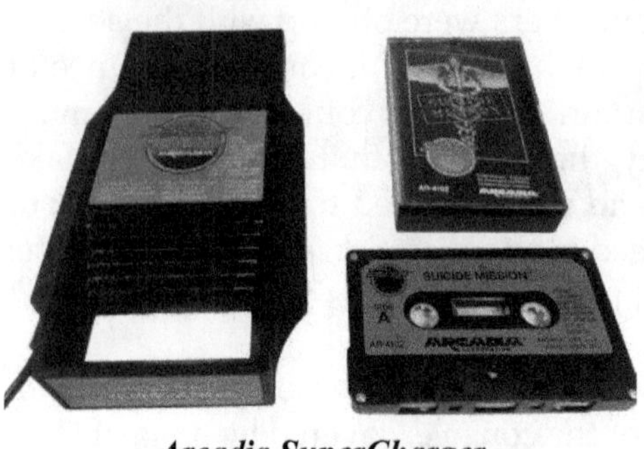

Arcadia SuperCharger

instead of the $25+ that the cartridge commanded. Games were loaded into the Supercharger via an attached cable that plugged into the earphone jack of a standard audio cassette player, in a procedure that took about fifteen seconds. Once the game was loaded, the 2600 interacted with the Supercharger as if it were a standard game cartridge. The game resided within the RAM of the Supercharger until the console's power was turned off.

Four games were released along with the Supercharger, and while all were rehashes of games that were already on the market, they did feature improved graphics and sounds, thanks to the additional memory. Although the games themselves weren't original, their titles were, as illustrated by the *Space Invaders*-inspired *Communist Mutants from Space*.

Because the games were on cassette tapes, Arcadia was able to offer previews of other Supercharger games. The previews loaded into the Supercharger like the games, but once loaded, they only displayed how each game played. They weren't playable themselves. However, at a time when people were paying astronomical prices to buy games sight unseen, these short previews were appreciated.

Approximately two months after the Supercharger was released, Arcadia changed its name to Starpath. This was because consumers confused the company Arcadia with a new console by the same name. To prevent any trademark infringements, and since the console had been on the market first, Arcadia chose to change its name.

Arcadia 2001

The console that forced Arcadia to change its name was the Arcadia 2001, a $100 system from Emerson, a manufacturer of inexpensive radios and televisions. The console had been designed to compete against the Intellivision and the Astrocade. While the system itself may have had the power to compete, the 8K games that Emerson released were lackluster at best. Since few of the games could be considered original, Emerson had the audacity to compare its titles against similar games by rival manufacturers. To its credit, Emerson did license several arcade titles, but they were obscure Japanese games that very few people in the United States had even heard of before their release.

Not everything about the Arcadia 2001 was negative, though. The controllers for the system were similar to those found on the Intellivision as they included a keypad and a disc control. However, Emerson also included a tiny handle with the unit that could screw into the center of the disc and, in effect, turn it into a joystick.

The Arcadia 2001 was also designed to be portable and included a twelve-volt DC power supply. Emerson hoped this feature would make the system attractive to boaters and campers and other fans of portable games. Unfortunately, since the unit didn't include a self-contained monitor, it still had to be hooked up to a television. This meant that anyone who wanted to use the console for portable gaming also had to bring along a portable television.

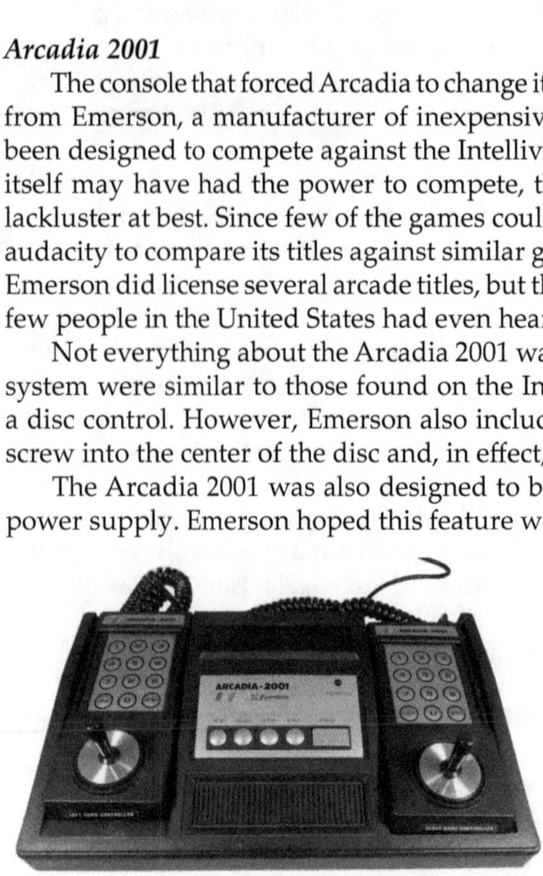

Emerson Arcadia 2001

Game & Watches

One portable device that didn't need a television was Nintendo's Game &

Watch series. On May 28, the company released *Oil Panic,* its fourth Game & Watch of the year, and there was a radical change to it that made it completely different from all of the Game & Watch units that preceded it. *Oil Panic* was the first in the *Multi Screen* series, Game & Watch devices that featured two screens instead of one.

The unit itself looked like it was comprised of two Game & Watch devices that were connected horizontally. The lower half looked like a standard Game & Watch device with a screen and control buttons. The upper half only had another screen. Although the two screens were not physically attached to each other, they made up one large virtual screen. If an object left the bottom portion of the upper screen, it reappeared at the top part of the lower screen. When the unit was not being used, the upper side could fold over and cover the lower side, protecting both screens.

Nintendo's next Game & Watch was released the following week on June 3. Another multi-screen game, *Donkey Kong* was the first Game & Watch that wasn't an original title. The controls on *Donkey Kong* differed from those on the previous Game & Watches. While the device had a standard button that was used so Jumpman could indeed jump, buttons were not used for Jumpman's standard movements. Instead, Gunpei Yokoi devised a new type of control that allowed Jumpman to move in any one of four directions. The *D-pad* (directional pad) was a cross-shaped button that could be easily pressed left, right, up,

Nintendo Game & Watch Oil Panic

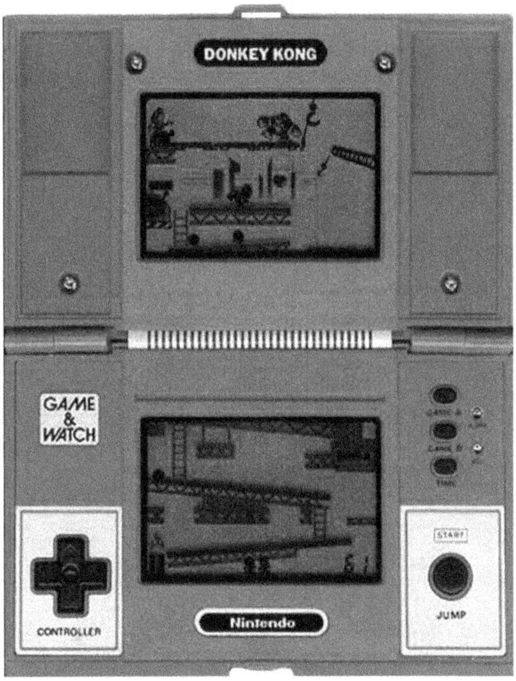

Nintendo Game & Watch Donkey Kong

or down with the player's left thumb.

Following the success of the Game & Watches, Bandai quickly released its own version. Like the Game & Watches, the Bandai units were powered by watch batteries, small cylindrical cells that were generally used to power wrist watches, calculators, and other small electronics. In mid-1982, Bandai introduced a new type of solar powered game/watch. The first six in the *LCD SolarPower* series resembled the Nintendo multi-screen units as they were also clam-shelled where the upper portion folded over and covered the lower part. However, instead of having a second screen built-into the upper half, the Bandai units had a solar panel.

Bandai released four more solar panel games during the latter portion of the year. These units differed from the prior ones as they contained two LCD screens, instead of

Bandai LCD SolarPower

one. But unlike Nintendo's multi-screen games where two separate screens worked in tandem to create a larger tableau, in the Bandai games one screen rested directly above the other screen. As they played, gamers could see both screens, and since one was directly atop the other, it gave off a primitive 3D effect.

Since companies were releasing handheld gaming consoles that also told the time, it was only natural that companies released watches that also played games. Nelsonic, a watch manufacturer, licensed *Pac-Man* from Namco and released a watch that could play the maze game on its face. General Consumer Electronics (GCE) followed with a trio of watches that played new non-licensed games. Game-Time included four simple games including a *Space Invaders* clone called *Alien Assault* and *Blast Away*, which was GCE's version of *Breakout*. The other two watches were Arcade-Time, which featured four arcade-themed games and a small built-in joystick, and Sports-Time, which had basketball, football, and soccer games built-in.

Programmable Table-Top Systems

Although the Game-Time watches were popular, it was with the *Vectrex*, which had been designed by Microvision designer Jay Smith, that GCE found its mark. The Vectrex was a tabletop console with its own built-in nine-inch black & white monitor that produced vector graphics just like arcade games such as *Asteroids*. GCE enhanced the graphics by borrowing from Magnavox's original Odyssey and including colorful overlays with every

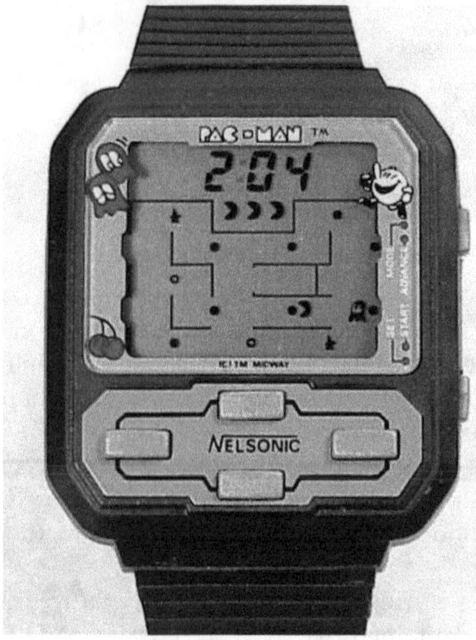

Nelsonic Pac-Man

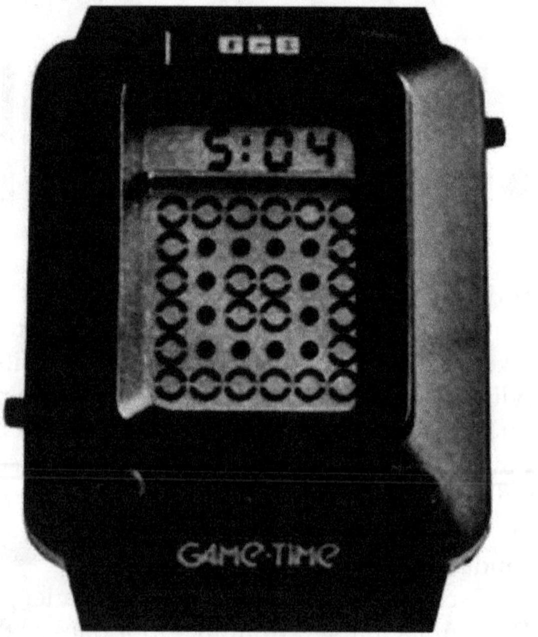

GCE GameTime

cartridge. The controller, which looked like a small rectangular box with a tiny metal joystick and four numbered buttons, plugged into the monitor.

The games themselves were of arcade quality thanks to the Vectrex's 8-bit microprocessor and 64K of RAM. Many of the games available for the system, including Stern's *Berzerk* and Konami's *Scramble*, were licensed. One game that GCE couldn't license was *Asteroids*, so instead GCE produced a similar game called *Mine Storm*, which was built into the machine.

Believing that GCE had a potential hit with the Vectrex, Milton Bradley purchased the company before the new tabletop was put on the market. GCE, operating as a new Milton Bradley subsidiary, released the Vectrex in October. However, this came at the expense of another Milton Bradley portable, the three-year-old Microvision. Although the Microvision cost much less than the Vectrex, its primitive LCD screen couldn't compare to the high quality vector graphics that the Vectrex offered. Milton Bradley quietly discontinued the Microvision and concentrated solely on the Vectrex.

Similar events occurred at Entex. The company removed its year-old Select-a-Game Machine and replaced it with the *Adventure Vision*a graphically-superior tabletop system.

Unlike the Vectrex, which utilized a vector monitor, the screen on the Adventure Vision was comprised of a single vertical line of 40 red LEDs. A 16-square inch rotating mirror inside the unit reflected the LEDs and simulated 6000 LEDS arranged in a 150 x 40 matrix, providing a three-dimensional visual effect against a black background. This effect, according to Entex, produced up to twenty times the resolution of other portable devices on the market. Unfortunately, although the screen was set back within the unit a bit, the graphics were difficult to see in heavy sunlight.

Entex released four games that were released on interchangeable cartridges. *Defender* was included with the unit and the remaining three were sold for $15 each. Regrettably, despite its sophisticated graphics, the Adventure Vision couldn't compete against the technologically advanced Vectrex, and it suffered the same fate as the Select-a-Game

GCE Vectrex

Entex Adventure Vision

Machine. Entex removed it from the market after only a year.

Intellivision Arcade Titles

Meanwhile, Mattel did its best to compete. In order to draw arcaders to the sports-friendly Intellivision, Mattel released a number of arcade titles for the console. Instead of licensing actual arcade games, Mattel designed Intellivision versions of games that were already available on other consoles. *Space Armada* was merely *Space Invaders* with fancier, more colorful graphics. Unfortunately, as players quickly discovered, it was not as challenging as *Space Invaders* because it couldn't play as fast, due to the Intellivision's limitations.

However, not all of the Intellivision games suffered from the console's limits. *Astrosmash*, which was based on both *Asteroids* and *Space Invaders*, was a winner in its own right. As in *Space Invaders*, the player controlled a cannon that moved across the bottom of the screen. Descending from the top of the screen was a number of variously shaped meteors. The player scored points by shooting missiles at the meteors and destroying them. However, a missile could only destroy the smallest meteors. As in *Asteroids*, the bigger ones broke apart into smaller fragments when they were hit. The player lost a cannon if a falling meteor hit it, and the game ended when all of the allotted cannons were lost. *Astrosmash* also differed from most games in that players *lost* points whenever a meteor hit the ground.

Mattel Intellivision Astrosmash

While many Intellivision owners were happy to be able to play arcade-type games on their console, many others were dismayed because Mattel chose to copy popular games, rather than actually go out and license them. Their disillusions intensified when Mattel announced that it had finally abandoned the long-promised Keyboard Component. Although specific reasons were never given, it had been assumed that the costs involved made the Keyboard Component too impractical, especially since prices for actual personal computers were dropping.

Those who purchased an Intellivision intentionally to upgrade to a computer were understandably upset and many complained directly to the Federal Trade Commission. The FTC received enough complaints against Mattel regarding the non-existent computer keyboard that it investigated the company for fraud. Mattel insisted that the Keyboard Component existed and it was still being test marketed. It also told the FTC that a small number of units actually made it to retail stores. However, in order to appease the FTC, Mattel Electronics offered Keyboard Components at a loss by mail order to anyone who complained about it not being available. However, this wasn't enough to satisfy the FTC, which ordered that Mattel pay a $10,000 a month fine until the Keyboard Component was available at the retail level in large numbers.

Mattel Electronics only produced 4,000 Keyboard Components and it didn't have any intention on manufacturing any more, even if it meant complying with the FTC's demand. The company had another idea. A different design division had developed the Entertainment Computer System (ECS), a computer system that was less powerful than the Keyboard Component. However since it would match the criterion of turning the Intellivision into a computer, Mattel felt it would satisfy the FTC.

Voice Modules

In mid-1982, Mattel introduced *Intellivoice*, a peripheral that added voice synthesis to the Intellivision. This adapter plugged directly into the console through the cartridge slot, and individual game cartridges then plugged into the Intellivoice. Although every game cartridge could be inserted into the Intellivoice module, only special games were capable of producing voices. Mattel released a trio of games that used voices to aid the player, rather than merely enhance the game. In *Bomb Squad*, the best of the three, the player had to disable a terrorist's bomb by using cutters, pliers, and a soldering iron. The Intellivoice acted as the player's partner, who directed the player where to work.

Mattel Intellivision Intellivoice

Coincidentally, Odyssey (which had broken away from Magnavox and became an independent division of its parent company, North American Philips), designed a voice module for the Odyssey[2,] which was called *The Voice.* The Voice sat atop the console and, like the Intellivoice, plugged into the cartridge slot. As in Mattel's voice module, only certain games were compatible with The Voice, although all cartridges could be inserted into the unit. However, while Mattel concentrated on developing action games for its voice module, Odyssey went with educational games to highlight its new peripheral.

Magnavox Odyssey[2] The Voice

Type and Tell was the first cartridge that Odyssey shipped for The Voice. Basically, all it did was act as an electronic-voice typewriter. The Voice would audibly repeat anything that was typed into the console via the keyboard. Critics blasted the cartridge, because it wasn't a game at all. Another complaint was that although the words were pronounced phonetically, they weren't necessarily pronounced correctly. Odyssey followed up with two more educational cartridges that at least resembled games, so kids could have fun while they learned. *Nimble Number N.E.D.* included three talking math games, and *S.I.D. The Spellbinder* used a talking *Space Invaders*-type approach to teach spelling.

Although The Voice could be inserted into a Videopac G7000 console, the unit was only released in the United States. However, owners of the Videopac were able to purchase their own exclusive peripheral. The *Videopac C7010* provided the Videopac console with the ability to play a game of chess, since the console alone didn't have enough RAM and computing power to do it on its own. Unfortunately, this didn't come cheap. The Chess module retailed at approximately DM 300 ($120), a price that was many times higher than the Atari 2600's *Video Chess* cartridge. However, for that price, chess fans were able to purchase a computer that played a serious game of chess.

Videopac G7000 owners were also able to turn their consoles into pianos. *Musician* was sold with an overlay that featured a 16-key piano keyboard, which sat over the unit's keyboard. When the console was turned on with the *Musician* cartridge inserted, the screen displayed musical staff line. When a piano key was

Philips Videopac C7010 Chess Module

pressed on the keyboard, the appropriate note scrolled along the staff bars. The software came with the "sheet music" to 14 songs including *Happy Birthday To You* and *This Old Man*, which allowed users to "perform" these songs on the console.

Musician was the first attempt to turn a videogame console into a piano tutor. Compositions entered into the console could be edited but the limited memory of the Videopac G7000 didn't allow them to be any longer than 81 notes. Also, since there wasn't any way to save songs that a user might compose himself, its usefulness as a piano replacement was very limited.

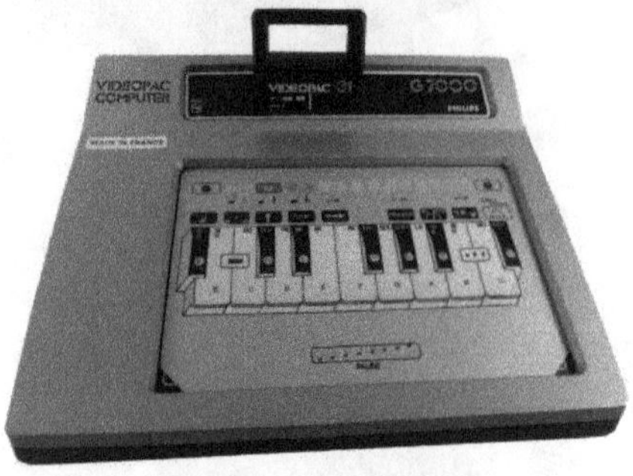

Videopac Musician

Although *Musician* and its keyboard overlay wasn't available for the Odyssey², Odyssey in the United States, along with Philips in Europe, did release a trio of *Master Strategy Series* games that came with their own overlays. The first game in the series was *Quest for the Rings*, which, at its most basic level, was a *Dungeons & Dragons*-type game in which players had to cooperate as they set off on a quest. This in itself was not a new genre for home videogames. Atari had started it with *Adventure*, and Mattel had refined it with *Advanced Dungeons & Dragons*. *Quest for the Rings* was different, however, because it integrated board games with videogames.

Packaged with *Quest for the Rings* were a game board, playing pieces, and an overlay that sat over the keyboard. The game was played on the game board, where the players had to search for ten mystical rings. Every time they reached a dungeon on the board, the action switched to the TV screen, where the players battled with monsters in an effort to get the rings. The keyboard overlays allowed instructions to be easily entered into the computer, so the Odyssey² was always aware of the action that took place on the board. Unfortunately, while most critics raved about how innovative the game was, very few found it entertaining.

Odyssey² Quest For The Rings

Odyssey³ Command Center

The *Master Strategy Series* games were the reassurance that Odyssey² owners needed from the company that the console wasn't being abandoned. However, even as Odyssey spent a lot of money to develop and publicize the voice module, it also announced a new console that would be available by mid-1983. The *Odyssey³ Command Center* featured a full-sized keyboard with real sculptured keys, which was a far cry from the Odyssey²'s membrane keyboard. The new console would contain increased screen RAM that could produce more intricate graphics than what was possible on the Odyssey². In addition, a Teletext decoder was planned, as well as an interface that could connect the Odyssey³ Command Center to a laserdisc player, which would give it the ability to play even more sophisticated games. It would be so advanced that Odyssey was unsure whether to market the Odyssey³ Command Center as a videogame console that people could use as a computer, or as a computer that could play games.

All existing Odyssey^2 cartridges would be able to play on the new Odyssey^3 Command Center, but naturally, they wouldn't offer enhanced graphics on the new console. Odyssey hinted that some of the popular Odyssey^2 titles might be reissued so they could play on the Odyssey^3 Command Center in the enhanced mode. All software for the Odyssey^3 Command Center would also be backward-compatible with the Odyssey^2, although they wouldn't display the improved graphics. It was reassuring to current owners of the Odyssey^2 to know that even if Odyssey concentrated solely on its new console, new software would still be available for the old one.

Odyssey^3 Command Center

But more important than having a steady supply of new games available was making sure that the games that *were* being released were fun and innovative. Odyssey's designers realized that consumers would simply buy an Atari system if all that Odyssey offered were clones of the existing Atari catalog. They came to the conclusion that instead of buying games that were similar to Atari's releases, gamers would simply buy an Atari and get the real ones. They had always known that the Odyssey^2's keyboard gave them the potential to provide more challenging games than its competitors, but they never fully utilized it. *UFO*, a space game released in 1981, allowed players to use the keyboard to type in their names next to their high scores. Still, this wasn't part of the game play, and didn't excite people enough to make them rush out and buy an Odyssey^2, especially since the high scores couldn't be retained after the console was turned off.

Japanese Imports

As the Intellivision, Arcadia 2001 and Odyssey^2 competed against each other in the United States, all three consoles were imported into Japan, joining Epoch's Video Computer System. The Intellivision and Arcadia 2001 were both imported by Bandai, the same company that had manufactured the Super Vision 8000, which was suspiciously similar to the Intellivision. The full story of how Bandai obtained the Japanese distribution rights for the Intellivision has not been disclosed but one theory is that when Mattel Electronics showed off its forthcoming Intellivision at a trade show in 1979, Bandai threatened to sue Mattel Electronics for a patent infringement concerning the controller pad. The lawsuit never happened and in 1980 Bandai was awarded the rights to be the sole Japanese distributor of the Intellivision. In 1981, with the Super Vision 8000 selling poorly, Bandai decided to discontinue manufacturing its own console and began preparing to import the Intellivision.

Bandai invested little in the Intellivision products that it imported. The software was sold in Japan in the same fashion as they were in the United States, in the same boxes that were completely in English. The instruction manuals and overlays were also in English. However, Bandai did include an additional instruction manual that was completely in Japanese.

The games themselves were also untouched and each opened with a splash screen that was completely in English. The only time a Japanese game was different from its American counterpart was in the case where the game title contained a licensed property. So while the baseball game was called *Major League Baseball* in the United States, it was simply *Baseball* in Japan.

In all, only 27 games were made available for the Bandai Intellivision and Bandai never introduced new software designed especially for the Japanese audience. Neither the

Bandai Arcadia Mobile Soldier Gundam

Intellivoice nor any of the games that supported it were available in Japan either. By 1984 Bandai would sell approximately 30,000 units before abandoning it completely.

Bandai put more care into the Arcadia 2001, which was called the *Bandai Arcadia*. Packaging for both the console and games were repackaged for the Japanese market. In addition, four games, including *Mobile Soldier Gundam*, were distributed in Japan exclusively.

In December, Kōton Trading Toitarii Enterprise began importing the Odyssey² into Japan where it sold for approximately $200. Apparently Kōton Trading Toitarii Enterprise invested less in the Odyssey² than Bandai had spent on the Intellivision. The packaging for both the hardware and software were the same as those in the United States, with the addition of katakana stickers on them. The full-color English manuals were replaced by cheap black-and-white Japanese manuals. Needless to say, the console failed to make an impact.

Home Pac-Man

Although the Odyssey² wasn't as popular as its competitors, it did boast one "must have" game that Odyssey had released at the end of 1981. The basic premise of *K.C. Munchkin*,[4] involved a little furry yellow creature named K.C. Munchkin, who moved around a maze while eating energy dots and avoiding pursuing ghosts. Although the game had definitely been inspired by *Pac-Man*, there were enough differences in it to prevent it from being a clone. For example, instead of featuring a maze full of stationary dots, the maze in *K.C. Munchkin* contained only twelve dots, and they were constantly

Odyssey² K.C. Munchkin

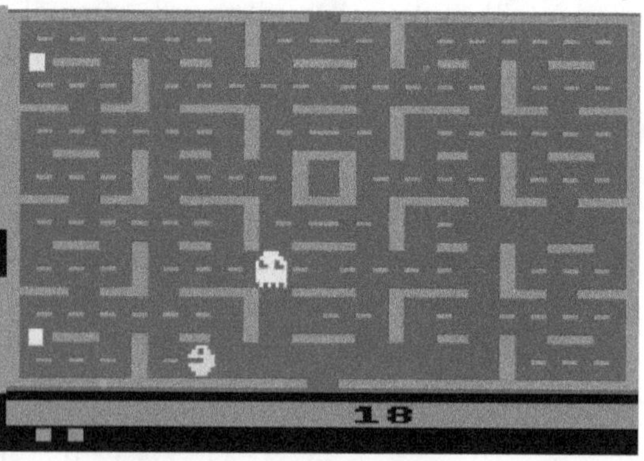

Atari VCS Pac-Man

moving. Much like the aliens in *Space Invaders*, the dots kept moving faster as their numbers decreased. The walls of the maze also moved. Despite these differences, the public felt that the game bared enough resemblance to *Pac-Man* to make them rush out in droves to buy Odyssey²s.

Atari agreed with them, and since it had licensed *Pac-Man* for the home, it wasn't happy with Odyssey's release. Odyssey was quickly sued for copyright infringement. The trial lasted several months, and in the end, two out of three circuit judges agreed with Atari. Odyssey was ordered to stop selling any more *K.C. Munchkin* cartridges, but stores were allowed to sell whatever remaining stock they had. The decision hurt Odyssey badly, because it had sold more copies of *K.C. Munchkin* in two months than it had any other Odyssey² cartridge in a year. The lawsuit forced other companies to take notice. Astrovision was sued for *Munchie,* a *Pac-Man*-type game that it was marketing for the Astrocade.

Atari had good reason to sue all of its competition. Even though Wall Street security analysts predicted that Atari would earn $200 million from *Pac-Man,* Atari knew that the public would scoop up any game that resembled *Pac-Man,* even it if wasn't the original licensed game. It didn't even matter whether the games were good or not. Besides, Atari wasn't willing to let anyone else share the profits from something that it had purchased the rights to.

On the other hand, most people assumed that if the Atari name was on the package, it would be a great game. So by that token, Atari believed it had nothing to worry about from other companies releasing their own versions of *Pac-Man.*

When Atari finally released its official version of *Pac-Man* for the 2600, it was one of the most highly anticipated games ever. Anxious people flocked to stores so they could exchange $35 for the experience of playing *Pac-Man* at home. But when they got home and turned on their televisions after inserting their *Pac-Man* cartridges, they were quickly disappointed.

The *Pac-Man* that Atari had released for the 2600 simply didn't resemble the game that was in the arcades at all. The maze looked nothing like what fans of the game had been accustomed to, and the sound was nothing more than irritating. Although Atari claimed that this was due to the 2600's limitations, many industry watchers speculated that the game was developed on the fly to get it into stores in time for the 1982 Christmas buying season. Tod Frye, who was not a fan of the original arcade game, was only given 4k with which to program it. Although the monsters blinked so terribly that they could barely be seen, and the joysticks couldn't control *Pac-Man* adequately, *Pac-Man* became the best-selling game cartridge to date simply because of its name, which had been what Atari had figured would happen. Approximately 70% percent of all households owning a 2600 purchased a copy of *Pac-Man,* accounting for seven million copies sold. While this number was indeed staggering, in reality Atari produced twelve million copies of the game, anticipating that people would go out and buy 2600s just to play *Pac-Man.* Some did, but the total number was nowhere near as many as Atari had expected.

Although *K.C. Munchkin* wasn't a *Pac-Man* clone, those who played both games declared that Odyssey had released the better game. In all probability, had Atari not caused Odyssey to withdraw *K.C. Munchkin* from the market, Atari would have lost many more sales. Once the poor reviews of *Pac-Man* began appearing, those who were in the market to buy a console just to have *Pac-Man* might have actually purchased an Odyssey² instead.

Soon, people began viewing Atari as a greedy corporation that was more interested in profits than in making people happy. The maze game that Atari released would have been a decent, playable game if it hadn't had the *Pac-Man* name attached to it. But by calling it *Pac-Man,* Atari represented it as something that it wasn't, because they knew full well that people would go out and buy it regardless. In the end, the company showed the public that it was not perfect, and people soon believed that not everything the company released was worth buying. Unfortunately, Atari didn't get the message.

Lawsuits

Atari's claim against Odyssey was only the first of several significant lawsuits in 1982. While Odyssey was defending itself from Atari over copyright infringements, it sued Mattel on another matter. Odyssey claimed that the Intellivision's sports games infringed upon its patents. In July, the courts agreed and forced a halt to the manufacture and distribution of those games. However, in October, another court granted a temporary stay of enforcement that allowed Mattel to proceed and sell the games until a further hearing could be held.

In August, Astrovision sued both Atari and Commodore Business Machines for copyright infringements over two Bally patents that covered a video display method called "bit-mapping". Astrovision claimed it was the exclusive licensee to these patents. Bally refused to appear as a co-plaintiff with Astrovision in the suit and had to be subpoenaed to appear as an involuntarily plaintiff.

Ironically, while both Atari and Commodore were being sued by Astrovision, Atari went ahead and sued Commodore over another matter. Atari claimed that Commodore had marketed joystick and paddle controllers for its VIC-20 computer that were identical to the joysticks and paddles Atari made for the 2600 and 400/800 computers. The Commodore and Atari controllers were interchangeable, and Atari sought to recover profits from controller sales that it felt it had lost to Commodore.

Atari also went after Activision shortly after the company formed in 1980, because it believed that the third-party's sales would cut into its profits. When the case was heard in 1982, all Atari got out of it was a disclaimer on Activision's boxes that said the game could be played on the VCS, something that Activision was already including.

The case was watched very closely as dozens of companies prepared to follow Activision's lead and jump aboard the third-party bandwagon. Imagic released its first trio of 2600-compatible games: *Trick Shot*, a pool simulation; *Star Voyager*, a space game; and *Demon Attack*, a *Space Invaders*-type game in which the object was to control the now familiar horizontally-moving cannon at the bottom of the screen, and shoot at the fast moving, bird-like creatures that were dropping bombs. Imagic made sure that its products stood out on retailers' shelves by packaging its cartridges in shiny, silver boxes. Games by Apollo released several more games in boxes that were similar to Atari's, and these games were significantly better than its first offering, *Skeet Shoot*. Another Texas company, Venturevision, sprung up and released a game called *Rescue Terra I*. Other previously unknown companies like Spectravision and Telesys also formed to release 2600-compatible games. However, not all of the new third-party companies appeared seemingly overnight. Established companies also wanted to get a share of the riches that the 2600 had to offer. Armed with lots of cash, these companies had the ability to license well-known titles. Among them was CBS, which had established a new division that it called CBS Electronics. CBS Electronics licensed several arcade titles from Bally, such as *Wizard of Wor* and *Gorf*.

Movies and Videogames

Parker Brothers was another major company that began licensing games for home use. In addition to acquiring arcade games like Sega's *Frogger*, Parker Brothers also licensed the movie *The Empire Strikes Back* and designed a game around it.

Even the cereal company Quaker Oats got into the act by purchasing US Games, a third-party company that had released a few 2600-compatible games under the Vidtec label. One of the first things that Quaker Oats did was license the movie *The Towering Inferno* from Twentieth Century Fox and turn it into a videogame.

Coincidentally, Twentieth Century Fox also went into the software business and set up Twentieth Century Fox Games of the Century, a division to market games that were based on Twentieth Century Fox movies and television shows. Ironically, the first four games that Fox released had nothing to do with either medium. In an attempt to quickly get games out on the market, Fox licensed four computer games from a computer software company called Sirius Software, which were then converted and released for the 2600.

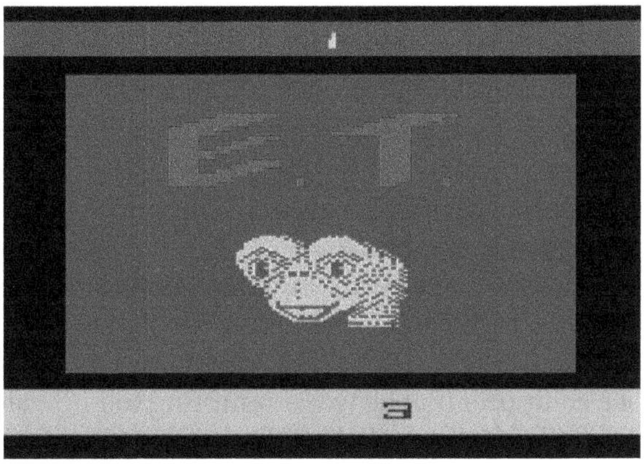

Atari 2600 E.T.

These were soon followed by original games based on the movies *Alien* and *Fantastic Voyage*.

Releasing movie-inspired games became a trend. The thinking was that if the movie was successful, then a game patterned after it would also do well. With this in mind, Atari licensed *E.T.* and *Raiders of the Lost Ark*. They would soon learn that a great movie didn't necessarily translate into a good game.

Pac-Man had been a major success for Atari, simply because of its recognized name. Atari figured that the same ploy could be used with *E.T.*: to use the name to sell the game. Unfortunately, Atari failed to realize that people had purchased *Pac-Man* because it was a game that they'd already known, and had been expecting to play the arcade game at home. Although the game wasn't quite what they anticipated, it still contained the basic features of the arcade version. Since *E.T.* wasn't a game to begin with, Atari should have designed a game that contained all of the ingredients that made the movie so successful. Atari gave designer Howard Scott Warshaw only six weeks to put something together. Unfortunately, there wasn't much he could do with the game within that time frame.

Most of the game's programming code was used in an elaborate opening title screen that displayed ET's picture. The remaining code was used for a game that followed the basic plot of the movie: help ET find pieces of his interplanetary telephone, so he could 'phone home' for a rescue ship. The game itself was repetitious and unimaginative, as ET kept falling into holes that the player had to help get him out of. Unfortunately, this happened too many times, and most players simply gave up.

The game received multiple negative reviews, and while Atari sold one million copies, another five million remained unsold in warehouses. The game would later be called one of the worst videogames of all time, and it would be erroneously blamed as one of the main causes of an upcoming videogame crash.

Atari finally got the message that neither its name nor its licenses guaranteed a best-selling game. With all the competition that it was now facing from the third-party producers, it was more and more important that the game was fun.

While the new market for movie-themed videogames opened new licensing possibilities for movie studios, they also brought headaches. Games by Apollo released a maze game that featured sharks, and called it *Lochjaw*. Universal Pictures quickly threatened to sue, because they felt that the title and theme infringed upon their copyrights for the movie *Jaws*. Rather than fight in court, Games by Apollo agreed to change the title of their game to *Shark Attack*.

Universal wasn't as successful when it went to court against Nintendo and Coleco over the *Donkey Kong* name. Universal, the owners of the *King Kong* name, contended that *Donkey Kong*, a game that involved a giant ape who kidnapped a beautiful woman and took her to the top of a high building, infringed upon its *King Kong* trademark. In addition, when Tiger, a manufacturer of handheld games, began a new software division called Tigervision, they licensed the *King Kong* name from Universal for their first videogame. The game, which was released for the 2600, was a *Donkey Kong* clone.

Coleco, which had everything riding on its ColecoVision and its *Donkey Kong* pack-in, quickly agreed to pay royalties to Universal. Nintendo wasn't as intimidated and refused to pay Universal a cent, especially after it discovered that Universal actually didn't own the *King Kong* name. Universal was ordered to pay Nintendo's legal fees, as well as restitution to the companies from which it had illegally collected royalties. In an ironic reversal, a judge ruled that Tigervision's *King Kong* was too much like *Donkey Kong*, and he ordered Tiger to pay Nintendo the amount that it had originally planned to pay Universal for licensing. The attorney who represented Nintendo was Howard Lincoln, the man who'd trademarked the *Donkey Kong* name in the first place. To show its appreciation, Nintendo of America offered Lincoln a senior vice-president position with the company and he jumped at the opportunity.

The marriage between videogames and movies took another step further when Walt Disney Productions released a movie called *Tron*. The movie was about a videogame programmer named Kevin Flynn (played by Jeff Bridges), who got sucked into the circuitry of a computer that he was attempting to infiltrate. Once inside the computer, Flynn found a world that was ruled by the Master Control Program (MCP). With the aid of a digital warrior named Tron, Flynn was able to defeat the MCP and escape from the computer and back into the real world.

In conjunction with the release of the movie, Bally released several *Tron* arcade games that duplicated some of the action of the movie. Mattel Electronics also released Intellivision and 2600 games that included *Tron* characters or scenes.

While the *Tron* games became popular in both the arcades and the home, the same couldn't be said about the movie, which received disappointing reviews. The arcade game actually out-grossed the movie. Amazingly, many kids who loved the *Tron* games didn't even know that they were based on a movie. Disney was about to pull the movie from the theaters when fans of the *Tron* videogames they discovered the movie and began flocking to see it. Although *Tron* never became the year's blockbuster as Disney had hoped, it did do well enough in the theaters to make it profitable.

More Pop-Culture Videogames

Movies, however, weren't the only licensed source of American culture that software vendors gobbled up for their games. Third-party start-up Data-Age designed a game around the rock group Journey and their latest album *Escape*. *Journey Escape* had gamers control different members of the band who had to avoid groupies and agents as they fled from a rock concert. Musical selections from the band's album *Escape* played in the background throughout the game. Parker Brothers designed games around *Spider-Man* and *The Hulk*, which they licensed from Marvel Comics. Atari, which released *Superman* a year earlier, published a comic book entitled *Yars' Revenge: The Qotile Ultimatum*. The book, which explained the background story of the *Yars*, was packaged with each copy of *Yars' Revenge*. Atari next joined forces with another Warner subsidiary, DC Comics, and produced a series of comic books called *Atari Force* that accompanied several games, including *Defender* and *Galaxian*. These comics had no relationship at all to the games they were sold with. Instead, they were about a group called *Atari Force*, which scoured the galaxy for a new planet for humanity to live on.

DC followed the pack-in books with a full-sized monthly comic book called *Atari Force*, which took place approximately twenty years after the adventures in the original pack-in comics. Atari then turned around and released an arcade game called *Liberator*, which was based on the *Atari Force* series.

None of the Atari comic books actually aided the player in how to play the game that the comic accompanied. This changed when Atari released the first of a quartet of games that made up the *Swordquest* series.

Originally conceived as a pair of games that were to be sequels to the popular *Adventure*, Atari decided to cash in on the popularity of Easter eggs and release four games that were somehow connected to one another (although each could also be played independently). Each game in the series consisted of multiple connected rooms, and

Yars' Revenge: The Qotile Ultimatum

DC Atari Force

the player had to wander through the rooms while collecting and dropping objects. If a certain object was dropped in a particular room, then a clue would appear that pointed to a certain page in the enclosed comic book. The gamer would then turn to that page and find a hidden word. Those who found all of the hidden clues could then enter a contest to compete for a $25,000 prize. There would be four contests in all (one for each game) and once all were completed, the four winners could then compete for a $50,000 prize.

The first two games, released in 1982, were *Earthworld*, and *Fireworld*. *Waterworld* and *Airworld* were to follow in 1983. Although over five thousand people entered the *Earthworld* contest, only eight of them had managed to find all five clues correctly. Those eight were then pitted against each other in a special contest where they had to find the most clues in ninety minutes, using a special different version of *Earthworld*. The winner of the *Earthworld* contest was Steven Bell, who won the *Talisman of Penultimate Truth*, which was valued at $25,000. More people correctly found all of the clues in *Fireworld*. Atari expected no more than fifty contestants for the runoff, but because more than fifty people solved the game, a preliminary round had to be held where the contestant had to write about what he liked about the game. The top fifty essays were then selected and those players then proceeded to the ninety minute contest where Michael Rideout won the $25,000 *Chalice of Light*.

Earthworld and *Fireworld* were two more Atari cartridges that sold millions and yet only pleased a fraction of the people who played them. Many people bought the games in the hopes of playing another *Adventure*, and found something that they couldn't even fathom. For people who weren't interested in solving Easter eggs, *Earthworld* was as dull and confusing as *E.T.* had been.

Multiplatform Games

Although many of the third-party software companies that focused on the Atari 2600 had sprung up practically overnight, this wasn't the case for all of them. Some companies that decided to release 2600-compatible games had been in business for decades, including

Mattel M-Network Astroblast

several of Atari's own competitors. As sales for the Intellivision began slipping against the 2600 in 1982, executives at Mattel Electronics, which in 1981 had accounted for 25% of the net sales for the entire company, began conceding privately that it could never take over the market that Atari dominated. Mattel then assumed an "if you can't beat them, join them" attitude by marketing *M-Network*, a new line of 2600-compatible games that were based on best-selling Intellivision games. *Astrosmash* for Intellivision became *Astroblast* on the 2600. Even though it didn't have the extraordinary graphics that was the signature of Intellivision games, the 2600's speed made *Astroblast* a better game than the original. M-Network also released baseball and football games for the 2600. Although they weren't anywhere as sophisticated as the Intellivision counterparts, they were light years ahead of the same sports games that were currently available for the 2600. Overall, M-Network managed to make the games look good, even though graphics wasn't one of the 2600's strengths.

Mattel Electronics' decision to design 2600 games, didn't mean that it was giving up on the Intellivision. The unit continued to sell and third-party vendors began supplying software for it too. Activision released *Stampede* and *Pitfall!* , two favorites from its 2600 catalog. Unfortunately, the games looked exactly the same as they did on the 2600. *Pitfall!*, which had looked marvelous on the 2600, was nothing special on the Intellivision. Imagic released *Demon Attack* for Intellivision and Parker Brothers came out with *Frogger*. Coleco, which was already distributing software for the 2600 and its own ColecoVision, released a number of games for the Intellivision, including *Donkey Kong*, and by doing so, became the first company that developed software for three consoles.

Imagic wasn't far behind Coleco in that feat. By releasing *Demon Attack* and *Atlantis* for the Odyssey² Imagic also marketed games for three separate consoles. Similarly, Parker Brothers developed several games for the Philips Videopac G7000, the European version of the Odyssey², but it never distributed these games outside of Europe. Unfortunately, these were the only third-party games for the Odyssey².

As companies released games for multiple consoles, they ran into the task of having the individual games take advantage of each console's strengths. For the Intellivision version of *Demon Attack*, Imagic was able to add an additional sequence at the end of the game, which challenged the player against a very powerful mother ship. This sequence was not available in the 2600 version.

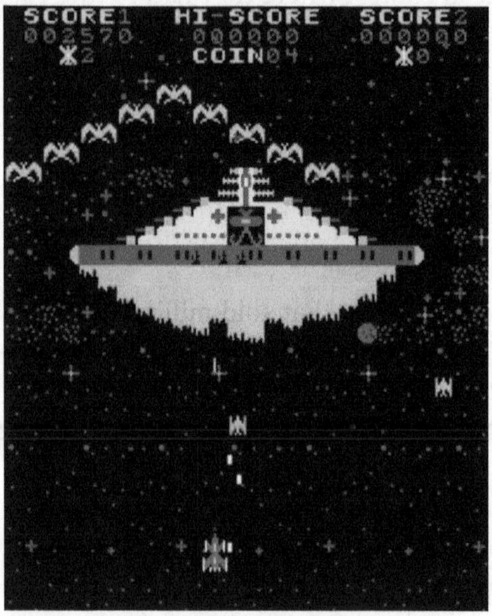

Centauri Phoenix

The Intellivision version of *Demon Attack* attracted the watchful eye of Atari, which wasn't happy with it at all. Atari viewed *Demon Attack* as a direct rip-off of *Phoenix*, an arcade game by Centuri that Atari had licensed for the home.

At the end of the arcade version of *Phoenix* was a mother ship that the player had to destroy in order to win. This mother ship represented the first appearance of a *Boss*, an opponent whose only function was to exhaust the skills that the player had built up throughout the game. Bosses acted as a final blockade to a goal and the only way to get past them was through a constant bombardment of firepower. Strategy alone usually wasn't enough to win against a boss.

Atari had planned to duplicate the Boss sequence in the home versions of *Phoenix*. Since the 2600 *Demon Attack* didn't have a boss at the end, Atari felt that it wasn't an exact copy of *Phoenix*. However, the Intellivision version of *Demon Attack* did include a boss in the guise of a mother ship and as far as Atari was concerned, *Phoenix* and the Intellivision *Demon Attack* were the same game. This meant that Imagic was making money at Atari's expense. Atari sued Imagic in late December and within a month the two companies settled out of court. Although the terms of their agreement were never disclosed, Imagic was still permitted to market its Intellivision version of *Demon Attack*.

X-Rated Gaming

As the home videogame industry turned ten years old, it was apparent that the teenagers who grew up playing the games during its first decade were still playing them as adults. It was only a matter of time before companies began developing games that they figured adult gamers would enjoy. Several X-rated videotape companies announced their intentions of releasing X-rated videogames. Cal Vista said that it was negotiating with Coleco to develop a line of adult games for the ColecoVision. Another company, VCX, announced that it would release ten adult games for the 2600 and Intellivision games by the end of the year. The first company to actually release X-rated videogames was Caballero Control Corporation, a company that distributed adult videotapes under the "Swedish Erotica" label. In conjunction with American Multiple Industries, they formed a videogame division called *Mystique*, which used the familiar "Swedish Erotica" label on its packaging. The company's first three games were released in October and carried a whopping $49.95 retail price. Atari quickly released a statement that condemned the games and promised that it was seeking a lawsuit to put an end to them.

Due to the memory restrictions of the 2600, the graphics didn't reveal enough to make the games sexually stimulating. Two of the games weren't even original, and only added sexual overtones to existing games. *Beat 'Em & Eat 'Em* was similar to Activision's *Kaboom!* except that the player controlled a horizontally-moving prostitute at the bottom of the screen. *Bachelor Party* was *Breakout*, in which a naked man replaced the ball and several naked women replaced the bricks.

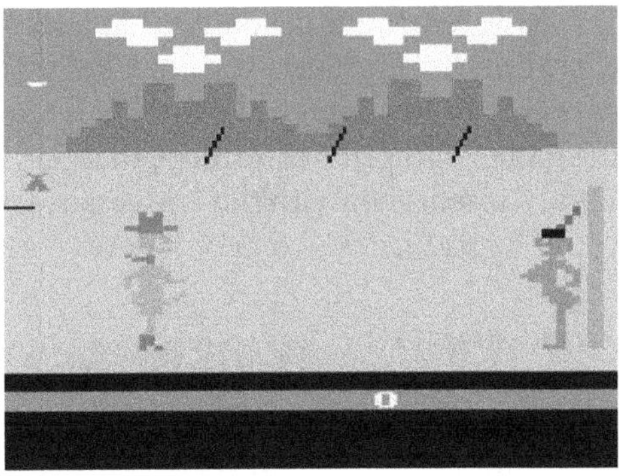

Mystique Custer's Revenge

Custer's Revenge was the only original game that Mystique released. The idea of this game was to get a sexually aroused General George Custer from the left side of the screen to the right, where a nude Native American maiden was tied to a post. Custer had to avoid falling arrows as he made his way across the screen. When he reached the maiden, he raped her with each press of the joystick button. Mystique's motto was, "When you score, you score!"

Custer's Revenge got more publicity than Mystique had intended when anti-porn and Native American activists began protesting that the game degraded women and Native Americans and promoted rape. Eventually, retailers refused to sell the game, and the whole event put a damper on the future development of X-rated games.

However, not all games aimed for adults needed to have sexual themes. Odyssey advertised its new Master Strategy Series game, *The Great Wall Street Fortune Hunt*, in the *Wall Street Journal*. Games by Apollo released a game called *Lost Luggage*, in which the player had to collect luggage from an airport carousel that had gone haywire. The company targeted *Lost Luggage* towards frequent travelers, who would appreciate the game's content.

Chapter 11

Lost Luggage represented a sort of renaissance for Games by Apollo, which turned one year old in October. After a slow start, the new releases showed rich promise for the young company, which began announcing ambitious plans, such as a 2600 game that talked without any need of a voice module. Other plans included the release of four games for the Intellivision and ColecoVision and two games for the Texas Instruments TI-99/4A computer. They even planned to translate several 2600 games for the Atari 5200 and 400/800 computers.

Unfortunately, none of these plans ever materialized. By the end of 1982, Games by Apollo had been forced to file for bankruptcy under Chapter XI.

Ever since Games by Apollo had been founded, it constantly drained money away from its parent company, National Career Consultants (NCC), which therefore suffered heavy financial difficulties. NCC simply didn't have any experience in the consumer market, just as Bally hadn't when it had launched its Professional Arcade. However, Bally had been a much larger company than NCC, and had more assets to spend on its new subsidiary. When Bally saw that it was in deeper than it could handle, it got out.

However, the problem was not entirely NCC's. When Games by Apollo had begun a year earlier, the software market had looked ripe and profitable, and there was room for an additional third-party vendor. Unfortunately, Games by Apollo was not unique, and many companies that saw how profitable the business could be jumped head-on into it. By the end of 1982, the market's growth had become completely saturated, because of all these companies competing against one another for the same shelf space in the stores. Games by Apollo found that it couldn't compete against giants like Atari, Parker Brothers and Coleco. Although the management of Games by Apollo seriously hoped that they could reorganize and release their new products, this never happened. The company became the first casualty of the videogame wars.[5] It wouldn't be the last.

A more serious casualty occurred on April 3 at the *Friar Tuck Game Room* in Calumet City, Illinois. Eighteen-year old Peter Bukowski was playing *Berzerk* when he suddenly succumbed to a fatal heart attack. It was unknown if it was actually the result of playing the game, or a prior condition, that had brought on the heart attack. However, Dr. Robert Eliot, a researcher with the University of Nebraska, released a study that said videogames could be hazardous to people who were susceptible to heart disease.

Twin Galaxies

Another arcade made national news, but for reasons less tragic than that of the Friar Tuck Game Room. *Twin Galaxies*, of Ottumwa, Iowa, had opened on November 10, 1981, by Walter Day, a former oil executive. The non-descript arcade only contained 22 games and wasn't known anywhere outside of Ottumwa. In its January 18, 1982 issue, *Time* magazine featured an article about the growing popularity of videogames. The article told about 15-year-old Steve Juraszek, who had achieved a world record score on *Defender*. Shortly afterwards, Tony Mattan of Ottumwa, broke Juraszek's record and he did it at Twin Galaxies.

Day called Williams to report the score, but was astonished to learn that Williams didn't keep such a scoreboard on its products. When he found out at Namco didn't keep such a scoreboard either, he decided to start one of his own. The *Twin Galaxies Intergalactic Scoreboard* was launched on February 9, 1982. Within six months, Day was receiving about nearly 75 phone calls per day, from people around the world claiming their high scores. Day soon had his high score list published in many magazines such as *Joystik* and

Electronic Fun.

With arcades making national news it was only a matter time before a game show featuring videogames debuted on television. This came in the form of *Starcade,* a show originally pitched to NBC, which premiered on TBS in December.

The show, which was used as a vehicle to show off new arcade games, combined standard game show question and answers with strategic game play. Two players competed on separate machines. The game started with a tossup question and the player who correctly responded first got to choose which game he wanted to play. He then had to accrue as many points as possible within a time limit. When time ran out, he then selected a machine for his opponent to play on, and collect as may points as possible within the same time limit. If a game ended during a player's session, then the score they amassed would go to their opponent. The player with the highest score at the end of three rounds was the winner. The show lasted one year on TBS and then went into syndication for a year.

Time - January 18, 1982

The year ended on sour notes. On December 7, Atari announced that sales of its 2600 didn't meet its predicted levels. The very next day Atari sued Coleco for $350 million, contending that Coleco's Expansion Module #1 contained circuitry that was nearly identical to the patented circuitry inside the 2600. Coleco immediately filed a $500 million countersuit, charging that Atari had violated antitrust laws by having their salesmen discourage retailers from selling Coleco products.

Whether Coleco's charge against Atari was true or not, Coleco had a very good year. Their sales had increased from $34.9 million in 1981 to $203 million in 1982. Their fourth-quarter earnings in 1982 were $15.3 million. They had lost over $600,000 during the same period the year before.

Atari and Mattel also had higher profits in 1982 than they did in 1981. However, their fourth quarter earnings weren't as cheerful as Coleco's. Mattel lost money during that quarter. Atari was in the black but its earnings weren't anywhere near the amount that had been forecasted. This sent Wall Street scurrying. Warner stock dropped seventeen points and trading of Mattel stock was suspended for more than 1½ days. Investors panicked from the news, affecting the stocks of other companies like Coleco and Toys "R" Us as well. Imagic had planned going public the following week but the news forced it to postpone its plans.

The naysayers came out in droves, and all of them began proclaiming the same bad news. They predicted that there was going to be a great shakeout in the videogame industry, and that it was going to come soon.

CHAPTER ELEVEN
1983

In January 1983, the talk that filled the Las Vegas Convention Center during the winter CES concerned the sudden drop in Atari's stock, and the rumors that a big industry-wide shakeout was inevitable. Most manufacturers were skeptical about this, especially since the industry seemed as strong as ever. This CES boasted a record number of exhibit booths from videogame manufacturers.

However, this larger turnout also meant that there would be a greater selection of new products for distributors, retailers and consumers to choose from. With retail space already filled with hundreds of games, new games, especially those from smaller, unknown companies, faced a hard road to the marketplace. The key to success for the smaller companies was to get their products noticed in any way they could. One new entry in the 2600-compatible market, a company called Zimag, announced its games on billboards along the route from the airport to the convention center.

And while some companies participated at CES with hopes that their products would be the next Christmas "must-haves," others realized that even a booth at the convention could no longer help them financially. Games by Apollo was in attendance with a large exhibit that had all of its previously released games on display. Unfortunately, there wasn't anyone available to demonstrate them. This verified the rumors that the company was heading toward bankruptcy, despite the denials by its president, Pat Roper, who was also absent.

Astrocade also had a booth without representation, which came as a surprise, because the company had never claimed to have financial difficulties. As fate would have it, the failure of Astrocade came at a time when the public was getting more and more interested in computers, and developers were looking at ways of turning their existing consoles into real computers. The Bally Arcade had been the first console that had the ability to upgrade to a computer, but because of its poor distribution and advertising, it had failed to catch on with consumers.

2600 Computer Upgrades

Despite Astrocade's failure, the market continued to shift towards computers. At the January CES, three third-party companies announced upgrades that could turn the 2600 into an actual computer. The *2000 Piggyback Color Computer* from Entex featured a full-size 70-key sculptured keyboard, 3K RAM that was expandable to 34K, built-in BASIC, and a retail price of $125. Additional peripherals included a modem, printer and disk drive. The Piggyback, which sat in front of the 2600, had a cartridge attached to it (via a ribbon cable) that plugged into the 2600's cartridge slot to connect the two systems. The Piggyback had its own cartridge port as well, but 2600-compatible cartridges couldn't fit into it. Instead, cartridges containing exclusive software applications, such as *Home Finance* and *Computer Typing*, which were exclusively designed for the Piggyback, plugged into this port. Since the Piggyback connected to the 2600 through the cartridge port, it would also have been compatible with the ColecoVision through the latter's 2600 adapter. However, Entex announced $7 converters that would connect the Piggyback directly to the ColecoVision.

Entex 2000 Piggyback Color Computer

Spectravideo's *Comp-U-Mate 2600* also sat

in front of the 2600 and connected to it via the cartridge slot with an attached cartridge. The $100 unit included BASIC, a music program and a drawing application, all of which were built into the unit. Unlike the Entex unit, the keyboard on the Comp-U-Mate 2600 featured membrane keys, which made typing a chore. To compensate for this, each "key" had an alternate function that allowed entire BASIC keywords to be typed at the touch of one button.

Spectravideo Comp-U-Mate 2600

Unitronics' *Expander* sat atop the 2600 and accepted tape-based 16K games that could be played with the unit's built-in tape deck. The Expander plugged into the 2600's cartridge port, instead of requiring a separate cartridge. The Expander also had its own cartridge slot, so that standard 2600 cartridges, including those designed specifically for the unit, could be played without having to remove the unit from the 2600. In addition, the Expander could turn the 2600 into a 16K computer (upgradeable to 32K) when a 64-key computer keyboard was plugged into the base unit. Unfortunately, the raised keys were made of rubber and hindered typing. Besides the keyboard, Unitronics promised peripherals, such as a printer and a modem. The company never announced a suggested retail price for the Expander, but claimed it would be inexpensive.

Unitronics Expander

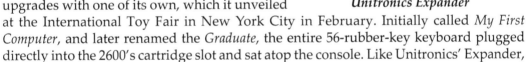

Atari responded to all of these computer upgrades with one of its own, which it unveiled at the International Toy Fair in New York City in February. Initially called *My First Computer*, and later renamed the *Graduate*, the entire 56-rubber-key keyboard plugged directly into the 2600's cartridge slot and sat atop the console. Like Unitronics' Expander, it also had its own cartridge slot, so it never had to be removed if someone wanted to play standard 2600 games. The $90 unit offered 8K RAM (expandable to 32K) and built-in Microsoft BASIC. Custom programs could be saved using an ordinary cassette tape recorder that could be attached via a cable supplied by Atari. The company also promised peripherals, such as a printer and high-speed storage, either through disks or wafer tapes. In addition to computer applications, Atari planned to release an entire new line of games for My First Computer that would take advantage of the increased memory.

Atari Graduate

The computer upgrades weren't limited to the 2600. Milton Bradley announced a 65-key keyboard that plugged into the controller port and added 16K ROM and RAM to the standalone Vectrex.[1] It also included built-in BASIC. Additional software, including a word processor, would be available on 120K tape wafers by early 1984.

Coleco Adam

It had been expected that Coleco would announce a computer upgrade for the ColecoVision at either the winter CES or Toy Fair. Instead, the company used the latter

Coleco Super Game Module

to introduce its Expansion Module #3. The *Super Game Module,* which would retail at under $120, would add one million bits of information to the ColecoVision. Games would be provided on wafers that were actually tiny cassette tapes that each contained thirty times more information than a 2600 cartridge. Unlike standard tape drives that normally took minutes to load a program, programs could load into the Super Game Module in less than ten seconds. Coleco announced that the games would be identical to their arcade counterparts and contain all screens, including intermissions. Because the games would come on tape, high-scorers would have the ability to save their initials. *Super Donkey Kong* would be shipped with the unit.

In May, Coleco announced that the Super Game Module wouldn't be released until August at the earliest, and would be shipped with *Super Buck Rogers: Planet of Zoom* and *Super Donkey Kong*. The Super Game Module was the big news for Coleco fans for the first half of the year, but that changed in early June at the summer CES in Chicago. It was there that Coleco first demonstrated its new computer, the *Adam*.

Crowds gathered around the computer, which was kept behind glass to keep the CES attendees from touching it. Coleco had promised that the Adam would have the same impact on home computing that the ColecoVision had on home gaming. The company stressed that the Adam was for people who wanted to buy a computer and have everything that they needed to make it fully operable when they arrived home. To reach this end, the Adam was packaged with several components: a 75-key sculptured keyboard, a letter-quality printer and word-processing program, and a Master Console that contained 80K RAM (expandable to 144K) and a digital datapack that was similar to an audio cassette tape, but was able to record and play back at very high speeds. One cassette had the ability to store 500K bytes of information, the equivalent of 250 double-spaced typewritten pages.

Rumors persisted that Coleco had trouble with its wafer system that had been planned for the Super Game Module, and this was why the Adam utilized the datapacks instead. The company insisted that the datapacks had been used because they were able to store more information. As far as software was concerned, the Adam would include two datapacks, *Smart BASIC* and *Super Buck Rogers: Planet of Zoom*. The entire system would retail at under $600.

Coleco Adam

The Master Console was essentially a computer with a built-in ColecoVision. It could accept all of the ColecoVision game cartridges, as well as the expansion modules. Existing ColecoVision owners could purchase a stripped-down Adam for $400 that excluded the ColecoVision feature, and could hook up to a ColecoVision through its expansion port.

As Coleco announced the Adam, it quietly put the Super Game Module onto the back burner and pushed its release date to 1984. The company claimed that since the Super Game Module and the Adam used similar datapack storage systems, the datapacks would be in short supply and Coleco wanted all of them available for the Adam. However, analysts and journalists believed that this was simply a marketing attempt by Coleco to make more money. Since the Super Game Module would only be available as part of the Adam package, gamers would have to spend $400 instead of $120. Naturally, Coleco denied these accusations.

A new company called Ultravision introduced its *Video Arcade System (VAS)*, which was a self-contained game system that played its own exclusive 16K, 32K and 64K game cartridges. Taking a cue from Coleco, Ultravision also offered an adapter that could play 2600-compatible games, and promised one for ColecoVision cartridges. It also promised a keyboard adapter that could turn the VAS into a 64K computer (expandable to 120K) that was compatible with Apple software.

Ultravision VAS with Keyboard Adapter

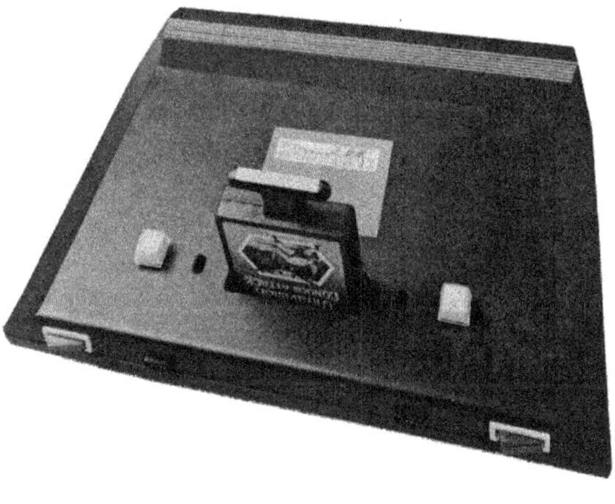

Ultravision VAS 2600 Adapter

Like the Arcadia 2001, the console operated on both AC and DC, which made it fully portable. It even came with a cigarette-lighter adapter, so it could be played in a car. This was not impractical, since the VAS also had its own built-in ten-inch color monitor and a VHF/UHF tuner. It even allowed for closed-circuit TV cameras to plug into it, thereby acting as a security monitor. The entire console, which weighed less than ten pounds, retailed for $500. The computer keyboard cost an additional $300.

In addition to the VAS, Ultravision announced a line of 2600-compatible software that they claimed would be more sophisticated than anything already on the market. Despite all of the publicity that Ultravision received in the videogame magazines, the VAS was never released, and only two 2600 games, *Condor Attack* and *Karate*, ever made it to the stores, albeit in very limited numbers. The games themselves were inferior, even by 2600 standards. *Condor Attack* wound up being a third-rate version of Imagic's *Demon Attack*.

Revamping the Intellivision

Following the release of its Expansion Module #1, Coleco was able to claim that the ColecoVision could play more games than any other system. Since the Intellivision had more games available for it than the ColecoVision, Mattel executives reasoned that if they could also release an adapter that could play all of the 2600 games, the Intellivision would have the bragging rights as the system that played the most games. However, before a 2600 adapter could be designed, the Intellivision needed to be revamped.

Because the Intellivision didn't have an expansion interface like the ColecoVision, Mattel's designers had to make use of the only input device that was available to them: the cartridge slot. Their plan was to design an adapter, which was essentially a 2600 clone that plugged into the Intellivision's cartridge slot. The adapter would receive its power from the Intellivision, and then pass its video signal through the main console to the RF modulator. Unfortunately, the designers quickly determined that they couldn't take this route, because the Intellivision didn't have an external video input, meaning that a video signal couldn't merely pass through the system.

To accommodate a 2600 adapter, the Intellivision console itself had to be redesigned. The result was the *Intellivision II*, a compact version of the original console. The new design accepted an external video signal on pin 2 of the cartridge port, which resolved the problem of the video pass-through.

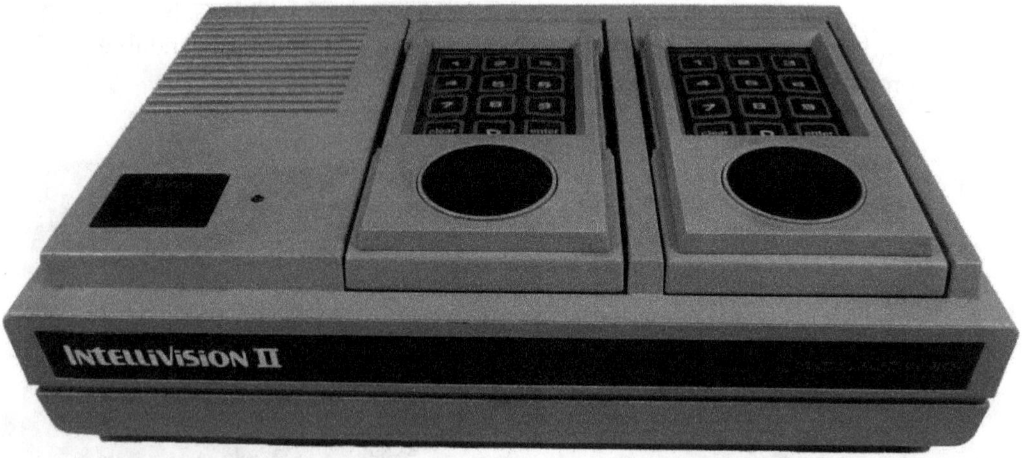

Mattel Intellivision II

The new console resembled a small, white, square box. The controllers fit snugly atop the unit, which they shared with a power button and an LED display (which signaled when the unit was turned on). The new design was aesthetically pleasant, and its designers followed a modular approach for the peripherals that were designed for it. The 2600 adapter, dubbed the *System Changer* upon its release, resembled the Intellivision II console, and when it was plugged in, the two units seemed to blend together.

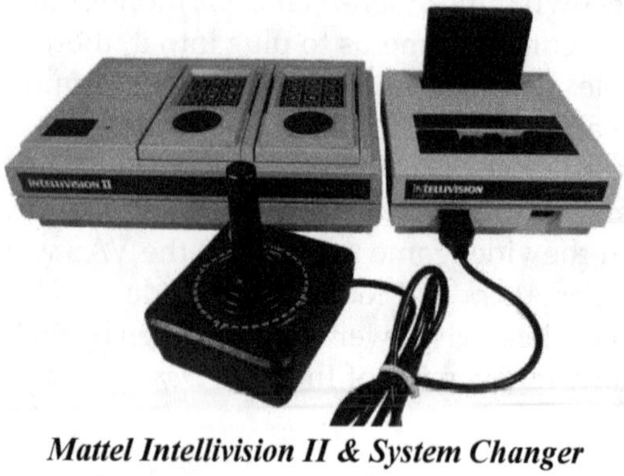

Mattel Intellivision II & System Changer

With the System Changer installed, the Intellivision II did indeed play more games than the competing ColecoVision, but as owners soon found out, the machine couldn't play the Intellivision games that Coleco had released! This had been done intentionally by Mattel to prevent unauthorized third-party games. Nonetheless, once the Intellivision II was released, Coleco's engineers were able to buy one and reverse-engineer it to circumvent Mattel's software lock-out.

Once the Intellivision II had the ability to receive an external video source, its designers were able to forge ahead and develop a computer add-on that could also use the console strictly as a means to funnel the video signal to the television. The long-awaited ECS plugged into the cartridge slot of the Intellivision II, effectively turning the latter into the real 16-bit computer that had been promised for years. Unlike the original, which was to have sold for over $700, the new Entertainment Computer System (ECS), which consisted of the Computer Adapter and a Computer Keyboard that plugged into it, had a suggested retail price of only $150.

In addition to the Computer Keyboard, the ECS accepted a 49-key piano keyboard called the *Music Synthesizer*, which turned the Intellivision II into a synthesizer. Several music-tutorial cartridges were displayed at CES along with the synthesizer, but only one would ultimately be released. *Melody Blaster* used the basic concept of *Astrosmash* to teach people how to play the piano. In this game, falling musical notes had to be shot down for points by hitting the correct keys on the piano keyboard.

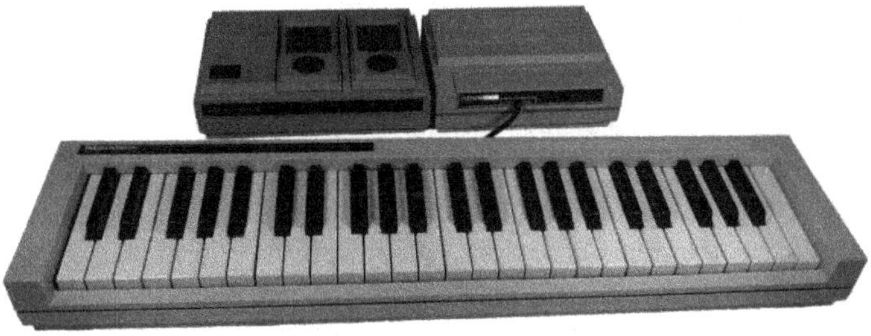

Mattel Intellivision II

with Computer Adapter ***with Music Synthesizer***

The ECS followed the same modular design as the 2600 System Changer and the Intellivision II console. A redesigned Intellivoice, following the same module design, was also shown at CES, but it was never released; in fact, the model displayed at CES was merely a piece of wood that had been carved and painted to look like an Intellivision II component. However, two prototypes of a brand-new International Intellivoice were actually built. These modules enhanced the original with additional ROM that contained voices in French, German and Italian. A special version of *Space Spartans* that could access the foreign languages was produced, but neither it nor the International Intellivoice was ever released. Mattel Electronics didn't give up on the Intellivoice concept, though.

1983

At the winter CES, in a private room that was off-limits to most attendees, the company previewed a new *Intellivision III* to select journalists. The new console promised to have 12K of ROM and 10K of RAM. Its graphics were astounding, and it could produce more colors on the screen at one time than any other available console, including the ColecoVision, which it had been intended to compete against. It would also be compatible with all of the existing Intellivision software. Mattel promised that the new Intellivision III would be available in the summer, with a retail price of $300.

Due to delays, the prototype that the press viewed was merely an original Intellivision that had been modified to display outstanding graphics. However, actual consoles that included the advancements needed to pit the Intellivision III against the ColecoVision could have been produced by the summer, as Mattel had promised. Unfortunately, Mattel didn't stop there. Additional features were haphazardly added to the original Intellivision III design, which sent the project off-track.

Mattel first decided to incorporate the ability to play Intellivoice games without a special adapter. It was also decided to improve the audio by including a stereo output jack, so gamers could connect the console to their audio systems and enjoy amplified sound effects. Finally, Mattel planned a new controller that would be a combination of the original Intellivision keypad and a real joystick. Unfortunately, the release of the Intellivision III would have been pushed beyond the summer to integrate these additional features. Everyone involved in the project, from the designers who'd conceived it to the

Mattel Aquarius

dealers who'd previewed it, agreed that by the time the system was released, it would be too late to successfully compete against the ColecoVision.

On June 1, shortly before the summer CES, Mattel Electronics released the *Aquarius*, a real computer that was designed exclusively for home use. The Aquarius had actually been conceived when Mattel Electronics officially axed the Computer Component and felt that it still needed a computer that it could sell in order to compete. Ironically, Radofin Electronics, a Britsh company that had manufactured the Intellivision for Mattel, just happened to have designed a stand-alone computer system that needed to be distributed. Mattel quickly purchased the marketing rights for the computer and released it as the Aquarius.

The basic Aquarius computer, which was sold with 4K RAM that was expandable to 52K, as well as built-in Microsoft BASIC, retailed for $160. There were also several optional peripherals, such as a printer, modem and disk drive. Like all good computers, the Aquarius could play games, and Mattel released Aquarius versions of several of its popular Intellivision titles. Of course, this narrowed the distinction between the Intellivision II and the Aquarius. Since one was a game machine that could perform computer functions and the other was a computer that played games, it was unclear what type of market Mattel Electronics was trying to capture. To make matters worse; the Aquarius didn't look like a respectable computer. Instead, with its bright blue buttons over white molding, it looked like an expensive toy. For Mattel, the system was a disaster.

Mattel Electronics showed few new products at the summer CES in early June. The company displayed the ECS and a few new peripherals for the Aquarius. The company promised to keep supporting the Intellivision and introduced games that featured SuperGraphics, a programming technique that increased the Intellivision's graphics by adding hi-res definition. The improvement was apparent in multiple and scrolling playfields, animated titles, and more colors.

Another announcement that Mattel made at the June CES was that it was scuttling the M-Network moniker from its 2600-compatible games. The company was concerned that consumers who purchased M-Network games weren't making the connection that the games had been released by Mattel Electronics, and they were worried about brand recognition. From then on, the 2600-compatible cartridges would be simply sold under the Mattel Electronics banner.[2]

Mattel Electronics finally released the long-awaited ECS in June, shortly after CES. Unfortunately, at approximately the same time, Mattel Electronics' president, Josh Denham, resigned from the company. Mack Morris assumed the president's office on July 12, and immediately placed the company's emphasis on software design. Nearly everyone connected to hardware development was laid-off less than a month later. In the wake of this restructuring, the ECS wound up receiving no publicity, and all development for the system was halted. At the same time, the Intellivision III was officially cancelled.

Only six games were ever released for the ECS. And of that number, one also utilized the Intellivoice voice module. *World Series Major League Baseball* was an update on the Intellivision's original launch title, *Major League Baseball*, which had been innovative with its use of voice synthesis, as the computer umpire screamed, "Yer Out!" *World Series Major League Baseball* had been even more innovative, as it had introduced camera angles. Rather than viewing the entire baseball diamond from above, this game was viewed as if multiple cameras were in front of the players. Playing the game was akin to watching an actual televised baseball game, and there were even an inset in the corner of the screen to display two images at the same time. This eventually became the standard for all sports videogames.

But the graphics weren't the only thing that made *World Series Major League Baseball* unique. The gameplay was based on the statistics of actual baseball players. And the videogamer acted as a manager by inputting batting and pitching statistics of the players on his team. This was another feature that would appear in nearly every sport videogame that followed.

Mattel Electronics stuck with the Aquarius for a brief time, primarily because the units were sitting unsold in warehouses. In October, the company finally made a deal with Radofin to take back all of the unsold computers. They actually paid Radofin to revoke their contract and return all ownership and distribution rights to the manufacturer. Radofin complied, with the intention of selling the remaining computers through a new distributor; but this never materialized.

Although Mattel promised that it would continue to develop new hardware and software, by November, they announced that it was considering closing down its electronics division before Christmas. The only thing that prevented this from happening at that time was the belief by company executives that such a move would damage the company's toy division.

Atari vs. Coleco

Since the 2600 was still the best-selling game console, many companies tried to profit from it. Coleco released a new console, the *Gemini*, which was basically a 2600 clone. Besides its styling, the only thing that differentiated it from the 2600 was its controllers, which incorporated both the paddle and joystick into one. In response, Atari quickly added the Gemini to the lawsuit that it already had pending against Coleco over the Expansion Module #1. Despite this, Columbia House, the company that ran popular record and tape clubs, took an interest in the Gemini and licensed it from Coleco for use in its new videogame club. Columbia House renamed the console to the Columbia Home Arcade and used it as a promotion to entice people to join the club. As an introductory offer, people who joined were able to purchase the Columbia Home Arcade for only $49.95, half the price that Atari charged for the 2600. Those who took advantage of this deal had to immediately purchase one cartridge for $20, and five more within the following two years for between $24.95 and $29.95.

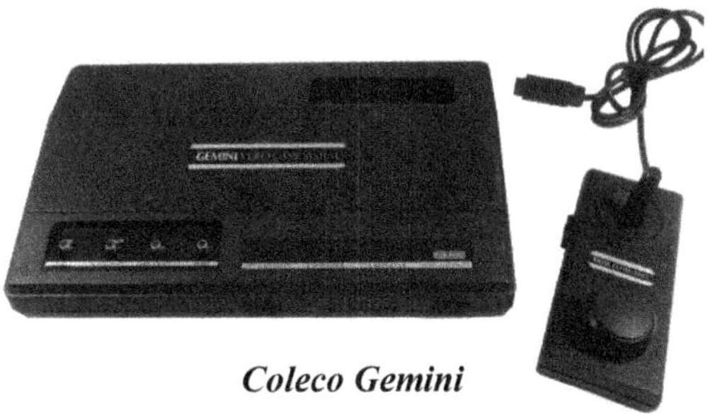

Coleco Gemini

In addition to the Gemini, Coleco also released a $50 voice module that had been designed by Ralph Baer, the inventor of the home videogame console. Unlike the voice modules that were sold by Mattel and Odyssey, the *Kid Vid* was a cassette player that hooked up to the Gemini or 2600 through a controller port. It played special audio tapes that were packaged with specific game cartridges. The audio tape ran while a child played a game, and at certain points, the tape stopped and would only resume when the child made the correct response on the TV screen. To make sure that kids aged three to seven would be interested in it Coleco went out and obtained licenses for such provocative children's fare as Dr. Seuss and the Berenstain

Coleco Kid Vid

Bears.

The lawsuit between Atari and Coleco took some time to settle. After Atari initially sued Coleco in late December 1982, Coleco countersued on charges that Atari had unfairly tried to monopolize the home videogame market by allegedly obtaining invalid patents and dealing with arcade companies so that it could buy exclusive licenses. Coleco also charged that Atari had spread false rumors about its competitors and their products, and had threatened its distributors and retailers against carrying competing merchandise. Additionally, Coleco claimed that Atari had violated U.S. laws when it had bought part of Namco (the Japanese company that had designed *Pac-Man*). And by doing this, Atari had an unfair advantage over hit games that Namco might create.

The two companies finally settled out of court in April, and Coleco agreed to pay Atari an undisclosed royalty for its Expansion Module #1 and Gemini sales. This opened doors for other companies to manufacture 2600 clones, just as Atari's lawsuit against Activision had paved the way for companies to sell 2600-compatible software.

Coleco's charges against Atari were never proven and were dismissed. Ironically, just as Atari and Coleco settled their differences, Parker Brothers filed an antitrust suit against Atari, on the grounds that Atari had tried to entice wholesale distributors into selling only Atari videogames by offering them between 25% and 40% discounts on the games that they bought. Parker Brothers claimed that it lost $15 million in business from 26 wholesalers who canceled orders because they decided to stock only Atari games. Parker Brothers' petition was denied.

Nolan Bushnell Returns

Atari was also involved in a lawsuit against Nolan Bushnell, the co-founder of the company. When Warner purchased Atari in October, 1976, Nolan Bushnell signed a non-competition clause prohibiting him from participating in any professional videogame-related activity until October 1983. In the weeks leading up to that date, a rash of publicity surfaced, stating that after the deadline passed, Bushnell would reenter the coin-op business with a new arcade company called Sente Technologies. Atari claimed that Bushnell had violated the terms of his contract by releasing this advance publicity. The two parties came to an agreement wherein Atari received the home rights to any arcade games that Sente created.

Ironically, like many other videogame companies, Sente had roots that began with Atari. In 1980, Ed Rotberg had programmed the arcade tank simulator, *Battlezone*. In December of that year, the U.S. Army approached Atari about converting *Battlezone* into a training simulator for soldiers. Atari went along with the idea, even though the Army wanted the prototype delivered by March, 1981, a mere three months later. Although he was against the idea of Atari getting involved with the military, not to mention the short time frame, Rotberg agreed to do the conversion only on the condition that Atari didn't team up with the military again.

Afterwards, disenchanted with Atari, he and two other Atari engineers, Howard Delman and Roger Hector, resigned in October 1981 and began their own development company called Videa. When Bushnell decided he wanted to reenter the videogame business, he approached Rotberg, Delman and Hector, and told them that he wanted to make Videa the videogame division of Pizza Time Theatre. He purchased the company for over $1 million and renamed it Sente Technologies.

Sente was primarily an arcade game company. However, Bushnell also became involved with a company that dealt with the consumer videogame market, which hadn't been included in Atari's lawsuit, because there hadn't been any advance publicity for it. The company, Androbot, introduced an exciting new peripheral for the 2600, a twelve-inch-high robot. Billed as the "World's First Real Life 3D Videogame Robot", *Androman* was joystick-controlled, via a remote-control infrared signal. The company planned to sell it along with a game cartridge, transmitter, game board, and a set of game pieces. Like Odyssey's *Master Strategy Series*, the game-play shifted between the TV screen and the game board on which *Androman* resided. After a certain number of points had been accumulated on the screen, *Androman* had to navigate through an obstacle course and make contact with the pieces that had been distributed around the game board.

Androbot Androman

Atari vs. X-Rated Games

Another Atari lawsuit was filed against American Multiple Industries, the manufacturer of the controversial X-rated game, *Custer's Revenge*. Atari feared that it would receive negative publicity if the third-party company was allowed to release its software. Because of the subject of *Custer's Revenge*, Atari received many negative letters from Native American and women's groups. As such, Atari wanted the game removed from the market, because it feared that the public would mistakenly believe that it had endorsed the game.

American Multiple Industries wound up filing an $11 million suit against Suffolk County, New York, on the grounds that the county had pushed to prohibit the game from being sold. The county argued that they enforced the ban because they believed *Custer's Revenge* was a danger to the health and safety of its residents.

The result was that the X-rated videogame industry received nothing but negative publicity. A second company, Gamex, released an X-rated maze game called *X-Man*, and discovered that distributors and retailers weren't interested in carrying it. Other companies, such as Multivision, had been preparing to enter the X-rated games market, but the negative publicity ended their participation. American Multiple Industries wound up selling the rights to its games to another company, PlayAround. This company rereleased *Beat 'Em & Eat 'Em* and *Bachelor Party*, along with three other titles, but decided against selling *Custer's Revenge*. On the innovative side, PlayAround sold both male and female versions of each game. It also packaged two games together in one cartridge. Billed as the **"WORLD'S FIRST 2-IN-1 ADULT VIDEO GAME CARTRIDGE,"** both ends of the cartridge could be plugged into the console, since each end contained its own ROM chip. Even though these cartridges didn't cost any more than a standard game cartridge, PlayAround received little distribution, and the games died quick deaths. Along with them died the controversy of the X-rated games, as no other company ever released another 2600-compatible X-rated game again.

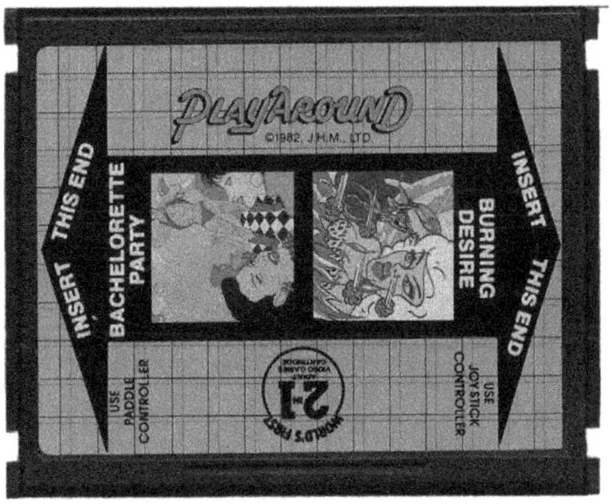

PlayAround 2-IN-1 Cartridge

Although X-rated games failed in the marketplace, they did prove that software vendors were willing to release something different to make their products visible in the stores. With the proliferation of increasingly more and more 2600-compatible games, the software companies did whatever they had to do to make their games unique.

Playaround wasn't the only company that released two-sided cartridges. another new

XONOX Double Ender

software company, XONOX, sold *Double-Enders*, cartridges that also had games on both ends. The name XONOX had been chosen because it was a palindrome; it read the same from either end, just like the cartridges had a game on either end. XONOX was a new software division of K-Tel, a record company that had made its name in the seventies and eighties by marketing record collections and then advertising them to death on television. XONOX felt that it would succeed where PlayAround had failed, because it marketed clean games that an entire family could enjoy. The company released two Double-Enders in 1983.

2600 Games on Tape

Starpath, the company that produced the innovative Supercharger, went one step farther and introduced a new type of game that was very different from others that were available. Multi-Load games loaded into the 2600 one segment at a time. After the player completed the first segment, the next one was loaded and the play continued from a new point. The Multi-Load games were more sophisticated and had better graphics than other 2600 games due to the additional memory of the Supercharger and the ability to load only portions of a game at a given time. *Escape From The Mindmaster*, the first Multi-Load game that Starpath offered, turned the player into a human rat who had been caught in an alien labyrinth. The maze was displayed from a first-person perspective and the movement was so fluid that it appeared as if the player actually walked through the maze. The object of the game was to find several hidden shapes and bring them to their correct places within the maze while avoiding a roaming monster. Once the pieces were correctly in place, the player advanced up a flight of stairs to the next maze. Each game segment contained two mazes and the player had to complete six mazes in order to win.

At Toy Fair, Amiga Corporation announced a memory-expansion device that was very similar to the Supercharger in both looks and purpose. The *Power Module* added 6K of RAM to the 2600, and had an additional feature that allowed two units to be interfaced together through a built-in modem. This gave two players the ability to compete against each other via the phone lines. Games were to be on cassette, and the Power Module was to be sold with *3D Ghost Attack*, the first three-dimensional home videogame (Amiga had planned to include a pair of special glasses) and *Depth Charge*, the first online interactive videogame.

Amiga Power Module

New Controllers

In addition to the Power Module, Amiga also debuted special controllers for the 2600 at Toy Fair. The *Joyboard* was a controller that players had to stand on in order to use. Instead of pushing a joystick forward, the player leaned forward on the Joyboard. This added an extra level of play to standard games, and Amiga developed a line of games that were specifically

Amiga Joyboard

designed for use with it. *Mogul Maniac*, a first-person skiing game, was packaged with the Joyboard. Amiga's other controller, the *Power-Stick*, was a tiny joystick controller that fit in the palm of the hand and was much more responsive than a standard Atari joystick.[3]

Another controller that was released for the VCS[4] was one that was new to the Atari console, but had already been available on another console. The *Video Command* from Zircon was the same controller that had already been available for that company's Channel F. The eight-directional knob at the top served the same purpose as the stick on Atari's joystick controller. Pressing the knob down like a plunger, served the same purpose as pressing the red firing button on the joystick controller.[5]

Amiga Power-Stick

Zircon International Video Command

Other companies also developed new innovative controllers for the various consoles. Coleco's *Super Action Controllers* for the ColecoVision put the player in physical contact with the action on the screen. Each controller looked like a pistol without a barrel. On top was an eight-position joystick, a twelve-button keypad, and a speed roller. On its handle were four trigger-like buttons, which precisely controlled specific areas of game play. The controllers had been designed especially for sports games and were sold with *Super Action Baseball*. Other sports games that Coleco announced for the Super Action Controllers were *Super Action Football* and *Rocky Meets The Champ*.

Coleco also offered the *Roller Controller*, a trackball controller for the ColecoVision. The Roller Controller could only be used with specific games and was sold with *Slither*, a *Centipede*-like game. Others were planned.

Atari responded by releasing the *Trak-Ball* Controller for the 5200. Like the Roller Controller, the Atari Trak-Ball could only be used with certain games that had been especially designed to work with it. To make the controller more attractive, Atari released *Centipede* for the 5200 since the arcade version used a trackball.

Coleco Super Action Controller

Coleco Roller Controller

Atari also released the *VCS Cartridge Adapter* for the 5200. Once this unit was plugged into the 5200's cartridge slot, it allowed the Super Console to play the hundreds of games that were available for the 2600. To help market the adapter, Atari launched an ad campaign which stated that the 5200 played more games than any other console.

Atari also released several new controllers for the 2600. The *Remote Control Wireless Joystick* had originally been sold by its manufacturer, Cynex, under the Game Mate 2 name. The set that Atari sold under its own name was the same one that Cynex sold. It consisted of two joystick controllers and a power base, which plugged into the controller ports of the 2600. The controllers resembled the standard Atari joysticks except that their bases were large and bulky.

Atari 5200 Trak-Ball

Atari VCS Cartridge Adapter

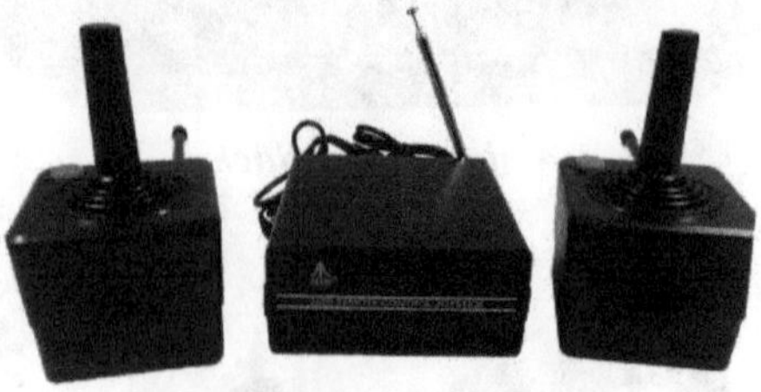

Atari 2600 Remote Control Wireless Joysticks

Atari 2600 Trak-Ball

Atari Kids Controller

The *Trak-Ball Controller* was a simple device that included the ball in the center and control firing buttons on both sides. The unit could be set to either *Trak Ball* mode or *Joystick* mode. In *Joystick* mode, which was universal and could be used by any game, moving the ball in any of eight directions had the game respond as if a joystick had been pressed. In *Trak Ball* mode, the ball could be rotated in a 360 degree motion and the speed was consistent with how fast the ball was rolled. No games for the 2600 were programmed to work in *Trak Ball* mode, while a handful of Atari computer titles, including *Missile Command*, could be played in *Trak Ball* mode.

Finally, Atari released a *Kid's Controller*, which looked like a blue book with twelve buttons on its cover. The controller was released in conjunction with a new line of Sesame Street games that Atari developed in partnership with the Children's Television Workshop (CTW). Each cartridge was sold with an overlay that fit onto the Kid's Controller and allowed very young children to easily manipulate the on-screen action.

Milton Bradley released two unusual

controllers for the 2600, which operated like standard joystick controllers, but were designed to give the impression that the player was part of the action. *Cosmic Commander* resembled the control panel of a spaceship, complete with a radar control gauge and flashing lights. *Flight Commander* looked like the cockpit of a jet fighter with an attached machine gun. Both controllers included raised cross-hairs so the player could take aim and fire at the on-screen targets, and both came with exclusive game cartridges (*Survival Run* and *Spitfire Attack* respectively). Unfortunately, the games simply weren't fun; with or without the special controllers. A third controller, *Tank Commander*, was shown at Toy Fair with the game *Tank Blitz*, but Milton Bradley wisely chose not to release it.

Milton Bradley Flight Commander

Milton Bradley Cosmic Commander

Milton Bradley had also designed a new game console in 1982 that it hoped would make it a contender against Atari and Mattel Electronics. This system would have provided voice recognition and speech synthesis. However, after Coleco released the ColecoVision, Milton Bradley figured that the market had no room for four separate consoles manufacturers. Milton Bradley then decided to turn this system into a peripheral for the Texas Instruments TI-99/4A computer, which Milton Bradley already produced software for.

The *MBX* made its debut at the winter CES. The system included a built-in keypad, a headset microphone and an analog 360 degree joystick controller that resembled a pistol. The system was a hit at the show and was eventually released near the end of the year.[6]

Milton Bradley planned to market a subset of the MBX controller for use on the Atari 2600 and other compatible systems. The company called it the *HD2000 Heavy Duty Joystick*. The HD2000, which would have been distributed by GCE, wouldn't have had the action buttons or the 360 degree rotation knob that were part of the MBX controller, but it would retain the pistol shape.

Atari took an interest in the MBX while Milton Bradley showed it at the winter CES and a deal was made at the show for Milton Bradley to design a version of it for the 2600 and 5200. As part of the deal Atari also took ownership of the HD2000 and released it as the *Space-Age Joystick* under the Atari brand.

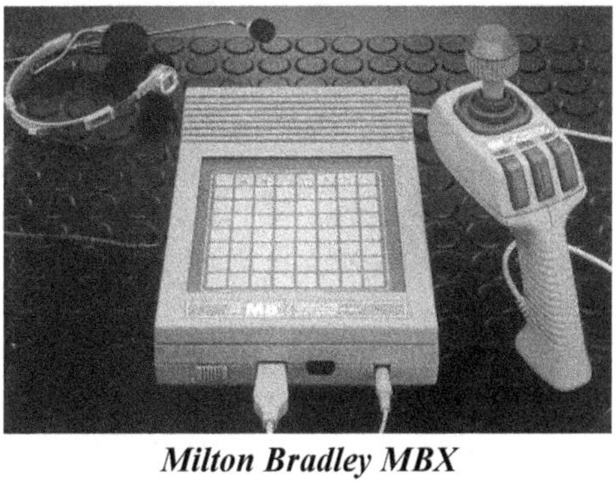

Milton Bradley MBX

Atari and Milton Bradley showed off their $100 *Voice Commander* at the summer CES. The Voice Commander was a plug-in peripheral

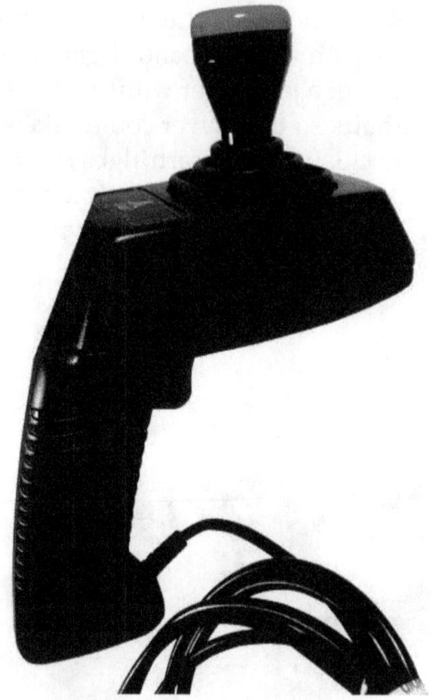

Atari 2600 Space Age Joystick

that acted as both a voice synthesis and voice recognition unit. Designed for both the 2600 and 5200, the module consisted of a headset and microphone that allowed players to control on-screen movement strictly by speaking. For example, in a game like *Asteroids*, the only thing the player had to do in order to send a ship into hyperspace, was say the word *hyperspace* into the microphone. Any word could be used since the unit had to be set up before it could be used. Pressing the joystick in the appropriate direction and saying the word that corresponded with that joystick movement into the microphone easily accomplished this. Milton Bradley agreed to manufacture the unit and 18 games for it over the following three years.

The controller was highly anticipated and was a big hit at the summer CES in June, where it was demonstrated using a special version of *RealSports Baseball*. However, in early August Atari sent out a press release stating that the Voice Commander was on "hold". No reasons for this decision were explained. By the end of that month, Milton Bradley filed a $43 million dollar lawsuit against Atari, charging the videogame company with breach of contract.

No matter how unique a controller might be, all they could do was dress up the way people interfaced with games. They couldn't change the way a game played. Unfortunately, players lost interest in a vast number of their games within a month after they purchased them and no type of controller could change that. However, at the summer CES, a company called Answer Software announced a device that could actually alter existing games. Like the computer upgrades for the 2600, the PGP-1 (Personal Game Programming) system plugged into the 2600's cartridge slot and had its own slot that accepted game cartridges. Once a game was inserted, any of its features, such as background colors, speeds, and even number of lives, could be modified.

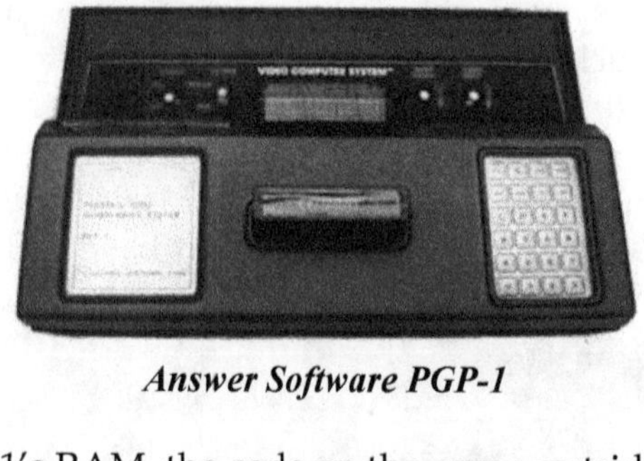

Answer Software PGP-1

The $200 PGP-1 worked by giving users the ability to delve into the binary code of the game program, and allowing them to change any of it. And since few consumers were fluent in binary programming, Answer Software developed a series of guides that instructed the user in how to modify many of the best-selling 2600-compatible games, as well as games to be released by Answer Software itself. And because all of the alterations to the program took place only within the PGP-1's RAM, the code on the game cartridge remained untouched.

Unfortunately, very few people were willing to pay $200 for a device that only allowed for temporary changes. Answer Software managed to sell a handful of PGP-1s, and its 2600-compatible game, *Malagai*, before permanently exiting from the videogame business.

Expanding Cartridge Memory

Some companies felt that if the amount of ROM in a cartridge could be expanded, a better caliber of game could be designed for them. At Toy Fair in February, two software companies announced that they had utilized new chips in their standard cartridges that enhanced the memory capabilities of the 2600.

CBS Electronics' chip, RAM PLUS, tripled the memory capacity of the 2600 and improved the graphics, control, detail, and complexity of a game. The company used RAM PLUS to develop sophisticated first-person games such as *Tunnel Runner,* which was a maze game similar to Starpath's *Escape From The Mindmaster.* As it turned out, Starpath's Multi-Load game had better graphics.

US Games called its enhanced chip RAM/ROM and designed complicated strategic adventure games around it. This new chip contained 8K of ROM and 2K of RAM, and the games that used it featured more sequential screens and sophisticated movement than standard adventures. US Games also developed a new controller that gave the user the ability to zoom in and out on the screen. The company licensed the popular cartoon character for its first RAM/ROM game, *Trail of the Pink Panther.*

Unfortunately, US Games never released *Trail of the Pink Panther* or any other RAM/ROM game. In March, the company filed for bankruptcy, due to the unforeseen, rapid over-saturation in the videogame market. Quaker Oats, the parent company of US Games, would have required a substantial investment for the company to remain in business. It chose not to do this.

Third-Party Failures

The US Games story began to get repeated elsewhere. After purchasing major licenses such as Mr. T, Mr. Bill, and Smokey Bear, Data-Age also went out of business. The games that were based on these licenses were never released. The remaining inventory of both Data-Age and US Games were sold to a salvage company called Kandy Man Sales, which in turn sold them to the public at bargain prices.

This dumping of games produced a domino effect. As dozens of games were unloaded at ridiculously low prices, casual consumers bypassed the newer and more expensive games in favor of the bargains. As their inventories increased, more and more companies dumped their stock in an effort to generate some income. This only added to the glut of product already on the shelves. As games were sold at clearance, manufacturers couldn't recoup the money that they spent on research and development, and this forced many of them to close down their operations.

By year's end, the shakeout hit most of the third-party software companies. Telesys, Spectravision, and Twentieth Century Fox all announced that they were leaving the videogame business. Some companies had just entered the business when they quickly discovered how over-laden the market had become. Among them was Avalon-Hill, which released three strategy games.

Sega Enterprises, Inc.[7] released several home versions of Sega arcade games for the 2600, as well as for the other popular consoles including the ColecoVision and the 5200. Because Sega was owned by Gulf & Western, which also owned Paramount Pictures, the company planned to release several games that were based on hit Paramount movies such as *48 Hours.* These games were abandoned when G&W decided to scuttle from the videogame business. In September, it sold its arcade operation, Sega Electronics, Inc.[8] to Bally. This gave Bally the first American right of refusal for Sega arcade games that were developed in Japan, including new games that utilized laserdisc technology. Sega Enterprises, Inc. remained in business in the United States to continue creating software for home console and computers.[9]

Movie-based games did make it to market, though, when Wizard Video released games based on the horror movies *Halloween* and *Texas Chainsaw Massacre.* Unfortunately, very few stores carried them.

Although its distribution was limited, Wizard had been lucky to get into some stores.

Other companies couldn't get their games into any stores at all. Zimag, the company that began the year with billboards to attract the throngs that attended the CES in Las Vegas, faded quietly. At February's Toy Fair, the Great Game Company announced a number of 2600-compatible cartridges that were all based on TV game shows such as *Jeopardy* and *Family Feud*. Not only had they never released, they were never even shown. Other companies, such as Broderbund and Sydney Software, also announced titles for the 2600 but failed to produce them.

Parker Brothers decided to continue marketing games but took a long look at the products that it was developing. After much thought, the company decided to abandon most of the games that were in development and to only release those that it considered to be the best of the best.

Imagic, which had hoped to go public at the end of 1982, put its stock offering on hold after Atari revealed that it made much less than it had projected. The public offering never happened, so Imagic received financing from the private sector in the spring of 1983. Despite this, in September, Imagic found itself in financial straights along with the rest of the industry. Because of a lack of sales due to the software glut, Imagic couldn't obtain major distribution for its new products. With limited distribution, Imagic could only get the new products into a few stores. Few people were aware of them anyway, since the company could no longer afford advertising. The lack of revenue forced the management to lay off nearly one-third of its 170 employees. By year's end, Imagic changed its course and decided to concentrate strictly on developing and licensing games for other companies. Since it no longer needed to manufacture products, Imagic laid off all of its sales and marketing employees.

Even Activision, the granddaddy of software companies, experienced a loss of business. By the end of the second-quarter the company had a net loss of $4 million, down from a $4.4 million profit for the same period a year earlier. To keep revenue flowing, Activision began releasing games for computers.

Starpath, the manufacturer of the acclaimed Supercharger, quietly closed down after Epyx, a computer software company, bought its entire design group. Epyx had no plans to enter the console game market and closed out the entire inventory of Superchargers and software.

Amiga changed its plans and scuttled the Power Module. In its place, the company announced cartridges that contained three ROM chips. Housed in the same super-long cartridge shell originally planned for the Power Module, Amiga called the new cartridges the Power-Play Arcade Series. Amiga also prepared to unleash a new 16-bit computer that it was developing.

Atari, the company that many people blamed for causing the shake-out because of its false projections, also suffered. In March, the company announced that it had eliminated 600 jobs in Sunnyvale, so that it could cut costs by moving its production facilities to Hong Kong and Taiwan.

In the following month, Atari announced that cartridge sales for the 2600 had risen 10% from the year before. They also projected that 10% of all households in the country were planning to buy a 2600 console within a year. Despite this optimistic forecast, Atari still closed its El Paso manufacturing plant, and discarded its existing inventory from that plant in an unusual way. Instead of unloading the consoles and cartridges to stores at bargain prices, the company loaded the entire inventory onto fourteen tractor trailers and took it to an Alamogordo, New Mexico landfill, where it was buried. Many speculated that Atari had dumped the games because it would have been too expensive to unload them through the normal distribution channels. Atari claimed that the games were defective and couldn't be sold.

In an effort to gain more sales, Atari began developing software for competing game consoles and computers. Famous games like *Pac-Man* and *Centipede,* which had previously been available only on Atari consoles and computers, were sold under the Atarisoft label for the Apple II, Commodore 64, Intellivision, and several other systems. Atari also announced that it had acquired the home rights to Nintendo's arcade hit, *Mario Bros.*

The fact that Atari began releasing software for the Intellivision didn't make the management at Mattel very happy. They quickly filed a lawsuit against Atari, charging it with hiring ex-Mattel employees in order to obtain trade secrets and develop and release Intellivision-compatible games in time for Christmas.

Interestingly enough, other companies, like Imagic, Coleco, and Parker Brothers, joined Atari and Activision in releasing software for the Intellivision. A new third-party company, Interphase, ignored the 2600 altogether and released two games for the Intellivision and ColecoVision: *Sewer Sam* and *Blockade Runner*. Interphase also released exclusive titles, *Aquattack* and *Squish'em Sam,* strictly for the ColecoVision.

Play the Original Arcade Classic in Your Own Home
TI 99/4A
PAC-MAN
FROM
ATARISOFT

AtariSoft

Probe 2000

Things looked more hopeful for Odyssey when the year began. The company displayed the new *Odyssey^3 Command Center* at the winter CES in January. Five months later, at the summer CES, the company announced *Probe 2000,* a new line of software for competing videogame and computer systems. The first Probe 2000 title would be *Pursuit of the Pink Panther*, a title that was quickly prepared after Odyssey had picked up the rights to the character when US Games folded.

As it prepared to roll out its Probe 2000 games, Odyssey decided to abandon its plans of marketing the Odyssey^3 Command Center in North America. This had been done because company executives felt that the new console wasn't technologically advanced enough to compete against the inexpensive computers that were already on the market. Although they were still marketing the Odyssey^2, company executives decided to concentrate on the new software line.

As Odyssey officials closed the door on the next-generation Odyssey^2, their counterparts at Philips went ahead and opened it. The company released the *Videopac G7400* in several European countries. The Videopac G7400 was backward compatible with the Videopac G7000, which meant that that these games would play on the new console but would look exactly the same as they did on the older unit. However, Philips began releasing many of its Videopac cartridges under the *Videopac* + banner and these games featured enhanced graphics when played on the Videopac G7400, but could also play on the Videopac G7000 with their original graphics. Philips released three games that could only play on the Videopac G7400, *Helicopter Rescue, Norseman* and *Trans American Rally*. This was essentially the same thing that Odyssey planned to do with the Odyssey^3 Command Center. Internally, the Videopac G7400 was basically the same console as the Odyssey^3 Command Center. However, the main difference between the two was the fact that the Videopac G7400 didn't feature sculptured keys as the Odyssey^3 Command Center was going to have. Instead, the Videopac G7400 looked almost like a Videopac G7000 with a narrower membrane keyboard.

By October, Odyssey had released only one game under the Probe 2000 banner.

Philips Videopac G7400

Probe 2000 War Room

Unfortunately, *War Room* for the ColecoVision would be the only Probe 2000 title that Odyssey would release. A severe chip shortage caused the company to scrap all of its other titles, since it couldn't hope to release them in time for the critical Christmas season. Following this disaster, Odyssey decided to abandon the industry that it had created altogether.

Alternative Ways of Distributing Games

As many companies folded due to the overabundance of games in the stores, others looked at other ways to deliver their products to consumers. Alternative methods of providing games had actually begun in 1980, when Mattel had partnered with General Instrument and formed PlayCable. Although the success of PlayCable diminished with the popularity of Intellivision, other companies began looking at the potential of delivering games by cable. In early 1983, Atari planned a joint venture with Time-Life that would have offered between 20 and 30 games a month. The games were to have been Atari's most popular titles, and the company intended to release one new game each week. Subscribers would even have the opportunity to test out brand-new games that Atari was in the process of developing. Unfortunately, due to Atari's ever-increasing financial troubles, the cable delivery system never got off the ground.

By February, another cable service, the Games Network, had signed up 470 cable companies to deliver its goods. Unlike the previous two services, which had required each subscriber to own a videogame console, the Games Network provided exclusive hardware that would play the games that it delivered. Originally, the company had anticipated to be fully set up by September, but this was later changed to December. Unfortunately, the shake-out had occurred by that time, and it caused the Games Network's executives to abandon their plans. The company never started up, and disappeared into game oblivion.

As computer enthusiasts knew, the phone lines were just as capable of delivering software into homes as cable. People who owned computers with modems had been dialing up networks for years. Videogame owners were awarded the same opportunity during the summer of 1983, when William Von Meister, president of Control Video Corporation (CVC), initiated a new online service called Gameline. Von Meister was well suited to partake in such a venture. He had previously founded The Source, which at the time had been the world's largest computer network.

FOCUS ON: CONTROL VIDEO CORPORATION

Following Gameline's demise, CVC borrowed $5 million from Bell South to form Masterline, an online service for Apple II and Commodore 64 computers. After this failed, Commodore decided that it wanted to create its own online service. Commodore bought shares of CVC and then licensed the technology of another service called Play-Net. Using Commodore's money, CVC paid off its investors and then closed the company; only to reform as Quantum Computer Services on May 24, 1985. Quantum then used the Play-Net technology and on November 1, 1985 introduced Q-Link, an online service for Commodore 64 computers.

When Commodore didn't whole-heartedly support its online service, and the Commodore 64 market began to wane, Quantum signed up with Apple in 1987 to distribute Apple Link, an online service for the Apple II. Unfortunately Apple wanted too much control of Quantum, which Quantum refused to relinquish. Apple paid Quantum $2.5 million in June 1989 to give up its rights to use the Apple logo and this in effect severed the deal between the two companies. The cutoff date to quit using the Apple Link name was October 2, 1989 and the company had to come up with a different name to use after that date. The new name chosen was America Online.

The secret behind Gameline was its *Master Module,* which resembled Starpath's Supercharger, and contained 8K RAM and a 1200-baud modem. When the Master Module was inserted into the 2600, it automatically dialed a toll-free number that connected it to a mainframe computer, from which the player could select games. After the game was downloaded into the Master Module's memory, the modem disconnected the line, and the game was then played on the 2600 like any other, with the Master Module substituting as a game cartridge.

The cost to use Gameline wasn't cheap. The Master Module retailed for $59.95. Next, a $15 registration fee was imposed the first time the player logged on. Finally, the player was charged one dollar for each session of a game that had already been downloaded. A session consisted of a set number of games, predetermined by CVC. Some games could be played twelve times per download, while others were set at eight. There were no restrictions on how long gamers could play an individual game. The program remained in the Master Module's memory until either another game was downloaded, the maximum number of games in a session were used, or the 2600 was turned off.

All fees were charged to a credit card. Parents were able to apply charge limits, so their kids wouldn't get carried away and continually download games.

The Gameline Master Module also contained a 2K CMOS (Complementary Metal Oxide Semiconductor) RAM chip. Unlike standard RAM, CMOS RAM required less energy and

CVC Gameline Master Module

could be powered by a small battery that was housed along with it. The advantage of this was that the data was retained even after conventional power, such as the power from the host console, was turned off. The Master Module used it to store players' names, Personal Identification Numbers, the module's serial number, and best contest scores.[10]

CVC planned other uses for the Master Module in addition to games. *Sportsline* would provide all sorts of sports information. *Infoline* would present all the latest news and stocks. *MailLine* would provide electronic mail and banking services to 2600 owners.

The games that were available through Gameline were supplied by companies that had signed up with the service. Their hopes were that a person would go out and buy the cartridge once the game had been sampled. Unsurprisingly, the larger and more successful companies, such as Atari and Activision, didn't feel the need to offer trial versions of their games; so they didn't take part. Ironically, all of the companies that had signed up with Gameline, including Imagic and Games by Apollo, were out of the videogame business by the end of the year, and unable to provide new games to Gameline. With nothing new to offer, Gameline eventually suffered the same fate that had befallen its suppliers.

In June, Coleco announced a joint venture with AT&T, where the goal of which was to modify existing cartridge-based games so two gamers could compete against each other via the phone lines. They took Atari's 2600 one-player *Star Raiders* and modified it so two players could compete against each other. Each player would pilot an individual ship, and instead of going after computer-controlled enemies, they would go against each other.

In its September 19, 1983, edition, *Newsweek* published an article revealing that Coleco and AT&T were collaborating. However, instead of mentioning the information from the June announcement, the latest news was that both companies planned to produce a service similar to Gameline, where a variety of games could be downloaded for all game systems. The modem was expected to sell for $100, and the service would cost $20 per month for unlimited downloads. The service was expected to start up sometime during 1984. It never did.

Basically, the idea behind the Gameline was relatively simple. Whereas a standard game cartridge contained a ROM chip that had the game program permanently burned into it, the Gameline Master Module contained a RAM chip, which was basically empty. Program information needed to be loaded into it, and CVC chose downloaded information via the telephone lines as the means to deliver the data. However, since RAM needs a constant power supply to preserve its data, the information would only remain within the Master Module as long as the system remained on.

It didn't take long for someone to figure out that blank cartridges could contain data besides the downloaded kind. In fact, two companies, Romox and Cumma Technology, used similar cartridge-filling methods to distribute games into blank cartridges.

In both cases, retailers could lease terminals that had access to hundreds of game programs. After paying a small fee, a customer placed a blank cartridge into a slot in the terminal and selected a desired game. The terminal then loaded the game program onto the chip inside the cartridge, which could then be used exactly like a standard cartridge. The blank cartridges could be reprogrammed over and over again, and the data was not lost when power from the host console was removed. This was because the cartridge contained an EPROM (Erasable Programmable Read-Only Memory) chip. Data on an EPROM could only be removed by subjecting the EPROM to strong ultra-violet rays. If the player wanted a new game loaded onto his cartridge, the terminal would first erase the old game program by bathing the EPROM in ultra-violet light, and then download the new code into it.

If the Romox system was used, a blank ECPC (Edge Connector Programmable Cartridge) had to be purchased for between $15 and $25, depending upon the memory requirements of the game system. Customers then browsed a Romox catalog, in which screen samples and instructions for every game offered could be viewed. After a game was selected, the retailer was paid between $1 and $20, depending upon the game. The retailer then inserted the ECPC into the correct slot in the Romox Programming Terminal (since several cartridge types could be loaded with data, and the contact pins of each cartridge varied, there had to be multiple slots to support them all). The desired game was then loaded onto the blank cartridge. At that point, the customer owned the cartridge and could play the game. Once the process was completed, the customer could use the ECPC as if it was a standard game cartridge. It could be kept and used whenever the customer wanted to play the game, or it could be returned to a retailer and reloaded with a new game program for the standard fee.

Cumma's process worked almost the same way. After purchasing the correct blank MetaCart, the customer placed it into Cumma's Metawriter. The Metawriter, which the company referred to as an "electronic vending machine", stood upright and displayed a fifteen-second preview of each game, as well as its instructions. The customer paid a fee of between $1 and $15, and the selected game was then loaded into the MetaCart. Finally, the Metawriter printed the game instructions on a slip of paper that the customer could take home. The benefit with this system was that the retailer didn't have to take part in the transaction with the Cumma system.

Although Cumma Technology was a new company, the people behind it weren't new to the industry. The vice-president of engineering was Al Alcorn, who had been the original designer of *Pong*. Two other Atari alumni, Nolan Bushnell and Joe Keenan, were major investors in the company.

Both Romox and Cumma planned to make money by selling blank cartridges, leasing Programming Terminals and Metawriters, and charging fees to software vendors for distributing their products. The software companies would benefit because they'd received a royalty each time one of their games was downloaded onto a blank cartridge. They'd make even more money if a consumer purchased the cartridge of a game that had been sampled from the ECPC or MetaCart.

Unfortunately for both Romox and Cumma, the retail price of videogame cartridges had dropped to a level that was far less than what a blank cartridge and a game program would cost the consumer. Cumma disappeared quite rapidly while Romox made it to some retailer outlets.[11]

While Romox and Cumma both had planned on creating a network of videogame vending machines, a third company brought the idea of blank videogame cartridges home. Vidco International marketed a device called the Copy Cart, which was basically a personal version of the Cumma Metawriter or the Romox Programmable Terminal. Marketed as a videogame recorder, the Copy Cart could copy the contents of one 2600-compatible cartridge onto the EPROM of a blank cartridge supplied by Vidco. Although Vidco stressed that the unit was intended only to copy its own videogames, the Copy Cart allowed users to copy any 2600 game that they wished without any royalties going to the vendors.

In most cases, the Copy Cart was impractical. The unit sold for $59.95 and included one Vidco game cartridge and one blank cartridge. Additional blank cartridges cost $15.95 each. People weren't going to pay $15.95 to buy a blank cartridge when most game cartridges were being discounted for $5 apiece. However, a few companies, such as Atari, were still developing new games and selling them at premium prices. Atari quickly filed a suit in Federal Court to block any sales of the unit. Atari won, and the Copy Cart was removed from the market.

Coleco Problems

As the videogame industry slowed down, Coleco set its sights on its new Adam computer. The company announced that it had taken advance orders for all 500,000 units that it expected to manufacture that year. Coleco announced in early August that the system would be on store shelves by the end of the month. When September arrived and the computers hadn't, Coleco stated that the delay was due to the FCC taking a long time to approve the computer. Meanwhile, despite Coleco's optimistic report that it had sold out all of its computers, many dealers were cautious about carrying it. Their prime concern was the low profit margin that the Adam carried. They were also skeptical that Coleco could deliver the finished product without any defects appearing soon afterwards. The retailers also feared that even if Coleco ironed out all of the unforeseen problems, customers might still hesitate to purchase a product that had a severe shortage of compatible software.

Coleco's own stockholders were also skeptical of the path that the company was taking. One stockholder, who had purchased Coleco stocks shortly after the Adam had been announced, filed a suit against the company. He claimed that Coleco hid many problems in an effort to get the computers to the stores quickly. He also charged that the company had sold 183,000 shares of stock in June, before announcing that it was suffering from engineering problems. From the day that Coleco first announced the Adam to the day that it revealed that it had to postpone its release date, Coleco's stock dropped from $60 a share to $30.

In November, Coleco announced that it would only be shipping 140,000 Adams, down from the original 500,000. By then, it had actually managed to ship a low number but retailers, even major department stores, only received a fraction of the units that they ordered. This was similar to what had happened in 1976 when retailers had received few of the dedicated game consoles that they had ordered because of a chip shortage. Ironically, at that time Coleco had shined, as it had been the only company capable of shipping full orders. Now it was Coleco's turn to look bad.

Table Tops and Handhelds

Coleco fared better with the stand-alone products that it released during 1983, tabletop versions of *Ms. Pac-Man* and *Zaxxon*. Coleco also sold a tabletop version of *Donkey Kong Jr.*, which had actually been manufactured by Nintendo. Nintendo also released the title itself in Japan as part of its new Game & Watch *Tabletop* series. Nintendo also released tabletop games in the United States including *Mario's Cement Factory*, *Popeye* and *Snoopy*. These games were a departure from the previous Game & Watch titles as they introduced a colored LCD screen. However, the screen needed to be illuminated from behind, so there was a plastic window at the top of the unit to allow light to shine through.

While they were part of the Game & Watch series, the tabletop games were no longer portable in the sense that they could be played everywhere as the units needed to rest on something. To bring the games slightly back to their roots, Nintendo introduced the *Panorama* line. These games took the color LCD screen found in the tabletop line and placed it back to back with the plastic window that allow light to shine through. The screen was stored inside the console but because it faced downward, it was attached to a hinge so it could be raised

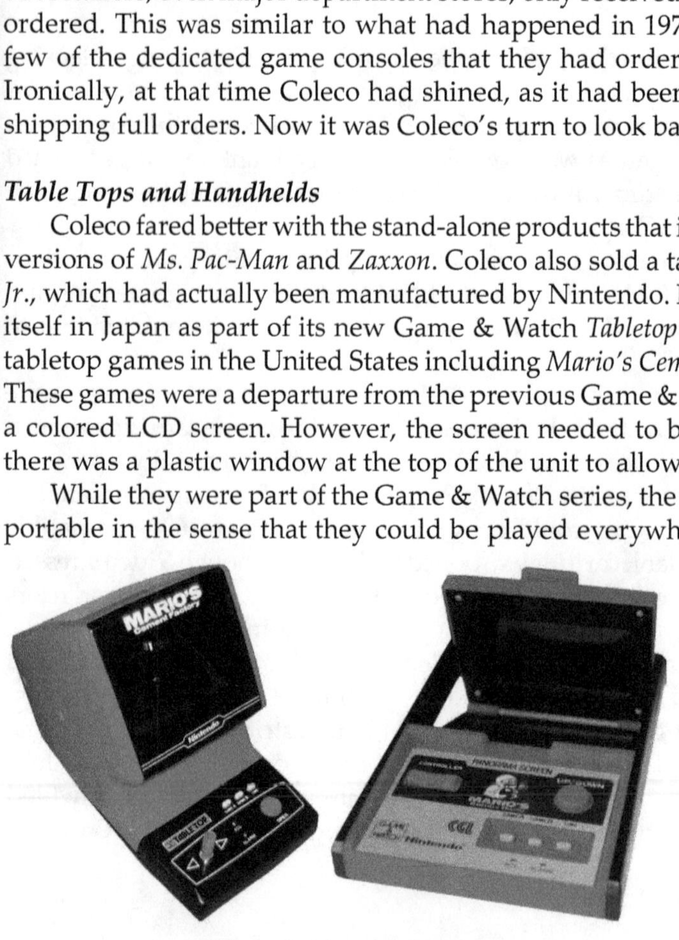

Nintendo Game & Watch
Tabletop ***Panorama***

out of the console. The player then viewed the actual screen through a mirror that was set within the gaming device.

Although the Game & Watch and other LCD games could be played in a lit room, the light sometimes created a glare on the screen. Nintendo's use in the tabletop and panorama games of funneling light to behind the screen helped eliminate this problem. But this merely illustrated a fact that all of the LCD games exhibited; they couldn't be played in darkness.

A company called Palmtex[12] introduced a new LCD handheld that alleviated the problem of playing in the dark. The *Super Micro* was a palm-sized programmable system that used individual game cartridges. The unit had a clam-shell design, which meant one side folded over the other like on the Game & Watch multi-screen devices. When open, control buttons and directional pads occupied the bottom half while the color LCD screen was on the upper portion. The clear plastic window was built into the outside part of the upper portion. The square-shaped cartridge, which also had a plastic window in its center, attached to the outside of the upper portion of the console. While in play, light passed through the plastic windows in the cartridge and the unit itself to illuminate the back of the screen. And if there wasn't enough light, the Super Micro was packaged with an additional battery-operated *lightpack,* which rested over the cartridge.

Palmtex Super Micro

The Super Micro was not well received. It had very limited distribution and only three cartridges were released, including *React Attack,* a maze game that was packaged with the device.

Another handheld that used interchangeable cartridges was the *Variety,* from VTech, a Hong Kong-based electronics company that had been founded in 1976 and had even released games for the Atari 2600 under the Technovision label. Each cartridge was self-contained with its own CPU. It also contained two separate LCD screens, one atop the other, similar to several of the LCD SolarPower handhelds that Bandai had released in Japan in 1982. The console itself was merely a frame to insert the cartridge into, which contained controlled and a battery compartment. Only six games were produced for this system, which disappeared almost as quickly as it was available.

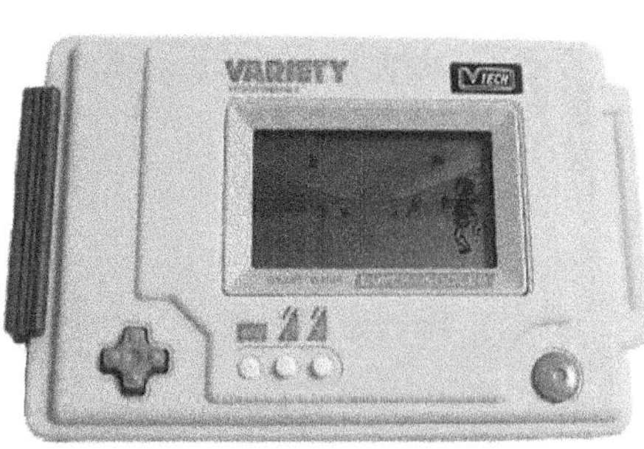

VTech Variety

New Arcade Games

In arcades, Midway introduced a new game called *Journey,* which had been loosely based on the *Journey Escape* game that had been available for the Atari 2600 a year earlier. In the arcade version, the five members of the rock group Journey had to go to a planet and find their lost

Midway Journey

1983

instruments. What made this game innovative was that the members of the band were portrayed with their actual digitized faces. This was the first instance where an on-screen character had a real face.

The technology behind this had been conceived by Ralph Baer in August 1981. Baer's idea was to have a digital camera take photos of a gamers face and then use the image on a character in a game. He took the idea to toy designer Marvin Glass where the concept was expanded to use images instead of initials next to a gamer's high score. Another idea was to create football videogames in which each player's image would be that of a real football player.

Marvin Glass built a prototype and sent it to Midway, who loved it. A game was built around it and placed in an arcade for test marketing, where it received favorable comments. But then shortly afterwards someone decided to drop their pants and have the camera take a photo of their posterior, instead of their face. That killed the customized portion of the project for good. But Marvin Glass still licensed the procedure to Midway, which soon released the *Journey* arcade game.

Midway also licensed Sega's *Astron Belt*, which had been the first laserdisc-based arcade game in Japan, since Electro Sport's 1981 horse racing game *Quarter Horse* had never been distributed in that country. But even if it had, *Quarter Horse* had been more of a betting simulator and didn't require any skill by the player. *Astron Belt*, on the other hand, was a true videogame as the action on the screen was manipulated by the player.

Astron Belt fell into the *Space Invaders* game genre as the player had to shoot down waves of invading enemy fighters while avoiding their shots and space debris. While the screen objects were computer generated and varied from game to game, the background, which the player didn't control, incorporated footage from several science fiction movies including *Star Trek II: The Wrath of Khan*.

Although Midway had licensed *Astron Belt* for release in the United States, it wasn't immediately imported because bugs had been discovered in both the hardware and the software. By the time *Astron Belt* reached the United States, a new laserdisc-based game had been released, which set the standard for laserdisc games that would follow.

The game, *Dragon's Lair* from Cinematronics, was in effect, an interactive animated movie that allowed players to go on a quest while controlling the action that took place in the movie. Because laserdiscs could display images randomly, players "told" the computer which scene to present by pressing the joystick in a number of directions. Although the response time was a little sluggish as the computer searched for the correct path, *Dragon's Lair* became a major hit in the arcades, mainly because of its uniqueness.

Dragon's Lair was the brainchild of Rick Dyer, a videogame veteran who had designed many handheld and tabletop electronic games for Mattel Electronics and Coleco. He had also been involved in designing the Intellivision and ColecoVision[13] consoles.

Dyer formed his own company, Advanced Microcomputer Systems, with the intention of designing a game system that utilized interactive movies. He first experimented with computer-controlled filmstrips, and then moved on to paper tape, before settling on laserdiscs that contained still images and narration. Once he was satisfied with this format, he created a graphic adventure game called *The Secrets of the Lost Woods*.

Dyer tried to find someone to market his system, but no one was interested. After watching the animated movie *The Secret of NIMH*, Dyer came to the conclusion that he needed quality animation in his game if it was to be successful. Dyer went directly to Don Bluth, the main animator of *The Secret of NIMH*, and explained what he wanted to do. Bluth was interested in the project, but Dyer couldn't afford someone of Bluth's stature. Instead, both men agreed to set up a new company called Starcom, where Dyer's Advanced Microcomputer Systems, which was renamed RDI Video Systems, owned one third, and Bluth's animation company owned another third. The final third went to

Cinematronics, the arcade-game maker that signed on to manufacture Dyer's new game.

Bluth followed *Dragon's Lair* with a second laserdisc game before the first even shipped. *Space Ace* wasn't nearly as popular as *Dragon's Lair* had been. Still, this didn't deter other arcade manufacturers such as Atari, Mylstar and Sega from releasing additional laserdisc games.

Cinematronics Dragon's Lair

Atari Ventures Outside of Videogames

Due to the oversaturation of videogames in the United States, most companies either filed for bankruptcy or simply discontinued their videogame lines. The remaining companies looked for alternate products to get them through the crisis. In January, Atari had announced a new line of computers to replace the aging-but-popular 400 and 800s. But even though the company touted that the new 1200XL would be completely compatible with the older models, early purchasers quickly discovered that it wasn't. While the 400 and 800 were being discontinued, they enjoyed a sales boom as people rushed out to buy them before they disappeared forever. Meanwhile, the word spread through the computer industry that the 1200XL was Atari's version of Ford's Edsel.

Atari announced in March that it was working on a secret venture called The Falcon Project. It was soon revealed that the Falcon Project was the code name for a new division, Ataritel, which would be Atari's entry into the home telecommunications market. Ataritel planned to offer telephones that would be equipped with video terminals and keyboards and would be useful for home security, appliance control, computer interface, and a way for Atari to deliver its videogames into homes via the phone lines. Despite the money that it constantly lost every day because of the great shake-out, Atari was very optimistic about its future. Ataritel was insurance that the company would survive, even if videogames didn't.

But Atari found itself amidst a controversy a few months later. News had leaked that on the day before Atari announced its infamous projected fourth-quarter loss, company head Ray Kassar had gone out and sold $250,000 worth of his Warner stock. Kassar resigned on July 7th amidst threatened charges for inside trading and was replaced by James Morgan on September 6th.[14]

Sega Computers and Consoles

In Japan, the videogame industry was free of scandal and oversaturation. It was impossible for too many games to be available for a set number of systems since the country didn't have any programmable consoles that everybody wanted to have a piece of. That was about to change.

Sega Enterprises, Ltd. decided to enter the home market by releasing an 8-bit entry-level PC called the *SC-3000*[15] in July for ¥29,800 ($124). The SC-3000 featured a flat, rubber keyboard. While this wasn't optimum for heavy-duty typing, many would-be game programmers liked the fact that the SC-3000 was one of the few personal computers that allowed them to program in machine language, as well as in *BASIC*.[16] Additional peripherals were also available that gave people the ability to save the games that they programmed. One was a data recorder, which saved programs to standard cassette tapes, and the other was an expansion

Sega SC-3000

unit called the *Super Control Station*, which attached to the SC-3000 by a special cable that had a cartridge on one end. Once the Super Control Station was attached to the SC-3000, users could save their programs on 3"-sized floppy disks. The Super Control Station also contained an RS-232C serial port and a Centronics parallel port, both of which allowed PC-compatible peripherals, such as printers, to be set up to the computer. The SC-3000 sold fairly well, with sales numbering in the tens of thousands.[17]

While Sega Enterprises, Ltd. was designing the SC-3000, it learned that Nintendo was planning to release a programmable gaming system. In response, Sega removed the keyboard from the SC-3000 and marketed the resulting console as the *SG-1000*.[18]

Sega released the 8-bit, programmable, ¥15,000 ($62) *SG-1000* on July 15. The system did fairly well thanks to the exclusive Sega arcade games that were ported to the system such as *Monoco GP*, a racing game that had appeared in 1979.[19]

Sega SG-1000

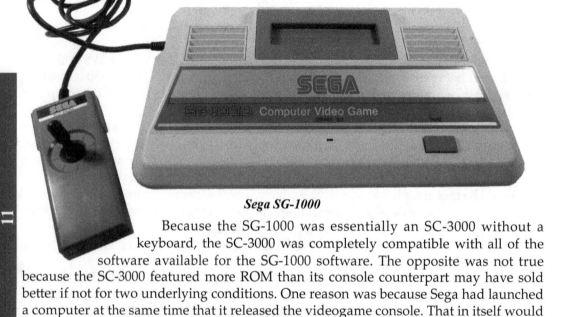

Because the SG-1000 was essentially an SC-3000 without a keyboard, the SC-3000 was completely compatible with all of the software available for the SG-1000 software. The opposite was not true because the SC-3000 featured more ROM than its console counterpart may have sold better if not for two underlying conditions. One reason was because Sega had launched a computer at the same time that it released the videogame console. That in itself would not have been a major factor except for the fact that

Nintendo's Famicom

On July 15, the same day that Sega's SG-1000 debuted, Nintendo also released its new gaming console. Like Sega, Nintendo had gained a reputation in Japan as a producer of arcade games. However, while the SG-1000 had been Sega's initial foray into home gaming, Nintendo had already released a handful of home consoles. Now Nintendo released its first programmable console, the ¥14,800 ($61) *Famicom* (FAMIly COMputer).
joystick controller that was used with all of the other Japanese consoles. Concerned that children might step on a joystick that was left on the floor, Nintendo elected to use the layout that was found on its popular Game & Watch series: a D-pad and two action buttons. The second controller also featured a built-in microphone so players' voices could be heard through the TV.

Nintendo Famicom Controller

Nintendo also released three games with the console. *Donkey Kong, Donkey Kong Jr.* and *Popeye,* all came on 24K ROM cartridges and featured graphics and game play that duplicated the arcade versions that they had been based upon. Unfortunately, despite its great graphics,[20] the console was faulty due

Nintendo Famicom

to a malfunctioning chip that caused frequent freezing during games. Nintendo recalled all of the sold units and suspended the production of new ones until the problem was fixed.

Additional Japanese Consoles

Nintendo and Sega weren't alone in releasing programmable consoles in Japan. Epoch, which had been selling its Cassette Vision for several years, released a new *Cassette Vision Jr.* The two systems were technically identical but the Cassette Vision Jr. was much more compact than its predecessor and included detachable controllers. The Cassette Vision Jr. also had a compact price of ¥5,000 ($21), which was more than half of what the original Cassette Vision had retailed for.

Epoch Cassette Vision Jr.

Gakken, a manufacturer of Japanese arcade and handheld games, released its own programmable console in Japan in October. The ¥8,800 ($37) *Compact Vision* was an odd looking system that had a T-shaped throttle control rather than a standard joystick or paddle. The throttle could move horizontally or vertically and had a fire button built into the handle. To keep the console steady while the throttle was being used, a handle was built-into the left half of the console, which gamers could hold on to while playing. A start button was also built into the handle.

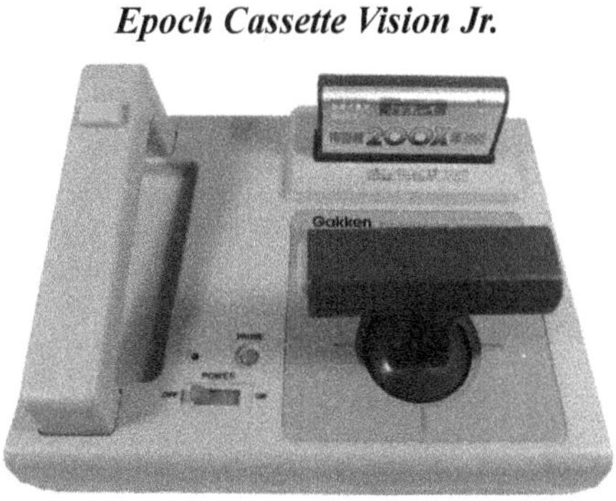

Gakken TV Boy

Problems with the Compact Vision were quickly apparent. Because of the configuration of the controls, a right-handed player had an easy advantage over a left-handed one. For a left-handed person to play, his hands would have to cross one another so his right hand could hold the handle and his left hand could operate the controller.

Another problem was that the console and its games had been designed for only one player at a time. Despite its low price, only six game cartridges were produced for the Compact Vision, and the console quickly faded from both store shelves and the minds of consumers.

Casio, a company known world-wide for its watches and calculators, also jumped into the videogame fray in October when it released its ¥14,800 ($63) *PV-1000*. The system came with one controller and had fifteen available cartridges. Unfortunately, Japanese consumers failed to be enamored by it and the PV-1000 disappeared from store shelves not long after its initial release.

Casio PV-1000

Additional American consoles were also available in Japan for the first time. With the success of the Intellivision, Bandai decided to also import the Vectrex and Emerson's Arcadia 2001.

Bandai's importation of the three American consoles proved that companies were willing to export their products to Japan. Atari was one company that wasn't. Although Epoch had been importing the 2600 into Japan, it hadn't done much in the way of promoting it. In 1983, executives at Atari decided to distribute a Japanese version of the 2600 themselves.

Rather than export the existing system into Japan, Atari designed a new version of its popular console, which it called the *2800*. Although it was completely compatible with the 2600, the 2800 sported a new sleek design with LEDs and buttons that replaced switches.

The controllers themselves were based upon the controllers for the non-released *Remote Control VCS*. Although it was connected to the console, it featured the combination joystick and paddle. The controller itself was slim and easily fit in the palm of a hand. And since each side of the base contained a red firing button, the controller was just as

Atari 2800

comfortable for lefties as it was for righties.

The 2800 sported four controller ports, instead of the two that were found on the 2600. This initially appeared odd because there weren't any games that required four joystick controllers. However, there were four-player games available that used the paddle controllers. This had not been an issue with the 2600 since two paddle controllers plugged into one port. However, the combination joystick-paddle controller for the 2800 required four ports so four controllers could be used for those games.

Approximately thirty cartridges were offered for the 2800 but they were the same games that were already available in the United States, right down to their English labels. However, the packaging and instruction manuals were in Japanese.

Despite the innovative new console, the games for the 2800 were the same as for the 2600, and unfortunately, they had been designed for a system that was six-years old. The Famicom and SG-1000 both had graphics that rivaled those from the 5200 and ColecoVision. The 2800 couldn't compete against them and was only sold for a short time.

Atari never released the 2800 in the United States under its own name. However, Sears decided to release the console in its stores as the Tele-Games *Video Arcade II*. The system was sold with two controllers and a *Space Invaders* cartridge.

Atari 2800 Controller

Atari and Nintendo Join Forces

While Nintendo's Famicom was being developed, the company's executives had aspirations of releasing the new console outside of Japan. Their dreams quickly faded when they came to the realization that they could never hope to compete against Atari, the worldwide leader in home consoles. But they sincerely believed that they had a superior product that they wanted everyone around the world to enjoy. So instead of attempting to compete against Atari, they decided to offer Atari the worldwide distribution rights to the Famicom outside of Japan. When approached with the offer, Atari was enthusiastic about the idea and pursued it. After Atari and Nintendo executives met in May at Atari's Sunnyvale headquarters, the Atari executives flew to Kyoto, Japan for their first look at the new console in development. There, they were told how Atari could manufacture the unit inexpensively and how Nintendo would receive royalties for every unit sold. Everyone was enthusiastic about the deal and they all promised to meet the following month at the summer CES to sign the papers. This little delay changed the course of history.

At the CES, Coleco had unveiled its new Adam computer, which it displayed behind glass, and chose to have *Donkey Kong* running on the machine. This created a problem because, although Coleco did indeed own the U.S. home videogame rights to the game, Atari owned the computer rights. Ray Kassar became enraged when he saw the display and threatened Nintendo with both a halt to the console deal and litigation for breach of contract.

Nintendo turned around and threatened Coleco with a lawsuit. Coleco tried to defend itself by arguing that although the Adam was a computer, it had the guts of a ColecoVision, which in turn made it a videogame console. Knowing that it couldn't win the case with such a poor excuse, Coleco promised to refrain from selling *Donkey Kong* specifically for the Adam.

The issue with Coleco gave Atari a reason not to sign with Nintendo for exclusive worldwide rights to the new console. However, by this time Atari was having problems of its own. It was only one week after Coleco's fiasco at CES that Ray Kassar was forced to resign and the Atari empire began to crumble. Before long, Atari had more pressing matters than acquiring the Famicom. The deal was off.

At first Nintendo's executives thought about the millions of dollars in royalties that they wouldn't receive and were mortified with the outcome. But as they thought about it they realized that Atari's problems might in turn be beneficial to them. Nintendo had initially sought Atari as a potential partner as an alternative to competing with the successful giant. Now Atari was falling apart and the coast was clear for Nintendo to market the Famicom in America on its own.

Meanwhile, Atari had its eyes set on a new gaming platform. On November 21, the company signed an agreement with Amiga, which allowed them to engage in discussions that would lead to a business relationship. Amiga had made its debut earlier in the year at Toy Fair where it announced several Atari 2600 peripherals, including the Joyboard and Power-Stick.[21] However, the sole purpose of these items was a means to raise money for the product that Amiga had specifically been founded to create: a 16-bit game machine/computer. Atari's agreement with Amiga gave Atari access to trade secrets regarding the 16-bit chipset that Amiga was developing.

Competitive Gaming

Japan may have been preparing to become the leading manufacturer of videogames, but the "Video Game Capital of the World" was right in the United States. Ottumwa, Iowa, the home of Twin Galaxies, had been given this title on November 30, 1982 by its mayor, Jerry Parker. The title was made official by Iowa Governor Terry Branstad on March 19, 1983, along with Atari and the Amusement Game Manufacturers Association, in a ceremony at Twin Galaxies.

On July 25, Walter Day and Twin Galaxies established the professional U.S. National Video Game Team (USNVGT), featuring the top gamers in the country. The original five members of the USNVGT were Billy Mitchell, Steve Harris, Jay Kim, Ben Gold, and Tim McVey. Their touring duties involved appearing at arcades around the United States and participate in the 1983 Video Game Masters Tournament.

Between the arcades and the consoles, videogames appeared to be the hottest form of entertainment. Within a year, that would all change.

CHAPTER TWELVE
1984

Thanks to the videogame shake-out of 1983, the January 1984 CES was much more subdued than the two of the year before. Ironically, despite the slump, 7 million game consoles and 75 million game cartridges had been sold during 1983, 15 million more cartridges than in 1982. Of that number, only 27% had been close-out titles selling for as low as $5 each. The remaining 73% consisted of popular titles that retailed for $30 to $40. Because the industry wasn't completely dead, the winter CES included half a dozen booths that featured videogames: a mere handful of the 30 companies that had attended the 1983 summer CES seven months earlier.

The general attitude towards the industry in 1984 was one of cautious optimism. Many retailers began filling their videogame shelf-space with computer software, which they believed was where the market was heading. However, since there were still many more videogame consoles than computers in homes, retailers still believed that they could earn some profits from videogames. As luck would have it, the only games that yielded any profit were hot, new titles, and very few companies remained to develop them. Those that were still around had to compete with the companies who had flooded the market with hundreds of discounted titles. One of the remaining companies, Activision, believed that once the salvaged titles made their way through the distribution chain, the way would once again be clear for new, exciting, and hopefully profitable cartridges.

Meanwhile, retailers predicted that the costs of the videogame consoles would continue to plummet. The retail prices for both the 2600 and Intellivision dropped to between $39 and $49 apiece, while the high-end machines like the 5200 and ColecoVision were in the $80 area. These new, lower prices made them more attractive to buy, and added to the demand for new software.

Console Reductions

Despite these efforts, the lower retail prices didn't help the manufacturers at all. In February, Mattel went ahead and closed down its Mattel Electronics division, a move it had been contemplating for some time. Despite Mattel's decision, Terrence Valeski, the division's Senior Vice President of Marketing and Sales, still had faith in the Intellivision. He figured that the three million Intellivision owners made up a formidable market for good software. With this in mind, he partnered with Ike Perlmutter and Bernard Marden, who were the owners of Odd-Lot Trading, a New York-based retailer of salvaged goods. Together, they bought the Mattel Electronics division for $20 million, and quickly renamed their new acquisition to Intellivision, Inc. They publicly promised that the new Intellivision games that Mattel had announced at CES in January would be on store shelves by the fall. Afterwards, the company would develop brand-new software for both the Intellivision and 2600. Mattel agreed to service Intellivision, Inc. products and to manufacture software for one year.

North American Philips made the same decision with its Odyssey division as Mattel had made with Mattel Electronics. However, nobody came to rescue the Odyssey when production of new hardware was halted.

Coleco also seemed to want nothing to do with videogames any longer, and put its first Adam computers into production at the expense of new ColecoVision units. Regrettably, the first units that came off the assembly line were loaded with bugs. Because Coleco had turned the Adam into a media event when it had initially announced the computer, the press was eager to report every difficulty that the company experienced. Although it wasn't unusual for a brand-new system to experience bugs, Coleco received more bad publicity than their competitors.

At the winter CES, Coleco informed the press that full production had resumed on the Adam. A few days later, an announcement went out stating that the company had cut its work force by 8% in a move to consolidate. Coleco had lost a lot of money by the end of 1983, because of the relatively few number of Adams that had shipped and hadn't been returned. In January, the price of the Adam went up from $600 to $750, which hurt its sales even further. Both retailers and members of the press grew skeptical about Coleco's ability to produce and sell a decent machine in mass numbers.

Initially, Coleco had promised to deliver 500,000 computers by the end of 1983, but this number was quickly reduced to 140,000. The actual number that Coleco produced and shipped was 95,000. Representatives stated that the company wanted to make sure that the product it shipped was of the highest quality possible, no matter how long it might take.

As it turned out, 60% of those first Adams were returned, because they were defective. Coleco assured the public that the actual return rate was only 5%, and that the real problem was how the instruction manuals had been written. Novice computer users simply couldn't understand how the system worked, and therefore returned it as defective.

Unfortunately, the problems didn't stop with poorly-written documentation. Many experienced computer users also had trouble getting some of their software to load. Others claimed that the output from the letter-quality printer was uneven, and that the printer was very slow and extremely loud. The word processor erased some text from memory when it shouldn't have, and there were reports of jittery screens and cursors that failed to move.

Even consumers who received perfect systems found minor inconveniences. For instance, the printer had to be turned on via a rear switch before any games could be played. This turned out to be a useless, annoying extra step for people who only wanted to play games.

Owners' annoyances with the system didn't end there, because after they turned the printer on, a game had to be loaded, and this proved to be a long and unreliable process. When Coleco had first announced its digital data device, it had promised that programs would load at very high speeds. In contrast, Adam owners soon discovered that it actually took several minutes for a game to load. Once loaded, the game could be played normally, although the data drive continued to advance the tape as it loaded the next level of play into the computer. If the gamer wanted to restart a game, he had to wait for the tape to rewind and then completely load it from the beginning again.

Milton Bradley

On January 1st, Milton Bradley began distributing the Vectrex Game System itself, after closing down its General Consumers Electronics Division. That had been done in an effort to reduce costs. However, in February, the company realized that the Vectrex had lost $18.7 million, and decided to discontinue the unit. All in all, the game company lost $31.6 million since purchasing GCE in 1982. The Vectrex became just another casualty in the videogame shake-out. It had originally been designed to sell at $200, but Milton Bradley had dropped the price to $150, and then to $100, in an effort to make it competitive. Even at that price, though, Milton Bradley couldn't sell enough of them profitably, and couldn't lower the price below $100 -- because of the high production cost of the built-in vector monitor. Despite this explanation, many industry watchers believed that Milton Bradley had an ulterior motive for dropping the Vectrex line: A merger was in the works between Milton Bradley and Hasbro, a company that had long shown no interest in joining the electronic gaming arena. That merger actually took place in May 1984.

Japanese Consoles

In March, the news from Japan was that Nintendo was seriously thinking about releasing an American version of its Famicom, which was selling briskly after Nintendo had recalled the original units and repaired their motherboards. Gaming analysts viewed this as a poor move on Nintendo's part. They felt that the Japanese company didn't know anything about the American market, except for its own will to dominate it. Meanwhile, on June 21, Nintendo expanded the capabilities of the Famicom when it released *Family BASIC*. This cartridge, which allowed users to program in a specialized dialect of the BASIC programming language, was sold with a computer keyboard. Nintendo also offered an optional cassette recorder, which was needed to save programs that were written with *Family BASIC*. By the end of 1984, the Famicom was the best-selling game console in Japan.

Nintendo Family BASIC

Nintendo Data Recorder

Despite the appearance of *Family BASIC*, Nintendo didn't have any plans to turn the Famicom into a full-fledged computer. Sega, on the other hand, had other plans.

Sega released its own computer keyboard for its SG-1000 console in July. With this keyboard, the SG-1000 console had the same computing power as Sega's SC-3000 computer. The keyboard also had ports that allowed the inclusion of the SC-3000's peripherals including a printer and a cassette drive for storage.

Although the keyboard would work with the SG-1000, it was released concurrently with an updated version of the console, the *SG-1000 II*. And although the ¥15,000 ($61) SG-1000 II was redesigned externally and looked nothing like its predecessor, the two units were functionally identical. The SG-1000 II could play all of the cartridges that had

Sega Keyboard

Sega SG-1000 II with Joypad

been designed for the SG-1000.

Besides its external appearance, Sega did make one change to the SG-1000 over its predecessor. Taking a cue from Nintendo, Sega replaced the joystick controller that had been packaged with the SG-1000, with a gamepad, that looked very similar to the "player II" gamepad that Nintendo packaged with the Famicom. The two gamepads were roughly the same size and shape, and both had D-pads[1] on their left sides and two control buttons on their right. The Sega pad did not include a built-in microphone but it did have a tiny hole in the center of its D-pad that allowed a finger-sized joystick to be screwed into it. Unlike Nintendo, Sega didn't have any plans of exporting its consoles to the United States.

By this time, Sega Enterprises, Ltd. was basically an autonomous, Japanese company. Its American parent, Sega Enterprises, Inc. had been reduced to a shell of its former business since Bally purchased the licensing rights to all of Sega's coin-op business in 1983. David Rosen was given the opportunity to purchase Sega Enterprises, Ltd. but declined because he didn't want to return to Japan on a full-time basis. Instead, in March, Rosen, Hayao Nakayama[2] and a Japanese conglomerate, CSK Corporation, bought the company and renamed it Sega Enterprises. Isao Okawa, the chairman of CSK, assumed the same position at Sega Enterprises.

Since Bally released Sega arcade games under its own name in the United States, the Sega name was not appearing on new arcade games in that country. This wasn't the case in Europe where Sega Enterprises, Ltd. opened a location. *Sega Europe, Ltd.* was based in the United Kingdom and was responsible for the sale of Sega arcade machines in Europe. Meanwhile the new games that Sega Enterprises, Inc. released for American consoles, weren't even home versions of Sega games. Instead, Sega licensed titles, including *Tapper* and *Spy Hunter*, from Bally.[3]

The Epoch name also wasn't appearing in the United States as Epoch didn't have any plans to export its console there. However its Cassette Vision, which had been available since 1981, was beginning to show its age, especially when compared to the newer consoles like the Famicom and the SG-1000.

In order to compete against the newer consoles, Epoch released a $149 console that it called the Super Cassette Vision. The 31 games available for the *Super Cassette Vision* had graphics that rivaled its contemporaries. However, since the Super Cassette Vision wasn't backward compatible with games from the prior Cassette Vision, owners of

Epoch's earlier console didn't have any particular reason to select the Super Cassette Vision over the Famicom or SG-1000 when they were ready to upgrade their videogame console. Still, Epoch did reasonably well with the Super Cassette Vision during the early days of the Famicom.

The Super Cassette Vision was also released in Europe under the brand name Yeno. It sold much better in Europe than in Japan probably due to the single reason that the Famicom wasn't yet available in Europe.

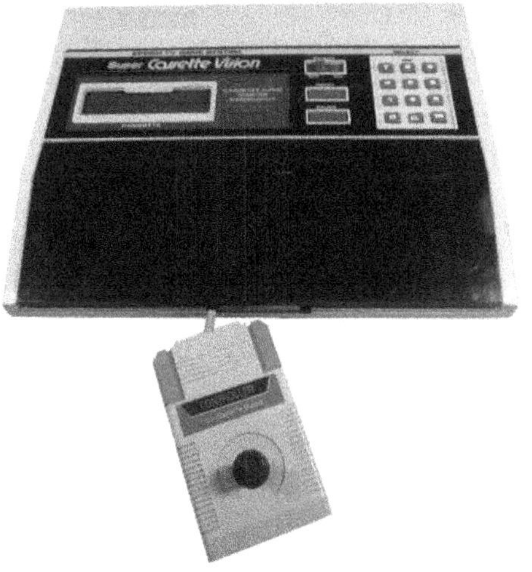

Epoch Super Cassette Vision

Game Pocket Computer

Epoch didn't have any competition against the second console that it released in Japan in 1984. The *Game Pocket Computer* was a handheld device similar to Milton Bradley's pioneering Microvision. Despite the term *handheld,* the Game Pocket Computer needed two hands to operate it. The size of a small book, the console was 8.5 inches wide and nearly six inches vertically. Positioned almost in the center of the unit was a 75 x 64 pixel black & white LCD screen, which gave the console far greater resolution than the 16 x 16 screen that the Microvision provided.

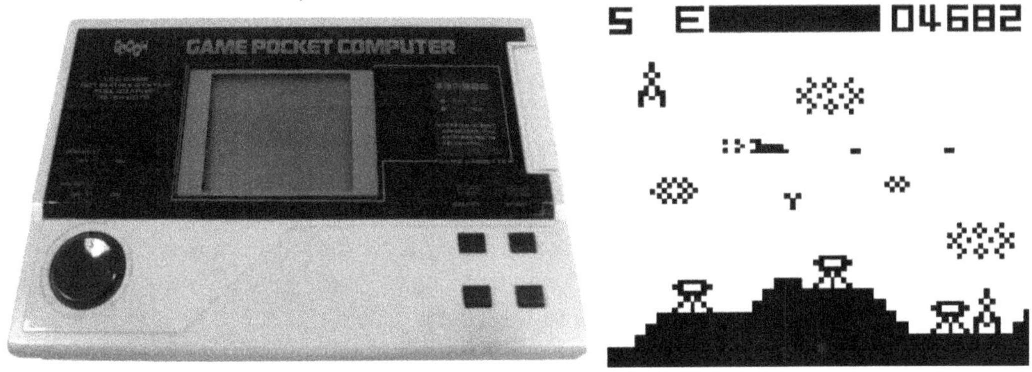

Epoch Game Pocket Computer

The Game Pocket Computer was the first programmable handheld unit released in Japan. Like the Microvision, games could be switched by changing game cartridges. Unfortunately, the system was a failure and disappeared from store shelves not long after it was released. It is unclear why the system failed since stand-alone handheld, and programmable consoles, were popular. The reason might have been because there wasn't any available software that made people rush out and buy a unit. In addition to a built-in puzzle game and drawing application, only five game cartridges were offered.

Meanwhile, Bandai, which was already manufacturing LCD handhelds that competed against Nintendo's Game & Watch series, released a new console called the *Digi Casse,*

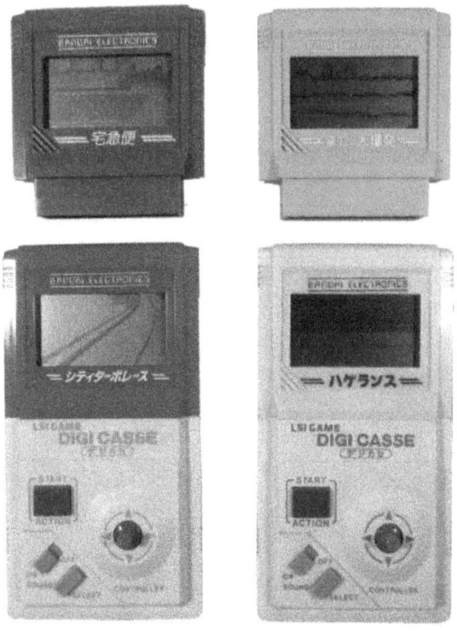

Bandai Digi Casse

1984

which was similar to the Variety, which VTech had released in 1983. Like the Variety, the cartridges for the *Digi Casse* contained the CPU and LCD screen. In fact, these cartridges looked very much like the LCD handhelds that Bandai was already selling, except that they didn't have any controls. The controls were in the base of the unit that the cartridge plugged into. Bandai released two different models of the Digi Casse, and each one was bundled with two cartridges. One unit included a tiny four-direction joystick, and the other had four buttons arranged in a crosshair formation. Oddly, Bandai distributed the Digi Casse the same way it did its other LCD handhelds, as two separate standalone units that each played two games. Additional game cartridges were never offered.

Atari's New Management

Atari, the company that had originally dominated the videogame business, was forced to restructure and move the majority of its operations overseas. All that remained of the mammoth company domestically was its management staff and its new Ataritel division.

Despite this, Atari had faith that the videogame industry still had life in it. Atari CEO James Morgan told the press at the winter CES that the company's new policy was to only display products that would be available within three months of their debuts. This was being implemented to gain credibility with merchants who had grown tired of Atari's habit of displaying vaporware, which was the term given to products that were shown but never ultimately released.

The first test of this new policy began in May when Atari announced the formation of a joint venture with Activision to deliver 2600 games into homes electronically. This was not the first time that Atari had formed such a partnership, although its prior joint venture with Time-Life had resulted in nothing. Atari and Activision stated that they wouldn't be using cable or telephone lines to transmit their games, but didn't specify the exact method that they were going to use. They projected that the system would be available nationally by the end of 1984.

Atari announced another partnership on May 8. The company signed a deal with Lucasfilm to produce two new games that featured extraordinary graphics and play action. The games, *Rescue On Fractalus* and *Ballblazer*, would be available for both the 5200 and the computers.

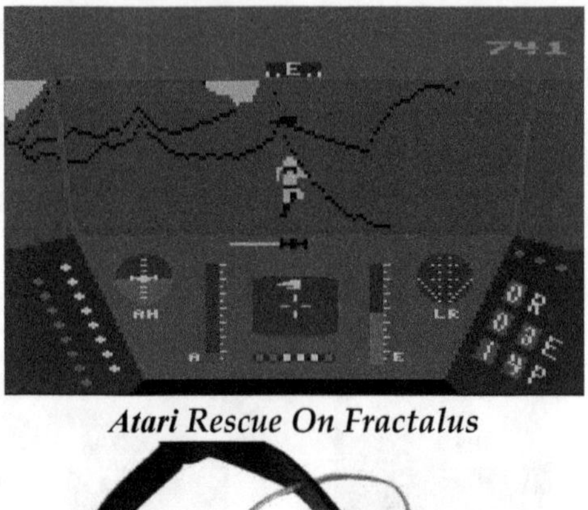

Atari Rescue On Fractalus

Atari announced some more products at the summer CES on May 21. All were to be released within three months according to Atari's new policy.

One was an extraordinary new controller called *MindLink*. This was actually a headband that detected electrical pulses in the head, and then transmitted these signals to a receiver connected to the controller port of the 2600, 7800 or Atari computer. The MindLink was to be sold with *Bionic Breakthrough*, a *Breakout*-type game in which players used their forehead muscles to control the on-screen action. Although other titles weren't specifically announced, Atari said that future MindLink titles would include programs that people could use to monitor their stress and relaxation levels, along with interactive ESP games.

Atari Mindlink

On the software side, Atari announced a new generation of cartridges that each contained a new chip (codenamed Sara) that expanded the amount of ROM in a standard cartridge. This resulted in enhanced graphics and more challenging game play. Atari also hired famed child psychologist Dr. Lee Salk to develop a series of games for toddlers; the first was titled *Peek-A-Boo*.

However, not every announcement that Atari made was positive. The company also broke the news that a lot of people had long expected: the death of the 5200.

Atari 7800

But the death of the 5200 was not going to leave a void in Atari's product line. The most surprising announcement that Atari made that day was the news that it was going to release the *7800*, an entirely new game console. Since 20 million game cartridges had been sold between January and April 1984, and over half of them had been sold at their full retail price, someone at Atari had figured that the public was still very interested in videogames and was ready for a new product. This prompted Atari to commission a market study, from which they learned that consumers wanted a videogame console that had

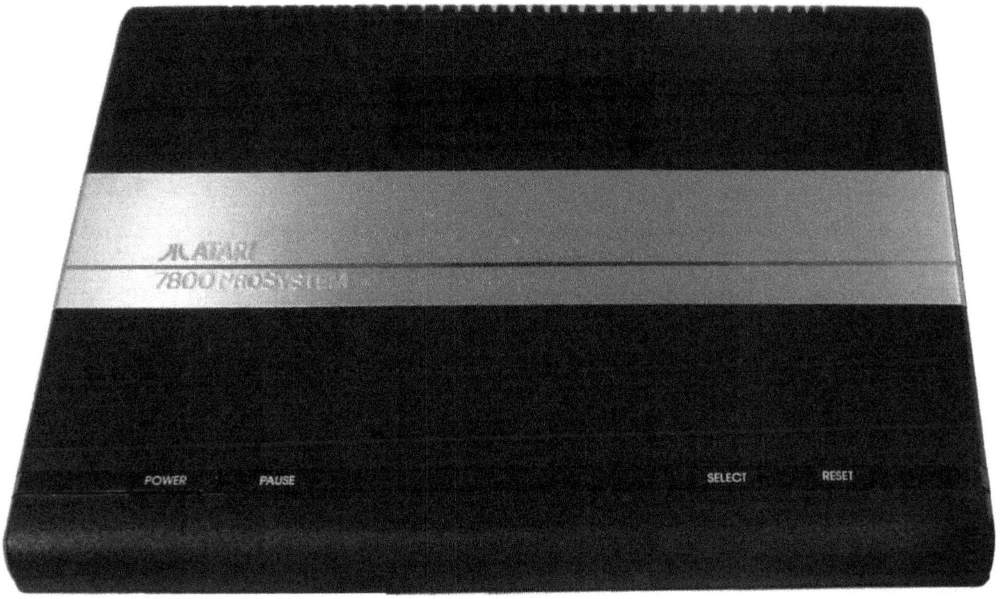

Atari 7800

a large base of challenging software, including arcade titles, and one that could expand with the technology. With this information in hand, Atari worked with General Computer Corporation of Massachusetts, and the result was the 7800.

According to Atari, the graphics on the 7800 were superior to any console already on the market. In order to achieve this, its designers developed a new 4K chip, which they called Maria. Maria was capable of moving 100 on-screen objects simultaneously, while providing 256 color shadings.

The Maria chip also served another purpose. Following the fiasco with the *Custer's Revenge* cartridge, Atari wanted to be certain that developers couldn't release unauthorized games

Atari Proline Controller

for the 7800. Atari had GCC add an encryption key to the console and its software. When a 7800 game cartridge was inserted, the Maria chip would ascertain that its checksum value was valid. If it wasn't, the system would remain in 2600 mode.

The 7800, which would retail at $140, would also be fully backward-compatible with the 2600. Games for the 2600 could be played on the 7800, but not vice-versa. But while it would play 2600 games, Atari wasn't going to include the classic 2600 joystick with the unit, Instead, it introduced the *Proline Joystick*, which was long and sleek and featured two controller buttons, so lefties didn't have a disadvantage.

Twelve games were planned for the 7800's launch, including the two new Lucasfilm games. The plan was to initially include a *Pole Position II* cartridge with each console, but it was later stated that the 7800 would have the game built in. Also built into the console was an expansion slot, which would permit the console to easily be upgradable like the Intellivision and ColecoVision.

Atari also planned to release a *High Score* cartridge that would allow players to record their names and high scores for up to 65 different games. Also planned was the *Terminal Cartridge*. This would contain a built-in modem and terminal emulator, and allow 7800 owners to access online services like CompuServe, and would even dial the phone just like the Gameline. To make accessing these online services easier, Atari also planned by year's end to release a $100 keyboard that would turn the 7800 into a 4K computer (upgradeable to 20K) that would be compatible with all Atari computer software. And for owners of the 5200, Atari promised a 7800 adapter that would be available at the same time that the console was released.

News of the 7800 had been received with excitement. Ironically, the same skeptics who had criticized Nintendo for thinking about bringing its Famicom to the United States now praised Atari for what they believed was the console that would renew the dying industry.

Atari began test-marketing the 7800 in southern California and New York in June. Unfortunately, June also brought events of quite a different nature that began occurring behind the scenes. Warner Communications began trying to unload the company that had turned into a great money drainer. The conglomerate began talks with Philips (the parent company of North American Philips), which had dumped the Odyssey earlier in the year. Philips displayed an interest in acquiring 50% of Atari. Videogame analysts soon began speculating what this marriage would create; since the 7800 included the expansion port, and Philips was the inventor of the laserdisc, it was conceivable that together, the two companies could design a home laserdisc-game player. Meanwhile, as talks went ahead with one company, they ceased with another. Atari announced that it had terminated its agreement with Androbot, leaving *Androman* unreleased.

Atari Changes

As it happened, the discussions with Philips never went anywhere either. In July, Warner Communications made drastic changes to Atari, Inc. It shuttered its new division, Ataritel, and renamed its arcade division to Atari Games.[4] It also kept 25% of its consumer division which included the computers and videogame consoles, before selling the remainder of it to Jack Tramiel, the founder and former president of Commodore.

On January 13, Tramiel had walked out of a Commodore board of directors meeting and never returned to the company. He soon started a new company, Tramel Technology,[5] to compete against Commodore. When he learned that Warner Communications was seeking to sell Atari, he purchased the company because it gave him instant access to factories and warehouses in Europe, which would make overseas sales much easier. However, he wasn't interested in the entire company. He only wanted the assets of the home computer and videogame divisions, which included the copyrights and trademarks, property, and inventory from the two sections. On July 1, Tramel Technology took ownership of these assets and within days Tramiel changed the name of that company to Atari Corporation.

Among the first things that Tramiel did after acquiring Atari was to place his three sons into top executive positions, and then suspend all development, so that he could evaluate what was going on. Next, he laid off nearly 90% of the staff, leaving approximately 100 people. For several months following the Tramiel takeover, information coming out of Atari was very scarce. The rumors that replaced the facts said that the new management was working on two new computers. One was a 16-bit that would sell for half the price of a PC or Macintosh, and the other was an 8-bit computer that would also include a cartridge slot for 2600-compatible cartridges. As it turned out, the 16-bit computer was real. Jack Tramiel held his first press conference on November 13, when he announced that Atari was going to produce high-quality, low-cost 16- and 32-bit computers that weren't intended to compete against the IBMs of the world.[6]

As far as gamers were concerned, the news wasn't good. The company apparently didn't have any plans to release the 7800 or any of the other new products that had been announced earlier in the year; in fact, nothing remotely concerning videogames was even mentioned.

Polygonal Graphics

Ironically, one of the last projects that the old Atari, Inc. released to the arcades reaffirmed the fact that the company's designers could be as innovative as ever: *I, Robot* was the first game that featured state-of-the-art 3D polygonal graphics, which was a technique that was nearly ten years ahead of its time. This bizarre game, designed by *Tempest* and *Missile Command* programmer Dave Theurer, borrowed features from earlier arcade games like *Galaga* and *Pac-Man*. The object of the game was to destroy the boss eye of Big Brother that watched over each level. In order to do this, the player controlled a robot that had to cross the red squares on the maze. This turned the squares blue and destroyed part of the shield that protected the eye. Some portions of the maze needed to be jumped, and if the player was in the act of jumping while the eye was red, the player would get zapped and lose a life. Other hazards abounded in the maze, such as birds, bombs, and flying sharks. There was also a time limit for helping the robot fulfill its task on each level. When the robot did destroy the eye, it would advance to a more difficult level, of which there were 99 in all, each with a unique layout.

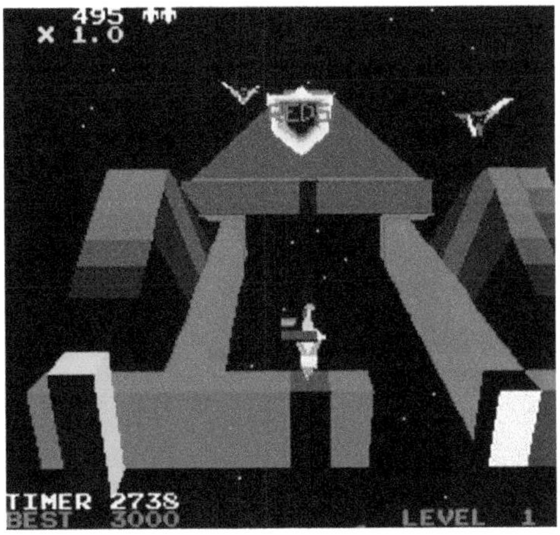

Atari I, Robot

I, Robot was the first game that featured camera-control options. When the game began, the camera zoomed in and out, and displayed the maze from different angles. More points could be scored as the player zoomed in closer, since it was more difficult to play when only a limited section of the maze could be seen.

I, Robot also offered an "ungame" mode called "Doodle City". For one credit (25¢), gamers were given three minutes in which they could move around the polygons from the "game" mode and create new shapes.

Alas, *I, Robot* failed in the arcades. One reason cited for the failure was that players were simply confused by the innovative 3D graphics. "Doodle City" didn't help, as mystified gamers paid 25¢ and learned that the mode they were in wasn't even a game. But there were also technical reasons for the game's failure.

Atari unknowingly used flawed RAM chips which, for brief moments, caused prior screens to blend with the current screen. This just made a confusing game even more baffling.

Finally, the game's failure was also blamed on the videogame crash. Atari failed to promote the game as the industry was falling apart around it. Only about 1,000 *I, Robots* were manufactured, and half of those were supposedly exported to Japan.

The Halcyon

As the home-videogame industry was dwindling, Rick Dyer's company, RDI Video Systems, decided to release the *Halcyon,* a laserdisc-based system.[7] The Halcyon had been in development for nearly five years, and had not been released earlier because market research had determined that it was ahead of its time. Following the arcade success of *Dragon's Lair,* which had used the Halcyon technology, Dyer felt that the time was ripe to finally release the home-gaming system. Dyer even felt that *Dragon's Lair* had been primitive when compared to the types of games that the Halcyon could produce.

RDI Halcyon

The Halcyon, with a staggering retail price of $2,500, went on sale in late 1984 at test sites on both coasts of the United States. Two games were also released with the system.[8] *Raiders Vs. Chargers* was a football simulation that utilized three seasons' worth of video footage to produce an embarrassingly simple game. The other game, *Thayer's Quest,* was similar to *Dragon's Lair,* but sadly didn't have the benefit of Don Bluth's outstanding animation. *Thayer's Quest* also featured demos of four other games that were scheduled to appear.[9]

The Halcyon was the first videogame console to utilize laserdiscs as its software media. Laserdisc had been used for games only once before when Optical Programming Associates released *The First National Kidisc* in 1981 for all standard laserdisc players. While the software itself received a Grammy nomination, it didn't do well sales-wiser on account of the laserdisc format's failure to catch on with the public. Despite the laserdisc's superior video and audio quality over videotape, laserdisc's couldn't be used for recording. So the public remained loyal to videotapes, resulting in the sale of nearly ten million units in the United States alone.

Parker Brothers took advantage of this number and released the first game on videotape, which could be played on ordinary VCRs. *Clue VCR Mystery Game* was a video version of the beloved board game. The hour-long tape featured 18 individual cases that had to be solved by two or more players.

Parker Brothers Clue VCR Mystery Game

The sad state of the videogame industry was reflected in the consumer magazines that served it. *Video Games* ceased publication in the spring, and then returned with a fall issue that proved to be its last. *Videogaming Illustrated* began the year with a new look and a new name: *Video & Computer Gaming Illustrated*. However, this new computer-gaming magazine only lasted through two issues before folding in March. *Electronic Fun With Computers & Games* became simply *Computer Fun* in April, but its last issue came out a month later. Only *Electronic Games* managed to stay afloat during 1984, but that victory was short-lived.

As 1984 came to an end, there were only three contenders left in the videogame-console race, and the futures of all three looked very uncertain. Atari, under the restructuring of Jack Tramiel, was very quiet about its plans for 1985, and didn't release any new products at all. Coleco continued to market the ColecoVision, but seemed to put the thrust of its development and money into the Adam. Finally, there was Intellivision, Inc., which continued to sell hardware and software. As the year closed, the company released a new cartridge that had previously been announced by Mattel: *World Series Major League Baseball.*

For all intents and purposes, the American videogame industry looked as good as dead.

CHAPTER THIRTEEN
1985

Although the great videogame crash had begun in 1983 and carried over into 1984, it wasn't until 1985 that its actual consequences became apparent. Atari had seemed to be out of the running ever since its new owner, Jack Tramiel, had announced that he wanted his company to be a dominant force in the computer industry. However, Atari's future was questionable. The company announced in April that it wouldn't attend the summer CES. Atari appeared to be experiencing financial problems, and industry watchers wondered if the company would be able to produce the inexpensive 16-bit computers that it had promised. Atari did manage to ship small quantities of its new 130XE computer, an 8-bit, 128K system that was a descendent of the old Atari 800. Meanwhile, the company experienced more layoffs, and the employees who remained discovered a 5-20% decrease in their paychecks.

During the same month, Coleco finally announced what had been expected for several months: the demise of the Adam. The company assured that it would continue developing new software for both the Adam and the ColecoVision. It fulfilled this promise by releasing several new cartridges, including *Jeopardy* and *Dragon's Lair*, the latter being the home version of the laserdisc arcade game that Coleco had paid two million dollars to secure the home rights to. Since the game was ultimately released on a standard cartridge, the conjecture that Coleco might release a laserdisc interface for the ColecoVision died. Coleco's future involvement in electronics was uncertain. After pouring millions of dollars into the Adam, the only thing that had kept the company from declaring bankruptcy was the unprecedented success of its Cabbage Patch Dolls during the preceding Christmas holiday.

If any more proof was needed that the industry was dead, one only had to look at the newsstands, where several competing videogaming magazines had coexisted two years earlier. By 1985, only *Electronic Games*, the pioneer of videogaming journalism, still remained -- and that was only for a brief time. The title of the magazine was changed to *Computer Entertainment* in May. The magazine was also given a complete facelift, which resulted in a more sophisticated look that would theoretically appeal to the average computer buyer. Unfortunately, it didn't, and the final issue of this magazine hit the newsstands in August.

Computer Entertainment

Not all companies were convinced that the market for games was over. Activision was one of them. In the summer of 1985, it released two new games for the 2600, *Cosmic Commuter* and *Ghostbusters*. The two games had limited distribution and didn't receive any advertising. Activision clearly had not intended on reclaiming its former glory with these two titles.

Magnavox vs. Activision

Meanwhile, Magnavox took Activision to court to demand royalties earned during the latter's glory days. Magnavox claimed that some of Activision's games infringed upon Ralph Baer's '507 patent, which basically covered when one on-screen symbol made contact with another on-screen symbol. Since its inception, Activision had never sought to license the '507 patent from Magnavox. Activision's lawyers argued that the '507 covered circuitry that had been available in 1970, and not microprocessor-based games. The judge argued that although microprocessor-based games came out after the '507 patent had been assigned; it didn't alter the nature of the games covered in the patent.

Activision next argued that since Atari did license the '507 patent, users of its 2600 console, which was the console that played most of Activision's games, had an implied license to play any game that was available for it. The court dismissed this argument and Activision was found guilty of patent infringement. However, the court also ruled that Activision's infringement had not been done willingly. Before releasing its first games, the company had sought help from a patent attorney who had not advised his clients about the '507 patent. In the end,[1] the Court found in Magnavox's favor and the industry was put on notice that the '507 patent, which vanquished in every suit that it was part of, covered certain software, as well as hardware.

INTV Corporation

When 1985 began, Intellivision, Inc. changed its name to INTV Corporation, but still hadn't shipped a single game. There was much speculation that the company was heading for bankruptcy. Ironically, near the end of the year, when the American videogame business seemed to be completely dead, INTV finally began to stir. In October, the company announced a brand-new Intellivision console. Priced at $59.95, the INTV System III would feature enhanced graphics, and would be compatible with all of the existing Intellivision software. INTV also planned to rerelease most of the original classic Intellivision titles, at prices ranging between $9.95 and $19.95 each. And in order to revitalize the consumer's stagnating interest in videogames, the company planned a mammoth advertising campaign.

INTV was not alone in its belief that the industry could be resurrected. Nintendo had sold 2.5 million Famicoms and 15 million cartridges in Japan during 1984. The company's management believed that it could achieve similar numbers in the United States, despite the reports of the industry's demise. Nintendo of America officially revealed its plans to market the Famicom in the United States and Canada at the winter CES in January.

Nintendo's NAVS

The unit that Nintendo of America displayed was not called the Famicom. Instead, the unit on display was called the Nintendo Advanced Video System (NAVS). "Advanced" was a key word, as the NAVS appeared to be a step up from the systems that the American companies could practically no longer give away. It even appeared to be more sophisticated than the Famicom, which it didn't resemble at all. For one thing, the unit was completely wireless. Its controllers, which were similar to the gamepads that were used by the Famicom, used infrared light to send and receive signals. Nintendo of America also displayed a light gun that would be sold with the unit, and would be used for target games such as *Hogan's Alley* and *Duck Hunt*. The graphics in these games looked absolutely beautiful, thanks to the NAVS' ability to display 52 colors. Each of the existing machines on the market could only generate 16 colors.

The console itself had a built-in keyboard, which made it look more like a computer than a videogame console.

Nintendo Advanced Video System

Although it wasn't designed to be a true computer, the unit would be sold with *Game BASIC*, a program similar to *Famicom BASIC* that would enable players to design their own games. An optional data cassette recorder was also displayed; this would be used to save the custom-written programs. For those who weren't creative enough to do this, Nintendo of America also planned an "Edit Series" of full action games that players would be able to modify, but not save.

Although it wasn't on display, Nintendo of America announced that a three-octave music keyboard would also be available. Unlike Mattel's Music Synthesizer, which could only operate when plugged into the Intellivision ECS, the NAVS keyboard would also be able to function by itself since it would use batteries and have its own built-in speaker.

Nintendo of America showed 25 cartridges at CES that were to be launched with the NAVS. This large library consisted of several sports games, such as baseball and tennis, as well as arcade classics from Nintendo's catalog, like *Donkey Kong*.

Nintendo of America's CES booth received a lot of attention. Retailers generally liked the new system, although they weren't about to risk carrying an unproven videogame system while all signs were showing that the industry was sinking. Industry analysts weren't as impressed with Nintendo of America's offering. They saw nothing in it that made it stand out from the rest of the pack. When Nintendo of America failed to attain an American distributor for the system, the company's management decided to redesign it into something that would win over the American critics, and in turn, the American consumers.

The Nintendo Entertainment System (NES)

At the summer CES in early June, Nintendo of America once again had a booth. However, the system that they displayed was substantially different from the one that had been shown five months earlier.

Nintendo of America had listened to the criticism that it had received for the NAVS, and had made many substantial changes in order to quell them. The first alteration was to the system's name, which became the *Nintendo Entertainment System (NES)*. This implied that the NES was not a mere videogame system like the others, or even an advanced gaming system. It was an entertainment system.

Both the music and computer keyboards were gone. In their place was a new peripheral, a ten-inch-tall robot called *ROB* (*Robotic Operating Buddy*). The Nintendo robot had the ability to assume sixty different positions as it responded to on-screen actions. *ROB*'s purpose was strictly to be a Trojan Horse. Since few electronic retailers wanted anything to do with videogame systems, Nintendo of America felt that it needed an angle to get the console into toy stores. *ROB* was promoted as a toy. The console itself appeared incidental, as it was marketed merely as the extra device required for *ROB*'s operation. Two games, *Gyromite* and *Stack-Up*, were designed to utilize the robot, and four more were planned to be released by the end of the year. However, Nintendo of America was certain that once people purchased the NES, they would be hooked on its games, and not its novelty robot. Nintendo of America's long-term plans for the NES didn't include *ROB*.[2]

Nintendo R.O.B.

Nintendo of America's strategy worked, at least as far as distributors were concerned.

Nintendo Entertainment System

Worlds of Wonder, a toy company that had made a name for itself by releasing *Lazer Tag* and *Teddy Ruxpin*, agreed to distribute the NES to toy stores. And if any retailer still expressed wariness about purchasing the NES, for fear that it wouldn't be able to move the units, Nintendo of America promised to buy back any unsold consoles from them. Nintendo of America was prepared to bear all of the financial risks associated with the system's launch.

Although a national and Canadian release of the NES had been scheduled for February 1986, Nintendo of America actually released it on October 18, in a test-market in the Metropolitan New York area. The $180 set contained the console ("Control Deck," in Nintendo jargon), two controllers, an NES Zapper light gun, *ROB*, and two "Game Paks," *Duck Hunt* and *Gyromite*. Fifteen addition Game Paks were available for sale individually.

However, one game that was supposed to be available during the NES's launch, wasn't.

In 1981, Shigeru Miyamoto had designed a follow-up to his classic arcade game *Donkey Kong*. Like its predecessor, the new game was set on a single screen, and featured multiple platforms. Partially inspired by *Joust*, the game could be played solo, or by two simultaneous players. The latter could choose to compete against each other or cooperate, but both were required to rid the platforms of multiple, assaulting creatures.

Miyamoto decided to use Mario, his hero carpenter from *Donkey Kong*, as the main character. However, as he was designing the game, a colleague told Miyamoto that Mario looked more like a plumber than a carpenter. Miyamoto agreed, and added a plumbing theme to his game. The platforms became pipes. For the second character, Miyamoto simply duplicated Mario and changed his colors, thereby creating an identical twin brother who was named Luigi. The game was simply called *Mario Bros*.

In 1983, Nintendo released *Mario Bros*. in arcades, where it wasn't very successful. If Nintendo hadn't been so eager to release a home console, the arcade game might have quickly been forgotten.

But Miyamoto didn't forget it. And when he was called upon to create a game for the new Famicom, he decided to produce a game that expanded on *Mario Bros*. Instead of a playfield where the action was limited to a single screen, Miyamoto created a landscape that was practically boundless. In addition to being fun to play, the game was also beautiful to look at. Featuring pastel colors, the game highlighted the best features of the Famicom.

Nintendo NES Super Mario Bros.

The game was called *Super Mario Bros*. It was released in Japan for the Famicom on September 13 and was slated to be released in New York on October 18. No word was given why the game was delayed, but it was finally available for sale around November 17.

By the end of 1985, Nintendo of America had sold 90% of the 100,000 units that it had produced. North America had once again embraced videogames.

Sega Competes

As the NES made a name for itself in New York, bolstered even further by the virtual lack of competition, its cousin, the Famicom, was the most popular gaming system in Japan. Sega Enterprises, Ltd. attempted to change this by offering lower-priced software. In this regard, they began releasing games on a credit card-sized piece of plastic called the *Sega My Card*. Developed by Mitsubishi Plastics, a Japanese chemical company, the Sega My Card could hold up to 32K of data[3] whereas a standard cartridge could contain up to 1,024K of code. The idea was to release smaller games on the Sega My Cards and larger games on the standard cartridges.

In order to use Sega My Cards on the SG-1000 and SG-1000 II consoles, Sega Enterprises, Ltd. released a ¥1,000 ($5) special cartridge called the *Card Catcher*. Sega My Cards could be placed into a slot in the Card Catcher, which could then be inserted into the cartridge ports of the two consoles.

Sega My Card

Sega Card Catcher

Sega Enterprises, Ltd. also released a new control pad for the SG-1000 II, although the differences between it and the original were very minor. The oval control buttons on the original were replaced with round ones, making the Sega control pad resemble the Famicom control pad even more.

But the new control pad wouldn't be around for long. On October 20, Sega Enterprises, Ltd. introduced the *Mark III*, a new console that came with control pads that were called *Joypads*. Physically, the only difference between it and the prior Sega control pads was that the Joypad featured a square-shaped D-pad. The console was backward-compatible with Sega's SG-1000 and SG-1000 II systems, and had a built-in card slot that could accept the Sega My Cards. New games that could only run on the Mark III were also produced on cartridges and *Sega My Card Mark IIIs*.

Sega Mark III

Sega My Card Mark III

The Mark III was a marginal improvement over its predecessors. Major differences included superior video and audio[4] as well as additional ROM.

Like its predecessors, the Mark III was not commercially successful. The Famicom commanded 95% of the Japanese videogame market. However, this did not dismay the executives at Sega Enterprises, Ltd., who were thinking about releasing a console in North America, and were now especially encouraged by the strong debut of the NES.[5]

JAMMA

Not all videogame news out of Japan was about the home gaming industry. JAMMA (Japan Amusement Machinery Manufacturers Association), a consortium made up of several arcade game makers including Namco, Sega, Taito and Capcom, introduced a new standard in arcade machines.

As long as a game was popular and generating income, arcade operators had no problem with keeping a machine, which took up valuable space within the limited confines of an arcade. However, if a machine didn't earn enough it had to be replaced by one that would. There were two ways to replace an unpopular game. One was by physically moving the cabinet out of the arcade and simply replacing it with a new one. The other way was by a tedious procedure that required rewiring of the PCB (printed circuit board), wiring harnesses and power supplies, which were usually custom-built.

JAMMA introduced a wiring standard so when a game needed to be changed, a PCB board simply needed to be replaced. The JAMMA standard used a 56-pin edge connector on the board with inputs and outputs common to most videogames, such as power and controller inputs and outputs for video and audio.[6]

Approximately $100 million game systems and cartridges had been sold in the United States during 1985. That amount was way down from the $900 million worth of videogames sold the year before. Most analysts believed that if Nintendo had not released the NES, the number would have been even lower. With Nintendo planning a national release in 1986, everyone agreed that the sales figure couldn't go anywhere but up.

CHAPTER FOURTEEN
1986

In Greek mythology, the Phoenix was a bird that lived for five hundred years. It finally died on a funeral pyre of its own making. From the ashes of the dead bird, a new and more powerful Phoenix rose, and it lived for another five hundred years.

Like the Phoenix, the videogame industry climbed from the embers of its own funeral pyre to begin a new and even more prosperous life. The talk among the attendees at the 1986 winter CES concerned videogames: the products that everyone had figured for dead.

To everyone's surprise, Nintendo of America's test marketing of the NES in New York resulted in a very good Christmas selling season for both the manufacturer and the retailers that carried the console. Videogame critics raved about the NES and *Super Mario Bros.* so much that consumers in other parts of the country bemoaned their inability to purchase it. Nintendo of America's booth at CES was overrun as retailers flocked to it to place orders.

With the success of the Famicom in Japan, and the expected duplication of that success in the United States, it was only inevitable that independent companies would begin producing their own software for the NES. It appeared to be 1982 all over again, as third-party companies scrambled to cash in on the success. However, although the flood of third-party software had nearly destroyed the industry three years earlier, independent NES software developers had the blessings of Nintendo. In fact, Nintendo of America even displayed many third-party titles at the CES in small satellite booths within its own exhibit.

Nintendo of America had done so well during its New York test-marketing, it feared it wouldn't be able to produce enough units in time for its planned national and Canadian release in February. In order to avoid an overall shortage, the company decided to prolong the rollout. In February, it began selling the system in Los Angeles, and followed that over the following five months with releases in Chicago, San Francisco and 12 other large cities. The company finally released the NES throughout the United States and Canada in September. By then, the NES was available in two configurations. The deluxe set was similar to the original set that Nintendo of America had launched in New York nearly a year earlier, but now retailed for $250. A new package, called the "Control Deck" set, only consisted of the console, the two controllers, and *Super Mario Bros.* And ultimately, it was this package that would ensure the success of the system and help to rejuvenate the industry.

The Nintendo Monopoly

Naturally, there was a reason for what seemed like madness on the part of Nintendo. The company, being well aware of what had caused the videogame shake-out of 1983, was determined not to let it happen again. In order to prevent third-party companies from flooding the market with inferior software, Nintendo developed a processor that prohibited the NES from playing cartridges that were manufactured by outside companies. Just as Atari had done with the Maria chip for the 7800, A special "lockout" chip inside the NES communicated with similar chips that were inside each legitimate cartridge. If their signals matched, the game was playable. If the NES couldn't detect a signal because the cartridge didn't contain the chip, then the game couldn't be played. Nintendo eventually designed three versions of the lockout chips: one for North American cartridges, one for UK cartridges, and one for cartridges distributed in the rest of Europe.

Nintendo was well aware that consumers demanded a vast selection of software when they purchased game machines. The company also knew that the best way to offer a varied and unique selection was by having third-party companies develop software. To prevent an overabundance of games, Nintendo granted licenses to software developers and then manufactured the cartridges for them, thus guaranteeing that the lock-out chip, or 'authenticating processor' as it was technically called, was inside the cartridge. Nintendo claimed several reasons for doing this. The first was that it wanted to avoid another videogame shake-out. By manufacturing all of the cartridges itself, Nintendo kept complete control on how much software reached the marketplace. It also claimed that it did this to prevent duplicate software from getting to the public. During Atari's heyday, there had been five different baseball games available for the 2600. Nintendo didn't want this to be the case with its machine. Part of the licensing process gave Nintendo complete autonomy to approve the games that its licensees wanted to develop. The bottom-line according to Nintendo, was that its licensing policy[1] was the public's guarantee that only good, playable games would be available for the NES. The company didn't want its customers confronting the problems that Atari owners had discovered: a surplus of inferior software. And consumers would know that the games on the store shelves had indeed passed Nintendo's strict conditions, because each licensed game had a gold "*Seal of Quality*" printed on its box. This Seal of Quality was meant to assure consumers that the game had gone through a stringent testing process and therefore had to be good.

Nintendo Seal of Quality

Nintendo didn't restrict only third-party publishers from manufacturing their own game cartridges. Even the games that were published by Nintendo and sold around the world were manufactured by Nintendo in Japan. Of course, all the games that were being released for the NES were available for the Famicom in Japan. However that changed on June 6 when Nintendo of America had released a title that had been developed by Nintendo in Japan, but was never released there.

Gumshoe had horizontally scrolling graphics that closely resembled those in *Super Mario Bros.* The premise of the game is that a detective must deliver five Black Panther diamonds in exchange for his kidnapped daughter. So the detective must go on a quest to find the diamonds. The gameplay was nearly the same as *Super Mario Bros.*, where the detective had to jump to get objects and avoid enemy creatures The game employed the NES Zapper light gun and the detective had to complete his quest before the player ran out of bullets. Shooting the detective would cause him to jump and catching a balloon would add bullets to the player's arsenal.

Nintendo NES Gumshoe

Famicom Disc System

Although American NES owners could purchase software that had would never be released in Japan, Japanese Famicom owners were able to purchase hardware that would get to America. On February 21, Nintendo released a disc-based system in Japan.

1986

Nintendo Famicom Disc System

The *Famicom Disc System* sat under the Famicom console and plugged into its cartridge port.[2] It allowed players to insert games that were stored on 128K proprietary floppy discs instead of cartridges. Nintendo announced that the disc system would be available in North America for the NES by the end of the year.

The disc system appealed to most people, because games sold on discs were less expensive than those on cartridge. A disc game cost roughly ¥3,000 ($16.50), compared to the ¥5,000 ($27.35) or more that each cartridge commanded. In addition, Nintendo and third-party companies provided kiosks where customers could purchase blank discs and have games written to them for only ¥2,000 ($11). While this was a great deal for gamers, cartridge retailers complained that it affected their bottom lines, and they weren't too enthusiastic about supporting it.

The first game released in the disc format was *The Legend of Zelda*, which featured a vast world that was so complex, it would take gamers weeks to complete. However, because data could

Nintendo The Legend of Zelda

be written to the discs, players could save their game sessions. Later, when they resumed playing, they would be at the section where they had previously left off, rather than back at the beginning.

Another advantage that the discs had was that they could store much more data than cartridges. Disc games were designed to be more complex than the standard cartridge titles, because there was so much room to store the additional game code needed to make them more complex.

Sharp Corporation licensed the Famicom Disc System from Nintendo, and on July 1, released its own version of the device. Called the *Twin Famicom*, the unit was a combination of both the Famicom and the Famicom Disc System. It could play Famicom cartridges and discs (although not at the same time). Like the Famicom Disc System, the Twin Famicom was only released in Japan.

Sharp Twin Famicom

Nintendo attempted to boost the Famicom Disc System with games that were released exclusively on disc. Many third-party companies, however, refused to support the system, because Nintendo demanded partial copyright ownership for any game that was developed for it. Before long, though, some advantages that the disc-based games had over the cartridges would become moot.

In October, Epoch released *Dragon Slayer*, the first game cartridge to contain a battery-powered CMOS RAM chip. This permitted players to save their games right on the cartridge itself. Surprisingly, *Dragon Slayer* was not a port of an existing Famicom disc game. In fact, the game wasn't even available for the Famicom. Instead, Epoch released it for its own Super Cassette Vision system.

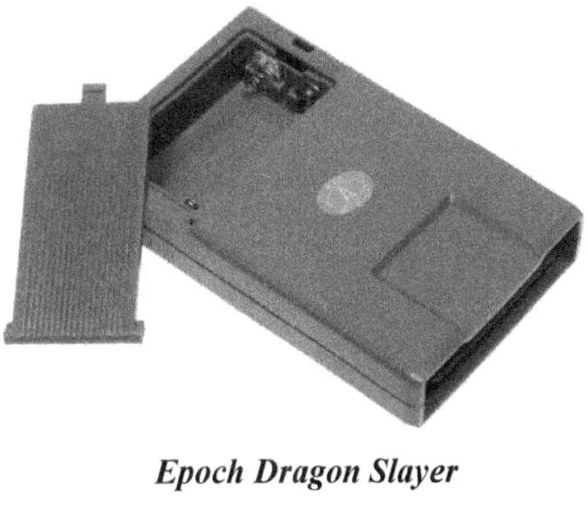

Epoch Dragon Slayer

As the prices of memory chips decreased, programmers were able to design cartridge-based games that were just as complex as those on discs. In November, Capcom released *Ghosts 'n Goblins*, the first 128K cartridge-based game.

Although Nintendo sold nearly two million Famicom Disc Systems in Japan, by the end of the year, the company felt that with the breakthroughs in cartridge technology, the disc-based system would no longer be as appealing to American consumers as they'd originally anticipated. The North American release of the disc system was scrapped.

Instead, Nintendo continued to concentrate on just rolling out the NES in North America. In June, the company offered two ways in which consumers could purchase a unit wherever it was available. The first was the $249.95 Deluxe Set, which was the configuration that Nintendo had been selling all along. It consisted of the console, two controllers, a Zapper light gun, *ROB*, and two games: *Duck Hunt* and *Gyromite*. A new $199.95 set was introduced, which contained only the NES control deck, two controllers and a *Super Mario Bros.* game cartridge. No matter how Nintendo packaged the NES, it consistently sold out. By the end of June, the company had sold over 200,000 consoles in the United States and Canada.

Bandai Family Trainer Mat

Packages of a different sort became available in Japan for Famicom owners in late 1986 with the release of a controller mat as part of a new *Family Trainer* bundle. The mat, which had been sold by Bandai, a Famicom licensee, included an *Athletic World* game cartridge. One side of the mat displayed eight control circles. An on-screen character in *Athletic World* did different things, depending upon which circle was stepped on. The opposite side of the mat displayed twelve numbered squares, which forthcoming games would use. The mat plugged into the second controller port of the Famicom, and worked in tandem with a standard controller that plugged into the first port.

Sega's American Console

Nintendo finished rolling out the NES in September. Coincidentally, during the same month, another Japanese company launched its console in North America.

Following Nintendo's American success during the 1985 holiday season, Sega Enterprises, Ltd. decided to once again maintain a presence in North America for home games. It quickly set up a new company, *Sega of America*, and rushed to get its Mark III ready for a grand premiere at the CES in June.[3]

By the time CES came around, Sega had changed the name of the console to the *Sega Master System*. Attendees at CES viewed a system that was very similar to the NES. It contained a Power Base console that featured 128K ROM and 128K RAM; two controller pads that suspiciously resembled those for the NES; a light gun and a game cartridge. Sega also promised a number of peripherals that would be available by Christmas, such as a track-ball Sports Pad controller, a Graphic Board for drawing pictures on the screen, and a 3½-inch disk drive.

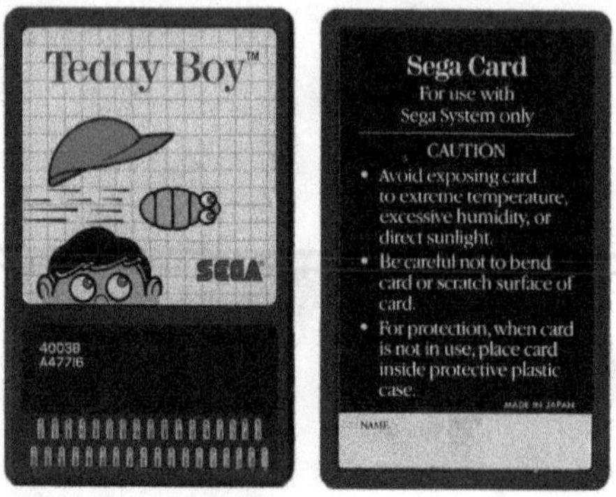

Sega Card

Like its Japanese counterpart, the Mark III, the $200 Sega Master System could play games from two different types of software. The first was the standard $30 *Mega Cartridge*, which could contain up to 1,024K of code. However, the console could not accept Mark III cartridges as the cartridges for the Sega Master System were

Sega Master System

designed differently. The Sega Master System also had a card reader that allowed it to accept the $25 credit card-sized *Sega Card* that contained 256K of code. And unlike the cartridges, the Sega Master System could play Sega My Cards and Sega My Card Mark IIIs that were imported from Japan.

Old is New Again

When Sega of America revealed the Master System at the summer CES, it was only one of several consoles that were on display. No one attributed this sudden glut of consoles to Nintendo. INTV Corporation claimed that it was due to a great 1985 with worldwide sales having reached $6 million. The company displayed its new $59.95 *System III,* which was basically Mattel's original Intellivision console with some slight cosmetic changes. The System III had been released nationally in May, along with several new game cartridges, such as *Pole Position.* In October, INTV Corporation released another handful of new games, including *Super Pro Football* and *Hover Force,* and announced that it would introduce a brand-new *System IV* game console and at least nine new cartridges at the upcoming winter CES in January, 1987.

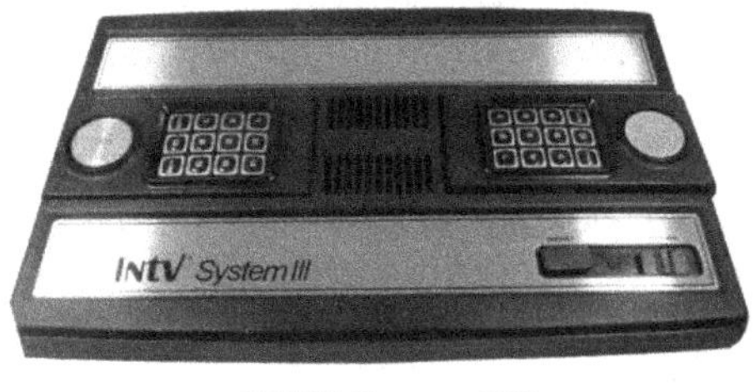

INTV System III

Many attendees at the summer CES may have thought that they had gone back in time to 1980. As the Intellivision sat on display in one booth, the 2600 was on display in another. Atari had initially planned to exhibit only its new line of computers, but those computers wound up alongside two game consoles that Atari had quickly assembled from its warehouses. The company quickly denied that Nintendo's success had anything to do with the resurgence of the 2600. Instead, Atari declared that its reason for reviving game consoles was that over one million 2600s had been sold in 1985, which proved that there was still a market for good, inexpensive systems.

The 2600 that Atari debuted at CES was a newly-designed unit called the 2600jr. The console was much smaller than the 2600, and had originally been planned in 1983 as a lower-priced 2600 that would appeal to younger game players. However, the sale of the company to Jack Tramiel in 1984 had caused those plans to be abandoned. When the 2600jr

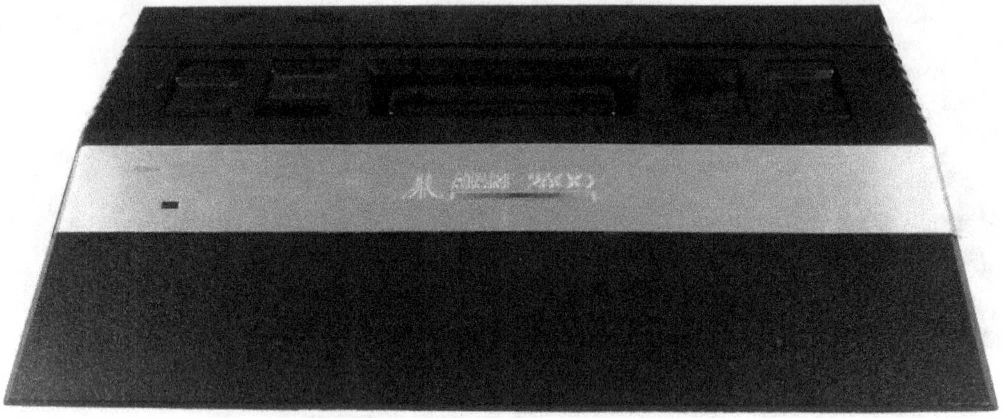

Atari 2600jr

was displayed at the summer 1986 CES, Atari claimed that the console was targeted for lower-income households, as an alternative against the newer, higher priced systems. The 2600jr was packaged with only a single joystick and one game cartridge, and retailed for under $50.

Atari also displayed its long-awaited 7800 console, which it had officially released in June. Atari under Warner had subcontracted the development of the 7800 out to GCC but when the sale of Atari to Tramel was finalized, GCC was still due payment. Tramiel had believed that Warner was responsible for the payment and that the console had been part of his purchase of Atari. After constant refusals by Warner to pay off GCC, Tramiel, eager to sell the stock of 7800 consoles that had been sitting in a warehouse since May, 1984, paid the GCC bill in May, 1985. But that payment only covered the consoles. Tramiel soon found himself negotiating with GCC for the three 7800 launch titles, *Joust*, *Ms. Pac-Man*, and *Asteroids* that were in the warehouse as well. In the end, Tramiel not only owned the stock of two-year old cartridges, but he contracted GCC to develop additional games as well. Unfortunately, products that Atari, Inc. had announced for the 7800 such as the High Score Cartridge and Terminal Cartridge, as well as the Mindlink controller for the 2600, had been canceled as soon as Warner Communications unloaded the company to Tramiel.[4]

Unfortunately, the new games that GCC needed to develop weren't available yet when Atari began shipping the console, so only the three original games were offered. This was a far cry from the fifteen titles that Nintendo had made available when the NES debuted. Atari quickly released an additional three titles, and promised that many more would be available during the following months. By September, only *Galaga* made it to the stores, and three previously announced titles disappeared from Atari's dealer list of upcoming games. 2600 titles were also disappearing from the dealers' list. Atari had announced in July that it was negotiating with INTV about licensing some Intellivision titles for the 2600. Atari was so confident that the licensing deal would go through that it even included the INTV game titles on its dealer lists of upcoming games. Unfortunately, the licensing never went through, and the titles were eventually removed from the list.

Even if Atari managed to release the games, the number of retailers that would actually carry them was uncertain. The old Atari had lost its credibility by displaying products that weren't anywhere near ready. Retailers didn't want to stake their profits on products if they didn't know when, or even if, they would receive them. Critics once again began accusing Atari of displaying vaporware at CES.

Although the ColecoVision wasn't represented at the 1986 CES, a Taiwanese company called Bit Corporation, which had previously produced games for the Atari 2600, released a console that it called the *Dina 2-in-1*.[5] The reason for this name was that the Dina was

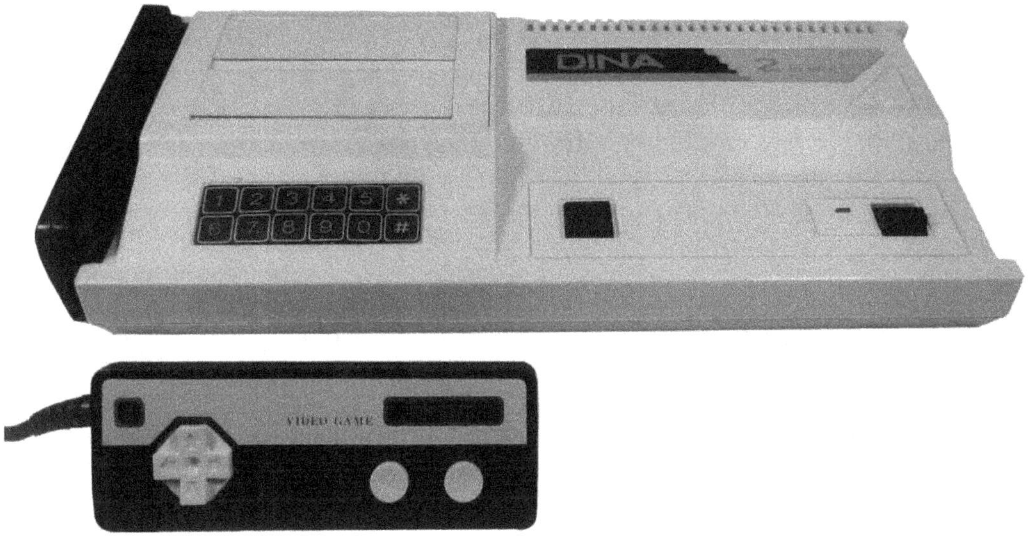

Bit Corp. Dina 2-in-1

compatible with both ColecoVision and Sega SG-1000 games, since both consoles had similar operating systems. The Dina had two cartridge slots that were uniquely structured for the software of each of the systems. It also included a built-in game called *Meteoric Shower*.

The Dina used control pads that were similar to the ones found on the Sega Master System and the NES/Famicom. Since the original ColecoVision used bulky controllers that utilized a numeric pad, a substitute numeric pad was built into the console. It also had a *pause* button that was used by the SG-1000 games. But the Dina wasn't compatible with everything from the original systems. The ColecoVision's Expansion Modules could not plug into the unit and many two-player ColecoVision games could not be played, since there was only one numeric pad built into the system and that corresponded to player one.

Tape and Disc Games

As the popularity of electronic videogames was being resurrected, a different form of videogame also appeared. Videotape games were similar to the laserdisc games although they couldn't offer instant access. However, since most people owned video cassette recorders rather than laserdisc players, videotape games offered the only interactive alternative to videogame consoles.

Parker Brothers had released *Clue VCR Mystery Game,* the first videotape game, in 1985. During the following year, Mattel and several other companies joined the throng. Unlike standard videogames, in which the action took place solely on the screen, the videotape games were more closely related to the Odyssey *Master Strategy Series,* wherein each game was played simultaneously on the screen and on a physical game-board. Unfortunately, unlike the Odyssey games, which could be played an infinite number of times and always be different, the videotape games were limited in their playability. Since the same videotape had to be used each time, it wasn't too long before the action became repetitious and the game was relegated to the closet. Some companies took the approach that the Mysterydiscs had used, wherein there was a multiple number of different scenarios, but the same problem arose when all these different versions had been played out.

Despite these drawbacks, the videotape games sold very well. As they grew in popularity, the superior videodisc games disappeared. In fact, the two Mysterydiscs wound up being the only bonafide game discs that were released. This was due to the general failure of the videodisc format, and not the quality of the games themselves. Since so few households owned videodisc players, it wasn't commercially practical for developers to create game discs that probably wouldn't sell.

Although the public virtually ignored the videodisc, it went crazy over the audio laserdisc that had been developed by Philips and Sony, and which had first been released in 1982. Like the videodisc, the audio disc utilized a laser beam to read information that the computer decoded and translated into something that the consumer could understand, such as music. Because the audio disc compressed an hour's worth of music data onto a five-inch piece of plastic and aluminum, it was called a *Compact Disc (CD).*

Since CDs were encoded with digital information, i.e. streams of bits, it didn't take long for developers to realize that computer information could be stored on these tiny discs just as easily as music. By 1986, companies duly began manufacturing CD players for computers. One CD-ROM (the name given to compact discs that were used to store computer code, rather than music) could store millions more bytes of data than a floppy disk. The only drawback with the CD-ROMs was that the user couldn't save data to them. This proved inconvenient to computer users who saw the CD as a mass storage device, but it was just the medium that software developers had been looking for. Before long, CD-ROMs that contained the entire Grolier's encyclopedia were available. For game developers, it looked as if there was no limit to what they could design. Since the CDs were capable of storing so much more data than even the Famicom Disc System could provide, there was no telling what kind of games they could devise.

CHAPTER FIFTEEN
1987

When 1987 began, videogame consoles were once again selling at a phenomenal pace. Atari sold 100,000 7800s in the six months since they had become available. Sega sold 125,000 Master Systems in only four months. Still, the clear winner was Nintendo, which sold 1,100,000 NES consoles in just fourteen months!

INTV also rode high on the resurgence of videogames. The company was faced with a large number of back-orders, because it couldn't produce software fast enough to satisfy the demand. But INTV wasn't content with its line of legacy games, and displayed nine new Intellivision titles at the winter CES in January. The company claimed that one in particular, *Tower of Doom*, was the most complex game ever designed for the system.

Also displayed was the new System IV, which looked exactly like INTV's System III and the original Intellivision. The system featured detachable controllers, a real-time clock, and fewer chips. In all actuality, INTV's System IV was actually Mattel's Intellivision III, which had been canceled in 1983. It was totally compatible with all previous Intellivision items, with the exception of the computer keyboard and its related software.

More Games On Tape

Interestingly, the Intellivision's former manufacturer, Mattel, debuted a new type of videogame at the Toy Fair in February. Their *Captain Power* line of toys consisted of $30 handheld spaceships that were used in conjunction with a live-action *Captain Power* TV series, which had begun airing in September, 1986. Viewers had to aim their toy spaceships towards the TV during certain segments of the show, and shoot the on-screen enemies. While they did this, their scores were tallied on an electronic scoreboard built into the spaceship. Controversy arose because parents had to go out and purchase *Captain Power* toys so their children could enjoy the show. Peggy Charon of the *Action for Children's Television* complained that it was "the height of arrogance" to make people go out and buy something so that they could "really watch the show the way it's designed to be watched." John Weems, Mattel's VP of Entertainment, countered by saying, "only a small fraction of the audience would ever own the toy line." Also noted was the fact that the show received good reviews from TV critics who didn't use the toys. In the end, a number of factors contributed to the series' cancellation after one season. Among them was the fact that it was very expensive -- approximately $1 million an episode -- to produce. And because some stations aired the show at ridiculous hours, such as 5 A.M., it received low ratings. Finally, the interaction between the show and the toys was very poor.

Mattel Captain Power

Several episodes of the *Captain Power* show were released on videotape. These tapes from Hi-Tops Video were for viewing only and couldn't be used with the Mattel toys. However, Mattel also released several videotapes on its own, and used packaging similar to that which the toys were sold in. These Mattel-issued tapes could be used with the *Captain Power* toys.

Worlds of Wonder also released live-action interactive videotapes. However, these were released in conjunction with the $99 *Action Max*, a brand-new videogame console that came out in September. Like the other systems, it came with a light-gun which was utilized in place of a controller.

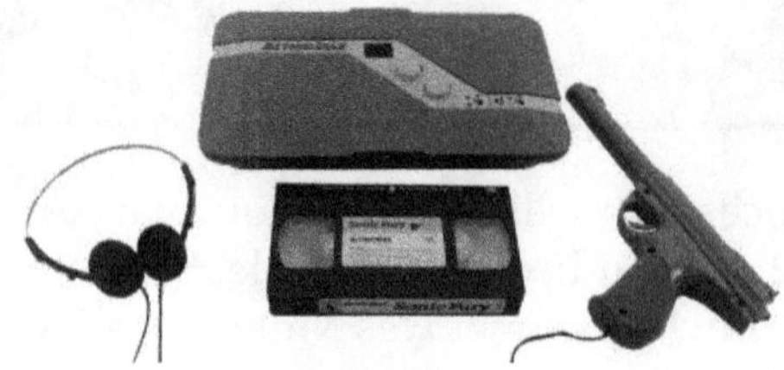

Worlds of Wonder Action Max

All of the games for Action Max came on VHS videotapes instead of cartridges, and the console had to be hooked up to a videotape player as well as a television. As the tape played, the gamer had to shoot at live-action targets that appeared on the screen using a light gun that connected to the console. A red light on the console lit up whenever a target was hit.

Action Max games suffered from the same fault as others on videotape: They became very predictable after only a few plays. Although Worlds of Wonder announced an ever-growing library of new titles, only a few were eventually released, due to financial problems that the company had acquired while developing the console. Action Max made it into stores, but without the benefit of any advertising, it eventually wound up in the discount bins.

Although the Action Max was available in North America and Europe, Japanese consumers couldn't purchase it domestically. Fortunately for them a similar unit called the *Video Challenger* was issued in Japan by a toy company called Takara.[1] Like the Action Max, the Video Challenger also used a gun (a "Challenge Blaster") that gamers aimed and fired at the TV screen, but in this case, the gun was the console! It also displayed a score that increased every time the player successfully shot an on-screen target. However, the player also had to avoid being shot from the on-screen characters or else the tally would decrease.

Takara Video Challenger

Video Challenger was also similar to *Captain Power* as it was tied to an anime called *The Headmasters* that aired on Japanese TV. Children could shoot at on-screen characters during the title sequence of certain episodes to score points.

Games for the Video Challenger were designed by key videogame developers such as Sega, Data East[2] and Konami. Despite this, the Video Challenger suffered the same fate as the other videotape-based consoles. They simply couldn't compete against mainstream videogame consoles like the Famicom. Due to the sequential nature of tapes, each game was repetitive and players simply lost interest after just a few plays.

Atari's XE Game System

Atari also introduced a new console in 1987, which came as a shock to many attendees of the winter CES. The company displayed a mock-up of a brand-new $129 game console that was incompatible with both the 2600 and 7800. The *XE Game System (XEGS)* was essentially an Atari 65XE computer without a keyboard. The system would include a standard 2600 joystick and a light gun. But the optional peripherals that were on display were what really made the unit confusing. These included a plug-in keyboard, a cassette-tape drive, and two disk drives. These peripherals essentially turned the computer-without-a-keyboard back into an actual computer. Once these peripherals were installed, the XEGS was compatible with all of the software available for the Atari 8-bit computers.

The big question was: Whom did Atari believe was the target audience for the new console? Consumers who wanted a computer could just go out and purchase a 65XE. Those who just wanted a game machine could buy a 7800. Atari explained that the XEGS was for people who weren't yet ready for computers, but might be interested in upgrading to one in the future. The only upgrades that they would need to purchase were the inexpensive keyboard and a storage device.

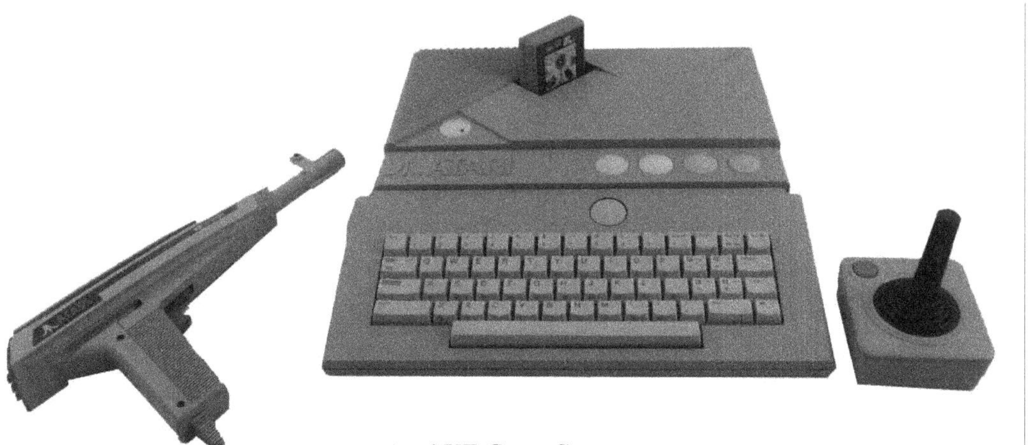

Atari XE Game System

The general response to the new game system from the CES attendees was one of amusement. Most felt that especially with Atari's history of displaying vaporware, the XEGS would never make it to store shelves. Since the unit on display was just a mock-up, many believed that Atari only showed it at CES in order to gauge the response. The company could then decide whether or not it should proceed with the product. When Atari asked the heads of several major toy stores whether they'd rather sell an $80 65XE computer or a new $150 game system, the majority of the responses was in favor of the gaming system.

Atari again displayed the XEGS at the Toy Fair the following month. There it was announced that the keyboard would be included with the console along with the joystick, light-gun and a game cartridge. The absence of the other computer peripherals that had been displayed at CES seemed to imply that Atari would no longer be marketing the XEGS as a gaming system that could be upgraded to a computer.

By the time of the summer CES in June, the XEGS was on Atari's release schedule. The production model carried a suggested retail price of $150, and came with all of the peripherals that had been displayed at the Toy Fair. Two new game cartridges, *Flight Simulator II* and *Bug Hunt*, a game that used the light-gun, were now included with the console, and *Missile Command* was built into it, along with *Atari BASIC*. Atari also intended to transfer 50 existing 800 and 65XE disk-based computer games to cartridges. And so gamers could access all of the disk games that weren't going to be transferred, the XEGS supported any disk drive that could be hooked up to an 8-bit Atari computer.

Atari released the XEGS in November, and the response was far less encouraging than the company had hoped. Critics tore the machine apart in their reviews. First they claimed that there was nothing new about it, especially since it was really an XE computer, which was basically a descendent of the nine-year-old Atari 800. They were also dissatisfied that the console came with the same ten-year-old joystick that had accompanied the 2600. They didn't rave about the software, either. Nobody was happy with the built-in *Missile Command*, since it was the same exact version that had been released for the Atari computers back in 1981. The critics argued that if Atari had really been serious about the XEGS, they would have at least selected a modern game to accompany the machine. *Flight Simulator II* received good reviews, but it was also an old game. The only thing new about it was that it was available on a cartridge for the first time. The only new game was *Bug Hunt*, which unfortunately contained a real programming bug. The entire screen flickered every time a shot was fired from the light gun.

Atari released other software for the XEGS, but this consisted entirely of old game cartridges, such as *Pac-Man* and *Asteroids*, which had been available for the computers for several years. Atari didn't even bother to change the games' original packaging. Instead, labels had been placed on the outer 400/800 packaging; these pointed out that the games were also playable on the XEGS.

Videogamers wanted the most advanced product with the most available software. The XEGS was far from being an advanced product. As far as software went, the XEGS could play the most games of any system, thanks to the vast number of titles that were available for the Atari 8-bits. The only problem was that most of the titles weren't new. The question most people wondered about was: How many new titles would Atari release in support of the system?

2600 Games Continue To Be Released

The 7800 didn't fare much better when it came to new software. Although Atari had displayed brand-new games for it at the summer CES, cynicism towards the company appeared when three new 7800 titles that were supposed to be available by the end of the summer failed to appear on their scheduled release dates. By that time, Atari hadn't released new software for the 7800 in over a year. New cartridges for the system didn't actually appear in stores until after Christmas. However, since the 7800 could accept 2600 cartridges, 7800 owners could at least purchase the new software that Atari released for the older system. The company announced many new games for the 2600 throughout the year, including new titles like *Jr. Pac-Man,* and older games that it had licensed from other companies. Atari bought the rights to *Donkey Kong* and four other titles from Coleco, and it licensed *Q*Bert* from Parker Brothers. At a time when Nintendo and Sega were releasing games that were at the forefront of technology, Atari was unloading four- and five-year-old games that, even when they'd been new, had been considered archaic in comparison with the same titles on other systems.

Surprisingly, Atari wasn't the only company releasing old games for the ten-year-old console. A new company called Froggo Games made several old titles available for the first time. *Karate* had been announced by Ultravision in 1983, but had never been released. Three other games, *Cruise Missile, Sea Hawk* and *Sea Hunt,* had been distributed in 1984 by a Japanese software company called Sancho, but they had never been released in the United States. Although the two remaining games from Froggo Games featured modified graphics, they had previously been released under different names by other companies. *Spiderdroid* had formerly been *Amidar* from Parker Brothers, and *Task Force was* Spectravision's *Gangster Alley*.

Mat Controllers

Oddly, even companies that had never developed games for the 2600 began releasing new titles for the system. Epyx, the computer software company that had taken over Starpath, put out 2600 versions of its computer hits *Summer Games* and *Winter Games*. And a company called Exus Corporation released two cartridges, *Jogger* and *Reflex*. These titles were included with the *Foot Craz Activity Pad* that plugged into the controller port. Like Bandai's *Family Trainer,* which had been released for the Famicom the previous year, the Foot Craz was a controller that had to be stepped on.

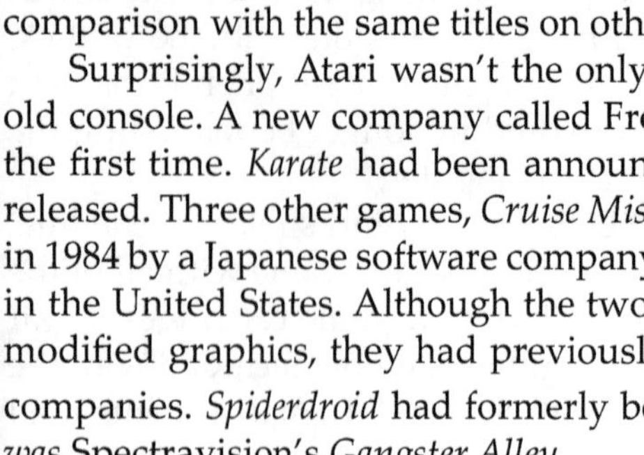

Exus Foot Craz Activity Pad

Ironically, Bandai released an NES version of the *Family Trainer* in North America, where it was called the *Family Fun Fitness* bundle. Bandai also released two game cartridges to go with the mat, *Athletic World,* and *Stadium Events,* which had its title changed from the original Japanese, *Running Stadium*.[3]

Not everything that Bandai developed for the Famicom made it to the NES. One such peripheral was *Karaoke Studio*, which Bandai released only in Japan on July 30. This unit, which had a built-in microphone, plugged into the Famicom's cartridge slot and sat atop the console. The unit also contained 25 songs that played through the Famicom, and displayed the lyrics on the TV screen. Players sang into the microphone and were given scores based upon the accuracy of their singing. On October 28, Bandai released a cassette that contained additional songs.[4]

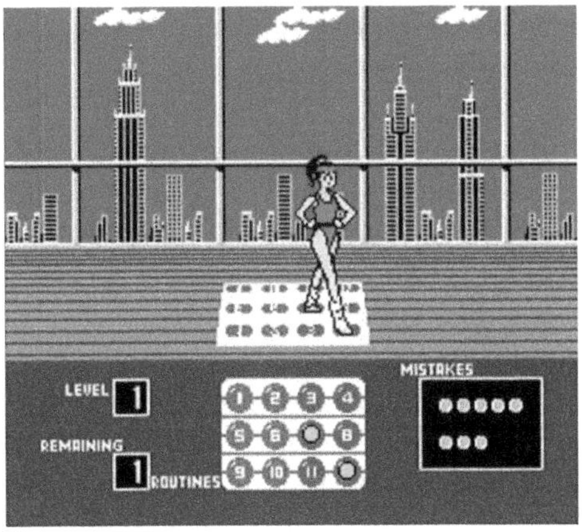

Bandai Aerobics Studio

But the Famicom didn't have a monopoly on exclusive hardware. In July, Nintendo released a new controller that was only available for the NES.[5] The *NES Advantage* featured a large joystick with a rounded top, and was meant to simulate a heavy-duty joystick using in arcade videogames. The stick sat within the left side of a large rectangular base that was meant to sit on a flat base, rather than being held, during play. To the right of the stick were two large red control buttons that had the same function as the red buttons on a standard NES controller. Above each of the red buttons were smaller white buttons that activated the turbo feature of the controller. When used, the turbo buttons duplicated the action of when a red button was pressed repeatedly. Above each white turbo button was a small gray dial that allowed the user to adjust the speed of the turbo. The NES Advantage also featured a *slow* button which caused the action on the screen to go in slow motion while it was activated.

Bandai Karaoke Studio

The NES Advantage plugged into both controller ports of the NES. It could be used by two players in games where the players took alternate turns. A switch determined whether the controller was used by Player 1 or Player 2.

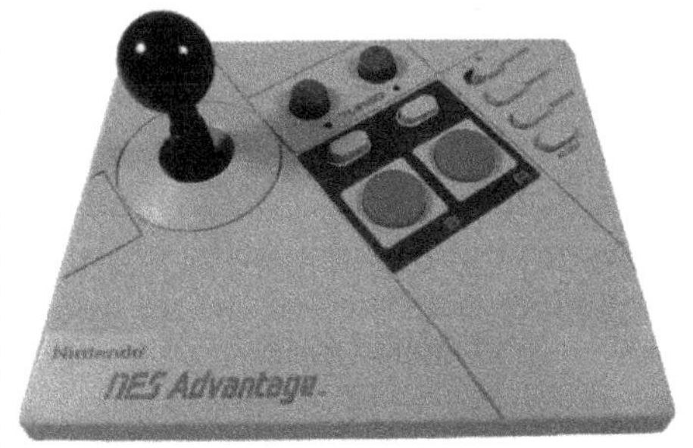

Nintendo NES Advantage

The Legend of Zelda

Although the NES Advantage couldn't be used with the Famicom, some Famicom games were being released for the NES. One such game was *The Legend of Zelda,* which had been released a year earlier in Japan as the inaugural title for the Famicom Disc System. At that time, the system boasted the perfect technology for *The Legend of Zelda,* since the game was much too large to fit in a standard cartridge. However, in the year since the game's Japanese release, two important breakthroughs had occurred: the inexpensive 128k RAM chip, and the CMOS RAM chip that was used to save game information. Utilizing both chips, Nintendo was able to release a rendering of *The Legend of Zelda* on cartridge that was virtually identical to the disc version.

The NES copy of *The Legend of Zelda* became an instant success in the United States. Its innovative, open-ended game play allowed players to direct Link, the on-screen hero, in any direction. There weren't any invisible barriers that prevented Link from getting to any point on or off the scrolling playfield. *The Legend of Zelda* went on to become Nintendo's second million-selling game.

Rental Issues

As Nintendo's games became more and more in demand, consumers found that they simply couldn't afford to spend a tidy sum of money on titles that might be bad or boring. With the dearth of videogame magazines, consumers no longer had the opportunity to read game reviews for every game that was available. Of all the entertainment software available, videogames were unique in the aspect that the buyer never necessarily knew what he was getting. While music could be heard on the radio and movies could be rented, videogames, which were less passive than the others, couldn't be previewed in any way.

Renting videogames became a profitable business for video stores in 1987. It is not known who rented out the first videogame cartridge, but the idea quickly spread from one video store to another. Most retailers favored the Nintendo compatible software since that was the unit that was in the most households. As the bigger chains such as Blockbuster Video became involved in the videogame rental business, Nintendo took notice and frowned upon it. Every title that was rented was one less cartridge sold and fewer profits to add to its treasury. Unlike movie companies that received a royalty for every rented videotape, the videogame companies received nothing from this practice.

Since it wasn't illegal to rent out videogame cartridges Nintendo couldn't stop the stores from doing so. However the company did score a victory in its war against the rentals by filing a suit with the U.S. District Court of New Jersey against Blockbuster Video.

Unlike a videotape that doesn't need any instructions on how to use it, most videogames played pretty poorly if they weren't played properly. Video rental store operators were faced with a dilemma. If they included the game's original instructions with a rented cartridge, the renter could conceivably lose the instructions and render the game basically unplayable. To get around that problem stores like Blockbuster included photocopies of the original instructions. By doing this they didn't have to worry about the instructions being lost since the original could always be copied again.

What the store owners neglected or ignored was the fact that the instruction manuals were copyright protected. Therefore any duplication of them without the permission of the copyright owners was a direct infringement of that copyright. Nintendo claimed that Blockbuster had violated its copyrights by photocopying the instruction manuals for inclusion with the rented cartridges.

The courts sided with Nintendo and forced Blockbuster and other companies to quit photocopying the instructions. However this didn't stop the companies from renting out the game cartridges. Before long the games contained rewritten instructions, which were printed on cards that were then glued onto the cartridge cases. Thus, there wasn't any danger of them getting lost unless a renter purposely ripped them off. Because the instructions were paraphrased, they didn't infringe upon the copyright owner's rights. On the negative side, they contained only the briefest of instructions and some didn't give players all the information that they would have received from the genuine instruction manuals. However they were better than nothing and a perfect way around Nintendo's attempted destruction of the rental market.

3D

Thanks to the achievements in technology, gamers who owned an NES were beginning to enjoy the same software as their counterparts in Japan who owned a Famicom. The same couldn't be said about the peripherals that Nintendo released for the Famicom.

One such item was the *Famicom 3D System*, which Nintendo released on October 21 in Japan only. This mechanical headset gave the illusion of 3D by using liquid crystal shutters that rapidly switched on and off to deliver two separate images, one to each eye. The system was never very popular, and was supported by only seven games -- a good reason why Nintendo chose not put out a version for the NES. One of the 3D games, *Highway Star*, did in fact make it to American shores for the NES. The American version, which was called *Rad Racer*, was packed with standard cardboard glasses that used red and blue plastic lenses.

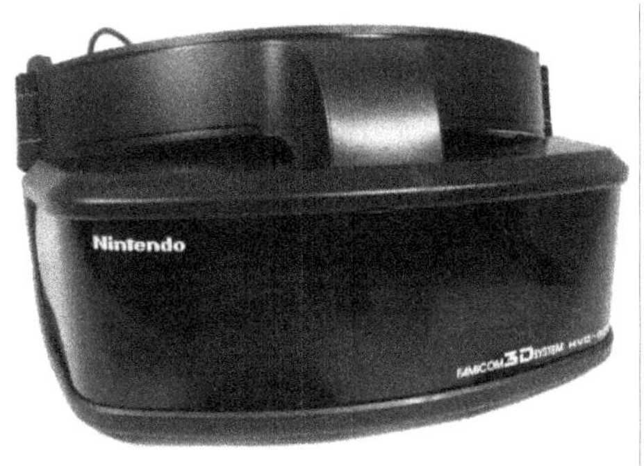

Nintendo Famicom 3D System

American gamers didn't completely miss out on 3D games. Those who owned a Sega Master System were able to purchase the *Sega 3D Glasses*, a device that was uncannily similar to the Famicom 3D System. The glasses plugged into a special Sega Card that came with them, which then could be inserted into the Sega Master System. The glasses were very comfortable, even after hours of play.

The *Sega 3D Glasses* was the first Sega product that had been distributed by Tonka Toys, a major manufacturer of toys and games (and the parent company of Parker Brothers). As the NES dominated 90% of the American videogame market, Sega CEO Hayao Nakayama decided in the summer that he didn't want to waste his company's time and money trying to sell a console that few people wanted. Instead of removing the Sega Master System from the market completely, Sega of America sold the US sales, marketing and distribution rights to Tonka. This was done because Nakayama felt that the toy company had a favorable reputation with retailers, and would be able to get the Sega Master System into more stores, where it could better compete against Nintendo. After the sale, Sega of America continued handling the warranties, and Sega of Japan[6] continued designing and manufacturing the software. The only problem was that Tonka had never marketed a videogame console before, and really had no idea how to do it.

Sega 3D Glasses

1987

As Tonka toiled with how to sell the Sega Master System in the United States, Sega of Japan released a new console on October 18, which it also called the Sega Master System. While the ¥16,800 ($118) Japanese model looked the same as its older American cousin on the outside, the two were slightly different. For one, the Japanese console featured a slimmer cartridge port. The Japanese cartridges were slimmer than those that fit in Sega Master Systems in North America. In fact, the dimensions of the Japanese cartridges were the same as those that fit the SG-1000 and Mark III consoles. So unlike the American console, which could only play game cartridges that were designed specifically for it, the Japanese Master System was backward-compatible with the Japanese Sega consoles that had preceded it. The console also had the Mark III's optional FM sound unit built-into it. The Sega 3D Glasses, which needed an intermediary Sega Card to connect with the American console, could plug directly into the Japanese Sega Master System.

Sega of Japan also released a new controller on March 15 that would be compatible with the Japanese Sega Master System as well as the Mark III. The *Paddle Control* was very similar to the Joypad, except that it featured a round knob, very similar to the knob on the Atari paddle controller, on the left in place of the D-pad. The unit only featured one control button on the face of it, and another along its top edge. The Paddle Control was packaged with *Woody Pop: Shinjinrui no Block Kuzugi,* a *Breakout*-type game that could only work with the new controller. The ¥1,200 ($8) Paddle Control was also sold separately as Sega of Japan released *Outrun,* a racing game that could use it but didn't require it. In November, Sega of Japan released *Alex Kidd: BMX Trial,* which did require the Paddle Control.[7]

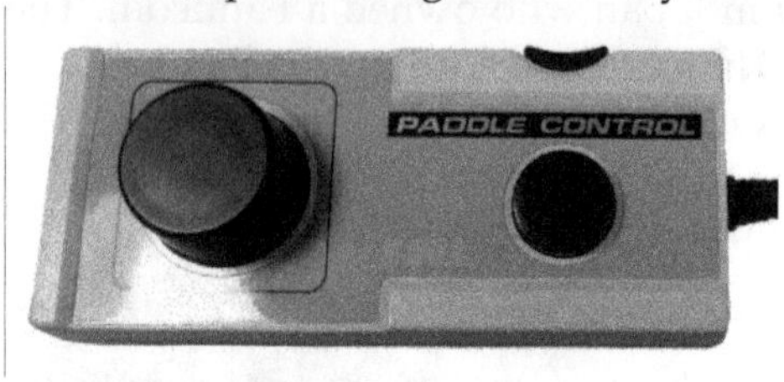

Sega Paddle Control

16-Bit Gaming

The Sega Master System wasn't the only new console that had been released in Japan in 1987. Hudson Soft,[8] a Japanese software company, designed a game console of its own, but didn't have enough capital to manufacture it. They teamed up with NEC, a major manufacturer of computers worldwide, which had been seeking to enter the console market. NEC built and released the system on October 30, which it called the *PC Engine.* They marketed the ¥24,800 ($178) system as the first 16-bit console.

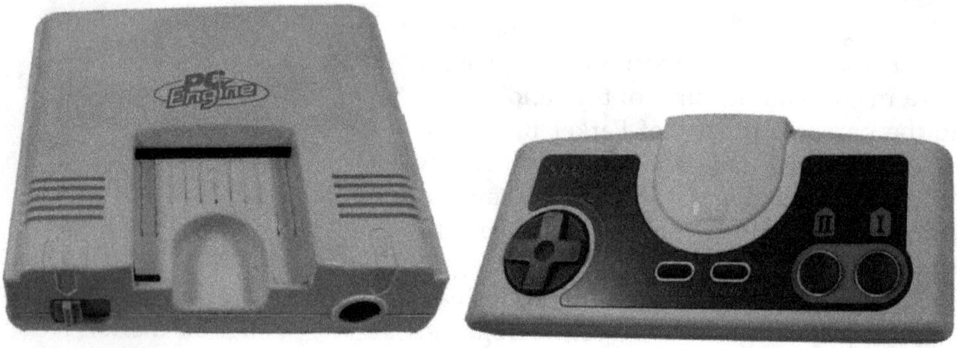

NEC PC Engine

In all actuality, the PC Engine wasn't any faster than any of the other systems on the market since it only had an 8-bit processor, the HuC6280, which was a custom-built processor based on the 6502. However, it did have a separate 16-bit graphic processor, which allowed it to display in much greater detail and with many more colors. Unfortunately, the picture that was displayed on the TV wasn't optimum as the PC Engine could only connect to the television using a standard RF cable.

NEC PC Engine HuCard

The games for the PC Engine came on credit card-sized cartridges called *HuCards* (Hudson Card), which were very similar to the Sega My Cards for the Sega Master System. However, while Sega used the cards as a means to provide inexpensive games to the system, the PC Engine used HuCards exclusively.[9]

The PC Engine was the smallest console released to date, measuring 5.5 square inches and only 1.5 inches high. However, a large expansion port at the rear of the console promised that there was more to come.

Upon its release, the PC Engine became well accepted in Japan, and even beat out the Famicom in sales. However, despite the popularity of the PC Engine, NEC didn't have any immediate plans to export the machine to the United States, where the existing videogame companies had all done well that year.

Shortly after the PC Engine hit store shelves, Sega of Japan announced its own 16-bit videogame console. The new nameless console would accept its own cartridges, as well as the existing software for the Japanese 8-bit Sega Master System. Unlike the PC Engine, which only featured 16-bit graphics, Sega of Japan's new machine would also boast a powerful 16-bit processor. Like NEC, Sega of Japan didn't say if and when the new machine would be available in the United States.

As the Famicom bowed to the PC Engine in Japan, its North American counterpart was second to nothing. The NES wound up being the best-selling toy of the 1987 holiday season in both dollars earned and units sold. Nintendo estimated that it had sold out its entire inventory of three million consoles throughout the year. Fifteen million cartridges, including six million from third-party manufacturers, were also sold during the year.

Atari also sold out its entire supply of 1.5 million consoles, but that number included the XEGS, the 7800 and the 2600.

Sega and Tonka didn't sell out their entire stock of Sega Master Systems, but they came close. The retail sales from August (when Tonka had taken over the distribution) through December totaled $90 million, 20% higher than anticipated. Many games were in such high demand that they had to be allocated.

New Breed of Magazines

The American videogame industry began to flourish once more, and magazines soon began reappearing to support the industry. The October issue of *ANALOG Computing*, a magazine for Atari computer users, began a new column called *Video Game Digest*, which reported the latest videogame news and software reviews for all of the videogame systems. Long-time gamers were pleased to see that the column had been written by Arnie Katz and Bill Kunkel, the two men who had founded the first American videogame magazine, *Electronic Games*. They posed a question to the readers asking whether the column should continue, or whether a separate magazine devoted to videogames should be started. Unfortunately, *ANALOG* disappeared from the stands after that issue. While the videogame industry appeared to be on the rebound, Atari computers were no longer popular.

The editors of *ANALOG* weren't the only ones who saw the need for a magazine about videogames. Steve Harris, one of the original members of Twin Galaxies' U.S. National Video Game Team (USNVGT), also felt the need for such a magazine. In order to raise funds to establish one, Harris and his friend Jeffrey Peters held a 1987 Video Game Masters Tournament, a national arcade-game championship that was sponsored by the USNVGT. Using proceeds from the tournament, Harris started a magazine that was devoted strictly to videogames.

Electronic Game Player, which was released in October, presented game strategies, previews of upcoming games, and features concerning the videogame industry. It was exactly the type of magazine that fans of the emerging videogame industry needed. Unfortunately for Harris, magazine distributors weren't aware of the renaissance that videogames were going through, and they remembered the number of videogame magazines that had failed only three years earlier. Few distributors were willing to carry *Electronic Game Player*, so the magazine appeared in only a few newsstands, and basically only on the west coast.

Publicists at Nintendo of America also bemoaned the fact that there weren't any

Electronic Game Player

NINTENDO® FUN CLUB NEWS

VOL. 1 NO. 1 WINTER 1987 $2.50

THE PREZ SEZ

Welcome to the Club!

A message from Howard Phillips – professional video gamesman and President of the Nintendo Fun Club

Super Mario Bros.™ enter amazing worlds to rescue princess

Princess held captive

Mario has special powers

Super Mario is poised to pounce on a deadly Koopa.

CAUTION!

NOW YOU'RE PLAYING WITH POWER

Nintendo Fun Club News

quality nationwide videogame magazines around. Without magazines, there weren't any print outlets in which they could advertise their new games. To rectify this, Nintendo of America established the *Nintendo Fun Club,* a free service that NES owners could join by merely returning a card that was packed with every new NES. The club was even promoted through a game! During an intermission in *Mike Tyson's Punch-Out,* one of the offered hints was to join the Nintendo Fun Club.

Included with the membership was a free subscription to the *Nintendo Fun Club News,* a quarterly multi-page newsletter that highlighted all of the new games that Nintendo was releasing for the NES.

Although magazine distributors may have thought otherwise, to those in the gaming industry, it seemed like the great shake-out of 1983 had never happened. Many dealers felt that with their hindsight concerning what had occurred in 1983, they were able to prevent another shake-out from taking place again.

The 1983 crash had been caused by an overabundance of software on the market. There now wasn't any danger of an avalanche of Sega or Atari titles because very few third-party games were developed for those systems. This was partly due to the fact that Nintendo-licensed developers were prohibited from designing software for competing systems. And as Nintendo had announced time and time again, it could regulate the number of cartridges that were available to the public, because of its licensing policies.

However, there was still a dangerous overabundance of hardware. By the end of 1987, there were four companies in the United States selling incompatible consoles. All of them used technology that was over ten years old. For 1988, the companies planned to bring out up-to-date hardware with the potential to make the current consoles obsolete.

Until then, it was business as usual. The companies intended to make every dollar they could from products that were about to become outdated.

CHAPTER SIXTEEN
1988

Nintendo's booth at the winter CES was alive with activity as it and twenty of its licensees displayed all of the new products that they planned to introduce during 1988. Because Nintendo manufactured and distributed the cartridges for all of its licensees, it also determined the release dates of all third-party software, and it was very good when it came to meeting these announced dates. Unfortunately, Nintendo ultimately couldn't meet the ambitious 1988 release schedule that it had set.

The reason for this was because a severe chip shortage caught Japan in its grasp. Nintendo was hurt dramatically by this. The shortage began early in the year, and lasted throughout most of it. This forced the manufacturers to delay production of many of their most awaited titles until 1989. One highly anticipated title was *Super Mario Bros. 2*, a sequel to the hit game that was still packed with all NES consoles. Nintendo had originally planned to release *Super Mario Bros. 2* in March, but the chip shortage pushed the date into September. When the game was finally released in limited quantities, many people lined up at stores hours before opening time in order to purchase one.

Nintendo's Tight Rein

Because of Nintendo's strict safeguards on software, many people in the industry doubted that there could be another shake-out on the scale of the one in 1983. Nobody ever considered that there could be a potential glut in hardware. However, with four incompatible systems in the marketplace, it was conceivable that an over-saturation might occur instead. But since Nintendo held such a tight rein on the market, the chances of it happening were very slim. The Sega, Atari and Intellivision consoles didn't sell in numbers that made third-party companies interested in them, so those companies didn't threaten to produce an overabundance of software.

However, despite Nintendo's stringent controls, there were ways to get around them. Licensees were getting more and more frustrated over Nintendo of America's rule that each vendor could only release a maximum of five NES titles a year. Acclaim Entertainment circumvented this rule by having its toy subsidiary, LJN, release games under its own label. Konami lobbied Nintendo of America to allow it to create a subsidiary in order to release additional games and Nintendo agreed. After Konami formed Ultra Games, two of its initial titles, *Metal Gear*, and *Teenage Mutant Ninja Turtles*, became among the top-selling games for the NES.

The only reason that Nintendo led the videogame race was because it had revived the industry, and had all of the major software titles behind it. Many critics insisted that the Sega Master System was slightly better than the NES in playability and graphics, but that didn't deter the majority of customers from buying an NES. As far as kids were concerned, peer pressure resulted in them purchasing an NES. How could a kid who owned a Sega expect to be popular when all of his friends had Nintendos? And to own an Atari was unthinkable! In fact, an entire new generation of videogame players didn't even know what Atari was. Sure, it was the company that made the neat games for the arcades; but for the home? Impossible!

What this new generation of gamers didn't realize was that Atari Corp. was a descendent of the company that had created the videogame industry in both the arcades *and* the home. In an effort to reestablish itself as a game company, Atari displayed only videogames at the summer CES. It tried to recapture its former glory by announcing that it had hired Nolan Bushnell to design new games for the 2600 and 7800. It also previewed 45 new titles for its three consoles.

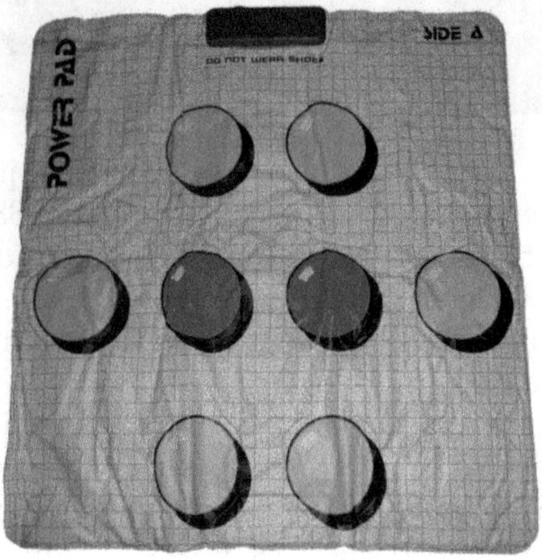

Nintendo Power Pad

If the announcement by Atari was supposed to scare Nintendo, it didn't work. Nintendo responded to the threat by buying the American rights to Bandai's *Family Trainer* pad and renaming it the *Power Pad*. It was then included in the *Power Set*, a $179.95 NES package that also included two controllers and a lightgun. *World Class Track Meet*, a track-and-field game that incorporated the Power Pad, *Duck Hunt*, and *Super Mario Bros*. were also included in the Power Set.

Nintendo announced that two more cartridges that used the Power Pad would be available by the time the new Power Set arrived in stores. It also promised that its new software would be compatible with the version of the Family Trainer pad that had been previously marketed by Bandai.

Nintendo NES Max

Another controller that Nintendo released was the *NES Max*. Like the NES Advantage that came out a year earlier, Nintendo released the NES Max only for the NES, and not the Famicom. And like the NES Advantage, the NES Max featured a pair of turbo buttons, although the speed of the turbo could not be adjusted.

The NES Max was approximately the size of a standard NES controller. Instead of a D-pad, the NES Max had a *cycloid*, which was basically a D-pad in the round that could be pressed in any direction. A moveable nub in the center of the cycloid was used for the player to rest his thumb on. He then aligned the nub to the part of the pad that he wanted to press, and could easily do so in a quick, fluid motion.

The NES Max also featured two grips along its bottom base, which theoretically made it easier to hold. This was a design feature that Nintendo would quickly abandon, but would revisit with successful results.

Despite the introduction of the NES Max, most players still preferred the standard NES controller. The gamepad was so popular that its design had been practically copied by Sega, which issued the similarly-designed Sega Joypad. Even Atari, the manufacturer of the iconic 2600 joystick, liked Nintendo's gamepad. When Atari released the 7800 in Europe, it did away with the Proline controller and replaced it with the *Atari Gamepad*. Atari's gamepad strongly resembled the Sega Joypad with a D-pad on the left and two control buttons on the right. And like the Sega Joypad, a tiny joystick could be screwed into the center of the D-pad. The Atari joystick, however, had a depressed top that allowed players to maneuver it with their thumb that could rest a top it.[1]

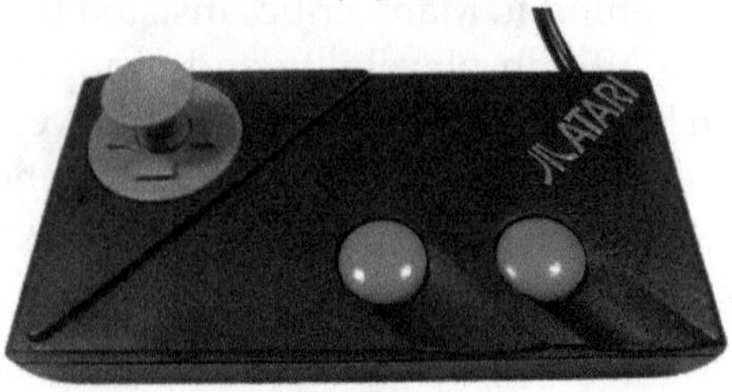

Atari Gamepad

Nintendo's huge share of the American market made it practically impossible for any other company to topple it. Since the competing consoles all had 8-bit processors, no console had a technological advantage over any other. The only thing that could scare Nintendo was a competing company's machine that was a vast improvement over the NES.

Games On CD

Beginning on April 8, NEC began releasing several peripherals for its PC Engine. The ¥3,500 ($28) *PC Engine AV Booster*, plugged into the back of the console, which only had an RF output, and supplied an audio/video output. Once the console was connected to a sound system, the stereo capabilities of the PC Engine could really appreciated, especially when NEC's *PC Engine Virtual Cushion*, a seat cushion with a built-in sub-woofer, was added.

NEC PC Engine AV Booster

Although the pad was the controller of choice for most consoles, NEC also released a joystick for the PC Engine. The *Turbo Stick* was NEC's version of the NES Advantage, complete with a large joystick on the left and turbo buttons on the right.

NEC PC Engine Turbo Stick

Surprisingly, the PC Engine only had one controller port, which only allowed for one gamer at a time. However, NEC released a *PC Engine MultiTap*, an adapter that supplied five controller ports. Once the MultiTap plugged into the console's single controller port, five controllers could then be plugged into it, allowing up to five people to play a single game at one time. NEC was the first company to offer such a device.[2] NEC provided another first when it released a mouse controller for the PC Engine, the first ever for a videogame console.

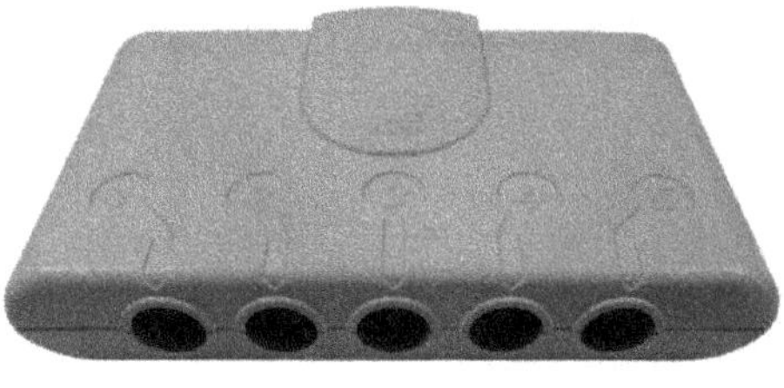

NEC PC Engine MultiTap

But it was the *PC Engine CD-ROM*^{2} that NEC released on April 12 that the PC Engine is best remembered for. While the ¥57,800 ($475) CD-ROM unit could also double as a stand-alone audio CD player, it had been designed specifically for videogame use. CDs were a great breakthrough in videogame technology. Prior to their introduction, the maximum amount of code that a game could utilize was 256K bytes. A compact disc could store 550 megabytes of data; or 2,000 times that of the most powerful cartridge. Since the CD could be accessed randomly and quickly, the PC Engine was able to load new information without the gamer being aware that such input was taking place. Because the disc was able to hold so much information, CD-based games offered the ultimate in complexity, detail and sound.

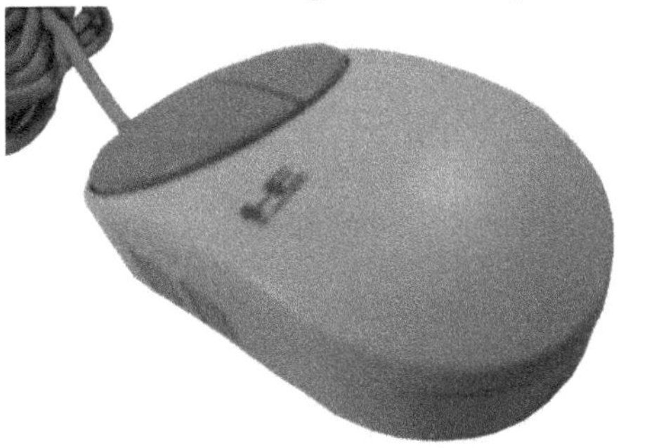

NEC PC Engine Mouse

The *PC Engine CD-ROM*^{2} connected to the console via an *Interface Unit*. The CD-ROM unit plugged into the left side of the Interface Unit and the PC Engine plugged into the right side through its expansion port. The Interface Unit included a cover and a handle that provided portability for the system inside. But the Interface Unit was more than

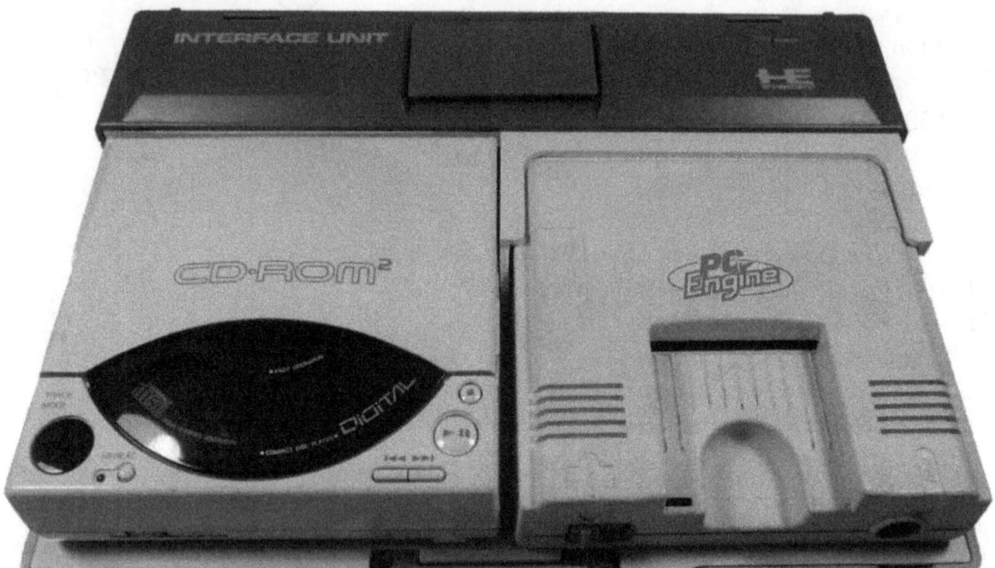

NEC PC Engine CD-ROM²

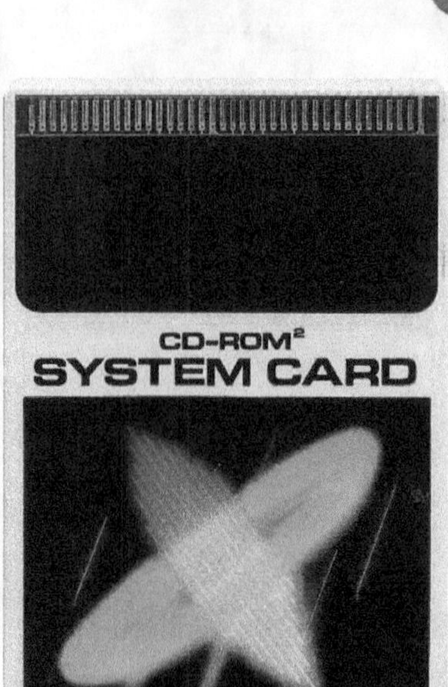

NEC PC Engine CD-ROM System Card

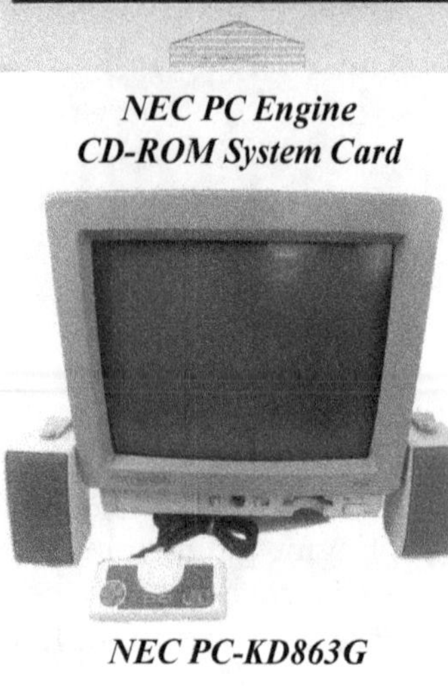

NEC PC-KD863G

something that just connected the PC Engine CD-ROM² to the PC Engine. Not only did it feature composite video and stereo output ports that eliminated the need for the PC Engine AV Booster, it also contained RAM that allowed games to be saved.[3]

The Interface Unit was originally sold separately from the CD-ROM player. This was done because Japan charged tariffs for audio devices but not computers, and the CD-ROM player was considered an audio device. In order to keep the price of the CD drive as low as possible, NEC opted to put all of its computer functionality into the separate Interface Unit, which would not be taxed.[4]

Once a PC Engine was connected to a PC Engine CD-ROM² unit, the HuCard port of the console was still needed. In order for the console to communicate with the CD-player, a special "System Card" was required. This card contained the necessary software that operated the CD Player, as well as additional cache memory that the console's CPU could access much faster than if it was stored in the console's normal RAM.

The PC Engine CD-ROM² wasn't the most expensive piece of hardware that NEC had to offer. On September 27, the company introduced its PC-KD863G. As Sharp had done with its My Computer TV C1, which was a TV set with a built-in Famicom, the ¥138,000 ($1,025) PC-KD863G was a computer monitor that housed a built-in PC Engine.[5]

The View-Master Interactive Vision

As NEC moved towards a software medium that supported random access and lots of storage, another

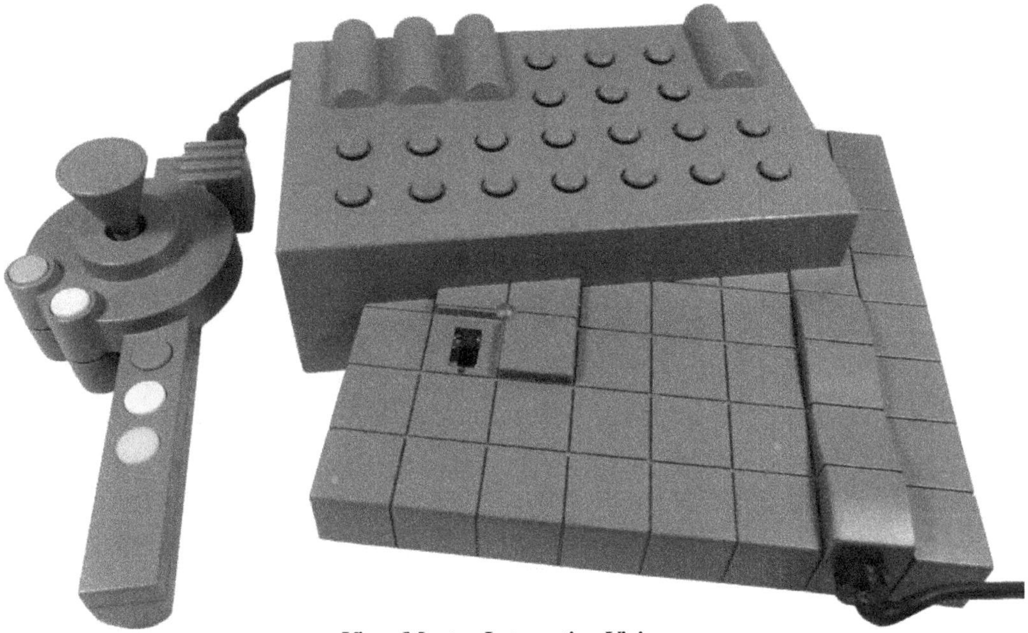

View-Master Interactive Vision

new tape-based system was introduced. But unlike Worlds of Wonder's Action Max and Takara's Video Challenger, which had both employed light guns for shooting onscreen targets provided by the videotape, the new *View-Master Interactive Vision* used videotapes to emphasize learning instead of violent action.

But there was a more important difference between the View-Master Interactive Vision and the videotape systems that preceded it. The Action Max and Video Challenger could not generate any computer images onto the screen. The videotapes for the View-Master Interactive Vision, on the other hand, had actual computer data encoded onto a track, that downloaded to the console while it played on a VCR. The result was a hybrid system that was a mix between a videotape game player and a true videogame console. While images from the videotape would always appear the same on repeated viewings, the games themselves were computer generated and therefore would differ on repeated plays. This was a huge advantage over the Action Max and Video Challenger, which would always be the same every time they were played.

But View-Master/Ideal even worked so that the portion from the videotape was not the same every time they were viewed. The tapes themselves featured two audio tracks, and the player selected which soundtrack would be used during the course of the play.

The View-Master Interactive Vision had been designed for children between the ages of three and eight. The unit utilized a controller that featured five color-coded buttons and a joystick, so children could highlight certain on-screen objects. Despite being named Game of the Year at one of the toy fairs where it was displayed, the system did not sell well at all. Thanks to poor marketing, few potential buyers even knew about it. And those who were aware of it refused to pay $130 for an educational product that only appealed to a very narrow target audience. Only seven tapes were released for the system, and all had been licensed by either Disney or *Sesame Street*.

Sega's Mega Drive

Sega of Japan released its 16-bit console on October 29. Initially, the system was going to be called the MK-1601, but this was changed to the *Mega Drive*, which represented the superiority and speed of the system's powerful Motorola 68000 processor. The Mega Drive also contained a Zilog Z80 processor, the brains inside the Mark III and Sega Master

Sega Mega Drive

System. The Z80 acted as a co-processor to the 68000. However, although the Mega Drive could technically play Sega's 8-bit games, the 8-bit cartridges weren't of the same design as the Mega Drive cartridges, and therefore couldn't be inserted into the 16-bit console. In addition, the Mega Drive had no place to insert the Sega My Cards or Sega My Card Mark IIIs.

Sega of America announced that it would release the 16-bit system in North America on January 9, 1989. Unsatisfied with how Tonka had distributed the Sega Master System, Sega tried to get Atari to distribute the console in the United States. However, the two companies couldn't agree on terms, so Sega of America decided to do it themselves.

Nintendo found itself one step behind Sega and NEC. Rumors circulated that Nintendo would announce its own 16-bit machine in November, but that month came and went without any news. Industry analysts felt that if Nintendo didn't come out with its own 16-bit system right away, it wouldn't have a chance in the upscale console market when it finally did decide to release one. Just like the NES had stolen the thunder from the other 8-bits because it had been the first of its kind, industry insiders speculated that the same principle would work against Nintendo in the 16-bit market.

Nintendo Famicom Tsūshin

Nintendo Goes Online

Nintendo of Japan's president, Hiroshi Yamauchi, wasn't immediately concerned with the 16-bit systems. Instead, he was looking into a way that would get adults interested in the Famicom as much as children already were. He wanted the Famicom to become a serious business device that adults would turn to daily. To this end, Nintendo of Japan released the $100 *Famicom Tsūshin*, a 2400-BPS modem that linked the Famicom to a standard telephone line. Once connected, users could access Nintendo's *Family Computer Network System*, an online service that promised to turn the Famicom into a terminal from which a number of online services could be accessed.

The Family Computer Network System, which was a joint project of Nintendo of Japan and Nippon Telegraph & Telephone (NTT), was similar to the online services that Control Video Corporation had planned for its Atari 2600-compatible Gameline. More than 300 banks signed up with the system and offered online banking services. Users could also subscribe to a securities-trading service run by Nomura Computing Center (NCC). And while games themselves were not offered on the Family Computer Network System, a *Super Mario Club* was formed, from which Nintendo of Japan distributors could access information about new Nintendo games for the Famicom.

Nintendo of America didn't have any immediate plans to bring the Family Computer Network System to the United States for the NES. Instead, its executives were preoccupied with a massive lawsuit that the arcade company Atari Games had filed against it.

Tengen

In 1987, after seeing the vast sums of money that could be made as a licensee of Nintendo, Atari Games had decided to enter the home-videogame business. The company had duly set up a subsidiary for this purpose. Since Atari Corp. already existed, Atari Games was barred from using the Atari name for the new company. Instead, they came up with a name for the new subsidiary that was also taken from the game *Go*. *Tengen* was a Japanese word that meant "the center point on a *Go* board". Tengen quickly became a Nintendo licensee, but was extremely unhappy with the terms of its contract, which only allowed it to release five games per year. And those titles had to be exclusive to the NES for two years. Tengen tried to change the terms of the license, and when that proved futile, the company reluctantly agreed to Nintendo's terms.

Tengen's agreement was made public, and throughout 1988, the company released three Nintendo-licensed titles: *Pac-Man*, *Gauntlet*, and *RBI Baseball*. Behind the scenes, however, the company was secretly looking for a way to bypass Nintendo's lockout chip

Tengen Vindicators & Box Note

Tengen Licensed & Unlicensed Cartridges

so it could produce its own software for the NES. Tengen's engineers were aware that the lockout chip could be disabled by zapping it with a volt of electricity. However, they were afraid that this might damage NES consoles and would subject them to lawsuits. They next decided to reverse-engineer the code inside the chip, but this proved fruitless.

Tengen's engineers realized that they would have to read the actual code that was used to program the lockout chip. Since Nintendo wouldn't provide this code, Tengen went to the United States Patent and Trademark Office, where a copy was on file. Tengen's lawyers told the Copyright Office that Nintendo was planning on suing them so they needed a copy of the code for the lawsuit. Surprisingly, the code was handed over without protest.

Once they read the code, Tengen's engineers fully understood what Nintendo's engineers had done, and they were able to write their own version of the lockout code. Once they had accomplished this, they were able to produce games for the NES that sidestepped their licensing agreement with Nintendo itself. By year's end, Tengen released *Vindicators*, its first non-licensed game for the NES. Most consumers were unaware of the change when they bought the game. Visually, the outside of the box for the non-licensed game looked very similar to the boxes for the three licensed Tengen games. However, in the lower-right corner, where the Nintendo Seal of Quality had appeared on each of the previous boxes, the *Vindicators* notice specifically read that the game was for the Nintendo NES and was not licensed by Nintendo.

What was inside the box was another story. When they opened it, gamers found a black cartridge that looked very different from the gray ones that the licensed games were housed in.

Tengen did, in fact, file a lawsuit against Nintendo, since its lawyers had cited that as the reason for which they'd needed the code from the Copyright Office. The $100-million lawsuit that the Atari Games subsidiary filed on December 12 charged that Nintendo held a monopoly over the game industry. After the lawsuit was filed, the public awaited a retaliatory move by Nintendo. The videogame giant remained quiet for the time being, anxious to let developments follow their own course and see where they led.

This battle that Atari Games waged against Nintendo for the right to manufacture its own home videogames was spurned by new confidence: the subsidiary had learned shortly beforehand that it now faced less competition in arcades: two leading coin-op companies had suddenly become only one. This was thanks to the July 10 purchase of Bally/Midway by WMS Industries, the parent company of Williams Electronics, Inc., one of the oldest arcade companies in existence.

A History of Williams

The company informally began in 1929 when Harry Williams purchased the franchise for a coin-operated game called *Jai Alai.* He founded the Automatic Amusement Company in 1932, after he designed his first game, *Advance,* which included the "tilt" feature that he'd invented. He followed this in 1933 with *Contact,* the first electrically powered pinball machine.

In 1935, Williams left the Automatic Amusement Company under the control of his father, and moved to Chicago, where he and his game-designing partner, Lyn Durrant, formed a new company called United Manufacturing. Williams left United Manufacturing in 1942 to start his own company, which he called the Williams Manufacturing Company.

During the fifties and sixties, the Williams Manufacturing Company was a leading pinball manufacturer, but it never became as popular as its leading competitor, Bally. The company changed its name again in 1958, this time to Williams Electronic Manufacturing Company.

In 1973, Williams Electronic Manufacturing followed the latest trend and released its first arcade videogame. *Paddle-Ball* was such a rip-off of *Pong* that even the cabinets were similar. *Paddle-Ball* was not a success and Williams Electronic Manufacturing stayed away from videogames until 1980, when it released *Defender,* which struck gold.

In 1974, when Williams Electronic Manufacturing diversified into different areas such as slot machines, lottery terminals, and hotels & casinos, a parent corporation called Williams Electronics, Inc. was formed. In 1987, in preparation for going public on the American Stock Exchange, the parent company changed its name to WMS Industries, Inc.

With the purchase of Bally/Midway, WMS Industries, Inc. became the world's leading manufacturer of arcade games. The company then used the Williams and Bally names exclusively for pinball machines and the Midway name for its arcade videogames.

Another company looking to diversify was Activision. In 1980, it had become the first manufacturer to produce third-party software for the Atari 2600. However, after four years of mounting losses that left it financially stricken, the company was ready to make changes. In January, 1987, the company's Board of Directors terminated founding CEO Jim Levy's employment and replaced him with Bruce Davis, who promised the Board that he would bring profitability back to the company. He made good on his promise six months into his tenure. By 1988, Activision had expanded and was ready to venture into business-application software. However, although the company experienced several minor successes, it couldn't release anything major and soon Activision, while technically profitable, was merely getting by. Davis felt that the Activision name was too associated with the games upon which the company was founded. And so in May he announced that the company was changing its name to *Mediagenic,* a move that most people associated with the company felt was stupid. Unfortunately, the company had factors going against it despite the name change. Shortly after the change, the Court rejected company's final appeal against the Magnavox lawsuit.[6]

The Return of Katz and Kunkel

On the print side, *ANALOG Computing* reappeared on the stands in April under new ownership. The new *Video Game Digest* column appeared for four months before the publishers of *ANALOG* decided to spin-off the column into a full-fledged magazine. *Videogames & Computer Entertainment,* which launched in November. Arnie Katz and Bill Kunkel, both of *Electronic Games* fame, were once again associated with a major videogame magazine.

Videogames & Computer Entertainment, as all magazines, depended upon advertising revenue in order to survive. In the case of videogame-related magazines, the majority of their income derived from NES licensees. Ironically, Nintendo itself didn't advertise in any of them. There were several reasons for this. The first was that by this time Nintendo

Video Games And Computer Entertainment

Nintendo Power

was so big that it didn't have to advertise. With a name that was quickly becoming synonymous with "game playing," there was no need for Nintendo to spend money on print advertising since its products were going to get covered anyhow. When Nintendo revealed new software titles at the CES shows twice a year, the magazines quickly mentioned them. CES was the only chance that the magazines writers had to preview the games, because Nintendo didn't send out advance review copies. On the other hand, the licensees hoped to have favorable reviews when their new titles were released so they were more than eager to send out advance copies.

But another reason why Nintendo didn't advertise in videogame magazines was because in August, Nintendo of America released its own magazine, which served as a liaison between the corporation and the gamers. *Nintendo Power* replaced the *Nintendo Fun Club News*, the free quarterly newsletter that had been initiated in 1987. *Nintendo Power* served two purposes. By making it available at newsstands, Nintendo of America expected to receive more exposure for its products than if the magazine continued to be available by subscription only. The company also generated revenue from the new magazine by having gamers pay for their copies instead of receiving them for free. Nintendo of America printed 3.6 million copies of the magazine's first issue, and a free copy was sent to all *Nintendo Fun Club* members, along with subscription offers.

Unfortunately, *Nintendo Power* was a little biased towards the games it reviewed. Unlike the magazines that didn't have manufacturers backing them, *Nintendo Power* viewed every Nintendo cartridge as if it were the greatest thing that had ever happened. Of course, *Nintendo Power* never mentioned the non-licensed NES games from Tengen.

Not all of the fledgling second-wave videogame magazines were successful. Steve Harris' *Electronic Game Player* failed to attract a national distributor, and ceased publication after its fourth issue. However, with the success of *Nintendo Power*, magazine distributors suddenly took notice of the potential of videogame magazines. Harvey Wasserman, a small magazine distributor from Chicago, offered Harris $70,000 to start up a new videogame magazine, for which Wasserman would have exclusive distribution rights. Harris took him up on his offer and began working on a new magazine.

The videogame market was alive and well, and appeared to be doing even better than it had done during its first heyday in 1982 and 1983. Nintendo of America had sold an estimated 11 million NES consoles in the three years since it had introduced the unit to North America. This was compared to the 30 million 2600s that Atari had sold in the ten years since that unit had been introduced.

The new era in videogames was expanding much more rapidly than anybody could have imagined. With the powerful 16-bit machines on sale in Japan, the foremost question on everybody's lips was: How long would it be before these consoles reached the United States?

CHAPTER SEVENTEEN
1989

When the 2600 ruled the videogame industry, many third-party companies tried to jump onto the bandwagon by releasing new peripherals for the console. In 1989, after the NES undeniably proved that it reigned, the past seemed to repeat itself as a new wave of third-party companies released new types of controllers for the leading game console. The first of these was unveiled to the public at the winter CES.

At first glance, LJN's *Roll & Rocker* appeared to be similar to Amiga's Joyboard, since both were plastic objects that had been designed for players to stand on. However, closer observation revealed that it wasn't a controller at all, even though it plugged into the controller port of the NES. A standard NES controller plugged directly into the Roll & Rocker, and its signals merely passed through the peripheral to the console. All the Roll & Rocker did was allow gamers to bobble in all directions, courtesy of its rounded bottom.

LJN Roll & Rocker

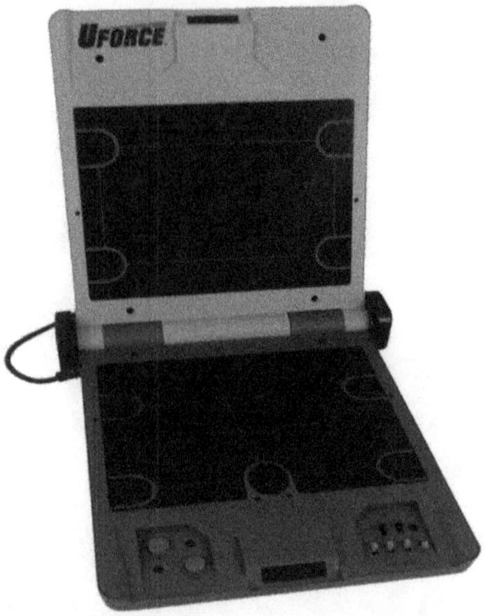

Broderbund U-Force

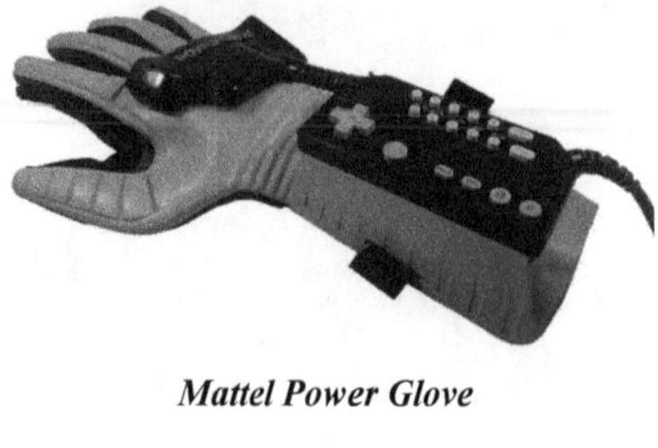

Mattel Power Glove

Innovative Controllers

The *U-Force* that Broderbund displayed at CES was a controller, though most attendees had a hard time recognizing it as one. Broderbund publicized it as a "Force-Field Controller" because it could detect the motion, velocity and direction of a gamer's hands as they were waved in front of the unit. This meant that the U-Force allowed gamers to control the on-screen action without having to hold anything in their hands. The U-Force recognized movements of the hands and sent translated signals to the NES, which duplicated the actions on the screen. It worked best in boxing games like *Mike Tyson's Punch-Out*, where an on-screen boxer instantly imitated the punches that the gamer had made in the air. For other games, a series of switches on the U-Force allowed gamers to configure it to fit their needs. The unit also included a T-bar that screwed into its base, so players would feel more comfortable using the U-Force with driving and flying games.

Broderbund planned to release the $69.95 U-Force in May. The company expected to sell between 500,000 and 750,000 before the end of the year.

Shortly following the U-Force's introduction, Mattel reemerged from videogaming isolation and released a controller that was very similar to Broderbund's remarkable innovation. The *Power Glove*, as its name implied, fit over a player's right hand (sorry, lefties) and controlled the on-screen action by the movements of the player's arm and hand.

Both controllers had taken years to develop, so it was totally a coincidence that Broderbund and Mattel released similar "hands-off" devices within a few months of one another. As it turned out, the Power Glove had been designed by VPL Labs for NASA, which had needed the technology to repair satellites out in space. The astronaut's hand movements inside the glove would send signals to a remote device that caused a robotic hand to move in the same manner. VPL Labs eventually licensed the glove to Abrams/ Gentile Entertainments, which then negotiated with Mattel to develop applications to bring the glove into the home.

Before the Power Glove could work, the gamer had to place a sensor device, which connected to the NES, atop the television set. This device monitored independent sensors inside the glove and determined the action that the gamer was undertaking. However, before a game could be played, the gamer had to input instructions into the glove that told the sensor device what every movement meant. A keypad containing its own microprocessor was attached to the glove for this purpose. Once the sensor device could understand what the individual movements meant, it forwarded this information to the NES, just like any other standard controller.

Because many games used different types of controls, Mattel programmed 15 different templates into the Power Glove. The company also released games that were specifically designed to use with the device. *Glove Ball*, for example, was a three-dimensional cross between *Handball* and *Breakout*. The player had to hit a ball into a wall of tiles and break the wall apart before he could advance to the next room. Instead of using an on-screen paddle, the player had to "hit" empty air with his open palm, as if a ball were coming at him.

Nintendo Goes Wireless

Nintendo itself experimented with wireless technology. Its *NES Satellite* permitted four people to play simultaneously even though the NES only had two controller ports. The NES Satellite had four controller ports and interacted with the NES console by sending infrared signals to a receiver that plugged into the two controller ports in the console. The only drawback was that the unit had to be in direct sight of the receiver in order for it to work. Although less than two dozen games were available for four-person play, many people used the NES Satellite just so they could play their NES without any wires.

The NES was not only popular with the third-party gaming companies. A new Saturday-morning cartoon show was developed that featured characters from hit Nintendo games. The *Super Mario Bros. Power Hour* featured both live action and animation. The live segments starred Mario and Luigi while the animated parts also featured Link, a character from another best-selling game, *The Legend of Zelda*.

As the NES's popularity increased, Nintendo of America sought new ways for it to capture an even larger share of the gaming marketplace.

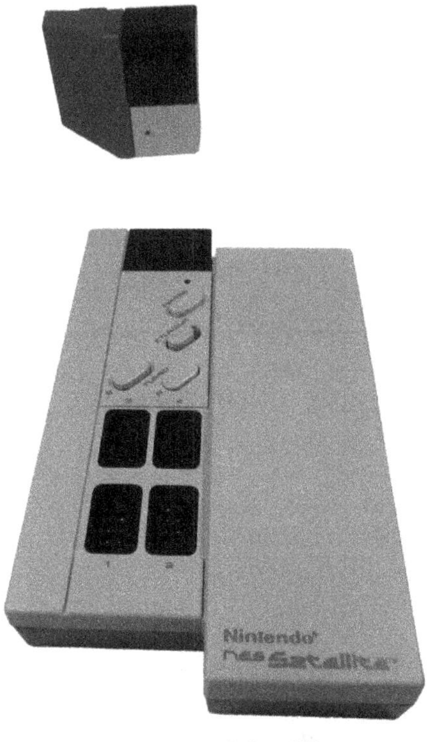

Nintendo NES Satellite

The company announced in August the formation of the *NES Network*, an American version of the Family Computer Network System that had been launched in Japan a year earlier for Famicom users. Like its Japanese counterpart, the new online service would allow people to trade stocks and perform home banking via their NES control deck and a modem. Nintendo of America expected the network to go live sometime in 1990, and anticipated that ten million homes would be connected to it by 1991.

In September, Nintendo of America and AT&T announced plans to form a joint venture to produce and deliver shopping, entertainment and information services. This was followed in October with the announcement that Nintendo of America and Fidelity Investments, the largest privately held investment manager in the United States, had begun a joint venture to make the NES Network a reality. Fidelity agreed to develop software that would give NES owners access to a number of financial services.

Unfortunately, the NES Network never materialized. Market research revealed that only about 7% of NES owners also had an account with a brokerage firm, and most of those who did already used their firm's own network for online trading. Nintendo of America tried to shift gears and have the NES Network offer services that provided chat groups and email, along with Nintendo game reviews and previews. Unfortunately, this wasn't a serious consideration for the company and the NES Network was shelved before it even got off the ground.

Nintendo of Japan's Family Computer Network System didn't fare much better, despite actually being in operation. Although millions of Famicoms were in use in Japanese households, the service only attracted 130,000 subscribers. While no one at Nintendo of Japan could state exactly why the system had failed, most critics speculated that the speed of the service was just too slow to make it practical for everyday use. Additionally, subscribers didn't like the inconvenience of their telephones being tied up in order for the service to work. Despite Hiroshi Yamauchi's hopes for the Family Computer Network System, the service only lasted about a year.

Unlicensed NES Games

While Nintendo of America tried to build its image so it could get the NES into more households, its competitors attempted to portray it as an evil monopoly that had built its huge empire at the expense of others. Atari Corp., the manufacturer of the 2600, filed a $250 million anti-monopoly suit against Nintendo. Atari charged that Nintendo had prevented its licensees from making their NES games available for other videogame consoles. Nintendo called the charge "absurd" and said that Atari was merely looking for an excuse "for its poor competitive performance" in the marketplace.

Meanwhile, Atari Games, which had filed its own anti-monopoly suit against Nintendo at the end of 1988, announced in early January that its software subsidiary, Tengen, had terminated its licensing agreement with Nintendo. Since Tengen had found a way to bypass Nintendo's lock-out chip, it was free to manufacture cartridges on its own, and therefore no longer needed to submit to Nintendo's outrageous policies.

Tengen wasn't alone when it came to manufacturing and distributing its own NES-compatible software. Color Dreams, which had been established in 1988, had succeeded in reverse-engineering the NES and discovered how to work around the lock-out chip without disabling it. The company released its first game, *Baby Boomer*, and because Color Dreams didn't have to pay Nintendo any licensing, manufacturing and distributing fees, it was able to sell its games for approximately ten dollars less than what the licensees usually charged for their games. Consumers learned pretty early that the games weren't necessarily bargains. Apparently, Color Dreams' labors to bypass the lock-out chip hadn't been completely successful and many consumers found that their Color Dreams games had trouble playing on their NES consoles. In many cases, they would have to restart their systems multiple times before any of the games could actually play.

Because the method that Color Dreams used to bypass the lock-out chip was perfectly legal, Nintendo couldn't prevent them from producing unlicensed NES-compatible cartridges. Tengen was another story.

Nintendo didn't respond to Tengen's licensee termination immediately. It finally fought back in November with a countersuit. Nintendo charged Tengen with breach of contract for severing its license, and copyright infringement for using Nintendo's own code to disable the lock-out chip.

In addition to the legal lawsuit that it filed against Tengen, Nintendo also resorted to illegal strong-arm tactics itself. The company warned many of its retailers that it would hold their shipments if they decided to stock Tengen's games. Most retailers who received this warning complied with Nintendo's threats, since their businesses would have been devastated if they couldn't sell Nintendo's products.

Tengen was permitted to keep selling its unlicensed games while the suit was pending.[1] Tengen released twelve unlicensed NES games throughout the year including unlicensed reissues of its three original games, *Pac-Man, Gauntlet,* and *RBI Baseball.* The final game that Tengen released in 1989 spurred yet another lawsuit from Nintendo.

In 1989, Nintendo and Tengen both released versions of an enormously popular, addictive Russian game called *Tetris*.[2] Both companies believed that they had exclusive rights to the game. Although Tengen didn't legally own any rights to the console version of the game, it tried to argue that Nintendo shouldn't have been allowed to release the game for the Famicom, since Nintendo didn't own the computer rights to *Tetris,* and it publicized the Famicom as a computer. But the judge didn't see it that way.[3] Tengen was ordered to recall all of its *Tetris* cartridges that were still on store shelves. In all, 268,000 cartridges were returned and destroyed, which made each surviving cartridge a collectible like Odyssey's *K.C. Munchkin.* Nintendo also tried to recover lost revenue, but Tengen appealed and the case dragged on in court.

Many considered Tengen's *Tetris* to be the superior of the two. Nintendo's choice of colors was confusing, and players couldn't distinguish between a dark blue block and a dark blue opening. This confusion didn't exist in the Tengen edition, which also included a two-player competition mode, in which two boards were displayed simultaneously. Nintendo's *Tetris* allowed two gamers to compete, but they had to take alternating turns. Even though the Tengen version was better by all accounts, it was the Nintendo version that had the Nintendo Seal of Quality on its box.

The fundamental purpose of the Seal of Quality had been to alert consumers that the game had been approved by Nintendo, in an effort to prevent poor quality or similar games from saturating the market. Unfortunately, by 1989 it was apparent that Nintendo's Seal of Quality no longer served that purpose. All games that were released by Nintendo and its licensees carried the Seal of Quality, whether they were good or not. And even Nintendo's reasoning behind its practice of licensing third-party companies no longer appeared to be true. Nintendo had always claimed that it licensed titles from the third-party vendors so that it could control the amount of product that was released to the marketplace, in order to prevent the conditions that had led to the crash of 1983. However, by 1989, Nintendo had over 40 licensees, and each was permitted to release two titles a year. Nintendo executives seemed unconcerned about whether or not retailers had shelf space for all those titles. Since Nintendo profited on every game that was sold, it didn't seem to matter which third-party titles got exposure and which didn't. However, for the small third-party companies that depended on the sales of their one or two titles to survive, the large number of games being released yearly for the NES was something for them to worry about.

Retailers were also concerned about the large number of NES games that were being released, since they couldn't stock them all. In addition, they also had to make room for software for the competing systems, such as the Sega Master System and the Atari 2600 and 7800, as well as new consoles that were being released.

The Genesis

Sega failed to release its 16-bit Mega Drive system in North America on January 9, as it had publicized. Later, while displaying the console at the summer CES, Sega announced that the system would be released in the fall. However, because the Mega Drive name was already being used in North America, Sega of America chose to call the new console the *Genesis*.

Although the Genesis that Sega displayed at CES looked exactly like Sega of Japan's Mega Drive, the Genesis could not accept Mega Drive cartridges.[4] Sega of America announced that it was working with 20 third-party publishers to develop games for the Genesis.

Sega Genesis

Sega Genesis with Power Base Converter

Sega also previewed the *TeleGenesis*, a modem for the console, which Sega didn't expect to hit store shelves until late 1989 or early 1990. Using the modem, players could compete against one another via the phone lines, a feature that Nintendo's Family Computer Network System didn't offer. The company also hinted about a keyboard adapter that would turn the Genesis into a home computer.

Sega released the $200 Genesis in New York and Los Angeles on August 14, 1989, and a month later in the rest of the country. The console came complete with one game cartridge, *Altered Beast*, and one controller. A second controller could be purchased separately for $20. Consumers generally were pleased with the console's speed, high resolution, and crisp stereo sound.

Sega released its first peripheral for the Genesis in October. The *Power Base Converter* allowed the Genesis to play the Sega Master System's 8-bit software. Although the games didn't look or play any better on the Genesis, Sega Master System owners at least had the option to upgrade their consoles without having to sacrifice any of their software.

The Power Base Converter plugged into the Genesis' cartridge slot and sat atop the console. It featured its own cartridge slot that accepted the Sega 8-bit cartridges, and another that accepted Sega Cards. The Power Base Converter did not feature any built-in Sega Master System components. When an 8-bit cartridge or Sega Card was inserted into the Power Base Converter, the data passed through the latter, and the Genesis' Z80 processor did all of the work. If an 8-bit cartridge or card was not inserted into the Power Base Converter, then the Genesis' 16-bit 68000 maintained control of the system.

The Power Base Converter was released in North America roughly nine months after it debuted in Japan on January 26. The ¥4,500 ($31.38) *Mega Adapter* had been designed so the 16-bit Mega Drive could play the cartridges and Sega My Card/Sega My Card Mark IIIs that were available for Sega's 8-bit systems.

The TurboGrafx-16

NEC America followed in Sega of America's footsteps, and released an unannounced American version of the PC Engine in New York and Los Angeles on August 29. The new

NEC TurboGrafx-16

American console was called the *TurboGrafx-16*, which emphasized the system's graphics capability.[5] However, like its Japanese counterpart, the TurboGrafx-16 was really an 8-bit system with a 16-bit graphics processor.

The TurboGrafx-16 was twice as wide as the PC Engine because it needed additional electronics for FCC approval. However, the CPUs within the two consoles were the same. Although games for the TurboGrafx-16 also came on HuCards, which were called *TurboChips*, the TurboGrafx-16 games and PC Engine games were not interchangeable. The TurboGrafx-16 was sold with a game called *Keith Courage In Alpha Zones*, and one controller, a *TurboPad*, that was similar to the PC Engine controller pad, with the addition of two turbo buttons. NEC America also released a *TurboStick* separately for the TurboGrafx-16. This was the same as the PC Engine's Turbo Stick with a slightly different appearance. NEC America also released a *Turbotap*, which was the same as the PC Engine's MultiTap.

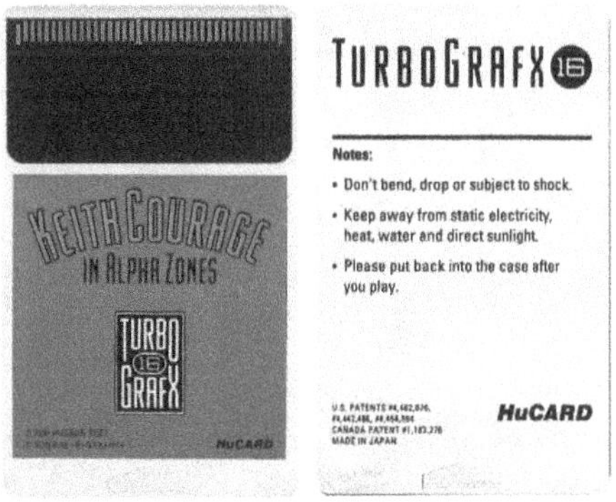

NEC TurboGrafx-16 TurboChip

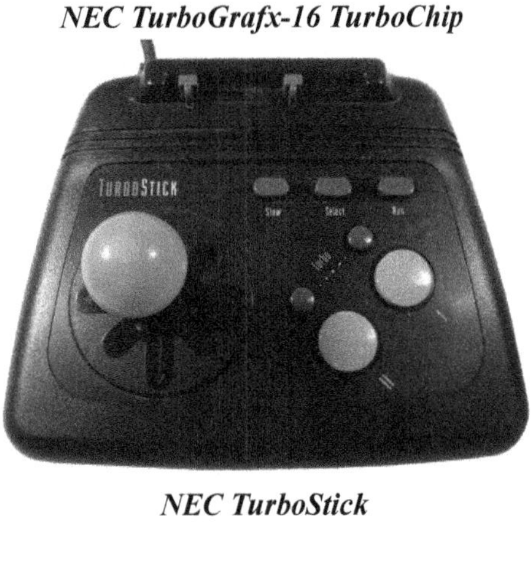

NEC TurboStick

Like the PC Engine, an expansion port was located on the rear of the TurboGrafx-16, and a wide plastic dust cover was used to cover the post when it wasn't being used. One peripheral that used the port was the *TurboBooster*, the equivalent of the PC Engine AV Booster.[6] However, the TurboBooster was twice as wide as the PC Engine

NEC TurboBooster

AV Booster so the entire console could slide into it.

NEC America wasn't as concerned about appearances with the *TurboGrafx-CD*, the American version of the PC Engine CD-ROM^2. This device, which was priced at $400 and didn't come with a game, but unlike the non-compatible HuCards, Japanese CD games could play on it.

NEC TurboGrafx-16 & TurboGrafx-CD

PC Engine Peripherals

The PC Engine Virtual Cushion and PC Engine Mouse weren't released for the TurboGrafx-16 and on September 29 were joined by additional PC Engine-only peripherals. The ¥24,800 ($178) *Print Booster* was actually a printer for the PC Engine. When used with the ¥9,800 ($70) *Illust Booster* drawing tablet and the ¥5,800 ($40) *Artist Tool* software, colorful drawings could be designed on the PC Engine and then printed out. An optional ¥5,000 ($36) *Photo Reader* could also be used in conjunction with the *Print Booster* to scan external photos.

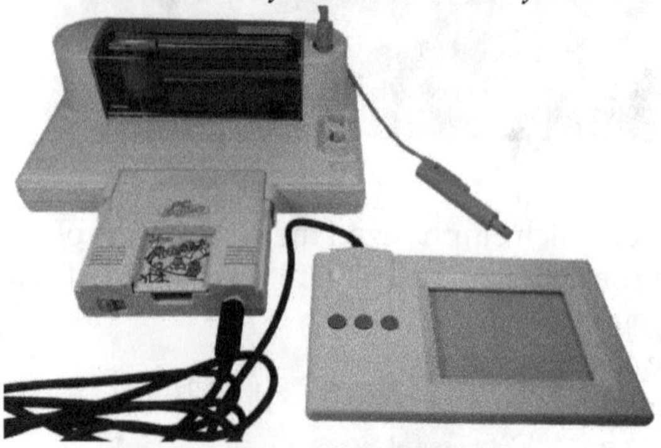

NEC PC Engine with Print Booster,
Illust Booster & Photo Reader

On August 8, Hudson Soft, the developer of the PC Engine, released a ¥2,600 ($19) peripheral that it called the *Tennokoe 2*. This unit plugged into the expansion port at the back of the PC Engine and gave users the ability to save games without the need of the expensive Interface Unit.[7] Two AA batteries were required to retain the saved information in memory. However, there were two catches. One was that the games themselves could only be saved if they had instructions in their code that specifically allowed them to be saved to the device.[8]

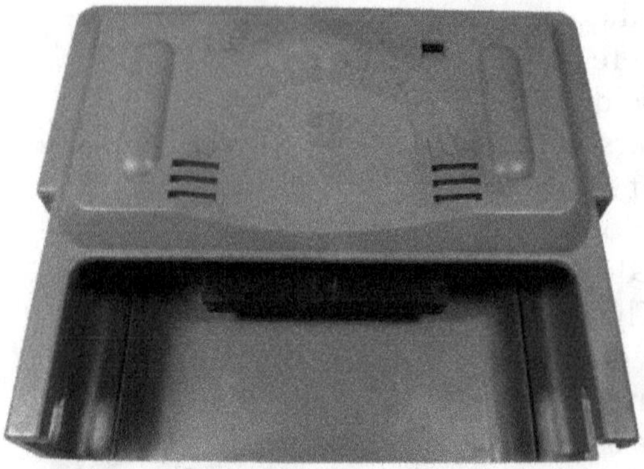

Hudson Soft Tennokoe 2

The other catch was that the saved games could not be viewed via composite video since the Tennokoe 2 plugged into the same expansion port that the AV Booster plugged into. NEC alleviated this problem in November when it released the *Backup Booster*. This unit looked and operated very much like the Tennokoe 2 except that it had the added advantage of having a composite video output.

The PC Engine Prospers

The PC Engine was so popular that NEC released several new Japanese models. These new consoles were all gray colored, unlike the white of the original PC Engines. On the low end of the retail scale at was the ¥18,800 ($130) *Shuttle*, a unit that derived its name from the fact that it looked like a spaceship. Released on November 22, the Shuttle was compatible with all of the HuCards but couldn't play any of the CD-based games.

NEC released two more consoles on December 8. The ¥24,800 ($172) *CoreGrafx* was basically a PC Engine that connected directly to a video monitor via composite audio-video cables rather than the standard RF modulator, without the need of the AV Booster. The unit also came with a new controller that included turbo buttons. The unit was also cosmetically different than the PC Engine as it had a circular indentation along its top that made it resemble a CD player.

NEC PC Engine Shuttle

At the top of the line was the ¥39,800 ($275) *SuperGrafx*. Originally called the *PC Engine 2*, this console featured 32K of RAM, four times the amount of memory that had been supplied in NEC's two other new consoles. This extra memory allowed the SuperGrafx to move 128 figures simultaneously on the screen. The SuperGrafx was also capable of providing twice as many background visuals than a standard PC Engine game, which gave it the ability to create 3D effects. Although the SuperGrafx could play all of the existing PC Engine games,[9] only games on special SuperGrafx HuCards could take advantage of the new features. However, these games could not be played on the PC Engine, Shuttle and CoreGrafx.

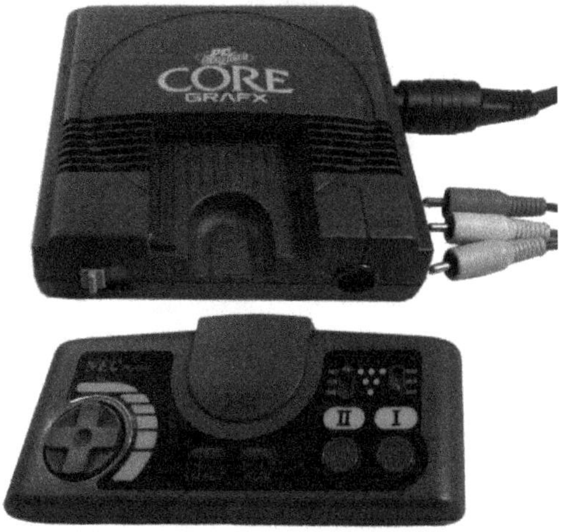

NEC PC Engine CoreGrafx

1989

In addition to the CoreGrafx and SuperGrafx machines, NEC also released the *Backup Booster II*. This unit was similar to the *Backup Booster* that had been released a month earlier, but the composite video output was removed, since both of the machines had built-in AV outputs anyway.[10] NEC also replaced the need for AA batteries by including an internal rechargeable nicad battery that was powered by the console.

NEC PC Engine SuperGrafx

The popularity of the PC Engine forced Nintendo to take notice. As long their 8-bit machine continued to outsell its competition, Nintendo executives had little interest in looking into a 16-bit console. But while the NES continued to outsell the Genesis and the TurboGrafx-16 in the United States, the story was not the same in Japan. Sega only sold 400,000 Mega Drives during the console's first year and didn't make much of a dent in the Famicom's sales. But by April, NEC had sold 1.5 million PC Engines in Japan, which amounted to approximately half of all the videogame-console sales in that country. This forced Nintendo to question if its 8-bit console's days were indeed numbered.

Unbeknownst to the public, Nintendo's president, Hiroshi Yamauchi, had assigned his Research & Development #2 team, the group that had been responsible for the Famicom, with the responsibility of designing a 16-bit system that would blow away the competition.

The Konix Multi-System

British-based Konix, a manufacturer of computer controllers, also tried to market its own 16-bit system. Its *Multi-System* was designed around the belief that the controller was the most important part of a videogame console. This resulted with a unit that almost resembled the ColecoVision Expansion Module #2. The Multi-System was small, with a large steering wheel built into it. Gamers could also add a manual stick shift and a foot pad to really simulate driving a car. The wheel itself was detachable and could be replaced by handlebars for motorcycle games. Additional controllers were also designed for the system. One was a light gun with attachments that turned it into a light rifle that even recoiled when fired. The most expensive controller, retailing for $375, was a chair that moved in different directions, so that the person sitting in it felt like he was actually piloting a plane or ship. The Multi-System mounted into the chair so it moved along with the player.

Konix Multi-System

Konix displayed the Multi-System and its peripherals at a London toy fair in February, and expected to get the unit into British stores by the end of August, with nearly 40 games available in time for Christmas from prestigious software companies such as Electronic Arts. The company also hoped to distribute it in the United States by early 1990, where it would retail at around $300. Instead of cartridges, the console had been designed to utilize 3½ inch discs to store data, because they were less expensive to produce. Each disc would retail for $25 and contained one megabyte of code. Konix even had discussions with both Mattel and Disney about distributing the console in North America, but nothing came out of those talks. Lucasfilm was mentioned as being a software developer for the system, and a potential manufacturer of the American version.

Unfortunately, the machine developed problems early. Its release date was first changed to October but then it was pushed back to early 1990. The software developers who had signed on had to stop, because they couldn't proceed any further without a completed console to work with. The truth of the matter was that Konix was running out of capital. In order to keep the project alive, the company sold its joystick line to a competitor, Spectravision, and pushed the console's release date back again, this time to late 1990.[11]

Control-Vision

Another project that suffered from a lack of funding was *Project Nemo*, a videotape-based videogame console conceived in 1985 by Tom Zito of Nolan Bushnell's company, Axlon. Zito had been a film major at New York University before he became Axlon's Vice President of Marketing. Zito's idea was to create interactive games combined with video footage. However, Zito's approach was closer to the path that Viewmaster took with its View-Master Interactive Vision than what Worlds of Wonder did with the Action Max. His idea was to have the computer create images over the background, which in the case of Project Nemo, would be a live-action movie.

After the project was approved by Bushnell, Zito assembled a team of videogame dignitaries, which included Steve Russell, the designer of *Spacewar*, David Crane, one of the four co-founding programmers of Activision and Rob Fulop, a co-founding programmer of Imagic.

Zito calculated that they would need $7 million to finance the project. Unfortunately, this was an amount that Axlon simply didn't have. Hasbro, the world's largest toy company,[12] which, until that point, had stayed away from videogames, stepped in with the needed funding in exchange for the exclusive rights to manufacture and distribute the final console, which was eventually called the *Control-Vision*.

Axlon developed a compression routine, wherein five full-motion video tracks and sixteen digital audio tracks could be crammed together on one videotape without any loss of quality. The system could also switch back and forth between the 21 tracks instantaneously. In addition to the video and audio, the videotape would also contain the program code. Hasbro claimed that the new system would be a cross between a movie and a videogame. Two movie/games, *Night Trap* and *Sewer Shark*, were produced at a cost of $4.5 million, and more games were scheduled to follow.

Hasbro had intended to market the Control-Vision directly against the NES. The $200 system was scheduled to appear on store shelves in early 1989, and retailers had pre-ordered 250,000 units. Unfortunately, a sudden demand for Video RAM (VRAM), which the Control-Vision used extensively, caused the price of the chips to jump from $30 to $80, which increased the wholesale price of the console from $105 to $155. Few retailers were willing to purchase the console at the higher price, which would have resulted in a higher retail price that potential customers would have balked at. Rather than selling the consoles at a loss to the retailers, Hasbro simply scrapped the project altogether.[13]

The Game Boy

While rival companies began developing 16-bit consoles, Nintendo released a new 8-bit system. This system had not been designed to compete against the new consoles, nor was it created to replace the aging Famicom.

Nintendo Game Boy

As early as 1987, Gunpei Yokoi worked on a product that combined the best features of the Famicom with the portability of his earlier Game & Watch handhelds. For two years Yokoi secretly worked on this project with his Research & Development #1 team, which Nintendo president Hiroshi Yamauchi believed would sell over 25 million units during its first three years, beginning in 1989.

Ironically, Yokoi was not the only person interested in creating a successful handheld console. Chris Stamper, co-founder of the software company Rare, Ltd., built a prototype of a handheld system that accepted NES cartridges. Believing that he had a hit product on his hands, he showed it to Minoru Arakawa and Howard Lincoln of Nintendo of America, who advised him to abandon his project since Nintendo was working on a handheld system of its own.

However, Stamper was not the only game designer who was working on a handheld gaming system. In 1986, two former Amiga programmers, RJ Mical and Dave Needle, began planning and designing a handheld system based around the workhorse 6502 chip. Unfortunately, the two men didn't have the capital needed to fund such a project, so they sought a videogame company that might be interested in it. The software company Epyx bought it from Needle and Mical in exchange for positions at Epyx and stock.

Epyx worked on the *Handy Game* project throughout 1987 and 1988. However, when the device was finally completed, Epyx began experiencing financial problems of its own. The company's CEO, David Morse came to the realization that the only way they could bring the Handy Game to market was by getting financial backing from another company. Morse and Needle made an impromptu visit to Nintendo's headquarters in Japan to make a pitch to sell their portable console. Nintendo's representatives showed little interest in the Handy Man. Instead, they brought out a pair of boxes, each containing a handheld videogame console. The Epyx contingent was the first group outside of Nintendo to sample the *Game Boy*.

The Game Boy was approximately the size of a Sony Walkman, hence its name. In fact, the Game Boy resembled the Walkman so much that Sony's head of R&D chastised his team for not developing the portable videogame console themselves.

The Game Boy featured a 2.6" LCD screen and interchangeable game cartridges. Its grey and green graphics were of a high enough resolution to allow for scrolling backgrounds. Built-into the console below the screen were the same buttons found on the Famicom's controller, a D-pad, "A" and "B" buttons and a "select" and "start" button.

Nintendo of Japan released the ¥12,500 ($95) Game Boy on April 21 and within two weeks all 300,000 available units had sold out. Four games were available at launch, *Super Mario Land*, a *Breakout* variant called *Alleyway*, *Baseball*, and a Mahjong-type game called *Yakuman* The games were provided on small gray cartridges called "Game Paks."

Nintendo Game Boy Launch Titles

The Game Boy featured real digital stereo sound, but the single speaker built-into the unit only produced monaural sound. Earphones that were packaged with the unit reproduced the sound in true stereo, and allowed gamers to play anywhere without disturbing those around them. Also included was a "Video Link" that allowed two players to connect their individual Game Boy consoles and compete head-to-head against one another. The only catch was that both players would also have to own a copy of the particular game. *Yakuman* was the only launch title that used the Link feature.

But that changed quickly. Nintendo of Japan released *Tennis* on May 29 and *Tetris* on June 14 and both used the Link feature. This version of *Tetris* featured an option not available in any other versions of the game. When it was used with the Video Link, the portable *Tetris* allowed two players to compete against each other on the same board at the same time.

Nintendo of America released the Game Boy on July 31 for $90, which included a copy of *Tetris*. With the exception of *Yakuman*, which was never released outside of Japan, the four other titles that were already available in Japan, were launched in North America with the console. Nintendo of America sold 40,000 Game Boy's on its first day.

Although the Game Boy was an undisputed success, people naturally found fault in it. The screen was too tiny to display the type of detail that players were accustomed to on the Famicom/NES. And because it was a portable system, many people strained their eyes by playing with the screen too close. And the biggest complaint about the Game Boy was the fact that it wasn't backlit. It had to be played in sunlight or in a bright room. Once under these conditions, the player had to struggle with the unit so that he could get enough light but not any glare.

The Atari Lynx

Approximately one month after Nintendo released the Game Boy in Japan, Atari displayed its forthcoming *Portable Color Entertainment System* at the summer CES. This was actually the Handy Game that Epyx had attempted to sell to Nintendo. After Nintendo had turned down the offer because they already had the Game Boy in development, Epyx approached Atari, which decided to go with it. The two companies signed an agreement where Atari would manufacture and distribute the hardware and Epyx would develop the software. Atari would then pay Epyx for each game that the latter produced. However, part of the contract contained a clause that specified that Epyx had 60 days to correct any bugs that Atari uncovered. Atari waited until near the end of this period to supply Epyx with a list of bugs it had found. Because Epyx couldn't repair these bugs within the time frame specified in the contract, Atari held back the payment that it owed Epyx, leading Epyx into further financial ruin, and eventually bankruptcy. At that point Atari agreed to pay Epyx only if Epyx turned over the full rights to the Handy Man to Atari. Epyx had no choice but to agree.

The Portable Color Entertainment System improved on the Game Boy in several ways. It featured a color screen that, when measured diagonally, was nearly an inch larger than the Game Boy's monochrome screen. This decreased the chances of eyestrain. And since the screen was backlit, the games could even be played in total darkness.

While both units were rectangular-shaped, the two didn't resemble each other at all. The Game Boy looked like a vertical rectangle, with the screen on the top and the controls directly below it. The Atari unit looked like a horizontal rectangle with the screen in the direct center. A controller pad was set on the left side of the screen, and two sets of A and B buttons were on the right. However, the unit could also rotated 180 degrees so the buttons were on the left and the controller pad was on the right, so "righties" didn't have an advantage over "lefties".

The two systems were also similar as they both could be linked together for cooperative fun. However, while the Game Boy could be linked to only one other Game Boy, the Atari Portable Color Entertainment System could connect with up to eight other units.

The Game Boy weighed 10.6 ounces and required four "AA" batteries. The system could operate on electricity, but a power adapter was optional. In comparison, the Atari

Atari Lynx

system weighed one pound, and because of its larger color screen, it needed six "AA" batteries. However, Atari planned to include a free AC adapter with each $189 unit.

In August, Atari and Epyx sponsored a three-day developer's conference to demonstrate the capabilities of the system, which by then was officially called the *Lynx*. More than 100 developers and third-party publishers attended, and many of them signed agreements with Atari and Epyx to develop software for the system. As an added bonus to Atari, many of these companies also displayed an interest in the 7800.

Atari released a small number of Lynxes in New York and Los Angeles on September 21. Unfortunately, delays prevented the company from shipping the portable system in large numbers to the rest of the country, and this forced shortages everywhere. Due to these delays, Atari postponed the Lynx's national distribution until the spring of 1990, which allowed the Game Boy to become the unchallenged sales leader in handheld consoles for the 1989 Christmas season.

New Magazines

With so many systems and games to choose from, videogame consumers in 1989 had a harder choice to make than their counterparts of 1983. To help them, several new magazines arrived on the newsstands in the wake of *Videogames & Computer Entertainment*'s success. The first arrived in March. *Electronic Gaming Monthly*, which focused on new releases, was the new magazine that Steve Harris had published with Harvey Wasserman's seed money. *Game Players*, a general videogame magazine, followed in April. Finqally, *GamePro*, which specialized in game reviews, became available in May.

Electronic Gaming Monthly

Gamepro

As the eighties came to a close, gamers looked towards the nineties with anticipation. When the decade had begun, Atari had been riding high, and Mattel was trying to make a name of itself with its advanced system. Nintendo and Sega were only known to Americans as Japanese arcade-game developers. It was a decade of lows and highs for an industry that at first people referred to as a fad.

As technology advanced at an alarming speed, people could only wonder what kinds of games they would be playing at the end of the nineties.

CHAPTER EIGHTEEN
1990

In 1989, sales of videogame consoles and cartridges totaled $3.4 billion; and that was just in the United States, where Nintendo controlled 80% of the market. Unfortunately for the competition, there appeared to be no stopping Nintendo. And even though their 8-bit consoles were technically inferior to the new systems that were appearing, the new software that was being released for it was breaking records. When software publisher Enix released *Dragon Quest IV* for the Famicom in Japan on February 11, the company sold 1.3 million copies of the ¥11,000 ($76) game on its first day in stores.

The story was the same in the United States. After Nintendo released *Super Mario Bros. 3* for the NES, the game went on to become the best-selling NES game of all time, with $500 million in gross sales.[1]

Jumping Aboard the NES Band-Wagon

Two "new" companies joined the ever-growing list of NES licensees. *New* is used loosely, because although these two companies were new to the NES, both of them were familiar to long-time gamers.

The first was Parker Brothers, whose last videogame cartridge had been released in 1984. The company released an NES game called *Heavy Shreddin'*, which involved the winter sport of snowboarding.

The other new Nintendo licensee was INTV Corporation, the company that had evolved from Mattel's electronics division. INTV announced that it would develop software for the NES, Game Boy and Genesis. The company also announced that it was ceasing production of the Intellivision, which had been available through mail order. New software for the ten-year-old console would continue to be available, but only via mail order.[2]

As the continued success of the NES proved that there was still a demand for 8-bit consoles, businesses around the world were willing to release anything that they thought might steer profits away from Nintendo. Two companies learned the hard way that just releasing a console didn't mean that consumers would necessarily rush out and buy it.

Amstrad

The first was Amstrad, which had been founded by Alan Sugar in 1968. The British company became successful in Europe by selling low-cost audio and video hardware. In 1984, Amstrad began selling a line of *CPC* home computers that were designed to compete directly against the Commodore 64. The first was the *CPC464*, which was sold with a monitor and a built-in cassette deck. It was replaced the following year by the *CPC6128*, which had a built-in disk-drive. In 1990, in order to compete against the newer 16-bit computers like the Atari ST and the Amiga, Amstrad released the *CPC464 Plus* and *CPC6128 Plus*, which added cartridge ports and slightly increased the functionality of the original CPC 464 and CPC 6128.

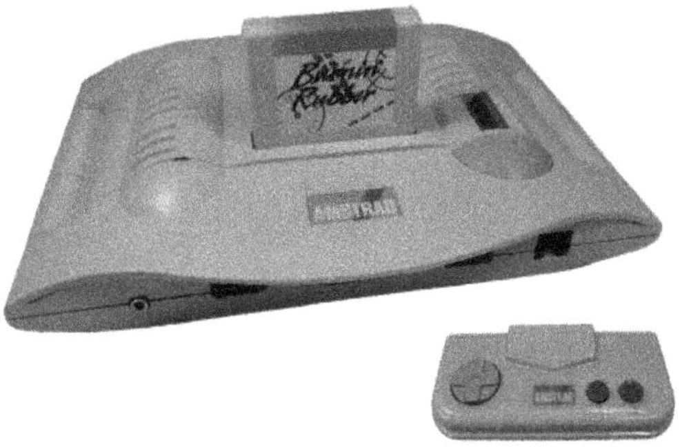

Amstrad GX4000

In June, Amstrad released a game console called the *GX4000*. The system was essentially a CPC6128 Plus computer without a keyboard or disk drive. The system retailed for £100 ($166) and was packaged with a driving game called

Burnin' Rubber. The cartridge could also play on the *Plus* computers.

Amstrad, whose advertising budget was nowhere near that of Nintendo or Sega, did little to garner interest in the Plus computers or the GX4000. Although the machines were built around an 8-bit processor, their graphics capacity allowed for 4,096 colors: even more than the Sega Mega Drive, which was released in Europe in November. However, rather than introduce new GX4000 games that took advantage of its capabilities, Amstrad merely dumped old computer games that already existed on tape or disk onto cartridges. To make matters worse, these cartridges sold for £25 ($42), while the same titles on disk or tape could be purchased for £3.99 ($7.50). The gaming public steered clear of them, and by August, the GX4000 was being sold for as little as £19.99 ($37), as dealers attempted to unload their stock.

The Commodore 64 Game System

Even while the unsold GX4000s were being discounted,[3] Amstrad's main competitor from the eighties followed in its footsteps. In December, Commodore also released a game system solely in Europe. The *Commodore 64 Game System* was basically a Commodore 64 without a keyboard. The system didn't have a chance, as dealers who couldn't sell the GX4000s had no plans to even attempt to sell Commodore's $189 system. Twenty-eight games were released for the system, and only nine of them were exclusive to the system. The remaining titles were cartridge versions of games that had been available on cassette for the Commodore 64.

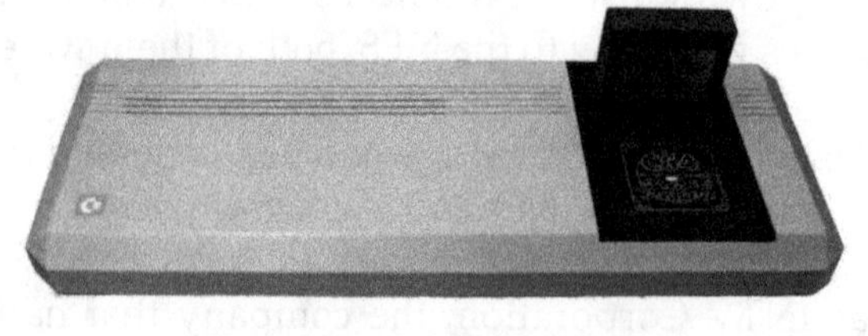

Commodore 64 Game System

Meanwhile, on November 3, Sega of Japan released the *Mega Modem*, a ¥12,800 ($100) modem needed to connect the Mega Drive to its new Sega *Meganet* online service. Unlike earlier videogame networks such as Nintendo's Family Computer Network System and Control Video's Gameline, the Sega Meganet allowed gamers to compete against each other head-to-head from different locations, as long as both had Mega Drives that were connected to the network. This was the first time that this feature was available for videogame consoles, although Amiga had announced a similar product for the Atari 2600 in 1983. In addition, when a special game cartridge called *Sega Game Library* was inserted into the Mega Drive, gamers could download and play Mega Drive games that were never sold in stores.

Sega Mega Modem

Sega Game Library

The service cost ¥800 ($5.50) per month with a six-month commitment. Sega of America planned to release the modem in the United States, where it was to be called the *TeleGenesis*. Unfortunately, the service failed to catch on in Japan and was eventually discontinued, resulting in Sega of America's decision to abandon its plans. However, early Genesis models were released with DE-9 expansion ports where the modem would have connected to the console. The port would be completely removed from later Genesis models.

The Sega Master System II

In the United States, Sega of America executives decided to give the Sega Master System another chance although the Genesis was selling steadily, They took the console's distribution rights back from Tonka, whom they blamed for poor marketing of the Sega Master System, and in January, released a newly designed console called the *Sega Master System II*. In an effort to lower the manufacturing costs and retail price of the console, the new design omitted several features from the original, such as a reset button and an expansion port that had never been utilized anyway. Also missing was a card slot; this not only prevented the Sega Master System II from being able to play Sega Card games, but also eliminated the use of the Sega 3D Glasses, since they connected to the system via the card slot.[4] However, all American Sega Master System cartridges could play on the new system.

Sega Master System II

Sega also released several new cartridges to accompany the new console: the first new Sega 8-bit games in several months. The emphasis on new software for the Sega 8-bitters was partly because Sega of America had a new president, who wanted to see his company take over a major part of Nintendo's business. Michael Katz, who had previously held major positions with Atari, Coleco, Mattel and Epyx, was someone who clearly knew the videogame industry inside and out.

Although Sega of America promoted the Sega Master System II, the console still sold poorly. And Tonka couldn't be blamed for the mediocre results this time. But the NES reigned in North America and the Genesis was also available so there were few reasons to purchase a Sega Master System II. However, the story was different overseas. Following its North American release, the Sega Master System II was released in Europe and Brazil where the original Sega Master System was actually more popular than the NES.

On November 30, at around the same time that the Sega Master System II was introduced to Europe, Sega went ahead and released the 16-bit Mega Drive, which wound up competing against the Sega Master System II. But the Mega Drive did not hinder the 8-bit system's sales. And the release of the *Master System Converter*, the European version of the Power Base Converter, only increased sales for Sega Master System software as developers realized that owners of the Sega Master System *and* the Mega Drive were potential customers.[5]

Nintendo's 16-bit Console

The Mega Drive/Genesis was selling extremely well in Japan and North America with virtually nothing competing against it. This didn't hinder NEC from signing up 21 third-party companies to develop software for its PC Engine/TurboGrafx-16. NEC America also proved how serious it was with the console by announcing that it would no longer manufacture televisions, video recorders or other electronic products for the U.S. market. This was so it could devote its operations to the TurboGrafx-16.

Even though the 8-bit Famicom was still holding its own against the 16-bit consoles in Japan, Nintendo of Japan finally released its own 16-bit system on November 21. The console was called the *Super Famicom*, a term that initially implied that the system was a Famicom and more.

Nintendo Super Famicom

Originally, Nintendo's plan had been to develop a 16-bit console that would accept 8-bit Famicom games. This was because they believed that people who already owned a Famicom would be less hesitant to purchase a new system that didn't require all new software. Unfortunately, the technology that was designed for the new console was so ahead of the Famicom's, that to make the Super Famicom backwards-compatible would have just been too cost-prohibitive. Without a ready-built consumer base to run out and buy the system, Hiroshi Yamauchi realized that the console would require exceptional software that would catch the interest of those who already owned a Famicom. He put Shigeru Miyamoto in charge of creating such software.

The Super Famicom featured *Mode 7*, a texture-mapping graphics mode that simulated a three-dimensional effect by allowing a background layer to be rotated and scaled.

Mode 7

Since neither the PC Engine nor the Mega Drive had anything like that, Miyamoto believed that the initial games for the system should take advantage of it. By the time the Super Famicom was released, Miyamoto and his team had two such games available, *F-Zero* and *Super Mario World*. A third game that took advantage of Mode 7, *Pilotwings*, would be available a month later.

The Super Famicom's controller was based on the Famicom/NES's controller as it featured the D-pad, select and start buttons, and "A" and "B" buttons. Additionally, it featured a third set of buttons, "X" and "Y", which were located parallel to the "A" and "B" buttons. But there was also a fourth set of buttons along the upper edge of the controller, one on the left and the other on the right. These buttons were referred to as *shoulder* buttons, and were easily accessed by the player using his index fingers.

Super Famicom Control Shoulder Pads

The ¥25,000 ($256) Super Famicom had first been announced in late October, and 1.5 million units were pre-ordered. Because the console was released on a Wednesday, kids skipped school and adults called in sick to work just for a chance to purchase the unit. Long lines formed outside stores that sold the console, which caused disruptions all around Tokyo. When word spread that Nintendo only had 300,000 available consoles, and that they had sold out in only a matter of hours, the crowds became unruly and eventually led the Japanese government to ask the videogame companies to restrict their console launches to weekends.

The Super Famicom sort of became available again on December 5, when Sharp released a television set with a built-in Super Famicom. The *Super Famicom Naizou TV SF1* was similar to the My Computer TV C1 unit that Sharp had released in Japan in 1983. Priced at ¥100,000 ($737) for a 14″ model and ¥133,000 ($980) for a 21″ model, the unit differed from the earlier Famicom model, as the cartridge slot was situated above the picture screen instead of below it. And while the My Computer TV C1 couldn't be used with Famicom peripherals such as the Famicom Disc System, the Super Famicom Naizou TV SF1 was designed so future Super Famicom peripherals would be compatible with it.

Despite the Super Famicom shortage, Nintendo concentrated on the future and announced that the Super Famicom would be available in the United States in November 1991.

Neo•Geo MVS

SNK's Neo•Geo

Many of the third-party publishers that had released games for the Famicom, such as Konami, Capcom and Enix, went on to produce games for the Super Famicom as well. However, SNK, a publisher of nine Famicom games, didn't have anything initially available for the Super Famicom.[6] Instead, SNK released an all-new type of system for the arcades. Its *Neo•Geo MVS* (Multi-Video System), which debuted in Japanese arcades on January 31, was the world's first cartridge-based arcade machine.

The Neo•Geo MVS was the next logical step in the arcade game evolution that began in 1985 with the JAMMA board. However instead of having PCBs (Printed Circuit Boards) that had to be switched in order to change games, the Neo•Geo MVS merely required a switch of a game cartridge, which was no different than changing a cartridge in a home console. The cartridges themselves were VHS-tape-sized and could contain up to 330 megabits of code. Arcade operators liked the system because each cabinet could hold up to six cartridges, which allowed them to offer more games in a limited amount of space.

Gamers also liked the system. Besides providing fun, colorful graphics that featured large, detailed characters, the Neo•Geo MVS offered a unique way for gamers to save their scores. The scores and positions of up to 27 games could be saved on 4K memory cards that could be inserted into the cabinets. Gamers could purchase the cards from the arcade operators and then use them in any Neo•Geo MVS machine in any arcade.

SNK Neo•Geo Memory Card

On the same day that SNK released the Neo•Geo MVS in Japanese arcades,[7] they also released a pay-per-play rental system that was designed to be used in hotel rooms. While the operating system of the *Neo•Geo Deck* was different from that of the Neo•Geo MVS, it accepted the same Neo•Geo MVS game cartridges. However, unlike the arcade version, the ¥68,000 ($471) Neo•Geo Deck could only accept one cartridge at a time. And although it played Neo•Geo MVS games, the unit did not have a memory-card reader, so games could not be saved.

SNK Neo•Geo Deck

To SNK's surprise, the Neo•Geo Deck was so popular among gamers that many of them were willing to purchase the system for home use. This led SNK to produce a home version, which they called the *Neo•Geo AES (Advanced Entertainment System)*. The ¥58,000 ($365) Neo•Geo AES was released in Japan on April 26.

The code used to write all of the Neo•Geo games was exactly the same, regardless of the

SNK Neo•Geo AES

system that they were played on. But while the cartridges that were used in both the Neo•Geo MVS and Neo•Geo AES systems were similar, they were not compatible. The arcade cartridges cost vastly more than their console counterparts, ranging between $500 and $1,200 per cartridge. To prevent arcade operators from purchasing the less expensive Neo•Geo MVS cartridges to use in their cabinets, SNK designed a different pin configuration, so the cartridges could only fit into the systems that they were designed for. On the other hand, SNK wisely included a slot for a memory card in the Neo•Geo AES and this was compatible with the Neo•Geo MVS, so games could be saved and restored on either system.

SNK Neo•Geo Cartridges
Top: MVS Bottom: AES

The controller that was sold with the Neo•Geo AES was nearly the same size as the console itself! The device had a heavy duty joystick and four control buttons arranged in the same order as they were on a Neo•Geo MVS machine. Although Nintendo and NEC had previously offered heavy duty controllers before in the NES Advantage and the PC Engine Turbo Stick, the Neo•Geo AES controller marked the first time that an *arcade-style* controller was modeled after a specific group of arcade machines.

Although, SNK advertised the Neo•Geo AES as a 24-bit machine, it actually used the same 16-bit processor as Sega's Mega Drive. It also had an additional 8-bit processor that was the same as the one in the Sega Master System. The dual processors allowed the Neo•Geo AES to display 4,096 different colors on the screen at one time.[8] And the Neo•Geo AES was no slouch when it came to audio. The system could produce sounds from fifteen different channels, seven of which were dedicated solely to digitized speech. This compared favorably against the Genesis's ten separate audio channels.

The Nintendo-Tengen Showdown

Since the Neo•Geo AES was based on the Neo•Geo Deck, which had originally been intended to be a rental unit, it might be assumed that SNK actively supported videogame rentals. Nintendo of America, on the other hand, was very much against it and lobbied Congress to pass laws forbidding the practice. Although Congress had planned to pass a bill outlawing the rental of computer software, the bill specifically excluded cartridge-based software, because cartridges couldn't be easily duplicated.

While Nintendo did everything it could to put an end to game rentals, Tengen promoted the idea. Tengen's belief was that if a game was good, it would be purchased whether it was available for rental or not. Rentals gave players the ability to try out games that they otherwise might overlook altogether. To promote the rental concept, Tengen began a campaign that rewarded consumers with a discount when they purchased a Tengen title that they first rented.

Tengen needed all the help it could get to sell its products. Because it wasn't a licensed third-party publisher, many retailers refused to sell their games, due to the pressure from Nintendo, which threatened to sue stores that sold Tengen's products. Very few retailers were willing to go up against Nintendo and jeopardize the revenue that they were enjoying just for the sake of carrying one specific software brand. Many of the retailers who did opt to carry the Tengen games kept them in separate displays away from the licensed titles.

Because of these alleged "strong-arm" techniques that Nintendo employed, and the anti-monopoly suits that were filed against it, the Federal Trade Commission began subpoenaing industry insiders to look into Nintendo's business practices.

While Nintendo questioned the legalities of Tengen releasing NES software, another battle between the two companies finally ended. The courts ruled that Tengen's version of *Tetris* was illegal but Tengen wasn't punished for releasing a title to which it had no rights. Instead, the courts placed the blame solely on Mirrorsoft for selling *Tetris* rights that it didn't hold in 1989. Mirrorsoft was ordered to pay Nintendo the revenue that it had lost from Tengen's *Tetris*.

As Nintendo completed its litigations with Tengen, another lawsuit loomed on the horizon. During the first half of 1990, several "multiple game" cartridges appeared. These high-memory cartridges were half the size of standard NES cartridges and contained up to forty games. As it turned out, the cartridges were counterfeit and contained illegal versions of licensed Nintendo games. In June, U.S. Customs agents seized 700 of these illegal cartridges in a sting operation in Wilmington, North Carolina. Besides the multiple-game cartridges, counterfeit copies of *Super Mario Bros. 3* were also appearing. In order to stop the flow of counterfeits that were entering the United States and Canada, Nintendo filed several copyright-infringement lawsuits against video rental stores, retailers, distributors and importers.

In October, legitimate licensed developers of NES-compatible games received some surprising news. Nintendo announced that it would allow them to manufacture their own cartridges. Nintendo claimed that it made this move because it believed that the quality of the games wouldn't suffer. However, many insiders believed that Nintendo was knocking down its equivalent of the Berlin Wall only because many of its licensees were becoming very dissatisfied with Nintendo's total control. Regardless of the reason, this was good news to consumers, since the licensees would be free to purchase components from whichever suppliers they wished, which would probably cost less than if they bought them directly from Nintendo. The savings would trickle down to the retail level and result in lower prices for new games. Of course, Nintendo wouldn't suffer, since the licensees still needed the all-important "lock out" chip that could only be purchased from Nintendo itself.

Changing The Code

Illegal cartridges weren't the only problems that Nintendo had to contend with. In April, a British company called Codemasters announced the forthcoming release of a code-altering interface device that it had designed.

The item, which Codemasters called the *Power Pak*, was similar to the PGP-1 that Answer Software had created for the Atari 2600. Both units allowed gamers to alter the characteristics of a game, such as speed or color, without permanently changing the game's original code. Gamers could change up to three features of an NES game by plugging their game cartridge into one end of the Power Pak, and then inserting the other end into the NES' cartridge slot. More than three features could be altered by plugging one Power Pak into another.

Camerica, a Nintendo licensee, originally planned to distribute the Power Pak in the United States and Canada. However, within a month after first announcing the device, Camerica signed Galoob Toys, a San Francisco-based international toy company, to handle the US distribution. Galoob renamed the unit *Game Genie* and planned to release it in June. The Game Genie wouldn't cost more than a standard NES cartridge and would be packaged with a booklet of codes for over 200 popular games.

Nintendo immediately sought a restraining order against Galoob to prevent the toy company from marketing the Game Genie. Nintendo claimed that the interface infringed upon its copyrights and shortened the lifespans of its games, thus rendering them unmarketable. Nintendo feared that gamers would rent a game like *Super Mario Bros.* and then use the Game Genie to simplify it, so they could easily reach the end. Nintendo found it highly unlikely that gamers would purchase games that they had completed.

Nintendo didn't get the restraint and quickly sought an appeal. It then won a temporary restraining order, which prevented Galoob from selling or even advertising the Game Genie. Although Galoob promptly appealed, the case, as well as the hundreds of thousands of Game Genies that Galoob had stored in a warehouse, were tied up for the remainder of the year.

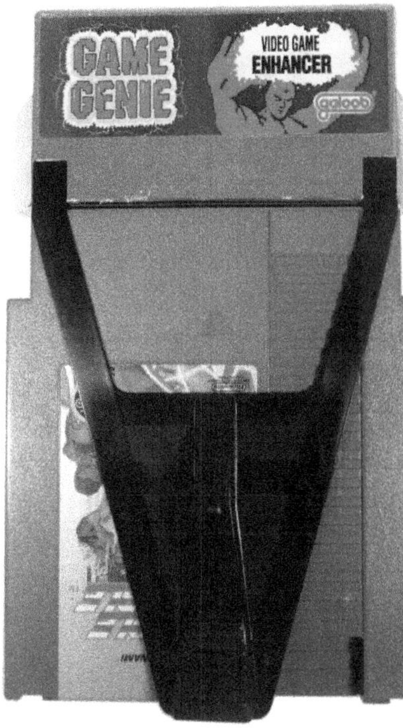

Galoob Game Genie

Guns and Pianos

Although the Game Genie was never released during 1990, several other NES peripherals did become available. The first was a replacement for the NES Zapper light-gun. Konami's *LaserScope* retailed for $40 and looked somewhat like a flight controller's headgear. The unit wrapped around the player's head and covered his ears like earmuffs. A slim microphone extended out in front of the player's mouth. Another extension came out over the player's forehead and rested in front of his eye. Attached to this eyepiece was a plastic shield with a set of crosshairs painted on.

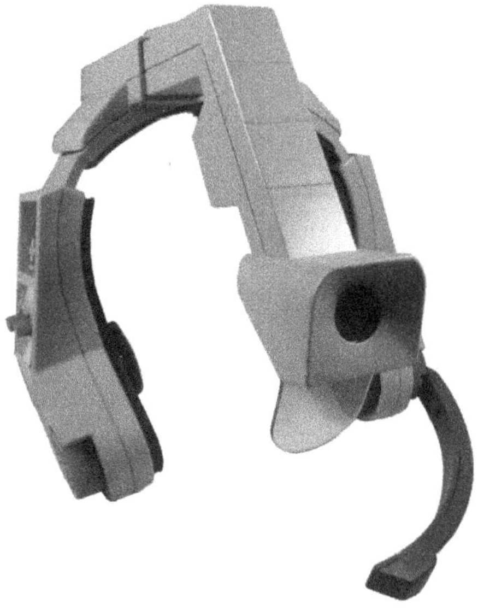

Konami LaserScope

Although the LaserScope was specifically designed to support one game *Laser Invasion*, which wasn't scheduled to be released until 1991, the device could be used with any NES game that worked with the Zapper. To fire a shot, the player moved his head until the crosshair of the eyepiece covered a potential target. At that point, the player said "fire" into the mouthpiece, and the LaserScope automatically fired a shot. Unfortunately, the unit often malfunctioned and fired merely from background noise. Due to this, the LaserScope received lackluster reviews and sold poorly.

For those who preferred standard controllers for their NES, Nintendo released another peripheral that allowed four people to play at one time. The *NES Four Score* was similar to the NES Satellite but it was connected to the NES via a cord that plugged directly into the NES' controller port. Because it lacked the wireless capability of the NES Satellite, the NES Four Score didn't require the six D batteries that were needed to power the older device.

The other new peripheral garnered much more excitement. The *Miracle Piano Teaching*

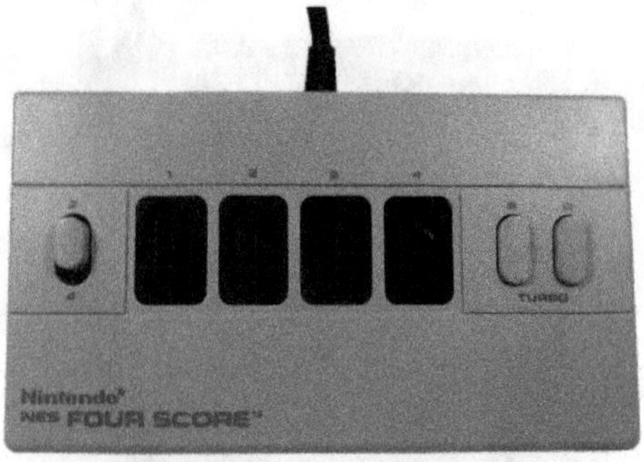

Nintendo NES Four Score

Software Toolworks Miracle Piano Teaching System

System from Software Toolworks was similar to the musical keyboard that had originally been promised by Nintendo when it introduced the NAVS in 1985. Unlike the musical keyboard that had been available for the Intellivision Computer during the final days of Mattel Electronics, the Miracle had been designed so that it could be hooked up to any audio system and work independently from the NES. In addition to the piano, the Miracle could imitate over one hundred other instruments. It could also play over one hundred songs that were programmed into it.

The Miracle was packaged with a special NES cartridge that featured games that made learning to play the piano as fun as playing *Super Mario Bros*. For starters, the screen displayed a keyboard with a musical scale above it. Every time someone pressed a key on the Miracle, an identical one on the screen flashed along with it. Once amateur Mozarts were familiar with the keyboard, they were ready to move on to the drills. One drill that taught students to learn notes combined Mattel's *Astromusic* with a traditional arcade shooting gallery. It featured a musical scale with ducks swimming across it. The player had to shoot the ducks by tapping the correct piano key. Another lesson taught rhythm by having the player control an on-screen robot who had to jump up and hit some power plugs at the correct moment.

The system was priced at $299, which made it comparable to the free-standing music keyboards that were already on the market. Software Toolworks promised to release additional cartridges that would concentrate on different music genres, such as country and rock.

The Miracle gave NES owners the ability to use their console for purposes other than games. Nintendo also sought practical non-gaming applications for the NES, and one result had been the NES Network that it had developed with Fidelity Investments in 1989. Unfortunately, Nintendo announced in October that it was severing its ties with Fidelity, as the latter company never developed the required user-interface. The NES Network was not abandoned, however. The online service that was available for the Famicom in Japan was successful, and Nintendo of America still hoped to duplicate that success in the United States sometime in 1991.

Game Boy Competition

Although the consoles sold steadily, 1990 wound up being the year of the handheld. Nintendo estimated that it would sell five million Game Boy units and 20 million cartridges, based on its wonderful sales figures at the end of 1989. Atari expected to challenge that number when it released its $179 Lynx nationwide in the spring. However, the Lynx wasn't the only competition that the Game Boy had to face.

Bit Corporation, the Taiwanese company that had released the Dina 2-in-1 system in 1986, and had since produced games for the NES/Famicom, released its own handheld console to challenge the Game Boy. The *Gamate* was very similar to the Game Boy. It featured a grey and green monochrome screen and the same number of controller buttons. However, unlike the Game Boy, the Gamate was held horizontally with the screen in the center. Another difference was that instead of cartridges, the games for the Gamate came on cards similar to the Sega My Cards. But although the Gamate was an original product from Bit, its games weren't. Like many of the games that Bit released for the 2600, the Gamate games were clones of popular titles from other systems.

NEC revealed a prototype of its own handheld videogame console at the first CES of the nineties. The unit looked very much like a Game Boy with a color monitor. Although specifics about the machine were lacking because of its premature showing, NEC officials said that an optional TV tuner would be available that would turn the unit into a tiny television set. Of more importance, the new unit would be compatible with the company's consoles and accept all the games that were released on cards, but not CDs.

Bit Corp. Gamate

In June, NEC released the portable console in Japan, where it was called the *PC Engine GT*. Earlier in the month, its American equivalent, the *TurboExpress*, was displayed at the summer CES. Although the company had a working model behind closed doors at the mammoth electronic show, they displayed prototypes in showcases to keep show attendees from touching the unit. NEC estimated the price of the device at between $199 and $249, which made it the most expensive portable.[9] The optional tuner was set to retail at $99.

NEC TurboExpress & TurboVision

NEC released the TurboExpress in August, and it was immediately compared to the Lynx. Since there were pros and cons with both systems, consumers didn't have an easy time choosing a color portable. While both units utilized credit card-sized cartridges, the NEC software was less fragile and easier to load. It merely plugged into the cartridge slot at the top-rear of the machine. The Lynx wafers had to be inserted into a compartment that was hidden behind a hinged door at the bottom left of the unit. Both portables needed six AA batteries but the Lynx turned itself off after four minutes of non-use to conserve power. Car cigarette lighters or AC adapters could also supply power to either machine.

The TurboExpress' 2.6 inch color LCD screen was slightly larger than the Game Boy's, but somewhat smaller than the one found on the Lynx. However, the resolution on the TurboExpress was much sharper since it had an active-matrix LCD. Each of the pixels, the dots that made up a picture, was controlled by its own transistor. Unfortunately, the LCD technology used in the screen was new and troublesome and many brand new units were frequently plagued with screens with bad pixels. The Lynx had its own problem as the motion on its passive-matrix LCD display caused visible trails, or "ghosting".

An important feature in a color portable was the range of colors that the screen could display. The Lynx could show an impressive 4,096 colors while the TurboExpress could only display 512. On the other hand, the NEC unit could display all of those colors at the same time, whereas the Lynx could only handle 16 colors at a time.

Both units came equipped with cables that could connect them to other units. The Lynx could link eight players at one time, while the TurboExpress could only connect two. In addition, each of the eight individual Lynx players could view a game from his own first-person perspective, a feature that was built into the Lynx itself.

The TurboExpress was smaller than the Lynx, but the Atari portable was priced less. Despite the higher price of the TurboExpress, it was definitely the better buy for those who already owned the TurboGrafx-16, since the software was compatible. However, since NEC sold fewer consoles than Nintendo or Sega, the majority of people shopping for a portable wouldn't have been influenced by this feature.

In October, Sega joined the handheld market when it released its ¥19,800 ($155) *Game Gear* in Japan. It was rectangular like the Lynx, but not as wide. Although its 3.2-inch screen in the center of the console was slightly smaller than the one on the Lynx, the Game Gear offered the largest handheld screen in Japan, since the Lynx wasn't available there. To the left of the screen was a directional controller pad, and to the right were two control buttons and a start button.

Sega Game Gear

Although the Game Gear used the same Zilog Z80 processor as the Sega Master System, the two units were not compatible. Sega felt that graphics that had been designed for standard televisions wouldn't display well on a tiny screen. However, many game titles from the Master System were redesigned to play on the Game Gear. Unfortunately, even had the Game Gear been compatible with the Master System, it might still had been a hard sell, since Sega's 8-bit consoles simply weren't popular in Japan. The Game Gear, like its Sega 8-bit console brethren, was poorly received.

Although the Game Gear sold disappointingly, Sega did manage to get it released. Other vendors weren't as fortunate. With the success of the Game Boy, many companies scrambled to release handheld units to compete against it. A start-up company called Hall of Fame Games announced that it had planned to release a monochrome portable game console priced much less than the Game Boy by Christmas, although an actual release date was never mentioned. The *PowerPro* was to be approximately the same size as the Game Boy, but designed horizontally like the Game Gear. The unit would have a 3.3-inch screen and use game cards similar to the Sega My Cards. Hall of Fame Games also claimed that it was developing a color portable.

Third-party software publisher Camerica announced similar plans. However, Camerica's planned monochrome and color units would also be able to play all of the available Game Boy games. As Christmas came and went, none of the rumored portables made appearances. For 1990 at least, Nintendo wasn't toppled in the portable-gaming market.

The year ended with more records, as the total worldwide sales revenues for hardware and software totaled over $4.1 billion, with 82% of that number coming solely from Nintendo's sales in the United States. Even with the Super Famicom being available for just a short time, and only in Japan, Nintendo still controlled 90% of the global market.

And Nintendo controlled much more than the marketplace. According to Marketing Evaluations, Inc., a company that developed a metric to determine the familiarity of each tested company's actual *brand,* as opposed to its products, Mario was better recognized by American children than Mickey Mouse. This infatuated the executives at Sega, whose unofficial mascot, Alex Kidd, was known by few other than those who actually played the Alex Kidd games. They too wanted a brand that would be recognized the world over in the same way as Mario. And so, in April, the company ordered its AM-8 development team to dream up a mascot, as well as design a game to feature it.

CHAPTER NINETEEN
1991

The year 1991 began on a great note when Nintendo of America announced at the winter CES that its total sales for 1990, $3.4 billion, had been a 27% increase from 1989. These numbers came from the sales of 7.2 million NES consoles and 3.2 million Game Boys. In addition, 60 million NES and 9 million Game Boy cartridges had been sold. The company proudly proclaimed that it controlled 87% of the home videogame market, and its consoles could be found in 30% of all American homes. Based on these figures, the new year looked extremely bright for Nintendo.

Unfortunately for Nintendo, the prosperity didn't continue. The company's anticipated sales for the NES plummeted by 46% during the first six months of 1991. The fact was that the eight-year-old NES was beginning to show its age. Although it still boasted the largest catalog of available software, its limitations were apparent when it was compared to the newer 16-bit consoles.

NEC Woes

Although sales for the NES plummeted, it still outsold the 16-bit TurboGrafx-16, which was technologically superior. Since the PC Engine had been so successful in Japan, NEC America cited two reasons why the TurboGrafx-16 was performing poorly in the United States. One was Nintendo's anti-competitive practices, which prevented its third-party licensees from developing games for any competing system for a period of two years after the game was released for the NES. Since this practice did not exist in Japan, the PC Engine enjoyed a larger catalog from more suppliers. One reason why the Genesis didn't suffer this same fate was because Sega was a game developer itself, whereas NEC wasn't.

The second reason was because NEC America followed the same marketing campaign that it had used in Japan for the PC Engine, where the company targeted metropolitan areas for its advertising. Since Japan was a relatively small country, the marketing that had been aimed towards cities, were also seen in smaller areas. Although NEC America targeted major cities in the United States, inhabitants of the numerous rural areas were unaware of the TurboGrafx-16, while ads for Nintendo and Sega were touted everywhere.

In May, NEC America made an effort to boost sales by reducing the TurboGrafx-16's retail price to $100, the same as the NES. NEC America also lowered the cost of many of its games. Despite the price reductions, and the console's unique, optional CD player, NEC America still couldn't manage to sway consumers to choose its console over the Genesis.

NEC PC Engine CoreGrafx II

NEC Triumphs

NEC managed to lower costs on its console when it released a new rendition of the PC Engine on June 21. The ¥59,800 ($143) *CoreGrafx II* retained the same dimensions as its predecessor, the CoreGrafx, as well as its composite AV output. Basically, the only differences between the two Core systems were cosmetic. The new CoreGrafx II sported a lighter gray paint job and had fewer indentations along its top.

NEC released another console three months later on September 21. The *PC Engine Duo* was

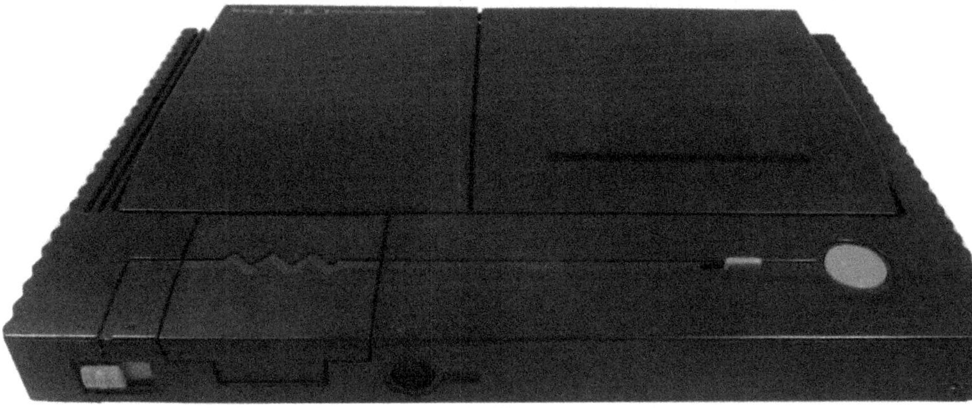

NEC PC Engine Duo

simply a PC Engine console with, the first time ever, a built-in CD-ROM player. And because the CD player was built-into the console, a system card wasn't required to tell the player how to act. Had such a card been needed, it would have been Version 3, which featured a RAM and BIOS update. The RAM available for the CD player was expanded to 256KB and the software that took advantage of this additional memory was called *Super CD-ROM^{2}s*.[1]

The new Super CD-ROM^2 games couldn't play on the older CD player that used earlier versions of the system card. But on October 26, NEC released a new Version 3

NEC PC Engine Super CD-ROM^2

System Card that would incorporate the new features and allow the Super CD-ROM² games to play on the older CD-ROM drives. At ¥9,800 ($75), the Version 3 System Card wasn't cheap, but it was less expensive than having to purchase a brand new peripheral in order to play the new games.

For those who did want to purchase a new CD-ROM player, NEC released a new one on December 13. The Super CD-ROM² was basically a PC Engine Duo without the PC Engine component. It featured the same color scheme as the CoreGrafx II, although any of the PC Engines, including the SuperGrafx could plug directly into it without an adaptor.[2] Since the ¥47,800 ($370) Super CD-ROM² had the Version 3 BIOs built-into it, a System Card was not required in the card slot of the PC Engine.

Like the PC Engine CD-ROM², the Super CD-ROM² offered memory so games could be saved, if the game had been programmed to allow game saves. However, too many game saves would eventually use up all of the available memory. In that case, the gamer would have to free up the memory be deleting some of the saved games. On September 6, Hudson Soft released a new HuCard that gave gamers another alternative to clearing space for saving games. The *Tennokoe Bank* was a HuCard that featured four banks of memory. While games were saved as files onto the storage device, the groups of files were saved in a bank of memory. The Tennokoe Bank could copy an entire bank of memory from the backup device (a CD-ROM² Super CD-ROM² player or a Tennokoe 2 unit) and save it to the HuCard itself. A complete memory bank could also be copied from the card back onto the backup device. However, this would erase any of the data already stored on the backup device. To prevent this, users could also swap one bank of memory from the card with the one on the backup device. The Tennokoe Bank increased the amount of storage area for saving games from one memory bank to five. And the purchase of additional Tennokoe Bank cards allowed users to save as any games as they liked without having to worry about running out of space.

Hudson Soft Tennokoe Bank

NEC PC Engine LT

NEC released yet another rendition of the PC Engine on December 13, the same day that it released the Super CD-ROM². But while most of the available PC Engine consoles could connect to the Super CD-ROM² without the need of an interface or adapter, the new ¥99,800 ($773) *PC Engine LT* required a special adapter to hook up to it.[3] The PC Engine LT was sort of a hybrid between a console and a handheld. It somewhat resembled a PC Engine with the same control buttons and pads, but it also had a built-in TV tuner and 4-inch screen. However, unlike the portable PC Engine GT, the screen was separate from the rest of the unit in a manner similar to

19

the multi-screen Game & Watches that Nintendo introduced nearly a decade earlier. Like those units, the screen section of the PC Engine LT connected to the body via a hinge, allowing it to fold over and cover the unit when not in use.

Neither the PC Engine Duo nor the PC Engine LT did well in the marketplace. The Duo's failure was due to the fact that most potential buyers already owned a PC Engine and the original CD-ROM², therefore all they needed to do was purchase the Version 3 System Card in order to play the Super CD-ROM² games. The high price of the LT, which was one of the most expensive consoles that NEC had to offer, led to its quick demise.

Sega TeraDrive

Although NEC called its console the PC Engine, the unit was not a personal computer. On May 31, Sega of Japan released a version of its Mega Drive that was also a 16-bit personal computer. The *TeraDrive* was an IBM computer that could also play Mega Drive games. The unit had a Mega Drive cartridge slot on top and two controller ports on its front. Sega released three models that ranged in price from ¥148,000 ($1,100) to ¥248,000 ($1,840). The low-end model came with 640KB of internal memory (expandable to 2.5MB) and one floppy drive while the high-end one had 2.5MB of internal memory (expandable to 5 MB) and data could be saved on a floppy disk or a 30MB hard drive.[4]

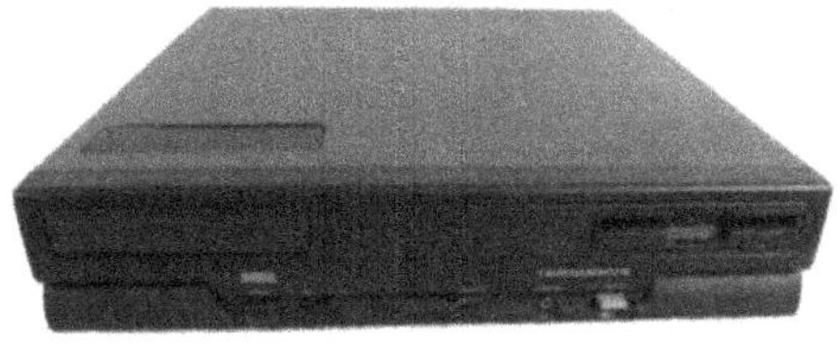

Sega TeraDrive

The TeraDrive didn't have a CD drive, so it couldn't read CD-ROMs. However, Sega decided to follow NEC's lead and add CD technology to its gaming consoles. The company released its JVC-manufactured *Mega CD* in Japan on December 12. The ¥49,800 ($370) CD-ROM player sat beneath the Mega Drive and the two units worked in tandem to provide games that had the potential to be faster and better looking than those loaded from standard cartridges. The Mega CD contained its own 16-bit 68000 processor that ran at 12.5 MHz, much faster than the Mega Drive's 7.5 MHz processor. Working together, the two CPUs eliminated any game pauses that could occur while the system loaded new information from the CD.

Sega Mega CD

The Mega CD also had two custom graphics chips that added more colors and sprites to the TV screen than the Mega Drive could accomplish itself. These chips also added scaling and rotation to Sega games; features that were already available on the Super Famicom.

With the Mega CD attached to it, the Mega Drive was an impressive system. Unfortunately, most software developers were unable to fully utilize the system. The developers were accustomed to designing games that fit within the memory constraints of a standard cartridge. It was very difficult for them to create a game for a media that could store the same amount of data as hundreds of cartridges.

In order to release CD games that couldn't fit on cartridges, Sega began concentrating on full-motion-video (FMV). Unfortunately, the processors in the Mega Drive and Mega CD weren't designed for FMV and the games ran slowly at an incorrect frame-rate and displayed grainy images in low resolution.

Despite the inadequacies of the Mega CD, many American gamers simply couldn't wait for the unit's North American release in 1992. Instead, they paid exorbitant amounts to purchase imported Mega CD units from Japan. However, they wasted their money because the Mega CDs weren't compatible with Genesis consoles.

Meanwhile, Europeans learned they would have to wait even longer than Americans for their Mega CDs. The problem with Europe was that it was comprised of many countries and each one had their own Sega distributor and launch dates varied among these distributors. In Great Britain, the distribution was carried out by Virgin Mastertronic,[5] who also sold the system in France and Germany. Sega realized it needed a tighter reign of its products in Europe and purchased the Mastertronic subsidiary from Virgin Mastertronic, which quickly changed its name to Virgin Interactive Entertainment. Mastertronic was then renamed *Sega Europe, Ltd.* and became Sega's operating branch for all of Europe.[6]

The Super Famicom CD Drive

In 1988, Sony had signed a contract with Nintendo for Sony to design a CD unit for Super Famicom. Part of that deal allowed Nintendo to create games featuring characters from movies by Columbia Pictures, which was owned by Sony. It also gave Sony the right to develop a separate stand-alone console called the *Play Station*, which would play both Super Famicom CD games and cartridges. This partnership was announced on February 6, when Nintendo said that it intended to release a CD drive for the Super Famicom sometime during 1991. Sony did not publicly announce its separate Play Station console at that time.

However, unbeknownst to Sony, Nintendo's president, Hiroshi Yamauchi, re-examined the contract and discovered that it gave Sony complete manufacturing and licensing control of all titles that would be produced for the Super Famicom CD. In

Nintendo/Sony SNES CD-ROM Development Kit

Sony Play Station

addition, Sony would be the "sole worldwide licenser" of all these games. This incensed Yamauchi, because Nintendo had always kept complete control of its games and earned much of its revenue from licensing. Yamauchi felt duped by Sony officials so in May, he secretly sent two employees, Howard Lincoln and Minoru Arakawa to Holland where they signed an agreement that allowed Philips to develop a CD-ROM peripheral for the Super Famicom. In return, all of the CD games would also be playable on a new console that Philips was planning to release later in the year. One caveat in the agreement was that Nintendo retained the rights to all of the CD games while Philips would be able to use select Nintendo characters, such as *Zelda* and *Mario*, for use in exclusive games for its new system.

Sony threatened to sue Nintendo but Nintendo assured them that although they wanted Philips to design the Super Famicom CD player, they were still partnering with Sony for the standalone Play Station console that would play the Super Famicom cartridges and discs. Sony believed Nintendo and so at the summer CES on May 31, Sony officially announced its intent to develop a videogame console called the Play Station, which would be available in 1993.

Sony expected Nintendo to announce the Play Station console as well at its press conference the following day. instead, what they heard was Howard Lincoln talk about Nintendo's new alliance with Philips. Lincoln then confirmed that in September, Nintendo would release the Super Famicom in North America, where it would be called the *Super NES (SNES)*. The company also disclosed that this new console would also have an optional Philips-built CD drive available for it. There was no mention of the Play Station.

Sony was shocked by Nintendo's announcement, but decided to move ahead with its stand-alone console that would accept Nintendo's 16-bit cartridges. However, since Sony was no longer developing the CD drive for Nintendo, the Play Station could not accept CD games manufactured by Philips. Sony decided to create its own CD player that would play games specifically designed for that system. Despite a lawsuit from Nintendo, Sony displayed a prototype of the Play Station at the Tokyo International Electronics Show in October, where the company announced that the system would be available in the summer of 1992.[7]

CD Promises

But American gamers would be getting their own CD-based system before that if the rumors that came out of Sunnyvale were true. Early in the year, word leaked out that Atari was developing its own 32-bit super videogame console, which it intended to release in September, coinciding with the release of the SNES. The system would run at 16Mhz, twice as fast as the Genesis and four times faster than the SNES. In addition to a cartridge port and CD drive, the system would also accept Lynx game wafers.

By May, Atari verified that the *Panther* was indeed a reality. However, since Atari didn't display it at the summer CES, many analysts wondered about the actual status of the machine. Their suspicions proved genuine a few weeks later, when Atari suddenly pulled an about-face and declared that work on the Panther had been discontinued. No reason was given, other than that Atari would be able to better concentrate on a new project that it called the *Jaguar*. By year's end, the only available information about the Jaguar was that it was a 64-bit system, and that an outside company was developing it with new technology that wasn't yet available in other systems.

SNK also experimented with an optional CD drive for its Neo•Geo. Although the console was holding its own in both Japan and the United States, its very steep price kept it from competing directly against Nintendo and Sega. SNK felt that providing software on an inexpensive CD, in addition to its very expensive Neo•Geo cartridges, would be a perfect boost for the system. Unfortunately, because the Neo•Geo was a pseudo-32-bit machine, SNK's prototype CD players couldn't deliver information as fast as the CPU could process it. Because of this, SNK didn't rush out and announce its CD player as quickly as the other companies. However, it promised that once it straightened out these problems, it would definitely release a CD player for the Neo•Geo.

American Neo•Geo

While CDs appeared to be becoming the medium of choice for software delivery, most established companies were still sticking with cartridges. SNK used cartridges that contained up to 330MB of information, nearly ten times the data that was stored on a Genesis cartridge, and more than half of the amount that could be stored on a CD.[8] Of course these high memory cartridges were very expensive.

On June 18, Americans learned just how expensive these cartridges could be when SNK of America released the Neo•Geo AES in the United States.

Originally SNK of America planned to sell the console, along with two controllers and a game, for $600. However this price was raised to $650 slightly before the launch when SNK of America decided to release the Neo•Geo AES in two different configurations. The $650 configuration was dubbed the Gold System and a less expensive $400 Silver System would only come with one controller and no games. The cartridges themselves carried a suggested list price of $199.

Multimedia

The CDs that were being used for videogame consoles and computers were called CD-ROMs. In addition to the audio files that standard music CDs contained, CD-ROMs also stored data, video, and still images. By 1991, the term "multimedia" became popular for such media that contained a variety of formats.

Manufacturers of computer hardware and software began asserting the benefits of multimedia, but consumers weren't as quick to embrace it. The problem was that although adding multimedia to a computer simply meant installing and configuring a sound card, a video card, and a CD-ROM drive, there was little standardization among PCs. If someone purchased a CD-ROM drive for the TurboGrafx-16, he knew that it would be compatible with that console. However, since PCs could be manufactured by anyone, there was no guarantee that a generic CD drive would work on a given computer, since the drives had specific memory and processing requirements in order for them to operate correctly. Unfortunately, most computers weren't configured to handle them.

MPC Logo

The Software Publishers Association (SPA) began a subgroup called the Multimedia PC Marketing Council, which consisted of several companies that included Microsoft, Creative Labs, Dell and Gateway. This group created a standard for PCs that could employ CD-ROM drives, which they called *Multimedia PC (MPC)*. Any PC manufacturer could license the MPC logo from SPA and display it on their computer, if it adhered to the MPC standards. Any PC displaying the MPC logo was guaranteed to be minimally configured to support multimedia.

Unfortunately, standardization within the PC industry was something that had never been taken seriously. Software developers continued to release games that could only run on the most powerful PCs, and various 3D video cards were manufactured with an extremely wide range of display capabilities. This was confusing to the consumer, and the idea of upgrading their computer into a multimedia computer was something they did not yet deem necessary.

Multimedia on PCs, with their long history of incompatibility, was something that just wasn't going to catch on in a big way. But some companies felt that multimedia was too important to ignore. They felt that if they could market multimedia devices that didn't look like computers, but were configured for multimedia to begin with, then they would be in the driver's seat with the next big appliance that everybody had to own.

In March, Commodore International was the first company to get a multimedia system onto store shelves. The $999 *Commodore CDTV* ("Commodore Dynamic Total Vision") was released by Commodore's new Interactive Consumer Products division, which was headed by Nolan Bushnell.

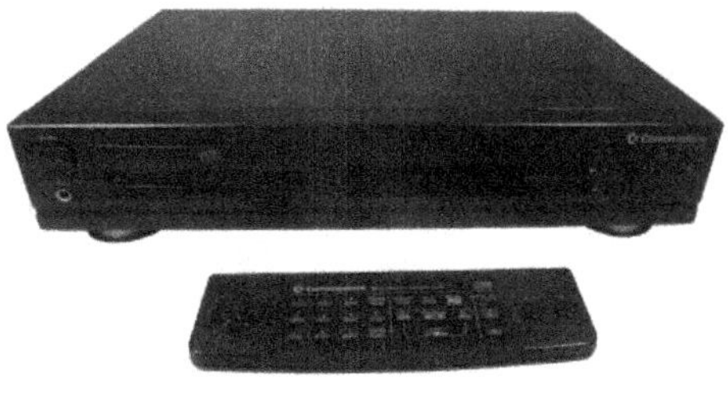

Commodore CDTV

The CDTV was essentially a modified Amiga 500, in which the floppy drive was replaced by a single-speed CD-ROM drive. It didn't look like a computer at all, and its styling was similar to that of a stereo component. The unit was sold with an infrared remote control, but it didn't come with a keyboard or mouse, although they could be purchased separately. Nearly one hundred discs were available for the unit upon its launch.

Although the CDTV was an Amiga on the inside, Commodore kept the Amiga name off the outside of the unit, so consumers wouldn't be confused into thinking that it was a computer. Oddly enough, the majority of the CDTV's advertising was in magazines catering to Amiga users, who had no interest in the CDTV at all, as they were mainly programmers and high-end software enthusiasts.

Philips, the company that had co-developed the compact disc with Sony, introduced its own multimedia player in October. Unlike Commodore's CDTV, which actually used a standard CD-ROM as its media, Philips' unit utilized a different media called *CD-I (CD-Interactive)*. And to add to the confusion, the name of the console was also called the *CD-i*.

Essentially, the CD-i and the CDTV performed the same functions, although the CDTV was a modified computer, while the CD-i was built from scratch right down to the specifications of the CD player itself. Both the CD-ROM used by the CDTV, and the CD-I used by the Philips CD-i, had been designed by Philips and Sony more than a half decade earlier.

Philips CD-i

The standard for the CD-ROM had been created in 1984, following the success of the audio CD. The standards for the CD-ROM specified that the disc contained a few bytes of data for a TOC (Table of Contents), header, sync, and ECC (error detection and correction). In addition, data and audio had to be stored on separate tracks. It also required that the CD-ROM could be read from just about all CD drives, no matter which company made it or what system it was on.

When Philips and Sony began their specifications for the CD-I in 1986, they found a way to combine the data and compressed audio onto a single track, which required less error correcting and allowed more room for data to be stored. Unlike the CD-ROM, which could be read from all drives, the CD-I could only be read from a drive that ran the Compact Disc Real-Time Operating System (CD-RTOS). And the first system to host this operating system was Philips' CD-i.

Philips didn't advertise the CD-i as a game machine, and the system was only slightly more successful than the CDTV, only because Philips pushed its unit harder than

Commodore did, with hands-on store displays. However, its retail price of $700 didn't help enamor it with consumers who only viewed it as an expensive game machine.

3DO

Trip Hawkins, the co-founder of Electronic Arts, the world's largest software company, viewed the CD as the future of videogames. And since it was a medium that was physically the same as audio CDs, Hawkins believed that it should be marketed in a similar fashion. While the videogame industry was centered around consoles that could only play games that were written specifically for them, the audio and video industries existed with multiple companies manufacturing and marketing their own hardware that played universal software. Hawkins' dream was for a single videogame standard that would play in multiple consoles marketed by different companies. To this end, he co-founded the *SMSG, Inc.* (San Mateo Software Group) along with several companies including Matsushita, Time Warner[9] and Electronic Arts. Their goal was to build a CD-based videogame system that would be manufactured by the partner companies and licensees in a fashion akin to the audio and video models. The name of the company was quickly changed to *The 3DO Company* to drive in the fact that their product was akin to the other two: Au***D***i***O***, Vi***D***e***O***, 3***DO***.

Nintendo's SNES

As Nintendo of America began gearing up for the September 9 release of the $200 16-bit SNES, many NES owners wondered if Nintendo would continue to support the 8-bit console afterwards. Nintendo had confirmed at the summer CES that the SNES would be compatible with NES games, but since the SNES used 72 pins to connect the cartridge to the console, and the SNES would use 62 pins, many critics questioned how the compatibility would be achieved. Nintendo later said that it would release an optional adapter that accepted NES cartridges and would insert into the SNES.

The SNES looked somewhat different than the Super Famicom. While rectangular in shape like its Japanese equivalent, the SNES was sharp boxy edge, where the Super Famicom was curved. And the square-shaped gray power switch and reset button on the Super Famicom were replaced by rectangular-shaped, purple buttons. The colorful control buttons on the Super Famicom were replaced with light and dark purple buttons on the SNES.[10]

Nintendo SNES

Most analysts agreed that Nintendo would sell out all two million SNESes that it had allocated for the United States. If the Super Famicom's history was any indication, then the Super NES would be successful from day one. Nintendo had sold out 300,000 Super Famicoms when it had debuted in Japan. Two weeks later, 400,000 additional consoles sold out in just one day. By early 1991, more than 1.5 million Super Famicoms had been sold. It took Sega and NEC over a year to jointly sell that number of 16-bit consoles in the

United States. Nintendo of America expected to double that number in just four months.

Nintendo of America was slightly off in its estimates. During the few months between the SNES' release[11] and the end of the year, the company sold 2.2 million of the consoles. The Genesis outsold the SNES that year with 55% of the total 16-bit sales. However, Nintendo still considered itself the victor, since Sega had an eight-month head start.

Sales for the SNES had been fueled in part by the game that came with it. Like the Super Famicom, the SNES was sold with *Super Mario World*. As with the Mario games that preceded it for the NES, *Super Mario World* went on to become one of the best-selling videogames of all time.

Another game that would later rank on "best games of all time" lists was released in Japan in November for the Super Famicom. *The Legend of Zelda: Triforce of the Gods* was the third installment in the highly-successful *The Legend of Zelda* series, and the first to be released for the Super Famicom. Whereas the second installment, *Zelda II: The Adventures of Link* (released in Japan in January 1987 and in the United States in December 1988), had strayed from the original game with a side view, *Triforce of the Gods* returned to an overhead view. The world in the game was so huge that the game's designers decided to use an 8-megabit cartridge at a time when most games only required 4-megabits.

Mascots

Super Mario World was the first 16-bit game to feature Mario, Nintendo's official mascot, who was the personification of videogames for millions of people around the world. It was also the first Mario game that was released after the introduction of Sega's own mascot, an intelligent blue hedgehog named Sonic.

Sonic the Hedgehog

Sonic the Hedgehog was released for the Genesis on June 23 in the United States, and in Japan three days later for the Mega Drive. In this *Mario Bros.*-type game, players controlled Sonic, who could travel at "supersonic" speeds. The game itself jumped off of store shelves almost as fast as its character. Sega took advantage of this popularity, and soon packaged it with the Genesis.

The game succeeded on many fronts. In Sonic, Sega had a mascot who could challenge Mario. And Genesis owners had a platform game that played much faster than anything that Mario appeared in.

Sega Lawsuits

As the Genesis developed a following in the United States, Sega began experiencing difficulties with third-party publishers, licensed and non-licensed alike. In June, RazorSoft, one of the Genesis licensees, wanted to release a game called *Stormlord*. Sega refused to manufacture it, because several female statues in the game were depicted without clothing. Sega requested for RazorSoft to change them but it refused, because it felt that the statues revealed no more than what was normally shown on television. Following this, Sega revoked RazorSoft's license. Undaunted, RazorSoft went ahead and released *Stormlord* on its own. Sega quickly sued RazorSoft for the unauthorized use of Sega's logo and trademarks, as well as for breach of contract.

Sega also initiated a lawsuit against Accolade, a third-party publisher that had reverse-engineered the Genesis in order to design unlicensed games for it.

Sega used a low-tech method to keep unlicensed companies from producing games that would run on the Genesis. Within the code of all valid games, the string '*SEGA*' was stored in a specific memory location. When the cartridge was inserted into the Genesis, the system would check to see if the word existed at the correct location. If it did, the message "**PRODUCED BY OR UNDER LICENSE FROM SEGA ENTERPRISES LTD.**" would display on the screen, and the game would begin. If the word was not found in the correct location, the game would not start.

While they were reverse-engineering the Genesis, the Accolade developers came across the *SEGA* string and figured that it might have something to do with getting games to work, so they imbedded the string into their own code. As they'd expected, when their games ran on the console, the screen displayed the message that the game had been produced by Sega, and then their game played.

Sega's lawsuit against Accolade was filed with two issues. The first was that Accolade did not have the right to reverse-engineer the Genesis so they could develop games that could play on the system. Sega's second issue was the trademark message that displayed at the beginning of each game. Sega contended that Accolade was purposely trying to pass their games off as having been either produced by or produced under license from Sega.

Accolade quickly filed a countersuit against Sega, citing "*restraint of trade, trademark infringement, and unfair business practices.*" Alan Miller, chairman and CEO of Accolade, charged: "Sega has consistently and unfairly pressured retailers and distributors around the world not to purchase videogame cartridges from Accolade." In addition, Accolade contended that Sega purposely displayed the message in order to pass Accolade's games off as its own.

At the hearing in April, the federal district court of San Francisco sided with Sega. Although Sega was granted a preliminary injunction preventing Accolade from selling any more Genesis game cartridges, the company had to post a one-million-dollar bond to cover Accolade's potential losses. Accolade quickly filed an appeal, hoping that it wouldn't have to recall the cartridges that were already in the stores.

In October, the Ninth Circuit Court of Appeals sided with Accolade on both issues. For the first, the court ruled that the reverse-engineering that Accolade had performed was considered *fair use,* since it constituted the only way in which they could gain access to "unprotected aspects of the program." In the second issue, the court ruled that Accolade had never intended to mislead consumers into believing that their games were actually produced or licensed by Sega, especially since the games' packaging specifically displayed disclaimers saying that the games were *not* endorsed by Sega. On the other hand, they found that Sega, while intentionally trying to squash competition, purposely claimed credit for the games with its startup message. Following the decision of the Appeals Court, Accolade quickly resumed its production of Genesis software.

Unlicensed NES Games

Nintendo was also having problems with its methods to prevent unlicensed publishers from cashing in on the continued popularity of the NES. Like Sega had done to Accolade, Nintendo sued Tengen, charging the third-party publisher with patent infringements in order to produce its NES-compatible cartridges. However, Tengen wasn't the only company that manufactured unlicensed cartridges for the NES and many critics accused Nintendo of making an example out of Tengen because it was by far the biggest. In its testimony, Nintendo proved that the three other non-licensed companies, American Video Entertainment, Color Dreams and Sharedata had not infringed upon its patented lock-out chip.

Although Nintendo didn't accuse these three companies of breaking any laws when they produced their unlicensed cartridges, Color Dreams wasn't taking any chances. It started a new company called *Wisdom Tree,* which began producing unlicensed, Christian-themed games to play on the NES. The belief was that Nintendo would never take a company to court if its sole business was developing religious, family-oriented games. Ironically, Wisdom Tree games sold better than the non-religious games from Color Dreams.

Wisdom Tree Unlicensed NES Game

Even though Nintendo deemed that the unlicensed games from American Video Entertainment, Color Dreams and Sharedata were legal, many retailers still refused to stock games from any of these companies, fearing reprisals from Nintendo. American Video Entertainment even sued Nintendo for $105 million, charging the company with violating antitrust laws. American Video Entertainment's main contention was that the lock-out chip forced the buying public into purchasing only Nintendo-licensed cartridges. One month later, American Video Entertainment accused Nintendo of making technical changes to the NES, which rendered the unlicensed games unplayable. Nintendo did not deny the tactic and responded to the accusation by saying that the changes were made in an ongoing effort to stop worldwide game counterfeiting. Afterwards, American Video Entertainment had nothing left to accuse Nintendo with. The costs pertaining to the frivolous lawsuit proved too much for the small publisher and forced it out of business.

On March 28, the United States District Court of the Northern District of California granted Nintendo a preliminary injunction that prevented Tengen from selling any more NES-compatible cartridges. The court ruled that Atari Games had lied to the Copyright Office so it could obtain a copy of the lock-out chip's source code. Tengen had to remove all of its NES-compatible cartridges from store shelves following the decision. Tengen quickly appealed, and the court allowed it to keep its games on the shelves while it waited for the appeal.

Nintendo Makes Amends

In April, NES owners learned that they would receive a $5 rebate coupon from Nintendo of America that they could apply to their next purchase of an NES cartridge. This came about because Nintendo of America had been charged with price-fixing. Allegations had been made that Nintendo of America had threatened retailers that if they charged customers less than $99 for an NES, they would receive late or unfilled shipments. Although Nintendo of America denied any guilt, in an effort to clear the matter quickly, the company agreed to send the $5 coupons to every registered NES owner who had bought the console between June 1, 1988 and December 1, 1990. The company also paid $1.75 million in administrative costs to Maryland and New York, the two states that had initiated the price-fixing investigation. An additional $3 million was paid by Nintendo of America to help with the enforcement of their antitrust laws.

The price-fixing suit arose from many allegations that Nintendo had used so-called strong-arm tactics in its attempt to create a monopoly in the videogame industry. As if in response to these charges, Nintendo began to loosen its iron grip. The first signs had come at the end of 1990, when the company announced that it was going to allow its licensees to manufacture and distribute their own games. Of course, Nintendo would still need to supply the licensees with the "infamous" lock-out chip, thus assuring that it would still profit from the deal. *Smash TV* became the first independently manufactured licensed game when it was released by Acclaim at the end of the summer.

In early 1991, Nintendo of America dropped the exclusivity clause that it required its licensees to use. Previously, in order to become a licensee, a company had to refrain from marketing a licensed title for any console other than the NES for a period of two years. This guaranteed that the games for the NES were unique. However, Nintendo of America only dropped this clause for games that were developed for the SNES. The standard contract remained intact for the 8-bit NES games.

Another lawsuit that Nintendo of America was involved in was against Galoob Toys and their Game Genie. By the end of 1990, Nintendo of America had successfully prevented the game-altering peripheral from reaching store shelves in the United States. However, Nintendo of America had failed to reach a similar injunction in Canada, where the unit had been distributed by Camerica since June 1990. Nintendo of America claimed that owners of the Game Genie had used the device to complete rented games and had no interest in purchasing them afterwards. But Nintendo of America couldn't prove that they had lost a single sale due to the Game Genie. In July, a U.S. District Court ruled that the Game Genie didn't infringe upon any of Nintendo's copyrights, and lifted the injunction that had banned Galoob from selling it. Although Nintendo of America promised to appeal, Galoob began shipping its long-awaited Genies in August. Shortly afterwards, the courts granted Galoob permission to pursue the nearly $15 million in sales that it estimated it had lost while Nintendo of America had kept the Game Genie off the market.

After Galoob released the Game Genie, the company announced that Codemasters was developing a Game Genie for the Genesis, which would be ready in time for Christmas 1992. Unlike its bout against Nintendo, Galoob didn't expect any trouble from Sega, and didn't receive any.

But Codemasters wasn't the first company to market a "game-cheating device for the Genesis. In November, another British company, Datel,[12] released the *Action Replay* for both the European Mega Drive and the Genesis. The device was similar to the Game Genie and an added bonus allowed Japanese Mega Drive cartridges to play on American Genesis consoles. Although unlicensed, the European Action Replay sold very well. The American version didn't fare as well.

Datel Action Replay

Acemore Game Action Replay

To make matters even more confusing in North America, another company, Acemore, announced a similar device for the NES. The *Game Action Replay*, which was unrelated to the similarly named Action Replay, allowed NES players to bring the action on the screen to a virtual standstill and then advance through the game one frame at a time, as if it were being viewed on a VCR. Games could also be played in slow motion. The Game Action Replay contained a lithium battery, which allowed games to be saved and then resumed from the exact same spot at a later date. The unit could save a total of five different game locations, either from one game, or from up to five different games, for up to six years.

Despite its age and inferiority to the 16-bit consoles, the NES was still the dominant gaming console in the United States. Therefore, third-party companies made sure that any peripheral that they released could be used with it. Other vendors sought innovative ways in which the NES could be used beyond gaming. At the end of September, Control-Data, a company that had made its name by developing early Super Computers, announced a modem for the NES. This modem would allow Minnesota residents to order lottery tickets online through their NES consoles. The state planned a six-month trial period beginning in the summer of 1992, when people could pay ten dollars monthly for the ability to order lottery tickets from their homes. Control-Data felt that if the service passed the trial, NES owners nationwide would eventually be able to use their consoles for other online services, such as CompuServe.

Naturally, the idea met with mixed reactions. Many people felt that it would give minors the ability to gamble, since they already had access to the NES. Control-Data claimed that adults who registered with the service would have to supply a password that could be withheld from minors in the household. In the end, the citizens of Minnesota felt that the state would be sending the wrong message to kids by releasing such a product. After hearing how the majority of the state's residents felt about it, the lottery commission quickly scratched its plans for the online lottery.

After achieving its victory against the Goliath-like Nintendo in Canada, Camerica decided to announce a trio of products that were sure to provoke Nintendo's ire. The first was, collectively, twenty unlicensed NES-compatible games. And unlike other unlicensed cartridges, each of these games would have a toggle switch that would allow them to be played on American and European NES consoles.

Camerica NES cartridge with toggle switch

Handheld Gold

The other two products that Camerica announced were never released at all, but they frustrated Nintendo all the same. One was an adapter that would allow Game Boy cartridges to be inserted into NES consoles so they could be played on standard television screens.

Camerica's other product that had Nintendo on edge was a portable NES player called *The Express*. Resembling a large Game Boy, the Express had a built-in color screen and didn't infringe upon any of Nintendo's copyrights or patents. Had the Express been released, it might have indeed challenged the Game Boy in the portable market. However, since it never reached the store shelves, the Game Boy continued to dominate the portable race, despite the fact that it was technologically inferior to the other consoles on the market.

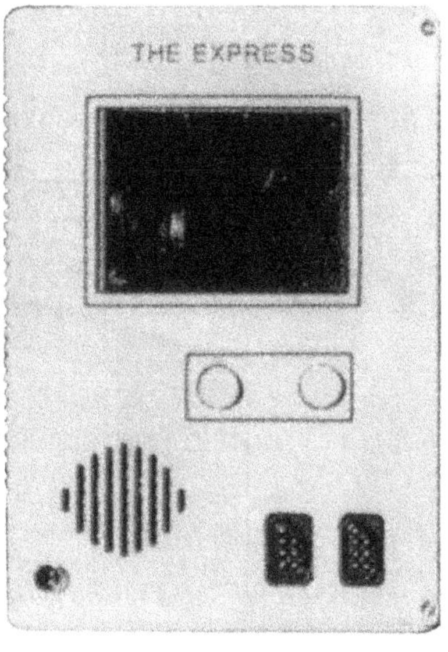

Camerica Express

The Game Boy's popularity was partly due to the Nintendo name, and partly due to the large amount of software that was available for it. While the ability to link two Game Boys together was a nice feature, many game designers felt that two wasn't enough. Nintendo released *F1 Race*, a first-person racing game, which came with an adapter that connected four Game Boys

Nintendo Game Boy 4-Player Adapter

Gametek InfoGenius Travel

Sharp Oz with Organizer Tetris

at one time. Bullet-Proof Software immediately announced a four-player football game to take advantage of Nintendo's new adapter, and also developed its own adapter that could support eight players at a single time.

Other companies sought practical uses for the Game Boy besides game playing. GameTek announced a line of *InfoGenius* cartridges that turned the Game Boy into an all-purpose information machine. One cartridge turned it into a portable spelling checker that could determine the correct spelling of over 70,000 words. Another offered a travel guide that included helpful information about twenty of the most popular American cities. GameTek also developed a number of cartridges for international travelers that allowed them to use their Game Boys as language translators. The company planned five languages: German, French, Italian, Japanese and Spanish. All of the InfoGenius cartridges retailed at $39.95 when they were released in the fall.

Coincidentally, while GameTek was turning the Game Boy into an electronic organizer, Sharp Corporation was turning its handheld electronic organizer into a game machine. For several years, the company had been selling the *Wizard*, a calculator-sized organizer that also functioned as a dictionary/thesaurus, time and expense manager and financial planner, with the help of different software cards. In October, Sharp introduced several game cards, such as *Organizer Tetris* and *Organizer Chess*.

With most of the portable sales going to Nintendo, Atari stepped up its campaign to make its Lynx color portable more visible to the public. In January, the company signed a deal with Flight Video, a company located in airports that rented out movies to fliers. Flight Video planned to open up outlets in twenty airports across the United States, where it would rent out a Lynx console and two games for $10 a day. Travelers could rent the Lynx before boarding their plane at one airport, and then return it at an outlet at another airport after they landed.

Sales for the Lynx doubled in 1991 from the previous year, prompting Atari Entertainment, the marketing arm of the company, to move from Sunnyvale to Lombard, Illinois. Atari announced shortly after the move that it was going to release a new, smaller and less expensive Lynx console in time for the summer. One graphics chip from the new console would replace four chips from the old unit, allowing Atari to sell the console for $99, which put it in the same price category as the Game Boy. However, when Atari actually did slash the price in April, it was still the original unit that was being sold. Atari was able to lower the price on the original model because for $99, all a consumer received was a Lynx console. Atari continued to market a $149 Lynx package that contained the console, a *California Games* game card, a power adapter, a multiple-player cable (standard with the Game Boy) and a coupon that was redeemable for an additional free game card. The new *Lynx II* finally began appearing in stores near the end of the year, *after* inventories of the original Lynx were depleted.

Atari Lynx II

The Lynx was popular, but its popularity came at the expense of Atari's sagging consoles. By the end of the year, Atari announced that it was discontinuing its 2600 and 7800 lines completely, so that it could concentrate on better supporting the Lynx.

One reason that the Atari Lynx was popular was because it didn't have any comparable competition. Unlike the Game Boy, it had a color screen, and unlike the TurboExpress, it was priced affordably. That changed in May, when Sega released its color portable Game Gear in the United States. For $149, buyers received the console and a game called *Columns*, a colorful contest that was similar to *Tetris*. Six games were available for the Game Gear at the time of its release, and Sega promised an additional thirteen titles by the end of the year.

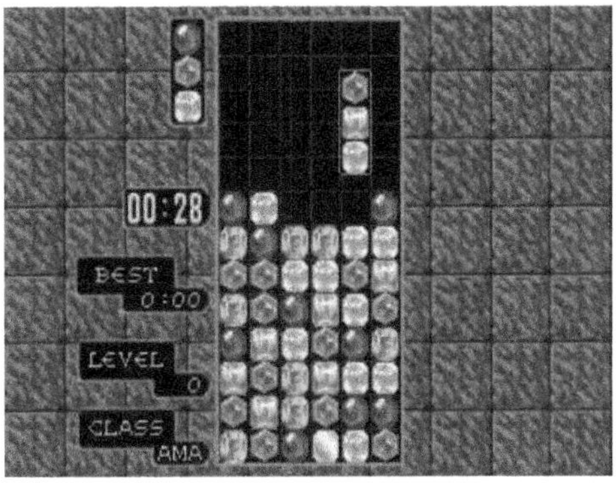

Sega Columns

The Game Gear hadn't done well in Japan, where it suffered from quality issues during its initial release. But the U.S. consumers were more receptive to Sega than the Japanese had been. However, since the Game Gear offered less software titles than the Game Boy, and its batteries wore out much faster, the American

Kalplus Master Gear Converter

Sega Game Gear TV Tuner

public bought the Game Boy in much larger numbers. The Game Gear did offer more titles than the Lynx, and Sega had a stronger marketing campaign than Atari, which helped make the Game Gear the number two handheld console in America.

Additional games became available for the American Game Gear when Hong-Kong based Kalplus introduced the *Master Gear Converter* on August 18. This small, $20 unit allowed American Sega Master System cartridges to play on the Game Gear.[13]

Other peripherals for the Game Gear included a battery pack, an AC adapter, a car AC adapter and a cable to connect two Game Gears together. And like NEC, Sega also introduced a peripheral that turned the Game Gear into a television set. The simply-named *TV Tuner* plugged into the cartridge port of the console and could capture both VHF and UHF signals. The ¥12,800 ($102) device, which was available in different TV standards in Japan, North America and Europe, also had an A/V input that allowed a VCR or even another videogame console to plug into it.

Arcade Virtuality

As home consoles were becoming more sophisticated, arcade manufacturers had to stay one step ahead and devise games that couldn't be played at home. Virtuality, a British company, introduced four virtual reality games into arcades. While the games were different, the basic play was the same. In each game, the player sat in a pod, an arcade cabinet designed to enhance the game's theme. One of the games, *Total Destruction*, had a racing theme, so the cabinet resembled a race car, complete with a steering wheel. In fact, *Total Destruction* was similar to first-person arcade games that had been around for years, such as Namco's *Pole Position*. In that game, a player sat in a cabinet and used a steering wheel as a controller, while viewing a race course on the screen in front of him. In *Total Destruction*, and the other games from Virtuality, there wasn't any screen in front of the player. Instead, players donned virtual reality goggles, which gave them the impression that they were immersed in the game.

Virtuality Pod

Sega Time Traveler

Sega's *Time Traveler* was another game that couldn't be played at home.[14] Devised by Rick Dyer, the creator of *Dragon's Lair*, *Time Traveler* utilized full motion video to present what was billed as the "*World's First Holographic Video Game*". Indeed, the live-action characters appeared to be holograms, presented in full 3D, and visible from any angle. The effect, however, was merely an optical illusion created from a huge curved mirror and a standard television set.

The game play itself was nothing out of the ordinary. However, the innovative presentation earned an average of one million dollars per week. Unfortunately, once the novelty wore down, players quickly grew tired of it. No other hologram game, either simulated or truly holographic, ever appeared again.

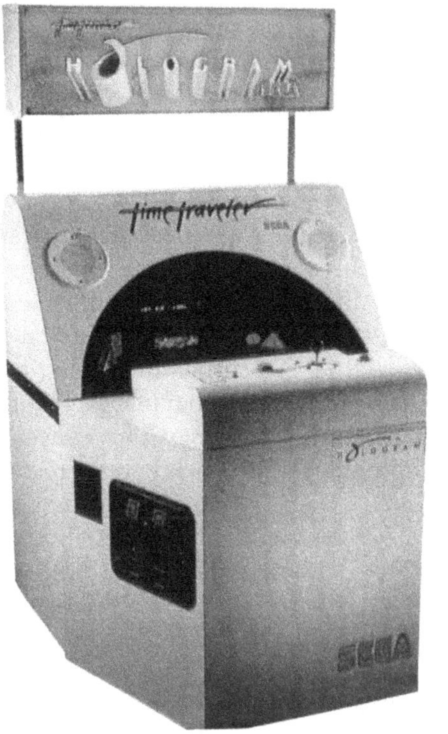

Sega Time Traveler Cabinet

While *Time Traveler* may have been a fad that spawned no imitations, Capcom's *Street Fighter II: The World Warrior* went on to become the best-selling fighting game of all time. *Street Fighter II* was a sequel to Capcom's 1987 arcade game, *Street Fighter,* which had introduced new play methods to the fighting game genre such as six-button configurations and command-based moves. *Street Fighter II* improved on these methods with a joystick and button scanning routine that sensed the controller motions that players were about to make, and responding with the correct moves. In addition, the game allowed players to choose from characters that had their own looks, fighting styles and moves. And thanks to a new chipset that Capcom had developed, the characters and background were highly detailed with animation that surpassed any arcade game before it.

Capcom Street Fighter II

Despite these improvements, there was little expectation that the game would be a hit. However, as word of mouth on the game spread, many arcades experienced long lines of gamers waiting to play the game. Since each of the eight characters had different fighting styles, gamers naturally wanted to try them all.

Beyond The Printed Page

By the end of 1991, the three major videogame magazines were doing so well that they all established "900" phone numbers. These numbers allowed players to call for information or game tips at rates ranging from one dollar to $1.75 per minute. The editor of *Electronic Gaming Monthly* proudly proclaimed in the June issue that the magazine was read by over a million readers each month. Although the circulation wasn't actually anywhere near that number, the magazine was so popular that each issue was passed around among many readers. In addition, *Electronic Gaming Monthly*'s publisher, Sendai Publications, launched two additional magazines to help fulfill the demand for information that gamers hungered for. *Mega Play* was aimed at Sega users, and *Super Gaming* was a magazine devoted to international gaming. As a leader in reporting international gaming news, Sendai also launched *World Net,* a network that various videogaming magazines around the world used for pooling their information. Meanwhile, Signal Research found its own niche in the gaming world by publishing a series of strategy guides that ranged from the Nintendo NES to sports games intended for children.[15]

GamePro, which had been the first magazine to install a "900" telephone number for gamers, set a new precedent on September 28, when it premiered a television show of the same name. Gamers no longer had to take their eyes away from their television sets in order to catch up on the latest gaming releases and reviews.

Videogame Culture

Videogames were hotter than at any prior time in their long history, a history that was partly displayed in St. Louis. On June 15, the National Videogame and Coin-Op Museum opened its doors. Visitors could view 75 arcade videogames and pinball machines. Among them was *Humpty Dumpty,* the first pinball machine to feature flippers, and, of course, the original *Pong.* The three-dollar admission price also included four free tokens.

Even the music that played in the games was popular. In 1991, the first of four yearly Orchestral Game Music Concerts was performed in Tokyo by the Tokyo City Philharmonic Orchestra. These concerts were recorded and later released on CD.

1991 also marked the end of home videogaming's second decade. It had been a volatile decade, which had begun with Atari leading an ever-growing industry. By the end of the decade, Atari was only a bit player. The industry now belonged to the Japanese and in particular to Nintendo, the company that had revitalized the dying industry and made it even bigger than it had been before.

But Atari wasn't prepared to surrender.

CHAPTER TWENTY
1992

As the third decade of videogaming began, the company that had led the industry during the majority of the second decade found itself no longer in the number-one position. This happened during the 1991 Christmas buying season, when Nintendo relinquished the throne to Sega, which had taken control of 55% of the 16-bit market. Most of the sales were attributed to the *Sonic the Hedgehog* game, which had attracted millions of new customers.

Both companies planned to release CD-ROM players during the year. And these CD-ROM players were the focuses of much of the attention at the annual winter CES held in January. Amazingly, the two units were to be very similar. Both would sit beneath their respective 16-bit consoles piggyback style, and both would run at 12.5 MHz and be capable of scaling and rotation. Nintendo claimed, however, that its CD-ROM player would contain eight megabits of RAM; two more than that of the Sega unit.

Nintendo used CES to officially announce that it had terminated its partnership with Sony. Philips used the show to affirm that it was working with Nintendo on a $200 CD-ROM drive that would be available for the SNES by January 1993.

Nintendo SNES with CD - Conceptional

Sega CD Consoles

Despite claiming that its CD-ROM player would be available for the Genesis before the end of 1992, Sega of America didn't display it at the winter CES, even though Sega of Japan had already released its Mega CD in Japan only one month earlier. Instead, Sega of America waited for the summer CES in May to officially unveil its $299 *Sega CD*. Technologically, the Sega CD was virtually the same as the Mega CD, although their software was incompatible.

On March 20, Sega of Japan released a ¥6,300 ($47) *Backup RAM* cartridge. This plugged into the cartridge slot of the Mega Drive to provide an additional 1MB over the 8KB of internal memory that was built-into the unit to save game information. Games could only be saved if they were programmed to include this feature.[1]

Mega CD Backup Ram

Sega's CD-ROM players offered the most advanced audio of any videogame console. JVC had helped Sega develop the audio, and in return, received permission to produce the Wondermega, a console that merged the Mega Drive and the Mega CD. JVC released the Wondermega under the Victor brand in Japan on April 1, with a retail price of ¥82,800 ($656), which was more than the combined price of the Mega Drive and Mega CD, but the Wondermega came with improvements over the individual units. JVC added Super VHS, which provided video output that was much more defined than anything else on the market. JVC also added a Digital Audio Processor and bass enhancer, which improved the audio over what was produced by the Mega CD. Also added to the console were several Karaoke features and MIDI (Musical Instrument Digital Interface) output. Although the unit could play standard music CDs, it did not have any standard physical control buttons

JVC Wondermega

such as *play* or *stop*. Instead, all CD functions were accessed through an onscreen menu. Even included in this menu was an *open* command, which was used to open and close the motorized CD tray.

Sega of Japan was so impressed with JVC's Wondermega that it released it under the Sega brand on April 24. At ¥79,800 ($630), it was slightly less expensive than JVC's model, but feature-wise, the two were essentially the same.

Sega of Japan also apparently liked the karaoke functions of the Wondermega so they made them available to owners of the Mega Drive and Mega CD. On November 18, the company released the *Mega CD Karaoke*, a ¥19,800 ($186) peripheral that provided the features of a karaoke machine, including a microphone, to the Mega Drive. Designed to sit along the left side of the Mega Drive/Mega CD combination, the Mega CD Karaoke connected to the Mega CD through the audio outputs in the rear of the unit.

Sega Mega CD Karaoke

Another off-shoot of the Mega Drive that Sega of Japan developed was the *Mega Jet*. This was a compact unit that passengers on Japan Airlines flights could rent. The Mega Jet didn't have a screen because it plugged into an LCD television that folded out from the seat's armrest.

The fact that JVC manufactured a console that used Sega software was a major blow against Nintendo. Although the Wondermega wasn't a runaway success, it still meant that there was extra revenue being made that Sega received and Nintendo didn't. And even without the Wondermega, Nintendo was increasingly losing market share to Sega. Nintendo's 16-bit system was trailing behind Sega's on both sides of the Pacific, and its CD-ROM player was not gaining traction.

In addition, Nintendo's ex-partner, Sony, announced that it was going to design games for Sega's CD-ROM player. However, the planned Sony-built console that would accept Nintendo's 16-bit cartridges was reevaluated. Sony's president, Norio Ohga, decided that this console wasn't in Sony's best interests, especially since it was becoming a Sega licensee. In June, Sony announced that the company planned to design its own videogame

Sega Mega Jet

console that utilized a CD-ROM player, but it wasn't going to be compatible with any existing software.

After Sony announced that it was going to enter the videogame business with its own console, many game publishers began getting nervous. With Sony and Nintendo coming out with CD-ROM players, and Sega and NEC already having CD-ROM players on the market,[2] the game publishers were concerned about all of the different CD formats that they would have to contend with. In October, the executives from Nintendo's largest licensees met with company president Hiroshi Yamauchi to convince him to collaborate with Sony again.

Meanwhile, Sega of America finally released its Sega CD at this time on October 15. Two of the first CD titles that were released exclusively for the Sega CD were *Night Trap* and *Sewer Shark*, the two titles that had been produced for Hasbro's failed Control-Vision system in 1988. Since the technology that enabled the games to work on videotape could actually work on any storage medium, Sega of America, anxious to deliver original products for its new CD system, readily released them.

Nintendo's CD Plans

Nintendo and Philips met with Sony, and the three companies agreed to create consoles that would use standard CD-ROM specifications worldwide. Philips would continue to manufacture the CD-ROM drive for Nintendo, while Sony would manufacture its previously-announced Play Station. Nintendo would control and license all games that would play on both systems. Sony would control all of the non-gaming media, such as educational software and movies that would play on its system. Sony's executives were ecstatic to again be partnered with Nintendo, whom they believed was going to be the victor in 16-bit gaming. Nintendo now announced an August 1993 shipping date, and still promised that its CD-ROM player would sell for $200.

However, even while they were announcing how great their forthcoming CD-ROM player would be, Nintendo's executives were actually losing their enthusiasm about it. Rather than compete directly against Sega, Nintendo decided it wanted to plan around the next generation of gaming.

Nintendo's definition of the next generation was the *Super FX* (SFX) custom chip that would be built into its new Super Famicom cartridges beginning in February 1993. This chip would be based on RISC technology and would display texture mapping, better shading and a real 3D effect, which in videogame terms, meant that characters could move in all directions, including forward and backwards, through an enormous landscape. Nintendo felt that its 16-bit CD-ROM player couldn't provide the new chip enough graphics power so Nintendo and Philips decided to center their CD-ROM development around a new custom 32-bit processor. The discs themselves would reside in plastic caddies and each disc would store 540 megabytes of data. The console would have a 56K-bit RAM memory chip that would be used to save game data.

Within a month of announcing the joint partnership between the three companies, Nintendo unexpectedly pulled the plug again; this time on both Sony and Philips. Nintendo's executives felt they could make higher profits with cartridge-based consoles, rather than CD-based ones. And with the forthcoming Super FX chip, they felt that their 16-bit console surpassed anything that was already on the market.

Nintendo and Sega Go To War

Throughout 1992, a price war had been going on in the United States between the 16-bit consoles from Nintendo and Sega. Nintendo of America fired the first shot in January when it lowered the suggested retail price of the SNES from $199.95 to $179.95. Sega of America quickly retaliated by lowering the price of the Genesis to $149 from $190, which also included a copy of *Sonic the Hedgehog*. The price reduction led to the sale of many more consoles for both companies, although by April, neither business took a decisive lead in 16-bit sales. However, Nintendo considered this a victory, since the Genesis had a two-year head start, a lower price and a much larger software library than the SNES.

In May, Sega of America decided to cut prices again, this time offering a Genesis for $100, with only one controller and no pack-in game. Nintendo of America quickly followed suit and lowered the price of an SNES with one controller and no game to $99.95. It also reduced the price of the full SNES package that included two controllers and a copy of *Super Mario World* to $149.95.

In order to lower the price of the Genesis, Sega also had to lower its own costs. This was done by replacing the console's motherboard with a new one that contained less circuitry. However, while they were in the process of upgrading, Sega's engineers also added circuitry that prevented unlicensed games, as well as some older Electronic Arts third-party titles,[3] from playing on the newly modified consoles.

Although the lower-cost models weren't compatible with all of the existing software, Sega vowed to rectify the problem with a new Genesis 2 and Sega CD 2, which it planned to release in 1993. These new units would be slimmer and sleeker than the current models, but they would be entirely compatible. Sega also announced at year's end that it was working on its own 32-bit home system that would be built around a RISC processor and would feature a built-in CD-ROM drive.

NEC America's Last Gasp

By reducing the base prices of their 16-bit consoles, Nintendo and Sega both seemed to be following NEC America's lead from 1991, when it had reduced the price of the TurboGrafx-16 to $100. Despite that price decrease, NEC America still continued to trail Nintendo and Sega in sales. In an effort to attract new customers, NEC America announced at the winter CES that it planned to release a new console called the *TurboDuo* sometime in the late summer or early fall. The TurboDuo, which had already been released in Japan the prior year as the PC Engine Duo, was simply a TurboGrafx-16 console with a built-in CD-ROM player that had four times the memory than the stand-alone one. This meant that the console could read information from the CD a lot quicker.[4]

On April 1, before the TurboDuo could be released, NEC America turned over the marketing of all of its videogame units to Turbo Technologies, Inc. (TTI). This was a joint-venture company between NEC America and Hudson Soft, the software company that developed the PC Engine.

In the late summer, TTI announced price cuts on its existing products. It reduced

NEC TurboDuo

the TurboGrafx-16 to $70, which included one game, *Keith Courage In Alpha Zones*. It also reduced the TurboGrafx-CD to $150. The $220 combination price for both the console and CD-ROM player was well below the price that Sega wanted for its Genesis and Sega CD player.

On October 10, TTI released the TurboDuo in the New York and Los Angeles areas for $300. TTI promised that the rest of the country would receive the unit in early 1993, when they also planned to release a peripheral that would allow gamers to use the TurboDuo's CD player as a CD-ROM drive for IBM or Macintosh computers.

By year's end, rumors began spreading that TTI was developing a 32-bit CD-based system that was based on a custom RISC processor. An availability date for this new system wasn't mentioned. Meanwhile, other CD-based systems were being released, but they were being marketed as multimedia players, a designation that completely confused consumers. In November, one week before Thanksgiving, Tandy released its own multimedia player called the *Video Information System (VIS)*. Like Commodore's CDTV, which had not been released in the United States, the VIS was built around an existing computer operating system, a special version of Microsoft's *Windows 3.1* called *Modular Windows*. The system was sold only at Tandy's Radio Shack stores and retailed for $699.[5]

While Tandy began filling Radio Shacks with its VIS, The 3DO Company began releasing information regarding its new machine, which it wasn't labeling as a multimedia device.

The 3DO was going to be the first videogame console that used CDs exclusively as its software media. With a 32-bit RISC processor, the machine would operate at a speedy

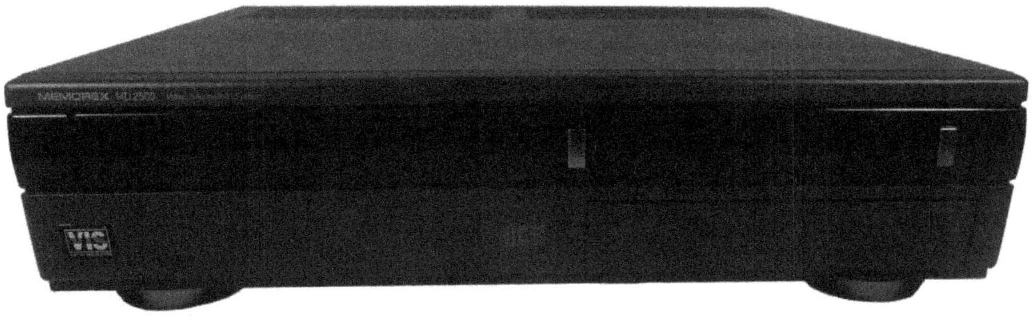

Tandy VIS

1992

25Mhz. Unlike other gaming machines, the 3DO would process compressed data, which would allow the CPU to retrieve more data from the CD in less time than with conventional data.

The 3DO console would have plenty of expansion ports, so it would be ready for any future technology. It would also have additional ports for players who wanted to add extra controllers or a MIDI keyboard.

The 3DO had plenty of backing. Behind it were giant corporations such as Matsushita (Panasonic), Time Warner and MCA. Third-party software support also seemed to be in the bag, as many companies were interested in the machine. Almost 470 people attended a 3DO developer's conference to see what the machine was capable of. Fifty third-party companies had already signed up to work on the machine by the time it was officially announced.

The Jaguar

Meanwhile, the oldest videogame company was also making its plans for 1993. Unlike 3DO, gaming pioneer Atari initially was highly secretive about its forthcoming Jaguar. In an early 1992 press release, Bob Schuricht, Atari's National Sales Director, claimed that the company was considering several configurations for the Jaguar, including both 32- and 64-bit architectures. But the press release was vague about how software would be loaded into the machine, citing just about every input device imaginable, from cartridges, CDs and diskettes to keyboards and modems. Atari wasn't taking any chances. It planned to use whichever technology the industry seemed to be heading towards. By not committing itself to any set technology, Atari planned its Jaguar to be at the forefront of the videogame industry, once it would finally be released.

By the end of the year, Atari's officials were finally willing to speak openly about the Jaguar. The system would be 64-bit and was scheduled for release sometime in the summer of 1993. It would contain a RISC-based processor and new custom chips that would allow for scaling, rotation and stereo sound. It would accept cartridge-based games that would contain more memory than SNES cartridges, but less than those for the Neo•Geo.

According to Atari, four game cartridges would be available when the Jaguar launched, followed by two new cartridges every month. Atari also planned peripherals, such as a keyboard and a modem. Surprisingly, the 64-bit system would be inexpensive. While Atari publicly hoped to sell the Jaguar for $99, it realized that $150 would be more realistic if a game cartridge were included.

As Atari geared up to release its newest console, it also said goodbye to one of its oldest. In June, after fifteen years, the company officially retired its VCS.

The Supervision

During the second half of 1992, the only console that was available from Atari was its portable Lynx. Information on sales for that unit were status quo, and the company didn't release any news regarding its plans in the portable market. And while none of the companies that were manufacturing handheld consoles had anything new to report, Atari's competitors all reduced the prices of their respective units. In January, Nintendo of America reduced the retail price of the Game Boy from $89.95 to $79.95. Sega of America responded in May by dropping the price of the Game Gear to $100. And TTI followed suit by lowering the price of the TurboExpress to $200. In addition, the price of the latter's TV tuner was reduced to $60.

Nintendo of America lowered the price of the Game Boy again in June, this time to $50, which didn't include a game cartridge or a video-link cable. For the same price, consumers could purchase a new portable unit called the *Supervision,* which had been released by Hong Kong-based Watara in several countries through a number of different distributors.

The Supervision looked very much like a Game Boy, although its monochrome LCD screen measured 2.76" X 2.76", which clearly made it the largest screen of any portable system. Its control buttons were also larger than the ones on the Game Boy and spaced a little farther apart. It also didn't feature the traditional Nintendo directional crosshair button. Instead, it mimicked the crosshair's appearance by having four separate buttons that served the same purpose, situated in a diamond-like configuration. Like the Game Boy, the Supervision offered stereo sound and the capability to link two units together.

The Supervision sold for approximately $50 and included one game, while additional cartridges sold for about $15. Watara promised more than 40 cartridges would be available but none of them by third-party vendors. By August, the company also planned to release a link that would connect the Supervision to a standard television set. Although the Supervision had a monochrome screen, the games would display in color on a color TV set.

Watara Supervision

The closest thing that Nintendo had to color Game Boy games was a rumor that had circulated around the winter CES about a color Game Boy in development. Knowledgeable sources claimed that the new unit would be backward-compatible, although existing standard Game Boy cartridges would still display in gray and white. They also said that Nintendo planned to keep the price of the color portable at $99. However, in order to achieve that, the screen would need to be of a lower resolution than either the Lynx or the Game Gear. Nobody speculated about when Nintendo hoped to get this unconfirmed unit into stores.

1992

Online Gaming

One feature that all of the portables shared was the ability to link one or more units together, allowing players to compete against one another head-to-head with their own unit in hand. Such a feature was necessary, since the tiny screens on the handhelds weren't congruent for multiplay. Console systems hooked up to television sets that many people could view at the same time so there was never any reason to link more than one console together.

Ever since Mattel had offered PlayCable for the Intellivision in 1980, many vendors had announced plans offering alternative methods of delivering games into homes. It was no different in 1992, when several companies announced their intentions to connect players via the phone lines and other methods.

Keith Rupp conceived the idea of linking NES consoles together via a modem in 1990. He sought investors and caught the eye of Nolan Bushnell. By 1992, they displayed a prototype 300-baud modem at CES, which they called the Ayota View. The response to the modem was positive.

Bushnell immediately took over all aspects of the company. It had been his insistence that the modem only be 300-baud in order to keep costs down, although Rupp realized that that speed was much too slow to support any serious gaming. This turned out to be irrelevant; when Bushnell had problems with another venture that he was involved in, he abruptly dropped out of his partnership with Rupp.

On his own, Rupp started a new company, which he called Baton Technologies, and quickly upgraded the modem, which he renamed the *Teleplay*, to 2400 baud. Rupp also realized that it didn't make sense for the modem to support only one console, so he had games designed that could play on several consoles. This way, a gamer with an NES could compete against someone playing on a Genesis.

Baton hoped to have its system ready by the spring of 1993. It was an uphill battle, however. Both Nintendo and Sega showed little interest in the modem, and Baton couldn't get an official license from either company. Although Baton proceeded with manufacturing the Teleplay, marketing it to stores was difficult without a license. That also created a *Catch-22* situation for Baton. Third-party software publishers were interested in making their games compatible with the Teleplay only if the unit was licensed.[6]

Another online system that was to begin operating in the spring was the *Games Channel*, which planned to supply games into households on a pay-per-play basis, via cable. The television set would receive the games and then the player would use his telephone to play them. Although users wouldn't need a game console to play, the Games Channel offered a $90 modem called the *Super Power American Competition Cartridge* (SPAC) for NES and Genesis owners. Players could "rent" games by downloading them into the SPAC via an 800 phone number. The SPAC could then be plugged into the game console like any standard cartridge. Games would remain in the SPAC for 72 hours.

A third system, the *Interactive Network*, used radio signals to deliver games into homes. For a one-time, $200 start-up fee, subscribers received a rechargeable battery and a Control Unit, a handheld device, half the size of a lap-top computer, which included a monochrome screen and a retractable keyboard. Afterwards, the monthly subscription fee was $15 for solo play or $35 for competitive play.

Once a person subscribed, T=the Control Unit received the information just like a radio. Game information came from FM radio signals and the Public Broadcasting System. Once they were tuned in, subscribers could access games and information. Competitive-play subscribers could plug their Control Units into their phone lines and compete head-to-head against other subscribers.

The Interactive Network hoped to release a Genesis-compatible Control Unit in 1993. This cartridge-sized Unit would plug into the Genesis like any other cartridge, and would offer the Interactive Network's services over the television instead of the small screen that was supplied with the Control Unit.

Target Practice

Sega did release a game that pit two or more players against one other but it had nothing to do with videogames. *Lock-On* was a laser tag game in which gamers fired infrared guns at headbands worn by other players. Each player's headband had an LED counter that started at "9". Each time a player was "hit", his counter decreased by one point. When it reached zero that player was out of the game. The last player remaining was the winner.

Sega Lock-On

Sega also released an infrared light gun that was used for videogames. The *Menacer*. Looking like a futuristic bazooka, the $60 Menacer was completely cordless. It worked in conjunction with a separate infrared controller that attached to the Genesis and sat on top of the TV. The Menacer was sold with one cartridge that contained six games.

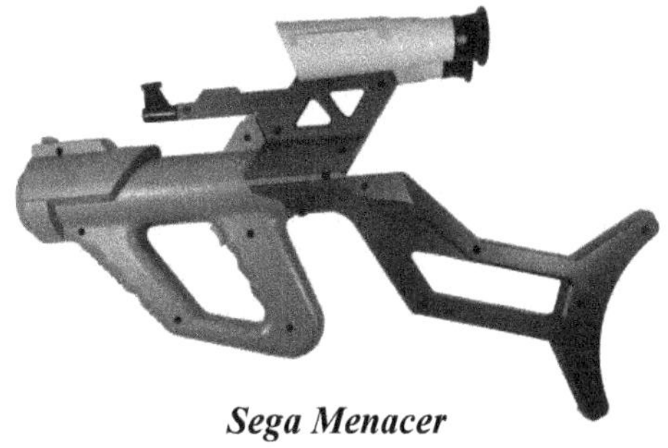

Sega Menacer

Coincidentally, Nintendo released a product that was almost identical to Sega's Menacer. The *Super Scope* also retailed for $60 and was also packaged with a cartridge that included six games. The Super Scope was released for the SNES in North America, and in Europe and Australia, where it was called the Nintendo Scope. The unit was also released in Japan, but interest in it was so light that Nintendo of Japan quickly withdrew it from the market.

Nintendo Super Scope

While both six-game cartridges were packaged with light guns, other companies were releasing stand-alone multigame cartridges. Camerica's Quattro series of cartridges each contained four games. American Video Entertainment planned the *Maxivision 30*, a $149 cartridge that featured 30 games,[7] and Active Enterprises offered the *Action 52*, a $199 cartridge with 52 games.

Street Fighter II

Although the multigame cartridges were expensive, the actual price per game turned out to be fairly affordable. On the other hand, Capcom designed a single game for the SNES that was expected to retail within the $75-$85 range.

The game was *Street Fighter II: The World Warrior*, the SNES translation of the most popular arcade game since *Pac-Man*. Capcom didn't just want to settle for a home rendition of the game; it wanted a home version that was nearly identical to its arcade counterpart. Soon after the game's development began, it was clear to the designers that they couldn't fit everything into an 8-megabit cartridge, which Nintendo had pioneered with *The Legend of Zelda: Triforce of the Gods*, or even a 12-megabit SNES cartridge. They finally decided to forge ahead into uncharted territories with 16-megabit cartridges. This proved successful, but the extra circuit boards within the cartridges contributed to the higher price of the game. Capcom was confident that despite the high price, *Street Fighter II* fans would come out in droves to purchase the game. And they were correct. After Capcom released the $70 *Street Fighter II* in June, the game went on to sell over one million copies by the end of the year. *Electronic Gaming Monthly (EGM)* called the SNES version of *Street Fighter II* the best game of 1992.

Capcom Street Fighter II for SNES

Just behind *Street Fighter II* on *EGM's* list was *Sonic the Hedgehog 2*, which was released worldwide in November. This title basically took the original game and improved on it by adding new, longer levels, brighter colors and a new character named *Tails*, who followed and assisted Sonic. While the overall game was applauded by most gamers and reviewers, an included simultaneous two-player version was equally disparaged. This version offered a horizontally split screen, on which one player controlled Sonic and the other controlled Tails. However, the split screen caused the CPU to work twice as hard, dramatically slowing down the action and displaying a lot of screen flicker.

While *Street Fighter II* and *Sonic the Hedgehog 2* were major successes for Capcom and Sega, it was Nintendo that scored with one of the top games of the year and of all time. *The Legend of Zelda: A Link to the Past* was the SNES version of *Triforce of the Gods*, which had been released in Japan in 1991.[8]

Illegal Software

With such memorable and best-selling titles being released, there was a lot of money being made in the videogame industry, both legally and illegally, which included the profits from an inundation of counterfeit games manufactured in Asia. Just like counterfeit watches and jeans, there were few differences between the counterfeits and the real products, except that the companies who developed the real games didn't receive any compensation from these sales. This problem had plagued the industry since the golden days of the Atari 2600, and cost game companies an estimated billion dollars per year. Several Taiwanese companies admitted in the May 1991 issue of *Asian Sources Electronics* that they manufactured over one million illegal Nintendo cartridges every month. The U.S. Customs Service agreed with this, citing that Taiwan had accounted for approximately 70% of all counterfeit electronics seized between October 1990 and March 1991.

In February, Nintendo lobbied United States trade representatives to do something about this problem. Most of the chips that were used in counterfeit cartridges were manufactured by United Microelectronics Corporation, in which the Taiwanese government had a 30% stake. Nintendo said that since Taiwan helped cause the problem, its government needed to take steps to end it.

Congress considered a bill that would serve harsh penalties to any person caught manufacturing or distributing over fifty pieces of illegal software. The offender would receive up to $250,000 in fines and five years in prison.

Bankruptcy

Even with the overwhelming influx of counterfeit games, most software publishers still enjoyed hefty profits. However, not all vendors were so fortunate. Two well-established companies found themselves in bankruptcy court.

The first was Mediagenic, formerly Activision, the first company to publish third-party software for videogame consoles. By 1991, the company was saddled with losses mounting $26 million, partly from lackluster sales that only amounted to $28 million and partly from the Magnavox lawsuit decision. Seeing an opportunity, venture capitalist Bobby Kotick assembled a team that invested $440,000 and wound up owning 33% of the company. Kotick then assumed Bruce Davis' role of CEO of the company. Using Electronic Arts as a model that could be improved on, Kotick eliminated the business software to concentrate on games. In early 1992, Mediagenic filed for Chapter 11 protection under the Bankruptcy Code in order to restructure. When the company emerged from bankruptcy in December, Kotick relocated the company from San Francisco to Los Angeles and changed its name back to Activision.

The other software company wasn't as fortunate. HAL, a software designer for the Nintendo systems, simply closed its doors during the summer as the result of poor Japanese videogame sales. Even though HAL's American subsidiary was still profitable, the company shut down its operations on both sides of the Pacific.

More Companies In Court

Other videogame companies continued to spend time in civil court for most of the year. In April, a U.S. District Court sided with Sega and ruled that Accolade had infringed upon Sega's copyrights when it created games for the Genesis. Accolade appealed, and in August, a U.S. Court of Appeals sided with them. This opened the door and allowed software developers to disassemble copyrighted programs, when no other means were available to sidestep code barriers -- as long as the disassembled code wasn't used in the new program. Sega attempted to appeal this verdict, but their case was dismissed in

October.

In addition to the Accolade suit, Sega was sued by an inventor named Jan Coyle, who claimed that he had developed the technology that Sega used in the Genesis to display its on-screen colors. The jury sided with Coyle on April 10. In an out-of-court settlement, Sega promised to pay the inventor $43 million. In exchange for this, Sega was free from any future problems with the patent.

Sega wasn't the defendant in all of the lawsuits in which it was involved. The company did win its 1991 suit against RazorSoft, after RazorSoft's president, Kyle Shelly, admitted that his company had indeed infringed upon Sega's trademarks and copyrights when it had released *Stormlord.* Following this admittance, RazorSoft remained an authorized licensee of Sega.

A trial between Nintendo of America and Atari Corp. began in February. In this suit, Atari. charged that Nintendo had illegally taken over 80% of the game market between 1986 and 1990, causing Atari. to lose $160 million in damages. Atari claimed that Nintendo used unfair business practices to force licensees into producing software only for the NES. This didn't only hurt the competition, it destroyed it. Nintendo responded to the suit by saying that Atari. was hurt by its own miscalculations and its attempts to compete cheaply. The jury agreed with Nintendo. After nine weeks, the trial ended when the jury decided that Nintendo had not harmed Atari. and didn't have any intent to monopolize the U.S. gaming market.

Later, in September, in a trial brought forth by Nintendo against Atari Games for copyright infringements, a U.S. Court of Appeals ruled that reverse-engineering was a legitimate business practice. However, it also agreed with Nintendo that Atari had indeed infringed upon Nintendo's copyrights. Atari quickly appealed the verdict, but lost and was forced to recall all of the unlicensed games for the NES that it had distributed under the Tengen label.

In December, the U.S. Federal Trade Commission closed its own antitrust investigation against Nintendo and didn't take any action against the company.

Nintendo wasn't as fortunate in another lawsuit. In July, the Ninth Circuit Court of Appeals sided with Lewis Galoob Toys and awarded that company the $15 million that it sought from Nintendo for lost sales of its Game Genie. Nintendo had barred the company from marketing the Game Genie from July, 1990 until Galoob's triumph in July, 1991.

Before the ruling, Galoob did get fully licensed by Sega, and blessed with its seal of approval. A Genesis Game Genie was announced at the winter CES. Also announced was a Game Genie for the Nintendo Game Boy. But although the unit was finished in time for the summer CES, Galoob did not display it for fear that Nintendo might hold up its production with another lawsuit. However, following the court's summer ruling, Galoob began production of the Game Boy Game Genie and even released a Game Genie for the SNES.

But while Galoob was only announcing a Game Genie for the Mega Drive/Genesis, Datel had already delivered with its Action Replay. Now the company was foraging ahead with a new cheat device called the *Pro Action Replay*, which altered game code like the Action Replay. As with the Game Genie, players had to input specific codes into the Action Replay in order to make it work correctly. The Pro Action Replay altered the program's code itself, by searching the console's RAM for specific addresses that held different game variables. The player inputted into the Pro Action Replay the features that he wanted activated, and the unit changed the appropriate variables into constants.

Datel also released version of the Pro Action Replay for the Sega Master System, NES and SNES. All of them continued to be unlicensed. And they all provided cross-regional support, such as allowed a European PAL SNES cartridge to play on an American NTSC console and vice versa. What the Pro Action Replay couldn't do was let NES cartridges

Innovation Super 8 Converter

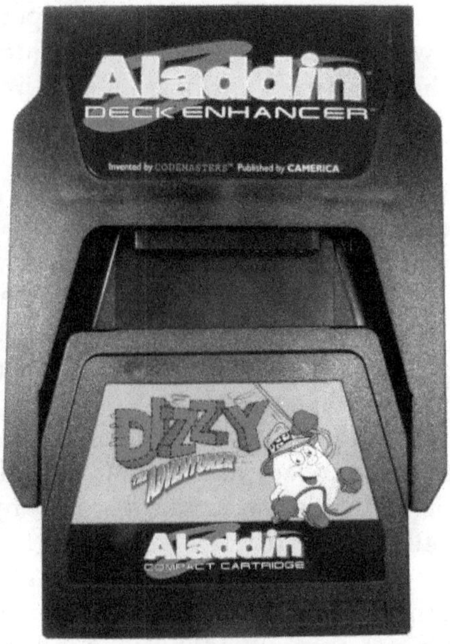

Camerica Aladdin

Bandai Datach Joint-ROM System

play on a SNES machine. But Innovation took care of that. The peripheral company released the *Super 8 Converter*, a $60 device that sat atop an SNES and accepted NES and Famicom cartridges.

Superchargers For The SNES

In mid-1992, Camerica, the company that originally had the North American rights to the Game Genie, announced the *Aladdin*, a new device by Codemasters that it felt would take the NES world by storm. The Aladdin; a $30 cartridge that contained an enhanced graphics SuperChip, a 64K graphics expansion chip and a battery to save games, was basically a modern version of Starpath's Supercharger. Accompanying the Aladdin were cartridges, called *game chips*, that would retail between $15 and $20. Once the Aladdin base unit had a game chip inserted, the two behaved together like a standard game cartridge; but the Aladdin combo was typically much cheaper. Camerica hoped that the Aladdin would be on store shelves by January, 1993.

On December 29, before Camerica could release the Aladdin for the NES, Bandai released a similar device for the Famicom. The *Datach Joint-ROM System*, which had been licensed by Nintendo, was an oversized unit that plugged into the cartridge slot of the Famicom. It then accepted individual ROM cartridges. But the Datach wasn't exactly the same as the Aladdin, as it also had a card-reader slot. Throughout a game, special cards could be slid through the reader. The Datach would then scan the bar code that was embedded in the card, which would then add additional features to the game. Not all games that used the Datach required the barcode reader. The system retailed for ¥7,800 ($63) and was packaged with one game cartridge, *Dragon Ball Z*, and several cards. Additional cartridges sold for ¥2,800 ($23), which was much less than a standard Famicom game would cost.

A second barcode game was also available for the Famicom. In 1991, Epoch had released a handheld device in Japan called the *Barcode Battler*. This unit had an LCD screen in its center and an action button on each side of the screen. At the lower portion of the unit was a card scanner. Players could scan bar codes from either cards that came with the device, or from every day products. The Barcode Battler would then create characters based upon the inputted codes. These characters would then battle against one another.

The Barcode Battler became very successful in Japan so in March, Bandai released a new model called the *Barcode Battler II*. This unit wasn't much different than the original except that it also featured an interface port. Nintendo of Japan took advantage of this port and in December it released a Famicom game called *Barcode World*. This game was packed with an adapter that connected to the Barcode Battler II's expansion port and the Famicom's controller port.[9]

Barcode Battler II with Famicom Adapter

Even the Game Boy succumbed to the lure of the barcode games. On December 25, Namcot (a Namco brand name) released the *Barcode Boy*, a barcode reader for the Game Boy. Although the Barcode Boy connected to the Game Boy console via a link cable that plugged into the handheld's expansion port, it covered the cartridge slot. Coinciding with the release of the Barcode Boy was the release of a battle game called *Space Battle*.[10] As with most other barcode games, the scanned barcodes were used to create and customize the fighting characters.

Namcot Barcode Boy

TV Videogame Shows

In January 1992, nearly a decade after *Starcade* first aired on American television, *Gamesmaster*, Great Britain's first videogame-related television program, launched on that country's Channel Four.

Unlike *Starcade, Gamesmaster* catered to console gamers. Gamers competed against one another playing console videogames, particularly the Mega Drive. *Gamesmaster* also had a segment where they reviewed new games that were being released. The show enjoyed a healthy relationship with the videogame industry. For instance, actual journalists from *Computer and Video Games* magazine reviewed the games. Videogame developers also helped out by adding special levels to their games that were used in competition on the show.

Videogame Demographics

The videogame industry as a whole seemed to be very steady. In a Christmas-time Gallup Poll of 500 children between the ages of 7 and 12, 63% named videogame systems when asked which gifts they really wanted. As a second choice, 54% chose portable systems. Finally, as a third choice, the winner was game software, according to 58% of the respondents.

Videogames weren't just popular among children. Adults, many of whom had been die-hard gamers during the original videogame golden age of the eighties, were also playing modern games. It wasn't unusual for commuters to be playing their Game Boys after a day at the office. With this in mind, a company called GEC-Marconi Inflight Systems signed a contract with United Airlines to install 6-inch diagonal video screens into the armrests of seats on all international Boeing 747s and 777s, so passengers could play videogames or watch movies at their seats. The companies hoped that the new service would begin by early 1993.

Electronic Games

Even the magazine editors realized that not all game players were teenagers and younger. Arnie Katz and Bill Kunkel, the two who were responsible for both *Electronic Games* and *Videogames & Computer Entertainment*, left the latter magazine in 1992 to join Decker Publications, a sister company of Sendai Publications, the publisher of *Electronic Gaming Monthly*. There they started a new magazine that they fondly called *Electronic Games*, evoking their first, but now defunct, magazine. *Electronic Games* was different from other magazines on the newsstand, as it catered to older game players, those who were in college and beyond. No longer did adult gamers have to read magazines that were targeted for children in order to keep up with the industry. *Electronic Games* didn't tell readers how to beat the games, but it did provide them with the insight behind those games.

Ironically, as the age bracket for games increased, Nintendo set its eyes on another type of game that appealed to all ages: baseball. In late December, 1991, the Seattle Mariners baseball team had been put up for sale. Rather than face the possibility of having an outside buyer purchase the team and move it out of state, Hiroshi Yamauchi, owner of Nintendo Company Limited of Japan, formed an investor group with several Seattle businessmen and called it *The Baseball Club of Seattle*. The group offered to buy the Mariners for $100 million. Yamauchi would own 60% of the team, and the other investors would own the remainder. Protests immediately came in from around the country from outraged baseball fans who didn't want another team owned by foreign interests. It was bad enough that two teams were owned by Canadians, but at least they were still located in North America. The fans looked at Yamauchi's offer as just another way in which the Japanese were taking over American businesses.

The Baseball Club of Seattle negotiated with Major League Baseball's Ownership Committee for several months. The deal was finally approved on June 30, but only after the Baseball Club of Seattle agreed to reduce Yamauchi's controlling interest to 49%. The rest of the investors then had a 51% controlling interest in the team. This way, at least the majority of the team was still American-owned.

Nintendo didn't need the Mariners to retain a strong presence. When the summer CES was held in Chicago, Nintendo's 76,000-square-foot booth was the largest in the history of the trade show. Around the same time, production began on *Super Mario*, a feature film starring Bob Hoskins and Dennis Hopper, based on the famous Nintendo character.

After beginning the year on a low note, Nintendo was now bigger than ever.

CHAPTER TWENTY-ONE
1993

By 1993, videogames were creating so much excitement that it seemed like the golden age all over again. Even the print media appeared to be revitalized. Future, a British media company that had been founded in 1985 by Chris Anderson, introduced two new videogame magazines during the year.

Gamesmaster premiered in January as a tie-in to the TV show that began a year earlier. The two were so closely related that everyone who worked on the magazine had also appeared on the show at least once. The magazine tried to copy the feel of the TV show. For example, the review section in the magazine featured the review booth that was on the show. Future's second videogame magazine of the year debuted in October. *Edge* was primarily aimed at adults, unlike most of the other videogames magazines available in Britain or the United States.

Gamesmaster

Edge

Although neither magazine was sold in the United States, Future began sowing the seed by purchasing an American company, GP Publications, the publisher of *Game Players Sega-Nintendo,* in November.

Meanwhile, in the United States, *Videogames & Computer Entertainment* shortened its name to *Video Games* in September, joining the year-old *Electronic Games* in having the same title as a magazine from the eighties.

While the magazines appeared to have stepped out of the early eighties on a merely superficial level, several new software titles brought games from the eighties to the computers of the nineties. *Microsoft Arcade* included the Atari arcade games *Missile Command, Asteroids, Centipede, Tempest* and *Battlezone.* Although classic games had been released for current systems before, *Microsoft Arcade* marked the first time that old games were viewed from an historical perspective. The manual that accompanied the disc contained histories about how the original arcade games had been developed.

Even though the games themselves had been rewritten for *Microsoft Arcade,* their graphics and gameplay were exactly the same on the modern computers as they had

Microsoft Arcade

been in arcades over a decade earlier. Microsoft had actually released two versions of *Microsoft Arcade*, one for *Windows 3.1* PCs and the other for Mac computers. That was something that hadn't changed since the time when the games on *Microsoft Arcade* had been new, the incompatibility among videogame consoles and computers. Fortunately, one company was attempting to change that.

3DO Appears

3DO, Trip Hawkins' company that planned to market a universal videogaming console, made its first appearance at the winter CES in January. While the unit appeared to be similar to the multimedia devices from Philips and Commodore, Hawkins stressed that the 32-bit 3DO was a videogame console first and foremost. Still, the unit would also be capable of playing educational software and displaying Kodak photo CDs. It also had one port that allowed the inclusion of a computer keyboard, and another that permitted several peripherals to "daisy chain" together. The console would also use this second port to support new peripherals that were being planned, such as a cartridge that would provide the ability to display full-motion video, and 3D goggles that were similar to Sega's LCD Master System 3D glasses. Finally, the 3DO was also being designed with a TV receiver so it could later take advantage of interactive cable television when that technology became available.

By the time The 3DO Company presented a prototype console at CES, they already had over 80 independent companies signed on to produce software for it. The unit seemed so impressive that over 500 people attended a 3DO press conference.

Although 3DO designed and developed the console, it licensed the manufacturing rights out to third-party companies. The first company to announce that it would be release a 3DO player was Panasonic, a subsidiary of Matsushita, one of 3DO's founding partners. Panasonic displayed its *FZ-1 REAL* (Realistic Entertainment Active Learning) 3DO player to a select group on May 13. By this time, there were over 200 third-party software licensees, more than for any other console. Most of the group agreed that the 3DO was well worth its high $700 price. Panasonic officially debuted the REAL 3DO player at the summer CES in June, where it displayed the hardware along with 35 software titles that were ready to be released. An additional 91 titles were said to be "in the works". Sanyo, which was still negotiating with The 3DO Company, displayed its own prototype 3DO player.

Despite the excitement that followed the 3DO's initial appearance, the response was less than enthusiastic when Panasonic released the first 3DO player in early October. Although by then there were over 360 licensed developers and 110 projects in various stages of development, the combination of the $700 retail price and the scarcity of available software kept away serious buyers. 3DO executives pointed out that new items were always expensive at first, but that the price eventually fell. Examples of this were VCRs and CD players, which had both cost over $1,000 when they were first released, but experienced drastic price reductions as time went on. The 3DO was simply another electronic device in that mold.

Another problem was that most consumers had no idea what a 3DO machine was. Although Trip Hawkins had always maintained that the 3DO was a game console before

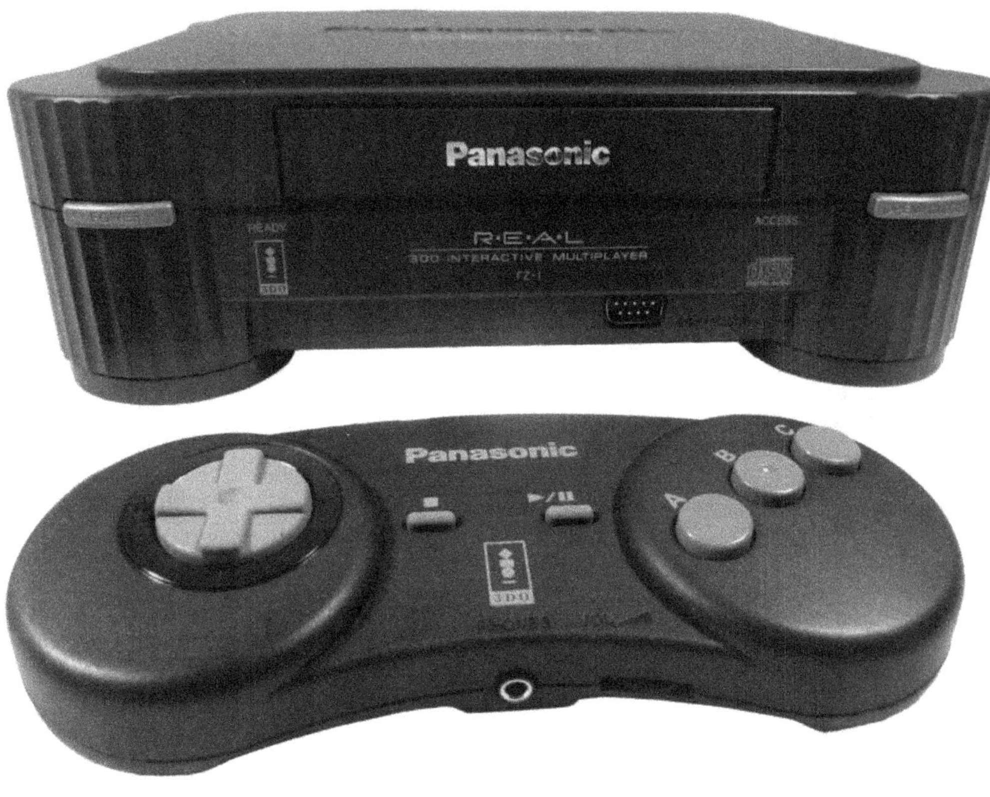

Panasonic 3DO

its release, Panasonic's marketing strategy blurred this distinction and only confused the issue. If it was a game machine, then it was outrageously overpriced when compared to the other consoles on the market. And most consumers knew little about multimedia machines to decide whether they needed them or not.

32-Bit CD Gaming Consoles

In September, one month before Panasonic released its 3DO console, Commodore began selling a new multimedia machine, which replaced the poorly received CDTV. The *Amiga CD*^{32} was a 32-bit, CD-based, multimedia game machine, but Commodore attempted to market it as a game console. The 14Mhz machine was capable of simultaneously displaying 256,000 colors from a palette of nearly 17 million. With an additional planned MPEG-1 cartridge, the unit could play full motion video and photo CDs in addition to the regular game discs and audio CDs. Like 3DO, Commodore claimed a slew of third-party developers. However, the Amiga CD^{32} already had a large amount of available software titles, because Commodore made the Amiga CD^{32} compatible with the CDTV multimedia system. The 3DO, which the Amiga CD^{32} had been designed to compete against, had virtually no software available when it came out. Another major selling point for the Amiga CD^{32} was its $400 price tag; $300 less than what Panasonic was selling its 3DO player for.

Commodore released the Amiga CD^{32} in Western Europe, Australia, and Canada on September 17. The company had also planned to release it in the United States; unfortunately, a deadline had passed in which Commodore had failed to pay a royalty for the use of a patent, and so a federal judge ordered an injunction that prevented Commodore from importing anything into the United States, including the Amiga CD^{32}s that were built in the Philippines.[1]

Amiga CD^{32}

Fujitsu FM Towns Marty

When the Amiga CD^{32} had initially been released, Commodore had marketed it as the "world's first 32-bit CD games console". While it did indeed hold that title in the regions that it had been sold, a 32-bit CD game machine had actually been released in Japan seven months earlier, by a company called Fujitsu, which, in 1989, had released the *FM Towns,* a 32-bit computer system that was the first in the world to offer a built-in CD drive. Fujitsu decided to duplicate that approach when it entered the videogame market.

The *FM Towns Marty* was released on February 20. It was basically an FM Towns computer in videogame clothing. Software for the FM Towns Marty was completely compatible with the computer. Internally, the two systems were basically the same, although the FM Towns Marty had some additional custom components. In addition, so that it could completely emulate the computer that it had been based on, the FM Towns Marty had a built-in 3.5-inch floppy disk drive.

The FM Towns Marty was only released in Japan. At that time, Japanese computer systems and their corresponding software were very expensive. Since it was essentially a computer, the costs for the FM Towns Marty were also very high; the product retailed at approximately $800. People were unwilling to pay the extra money for a console that was basically a computer system that could only play games. And although it had a 32-bit operating system, gamers were willing to forego the FM Towns Marty and purchase the 16-bit Sega Mega Drive or Nintendo Super Famicom, which both cost much less.

The SNES ND Drive

Whether they were marketed as videogame consoles or multimedia consoles, all of the new systems had built-in CD-ROM drives. It was obvious that CD-ROM was the way to go. And yet the world's number-one console, the Famicom/NES, still didn't have a CD drive. In the United States, where the Genesis had such a drive available for it, sales of the Genesis began surpassing those of Nintendo's consoles for the first time.

In May, Nintendo finally revealed specs for a CD-ROM player. The SNES *ND Drive* would be built around a 32-bit RISC co-processor, so called because it would work in tandem with the SNES' 16-bit processor. The ND Drive would hook up to the SNES via a cartridge called the *ND System Cart,* which would plug into the SNES' cartridge port. The ND System Cart would contain chips that would give the SNES the 32-bit processing capability it would need to access the CD games. It would also expand the available memory in the SNES, and process data much faster. A cord would attach the cartridge to the ND Drive, which had the same dimensions as the SNES. This set-up allowed the game console to sit on top of the CD player, much like the Genesis did with its Sega CD.

The CDs would be packaged in individual plastic caddies that kept them out of harm's way. A security device to prevent illicit duplication of the CD would be built into the caddies, along with 256,000 bits of memory, which would allow players to store game data. The CDs would also play on Philips' CD-i multimedia machine.

The ND Drive would contain a CD-ROM decoder called *HANDS* (Hyper-Advanced Nintendo Data-Transfer System), which would do the job of reading the main memory, and handle some data conversion. This would free the co-processor and allow it to do its own work without interruption. HANDS would also enhance the SNES' audio system.

Although Nintendo didn't mention an actual release date, it did state that the CD drive would be available sometime in the fall of 1994, and would retail for approximately $200. The company promised that the drive would be on display at the 1993 summer CES, which was only a few weeks away.

The announcement of the ND Drive made SNES owners happy. After they learned in 1992 that Nintendo was abandoning its 16-bit CD-player, many owners were left second-guessing whether or not they should have bought a Genesis, which already had a CD player. Now it appeared that they were going to get one after all - and that it was going to be a 32-bit unit to boot!

Unfortunately, their delight was short-lived. First, the CD drive was never shown at the summer CES, despite Nintendo's promises that it would be. Instead, Nintendo chose to announce new games for the SNES that took advantage of its new Super FX chip that greatly improved visuals and sounds.[2] But the big blow for SNES owners transpired on August 23, when Nintendo announced that it was teaming up with Silicon Graphics, one of the world's leading visual computer-technology companies, to create a new, 3D, 64-bit game machine that was code-named *Project Reality*. Unlike previous machines that Nintendo had developed and manufactured itself, Silicon Graphics would manufacture the console and Nintendo would pay a royalty for every unit sold.

The new system would feature the Nintendo-designed *Reality Immersion Technology* that would allow players to become part of the games; sort of like virtual reality on a standard television set. The microprocessor in the console would have a clock speed of over 100MHz! And the unit would feature real-time 3D graphics and CD-quality audio (although it would not incorporate a CD drive) and generate more than 100,000 polygons per second. Nintendo hoped to have the new console in stores by Christmas 1995, with a retail price under $250. The company also planned to introduce the Project Reality technology in its arcade games sometime in 1994.

Nintendo planned to sink all of its development money into Project Reality at the expense of the ND Drive, which had finally been declared dead once and for all. The prospect that the SNES or its software would remain current diminished when Nintendo further announced that Project Reality would be incompatible with all prior Nintendo consoles. However, Nintendo promised that Project Reality would be compatible with any *future* projects, as if this would console the 8.6 million owners of the SNES, who had just learned that the console that they'd invested in had been suddenly deemed obsolete.

When Nintendo decided to go ahead with Project Reality at the expense of the ND Drive, it finally severed the long-teetering Nintendo/Sony relationship. Sony, which had never been too happy with its agreement with Nintendo, surprised the videogaming world in May when it purchased Psygnosis, a Liverpool-based game developer. The reason for the purchase became clear in November when Sony officially announced the formation of a new division called *Sony Computer Entertainment* (SCE).

The first project by this new company was to release its new CD-ROM-based game console in Japan at the end of 1994, and in the United States and Europe the following year. According to SCE, this new console, code-named *PS-X*, would employ a 32-bit RISC chip and have graphic capabilities that would be able to generate 360,000 polygons per second, as well as 16.77 million colors.

Shortly following the news of the PS-X, SCE announced that it had signed with Namco to develop software for the new system. It also said that it had contacted many 3DO developers, and that several were seriously interested in creating software for the PS-X.

The Duo

As anticipation for a new, CD-based videogame system from SCE increased, interest in the original CD-ROM playing game machine began to subside. NEC did its best to keep its PC Engine and its off-springs alive in the minds of consumers seeking to buy a CD-based system. In March, the company released the *MemoryBase 128*, a new memory unit that could save banks of data like Hudson Soft's Tennokoe Bank. But whereas the Tennokoe Bank had 8000 blocks of memory divided into four 2000-block banks, the MemoryBase 128 had 128,000 memory blocks that were divided into 64 2000-block banks. Unfortunately, all of this memory could only be used with specific games that were compatible with the device. The MemoryBase 128 plugged into the controller port and by that nature, wasn't capable of producing an onscreen menu that let gamers transfer data around. So only games that had code that allowed for data transfer with the unit, could take advantage of it.

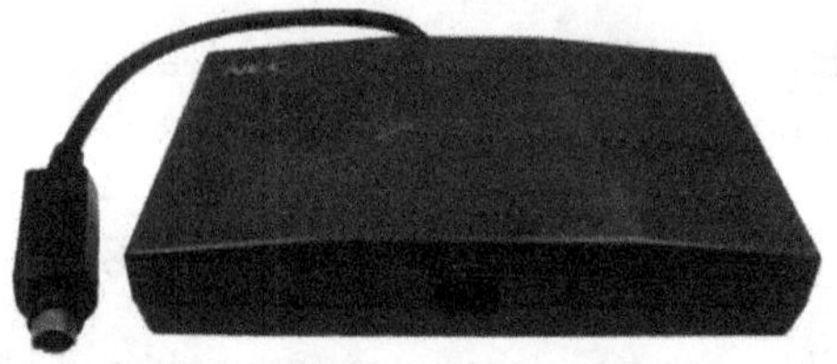

NEC PC Engine MemoryBase 128

Concurrent with the release of the MemoryBase 128, was a new console that it could be used with. The *Duo-R* was merely a less-expensive version of the Duo. The console retailed at ¥39,800 ($340), approximately $100 less than the console it replaced. To reduce the price, NEC removed the headphone jack connector and a switch that allowed the CD-ROM lid to lock. The shape of the Duo-R was also slightly different than the Duo. But to the eye, the biggest difference was that the Duo-R was white whereas the Duo had been black. This was another cost-cutting measure as the plastic used for the Duo-R was flimsier than that used in the Duos.

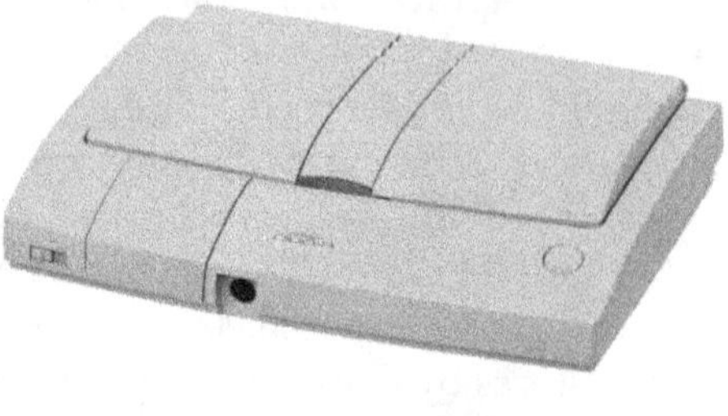

NEC PC Engine Duo-R

On August 20, another way to play PC Engine software was introduced in Japan. On that date, Pioneer, the company that had kept the laserdisc industry alive by manufacturing laserdisc players when no one else bothered, introduced a new, revolutionary machine that could play a number of different media, including PC Engine HuCards and CDs. The oversized, ¥89,800 ($856) *LaserActive CLD-A100* was a Pioneer laserdisc unit that could play standard laserdiscs and CDs. The unit became available in the United States on September 13 with a retail price of $970.

The LaserActive CLD-A100 was expandable. Individual expansion modules, or PACs, could be purchased and inserted into an expansion port of the Laserdisc unit like a drawer. The Karaoke PAC was a $350 add-on that could also play *LaserKaraoke* laserdiscs and included two microphone inputs and controls for volume and tone.

Pioneer LaserActive

Also available, for $600 each, were two PACs that could play videogames. The *LD-ROM^2 PAC* was produced from a collaboration between Pioneer and NEC and could play games from

PC Engine HuCards and CD-ROM^2 and Super CD-ROM^2 discs. In addition, it could also play games from exclusive *LD-ROM^2* videodiscs. These were LD-ROMS (Laserdisc ROMS), which was based on a proprietary optical format that Philips had developed that could store analog video and computer data for interactive applications.[3] All of the games, whether they be from HuCards, CD-ROM^2, or the new LD-ROM^2 discs, all used the standard PC Engine controller, which came with the PAC.[4]

The other $600 PAC was the Mega LD PAC, a similar module that played Sega Mega Drive games. The PAC could play Sega Mega Drive cartridges and Mega CD games. And exclusive games were provided in the form of *Mega LD* videodiscs. Like the *LD-ROM^2 PAC*, the Mega LD PAC was packaged with its own Mega Drive controller.

64-Bit Consoles

Although Nintendo had announced its plans for the 64-bit Project Reality, most of its competition was just foraying into 32-bit territory. However, if Nintendo thought that it would have the only 64-bit console on the market, it was wrong. Throughout the year, Atari Corp. began rolling out its latest console, the Jaguar, which was highly touted as a 64-bit system. Atari even went as far to beckon consumers to "do the math" so they could see for themselves that it was a better buy than the 16- and 32-bit systems. However, the 64-bit moniker was something of a misnomer as the Jaguar's main processors were actually 32-bit. But the system also included a 64-bit object processor, which controlled several graphic architectures and a 64-bit *blitter*, which was used for high-speed logic operations.

Although the Jaguar hadn't been physically displayed at the summer CES, a video of the new machine was shown that highlighted its strengths. Atari proudly proclaimed that third-party developers who compared the 3DO and the Jaguar all favored the latter. And while the Jaguar promised to step up to full multimedia capabilities, Atari was careful to label it as a game console. And even though Trip Hawkins had made the same claim with the 3DO, the Atari name was still synonymous with games to many.

All speculation about the machine came to an end in mid-August when Atari officially unveiled the Jaguar at a press conference at its Sunnyvale headquarters. The conference had originally been intended only to gaming journalists but Atari president Sam Tramiel decided to open it to all journalists after he learned that 3DO had spread inaccurate information about the Jaguar to the press. This worked to his advantage, and the Jaguar was featured in virtually every newspaper in the country.

Atari planned to release 50,000 units in New York, San Francisco, London and Paris in October, followed by a national and European release the following spring. The official word about the machine was that it would be cartridge-based, although an optional $200 CD-ROM player would be available in the spring. A 32-bit expansion port would also be available to support cable and phone networks, as well as a modem. The console would cost around $200, and would be sold with one cartridge and a ten-button Power Pad Controller.

Shortly after the press conference, Atari officially announced that it had joined forces with IBM to manufacture the Jaguar. Actually, Atari had signed a 30-month contract with the monolith computer company to build, package and distribute the console. This deal brought the manufacturing of videogame consoles back to the United States, since the new Jaguars were being built in Charlotte, North Carolina. It also marked the first time that IBM ever manufactured a product for a company other than itself.

When the Jaguar was actually released on November 15,[5] the initial group of consoles sold out quickly, even though the console was priced at $250, higher than originally declared. Despite this promising start, many journalists were skeptical about Atari's ability to deliver software. The portable Lynx had been Atari's shining glory when it debuted in 1989, but by 1993, its lack of software made it practically a memory. Sales had been so

Atari Jaguar

poor that Toys "R" Us quit selling it altogether. Atari promised that the Jaguar wouldn't suffer a similar fate, and released a list of over twenty third-party developers that were working on Jaguar games.

The company also announced stunning peripherals that would be available for the console. One device allowed the Jaguar to act as a server that could feed multiplayer games to linked Lynxes. Another was an MPEG-2 video compression cartridge that would give the Jaguar the ability to play laserdisc quality CD movies. And finally, there was a virtual reality helmet.

Virtual Reality At Home

Atari's proposed virtual reality helmet had been planned to compete against the *Sega VR*, a virtual reality helmet for the Genesis that Sega had shown at the winter CES.

Sega brought its Master System LCD 3D glasses up several notches. The Sega VR was a visor that consisted of a stereoscopic video display and stereo headphones. Since the unit plugged directly into the Genesis' video and audio outputs, gamers didn't need TV sets to play games. When using it, they were given the illusion that they were completely immersed in the game, and felt like they were totally removed from the rest of the world.

Sega planned the Sega VR for a 1993 release, but the year ended without appearing in stores. However, Sega did release a different kind of peripheral that literally placed gamers in the center of the game play.

The *Activator* was similar to Mattel's Power Glove and Broderbund's U-Force Controller, two peripherals that had been released for the NES in 1989. However, while those NES controllers could only duplicate moves that the gamer's hand made, Sega's Activator simulated action made by the player's entire body.

The Activator consisted of eight interlocking modules that formed an octagon. It sat on the floor, and the player stood within its center. When the unit was powered on, each of the eight modules sent infrared beams towards the ceiling. By breaking any of the infrared beams with his hand, foot or head, the player sent signals back to the Genesis that were comparable with pressing the controller buttons.

Sega released the Activator in November. Although no games were specifically designed for the $80 device, Sega did include a booklet that revealed which moves gamers had to make in order to play many popular games.

A virtual reality helmet was also displayed at the summer CES for the SNES, from a third-party developer called Virtual Maxx. The helmet contained a tiny TV monitor that displayed the game when the helmet was plugged into the SNES. The player merely had to turn his head a certain way to control the on-screen figures. Unfortunately, like Sega's Activator, the helmet was really only an innovative controller. In order for it to have a shot as a virtual reality contender, it needed new first-person software to be developed for it, and that wasn't in the plans.

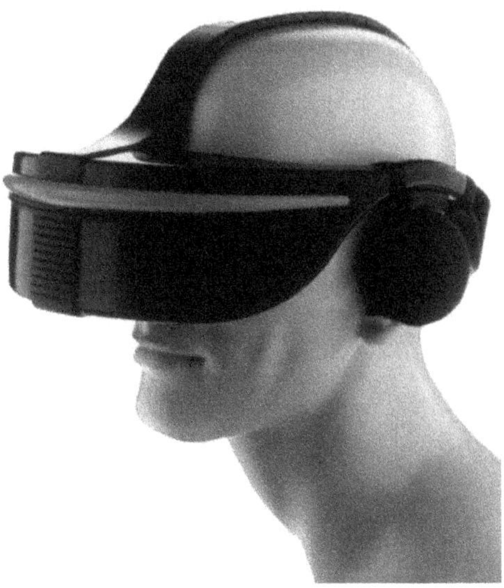

Sega VR

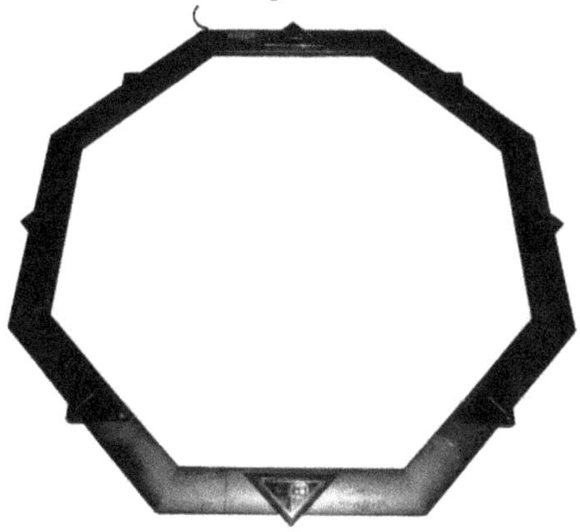

Sega Activator

Nintendo 8-Bits Still Relevant

Another new peripheral for the SNES was announced by a British company called Hornby of England. The *Superdeck* allowed the 16-bit console to play all of the NES 8-bit cartridges without violating any of Nintendo's patents. Hornby expected it to be available in England in the fall for around £40 ($60). Both Camerica and Innovation showed interest in importing the device to the United States, where they would sell it for $70. However, since brand-new NES consoles were already retailing for that price, no one expected the Superdeck to be a strong seller in the United States, unless Hornby could somehow lower its costs. Even if Hornby managed to do so, it wouldn't have made much of a difference. On October 15, Nintendo of America released a new NES that retailed for $49.95.

The new console had been completely redesigned, and mostly improved. One of the biggest problems that faced the original console was its cartridge-loading mechanism. In order to insert a cartridge, the gamer had to first open a lid, and then slide in the cartridge, pressing it down on a spring-mounted tray until it locked into place. With continued use, the mechanism eventually wore out in many instances. The new console removed this problem with a top-loading cartridge port.

Two controllers came with the unit, and they were redesigned to match the controllers that fit the SNES. Unfortunately, the new controllers were incompatible with R.O.B.

Some features had to be eliminated in order to lower the costs. One was the infamous lockout chip. The new NES allowed unlicensed games, as well as licensed games from other regions.

The other feature that was removed was the ability to use RCA video cables to connect the console to the television. The only way to hook the unit up to a TV was through an RF connector.

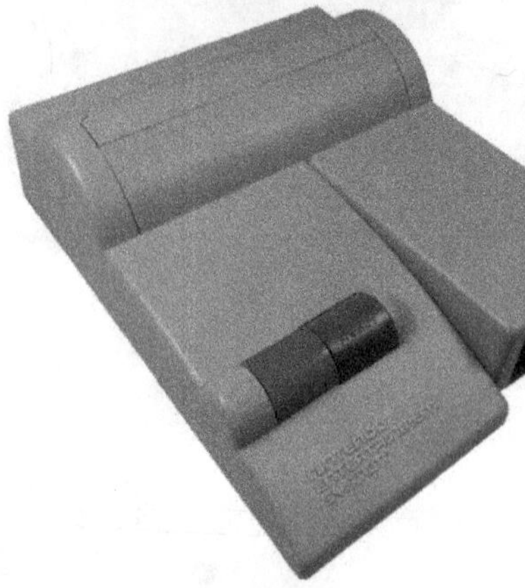

Nintendo NES 2

Nintendo AV Famicom

Nintendo of Japan quickly followed suit and released a redesigned Famicom on December 1. Externally, the ¥6,800 ($63) unit looked almost the same as the new NES, except in the area where the cartridge was inserted. While the area on the NES was rounded, Nintendo of Japan opted for it to be flat, so that it could accept the RAM cartridge required by the Famicom Disc System.

Nintendo of Japan followed Nintendo of America's lead and offered removable controllers for the new Famicom. The controllers for the original Famicom had been hardwired, unlike those found on the original NES. The microphone on the right controller was removed, since this had been a feature that had long been under-utilized.

Curiously, the redesigned Famicom exclusively used composite video to connect to a television, unlike the redesigned NES that used an RF modulator. This was ironic, since the original Famicom connected using the RF modulator and the original NES used the video output.

New Sega Consoles

Nintendo wasn't alone in releasing revamped versions of its console. Sega of Japan did the same thing on April 23, when it released the newly-redesigned *Mega Drive 2*. The new model, which retailed at ¥12,800 ($115), was lighter than the original and consumed less power. While the new model was missing the headphone jack and volume control that appeared on the original, it supported stereo. Sega of America followed suit and released a newly-designed version of the Genesis that was almost cosmetically identical to the Mega Drive 2. The only difference was that the Mega CD had an on-off switch, a blue reset button and red covers over the cartridge slot. The new Genesis had an on-off *button* that was black as was its reset button and the cartridge slot lids were black as well. Oddly, while Sega of Japan added a numerator to the end of the console's name, Sega of America didn't and officially called the new model the *Genesis*. However, the public immediately dubbed the console the *Genesis 2*.

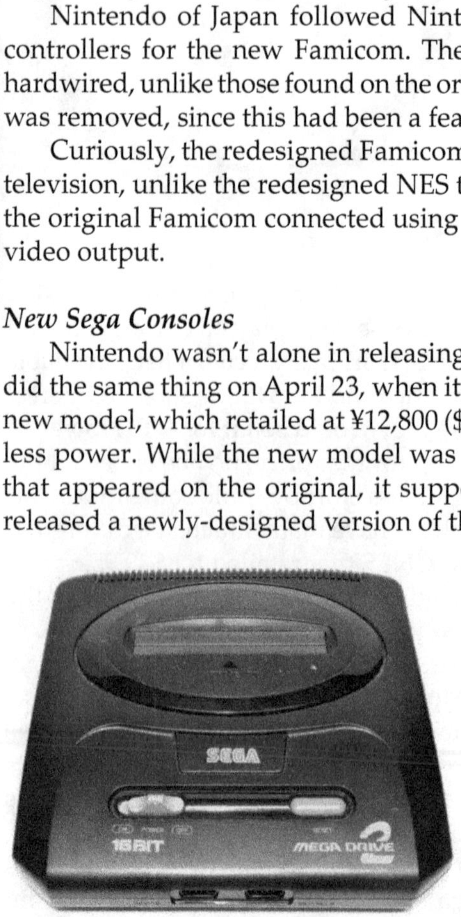

Sega Mega Drive 2

Accompanying the newly-designed consoles were new CD drives. The Japanese *Mega Drive*

2 and the new American Sega CD both featured a lid that pop-opened at the press of a button so discs could be inserted or removed. This replaced the motorized front-loading drawer that was on the original model, and helped reduce the Japanese retail price from ¥49,800 ($449) to ¥29,800 ($269) and the American price from $400 to $229. The new CD player sat alongside its respective console, rather than beneath it. Sega also packaged an optional extender plate with the console that allowed owners of the original system to use the new CD player. However, the original CD player wasn't compatible with the new CD drive. Cosmetically, the Japanese and American models were the same except that each had an eject button that was the same color as its corresponding console's reset button.

Sega Genesis 2 with Sega CD 2

Despite the formation of Sega Europe in 1991, shipments within Europe were still sporadic. Great Britain, Italy and Germany received their Mega CDs in April, while France and Spain didn't get theirs until September. And those countries that did receive the earlier shipments, received the original Mega CD, even though the less expensive Mega CD 2 had already been announced in Japan. Although many people chose to wait until October for the newer, less-expensive model to appear, 60,000 original units were sold in Great Britain alone. And while many of them went into households with original Mega Drives, many of them also were paired up with the new *Mega Drive II*. When the redesigned CD player arrived in Europe, it was called the *Mega CD II*. The European console and CD player were cosmetically identical to the redesign-designed Genesis and Sega CD except that it had red on-off and reset buttons on the console and a red eject button on the CD player.

European consumers had one problem with the Mega Drive II that customers in other regions weren't concerned about. The problem was with the Master System Converter, the device that allowed the Sega Master System games to play on the Mega Drive. Technically, it could work with the Mega Drive II, since data only passed through it. However, because the casing of the Mega Drive II had been redesigned, the Master System Converter couldn't be inserted firmly into the Mega Drive II, rendering it obsolete. This wasn't a major problem in Japan or North America because the hadn't been a big seller. But

Sega Mega Drive II

Sega Master System Converter II

JVC Wondermega M2

the Master System had been popular in Europe and most people didn't want to have to give up their 8-bit games. So to appease this group, Sega released the Master System Converter II. This unit looked much like an oversized cartridge and fit directly into the cartridge slot of the Mega Drive II (as well as the original Mega Drive). A Master System cartridge could then be inserted into the top of the unit. At £29.99 ($45), the Master System Converter II was £10 ($15) than the original Master System Converter. However, it was missing the slot that allowed Sega My Cards.

As if to coincide with the release of the Mega Drive 2, JVC released a newly-designed Wondermega, the *Wondermega M2*, on July 2. Pricing it at ¥59,000 ($520), ¥23,800 ($221) less than the original, JVC followed Sega's lead and removed the motorized drawer from the CD drive, and replaced it with a pop-up lid. Also included were wireless controllers with the wireless functionality built into the console. Absent from the new Wondermega M2 were the MIDI and Super VHS outputs that had been available on the original.

While Sega was redesigning the Mega Drive/Genesis, Sega of America's 27-member *Away Team* had been quietly developing a new 32-bit game system, code-named *Aurora*. Although the project was supposed to be top secret, Sega of America president, Tom Kalinske, publicly referred to it many times. When the 3DO had been released, Kalinske inappropriately bragged that "we have a more powerful machine waiting in the wings, but the time's not ready yet." He also boasted throughout the year that Sega of America could release its new system on demand if it wanted.

But the reason it wasn't released right away was because Sega didn't want a CD console that retailed for more than $500. Another reason that Sega didn't want to rush the new console to market was because it wanted to promote the already available Sega CD for the 16-bit Genesis. Sega believed that as new technology became available, the Sega CD would only get better with time. *Cinepak,* a new technology that was already available, improved the performance of the Sega CD in the area of full-screen, full-motion video by increasing the number of on-screen colors from 64 to 512. Although Sega hadn't yet used Cinepak in any available software, it planned to use the technology in CD titles that were in development.

Despite Kalinske's boasts, the 32-bit project had not been going well. Initially, the new console had been designed with a single central processor. However, when the team learned about SCE's PlayStation, they decided to enhance their own console to make it even more powerful by adding a second CPU and several other processors late in the design process. Unfortunately, they didn't have time to design custom chips, so they used chips that were commercially available. This made the design more complex, because the chips hadn't been designed to work in tandem.

Sometime during the summer, the corporate minds at Sega of Japan realized that Sega of America couldn't release the new console on demand after all, so they decided to get into the act. On September 21, the company joined forces with Hitachi to quickly manufacture the new console's 32-bit RISC processor. Sega of Japan then announced that the console, now called the *Saturn,* would be available in Japan by the fall of 1994, and that JVC and Yamaha would join Sega in the distribution of the console.

The Saturn was to be built around a customized 68030 processor. This was bad news for owners of the Sega CD, which utilized a 68000 processor. The different chips made the Saturn incompatible with the Sega CD games. Although it was possible for Sega to include a set of 68000 chips in the Saturn to make it backward-compatible, that would have dramatically increased the cost of the unit. Sega wanted to keep the price as low as possible, so that it could compete against the Jaguar and whatever Nintendo might come out with. Game designers on both sides of the Pacific became worried. Japanese Mega CD developers were afraid that the Mega CD would be dumped in favor of the new machine, and American Sega CD designers were concerned about how the new console's American release date of mid-1995 would affect their sales. They worried that during the Christmas 1994 buying season, consumers would forego buying any new Sega CD systems in anticipation of the new one.

In October, Sega of Japan announced that the Saturn would include a 64-bit video-processing chip. Based on this information, the press soon began calling the Saturn a 64-bit system. To alleviate any confusion that this tag might create, Sega immediately began referring to the Saturn as a *multi-processor* system: an accurate moniker, since the Saturn contained seven different processors.

By this time, all of the news about the Saturn had come out of Japan. Sega of America was now being very silent about the new console that it had started, because it wanted to keep the Genesis/Sega CD market alive as long as possible.

As the year came to an end, Sega of Japan was also quiet about the new console, and journalists began to speculate about whether the Saturn even existed. However two third-party companies, Acclaim and Virgin, were already developing software for it, which lent some credence that it was real after all.

Sega For Kids

Sega of Japan did manage to release a brand-new console in June, one that received little fanfare. The *Pico* was a small computer for children aged 3 to 7. It opened like a PC Notebook, but had to be connected to a TV set, because it didn't have its own monitor. Its software resembled books that could be inserted into the computer. As the pages of the book were turned, images on the TV screen changed. The Pico also had an attached stylus that children could use to animate on-screen characters by touching their corresponding images in the book.

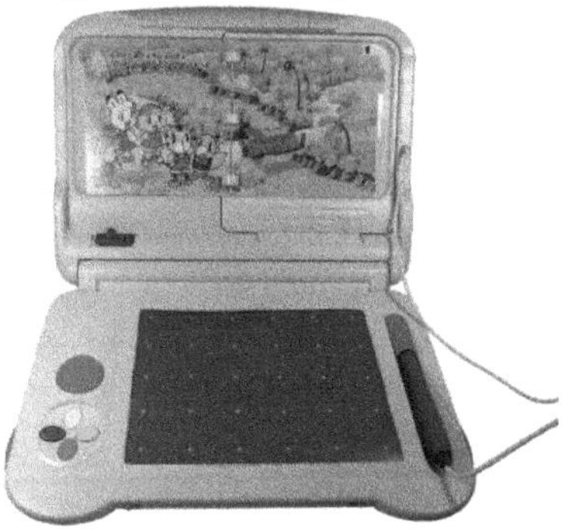

Sega Pico

The ¥13,440 ($139) Pico included four software books. Additional books were in development by third-party companies, such as Bandai and ASCII. Sega planned to release the Pico in the United States sometime in 1994.

Meanwhile, Sega continued to improve on the technology for its 16-bit consoles. In June, the company announced that it would be using Ramtron International's *FRAM* (Ferroelectric Random Access Memory) chips in its games. These unique chips could store external information, such as high scores and game saves without the need for a separate lithium battery inside the cartridge shell. And as Sega was accepting delivery of 100,000 FRAM chips from Ramtron International, it announced that it was developing a new chip that enhanced game speed. The chip would first be used in a game called *Virtua Racing*.

Cougars And Ducks

Nintendo, being the world's number-one videogame company, made successful products that other companies wanted to emulate. Watara introduced a new version of the Supervision that had the screen built into a pivoting base which allowed the player to merely tilt the screen if there was too much glare. QuickShot, a controller manufacturer, distributed this version in England, and a company called Goldnation USA distributed it in the United States.

Watara Pivoted Supervision

On the heels of Watara's Supervision came another handheld console that was meant to capitalize on the Game Boy's success. Like the Supervision, this device was distributed by different companies in several European countries, where it was marketed as the *Mega Duck*. In South America it was distributed by a company called Cougar, who called it the *Cougar Boy*. Aside from the name differences, the two handhelds were identical. And they were also very similar to the original Supervision, with the placement of control buttons all in roughly the same locations. But while the internal components of the Mega Duck/Cougar Boy were basically the same as the Supervision, the games for the two systems were not compatible, as the Supervision's cartridges were slightly wider.

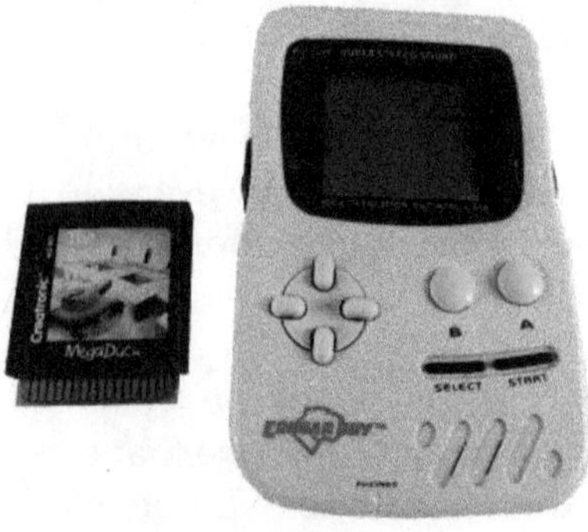

Cougar Boy

Bandai, the Japanese electronics-toy company that had released early videogame consoles in 1977, decided to re-enter the market. In June, it displayed a portable Super Famicom that it called the *Home Entertainment Terminal* (HET). The HET had a four-inch color LCD screen, a TV tuner and the capability to connect with different peripherals, such as a printer, modem, fax machine and CD-ROM player. Bandai never announced a release date, and many critics were skeptical whether or not the unit would ever see the light of day. Besides, rumors began coming out of Nintendo near the end of the year that it too was planning to release a portable SNES.

Taking Bandai's idea down a level, Innovation developed a handheld unit that could play NES games. The *Top Guy* resembled a Game Gear, but it allowed NES cartridges to be inserted into a slot at its top (hence its name). It also included a cord that could connect it to a TV set, and a port that accepted NES controllers. As with the Bandai unit, there was no mention of when the *Top Guy* would be available.

New Code-Altering Devices

While Innovation wasn't in any rush to get the Top Guy into stores, in the summer it began to manufacture its own version of the Pro Action Replay, which it called the *Game Wizard*. The Game Wizards were functionally identical to the Pro Action Replays, but since they were built in the United States, their retail price was considerably less than the imported Pro Action Replay.

In late 1993, ads began appearing in the videogame magazines promoting a new code-altering device for the SNES called the *GameMage*; from a company called Select Solutions. The ad said that the GameMage remembered codes that, when entered once, never had to be entered again. Curiously, none of the magazines chose to review this unit.

As a plethora of new code-altering devices began appearing, Camerica, the Canadian importer of the Game Genie, went full steam trying to push the Aladdin. It was displayed at the winter CES and received kudos from the press. Unfortunately, sales for the NES began diminishing as the 16-bit SNES and Genesis sales increased. There was no longer an NES customer base large enough to support the Aladdin. Camerica had too much money invested in the Aladdin that it couldn't recover, the company just suddenly closed down. Codemasters, the British designers of the Game Genie and Aladdin, announced that it would take over Camerica's business in North America, but that it couldn't release the Aladdin in time for Christmas 1993.

Meanwhile, Codemasters was busy with the Game Genie. The company announced in September that it was developing a Game Genie for the Sega CD. Many people thought that this would be impossible, because of the high volume of I/O that the CD-drive had to make. In brief, the new Game Genie would catch the data sent from the Sega CD before it could reach the Genesis at the point where the Sega CD connected to the Genesis' expansion port. Codemasters didn't say when the new Game Genie would be available, since it was still in development.

Codemasters also announced that it was beginning production of its new *Game Genie 2*, a unit that worked like the Pro Action Replay, which searched the console's memory for specific addresses rather than having the player input the altering codes. Although the new device was ready in time for Christmas, Galoob decided to hold off its distribution until 1994, citing that it was too late to set up an advertising campaign and national distribution in time for the holidays. Meanwhile, Galoob released a Game Genie for the Game Boy early in the year, and followed that with one for the Game Gear.

Software publishers weren't happy with the idea of another Game Genie. However, most felt that it didn't hurt their businesses because most of their games were sold before the codes could be released. However, others claimed that they had lost sales because potential customers no longer found the games challenging after renting and solving them with Game Genies. Rumors spread that one software company, Sunsoft, "cheat-proofed" its games. Sunsoft denied these accusations.

Nintendo's Victories In Court

Nobody was against the Game Genie more than Nintendo of America. In March, the company learned that the U.S. Supreme Court had rejected its appeal of the decision that allowed Galoob to sell the code-altering device in the United States. Despite this loss, Nintendo still refused to admit defeat, and sought other legal ways to get out of paying the $15 million that had been awarded to Galoob.

Meanwhile, Nintendo was awarded $24 million from two Taiwanese companies that had been caught counterfeiting its games. One of the companies, believed to be among the largest counterfeiting rings in Taiwan, was called the *Nintendo Electric Company*.

Nintendo was also the winner in a suit against Atari Games (Tengen). The U.S. District Court in San Francisco ruled on July 29 that Atari's games infringed on Nintendo's patents for the NES' lockout system. However, Atari immediately filed appeal papers that questioned the validity of Nintendo's patents and whether Atari committed *willful* infringement or not.

In October, Jack Tramiel's Atari Corp. filed a lawsuit against Sega, which charged that the latter had infringed upon Atari's patents regarding horizontally scrolling games, especially *Sonic the Hedgehog*. Although Atari met with Sega regarding the problem, the company felt that the meetings went nowhere, and so it resorted to a lawsuit.

The Sega/Atari conflict came just when Sega began recovering from its long and drawn-out lawsuit against Accolade. In March, the Ninth Circuit Court of Appeals refused Sega's request for another hearing on the case. Atari chose not to attempt to sue Accolade on other grounds; instead, the two companies finally settled out of court in May. According to the settlement, both companies agreed to pay their own court costs, and Accolade became a legitimate licensee of Sega.

Alternative Ways To Distributing Games

Accolade became a Sega licensee just when Sega was about to take part in a new venture. In May, the two largest cable companies in the United States, Time-Warner and TCI, joined forces with Sega of America to form the *Sega Channel*, a cable service that was reminiscent of Mattel's PlayCable for the Intellivision. For a monthly $10 fee and an unspecified one-time price for a decoder that plugged into the Genesis' cartridge port, gamers would be able to download approximately 50 games to their Genesis consoles via cable. In addition to a selection of current games that would be updated every month, Sega of America also planned to include Japanese games that normally wouldn't be available in the United States. The Sega Channel would also preview forthcoming games, and host gaming contests for subscribers.

Sega Channel

Sega originally planned to begin test-marketing the new channel in selected cities in August, with the entire system going online by January 1994. This of course wasn't the case. In December, Sega announced that it had signed up with General Instrument and Scientific Atlanta to design and manufacture the equipment that was needed to deliver the games. The new schedule planned for test-marketing to begin in March 1994, with the system going nationwide by the fall.

Meanwhile, in November, Sega of Japan already began test-marketing its own similar system. The Japanese system employed a battery-powered game-receiver cartridge that could save data. Sega of Japan confirmed that if the test-marketing in nearly 500 households was successful, the system would be ready nationwide sometime in 1994, and would cost users between $19 and $29 a month.

Sega also teamed up with AT&T and P.F. Magic, an interactive entertainment company, to develop games that allowed gamers to compete against one another via the phone lines. AT&T's first excursion into the videogaming industry was a Genesis peripheral called the *Edge 16*, which was basically a 4800 baud modem that plugged into the Genesis' cartridge port. Game cartridges could then be inserted into a port in the modem. Once connected, players could call up their friends on the phone and compete against each other. In a way, it was like the Game Boy's Video Link, as each player had to own a copy of the game cartridge.

AT&T planned to release the Edge 16 in the summer of 1994, and promised to develop interactive software in time for the unit's debut. Other software developers, such as Tengen, GameTek and Sega, also planned software.

Once it sunk its teeth into the videogame world, there was no stopping AT&T. In September, Sierra On-Line sold AT&T its controlling interest in the *Sierra Network*, an online entertainment service available to PC owners. AT&T changed the name of the service to the *ImagiNation Network* and promised to upgrade it, so it would also be available to 3DO (which AT&T also had a stake in) and Genesis owners via the Edge 16.

Meanwhile, the Games Channel, which was introduced in 1992, hoped to get online nationally in the fall. As with the Sega Channel, players subscribed by paying a monthly fee ($10 for 20 hours or $20 for 60 hours), which gave them the privilege of being able to download games via the telephone lines. The Games Channel offered games for the NES,

SNES and Genesis.

Nintendo of Japan wasn't sitting on its laurels as other companies began to offer alternate ways of distributing games into the home. In May, the company bought Japan's only satellite broadcasting company, and immediately began formulating plans on how to use it for games. Nintendo planned to develop special games that would take advantage of the satellite network and allow all of its subscribers to compete against each other simultaneously. Some ideas that were considered included timed high-score contests and quiz games. Nothing was ever finalized, since Nintendo still wanted to study comparisons between satellite broadcasting and standard cable and phone methods. Nonetheless if Nintendo decided to go ahead and use the satellite to deliver games, it hoped to have the system up and running by early 1994. Although plans for the satellite network didn't expand outside of Japan and Nintendo of America didn't show any interest in it, the *San Francisco Chronicle* published a rumor in June claiming that Nintendo of America planned to start an interactive TV network that would feature entertainment, games and shop-at-home services. The service was supposed to start up by the end of the year, but when December 31 came around, it was still only a rumor.

There was another way to get games into homes without selling them, and that of course was the rental market. Blockbuster heavily promoted the renting of games, and Electronic Arts even released a Genesis game strictly for the rental trade, *John Madden Football Championship Edition*. More and more video rental outlets began carrying videogames as the lines between videogames and motion pictures diminished. Although there had been videogame tie-ins with movies ever since Atari released *Superman* for the 2600, a new videogame was introduced in 1993 that actually incorporated movie footage into the game. Virgin's *Demolition Man* for the 3DO, which was scheduled to be released in February 1994, also included scenes starring Sylvester Stallone and Wesley Snipes that were filmed exclusively for the game.

Movies with videogame-related themes had been around since Walt Disney Productions released *Tron* in 1982. However, there had never been a movie based on a *specific* game. That changed on May 28, when Disney released *Super Mario Brothers*, starring Bob Hoskins as Mario and John Leguizamo as his brother Luigi. Unfortunately, the success of the game didn't carry over to the movie, which only grossed half of its $42 million budget.

Games On Planes

Since movies were offered on airlines, it was only natural that videogames would wind up there as well. In early 1993, Sega signed a deal with Matsushita to manufacture and sell videogame systems that would fit in the backs of airplane seats. Meanwhile, In-Flight Phone International, the company that had originated Flightlink, received a hefty investment from Mercury Communications of London. In-Flight used this investment to start In-Flight Phone Europe and to expand Flightlink service to international flights to Europe. By year's end, In-Flight Phone Brazil Corporation was started to provide Flightlink services to South American destinations. More and more airlines signed up as the service expanded. In-Flight also signed a deal with Epyx to provide the latter's games on the planes. Previously, the service only provided simple games; such as *Tic-Tac-Toe* and *Reversi*. In addition to the videogames that cost the player a one-time charge of three dollars, In-Flight also provided phone and fax services, stock quotations and a radio that offered news, sports and music.

Naturally, Nintendo of America couldn't be left out of the fledging airline gaming market. In early fall, the company unveiled the *Nintendo Gateway System*, an interactive service that provided SNES games, movies, travel information and other services to airplane passengers. Nintendo of America also installed the service on cruise ships and several hotels.[6]

Ironically, as more and more airlines began carrying videogames for their passengers, the FAA was deciding to ban passengers from bringing their own portable games onto planes. They believed that electronic units such as portable game machines, portable computers and cellular phones clashed with the planes' navigational systems. Eventually, these systems were banned from use only during take-offs and landings. However, this would only be the beginning of the U.S. government's attempts to control where and how videogames were played.

Violence In Videogames

Ever since Steve Russell programmed *Spacewar* in 1962, videogames tended to be violent in nature. This was reaffirmed in 1974 when Kee Games released *Tank* in the arcades. As the games became more and more sophisticated, the level of violence also matured. By 1993, the graphics were so detailed, with live-action footage in some cases, on-screen characters discharged what looked like actual blood when they were killed. As they had done for the previous twenty years, parents complained to the videogame companies that this violence had to stop.

A USC professor named Marsha Hunt claimed that violence in videogames was more harmful to children than the violence found on TV. While parents didn't want to buy violent games for their children, there was no way that they could measure how vicious a game was without first renting it and trying it out. There had to be a better way.

On May 24, Sega finally responded to the pleas of the parents and announced that beginning in August, all of its games would be rated in a fashion similar to that of motion pictures. And the ratings would appear prominently on the packaging.

Sega formed an executive advisory *Videogame Rating Council* (V.R.C.) that worked with consumer groups to set the ratings on all licensed games that were playable on its consoles. The games themselves were rated on their basic rules, their graphics and their audio content.[7]

The V.R.C. came up with three ratings: **GA** for General Audiences, **MA-13** for more mature audiences, with parental discretion advised, and **MA-17** for adults only not appropriate for minors.

When the ratings were first enacted, only one game, *Night Trap*, received an MA-17. This was a game that Great Britain and Australia deemed so violent that they wouldn't allow it imported into their respective countries. Toys "R" Us removed the game from its shelves on December 16, and Kay-Bee Toys followed suit the following day; but both stores said that the game was removed in response to complaints from the public about its violence, not because it carried an MA-17 rating.

The fact was that even if a game received an MA-17 rating, there weren't any laws that required store owners to enforce it. Despite the rating, anybody could still buy the game. Even Sega CEO Tom Kalinske was aware that the ratings had no legal power behind them to prohibit anyone from buying certain games. However, he hoped that people used the ratings as a guide to decide which games to purchase. Kalinske admitted that Sega was developing games to appeal to different age groups, and he was particularly concerned that parents buy games appropriate for their child's age.

Sega suggested that the other videogame manufacturers should follow its lead and offer similar rating systems. Nintendo immediately condemned Sega's rating system, and declared that it had only been started so Sega could justify the sales of increasingly violent games. Nintendo, on the other hand, felt that it didn't need a rating system, because its game-development guidelines already banned very violent games, along with nudity, sexual violence, profanity and drug use. Nintendo claimed that every one of its games was rated **G** and appropriate for all ages.

The big test came on Monday, September 13, when software developer Acclaim released the home edition of *Mortal Kombat* for virtually every home-gaming platform in the United States. *Mortal Kombat* had been a hit in the arcades, mainly because of its realistically-detailed graphics. Fighters in the game could be decapitated, and blood would flow rampantly. If the home edition was anywhere near as gory as the arcade one, the game would definitely be a candidate for an MA-17 under Sega's guidelines.

Nintendo would not permit the SNES and Game Boy editions of *Mortal Kombat* to be as violent as the arcade version. Acclaim was forced to substitute blood with sweat and the most dangerous moves in the game were either removed or changed. However, despite Nintendo's claim that all of its games would be rated **G** if rating guidelines had been in place, the water-downed *Mortal Kombat* should still have been rated PG-13 at the least.

The Sega versions of the game were a bit different. Unlike the Nintendo versions, which people expected to be squeaky clean, the Genesis and Game Gear versions of *Mortal Kombat* were so innocent that the warriors couldn't even sweat, let alone bleed. Sega assigned MA-13 ratings for these versions. However, it was soon discovered that players could enter secret codes that would allow the warriors to bleed freely, and even get decapitated if need be, features that weren't mentioned in the game manual. Videogame magazines and newspaper articles soon printed the secret code[8] that made them accessible to every potential buyer. Although Sega claimed consumers should use the ratings as a guide when purchasing games, it was apparent that the games weren't rated as aggressively as they should have been. Despite the violence, or perhaps because of it, *Mortal Kombat* became the top-selling game of the year.

The brutality in *Mortal Kombat* may have gone too far. Before long, government officials began criticizing the amount of violence in the games, and *Mortal Kombat* was a title that was always cited. On November 15, the Attorney General of California, Dan Lungren, wrote to several game developers and stores and asked them to stop designing and selling games "that portray graphic and gratuitous violence."

Although Lungren made it clear that he was against regulating the videogame industry, he hoped that the manufacturers would use "sensible discretion" in their games. Several of his peers weren't as willing to depend on the manufacturers. Two senators, Joe Lieberman of Connecticut and Herb Kohl of Wisconsin, informed the press that they planned to introduce a bill to Congress that would force the manufacturers to adopt a rating system. If their bill passed, the companies would have one year to develop an across-the-board rating system. If they couldn't do it themselves, the government would step in and do it for them.

The manufacturers responded in the same way they had when Sega began its own rating system. Nintendo reiterated that a rating system wasn't needed, as long as the companies were responsible for what they released. However, while Nintendo continued to insist that its games weren't violent, Sega admitted that it did release violent games, because adults also played videogames and their gaming tastes were a lot different from what kids wanted. Why should adults be restricted to games that were meant for kids? And its rating system was the first line of defense to keep the violent games out of children's hands.

As the year came to an end, the issue of rating videogames remained unresolved. However, the battle lines had been drawn, and the matter would have to be settled conclusively!

CHAPTER TWENTY-TWO
1994

Due to the congressional hearings in late 1993, the subject of game ratings was on the minds of most people involved in the videogame industry in 1994. At the winter CES in January, much of the talk around the videogame exhibits were centered on the subject. Separate meetings were held between representatives from several hardware and software manufacturers, the Better Business Bureau, the Software Publishers Association and the Motion Picture Association of America. The purpose of these meetings was to come up with some sort of rating standard among all of the companies before the US Government took over, once its one year deadline ran out.

Until a standard was decided upon, some companies decided to adhere to their own rating criteria. Sega had been the first to do this, when the debate had first flared the year before. In early 1994, 3DO became the second company to impose its own four-tier rating system. Games designated with an "E" were meant for everyone. A game that had a "12" on its box suggested parental guidance for ages 12 and under. Likewise, a "17" rating suggested parental guidance for ages 17 and under. The final rating, "AO", was printed on boxes for games that were meant for adults only.

In March, Senators Lieberman and Kohl met with Jack Heistand, Sr., a Vice-President at Electronic Arts who also acted as the chairman of the Interactive Digital Software Association (IDSA), a new organization of videogame companies that included Acclaim, Atari Corp., Electronic Arts, Nintendo, Philips, Sega and 3DO. Heistand presented the senators with a 13-point plan to institute an across-the-board rating system before the 1994 holiday season.

Ken Wasch, the executive director of the Software Publishers Association (SPA), met with Senator Lieberman in early summer to discuss their latest plans. Lieberman was against separate rating standards for different gaming consoles, and ratings that were set by the software publishers themselves. He was in favor of rating educational games.

While the Senate was busy with the idea of the federal government mandating the ratings of videogames, California was trying to control videogame violence at the state level. Three bills were drafted as means to this end. One allowed the creation of a California Videogame Rating Administration. A second demanded that retailers lock games with mature themes behind a counter. The final bill allowed victims of violent crimes to sue stores that sold violent games if they could prove that the games directly led to the violent attacks.

ESRB Rating

By July, the IDSA proposed the formation of the Entertainment Software Rating Board (ESRB), which would be the sole entity for rating videogames in North America.[1] Manufacturers had to submit their games to the ESRB in order to receive ratings that were similar to those in the system that Sega had utilized. Large letter icons on the game boxes signified the games' rating. "EC" stood for "Early Childhood", which meant that the game was adequate for children aged three and up. "K-A" stood for "Kids To Adults" and was appropriate for children six and over. "T" was for "Teenager" and was for ages 13 and up. "M" was for "Mature" audiences 17 and over. Finally, an "AO" rating meant that the game was for adults only. Accompanying content descriptors would also note the game's content of violence, sex, profanity, and other factors that led to a game's rating.

Developers of computer software didn't like the rating system set up by the ESRB, so the SPA established the Recreational Software Advisory Council (RSAC) to rate computer games based on publishers' descriptions. The RSAC was composed of three groups: a Governing Board, an Advisory Board and a Ratings Review Board. The ratings themselves fell into five levels. The most general level entailed games that were suitable for all audiences. If a game was not suitable for all audiences, then an icon on the box displayed a rating based on a game's violence, sex and language, with each aspect given a score from one to four.

By November, both rating systems were in place. The videogame industry followed the ESRB ratings, while the computer industry followed those set up by the RSAC. Retailers didn't care which system was utilized, as long as the games were rated. Although adhering to the rating system was voluntary, Toys "R" Us and many other stores opted to only sell games that had been rated.

Ironically, one of the first games to be rated by the ESRB was *Night Trap,* the game that Sega had removed from store shelves in 1993 because it had been deemed too violent. The ESRB assigned an "M" rating to the new version of *Night Trap.* The game was also rereleased in the United Kingdom, where it was given a "15-17" rating by the new European Leisure Software Publisher's Association. This signified that the game was not suitable for children under 15.

The videogame industry had thus put into place a rating system within the year that Congress had allotted it. But this didn't stop Senators Lieberman and Kohl. By December, the two were working on plans to force game manufacturers to display the ratings in all of their TV commercials.

Although the videogame companies appeared to be working together via the IDSA, this wasn't quite the case. It turned out that at a December, 1993 Senate press conference, the assembled crowd viewed a videotape that Senator Lieberman had informed them was a scene from Sega's home version of *Mortal Kombat.* Actually, the scene had been taken from the arcade version, which was much more graphic than any of the home editions. It was later revealed that Nintendo of America had supplied the tape, in an effort to show that its version of the game wasn't as violent as others.

Ironically, while Nintendo was trying to prove that it only produced "innocent, wholesome" games, the company sent new guidelines to software developers that surprisingly allowed violence in its games.

Sega, on the other hand, suddenly wanted its name associated with family entertainment, so it established a subsidiary group late in the year called *Deep Water.* The analogy used to explain the new company's name was that swimming children were not allowed to venture into deep water. They wouldn't be allowed to enter Deep Water when they selected videogames, either. For this reason, Sega chose a lurking shark in the logo of the new label. In other words, Deep Water was off limits to kids.

The purpose behind Deep Water was so Sega could keep its family-friendly image and still release adult-oriented videogames. All games with a rating of "M" or "AO" would be released under the Deep Water banner, while all other games would come out under the Sega name.[2]

Sega Deep Water Logo

Nintendo's Next Move

While Deep Water and its shark seemed mysterious to many people, something even more perplexing was lurking over at Nintendo: Project Reality. In February, Nintendo once again said that its new unit would be cartridge-based, but that it would now include an expansion port, so a CD player could be added later if Nintendo decided to release one. The cartridges themselves would each contain 100 megabytes of data. Although this was five times the amount of data that SNES cartridges were capable of storing,[3] the retail price for the new cartridges would remain the same as the old ones. The company also admitted that several software titles for the new machine were already in development.

Although the $250 home system was expected to be released sometime in 1995, the first games were to begin appearing in arcades by the end of the year. Nintendo had joined forces with WMS, the parent company of Williams Bally/Midway. They formed a new company called Williams/Nintendo, Inc. to release arcade games based on the Project Reality hardware. They announced that their first arcade game would be *Killer Instinct*, a gory, futuristic fighting game, which had been created by Rare, Ltd., a British company that had signed an exclusive development deal with Nintendo. Although Rare was relatively unknown to most people, its dealings with Nintendo went back nearly a decade. In 1985, Rare had been the first company outside of Japan to develop games for the NES.[4]

Rare *Killer Instinct*

By the time summer came around, Nintendo had renamed its new system Ultra 64. Nintendo announced that the Ultra 64 would utilize Rambus memory chips, which would allow the system to run at 500Mhz, five times faster than the originally stated clock speed. Despite this improvement, Nintendo promised that the unit would still be priced at $250.

Nintendo also signed a contract with Alias Research to create 3D graphics-development tools for the Ultra 64. Previously, Alias software had been used in movies such as *Jurassic Park* and *Terminator 2*. Nintendo bought so many Alias Power/Animator licenses that it became the largest 3D developer in the world.

In late December, Nintendo signed GTE Interactive to "jointly develop, market, publish and distribute videogames." Although the two companies worked together to produce an unreleased SNES game *FX Fighter*, most analysts took notice of Nintendo's recent marriage to GTE for a different reason. GTE was the largest local telephone company in the US, and it was no secret that Nintendo wanted to take part in some sort of in-home electronic delivery service. It was GTE's responsibility to accomplish this.

While Nintendo was exploring ways to get its games into homes electronically, its electronic gaming service for commercial businesses was improving. By the middle of the year, the Nintendo Gateway System was available on three airlines, comprising a total of 5,000 seats. Nintendo expected that number to triple by the end of the year. Approximately 10,000 hotel rooms were also served by the system, and that number was expected to multiply ten-fold, thanks to a deal that Nintendo had signed with COMSAT Video Enterprises, a company that provided movies to 170,000 hotel rooms around the United States. The deal between the two companies allowed COMSAT to offer the Nintendo Gateway System to thousands of hotel guests.

After succeeding with the commercial electronic delivery of games, it was important for Nintendo of America to introduce a similar system for delivering games into homes. However, Sega of America beat them to it when it finally began testing the Sega Channel on twelve cable systems in March. The political atmosphere regarding videogames was apparent as the cable system included an added feature that allowed parents to block out games that were rated MA-13 or MA-17.

Since cable wasn't available in all homes, alternative methods of delivering software were developed. Work on AT&T's phone-based Edge 16 continued, and AT&T announced that the modem would be available for the 3DO as well as the Genesis. Several developers, such as GameTek, P.F. Magic, U.S. Gold and Sega, presented software for the modem early in the year. An additional dozen entertainment companies pledged to support the $149 system, which was now to be released in the fall of 1994. Thanks to AT&T's VoiceSpan technology, players competing in a game via the Edge 16 would also be able to talk to each other as they played.

The Catapult and XBand

In the fall, around the time that the Edge 16 was to be released, AT&T suddenly announced plans that it was dropping the unit. The company decided to focus its energies into developing new telephone technologies. However, an AT&T spokesman said that it was always possible that the company might yet enter the gaming market at a later time. He also noted that the technologies behind the Edge 16 modem could be sold to another company that might release it to the public.

The sudden demise of the Edge 16 didn't mean the end of modem-based gaming. In the early summer, a company called Catapult introduced a modem for Sega and Nintendo systems.

The modem, which was also called the Catapult, allowed gamers to choose from a local network of players to compete against. The network displayed the scores, skills and rankings of the individual players, but their identities remained unknown. A player could also arrange to compete against someone outside the local calling area.

Catapult XBand for Genesis

Catapult announced that the modem would be priced around the same as a game cartridge, and the service would cost $7.95 for 32 game plays. Each additional game play would then cost 15¢. Payment would be made via a debit card that would be slid through a card reader in the modem, and parents could control the amount of time that their children spent online. As was the case of the Edge 16, all of the competitors in a specific game had to own a copy of the game cartridge.

Once online, users of the system could send and receive messages to one another. Because of software limitations, Nintendo and Sega owners could communicate with each other, but they couldn't compete against one another in games. The system also featured *Bandwidth*, an online newspaper that provided gaming, entertainment and sports news to subscribers.

Catapult began testing its system in five cities in September and the network officially went online on November 17. Catapult planned to release a Sega-licensed modem by Christmas, and the Nintendo modem in 1995. By this time, Catapult also promised email services via the Internet.

When the system was actually released for the Genesis at Christmas, its name had been changed to *XBand*. For many, the XBand network was their first experience with online networks, something that was becoming more and more popular, thanks to CompuServe, America Online and Prodigy. However, the XBand provided services that couldn't be found on its computer counterparts. XBand users wouldn't lose their connections with the network if an extension phone was picked up. Likewise, call-waiting, the bane of many online users, wouldn't disrupt the service either. If a call came through while someone was online, an on-screen message would alert the player, and he would have the option of taking the call or continuing to play. Finally, if the telephone cord accidentally came loose from the modem during a gaming session, the game would merely pause and wait for the connection to be restored.

Since it had email capabilities, XBand users needed a way to "write" messages. Since the gaming consoles didn't have physical keyboards, the XBand could generate an on-screen virtual keyboard. This proved to be a very slow and cumbersome process, as users had to "point" to the on-screen keys by navigating a cursor. Catapult announced that it would release a real keyboard for the XBand sometime in 1995.

In December, Nintendo of Japan announced that a Japanese radio network would begin transmitting Nintendo game previews beginning in April, 1995. Subscribers to the service would need a $140 adapter pack that could download the games during a three-hour period every night.

Jaguar Online

Owners of Genesis and SNES systems weren't to be the only ones who would have access to online gaming. In September, Atari Corp. announced a Jaguar Voice/Data Communicator modem, which would also allow players to compete against one another over the phone lines. While playing, the gamers would wear headsets that would permit them to talk with the person they were competing against, and also provide call-waiting tones to let them know if another call was coming in. Unlike Catapult, which developed its own gaming network, Atari expected its games to be played over existing online networks. The new modem was set to retail for under $100, and although Atari hoped that it would be available in time for Christmas, the unit was delayed into 1995.[5]

Atari did release the *Jaglink*, a device that allowed two Jaguars to be linked together for multiplayer competition. Unfortunately, at the time of the Jaglink's release, only one game, *Doom*, could be used with it. In order to play, both consoles required their own copy of the game, and each had to be connected to its own TV.[6]

Atari Jaglink

It was important for Atari to release peripherals for the Jaguar that were similar to those that had been available for the older, more popular machines. Atari had begun the year on an upbeat note, as all of the 20,000 machines that had been available in the test-market areas sold out in one day. Atari expected to sell 500,000 units in 1994, once the unit was distributed nationally. To keep the public enticed, Atari promised that a $200 CD player would be released sometime during the year, and a virtual reality helmet would follow shortly afterwards. Atari claimed that 35 developers had been licensed to create games for the new system, and that three new games would be available each month, beginning in April. In all, 30 games would be available by Christmas. In actuality, only 20 games made it to market by the end of the year. And the highly waited Jaguar CD-ROM player failed to materialize by that time.

The Fall of Commodore

While Jack Tramiel's Atari wasn't selling as many Jaguars as it had hoped, it was still doing better than a former Tramiel company. In late May, Commodore International was forced to declare bankruptcy.

Commodore had been founded in 1958 by Tramiel, a young Holocaust survivor who had emigrated to the United States following the end of World War II. Tramiel began his company by assembling typewriters, and later began manufacturing electronic calculators. In 1976, the company purchased MOS Technology, the company that had developed the 6502 chip, which had been used in the early Atari and Apple computers.

Commodore had been one of the earliest companies to manufacture a personal computer. Its Commodore PET had come out in 1977. After Apple formed the same year, Commodore tried to purchase the new company, but the two couldn't reach an agreement. However, it was this interest by Commodore that inspired Steve Jobs to pursue grand ideas for his own company, and he quickly sought money and people to help make it grow.

In 1980, Commodore released the VIC-20, which was the main competitor with the Atari 400. In 1982, Commodore released the Commodore 64, a 64K computer that competed with the Atari 800XL, following the latter's release in 1983. Neither computer was taken seriously and both were widely purchased as game-playing machines. Of the two, the Commodore 64 reigned in sales.

In 1990, Commodore's new Interactive Consumer Products division, which was headed by Nolan Bushnell, released the first home multimedia system, the CDTV (Commodore Dynamic Total Vision). There wasn't much interest in the $999 system. Commodore lowered the price to $599 two years later, but by then, the CDTV had a lot of competition and failed to catch on. In 1993, Commodore decided to enter the videogame arena with the Amiga CD^{32}, which had been released late in the year. Despite good reviews, the unit also failed to catch on, because potential customers were confused by the avalanche of similar competing hardware, such as the 3DO and the CD-i.

Once Commodore declared bankruptcy, its remaining assets were handed over to a Bahamian accounting firm, Touche Ross. By year's end, two companies declared war upon each other in an effort to gain control of the once mighty corporation. The managers of Commodore's still-operating United Kingdom office wanted to purchase the remnants of the company and run it from England. Their plans included tripling the American R&D group and creating a RISC-based Amiga. However, the UK team couldn't secure funds from the Far East, which put a damper on their plans. Meanwhile, the president of Miami-based CEI (Creative Equipment International) was so certain that he would gain control of Commodore that he already had a manufacturing company getting ready to mass-produce new Amigas.

3DO Issues Licenses

1994 marked the first full year through in which the 3DO was out in the marketplace. Panasonic, the only company that began the year with a 3DO player, announced in March that it was lowering the price of its console from $700 to $500. The company claimed that the price reduction was due to "improvements in technology, and an expansion of production scale resulting from the introduction of the multiplayer feature in Japan and Europe." Panasonic also said that it had experienced a strong Christmas selling season.

Meanwhile, Sanyo announced that it would join Panasonic and manufacture its own 3DO player. Around the same time, 3DO announced that it had issued licenses to Goldstar and Samsung, enabling them to manufacture the players as well.

March also brought the 3DO into Japanese stores for the first time, as 70,000 units were shipped to 10,000 retail outlets in the tiny country. By May, over 120,000 consoles had been sold worldwide, and the 3DO Company proudly announced that it had pressed its one millionth disc for the system. The company also announced that it had signed a deal with Toshiba to market 3DO machines. Toshiba planned to develop portable 3DO players that could be used in cars to provide navigational information.

The year appeared to be going well for 3DO, which actively promoted the console by going "on tour" and displaying it at prime spots in shopping malls and college campuses. Whatever 3DO was doing, it was working. In August, the company announced that 200,000 consoles had been shipped. A month later, that number rose to 300,000. While other console manufacturers felt a decline in business during the third quarter, 3DO's sales were the best in its short history. By the end of the year, Goldstar released its 3DO console in North America, which brought the total number of 3DO consoles sold up to 500,000. Sanyo released a console in Japan, and planned to do the same in the United States in 1995, along with Samsung and Toshiba. To further the appeal of the 3DO, Creative Labs released a 3DO board for PC computers. After a slow start, the 3DO finally appeared to be taking off. In fact, it seemed to be doing so well that the company announced in the late summer that it was planning a 64-bit 3DO console that would be available in the fall of 1995.

The new system, which was to be called the M2, would have a clock speed of 68 MHz and would be compatible with the existing 32-bit software. And the current 32-bit machine would be able to accept the new M2 software with the help of the *M2 Accelerator*, a cartridge that would boost the power of the original machine to that of the new console.

However, not everything was as rosy for the 3DO Company as it appeared. AT&T decided not to manufacture a 3DO console as it had originally planned, and in October, 3DO raised its licensing fee from $3 to $6 per game. In a June article, *Newsweek* magazine reported that the Panasonic console was selling poorly in the United States. It also mentioned that software developer Spectrum Holobyte had suspended its development on a *Star Trek: The Next Generation* 3DO game.

Another system that had started slowly was Philips' CD-i. Although the multimedia system had been around since 1991, the $499 unit failed to catch on with the buying public. Since its inception, Philips had always resisted labeling the CD-i as a game machine. In 1994, Philips took a good look at the industry and realized that it should have promoted the CD-i as a gaming console all along.

Philips redesigned the console so that it looked like a gaming machine, and lowered its retail price to $299. To further target gamers, Philips began packaging a game called *Burn: Cycle* with its consoles in November. Unfortunately, most critics pointed out that as a game machine, the CD-i wouldn't be able to compete against new 32-bit super machines that were going to be released from SCE and Sega However, since those machines weren't yet available in the United States or Europe, Philips executives were optimistic that they could sell one million units by the end of the year.

Neo•Geo CD

After trying to develop a CD player for their Neo•Geo, SNK of Japan announced in June that instead of releasing an add-on CD peripheral to their existing Neo•Geo, it was coming out with an entirely new front-loading CD-based console, which would be sold in Japan before Christmas with a retail price of $475. SNK also announced that all of its existing cartridge-based software titles would be reissued on CD. These titles would sell for $45, and new original games would retail for $80: much lower than their cartridge counterparts.

The front-loading Neo•Geo CD system was actually released in Japan in September with a retail price of ¥52,500 ($525). Although the system sold very well, there were many users who were unhappy with the unit's slow loading time. Unlike other systems that only loaded parts of a game into the console's RAM, the Neo•Geo CD loaded the entire game. Coupling this complete load with the console's slow, single-speed CD player made the loading time unbearable to many users.

SNK Neo•Geo CD (Front Loading)

In an effort to quicken the load times, SNK had reduced the size of some games from their cartridge counterparts but this only reduced the over-all quality of the games. And although the machine was supposed to be an exact duplication of the earlier cartridge-based system, this wasn't exactly true. The new model didn't have a memory card slot so games that were saved from the cartridge console or the arcades couldn't be brought into the new model. The CD console didn't have its own memory card either, but up to 25 games could be saved in internal memory.

In December, SNK released a new, less-expensive top-loading Neo•Geo CD in Japan. Unfortunately, the top-loading model also came with the same single-speed CD drive, which impacted the games. The system was also released in Europe at that time. SNK of America announced that a top-loading Neo•Geo CD console would arrive in the United States in the spring of 1995. However, according to the company, the unit would include a double-speed CD-drive and would retail for under $400.

With the Neo•Geo CD, SNK abandoned its original model of having switchable arcade cartridges playable on home consoles. The CDs that SNK released were for home use only. However, Capcom, another Japanese arcade company, liked SNK's original idea and released its own home system that could play its arcade games.

Capcom's system used interchangeable arcade boards. Each board contained the circuitry for a unique game, and the boards could be switched in the arcade cabinets. The boards themselves were housed in cartridge-like plastic shells that could plug into the console, which was called the *CPS Changer;*[7] and the arcade boards plugged directly into it. Actually, the CPS Changer plugged into the cartridge, which was substantially

SNK Neo•Geo CD (Top Loading)

larger as it contained most of the components, including the CPU, that were required to run the game. The CPS Changer was basically an adapter that only featured the essentials needed to play the game at home, such as a composite video output, a power input and two controller ports. The system sold for ¥39,800 ($350), which included one *Street Fighter II: Hyper Fighting* arcade board. Additional arcade boards could be purchased for ¥20,000 ($176) apiece.[8] Also included was the *Power Stick Fighter*, an arcade-style joystick from Capcom.

Capcom also offered a slightly less expensive set that didn't include the Power Stick

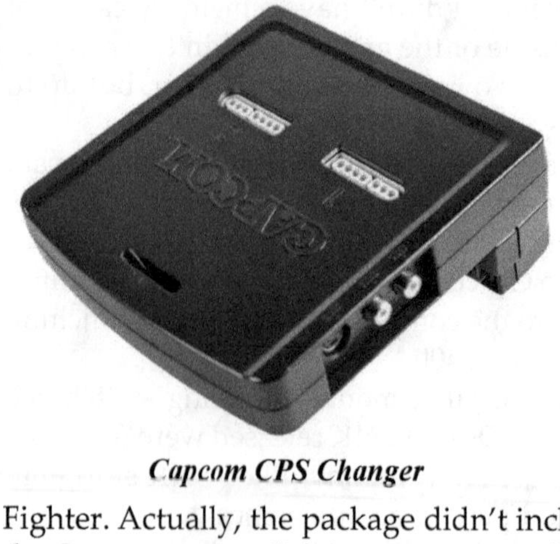

Capcom CPS Changer

Capcom CPS Changer Cartridge

Fighter. Actually, the package didn't include any controller at all. This was not because the Capcom games didn't require controllers. Instead, Capcom had designed it so it could use Super Famicom-compatible controllers which were readily available. In fact, Capcom specifically designed the Power Stick Fighter to be used with the Super Famicom version of *Street Fighter II*. Capcom soon released several adapters that made the Power Stick Fighter work on virtually every console and computer that was available at the time;

even on consoles that didn't have *Street Fighter II* ports for them.[9]

The Power Stick Fighter, which was released in Japan and the United States, wasn't the only arcade-style controller that was released for the Super Famicom/SNES. The *Super Advantage*, which was released in the United States, looked like a Nintendo product, from its packaging to its shape and coloring that resembled an SNES. But the controller had actually been released from Asciiware, which was a Nintendo licensee. Asciiware had also manufactured the original NES Advantage, which had been released by Nintendo. However, while many users decreed the NES Advantage to be one of the best controllers for the NES, they didn't feel the same about the Super Advantage. Complaints about its buttons ranged from their stickiness to their layout, which wasn't "*Street Fighter II* friendly." Ironically, the buttons were color-coordinated with the controller buttons found on the Super Famicom controllers.

Nintendo did release an arcade-style controller of its own for the SNES, but only in Europe. The Nintendo *Score Master* appeared to be well built and its correctly colored control buttons were in the correct *Street Fighter II* positions.

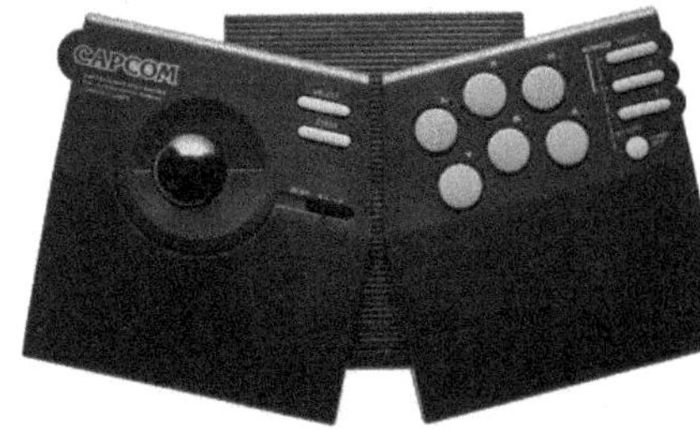

Capcom Power Stick Fighter

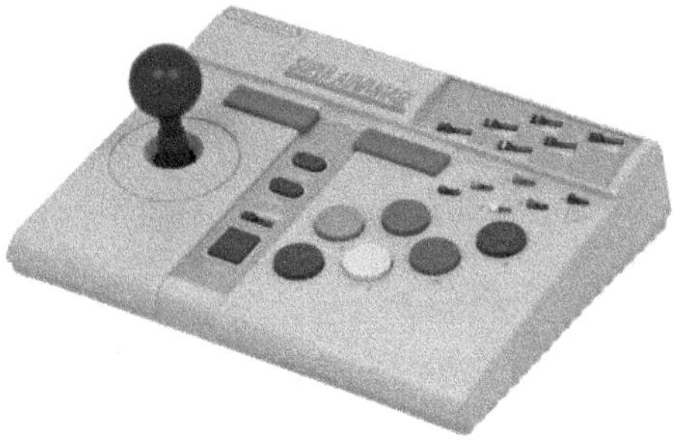

ASCII Super Advantage

Nintendo Score Master

NEC Goes Arcade

As it could with most other consoles, the Capcom Power Stick Fighter could be adapted to play on NEC's PC Engine. Capcom had released *Street Fighter II* for that system in June, 1993. In addition, NEC had released the *Avenue Pad 6*, its own six-button controller specifically to be used with the game. However, this pad was not an arcade-style controller, so players using it couldn't get the true arcade flavor when playing the game. But the PC Engine copy of *Street Fighter II* wasn't arcade-quality anyway.

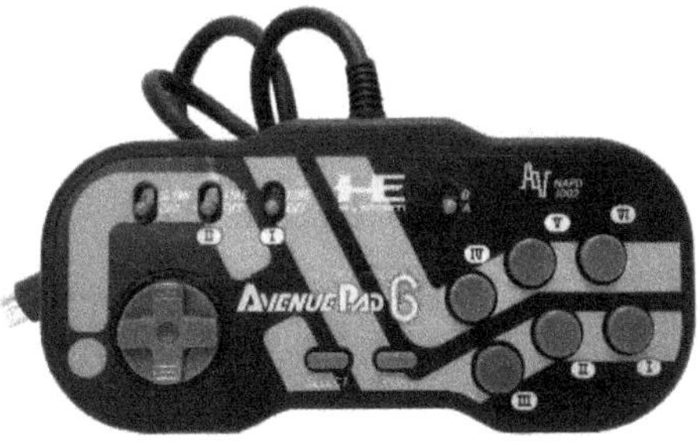

NEC Avenue Pad 6

NEC decided to release a new brand of games that could be played on the PC Engine that would be arcade-quality. On March 12, the company released two new system cards that would increase the RAM of its machines and play games from specific *Arcade CD-ROMS*. The *Arcade Card Duo* sold for ¥12,800 ($122) and was used in the standalone machines such as the PC Engine Duo and PC Engine Duo-R. It increased the console's built-in RAM to 16M. The *Arcade Card Pro* cost ¥17,800 ($169) and was used for the consoles that needed to be connected to the CD-ROM² and Super CD-ROM² units. It increased the system's internal RAM to 18M.

NEC released a new console on June 25, which could also accept the Arcade CD-ROM games by using the Arcade Card Duo system card. The *PC Engine Duo-RX* was basically a Duo-R packaged with a 6-button controller that was slightly different from the *Avenue Pad 6*. However, at ¥29,800 ($297), it was ¥10,000 ($100) less expensive than the Duo-R.

TTI had no plans on releasing the Duo-RX in North America and in early May it announced that it would abandon the North American market altogether although it planned to continue to support the with new software. On June 1, a new company called *Turbo Zone Direct* was established to sell old and new software for the TurboGrafx-16 and the TurboDuo, as well as provide service to repair them through a contract with NEC through 2001.[10]

NEC PC Engine Duo-RX

The Duo-RX was NEC's last hurrah for the PC Engine line. But the company wasn't abandoning the Japanese videogame scene as it had done in North America. On December 23, it released a new 32-bit CD-based console called the *PC-FX*, which was completely incompatible with the PC Engine. The only similarity that the ¥49,800 ($497) system shared with any PC Engine-related console was its six-button control pad, which was similar to, but not the same, as the pad that came with the Duo-RX. NEC didn't expect the machine to be a major seller, anticipating sales of only 50,000 units during its first year. The company didn't have any immediate plans to bring it to the United States.

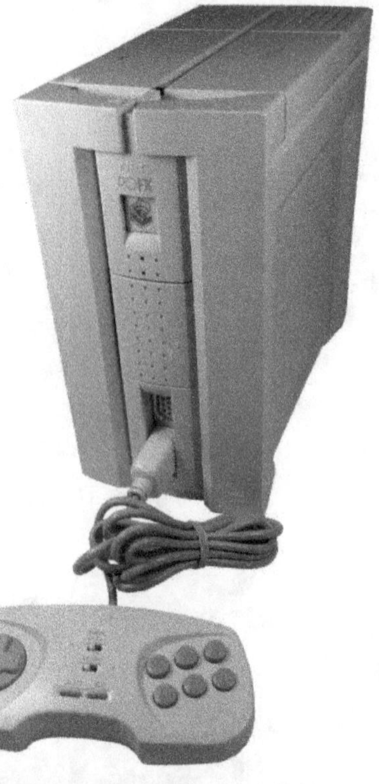

NEC PC-FX

Computers and Consoles

Although the PC-FX was not backwards-compatible with the PC Engine line, NEC, which was a computer company, offered an internal card for its PC-98 computers that would let them play PC-FX software.[11] The PC-FX, which looked like computer hardware, could be used as a CD-ROM drive for the PC-98 computers. And for those who didn't yet own a computer, NEC had plans expansion for the PC-FX that would indeed turn it into a computer.

The PC-FX wasn't the only Japanese videogame console that had been based on computer architecture. Another was the FM Towns Marty. Fujitsu replaced it with the *FM Towns Marty 2* in November. Like the Duo-RX, the new Marty was basically the same as the original one, although priced at ¥66,000 ($667), it cost approximately $130 less than the first. The only difference was that the FM Towns Marty 2 had a dark grey cabinet.

Fujitsu FM Towns Marty 2

Fujitsu released a third *Marty* system right on the heels of the FM Towns Marty 2. As its name implied, the *FM Towns Car Marty* was designed to be used in an automobile along with an optional TV monitor. The $3,500 unit looked more like a Commodore 64 disk drive than a videogame console. On the other hand, the FM Towns Car Marty did more than just play games. It also behaved as a global positioning system (GPS), and allowed users to track their positions as they drove.[12]

Fujitsu FM Towns Car Marty

Bandai Playdia

The Playdia and the Pippin

On October 23, the Japanese toy company, Bandai, released its first game console since the TV Jack 8000 in 1984. The ¥24,800 ($253) *Playdia* had been designed for young audiences and most of the approximately 40 titles available were educational. All of the software for the CD-based system consisted of interactive full-motion videos, although the system had the capability to play back video CD movies, audio CDs, karaoke and interactive videos. As far as playability was concerned, all the gamer had to do was press a directional button on the controller in response to on-screen menu prompts. The controller itself was wireless. Although wireless controllers had been available before, the Playdia was the first console to be packaged with one.

Unfortunately, Bandai lost money on the Playdia. In order to recoup some of its losses, Bandai began releasing *Idol* CDs, which were full-motion videos in which attractive young women removed their clothing according to the player's wishes. While Idol CDs were nothing new in Japan, it was curious that Bandai chose to release them for a system that had been designed for children. Still, the marketing worked, and Bandai managed to make a small profit off of the Playdia.

On December 13, Apple Computers announced the *Pippin*, a new 64-bit CD-ROM player built around a 66Mhz PowerPC 603 RISC microprocessor and Mac operating system. According to Apple, the Pippin would be compatible with Mac software and include a quadruple-speed CD-ROM player. Apple also planned to release a slew of peripherals, such as a keyboard, a mouse and floppy and hard disk drives for the unit. Built into the machine would be a telephone port so players could compete against or communicate with each other via the phone.

Apple planned for Bandai, which had distributed American videogame consoles in Japan during the early '80s, to release the $500 Pippin in Japan in the summer of 1995. In the fall Apple would release it itself in the United States, where it was expected to sell for between $300 and $500.

New Sega Systems

The 1993 Christmas season had been a good one for Sega. Not only did the Mega Drive/Genesis outsell the SNES, but the Game Gear's sales had increased over 200% from the previous year, giving it an installed base of nearly four million households. Lastly, the CD unit was in nearly one million households. Although the Mega Drive/Genesis outsold its competitors by almost 5-to-1, Sega didn't rest on its laurels, as far as new products were concerned.

On March 10, Sega of Japan released a commercial version of the *Mega Jet,* the semi-portable version of the Mega Drive that had been used by Japan Airlines. Although the ¥15,000 ($145) device sported a compact size, its lack of a screen and its need for an AC adapter prevented it from being a true portable unit.

The Mega Jet wasn't released in the United States. Instead, North America received the $400 *CDX*, a compact unit that combined the Genesis and the Sega CD. The console was the size of a portable CD player and weighed only 1½ pounds. It featured a lift-up top, so Sega CDs could be placed onto a platter, as well as a cartridge slot for Genesis games. Despite its tiny size, the unit was completely compatible with both Genesis and Sega CD software.

Although Sega touted the CDX as a portable, it really wasn't when compared to the Game Boy and Game Gear. It was only portable in the sense that its small size made it

Sega CDX

easy to carry around. Since it didn't have its own monitor, its only true portable use was in doubling as a portable CD player. However, its $400 price tag made that impractical. Sega only sold 5000 units, and never released the CDX within Japan.[13]

In September, JVC released the Wondermega M2 in the United States, where it was called the *X'Eye*. The $499 X'Eye was virtually the same unit as the Wondermega M2 although it didn't come with the wireless controllers. JVC attempted to emphasize the multimedia capabilities of the X'Eye by packaging it with *Compton's Multimedia Encyclopedia*, a Karaoke disc and a Sega CD disc. Regardless of whether it was a multimedia device or not, the system didn't sell well in either country, mainly since it retailed for $500, $100 more than the CDX/Multi-Mega, which itself wasn't flying off store shelves.

JVC X'Eye

Even though work was progressing behind the scenes on the 32-bit Saturn, Sega didn't want to lose the huge base of Genesis owners that it had established in the United States. Although Sega anticipated that many Genesis owners would purchase the new Saturn, they also expected that a large majority of them would simply just relegate their consoles to closets when Sega stopped supporting the machine. Sega knew that it had to somehow keep the Genesis timely, even as the company marketed a more powerful system.

Sega had originally planned two new 32-bit machines: the CD-based Saturn and a cartridge-based Jupiter that would have an optional CD player available for it. Sega realized early, however, that it would be unwise to sell games in both cartridge and CD formats, since the cartridge versions would be economically inferior to the less expensive CDs. Sega decided to abandon the Jupiter and added a cartridge slot to the Saturn that could be used to save data, or for future expansion.

As Sega planned to keep supporting the Genesis, it was decided to incorporate the Jupiter technology. The result was the *Mars*, a 32-bit cartridge-based system that would sit atop the Genesis.

Sega of America announced in mid-March its plans to release the Mars, which by that time had been renamed the *Super 32X*. The new system, which included two Hitachi SH2 RISC processors and a brand-new video digital processor, would plug into the Genesis cartridge slot. Sega touted that the new system brought near-Saturn quality games to the Genesis by providing a faster processing speed, high-color definition, texture-mapping, enhanced scaling and rotation, improved polygon graphics and an ever-changing 3D perspective. The Super 32X would be priced at an affordable $150 and give existing Genesis owners the ability to purchase the newest games without having to purchase an entirely new system.

What wasn't mentioned was whether or not the software for the Super 32X would be compatible with the forthcoming Saturn. Since the Super 32X was to be cartridge-driven, while the Saturn would be using CDs, compatibility was unlikely. However, speculation was that at least Sega of America would add a cartridge port to the American Saturn to make them compatible.

Sega of America unveiled the new system at the summer CES in June, where it was unofficially called the Genesis 32X.[14] By the end of the summer, Sega raised the price of the Genesis 32X to $160 and announced that a game cartridge would not be packed in.

Sega 32X

Instead, Sega planned to include six $10 coupons that could be used towards the future purchase of Genesis 32X software.

The Genesis 32X was released in the United States on November 21. Demand for the unit was so high that Sega couldn't keep up with it. By Christmas, only 350,000 had actually been shipped, even though retailers had ordered one million units. After going on an around-the-clock production schedule, Sega managed to deliver a total of 600,000 units by the end of the year.

With the Genesis 32X out of the way, Sega of America began releasing information about its next console, which was planned for late 1995. Surprisingly, it wasn't the Saturn. Instead, Sega announced the *Neptune*, which was a combination of a Genesis and 32X that would sell for under $200 and would not include a CD-ROM player.

Sega of Japan, meanwhile, focused on the 32-bit Saturn, which they heralded as the machine that would set the standards for all future home videogame consoles.

Sega had displayed games for the Saturn early in the year at the winter CES, where little was revealed about the machine other than that it would be able to produce 1,024 on-screen colors (the SNES could only produce 256), and that its processor would run at 24Mhz (the next fastest machine, the Neo•Geo, ran at 14Mhz). Other questions remained unanswered, such as whether the Saturn would be compatible with Sega's 16-bit software. The main consensus was that it wouldn't, because otherwise, the Saturn would have to employ custom chips that would drive up its price, which was already set at an alarming $430.

Then there was a show-sweeping rumor about Sega and Microsoft forming a partnership. This rumor stemmed from private talks that had taken place between the two companies. Other rumors implied that Microsoft had designed the Saturn's operating system, along with several games for the new console.

Only software had been previewed at the CES in January. The actual hardware didn't appear in public until June 2, at the Tokyo Toy Show. Unfortunately, the silver-wood consoles that were displayed weren't playable; but incomplete games could be played on Saturn circuit boards. Critics were impressed by the little they were shown. Sega of Japan assured the press that the system and software would be available in Japan in November. Sega of America refused to publicly comment when the Saturn would be available in the United States, because it didn't want to jeopardize its Genesis 32X sales. However, in private, it spoke of an April 1995 launch.

But because many of the third-party vendors would be releasing their new Genesis 32X software in the spring, Sega of America really wanted to push the Saturn's American debut into the latter part of the year, to profit from the Genesis as long as possible. Nearly eight million Genesis consoles had been sold in 1994, and Sega of America wanted to assure its customers that it would stand by the Genesis for many years to come.

Sega of Japan released the Saturn on November 22, and approximately 170,000 machines, Sega's complete inventory, were sold that first day with a retail price of ¥44,800 ($457). The Saturn was heralded as the best system on the market, and featured an expensive television-ad campaign to make sure the public knew it. In a move similar to one by 3DO, Sega licensed the console to three other companies (JVC, Hitachi and Yamaha), who would sell it under their own brand names. Hitachi also signed a deal with Sega to distribute the Saturn to electronic stores, much like JVC had done for the Mega Drive with its Wondermega.

Sega of Japan Saturn

The Japanese Saturn console did have a cartridge slot, although at the time of its release, the only thing that plugged into it was a ¥4,800 ($47) *Saturn Backup Memory* cartridge used to save games. The console also had a five-pin port that was simply labeled "communications connector". No one knew what this meant, and very few even cared to speculate. Practically every system beginning with the Atari 7800 had contained such an expansion port, and none of them had ever been utilized. Finally, the console was sold with *Virtua Fighter*, a hit Sega arcade game.

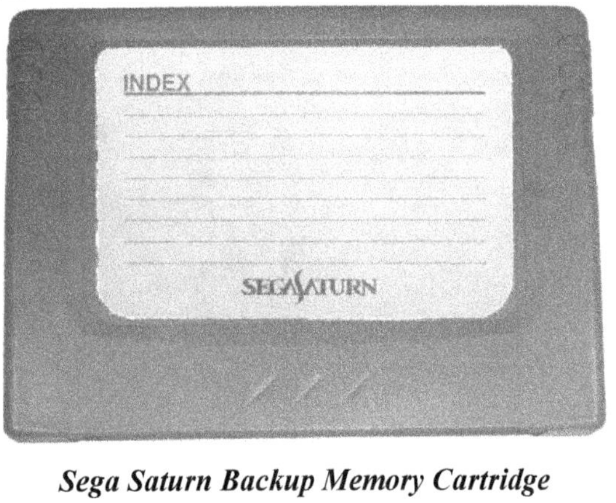

Sega Saturn Backup Memory Cartridge

Although Sega of Japan seemed to have a hit on its hands with the Saturn, on December 3, it went ahead and released the ¥16,800 ($168) *Super 32X*, one day before it came out in Europe. The release of the 32-bit hybrid in the United States and Europe made sense, since the Saturn was still nearly a year away. But in Japan,

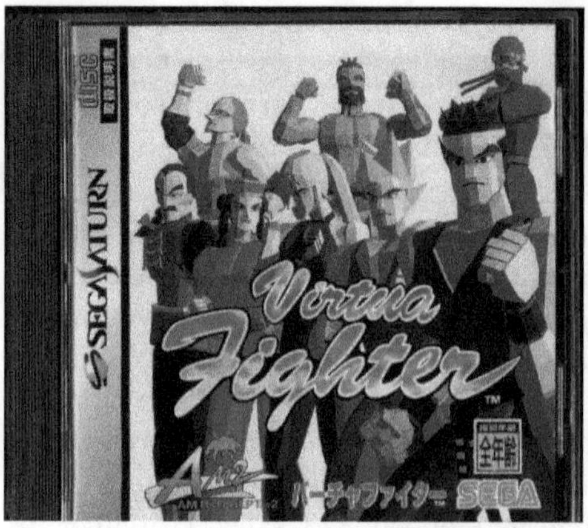

Sega Saturn Virtua Fighter

where the Saturn was already being sold, the appearance of the Super 32X just left many would-be customers confused. Did it mean that Sega didn't have faith in the Saturn and was trying to appease its 16-bit owners by giving them the ability to upgrade? And for those who owned a Mega Drive: should they purchase a Saturn or a Super 32X?

Or should they just wait and see what SCE had to offer?

The PlayStation

Excitement for the PS-X had begun in April, when SCE began releasing patchy information regarding the new console. SCE officials announced that the unit would be released in Japan in November, followed by releases in the United States and Great Britain in September 1995. The reason for the lag of nearly a year was to give developers in those countries time to create extraordinary games that would appeal to their customers.

On May 18, SCE formed a new company called *Sony Computer Entertainment America (SCEA)*, which would be responsible for the system in the United States. Shortly afterwards at a conference held for the Japanese press, the company announced a new name for its videogame system. The new name was actually an old one. The system would now be

SCE PlayStation

called the *PlayStation*, the same moniker that Sony had used when it had planned to create a videogame console in tandem with Nintendo.

SCE used the press conference to demonstrate the capabilities of the PlayStation. One special feature was a serial port that allowed two PlayStations to be hooked up to each other, enabling players to compete against each other on their own separate monitors. The PlayStation also had a parallel I/O port that SCE chose not to talk about. Critics speculated that it would probably be used to connect a modem to the console.

The PlayStation's controller was somewhat similar to the Super Famicom's. There were four control buttons on the right, which SCE elected to label by color-coded shapes, rather than letters.[15] Select and Start buttons were located in the center of the controller. And although it didn't have a D-pad, the controller featured four directional buttons that were arranged in a cross formation. The controller also had two sets of shoulder buttons.

SCE PlayStation Controller Symbols

Like the Super Famicom controller, the face of the PlayStation controller resembled a dog bone, with two rounded sides and a slim body connecting them. But each of the rounded sides on the PlayStation controller had a long grip extending downwards, making the controller look more like Nintendo's NES Max.

The most spectacular parts of the PlayStation were hidden. SCE had teamed up with LSI Logic to design a chip that shrunk its MIPS R3000A-compatible 32-bit RISC CPU to 1/200 the width of a human hair. The reduced circuitry allowed the PlayStation to require less power for it to manipulate data much faster. This let the PlayStation create sophisticated, 3D geometric graphics that rivaled workstations costing tens of thousands of dollars. The system could also produce full-motion video.

Like the 3DO and CD-i, PlayStation software was only available on CDs, which were black on their data sides instead of silver, to make them stand out. Skeptics pointed out that this wasn't necessarily a good thing. Although CDs could store much more data than cartridges, the drawback was that information could be retrieved from cartridges much faster. SCE promised that the PlayStation's access time would be negligible and without any flicker or slowdown.

By July, SCE began promising that 82 PlayStation games would be released in Japan during 1995. SCE executives had so much faith in the machine that they projected Japanese sales of three million units by 1996.

Just prior to Sega of Japan's November 22 release of the Saturn, SCE announced to a large Japanese press that the PlayStation would debut in Japan on December 3, with a retail price of ¥39,800 ($402). Eight games and a mouse would be available for the launch, and SCE was confident that an additional fifteen titles would be available before the end of the year. However, the console itself would be sold without any bundled software.

SCE shipped the PlayStation on the promised date. The company used a distribution company called HappyNet to get the machines into game stores, a market that it never had to deal with before. Only 4,000 stores were able to acquire the 100,000 units that were shipped, and sales of the PlayStation were limited to one per customer.

By year's end, the sales battle in Japan between Sega and SCE was going full gear. All of the Saturns that had been initially shipped had been sold out while a few PlayStations remained on store shelves. Many critics felt that the PlayStation was the superior machine, and that the only reason it lagged behind the Saturn was because it didn't have any killer

Two PlayStation Launch Titles

games on the level of *Virtua Fighter*. Both companies were positive that their machines would dominate the industry. It was up to the Japanese consumers to decide which one would.

The buying public couldn't seem to make up its mind. A Japanese gaming magazine called *Famicom Tsūshin* polled its 750,000 readers and asked them which machine they wanted to buy. While 22% of the readers favored the Saturn, nearly twice that amount, 41%, said they would buy a PlayStation. These numbers didn't jive with the figures that were coming in from the retail stores, where the Saturn, with 500,000 units sold, outnumbered the PlayStation by 200,000 systems. However, most of the hardware companies were doing well. 3DO surprised most critics when it announced that it had over 350,000 consoles in Japanese homes. SNK sold over 100,000 Neo•Geo CD players, and even the brand-new NEC PC-FX, which went on sale during the final week of 1994, sold 70,000 systems before the end of the year.

Only Atari did poorly. By Christmas, the company had sold only 2,000 Jaguars in Japan. This number did nothing to help Atari achieve the two-million mark that it had hoped to reach in 1995.

Sega Pocket Arcade

Sega's Non-Video Products

Although Sega hoped that its new Saturn would reign supreme in the videogame world, the company wasn't putting all of its eggs in one basket. During 1994, Sega merged with Yonezawa Toys, Japan's largest toy company, to start a new company called *Sega Yonezawa* to create electronic products other than videogames.[16] Sega of Japan shifted its Pico, the "computer that thinks it's a toy," over to the new division Since *Sega Yonezawa* didn't operate outside of Japan, in November, Sega of America released a $139 Pico under the Sega banner in the United States, where they licensed many popular characters, such as Mickey Mouse and Winnie the Pooh to help make it a hit. To appease older children, Sega also released a few items that were not available in Japan. The *Pocket Arcade* handheld units were developed by Tiger. This was a group nine dedicated LCD devices that sold for $25 apiece. In each unit, the screen was protected when it wasn't being used by being either being stored in the unit itself and popping out when needed, or with a plastic cover that flipped open for play. Some Pocket Arcades, such as *Ecco the Dolphin* and *Columns* were based on Sega console games.

Sega also released the *IR7000*, an $80 pocket organizer that contained a database for addresses and phone numbers, a calculator, an alarm clock, a currency converter, and a memo pad. The device was manufactured by Casio, which had also released two similar products under its own brand called *Secret Sender 6000* and the *My Super Magic Diary*. All three devices allowed their users to compose texts and transmit them across the room to someone else's unit via infrared technology. However, unlike the two Casio units, the *IR7000* also included a game called *Brain Drain* that could be played alone or against another person up to thirty feet away.

Sega IR7000

Sega also released an electronic toy that it had manufactured. *Pods* was a $50 machine that recorded the player's movements and sent out sounds and flashing lights. Sega referred to *Pods* as "futuristic Simons."

Sega also announced that it would release 21st-century walkie-talkies, called *Beamers*. Each of these palm-sized units allowed two people to transmit up to 16 seconds' worth of messages to one another from a distance of up to thirty feet. The Beamers were never released.

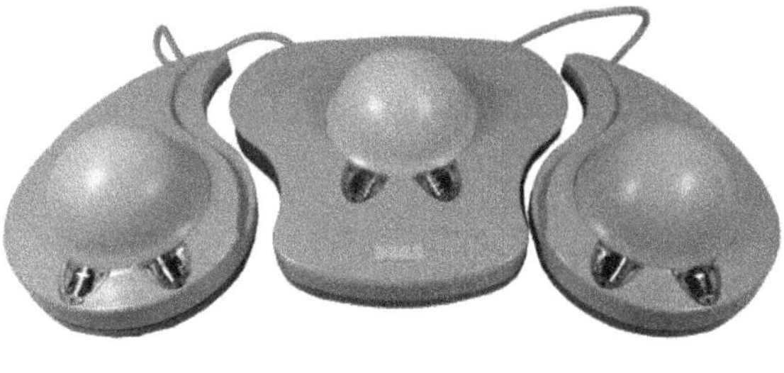

Sega Pods

1994

Additional Sega Ventures

Personal electronics wasn't the only industry that Sega was venturing into. Early in the year, the company signed a contract with MCA to create an entertainment attraction at MCA's Universal Studios in Hollywood. Surprisingly, on July 1, Sega opened a similar type of exhibition at Universal's competition, Walt Disney World. Sega had signed a three-year contract with Disney to display 140 Genesis, Sega CD and Game Gear products at the new *Innoventions* area inside Epcot Center. Sega's use of Epcot Center may only have been a trial run into the theme-park business. On July 20, the company went ahead and opened its own theme park, Joyopolis, in Yokohama, Japan. In addition to featuring Sega arcade games, Joyopolis also had amusement rides that were based on Sega intellectual properties.

Sega also expanded into new areas of the arcade industry when it purchased Data East Pinball., the second-largest manufacturer of pinball machines. Sega didn't have any plans to change the Data East name, but the acquisition made them a dominant force in the arcade industry.

Despite all of the new areas that Sega was entering, the most unexpected Sega purchase in 1994 was an interest in a competing videogame company.

Sega's purchase of 7.4% of Atari Corp.'s outstanding stock began in 1993 when Atari sued Sega for patent infringements. Sega countersued and the two companies squabbled into 1994. Their bickering finally came to an end on September 28, when the two companies agreed to settle out of court and drop all charges against each other. Under the terms of their agreement, Sega was permitted to purchase 4.5 million shares of Atari stock valued at over $40 million.

Other parts of the agreement had Sega pay Atari $50 million for non-exclusive worldwide rights to 70 of Atari's patents. The two companies also agreed to license games from each other for use on their respective videogame consoles.

Both companies admitted that they had made out in the bargain. Sega had the lawsuits against it dropped and had access to Atari's excessive library of patents. Atari benefited, because it now had an additional $90 million, a portion of which would be used for marketing. This money had been sorely needed, as Atari had announced that it had lost $22.6 million during the fourth quarter of 1993, which it had attributed to the start-up costs of the Jaguar. However, eight months later, Atari reported an additional $3.9 million loss that it blamed on the costs needed to promote the Jaguar.

Sega wasn't the only company with a stake in Atari Corp. Time Warner, which had previously owned the entire company, still retained 25% of it. In March, the conglomerate increased its stake by purchasing an additional 2%.

In addition to its victory against Sega, Atari Corp. succeeded in a lawsuit against Nintendo. Atari contended that Nintendo had illegally utilized its "114" patent, which covered horizontal-scrolling routines. The outcome of the lawsuit allowed Nintendo to license the technology from Atari Corp.

Changes To Atari Games

The arcade company, Atari Games, also had a lawsuit pending against Nintendo. This suit was over certain patent infringements, but Atari Games wasn't as fortunate in its outcome as Atari Corp. had been. Lawsuits between the two companies had scuttled back and forth for several years, and by late April, the two companies had finally resolved their differences and settled out of court. Both issued statements that they were glad that the lawsuits were over, and that they were looking forward to working together in the future. Whoever came out on top was anybody's guess, but both companies were winners, as Tengen once again became a Nintendo licensee. In the end, however, Tengen was not a winner. The many years of lawsuits left the company financially ruined.

Meanwhile Namco decided to finally get rid of its share of Tengen's parent, Atari Games. It sold its 40% ownership back to Time Warner, which gave it full control since it already owned 40%. Time Warner made the decision to consolidate all of its interactive divisions, which also included Warner New Media under one banner, which was called *Time Warner Interactive*. Although the division retained the Atari Games identity for its arcade games, they chose to use the Time Warner Interactive name for its home products, so the Tengen and Warner New Media brands were officially disbanded.

Shortly after Time Warner Interactive was formed, Atari Games announced that it was going to use Atari Corp.'s Jaguar in its coin-op games. Following this decision, all games would then be developed for both the arcade machines and the home Jaguars. After ten years of separation, the two Ataris were once again working together.

Arcade players weren't to be the only new audience that could play Jaguar games. In May, Atari Corp. licensed the Jaguar technology to a company called Sigma Designs, which had developed a card that allowed PC owners to play Jaguar games on their home computers. Although the $500 board was announced to be in the stores in time for Christmas, it was never released.

More Nintendo Lawsuits

The victor in a different lawsuit against Nintendo was more easily identifiable. In a $400 million suit that had been underway since February 1986, a company called Alpex Computer Corp. was awarded a judgment against Nintendo for patent infringement. In 1974, Alpex had designed a new technique that allowed game consoles to use replaceable, ROM cartridges to play multiple games. Even before Alpex was issued U.S. Patent No. 4,026,555 on May 31, 1977, Alpex licensed the technology to Fairchild, who used it to produce the first cartridge-system, the Channel F.[17] Alpex went bankrupt in 1984, but its patents didn't expire until May, 1994.

The specific technology, as the patent was awarded, worked by bit-mapping, where an entire image was produced, bit-by-bit, before it was displayed on the screen in specific memory locations. Alpex claimed that Nintendo used its technology in the NES, which had first been released in 1985. In June, 1994, a jury agreed with Alpex, and two months later, Nintendo was ordered to pay more than $253 million, a figure based on all of the sales of the NES through 1992.

Nintendo argued that it had not infringed upon Alpex's patents, because it had used a different technology. The patent clearly outlined the use of a RAM memory map for each of the 32,000 pixels in the television's horizontal scanning lines, while the NES used shift registers that only used a maximum of 64 pixels.

During the trial, Alpex had specifically distinguished its patent from a prior one that used shift registers. Nintendo claimed that the jury reached its verdict much too quickly to have understood all of the testimony and evidence.[18]

Ironically, Fairchild Semiconductor, the company that had been the first to license the Alpex technology, was also involved in a lawsuit with Nintendo. Fairchild contended that Nintendo had used its patented method of "loading and locking" game cartridges into a game console. The court sided with Nintendo. Fairchild appealed the case, but the U.S. Court of Appeals upheld the prior decision in favor of Nintendo.

Courts all over the United States seemed to be ruling in Nintendo's favor. In Los Angeles, a Federal judge sided with Nintendo in a patent-infringement case that had been filed by an individual named Edward Gussin. Gussin had been awarded a U.S. patent on September 21, 1993 for a device that allowed users to electronically draw and color on a color television screen. Gussin claimed that his patent had been infringed by the SNES when it was using the *Mario Paint* program, which in effect allowed the SNES to perform the same function as his invention. However, as Nintendo pointed out in its testimony, Gussin's patent was awarded for, and covered, a dedicated device. Since the SNES was not dedicated, and *Mario Paint* was software, it was an easy win for Nintendo.

Nintendo wasn't always the defendant. In September, the company filed a suit against TSMC, Taiwan's largest chip manufacturer. Nintendo claimed that TSMC's chips had been found in counterfeit SNES machines. Without accepting guilt, TSMC responded that since its customers owned the product designs and tooling that it used when manufacturing the chips, it had no way to identify whether or not the information in the chips it made violated anyone else's patents.

Meanwhile, Taiwan's second-largest chip manufacturer, United Microelectronics Corp. (UMC), settled with Nintendo, for doing basically the same thing that TSMC had been charged with. After the settlement, UMC claimed that it would be more careful to avoid infringements in the future.

Sega also scored a victory in the fight against videogame piracy. In its case, an injunction

Nakitek GameSaver

was granted against the MAPHIA computer bulletin board, which offered to download Sega games. The injunction prohibited the electronic copying and distribution of copyrighted Sega games.

Ironically, a device that *legally* copied games was released in the United States. Nakitek's GameSaver was a cartridge that enabled SNES players to save where they were in a game. Then the next time they played they could easily get to the spot where they left off. It also allowed a game to be played in slow motion.

Fight Games Fight It Out

The hardware manufacturers weren't the only companies involved in lawsuits. Another major lawsuit of 1994 involved two arcade companies: Capcom and Data East. Capcom claimed that Data East's arcade game, *Fighter's History*, infringed upon its own *Street Fighter II*. While setting an October 31 trial date, the judge declared that since there were many similarities between the two games, Data East couldn't deny that it set out to copy the successful *Street Fighter II* when it began designing *Fighter's History*. However, before the case reached a jury, the judge stated that there weren't any triable issues in the areas that Capcom claimed copyright infringement. The case was eventually dismissed after Data East received two partial summary judgments against Capcom. Data East was especially happy with the result and claimed that if Capcom had been victorious, it would have had a virtual monopoly on all fighting-type videogames. Ironically, it had been Data East that had established the fighting game genre when it released *Karate Champ* in 1984.

But Acclaim was proof that Capcom didn't hold a monopoly on fighting games. The former company managed to break all records with *Mortal Kombat II*, the follow-up to the violent game that had sent Congress scrambling. Following its much publicized release in early September, *Mortal Kombat II* became the biggest-selling videogame in history, earning over $50 million during its first week. Even *The Lion King*, the top-grossing movie of the year, didn't earn that much during its first week.

Sensational Games For the SNES

Mortal Kombat II had been released for a multitude of gaming consoles and computers, and this played a considerable part in the game's staggering success. However, despite its huge achievement in sales, the game would be in the spotlight for a very short time. Within three months of *Mortal Kombat II*'s dazzling debut, a new title was released that shattered its sales records. And this new game was available for only one console, making that accomplishment even more amazing.

Nintendo Donkey Kong Country

The game was *Donkey Kong Country* for the SNES, and Nintendo sold over 500,000 copies of it within a week of its November 21 release, making it the fastest selling game at that time. It had been designed on Silicon Graphics workstations, and provided outstanding graphics and a sophisticated 3D effect on the SNES. Nintendo forecasted selling over six million copies of the game.[19]

Donkey Kong Country was the hit that Nintendo of America desperately needed. Prior to the game's release, the company had announced that its income for the first half of the year fell 18% from the same period a year earlier. Nintendo of America had blamed the drop on poor sales and a strong Japanese yen.

While *Donkey Kong Country* was the must-have game for the SNES, it certainly wasn't the only game that everyone had to own. More than a month before it was released, another must-have game for the SNES came out for the first time in the United States. *Final Fantasy III* was the American version of *Final Fantasy VI*, which had been released in Japan in April for the Super Famicom. The game was an immediate hit, garnering enthusiastic reviews from the day it debuted. *GamePro* magazine rated it 5/5, while *EGM* rated it 9/10, and named it their game of the month. At year's end, *EGM* also awarded the following: Best Music for a Cartridge-Based Game, Best Role-Playing Game and Best Japanese Role-Playing Game.

With the releases of *Final Fantasy III* and *Donkey Kong Country*, Nintendo of America finally had the ammunition it needed for the SNES to be a worthy opponent of the Genesis. And even before these games were available, Nintendo of America took strides to brighten its public image. Following 1993, a year when Sega was more popular, Nintendo of America realized that its name was no long synonymous with outstanding games. In late summer, the company began a $10 million ad campaign that included major advertising in all of the videogame magazines, as well as in newspapers and on television, to win back its customer base.

Nintendo of America also changed its policy with its licensed developers. Previously, its attitude was that they had to follow by its rules or they could forget about manufacturing games for the NES and SNES. Now that those machines weren't number one and the developers were free to go elsewhere, Nintendo had to change its policies towards them. Nintendo started paying top dollars for outside developers and began offering incentives of up to 15% of sales to companies that could produce a best-selling game for the SNES. Despite the fact that its popularity was waning, Nintendo still managed to take the lead spot in an annual ranking of excellent Japanese companies for the fourth year in a row. Meanwhile, its toughest competitor, Sega, dropped to number thirteen.

As new games such as *Donkey Kong Country* came out for the SNES, and the onslaught of new generation machines on the horizon, the enthusiasm for the 8-bit machines completely died. Nintendo realized that it was time to retire its revolutionary ten-year old 8-bit console. On June 24, Hudson Soft released *Adventure Island IV*, which was the final game released for the Famicom. The NES didn't last much longer. On December 10, Nintendo of America released *Wario's Woods*, which was note-worthy for two reasons. Not only was it the last official release for the NES, but it was also the only game for the NES that carried an ESRB rating (K-A).

Although interest in the Famicom/NES was gone, one company believed that there was still some life left in the 8-bit games. In the spring, a British company called Fire International released a £39 ($58) peripheral called *Tri-Star*, which let NES and Famicom games play on the SNES. Although the unit did fairly well in Great Britain, that success was not replicated in the summer when the Tri-Star was released in the United States.

Game Boys: Super and Color

Even though gamers apparently weren't interested in playing their NES games on their SNES consoles, Nintendo thought they might like to use their 16-bit systems to play their Game Boy games. The *Super Game Boy, a* $60 SNES cartridge with a built-in Game Boy interface, was released by Nintendo in June. After any Game Boy cartridge was plugged in, the game could be played in four shades of color on a standard TV set. Nintendo also began releasing new Game Boy cartridges specifically for play on the Super Game Boy. When played on a standard Game Boy, these games didn't look any different from the

Nintendo Super Game Boy

older Game Boy titles that were already on the market. However, they displayed 256 colors on a TV screen when they were played through the SNES. The first new Game Boy cartridge that Nintendo released that took advantage of the Super Game Boy was the original *Donkey Kong*.

The Super Game Boy had been released to enhance the popularity of the Game Boy, which had been on the shelves for five years and was beginning to show its age. However, with the number of units sold around the world exceeding 40 million, and over 400 game titles available, Nintendo believed that there was still life left in the system. In late 1994, the company announced a new Game Boy that would be available the following year. And from its name, the *Game Boy Color*, consumers believed that it was the system that they had been waiting for for five years.

Introducing the Virtual Boy

The Game Boy Color joined another system that Nintendo had introduced in April. At that time, Nintendo had announced the spring 1995 Japanese release of a new 32-bit home game system that would feature virtual reality applications. The company was very tight-lipped about this new system, and only called it by its code name, the VR-32. Little was revealed about this new system, apart from the under-$200 price tag and the built-in monitor.

On November 14, Nintendo of Japan was more forthcoming when it unveiled the VR-32 at its annual Shoshinkai trade show. At that time, it was revealed that the new 32-bit virtual reality system was actually a portable unit with the unimaginative name of *Virtual Boy*. Like the new, bigger consoles that were being announced, the Virtual Boy contained a 32-bit RISC chip that operated two "mirror-imaging" screens, each containing red LED on a black background. Players didn't have to use "virtual reality" glasses in order to see the 3D images. In order to maintain the "virtual feel", Nintendo made the double-gripped controllers external from the unit. The portable unit also featured true stereo sound.

The Virtual Boy was the brainchild of Gunpei Yokoi, a leader of one of Nintendo's four Research & Development teams. Yokoi had the distinction of being one of Nintendo's oldest and most respected engineers, and had played an important role in turning Nintendo from a maker of Hanafuda cards to a major force in electronic games. He was also responsible for the early Nintendo Game & Watches, as well as the phenomenal Game Boy. Nintendo was betting that Yokoi's design team had come up with another runaway blockbuster.

The Shoshinkai, where the Virtual Boy made its debut, was a yearly affair that Nintendo set up to show its distributors its new products. Far from wowed by the new unit, the attendees at the show were stunned and dumbfounded. They didn't know what to make of the it since it wasn't portable and was difficult to use. Another complaint was similar to the one used against Atari's abandoned Cosmos unit; the 3D effect didn't add anything to the gameplay.

Still, Nintendo assured the attendees that the Virtual Boy would sell three million units in Japan during its first year, from April 1995 to March 1996. With the unit retailing for ¥15,000 ($170) and the cartridges going for around ¥6,000 ($68) apiece, the attendees didn't actually believe in Nintendo's promises. The press was even less kind. Calling the new unit the Virtual Dog, the American reporters who attended the Shoshinkai predicted a quick death for the Virtual Boy.

The technology that was used in the Virtual Boy had been developed by Massachusetts-based Reflection Technologies, Inc.[20] In late 1994, Nintendo obtained a minority interest in the company, marking the first time it had ever taken an interest in an American business. Nintendo also acquired the exclusive worldwide videogame rights to Reflection's virtual display.

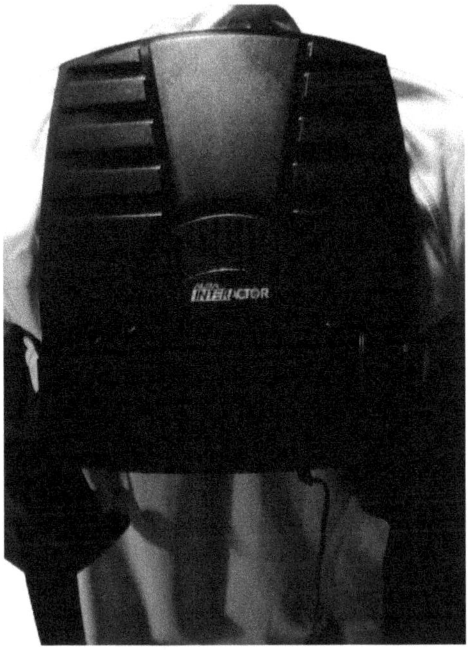

Aura Interactor

Although Nintendo had the rights to Reflection's method of virtual reality, other companies were free to ponder upon their own technologies. The first virtual reality product to be announced in 1994 was the *Interactor* Interactive Vest that Aura Systems had developed. The Interactor didn't provide virtual reality in the truest sense, but it helped augment the virtual reality experience. Worn like a real vest, it enhanced sound vibrations, so the gamer could actually feel the sounds that took place during a game. Aura released the vest in the late summer with a retail price of $100.

LifeFitness Lifecycle 3500

LifeFitness, a leading manufacturer of exercise bicycles, teamed up with Nintendo of America and came up with the *Lifecycle 3500*, an exercise bike that hooked up to a standard SNES. The $800 bike was sold with the Lifecycle Exertainment, a unit that plugged into the bottom of an SNES. That unit was then connected to another, which plugged into the bike. Special game controllers, which attached to the bike's handlebars, were also included. The front of the bike attached to a kiosk which contained a built-in TV monitor.

The bike could only be used with SNES games that were specifically designed for the Lifecycle 3500. The games had a Program Manager built into them, which monitored the cyclist's performance while calculating distance, time elapsed and calories burned. Unfortunately, only two games were ever available for the system. *Mountain Bike Rally* was packaged with the bike, and *Speed Racer* was available separately. *Pac-Man* and *Tetris* were announced but never released. The combination of the lack of new games and the system's high price doomed it.

Virtual I/O's $250 *PDS Gamer* was a headset that consisted of two LCD television panels that sat in front of the eyes. It also featured a set of stereo headphones. When playing a game while wearing the PDS Gamer headset, a person would be totally immersed in the game, in the sense that all he could see was the screen in front of him, and all he could hear were the game sounds. Unfortunately, this wasn't a true virtual reality environment, since the gamer would still see the same screen in front of his eyes no matter which direction he turned his head. And he wouldn't feel the action that was happening in the game.

Virtual I/O's *The Gamer!* was much closer to true virtual reality. The $399 device, which Virtual I/O planned to release in 1995, was a headset that used real-time head tracking to simulate a true 360 degree world. Virtual I/O promised that the new device would work with all of the game consoles.

In late 1994, Anaphase Unlimited introduced *The Glove*, which was similar to Mattel's Power Glove. Commands to the console were as simple as a turn of the hand. However, while the Power Glove had been available for only one console, the NES, The Glove was available for both the SNES and the Genesis.

Around the same time that The Glove was introduced, another virtual reality device, which was also compatible with both the SNES and Genesis, began making the rounds. The $69 *Batter Up* from Sports Sciences was a virtual reality baseball bat that plugged into the console's controller port. After an on-screen player pitched the ball, the real-life player would swing the Batter Up. The bat would then figure out whether the ball had been hit or not. If it decided that the ball had indeed been hit, it then calculated exactly what kind of hit had been made.

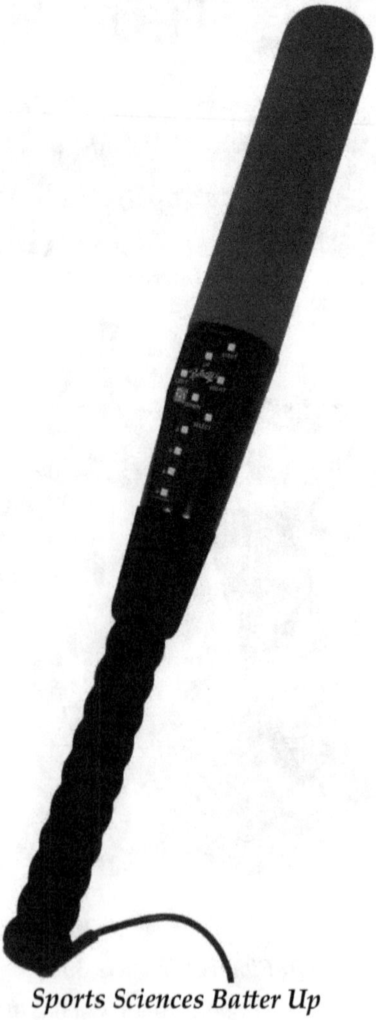

Sports Sciences Batter Up

Although it had promised a virtual reality device for the Jaguar in 1993, by the end of 1994, Atari still hadn't delivered one. However, the company announced that it had teamed up with a British company called Virtuality to release a $200 virtual reality helmet for the Jaguar in time for Christmas 1995. Neither company released any details at the time but both were confident that the Jaguar and the virtual reality helmet would be megahits.

The story was the same with Sega, which had also touted a virtual reality unit for the Genesis in 1993. By the end of 1994 the company realized that it couldn't satisfactory produce the unit within a realistic price margin. When Sega began backing away from its virtual reality helmet a company called RPI Advanced Technology Group began talking about $250 virtual reality glasses that would interface with the Sega Channel. The glasses had been created to aid in 3D stereo television programming. In addition to the Sega Channel, RPI also targeted their HMS-EYE glasses for TV networks such as Fox and NBC.

Sega's Modular Cartridges

Although Sega couldn't deliver virtual reality, it did take many people by surprise when it release a home version of its arcade hit, *Virtua Racing*, which had arrived in arcades in 1993. Due to the complexities of the game, a home version had seemed improbable. In order to make it happen, Sega derived a new chip called the *SVP* (Sega Virtua Processor) to expand the 3D capabilities of its 16-bit consoles. Unfortunately, the chip was very expensive. In an effort to lower the price and generate more sales, Sega introduced a modular cartridge. The idea behind it was simple. Since the SVP was the most expensive component in a cartridge, the consumer shouldn't have to buy it over and over again in every cartridge that he purchased. Instead, for $50, he could buy a modular cartridge that contained only the SVP chip. Later, as new SVP games were developed, the player could buy the $50 game cartridges and plug them into the modular cartridge. This was the same approach that Starpath had used with its Supercharger in 1983, and Camerica with its Aladdin in 1992.

Sega *Virtua Racing*

Unfortunately, Sega wasn't able to make the new modular system available until the summer, so *Virtua Racing*, which was released in the spring, wasn't sold as a modular cartridge. The game retailed for $100, making it the most expensive Genesis game ever.

Sega then took another look at producing modular cartridges for games that would use the SVP chip. However, in the end they could find no justification in the project as popularity in their 16-bit machine was diminishing and the new 32-bit Saturn was going to be available in Japan by the end of the year. In the end, Sega scuttled the modular cartridge project.

As it turned out, before the end of the year Sega did release a modular cartridge after all. But it wouldn't be for the reasons it had originally intended.

Virtua Racing wasn't the only game that Sega rushed out into the marketplace before it was completely ready. *Sonic the Hedgehog 3*, which came out in North America on February 3, was also released prematurely.

1994

Originally, *Sonic the Hedgehog 3* was to contain one large game that introduced a new antagonist called *Knuckles The Echidna*. During latter stages of the game, the player would be able to assume the role of Knuckles. Unfortunately, in its original form, the game would have been very large and expensive, and probably would have required the SVP chip. Also, for PR reasons, Sega of America wanted the game released on February 2, Groundhog Day, which they were preparing advertising campaigns renaming it *Hedgehog Day*. However, the development team couldn't get the game finished in time so only half of it was released on the required date.[21]

Sega *Sonic & Knuckles* with *Sonic 3*

The second half of the game, *Sonic & Knuckles* was released on October 18. The game was playable by itself but it wasn't cased in a standard Mega Drive/Genesis cartridge. Instead, a door at the top of the cartridge could slide back to reveal a slot in which another cartridge could plug into. When the *Sonic the Hedgehog 3* cartridge was plugged into it, a new game, called *Sonic 3 & Knuckles*, would load. This was the original game that Sega had planned.

Sega called the method of joining the two games together to form a different playable game, *Lock-On Technology*. When the *Sonic the Hedgehog 2* cartridge was locked-on the *Sonic & Knuckles* cartridge, a game called *Knuckles the Echidna in Sonic the Hedgehog 2* could be played. This was basically *Sonic the Hedgehog 2* but the Sonic character was replaced by the Knuckles character. When the original *Sonic the Hedgehog* cartridge was locked-on, a screen appeared that said "No Way", indicating that there wasn't a new game to be played. However, if the combination of pressing the "A", "B" and "C" buttons were pressed while at the "No Way" screen, a new game called *Blue Sphere* could be played.

New Leaf

Sega sought other ways to make Genesis and Game Gear software more affordable and accessible. The company teamed up with Blockbuster Video and began test-marketing a new videogame rental system that had been developed by New Leaf Entertainment, a joint venture between Blockbuster and IBM. Originally designed as a method to produce music on compact discs, the New Leaf system allowed retailers to store games electronically. When someone wanted to rent a certain game, the code was downloaded to a special Genesis or Game Gear cartridge. By utilizing this system, stores could stock every game that had ever been released for either system without sacrificing any shelf space.

New Leaf Genesis Cartridge

Actually, the New Leaf technology wasn't much different from the Romox and Cumma Technology systems that had been introduced in 1983. Those had failed because they had been designed as alternatives to buying game cartridges, and they required blank cartridges that cost more than the heavily discounted games. By 1994, the cost to purchase games had increased dramatically, and the new system had been designed with the rental market in mind. A game renter was imposed a hefty fee if he decided to keep the reprogrammable cartridge.

In August, Sega and Blockbuster began test-marketing the New Leaf system in ten Blockbuster stores in South Carolina. Initially, the system only downloaded Sega-published games. However, it was anticipated that more and more third-party companies would sign up to have their games included.[22]

By 1994, the videogame rental market was a $1.5 billion dollar industry, and everybody wanted a stake in it. Despite Nintendo's 1990 lawsuit against Blockbuster, the former realized that it could no longer ignore the rental market, so it decided to include rental stores in its distribution chain. By doing this the rental stores were entitled to participate in the same promotions that Nintendo offered the retail stores. Blockbuster and West Coast Video were among the first stores to participate in the new program.

Blockbuster's interest in videogames went beyond the rental market. The company spent $30 million in early 1994 to purchase nearly 20% of Virgin Interactive Entertainment. Blockbuster picked up an additional 55% of the software company five months later, and had the option to purchase an additional 10% if it chose to. Virgin's remaining stock (1.5 million shares) was owned by toy company Hasbro, which had bought it right before Blockbuster's initial purchase. In September, Hasbro turned around and offered to trade its Virgin stock for 1.3 million shares of Blockbuster stock. Following this trade Blockbuster and Hasbro agreed to form an interactive partnership.

Nintendo's reasoning against renting games was that it feared that consumers would rent a game and then use a device like the Game Genie to conquer it and thus eliminate any chance of purchasing it.

Code-Altering Devices Keep Coming

Although Nintendo had finally accepted game rentals, it never graced the peripherals that would render the games easily winnable. And newer versions of those peripherals were constantly being released.

Innovation introduced one for the SNES at the end of 1994. The *Game Wizard* was similar to the Game Genie, in the sense that a player could enter codes to alter games. However, while the Game Genie forced players to use the codes that were printed in the unit's instruction manual, the Game Wizard allowed them to scan a game's actual program code to find new instructions. As a bonus, the Game Wizard also permitted Super Famicom cartridges to play on the SNES.

At the end of 1993, Codemasters had announced the Game Genie 2, a device that would have been similar to the Game Wizard. At the time, Codemasters was very optimistic that the device would be available by the end of 1994. Unfortunately, Galoob, the American distributor of the Game Genie, did not share that optimism. They didn't see how the unit could be completed by the summer of 1994 in order for it to have a Christmas 1994 release. Instead, Galoob estimated that the Game Genie 2 would be available sometime in 1995.

Codemasters had also announced in 1993 that it had been developing a Game Genie for the Sega CD. That project was scrapped in 1994. Despite a lack of new products, Galoob still managed to have a good year, due in part to the $16 million in damages that Nintendo was forced to pay after its failed lawsuit. After receiving the settlement, Galoob turned around and decreased the prices on its various Game Genies.

Another innovation by Codemasters was the *J-Cart*. This was a standard Mega Drive/Genesis cartridge that featured two controller ports, which allowed four-player competition without the need of an additional multi-tap unit.

Codemasters was the only company that used the J-Carts for multiplayer games. Of the six games that it released on J-Carts, only one, *Pete Sampras Tennis,* was available for the American Genesis. The remaining five titles were only released in Europe for the Mega Drive.

Codemasters J-Cart

Fox Returns To Gaming

Blockbuster wasn't the only media company that was anxious to break into the booming videogame industry. After a twelve-year hiatus, movie studio Twentieth Century Fox decided to jump back in. The company called its new division Fox Interactive, and began operating in November. As Twentieth Century Fox Games of the Century had done in 1983, Fox Interactive planned to design games that tied in with Fox movies and TV shows. Their first game, *The Pagemaster*, came out on November 23, the same day that its movie counterpart reached the theaters, marking the first time that a movie-based game was released simultaneously with the movie.

Twentieth Century Fox wasn't the only movie studio that decided to release videogames. Paramount Pictures, which had been a sister company of Sega in the early eighties, decided to release videogame software once again. A third movie studio, Universal, announced plans to do the same thing. Although Universal hadn't taken part in the initial wave of videogame mania during the eighties, its parent company, MCA, had planned such a venture.

While these movie studios planned to develop games as third-party companies for multiple consoles, another studio, MGM, announced in April that it had partnered with Sega of America to create products that melded live-action video with computer technology. This would be applied to Sega's games and MGM's movies and Television shows.

And as the movie studios were getting into games, movies that were derived from games continued to be made, despite the disastrous release of the wide-screen version of *Super Mario Brothers* in 1993. On November 4, 1994, a live-action version of *Double Dragon* was released. The $7.5 million budget of this movie was considerably less than that of *Super Mario Brothers,* and yet the film still lost money at the box office, grossing a mere $2.3 million.[23] While many reviewers praised the movie's special effects, the overall consensus was the storyline was simplistic and the dialogue was bad.

But bad reviews didn't necessary seal the fate of a movie. On December 23, Universal Pictures released *Street Fighter,* which was based on the Street *Fighter II* game. Like the two videogame-inspired movies that preceded it, *Street Fighter* was plagued by bad reviews.[24] The *Washington Post* reported that the only thing notable about the movie was that it was the last film that actor Raúl Juliá starred in before he died. However, despite the poor reviews, *Street Fighter* managed to accomplish something that its predecessors had failed to do - it actually made a profit at the box office.[25] The movie's $35 million budget was returned three-fold to its producer, Capcom, the same company that had created the *Street Fighter* videogame.[26]

Magazines Reach Their Peak

Interest in videogames reached an all-time high during 1994. In January, *GamePro* became the first videogame magazine to sell 500,000 copies of a single issue. *EGM* broke a different type of record when its December issue contained 404 pages. So much news concerning videogames was coming out that *EGM*'s publisher, Sendai Publications, decided that one monthly magazine a month wasn't enough to contain all of this information. For a while, the publisher thought about releasing the magazine on a biweekly schedule, but that was problematic, since each issue would therefore only have a shelf life of two weeks. Instead, the company introduced an all-new monthly magazine called *EGM²*, which was published two weeks after its sister publication, *EGM*. Now Sendai had two magazines sharing shelf space every month.

Most videogame magazines were geared towards teenagers and pre-teens. Following the success of the adult-oriented *Electronic Games,* new magazines were published that attempted to go after an older audience. The first of these was *Electronic Entertainment* (*E²*), which debuted in January by Infotainment World, the same company that published *GamePro. E²* immediately gained respectability in the gaming world by providing a monthly column by Nolan Bushnell.

During the year, Chris Anderson, the owner of British-based Future, sold the company to Pierson. He still retained the American GP Publications that he had purchased in 1993. Following the sale, Anderson moved himself, and the entire North Carolina-based

EGM²

Electronic Entertainment

Next Generation

publishing company, to California, where he renamed it *Imagine Publishing*. By the end of the year, Imagine premiered a new magazine called *Next Generation,* which offered a format that was amazingly similar to the British *Edge. Next Generation* quickly established a niche with adult gamers.

The interest in videogames also spread to prime-time television. On November 5, TBS presented *Cybermania '94: The Ultimate Gamer Awards*. Hosted by Leslie Nielsen and Jonathan Taylor Thomas, the show tried its best to imitate highly-rated shows like the Academy and Grammy Awards. Unfortunately, the program clearly missed its mark, as D-list celebrities announced the names of games that they obviously had never heard of. If the show had been hosted by game programmers and gaming executives, it might have had fewer ratings, but would have been more believable.

CES-Interactive

The major success of video and computer games brought changes to the rest of the electronic industry. For the first time in over twenty years, the Electronic Industries Association (EIA) decided not to hold its annual summer CES in Chicago. The EIA announced that the show would be renamed *CES Interactive (CES-I)* and would be held in Philadelphia during May 11-13, 1995. The purpose of the new name was to highlight the fact that it would be meant for multimedia and videogame hardware and software only. The winter CES in Las Vegas would remain unchanged.

Shortly following the announcement of CES-I, Infotainment World announced that it was establishing its own electronics show in Los Angeles. The conflict began when it was disclosed that its *Electronic Entertainment Expo (E^3)* would be held during the same three days as CES-I.

By September, both groups had claimed that their shows would take place, and both boasted an impressive list of attendees. CES-I had Nintendo and Microsoft on its side, while E^3 had Sega, SCE, Atari and 3DO. Other companies signed up for both shows, with the intention of deciding at a later date which show they would actually attend.

In October, Nintendo reversed its decision and announced that it was going to attend E^3 instead of CES-I. Following Nintendo's defection, the EIA decided to throw in the towel and scrap the 1995 CES-I altogether, citing that it was best for the industry if there was only one show. The EIA then began its plans for a 1996 CES-I.

The year ended quieter than it had begun as the talks of game ratings had now been silenced. However, in the distance, the soldiers were lining up and quietly preparing for battle. As America was awaiting the release of the Saturn, PlayStation and Virtual Boy, 1995 was gearing up to be one of the most decisive years in the history of videogaming.

CHAPTER TWENTY-THREE
1995

The annual winter CES, which was held during the first week of January, was highly anticipated. It was expected that Sega's Saturn and SCE's PlayStation would both make their American debuts at the show. And there was optimism that Nintendo would display its Ultra 64 for the first time.

Play It Loud! color Game Boy

Nintendo didn't unveil the Ultra 64 at CES as hoped but it did spotlight two other new consoles, including one that had launched during the week before the show. This was the highly anticipated color Game Boy. However, most of those who had eagerly awaited its arrival wound up highly disappointed. The name *color Game Boy* was just a teaser, as the new Game Boys were simply the same devices that had been available since 1989, with one important difference: These new *Play It Loud!* Game Boys were housed in red, green, black, yellow, blue, white and even transparent casings. They were indeed color Game Boys. The only problem was that it was the unit, and not the display, that featured color.

While Nintendo had used CES to promote the color Game Boys that were already available, it also used the show to launch new software that would be available for them. Among the games that Nintendo planned to release during the year was the classic *Space Invaders*, as well as *Donkey Kong Land*, a Game Boy version of *Donkey Kong Country*.

Nintendo also used CES for the American debut of its new Virtual Boy, and most American journalists and retailers finally got their first hands-on look at the device. The console was totally unlike anything that they had ever seen before. It wasn't a console that plugged into a TV, and it wasn't a portable handheld that could be taken anywhere. The closest console that it could be compared to was the Vectrex, but even that had its own monitor that let non-gamers watch what the player was doing. This couldn't be done on the Virtual Boy, which the gamer had to look into to use. And although the console was attached to a stand that raised it, gamers had to hunch over the unit in order to be able to look into it adequately.

The Virtual Boy displayed its images only in red and black, but that was a minor detail that many people overlooked. After all, the Game Boy had only displayed in only two colors as well, and it went on to sell over 40 million worldwide. This was more than twice the number that the two color portables, the Sega Game Gear and the Atari Lynx, had sold together.

Most CES attendees who had also expected to get their first look at SCE's PlayStation and Sega's Saturn were out of luck. Although both companies did show their new consoles at the show, neither unit was exhibited on the main floor where the vast majority of attendees could actually see them. Instead, they were hidden behind closed doors that only opened to selected people in the industry.

No details about either console were made public until March 9, when Sega of America issued a press release that formally announced its intentions for the Saturn. Basically, the company was going to release the console in North America with a retail price of $399.99 on September 2. That day, a Saturday, was quickly dubbed "Saturn Day."

SCEA soon responded with its own details about the PlayStation. It would launch in the United States on September 9, exactly one week after the Saturn's American debut. Its retail price would be $299.99.

Although Sega of America was relieved that SCEA wouldn't release the PlayStation before the Saturn, they were nonetheless unhappy that they were only going to have a one-week head start to get their system into the hands of gamers. Although Sega of America never believed that SCEA could sell the PlayStation at $300, since the Japanese model was selling for the yen equivalent of $400, they had to accept the slight possibility that SCEA might do so. And if that was the case, many consumers would probably sit out the one week difference and purchase the PlayStation, if only because it would cost at least $100 less than the Saturn. Sega would be the only game in town for one week, and its executives wondered if that would that be enough time. They didn't think so.

The Electronic Entertainment Expo

SCEA and Sega of America had waited to officially debut their consoles at the new Electronic Entertainment Expo (E^3), which was held in Los Angeles over a three-day period, beginning on May 11. More than 28,000 people in the videogame industry attended and they weren't disappointed, as 350 companies displayed more than 1,300 games.

At the expo's very first keynote speech, Tom Kalinske told the crowd that the Saturn's previously announced September 2 release date had simply been a decoy to throw SCEA off. To everyone's surprise, the Saturn was actually being released in very limited numbers to four retail chains that very day. Within a few days, 30,000 Saturns had been released to Toys "R" Us, Electronics Boutique, Babbage's and Software, Etc. The system carried a $400 retail price without a packaged game.[1] For an additional $50, it was bundled with *Virtua Fighter*. An additional ten games were available for purchase immediately.

This was a move that Tom Kalinske didn't really want to make but Sega in Japan was calling the shots. With the Saturn already for sale in Japan, Sega of Japan didn't have any interest in continuing to support the Mega Drive. The console had never been a top seller in Japan, always falling in third place behind the Super Famicom and the PC Engine. But that hadn't the case in North America where the Genesis was favored over the SNES.

SCEA's president, Steve Race, had originally planned a keynote speech that would confirm that the PlayStation would be available on September 9 and would retail for $299. And although the console would not come with a free game, twenty games would be available for the launch. An additional thirty titles would be out by Christmas. In addition, a unique memory card would be available for the console in September. The memory card would plug into the front of the console and let players save their games at any time. That was what Race was originally going to talk about. However, after hearing that the Saturn would retail for $400, Race simply said "$299" to the packed-crowd and then famously walked off the stage.

Sega Blunders

Sega of America had hurt itself by jumping the gun in its efforts to beat SCEA. Third-party software was not available in time for the new release date, since the third-party developers and publishers had never been informed about the premature launch. These vendors viewed the early launch as a way for Sega of America to boost sales by only having its own titles available. And these software companies weren't the only ones that were angry with Sega of America. Major retailers, such as Walmart and Kay-Bee Toys, that hadn't been included in the early launch, were just as angry. Even after Sega of America

1995

Sega of America Saturn

increased the Saturn's distribution to all retailers, Kay-Bee Toys refused to carry it.

The American Saturn appeared to be nearly the same as the one previously released in Japan, with some minor cosmetic differences. It was black instead of gray, and its controller was redesigned with larger buttons and a longer cord. Like its Japanese counterpart, the American Saturn had a cartridge slot, even though Sega of America didn't have plans to create any cartridge-based games. However, like its Japanese counterpart, the company did release a Saturn Backup Memory. Meanwhile, Datel Electronics came out with a practical use for the cartridge slot. Its *Pro Universal Adapter* allowed any Saturn CD to play on any Saturn, no matter where in the world it was purchased. This was good news for people who had purchased the Japanese Saturn before the console was released in the United States.

The Saturn from Sega was the only Saturn available in North America. However, that

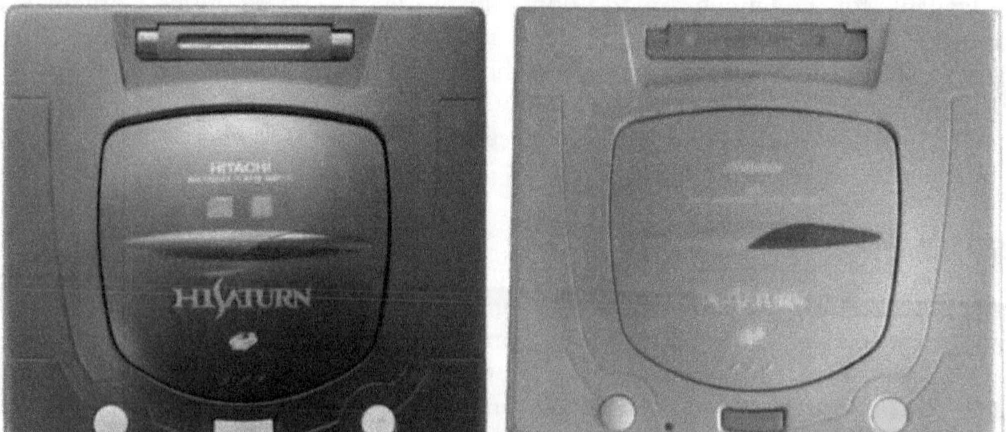

Hitachi HiSaturn (l) and JVC V-Saturn (r)

wasn't the case in Japan where two companies in addition to Sega built and sold their own Saturn consoles.

One was JVC, whose *V-Saturn* came out the same day as Sega's model in November, 1994 at the very same price. Aside from the branding, there was virtually no difference between the Sega Saturn and the JVC V-Saturn.

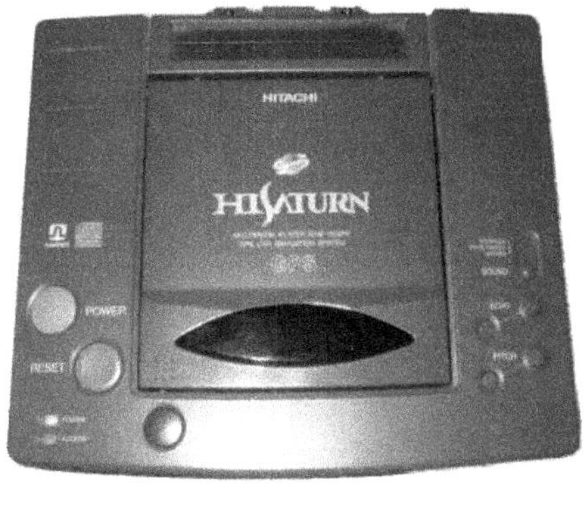

Hitachi Game Navi HiSaturn

The third Saturn was distributed by Hitachi, the company that supplied many of the Saturn's chips. Hitachi introduced its ¥64,800 ($743) *HiSaturn* on April 1. This model featured built-in MPEG-1 decompression, which allowed for the inclusion of full motion video in games and the ability to play back video compact discs (VCD).[2] The Sega Saturn did not have this feature until June 23 when Sega of Japan released a ¥19,800 ($518) *Movie Card*. Sega Europe released a similar £170 ($267) *Video CD Card* in October.

Hitachi released a second HiSaturn on December 6 that was even more expensive than their first. The *Game Navi HiSaturn* retailed at ¥150,000 ($1,479) and was totally unlike any of the Saturns released from any company. Hitachi billed it as a "portable multimedia player." To that extent, an optional ¥45,000 ($444) LCD screen was available that plugged into the back of the console. Besides having a place for the screen to plug into, the Game Navi HiSaturn also differed from standard Saturns as it also had two karaoke microphone ports[3] and a port for an unreleased TV tuner. Finally, there was also an additional port to insert a GPS antenna. Like Fujitsu's FM Towns Car Marty, the Game Navi HiSaturn could also be used as a GPS navigator. The GPS unit itself sat atop the console itself, which unlike other Saturns, was flat above the CD door. The console was also slightly smaller than standard Saturns so it could sit above a car's dashboard connected by Velcro strips.[4]

On June 14, Sega of Japan dropped the price of its Saturn by more than half. The console then sold for ¥34,800 ($413) and was bundled with a copy of *Virtua Fighter Remix*.

SCE lowered the price of the PlayStation by releasing a new version of the console that sold for ¥29,800 (US $350), ¥10,000 less than the original model. The new console lacked an S-VHS video output port, which had been available on the original console. Since SCE already offered an optional S-VHS cable, anyone who really wanted the S-VHS port could simply buy the cable separately.

SCE had removed the S-VHS port in order to avoid a legal conflict with the International Trade Commission (ITC). Atari's Sam Tramiel had contended that SCE would infringe upon ITC rules when it released the PlayStation in the United States by "dumping" the console at $299. This was the term for selling identical products in more than one country, and pricing the units at significantly different amounts within the different countries. Since Japanese consumers were less concerned about price and more interested in quality, manufacturers were retailing their products much higher in Japan than elsewhere. Consumers in the United States were cost-conscious. Tramiel argued that SCE would lose money by selling the PlayStation at $299, which would be more than recompensed by software sales.

By removing the S-VHS video outputs from its newer consoles, SCE was able to sell a less expensive PlayStation in the United States without breaking any laws. But meanwhile, throughout 1995, SCE didn't have any plans on releasing outside of Japan. Sega again jumped the gun on SCE in July by releasing the Saturn in Europe.

On August 7, SCEA announced that Steve Race had resigned after disagreements with other SCE divisions concerning the long-term pricing of the PlayStation. He was quickly replaced by Martin Homlish, who had been the vice-president of another Sony division. Soon afterwards, SCEA began a pre-registration service, and promised those who signed up that they would have a PlayStation and a free demo CD available for them on September 9, SCEA's planned launch date.

New Consoles In America

Sega of America released the Saturn nationwide on September 2, its original release date, and one week before the PlayStation's scheduled U.S. launch. The price of the unit remained at $400 for the unbundled console or $450 with *Virtua Fighter.* SCEA was going to initially release the American PlayStation with a twelve-game demonstration disc, rather than a playable game. At the eleventh hour, the company decided to also sell a $349 package that included the console and a` pack-in game, *Ridge Racer*.

Sega of America had sold approximately 80,000 Saturn consoles during its four-month head start. SCEA had presold 100,000 PlayStations during the three weeks prior to the system's release. This didn't give SCEA executives any reason to celebrate. As Chip Herman, SCEA's VP of marketing, pointed out, the summer months were historically slow for the videogame industry. And coupled with that was the fact that the Saturn had initially only been available in limited outlets. Executives from both companies knew that the actual selling season wouldn't begin until the weeks approaching Christmas. That was when the real war between the two systems would erupt.

By October, sales figures began to show which system consumers preferred. While Sega of America announced that it had sold 120,000 Saturns after six months, that number didn't come close to SCEA's claim of 200,000 PlayStations in just over two months. Sega of America, obviously worried about these figures and on October 2 dropped the price of the non-bundled Saturn to $300, the same as the PlayStation. A bundled game still cost $50 more but the game was changed to *Virtua Fighter Remix*. The company also began a massive television campaign to advertise the system.

Another problem that Sega of America faced was that there was a lack of great games available for the Saturn. This changed in November, when Sega of America released Saturn versions of its arcade blockbusters *Virtua Fighter 2* and *Sega Rally*. Unfortunately, games like these took developers nearly two years to create, while equivalent games for the PlayStation were taking only six months.

Sega had plans to make the Saturn more than just a game machine. The company was developing a $150 peripheral that would link the Saturn to the Internet. The company conceded that it was also developing a 64-bit console, code-named *Eclipse*. Eclipse would incorporate new DVD (Digital Video Disc) technology and would also be compatible with current audio CDs and CD-ROMs. In order to avoid a fiasco similar to the one that it had stirred when it tried to sell the Sega CD with the superior Saturn just around the corner, Sega announced that Eclipse would be downwardly compatible with Saturn software. It wasn't scheduled to appear until 1998.

Sega PriFun

But it was doubtful that the Eclipse's planned compatibility was currently going to help Sega sell any consoles. SCEA announced on December 6 that in the less than three months which the PlayStation had been available in the United States, the company had sold approximately 300,000 consoles. By that time, the Saturn was lagging far behind. With only 130,000 consoles sold, Sega of America had sold only half the units that SCEA had, and had taken more than twice the time.

Printer Fun

Although the Japanese Pico had been moved to the Sega Yonezawa division, Sega of Japan still developed hardware for it. The *PriFun* was a small printer that could print out screen shots from the Pico and the Saturn. An optional *Pause Pack* that connected to the console, caused the game to pause, during which time a full color image of the screen could be printed from the PriFun on special thermal paper.

In addition to the 4 x 6 inch photos that the PriFun produced, it could also print out stickers. Stickers were a new fad in Japan and many companies were devising different ways that they could be part of it.[5]

In October, Casio jumped on the sticker bandwagon with a new 32-bit Japanese console called the *Loopy*. This was Casio's first videogame system since it had released the unpopular PV-1000 in 1983. This time around, Casio decided to focus on a certain segment of the population that was usually ignored by videogame manufacturers: young girls.

Casio Loopy

The Loopy had its own thermal color printer built-in to it that allowed players to create stickers from game screenshots, just like the Sega PriFun. But with the inclusion of an optional peripheral called *Magical Shop* the Loopy could also hook up to external devices such as video recorders, from where it could grab additional images to print on stickers. Kanji text could also be added to these images.

Only ten games were released for the Loopy, and most of them consisted of games where the player's female character had to develop a romantic connection with one of the on-screen male characters. The remaining games allowed girls to dress up their own on-screen characters.

The Loopy was not successful and was not released outside of Japan. It disappeared after a short time and marked Casio's departure from the videogame console market once and for all.

More Japanese Console Failures

But the Loopy wasn't the only console that represented a company's exit from the industry. NEC was another that tried several times. Its latest console, the PC-FX, had been released in Japan at the end of 1994. Unfortunately, its sales during 1995 had been relatively poor. Even though NEC had never anticipated that the PC-FX would be a major seller in Japan, it never expected the console to sell as poorly as it did. NEC's original intent had been to release the PC-FX in the United States if it sold moderately well in Japan. Since it didn't, the plans were scrapped to release the PC-FX outside of Japan, and eventually, it faded into obscurity.

Another CD-based system that appeared to be on the verge of failure was Philips' CD-i multimedia system. The marketing personnel at Philips appeared to realize this. Although Philips had the console on display at its booth at E^3, no one appeared to be pushing it. Instead, Philips concentrated on CD-i software because the company's Philips Media division began translating its CD-i games to play on PCs and the Sega Saturn. In July, the division purchased 20% of Infogrames, the largest videogame developer in France. To the world, it looked like Philips was abandoning its hardware and gearing itself up to become a major presence in the software market.

Strangely enough, Philips announced in late summer that it was releasing a modem for the CD-i. Although the company didn't have any CD-i-related applications on the Internet, it promised that there would be many by the time of the modem's release in late 1995. Philips planned to release the modem in Great Britain first and then in the rest of Europe. The United States would follow Europe, but no actual time-table was announced. The modem appeared to be a last-ditch effort by Philips to get people interested in the CD-i, since the company had warehouses full of unsold consoles that it wanted to unload. Although Philips had originally marketed the console as a multimedia system, it began promoting the CD-i as a gaming console with nearly 200 titles available.

3DO Price Decrease

Although the 3DO continued through the hard times that it had experienced since its launch, the console managed to persevere and by 1995, over a half million consoles had been sold around the world under various brand names. In June, when Goldstar changed its name to LG Technologies, and released its 3DO console in the United States, it offered a $50 rebate on each unit. This effectively lowered the price of the console to $299. After LG Technologies ended the rebate promotion, it permanently lowered the retail price of the console to $299. Panasonic immediately followed suit, and sales of its own 3DO console unit went up. 3DOs actually outsold the new Saturn in some stores.

The 3DO Company assured its customers that their 3DO consoles would always be on the cutting edge of technology, no matter what was released by Sega or Nintendo. To this end, the 3DO Company announced that its M2 upgrade, which would make the 3DO ten times as powerful as the Saturn or PlayStation, was on schedule and would be available by the end of the year. Specs for the M2 were released and they truly were spectacular. The 64-bit system would have ten custom coprocessors that worked in tandem with a 528 megabyte-per-second CPU. It would be capable of generating one million polygons per second (the PlayStation produced up to 360,000 polygons per second).

The 3DO Company claimed that the M2 would be the world's first true 64-bit 3D machine. It would also include MPEG-1 video compression that would allow it to play full-motion digital video. The hardware itself would have slots for memory cards so players could save their games.

The competing manufacturers weren't too worried about the proposed capabilities of the M2. They all figured that its success or failure would depend upon two points: the number of good games that were available and the price. The 3DO Company didn't specify a retail price for the unit, because Panasonic and LG Technologies would determine how much their particular models would be, but most analysts agreed that it would have to be in the same area as the existing systems, which was somewhere between $149 and $300.

By the end of the summer, the release date of the M2 was pushed back to early 1996, and many people began wondering if it would actually ever see the light of day. Although 3DO Company executives claimed that the M2 would always be the company's top priority, they still began looking into other avenues, such as software design and the Internet. In early November, it was revealed that the 3DO Company no longer had any interest in the M2. They sold the technology to Matsushita, the parent company of Panasonic, for $100 million. Following the sale, the 3DO Company in essence became a software company.

Following the sale, Matsushita announced that it was going ahead with its M2 technology, and the new hardware would be available by autumn 1996. Still, videogame analysts wondered exactly what Matsushita's plans were. Although they were certain that the company would release the M2 as promised, they saw two scenarios that could take place. One had Matsushita using the M2 as a launching vehicle for its new DVD technology. More probable was that Matsushita would license the M2 technology out to other manufacturers, just as the 3DO Company had done. By the end of 1995, nobody had a concrete answer, and the fate of the 3DO console was suddenly in limbo.

Whether the M2 was released or not, LG Technologies found itself in a lose-lose position. If it hoped to release the M2 Accelerator for its 3DO machine, it would need to obtain a license from Matsushita, a costly process that its sole 3DO competitor, Panasonic, didn't need to do. The company continued to sell its 32-bit 3DO consoles, but lowered the price to $199 toward the end of the year. LG Technologies claimed that it had streamlined its manufacturing process, but most people believed that the company just wanted to dump the consoles.

The Apple Pippin

The original business model for the 3DO Company had been to design a console that other companies would manufacture, and then design and sell software for it. As the console manufacturers were left with large inventories and the 3DO Company moved strictly towards software design, it was apparent that the original business model didn't work. Still, that wasn't enough to keep another company from trying it.

Apple planned to market its Pippin in the same fashion that the 3DO Company sold its 3DO console: by licensing out the technology to other companies, who would manufacture

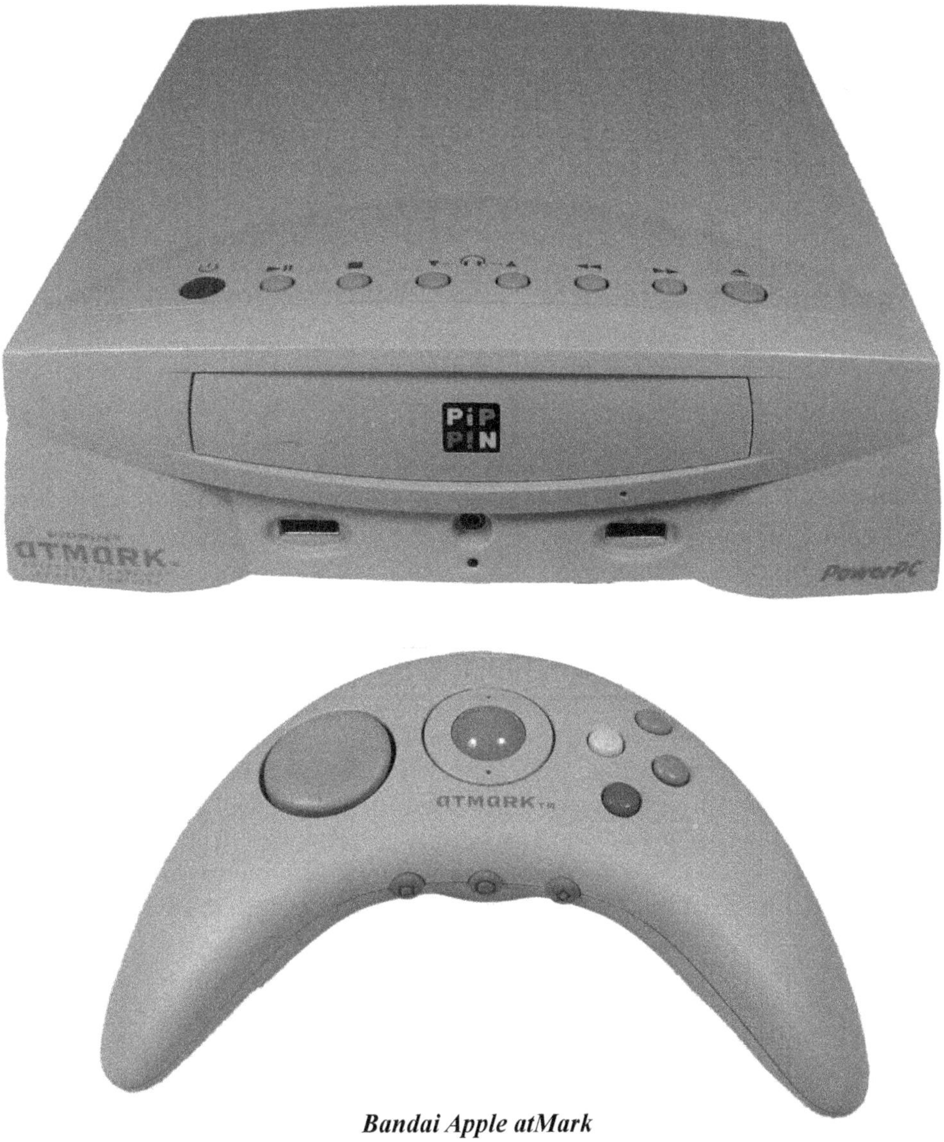

Bandai Apple atMark

it. Unlike the 3DO, which had not been built around an established computer, The Pippin already had a large amount of available software, since Apple's PowerPC software was compatible with the Pippin. In addition, Mac software that wasn't compatible with the PowerPC could be easily converted by software developers in less than two hours. Interestingly, the Pippin hardware would not contain its own operating system. Instead, the operating system would be included on every game disc that was sold. By doing this, developers would be able to "tweak" the operating system to fit their own special needs.

From the beginning, Apple had a licensing partner, the Japanese toy company, Bandai. Although the latter had released the poorly received Playdia in Japan a year earlier, Bandai was willing to ignore its own past as it had big plans for the Pippin. It was going to market peripherals like a keyboard and a hard drive, which would essentially turn the Pippin into a Mac computer with a minimum of 2MB of RAM. In order to keep the Pippin distinct from the Mac, Bandai planned to offer a Geoport, a modem device that would allow players to interact from different places. Bandai toyed with the idea of using the Geoport to let the Pippin hook up with an online service.

This idea germinated as soon as the failure of the 3DO became apparent. Since it appeared that consumers weren't interested in a multimedia console, Apple and Bandai decided to switch gears and market the Pippin as a game console that allowed users to surf the Internet.

Although the first website appeared in 1991, it was a simple text-only interface that was used to educate physicists on how the hyperlink concept worked. From that point on, the World Wide Web slowly grew, but it was pretty much limited to educational and governmental agencies. However that changed in 1993 when a web browser called *Mosaic* was developed by students at the University of Illinois. Mosaic allowed people to access the World Wide Web through a graphical interface by merely pointing and clicking with a mouse. An advanced browser called the *Netscape Navigator* followed in mid-1994, and pretty soon, Internet providers were popping up everywhere. While the first web sites consisted of text, they were soon replaced by colorful pages that contained graphics.

In mid-1995, commercial online companies such as Prodigy, America Online and CompuServe began providing access to the Internet. Once they did, millions of computer owners began to "surf the web." Once this vast number of people gained access, most companies realized that they had to have presences on the Web.

However, although surfing the Internet became a popular pastime, the one drawback was that a computer was needed to do it. Apple executives decided that since the Pippin already had a modem available, they could have the Internet console market solely to themselves.

Before the Pippin was released, Bandai's marketing team decided to rebrand the unit as an Internet console. They changed the name of the system to emphasize that it was for Internet surfing. The Japanese console was rebranded as the Pippin ATMARK, which was the name of the "@" symbol used in email addresses. It was released on march 28. The North American console was called the Pippin @WORLD and released on September 1. To further distinguish between the two otherwise identical systems, the Japanese console was housed in a white case while the North American one was black.

The system was sold with a 14.4-baud modem, a game-system type controller, and four software CDs. An optional keyboard was also available. Because it utilized a Macintosh processor, the software could actually play on a Mac. While its price was still pretty steep for a game machine (¥64,800 ($726) in Japan and $599 in North America), Bandai hoped to target households that wanted Internet access without the expense of getting a computer. While it was a high price to pay for a videogame console, it was a relatively inexpensive way to access the Internet, since computers generally cost three times as much.

Neo•Geo CD Problems

SNK of America had also used the first E³ to debut its new top-loading Neo•Geo CD, although it didn't announce an American release date. This was due to a dispute between SNK of America and its Japanese sibling, SNK of Japan. After it had become apparent that the single-speed drive in the Japanese Neo•Geo CD was just too slow for loading games, it had been announced that the model released in the United States would contain a double-speed CD drive. However, SNK of Japan had produced too many of the top-loading consoles with single-speed drives for the Japanese market, and they were sitting idly in a warehouse. SNK of Japan wanted to release those units in the United States, while SNK of America was strictly against it. But the cost to convert these single-speed drives into double-speed drives was more expensive than the corporate parent, SNK, was willing to spend. In the end, SNK of Japan won out, and the single-speed Neo•Geo CD was released in North America in October with a retail price of $350.

SNK Neo•Geo CDZ

Once all of the single-speed consoles were sold, SNK would then make a decision on the drive speed of all subsequent models. On December 29, SNK of Japan released a new console that dealt with the slow loading time problem. But SNK only addressed the problem in the new *Neo•Geo CDZ* by increasing its cache RAM, rather than employing a new higher-speed CD drive. So like the first two Neo•Geo CDs, the Neo•Geo CDZ only had a 1x CD drive.

The Neo•Geo CDZ was only released in Japan. SNK of America opted not to market the console because it realized that the system couldn't compete against the Saturn or PlayStation. However, since the Neo•Geo CDZ did not feature a region lock, American enthusiasts were able to import the system and use it without any difficulty.

Ultra 64 Rumors

Meanwhile, Nintendo kept everyone in suspense about its new console, the Ultra 64. During the early part of the year, the console was pretty much still a rumor, since no one outside of the company had ever seen it. It was believed that since the system would be cartridge-based, it could never compete price-wise against the CD-based 32-bit systems from Sega and SCE. Although many people in the industry had expected Nintendo to show it off in some form at the CES in January, it never happened.

By late March, the unofficial word from Japan was that the system had been completed and that it would be displayed in May at E³. The rumor was that the system would be released in the United States on Labor Day (September 4), which would put its release ahead of the Saturn's and PlayStation's. However, before that date could be officiated, it was quickly changed to the day after Thanksgiving: November 24. The console would sell for under $250.

On May 5, Nintendo of America head, Howard Lincoln, announced that the Ultra 64 would be delayed until April 1996, thereby missing the 1995 Christmas season. This delay was to allow software developers additional time to produce the best games possible. However, rumors persisted that Nintendo of Japan had ordered that the Ultra 64 be delayed, so that the new console could make its official debut at the annual Shoshinkai show in the fall, and would then go on sale on December 1. This rumor went unsubstantiated, since Ultra 64 development systems hadn't even been delivered to developers until early August. Unfortunately, the software companies didn't know exactly what their status was. Only three companies, Acclaim, Virgin and Williams, were officially deemed licensed game publishers by Nintendo. Most of the remaining developers were hesitant to begin anything until they knew exactly who would be publishing their games. And this was something that they couldn't discuss publicly, since written into their licensing agreement with Nintendo was a clause that prohibited the actual developers from discussing any details about unannounced projects with anyone outside the development team, including other company employees.

Some information about the console was finally revealed in late October. The Ultra 64 console would have four controller ports. This would be the first time that a system had four built-in controller ports since the Atari 5200.

The Ultra 64 controller would feature the familiar D-pad that had been around since the *Game & Watch* days. Unfortunately, the digital D-pads only permitted onscreen objects to move in one of 8 directions. In order to allow players to precisely move their on-screen objects in *any* direction, the controller would also include an analog stick.

The back of the new controller would include a slot, which was not explained by Nintendo. Speculation was that it would be used for a memory card, so games, and even the series of controller movements, could be saved. Nintendo planned to sell the controllers in designer colors.

As Nintendo finally went public with information about the console, it also announced that the name of the system was being changed, at least in Japan. The company had always intended to call the Japanese version the Ultra Famicom. Unfortunately, since the word "Ultra" had already been trademarked in Japan, they settled on the *Nintendo 64*. Nintendo of America continued to call its forthcoming console the Ultra 64.

The Nintendo 64

As predicted, the Nintendo 64 made its debut on November 24 at the annual Shoshinkai show in Chiba, Japan. Along with the system were two playable games, *Super Mario 64* and *Kirby's Air Ride*, and several more were shown from videotaped footage.

Nintendo head, Hiroshi Yamauchi stated at a press conference that the release dates for the system had been pushed back, due to a lack of ready-to-ship games. The Japanese release date had been changed to April 21, 1996, and the U.S. release date was pushed to September 1996. Many analysts and developers doubted that Nintendo could meet the proposed April date. One of the playable games that was displayed, *Super Mario 64*, was only 50% complete, and it had taken its designers eighteen months to reach that point! The analysts figured that in order for Nintendo to meet its April 21 release date, the second half of the game would have to be completed by mid-February, which was less than two months away. Nintendo executives, however, didn't appear to be concerned about this. And one thing that they didn't deny was the rumor that since September, the company

Nintendo N64

had been quietly manufacturing Nintendo 64s, which were sitting in a warehouse all boxed and ready to go.

The biggest complaint about the Nintendo 64 was the fact that it was cartridge-based. Many analysts questioned this decision, because cartridges cost more than three times as much as CDs to produce, and such costs were always passed on to consumers. Sure enough, the game cartridges were expected to retail for $60-$70, the same price range at which the SNES cartridges were selling. Nintendo reasoned that as long as the games were original and fun, there would be a ready market for them no matter how much they cost. Some analysts theorized that the choice to use cartridges would cause developers to be much less anxious to create new games for the Nintendo 64, since they had become accustomed to creating CD games that had virtually unlimited memory restrictions. Still, Nintendo remained positive about the system and pointed out that by eliminating a CD player, they were able to keep the retail price of the Nintendo 64 below $250, a price point that they had promised throughout the system's entire development.

Although the N64 would include an expansion port, Nintendo assured that it wouldn't be for a CD upgrade. Instead, the company was developing a *Magni-Disc*, a 64MB magnetic disk drive that was different from computer disk drives. Nintendo referred to the peripheral as a *Bulky Drive*.

It was important that owners of the N64 had the same features that owners of the PlayStation and Saturn enjoyed, such as the exchanging of game data, since critics were still skeptical about the company's decision to stick with game cartridges. Nintendo continued to contend that the access time for cartridges was much faster than it was for CDs, but it couldn't dispute that a CD could still contain eighty times as much data as an N64 cartridge. CDs were also cheaper and faster to manufacture than cartridges. Sega and SCE could make new games in smaller quantities, because they knew that they could quickly produce more copies if the games were to become hits. This wasn't the case with cartridges. If Nintendo manufactured too few of a given title, it would take weeks for the supply to be replenished.

The Bulky Drive and the Expansion Pak amounted to a mere compromise between the two technologies. Although the new Nintendo discs wouldn't be as durable as standard CDs or be able to store as much data, they would be writable, which would put Nintendo ahead of the competition that merely had read-only software. Nintendo hoped to have this peripheral available by the end of 1996.

Since the N64 would not be available in 1995, Nintendo of America continued to push its SNES workhorse. The company had displayed new SNES software in January at CES, but there had been nothing in the group that excited the media. Industry insiders predicted that 1995 would be the last hurrah for the 16-bit console, and that it would then follow its predecessor, the NES, into history. However, Nintendo hadn't used the winter CES to show games that would be released in the latter part of the year such as *Super Mario World 2: Yoshi's Island*, which Nintendo of Japan released in August, with Nintendo of America following in October.[6] As long as games like *Super Mario World 2: Yoshi's Island* continued to be developed and released, the Super Famicom/SNES would have a healthy future.

The same couldn't be said for the NES. Nintendo of America used the winter CES to announce that it was officially retiring the machine.[7]

Sega's 16-Bit Commitments

Despite the release of the Saturn, Sega of America was eager to prolong the lifespan of the Genesis. This was something that Sega of Japan had no intention of doing, since the Mega Drive hadn't sold well in Japan, coming in third behind the Super Famicom and the PC Engine. But the Genesis was still popular in North America. While Sega of

Japan was developing the Saturn, Sega of America was working on the *Venus*, a portable Genesis. The Venus was basically a Mega Jet with a built-in 3.25 inch, color, LCD screen. It had an audio/video jack that allowed it to be hooked up to a monitor or television set like a standard Genesis console, or it could be played without one using its built-in screen. Sega of America had originally designed the Venus to have a touchscreen interface. Unfortunately, although the technology was available, it would have been much too expensive to incorporate, as it would have added $100 to the unit's $180 retail price.

By the time Sega of America released the unit on October 13, the name of the console was changed to the *Nomad*. But while the Nomad had a library of more than 500 games already available upon its release, the public wasn't particularly interested in a portable

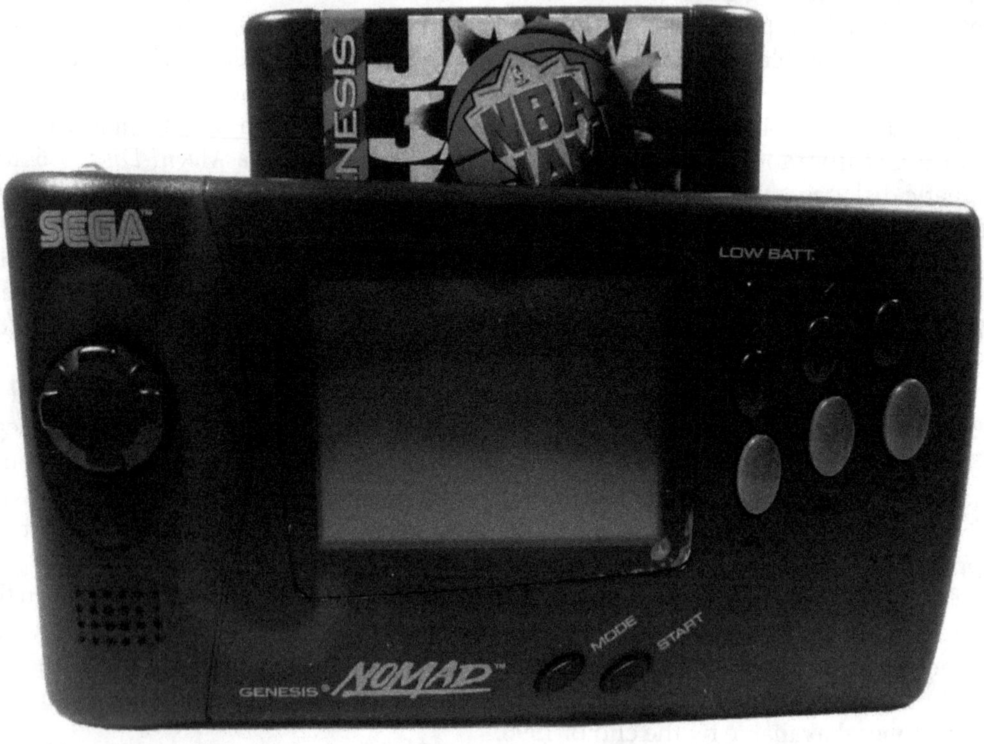

Sega Nomad

Genesis at a time when the 16-bit work-horse was handing its reigns over to a 32-bit successor.

Those who did purchase the unit discovered that it wasn't 100% compatible with the Genesis. At least 13 games, including *Sonic the Hedgehog*, either had trouble running on the Nomad, or didn't run at all. And the Genesis peripherals, such as the Sega CD, 32X and SMS Power Base Converter, wouldn't work on it either. Technically, these devices were compatible with the Nomad. However, their shapes, which were designed to work with the Genesis, restricted them from plugging into the Nomad. Depending upon the volume and screen settings, six alkaline AA batteries would only last approximately two hours. Sega of America offered a power adapter but it had limited distribution, and retailed at $79 when it could be found.[8]

Sega of America had publicly stated that the 32X wouldn't work on the Nomad, even though it was technically capable of doing so. On the other hand, some owners of the 32X discovered that it wouldn't even work on their Genesis consoles. In fact, so many consumers complained to Sega about this that the company published a set of simplified instructions that they hoped would make the installation easier. Unfortunately, that didn't end the 32X compatibility problems. As it turned out, the the 32X also couldn't work with some older TV sets. Sega had to inform the owners of these TVs that they had to purchase an adapter from an electronics store.

32X owners were also unhappy with the low amount of software support that the 32X received. Although the unit had rocketed out of the starting gate in 1994, with demand exceeding supply, sales had slowed down considerably during early 1995 as many prospective customers decided to wait for the new Saturn. Since hardware sales were low, software sales suffered as well, causing many third-party software companies, Capcom and Konami among them, to abandon their 32X projects. Although Sega denied that there was any problem, a noticeable sign of trouble emerged during the summer, when the company postponed the release of its *Neptune* console, a combination of the 16-bit Mega Drive/Genesis and the 32X, until early 1996. Despite this, Sega promised that 40 new 32X games would be available in time for Christmas. However, long before Christmas, Toys "R" Us, the world's biggest toy store, failed to include the 32X in its stock directory, which pretty much meant that there was no market for the device. Even Tom Kalinske admitted that his company hadn't lived up to the promises that it had made to the consumers who had invested in the product. The bottom line was that the 32X hadn't been profitable, and Sega had much more invested in the Saturn.[9]

Sega Neptune

Another product that lost support from Sega was the Mega CD/Sega CD. Although Sega had publicly stated that it ceased production of the unit in December in order to increase production of the Saturn, the company had actually discontinued all advertising for the Mega Drive/Genesis peripheral following Christmas, 1994. Although Sega had never realized the potential for CD-drive peripheral, many consumers had hoped that the company would design the Saturn to be backward-compatible with it, but Sega refuted the idea. Sega of America managed to salvage one legacy of the Sega CD when they decided to use the Sega CD's oversized jewel boxes as the packaging for Saturn software.

SegaSoft

The Saturn may have been Sega's top priority, but it wasn't the company's only concern. Sega began looking at the PC market very seriously after a company called Nvidia Corporation created a new chip that featured a new graphics-processing system. This, and the introduction of *Windows 95*, opened up an entirely new market for Sega. The earlier *Windows 3.1* operating system and its SVGA graphics weren't friendly towards the action-oriented games that Sega was known for. With the new available technology, Sega decided that the time was ripe to enter the crowded world of computer software.

Sega established a new software division that it called SegaSoft. In addition to PC and Mac games, SegaSoft was responsible for the development of Saturn software. There was also a rumor that the group would develop Sega games for competing consoles, such as the SCE PlayStation, but nothing ever came out of that. But games weren't the only things that were on the minds of the SegaSoft developers. The group was also developing computer peripherals, such as a card that would allow Saturn controllers to work on PCs.

In order for its future games to be state of the art, an investment group that Sega belonged to financed several million dollars into Integrated Computing Engines (ICE), a company that researched and developed computer and virtual reality technology. Sega's hope was that it could make a deal with ICE that would give it the rights to use the latter's technology in its upcoming games.

Sega also signed a deal with SNK, the manufacturer of the competing Neo•Geo system. This allowed the two companies to develop each other's best games for their own machine. Although many wondered which games would be swapped, neither company had any intention of officially selecting the games until they met in January, 1996.

On February 10, Sega of America signed an agreement with Tiger Electronics in which Tiger would manufacture, distribute and sell Sega's non-videogame products such as the *Pods* that had been introduced in 1994. Tiger also gained world-wide rights to the *Pocket Arcade* games. Eleven games were released in the fall under the *Sega by Tiger* banner. Two titles, *Ecco the Dolphin* and *Bug!* were the only returning titles but they were somewhat different from the ones that had been released solely by Sega in 1994 as they included a D-pad as part of their controls. The deal with Tiger did not include the *Pico.*[10]

Outside of the videogame realm, Sega continued to develop more theme parks where its games could be showcased. Sega and MCA teamed up with the new company DreamWorks SKG to develop and open 150 Interactive Entertainment Centers (IECs) around the United States by 2000. The centers would feature interactive attractions, simulators and the newest games. The first IEC was planned to open in July 1996 in Seattle, near the home of Nintendo of America. The largest would be a 50,000-square-foot center that was targeted for Las Vegas. Sega actually *needed* to open such a venue in order to get its latest arcade games played. These new machines, such as the driving simulator *Virtua Racing*, cost in excess of $18,000. Unless the game was very successful, it was very difficult for a typical arcade to afford to bring in a machine at that price. Even if the machine was leased from a distributor, it was still too expensive to render a return on the investment. Although a single game cost a dollar to play, the chances of it ever breaking even were very slim. The bottom line was that only an arcade owned by Sega could showcase such an expensive machine.

Tiger Sega Pocket Arcade II

E2000

Sega wasn't the only company that planned an interactive center. On May 10, Nolan Bushnell, the co-founder of Atari, announced plans to start *E2000*, a virtual-entertainment center that would include a futuristic restaurant, video rides, immersive theaters and interactive gaming rooms. The first E2000 was scheduled to open in northern California in September, with a dozen more opening throughout 1996.

Unfortunately for Bushnell, old debts came back to haunt him. He had owed the investment company Merrill Lynch millions of dollars for loans he borrowed during the eighties. Bushnell had paid the firm back all but one final payment of $500,000, and it was due in June. But for some reason, in February, Merrill Lynch sued Bushnell for $3.5 million. The investment company later admitted that the suit they had filed was erroneous, but by then, the damage had been done. E2000 investors changed their minds and took back the $2.5 million that they had fronted Bushnell for the interactive-entertainment center. E2000 never opened a single location.

Jaguar CD

Like its co-founder, the current incarnation of Atari wasn't doing well. The company struggled to increase the attractiveness of its cartridge-based Jaguar. Although Atari had claimed that by the end of 1994 it had sold between 150,000 and 200,000 units, the bottom line was that the eighteen-month head-start that Atari had on the other companies by releasing its 64-bit system in late 1993 had done little to win it any popularity, and the initial cartridges were scarce and not very good.

In order to popularize the Jaguar, Atari produced a slew of brand-new games based on old titles from its vast catalog. The "2000" series were games from the eighties that had been updated for the nineties: *Tempest 2000, Defender 2000* and *Breakout 2000*. When *Tempest 2000* was released, it was hailed as the best game for the Jaguar. So it could further entice consumers to buy the Jaguar, Atari lowered the price of the console to $149 in the late summer.

Atari Defender 2000

Atari Jaguar with CD Player

Throughout the year Atari announced new products that would enhance the Jaguar. In the forefront was the *Jaguar CD*. Although it was originally promised for late 1994, its release date was changed many times during 1995. The $200 unit was actually released on September 15, six days after the American release of SCE's PlayStation.

Manufactured by Philips, the Jaguar CD sat above the Jaguar console, where it was inserted into the console's cartridge slot. The peripheral had its own cartridge slot, so the unit did not have to be removed from the console for a cartridge game to be played. Built into the CD player was a program called the Virtual Light Machine, which produced startling on-screen light effects that were in sync with the music from audio CDs, sort of a modern update of Atari's 1976 poorly received *Video Music* console.

Even before the CD player was available, Atari was already planning the *JagDuo*, a Jaguar console with a built-in CD player. Atari hoped originally hoped to release this unit in the fall for $350. However, by that time both the Saturn and PlayStation had available at much lower prices. The JagDuo was scrapped.

Unfortunately, the JagDuo wasn't the only Jaguar-related item that failed to materialize. Other vaporware products included an MPEG video cartridge that would allow the console to play full-motion video movies, and a cartridge that could save game scores. The company also planned a virtual reality headset that had been developed by London-based Virtuality, a company that had become a leader in virtual reality entertainment. Virtuality designed a VR peripheral for the Jaguar, which Atari announced would be available in time for Christmas for under $200. However, many critics doubted that Atari could deliver such a VR unit for under $300, let alone $200. Atari tried to sooth the skeptics demonstrating a working unit at E^3. However it was quickly revealed that the model Atari used at E^3 was actually a Virtuality arcade system boxed in Jaguar housing.

Despite this deception, Virtuality did create a working prototype model of the VR unit. However, the red VR headset had low resolution, and Atari wasn't satisfied with its quality. While Virtuality went to work on a blue, high-resolution headset, Atari severed ties with the company, claiming that Virtuality couldn't produce a high-resolution VR headset at the $200 price point that it wanted.

Missile Command 3D was the only game that was the only game that would have been compatible with the VR headset. Unfortunately, the VR headset was not released, which left few people excited about the Jaguar. The system had few "must-have" games and the majority that had been released appeared to be rushed and buggy. Near the end of 1995, Atari announced that it would lay-off twenty employees. The company was quick to state that the lay-offs were due to software projects that had been scrapped, and not because of any poor performance by the Jaguar. Still, many wondered why Atari would even cancel one title, let alone three, when there was such a scarcity of Jaguar games in the first place.

Next, Atari announced that it would develop games for the PC and other consoles, such as the Saturn and the PlayStation. This seemed like *deja vu* to many longtime gamers, who remembered the Atarisoft label from the original Atari company. The press wondered if Atari would be abandoning the Jaguar, but Atari insisted that Jaguar sales were healthy, and that it merely made sense to cover all of its bases.

Virtual Reality Turns To Toast

Atari wasn't the only company that killed its virtual reality system in 1995. Hasbro, one of the world's largest toy companies, had been secretly working on a virtual reality console, codenamed *Toaster*, since 1992. Initially, Hasbro planned for the system to appear on store shelves as the *Hasbro VR* during the first half of 1996, with a price that would be comparable to the Nintendo 64. Abrams/Gentile Entertainments, the company behind the Mattel Power Glove for the NES, was even developing a new Power Glove for the Hasbro VR, which was rumored to have microphones built into headsets and have Internet capabilities. Although little was revealed about this console, many videogame insiders were very excited about it, and the one game that was leaked. *Nero Zero*, which was being created by 3D Creations and KATrix, was to be a first-person virtual reality game. Unfortunately, in September, Hasbro announced that it was scrapping its plans for the virtual reality device after sinking $59 million into its development. The company cited that the chips cost too much to allow an affordable retail price.

Hasbro VR Toaster

Although the Hasbro VR Power Glove died along with the system it was meant to support, a different type of glove controller did appear in the fall. The *Game Glove* from Anaphase Unlimited was a standard work glove with cords that attached to a game console. The player could control the action on the screen by moving his hands and fingers. Unlike previous glove controllers, the $90 Game Glove was generic, meaning that it could work with any game console. Only the cords that connected the glove to the console were different, and players could buy the cords for their specific machines. At the Game Glove's launch, there were cords for the SNES, Saturn and PlayStation. Nintendo 64 cords were in development.

Another new virtual controller that was announced in 1995 was the *Bird* from VIR Systems, an Australian company. This controller closely resembled Datasoft's Le Stick from 1981. In fact, the only difference was that while Le Stick had used mercury inside incline switches, the Bird utilized accelerometers and gyroscopic technology to sense every movement and then relay the information back to the game console via an infrared link. While the device had been displayed at the winter CES, there weren't any immediate plans for its release in the United States, where VIR Systems didn't even have an office set up. However, the company did plan to license its sensing technology to other manufacturers.

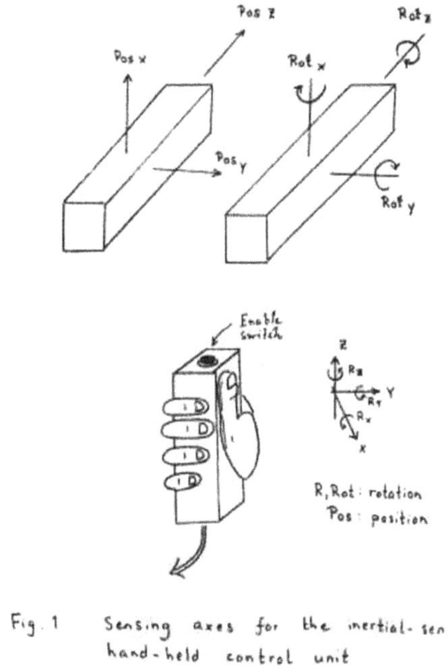

VIR Systems Bird Controller

Sega, which had been promising a virtual reality system for the Genesis for a year, quietly killed its project without much of an explanation. Sega officials soon began promoting a virtual reality system for the Saturn that they hoped to release either in late 1995 or early 1996. It was widely believed that this was the same system that had been planned for the Genesis. Since the Genesis was reaching the end of its practical life, the virtual reality system was, according to the theory, merely shifted to the Saturn.

Virtual I/O, the company that had developed the virtual reality glasses for Sega, was also working on a standard virtual reality headset that would be compatible with all of the videogame consoles. At the end of 1995, Virtual I/O began talks with SCE to develop

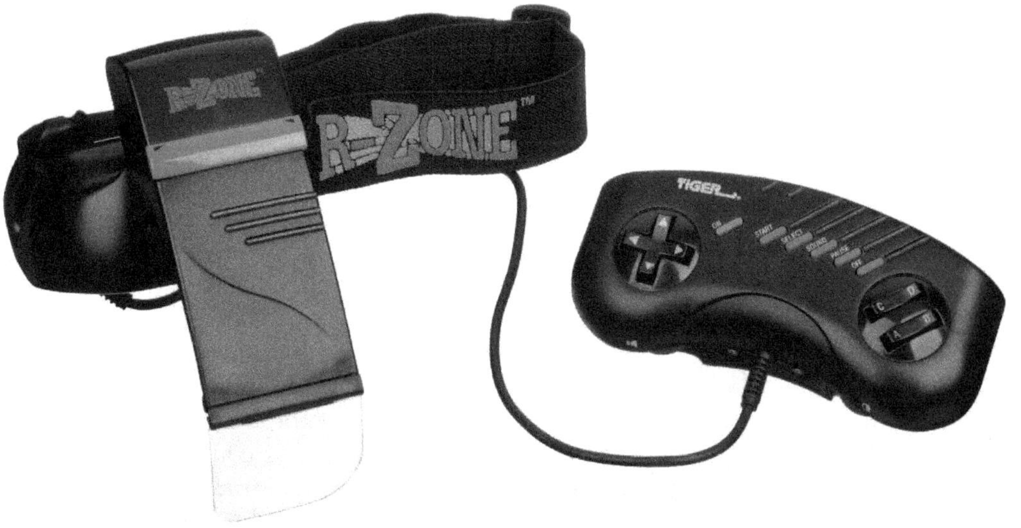

Tiger R-Zone Headgear

a video headset exclusively for the PlayStation. While this headset wouldn't incorporate virtual reality technology, it would give gamers the impression that they were playing videogames on an 80-inch screen. Virtual I/O acknowledged that a product would be released before April 1996.

One "Virtual Reality" device did reach the marketplace in time for Christmas. Tiger Electronics' R-Zone was a programmable system that attached to a player's head and projected red-shaded LCD images onto a plastic screen that sat in front of the player's eyes. While the games were low-quality, the price of the unit was low as well. The R-Zone cost only $30.

Release of the Virtual Boy

Nintendo of Japan released the Virtual Boy on July 21 to a less-than receptive consumer base. The company did little to support the system, which retailed for ¥15,000 ($169) and didn't include any pack-in software. Nintendo of America, on the other hand, began planning new advertising strategies for the Virtual Boy before its August 14 release date. The console's singular unique feature was its 3D screen, which couldn't be highlighted in two-dimensional print or television advertising. Nintendo needed to devise a way that potential customers could actually fully experience it before they purchased the console. As a means to this end, Nintendo worked out a deal with Blockbuster Video. Through the end of 1995, Blockbuster would rent out two game cartridges and the Virtual Boy console for a two-night period for only $10. In addition, the renter would receive a $10 coupon towards the purchase of a brand-new Virtual Boy. And unlike the Japanese version, the American Virtual Boy was packaged with a copy of *Mario's Tennis*.

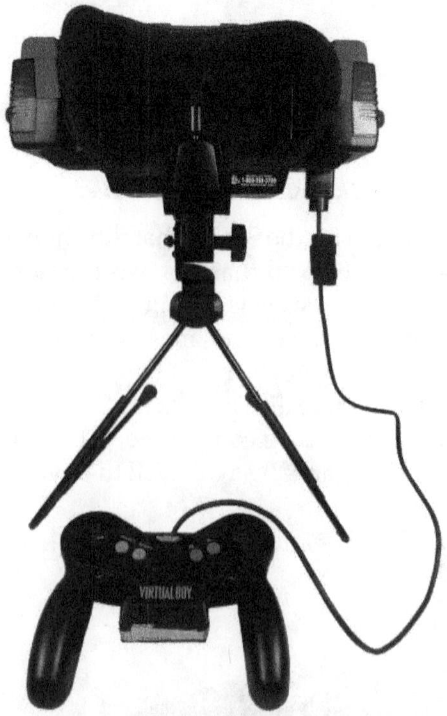

Nintendo Virtual Boy

Nintendo Mario's Tennis for Virtual Boy

Nintendo of America continued to promote the Virtual Boy after its release. The company set up tents at several Blockbuster locations around the country over the Labor Day weekend and allowed gamers to try the system up close without even having to rent it. After playing it, many people actually changed their first impressions of it. However, they didn't change their minds enough to actually buy one.

Many potential customers felt that the $180 console was just too expensive. They were hesitant to spend so much money on a new system that had nearly no support from third-party vendors, and had to be played solitarily. Nintendo of America tried to confront both problems. The company announced that it would release a new controller that would allow players to hook up two Virtual Boys for head-to-head competition. When this announcement failed to increase sales, Nintendo announced that it would reduce the price of the Virtual Boy by twenty dollars, claiming that it could do this because the yen/dollar ratio had improved. Few people believed this, especially when some retailers were already discounting the Virtual Boy at $99 in an effort to get rid of them.

And then there was a health problem that Nintendo couldn't control. Many Virtual Boy gamers experienced headaches after long gaming sessions. But more serious were cases of epilepsy. While games in the United States carried disclaimers that they could cause epileptic fits, the Virtual Boy, due to its self-contained screen, made epileptic gamers even more prone to fits than standard game consoles. Naturally, this was written in the press, which made the Virtual Boy even less accepted by consumers.

By the end of December, Nintendo of Japan decided to pull the plug on the unpopular system. With a five-month lifespan, the Virtual Boy became one of the greatest failures in videogaming history. Although Nintendo of America decided to carry the console into 1996, the damage had already been done, as far as the corporate headquarters in Japan was concerned. And unfortunately, they would make sure that someone paid for that damage.

Sega Channel

Although the Internet had been around in one form or another since 1969, it wasn't until 1995 that the vast majority of computer users were able to access it. This was because the main online services, such as America Online, CompuServe and Prodigy, finally linked to the World Wide Web. Unfortunately, videogame consoles still weren't capable of any Internet access. However, as they had been doing ever since Ralph Baer decided he wanted videogames to be delivered via cable, videogame companies still sought ways to transmit games directly into homes.

Sega was ahead of the other companies with its Sega Channel. By the beginning of 1995, the beta testing of the new online service had been completed and it was firmly in place on over eighty cable systems nationwide. By year's end, the system was so successful that it expanded into Canada.

The Sega Channel was very similar to the Intellivision's long-forgotten PlayCable. As with the former system, subscribers received a special adapter that plugged into the console's cartridge slot. For a monthly fee of $14.95, Sega Channel subscribers had access to fifty games, which they could download to their Genesis or Mega Drives in less than a minute. The game would then remain in the console's memory until the unit was either turned off or another game was downloaded.

The Sega Channel had more than just Sega-published games. It also offered licensed games from third-party vendors like Electronic Arts and Konami. Some games, such as *Ozone Kid*, were only available to subscribers. Other games had to be altered so they would completely download before the transmission timed out. One example was *Super Street Fighter II*, which needed to have several characters removed. In early fall, the Sega Channel offered *Express Games*, an additional service that would cost Sega Channel subscribers another $2.95 a month. For that price, they would also be offered brand-new games for downloading at the same time that they were released to retail stores.

The Sega Channel also provided hints on how to get through Sega games. An online Game Guide listed all of the games that were available through the service, along with passwords and codes. An online News Link provided subscribers with information concerning gaming contests and news.

If the Sega Channel was the '90s version of the Intellivision PlayCable, then the '90s equivalent to the Gameline was Catapult's XBand modem. While the Sega Channel delivered games via cable, the XBand used the phone lines to distribute games. However, the XBand went beyond the capabilities of the Gameline, which had only been able to deliver games. The XBand allowed gamers in two different locations to compete against each other in the same game. The only problem was that in order to play games against opponents who weren't local, one gamer might have had to call another long-distance.

That could become costly especially if a game lasted a long time.

The XBand was released in June. In July, the two companies decided to join forces, and beginning in August, the XBand modem was linked to the Sega Channel adapter. Of the fifty games that were available through the Sega Channel, the top five or ten were set up for remote play via the XBand. Without raising the basic monthly subscription fee, the Sega Channel included twenty connections to the XBand Network. An added bonus allowed users to send email to one another. However, email was only the tip of the Internet iceberg. Catapult hoped to have World Wide Web access via the XBand Network available by November.

Unfortunately, that goal was never achieved. After Sega released the Saturn in the United States, the spotlight was removed from the 16-bit Genesis. Although the Sega Channel was still popular, people wondered how it would survive once the next-generation machines grew more popular. Many speculated on whether or not the Saturn would embrace the Sega Channel, but most videogame analysts doubted that it would happen. The games for the Saturn were just too large to download quickly.

Sega of Japan found another solution for the online distribution of games to the Saturn. At year's end, the company announced that it would be releasing peripherals in April 1996 that would connect the Saturn to the Internet. The peripherals, which would include a modem and keyboard, would cost around $200. Sega of Japan also planned to move the Saturn beyond videogames. In December, the company signed a deal with automaker Nissan to place Saturn consoles in 3,000 Nissan dealerships. These systems would play interactive Video CDs that would feature car information and also connect with Nissan's home page on the World Wide Web.

Sega of America didn't have plans to place the Saturn in car dealerships. They were also skeptical about whether an Internet Connection was even feasible in the United States. The company decided to take a wait-and-see attitude, and observe how the market fared before it went ahead and released the peripherals.

While Sega was delivering games via cable and phone lines, Nintendo used satellites. Nintendo of Japan signed a contract with St. Giga, a Japanese satellite channel, to broadcast games to the Super Famicom beginning on April 24. Customers first had to subscribe to St. Giga's Broadcast Satellite (BS) system, which required a BS tuner and a satellite dish. They would also have to purchase a ¥16,000 ($175) Satellaview system from Nintendo via mail order. The Satellaview unit sat under the Super Famicom in the same fashion that the original Mega CD sat under the Mega Drive. A special BS-X broadcast game pack that plugged into the Super Famicom's cartridge slot provided decoding software.

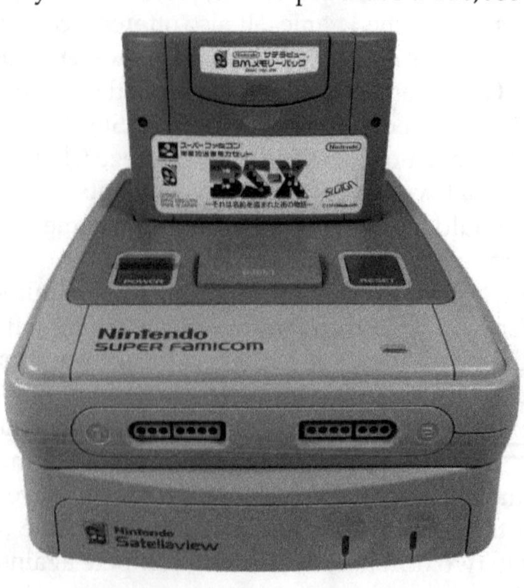

Nintendo Super Famicom with Satellaview & BS-X Game Pak

Once everything was set up, the user could download games that were broadcast by Nintendo nightly between 4 and 7 PM. Games would be channeled through the BS-X Cassette, which contained 256K of memory and was capable of saving games. Consumers could also purchase an optional memory cartridge that plugged into the BS-X and provided an additional 8MB of memory.

Nintendo of America had no intention of bringing the Satellaview to the United

States. Fortunately, SNES owners had another option that at least allowed them to play some games online against players in other locations.

In mid-June, Catapult test-marketed an XBand modem for the SNES in five cities. The system was so popular during the testing that the SNES XBand was released nationwide in September.

The SNES model sported new features that weren't available on the Genesis model, including the ability to practice a game while waiting for an opponent, and letting the user switch between local and long-distance access. Testers of the new modem liked these new features so much that Catapult planned to upgrade them into the Genesis model as well. This was a fairly simple process, since the operating-system could be modified by downloading it into the XBand where it was saved within the modem's battery-powered RAM.

Catapult also teamed up with MCI and offered a new "XBand Nationwide" program that allowed long-distance gaming for the relatively low price of $3.95 per hour. This novel approach finally made multiplayer gaming affordable.

Catapult next began working on an XBand modem for Nintendo's forthcoming 64-bit console. However, Nintendo of Japan also sought a way to link the new console to a network. The company teamed up with two software companies, Square of Japan and Just System Corp., to develop a peripheral that would give the Nintendo 64 full network capabilities. By the end of 1995, the alliance hadn't gone beyond a basic plan towards where they wanted to head. They felt they could develop an interactive network where gamers could compete against one another, and which could later expand into home shopping and home banking. The team even thought about using the Catapult XBand as a way of getting onto the network.

Nintendo of Japan also began having discussions with Netscape Communications, the leader in World Wide Web browsers. While Nintendo's partnership with Square of Japan and Just System Corp. had been formed for the purpose of building a private online network, the talks with Netscape seemed to show that Nintendo was willing to link the Nintendo 64 to the mother of all networks, the Internet.

In January, GTE Interactive Media, a subsidiary of GTE Corporation, which operated local telephone and cellular companies around the United States, had joined with Nintendo of America to develop games for the SNES and the new 64-bit console. Both companies used CES to preview their first collaboration, *FX Fighter,* a 3D fighting game for the SNES that used Nintendo's FX2 graphics-enhancer chip. Although the two companies announced only games for the consoles, Howard Lincoln, Nintendo of America's chairman, did say that they were in discussions with GTE Corporation about creating games that could be played over the phone lines.

Nintendo's Going-Ons

Besides forming partnerships with other companies, Nintendo was also busy investing in them. In April, the company paid $39.5 million to acquire a 25% interest in the software development company Rare, marking the first time that Nintendo had ever invested in a non-Japanese development company. Rare had enjoyed a good working relationship with Nintendo for over a decade. In 1984, Rare began developing programming tools for the Famicom. It followed up by becoming the first company outside of Japan to be licensed to develop Famicom software. Rare also developed Nintendo-compatible games for other third-party companies, such as Acclaim and Konami. In 1992, the company started an arcade division, and was responsible for such arcade hits as *Battletoads* and *Killer Instinct.*

Rare had become well-known in 1994, when it developed the SNES megahit *Donkey Kong Country* using Advanced Computer Modeling, its exclusive 3D technology. After the game sold 7.4 million copies worldwide by mid-1995, the two companies began looking for ways to outdo *Donkey Kong Country*. In September, Nintendo released an SNES version of *Killer Instinct*, which went on to sell over 150,000 copies in less than two months, making it the fastest selling game of 1995.

During the same month, Williams released an SNES version of the hit computer game, *Doom*. It received a "Mature" rating from the ESRB, marking the first time a Nintendo-licensed game ever received such a rating.

Nintendo sold its one billionth videogame cartridge in October. Nearly half of those sales had been from the Famicom/NES catalog, while 27% were from the Super Famicom/SNES library. The remaining 23% was comprised of Game Boy titles. Japanese consumers had purchased 44% of the cartridges, Americans had bought 42%, and the remaining 14% had been distributed around the rest of the world. This amounted to approximately three games per second for twelve years!

Although Nintendo's figures were extraordinary, they could have been even better. Unfortunately, the videogame manufacturers claimed to lose billions of dollars of revenue to counterfeit games. During the winter CES in January, it had been brought to Nintendo's attention that counterfeit copies of *Donkey Kong Country* were being distributed.[11] After an investigation, Nintendo of America determined that Samsung Electronics, a major supplier of ROM chips, had produced chips with counterfeit *Donkey Kong Country* software burnt into them, and then shipped them to two pirate operations in China that were owned and operated by the Chinese government.

Nintendo, which used Samsung to supply its ROM chips, immediately shut down all of its associations with the Korean company. Naturally, Samsung declared its innocence, even though the counterfeit software had indeed been stamped into its ROM chips. However, as pointed out by a Samsung executive, Nintendo's action against Samsung was the same as if a company took action against a computer diskette manufacturer because counterfeit programs were found on one of its diskettes.

Nintendo of America sought several things in its lawsuit. It wanted:

- all of the counterfeit software destroyed
- Samsung to provide information on the counterfeiting network
- more safeguards to prevent similar events from happening in the future
- monetary compensation for the lost sales, estimated to be in the billions

Samsung immediately filed a countersuit against Nintendo of America, citing that the company had defamed its good name. Samsung also wanted monetary compensation as well, as an injunction against Nintendo of America's lawsuit.

Samsung claimed that it had a history of fighting piracy and had even discussed with Nintendo about ways in which it could be prevented. One way to do it was by monitoring the code that was to be burned into the ROM chips, which was sent by Samsung's clients. Sega of America, another Samsung client, provided Samsung with a program that screened the ROM chips for any Sega code. Nintendo of Japan had been agreeable with this method, but Nintendo of America had not. Instead, it wanted Samsung to shut down the manufacturing of all of its ROM chips and to provide Nintendo with information about all of its clients. Samsung refused.

Nintendo of America, of course, had a different story. It claimed that it agreed with the screening process, but wanted it to be done by an independent third party.

Suddenly in April, the two companies announced after negotiations that the suit was over and Samsung could once again resume etching ROM chips with software. Both companies declined to discuss the case any further, although Nintendo conceded that Samsung was not the source of the counterfeiting.

Nintendo wasn't alone when it came to counterfeiting. Phony Sega hardware and software was confiscated during a raid in Beijing, China in the spring. The counterfeiters had planned to sell the pirated goods in China and Russia.

While Nintendo and Sega were the victims in the counterfeiting schemes, both companies were found guilty of monopolistic practices in an unrelated British lawsuit. The Monopolies and Mergers Commission came to the conclusion that both Nintendo and Sega were purposely restricting the number of titles that third parties could release. This allowed them to control the prices of the games, as well as limit the amount of software that was available to the consumers. The Commission recommended that the practice be stopped, so greater competition could appear in the marketplace.

Industry Ups and Downs

For the first time in eighteen years, the 1995 winter CES was to have been the only one held during the year. The Consumer Electronics Association (CEA), which hosted the event, had planned a new show called CES Interactive (CES-I) that was supposed to be held in Philadelphia during May 11-13. However, as it turned out, those were the same dates that the first E^3 was held. Because the majority of the vendors who would have exhibited at CES-I had to back out in order to attend E^3, The CEA was forced to cancel the show.[12]

Although 1995 had begun with slow videogame sales, they picked up after the release of the Saturn and PlayStation. All in all, 1995 had been a good year for most of the software companies, and more planned to jump onto the bandwagon. Mattel announced that it was once again entering the videogame foray, with its new Mattel Media division. The most successful company was Acclaim, which had posted revenues that were more than $100 million higher than the previous year's.

Unfortunately, not every company enjoyed a profitable year. Sunsoft was hit by major layoffs that affected most of its staff, leaving mostly high-level executives. While all games in development were put on hold, a Sunsoft spokesman assured that the company was not going out of business and would once again release games, once the industry had been re-evaluated. Enix America Corporation, a company that was known for publishing NES and SNES games, closed its doors in November, after its Japanese parent company decided to quit releasing games in North America because of poor sales.

The business of software enhancements wasn't as lucrative as it had been either. With the Sega 32X out of the running, Codemasters never released its rumored 32X Game Genie. A Game Genie for the Saturn or PlayStation didn't even reach the rumor stage, and it was doubtful that one would ever be released.

While Codemasters was strangely silent, some activity was happening at Datel, the makers of the Pro Action Replay. In September, the company released the Ultimate Game-Buster Action Replay (UGBAR) for the PlayStation. This was a memory card with fifteen slots that contained cheats for several games. If a player loaded a particular game that was supported by the UGBAR, he would then receive optional onscreen instructions on how to load the cheats.

At year's end, Datel joined forces with InterAct Accessories to produce a Pro Action Replay for the Saturn, PlayStation and Nintendo 64 upon its release. The new unit was called the *GameShark* and worked with game codes in the same fashion as the previous Pro Action Replay.[13]

Interact GameShark for PlayStation

Retro Games Return

As the new breed of games became more sophisticated with the advances in hardware, many critics argued that they were pretty to look at, but had no substance. Another problem was that it seemed as if all the new games were merely rehashes of old ones. To drive the point home, one only had to mention Atari's best contemporary game, *Tempest 2000*, which was merely an update of an old classic game from the early eighties.

However, Atari wasn't the only company that was actively making use of its back catalog. Activision, which had been around since 1981, also opened its library of classic videogame titles to a new generation of gamers.

Actually, Activision's first classic rerelease was buried within a brand-new game. *Pitfall: The Mayan Adventure* was an updated version of the classic *Pitfall!*, which had been released for several consoles including the SNES and Genesis. However, hidden somewhere in the new game was the original *Pitfall!* exactly as it had appeared on the Atari 2600 and Mattel Intellivision over a decade earlier.

Activision Atari 2600 Action Pack

Edtris 2600

Activision followed this with the release of three *Atari 2600 Action Packs*. These $29.95 CD collections for PCs and Macs contained most of the games that Activision had released for the 2600, including *Pitfall!*. The third collection even included some classic Atari-brand games.

The games themselves used the exact same code that they had used when originally released. An emulator program was supplied that translated the native code into something that the computer's operating system could understand. And since the original Atari controllers couldn't be used on the computers, the emulator converted the controller commands in the code into keyboard actions. For instance, pressing the space bar on the computer provided the same response that pressing the red firing button did on the controller.

In addition to the games, the Activision collections contained on-screen histories of the individual games, as well as scans of the original instruction manuals. The positive reviews for the collections were practically unanimous. While the games were graphically simple, they were still fun to play.

As a new generation of gamers was introduced to the Atari 2600 games via their computers, hundreds of gamers who still used their 2600 consoles were thrilled to discover that a brand-new game had been released for the eighteen-year-old system. *Edtris 2600* was a version of *Tetris*, which had never been released for the 2600. Ed Federmeyer, the software engineer who wrote *Edtris 2600*, called this new game for an old system a "homebrew".[14]

And while the old Atari 2600 was getting a second chance, it appeared that Jack Tramiel's former company, Commodore, was going to get one as well. In April, a German company called Escom bought the Commodore name and patents for $10 million at a bankruptcy auction. At a press conference, an Escom spokesperson said that the company planned to revive Commodore's entire line, including the Amiga. However, Commodore and Amiga would become two distinct entities with separate product lines. The Commodore name would be affixed to PC clones, while a new subsidiary, Amiga Technologies, would be created to handle the Amiga line. Escom also signed a deal with a Chinese company to build low-cost Amigas and Commodore 64s for sale in China.

Magazine Changes

As classic games began to take on a new life, the 'new' *Electronic Games*, a magazine that had been associated with the early days of gaming, was getting a facelift. As the editorial page of the July issue stated, it was the "End of an Era." In August, *Electronic Games* was reincarnated as *Fusion*, a magazine that was to focus on all aspects of electronic entertainment including virtual reality and the Internet. *Electronic Games* had been devoted to all electronic entertainment for some time, but the title of the magazine had been a misnomer; thus the change.

Another magazine went through a less obvious title change. *Game Players Sega-Nintendo*, which many thought was a magazine that focused strictly on Sega and Nintendo, dropped the two company names from its title and became *Game Players*.

As *Game Players* emerged as a magazine that wasn't console-specific, a new British magazine appeared in October that was. *Play* was an independent periodical from Live Publishing that focused on the new PlayStation. One month later, Future Publishing introduced the *Official UK PlayStation Magazine* with support from SCE Europe (SCEE). Each issue of the magazine included a CD that contained game trailers and playable demos of forthcoming PlayStation games. At around the same time that the magazine first appeared, two new PlayStation magazines were also introduced in the United States, although neither was sanctioned by SCEA. Ziff-Davis published *PSX* (PlayStation Experience) and Dimension Publishing put out *Dimension PSX*.

While the purpose of any magazine is to entertain and report the news, one magazine, *Diehard GameFan*, lost a lot of its credibility that it may have had after it printed an offensive review in its September, 1995 issue. The review was for *College Football USA '96*, a Genesis game from Electronic Arts. Unfortunately, the text was the farthest thing from a review. Instead, it was an offensive and unintelligent attack against the Japanese. An apology immediately appeared on the editorial page of the following issue, with a renunciation claiming that the magazine had been sabotaged.

1995 had been a roller coaster of a year that had been dominated by the battle between Sega and SCE. However, although the skirmishes between the two companies didn't produce an all-out winner, they were just a prologue to what was in store for 1996, the year when the sleeping giant was once again about to awake.

CHAPTER TWENTY-FOUR
1996

During the earliest days of the home videogame industry, new products had always been showcased at CES, the twice-annual trade show that focused on all aspects of consumer electronics, which was not open to the public. As the videogame industry grew larger, it needed a trade show of its own, and so E^3 was created. But E^3 was something of a redundancy. Since the majority of gaming companies were Japanese, why did they need to debut their games and systems at an American venue? IDG and the IDSA, the forces behind E^3, attempted to rectify this with a Japanese E^3 that was held in Tokyo in early November. *E^3: Tokyo 96,* as it was called, received little cooperation from the console manufacturers - Nintendo was the only one that attended - and the show was deemed a failure. E^3 was never held in Japan again.

But one reason why E^3: Tokyo 96 failed was because Japan already had its own major gaming show. Organized by the Computer Entertainment Supplier's Association (CESA) and Nikkei Business Publications, the *Tokyo Game Show* was held twice a year, in the spring and the fall. And unlike E^3 and other trade shows, the Tokyo Game Show was open to the public during the last two days of the multi-day event. Before long, the Tokyo Game Show became the show of choice for manufacturers to show off their new products. This made perfect sense since most Japanese videogame items were released in Japan before the rest of the world.

Price Wars

As 1996 began, Sega and SCE revealed their total sales figures for the prior year. Sega of America reported that it had sold 400,000 Saturns in North America since May 1995. SCEA outdid that by claiming sales of 800,000 PlayStations since September.

The situation was different in Japan, where the Saturn outsold the PlayStation. Despite this edge, Sega of Japan lowered the price of the Saturn on March 22 to ¥20,000 ($189), a price that made the 32-bit console even less expensive than Nintendo's 16-bit Super Famicom. The price decrease came with a console that was slightly changed from the original, and cost less to produce. The new Saturn had round buttons instead of oval, and an "access LED" that appeared on the original model was removed. In an effort to appeal female game players, the new console was white.

The newly designed Saturn was sold in all regions, although the white one stayed in Japan. The rest of the world received black consoles that were other-wise no different from the Japanese one. The only difference appearance-wise between the North American model and the European one was the color of their Power and Reset buttons. Sega of America lowered the price of the new Saturn by $50 to $249 on April 1. A console bundled with *Virtua Fighter Remix* was also sold for $50 more.

Redesigned Japanese Sega Saturn

Redesigned American Sega Saturn

Although the Saturn's sales lagged behind the PlayStation in America, Sega of America insisted that it wouldn't lower the price of its Saturn any more to match Sega of Japan. Despite this, many analysts predicted that it was inevitable for Sega of America to lower the price of the American console even further. SCEA apparently also felt that it was going to happen. On May 16, the first day of the Electronic Entertainment Expo (E^3), the company surprised the industry by announcing that it was immediately lowering the price of its PlayStation to $199. A day later, Sega of America announced that it would also drop the price of its console to $199 to match the PlayStation.

Both systems experienced sales increases once their prices dropped under $200, but the PlayStation still outsold the Saturn. One reason for this was due to a deal that SCEA had signed with Kay-Bee Toys and Circuit City, which made the PlayStation the exclusive 32-bit system that these stores sold. Neither chain had been happy in 1995, when they were left out of Sega of America's initial surprising Saturn release, and this was their way at getting back at Sega. Although the stores didn't officially call their action a boycott against the Saturn, the result was the same, with Sega being shut out from over 1,500 stores.

The Nintendo 64

Despite the overwhelming success of the PlayStation over the Saturn, SCE executives knew that they couldn't sit back and enjoy their victory. They still had Nintendo to contend with and they knew that the competition would be fierce. Throughout the entire year, even before its release, the Ultra 64 was the top videogame-related story of 1996.

News concerning Nintendo's 64-bit console began early in the year, when the company announced that the system was going to be called the *Nintendo 64 (N64)* everywhere in the world. While the "Ultra" trademark was not a problem outside of Japan, the consensus among the head executives at Nintendo was that they wanted to have a product with a single name and logo worldwide.

Ironically, while Nintendo was stressing a single unity, it was going in the opposite direction with its release dates. Originally, Nintendo intended to release the N64 worldwide on April 21. But by February, the company's marketing people realized that it just wasn't feasible to proceed with this plan. To do so would have strained Nintendo's distribution system. Although all countries would receive shipments, the supply of consoles would be too limited to be available to most consumers. Instead, Nintendo decided to release the N64 on April 21 only in Japan. The United States would get its first shipments on September 30, and Europe and the rest of the world would receive their systems sometime in the fall.

Although the reason behind the delay was plausible, many critics were skeptical about its truthfulness. Rumors persisted that Nintendo had actually been manufacturing the system since September 1995, and that thousands of units were already sitting in a warehouse. Many suspected that the real reason Nintendo wasn't in a hurry to release the consoles was because there was a dearth of software to accompany them. While this wouldn't necessarily trouble Japanese consumers, American buyers expected a wealth of titles to be available with a new system.

Knowing that Americans would be very disappointed with this setback, Nintendo of America placed a full-page ad in *USA Today* that explained the system's delay and assured potential buyers that it would be well worth the wait. By printing the ad, Nintendo of America had committed itself to release the new console on September 30 in North America.

Unfortunately, such a commitment hadn't been made by Nintendo of Japan. Although the company assured everyone that the console would indeed be available on April 21, that launch date became an impossibility due to an unexpected shortage of semiconductors. Of the 500,000 N64s that were planned, only 200,000 could be available on time. Nintendo had no choice but to push back Japan's release date two months to June 23.

In April, Nintendo began announcing how the N64 would be sold. The ¥25,000 ($231) package would contain a console, one gray controller and an AC adapter. A game would not be included. The fact that Nintendo specified that the controller would be gray was of some importance, because the company planned to sell additional controllers in designer colors such as black, blue, green, gray, red and yellow for ¥2,500 ($25) each. The new controller itself differed dramatically from the Super Famicom controller. It featured two grips like the NES Max. However, a third grip extended from the unit's center, giving the controller an "M" shape. In the direct center of the controller was a red reset button, and beneath it was an analog thumbstick. The standard D-pad was on the left and six control buttons were on the right. Four of these control buttons were designed to be used to manipulate how the first-person 3D games were viewed, but developers could use them for other purposes. A set of shoulder buttons were located at the rear of the controller, and a "Z" trigger button was positioned on the underside of the center grip. The controller also featured an expansion slot, where additional accessories could be added.

Nintendo N64 Controller

One such accessory was a *Controller Pak*, which would be used as a memory card to save important game data. Memory cards were becoming a required peripheral for the PlayStation because they played CDs that couldn't save data.[1] Since the days of the Famicom, cartridges had been produced that could save game information. However, data stored on a cartridge could not be exchanged by one gamer to another, something that could be done with the memory cards for the PlayStation and Saturn. The Controller Pak allowed gamers to save their game data and then exchange it with other people who owned the same game.

Nintendo N64 Controller Pak

The N64 made its American debut at E^3 in May. Visitors to the Nintendo booth were given a tour that showed them all of the playable games. The consensus among visitors was that Nintendo had another hit on its hands, and *Super Mario 64* was their hands-down favorite game.

Super Mario 64, like the *Super Mario Bros.* games that preceded it, had the player control Mario as he made his way through several worlds. However, unlike the platform games that came before it, *Super Mario 64* was three-dimensional. Mario seemed to be able to venture anywhere in any direction. While creating the game, Shigeru Miyamoto's self-appointed task wasn't to invent a completely new one. To make the best use of the N64's technology, he decided to use an existing genre and retool it. The result was hailed as revolutionary. *Next Generation* magazine called it *"the greatest videogame ever made."*

Nintendo Super Mario 64

After seeing what a game looked like on the

N64, the attendees at E³ wanted to see what the Bulky Drive would add. Unfortunately, they were informed that the storage device wouldn't be unveiled until the Japanese Shoshinkai show in November. Still, Nintendo revealed that the device would be based on optical technology rather than magnetic, and that it would cost less than had been expected. However, while Nintendo insisted at E³ that the bulky drive would ship on time in early 1997, within a few weeks that date was pushed back to the fall of 1997.

One date that had already been pushed back was that of the N64's release in Japan. During the week preceding the launch date, Nintendo began supplying retailers with N64 kiosks that allowed potential customers to demo the new machine and *Super Mario 64*. Lines began forming immediately, while neighboring SCE and Sega kiosks went empty. Everyone wanted to try the game, and while most who did were floored by it, the ever-present skeptics reminded game magazines that since *Super Mario 64* had been in development for over 2½ years, much longer than other game, it better be a good game. Still, *Super Mario 64* was the first game that people saw for the console and it showcased the capabilities of the N64 perfectly.

Nintendo of Japan released 300,000 N64s. Since eighty percent of those machines had already been presold, not many retailers received any systems that they could sell to people who hadn't preordered them. The few stores that did have extra systems to sell were swamped by customers. One Japanese retailer, Laox, had 300 consoles to sell. By 2 AM on the morning of June 23, thirty people were camped out in front of the store. As the morning progressed, the line kept getting longer. The store finally opened an hour early, and all of the consoles sold quickly. While Laox was almost unique because it had N64s that it could sell, lines had formed at most stores as people waited just to pick up the N64s that they had preordered.

The initial 300,000 units sold out in one day, and Nintendo followed that with the delivery of another 200,000 units on June 26. That shipment also sold out in one day. After a third delivery of 200,000 was shipped on June 30, Nintendo distributed an additional million during July and August. After that, it geared up for the American release.

In most cases, people who purchased an N64 also purchased a *Super Mario 64* cartridge. Only two other games were available, *Pilotwings 64*, an updated version of a Super Famicom game, and *Saikyō Habu Shōgi*, a strategy board game popular in Japan that was similar to chess.

Although Americans still had to wait three months before the N64's release, several enterprising retailers decided to import the Japanese model into the United States. Those gamers who couldn't wait until the end of September were able to purchase a Japanese

Nintendo 64 Launch Titles

model with *Super Mario 64* and *Pilotwings 64* for $750!

Nintendo made two announcements concerning the new machine's American launch during the month before the scheduled September 30 release date. First, because September 30 fell on a Monday, Nintendo had decided to push the release date ahead one day to the 29th, so children (and adults) wouldn't have to cut school (or work) just so they could purchase consoles.

The other good news from Nintendo concerned the machine's retail price. During the entire development cycle of the N64, Nintendo had promised that the N64 would retail for under $250. But when Nintendo officially announced that the N64's list price would be $199, most critics were surprised. And instead of welcoming this news, they began analyzing why Nintendo was setting that price.

Most believed that Nintendo was running scared, and had lowered the price at the last minute. In Japan, despite the best launch in history for any system, sales for new N64s were beginning to slacken. Analysts attributed this to the lack of new game titles. Many believed that Nintendo of America had lowered the price to $199 so the N64 would be price-competitive with the Saturn and PlayStation, which by then were also selling at that price. The truth was that Nintendo had intended all along to release the console at under $200, although it had never publicly reported this. They had finally made the announcement at the last possible moment so that Sega and SCE wouldn't have enough time to form an immediate counter-attack with the prices for their own systems.

As promised, the N64 was officially released on North American shores on September 29. In actuality, the system actually began appearing in stores on September 24. In order for all retailers to have consoles ready to sell on the 29th, Nintendo began shipping the consoles to stores a few days early. Although Nintendo requested that retailers not actually sell their supplies until the 29th, anxious storeowners began selling them as soon as they had them in stock. As word spread that some stores were selling the consoles early, other stores began doing the same. Once the dam burst, there was no holding the floodwaters back, and Nintendo finally gave an official nod to the rest of the retailers to begin selling their inventories on the 25th, four days early. As had been the case in Japan, the 500,000 units that had been allocated for North America were all gobbled up immediately from preorders. However, unlike the Japanese launch, when only three games were initially offered, Americans were only able to purchase *Super Mario 64* and *Pilotwings 64*, along with the console. A third-party title, *Cruis 'n USA*,[2] was a third game that had supposed to have been available immediately. However, Nintendo had not been happy with the finished game and forced Williams to go back and revamp it. While North American gamers had fewer games to choose from, one of the games offered more than its Japanese counterpart. The American *Super Mario 64* had some small enhancements, such as extra voices and sounds.

While nobody could predict how the N64 would fare against the PlayStation and Saturn in the long run, many comparative sales figures were offered. It had taken Sega nearly a year and SCE approximately three months, to sell 500,000 of their respective consoles. Nintendo had sold that many N64s on its first day. And since Nintendo had sold that number of machines through preorders, it was assumed that if the company had made the inventory available, the total number would have been much higher. But there were still two questions that haunted Nintendo immediately following the N64's release: could the console survive with a shortage of available software, and could its cartridges compete with CDs?

As for the lack of software, Nintendo was quick to point out that it preferred quality over quantity. And as far as the debate over cartridges vs. CDs went, *Super Mario 64* proved what could be done in a cartridge-based game. It was extensive, beautiful and fun, and it played seamlessly without any wasted loading time.

The demand for the N64 in America was greater than Nintendo had anticipated. Initially, Nintendo had planned to ship 600,000 N64s to North America during the console's first year. However, because of the overwhelming demand for the 64-bit game machine, Nintendo decided to raise that number to 1.2 million. Because the company couldn't increase its production facilities, the additional consoles had to come from other sources. Nintendo decided to use 300,000 units that had originally been slated for Japan, and send them to North America. The remaining 300,000 came from a different stockpile that had originally been assigned for distribution in Europe at year's end. In order to accommodate its North American customers, Nintendo pushed back the release date of the European N64 to sometime in 1997.

Even with the infusion of additional consoles, not everyone was able to purchase one. Fortunately, people were able to get a taste of the new console from rental stores. The Video Software Dealers Association reported that *Super Mario 64* had generated $52,000 in rental fees during its first week of release. On average, one copy of *Super Mario 64* was rented every minute for an entire week straight.

By all accounts, the N64 was a winner. Statistics showed that the system had accounted for 51% of all videogame consoles sold in the United States during the month of September, even though it hadn't even been released until the final week of the month. By the end of November, Nintendo had sold over 750,000 N64 consoles in the United States alone, making the N64 the fastest-selling system up to that point.

With the launch of the N64 behind it in Japan and North America, Nintendo focused on the future. In November, the company held its annual Shoshinkai show, which focused on the peripherals and software for the N64. A total of 38 games in various forms of development were displayed. Nintendo finally showed off its highly touted Bulky Drive, which was now officially called the *64DD*. The drive had a disk version of *Super Mario 64* playing on it, to prove that the loading time for the disk drive was minimal compared to the cartridge version.

The 64DD would also allow players to save and customize games. The information would be stored on a magnetic disk that would be slightly larger than a 3½" computer disk, and which would hold 64 megabytes of data. The disk would be inserted through a slot in the front of the drive, which would sit under the N64 in the same manner that the original Mega CD/Sega CD sat beneath the Mega Drive/Genesis. A memory expansion RAM pack that would be sold with the 64DD and would insert into the N64's memory expansion slot, providing the N64 with four additional megabytes of main memory that could be used by cartridges, disks or a combination of both. Nintendo announced that one of the first games that would use this *Expansion Pak* would be an N64 version of *The Legend of Zelda*. Perrin Kaplan, Nintendo's Director of Corporate Communications, announced at the show that the 64DD was scheduled to be released in Japan in late 1997.

Another new peripheral shown at Shoshinkai was a ¥1,400 ($13) "Jolt Pack", which plugged into the memory-card slot beneath the controller. It caused the controller to vibrate along with the action on the screen. Nintendo promised other types of controller-enhancement paks in the future, including one that would convert the controller into a light gun.

Keeping the 16-Bitters Alive

Nintendo had planned to close shop on its 16-bit console after the N64 caught on. This plan was curtailed after the 16-bit systems and corresponding software sold surprisingly better than expected during the Christmas 1995 season. This was attributed to the fact that many holiday shoppers found the newer 32-bit systems to be too expensive. Together, Nintendo and Sega sold four million 16-bit consoles, four times the number of 32-bit systems that had been sold. The unexpected demand for the older consoles was so gr that Nintendo and Sega were both caught off-guard and simply didn't have enough 16-bit systems to fill the need. Both companies claimed that they could have easily sold an additional 200,000 16-bit consoles if they had only been prepared. But they couldn't have known, since sales for both the SNES and Genesis had dropped dramatically in 1995 from prior years, signaling that their time was nearing a close. Nintendo of Japan had even been prepared to cut the price of the Super Famicom and its software by 23%, just so the cartridges would be cheaper than the N64 games when the latter became available. Nintendo of Japan had also decided to cut Super Famicom licensing fees by 30%.

One of the companies that benefitted from these lower fees was Bandai, a long-time Nintendo licensee that produced both software and peripherals. One such peripheral had been 1992's *Datach Joint-ROM System,* which connected inexpensive ROM cartridges with the Famicom. On June 28, Bandai released the *Sufami Turbo,* which was a similar-type device for the Super Famicom. The *Sufami Turbo* differed from the *Datach* in two respects. For one, it didn't feature the barcode reader. It also had two built-in cartridge slots so it could accept two ROM cartridges at a time. The main game was placed in the slot on the left side of the *Sufami Turbo* cartridge, and it could share data with a cartridge in the right slot.

Bandai Sufami Turbo

Although Sega of America's Genesis enjoyed an unexpectedly healthy Christmas season, its peripherals weren't as successful. Following the Christmas holidays, the company had officially announced that it would cease production of both the Sega CD and the 32X, so it could better concentrate on its other lines: the Saturn, Genesis and Pico. The retail price of the 32X was immediately slashed to $20, and the Sega CD was lowered to $50. Software for both systems was also heavily discounted.

Despite the surprising sales of the Genesis, the lower-than-expected Saturn sales forced Sega of America to lay off ten percent of its 400 employees at the beginning of February.

Someone had to take the fall for the Saturn's poor showing in the United States. Tom Kalinske, Sega of America's CEO, announced his resignation from the company on July 15, effective October 1. All sides claimed that Kalinske hadn't been forced out, and he even remained on Sega's board of directors. Kalinske was replaced by Shoichiro Irimajiri, a former CEO of Honda of America, who had been with Sega of America since 1993. In addition, Ted Hoff, who had formerly been the CEO of North American Operations with Atari, joined Sega of America as the executive vice-president in charge of sales and marketing. Bernie Stolar, who had previously been with SCEA and was a major player in the launch of the PlayStation, joined Sega of America as it new executive vice-president of product development.

SCEA was also going through major personnel changes. Martin Homlish, who had replaced Steve Race as the head SCEA, resigned early in the year after only five months on the job. Although Homlish left the computer division, he still stayed with Sony in a different capacity. He was replaced by Shigeo Maruyama, who also retained his former position as executive vice-president of Sony Computer Entertainment of Japan (SCEJ). At the same time, Olaf Olaffson, an SCEA technologist who had fought with Steve Race to keep the PlayStation's initial price at $299, also moved to another division within Sony.

In August, SCE removed all of its executive vice-presidents. While many critics viewed this managerial overhaul as an advanced tactic by SCE to prepare for its eventual battle against Nintendo, several Sony insiders admitted that this type of reshuffling was normal within the Sony empire.

Hit PlayStation Games

Gamers on both sides of the Pacific were in love with their PlayStations, but the titles that they had to choose from varied between Japan and North America. Most games were developed in Japan first and released in North America months later. Also, games from a particular region were only playable on the console from the same region.[3] However, American users discovered a special disc-swapping technique that allowed them to play Japanese games on older PlayStations. Electronics Boutique began a pilot program, wherein they sold two Japanese titles, *Ridge Racer Revolution* and *Battle Arena Toshinden 2,* in its American stores, despite the label on each game that read: "**For Sale and Use only in Japan.**" Even though the Japanese discs retailed for $89 each, the stores sold out of them as soon as they were available. The program only lasted a month, ending when SCEA pressured Electronics Boutique into concluding it. SCEA itself had been approached by third-party company Takara to ban the practice, since it had scheduled to release *Battle Arena Toshinden 2* in North America.

One PlayStation title that was a hit on both sides of the Pacific was a platform game called *Crash Bandicoot,* in which the player controlled a mutated marsupial who searched for his girlfriend, Tawna. This game, which was developed in the United States and released for the PlayStation on August 31, was raved by critics and gamers alike for its graphics and visual style. It was released in Japan on December 6, and became the first foreign-designed game to become a hit in that country, where it sold 500,000 copies.

SCE Crash Bandicoot

With *Crash Bandicoot,* SCE also obtained something that Nintendo and Sega had possessed for years; a mascot.

PlayStation Expo

The PlayStation became so popular that SCE decided to set up its own Shoshinkai-type exposition to highlight it. The *PlayStation Expo* was held in Japan in early November, shortly before Nintendo's Shoshinkai. Although it was a trade show, the three-day show was open to the general public, and gamers stood in line for nearly two hours to get in. In all, over 70,000 visitors attended the exposition for the chance to see new PlayStation software and hardware.

One piece of hardware that SCE planned to make available was a new PlayStation console. While this new unit resembled the old one on the outside, it contained fewer parts, which allowed SCE to increase its manufacturing output by thirty percent.

SCE also announced that it was going to release a special white version of the PlayStation in Taiwan and Singapore. The machine was completely compatible with the existing PlayStation that was available everywhere else, but it also had the extra ability to play full-motion VCDs, which were very popular in those countries. SCE planned to sell these white systems for $279.

SCE also displayed a new PlayStation controller that would include analog joysticks, which were already available on the N64. Also built-in was a biofeedback vibration feature that was similar to the optional N64 Jolt Pack, which hadn't yet been introduced. The new controller was scheduled to be released before the end of the year.

But this wouldn't be SCE's first foray into analog controllers. On April 25, SCE had released the ¥3,000 ($24) *Analog Joystick* in Japan and, shortly afterwards in the United States. But a gamer could not simply hold the Analog Joystick in his hands as he played as he could with the standard PlayStation controller. The controller was nearly as wide as the console itself.

The Analog Joystick looked as if it could be used in simulation games, and its two large sticks resembled the controls used in Coleco's 1977 *Telstar Combat* console. While the controller did have a digital mode, which could be used for all PlayStation games, the analog sticks were only compatible with a handful of games. This combination of a lack of compatible software, and its bulkiness, left the Analog Joystick rather unpopular.

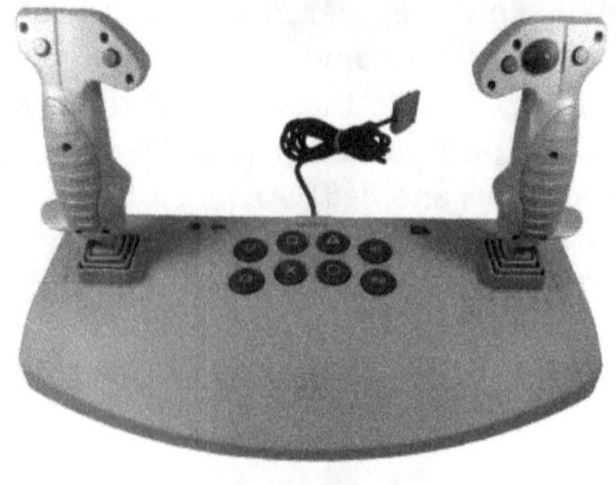

SCE Analog Joystick

Sega also released an analog controller for the Saturn. Its *3D Control Pad,* which came out on July 5, was bundled with the *Nights Into Dreams* game. The controller was round and resembled a CD player. While it featured the same six buttons and D-pad as a standard Saturn controller, it also had a separate analog thumbstick that was similar to the joystick nub that Atari had added to the D-pad of the European 7800's Gamepad controller. Despite its non-conservative shape, the 3D Control Pad was found to be very comfortable and responsive by most of the gamers who used it. Unfortunately, it wasn't enough to make people run out and buy Saturns.

Sega Saturn 3D Controller

The End of Home Atari

Sega was not the only videogame company that was having problems and laying off employees. Atari Corp., which had cut the price on the Jaguar to $99 right before the Christmas 1995 holiday, now struggled to keep its credibility. Following the layoffs of twenty essential Jaguar game designers, Atari announced that development for Jaguar games would continue as usual. When Ted Hoff, Atari's CEO of North American Operations, left the company on January 18 to join Sega of America, he remarked that he couldn't see how Atari could function in the game business in the state that it was in. Atari dismissed his statements by saying that they had been in the game business long before Hoff had joined the company, and that they could continue well enough without him. While sources within the company indicated that the Jaguar was no longer being manufactured, Atari's official position was that it would still support the Jaguar and Atari Interactive, its new line of computer software that had been launched in January. However, financial papers that had been released to stockholders confirmed that new Jaguars hadn't been manufactured since the summer of 1995.

Following this revelation from Atari, there was an eerie silence from the company, reminiscent of 1984, after Jack Tramiel had taken over the company. Reports soon came out of Sunnyvale that the company was operating with a skeleton staff and was about to exit the videogame business. The company didn't release any statements to refute this.

Atari announced on February 13 that it had merged with JTS Corp., a manufacturer of computer hard drives. The company had been founded in 1994 by Jugi Tandon, the inventor of the double-sided floppy disk drive, and Tom Mitchell, a co-founder of Seagate, a leading manufacturer of hard drives. The intent of the company was to develop a new

3″ drive for laptops.

Although JTS had good products to sell, it didn't have much capital to stay afloat. Atari, on the other hand, had money, but its products were selling poorly. Although Atari injected $25 million into JTS, and Jack Tramiel gained a seat on JTS' board of directors, the once mighty Atari became a mere subsidiary of the disk-drive company.

After the merger was finalized on July 30, JTS announced that it planned to allow Atari to continue as a wholly owned subsidiary. But within weeks of this announcement, the majority of the remaining Atari employees were let go and the company's inventory was sold off to liquidators.

The End of the 3DO

Had it not been for the collapse of Atari, few would have paid attention to the Jaguar's demise. However, the Jaguar was not the only console that died in 1996.

Following the Christmas 1995 price slash of its 3DO player, Goldstar decided to exit from the game business. It cited that when its 3DO player was $199, it had lost $100 on every one sold. It was common for manufacturers to lose money on their hardware, because they usually recouped the loss with the software. However, Goldstar claimed that it was unable to do this, because it had entered the software market too late to gain a foothold against the other 3DO developers.

Another reason that Goldstar decided to get out was due to the sale of the M2 technology to Matsushita, which claimed that the M2 upgrade would not be compatible with the Goldstar machine. Panasonic, the division of Matsushita that manufactured the 3DO console, announced a drop in the price of its 3DO player to $199 to match Goldstar's. Most critics viewed this price decrease as a sign that Panasonic was planning to dump its 32-bit player. By April 1996, sales for 3DO players were well behind those of the PlayStation and Saturn. Developers for 3DO games saw the writing on the wall and stopped developing games for the system. Even Studio 3DO, the software division of the 3DO Company, announced that it wouldn't develop any more 3DO games. The only company that continued to release 3DO software was Panasonic itself.

The final nail in the 3DO's coffin came at the end of 1996, when Electronics Boutique began selling off its stock of Panasonic 3DO players for $99. The end of the 3DO had come, allowing Panasonic and Matsushita to direct all of their energy to the development of the M2.

Matsushita had discussions with Konami for the use of the M2 technology. In February, the two companies signed a deal whereby Konami would use the 3DO technology in its arcade games. These games in turn would be converted for the home M2 console. Konami expected to have its first M2 game available in the arcades by the end of the year.

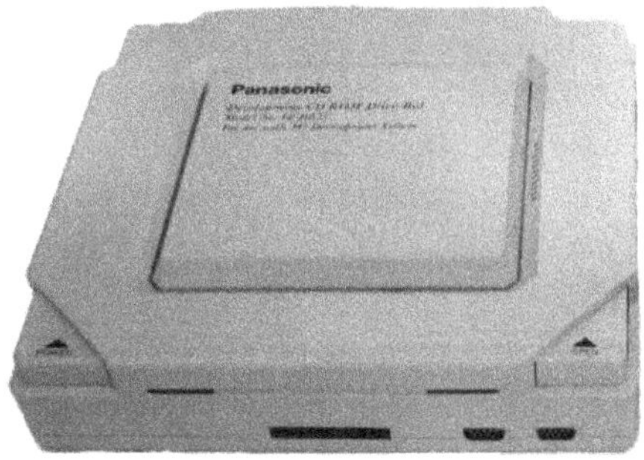

Panasonic M2

Through 1996, the M2 became one of the most secretive videogame projects ever. The Japanese newspaper, *Yomiuri Shimbun,* reported early in the year that Sega and Matsushita were going to join forces, but neither company confirmed this. Actually, there had been rumors long before Matsushita acquired the rights to the M2 that Sega and the 3DO Company had reached an agreement where Sega would use the M2 technology. The 3DO Company wanted to publicize this news quickly, in the hope that it would generate interest in its staggering stock. Sega, on the other hand, didn't want it to be made public until after Christmas, so that the holiday sales of the Saturn wouldn't be jeopardized.

As reported by *Yomiuri Shimbun,* Sega had wanted to join forces with Matsushita to create a new M2-based, 64-bit game console to compete directly with the N64. Although Sega and Matsushita both denied this news, it was revealed that Sega of Japan had possession of a prototype M2 system for "feasibility studies." Sega's vision was that it would be the exclusive distributor of the console that would display its brand name, and that the console would be manufactured by Matsushita. But Matsushita wanted a 3DO-type game console that would be sold by many companies. Another reason why Sega backed away from the talks was because its technicians apparently weren't truly impressed with the M2 technology. Because of these issues, the unofficial talks came to a real end by the summer, which allowed Matsushita to claim the prize for $100 million.

There was little news from Matsushita concerning the M2 following the breakdown of its talks with Sega. Matsushita and Panasonic ceased developing games for the new platform, while Studio 3DO and Interplay continued to do so. However, just when people began to believe that the M2 would never see the light of day, Matsushita suddenly announced the system's specifications.

The word from Tokyo was that the M2 would incorporate two of the 3DO Company's custom chips, rather than one as had been previously disclosed. This would provide the M2 with the power to generate over one million polygons per second, more than double that of the PlayStation. The system would also include a 4x-speed CD-ROM player.

However, this news only brought more questions. Panasonic's official line was still that there would be an M2 upgrade for the existing 3DO console. But how could that be possible if the new system was going to have a 4x-speed CD-ROM player and two custom chips? And since these chips cost $150 each, how did Matsushita expect to release the M2 console for under $300? Many critics speculated that the company would simply sit back and wait for the price of the chips to plummet. But if that was Matsushita's intention, how long could it afford to wait? Interplay, which had been developing an M2 game called *Clayfighter 3*, couldn't afford to wait any longer. It abandoned its M2 game design and focused its energies into developing N64 software.[4]

Meanwhile, Matsushita created a new division called Panasonic Wondertainment to develop games for the M2. By the end of the summer, Matsushita announced that it would display the console at the new E³ in Tokyo in the fall, in anticipation of releasing the console in Japan during spring 1997, and in the United States the following fall. Matsushita expected to sell three million M2 consoles during its first year.

The Japanese E³ came, and Matsushita did not display the M2 consoles as it had planned, although the company affirmed that the new system was still on track for release during the first half of 1997. Another promise from Matsushita was reversed shortly afterwards, when the company announced that the new 64-bit system would not be backward compatible with the 3DO after all. Still, despite the broken promises from Matsushita, most believed that the console would eventually arrive. After all, everyone knew that the world's largest consumer-electronics company wouldn't make a $100 million investment and then just abandon it.

More Consoles Begin To Fall

If Matsushita was deciding to abandon the M2, it was in good company. The future of SNK's Neo•Geo was also in question. Although the elite system, which had always been more expensive than others, was able to play arcade-quality games, the dividing line between arcade and home games became narrower as newer and newer 32- and 64-bit systems arrived. While SNK didn't publicly announce any intentions to faze out the Neo•Geo, the company quietly returned to the role that it had before it had introduced the console: developing games for competing systems, including the Saturn and PlayStation. The Saturn version of one planned SNK game, *King of Fighters '95*, was to utilize both a CD and a cartridge. By mid-year, SNK had developed a cartridge that boosted the Saturn's memory by 1 meg and reduced any applicable game's loading time. The downside was that this memory cartridge only worked with games that were specifically designed for it.

With all the third-party work that SNK was doing, many analysts wondered what it meant for the future of the Neo•Geo. However, SNK continued to support its own player throughout 1996.

In the late summer, Philips officially announced that it was abandoning its CD-i after having lost over one billion dollars on the system since its introduction in 1991. Philips downplayed the announcement by stating that it would incorporate the CD-i into a forthcoming DVD system.

From its inception, one of the problems with the CD-i was the fact that Philips didn't want to label it as a game machine. By typecasting it as a "multimedia device," Philips lost out on many consumers who only wanted to purchase videogame consoles.

Pippin Hits America

As Philips closed up shop on its multimedia system, Apple Computers was eager to fill its place. On March 13, Apple and Bandai demonstrated the Pippin @WORLD console in New York, in order to recruit software developers. Bandai finally released the console in North America on September 1 to a lackluster reception. While the system could play decent games, Apple fell short of calling it a game console and emphasized its ability to access the Internet and play multimedia CD-ROMs, features that were available on computers costing thousands of dollars. But the truth was that the @WORLD was a console, and with its $600 price tag, and lack of dedicated graphics chips, it simply couldn't compete against the PlayStation and Saturn. Bandai would only release 18 titles for the @WORLD, as opposed to the 80 titles that it had released for the ATMARK in Japan. But both systems were doomed. After selling only 42,000 units in North America, Bandai returned the unsold black consoles to Japan, where they were offered for sale as ATMARKs.[5]

Internet Gaming

Apple's original plan for the Pippin was to market it as an inexpensive way for people to get onto the Internet without forcing them to purchase expensive computers. Unfortunately, by the time the console was released in the United States, consumers already had alternatives. One of the first companies to actually get such a product into stores was Philips, which in late summer released a $329 box that hooked up to standard television sets and provided World Wide Web and email capabilities. Sony Electronics followed a month later with a similar $350 Internet box that could hook up to a television. However, many retailers that these Internet boxes couldn't be true mass market items until they were priced under $200.

In both cases, this connection was made via the standard audio/video or RF connections. It also hooked up to a phone jack, because it used a high-speed internal modem and the phone to send and receive data. The box automatically dialed up and connected with an Internet service provider called *WebTV*.

WebTV was the first company to provide Internet connections to TV set-top Internet boxes, but other companies were quick to join the fray. Netscape, the company that provided the number-one Web Browser for computer users, formed a new company called Navio Communications to utilize its Netscape browser for emerging platforms other than standard computers. Nintendo, SCE and Sega all signed up to the new company, although nobody was exactly sure how they were going to incorporate the Internet into their game machines. Nintendo had vague plans to use an Internet gateway with its forthcoming 64DD storage drive, even though the system hadn't been designed with an internal modem.

Sega Saturn Modem

Sega Saturn Keyboard

Sega Shuttle Mouse

Sega Saturn Floppy Drive

Sony, which had released its WebTV Internet box as a stand-alone unit, had no plans to incorporate the technology into the PlayStation. Its goal was to provide Internet access to everyone, not just videogamers. Sega decided to go another route.

On July 27, Sega of Japan surprised everyone and released the ¥16,125 ($150) *Saturn Modem*. This was a 14.4-baud modem cartridge that plugged into the Saturn cartridge port and featured a slot where special Sega game credit cards, which were needed to set up Internet provider accounts, could be inserted. A CD containing Web browser software was also provided with the modem. In order to 'type' into the browser, a Saturn controller was required to move an arrow around an on-screen keyboard. Fortunately for those who found this method very tedious, Sega also offered an optional *Saturn Keyboard*, as well as an optional *Shuttle Mouse*.[6]

The system had been designed to merely browse the Web or send email. Little provision had been made for receiving and saving email. The Saturn had only 500K of RAM in which it could store downloaded data, but this, of course, was lost the moment the power was turned off.[7] To alleviate this problem, Sega of Japan also released a ¥9,800 ($90) *Saturn Floppy Drive* that connected to the Saturn's rear extension communication terminal. The drive utilized standard 3.5" computer discs that could store 1.44MB of data, more than twice the amount that could be saved on the Saturn Backup Memory cartridge. The floppy drive had been designed to be used instead of the console's internal memory. Unfortunately, it could only be used by games that specifically supported it, and there were only a few of those.

One item that the Saturn lacked was a professional printer to print out emails. However, software manufacturer Koei, offered the ¥29,800 ($275) *Saturn Word Processor* set, which included a word processing program called EGWORD, a Canon printer, and an interface cable that connected the printer to the console. However, since most people couldn't print out their emails, they had to be read from the television screen, which was problematic. Computer Internet browsers had been designed to display text and graphics on high-resolution computer monitors.

Designers of videogame browsers faced the problem that the console might occasionally be hooked up to a low-resolution TV set. A browser called *Planet Web* was designed for the Saturn, with a display that would look good on any TV or monitor.

Sega of America released a $200 *NetLink* modem on October 31. The Netlink transferred data at 28.8 megabits per second, twice the speed of its Japanese sibling. It was also missing the credit-card slot that was found in the Sega Saturn Modem since credits were not needed to play games online in the United States. Sega hoped to sell 100,000 NetLinks in time for Christmas. In order to make the idea of surfing the Internet even more desirable, Sega planned a number of online games that would allow gamers from around the country to compete against each other in real time.

Sega NetLink

Sega of America did not offer an actual Saturn-compatible keyboard to accompany the modem, as Sega of Japan had done. Instead, it sold a $20 *NetLink Keyboard Adapter*, which was used to connect any standard PC PS/2 keyboard to the console. A *NetLink Keyboard* was also available, but it was only sold as part of a NetLink bundle, and was not available separately. However, it was nothing more than a Sega-branded PS/2 keyboard that still needed the NetLink Keyboard Adapter to connect it. Sega of America also offered a $25 *NetLink Mouse* but it was the same as Japanese Shuttle Mouse.

Sega NetLink Keyboard with Adapter

The design of the NetLink modem was a team effort by Sega and two other companies: Nisho Iwai and Catapult. Because of Catapult's involvement, it had been widely assumed that the XBand Network would be utilized for the Saturn's venture into online gaming. Unlike the 16-bit version of XBand, on which gamers could only compete against players with the same console, the Saturn version was supposed to allow players to compete across platform lines. Unfortunately, not all games could be played from different consoles since the software had to be custom-written for each console to incorporate the online features.

One of the new platforms that Catapult was designing its network for was the PC. In addition to games, the XBand PC would also offer chat rooms and other online conveniences that were found on other services, such as America Online.

The Saturn Cartridge Slot

The Saturn modems plugged into the Saturn's cartridge slot. This was appropriate since no one expected cartridge-based games on a disc-based console. Discs held more game data and were cheaper to manufacture and therefore less expensive than cartridges. On the other hand, data loaded from cartridges more quickly than from discs. On March 28, SNK released a game that used both.

The bulk of the *King of Fighters '95* code resided on the disc. However, to save time, data that needed to be accessed frequently was stored on a ROM cartridge that was packaged with the CD. However, there was a price for this efficiency. The game retailed for ¥7,800 ($73), much higher than other Saturn games.[8]

On September 20, Sega of Japan released a cartridge that expanded the amount of work RAM that the Saturn used. The ¥5,800 ($53) *Extended RAM Cartridge* plugged into

Sega Saturn ROM Cartridge ***Sega Extended RAM Cartridge***

the cartridge slot and provided an additional 1MB of random access memory. With this extra RAM, developers were able to create more extensive games that used additional data and save data that needed to be accessed frequently on the cartridge. The Extended RAM Cartridge was similar to the N64's Expansion Pak. However, on the N64, games could be saved to the Controller Pak even when the Expansion Pak was in use. This could not be done on the Saturn as the Extended RAM Cartridge shared the same cartridge port at the Saturn Backup Memory cartridge.[9]

The Extended RAM Cartridge eliminated the need for a Saturn game to be released on a ROM cartridge since it did pretty much the same thing. Only one more game that used a ROM cartridge was released for the Japanese Saturn, since it had been completed before the release of the Extended RAM Cartridge.[10]

24

Arcades Hit Hard Times

Arcade game developers were also eyeing the Internet. On August 22, Aristo International displayed its first arcade games that incorporated Internet technology.

Aristo's plan had been to be a leader in the out-of-home Internet market, and it had the personnel behind it to do so. While Aristo was a name that few people had ever heard of, the company had as its Director of Strategic Planning someone who was well known to all in the videogaming community: Nolan Bushnell.

Aristo had developed a line of arcade sports machines called *TeamNet*, on which teams of four players at one location competed against teams at other locations via the Internet. The first four *TeamNet* games available were hockey, air hockey, soccer and football. Aristo also released a series of arcade games that were designed to be played online by a single person. The *TouchNet* machines offered solitaire games as well as chat rooms and were targeted for bars and restaurants, as well as standard videogame arcades.

As the Aristo games were targeted to adult audiences, another company planned to enter the arcade arena with videogames designed for children. The company was Mattel Media, a new division of Mattel. Mattel Media planned to produce PC and arcade games that were based on its well-known toys, such as Hot Wheels.

Although the introduction of new companies entering the arcade foray was always a good thing, the truth was that the arcade industry was going through a very unstable time. Taito, the company that had produced *Space Invaders*, announced early in the year that it would close its American offices. At the same time, the company signed a deal with Acclaim, allowing the latter to produce home versions of Taito's new arcade games. So while the home versions of these games would be sold in the United States thanks to the Acclaim deal, the arcade games that they would be based on wouldn't, because Taito no longer had an American distributor to import them into the country.

American Laser Games announced that it was leaving the arcade business so it could devote its energies to producing Saturn and PlayStation games. When that didn't pan out, the company switched gears again and announced that it would concentrate solely on computer games for girls.

In March, Time Warner also decided that it was time to abandon the arcade business, and sold its Time Warner Interactive subsidiary to WMS Industries. Atari Games, which was the arcade division of Time Warner Interactive, was included in the sale. WMS Industries retained the Atari Games name, and it became a separate arcade division under the WMS umbrella.

Videogame companies weren't the only arcade companies that were suffering. In late summer, Gottlieb announced that it was closing its doors. Although Gottlieb had had videogame hits such as *Q*Bert,* its reputation as a pinball company went back decades. However, the extreme fall in pinball sales forced the closure, leaving Williams and Data East Pinball as the sole pinball companies.

Fortunately, the entire arcade industry was not falling on hard times; many companies were beginning to prosper again. Several Japanese companies all reported that they were doing better in 1996 than in prior years. Sega's coin-op sales were up 29.1% worldwide, while Namco's were up 31.2%. Although Tecmo was still in the red in 1996, its overall losses were lower than they had been during the preceding few years. Jaleco Limited and Konami reported profits for fiscal 1995 after several money-losing years. Things were going so well for Konami that the company was able to sign a deal with Matsushita to develop M2-based arcade games.

Home Software Shutdowns

Some third-party developers of console games were also going through hard times. In the late spring, Squaresoft USA, which had been based in Redmond, Washington, announced that it would be closing its doors. However, its Japanese parent, Square of Japan, disclosed that although it was shutting down its Squaresoft USA division, it would still maintain its U.S. office in Los Angeles. This news was followed a month later by the announcement that JVC would close its software-development division. Data East announced late in the year that it would also close down its home-game division in the United States. Mindscape followed with similar news. Although the veteran software company wouldn't close its doors, it had to lay off twelve game designers in an effort to cut costs.

Acclaim also had to lay off employees. After a 40% drop in sales of its cartridge-based games, the company decided to leave the 16-bit cartridge-based business altogether and concentrate solely on CD-based and N64 games. Unfortunately, this decision didn't turn Acclaim's fortunes around quickly enough, and seventy employees had to be let go. None of them had been involved in game design, and Acclaim downplayed the news by announcing that thirty new games would be available in the following months.

One other company announced that it would be leaving the software business, and its reasons had nothing to do with financial problems. That company was SCE.

In May 1993, SCE had purchased Psygnosis, a British designer of Genesis games, for less than $30 million. When SCE began working on the PlayStation, Psygnosis switched gears and began developing games exclusively for the PlayStation, producing hit games such as *Wipeout* and *Destruction Derby.*

In early 1996, Psygnosis announced that it would begin releasing games for the Saturn, as well as any other popular console. Critics questioned why corporate Sony agreed to this, since the PlayStation had an advantage with popular, exclusive games.

It became apparent in late May when Sony announced that it was putting the software company up for bids that SCE was not happy with Psygnosis' move to offer games for competing systems. Before long, bids came in from top software companies, such as

Acclaim and Electronic Arts.

Initial reports suggested that the bidding had reached $300 million, but this wasn't quite accurate. Actually, SCE sought $300 million for the company, an amount nobody was willing to pay. In the end, SCE decided not to sell Psygnosis after all, and the software company was free to release software for competing systems as it had intended.

In a similar move, SegaSoft announced that it would produce PlayStation games. Although Sega of America officials were concerned about this, SegaSoft officials explained that they were independent from other Sega divisions and could produce software for any system they wanted. An investigation by *Next Generation* seemed to prove this statement correct. It revealed that SegaSoft was only 40% owned by Sega, and that the remaining 60% belonged to CSK Corporation. SegaSoft had a responsibility to all of its stockholders to make money in any way possible.

However, further investigation by *Next Generation* uncovered more. Apparently, Sega itself had been owned by CSK since 1984, so SegaSoft wasn't as independent from Sega as its executives wanted people to believe.

As SegaSoft entered PlayStation territory, many people felt that Sega was abandoning the Saturn in favor of commercially safer systems. However, the Saturn enjoyed healthy sales in Japan and Europe, so Sega wasn't about to jump ship on its console. In addition, Sega wouldn't allow any of its exclusive licenses to be available on the PlayStation.

Along with developing games for the PlayStation, Sega also began converting its popular arcade and home games to PCs using Microsoft's *Windows 95* operating system. *Sega Entertainment* was established on March 29 as a joint venture between Sega Enterprises and Softbank, the largest distributor of software in Japan, for this purpose. The company released its first game later in the year. *Sonic CD* marked the first time that Sega's popular hedgehog appeared on a personal computer.

If anyone was really worried that Sega was abandoning its Saturn, all he had to do was check into a Japanese hotel and turn on the TV. In the summer, Sega and Toshiba joined together to deliver Saturn games to hotel rooms. Sega announced that seven Saturn titles would be available initially and 40 more would follow.

Sega Subsidiaries

The deal with Toshiba was proof that Sega's home videogame division was branching into newer territories. However, there were several divisions of the company that had nothing to do with videogames. The Sega Foundation, for example, donated $250,000 to start a new multimedia learning center in Los Angeles. The money was used to purchase computers that would provide underprivileged people with exposure to the Internet and other high-tech applications.

Sega continued with its plans to develop interactive theme parks with MCA and DreamWorks SKG. The new entertainment centers would fall under a new division called *Sega Gameworks.*

The Sega Gameworks theme parks were based on the Joyopolis theme park in Tokyo. Sega also built similar parks in London and Toronto under the *Segaworld* name, although these weren't merely vessels for Sega to unveil new, expensive arcade games. London's Segaworld featured six virtual reality rides that had cost Sega nearly one billion dollars to develop. Unlike rides at Walt Disney World and other theme parks, Segaworld's interactive rides were unique, and the company promised that no two visits to any of the attractions would ever be the same. On several of the rides, visitors got to wear Mega Visor Displays that projected a virtual reality image to the wearers. The display changed as the wearer looked in different directions.

Sega scheduled to build the first US Sega Gameworks parks in late 1996 in Seattle and Las Vegas. However, Americans received their first glimpse of what Sega Gameworks had to offer early in the year, when Sega opened its *Sega City* center in Irvine, California. While Sega City didn't offer the rides that would be available in the larger parks, it did offer state-of-the-art, "deluxe" arcade machines. While most of the games were known to frequent arcaders, they were presented in new and exciting ways. For instance, gamers playing *Sega Rally* could sit in an imitation racing car that would tilt and shake according to what was happening on-screen. In addition, Sega City was not restricted to carrying only Sega arcade machines. Parents accepted the park because it didn't resemble a standard arcade. The decor was well lit, and "Game Specialists" monitored the floor to make sure gamers understood the games that they were playing.

As Sega continued to diversify, the summer brought an announcement that Sega Gameworks had teamed up with the Cineplex Odeon movie chain to open a string of entertainment centers called *Cinescape*, which would adjoin the movie theaters. The Cinescape centers would feature state-of-the art arcade games, Internet stations, and bars and restaurants. They would be based in Canada, and the first one was planned to open in 2000.

In October, Sega of Japan released the *Digio*, a digital camera that was priced at $270, $100 less than its nearest competitors. The images that were taken by the camera were available immediately after downloading them to a computer, on which they could be manipulated and printed. For those who didn't own computers, Sega planned to set up service areas in its arcades and theme parks where the downloading and printing could be done.

Another new product that Sega planned to release in Asia was a stand-alone called *TV-Mail*. This console would allow young children to electronically write and draw on the TV screen, and to send and receive email and faxes.

Videogame Museums

Although the Sega Gameworks theme parks were great places to showcase brand new arcade games, many people still yearned for the old classic games that were slowly disappearing from arcades. The National Videogame and Coin-Op Museum in St. Louis seemed like the ideal place for people to find the machines that they were nostalgic for. Unfortunately, after five years, the museum closed its doors in 1996, due to a lack of money and a lack of general interest in the exhibit.

While the museum was a good idea, there was one basic problem with it. It was located in St. Louis, and few people were willing to travel there just to see videogame history. They would, on the other hand, go to an exhibit on videogames if it were to travel to their locality instead. This was the concept behind the Electronics Conservancy's *Videotopia*.

Videotopia was a traveling museum exhibit that opened at the Carnegie Science Center in Pittsburgh on June 15 (exactly five years after the National Videogame and Coin-Op Museum had opened) for a three-month run. With Nolan Bushnell and Eugene Jarvis (the creator of *Defender*) among its list of advisors, the exhibit's "Ultimate Arcade" displayed most of the classic arcade machines, from *Computer Space* and *Pong* to new, emerging classics like *Alpine Racer* and *Daytona USA*. All were available for play. Each machine was captioned with its particular history, along with American events that had occurred during the particular machine's heyday.

Videotopia not only provided a place where people could play games, but it also served to educate people about videogames. One exhibit displayed the technology behind videogame controllers. There was also a playable *Pole Position II* that had much of its cabinet replaced by Plexiglas, so visitors could view the inside of an arcade machine. Scattered around the exhibit were "Power-Up Stations," where visitors could answer questions about videogame history and be rewarded with game tokens for correct responses.

Videotopia featured more than the arcade side of the industry. Most of the home game consoles from the Odyssey through the Virtual Boy were on display, alongside their individual printed histories.[11]

DigiPen

Museums like Videotopia weren't the only places where people went to learn about videogames. They also went to more traditional places such as schools.

As videogames continued to grow more sophisticated, it was only a matter time before schools began adding classes in videogame history and design. In 1988, Claude Comair had founded DigiPen Corporation, a software house located in Vancouver, which specialized in computer simulation and animation. In 1990, because the company was having a hard time finding qualified designers, Comair decided to offer a dedicated training program in 3D computer animation. By the end of that year, the company partnered with Nintendo of America to establish a program for people who were interested in programming videogames as a career. The DigiPen Applied Computer Graphics School opened in 1994, with a two-year program that provided a degree in the "Art and Science of 2D and 3D Video Game Programming." Finally, in May 1996, after the Washington State Higher Education Coordinating Board granted the school accreditation to award associate and bachelor degrees, DigiPen became the first university in the world dedicated to computer and videogame development.

Rappers and Raiders

As younger gamers in Japan spent the year getting to know 151 new characters, older male gamers in Europe and North America were getting familiar with one new female character.

Lara Croft was a British archaeologist who starred in a new game from Eidos Interactive called *Tomb Raider*. She was intelligent, athletic, and, most importantly, beautiful, with physical attributes that made many players forget that they were looking at a videogame.

Eidos Tomb Raider

Lara Croft could do things that Mario simply couldn't, including carrying and firing guns. And while many players didn't fantasize that they were the on-screen character, they sure wished they were with her in her adventures. Although there had been many female videogame characters prior to Lara Croft, she arguably became the most culturally iconic one since Ms. Pac-Man.

Lara Croft's appearance in *Tomb Raider* helped make the game a blockbuster, but *Tomb Raider* didn't become successful simply because of Lara Croft. It also advanced the 3D platform that had been made popular by *Super Mario 64*, which was only available for the N64. Although *Tomb Raider* wasn't available for the N64, there were versions for the PlayStation, Saturn and PC (and later, the Mac), with the PlayStation being the one that really took off, and eventually helped SCE sell more consoles.

But *Tomb Raider* was not the sole reason people purchased PlayStations. In March, Capcom released *Resident Evil* exclusively for the PlayStation. *Resident Evil* was somewhat similar to *Tomb Raider*, as the player controlled an on-screen (male) character through a 3D world, in this case a haunted house. As in *Tomb Raider*, the player had to solve a number of puzzles while avoiding unsavory characters. However, in *Resident Evil*, players didn't have as many weapons at their disposal as Lara Croft had. And inspired by horror fiction, the game was outright scary. *Resident Evil* spawned a new sub-genre, the survival-horror game.[12] By the end of September, over one million copies of the PlayStation version had been sold.

Tomb Raider and *Resident Evil* were new games that became megahits and would produce several sequels. But even titles in established series were finding their ways exclusively to the PlayStation. In January, developer Square announced that the latest installment in its *Final Fantasy* series, *Final Fantasy VII,* would be released only for the PlayStation. The game had originally been intended for the SNES, but was moved to the N64 after Nintendo announced that machine. But because the N64's cartridges lacked the required storage space needed for *Final Fantasy VII,* Square went on to develop the game for a CD-based system.[13]

And while Square was preparing to introduce the *Final Fantasy* franchise to a new platform, SCEJ used the PlayStation to introduce *PaRappa the Rapper*, along with an entirely new gaming genre.

PaRappa the Rapper was basically an animated MTV video. In it, a dog named Parappa rapped and danced in order to win the love of Sunny Funny. Meanwhile, a small icon scrolled across the top of the screen, passing over the symbols that were found on the PlayStation controller. The object of the game was to press the correct corresponding buttons at the correct time. If the player couldn't keep up with the beat, then he would be rewarded with a POOR rating. Keeping up with the beat guaranteed a GOOD rating.

SCE PaRappa the Rapper

The genre started by *Parappa the Rapper* was called *rhythm game* or *rhythm action.* While there certainly had been prior games in which the player had to repeat on-screen sequences, never before had the element of rhythm been required.[14]

Pocket Monsters

Another new genre debuted on the Game Boy in Japan on February 27, which helped to affirm the portable console's longevity. *Pocket Monsters* was basically a modern take-off on the children's game "Rock, Paper, Scissors." Gamers assumed the roles of trainers who used their Game Boys to search and collect as many of the 151 different creatures as possible. Since some Pocket Monsters were harder to find than others, gamers could trade captured monsters with their friends by connecting two Game Boys via the video-link cables. Trading was essential, since Nintendo marketed the games on two separate cartridges: *Pocket Monsters Green* and *Pocket Monsters Red.* While the two games were basically the same, only half of the *Pocket Monsters* species could be found in either set, so in order for a gamer to collect all of them, he either had to purchase both cartridges, or trade *Pocket Monsters* with his friends.

Nintendo of Japan released a third *Pocket Monsters* set on October 15. *Pocket Monsters Blue* was available only by mail-order to subscribers of the *CoroCoro,* a popular Manga comic book that had been around for nearly twenty years. *Pocket Monsters Blue* featured updated artwork and new dialogue, and incorporated most of the monsters that were available in both *Pocket Monsters Red* and *Pocket Monsters Green.* However, a few were left out of the blue release to keep them exclusive.

Nintendo Pocket Monsters Red & Green

FOCUS ON SATOSHI TAJIRI

Before December 1997, few people outside of Japan heard of Pocket Monsters. However after the December 16 broadcast of a Pocket Monsters anime (a form of Japanese animation) that left 650 children suffering from epileptic seizures, the world learned quickly about Pocket Monsters. The seizures had been caused by excessive flashing on the TV screen and the anime's production crew quickly made sure that such a problem would never happen again.

Pocket Monsters were the brainchildren of Satoshi Tajiri. The collection of 150 creatures were inspired by Tajiri's childhood hobbies: watching Godzilla movies on Japanese television and catching insects, which he placed in jars where they battled each other as if they were the Japanese monsters that he worshipped.

Another love of Tajiri's was videogames. After getting hooked on *Space Invaders* in 1978, Tajiri was dismayed because he couldn't find enough information about videogames in the media. To fill the gap he created his own fanzine, *Game Freak*. By the time he was eighteen, Game Freak had a circulation of 10,000 copies and was a true magazine with each issue being printed, rather than photocopied. By that time the magazine also had other writers besides Tajiri and the group would get together and talk about games. The conclusion was that the then-current crop of games weren't very good so they decided to design their own. Game Freak then went from being a magazine to being a game design company. This wasn't just a whim on Tajiri's part. When he was sixteen he won a contest for a game idea that Sega had sponsored. He then spent two years learning how to program and then another year programming his first game, *Quinty*.

From the beginning Tajiri wanted to create a world where monsters could be caught and trained to battle other monsters. After Nintendo first released the Game Boy in 1989, Tajiri saw it as the perfect vehicle for his game to play on. He then spent the next six years designing and developing his idea. The result was Pocket Monsters, which Nintendo released on two separate cartridges in 1996. The games sold four million copies and broke all sorts of records.

Pocket Monsters brought new life to Nintendo's seven year old Game Boy and spawned an entire industry that included trading cards, toys, and, of course, the hit anime that introduced them to the world outside of Japan.

The combination of the three sets made *Pocket Monsters* the number-one Japanese console game released in 1996, and the only Game Boy title in the Top 30. Plans were made to release the sets in the United States and elsewhere. Unfortunately, this would prove to be a larger task than the developers anticipated. First, each of the individual monsters had to be renamed for Western audiences, based on their appearance and characteristics. Afterwards, Nintendo trademarked each of these 151 new names, to be sure that they were unique. When it came time to translate the text from Japanese to English, programmers discovered that the code was so delicate that they couldn't simply change the text in the source code. Each game had to be completely rewritten. This would be a lengthy process, so *Pocket Monsters* wouldn't be available in the United States until 1998.

Pikachu Pocket Monster Playing Card

Pocket Monsters could also be traded without a Game Boy. In October, a Pocket Monsters trading card game was distributed in Japan. Like everything else connected to the Pocket Monsters, the trading card game was a major success.

Game Boy Pocket

Pocket Monsters was a welcome and much needed hit for the aging Game Boy. Sales of the seven-year old handheld had been declining, and Nintendo had been seeking ways to expand its lifespan. The way they had decided to do so was by redesigning it as a smaller and more efficient unit that contained fewer components and was less expensive to manufacture and sell.

The *Game Boy Pocket* was much slimmer than the original, and just a bit thicker than the cartridge that was inserted into it. The screen on the new machine was the same size as the original, but it had been redesigned and was easier on the eyes. Most notable was the screen that had a true black and white display, instead of the greenish-grey of the original. It also consumed less power. The Game Boy Pocket only used two AAA batteries, whereas the original needed four AA batteries. Nintendo of Japan released the new ¥6,800 ($63) Game Boy Pocket in nine colors on July 21, 1996. Nintendo of America followed suit with a $60 unit in seven colors on September 3.[15]

Nintendo Game Boy & Game Boy Pocket

Even as Nintendo publicized its new Game Boy Pocket, the company was quietly developing a system that would replace it. In March, rumors began leaking that Nintendo was working on Project Atlantis, a handheld system with a 3-by-2 inch LCD color screen that would not be compatible with any other system. Nintendo verified the rumors when it publicly announced that RISC Machines (ARM), a British company, had been contracted to develop the system. Among the requirements was a custom chip that would have batteries last 30 hours.

Initially, Nintendo had hoped to release the new portable in at least one territory by the end of the year. However, after Nintendo saw that the new Game Boy Pocket's sales were much higher than had been anticipated, the company decided to push back the release of the color portable until the Game Boy Pocket's sales began to slow down. Nintendo estimated that this could take as long as two years, so a new tentative date for the color portable was set for Christmas, 1997. Meanwhile, at least one specification was changed along with the new release date. The battery life of the machine was reduced dramatically to eight hours.

Tiger Super Screen

While Nintendo's color portable was delayed, Tiger Electronics released their own, which sold for only $30. Actually, the system that Tiger launched was similar to the R-Zone projector that it had released in 1995. The *Super Screen* was a handheld unit that used the same R-Zone cartridges and displayed them on a large, magnified screen. Tiger announced another model called the *Data Zone*, which, although it would never actually be released, would combine the Super Screen with a planner-like data organizer.

Tiger R-Zone Super Screen

Gunpei Yokoi's Folly

The success of the Game Boy Pocket was a refreshing surprise to Nintendo executives. They needed this triumph to compensate for the failure of their other stand-alone unit, the Virtual Boy, which had been released in late 1995 to an unenthusiastic marketplace. Many of those who had bought the stand-alone unit suffered from headaches following just a single gaming session. Parents were reluctant to purchase a system that came with a warning to keep it away from children under seven because it could cause eyestrain. Others didn't like the unit because of its lack of competitive game play. It wasn't fun playing a game that no one else could even see.

Despite these setbacks, Nintendo of America decided to give the Virtual Boy a second chance in early 1996. The company began a new ad campaign to promote the unit, and released a new game cartridge on February 26: *Nester's Funky Bowling*. The game did nothing to improve the Virtual Boy's popularity and so Nintendo of America finally cancelled the system without any fanfare on March 2. The company then released one final game, *3D Tetris*, on March 22. Stores quickly began selling their stock at clearance prices. Blockbuster began selling its supply of used rental Virtual Boy consoles for $30 each, and software for $10 but only die-hard videogame collectors seemed to be interested in the unit even at those prices.

Nintendo blamed the failure of the Virtual Boy on the person who was responsible for bringing the technology to Nintendo, Gunpei Yokoi. While other company executives had been doubtful about the Virtual Boy from the beginning, Yokoi had been optimistic about the system's prospects, and his assurances had been all Nintendo needed to move the project forward. Nintendo couldn't be faulted for listening to Yokoi, who had been a designer with the company for nearly thirty years. Yokoi's greatest achievement was the Game Boy, which had sold over 48 million units around the world. Unfortunately, executives had short memories, and when the Virtual Boy failed to sell more than 50,000 units, it was Yokoi who had to bear the blame. In September, he left Nintendo in disgrace and started his own R&D company, which had nothing to do with videogames at all.

Virtual I/O

In spite of its name, the Virtual Boy didn't make the user feel like he was totally immersed in a virtual world. But other companies continued to market virtual glasses that really weren't that much different from the Virtual Boy.

At the winter CES on January 5, Seattle-based Virtual I/O announced its $399 *Virtual TV*, a headset that, when worn, displayed an image in front of the viewer's eyes that gave the impression of viewing a 62-inch television from eleven feet away. Although the headset also had two built-in stereo speakers, it didn't offer a true virtual reality experience, since it didn't have a tracking system that caused the video image to shift when the viewer turned his head. Virtual I/O did market a $799 headset for PCs called the *Virtual i-Glasses*, which was capable of head tracking.

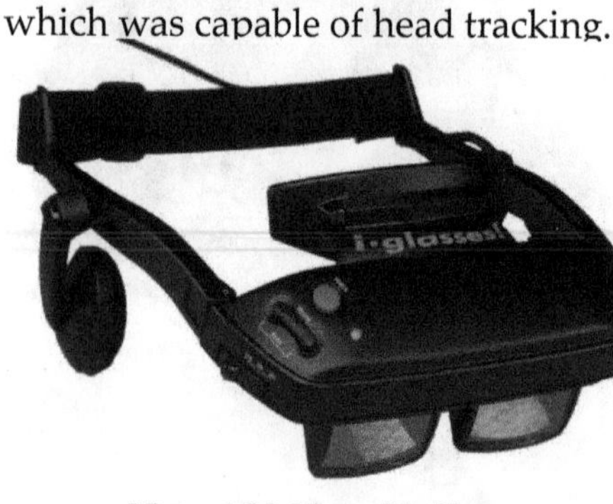

Virtual IO Virtual i-Glasses

Virtual I/O had another surprise at E³, where it announced that it planned to release a headset similar to the Virtual TV that would be exclusive to the PlayStation. Although SCE conceded that it would license the headset and market it under its own name, the unit was never released and neither company referred to it again.

Virtuality also marketed a virtual headset similar to the Virtual TV. Atari originally had planned to license its technology and release it as the Jaguar VR in 1995, but eventually severed the deal. In its place, Takara, a major Japanese toy company, stepped in and planned to release the headset for $360. Like the Virtual TV, the model that Takara planned to market did not feature a tracking control, although Virtuality admitted that it might also release a higher priced model equipped with a tracking feature.

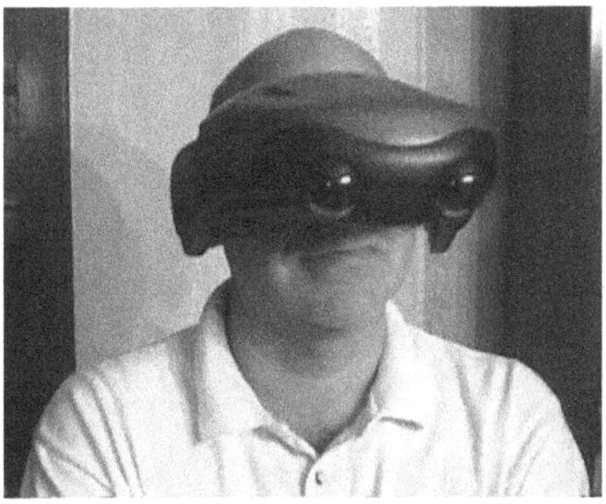

Atari Jaguar VR

Namco signed a deal with Virtuality to create a new virtual reality arcade game based on the old arcade classic *Pac-Man*. The new game, *Pac-Man VR*, placed the player in the guise of Pac-Man as he navigated the maze from a first-person perspective. The game also allowed up to four players to participate at one time, by giving them the ability to see and talk to one another as they went through the maze scooping up power pills and avoiding ghosts.

Arcade Classics Return

As Virtuality was bringing an old classic back to arcades in a new way, other companies were releasing classic arcade games for new formats. Following the success of Activision's *Atari 2600 Action Packs*, several companies began releasing compilations of classic arcade games.

Williams released its *Williams Arcade Classics* early in the year. Among the six games included in this collection were *Defender* and *Joust*. What made this collection particularly interesting was that the games used the original program code, which ran through an emulator so they could be played on different platforms. Besides being available for the PC and the Mac, *Williams Arcade Classics* was released for the 16- and 32-bit game consoles.

Williams Arcade Classics

The CD versions of *Williams Arcade Classics* also included histories of the featured games. Unlike the text history that had been included on the Activision CDs, *Williams Arcade Classics* contained multimedia interviews with the designers, as well as photos of early game designs.

Williams' sister company, Midway, released a PlayStation CD that spotlighted Atari's classic arcade games. *Arcade's Greatest Hits: The Atari Collection* contained six of Atari's most famous arcade games, including *Asteroids* and *Tempest*. In the spirit of *Williams Arcade Classics*, the games on the disc featured the original code running through an emulator, and also contained multimedia histories of the games.

Midway, which had released *Pac-Man* in the United States, did not release a version of that game for the home market. Instead, Namco released it for the PlayStation in a collection called *Namco Museum, Volume 1*. This package contained seven games, but did not include interviews with the game designers. Unfortunately, little thought of the American audience was put into the CD when it was released in the United States. The displayed marquees on several of the featured machines were displayed in Japanese.

The major gaming companies were not the only ones that were releasing CD compilations of classic games. In mid-1996, a limited CD called *Stella Gets a New Brain* was released via mail-order only.

Stella Gets a New Brain was a compilation of all the Starpath games that had originally

Cyberpunks Stella Gets a New Brain

been available on cassette tape for the Starpath Supercharger during the early eighties. The CD was put together by Cyberpunks, a group of four classic-gaming fans who had secured the rights to all thirteen Starpath games from Bridgestone Multimedia, the company that had owned the rights to them. However, their contract with Bridgestone only allowed them to produce a limited number of the CDs on a non-profit basis. They also managed to secure rights to include an unreleased Atari 2600 game called *Polo*.

Congress Rates the Industry

While many were retreating to what seemed like the innocent videogames of the early eighties, the nineties controversy over violent games continued. Senators Joe Lieberman and Herb Kohl, the forces behind the videogame ratings, met with the press at the end of the year. The timing of this press conference coincided with the first anniversary of the rating systems, and the two senators were eager to let the world know how they felt about them.

All in all, the senators were happy with how the videogame industry had enacted the ratings. Using standard report-card grading, the senators gave the system an "A". Most of the software that had been produced after 1993 prominently displayed the ESRB rating code. The senators also gave the videogame manufacturers an "A" for their complete cooperation in establishing the codes.

The senators were less happy with computer-game developers that used the IDSA rating codes. They felt that the IDSA ratings were more difficult to understand, and gave it a grade of "B-".

Retailers received a "C" from the senators for their lack of cooperation. Of the nine retailers that were visited, only Toys "R" Us agreed to ban unrated computer games. Furthermore, the senators discovered that store clerks were unfamiliar with the rating codes and could not explain what they meant when asked about them.

On the whole, the senators were satisfied with the way in which the home videogame industry had responded to the demand for ratings. They were less than enthusiastic about the lack of ratings in the arcade industry, and awarded a "D" to both the arcade-game manufacturers and the arcade owners. Since arcade games didn't come in cardboard boxes that ratings could be printed on, there wasn't any way for their ratings to be displayed, if they were rated at all. Arcade trade groups took care of this problem by printing rating stickers that were distributed to arcade owners. It was then up to the discretion of each arcade owner whether he wanted to display them or not. The US game companies called for more permanent ratings and appealed to the Japanese manufacturers to include on-screen ratings during each game's attract mode.

While the Americans were concerned about violence that was attributed to violent games, the Japanese released a 1994 study that showed that videogames were unhealthy for other reasons. The study's organizers had interviewed 5,400 junior high school students and learned that 30 percent of the students who regularly played videogames eventually developed health problems, which included dizziness and stiff shoulders. The industry reacted by saying that gamers should take frequent breaks while playing.

Ironically, many school districts began embracing videogames. SCEA partnered with Lightspan, a San Diego-based provider of educational software, to produce *Lightspan Adventures*, a series of 80 'adventures' that featured on lessons in reading, language arts and math for students in grades K-6. The lessons were 'played' on PlayStation consoles, and if a student didn't own one, the school districts were able to purchase consoles for $100 each, which could be lent out to students for the school term. Students were not charged for the use of the hardware or software.

Lightspan Adventures

Game Guru

Gamers could certainly spend less time playing by completing the games more quickly. One way to do this was by cheating. Although Codemasters no longer produced the Game Genie, other companies quickly took its place with their own versions of game-altering devices.

The Game Guru was a 3DO CD that featured codes for 39 games. The games had to be saved within the 3DO's internal memory before the Game Guru could be used. Once they were saved, the Game Guru merged the cheat codes with the saved code.

Saturn and PlayStation owners had the GameShark from InterAct. Unlike the earlier Game Genies, long strings of codes didn't have to be entered into the GameShark. Players just had to enter a code once and it was saved for them. In addition, the GameShark was sold with cheat codes already loaded. Once it was inserted into the game console (via the cartridge port on the Saturn or the I/O port on the PlayStation), it bypassed the system's normal start-up procedures. Players could then access a menu from where they could choose the codes that they wished to use.

Unlike the Game Genies, which existed only to alter code, the GameShark could also double as a game saver. And it didn't need a battery to save the games, since it utilized flash memory. This decreased the danger of losing the saved information.

When the original Game Genie had been released, Nintendo had fought hard to stop the selling of it. Nintendo originally won the suit, and Galoob, its American distributor, received a restraining order to prevent it from selling the unit in the United States. Eventually, Galoob appealed the verdict and won the right to sell the Game Genie in the United States.

New Magazines

As the videogame industry went through a constant state of flux, a major overhaul was occuring to the magazines that reported the gaming news, when publishing giant Ziff-Davis purchased the Sendai magazines. *EGM²*, which had originally been launched because there had been just too much videogame news to fit into a monthly *EGM* issue, became a strategy magazine. *Fusion*, the magazine that had been the new incarnation of *Electronic Games*, had not been well-received by the videogaming readers, and morphed into *Intelligent Gamer*, a totally new magazine that was well-written and interesting, even to adult readers. Unfortunately, that apparently wasn't enough to attract readers, and *Intelligent Gamer* ceased publication at the end of the year with the January 1997 issue.

Intelligent Gamer was similar in content to *Ultimate Gamer*, a magazine that had been published by L.F.P., which had ceased publication with its January 1996 issue. L.F.P. was the company that had started the second wave of videogame magazines when it began publishing *Videogames & Computer Entertainment* in 1988. That magazine became *VideoGames*, which in 1996 was also purchased by Ziff-Davis, who then immediately put it to rest with the August 1996 issue.

While the videogame industry had magazines that covered it, it didn't have a professional organization that advanced it, such as the movie industry's Academy of Motion Picture Arts and Sciences and the record industry's National Academy of Recording Arts & Sciences. That changed in 1996, with the formation of the *Academy of Interactive Arts & Sciences.* The goal of this not-for-profit organization was to promote and advance the interactive entertainment community. And like the other industry organizations, it planned to reward excellence with a yearly awards show.

1996 had been a year that belonged to no videogame company in particular. Classic gamers would remember it as the one when Atari died. Newer gamers would remember it as the year when the N64 was finally released in the United States. It was also the year when newcomer SCE established itself as a serious videogame company, while the veteran Sega began to show that it wasn't perfect after all. As the year came to a close, the three surviving companies continued to battle, but no company could claim that it had a commanding lead over the others.

That would have to wait until 1997.

CHAPTER TWENTY-FIVE
1997

During the first few months of 1997, there wasn't any clear global leader in the videogame console war. Sega's Saturn was doing well in Japan, but the games that made it popular in Japan weren't found appealing by Western audiences, and many notable titles were never released outside of Japan. In North America and Europe, the Saturn found itself running third in a pack of three contenders.

Between SCE's PlayStation and Nintendo's N64, it was unclear which console was more popular. Both SCE and Nintendo alleged to have sold approximately 1.7 million consoles each in the United States by the end of 1996. However, the Sega numbers reflected a console that had been around for eighteen months. Nintendo had achieved nearly identical sales figures in only three months. The system established itself as the fastest selling videogame console of all time, up to that point. Nintendo claimed that the demand for the N64 had been so great that it could have sold almost a million more consoles if it had been able to manufacture them. N64 software was also in very high demand, and even titles that hadn't received good reviews were scarce on store shelves.

SCE's sales were just as great. The company announced that it had an American base of 3.2 million consoles. One million of these PlayStations had been sold during the 1996 Christmas season, and the average consumer purchased a remarkable five games for every console sold. Upon hearing these figures, Nintendo's president, Hiroshi Yamauchi, merely shrugged at SCE's success and declared that most of SCE's games were "silly and boring."

Yamauchi's comments may have been made out of frustration and jealousy. Shortly following the holiday season, N64 software developer Enix announced that it would release its widely anticipated role-playing game *Dragon Quest VII* for the PlayStation, instead of the N64, as had previously been announced. This was a great blow to Nintendo, which didn't have a major role-playing title. Enix, which continued to remain an N64 developer, announced that the change had been made for purely economic reasons. The PlayStation offered a larger market, and CDs were cheaper to mass-produce than cartridges.

The real truth behind the numbers began to emerge after Christmas. Statistics showed that the N64 had the potential to dominate the videogame wars. However, because SCE had a two-year head start, it naturally had more consoles already in homes than Nintendo. But these figures showed that Nintendo was catching up. While SCE was selling the PlayStation at an average of 195,000 units per month, Nintendo was up to 383,000. Sega was at a distant third, with average sales of only 77,000 Saturns per month, already igniting frequent questions concerning the future of the console. Despite these numbers, each company, including Sega, was optimistic about its future.

The first shot in the videogame war of 1997 was taken on February 21, when the Tokyo newspaper *Mainichi Shinbun* quoted Nintendo of Japan head Hiroshi Yamauchi, who stated that his company would lower the price of the N64 from ¥23,090 ($187) to ¥16,917 ($137) on March 14. Yamauchi explained that Nintendo could do this because of lower costs associated with the mass production of the Nintendo 64.

This price decrease would not take place in the United States, where the N64 was selling in record-breaking numbers and where it would remain at $199.

As expected, SCE quickly followed suit, and on February 27 announced its own price decreases for the PlayStation. SCE intended to immediately lower the price of the console to $200 in the United Kingdom and Australia. But this was just the beginning. Less than a week later, on March 3, SCEA announced that in addition to lowering the price of the US PlayStation to $149, it would also be dropping the price of new software to $50. And

PlayStation Greatest Hits

to make the system even more competitive and irresistible, SCE introduced a line of "Greatest Hits" games, which consisted of titles that had sold more than 150,000 copies and had been available for over a year. The "Greatest Hits" games would each sell for $25.[1]

Although SCE's price decrease had been expected following Nintendo's prior move, the immediacy of it was totally unexpected by both Nintendo and Sega. George Harrison, Nintendo of America's vice-president of marketing, initially proclaimed that the SCE price drop didn't faze his company in the slightest, and that Nintendo of America had no plans in doing likewise. According to Harrison, Nintendo had expected the price decrease from SCE, since the N64 had been outselling the PlayStation during every month since its introduction.

George Harrison had spoken too soon. Nintendo of America lowered the price of its N64 to $149 on March 17.

Net Yaroze

No sooner had Nintendo lowered its price on the N64 to compete with the PlayStation, rumors emerged from the SCE camp implying that the company was planning a new 64-bit powerhouse to replace the PlayStation. SCE didn't deny the existence of the new PlayStation, which would contain additional RAM, an R4000 chip and a DVD player. The new system, expected to appear sometime in 1998, would be completely compatible with
25 software for the existing PlayStation. Another circulating rumor revealed that some of the specifications for the new console, such as the additional RAM, were being reworked into new models of the current PlayStation. Again, SCE didn't sanction the rumor, but admitted that the PlayStation was constantly being updated. However, all the new models that were released in Japan beginning in August, and in the rest of the world beginning in December, included a feature called *Soundscope*, which was very similar to the Jaguar's *Virtual Light Machine*.

Since the PlayStation was going to be around for at least another year, SCE continued to support it. In March, SCE released the Net Yaroze, a $750 specialty console that allowed even novices to design PlayStation-compatible games on their home computers. The Net Yaroze, whose name meant "Let's do it together," was a standard SCE PlayStation[2] that came with a serial cable that attached it to a PC or Mac, and a CD that contained several hundred programming libraries, a C compiler, and many more development tools. These tools allowed ordinary gamers to program games on their computers that could then be played on their PlayStation consoles.

Owning a Net Yaroze gave its users access to a website that made their games available to other Net Yaroze owners and gave them access to games programmed by other users. In addition, SCE took an interest in the games that its users created, and had the first right of refusal of any games that were created. If anything spectacular came along, SCE had the right to market it.

Even gamers who weren't interested in developing PlayStation games liked the Net Yaroze as it was also capable of playing PlayStation games from around the world. Regular PlayStation consoles could only play foreign discs after a special chip was inserted, a process that voided the PlayStation's warranty.

Sega's Pricing Pressures

Even though Sega subsidiaries in the United Kingdom and Australia followed the leads of their competitors and lowered the price of their Saturn consoles, Sega of America held firm and refused. Executives of the company believed that the long-term success of the Saturn depended upon quality software, not the price of the hardware. Optimism turned into realism, and Sega of America eventually lowered the Saturn's price to $150 on June 3, a price that would not include a packed-in game. However, Sega of America also introduced a new $170 package that would come with one game. Sega also took a cue from SCE and lowered the price of its software so that no new game would cost over $50. Sega even lowered the price of the Genesis by $20!

Sega's lower price points brought new life to the floundering system. However, while most analysts agreed that Sega had done the right thing by lowering its prices, it was much too late in the game to make a difference.

By the end of the summer, things looked even bleaker for Sega of America as SCEA began signing exclusive contracts with companies that had previously designed games for both systems. Shiny signed first and began developing its game *Wild 9s* only for the PlayStation. SCE next approached Eidos. Even though Eidos' *Tomb Raider* had been the best selling Saturn game of all time, the sales figures from that version couldn't come close to the PlayStation version. Sega's executives weren't too concerned about the exclusive PlayStation games, however. As far as they were concerned, any game from Sega's arcade division was a Saturn exclusive.

Ironically, the woes that Sega of America was experiencing were not felt in Japan, where the Saturn sold in great numbers. The system was so popular that Sega of Japan announced that it intended to sell exclusive Saturn software through vending machines at 7-11 Japan, the country's largest convenience store. The first would be *Digital Dance Mix*, which would feature 3D animations and hit songs by a Japanese singer named Namie Amuro.

Yet despite Sega of Japan's success with the Saturn, behind the scenes the company was already developing a new system to eventually replace it.

Rumors concerning a new Sega 64-bit console with a built-in modem and a six- or eight-speed CD-ROM drive began circulating early in the year. Many analysts felt that Sega of America would forego the Saturn in favor of this newly rumored console but Sega put the story to rest by stating that they wouldn't release a new console in 1997. They intended to "stand by the Saturn" by producing less software. What this paradox meant was that Sega planned to release a small number of high-quality games, rather than a large number of mediocre ones. Sega also promised more original titles instead of arcade standbys.

Despite Sega's denials, it had been revealed in March that throughout 1996, Lockheed Martin had submitted several plans for a new Sega console. The truth finally came out in May, when Bernie Stolar, CEO of Sega's North American Consumer Business Operations, announced in an E^3 interview with *Electronic Gaming Monthly (EGM)* that the "Saturn [was] not in (Sega's) future." This statement implied that Sega of America would be devoting all of its emphasis on its next system, which wouldn't be available for at least another eighteen months. This statement irked Victor Ireland, president of one of Sega's biggest software developers, Working Designs. Ireland contended that Stolar's statement would in effect kill the Saturn market in North America.

Ireland had other gripes with Sega of America. Although Working Designs was one of Sega's staunchest supporters, their booth at E^3 was outside of Sega's perimeters and buried deep in the back of the exhibit hall, where very few attendees ventured. Ireland decided to quit supporting the Saturn, even though Working Designs and Sega of America had a decent relationship going back to the early days of the Sega CD.

Sega of America felt that Working Designs' desertion wouldn't impact it at all. The majority of the games that Working Designs had released for the American Saturn were conversions of Japanese games licensed from Sega of Japan. Sega of America felt that another company would simply take Working Designs' place and convert Japanese games for the American market. They couldn't have been more wrong.

Working Designs was not the only company that defected from Saturn development. In a bold move that more or less signaled the inevitable death of the Saturn, SegaSoft announced early in the year that it would limit its development of Saturn games and concentrate on online PC games. With this announcement, the Sega division laid off ten percent of its employees.

But not all companies were giving up on the Saturn. On August 9, Waka Manufacturing, a maker of computer adapters and components, decided to enter the Japanese videogame industry with a Saturn game called *Saturn Music School*. This was an ¥8,880 ($72) game that taught users how to play a piano. Included in the package was a MIDI Interface Box that connected the Saturn to any MIDI piano keyboard, which was needed to play the game. Waka Manufacturing also offered a limited ¥22,400 ($191) set that included an actual Yamaha CBX-K1 keyboard.[3]

Yamaha CBX-K1 Keyboard

Sega Competes Against Itself

The Saturn was doomed, at least in the United States. And since the system was successful in Japan, Sega of America was on its own to replace it. Fortunately, the company had already begun designing its own console, code-named Black Belt.

The console would be powered by Hitachi's new SH-4 processor, which had been designed especially with videogames in mind. The SH-4, which wasn't even on the market yet, promised to have a speed of 200 MHz and the ability to compute 350 million instructions per second. While the new console would be more powerful than the N64, it would still only have a 32-bit processor. Like the Saturn, the Black Belt would use a CD-ROM drive. Sega didn't have any plans to make it DVD-compatible.

The console would also incorporate 3Dfx Interactive's Voodoo Graphics, which had become very popular with PC gamers. The Black Belt would feature a modified version, with 128-bit architecture that 3Dfx Interactive touted as very developer-friendly.

Finally, the new system would borrow something else from the computer world. Thanks to an agreement between Sega and Microsoft, the massive software company would provide some portions of the Black Belt's operating system.

While the Black Belt sounded like it would be a worthy successor to the Saturn, it turned out to be a project that Sega of America was developing independent from its sibling, Sega of Japan. This was problematic because Sega of Japan was also secretly working on a replacement for the Saturn.

Sega of Japan's new console was called the Dural, and it utilized NEC's PowerVR chip. Although the PowerVR chip wasn't as powerful as the Voodoo Graphics, it used a new technology called Highlander, which was five times faster.

Sega of Japan was caught in a dilemma. While both chipsets were excellent, Sega could only use one worldwide. The Japanese design team threatened to quit the company if the PowerVR technology wasn't used. In the end, Sega went ahead with the Dural system that its Japanese team had developed. Following this decision, most of the American design team immediately quit the company in retaliation and quickly found jobs elsewhere.

Greg Ballard, head of 3Dfx Interactive, admitted that he was disappointed with Sega's decision. He downplayed the incident and claimed that Sega would have only represented ten percent of his company's overall projected 1998 revenue. Sega of America still planned to pay 3Dfx Interactive anyway, to continue developing the technology for its own use. By doing this, Sega could retain the rights to the technology and prevent other companies, including SCE, which had expressed interest in it, from utilizing it. Sega of America even invested in 3Dfx Interactive itself.

In September, Greg Ballard's company filed a breach-of-contract lawsuit against Sega, contending that Sega had deceived 3Dfx Interactive by becoming an investor to learn its proprietary secrets. Sega responded that it invested in many companies and in all cases, never disclosed any proprietary information that it was privy to. The lawsuit also named NEC, which 3Dfx Interactive contended had interfered with the contract that it had with Sega.

Once Sega of Japan went ahead with the Dural, it began releasing public information about the new console, which it planned to have in stores by late 1998. Powered by Hitachi's 200 MHz SH4 chip, the Dural would produce graphics at an astounding 1.5 million polygons per second, thanks to the PowerVR chip. Yamaha would design a sound chip that could produce 64 different voices at one time. While the Dural would incorporate standard CD-ROMs, the special dual-speed drive would also be able to read data from unique Dural discs that could each hold up to one gigabyte of information. These discs were called *GD-ROMS*.

All of the work that Sega of America had put into the Black Belt had not been lost. The rumored Microsoft operating system became a reality for the Dural. In September, the Japanese newspaper *Nihon Keizai Shinbun* officially announced that Microsoft would provide a *Windows CE* operating system. Such an OS would make it easy for programmers to port computer games over to the console and *vice-versa*. This also allowed third-party software companies to immediately begin designing games for the Dural. Sega, learning from its past mistakes, was very determined to offer a system that was "designer-friendly." The Saturn, which had been a very difficult system to program, had lagged terribly in popularity while the top-selling PlayStation was a developer's dream. The designers of the Dural knew that this wasn't just coincidence.

Surprisingly, the operating system would not reside within the machine. Instead, each game disc would include the latest version of the operating system, which would automatically load when the disc was inserted. According to Sega, the advantage of this was that developers could design games that exploited the features and enhancements of the latest version of the operating system, and would not have to worry about compatibility issues.

Sega's goal was to release the $199 Dural by October 1998. The company was certain that it had corrected all of the mistakes that it had made with the Saturn, a system that most critics believed would, during 1998, go the way of the Sega CD/Mega CD and the 32X.

Meanwhile, until Sega released its new machine, it had to deal with the ramifications of the Saturn's poor retail performance. In the fall, Sega of America sent letters to several distributors, stating that they would no longer be part of Sega's distribution network. The company claimed that only ten distributors, five percent of its overall network, were removed as Sega sought to reallocate its services in a cost-saving measure.

By year's end, the Saturn commanded less than 2% of the console market share, down from the 20% that it had held only a year earlier. In all, Sega of America lost $267.9 million and was forced to lay off 30% of its employees from its California headquarters, souring an already dismal Christmas season.

Sega Channel Signs Off

Sega of America wasn't the only division of Sega that was experiencing problems. On November 25, the Sega Channel announced that it would cease broadcasting in June 1998. This came as a surprise, since the year had begun on a healthy note with a January announcement that the service would be increasing the number of available games from 50 to 70, and that new games would be updated biweekly instead of monthly. The service had also signed with Disney Interactive to offer Genesis games that weren't even available in stores. Unfortunately, the Sega Channel never really caught on with the majority of Genesis owners. Only 150,000 of the twenty million Genesis households that could receive the Sega Channel actually subscribed to it. And as the Genesis moved closer to extinction with the success of the PlayStation and N64, the subscription base for the Sega Channel kept decreasing.

Catapult's XBand was also facing problems. First, it received little support from game developers. Only *Weaponlord*, a fighting game for the SNES and Genesis from Visual Concepts supported the XBand outright. All the other games that were available to play through the XBand had to first be reverse-engineered by Catapult in order to hack versions that could be played online.

But the XBand also suffered with a very low-response time in its games, which only frustrated its users. Eventually it suffered from the same problem that plagued the Sega Channel; a lack of subscribers. Catapult turned to Japan as a new market, but ironically faced competition from Sega's NetLink, which used the same technology as the XBand.

By March 16, Catapult limited the XBand's service, so gamers could only compete against players within their own area codes. By the end of April, the service was shut down completely.

The demise of the Sega Channel and XBand didn't affect Sega of Japan, since it was more interested in its online service for Saturn owners. In January, Sega of Japan announced that it had joined forces with Nippon Telegraph and Telephone to develop a videophone called the *SS Phoenix*. This was a unit that contained a microphone and camera, and which plugged into the Saturn's cartridge port and connected to a standard telephone line. Once the unit was set up, it allowed users to call up other SS Phoenix owners; and let them see each other on their TV screens as they talked. Sega of Japan planned to release the unit for under $400.

Meanwhile, Sega of America, which was struggling with selling the Saturn itself, tried new ways to push its online platform, the NetLink. Unfortunately, Sega of America had only sold 15,000 NetLink units by mid-1997. The company announced early in the year that new NetLink-compatible games would become available, with the hope that by offering the new NetLink-compatible games, many more people would go out and purchase the unit.[4] Sega even offered a special price. At E^3, the company announced that it would release a NetLink bundle that would come with a Web Browser and NetLink versions of *Virtual On* and *Sega Rally* for only $100.

More Third-Party Suffering

Software publishers were also suffering. After laying off seventy employees in 1996 in an effort to save costs, Acclaim experienced a minor success in March when it released *Turok: Dinosaur Hunter* for the N64. Unfortunately, the game wasn't enough to keep the software company from spiraling downwards, and 115 more jobs had to be cut in May.

GameTek, a familiar software name since the NES days, also began experiencing lower-than-expected sales. Sales became so poor that the company was forced to file for Chapter 11 Bankruptcy Protection shortly before the Christmas buying season.

GTE Interactive decided to exit from the software market in early spring to concentrate on its core business of telecommunications. While it had never been a major player in the videogame arena, GTE Interactive's departure from the industry meant the layoffs of approximately eighty employees.

Capcom also found itself in trouble, because it hadn't been granted permission to release games. While its *Mega Man* series was popular in Japan, it didn't enjoy the same level of success in the United States. When Capcom decided to release its two Japanese games *Mega Man X4* and *Mega Man Battle and Chase* in the United States, SCE decided to activate its veto power and nix the games. While SCE had the right to veto any game, this action became a source of friction between the two companies. Within four months, Capcom began experiencing financial problems due to lower-than-expected sales of some its other games.

Even companies with deep pockets found themselves bleeding money. Disney Interactive ceased all in-house development and laid off 20 percent of its staff, so it could begin concentrating on developing games for other publishers.

But not every software company was having a rough time. Konami, Bandai and Namco all reported increases in profits over 1996. Telegames, a company that primarily dealt in orphaned systems, surprised many and released eight new games for the Atari Jaguar and Lynx. Nintendo was quick to announce that its *Star Fox 64* had become the "hottest" videogame for any system after it sold 300,000 copies within five days of its June 30 introduction. Purists were quick to point out that this record only applied in the United States, since Square had sold over 2 million copies of *Final Fantasy VII* during the three days following its January 31 Japanese release. The argument became moot anyway, following the North American release of *Final Fantasy VII* on September 7, when over 330,000 copies were sold during its first weekend.

Studio 3DO

One company that hoped to publish games in record numbers was Studio 3DO. On June 24, the 3DO Company sold the remainder of its hardware business to Samsung for $20 million. Afterwards, the 3DO Company, through Studio 3DO, was solely a software developer.

Although the 3DO Company had sold the M2 to Matsushita, Studio 3DO still developed software for the unreleased console. In May, it announced that it would release *Battlesport*, a game that had already been available for the 3DO and N64. Greg Richardson, president of Studio 3DO, explained that the games that his company was already working on for the M2 were easy to translate to the N64.

Studio 3DO finally unveiled its M2 products for the press at the same time that it announced its N64 lineup. With a blanket covering the actual M2 hardware, Studio 3DO demonstrated its first M2 product, *World Championship Racing*. The initial reaction was that the graphics were smoother than those of the N64, and the loading time from the CD was very quick.

But even though M2 games were actually being demonstrated, most critics doubted that the console would ever be released. One reason was that there was a lack of software. In October 1996, Matsushita had announced that the M2 would have more available titles at its launch than the N64 had. Eight months later, the reality was that only three companies were developing games for the system. And these companies didn't even know Matsushita's intentions, since the development model that they used had been supplied by 3DO before the Matsushita purchase. Whether or not the electronics giant improved on 3DO's original design was anybody's guess. Although the original M2 technology had blown away the current available systems, the longer Matsushita held out from releasing the system, the less impact it would make in the marketplace.

When the M2 didn't appear at E^3 in June, speculation of its death continued. In July, a Japanese newspaper, *Nihon Kogyo Shinbun*, reported that a high-ranking Matsushita official had mentioned during an interview that the M2 had been terminated and the entire console division of the company was being disbanded. Matsushita immediately issued a statement that claimed the interviewer had misunderstood the official, and that the M2 and ten games were ready to ship. But it wasn't shipping to stores, because Matsushita felt that there were just too many systems already on the market to try and introduce a brand-new system.

Shortly following Matsushita's announcement that the console was alive and well, the company's president, Yoichi Morishita, stated that the M2 would not be released as a videogame console after all. Although Morishita was confident that the M2 was superior to the current systems, he felt that the other manufacturers would catch up and surpass the M2's technology within a year. Morishita hinted that the M2's technology might resurface one day, but that if it did, it would be part of an all-purpose multimedia console, the type of console that the 3DO and Philips CD-i had originally been designed to be.

The M2 resurfaced in October, a scant three months later. At that time, Matsushita announced that it was accepting orders for the new incarnation of the console, which was now aimed at the industrial multimedia market. But the possibility of the M2 coming out as a videogame console was still not put to rest. As one Matsushita executive remarked, since the videogame market changed in five-year cycles, and it was feasible that the M2 could still be released commercially if the market warranted it. In fact, the M2 appeared just a month later at Comdex and Japan's Digital Media World Expo. This time, it was displayed as an all-purpose multimedia system. Ironically, most of the software that was demonstrated with it were games.

Project X

Although Matsushita was under the impression that the time wasn't ripe for a new console to go up against the established three, the founders of an unknown three-year-old company called VM Labs felt differently. In late September, word began leaking that the company was going to produce a new game console to be available in late 1998. Behind the new system, which was dubbed "Project X," were Richard Miller, a former R&D head for Atari who had created the chipset for the Jaguar, and Jeff Minter, a renowned programmer who had designed the Jaguar's *Tempest 2000*.

In November, VM Labs decided to quench all rumors and Miller officially announced the existence of Project X. Although he wouldn't offer the specifics of the new machine, he did promise that it would be more powerful than the current crop of consoles. He also admitted that Project X would be manufactured by more than one company, in the same fashion as the 3DO console had been. Miller claimed that many developers and publishers were interested in supporting the new console, although he didn't name any of them.

While many critics were skeptical about a new company introducing a new system to an already crowded marketplace, Bill Rehbock, VM Labs' Vice-President of Third-Party Development, pointed out that SCE had run into the same problem when it first announced the PlayStation as an individual unit. At that time, there had been no less than six consoles already on the market. Rehbock knew a lot about SCE. He had left that company and its number-one game console to join VM Labs, because he felt that the Project X hardware was a winner.

Intellivision Returns

As VM Labs forged ahead with its talented crew of Atari alumni, a pair of Mattel Intellivision ex-programmers, Keith Robinson and Stephen Roney founded a different type of company called Intellivision Productions Inc. Robinson, who was also a successful cartoonist, had also drawn the box art for the Intellivision games that had been released by INTV. Robinson and Roney believed that there was still interest in Intellivision games despite the closing of INTV in 1991. In 1995 they built a website dedicated to the history of the Intellivision, and high traffic to that site proved to them that they were right. Robinson was able to purchase the rights to most of the Intellivision library and the goal of Intellivision Productions was to release these games in new formats, such as for the current consoles or as handheld devices.

Sega and Bandai Plan to Wed

On January 23, Sega made the startling announcement that on October 1, it planned to merge with Bandai, one of Japan's largest toy companies. The new company, Sega Bandai Limited, planned to be a major powerhouse in interactive-related businesses, and claimed a combined net worth of over five billion dollars. Sega's president, Hayao Nakayama, predicted that the new company would be the world's second-biggest entertainment company, right behind the Walt Disney Company.

Although most details weren't initially worked out, the merger looked good on paper for both companies. At the time, both appeared to be floundering. Bandai owned the rights to many popular licenses, including the *Power Rangers*, but profits from the latter had been on the downswing since 1995. Sega's hope was that many of Bandai's popular licenses could be converted into popular videogames. Bandai, on the other hand, wanted to use many of Sega's popular characters, such as Sonic, in ventures outside of videogames.

Since Bandai was a third-party developer of PlayStation games, conflict-of-interest questions naturally arose. A Bandai spokesman claimed that the company would continue developing PlayStation games, because they were profitable.

Another question concerned the fate of Bandai's Pippin player. Bandai wanted to continue with the system, but Sega was against it. Since the Pippin was marketed as an Internet device, it was in direct competition with the Saturn's NetLink. During one of Bandai's numerous board meetings, the decision was made to simply abandon production of the Pippin altogether. It hadn't been a hard decision to make, since the console had been doing so poorly. In the United States, the @WORLD had worse sales numbers than the Saturn, and only 18 software titles were available. In Japan, approximately 80 titles were available for the ATMARK, but the system lagged well behind the Saturn and the other consoles.

With the lack of support from Bandai, Apple announced at the end of January that it too would no longer support the Pippin.

Although the Pippin question had been settled, the Bandai board continued to meet, but still couldn't come to any sort of agreement. Bandai president Makoto Yamashima admitted that his company had missed important deadlines, but didn't mention why. Sega's spokespeople didn't acknowledge the delays, but stressed that the two companies had to act as one in order for both to survive in the changing marketplace.

Bandai's board finally sat down and agreed to the merger on May 26. Unfortunately, approximately 80% of Bandai's mid-level managers had been against the merger altogether, because they felt that the cultures between the companies were completely different. The board was also concerned that profits for the new company would be very meager during its first year of operation. On May 28, the board met again, but this time they voted against the merger. Afterwards, Yamashima, who had been leaning towards the merger, took full responsibility for its failure, and tendered his resignation from Bandai.

Although Bandai announced publicly its reasons for going against the merger, industry analysts felt there were other factors that had been weighed. One unconfirmed rumor involved a merger between Matsushita and Sega. Many critics believed that Matsushita wanted Sega's help in the development of the long-awaited mysterious M2 console, and that this may have scared Bandai off.

But a more plausible reason why Bandai backed out was that the toy company felt that it simply no longer needed Sega to help turn around its sluggish sales. On November 23, 1996, Bandai had released a new electronic toy that would go on to fortify the company's fortunes all by itself.

Tamagotchi

The toy was called the *Tamagotchi*, Japanese for "loveable egg." The Tamagotchi was a small, plastic egg-shaped unit attached to a keychain, with a tiny dot-matrix screen and three buttons. When the device was turned on, a virtual on-screen pet "hatched" from an egg. It was then the duty of the pet's owner to keep it alive and pampered. The virtual pet used a system of beeps around the clock to tell when it wanted to play or eat. If the pet was neglected, it would eventually "die" and a new pet could be hatched at the press of the reset button.

Bandai Tamagotchi

The Tamagotchi quickly became a national obsession in Japan. Although it had been designed for children, many adults purchased it for themselves. Other adults took on the responsibility of raising their children's pets. The demand for the unit quickly exceeded the supply, and before long, the $16 Tamagotchi was being sold for hundreds of dollars.

By the time Bandai was ready to release the Tamagotchi in the United States in May, 20 million of them had been sold worldwide. However, one modification had been made before Bandai released the toy in the United States. After one Japanese girl committed suicide because her virtual pet died, Bandai executives decided to change the story-line for the American version. Each of the Tamagotchis that were to be sold in the United States hatched a creature from another planet, where it would simply return if it wasn't cared for adequately.

F.A.O. Schwartz, the first American store to carry the Tamagotchi, sold out its initial supply of 30,000 in just three days. Bandai knew it sat upon a gold mine. At E^3 in June, the company announced that it was developing PC and Game Boy versions of the Tamagotchi.

Following the Tamagotchi's success, Bandai's competitors wasted little time creating their own virtual pets. Tiger Electronics released a series of $13 virtual toys called *Giga Pets*, virtual cats and dogs with which people could really relate. However, there were also absurd Giga Pets, such as a baby Tyrannosaurus Rex for a *Jurassic Park II* tie-in. By the end of the year, Tiger also released *Star Wars* Giga Pets, which allowed people to take care of familiar characters such as Yoda and R2-D2.

Tiger Giga Pets

The $18 *Nano*, which was released by Playmates in June, allowed buyers to care for kittens, puppies and even human babies. Mistreatment of the pets (or children) would cause the virtual entity to run away.

By September, the stores were saturated with virtual pets. While most analysts believed that the trend would carry the toy companies through the Christmas season, the assumption was that the virtual toys were fads, and that their popularity would eventually diminish.

Handheld Classics

Stores were also saturated with dedicated handheld, LCD retro-gaming consoles. MGA

Entertainment, a California-based toy company, released the *Classic Arcade Collection*, six individual units that were each slightly smaller than a Game Boy Color console. Titles in the series included *Ms. Pac-Man, Asteroids, Missile Command, Centipede, Pac-Man* and *Super Breakout*. MGA also released the latter three titles in a series called *Keychain Game*. These units were smaller than those in the *Classic Arcade Collection* and each had an attached keychain.[5]

Tiger's game.com

Tiger also introduced an LCD games-on-a-keychain series. *Joust, Defender* and *Kaboom!* were released under the *K Games*[6] banner.

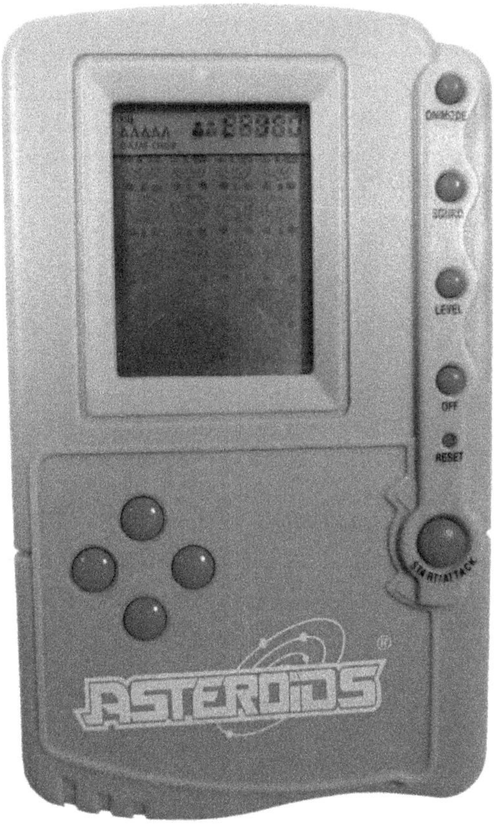

MGA Classic Arcade Collection

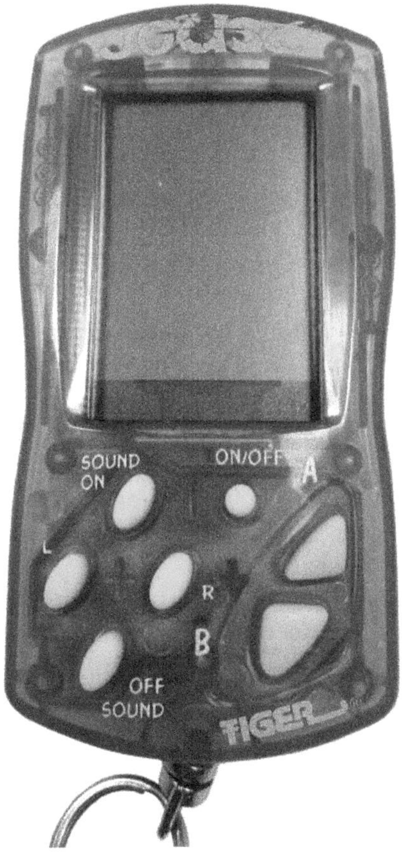

Tiger K Games

Tiger also continued to market its R-Zone series of cartridge-based games. The company discontinued the Super Screen and released the *R-Zone X.P.G. (Xtreme Pocket Game)*, a handheld version of the R-Zone, which used the same cartridges.

Although Tiger Electronics had a booth at E³ that June, neither the R-Zone nor the Giga Pets were on display. Instead, Tiger concentrated all of its publicity on the *game.com*, a new, handheld, duel cartridge-based system that it had developed.

The $70 game.com employed a primitive monochromatic LCD screen like the Game Boy,

Tiger R-Zone XPG

Tiger game.com

its targeted competition. However, the game.com also employed a few extras, such as a built-in solitaire game and a bundled cartridge called *Lights Out* that was based on a best-selling 1995 Tiger electronic game of the same name. In addition to games, the system contained several built-in applications including a calculator, an address and phone number database and a calendar. An unusual feature of the game.com was the inclusion of a stylus and touchscreen technology. While the stylus could be used to select menu choices, its main purpose was to compose messages. This was extremely important, because Tiger planned to offer a special cartridge that connected with a standard PC modem to give game.com users online access. Tiger partnered with Delphi to provide an online, text-based email service. Messages could be composed and then transmitted. But while the system was able to receive email, it lacked the capability to store data, so messages could not be saved or printed.

Tiger's plan was for this lack of storage to be temporary, and the company hoped to release an optional RAM cartridge. In addition to storing emails, the RAM could also be used to save updated versions of games, which would employ new codes and secret levels that could be downloaded from the Internet.

Tiger hoped to get people to buy the game.com by developing games that they would be interested in. Tiger went out and licensed well known titles, such as *Batman and Robin* and *Jurassic Park*, in addition to recognizable games like *Williams Arcade Classics* and *Mortal Kombat*. The company also launched an ambitious full media blitz and inserted their catalogue into the bindings of the current videogame magazines.

SNES 2

Tiger had designed the game.com to compete with Nintendo's Game Boy, which had been around since 1989 and still amazed the company's executives by remaining popular. Nintendo announced late in the year that its overall sales for the first six months of 1997 would top ¥180 billion ($1.5 billion), and the company attributed this to the continued success of the eight-year old Game Boy and its year-old successor, the Game Boy Pocket. In April, Nintendo took advantage of this popularity by introducing a new line of vivid Game Boy Pockets that were similar to the colorful Play It Loud! Game Boys that had

FOCUS ON GUNPEI YOKOI

Gunpei Yokoi, the inventor of the Game Boy, died tragically on October 4, 1997, following a minor car accident in Tokyo. After stepping out of his car to inspect the damage, he was hit by another car and was killed instantly.

Although Yokoi had left Nintendo in 1996 after the failure of his Virtual Boy, the executives at Nintendo were saddened by his sudden death and paused to reflect how much he meant to the company. They realized that much of Nintendo's success as a videogame company was due to Yokoi.

Besides the Game Boy and Virtual Boy, Yokoi had a hand in most of the products that Nintendo released. Among his inventions were the pocket Game & Watch series, which included another of his innovations, the cross-key directional pad that Nintendo introduced on the NES controllers. The directional pad was part of every console that Nintendo released. The controller eventually replaced the joystick as the standard controller and although it later appeared on controllers by Sega and Sony, the actual design had been patented by Nintendo.

been introduced in 1995.

Because the Game Boy continued to sell, Nintendo had placed its proposed Project Atlantis color portable on hold. However, in mid-1997, the company announced that it was once again ready to tackle the new handheld system, and that development kits would be sent to third-party developers by the end of the year. Nintendo also revealed that the Atlantis would operate off a 32-bit StrongARM CPU and allow up to thirty hours of play without needing its batteries changed.

Surprisingly, on October 20, Nintendo of America released a new console in the United States. Unofficially dubbed the *SNES 2*, it was actually a redesigned, slimmer version of the SNES. In addition to containing six fewer chips than the original, the SNES 2 also lacked an eject lever, LED power light and RF modulator. This allowed Nintendo of

Nintendo SNES 2

America to sell the console at $100. The company also rereleased a slew of old SNES favorites, such as a *Tetris/Dr. Mario* combination cartridge and *Donkey Kong Country*. Curiously, the release of the SNES 2 occurred four months after Nintendo had announced that it would cease development for the 16-bit system.

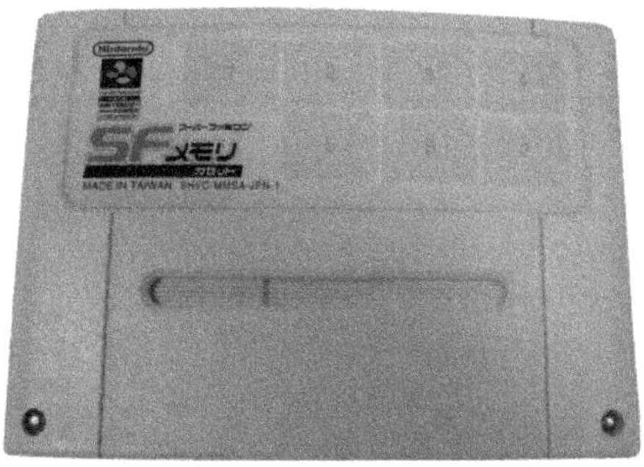

Nintendo Power blank cartridge

Nintendo of Japan was also actively supporting the Super Famicom. On September 30, the company launched a new service called *Nintendo Power*.[7] After first purchasing a blank

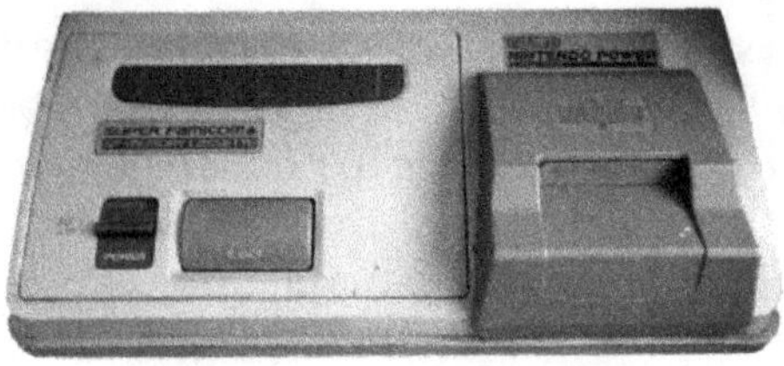

Nintendo Power Flash Writer

Super Famicom[8] cartridge for ¥3,980 ($35), consumers could then buy games that could be downloaded to it. Basically, it was the same type of system that Nintendo of Japan had previously used in 1987 with its Famicom Disc System. Sega had also tried a similar method with RAM cartridges in 1994, when it had partnered with New Leaf Entertainment and Blockbuster for a new method of renting games.[9]

The *SF Memory Cassette* could be purchased at the Japanese convenience store, Lawson, and several other stores for ¥3,980 ($33). Software for the blank cartridge, however, could only be purchased at Lawson, which was the only store that had the equipment that could load games onto the cartridge. The games themselves cost between ¥1,050 ($9) for older titles and ¥2,100 ($17) for new releases. Additionally, exclusive games that were only available through the Nintendo Power service cost ¥2,625 ($22). These prices also included the games' instruction manuals, which were printed at the store. An SF Memory Cassette could store as many as seven games.

64DD

The press and the public weren't particularly interested in the new SNES. What they wanted was news concerning Nintendo's long-promised 64DD bulky drive. Following the 1996 Shoshinkai show, many analysts firmly believed that the 64DD would finally be released before the end of 1997.

When the year began, many developers thought that the 64DD would be used as Nintendo's gateway to the Internet. They speculated that the 64DD would either have a built-in modem or an expansion port that would link to a modem. Although Nintendo didn't use E^3 to confirm or deny any of these rumors, the company did use the show to announce that the flagship game for the 64DD, *Legend of Zelda 64*, was going to be released on a standard cartridge for the N64. This came as a shock to many, since Nintendo had used the same game to highlight the advantages of the 64DD. The fact that the game was being released on a cartridge made it appear that the 64DD was not going to be released after all. Nintendo of America's VP of Marketing, George Harrison, assured the press that this was strictly a marketing decision. Company executives believed that a great title like *Legend of Zelda 64* needed to be available to all N64 owners, not only to those who would own the 64DD. According to Nintendo, the cartridge version would be released simultaneously with the 64DD version at the end of 1997.

That plan changed in late May, when Nintendo announced that the release date for the 64DD would be pushed back to March, 1998, due to delays in the development of both the bulky drive and the disks for it. It would eventually be launched with four titles, *Legend of Zelda 64* among them, and would cost approximately $100. The release date of the cartridge version of the *Legend of Zelda 64* cartridge was still set for December of 1997.

Nintendo Space World

In November, Nintendo held its annual Shoshinkai show, which was renamed *Nintendo Space World*. A playable version of *Legend of Zelda 64* was displayed, and most attendees agreed that the game was even better than Nintendo's previous tour de force, *Super Mario 64*. The bad news was that the release date of the 64DD, which was displayed at the Nintendo Space World as little more than an unplayable mock-up, was once again pushed back, this time to June, 1998. No mention was made of a U.S. launch at all. Rumors circulated that Nintendo was pulling people from the 64DD to work on *Pocket Monsters* for the Game Boy, and this was why the 64DD was constantly delayed. Others felt that there no longer was a need for such a device. When it had been first announced, the 64DD seemed like a good idea, because it appeared to give the N64 an advantage over its CD-based competitors by offering disks that could each contain up to 64 megabytes of storage, including space for the user to store data. However, with the *Legend of Zelda 64* cartridge containing 32 megabytes of data, the largest-capacity cartridge produced by Nintendo, the difference between the cartridge and the 64DD disk wasn't really that much. While many players liked the idea of storing data, they weren't thrilled with having to purchase an entirely new peripheral in order to do so. In addition, disk users would have to contend with access time, a minor annoyance that didn't occur with cartridges.

Other types of peripherals, such as InterAct's *GameShark*, were easier to deal with. With versions of the GameShark already available for the Saturn and the PlayStation, the code-altering accessory was released for the N64 in late summer. The N64 GameShark had more in common with Galoob's Game Genie than its PlayStation and Saturn counterparts. This was because the N64 cartridge had to be inserted into the GameShark, which then had to be placed into the cartridge port of the N64.

Thanks to the judgment against it in the 1993 Game Genie lawsuit, there was little that Nintendo could do to prevent code-altering devices like the GameShark. Instead, Nintendo decided to take legal action against publishers of unauthorized N64 game-strategy guides, specifically Prima Publishing, which Nintendo cited as a chief offender. As the year came to an end, Prima hoped to find an agreeable resolution with Nintendo.

In addition to suing legitimate businesses like Prima, Nintendo also targeted illegal companies that were manufacturing counterfeit games, a practice that cost the videogame industry $810 million annually. In June, Paraguay police raided a warehouse and discovered thousands of bootlegged N64 and SNES cartridges. Closer to home, Nintendo of America filed a lawsuit against Bung Enterprises Ltd. of Hong Kong and Carl Industries, Inc. of California, charging them with illegally producing and distributing a gadget that threatened Nintendo's business. The *Doctor V64* was a device that had a built-in CD-R (CD Recordable) unit that had the ability to copy game code from N64 cartridges. Once a game had been copied to the CD-R, the user merely had to attach the Doctor V64 to his N64 console and play the game from the CD-R instead of the cartridge.

All of the videogame companies were unsure how they would handle the illegal products coming out of Hong Kong. Their main concern was that Great Britain returned control of Hong Kong to China at the end of 1997. China, on the other hand, was having its own battle with videogames. In an effort to reduce the flood of foreign games that were entering the country, the Chinese government began pushing patriotic games that promoted China's image.

Nintendo Unlicensed

Ever since Nintendo had jumpstarted the ailing videogame industry with its Famicom, software developers had been dependent on the console manufacturers. They had to sign exclusive contracts with the manufacturers and then pay licensing fees for the rights to develop games for particular systems. The publishers then had to rely on the console manufacturer to assemble the games. Publishers had to pay the manufacturers up front to assemble a predetermined amount of games. If they ordered too many copies of a game that ultimately failed, they were in a position to lose a lot of money. On the other hand, if the game was a success and they didn't order enough, they would again lose money from lost sales.

Still, the market was so lucrative that many companies were willing to take the risk. This way of doing business had been practiced for over ten years and had been adapted by all of the hardware makers. However, when a system became too successful, its manufacturer was deemed a monopolist. This was the stigma that had always been attached to Nintendo.

All this ended in mid-1997, when Nintendo had to change the way it conducted business with European companies. Under strict new laws that were passed by the European Economic Commission to promote competition within Europe, Nintendo could no longer award licenses to European software companies to develop Nintendo-compatible games. And since developers no longer needed licenses to create them, they no longer had to create games exclusively for the N64. Another aspect of the law prohibited Nintendo from being the sole manufacturer of cartridges for its console. The only exception pertained to games that featured Nintendo trademarks.

The new European law didn't affect Nintendo's dealings in the rest of the world. However, analysts predicted that other regions would eventually feel the results. Once the Europeans were free from the licensing and manufacturing restrictions, lower production costs were expected, leading in turn to lower prices. However, if the prices of the European software did indeed drop to less than what those products sold for elsewhere, a gray market would develop as non-European stores and distributors would scramble to acquire their games from lower-priced European sources.

With the absence of a licensing policy, Nintendo's revenue would depend upon its own products and not those of third-party developers. Unfortunately, by the end of the year, Nintendo was not in a good position with its own products. In June, the company had announced five new high-profile N64 games at E^3 that were targeted for a holiday release. Two of those titles, *GoldenEye 007* and *Tetrisphere*, were released in August and were no longer new enough to create a holiday frenzy. The remaining three, which included the highly anticipated *Legend of Zelda 64*, were delayed until after the holidays.

Nintendo's problems were analyzed in time for the N64's first birthday on September 29. At that time, *Electronic Gaming Monthly* took a look back to see what Nintendo had accomplished during the prior year. *EGM* found Nintendo's hardware and software to be exceptional, but also felt that the company lacked in competitive pricing and third-party development. This was partially due to the high cost of cartridges. A third-party developer had to pay as much as $35 per cartridge to produce an N64 game. By comparison, the production of a PlayStation title only ran $7. Following the report, Nintendo, in an effort to spur development and bring out more titles, reevaluated the costs that developers accrued and cut that amount in half. All in all, *EGM* was pretty much satisfied with the N64, and anticipated that the situation would improve with the release of the 64DD.

Changing of the Guards

Someone else who anticipated the release of the 64DD was Hiroshi Yamauchi, the 69-year old president of Nintendo of Japan. In September, Yamauchi told the Japanese newspaper *Asahi Shimbun* that he would retire sometime in 2000. His goal was to step down after the release of the 64DD. Yamauchi believed that the 64DD would be revolutionary to the gaming industry, and he wanted to remain in charge long enough to lead that revolt.

Yamauchi's announcement came several months after SCEA had named a new CEO to replace Shigeo Maruyama, who had moved on to a management position with SCE. Maruyama was replaced by former SCEA executive vice-president, Ken Kutaragi, who was also known as the "Father of the PlayStation." Kutaragi also retained his former duties in SCE's research and development department.

Reality Quest The Glove

One part of SCE that Kutaragi wasn't involved in was third-party development. Because the PlayStation was such a hot-selling console, developers went out of their way to develop controllers that would separate them from the rest of the pack. One company succeeded. Reality Quest's *The Glove* was similar to Mattel's *Power Glove* for the NES.[10] It wrapped around a player's wrist and offered one-handed play. Reality Quest initially released its PlayStation Glove version in the fall with a retail price of $89.95, and planned to release Saturn and N64 versions.[11]

Vibrating Controllers

On April 27, Nintendo of Japan released a new peripheral for the N64, which would soon become a standard for all consoles. The *Rumble Pak,* which had originally been called the Jolt Pack, plugged into the expansion slot of the N64 controller, in place of the Controller Pak. When used with games that supported it, the Rumble Pak caused the controller to vibrate during certain actions, enhancing the gaming experience.

Nintendo Rumble Pak

Nintendo of Japan bundled the Rumble Pak with its new *Star Fox 64* game. The rumble effect gained instant success, and in July, the company rereleased *Wave Race 64* and *Super Mario 64,* the titles that had originally been launched with the N64, to support the Rumble Pak. At that time, Nintendo of Japan released the peripheral alone for ¥1,400 ($11) without *Star Fox 64,* and Nintendo of America released it in the United States for the first time, bundled with *Star Fox 64* and packaged by itself. Another launch occurred in October in Europe. Before long, most new games developed for the N64 supported the Rumble Pak.

But SCEJ had jumped the gun on Nintendo by two days when it released a new controller with a built-in vibrating feature similar to the Rumble Pak. However, unlike the Rumble Pak, which needed batteries that added to its weight, the vibrating feature in the SCE controller derived its power directly from the PlayStation console. The *Dual Analog Controller* looked like the standard PlayStation controller that it replaced, with the addition of two analog thumbsticks and a button that switched the controller between analog and digital modes. Unlike the Analog Joystick that had been released in 1996, which was suited for simulators, the Dual Analog Controller worked best with fighting games. Indeed, two fighting games, *Tobal 2* and *Bushido Blade,* were released on the same day as the controller.

SCE PlayStation Dual Analog Controller

When SCEA released the Dual Analog Controller in the United States in August, the vibrating feature was removed. According to SCE, the motor that created the vibration was unstable and had the potential to damage the PlayStation console. However, another theory concerning the lack of the rumble feature was that SCE feared a lawsuit from Nintendo over it although Nintendo claimed that the patent for the technology had actually been filed by two Atari Games developers back in 1991.

Whatever reason SCE had for removing the rumble feature from the Dual Analog Controller became moot on November 20 when SCEJ released its new *DualShock Analog Controller*. Externally, the DualShock Analog Controller closely resembled the Dual Analog Controller. But it was what couldn't be seen that made the controllers vastly different from each other. The new controller employed two vibration motors. One was a weak buzz, while the other was a strong vibration not unlike the one generated by Nintendo's Rumble Pak.

E^3 Moves Deep South

Since its inception in 1995, E^3 had become the industry's official showplace. In 1995 and 1996, the massive exhibition had been held at the Los Angeles Convention Center. Although it was several hundred miles from Silicon Valley, Los Angeles was considered an ideal spot because of its close proximity to most videogame companies operating on the West Coast. Attendees traveling in from other parts of the country and world found Los Angeles to be a fairly easy travel destination.

Despite its success, the IDSA decided to change E^3's location. Instead of the West Coast, the show moved to Atlanta's Georgia World Congress Center for a two-year run beginning in June. Following the show, the IDSA claimed that it had been a success, despite the fact that its attendance had dropped 40% from the prior year. While some claimed that the drop in attendance was due to a declining number of videogame developers, most attributed it to the fact that it just cost too much money for the Pacific-based companies to send their employees and equipment to the East Coast.

Gameworks

Videogame arcades experienced a resurgence in 1997, thanks to the opening of several new mega-arcades. Gameworks, the massive arcade that was a joint venture between Sega, Universal Studios and DreamWorks SKG, opened its doors in Seattle with a grand Hollywood-like gala on March 15. It was quickly followed by one in Las Vegas and a third outside of Los Angeles with nearly 100 additional centers planned by the year 2002.

While each site would have at least one unique attraction, they would also have similar sections that would appeal to different types of gamers. One section would feature classic arcade games, while another would have brand-new, cutting-edge machines that would be on display for beta testing.

Some of the cutting-edge machines contained SNK's Hyper Neo•Geo 64 arcade system board, which was released in September. This board enabled SNK to deliver advanced 3D games into arcades and eventually into the home on a console that was to replace the Neo•Geo AES. Such a console was never released, and although the games that SNK released in the arcades looked impressive, they never became popular. SNK would eventually release only seven games for the system, before abandoning arcades for good.

Rhythm Games

In Japan, *Pocket Monsters* were so successful that an animated cartoon starring them premiered on Japanese television on April 1. Although the series was an immediate hit, one episode caused controversy and worldwide headlines. While viewing the 38th episode on December 16, over 700 children suffered seizures, thanks to the strobe effect of a red and blue flash. The show was then taken off the air for four months and returned on April 16, 1998. The culpable episode was never aired again, nor did it ever appear on subsequent home-video releases of the show.

Although the *Pocket Monsters* cartoon weren't shown on American TV sets in 1997, Americans did receive a cartoon-like videogame imported from Japan.

On November 19, Americans were introduced to rhythm-based games when *PaRappa the Rapper* was released in the United States. One month later, the rhythm-type game genre invaded Japanese arcades with the introduction of Konami's unusual *Beatmania*. In this one- or two-player game, players assumed the role of club DJs who had to win the praise of their audience by correctly pressing the correct controls as dictated by events on the screen.

The controls were made up of five buttons, three white and two black, and a turntable. The arcade machine had two sets of these controls, one for each player.

The screen displayed two sets of four vertical columns, each column separated by vertical gray lines. Beneath the three left-most columns were five buttons that resembled the keys on a piano. A white key was at the bottom of each the three columns, and two black keys were beneath the two vertical gray lines that surrounded the center columns. These five keys corresponded with the five buttons on the control panel, while the physical turntable corresponded with its own onscreen icon that was beneath the column on the right.

During the game, as popular songs blared through the cabinet's speakers, various blocks descended along the columns and gray separator lines. The player's job was to press the correct button just as the shape hit the corresponding key at the bottom of the screen. If a shape fell down the fourth column, the player had to rotate the turntable. The object of the game was to hit the correct buttons at the same moment that the onscreen shapes hit the corresponding key.

Beatmania was an instant hit in Japan, and several new editions (mixes) featuring new songs were introduced during the following years. However, this success did not spread to the rest of the world.[12]

Konami Beatmania

Konami Beatmania

Digital Poison

Beatmania was a fun, innocent game that was a far extreme from the stereotypical violent games that were causing ire across the United States, where the ongoing debate regarding the content of many games continued to rage. After Arizona proposed a bill that would prohibit minors from playing violent games, opponents of game ratings were troubled by Arizona's definition of violence. According to the bill, it was defined as "graphic, bloody depictions of torture, sexual assault, cannibalism, mutilation, murder and urination or defecation that occurs in a morbid or violent context." The proposed law made it a misdemeanor to distribute or even display violent (as defined in the bill) videogames to minors. And the bill wasn't limited to videogames; videos and magazines were also included. Unlike previous laws that put the onus of ratings on the software publishers, Arizona's proposed bill made it the retailer's responsibility to keep the violent games away from minors. Fortunately for retailers throughout the state, the bill was not approved when it was brought before the Rules Committee for the third step in the four-step process.

At the Federal level, the National Institute On Media and the Family (NIMF) teamed up with Senators Kohl and Lieberman, the two who had been responsible for game ratings in the first place. They issued their annual report card on how the industry had complied with their suggestions. On the whole, the Senators were pleased. By the end of 1997, most software packaging prominently displayed the ratings. However, the Senators weren't happy with retailers, because most stores didn't have a policy that restricted minors from obtaining games with mature themes; this was the very same problem that Arizona had attempted to rectify with legislation. The Senators did not rate the arcade industry, which was still in the process of implementing its own rating system.

Although the Senators were happy with the industry on the whole, they did use the term "digital poison" to describe violent computer games such as *Quake* and *Postal*. Doug Lowenstein, president of the IDSA, defended the games by saying that not all games were intended for children. Statistics showed that 73% of PC gamers and 46% of console gamers were over the age of 18. The whole reasoning behind the ratings in the first place was to alert consumers, especially parents, as to whether a game was suitable or not for a child.

When 1997 came to an end, sales for videogame software and hardware in the United States had reached $5.2 billion, a new record high. Much of these sales were attributed to SCE, which in April had released figures that proved that the PlayStation was the world's most popular system. Five million PlayStations had been sold in Japan, four million in the United States, and 2.2 million were sold in Europe. SCE proudly declared in August that the 20 millionth PlayStation had been sold and the sales numbers that SCE had released in April nearly doubled by October. Demand for the PlayStation was so high that SCE had to increase its monthly production to two million systems. Even though other companies had sold consoles in similar mass quantities before, the amazing thing about the PlayStation was that it had been built by a company that didn't have any prior videogame experience.

The popularity of the PlayStation naturally inspired magazines that covered the console. In September, Imagine Media, which published *Next Generation*, introduced a third PlayStation magazine to the United States, which it called *PSM (PlayStation Magazine)*. However, in November, SCEA threw its support behind the competing *PSX*, and allowed Ziff-Davis to change the name of the magazine to the *Official US PlayStation Magazine*. From that point on, each issue of the magazine also included an SCEA-sponsored CD that contained game trailers and playable demos. Meanwhile, the PlayStation's official magazine in the United Kingdom, *Official UK PlayStation Magazine*, which boasted a monthly circulation of 150,000 copies, was considered the world's best-selling videogaming magazine.

The future of the PlayStation looked sunny. Analysts believed that the console's popularity would carry it through 1998.

CHAPTER TWENTY-SIX
1998

When 1998 began, SCE and Nintendo were claiming that they were number one, and technically they were both correct because they used different accounting methods. In terms of revenue, Nintendo controlled 53% of the industry with SCE at 39% and Sega at 7.6%. However, the N64's cartridges retailed higher than the PlayStation and Saturn CDs but Nintendo hadn't factored that into the equation. Nintendo's figures also included income that it still generated from the Super Famicom/SNES, which commanded 67% of the 16-bit market, and from the Game Boy, which dominated an overwhelming 85% of the handheld market.

SCE was more interested in quoting actual sales figures. Nintendo had sold 3.35 million N64 consoles in North America throughout 1997, compared to the 3.8 million PlayStations that SCEA had sold between October and December alone! In total, 4.9 million North American households owned N64s. The PlayStation, which had been available an additional year, could be found in 47.3 million North American homes.

This rivalry between SCE and Nintendo continued through the first half of 1998. On May 6, several weeks before the opening of E^3, SCE released its DualShock Analog Controller in the United States, and began packing it with the PlayStation shortly thereafter. To clear out its supply of consoles that still included the original controllers, SCEA temporarily lowered the retail price of the PlayStation from $149 to $130. But this reduction only applied to the consoles that still had the original controllers packed in. Even so, Nintendo, which had once stated that it would match any competitor's price-decrease within 24 hours, followed through and temporarily lowered the price of the N64 to $130 to match SCE's fire sale. Both companies claimed that these temporary prices would only last through September. But when September came, SCE retained the $130 price even for consoles that were packed with the DualShock Analog Controllers. Nintendo retaliated by also keeping its $130 price and throwing in a coupon that was good for $10 off any Nintendo software or peripheral.

The 64DD No-Show

But as Nintendo kept in line with SCE to get its N64 into homes, it was having less luck getting its N64 peripheral at the door. The 64DD was not on display at E^3, and games like *The Legend of Zelda: Ocarina of Time,* which had been scheduled to appear in the 64DD format, were shown only in cartridge form. Despite the notable absence from E^3, Nintendo still intended to release the 64DD in Japan during the summer, and delaying its U.S. release until after Christmas. This timetable changed dramatically as the year progressed. Within a month after E^3, the summer release date for Japan was cancelled. Then, in October, Nintendo formally announced that the Japanese 64DD release would be delayed until June, 1999. In a related statement, Nintendo announced that it would not hold its annual Spaceworld exhibition that November. The company decided to delay the show until shortly before the 64DD's release.

The most anticipated game for the 64DD was *The Legend of Zelda: Ocarina of Time.* With the 64DD constantly being pushed back, a decision was made to release the game on cartridge. Because of the game's scope, it was released on a 32-megabyte cartridge which, to date, was the largest-capacity cartridge produced by Nintendo.

No matter which format it was available in, the public clamored for *The Legend of Zelda: Ocarina of Time*. Over 325,000 advance orders were placed before the game's actual Japanese release on November 21 (November 23 in the United States). In just six weeks, *The Legend of Zelda: Ocarina of Time* became the best-selling game of 1998 and generated more revenue than any movie released during the same period. Nintendo shipped over 2.5 million copies by the end of the year and predicted that it would sell more than 6 million copies worldwide by the end of March, 1999.

Unfortunately, the overall outlook for the N64 didn't appear bright, even with the success of *The Legend of Zelda: Ocarina of Time*. In Japan, the cartridge-based system lagged behind the PlayStation and Saturn in sales. Although *The Legend of Zelda: Ocarina of Time* had finally been embraced by the buying public, many other long-awaited titles constantly missed their scheduled release dates. Nintendo desperately needed new, quality products to make the N64 more attractive, especially in light of the constant delay of the 64DD.

After Nintendo released the three-dimensional *Tetrisphere* for the N64 in North America in 1997 and in Europe in February, by November 13 it was Japan's turn. But Japanese consumers weren't offered *Tetrisphere* on that day. Instead, SETA released *Tetris 64*, which was basically the original game of Tetris for play on the N64. However, *Tetris 64* did have one variant of the game that wasn't available anywhere else. *Bio Tetris* was the standard game of *Tetris* that sped up or slowed down, depending upon the player's heart rate, which the game knew, thanks to a supplied biosensor.[1] One end of the biosensor plugged into the console, while the other end clipped onto the player's ear to measure his heart rate.

Nintendo 64 Bio Sensor

SETA Morita Shogi 64

Nintendo Mario no Photopi

Bio Tetris didn't really increase the playability of the standard game. However, *Tetris 64* was notable for being the first version of *Tetris* that allowed for four-player competition. Unfortunately, although the game was presented completely in English, it was only released in Japan.

Earlier in the year, on April 3, SETA had released another unusual game for the Japanese N64. *Morita Shogi 64* was an update to 1996's *Saikyō Habu Shōgi*, one of the N64's three launch titles. The game cartridge actually doubled as a modem and allowed people to play Shogi against competitors online as long as both players had a copy of the game plugged into their N64 consoles. Because it was a chess-like game, there wasn't any noticeable delay, which was usually associated with online gaming. An action game with constant movement couldn't hold up as well as a strategy game, so the question of whether SETA would use the technology in other games was up in the air.[2]

Another N64 release that came with a unique cartridge was *Mario no Photopi*, which was released by Nintendo of Japan on December 2. This was not a game. Instead, the ¥9,800 ($74) product let users edit pictures that could be created within the application, or imported into it. The edited pictures could then be saved, but not to the Controller Pak. Instead, the *Mario no Photopi* cartridge had two slots, in which SmartMedia cards could be inserted.[3] Pictures could be read from or saved to a 2MB SmartMedia card, one of which was packaged with the program.

Neither *Morita Shogi 64* nor *Mario no Photopi* were released outside of Japan. Neither was *Tetris 64* with its unique four-player mode. However, on December 18 Nintendo of Japan released another four-player game that would eventually be distributed around the world. In fact, *Mario Party* was one of a few games that would receive rave reviews as a multiplayer game, while the single-player mode left a lit to be desired.

Mario Party was similar to a virtual board game and consisted of 59 mini-games. Up to four players took turns rolling a dice and moving the number of spaces shown in a quest to collect stars. The player with the most stars after all the rounds had been completed was the winner.

Nintendo didn't release *Mario Party* outside of Japan in 1998.[4] But Nintendo of America did get to exclusively release an N64 peripheral in December. The $30 *Expansion Pak* fit into the N64's "Memory Expansion" slot and increased the N64's internal memory from 4 to 8 megabits. Although this additional memory had originally been intended to support the 64DD, it was welcomed by many N64 game designers, who previously had to cut features from their games because the N64 simply couldn't provide enough storage memory to support them. The additional memory also enabled new N64 games to display in much higher resolutions. And while these games could be played without the Expansion Pak, they just looked many times better with it. Designers were pleased with how easy the additional memory was to work with. Unlike other game consoles that had certain parts of memory reserved for specific features, all memory locations in the N64 could be used for whatever the developers wanted.[5]

Nintendo 64 Expansion Pak

1998

And while Nintendo of Japan aggressively pushed the N64, it quietly released another console with little fanfare. Few in Japan were aware about the March 27 release of the *Super Famicom Junior*. This ¥7,800 ($60) console was basically the same model that Nintendo of America had released in 1997, with a few minor cosmetic differences.

New Game Boy Consoles

In addition to the hundreds of Super Famicom games that were already available, people who bought the new Super Famicom Junior also had had access to the hundreds of Game Boy games that could also be played on the console with the help of the Super Game Boy.

Nintendo Super Famicom Junior

While the Super Game Boy was basically a Game Boy console in cartridge form, it was missing one key feature that was available on the handheld models: the ability to link the game in play with another Game Boy. Nintendo of Japan alleviated this problem on January 30 when it released the *Super Game Boy 2*. This ¥5,800 ($46) unit closely resembled the original model except that the cartridge was made of a translucent blue plastic. And it could also accept the link cable that let it connect to other Game Boys, allowing for two-player simultaneous gaming. Nintendo had no plans to release the Super Game Boy 2 outside of Japan.

Nintendo Super Game Boy 2

The *Super Game Boy 2* was the first of several new Game Boys that Nintendo released throughout the year. The second appeared on April 14 when Nintendo of Japan released the *Game Boy Light*. This ¥6,800 ($52) handheld was basically a Game Boy Pocket with a built-in backlight. Although this was a feature that many Americans had wanted for a long time, Nintendo didn't plan to release the Game Boy Light outside of Japan. And the reason for that was because Nintendo was more interested in releasing another product that the gaming public and game developers had been clamoring for: a Game Boy with a color screen.

Nintendo showed off the *Game Boy Color*, safely protected behind plastic, at E[3] in May. Unlike the company's prior attempt at a color portable, the 32-bit Atlantis, the Game Boy Color was an 8-bit unit like its predecessors. It was also compatible with all of the existing
26 monochrome Game Boy games. While these games would display in shades of gray on the Game Boy Color, gamers could activate a palette and assign several colors to the old

Nintendo Game Boy Light

Nintendo Game Boy Color

games. New color games were developed for the Game Boy Color that would also play on the old units where they would naturally not display in color.

The new screen was capable of displaying up to 54 simultaneous colors from a palette of 32,000. Although the color graphics were the main showcase of the Game Boy Color, there were other features that set it apart from the previous models. Even though the new unit used the same Z-80 chip as the original, it ran at twice the clock speed. The unit also had an infrared port near the cartridge slot that would be used for linking systems together, without the need of a cable. The screen buffer was doubled from 8k to 16k, and RAM was raised to 32k from the original 8k. Nintendo explained that any new color games that were designed to be compatible with the existing Game Boy and Game Boy Pockets couldn't take advantage of these new features. However, a new line of color games that would benefit from the new features was being developed, but these would only play on the Game Boy Color. Nintendo offered different colored cartridges to let consumers tell which games played on which machine. The standard monochrome games would continue to come in gray cartridges. The new color games that could play on the old systems would come in black cartridges. Finally, the games that would only play on the new Game Boy Color would be housed in clear cartridges that were also shaped a little bit differently than the other two types.

Nintendo released the highly anticipated ¥9,000 ($75) Game Boy Color in Japan on October 21, and in North America on November 18, where it retailed for $80.

Pokémon

The main reason why Nintendo of Japan created and released the Super Game Boy 2 was to appease the many fans of Pocket Monsters who complained that they couldn't trade Monsters between their Super Game Boy and Game Boy.

Pocket Monsters were huge in Japan and more than 8 million copies of Pocket Monsters games had been sold there. They had become such a phenomenon that on April 25 Pocket Monsters Centers were opened in Tokyo and Osaka. These stores sold all officially-licensed products that were remotely related to the Pocket Monsters, such as dolls and card games.

American analysts thought that if the Pocket Monsters were released in the United States, they could never reach the same level of popularity because of cultural differences between the Japanese and the Americans. However, in May, the major news at E^3 was that Nintendo would be releasing Pocket Monsters in the United States in September. However, the name Pocket Monsters had to be changed because it was too close to a franchise created by the Morrison Entertainment Group in 1990 called *Monster In My Pocket,* which was made up of strange creatures that were also featured in toys and trading cards. In fact, Konami had even published a *Monster In My Pocket* game for the NES in January, 1992. The new name for the American Pocket Monsters was *Pokémon,* which was merely an abbreviation of Pocket Monsters.

Many critics felt that Nintendo was taking a big risk by releasing Pokémon in the United States. They were certain that American children would not embrace the characters in the manner that the Japanese kids had. Despite this, Nintendo

Konami Monster In My Pocket

planned a major marketing blitz to ensure that Americans would warmly welcome the Pokémon upon their September release. In late August, Nintendo dispatched a fleet of ten bright, yellow Volkswagen Beetles that had wings and fins added, to make them look like Pikachus. An SNES and Super Game Boy was on board each car, so when they appeared at local events, the Pokémon games could be shown to the crowds.

Nintendo of America released *Pokémon Red* and *Pokémon Blue* on September 30. The American games were English-translated versions of the earlier Japanese *Pocket Monsters Red* and *Pocket Monsters Green*, and included the updates that were found in *Pocket Monsters Blue*.

Pikachu was the most popular of the 151 Pocket Monsters, which had taken Japan by storm and Nintendo used it to its advantage. On March 27 Nintendo of Japan released a small stand-alone device that was similar to the Tamagotchi. The purpose of the *Pocket Pikachu* was to help people exercise. The device doubled as a pedometer and the person who wore it was awarded one "watt" for every twenty steps he took. Watts were used to buy the on-screen Pikachu gifts, so the more watts accumulated, the happier the Pikachu became and the more activities the creature partook in. However, if the Pikachu wasn't provided with gifts, it would become angry and eventually ignore the walker. The Pocket Pikachu was renamed *Pokémon Pikachu*, when it was released in the United States on November 2.

Nintendo of Japan also released a pink-encased version of the Pocket Pikachu, which was called the *Pocket Hello Kitty*. Actually, Sanrio, the holder of the Hello Kitty franchise, had licensed Nintendo to manufacture the Pocket Hello Kitty unit. The basic idea between the two units was the same. Using the Pocket Hello Kitty the player had to walk to accumulate "Kitt" points, which could be used to acquire items.

Nintendo Pocket Pikachu

Nintendo Pocket Hello Kitty

Nintendo of Japan released a new Pocket Monsters game for the Game Boy on September 12. *Pocket Monsters Pikachu* was a combined, enhanced version of *Pocket Monsters Red* and *Pocket Monsters Green*. One change to the new game was that Pikachu became the only Pocket Monster that a player could start with.

Pocket Monsters Stadium was released on August 1. Originally designed for the 64DD, Nintendo decided to scale back the game and release it for the N64. Because of this, gamers could only select 42 of the full 151 Pocket Monsters to battle in an onscreen arena. However, this marked the first time that the Pocket Monsters could be played on a gaming console.

Pocket Monsters Stadium was packaged with the *64GB Pak*,which plugged into the expansion slot of the N64 controller. Pocket Monsters Game Boy cartridges could be inserted into a slot in the 64GB Pak. Pocket Monsters from the game cartridge, could then be loaded into the *Pocket Monsters Stadium* game. Two gamers playing *Pocket Monsters Stadium* could also trade among themselves as long as both had a 64GB Pak plugged into their controller.

Nintendo N64 64GB

The 64GB Pak was also needed so people could play Pocket Monsters Game Boy games on their TV sets, without using a Super Game Boy. Within *Pocket Monsters Stadium* was a *Game Boy Tower* location that could be unlocked by completing certain matches. Once inside the Game Boy Tower, the Pocket Monsters game that was in the 64GB Pak would appear on the screen just as if it was being played on the Super Famicom via the Super Game Boy.

Nintendo of Japan released another new N64 Pocket Monsters title on December 12. In *Pikachū Genki dechū*, the player befriended a Pikachu that was found in the wild, and attempted to domesticate it. Throughout the game, the Pikachu had to perform a variety of chores at the player's command while partaking in a series of activities, such as fishing and picnicking. The unique aspect of this game was that the player used verbal commands to instruct the Pikachu in what to do.

Pikachū Genki dechū required the N64 *Voice Recognition Unit (VRU)*, which was packaged with the game and allowed players to "talk" to their Pikachus. The player wore a head-mounted microphone that plugged into the VRU, which itself plugged into the fourth controller port of the N64. Players spoke their commands into the microphone, and the on-screen Pikachu could recognize approximately 200 commands. At the end of the game, the player had to release the Pikachu back into the wild. This was accomplished by returning the creature back to the woods, where it had originally been found, and saying "Sayounara" (goodbye) into the microphone several times.

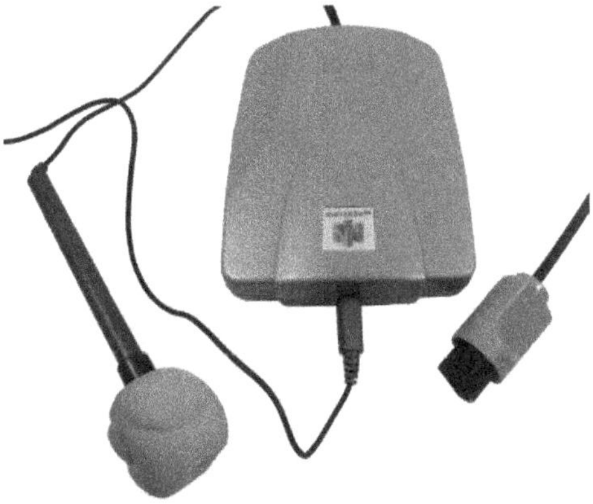

Nintendo N64 VRU

Mewtwo Strikes Back!, a full-length Pocket Monsters cartoon, debuted in Japanese movie theaters on July 18. Not long afterwards, on September 8, the popular Pocket Monsters television cartoons were dubbed in English and began appearing daily on American TV (the seizure-inducing episode would not air) under the Pokémon name. The Pokémon characters were heavily licensed and began appearing in electronic games from Tiger, and as plush figures from Hasbro. In December, Wizards of the Coast, the makers of the

Magic: The Gathering card games, began offering an American version of the popular Pocket Monsters card game which, like all Pocket Monsters-related things, was an enormous success in Japan. The American version was no different, and the demand erupted into a collecting frenzy. Meanwhile, in Japan, Nintendo of Japan released *Pokémon Card GB*, a Game Boy Color version of the Pocket Monsters trading card game. The game included digital versions of all of the cards that were available, and was even packaged with a new exclusive card. *Pokémon Card GB* was the first Pocket Monsters game that had been designed specifically for the Game Boy Color.

Game Boy Peripherals

While Pocket Monsters/Pokémon was arguably the greatest thing for the Game Boy since *Tetris*, it wasn't the only thing that was released that enhanced the appeal for the portable system. On February 21, Nintendo of Japan introduced the ¥5,800 ($46) *Pocket Camera*.

Nintendo Game Boy Camera & Printer

The unit looked like a cartridge with a round ball on top, which actually housed a low-res black and white camera. Photos taken by the camera could be edited on the Game Boy screen or traded with other gamers by transferring them from one Game Boy to another. Although the camera was capable of saving up to 30 photos, gamers could also save their photos by printing them out on an optional ¥5,800 ($46) *Pocket Printer*, which became available the same day as the *Pocket Camera*. To capitalize on the Pocket Monsters phenomenon, Nintendo released the $50 camera and $60 printer in North America on June 1 and in Europe and Australia three days later. Outside of Japan the set was called the *Game Boy Camera* and the *Game Boy Printer*.

Nintendo of Japan also issued a special, limited-edition, bright-yellow Pikachu camera and printer on September 12. The *Pocket Monsters Pikachu* game that was released supported the Pocket Printer and allowed gamers to print out "so-called" Pokédex entries onto stickers, which were so popular in Japan

At the time of the product's release, the *Guinness Book of World Records* declared the Game Boy Camera to be the world's smallest digital camera.

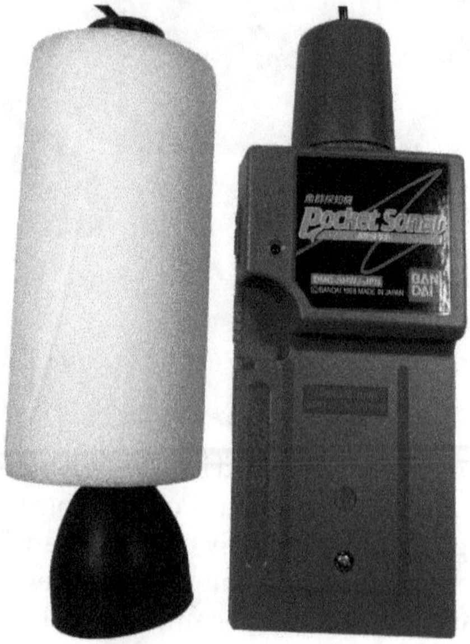

Bandai Pocket Sonar

On July 24, Bandai released a Game Boy peripheral that was only available in Japan. The ¥14,800 ($115) *Pocket Sonar* turned the Game Boy into a device that helped fishermen find fish. Developed by Bandai and Honda Electronics, the Pocket Sonar consisted of an oversized cartridge that plugged into the Game Boy, and a sonar unit that went in the water. A wire connected the sonar unit to the cartridge. When the sonar unit sat upon the surface of the water, it could detect fish up to 30 meters deep. The data was then sent to the Game Boy, which displayed it on its screen. And for would-be fishermen who weren't near water, a fishing game was also included.[6]

Sega's New Console

As Nintendo and SCE volleyed for the top position, it was plain to see that Sega was no longer in the running, even though the Saturn was outselling the N64 in Japan. North American sales for the Saturn had fallen so dramatically during 1997 that Sega of America decided to completely stop supporting it. Just before Christmas 1997, distributors and retailers were warned to place their final Saturn orders, because the merchandise wouldn't be available afterwards. The company cut 30% of its work force in January, as retail stores began discounting Saturn software for as low as $5. By March, the price of the remaining consoles was lowered to $100. Although they were denied by Sega of America, rumors persisted that the console would cease shipping after March 31.

Despite the gloomy atmosphere at Sega of America, the executives at Sega Enterprises in Japan were determined to begin 1998 optimistically. Sega's chairman, Isao Okawa, officially announced at a New Year's Eve party that Sega and Microsoft were jointly working on Sega's new system, the *Dural*. Before the end of January, that name was changed to *Katana* (an extremely sharp, short, Japanese sword typically carried by warriors). Sega announced that the Katana would be available in Japan by Christmas 1998, and in the rest of the world in September 1999. The announcement also added that the console might be sold in Japan by NEC and Hitachi under their own brand names, as well as by Sega.

Even with the confident news concerning a new console, Hayao Nakayama, president of Sega Enterprises, suddenly resigned in February. Many believed that Nakayama stepped down because of fallout from the failed Sega/Bandai merger of the year before, and the lackluster performance of the Saturn. He was replaced by Shoichiro Irimajiri, Sega of America's CEO.

Irimajiri's former position was filled by Bernie Stolar, who also assumed the role of Chief Operating Officer. Stolar continued promoting the Katana and announced that the console's American release would be backed by a $100 million marketing campaign: the most expensive in gaming history. Stolar was overly optimistic that Sega would claim 50%

Sega Dreamcast

Sega Dreamcast controller

Sega Dreamcast VMU

Sega Dreamcast VGA Cable

of the market share, following the introduction of the new console.

On the evening of May 27, the night before E^3 opened, Sega held a press conference to announce that the new console's name was changed from Katana to *Dreamcast*, which was a combination of *dream* and *broadcast*. Surprisingly, with all the press coverage surrounding the new console, Sega of America chose to not display it on the main floor at E^3, although reminiscent to the Saturn's American debut, it was shown behind closed doors.

The Dreamcast was a departure from previous Sega consoles in several ways. First, the Sega name and logo were missing from it. In an interview with the British *Sega Saturn Magazine*, Irimajiri stated that market research concluded that casual gamers did not view Sega as a favorable brand name. The company wanted the Dreamcast to stand on its own merits and, if the market research was correct, didn't want it hampered by the Sega name. Ironically, the same research revealed that the Sega name carried much more weight when it came to software so therefore, the company was going to focus its brand-name marketing on that aspect of the business.

Other differences between the Dreamcast and the Sega consoles that preceded it included its analog/digital controller, which featured two ports for expansion packs. The first of the expansion packs was to be available immediately and was called the Visual Memory System (VMS), which Sega touted as the "world's smallest portable game card." This wasn't exactly true, since the VMS wasn't really a memory card. While it could store game data, it contained action buttons, a directional pad, and its own small LCD screen. Unlike standard memory cards, it could be used as a stand-alone gaming unit. Sega announced that graphically primitive stand-alone games would be available for the device. But the VMS could also be used to program special features, such as secret moves for Dreamcast fighting games. Two VMSs could also be docked together, so gamers could transfer data between the two.

Another innovative feature of the Dreamcast was its ability to connect to the Internet. Sega of Japan planned to package the Japanese console with an internal 33.6K modem, so gamers could access an online gaming network that was being set up. The company promised that the modem would be upgradable, so users could switch to broadband or cable modems as they became available. Sega of America opted not to include an internal modem with its version of the Dreamcast, but planned to release an external modem, although it was undecided whether the modem would be included with the unit or sold separately.

The Dreamcast hooked up to a standard television using a stereo AV cable that was supplied with the console. One end of this cable consisted of standard audio and video RCA jacks that plugged into the TV. The other end plugged into an "AV terminal" in the back of the console, which looked very much like a USB slot. Sega of Japan also offered an optional *Dreamcast VGA Box* that offered higher video resolution.[7] This peripheral also plugged into the AV terminal on the Dreamcast but since it only had RCA jacks built-into it, RCA audio and video cables had to be purchased separately.

Dreamcast software would be stored on GD-ROMs, rather than CDs or DVDs. The GD-ROM, which stood for ***G****igabyte* ***D****isc* ***R****ead-****O****nly* ***M****emory*, was a proprietary format developed by Sega and Yamaha. It was similar to a CD-ROM, except that information could be packed more closely together, resulting in more storage space. The GD-ROM held a maximum of 1.2 gigabytes, compared to a CD-ROM's maximum of 900 megabytes (.9 gigabytes). Originally, Sega ruled out CD-ROMs for storage, because Dreamcast games were going to exceed the maximum available space, and because CDs were prone to piracy. The company briefly considered using DVDs, but decided against them because they were too costly to produce at that time.

Sega planned to release the Dreamcast in Japan on November 27 with a retail price between ¥20,000 ($147) and ¥30,000 ($220). American gamers wouldn't be able to purchase the unit until the fall of 1999.

In October, with only a month remaining before the launch of the Japanese Dreamcast, the console and its online capabilities was shown publicly for the first time at the Sega New Challenge Conference in Tokyo. Sega proudly displayed its Internet home page, which it called *Dricas*: shorthand for Dreamcast. Dricas offered a number of features, including an email system called *Dream Flyer*, and a virtual newspaper called *Daily DC News*. No mention was made regarding which web browser the Dreamcast would use, or whether the system would even be packaged with one or not. However, the company's plans included WebTV compatibility and online multiplayer games, beginning with *Sega Rally 2*.

Several peripherals were also revealed, including an arcade stick, racing controller, steering wheel, fishing rod and a keyboard. As far as software for the console went, Sega promised that it would release one new game a week beginning with the system's launch through the end of the year.

Advertising for Sega and the Dreamcast proliferated. The Dreamcast logo was everywhere at the Tokyo Game Show, which followed the New Challenge Conference. Dreamcast-branded bags were even handed out at local train stations. Despite all of the emphasis on the Dreamcast, Sega of Japan set aside a small portion of its Tokyo Game Show booth for the still-supported Saturn.

Everything appeared to be moving flawlessly for Sega in the weeks leading up to the November 27 launch. However, in early November, a problem occurred on the PowerVR production line that resulted in the completion of far fewer chips than what Sega had ordered. The consequence of this was that fewer consoles were available at launch time than originally expected. Anticipating shortages, some local Japanese stores informed gamers who had reserved Dreamcasts that they probably wouldn't receive their consoles right away. With the prospect of less Dreamcasts on the market than anticipated, Sega changed its software release plans. Instead of a new title each week until the end of the year, the company decided to release three groups of games: one at launch, one right before Christmas, and the last on January 14, 1999.

Despite the fears of shortages, Sega delivered the Dreamcasts on November 27 as promised. Lines formed outside major stores in the Akihabara district of Tokyo. Everyone who had preordered a Dreamcast was able to purchase one for ¥29,000 ($236), which was just under the high-end price that Sega had quoted in May. Even the occasional customer who hadn't preordered was able to take one home.

Sega Dream Passport

Each Dreamcast that Sega sold was packaged with a fully-functional web browser called *Dream Passport*, which let users surf the Internet and check email.

By the end of the day, Sega had delivered all 150,000 consoles that it had available, but it estimated that it could have sold an additional 300,000 consoles if it had them. Four games were also offered at the launch, with *Virtua Fighter 3tb* being the most popular. On average, one copy of the fighting game was sold with every console.

Sega Dreamcast Virtua Fighter 3tb

The Dreamcast launch nearly paralleled that of the Saturn's almost four years earlier. By the end of the day on November 29, 1994, Sega of Japan had shipped 150,000 Saturns, along with an almost equal number of *Virtua Fighter* games. Sega executives hoped that the comparisons between the two systems ended there.

Sega Naomi

While the Dreamcast wasn't officially available in the United States in November, its architecture was, at least in arcades. Introduced at Japan's JAMMA 98 trade show in September, Sega's new *Naomi (New Arcade Operation Machine Idea)* arcade board contained what was basically a sister chipset to the Dreamcast. Naomi allowed Sega to distribute high-quality arcade games for a third of the price of its predecessor, the Model 3. The compatibility between the Naomi and the Dreamcast meant that games played in the arcade could be saved and brought home to the Dreamcast in a fashion similar to what SNK had done with its Neo•Geo systems. Although Sega didn't specifically announce any games that would take advantage of this feature, the company did explain that the data-saving procedure would be done via the VMS.

Since the Naomi was basically the same chipset as the Dreamcast, it was also powered by NEC's PowerVR2 chip. This was the chip that Sega chose instead of the one from 3Dfx, which then initiated a lawsuit between the two companies. In August, Sega and 3Dfx announced that they had reached a confidential agreement concerning their lawsuit.

Genesis 3

Ironically, as Sega of America braced for its Dreamcast debut, a new version of the Genesis was quietly released in American stores. Dubbed *Genesis 3*, the new console was the size of a portable CD player and was fully compatible with all of the existing Genesis cartridge-based games. Interestingly, the Genesis 3 hadn't been released by Sega at all. Majesco, a New Jersey-based software distributor, licensed the Genesis name from

Sega and released the console on its own with a retail price of $50. The Genesis 3 was only the beginning for Majesco, which planned to release new, inexpensive Saturns, Game Gears and Picos in 1999.

Sadly, purchasers of the Genesis 3 couldn't be able to access the Sega Channel, as Sega shut down the online service on July 31. Sega considered the 16-bit console dead and buried and decided that there was no point in continuing development using the 16-bit technology.

Sega Genesis 3

Project X Questions

Sega, with its new and old systems appearing on store shelves, wasn't the only potential competition that Nintendo and SCE had to contend with. VM Labs' Project X was still waiting in the wings.

After being something of an anomaly for three straight years, Project X finally came out of hiding in January at the winter CES. VM Labs finally permitted a select group of people to actually witness a demonstration of the hardware that had long been written off as vaporware by industry skeptics. While the guests found the hardware to be impressive, VM Labs still was tight-lipped about the system. Company spokesmen stated that the console would be manufactured by several companies, whose names couldn't yet be revealed. Third-party support for the system was ensured, as development kits (which cost only 1/3 of a PlayStation development kit) had been sent out to twelve developers (whose names were also confidential). Game development was promised to be relatively easy, as demonstrated by a CES presentation during which engineers were able to take the source code of *Doom* and have it run on Project X in a mere two days. Even more impressive was the fact that the playable version of *Doom* only utilized 15% of the system's resources. At least six games were expected to be available when the console finally made its grand debut in late 1998. VM Labs optimistically revealed that it expected to sell millions of units by 1999.

Many unanswered Project X questions from CES were answered at E^3 in late May. Instead of being a new stand-alone game console as had been expected, Project X was going to be a chip that would enhance the capabilities of DVD players, including the ability to play games. The inexpensive chip would be powerful enough to serve as the DVD unit's MPEG-2 decoder, and would replace the MPEG-2 decoding hardware that DVD players currently used. VM Labs insisted that the manufacturers of DVD-players would pay very little, if anything, for the chips. VM Labs expected to make its money by charging third-party developers royalties for the software that they created to use on the Project X-equipped DVD players. VM Labs seemed to be offering highly advanced DVD players that would cost no more than standard DVD players. The system interested many of the top names in software, such as Hasbro Interactive, Activision and Capcom, and the first Project X-enhanced DVD systems would begin appearing in early 1999.

By year's end, VM Labs announced that it had shed the Project X moniker and replaced it with an official name for their chip. The *Nuon* name "reflect[ed] the wide-reaching power of a technology capable of introducing millions of consumers to interactive entertainment through their television sets," according to VM Labs' CEO, Richard Miller.

Games On DVD

While DVD players with Nuon chips would be able to play specially designed videogames, even DVD players without them would be able to play games. Canada-based

Digital Leisure released *Dragon's Lair*, the first game that could be played on any DVD player.

Although *Dragon's Lair* had been released for the home many times over the years, the DVD version was the first to be completely faithful to the original arcade laserdisc version. The disc also included exclusive interviews with Don Bluth and Rick Dyer, the original designers of the game.

Replacing the PlayStation

Throughout the year, as Sega readied its plans to release the Dreamcast, SCE began slowly revealing its plans for a successor to the PlayStation. Early rumors for the new console indicated that it would be backward-compatible with the original PlayStation, causing critics to began weighing the merits and pitfalls of such capabilities. On the plus side was the fact that one could own a pre-existing library of games as soon as he bought the new console. However, history showed that backward compatibility didn't necessarily spawn success. A good example of this was the Atari 7800 which, to date, was the only console that offered built-in backward compatibility. Even though it could play nearly all of the games that had been made for the 2600, the 7800 had never achieved popularity. On the other hand, the 7800 hadn't been released until after the NES successfully entered the American market, by which time the Atari 2600 became passé.

If the rumors were true and SCE did decide to release a backward-compatible console, it ran the risk of selling a product that contained features that nobody would use. Developers might continue to release games that would play on all PlayStation systems and ignore the new features that would set the new console apart from the old one. If that happened, then there would be little need to purchase the new console, since all of the new games would still play on the old one.

In addition to compatibility, another issue that SCE had to decide about was whether the new system would be CD or DVD-based. SCE polled its developers to see what they thought.

In order to regain much of the thunder that Sega was receiving for the Dreamcast, SCE began discussing the follow up to the PlayStation publicly at E^3. SCE made developers happy by promising 3D graphics that would rival those on the Dreamcast and allow developers to create products that would have a similar look on both machines. On the whole, developers liked what they heard about the new system's capabilities, although they felt that development for it would be more difficult than for the Dreamcast. And since the new system wouldn't incorporate the Windows CE operating system like the Dreamcast, PC games would be more difficult to port over.

Despite all of the hoopla, SCE's next generation system was still in the planning stages, and the company couldn't even cite when it would be available. SCE didn't have any intentions to release a new system until after sales began to slow down on the original PlayStation. Most analysts didn't expect to see the new system until 2000 at the earliest.

With the new console still years away, SCE had other new hardware up its sleeve that it planned to release in Japan by the end of the year. A $30 PDA (Personal Digital Assistant) was announced in February and was similar to Sega's VMS. The PDA could plug into the PlayStation like a standard memory card, and gamers could then load characters from games into the PDA. They would even be able to train these characters when a PlayStation wasn't available. The PDA also contained an infrared function, so gamers could trade characters with one another easily.

However, the PDA wasn't meant to be merely a PlayStation peripheral. Like Sega with its VMS, SCE planned to release simple games that would play only on the PDA. Software would be available on standard PlayStation discs that could be loaded into the PDA via the game console. SCE planned to have twelve titles available upon the PDA's release. At least one third-party company, Square, planned to support the PDA.

In November, SCE announced a name for the PDA, the *PocketStation*. A December 23 Japanese release date was established. However, two weeks prior to that date, SCE felt that it couldn't produce enough PocketStations in time to satisfy the anticipated launch demand. SCE decided to delay the release until January 23, 1999 to avoid shortages.

SCE PocketStation

SNK Neo•Geo Pocket

The Neo•Geo Pocket

The astounding success of Nintendo's Game Boy had naturally led to the release of competitive handheld portables. Although several systems, including the Atari Lynx and Sega Game Gear, had been released over the years, none could ever gain a foothold in the market. Of course, other companies believed that they could fare better. SNK, the maker of the Neo•Geo consoles, decided to enter the Japanese handheld market in October with a small, monochrome portable called the *Neo•Geo Pocket*.

Early prototypes of the Neo•Geo Pockets looked like slightly larger versions of the Sega VMS. This was probably not coincidental, since the Neo•Geo Pocket had originally been designed to link to the new Dreamcast, as well as with other Neo•Geo Pockets. The final model, that was released on October 28 and cost ¥7,800 ($66), was a horizontally-held console similar to the Game Gear. Although the initial release didn't include any games that were Dreamcast-compatible, SNK revealed that it would release a Neo•Geo Pocket version of *King of Fighters* that would work in tandem with the Dreamcast version.

Initially, SNK didn't plan to bring the Neo•Geo Pocket to the United States. This changed shortly following the handheld's Japanese release, when SNK announced that it would the unit in the United States in April 1999.

WonderSwan

SNK was not the only company that planned to compete against Nintendo in the handheld arena. In May, Bandai, the distributor of the Tamagotchi, announced that it would also release a monochrome handheld system. Bandai system's 2.5-inch screen would have twice the visual capacity of the Game Boy. This would provide the console with limited full-motion video and give the illusion that several characters were moving independently. Bandai expected the system to be available in Japan by the end of the year, and predicted that sales would reach $304 million by March, 1999. Like SNK, Bandai initially didn't plan to release the new system in the United States.

The Bandai system, which had been designed to compete with the Game Boy, had been partly designed by Gunpei Yokoi, the designer of the Game Boy, through a partnership between his Koto Laboratory and Bandai. Yokoi tragically died before he could complete the system, so his designers finished it for him. They designed a puzzle game for the console called *Gun Pey* in his memory.

Bandai officially showed the new handheld on October 8, by which time it was officially called the *WonderSwan*. Bandai had signed over 30 third-party companies to design games for the console, Most of the games were targeted at a Japanese audience but Bandai hinted that if software suitable for American gamers were made available, it might release the console in the United States.

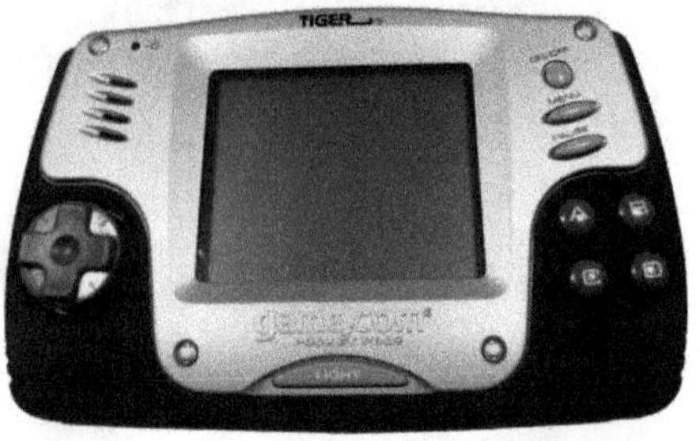

Tiger game.com Pocket Pro Backlight

Hasbro

Although SNK's Neo•Geo Pocket wasn't available in North America, Tiger Electronics' unpopular game.com was. Surprisingly, Tiger rereleased the unit in a smaller, compact edition called the *game.com Pocket Pro*. This new $50 unit contained the same features as the original, but was smaller due to the omission of the second, mainly unused cartridge port. Without it, the game.com Pocket Pro lost its ability to access the Internet or be used for email. However, added to the console was a "light" button that provided a frontlight to the screen,[8] a feature not available on most Game Boys. Tiger also released several new titles such as *Sonic Jam*, *Resident Evil 2* and *Monopoly*.

Tiger had been able to easily obtain the rights to *Monopoly*, because the company was purchased by Hasbro for $335 million during the first quarter of the year. Hasbro was already the parent company of Parker Brothers, which owned *Monopoly*. *Centipede* became available for the game.com in a similar fashion. In a highly publicized purchase, Hasbro Interactive, Hasbro's game subsidiary since 1995, purchased Atari's remaining assets from JTS for $5 million. This sale gave Hasbro ownership of more than 75 classic Atari titles, including *Asteroids*, *Missile Command* and *Pong*. Also included in the sale were the various consoles that Atari had marketed over the years such as the 2600, 7800 and Jaguar, as well as the Atari line of computers. What wasn't included in the sale were the Atari arcade games, which were owned by Williams. In the case of pre-1984 games that appeared in both arcade and home versions, Williams retained the arcade rights and Hasbro Interactive acquired the home rights.[9]

Many classic gaming fans hoped that Hasbro Interactive would rerelease classic games for the 2600 and Lynx, but Tom Dusenberry, Hasbro Interactive's president, stated that the company planned to "bring these classics back to life by updating them with the latest technology and interactive game design." Dusenberry hoped to duplicate the success that Hasbro had enjoyed following the release of an updated version of *Frogger*, which had been released by Hasbro the previous year and had gone on to become one of the top five PlayStation games of 1998. *Centipede* was the first Atari title that Hasbro Interactive updated, with versions available for the PC and PlayStation.

Hasbro Interactive's purchase of Atari caused the Securities Exchange Commission (SEC) to take a second look at JTS. In order to receive SEC approval for the 1996 merger of JTS and Atari, JTS had to promise to keep Atari afloat. However, according to rumor, after the two companies merged, JTS paid its executives back bonuses with Atari money. At the same time, Atari severed its existing contracts with Jaguar developers, and no new Atari R&D was instituted. The merger with JTS had allowed Atari to stay in business longer than it might have without JTS. However, without any sales or R&D, it was questionable whether Atari was really still in business or not. This is what the SEC wanted to find out.

Regardless of what the SEC discovered, Hasbro Interactive's purchase of Atari made many classic fans happy, since this meant that the Atari name and logo would continue.

They were also happy that Activision decided to release its popular collection of Activision 2600 classics for the PlayStation. Unfortunately, the result was less than what the fans had hoped for. The interface was poorly designed, and the PlayStation controller did not work well with the 2600 games.

The original 2600 games had been written in a form of assembly language that could only be understood by computers with a 6507 CPU. Since the PlayStation's R3000A RISC processor couldn't understand the original code, there were only two ways that Activision could get the old games to play on the new system. One was by rewriting the games altogether. This method required the programmer to study the original game's look and feel, and write a version of it in a language that the PlayStation could understand. The danger of this was that unless the programmer was thoroughly familiar with the original game, important aspects of the game, such as Easter eggs, might not be programmed into the new version.

ROM Legalities

The second method was to emulate the original code, that was saved as binary files called ROMs. An emulator was a program that could read the original 6507 code and convert it into something that the PlayStation could understand. The danger of using emulators was that any bug that existed in the original design would be carried over into the translated code. However, from a nostalgic point of view, the emulated version was the way to go, since it allowed gamers to play the actual game just as it had originally been written.

Since Activision owned all of the games that were featured on the collection, the company was free to do whatever it wanted with the ROMs. Unfortunately for the publishers like Activision, ROMs for virtually every game that ever existed were freely available on the Internet. Various emulators, which could translate the different ROMs to play on computers, were also available. This led to a legal tug-of-war between those who believed that the old games should be preserved and freely distributed, and those who believed that only the legal copyright holders should have access to the ROMs.

All sides agreed that the emulation programs were perfectly legal. Anyone with the know-how could sit down and write an emulator for any computer that he wished. The legalities came into play with the software that needed to be emulated. The general consensus was that any game that was no longer commercially available was ripe for emulation. The games from companies that were no longer in business were prime candidates.

In actuality, this wasn't true at all, and the IDSA was quick to seek out and shut down any Internet sites that were illegally distributing ROMs. People failed to realize that games were protected by copyright laws, whether they were still being distributed or not. Current copyright laws protected any game that had been written after 1978 for 75 years following its publication (or 100 years after its creation date - whichever was longer).

Although the actual legalities were in question, the general rule of thumb was that someone could possess a ROM image only if he owned the original game. But someone who owned an Atari 2600 version of *Defender* didn't have the right to the ROM image of the arcade *Defender*. Although it was highly unlikely that the IDSA would file suit against individuals for owning illegal ROMs, the organization did go after the distributors of the questionable titles.

Illegal Violent Games

While the IDSA was in favor of getting rid of disputed ROMs, the organization took the opposite view concerning the removal of violent videogames. Following fatal school shootings in Jonesboro, Arkansas and Springfield, Oregon, two Florida politicians proposed a ban on all graphically violent videogames. The IDSA quickly responded with a warning that such a law would be a "serious threat" to all videogames in Florida. And, as they pointed out, when a bill became a law in one state, it wouldn't be long before other states followed suit.

The problem began early in the year, when Florida Representative Barry Silver and Senator John Grant began pushing the *Children's Protection from Violence Act*. This law would "prohibit the public display of videogames that contain[ed] graphic violence in specified places." According to the bill, people under 18 would be restricted from entering establishments that offered graphically violent arcade games for play. Graphic violence was described as "the depiction or representation of death or severe injury, including, but not limited to, decapitation, dismemberment, repeated instances of bloodshedding, or grotesque cruelty." It would be up to the business' operator to keep the minors out.

While the bill had been written primarily to remove dubious games from public areas such as movie theaters and family arcades, the IDSA was deeply troubled with its wording, which had been constructed in such a way that it could also apply to home games. If such a law were enforced, then any questionable game had to be removed from store shelves before minors could be allowed to enter.

Although the IDSA was troubled with the bill, it was also confident that the bill would never pass. The videogame industry, which was already cleaning up its act through the use of warning labels, did not need to be dictated by a state government on what could and could not be displayed. Furthermore, the bill was unconstitutional. This had been proven in 1989, when Missouri tried to pass a similar law that would have prevented minors from entering video stores that rented and sold violent videotapes. In addition to deciding that that bill was unconstitutional, the Federal Court had ordered Missouri to pay the plaintiff's[10] attorney fees, which amounted to $200,000. Although videotapes, like videogames, had rating guidelines printed on their packaging, there weren't any laws that required stores and movie theaters to enforce these ratings. While some states made moves to create laws that required mandatory enforcement of the ratings, these attempts had been decreed unconstitutional.

The IDSA felt that the Florida bill was merely a rehash of the Missouri law, and that the result would be the same if the law was passed. Fortunately, it never came to that. The bill died in May.

With similar bills being proposed nationally by politicians who had no idea what videogames were all about, members of the videogaming industry decided to form a political-action confederation (PAC) to stick up for their interests in Washington and at the local levels. The group called themselves GamePAC, and their purpose was to "form a grassroots organization to monitor Congress and the federal bureaucracies, state legislatures and local governments, and in turn notify" members of GamePAC "so that they can then voice their opinion to these entities."

Despite this new voice in Washington, the arcade industry suffered a major defeat when Walmart, one of the industry's top customers of arcade games, announced that it would remove all violent arcade games from its stores. Fifty titles were scheduled to be removed from the stores by the end of the year, so Walmart could maintain its image as a family store.

Even though the industry had experienced setbacks such as the proposed Florida law and the Walmart ban, the two senators who had originally been responsible for game ratings were very happy with the results. At a July press conference Senator Herb Kohl thanked and praised game makers and arcade owners for posting game ratings. Kohl said that because of this goodwill act on the part of the arcades, no new laws needed to be enacted to force the arcades to monitor games with mature themes. Kohl warned, however, that boycotts would be considered at arcades that failed to voluntarily enforce the ratings. Kohl was joined by Senator Joseph Lieberman at a November press conference that had been set up by the citizens group, NIMF. Senator Lieberman declared in a speech that the industry had developed a "split personality." This alluded to the fact that although most of the industry had complied in the effort to clean up violent games, there was still a small fraction of developers releasing games that were more violent than ever. These games went beyond the usual killing and carnage by including graphic scenes of torturing and maiming. Despite this, the group released its *Fourth Annual Video and Computer Game Report Card* in December that awarded the gaming industry with an "A for Effort" in its attempts to enforce the ratings. Unfortunately, it was pointed out once again that not all arcades were cooperating.

Videogame Organizations

The United States wasn't the only country with a rise in violence that had been credited to videogames. Japan, where violent acts were rare in the first place, began seeing a rise in teen violence. To counteract the wave of negative criticism, the Japanese companies formed a trade organization called the Computer Entertainment Supplier's Association (CESA), whose goal was similar to that of the IDSA in the United States. It provided a unified voice that spoke for the entire industry.

Meanwhile, the organization that promoted videogame entertainment, the Academy of Interactive Arts & Sciences, made good on its promise and staged its first annual Interactive Achievement Awards ceremony to recognize the best games from the prior year. Awards were given in several categories, such as best adventure or action game for both consoles and computers. *GoldenEye 007* for the N64 was named the best overall game of the year.

Dancing Revolution

The Interactive Achievement Awards recognized the year's best console and computer games, but not arcade videogames. For years, arcades had been consistently stereotyped as breeding grounds for violence, but fortunately, they began changing for the better. Disney followed Gameworks' lead and opened DisneyQuest, a five-story entertainment center at Walt Disney World. While similar to those at Gameworks, the attractions at DisneyQuest featured Disney characters and themes. Disney planned an additional twenty DisneyQuest centers around the country, with the first scheduled to be built in Chicago in 1999.

Although big seemed to be better, Gameworks began opening smaller entertainment centers. The new Gameworks Studios were one-third the size of the regular Gameworks centers, yet featured big, brand-new arcade games that were just too expensive for older, smaller arcades to support. Just as the movie industry had to find unique ways to get people away from their TVs and into theaters during the fifties, arcade manufacturers were facing the same dilemma. One calamity resulting from this shift to the home was the closing of Acclaim's coin-op division early in the year.

Meanwhile, another Japanese arcade company continued churning out machines that the public clamored to play. Following the success of *Beatmania,* Konami released *Beatmania 2ndMix* in March. The new version followed the same game play as the original, but included a new mix of songs. In September, Konami released *Beatmania 3rdMix*.

With the success of *Beatmania,* Konami changed the name of its division that developed its rhythm games. What had been formerly known as G.M.D., which stood for "Games & Music Division," soon became *Bemani,* in honor of *Beatmania.*

On September 29, *Bemani* introduced a new Japanese arcade game that was a take-off on *Beatmania. Pop'n Music,* which offered colorful animated graphics, had nine vertical

Konami Pop n' Music

Konami Dance Dance Revolution Controls

Konami Beatmania Pocket

ASCII Beatmania Controller

columns, each colored differently. Nine large buttons sat on the cabinet, each corresponding with one of the columns on the screen. As notes randomly fell down the columns, the player had to tap the corresponding button as the note hit the bottom. The system would let the player know how accurately timed the tap was by flashing a word judgment such as "Great" or "Poor" on the screen.

While *Beatmania* and *Pop'n Music* were big draws in Japan, they made little impact outside that country. Konami's third rhythm game, released in Japan on November 21, was the charm.

As in the prior two games, the object of *Dance Dance Revolution* was to press the correct controller button that corresponded with a note on the screen. However, in this case, the "controller" was on the floor and players had to stomp the buttons with their feet.

The player stood on a "stage" in front of the cabinet. The stage consisted of nine tiles, arranged in a 3x3 square. The player stood in the center. The tiles directly surrounding the player featured arrows pointing away from the player. The four corner tiles were unused and unmarked.

On the screen, arrows scrolled upwards and passed over a set of stationary "guide arrows." When the two arrows met, the player had to step on the stage tile containing the arrow that corresponded to the one on the screen. As in *Pop'n Music*, players were awarded judgments for their accuracy.

Dance Dance Revolution was a game that was almost as fun to watch as it was to play. Spectators would stand around *Dance Dance Revolution* cabinets and gawk at the players simulating dancing as they attempted to keep up with the arrows on the screen.

As *Pop'n Music* and *Dance Dance Revolution* took over Japanese arcades, Konami introduced two Japanese home versions of *Beatmania*. One was a handheld model that featured an LCD screen, along with five buttons and a tiny turntable. The other version was used with the PlayStation. While the standard PlayStation had enough buttons to adequately play the game, the game was packaged with a special controller manufactured by ASCII, which mimicked the button-and-turntable layout of the arcade version.[11]

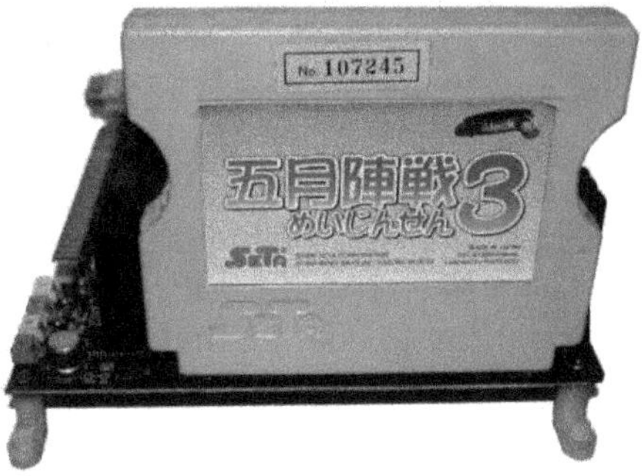

SETA Aleck 64 Cassette

As the rhythm games swept Japan, a new type of arcade system debuted in that country. The *Aleck 64* was an arcade system that was based on the N64. It had been designed by SETA under license from Nintendo. Games were available on ROM cassettes that could be easily switched.[12]

In the United States, the number of quarters that were dropped into arcade games, actually dropped themselves. Ironically, this occurred while the gaming industry experienced a record year, as Americans spent $6.3 billion on game consoles and software, a 20% increase over the previous year. As the technology for the home systems improved and rivaled that of the arcades, much of the money that had formerly been spent on arcade games was now used to purchase software. Unfortunately for the arcade industry, this was a trend that appeared to be continuing as the year came to a close.

CHAPTER TWENTY-SEVEN
1999

The MacWorld Expo show, which was held from January 4 through January 8 in San Francisco, was the first major game-related event of 1999. Even though Apple's Mac had never been noted for its games, Steve Jobs, the company's co-founder and interim CEO, wanted to change that. Jobs was "totally committed to making the Mac the best gaming platform in the world." He hoped to do this with a new line of super-fast Mac G3 computers and partnerships with notable software companies like id, Activision and Eidos.

Although Jobs' promise had been specifically aimed at the PC market, there was also an implication that he planned to go after the dedicated consoles like the N64 and the PlayStation. During a keynote speech, a representative from a software company called Connectix addressed the Expo crowd about his company's newest product, the *Virtual Game Station (VGS),* which was an emulator that allowed nearly 100 PlayStation games to run on the Mac G3. While the Connectix representative demonstrated several PlayStation games on the Mac, including *Street Fighter* and *Crash Bandicoot: Warped,* the crowd witnessed games that looked like they were being played on an actual PlayStation console. Although it wasn't yet officially available in stores, Connectix sold copies of the $50 VGS at the MacWorld Expo.

Connectix Virtual Game Station

SCE did not endorse or authorize the VGS, and socked Connectix with a copyright-infringement suit at the end of January. The lawsuit was confusing, since the VGS didn't actually infringe upon any of SCE's copyrights. Furthermore, according to Connectix CEO Roy McDonald, a legal precedent had determined that software that emulated hardware didn't violate any patent laws.

Critics were also confused about why SCE was so dead-set against the VGS in the first place, since SCE and the third-party publishers would probably benefit from it. Because the emulator couldn't use imported or pirated games, people would have to purchase the legal software. Sony claimed that the VGS violated its intellectual property rights and displayed the games in a way that could potentially tarnish the PlayStation brand name. Indeed, PlayStation games playing on the Mac using the VGS were prone to numerous bugs, limited compatibility and an inclination to crash often.

Despite the lawsuit, Connectix continued to sell the VGS throughout the winter. In the spring, the court discovered that the VGS did actually copy the PlayStation's BIOS and did indeed violate some of SCE's copyrights. A preliminary injunction ruled in SCE's favor and forced Connectix to stop delivering the VGS. Representatives from Connectix vowed that shipments would resume once the courts studied the evidence further.

SCE was determined to prevent Connectix from selling the emulator in any way that it could. In the end, SCE simply purchased the VGS from Connectix and quickly discontinued it.

SCE had less success against Bleem! which, on April 15, began marketing a similar PlayStation emulator under its own name. Although SCE submitted numerous requests for restraining orders to keep Bleem! off the market, they were all denied by the court.

Bleem! cooperated fully with the courts, and even handed its source code over to SCE, who couldn't find any evidence of copyright violations. Consumers who purchased Bleem! when it was released at the end of July found it to be just as buggy as the VGS was. Bleem!'s excuse was that its product was still a work in progress and would improve as patches were released.

bleem!

The Future PlayStation

The fact that people were purchasing emulators so that they could play PlayStation games on their computers was one indication of how popular SCE's freshman attempt at a videogame console actually was. But even as PlayStation games were being played on devices that they hadn't been intended for, SCE was "secretly" working on the details for the follow-up to its four-year-old console. The secret was officially announced on February 16, when Ken Kutaragi, the "father" of the PlayStation, presented specifications for a new chip at the annual IEEE International Solid State Convention in San Francisco. The chip, a joint project between SCE and Toshiba, was more powerful than any other on the market. Code-named the Emotion Engine, it actually consisted of four processors, including a built-in MPEG2 decoder and a 128-bit RISC CPU that clocked at 300MHz. Although Kutaragi didn't come right out and say it, everyone in attendance knew that this chipset was the successor to the PlayStation.

On March 2, SCE officially announced that the chipset that Kutaragi had shown was indeed for the "future PlayStation." In addition, the Emotion Engine was going to be joined by the CPU from the original PlayStation, which would handle all I/O functions, and would render the new console backward-compatible with the original's software.

While SCE lauded the new system as the most powerful console ever built, developers quickly learned that harnessing all of its power would not be easy. At a developer's conference in San Mateo, California, they learned that the new PlayStation would be able to do anything they wanted. They just had to figure out how to make it happen. Even though SCE would deliver development libraries, the developers would still have to program their own Assembly-language subroutines to really take advantage of the new console's power. This had been discouraged with the original PlayStation. Although most developers were certain that the first generation of games for the new system would be on par with games for the Sega Dreamcast, they speculated that the games could only improve as they learned more about the system.

Chip production was set to begin in the summer, at the rate of 10,000 chips per month. SCE estimated that it would have 1.44 million systems ready in time for a Japanese launch before the end of the year. One magazine was skeptical of these numbers. *Next Generation* printed a sidebar in its May 1999 issue that speculated that SCE might experience shortages upon its launch.

Because SCE didn't yet have an official name for the new system, it was simply referred to as the "future PlayStation." The press, on the other hand, had been calling it the PlayStation 2. SCE agreed with them and on September 13, announced that this would be the console's official name. SCE also announced that the system would be released in Japan on March 4, 2000 and would retail at ¥39,800 ($370), which was approximately the same price that the original PlayStation had cost in 1994.

Although it shared the same launch price as its predecessor, the PlayStation 2 looked

SCE DualShock 2

nothing like the original. SCE's intention had been to sell a set-top box that bridged the gap between videogames and other forms of home entertainment. Towards this end, the PlayStation 2 resembled a cross between a stereo component with a front-loading tray that accepted DVDs and CDs, and a computer with USB ports in the front and slots for modem and Ethernet cards in the back. Unlike Sega and its Dreamcast, SCE didn't plan to release the PlayStation 2 with a built-in modem, due to the fear that it would be obsolete by the time the company was ready for networking in 2001. SCE planned at that time to offer broadband technology through the Ethernet connection or a cable modem. SCE also planned to release an optional disk drive that would allow gamers to download and store game data and demos. Options that would be available at launch included a DualShock 2 Analog Controller and a memory card with 8MB of memory.

Games for the new system would be delivered in both CD- and DVD-ROM formats. CD-ROMs would be read at 24x, 12 times faster than on the original machine. DVD-ROMs would be read at 4x. The CD-ROMs would have blue undersides to differentiate them from the black PlayStation discs. DVD-ROMs would be silver. Unlike PlayStation games that were packaged in standard CD jewel-cases, the PlayStation 2 discs, regardless of whether they were CDs or DVDs, would be packaged in plastic Amaray cases, which were becoming the standard in the DVD industry.

An unprecedented 172 developers from Japan, the U.S. and Europe initially signed on with SCE to develop games for the PlayStation 2. Unfortunately, SCE had trouble keeping most of them happy. As the year progressed, many developers, particularly those outside of Japan, complained that they weren't receiving software-development kits (SDKs) from SCE. The select developers that did receive the SDKs complained that they had received "preliminary" kits that didn't represent what the final console would be like. SCE acknowledged that the full development kits wouldn't be available until 2000, and this made many developers nervous, because they anticipated that they wouldn't have any titles available in time for the PlayStation 2's launch.

SCE's Interesting Releases

Even though SCE was setting its sights on the PlayStation 2, it promised that it would still support the original PlayStation. To this end, SCE continued to release interesting games. Among them was *Vib Ribbon*, an odd game that was released in Japan on December 12. The graphics in *Vib Ribbon* were simplicity itself. The black screen was made up of white lines that looked like a child had drawn them with chalk and resembled the old vector graphic games such as *Asteroids*. The "ribbon" in the title was a white line that stretched across the screen. The object of the game was to guide a rabbit named Vibri along the ribbon and avoid the 18 obstacles that would be encountered by pressing one of the four buttons on the PlayStation controller. The player started with three lives[1] and lost one every time an obstacle was struck, and gained one if he reached the end of the level. The game ended when the player lost all of his lives.

Vib Ribbon was so ridiculously simple that the entire program loaded into the PlayStation's RAM without any need to constantly read the CD and load new information. This was the first PlayStation game that could do this but it was a good thing and not a step backwards. The game had been designed by Masaya Matsuura who had previous designed *PaRappa the Rapper*, which had launched the rhythm game genre. And like the previous effort, *Vib Ribbon* was also a rhythm game. In order for Vibri to pass an obstacle, the correct controller button had to be pressed in accordance with the music. Like *PaRappa the Rapper*, the game was packed with music. However, since the gamed resided in RAM, the game disc could be replaced with any CD that contained music tracks, and so a player could, for the first time, play a rhythm game with his own customized track list.

SCE Vib Ribbon

SCE finally released the $25 PocketStation in Japan on January 23. The tiny handheld sold out immediately, and SCE soon claimed that in order to fulfill the unexpectedly high demand for the PocketStation in Japan adequately, it would have to postpone the U.S. and European launches. Those outside of Japan weren't missing much. The gamers in Japan who purchased the PocketStation quickly learned that it consumed batteries very quickly and that it did little more than a standard memory card.

But the PocketStation was more than a standard memory card. The unit featured an LCD screen through which minigames could be played. On October 28, a third-party, Japanese developer released a package that added personality to a PocketStation. *Pokeler* from Atlus accessed the PDA functions of the PocketStation. However, it also came with tiny plastic pieces such as arms and legs. These pieces attached to the PocketStation, just like pieces attached to Hasbro's *Mr. Potato Head*, which made it look like a tiny robot.[2]

Atlus Pokeler

After the PlayStation 2 became official, SCE announced that it was going to revamp the PocketStation so it could be used with the new console. This decision effectively canceled all release plans for the PocketStation outside of Japan. SCE's plans were to upgrade the PDA by adding more memory and increasing the battery power.

While some critics felt that the PocketStation was SCE's entry into the portable-gaming market, SCE was actually pursuing other avenues into that area, which had always been dominated by Nintendo's Game Boy. One route had SCE looking into SNK's Neo•Geo Pocket. However, this seemed very unlikely, since SNK was courting Sega in a bid to link the Neo•Geo Pocket with the Dreamcast.

SCE's second possibility was to manufacture a portable version of the original PlayStation. This could be accomplished by shrinking the PlayStation to a size that would be similar to Sony's popular audio Discman player. A small, 2.25-inch screen could attach to the lid of the player, and power could be supplied by a lithium battery.

SCE never disclosed when or if a portable PlayStation would reach store shelves. However, the company did continue to make changes to the original PlayStation that were less obvious. In the late summer, SCE announced that it would remove the I/O ports from future PlayStation models. Many analysts believed that this was a strategic move by SCE to lower the price of the console to under $100. Since the I/O ports had never been used by SCE, the decision was practically a no-brainer. Unfortunately, it wasn't so cut and dried for the third-party vendors that produced peripherals that utilized the ports.

InterAct, for example, used the I/O ports for its highly popular GameShark. Questionable peripherals, such as the Game Wizard Pro, a device that allowed gamers to get around territorial lockout switches so Japanese discs could play on American consoles, also used the I/O ports.

On August 23, SCE reduced the price of the PlayStation to $99, an amount that many financial experts believed put it in the category of "impulse buy". Nintendo quickly followed SCE's lead and lowered the price of the N64 to $99 to match the PlayStation.

9/9/99

The price decreases for the PlayStation and N64 went into effect only two weeks before the Dreamcast's U.S. debut. Sega claimed that it wasn't bothered by the $99 price, which it claimed wouldn't change the Dreamcast's expected market share. Casual gamers might be swayed by the lower price. Sega was after the hard-core gamers.

As Sega of America geared up for the September launch of the Dreamcast, it also analyzed the console's impact on Japanese consumers. Although the Japanese launch had been less than stellar, executives at Sega Enterprises were confident that they would have an installed base of four million units by the end of 1999.

Chief Operating Officer Bernie Stolar referred to the Dreamcast as "a living organism that can grow as the player grows." According to Stolar, the system would "change and evolve with the gamers' needs, demands and wants." One way to make the console evolve was by offering a variety of peripherals.

Two storage devices, one external and the other internal, were announced. The external one was a Dreamcast version of Iomega's popular Zip Drive, which Sega and Iomega had joined forces to produce. Although a prototype had been displayed, neither a release date nor a retail price was announced. The internal device was a hard drive that

Sega planned to release so online users had a place to save their email. A camera and a microphone were also planned so online gamers could see and talk to the people they were competing with.

The new peripherals emphasized online gaming because Sega viewed it as videogaming's next frontier. Dreamcast owners were pioneers, since they had, at least for the time being, the only videogame console that could directly connect to the Internet. Sega of America's plan was to offer the *Dreamcast Network*, an online gaming site, and on December 14, Sega of America announced a partnership between SegaSoft and Excite@ Home, a high-speed cable Internet provider, who would both be collaborating on the website. Even though the Dreamcast Network wouldn't be available until 2000, And to make web surfing from a console as easy as it was from a computer, an optional $25 keyboard would be available. Sega would even provide the keyboard free to those who subscribed to AT&T's Worldnet, Sega's ISP (Internet Service Provider) of choice.

Sega planned for most of its games to benefit from online access in one way or another. For instance, *Sonic Adventure*, one of the U.S. launch titles, which had already been released in Japan at the end of 1998, allowed players to upload and download game data between the Dreamcast and Sega's website.

Americans would have a faster online experience than the Japanese. Bernie Stolar told an audience at the Game Developers Conference in March that the American Dreamcast would include a 56K modem instead of the 33.6K model that had been offered to the Japanese.[3] What he failed to tell them was that Sega had asked Microsoft and NEC to absorb the cost of the modem, so that the price of the Dreamcast could be under $200. If the two companies refused, the modem would have to be sold as an accessory. When Stolar announced in April that the American Dreamcast would be launched on September 9 (9/9/99) and would retail for $199, he didn't mention whether the modem would be included or not, because he didn't yet have a firm commitment from his corporate partners.

In May, Sega of America officially announced at E^3 that the 56K modem would be included with the $199 Dreamcast. However, that was just the beginning. At a later date, Sega planned to offer a cable modem or an Ethernet connector, either of which would replace the 56K modem.[4]

In addition to the faster modem, some peripherals for the North American Dreamcast would be named differently than their Japanese counterparts. In North America, the memory device would be called the *Visual Memory Unit* (VMU), instead of the Visual Memory System. The reason for this was because the *VMS* acronym was trademarked in the United States by the Digital Equipment Corporation for its computer operating system.

Another product that would fit into one of the controller's expansion ports was the *Jump Pack*, which was called the *Puru Puru Pack* in Japan and the *Vibration Pack* in Europe. The Jump Pack was similar to Nintendo's Rumble Pak and provided force feedback to the controller in compatible games.

Sega Dreamcast Jump Pack

Sega had much riding on the Dreamcast's American launch. The company had experienced a $378 million net loss during the fiscal year that ended on March 31. In order to save money, the company combined its arcade and consumer divisions and planned to close many Japanese arcades. Sega employees also felt the pinch. The company announced that it would lay off 25% of its employees and reduce the salaries of its executives.

Unexpectedly, three weeks before the U.S. launch, Bernie Stolar was fired from Sega of America. Apparently, Sega of Japan had never been happy with the Dreamcast's $199 price, an amount that had been set by Stolar. Sega of Japan wanted the Dreamcast to retail for $249, so the company could make an immediate profit. Stolar was replaced with Toshiro Kezuka, who had formerly been in charge of domestic sales and distribution for Sega Enterprises in Japan. Sega was certain that Stolar's departure would not affect the Dreamcast's launch.

The Dreamcast launched in North America on 9/9/99, as promised. And unlike the Japanese launch, when only four titles were offered, 18 games were offered including the long awaited *Sonic Adventure*. Generally, system launches in the United States never produced the frenzy that was typically felt in Japan, with long lines outside of electronics stores that opened at midnight. The year-long hype for the Dreamcast changed that. While one hundred thousand people had preordered the PlayStation in 1994, three times as many had pre-ordered the Dreamcast. Stores opened at midnight on September 9 to waiting crowds. All in all, during the 24-hour period of September 9, sales of the Dreamcast totaled nearly $98 million, which set an entertainment-industry (which included games, music and movies) record for the highest gross in a single day. The launch went so well that Sega executives who had forecasted that one million units would be sold by the end of the year went back to raise their projections.

Unfortunately, the launch did not go off without a hitch. Complaints about defective discs began arriving on Sega's customer-service hotline immediately. A quick investigation revealed that all of the defective discs had been pressed on a single duplicating machine at a Sanyo plant in California. The discs hadn't fit in their molds correctly, which resulted in missing data. What made it worse was that the defect was found among Sega's most eagerly awaited launch titles, including *Sonic Adventure*. Although the problem had been caught relatively quickly, it still put a damper on Sega's nearly flawless launch. In order to satisfy the public, Sega and the third-party publishers that had produced the defective discs changed their return policies. Activision even went so far as to set up a toll-free phone number that could be used by anyone who had bought a defective copy of *Blue Stinger*. Everyone who called the Activision hotline immediately received a pristine copy of the game along with a postage-free envelope so they could return the defective disc.

Another problem that Sega experienced was a temporary shortage of consoles and peripherals. Within a week after the launch, the stores were again stocked, and Sega went on its way to sell its first million consoles.

From the beginning, Sega of America had a five-phase plan in the development of its online network:

Phase 1: E-mail, Game Tips
Phase 2: Enhanced Gameplay Elements
Phase 3: E-mail Based Games
Phase 4: Fully Networked Games and Parlor/Puzzle Games
Phase 5: Full 3D Multiplayer Games and the Ultimate Online Video Gaming Destination

The Dreamcast launch fulfilled the first two phases. Phase 1 was accomplished with the web browser that accompanied the console, which allowed users to the surf Internet and use email. Phase 2 was accomplished with games like *Sonic Adventure*, which allowed users to download new characters.

Sega Europe planned to release the Dreamcast on September 23, but it was pushed back to October 14 in order for Sega Europe's online network, *Dreamarena*, to be completed. The European Dreamcast was bundled with a 33.6kb modem like the Japanese one, and came with a software package called *Dream Passport*, which was used to access the Internet. Unfortunately, even with the delay in the launch, Dreamarena's infrastructure was inadequate to handle the influx of people who were trying to sign onto the network. Sega Europe was also accused of misleading advertising since ads for the Dreamcast mention online gaming and games weren't planned to be released until 2000.

Microsoft Xbox

Until Microsoft optimized its *Windows CE* operating system for the Dreamcast, it had never had anything to do with videogame consoles. Although Microsoft's part in the overall development of the Dreamcast was relatively minor, the software giant had gotten its feet wet in the lucrative videogame hardware industry, and apparently liked what it saw. By the end of the summer, rumors began to stir that the company was about to jump headfirst into the deep end. Microsoft was going to build its own videogame console.

The rumors were, of course, true. In February, Bill Gates had signed off on the project. Microsoft then spent the rest of the year denying what would become one of the worst-kept secrets in the videogame industry.

The initial reports were quite detailed for something that was only a rumor. The system would be code-named *Xbox*[5] and would employ a *Windows CE* operating system similar to the Dreamcast's. It would contain a 500MHz Intel processor and a graphics chip supplied by either Nvidia or 3Dfx. Microsoft would not actually manufacture the Xbox. That job would most likely be subcontracted to a computer company like Dell or Gateway. And like a PC, the system would have an open architecture, for which developers could freely design and release games without having to pay any royalties. The system would be DVD-based, and all Xbox software would run on PCs that had the *Windows* operating system. Finally, the system would be released in the fall of 2000 and would retail for under $300.

Additional details were leaked to the press within a month after the initial rumor first broke. The Xbox would have an AMD processor instead of the Intel, and it would include a 4GB hard drive. While Microsoft continued to deny the existence of the Xbox, other companies were more forthcoming. Sega of America executives admitted that they had known about the Xbox for a while, and that they were pleased with it because it would complement the Dreamcast. Since they both used a *Windows* operating system, developers would have little trouble porting games between the Dreamcast and the Xbox, as well as the PC.

Another rumor spread that the Xbox would wirelessly connect to any TV. This meant that if someone wanted to use the Xbox in a room where the TV was being used by someone else, the gamer merely had to go to a second TV to play. A wireless adapter would send video from the Xbox to the secondary TV, and from the game controller back to the Xbox.

By the end of the year, there still wasn't any confirmation from Microsoft regarding the validity of the rumors, despite all of the publicity that the Xbox was receiving from mainstream publications like the *Wall Street Journal*, as well as the videogame magazines. According to a Microsoft spokesman, the Xbox was just a rumor, and Microsoft did not comment on rumors. Most analysts agreed that Microsoft was merely biding its time and waiting for the right moment to make an official announcement. Many felt that Bill Gates would surprise the world about Microsoft's involvement with the Xbox during his keynote speech at CES in January, 2000.

Nintendo Dolphin

On May 12, the day before the opening of E^3, Howard Lincoln officially announced Nintendo's new console, which was code-named *Dolphin*. This would be driven by an IBM 400MHz Gekko processor, which was an extension of IBM's PowerPC computer architecture, and was small enough to sit on a human fingertip. The individual transistors in the chip would use copper connectors instead of the traditional aluminum; the former would result in smaller chips that would be less expensive to produce and would require less power. Lincoln assured the press that the Dolphin would be the "most powerful of any current or planned home videogame system."

Nintendo intended to release the new system in time for Christmas 2000, to directly compete with the PlayStation 2. Lincoln made it a point to inform the press that due to its capabilities, the Dolphin would "equal or exceed the PlayStation 2." The console's 200 MHz graphics engine was being developed by Art-X, a company whose head, Dr. Wei Yeng, had designed the N64's graphics chip when he had been with Silicon Graphics. NEC, in a deal worth $2.86 billion, would manufacture the chips.

Lincoln further revealed that the new system would be DVD-based. Matsushita, who was developing the DVD drive, would manufacture the drives and the software. Matsushita would also manufacture, under its Panasonic brand, other consumer devices that would use the Dolphin technology. In a move reminiscent of VM Labs' integration of its Nuon technology, Panasonic planned to release DVD players that would be able to play Dolphin games, beginning in fall 2000.

While the Panasonic machines would play standard DVDs and audio CDs, as well as Dolphin games, Nintendo's Dolphin console would not. Nintendo was experimenting with a proprietary disk system that could store 1.6 gigabytes of data. With the absence of a cartridge slot, the new console definitely would not be backward-compatible with the N64.

Lincoln made it clear that Nintendo was strictly a game company and he stressed that the Dolphin's inability to perform functions other than playing games would theoretically keep the price of the console down. Although the price wasn't revealed, Lincoln promised that the Dolphin would be sold at a "very aggressive mass-market" price.

During the six months following E[3], there was little news from Nintendo regarding the Dolphin. Factor Five, a developer of proprietary sound tools, was added to the list of developers working on the Dolphin hardware, and S3, Inc. was employed to add an advanced texture-compression technology. Unfortunately, no one outside of Nintendo would be able to view the completed product for nearly a year, after which Nintendo planned to publicly debut the Dolphin at its annual *Spaceworld* show in August, 2000. Nintendo still stood behind its Christmas 2000 release date, although several anonymous developers began hinting that the date was totally unrealistic. Meanwhile, Matsushita announced that it would not release its Dolphin-compatible DVD consoles in the United States.

64DD is Delivered

As Nintendo prepared for a new-generation console, it still had some unfinished business with its current one. On December 1, after two years of promises and delays, Nintendo of Japan finally delivered its 64DD peripheral. However, because of the long delay, Nintendo expected the 64DD to be a failure in the marketplace, and made it available primarily through a service called RandNet. Only a very limited number of 64DDs were available in retail stores, which more than guaranteed the peripheral's fate. The system was canceled outside of Japan.

RandNet was an online service for the N64 that had been created by Nintendo of Japan and Recruit, a Japanese media company, to perform the same function that the Satellaview had done for the Super Famicom.[6] A RandNet Starter Set came with a new 64DD and included a telecommunications cartridge that connected to a phone jack, a disk that contained a web browser and an Expansion Pak that boosted the N64's internal memory to 8MB. A subscription to the service cost ¥2,500 ($28) per month and allowed subscribers to compete with other gamers online, play unreleased games, surf the Internet, access online message boards and send and receive email. Downloaded information could be saved on disks through the 64DD.[7]

Nintendo 64 with 64DD

Nintendo 64DD Modem

Nintendo Mario Artist with Mouse

Two disks launched with the 64DD. One was *Kyojin no Doshin* (*Doshin the Giant*), a God simulation. The other launch title was *Mario Artist: Paint Studio.* which was a program that allowed budding artists to draw on the screen and save their art to the disk. It was the first in a series of *Mario Artist* programs that would include a 3D computer graphics editor and an animation studio.[8] Similar to the earlier *Mario Paint,* which had been released for the Super Famicom/SNES, *Mario Artist: Paint Studio* was sold with an N64 mouse, which could be used by other *Mario Artist* titles, but was never incorporated into any other N64 program.

While the 64DD and the RandNet service were confined to Japan, American gamers were also offered a peripheral that could get them online through their N64s. InterAct introduced its *Sharkwire* at E^3 in May, and then test-marketed in several American cities throughout the year.[9] It consisted of a modem cartridge and a full-size keyboard that plugged into the N64. Basically, it wasn't much different than Sega's NetLink for the Saturn. However, where the NetLink had cost $200, the Sharkwire retailed for only $80.

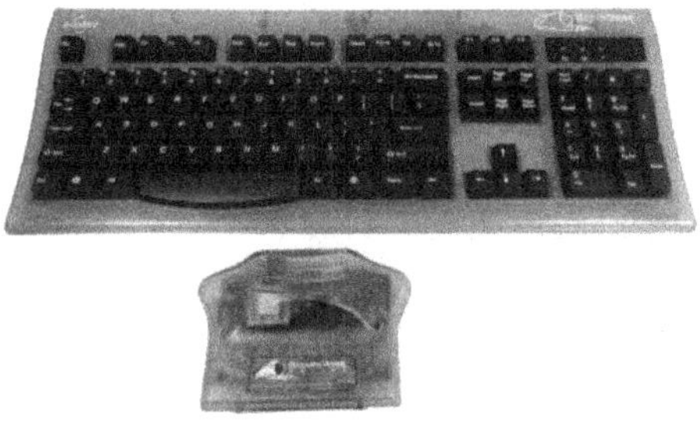

Interact Sharkwire

Unfortunately, the Sharkwire provided only limited online support. While the standard modem speed was 56k bits per second, the Sharkwire modem was only capable of 14.4k. That speed was much too slow to browse the Internet or play online games. However, the Sharkwire didn't offer either service to its users. Instead, Sharkwire users signed onto Sharkwire Online, InterAct's personal website. Sharkwire Online was text-based, so the slow modem speed didn't interfere too much. And since Sharkwire users could only sign onto that website, there wasn't any danger of them trying to access anything else on the Internet, although certain sponsored sites, such as Fox Sports and Electronics Boutique, were accessible. InterAct provided a gaming community that users could access for $10 a month, which let them keep in touch with other N64 owners, and which included an email service. Unfortunately, users didn't have any way to save anything they downloaded, including their email.

Game Boy Advance

In early 1999, Nintendo's known plan was to slowly phase out the old line of monochrome Game Boy Pockets and focus on the Game Boy Color, which had sold more than 8 million units in approximately six months. However, this plan seemed to be in question when, in May, rumors began emerging out of Japan that Nintendo was developing a new color handheld that would feature a bigger backlit screen.

The rumors proved to be true and in August, Nintendo began disclosing details regarding the new handheld at its annual Japanese Spaceworld show. Tentatively called the *Game Boy Advance*, it would contain a 32-bit RISC processor which, in addition to running games that could only play on the new system, would also be backward-compatible with all of the prior Game Boy and Game Boy Color cartridges. However, despite the original rumors, the new system would not be backlit.

The processor was being developed by ARM Corp, a British company that developed CPUs for cellular phones. Not surprisingly, the Game Boy Advance would have the ability to hook up with a cellular phone to connect to the Internet, which would then give gamers the ability to access email, download games, chat and partake in some type of online gaming system. Nintendo was also developing a digital camera that would allow network gamers to see each other while playing.

The release date for the Game Boy Advance was scheduled to parallel that of the Dolphin. It was usually risky for a company to launch two new consoles during the same time frame, since most households would probably only buy one of them. Nintendo had the incentive to do so because the two consoles would be joined at the hip. In other words, Nintendo planned for the Game Boy Advance to hook up to the Dolphin in some capacity.

WonderSwan

Bandai hadn't released its WonderSwan in 1998 as it had announced. Instead, the monochrome launched on March 6, with a retail price of ¥4,800 ($39), which was ¥3,000 ($24) less than the similar Neo•Geo Pocket. In September, Bandai displayed the

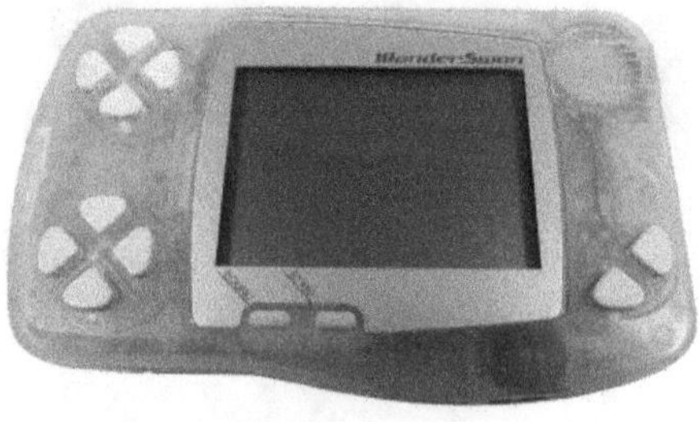

Bandai Wonderswan

SNK Neo•Geo Pocket Color

WonderSwan at the Tokyo Game Show along with new peripherals that were scheduled to arrive in 2000. One item shown was a infrared adapter that would connect the WonderSwan with SCE's PocketStation. Another peripheral would connect the WonderSwan with the Internet.

Neo•Geo Pocket Color

However, no matter what Bandai did with the WonderSwan, it appeared to be one step behind SNK's Neo•Geo Pocket. On March 16, ten days after Bandai released the monochrome WonderSwan, SNK launched a ¥8,200 ($69) *Neo•Geo Pocket Color*. Like the Game Boy Color, the Neo•Geo Pocket Color was compatible with all of the monochrome Neo•Geo Pocket's games, and new color games would also play on the original system.

SNK had planned for its Neo•Geo Pocket Color to compete with the Game Boy Color, feature to feature. The Neo•Geo Pocket Color ran on two AA batteries for 40 hours, twice as long as the battery life of the Game Boy Color. SNK also bragged that the Neo•Geo Pocket Color sported near-arcade graphics, thanks to its 16-bit CPU. In addition, SNK threw in some extras, such as a horoscope generator, calendar, alarm and world clock.

SNK also released a *Wireless Communication Unit* that plugged into the system. This device allowed gamers within close proximity of one another to compete against each other as long as each one had a Wireless Communication Unit and a copy of the game. The Wireless Communication Unit sent signals via radio waves and allowed up to 64 players to compete at one time. Of course, a special link cable was also available that could connect two Neo•Geo Pocket consoles together so games could be played by two players simultaneously.

A different type of link cable was also available. The *Neo•Geo Pocket/Dreamcast Setsuzoku Cable*, which was only issued in Japan. could connect a Neo•Geo Pocket Color with a Dreamcast and allow gamers to transfer data, such as new characters, between the two systems. The first games to offer this compatibility were the Dreamcast's *King of Fighters: Dream Match 1999* and the Neo•Geo Pocket Color's *King of Fighters R-2*.[10]

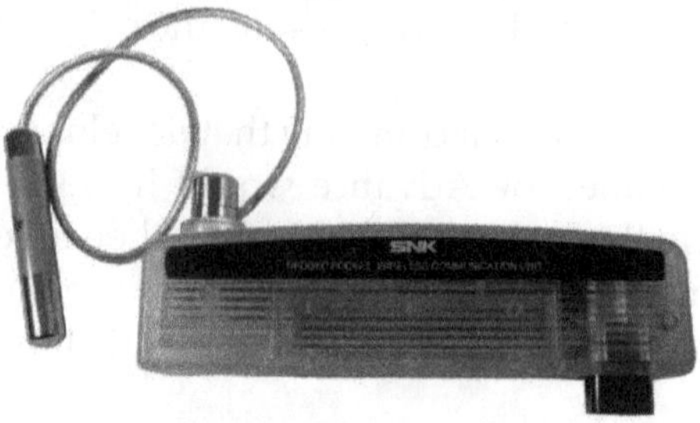

SNK Neo•Geo Pocket Wireless Communication Unit

SNK had initially announced that the Neo•Geo Pocket Color would be available in the United States in September. However, it jumped the gun and offered the console to Americans through its website in April. The $70 Neo•Geo Pocket Color actually reached American store shelves on August 6.

And yet, while Americans were finally able to purchase a handheld from SNK, they were not to get the latest model that their Japanese counterparts were offered. On October 21, SNK

SNK New Neo•Geo Pocket Color

introduced the *New Neo•Geo Pocket Color* in Japan. This unit, which was completely compatible with the previous Neo•Geo Pocket Color, was actually 13% smaller and had improved sound output. The price was slightly improved as well as it retailed for ¥6,800 ($64).The Neo•Geo Pocket Color was not released outside of Japan.

While Americans weren't recipients of the link connection between the Neo•Geo Pocket Color and the Dreamcast, they did benefit from another result of the agreement between SNK and Sega. This was the release of Sega-brand games for the Neo•Geo Pocket Color. The first was *Sonic the Hedgehog Pocket Adventure*, which was released in North America and Europe in December.[11]

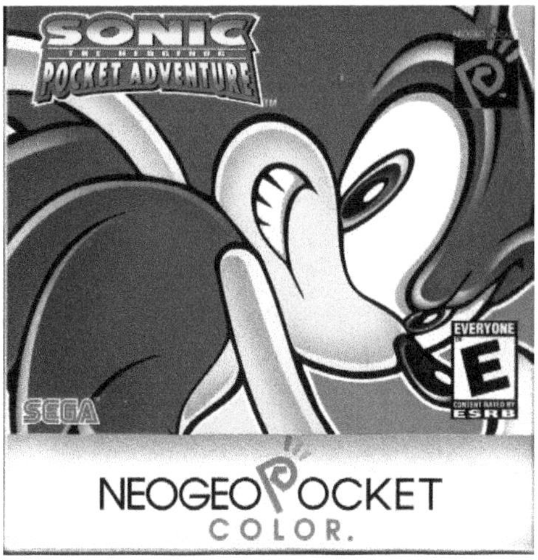

Sonic the Hedgehog Pocket Adventure

However, a May announcement by Sega Enterprises president Shoichiro Irimajiri had suggested that the Neo•Geo Pocket Color wouldn't be the only portable recipient of Sega games. According to the Japanese newspaper *Nihon Keizai Shinbun*, Irimajiri had said that his company would also begin developing software for the Game Boy Color and the WonderSwan. Irimajiri's reasoning behind this business decision was sound. Since Sega didn't have any plans to reenter the handheld market for the time being, it could develop games for the competitor's systems without actually having to compete with them.

Sonic Jam was already available for Tiger Electronics' poorly received game.com Pocket Pro. Unlike SNK, which had released a color version of its handheld to better compete with the Game Boy Color, Tiger Electronics didn't have any intentions of doing such a thing. Instead, the price of the monochrome unit was lowered to $30 and the frontlight option was removed. In its place, Tiger offered the system in five colors, including pink and orange. Three additional cartridges from the Hasbro catalog, *Centipede*, *Frogger* and *Scrabble*, were released. Unfortunately, this wasn't enough to get people interested in the console.[12]

Tiger game.com Pocket Pro - no frontlight

Pokémon All Over

Whether a handheld system was good or bad wasn't ultimately as relevant as it would have been if it didn't have to compete with Nintendo's juggernaut. Even though the original Game Boy was ten years old, its popularity showed no signs of abating. Fueling most of the interest in the device was the Pokémon phenomenon, which was so popular that it was featured in a cover story in the November 22 edition of *Time* magazine.

Time Magazine - November 22, 1999

Nintendo released several new Pocket

Nintendo Pokémon Pinball

Monsters/Pokémon games throughout the year. *Pokémon Pinball* came out in Japan on April 14, and in North America on June 28. This was the first handheld game to have a built-in rumble option. Because the Game Boy Color didn't have an extra slot where a Rumble Pak could be inserted, the feature was built into the cartridge. The cartridge itself was oversized and required one AAA battery in order for the rumble feature to work (although the game could still play without it).

On October 19, Nintendo of America released *Pokémon Yellow,* the American version of *Pocket Monsters Pikachu*. Over one million copies of *Pokémon Yellow* were sold within two weeks of its release. A special yellow Game Boy Color console, which had been available in Japan for two years, was finally released in North America. The $110 unit was bundled with *Pokémon Yellow.*

Nintendo also released new Pocket Monsters/ Pokémon games for the N64. *Pocket Monsters Snap* came out on March 21, while its American counterpart, *Pokémon Snap,* became the first Pokémon title for the American N64 when it was released on June 30. The first Japanese Pocket Monsters N64 game, *Pocket Monsters Stadium,* was rereleased as *Pocket Monsters Stadium 2* on April 30. The game was updated so that all 151 Pocket Monsters were available for battle.

Like the original *Pocket Monsters Stadium, Pocket Monsters Stadium 2* was compatible with the N64 64GB Pak. Nintendo released several games in Japan that incorporated the device. *Mario Golf,* for example, was available in both N64 and Game Boy Color editions and characters from either version could be transferred to the other. But while characters could be saved on the Game Boy Color, they could not be saved on the N64.

Mario Golf was released in North America for the N64 and Game Boy Color on June 30. Nintendo of America also released the 64GB Pak simultaneously but changed its name to the *Transfer Pak. Mario Golf* would be the only game released in North America during 1999 that used the Transfer Pak.

The 64GB Pak wasn't used only used to transfer data between a Game Boy Color cartridge and the N64. Japanese users could also plug the Japanese Game Boy Camera into the 64GB Pak to save or retrieve photos while using the 64DD game *Mario Artist: Paint Studio.*

But while the 64GB Pak was optional for most of the games that could use it, it was necessary for the playing of *Pocket Monsters Stadium 2,* wherein Pocket Monsters could be transferred from the *Pocket Monsters Green, Red* and *Blue* cartridges and then battle on the N64.

Although *Pocket Monsters Stadium 2* allowed gamers to use all of the Pocket Monsters in battle, it was determined that 151 creatures weren't nearly enough. And so, on November 21, Nintendo of Japan released two new cartridges for the Game Boy Color, *Pocket Monsters Gold* and *Pocket Monsters Silver*. These sets introduced 100 additional monsters in total. The sets were also backward-compatible with the original generation, so it was mandatory to collect the 151 from the initial sets, in order to collect them all.

Nintendo of Japan also released its *Pocket Pikachu 2 GS* on November 21. This handheld unit was similar to the *Pocket Pikachu* that came out in 1998. New features included a color screen and the ability to transfer data between two of the units via an infrared port. But the *Pocket Pikachu 2 GS* could also communicate with a Game Boy Color through the new *Pocket Monsters Gold* and *Pocket Monsters Silver* games.

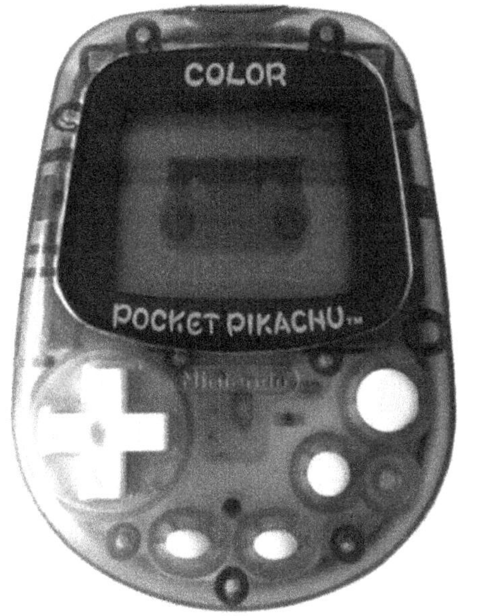

Nintendo Pocket Pikachu 2

Pokémon: The First Movie was released on November 10 in theaters throughout North America. When a Los Angeles radio station offered chances to win movie tickets, Warner Bros. was inundated with more than 70,000 calls, which forced the studio to shut down its voicemail system for a short time. And as if children needed any enticing to attend the movie, one free, exclusive Pokémon trading card was given to each attendee. This caused another problem for parents. Wizards of the Coast produced four different cards for the movie, but the theaters only handed out one per customer. This meant that many children attended the movie at least four times just to get the individual cards that they needed.

In November, Burger King began its most ambitious Kids Meal promotion ever. As a tie-in with the movie, the fast-food chain included one Pokémon character with each Kids Meal. Unfortunately for collectors, Burger King produced 59 different Pokémon toys,[13] and the promotion only lasted eight weeks. And since each Pokémon was packaged in a sealed, plastic Pokéball, patrons couldn't request specific toys with their meals. Individual Burger King outlets ran out of the giveaways very quickly as people kept returning over and over again, each hoping to collect a complete set.

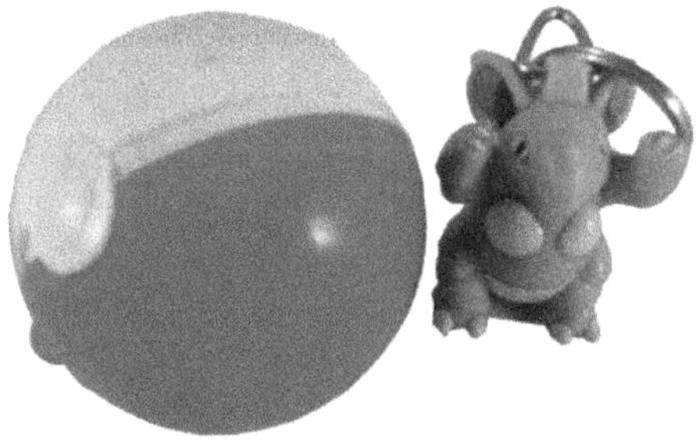

Burger King Pokéball

Unfortunately, the Burger King promotion wasn't without mishap. In December, a 13-month-old girl in Sonora, California terminally suffocated when half of one of the spherical containers had become stuck over her nose and mouth. Burger King refused to recall the balls until it could be proved that the Pokéball had caused the baby's death. After an 18-month-old Kansas girl got her nose and mouth stuck in a Pokéball half, and was fortunately saved by her father, Burger King recalled the Pokéballs, offering free fries for every Pokéball turned in.

Wizards of the Coast's Pokémon trading cards were being collected with the same intensity as the Burger King toys. While kids bought the cards and actually played the game, most were caught up in the quest of trying to "get them all."[14] This wasn't easy, since some cards were rarer than others. The packaging that the cards came in said that the odds of getting a "premium" card were one in thirty-three. This led to a racketeering charge by parents in New York and California against Nintendo of America and Wizards of the Coast.

According to the suit, which had been filed by a San Diego law firm, the buying of Pokémon cards was akin to illegal gambling. Children purchased multiple eleven-card packs with the hope that they'd find some of the rare premium cards inside. The law firm asserted that this was nothing more than "a lottery disguised as a kids' game." Nintendo viewed the lawsuit as frivolous, especially since this was the ninth such suit that the same firm had filed against various trading-card companies.

Although the cards were not declared illegal, they were banned by many school districts around the country. School officials found that the cards were constantly the cause of fights and general disturbances.

Voice Commands

Nintendo of America had been involved in another lawsuit in 1999. On February 8, the company released *Mario Party* in North America. While the game received positive reviews, some of the mini-games required the controller's analog stick to be rotated very quickly. Some players incorrectly used their palms to rotate the sticks, and this resulted in blisters. Many wound up with broken controllers, because the analog stick just wasn't sturdy enough to take on the constant movement. Several parents sued the company, either for the hurt hands or the broken controllers and Nintendo of America was found guilty of both charges. As a penalty, the company had to reimburse those who had broken their controllers. Nintendo also had to give gloves to anyone who had hurt his hands while playing the game. Despite the unexpected lawsuit, *Mario Party* was a much needed hit for Nintendo and the N64.

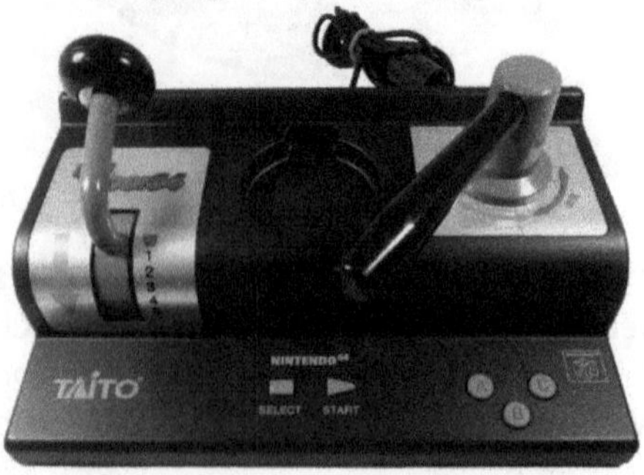

Taito Densha de Go! 64 Controller

Of course, not all games released for the N64 were hits. On July 30, Taito released *Densha de Go! 64* for the Japanese N64. This game was a simulation wherein the player had to control a train that was based on an actual Japanese passenger train line. Using a special train-driving controller that was only used for this game, the player had to follow a train timetable accurately and stop at specific spots within train stations.

In addition to the special controller, *Densha de Go! 64* also utilized the N64's Voice Recognition Unit (VRU), which had been released a year earlier for *Pikachū Genki dechū*. Unlike the former game, the VRU wasn't required to play *Densha de Go! 64*. However, it gave the player the ability to announce upcoming stations to the "passengers." The VRU was never utilized again in an N64 game.

Sega Dreamcast Microphone

Ironically, on July 29, the day before Taito released *Densha de Go! 64* for the N64, Sega of Japan released *Seaman* for the Dreamcast.[15] This game utilized the *Dreamcast Microphone*, which plugged into the Dreamcast's VMS and acted as a voice-recognition unit.

Like *Pikachū Genki dechū*, *Seaman* required the player to use verbal commands to guide a virtual creature. In this case, the creature was an animated fish with a human face. However, the game was more akin to the *Tamagotchi* genre, wherein the "player" had to care for the pet by feeding it and keeping it company, and answer its questions, which was where the Dreamcast Microphone came in.[16]

While *Seaman* let gamers care for a fish, *Sega*

Bass Fishing, which was released in Japan on April 1, and as a launch title for the American Dreamcast on September 9, allowed players to catch them. Based on the 1997 Sega arcade game of the same name, *Sega Bass Fishing* perfectly displayed the graphical capabilities of the Dreamcast, showing realistic-looking fish swimming in their natural habitat. The gamer took the guise of a fisherman who simply sat in a boat and fished. Although the game could be played with a standard Dreamcast controller, Sega released a fishing controller that looked like an actual fishing rod, which used motion sensitivity to cast a line. The unit, which had no actual line, vibrated when a fish was caught, and included a reel winder on its side for reeling in the captured fish.

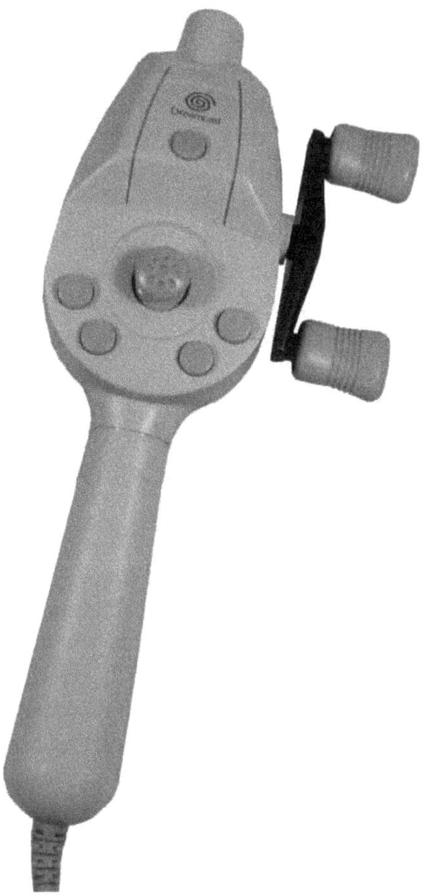

Sega Bass Fishing Controller

Sega Bass Fishing was not the first fishing game for home videogame consoles – there had been scores of such games since Activision first released *Fishing Derby* for the Atari VCS in 1980. But *Sega Bass Fishing* was the first game that used a fishing controller. It would not be the last.[17] On September 16 Agetec released *Bass Landing* for the PlayStation. This was a third-party fishing game that was bundled with a fishing controller that looked similar to the one from Sega. In a December review of the game, IGN compared it to the "flood of fishing games on the market." IGN found that there was nothing to distinguish one fishing game from another and they were all "basically mediocre." But it determined that Bass Landing was the one exception, with a combination of 3D graphics and realistic sounds that helped "set it apart from the opposition." And while IGN found *Bass Landing* exceptional while using the standard PlayStation controller, the game was even more rewarding and realistic when using the fishing controller.

Agetec PS1 Fishing Controller

Although the N64 also had fishing videogames in its catalog, none of them had been bundled with a fishing rod controller.

Multi-Language Games

While school districts were upset with Nintendo because of Pokémon, the government of Quebec, Canada was angry with Nintendo and the other videogame companies for a different reason. A Quebec charter decreed that any company that performed business in French-speaking Quebec had to sell products with the French language on its packaging. Any other language, including English, could be included as an option. To alleviate any problems, most companies simply printed their packaging with both English and French text. Videogame companies were the exception. Canada and the United States received the same products, and all were in English. And unlike a standard product, for which the manufacturer only had to worry about the packaging, videogames had the unique problem of the English language text's appearance within the product itself.

Many American companies that wanted to sell products in Quebec got around the dual languages by importing their products from France. That couldn't be done with videogames, which used different television standards. Canada, like the United States and Japan, used the NTSC broadcasting standard. Because France used the SECAM standard, French games could not play on Quebec sets.

In order to change the companies' negligent policies towards Quebec, the province's government threatened to sue if the policies weren't changed by the end of the year. Meanwhile, Quebec gamers and retailers alike were unhappy with this demand. Most worried that French Quebec editions of games might contain bugs that would occur during the translation process that wouldn't appear in the native-language versions. They also feared that the release of a translated game might lag several weeks behind that of the native-language version, forcing many customers to import the original edition, rather than wait for the French edition.[18]

SIRAS

Other policies that were being changed included the way in which retailers sold consoles. During the early nineties, Nintendo and other console manufacturers had noticed a particularly high return of systems to the retailers from consumers. Because no type of tracking system was in place, there was no way for a retailer to tell if a console returned to his store had indeed been purchased there. In order to maintain good customer service, retailers would accept the returns in exchange for store credit when sales receipts couldn't be produced, but even a receipt was no proof that a returned machine was actually the same one indicated on that receipt. As far as the retailer was concerned, the customer may have purchased a new console to replace a damaged one that was of out of warranty, and then simply returned the latter. There was no way to know, and as long as it was returned in what appeared to be pristine condition, it was accepted.

Nintendo began to research systematic methods that might allow for the regulation of returns while providing the retailers with complementary, easy-to-use, gate-keeping tools at the store level. The result was a patented business methodology, which was so successful that Nintendo started a Redmond, Washington-based business called SIRAS to provide this service to any company that needed to track its merchandise.

SIRAS' patented electronic registration system used the combination of a product's UPC and unique serial number to identify the product's "fingerprint." These numbers were then scanned during each break in the product's delivery channel. If a console was stolen from a Toys "R" Us warehouse, for instance, and later returned to a Best Buy without a receipt, not only would Best Buy know that the console hadn't been purchased there, but authorities would also know that the specific console had been stolen from Toys "R" Us.

SIRAS was so successful in streamlining the returns process that other manufacturers, including SCEA, signed up to use it.

Music Mania

As Nintendo and the other console manufacturers basked in their successes, the arcade companies prepared for troubled times. In early spring, Midway announced that its revenues from coin-op sales were down 25% from the same period one year earlier. Meanwhile, Namco's chairman, Masaya Nakamura, pinpointed two reasons for the arcade's failures: the high quality of the home systems and the success of online gaming through the Internet. Nakamura warned that the arcade industry had to be innovative in order to survive.

In Japan, Konami had found success with its Bemani franchise. On February 16 it introduced a new game that was similar, but different. *GuitarFreaks* once again consisted of playing a song by hitting the correct buttons on a controller that corresponded with the notes on the screen. This time, the controller resembled an electric guitar that consisted of three buttons and a switch. A guitar icon also floated on the screen, and when it reached the correct point, the gamer had to raise the guitar controller and produce a "wailing bonus."

Konami followed *GuitarFreaks* with a companion game called *DrumMania*. It borrowed the same general game play as Konami's prior rhythm games, but used a drum kit as its controller. Arcade owners also had the option of linking a *GuitarFreaks* cabinet with *DrumMania*, allowing for cooperative play. However, despite their success within Japan, neither *GuitarFreaks* nor *DrumMania* were distributed outside of the country. Konami test-marketed *GuitarFreaks* in a few U.S. arcades, but the reception was low so the company never attempted to make it commercially available.

Konami Pop'n Music Controller

Konami also released several home editions of its Bemani games in Japan only. *Pop'n Music* was released for the PlayStation on February 25. A controller with nine multi-colored buttons that resembled the arcade version was released the same day.

On July 29, Konami released a PlayStation version of *GuitarFreaks*. The home edition followed the same game play as the arcade version and was packaged with its own guitar controller, although the standard PlayStation controller could also be used.

Konami did find international success with *Dance Dance Revolution*, which the company introduced to American arcades in March. The addicting nature of the game brought would-be dancers into arcades and kept them there. And as in Japan, the game was as much fun to watch as it was to play. Meanwhile, a home version of the game was released in Japan for the PlayStation on April 10. Like the previous home versions of Konami's rhythm games, a special controller was needed in place of the standard controller to mimic the arcade experience. In the case of *Dance Dance Revolution*, it was a dance pad, similar to the old Bandai Family Trainer Mat for the Famicom.

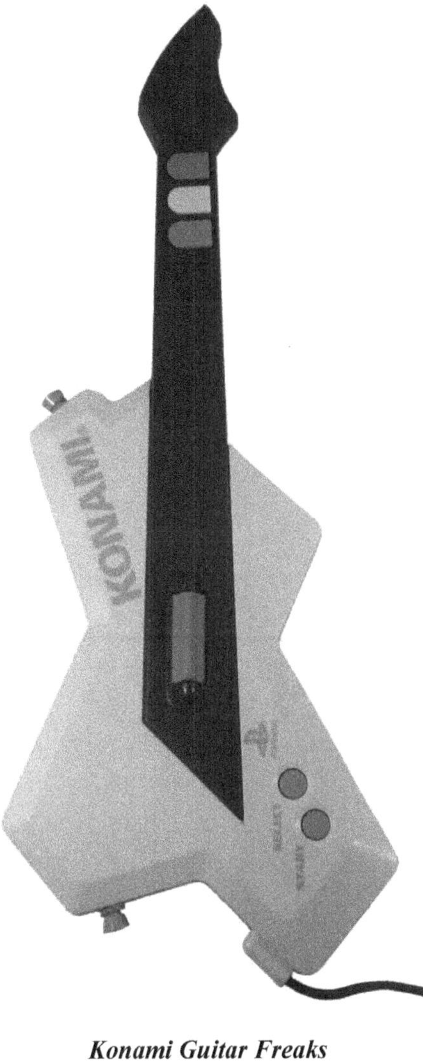

Konami Guitar Freaks

Arcade Centers

Unfortunately, the few spectacular must-have arcade machines that were created were so complex, their cost was too prohibitive for smaller arcades and distributors to acquire. A machine that cost $10,000 required ten thousand plays at $1 each just to break even, and if a game was not a hit, the small-arcade owner had no hope of ever recouping his investment. The family-owned arcades were gradually replaced by large amusement centers, such as *Dave and Buster's* and Gameworks, which offered dining as well as entertainment. These new arcade centers catered to adults, as well as to children and teens. In fact, Gameworks began installing large bars at its newer facilities to attract more adults.

Ron Benison, the CEO of Gameworks, compared his centers to movie theaters. Critics had forecasted for years that videotapes and home viewing would cause the eventual extinction of the movie theater. Despite those gloomy predictions, movie theaters were experiencing record attendance. Benison felt that the same critics had predicted the fall of the arcade because of the success of home games, and his goal was to prove them wrong. One way that Gameworks kept people coming back was by featuring exclusive games that couldn't be found anywhere else.

Good arcades could not exist without good games, and many questioned whether the arcade-game companies were doing their part. Sega was accused of ignoring its arcade business as it concentrated on its home system. Sega of Japan's CEO denied these accusations at a summer meeting with members of the U.S. arcade industry. As proof, one only had to look at the 200,000 Naomi arcade boards that Sega had sold during 1998, its first year. Fifteen arcade manufacturers had ordered the board, and while Sega wouldn't reveal who they were, the company planned to support them by releasing 30 Naomi games within a year of the board's release. Sega later improved on the Naomi design by adding the capability to allow satellite downloading of new software.

Of course, not all arcade-game manufacturers were going to use the Naomi system. SCE confirmed in July that a number of manufacturers, including Namco and Taito, would use the PlayStation 2 hardware.

Williams Pinball 2000

Home videogames were not the only cause of the downfall of the arcades. Although videogames pretty much dominated the arcades, they usually shared some floor space with the original arcade money generators -- pinball machines -- which had collectively been a mainstay in arcades for most of the twentieth century. However, once *Space Invaders* began descending, the glory days of the pinball machines were over. As videogames became more and more dominant, pinball companies began merging and disappearing. Bally, once the prestige name in pinball, was acquired by Williams, along with Gottlieb. Attempts to merge videogame and pinball technology were tried (*Baby Pac-Man*), but they were rarely successful.

In 1999, Williams tried to regain some of its previous eminence by releasing an extraordinary new pinball line that it called *Pinball 2000*. Unlike the previous attempts at linking videogames with pinball, which switched back and forth between the two, *Pinball 2000* actually integrated the two.

Pinball 2000 tables looked almost like a standard pinball table, but they also featured a video monitor in the playing area. Video images were projected into this area, and players had to shoot at virtual targets in addition to the physical ones.

While Williams planned for *Pinball 2000* to be challenging for players, it also designed the series to be easy for arcade operators. The game play was completely controlled by a CPU that was housed in the back of the table, allowing for the machine to be completely upgradeable. For the first time, arcade operators could improve a pinball machine by merely changing the software and replacing the easily removable playing field. Williams initially released two *Pinball 2000* games, *Revenge From Mars* and *Star Wars: The Phantom Menace.*

The *Pinball 2000* line received kudos from the press, and in the summer, Williams declared the line a success. Despite this, on November 19, WMS Industries, the parent company of Williams, abruptly shut down the pinball division. Even though the *Pinball 2000* line proved to be successful, company executives at Williams realized that it wouldn't earn the type of revenues that their investors demanded.

Sega also decided to exit the pinball business and sold it pinball division to the president of Sega Pinball, Gary Stern, who was the son of Sam Stern, the founder of Stern Electronics, and a former vice-president of Williams. Gary Stern renamed the company *Stern Pinball.* With the end of Williams, Stern Pinball became the only pinball manufacturer still in existence. Stern's targeted audience consisted of people who frequented bars and pubs, not arcades. Although videogames won in the big picture, pinball machines were down but not quite out.[19]

Employees at Williams weren't the only WMS Industries workers who lost their jobs. Atari Games, which had been owned by WMS Industries since 1996, slowly gave up its status as an independent game designer. By 1998, the once grand company began developing less and less titles and sharing hardware with its sister company, Midway. During 1999, it lost everything that had made it an independent company within WMS Industries, including its own management, sales, marketing and distribution. All that remained of Atari Games was its designers and its location in Milpitas, California, where it had access to Silicon Valley programmers. While new games would still be released with the Atari logo, Atari Games became a brand name under Midway in the same fashion that the Atari without "Games" in its name was really a brand name under Hasbro Interactive.

Retro Gaming

Atari had merely been one among Hasbro Interactive's recent acquisitions. During the latter's buying spree, a French company called Infogrames was doing a similar thing. Infogrames had been founded in 1983 by Bruno Bonnell and Christophe Sapet. In 1996, the company began purchasing European and Australian software companies, including Ocean Software and Philips Media. Finally, in 1999, the company made its move into the United States with its purchase of Accolade and GT Interactive. And for a while, it was content with what it had.

Hasbro Interactive, meanwhile, believed that there was still interest in classic games. During 1999, it released an updated version of *Pong* that played on the PlayStation, along with a PC compilation of classic arcade games that included the original versions of *Pong, Asteroids* and *Centipede.*

Hasbro Interactive wasn't intent on just releasing games from the Atari catalog. The company announced in April that it had secured a license from Namco to distribute 13 classic titles, beginning in 2000. Among the games were *Pac-Man, Ms. Pac-Man* and *Dig Dug,* which were to be available on PCs, and *Galaga, Galaxian* and *Pole Position,* which would be released for PCs and several gaming consoles.

Nintendo and Sega were also reissuing classic games, but in a different way. Between November 24 and December 10, Nintendo released *Donkey Kong 64* in North America, Europe and Japan. Two classic-style games were included within the new game. The first was a game called *Jetpac*, which had originally been released in 1983 for the Commodore VIC-20. Acquiring fifteen Banana Medals in *Donkey Kong 64* awarded the player with a chance to play *Jetpac*. And if he won that game, he would receive a Rare coin. In another part of the game, gamers could play the original *Donkey Kong* arcade game from 1981. Winning that game would reward them with a Nintendo coin, which could then be used to buy essential combat items. *Donkey Kong 64* used the N64's Expansion Pak. However, while other games used the memory boost to enhance the game play and graphics, and could be played without it, *Donkey Kong 64* was the first one that required it.

Shenmue, which cost $47 million to produce, was released for the Japanese Dreamcast by Sega of Japan on December 2.[20] In this game, the player assumed the role of Ryo Hazuki, who needed to seek information to ultimately avenge the killing of his father. The action took place in the city of Yokosuka, Japan, four sections of which Hazuki had free access to. The virtual city was as close to the real thing as possible. Life there continued even while the game was turned off. And the city was filled with small details, such as vending machines and stores from which Hazuki could make purchases. The city also had arcades. And featured in those arcades were two working versions of the Sega games *Space Harrier* and *Hang-On*. Unlike *Donkey Kong 64*, which included the classic-style games as part of the overall experience, the playable arcade games in *Shenmue* were for amusement purposes only.

Retro games were also making headlines. On July 3, 33-year old Billy Mitchell became the first person in history to achieve a perfect score in *Pac-Man*. In six hours, Mitchell scored 3,333,360 points, the maximum that could be attained. Mitchell, who also held the world record for *Donkey Kong*, did not go unnoticed. His feat was written up in several mainstream magazines, including *Time*. Namco, the manufacturer of *Pac-Man*, flew him to Japan, where he received an award that certified him as the "Player of the Century."

As further proof that the classic games still supported a very large fan base, the pioneers of the videogame industry gathered together in August in Las Vegas for the first annual *Classic Gaming Expo* (CGE). CGE was the brainchild of John Hardie and Keita Iida, two New York-based videogame collectors who had conceived the idea a year earlier during an annual *World of Atari* conference. Unlike the trade-only E^3, which it was wrongly compared to, CGE was open to the public, and celebrated the classic games and the people who had designed them.

CGE '99 Program

More than 600 people from around the world attended the two-day show. Among the highlights were question-and-answer sessions where fans could interact with the celebrated guests. Ralph Baer even set up his "Brown Box," the legendary Odyssey prototype which, amazingly, still worked after more than thirty years. Several lucky fans were even allowed to play against Baer at his own game. Classic home consoles and arcade machines were set for free play and were scattered around the room. Walter Day of the Twin Galaxies Intergalactic Scoreboard held contests throughout the exhibition, so people could try to get their names in the latest edition of his *Official Video Game & Pinball Book of World Records*. Along with Day was Billy Mitchell, the world-record holder for *Pac-Man*. Also packed around the room were vendors who sold brand-new copies of old games.

Other videogame legends who attended the show included Dave Nutting, Jerry Lawson, Jay Smith, David Crane and Howard Scott Warshaw. Fans of the original *Electronic Games* magazine were offered the opportunity to meet its originators, Bill Kunkel, Arnie Katz and Joyce Worley. All in all, the show was a great success, and plans were laid to make it a yearly event.

While CGE honored retro games and the developers that had created them, modern game developers attended their own exhibition that was held in Long Beach, California in May. The *Computer Game Developers Conference* (CGDC) had been started by former Atari developer Chris Crawford in 1988 at his San Jose home. Twenty-seven designers attended the first one. That number swelled to 125 the following year, so Crawford had to hold it at a Holiday Inn instead. The attendance continued to grow each year. For the 1999 show, the name was changed to *Game Developers Conference (GDC)* to reflect the large number of console gaming developers that attended. Two of its keynote speakers were Nintendo's Shigeru Miyamoto and Sega of America's Bernie Stolar, who represented the console community.

Console-Specific Magazines

The legacy of the *Electronic Games* founders continued and all new magazines were always inevitably compared to it. Throughout the years, several magazines such as *GamePro* and *EGM* still followed its format of covering all systems, but through the years, new magazines appeared that exclusively covered one system or company. The latest of these magazines was the *Official Dreamcast Magazine* which debuted in the United States at E^3 with a preview edition. The magazine, which began regular issues at the same time that the Dreamcast was released was published by Imagine Media, the same company that published *Next Generation*. Each bi-monthly issue was accompanied with a sample GD-ROM that contained demos of upcoming Dreamcast games. In Great Britain, a similarly-named magazine was released on a monthly basis by Dennis Publishing.

Violent Games Spawn Violence

CGE honored games from an era when the most violent game involved the player running down on-screen gremlins (*Death Race*). Unfortunately, that innocent time was long gone. After a 1998 schoolyard shooting in Jonesboro, Arkansas, the state Senate proposed a bill that would make it illegal for a minor to enter an establishment where a violent game was sold or displayed. The bill was forwarded to an interim study commission on March 31 that, in effect, killed it. The IDSA seemed to have gotten the message out that videogames were not responsible for the killer's behavior. In fact, of the 5,000 games that had been rated since 1994, less than 7% had been rated as violent. Less than 1% were deemed for adults only, and they were all PC games.

Just as America began turning away from the issue of videogame violence, tragedy struck again. After two teenagers shot and killed twelve fellow students and a teacher at Columbine High School in Littleton, Colorado in May, videogames were again blamed. This time, it was discovered that the two killers had been fans of *Doom*, the violent PC game that had been around for five

Sega Dreamcast Gun

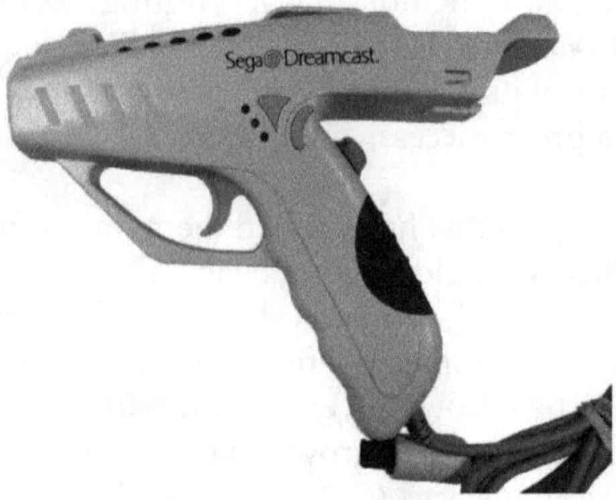

Mad Catz Dream Blaster

years. At E^3, which was held in Los Angeles one week after the shootings, exhibitors were more cautious about the types of games they showed. Most new violent games were not displayed to the convention public. Sega of America, which was gearing up for its U.S. Dreamcast launch, decided not to release the *Dreamcast Gun* an official Sega-branded light-gun that had been intended to accompany its launch title, *House of the Dead* 2. The same gun was available in Europe and Japan, but those who imported them into the U.S. discovered they wouldn't work with the American version of the game. Although the imported copies of the Dreamcast Gun were fully compatible with the American Dreamcast, the American copies of *House of the Dead* 2 had been coded to disable the gun, no matter where it was from.

Oddly, Sega of America had licensed peripheral maker Mad Catz to produce a less expensive version of the Dreamcast Gun. Mad Catz's Dreamcast-branded *Dream Blaster* was permitted to be sold in the United States and wasn't disabled in the American games like the Dreamcast Gun.

Despite the publicity proclaiming that America was out of control because of violent videogames, other countries were also experiencing violence that videogames were blamed for. In November, a 24-year-old medical student opened fire in a crowded Brazilian movie theater, killing three and injuring eight. After he was arrested, the suspect said he got the idea from a PC game called *Duke Nukem*.

In the wake of the shootings, a Brazilian judge banned six violent videogames from store shelves. Among them were *Duke Nukem*, *Doom* and *Mortal Kombat*. Stores that didn't remove the banned games faced daily fines of $10,000. The judge who ordered the ban also ordered the federal government to institute a gaming-rating system within four months.

Despite the negative publicity, the videogame industry enjoyed another record year in 1999. Videogame software grossed $3.75 billion, and consoles weren't far behind, as they grossed $2.9 billion.

The videogame industry was bigger than ever. And as SCE geared up for the release of the PlayStation 2, widespread expectations were that it could only get better.

CHAPTER TWENTY-EIGHT
2000

The world did not end at midnight on January 1, 2000. Despite all of the doom-and-gloom forecasts concerning the Y2K bug, most date-sensitive devices, including PCs, continued to operate just as they had been programmed to. But while civilization continued on its merry course, the PC gaming industry appeared to be on the verge of collapse.

Throughout their history, computer games had always been the bigger cousins to console games. In the early days of computers, games on PCs looked better than they did on the lower-memory consoles. Second-generation consoles like Atari's 5200 and the ColecoVision upped the ante and brought the console games to an even plane with PC games. But as the costs of home computers began plummeting during the early eighties, the school of thought was that the powerful low-cost computers would eventually force the console makers out of business. After all, computers could run other applications, instead of just games. With everything being even, it just made sense to buy a computer instead of a console.

Of course, that never happened. As processing power and memory increased on the computers, software companies began designing games that demanded all of the processing power and storage that the computers could muster. Unless people owned a computer that was upgraded to the hilt with the latest peripherals, they could never be sure if a game would play on their computer adequately. This had never been a problem with videogame consoles. If a PlayStation game was purchased, there was no question that the PlayStation console could handle it.

As processor speeds continued to increase, software companies finally realized that they could no longer design games that could only be played on the most powerful computers. By doing so, they ignored the majority of consumers who didn't upgrade their computers every time a better one came along. Software designers needed to make sure that their games were compatible with older systems as well.

Xbox According To Gates

But there was a glimmer of hope for the future of PC games. Microsoft's "secret" Xbox was on the horizon, and if the rumors were correct, games developed for the Xbox would essentially be the same as those for the PC, since the two would have similar operating systems. Nonetheless, there was one major problem concerning the Xbox. When the year began, Microsoft still hadn't confirmed that the console even existed.

The many industry insiders who had believed that Microsoft would officially announce the Xbox in January at the winter CES had been wrong. However, the "secret" was informally disclosed in February, when Microsoft held private talks with many of the top PC software developers in order to sell them on the Xbox. Despite the lack of an official statement from Microsoft, the developers confirmed that the Xbox was indeed real and was set to be released in 2001. And from what they'd learned, they believed that it would be more powerful than anyone had dared to imagine.

The extent of the Xbox's power was officially revealed on March 10 at the Game Developers Conference (GDC). And it was Microsoft's CEO Bill Gates who announced the intriguing details.

According to Gates, Microsoft had put to good use information that it had gleaned from developers. It also paid attention to what consumers wanted in a game machine. One thing that they definitely didn't want was a PC that played games. Gates quickly quelled the notion that the Xbox would be a wolf in sheep's clothing. Even though it would have some similarities with PCs, the system would definitely be a game console that Microsoft expected to have on the market for approximately four to five years. Contrary to earlier rumors, the Xbox would have a closed architecture, and third-party developers would have to pay licensing fees. And like Nintendo and SCE, Microsoft would have the right to approve the quality of the games from the third-party licensees. But unlike the other console manufacturers, Microsoft planned that all games would play on every Xbox around the world, without any regional lockouts.

Initially, Microsoft shopped for PC developers who could quickly convert their PC games to the Xbox, thanks to the similar architectures of the two machines. However, Gates stressed that not all PC games were suitable for a game console.

The fact that the Xbox would be powered by a 600Mhz Intel Pentium III processor certainly didn't quench the belief that the console would be a PC in disguise, even though Gates clarified that the Xbox was indeed a real gaming console with "no boot time or software installation." And the presence of an 8GB hard drive didn't mean that the Xbox was really a computer, either. Gates explained that the games that would play on the Xbox demanded storage. Games would run faster, because large audio and video files that would be needed in any given game could load onto the hard drive while the game was in progress. Game statistics and demos that could be downloaded from the Internet would also be stored on the hard drive. As far as the gamer was concerned, the hard drive would be transparent and wouldn't be used to store and access files in the traditional sense.

Gates promised that the graphics on the Xbox would blow away its competitors. The custom Nvidia graphics chip would be capable of generating 150 million polygons per second. This was more than double of what SCE claimed the PlayStation 2 would be able to generate, and completely ridiculed the 12 million polygons per second that the Dreamcast could create.

Microsoft's console would contain 64MB of memory, which would be shared by the CPU and the graphics processor. The benefit of this was that programmers could allocate any portion of memory to use in any way that they wanted.

Since the Xbox was a game machine, Gates placed less emphasis on its non-gaming features, such as the ability to play DVDs and connect to the Internet. While a modem would not be included with the console, an optional one would be available for purchase.

The prototype that Microsoft showed off at the GDC, and later at E^3, resembled a large "X". Microsoft stressed that this was simply a way to display the chipset in a presentable manner, and wasn't meant to portray the final console at all.

Microsoft announced on September 20 that it had signed with more than 150 publishers to develop games for the Xbox. Most of the major software developers were represented, although the absence of Electronic Arts, the world's largest software company, was highly conspicuous. On the other hand, several Japanese developers had signed on. This was a major achievement as it had been in question whether or not the Japanese companies would embrace the American console.

One particular Xbox developer stood out among the others. On June 19, Microsoft announced that it had purchased the nine-year-old Bungie, Inc., a San Jose-based developer of Mac games. Two years earlier, on July 21, 1999, Steve Jobs had announced that *Halo*, a real-time, third-person shooter that Bungie was developing, would be released simultaneously for both Mac and *Windows* computers. The game had received major acclaims by all who saw previews of it. Microsoft realized that it could use such a game as a launch title for the Xbox. After the corporate giant bought Bungie, *Halo* became an exclusive title for the Xbox, and was changed to a first-person shooter.

By year's end Microsoft announced that Electronic Arts was also on board to develop Xbox games. This was seen as a major endorsement for the forthcoming console. And while Electronic Arts was also developing games for the PlayStation 2, it had no plans to do the same for the Dreamcast.

All along, *Xbox* had been the code name for the new system. Microsoft used the GDC to announce the console's official name once it was in production. The official name of the system was *Xbox*.

Indrema

Microsoft wasn't the only American company that planned to release a new videogame console. However, unlike Microsoft, which had years of experience and billions of dollars behind it, the Indrema Corporation was a small start-up that began in January. While playing *Quake* one night, future Indrema CEO and founder John Gildred came to the realization that while innovations were occurring for PC-based games, the same could not be said for their console cousins, due to obstacles that had been put in place by the console manufacturers. Indrema's goal was to develop the first open-source videogame console, one that would allow independent game developers to easily create and bring to market new programs.

Indrema's planned console would serve several functions. In addition to playing games, it would be capable of playing DVDs and CDs. It would also act as a digital video recorder (DVR). Recordings would be saved on an internal hard drive that would range in size between 8GB and 50GB. The hard drive would also store MP3 files that would be playable on the unit. Nvidia would provide a graphics chip that could generate 120 to 150 million polygons per second and would also be accessible by the end-user. If a newer, more powerful graphics processor became available, the user would be able to easily replace the old one with a new one, a first in videogaming history. Games would be stored on 10GB discs.

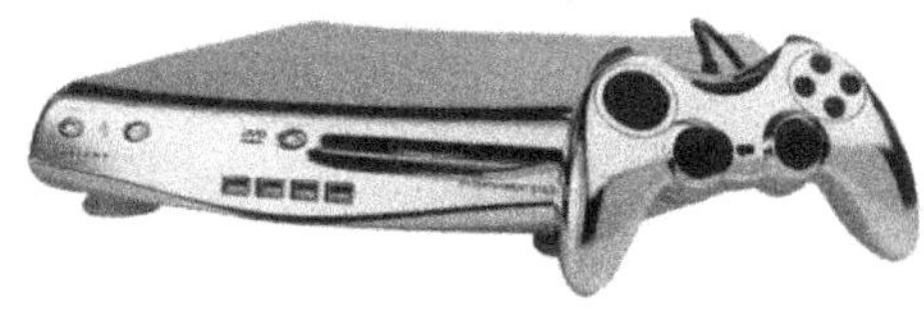

Indrema L600

The brains of the system would be a 600MHz CPU. The operating system would be Linux. Unlike *Windows*, Linux had an open-source architecture that made it accessible to anyone who wanted to use it. Indrema's goal was to attract independent developers by enticing them with a free developer's kit. Coupled with a low royalty rate, developers wouldn't have to spend as much money to develop for Indrema's console as they would for a PlayStation 2. The result would be high-quality, low-priced games.

According to Indrema, its first console, the *L600*, was targeted for release during the spring of 2001.

Nuon Games

The Xbox had not been the first videogame console to have an "X" in its code name. When VM Labs had initially announced its videogame system in 1997, they called it *Project X*. Eventually, after Project X evolved into a chip that would enhance DVD players, VM Labs settled on the name *Nuon*. Still, after years of publicity, the company hadn't shown to the world exactly what it planned. That finally changed in January when the company at last revealed its products at CES.

As divulged in 1998, Nuon-equipped DVD players allowed viewers to zoom in on any area of the screen without any appreciable loss of quality. Specially enhanced DVDs

Samsung Nuon Player

were planned that would allow viewers to see data about movies that they were watching. Nuon machines could also play videogames, and VM Labs officially announced several of them at CES. One promised title was *Tempest 3000*, which had been designed by Jeff Minter, who had also designed *Tempest 2000* for the Atari Jaguar. And like the Jaguar, the Nuon machines included Minter's popular *Virtual Light Machine* program, which displayed psychedelic effects on the screen in sync with the music.

Although the first enhanced DVDs weren't scheduled to appear until 2001, Nuon-equipped DVD players began selling in 2000. The first, a $400 Samsung model, came out in June. The DVD player was packaged with a game controller, a test disc, and an Infogrames game called *Ballistic*. Toshiba followed in September with a $350 unit that didn't include a controller, but was sold with *The Next Tetris*.

Sony's Trojan Horse

Nuon consoles were basically DVD players that played games. The *PlayStation 2 (PS2)* was a game machine that also played DVDs. And it was the console from the three major hardware manufacturers, Nintendo, Sega and even SCE, that could play DVDs.

While the Xbox garnered much attention throughout the year, it was nothing

SCE PS2

compared to what SCE mustered. The PS2 was written up in mainstream publications that usually ignored videogames. The *Wall Street Journal* called it "Sony's Trojan Horse," a device that would enter households as a videogame console but wind up being an all-purpose entertainment system. Trip Hawkins, who had failed in a similar attempt with his 3DO console, said that the "PlayStation 2 [would] do for entertainment what Johannes Gutenberg's movable type did for printing." With more hype preceding it than any other gaming console in history, SCE released the PS2 on March 4 to record crowds in Japan, where excitement for the new console began to intensify one week prior to that date. In Akihabara, Tokyo's electronic district, people began camping outside shops on March 1, knowing that stores would distribute the PS2s on a first-come, first-served basis.

But the demand for the console was so much higher than the supply that some people resorted to unscrupulous means in order to obtain them. There were many reports about people being mugged for their ¥39,800 ($369) consoles. One group of teens even attempted to rob a stockpile of consoles from a store. They didn't succeed, and were arrested. And one young man jumped off a building after learning that he would not be able to purchase a console. Fortunately, he survived with minor injuries.

Such actions had previously been unknown in Japan, where youths usually waited in line patiently and orderly. However, the PS2's hype was just too much to ignore. To make matters worse, SCE didn't even have enough consoles to go around. While the company had planned to have two million PS2 consoles available at launch, only half that number was actually on hand, and only 600,000 even went to stores, which had to actually stop taking advance orders, because SCE couldn't produce enough consoles to meet the demand. The rest had been allocated to SCE's website, which crashed from an overload of visitors as soon as the consoles went on sale. Despite the shortage of PS2 consoles, SCE still managed to sell close to one million PS2s during the first two days of its availability, making its launch the most successful in Japanese history to date.

SCE's problems also extended to its peripherals. It was quickly discovered that many of the 8MB memory cards did not function correctly. Saved information was somehow erased from the card and replaced with useless data that couldn't be copied or deleted. To make matters worse, since the memory card was needed to operate the PS2's DVD player, a defective one rendered DVD movies unplayable. Although this was a small problem that was resolved fairly quickly, it caused SCE's stock price to fall a few points after it was reported.

People who purchased the early PS2s discovered that it hadn't been a good idea for the DVD drivers to reside on the memory card. Although the drivers could be reinstalled if they were accidentally deleted, it was a hassle that consumers shouldn't have had to go through. Before long, it was discovered that there were other glitches with the console's ability to play DVDs.

The Japanese PS2s were set up so they could only play Region 2 DVDs. This included all Japanese discs and a few European ones. Region 1 DVDs, which included those sold in the United States, were not supposed to play on it. On the heels of the defective memory cards, SCE learned that there was a bug in the DVD driver. In true Easter-egg fashion, gamers discovered that they could play Region 1 DVDs on their Japanese PS2s if they plugged a regular PlayStation controller into the PS2's left controller port and then followed a few easy steps. SCE quickly issued a fix to what it deemed a problem.

What SCE did not consider a problem was the fact that the DVD features could only be accessed through the PS2's wired controller. However, the reality was that most people didn't watch movies from a distance of only a few feet from their TV sets. Several third-party companies quickly came to their rescue with wireless remote controllers.

Once the initial Japanese launch was out of the way, SCE was able to set its sights on the PS2's American release, scheduled for October 26. Bloomberg L.P., a news agency, leaked the story on April 14 that SCE, in an attempt to get a jump on the Xbox, would include a hard drive and a modem in the American console. SCE wouldn't comment on this information, but Microsoft executives were quick to positively react. Microsoft had refrained from including a hard drive with the Xbox, because it felt that many people wouldn't then be able to distinguish the console from a computer. SCE's plan to embrace a hard drive would, it was presumed, prove that the storage device was no longer relegated only to computers.

The Bloomberg story turned out to be false, and SCE wouldn't be including a hard drive and modem with the American PS2. However, unlike the Japanese PS2, the American one would have an expansion bay in its rear that would eventually house an optional hard drive or Ethernet adapter.

In May, SCE used E^3 to highlight the changes between the American and Japanese consoles. The most notable was the fact that the DVD driver would be built into the console and not into the memory card. Since the memory card would no longer be required, it wouldn't be packaged with the system, and this would reduce the retail price to $299, $70 less than what the Japanese were paying.[1]

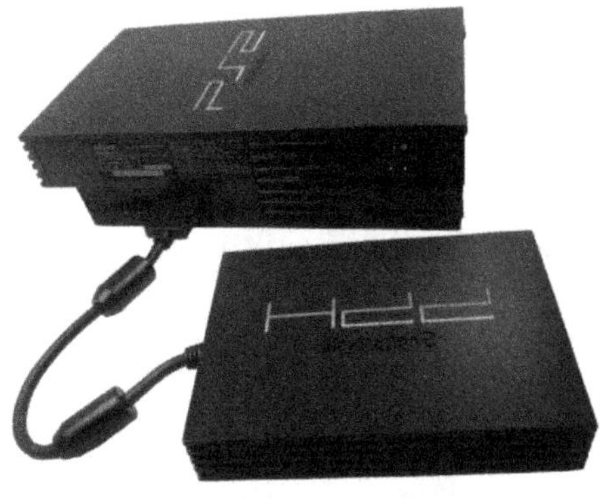

Japanese PS2 and Hard Drive

Within a month after announcing that the American PS2 would have room for an internal hard drive, SCE showed an external hard drive for the Japanese console. The HDD (Hard Disc Drive) had its own power supply and plugged into the PS2's PCMCIA slot. Because SCE was evasive about mentioning details such as how much data could be stored on the drive, speculation arose that the company might offer several hard drives with various capacities.

SCE PSone

When SCE president Ken Kutaragi announced the PS2 HDD, he also introduced the *PSone*, a replacement for the best-selling PlayStation. The PSone was 1/3 the size of the original console and was designed for mobile use. An optional 4-inch LCD screen would be available in 2001. While SCE stressed that the PSone would not be a handheld unit like a Game Boy, it would be portable in the sense that it could be played in a car with an optional car power adapter. An adapter would also be available so cell phones could plug into the console and allow users to connect to a network for online gaming.

The ¥10,599 ($99) PSone was released in Japan on July 7.[2] Although most developers were by then concentrating on the PS2, innovative software was still being released for the original PlayStation. On July 27, a company called Global A released *The Maestro Music*, which had the player leading musicians in a virtual orchestra. A "baton controller", which plugged into a controller port of the console, was packaged with the game disc. This device, which had a long wand attached to it, resembled a conductor's baton. The player waved the unit in beat to the musical notes that passed by on the screen. Built inside the controller was a motion detector that registered the waving effect and sent the data back to the console.[3]

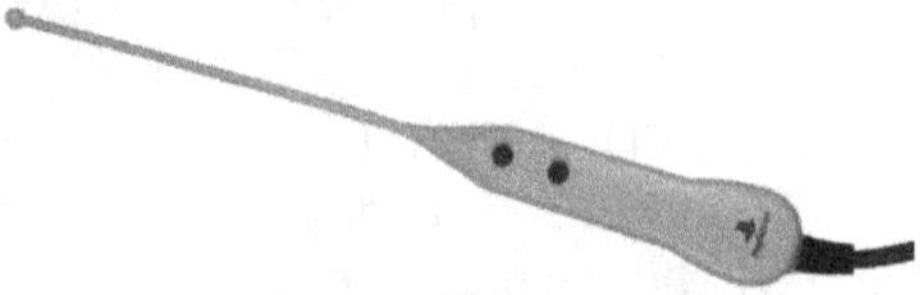

Global A The Maestro Music

The Maestro Music took advantage of the growing genre of music-based games that Konami had introduced with games like *Beatmania* and *GuitarFreaks*. Meanwhile, Konami continued to release more home versions of its popular *Bemani* games. One of the launch titles for the Japanese PS2 was *Drummania,* a home version of Konami's 1999 arcade game. The game was basically similar to the Bemani games before it, *Beatmania* and *GuitarFreaks*. Bars descended in up to six columns, where five of the columns represented a different drum pad and the sixth column represented a foot pedal. The player had to

Konami Drummania screenshot

Konami Drummania controller

hit the appropriate pad (or foot pedal) when a bar in a corresponding column reached the bottom.

As with the prior Bemani home games, *Drummania* used a special controller. In this case it was a $130 five-pad drum kit that plugged into the PS2's left controller port. And while *Drummania* was a one-player game, another player could compete by inserting a *GuitarFreaks* guitar into the PS2's right controller port.

Konami Keyboardmania controller

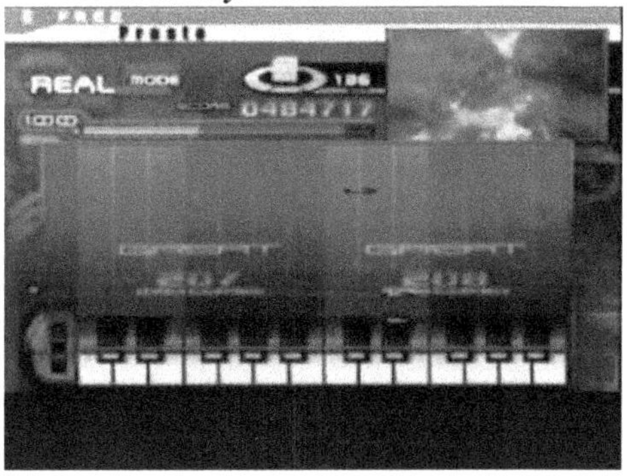

Konami Keyboardmania

Konami released another Bemani game for the Japanese PS2 on September 21. *Keyboardmania* was similar to the prior Bemani games except that it featured 14 columns of falling objects, where each column represented a white key on a special keyboard controller. When an object in a specific column reached the bottom of the screen, then the matching white key on the piano controller had to be pressed. If an object descended along the line between columns, then a black key needed to be pressed. Special arrows also descended and the direction that the arrow pointed determined in which direction a special "effector wheel", which was located on both ends of the controller, had to be scrolled.

PS2 Shortages

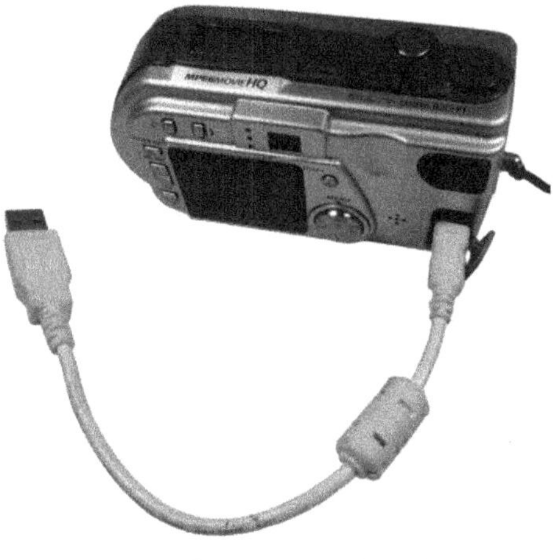

Sony CyberShot DSC-P1

Sony released two peripherals that allowed users to manipulate photos, on their PS2 much in the way that they could with the Game Boy Camera. The ¥99,800 ($950) *CyberShot DSC-P1* camera, which came out on October 20, could connect directly to a PS2 via a USB cable. An SCE-developed application called *Picture Paradise*, would then upload photos from the camera into a supported game, where the images would become part of the game. Picture Paradise was not an application that users could purchase and install. It was built-into compatible games. Among the supported titles was Konami's *Jikkyou World Soccer 2001*, in which the player could paste a photo of his face onto a custom character.[4]

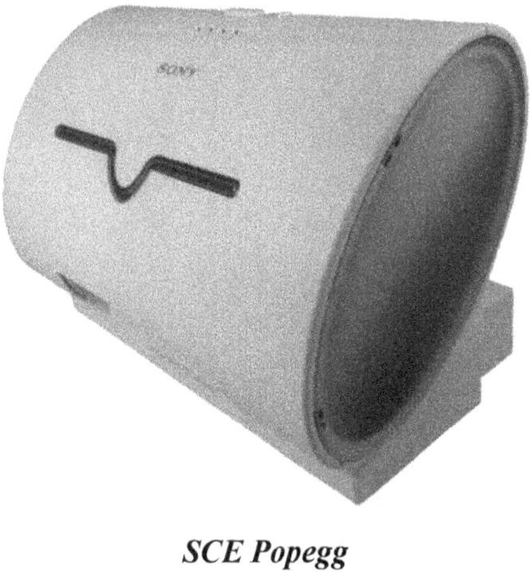

SCE Popegg

Beginning on November 15, people were also able to edit the digital photos that they uploaded to the PS2, thanks to *PrintFan*, a new software program that SCE released in Japan. They could print the photos as well. *PrintFan* was packaged *Popegg*, a color ink-jet printer.

Even though the camera was released in the United States, the *Printfan* package wasn't, so those in the United States who wanted to use their PS2s to edit their photos were out of luck. Not that it really mattered since American people who had planned to purchase a PS2 when it became available, learned that the console would be just as elusive to purchase in the United States as the Japanese-only *Printfan*.

SCEA reported the bad news on September 27, just prior to the PS2's North American launch. Instead of having one million consoles available on October 26 as promised, only half that number would actually be ready to be sold. This was on account of a shortage of some of the console's components. SCEA promised that 100,000 additional consoles would be released each week through the end of the year. This new shipping schedule would actually provide an additional 300,000 consoles by the end of the year.

The hype for the PS2 ran very high during October. With the notion that the consoles would be impossible to get, even people who never had any interest in the system wanted one.

A line began forming in front of SCE's Metreon store in San Francisco on October 24. There were one thousand people in that line twenty-eight hours later when the store opened at midnight to begin dispensing the PS2. Half of those people went home empty-handed, since the Metreon only had 500 consoles to sell. More people went home frustrated elsewhere in the country since most stores only received twenty-console allotments and had to contend with crowds of 100 or more. As people realized that they wouldn't be getting a PS2 even though they had pre-ordered, the crowds became unruly, with fistfights breaking out between people on line. In some instances, people who did receive a console had to be escorted from stores to prevent them from being stolen.

Not everyone who went home with a PS2 intended to keep it. Within hours, eBay was flooded with PS2 auctions, with prices for the $299 console ranging from $650 to more than $1,000.

Although spectacular launches were common occurrences in Japan, this had never happened before in the United States. Most mainstream newspapers and TV news covered the launch, and the additional hype made the PS2 desirable to anyone who read or heard about it. Unfortunately, they were nearly impossible to find during the 2000 holiday season.[5]

Dreamcast Network

Although the hype around the PS2 made it seem like it was the only system available, Nintendo and Sega were quick to prove that it wasn't. Dreamcast sales were pretty good, and Sega continued to release fun and innovative games for the system. One of the more addicting games arrived in 2000 in the form of *Samba de Amigo,* an arcade port that came out in Japan on April 27, and followed in North America on October 16. In this rhythm game, the player had to shake a pair of maracas at certain intervals. Following the lead of the original arcade game, Sega actually released a pair of *Maraca* controllers to go with this game. This peripheral was not used in any other Dreamcast game.[6]

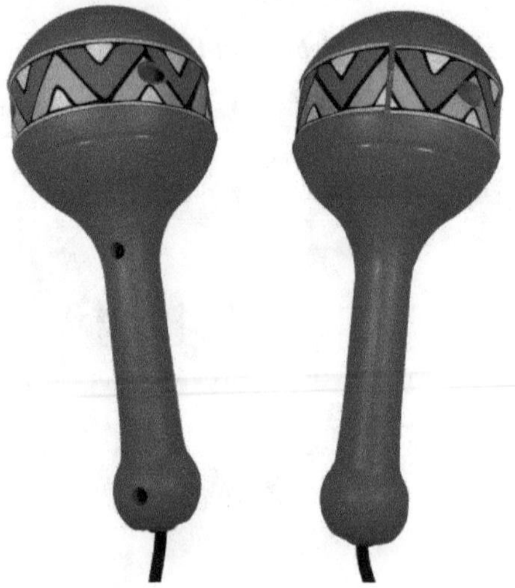

Sega Samba de Amigo Maraca controller

Meanwhile, another Dreamcast peripheral wasn't being used for games at all. Every American Dreamcast had been sold with a 56k modem that could be used to surf the Internet or check email. However, it couldn't be used for games until Sega's planned gaming network went online. This was Phase 5 of Sega's 5-phase plan and it wasn't scheduled to happen until the second half of the year. In the meantime, the company didn't waste any time getting through the third and fourth phases.

On January 12, the company released *Sega Swirl*, a free game that was included on the Dreamcast's *Web Browser 2.0* disc and on a demo disc that came with the *Official Dreamcast Magazine* in both the United States and Great Britain. *Sega Swirl* was a puzzle game, similar to *Tetris* and *Columns*. The screen filled with different colored swirls and the player had to remove a swirl by clicking on it. This would remove the selected swirl as well as any other swirls with the same color that were connected to it. The game could be played solitaire in the "Level Challenge" or the "Versus Challenge" where up to four players took turns removing swirls. The more swirls removed on a turn earned more points.

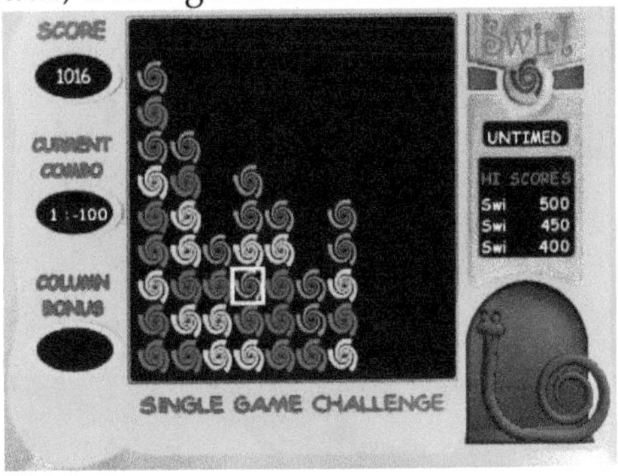

Sega Swirl

Sega Swirl also offered an "Email Challenge" level. This was similar to the "Versus Challenge" except that players used the Internet connection of the Dreamcast to make moves. After one player made a move, the Dreamcast automatically sent an email to the other player's console. When it was received, the console would display the move that the first player made, and then wait for the second player's response. Although this wasn't true online gaming, it did permit two players in different locations to play against one another in the same game.

Phase 4 of Sega's 5-phase plan occurred on March 7, when Sega of America released *ChuChu Rocket!*, a game that had been available for the Japanese Dreamcast since November 11, 1999. This was a maze game in which up to four players could compete. Sega of America used the game to emphasize the online capabilities of the Dreamcast. And since up to four players could compete at the same time, it is credited as being the first multiplayer[7] online game for a home console.[8]

Sega of America went through its second major organizational change in just over six months shortly after the release of *ChuChu Rocket!*. Toshiro Kezuka, the man who had replaced Bernie Stolar as Sega of America's president just prior to the Dreamcast's launch in September 1999, returned to Sega of Japan. On April 24, Peter Moore, a vice-president at Sega of America, replaced Kezuka as president.

Moore attended his first E^3 as Sega of America's president two weeks later, on May 11. The company used the show to announce several new Dreamcast peripherals including a mouse and an MP3 player. In order to make the Dreamcast even more enticing, Sega offered a rebate of $50 to anyone who signed onto the Dreamcast Network between June 4 and August 31, for at least one month.

Following E^3, Sega of America changed the name of the Dreamcast Network to *SegaNet* and set the launch date for September 7. In addition, Sega started a new subsidiary called Sega.com that would function as an Internet Service Provider (ISP) for both Dreamcast and PC owners. To lure people to sign up for the monthly $21.95 service, a rebate program was announced that would award two-year subscribers with a free Dreamcast. Existing Dreamcast owners who signed up for the service were given $200 in place of a console. While potential Sega Network subscribers weren't required to sign up with Sega.com, it was recommended, because not every ISP was accessible from the Dreamcast. One such ISP was America Online (AOL), the largest ISP in the world, with 20 million subscribers.

As Sega of America prepared for its new network that would be powered by its 56KB modem, many Dreamcast gamers in Japan were able to navigate Dricas, Sega of Japan's network, at nearly 2000 times that speed. On July 15, Sega of Japan released a ¥6,470 ($60) *Dreamcast Broadband Adapter*. Unlike the LAN Adapter that had been released in 1999 and

Sega Dreamcast Broadband Adapter

only operated at 10MB, the Broadband Adapter could transfer data at up to 100 megabits per second.

On September 1, the day after the $50 rebate ended, Sega of America announced that the price of the Dreamcast would be permanently reduced $50 to $149. The price change naturally affected Sega's $200 rebate program for signing on with SegaNet. A new program went into place immediately that offered a $150 rebate to those who signed up to SegaNet for 18 months. Finally, Sega offered a free 50-hour network trial period to anyone who purchased *NFL 2K1* or *Quake III Arena*.

On September 7, Sega of America released *NFL 2K1*, the first Dreamcast game that took full advantage of the Dreamcast's online abilities. The release coincided with the launch of SegaNet.

SegaNet was a network that had been conceived strictly for online gaming. However, the $21.95-per-month subscription to SegaNet wasn't required in order for gamers to compete online. While gamers were free to dial up their own ISPs, SegaNet was built to provide high-speed gaming with a minimum of latency, and Sega games were designed to take full advantage of what the network offered.

Despite a few initial glitches, the startup went reasonably well, and most gamers discovered that playing *NFL 2K1* against online opponents was a fun experience. Sega officials were highly optimistic that the Sega Network would be a success.

As gamers in the United States were experiencing online console gaming for the first time, Japanese consumers were discovering where Sega was taking the Dreamcast. Sega of Japan introduced several new peripherals that enhanced the online gaming experience in one way or another. None of these products were released outside of Japan.

Sega Dream Karaoke

The *Dream Karaoke* was a karaoke machine that sat under the Dreamcast, in the same way that the original Sega CD/Mega CD had sat beneath the Genesis/Mega Drive. Two microphones plugged into the front of the unit, which allowed for duets, and the volume of each microphone could be controlled separately.

The downside of the Dream Karaoke was that songs had to be downloaded from Sega's Karaoke Service website. And since the unit had no way to save the songs after they'd been downloaded, would-be entertainers had to download the same song multiple times if they wanted to sing it on separate occasions.

The *Dreameye* was a digital camera that Sega of Japan released on February 16. This could be used for both still photos and videos. It connected to the Dreamcast through a controller port and could be used to create video e-mails, or for teleconferencing. The camera was packaged with the same microphone that was sold with *Seaman*, and it allowed people to video chat with one another via the Internet.

The camera also came with software that allowed users to edit their photos. The photos could be saved on the Dreamcast's VMS. But unlike the PS2, which had the new

Popegg printer, there was no way to print photos directly from the Dreamcast.

Sega also announced a partnership with Motorola, which would bring the Dreamcast technology to cellular phones. Software, which was to be developed jointly by both companies, would allow people to use their cell phones to connect to the Internet, from where they would be able to download games and other media.

Sega Dreamcast Dreameye

Sega wasn't alone with the idea to connect its console to the Internet via a cell phone. On August 1, SCE announced that it would team up with NTT DoCoMo of Japan to develop a wireless network that would allow PS2s to connect to i-mode cell phones.[9]

Mobile Handheld Gaming

Bandai had the same idea with its *Mobile WonderGate*, a modem that linked a WonderSwan to a cellular phone. Bandai released the ¥4,800 ($44) Mobile WonderGate on July 14 and only to Japanese mobile communication carriers, rather than the retailers who sold the WonderSwan. While the peripheral was created primarily so users could surf the Internet from their WonderSwan consoles, games were also developed that used the online capabilities to some degree. Capcom's *Pocket Fighter* had a feature that ranked players from all over Japan, and Namco's *Final Lap 2000* allowed users to download new original courses, or to share edited courses with other players over the network.

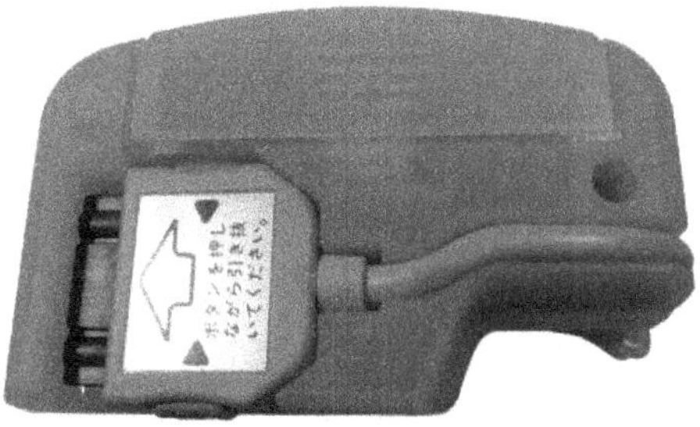

Bandai Wonderswan Mobile Wondergate

Nintendo of Japan intended to release a similar device for the Game Boy. The first game that would use this new technology was *Pocket Monsters Crystal Version*. This was an enhancement of *Pocket Monsters Gold* and *Pocket Monsters Silver*, a Pokémon Communications Center was added in place of the Pokémon Center, which had appeared in the prior games. The Pokémon Communications Center was a place that gamers could enter to perform several functions that utilized the mobile capability including linking up with other players and reading about their adventures, and obtaining a GS Ball (a gold Pokéball) that would be used later in the game. Players could also trade with or battle against other players by linking together over the Internet.

Nintendo's plan was to release the mobile adapter on December 14 along with *Pocket Monsters Crystal Version*. However, the company announced at the end of October that the adapter was being delayed until January, 2001. The game was released on that date as planned but of course the online aspect of the game could not be accessed.

Game Boy Peripherals

Although the Internet wasn't available to Game Boy owners for online gaming outside of Japan, InterAct provided a product that allowed them to use their Game Boys to connect to the Internet to send and receive email.

The *Shark MX* was essentially a cartridge with a built-in modem. A standard telephone cable plugged into a phone jack in the cartridge. For a fee, users could subscribe to the service provided by Internet, and then dial a toll-free number that gave them access to their email. They could compose email on an onscreen keyboard by manipulating a cursor with the Game Boy's "A" button. It was a monotonous way to write email, but it was meant

InterAct Shark MX

for novices who had no other email connections. The device also provided Game Boy users with a calculator, calendar and address book.

The Shark MX was a great innovation, but it was late in coming. By the time it came out, Nintendo had already released information about the Game Boy Advance, its next-generation Game Boy Color that would feature a wireless connection to the Internet.

The 32-bit Game Boy Advance, which would provide Super Famicom-quality graphics, would be roughly the same size as a Game Boy Color, but would be held horizontally instead of vertically. Like the Super Famicom controllers, the unit would feature two shoulder buttons, the first handheld unit to include them. The screen would be wider than the one on the Game Boy Color and wouldn't be backlit either. The absence of a light would allow the Game Boy Advance to run 15 hours on two AA batteries. While the unit would not have an infrared communications port like its predecessor, a link cable would be available to hook up as many as four units. Of special interest was the fact that if two or more Game Boy Advances were linked together, only one copy of a game was needed. When earlier Game Boys were linked together, each one needed a copy of the game that was being played. The Game Boy Advance would also connect with Nintendo's forthcoming Dolphin in some fashion, while maintaining compatibility with all of the Game Boy cartridges that had preceded it.

Originally, Nintendo had expected to release the Game Boy Advance in the fall of 2000. Nintendo decided to delay its launch until 2001, simply because the Game Boy Color was selling too well to be replaced. Since the Game Boy Color didn't have any real competition in the marketplace, there wasn't any reason for Nintendo to jump the gun and change things.

The Game Boy was actually doing better than anybody's expectations. In June, after the unit had been available for 11 years in several incarnations, Nintendo sold its 100 millionth Game Boy console, making it the most popular game console in videogame history. In fact, thanks mostly to the success of Pokémon, Nintendo managed to sell 17 million consoles just between June, 1999 and June, 2000.

Due to the unprecedented success of the Game Boy, third-party companies continued to release new games and peripherals. On August 23, Nintendo of Japan released a game called *Kirby's Tilt 'n' Tumble*. Within the cartridge was a motion detector that sensed the angle that the Game Boy console was held. This angle determined in which direction Kirby would move on-screen. Nintendo announced that the technology would be used in many Game Boy Advance games to come.[10]

But not everything released for the Game Boy Color was game-related. The Singer Corporation released a new sewing machine called the *Izek*. Included with the $500 machine was a Game Boy Color unit. A special Izek cartridge, which was only available with the sewing machine, contained over 84 stitch patterns. The Game Boy Color connected directly to the sewing machine, which then had access to the patterns on the cartridge. People could also create custom patterns that could be saved on the cartridge. And for those who insisted on playing games on the Game Boy Color while sewing, the Izek worked independently when the handheld console was detached from it, although it didn't have access to the preset stitch patterns.

Whereas playing a Game Boy while sewing might be somewhat difficult, a new unique Game Boy peripheral was shown at E³ in May that allowed people to at least listen to music while they sewed. The *Songboy* turned the Game Boy into a portable MP3 player. The Songboy itself was an oversized cartridge that plugged directly into the Game Boy. MP3 files could be downloaded to a PC from the Internet and then loaded into the Songboy via a USB connection. The $79 Songboy could store approximately sixty minutes worth of music within its 32MB of memory. And if that wasn't enough, an additional 32MB of memory would be available.

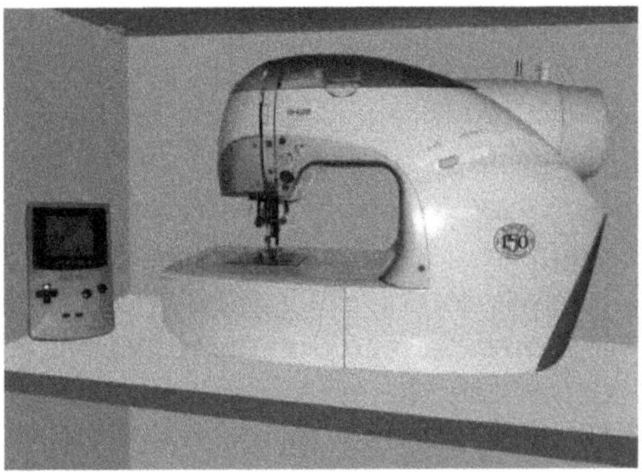

Singer IZEK

The Songboy didn't just funnel music through the Game Boy. Thanks to the handheld's screen, additional features such as viewable song lyrics or album-cover visuals were also possible. The Game Boy could even double as a recorder, since the Songboy had a built-in microphone.

Songboy.com, the company behind the peripheral, had applied to become an official Nintendo licensee. Nintendo not only denied the request, but turned around and sued Songboy.com for infringement of its intellectual property rights. The suit became even more vicious when Ron Jones,[11] who had invented the Songboy and was head of Songboy.com, commented that the lawsuit was a biased attempt by Nintendo to stop Songboy.com because it was a black-owned company.

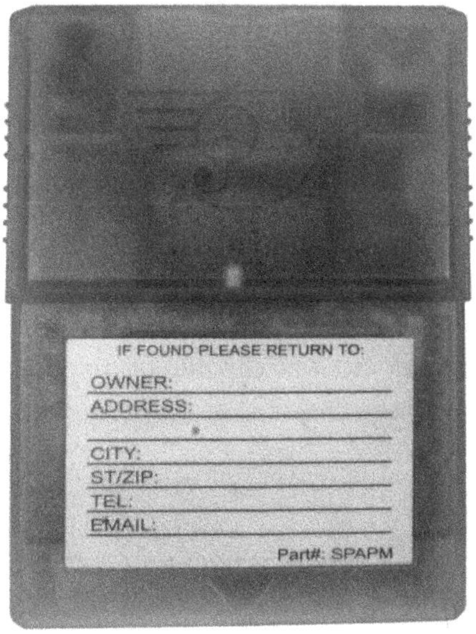

Songpro Songboy

The two companies battled each other throughout the summer. In August, representatives from both companies finally faced each other in a meeting sponsored by Reverend Jesse Jackson. It was there that they were able to reach an amicable decision. Songboy.com agreed to change its name to SongPro.com, and the name of its product was changed to SongPro. In turn, Nintendo agreed to officially license it.

SNK Scales Back

The Game Boy wasn't the only handheld system that Songboy.com had initially intended to support. In addition to the Songboy, the company used E³ to introduce the Songjones, a version of the Songboy that was compatible with the SNK Neo•Geo Pocket Color. Unlike the Game Boy version, the Songjones never made it to market. And this wasn't due to any fault of Songboy.com.

In January, SNK was acquired by Aruze, a manufacturer of Pachinko machines, with the sole intention of using SNK's intellectual properties, such as *King of Fighters*, in its Pachinko machines. Following E³, where SNK had a large exhibit, Aruze decided to confine its focus to Japan. On June 13, Aruze closed down its entire overseas operation, and immediately asked Western retailers to return all unsold SNK products. These included not only the Neo•Geo Pocket Color hardware and software, but also any third-party SNK software for the Dreamcast and PlayStation. SNK intended to repackage the recalled merchandise and sell it in Japan.

In the United States, the closure of SNK took its personnel completely by surprise, especially since a new five-year lease had just been signed for its Torrance, California headquarters. The response at E^3 to the Neo•Geo Pocket Color had been overwhelming, and at least four third-party companies intended to begin developing games for it. SNK's American sales department had even requested a $10 million advertising budget from Japan to promote the handheld. Instead, it received notice of the closure.

Aruze claimed that the foreign subsidiaries were being closed because its executives felt that the Neo•Geo Pocket Color couldn't compete in a market that was more than 80% dominated by the Game Boy Color. Many believed that the closures had actually occurred because SNK didn't really need to have the overseas branches open. Much of SNK's foreign business was with die-hard gamers who imported the games from Japan because they couldn't wait for the domestic releases. This business would continue and prosper, since the Japanese exports would now be the only SNK games available.

Wonderswan Color

With the death of the Neo•Geo Pocket Color in North America and elsewhere, Nintendo had absolutely no competition in the handheld market. This wasn't the case in Japan, where the Neo•Geo Pocket Color still flourished along with Bandai's monochrome WonderSwan which was so popular that Bandai released a ¥6,800 ($65) color version on December 9. The *WonderSwan Color* was completely backward-compatible with the original and was capable of displaying 241 colors on the screen at a time. It could play for twenty hours on one AA battery and featured a USB port, so it could hook up with cell phones, PCs and the PS2. Bandai sold 300,000 units in its first two days, many of them because *Final Fantasy* was one of the launch titles.

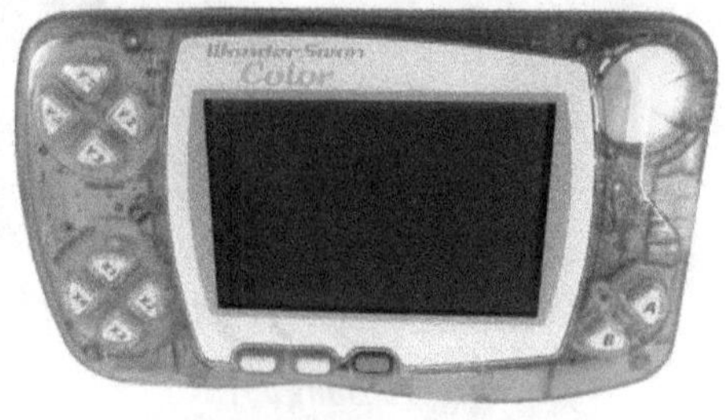

Bandai Wonderswan Color

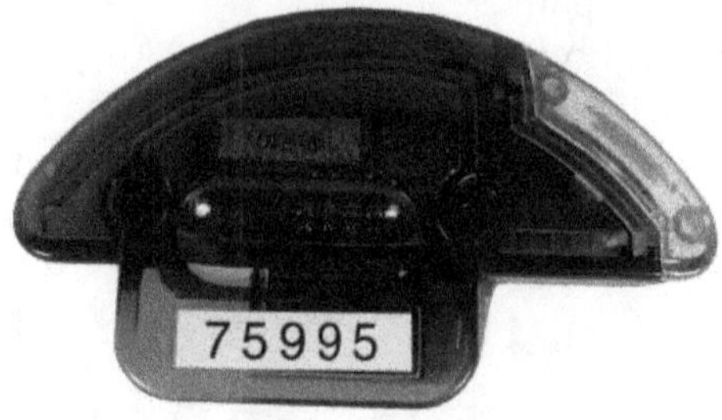

Bandai WonderWave

Bandai Wonderborg

Bandai also released peripherals for the WonderSwan and WonderSwan Color. The *WonderWave*, which came out in February, was a wireless adapter that plugged into the end of a WonderSwan console. Once installed, it could send data to a nearby WonderSwan via an infrared light.[12] But the WonderWave was also Bandai's answer to the cable that SNK released that linked the Neo•Geo Pocket to the Dreamcast. In this case, the WonderWave could be used to transfer data with SCEJ's PocketStation. This data could then be used in certain Bandai PS2 games.

Bandai also released the *WonderBorg*, a robot beetle that, once assembled, could be trained. This was done through a *Robot Works* cartridge that was packaged with the WonderBorg. Once this cartridge was inserted into the WonderSwan, the user could send instructions via the WonderWave to the robot about how to react to specific situations. An additional program was included to treat the WonderBorg as a pet, similar to the *Tamagotchi*, which Bandai had introduced in 1997.

While the original monochrome WonderSwan never made it to the United States, the word from

Bandai was that the WonderSwan Color would, although not in 2000. As a sign that the company meant it, the WonderBorg was packaged with both Japanese and English instruction manuals.[13]

The GameCube

In early January, executives at Nintendo insisted that the Dolphin would appear during 2000. Most critics, both inside and outside of Nintendo, were highly skeptical, and several reasons were cited. Chief among them was the fact that the second- and third-party developers weren't anywhere near completing their first Dolphin games. It didn't help that the development kits that were used by the licensees weren't representative of what the final Dolphin would be like. Nintendo acknowledged this and promised that it would send out updated development kits beginning in April. Once Nintendo admitted that it hadn't yet shipped the current development kits, it had no other choice than to confess at the GDC in March that the Dolphin would not appear in the United States and Europe until the first half of 2001. A holiday 2000 release was still expected in Japan.

Attendees at E^3 in May were disappointed when they learned that Nintendo wouldn't be showing off either the Dolphin or the Game Boy Advance. Prototypes of these new consoles weren't even displayed privately behind closed doors to select members of the press, as was usually the custom when a company had a hot new system coming out. Instead, Nintendo concentrated on promoting its N64 and Game Boy Color lineup, which included several new Pokémon titles.

Nintendo preferred to debut its new consoles at its own Spaceworld show, which was to be held in Japan on August 25. However, even that date wasn't official. Several developers suggested that Spaceworld might be pushed back to November if Dolphin software wasn't ready by August. This scenario became more and more realistic when July passed and Nintendo still hadn't sent out the all-important, updated development kits to the second- and third-party developers.

Despite the anxiety felt by the developers, Nintendo intended to hold Spaceworld at the end of August as originally planned. Prior to the show, Nintendo went and changed the name of its new console. Dolphin was out and *Star Cube* was in. That moniker wouldn't last long. By the time Spaceworld actually opened on August 25, the name of the new console was officially the *GameCube*.

The name was appropriate. When the press saw the console for the first time at Spaceworld, what they saw simply looked like a cube that played games. Measuring a mere 6 inches x 6 inches x 4.3 inches, the GameCube contained nearly the same specifications that Nintendo had outlined for the Dolphin over a year earlier. The Gekko microprocessor would run at 405Mhz, and the graphics chip would generate 6 to 12 million polygons per second.

Nintendo finally abandoned the cartridge format with the GameCube, but like Sega, it chose to go with a proprietary optical disc. The 8CM discs, based on Matsushita technology, was roughly half the size of a standard 5-inch CD or DVD, and could store up to 1.5GB of data, which was roughly 190 times the amount of data that could be stored on an N64 cartridge, and twice as much as on a standard CD. Nintendo predicted that its format would eventually become a standard, and that its small size would be attractive for future handheld consoles.

Like the other videogame consoles that would grace the 21st century, the GameCube would have the optional ability to hook up to the Internet. Modular 56k or broadband modems would plug into a socket on the underside of the console.

While Nintendo revealed much about the GameCube including release dates of July 2001 in Japan and October 2001 in North America, it didn't announce everything. The company specifically left out details that it wouldn't make public until the 2001 E^3, for fear that the competition might "borrow" them. Game titles for the GameCube were also conspicuously absent at Spaceworld.

Even though the GameCube wouldn't be available until 2001, Nintendo still managed to release a "new" console at the end of 2000. The *Pikachu Nintendo 64* was a redressed version of the N64. The console was available in two colors In Japan, blue or orange, while the rest of the world received one with a second shade of blue. The console featured a Pokéball that doubled as an on-off switch, and a raised Pikachu whose cheeks lit up when the power was turned on.

Nintendo Pikachu N64

The Pikachu N64 was Nintendo's attempt to use the Pokémon franchise to keep the N64 alive, since sales of the console had plummeted following the release of the Dreamcast. The few third-party companies that had invested in the N64 were abandoning it. One of them, Acclaim, had announced early in the year that it would release its final five games for the N64 during 2000. Nintendo, on the other hand, didn't plan on forsaking the console. At E^3 it had announced several new outstanding games, including *Pokémon Puzzle League*, a *Tetris*-type puzzle game.

It made sense for Nintendo to continue releasing Pokémon-related products. The company had seen its sales rise in record proportions after Pokémon had been introduced. In 1997, handheld games had only accounted for 6% of the total videogame sales in the United States. Following the release of *Pokémon Red* and *Pokémon Blue* in September 1998, handheld sales jumped to 8%. And that number climbed to 18% in 1999 when Pokémon products were available for an entire year, during a period when overall videogame sales actually fell slightly. During the first five months of 2000, Nintendo of America reported a 220% gain in sales on Pokémon-related games over the year before. And that was before even October 15 when the company released *Pokémon Silver* and *Pokémon Gold* for the Game Boy Color, the American versions of *Pocket Monsters Silver* and *Pocket Monsters Gold*. And on the following day Nintendo of America released the *Pokémon Pikachu 2 GS*, which could transmit data to the two new *Pokémon* games.

A different version of the *Pokémon Pikachu 2 GS* unit had been released in Japan on July 28. The *Pocket Sakura* was packaged in deluxe editions of the game *Sakura Taisen GB*.[14] *Sakura Taisen* was a popular RPG series that appeared on a number of game consoles. Like the *Pokémon Pikachu 2 GS*, the *Pocket Sakura* acted as a pedometer and sent data back to the game, which increased a character's strength.

Nintendo Pocket Sakura

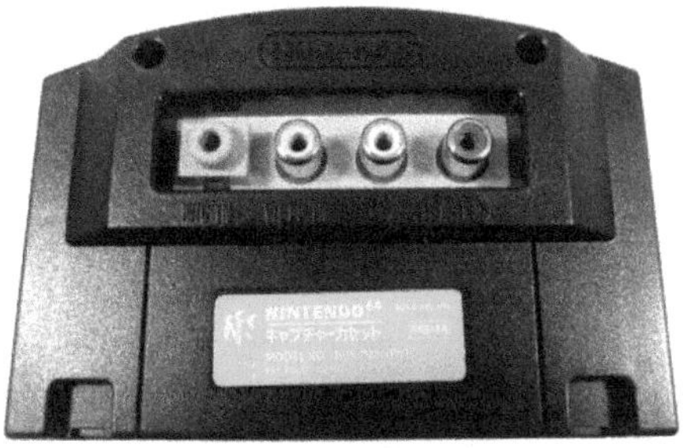

Nintendo Capture Cartridge

Marketing Pocket Monsters-related games for Nintendo of Japan was akin to printing money. Unfortunately, not everything that the company released turned to gold. Following the late 1999 release of the 64DD, Nintendo released additional software for the unit throughout the year. Two disks were released on February 23. *SimCity 64* was an updated version of the popular city-planning game. *Mario Artist: Talent Studio* let people build onscreen characters that they could then apply real faces to. These faces could be imported from external sources such as videotapes or the Game Boy Camera through the *Nintendo 64 Capture Cartridge*, which was bundled with the disk. The *Nintendo 64 Capture Cartridge* could also be used with the previously-released *Mario Artist: Paint Studio.*

Nintendo of Japan issued the *F-Zero X Expansion Kit* on April 21. This disk could only be used with the *F-Zero X* game that had been released for the N64 in 1998. When the game was played, portions of it could detect whether the expansion disk was connected or not. If it was, players were able to create and save additional tracks and cars, in addition to other new features. In May, two 64DD games were released, *Japan Pro Golf Tour 64* and *Doshin the Giant: Tinkling Toddler Liberation Front! Assemble!*. June and August saw the release of two final *Mario Artist* titles: *Communication Kit* and *Polygon Studio*. And that was it. In all, only ten disks were released altogether, of which only four of them were games.

By October, there were only 15,000 subscribers to the Randnet service, not enough to sustain it. Nintendo announced that it would be shutting down the service as of February 28, 2001 and offered to buy back any of the network-related hardware such as the Nintendo 64DD Modem. It also provided free service to the network from the date of the announcement to the day it was shut down.

More Speech Recognition Games

Dozens of titles had been scheduled to be developed for the 64DD. Many of them were eventually released on N64 cartridges or switched to a different console altogether. One title that was completely discontinued was *Sound Maker*, a fifth title in the *Mario Artist* series.[15] According to Shigeru Miyamoto, this program would have let users create music and melodies, which could be saved to a disk. Conceivably, this program would have used the N64's Voice Recognition Unit (VRU), which had previously been included with *Densha de Go! 64* and *Pikachū Genki dechū*, Those two games wound up being the only Japanese titles that embraced it.

Nintendo of America released *Hey You, Pikachu!*, the American version of *Pikachū Genki dechū*, on November 6. Like its Japanese counterpart the game was sold with the Voice Recognition Unit (VRU). However, in North America, this would be the only game that used it. In *Hey You, Pikachu!*, gamers talked to Pikachu and had him respond to their voice commands.

Hey You, Pikachu! was the first voice-recognition game to be released by Nintendo of America but it wasn't the first such game to be released in North America. Sega of America had actually beat Nintendo of America to it when it released *Seaman* on August 8.

Sega's long-term plan was to use the microphone that came with *Seaman* for other applications, such as *Dreamcall,* which allowed for two Dreamcast owners to chat over the Internet for free. But since games were Sega's prime business, the company also looked into ways to incorporate *Dreamcall* into its games. One idea was to allow players competing in online games on SegaNet to talk to each other. Sega of America planned to release *Alien Front Online,* the first game that had this feature, in the fall.

On December 7, voice-recognition games also became available on the PS2 in Japan. On that day, Taito released its *Taito Speech Recognition Controller,* which consisted of a triangular device that a headset plugged into, which itself plugged into one of the PS2's USB ports. The controller sold for ¥4,980 ($45) alone, or bundled with a game, *The Greatest Striker,* for ¥9,800 ($89). *The Greatest Striker* was a soccer game in which gamers could tell the system to navigate through menus. Once the game began, verbal commands such as "pass" or "shoot" could be used to make the players on the field perform. Over 40 commands were built into the system. A second game, a Mahjong simulation called *Mahjong Declaration* followed on December 14. Neither the voice-recognition system, nor the two games that utilized it, were became available outside of Japan.

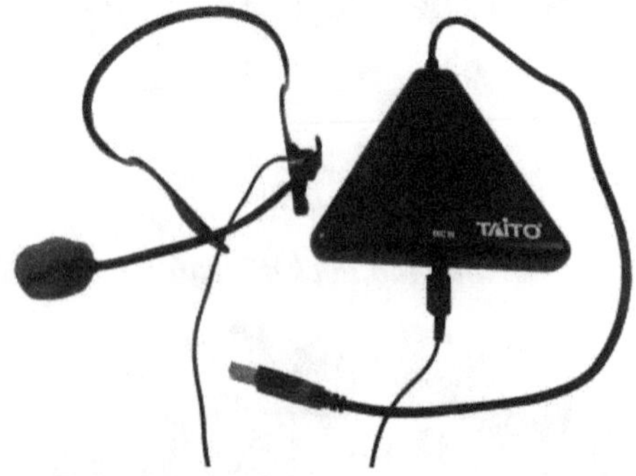

Taito Speech Recognition Controller

Cross Console Gaming

Because it used cartridges, software for the N64 generally cost more than it did for the other consoles. And while Dreamcast and PlayStation games were competitively priced, the profit for SCE was somewhat higher, since Sega had selected a proprietary disc format for the Dreamcast. Thanks to a new licensing structure that SCE put into effect in April, the prices for its games were about to come down.

The new plan allowed third-party publishers to pay lower licensing fees. According to SCE, this opened the door for new low-cost titles that would keep the PlayStation popular. Once the new price structure went into place, several companies released brand-new $10.00 PlayStation discs. Although the majority of these low-priced games didn't look or play as well as the higher-priced titles from better-known companies, they still managed to sell decently.

One reason people may have been buying PlayStation discs was to play them on their Mac computers. On February 11, the U.S. 9th Circuit Court of Appeals reversed the ruling that had prevented Connectix from selling its Virtual Game Station emulation software, which allowed PlayStation games to be played on Macs.

PlayStation games could be played on Sega Dreamcasts as well. Bleem! announced a new emulator at E^3 that made this happen. The company planned to sell four $20 *Bleempaks,* each of which was a disc-based emulator that would let a Dreamcast play 100 different PlayStation titles. Although Bleem! garnered much attention for the Bleempaks at E^3, they weren't available for sale by the end of the year.

Another way American Dreamcast owners could play more games on their consoles was by purchasing Japanese imports. The only problem was that none of these imported games could play on a domestic Dreamcast without the installation of a modification (mod) chip, which voided the console's warranty. This procedure eventually proved to be unnecessary after it was discovered that by inserting a GameShark CDX into a Dreamcast and pressing "Start Game" without activating any codes, the console was put into a state in which it could accept any Dreamcast CD, regardless of the region that it originated from.

And then, of course, there were counterfeit copies of games. However, thanks to Sega's anti-piracy actions, there were far fewer unscrupulous people selling bootleg copies than there would otherwise have been. Sega had been responsible for the shutdown of over 60 websites and 125 online auctions that had sold counterfeit material.

Battle Against Violent Games

Meanwhile, the battle concerning violent videogames raged on. In April, federal Judge Edward Johnstone dismissed a lawsuit against 25 entertainment companies that had been filed by the families of three girls who had been killed at a 1997 school shooting in Paducah, Kentucky. The prosecution charged that the shooter, Michael Carneal, had imitated the violence that he'd found in movies and games that had been released from a multitude of entertainment companies, including Nintendo, SCE and Sega. The judge ruled that Carneal's actions were tragic and appalling, but that there was no way that the companies could be held responsible.

Despite this ruling from at least one judge that videogames weren't responsible for violent behavior, most retailers weren't taking any chances. In May, following an Illinois sting operation wherein 32 children were able to buy M-rated games from every store that they entered, Illinois Attorney General Jim Ryan wrote to the leading department stores and asked them to stop selling M-rated games to minors. Sears and Montgomery Ward complied by removing all games that had Mature-rated content. These stores received kudos from Senator Joe Lieberman, and he implored other stores to follow suit and not sell M-rated games to people under 17. Walmart and K-Mart responded to Lieberman's request by announcing that they would check the ID of anyone who wished to purchase an M-rated game. These two stores didn't go all the way and completely remove the games, because they felt that the games were legal and should be available to adult customers who wanted them. Toys "R" Us already had a similar policy in place.

As kids around the country were being banned from buying mature games, kids in Indianapolis found that they couldn't play violent games in arcades. Indianapolis became the first city in the country to officially ban minors from playing games with graphic violence or sexual content. The law called for mature games to be separated from other games in any arcade by at least ten feet, and placed behind a curtain or wall so minors couldn't even see them. The new law was challenged by two game-industry groups, but the Mayor of Indianapolis was confident that it would hold up in court.

So, game content was still a major concern. However, in light of the Columbine shootings, developers were more in tune with the level of permissible violence, even if a "Mature" rating was assigned. The 2000 E³ was more subdued than in previous years, and few companies wished to display games that had extraneous violence.

One company, Rare, even went the extra step and removed a non-violent feature from a game, due to concerns that people might perceive it the wrong way.

Perfect Dark was a first-person shooter that Rare released for the N64 in May in North America and elsewhere later in the year. Originally, the game had utilized the N64 Transfer Pak, so players could snap photos of people with their Game Boy Cameras. Those facials could then be transferred to the N64, where they would become the actual faces of the characters in the game. However, in light of the violence that had penetrated the schools, Rare decided to remove this feature, which it thought could be deemed overly-violent. The version that was eventually released allowed players to transfer unlock codes for the

N64 version from the Game Boy version.

However, despite the ratings that were imposed on games, children were still learning about the "Mature" ones. An FTC report issued in September found that the game companies targeted minors by placing ads for "Mature" games in inappropriate places, such as magazines that catered to teens. Peter Moore of Sega didn't completely agree with the report. While he conceded that the companies shouldn't place ads for violent games in a magazine like *Sports Illustrated for Kids*, he didn't see a problem when the ads appeared in the general videogame magazines.

Hard Times

The videogame magazines themselves experienced a bad year, as four U.S. magazines closed down. *Diehard GameFan* and newcomer *Incite* had been directed at consumers, and *Games Business* and *MVC* had been trade publications. While the deaths of the consumer magazines didn't leave much of an impression upon readerships that still had four other general videogame magazines to choose from, the loss of the trade magazines made a larger impact. Only *Gameweek*, the first of the videogame trade magazines, remained.

Meanwhile, with the release of the PlayStation 2, the magazines that covered the PlayStation changed their focus. In the United Kingdom, Future Publishing elected to launch a brand new magazine in November dedicated to the PlayStation. The *Official UK PlayStation 2 Magazine* was sold alongside the *Official UK PlayStation Magazine* which continued to support the original PlayStation. But in the U.S., the *Official US PlayStation Magazine*, which was published by Ziff-Davis with complete cooperation from SCE, began covering the new console alongside the old one in its December issue.

But Ziff-Davis, which also published *EGM*, wasn't banking on the future of its tech magazines. to supplement its computer magazines. The company had started ZDTV in 1998, the first 24-hour cable network to provide programming about computer and technology issues. Despite prophecies of doom from industry critics, the network thrived, and on October 21, 2000, it was renamed *TechTV*.

Magazines weren't the only businesses in the industry that were having hard times. Hasbro Interactive, the software division of Hasbro, also found itself in dire straits. The company announced in December that it was pursuing a deal wherein France-based Infogrames would buy it for $100 million in cash and stock. Among the assets that Infogrames would receive were all of the Atari patents and titles.

But if any company symbolized the fickleness of the buying public, it was Sega Enterprises. Sega had entered 2000 after losing nearly $100 million in 1999. The company had initially experienced healthy Dreamcast sales, but that changed considerably once SCE released the PS2 in Japan. In mid-summer, as mounting losses continued, Sega's president, Shoichiro Irimajiri, took responsibility and stepped down from his position. He was replaced by Isao Okawa, who had been the chairman of CSK Corporation, Sega's primary stockholder. One of first things that Okawa did as president was to give Sega of America's Peter Moore an ultimatum. Moore was given $500 million from Okawa's personal fortune and one year to make the Dreamcast healthy again. After that, the fate of the Dreamcast, as well as Sega, was anybody's guess.

Nobody within the company wanted the Dreamcast to fail, especially so soon after the failure of the Saturn. Meanwhile, the last official game for the Saturn, MediaWorks' *Yuukyuu Gensoukyoku Hozonban Perpetual Collection*, was released in Japan on December 4.

But even as the Dreamcast was given a new lease on life in the United States, the outlook for Sega Enterprises was miserable. After the overall corporation had been called "the least profitable company in Japan" by the Japanese newspaper *Nihon Keizai Shinbun*, executives at Sega of Japan met on November 15 to announce that Sega planned to become the number-one network-game service provider before 2003. At that time, Sega would split up into three separate businesses. One would run online videogame content, the second would provide broadband online services, and the third would concentrate on entertainment centers that would feature Sega's arcade games. On the software side, Sega would support several consoles by licensing its hit titles to third-party developers. Bandai expressed interest in bringing Sega games to the WonderSwan Color, and there were rumors that Acclaim would team up with Sega to develop Sega titles for the PS2. And on the hardware side, Sega intended to keep supporting the Dreamcast. Sega's intention was to license the Dreamcast technology to other companies, in order to incorporate it into platforms such as DVD players, cellular phones, and PCs. The goal was to raise Sega's market share from 4.2% to 25%.

The newspaper accounts in the United States were quite different. On December 27, *The New York Times* published a story that said Nintendo was negotiating to purchase Sega for around $2 billion. Executives from both companies emphatically denied that such actions were taking place. *The New York Times* published another article two days later, stating that Sega was having talks with Microsoft and Electronic Arts. Again, all the parties mentioned in the article denied it.

Regardless of what the newspapers said, Sega appeared to be off to a good start with its new console. With PS2 shortages abundant, many people settled on the Dreamcast, which numerous videogame critics favored anyway. But it would be a minor victory. As the year came to a close, the rumor mills were already reporting that the Dreamcast's days were numbered, despite Moore's ultimatum.

And in the world of videogames, the rumor mills were usually correct.

CHAPTER TWENTY-NINE
2001

Rumors began circulating during the last few months of 2000 that Sega was going to pull the plug on the Dreamcast. This was confirmed on the morning of January 31 when Sega of America president Peter Moore announced, in a worldwide teleconference, that Sega was exiting the hardware business and would reestablish itself as a "platform-agnostic third-party publisher."

Sega decided to announce the news at the beginning of the year, so it could limit its losses to the previous fiscal year. Meanwhile, it had nearly a whole year before the 2001 holiday season, during which it could establish itself as a venerable third-party developer and publisher.

Although Sega would continue to sell and support Dreamcasts throughout 2001, the company would not manufacture any more consoles after March 31. And Moore announced that as of February 4, Sega would reduce the price of the Dreamcast to $99.95 in order to sell out the remaining stock as soon as possible.

Sega's reason to eliminate the Dreamcast was plausible. Although the company had developed highly popular and innovative games such as *Crazy Taxi*, it was restricted in the potential number of games that it could sell, because it was limited to releasing them only for the Dreamcast. While Sega had sold 1.8 million consoles during the six months that followed the Dreamcast's September 1999 launch, the company only sold an additional 1.35 million units during the nine months afterwards.

Sega only made a profit on the software, so it couldn't earn enough from the console-exclusive titles to maintain a profitable position. The Dreamcast only had an installed base of slightly over three million units. By unloading the hardware, Sega was free to design games for all of the systems, not just the one that was in third place among the consoles.

Sega estimated that phasing out the Dreamcast would cost the company approximately $689 million. Fearing that this projected loss would panic many Sega shareholders and cause them to dump their stock, Sega president Isao Okawa turned over $730 million of his own personal shares back to the company to ensure that Sega stayed on its feet. Ironically, Okawa had wanted Sega to exit the hardware business as early as 1994, even before the release of the Saturn.

Sadly, Okawa's large donation would be his last. The self-made billionaire, Japan's wealthiest citizen, died from heart failure on March 26, at the age of 74.

Although it had been Okawa's desire that Sega drop the Dreamcast and solely become a software developer, the Dreamcast continued to sell for several months after he died. This was due to two price cuts that Sega instilled to ensure that the units would sell. The price was first reduced to $80 in the summer, and then again in mid-November to a remarkable $50. This price guaranteed that any remaining consoles would be sold by Christmas. The final shipments of new Dreamcast consoles were actually sent to American retailers on November 23.

New Dreamcast software continued to be released as long as the consoles were selling. This was especially true in Japan, where the system suddenly gained the large following that it couldn't get before it was cancelled. And when Sega of Japan ran out of new consoles, it began selling refurbished ones.

Sega of America quietly released the Dreamcast Broadband Adapter on January 10. However, since the company was planning to cancel the Dreamcast, the adapters were only available through Sega of America's online store. Many of the $60 adapters that had been purchased were quickly placed on eBay, where they commanded prices of more than $100 apiece. Unfortunately, not all of the Dreamcast's online games supported broadband.

NFL 2K1 and *NBA 2K1*, for example, could only be played online via dial-up.

One of the last Dreamcast games that Sega of America released that supported online gaming was *Alien Front Online*. It came out on August 19, five months after the company stopped producing new Dreamcast consoles. Shortly afterwards, Sega decided to shut down its SegaNet ISP service. Current subscribers were transferred to an Earthlink account for the same $20 monthly fee. However, Sega shut down its free online servers on November 1, forcing gamers to pay an additional $10 per month to play any of its online games. The result was that a lot fewer people played the games than would have normally. And since less people were online to play, there was a smaller chance that someone who wanted to play would find someone to play against. But this was only for a short time. Sega eventually shut down all of the Dreamcast's online servers for good. Gamers could still compete in online games against one another, but they had to connect to their own ISPs to do so.

Alien Front Online was the only U.S. Dreamcast game after *Seaman* to employ the microphone peripheral, which gamers used to voice-chat with other online gamers as they played. Although voice-chatting had already been available in computer games for a short while, this marked the first time it was available through a game console. Unfortunately, this feature could no longer be used once Sega had shut down its servers, even when gamers connected through their own ISPs.

Majesco Game Gear

Ironically, as Sega eased out of the hardware business, one of its older consoles was given a new lease on life. On February 21, Majesco announced that it had acquired the rights from Sega to manufacture the Game Gear, as it had previously done with the Genesis. The announcement said that the new console would be available exclusively at Toys 'R' Us and that Majesco was going to support it by releasing new original Game Gear software that would retail for $15, along with ten classic games that included *Sonic Spinball* and *Pac-Man*.

Majesco Game Gear

Majesco's Game Gear differed from Sega's in several respects. It was black instead of gray, and had a purple start button instead of Sega's blue one. Taking advantage of a decade's worth of technology, the new Game Gear featured a screen that responded quicker to a player's actions. And while the new handheld was completely compatible with all the games that had been released for the original, two peripherals, the Master Gear Converter, which allowed Sega Master System games to play on it, and the TV Tuner,[1] were not compatible with it.

While Majesco didn't have any illusions that the Game Gear might outsell Nintendo's Game Boy Color, the former's $30 price made it a nice inexpensive alternative.

By the time of Moore's announcement that Sega would be leaving the console business, the company had confirmed that it would be releasing several titles, including *Virtua Fighter 4*, for the PS2. Most games would be published under the Sega name, but some would also be licensed to Acclaim. Sega games were also being converted to new markets, such as Palm Pilots and Motorola cell phones. On August 30, Sega formed a partnership with Synovial, Inc., a multimedia wireless provider, to develop a *Virtual Game Gear* that would recreate the Sega Game Gear experience on handheld devices such as PDAs, cellular phones and Internet devices. It was initially available for Pocket PC devices and shipped with several classic Sega games, including the original *Sonic the Hedgehog*. Additional games were to be offered that users could purchase and download from the Internet.

Sega also signed an agreement with Pace Micro Technology, a manufacturer of set-top boxes. This deal would integrate Dreamcast technology with Pace's boxes, and allow the owners of those boxes to play Dreamcast games, either online or by downloading them. The first set-top boxes were expected to hit the market in 2002.

The Sony/AOL Alliance

With the Dreamcast out of the way, online gaming through consoles came to a halt, as the PS2 was not yet set up for it. But this was going to change. On April 18, SCE released a new PS2 model in Japan. Like its American counterpart, the new model featured an expansion bay in the rear, rather than the unused PCMCIA card slot. Then, a month later, SCE announced what the expansion bay would be used for.

SCE used E³ to announce an alliance with AOL that would give PS2 owners the ability to send and receive Instant Messages (IM) using their consoles. In order for them to do this, they would also have to access an online network. SCE displayed its network adapter, which would provide both a broadband and 56k dial-up connection to the Internet. This network adapter would also be key in providing PS2 gamers with online gaming. SCE also showed a 40-gigabyte hard drive, which would plug into the unused expansion bay, and would be used to store games and other information downloaded from the Internet.

In addition to allowing online gaming through the PS2, SCE planned that the PS2 would behave more and more like a personal computer. In addition to the hard drive, the company also announced a keyboard and mouse that would be available in November. A desktop LCD monitor was planned for the coming winter.

SCEJ announced on June 28 that it would be lowering the price of the Japanese PS2 from ¥39,800 ($319) to ¥35,000 ($280). The reason was to strengthen the console's market position before the arrival of new consoles from Nintendo and Microsoft.

SCE released the hard drive and network adapter in Japan on July 19 through a PlayStation website. Two types of drives and adapters were available. The majority were external units that plugged into PCMCIA (Personal Computer Memory Card International Association) slots, or PC Card slots,[2] in the rear of the console. The hard drive received its power by plugging it directly into a standard electrical outlet. A small number of the hard drives were internal models that sat inside the console's expansion bay. These were for the newer Japanese consoles that SCE had only begun selling in April, and which were the same as the American PS2s. These hard drives plugged into, and received their power

SCE PS2 with Internal Drive

from, the separate network adapter, which itself plugged into the console. The Japanese network adapter, which was packaged with the hard drive, was slightly different. Unlike the one that had been displayed at E[3], it only supported broadband. The external hard drive and PC Card retailed for ¥19,000 ($158), while the internal one with the network adapter sold for ¥18,000 ($149). Although the hard drive had originally been designed to be used as a place to download data from the Internet, this was no longer the case since the PS2 didn't yet have a network to connect to. Instead, the hard drive was used to back up data from memory cards. In addition, several dozen games stored data on the hard drive to help reduce their load times.

As 2001 neared its conclusion, AOL and SCE revealed more terms of their partnership. While on the surface, the two companies were jointly developing an Internet browser that would provide PS2 owners with a variety of services, SCE's real intent was to create a network that would tie together many different SCE products, including the PS2.

Unfortunately, SCE's entrance into online gaming didn't go according to plan. The key to everything was SCE's network adapter. Originally scheduled for a November release, the $40 unit, along with the network itself, was pushed back to spring, 2002. The American release of the $150 hard drive was also pushed back, and a new date wasn't announced. Meanwhile, the first PS2 game that could be played online was released on October 28. SCE stressed that this game, *Tony Hawk's Pro Skater 3*, could be played online without the need for an adapter. Players could merely use any USB modem that connected to the Internet through their own ISPs. This game was the exception, however. All other online games that SCE planned would require the use of the adapter.

Details of the planned network were sketchy. Marketing personnel within Activision, which had published *Tony Hawk's Pro Skater 3*, said that the online service would initially be free to all users.

Although SCE's plans to get into online gaming in a major way were delayed, the company had announced on February 21 that it had made a deal with Namco and Sega to provide an advanced version of the PS2 with networking capabilities to Japanese arcades, so players in different locations could compete. A limited test of the new system was expected to occur before the end of the year, prior to the system's nationwide release in 2002.

While PS2 owners couldn't get online with their consoles, PSone owners in Japan were given the ability to do so. On May 24, SCEJ released *Doko Demo Issyo*, a ¥2,800 ($26) package that included a cable that plugged into a PSone controller slot and connect it to an i-Mode cell phone.[3] *Doko Demo Issyo* included a calendar program that allowed users to send and receive emails, maintain a task schedule and send business cards, using the i-Mode cell phone to link the console to the Internet. A popular PocketStation game, *Moissho*, was also included, which users could play while competing against others.

SCE's networking plans didn't faze Microsoft. According to Seamus Blackley, the "father" of the Xbox, 90% of the people polled wanted to play games on consoles, and leave their web-browsing

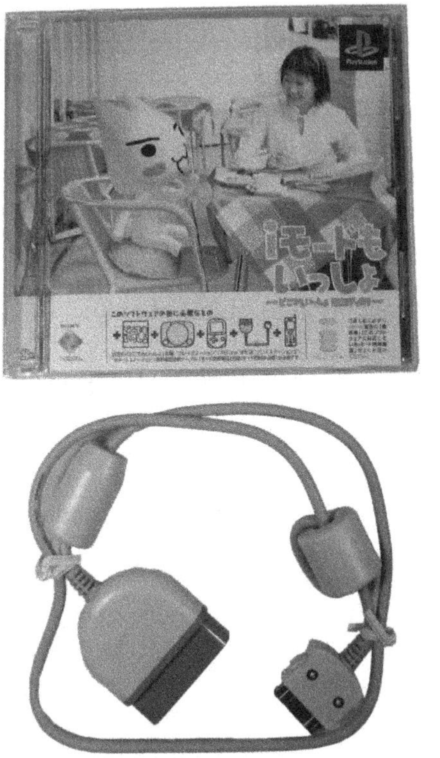

SCE Doko Demo Issyo

and instant messaging to their computers.

Meanwhile, SCE wasn't too concerned about the competition, either. By this time, the Dreamcast was dead, and even though Sega still supported it, the realization was that gamers would abandon it when other online avenues became available. Although it was public knowledge that the Xbox would provide online gaming, Microsoft announced that its gaming network wouldn't be up and running until mid-2002. SCE planned to have its network ready long before that.

Presenting the Xbox

The Xbox was officially unveiled on January 6 at the winter CES, during the final 15 minutes of Bill Gates' 45-minute keynote address. Only those assembled at the speech got to see a non-working model, as it wasn't displayed at Microsoft's booth. Giving attendees the chance to see it up close was planned to occur at E^3.

But what the audience did see was a console that was wider than the PS2, and big enough to house a 733 MHz processor, a 250 MHz graphics processor, four controller ports and an Ethernet port. It was made clear that the console would not support 56k dial-up. An 8GB hard drive, which would be used for storage and not limited to online play like the PS2's, would be included with the system. And while the Xbox would be able to play DVDs, this would require an optional remote control, unlike the PS2, which used a standard controller.[4]

The actual controller that Microsoft showed was one that did not win the hearts of the press that viewed it. It featured eight buttons, two analog sticks and triggers and a pressure-sensitive directional pad, which rendered it bulky and hard to hold comfortably. *Game Informer* dubbed it "The Blunder of The Year."[5]

The release date and retail price of the Xbox were announced on May 16 at E^3, during an early-morning presentation. The console would be released in the United States on November 8, and would sell for $299. Between 600,000 and 800,000 units would be available for the launch, and a total of one million systems would be produced by the holidays. A specific Japanese release date was not announced, but a Microsoft spokesman assured that it would happen before Christmas.

Microsoft disclosed little at E^3 about its online intentions. It was revealed that it would be initially possible to link several Xboxes together to form a LAN (Local Area Network), but that would only allow gamers to compete against those who were on their own limited networks. Microsoft promised an experience that would be easy for gamers when the Xbox did go live more than a year down the road. This included online storage of games and one bill, no matter how many different companies published the games that an individual might play.

One valid concern was the amount of support that the Xbox would receive from Japanese developers. Although Microsoft itself had opened a Japanese development center, where it employed approximately one hundred programmers, it was uncertain about the level of involvement from the third parties. Square, the developer of the *Final Fantasy* series, was unhappy with Microsoft's plan for one-stop billing, because it received a lot of revenue from its own online subscription service.

Sega Software

Ironically, one major Japanese developer that did sign up to create Xbox games was Sega. And although Sega wouldn't actually publish any games for the Xbox until 2002, Sega made good on its promise to become "platform agnostic". Sega-branded games began coming out for non-Sega consoles throughout the year. Aside from a pair of handheld games,[6] this marked the first time that Sega published titles for a non-Sega videogame system since 1984. Sega released *ChuChu Rocket!* for the Game Boy Advance in Japan on

March 21 and in North America on June 11. The Dreamcast version of *ChuChu Rocket!* had been the first multiplayer online game. The Game Boy Advance version featured the same game play as the Dreamcast version, including multiplayer competition. However, in order to accomplish this, up to four Game Boy Advance consoles had to be linked together.

Sega ChuChu Rocket!

But Sega of Japan didn't just port previously-released Dreamcast titles to the non-Sega consoles. Its first PS2 game, *Rez*, was released in Japan on November 22, the same day that the game came out for the Dreamcast.[7] *Rez* was a rail shooter[8] that had very limited human interaction. Players manipulated an aiming reticule that could lock-on and destroy enemies and projectiles. But Rez wasn't developed simply as a rail shooter. It was designed to be a visual and aural experience. The action in *Rez* was accompanied by electronic music that became more intense as the game progressed.[9] A special edition of the PS2 version was bundled with a *Trance Vibrator*, a device that plugged into the PS2's USB port and vibrated in tune with the music.[10] In theory, players would place the Trance Vibrator beneath a pillow that they might be sitting on so they could physically enjoy the explosion of sound that was coming from the game.

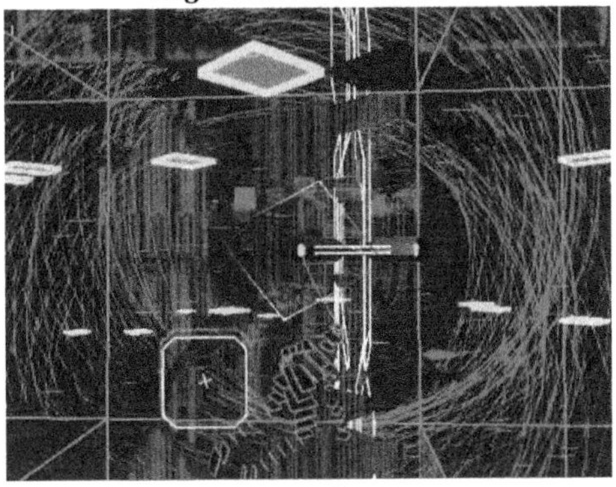

Sega Rez

Months before their arrival in Japan, Sega of America had used E[3] to announce its software lineup for the PS2 and for Nintendo's new console, the GameCube, which had made its first American appearance at the massive industry-only event. And although Sega was developing games for multiple consoles, it unofficially announced that it was developing a new Sonic game exclusively for the GameCube. Among the games that Sega displayed at the show was *Phantasy Star Online*. Surprisingly, gamers who played this on their non-Sega consoles would be able to compete against those who played it on their Dreamcasts. In order for this to happen, users would have to connect to Sega's own network.

While a version of *Phantasy Star Online* was being developed for the GameCube, Nintendo was very closed-mouth about its online plans. Although the company displayed a dial-up *Modem Adapter* and a separate high-speed *Broadband Adapter*, each of which plugged into

Sega Trance Vibrator

the bottom of the GameCube, the company expressed no firm plans concerning an online network that would support a worldwide audience. Nintendo director Satoru Iwata told *Electronic Gaming Monthly* that "right now, we feel that we're a profitable company offline, and there's no need for us to run to the online market to try and boost our profits at this

Nintendo GameCube Modem Adapter (l) and Broadband Adapter (r)

point."

Nintendo officials didn't appear to be too concerned about the forthcoming Xbox, either. On the night before Microsoft had announced its launch intentions, Nintendo's legendary designer, Shigeru Miyamoto, announced to a packed crowd that the GameCube would be available in the United States on November 5, three days before the Xbox. Nintendo planned to ship 1.1 million consoles on that day in the United States alone. Meanwhile, the company intended to ship 500,000 units in Japan on that country's launch date, September 14, with an additional 900,000 consoles following before the end of the year.

Nintendo did not appear to be going after the same audience sought by SCE and Microsoft. While the two companies were doing all they could to make their consoles function more and more like multimedia players, Nintendo didn't promise anything but games. Unlike its competition, the GameCube would not be capable of playing DVDs or CDs, since it used small 3.5-inch proprietary discs. However, at E^3, Nintendo displayed a unit from Panasonic that could play standard 5-inch DVDs as well as the smaller GameCube discs. The *Q*, as it was called, would only be available in Japan. It was the result of a deal that had been made between Nintendo and Matsushita, the parent company of Panasonic, when Nintendo first contracted Matsushita to produce the GameCube's optical drive. Since Nintendo had no intentions for the GameCube to be anything other than a gaming console, and since Matsushita wanted to market a Nuon-type device that was a DVD player that could also play games, there was little chance of the two consoles competing against each other. The Q was released in Japan on December 13, where it sold for ¥39,800 ($305).

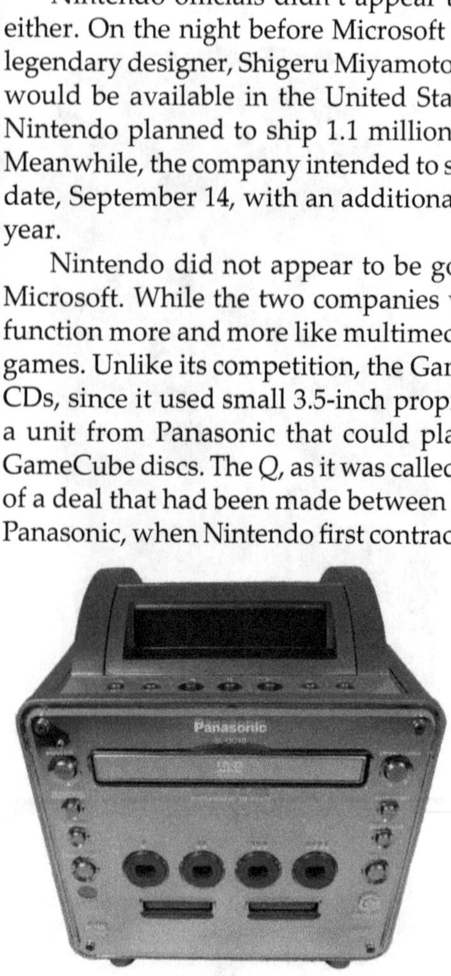

Panasonic Q

Nintendo waited until May 21, two days after E^3 closed, before it announced that the GameCube would sell for $199.95. A Nintendo spokesman admitted that because the console used several expensive components, the company might lose money on each unit that it sold, something that had never happened with any of its prior consoles.

Console Launch Delays

Throughout the summer, the world anxiously awaited the releases of the Xbox and the

Nintendo GameCube

GameCube. Then on August 23, at its Spaceworld convention in Tokyo, Nintendo dropped a bombshell. The GameCube's American launch was going to be pushed back two weeks to November 18, because Nintendo couldn't guarantee that it could ship 700,000 units in time for the original launch date. The company did not want the launch to be plagued by a massive shortage, as SCE had experienced when it had released the PS2. The downside for Nintendo was that the American GameCube would now be released after the Xbox.

Nintendo GameCube Controller

Shortly after Nintendo announced the GameCube's delay, Microsoft had similar news to share. In this case, the release date for the Japanese Xbox was going to be pushed back to February 22, 2002 in order to ensure that there would be enough units available in the United States -- not only on the launch day, but also throughout the following six weeks leading into the holiday selling season.

But even after the Japanese launch date was changed, the likelihood that Microsoft could deliver enough Xboxes to support North America was still uncertain. Following in Nintendo's footsteps, Microsoft cited that in order to prevent shortages such as SCE had experienced, it needed to push back the Xbox's North American release by one week to November 15, three days before the GameCube's scheduled launch date.

The GameCube launched in Japan on September 14, as planned. The frenzy that had occurred when the PS2 was released was not repeated. In the end, the lines for the GameCube were not long, and everybody who wanted to purchase the console got one. While Nintendo had expected to sell 500,000 consoles during the GameCube's first weekend, the actual number was around 300,000, and most of them had been preordered, a move that Nintendo had encouraged to avoid the insanity that accompanied SCE's launch. Only three games, *Luigi's Mansion, Wave Race: Blue Storm* and *Super Monkey Ball* were available. It was unclear whether the lack of software was one of the reasons for the

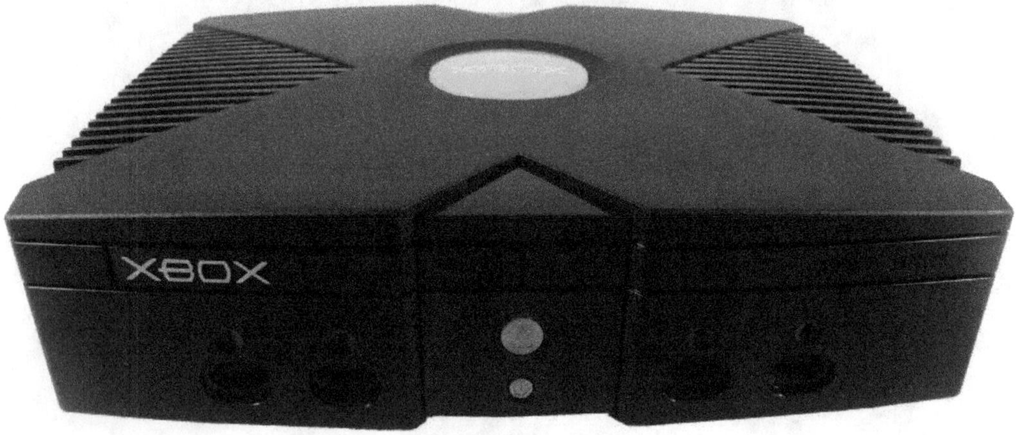

Microsoft Xbox

Microsoft Xbox Controller

console's lackluster debut. But Nintendo did plan to have fifteen titles available for the system's American release.

The Xbox launch began at 12:01 AM on November 15 in New York, where Bill Gates sold the very first console at the Toys "R" Us in Times Square. By the end of that day, it was estimated that Microsoft had only delivered approximately 400,000 consoles. Although this was half the number that Microsoft had promised, it was still more than the 300,000 PS2s that SCE had available a year earlier. And as with the Japanese GameCube's launch, everybody who wanted to purchase an Xbox went home with one. There were no shortages. And because the consoles were being manufacturered in Mexico, stores could quickly get their supplies replenished when they ran low. Microsoft sold nearly one million consoles by the end of the year.

At midnight on November 18, 700,000 GameCube consoles went on sale. Nintendo claimed that it had sold 329,000 units by the end of that day, whereas Microsoft had sold 292,000 Xboxes on its first day. Nintendo sold 500,000 GameCubes after five days, which made it the biggest console launch in U.S. history. And by the end of the year, Nintendo had sold 1.3 million consoles. Of course, such numbers didn't reflect the overall success of a console, as had been proven by the Dreamcast, which had experienced the most successful launch in history when it had been released two years earlier.

The Game Boy Advance

With all the hype dedicated to the two new consoles, it was easy to overlook the fact that Nintendo also released a new handheld unit during the year.

The year began with Nintendo claiming that it would produce 24 million Game Boy

Advance (GBA) handheld systems during the device's first year on the market. Nintendo of Japan planned to ship one million of the ¥9,800 ($85) units on the system's Japanese launch date, March 21. Twenty-one games were expected to be available on that day, including *Super Mario Advance*, which was a handheld version of *Super Mario Bros. 2*. However, by January 29, the company had already received preorders for 2.7 million consoles.

Many well-known third-party publishers were on board to produce games for the new handheld, including Konami, Namco, Hudson and Sega. However, it was revealed that many of these companies were hesitant to produce games that could be linked between two or more consoles but only requiring one cartridge. While the obvious reason was that the publishers were afraid that this would impact their sales, there was a technical reason as well. Publishers cited that the limited amount of RAM in the GBA would cause some lag time and interfere with the game, as both consoles read data from the linked cartridge.

On March 7, Nintendo of Japan held a special GBA preview event in Tokyo for retailers and the media. They announced a new peripheral that would be available for the upcoming handheld. The *Pokémon Card e-Reader* was a card reader that would plug into the cartridge slot of the GBA. *Pokémon* trading cards would be printed, with data stored as dotted barcodes along the cards' sides. When a card was slid through the e-Reader, the data would be read and stored within the GBA's memory. Depending upon the type of card used, special *Pokémon* trainers or enigma berries would be loaded, which could then be used while playing two new GBA *Pokémon* games, *Pokémon Ruby* and *Pokémon Sapphire*, that were going to be released. The *Pokémon Card e-Reader* wasn't that different from the Barcode Boy that Namcot had released for the Game Boy in 1992.

Nintendo did not announce either a release date or a retail price for the Pokémon Card e-Reader during the GBA Preview Event. But it did have a launch date for the American GBA. Nintendo announced that the date was being pushed forward a month to June 11 and promised that one million units would be available on that day.

On March 21, Nintendo of Japan had 650,000 GBA consoles available for those who hadn't preordered. They sold out that day. Within the following week, the company shipped an additional 450,000 consoles to retailers, and they too sold out as fast as the stores could get them.

The GBA had an astounding launch with 25 titles available the first day. Four of

Nintendo Game Boy Advance

them[11] prominently featured the "Mobile System GB" logo on the front of their boxes, indicating that the games were compatible with the *Mobile GB Adapter*, Nintendo's modem that would link the Game Boy Color and GBA with a cellular phone and provide online gaming with compatible titles.

Mobile System GB Logo

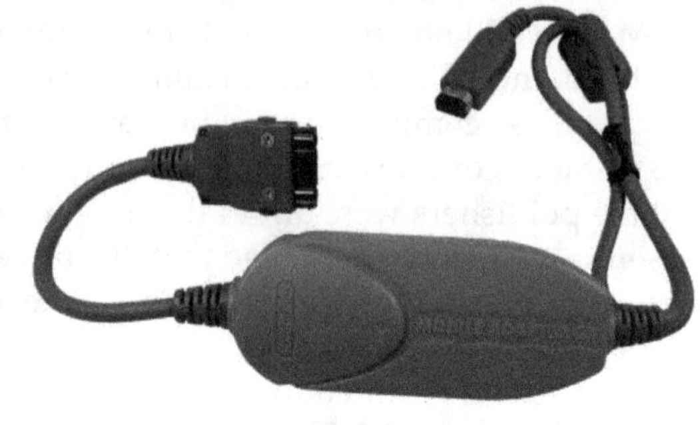

Nintendo Mobile Adapter GB

Nintendo of Japan had finally released the ¥5,800 ($52) Mobile Adapter on January 27. Unfortunately, the reception for the device was lackluster. By the time the GBA was released, Nintendo of Japan had sold only 80,000 Mobile Adapters. Initially, it was believed that sales for the adapter had been stagnant because the only game that worked with the unit, *Pocket Monsters Crystal Version*, was a kids' game and most kids didn't own a mobile phone. Unfortunately, even the new GBA games that utilized the mobile service failed to increase sales. On May 11, Nintendo of Japan released a second mobile-compatible game for the Game Boy Color. Even though Nintendo of Japan packaged the Mobile Adapter with *Mobile Golf*, the online gaming device still failed to make an impact.

Nintendo reduced the price of the Mobile Adapter by ¥2,000 ($16) on July 19, which brought it down to ¥3,800 ($31). Throughout 2001, fifteen GBA and three Game Boy Color titles were released that used the Mobile Adapter for online play, but the device and service failed to catch on.[12]

Nintendo had originally planned to also release the Mobile Adapter GB outside of Japan. However, this idea was scrapped due to the absence of global cellular phone standards.[13]

The GBA was released in the United States on June 11, where it retailed for $99.95. Fifteen games were available immediately, including *Super Mario Advance* and *Tony Hawk's Pro Skater 2*. The GBA's box prominently displayed that it was a 32-bit system, to remind consumers that although it played SNES-quality games, it was capable of much more.

Also displayed on the box was the fact that the GBA had a wide screen, 2.9 inches measured diagonally compared to the Game Boy Color's 2.6-inch screen. And since the GBA was backward-compatible with the games that fit comfortably within the confines of the Game Boy Color's smaller screen, users could select the way they wanted these games to display on the new device. Pressing the "L" or "R" button toggled between a stretched mode where the display filled the entire GBA screen, and a letterbox mode, in which the display had the original Game Boy Color dimensions, with black horizontal bars running above and below the display. Like all Game Boys that preceded it, the GBA was region-free, which meant that GBA software purchased anywhere in the world would play on any GBA.

GBA cartridges were roughly half the size of those for the prior Game Boy models. Because their widths were the same, both could be inserted into the same cartridge slot of the GBA. However, when a GBA cartridge was inserted, the top of it was flush with the top of the console, and otherwise didn't show. The earlier Game Boy cartridges stuck out from the top of the device.

Although scores of American buyers didn't line up at stores for hours as the Japanese had done during their GBA launch, stores began running out of them very quickly. Within two weeks after the launch, Nintendo of America reported selling approximately one million units.

Sega's mascot, Sonic the Hedgehog, made his first appearance on a non-Sega console on December 20, when Sega of Japan released *Sonic Adventure 2 Battle* for the GameCube. Like *ChuChu Rocket!* this was a game that had already been available since June on the Dreamcast.[14]

Game Boy Advance/GameCube Compatibility

Sonic Adventure 2 for both systems featured Chao, which were like virtual pets. In the Dreamcast version, players could load their Chao into their VMUs, where they could be used in a mini-game called *Chao Adventure*. In the GameCube version, a single Chao could be loaded from the GameCube to the *Sonic Advance* game in the GBA via the *GameCube-GBA cable*.

Nintendo Gamecube & Game Boy Advance

The *Sonic* games were the first to utilize this cable, which Nintendo touted as the GameCube's version of the N64's Transfer Pak. In addition to moving characters between systems, the cable also allowed, according to Nintendo, for forthcoming mini-games to be passed to the GBA from the GameCube, and for the GBA to act as either a GameCube controller in some games, or to behave as an additional GameCube screen in others.

Nintendo of Japan released another game that used both the GameCube and the GBA. Although *Animal Forest* had originally come out for the N64 on April 14, an enhanced version for the GameCube was released in Japan eight months later. Technically, this wasn't a game. The protagonist lived his life mingling with neighbors, decorating his house, collecting hidden objects, and earning money. The more money earned, the more goods that could be purchased, or given away as presents.

Although *Animal Forest* was a one-player game, up to four players could move into a single village, which was stored on a memory card that came with the game. And when a second memory card was inserted into the GameCube, it gave the player access to another village, with plants and fruits that were not indigenous to the player's own village. Rare items brought from a neighboring village fetched more money on the open market than the local goods. When a GBA was connected to the GameCube, the player could then use the GBA to explore an island. As with the items collected in neighboring cities, stuff brought back from the island commanded high prices from the general store.

Other hidden items that could be collected were Famicom consoles, and Famicom games that could be played on them. When these games were found, they could be downloaded to, and played on, the GBA.

On December 1, Nintendo of Japan released the ¥5,800 ($47) *e-Reader*, the card reader that it had displayed at the Tokyo GBA preview in March. With the *Pokémon* tie-in removed from the unit's official name, the e-Reader became a device that loaded bonus features into the GBA for several types of games, including the *Pokémon* series.

Nintendo e-Reader

Nintendo Pokémon Mini

Although the *Pokémon* emphasis was removed from the e-Reader, Nintendo was in no way deserting its profitable franchise. On the contrary, the company released a brand-new programmable handheld that had been specifically designed to play Pokémon-themed mini-games. The *Pokémon Mini* went on sale in North America on November 16, one month before it was available in Japan. The $40 device, which was the smallest cartridge-based system that Nintendo had ever produced, was sold with one game, *Pokémon Party Mini*, and also featured built-in rumble support and an alarm clock. And while it featured an infrared sensor that allowed up to five units to link together, only two of the four games available in America supported this feature. Six additional games were available in Japan, but Nintendo decided not to export them to the United States, because of a lack of interest in the unit.

Besides the opinion that the mini-games simply weren't fun upon repeated playing, there was another reason for the unit's lack of interest. The *Pokémon Mini* was first sold in the United States during the three-day span between the release of the Xbox and the GameCube, when the media concentrated on those two consoles. The Pokémon Mini's release date corresponded with the grand opening of a Pokémon Center store in New York City's Rockefeller Center, the first such store outside of Japan. The Pokémon Mini could only be purchased at the Pokémon Center, or by mail order, which made this niche product even harder to obtain, especially for those who were spurred by impulse buying.

Game Park

While the American Pokémon Mini could only be found in New York, another brand-new handheld game player could only be found in South Korea. Game Park, a South Korean company, released a domestic handheld console because it was illegal to import them from Japan.

Following World War II, the Korean government enacted a law that prohibited the importation of Japanese electronics. Because of this, most Koreans played games on computers. Since licensing was permitted, Samsung manufactured a Saturn console under license from Sega, and Hyundai manufactured an N64 console under license from Nintendo. Both consoles were intended to be sold only in South Korea. But while they sold moderately, they could not break the stronghold dominated by the computer games.

In 1996, the South Korean government decided to finance a company that could create a new console to compete with the Japanese. Game Park was created, and received funding from the South Korean government. The company decided to enter the handheld market, where there was less competition.

Game Park's developers initially used the original Game Boy, a vertical-standing console with the screen on top and control buttons beneath it, as a model. A metallic unit was completed in time to be displayed at the 2000 Tokyo Game Show, where it failed to attract any attention. The device was then redesigned. The metal was switched to plastic, and the shape became horizontal instead of vertical. In the end, the Korean handheld looked slightly like the new GBA.

Game Park GP32

The device was called the *GP32* (Game Park 32-bit). But while the GP32 resembled the GBA with its 32-bit processor and lack of a back light, there was a significant difference between them. All of the programmable handheld consoles that preceded it had used software that was stored in proprietary cartridges. The GP32 used *SmartMedia*, the flash-memory cards that had been introduced by Toshiba in 1995. Since blank SmartMedia cards were widely available commerically, game developers could easily write games and save them on the cards, and then test them on actual GP32s. Game Park encouraged homebrewers to produce games and offered free development tools from their website. The only catch was that the GP32 could only run encrypted games. However, a free "launcher" was built into the unit's firmware that permitted developers to run unencrypted software.

In addition to the SmartMedia cards, which could each be purchased for much less than a GBA cartridge, software could also be downloaded from Game Park's website. This effectively cut the price of new software to an economical $10.

The GP32 was a success within South Korea when it was released on November 23. Soon, plans were made to export the device elsewhere.

The PSone Monitor

Although SCE didn't release a new console in 2001, it did begin promoting its redesigned PlayStation, the PSone, as a portable unit. This was not the first time a gaming console was labeled as a portable. Both Emerson's Arcadia 2001 and Fujitsu's FM Towns Car Marty were consoles that had come with car adapters. The problem with both of these units was that they still required TV screens. The same was true for the PSone until early in the year when several third-party companies, including InterAct, Pelican and Innovation, began selling LCD monitors for the console. Innovation and InterAct also sold rechargeable batteries, which made the PSone truly portable.

SCE announced its own PSone monitor at E³, and on November 28, began selling a $129 5-inch LCD screen with built-in stereo speakers. But while SCE also sold a car adapter, it did not market a rechargeable battery.

Another peripheral that SCE showed at E³, and released in August, was a DVD remote control for the PS2. This $20 device was sold with an infrared receiver that plugged into a controller port, and a DVD-upgrade BIOS disc, which copied DVD drivers onto a PS2 memory card. Everyone applauded the release of the remote control, especially those who had purchased the PS2 as an inexpensive DVD player. Still, the question of why it had taken SCE over a year to

SCE PSone Monitor

SCE PS2 DVD Remote Control

release it persisted, especially since the company had been selling stand-alone DVD players that came with remote controls since 1998.

But at least PS2 owners had the option of purchasing a remote-control unit to watch DVDs. Xbox owners did not have that luxury. They were required to purchase a $30 remote control if they wished to use the Xbox as a DVD player. The standard controller could not be used for that purpose.

The Only Game In Town

As the PSone continued to breathe new life into the PlayStation franchise, its successor, the PS2, outsold its two rivals. This wasn't enough for SCE. On November 27, the price of the console and all of its software was lowered in Japan by 15% in an effort to increase sales for the holidays. The price of the console dropped to ¥29,800 ($240), while the price of the American PS2 remained unchanged at $299.

Sega had cited that the competition from SCE was a major reason for its abandonment of the Dreamcast. Meanwhile, companies that actually derived their income from the PS2, from developers to retailers, also grumbled about SCE's tactics. While SCE claimed that the PS2 was an easy system to develop games for, many developers disagreed. Lorne Lanning, president of Oddworld Inhabitants, complained that the system was counter-intuitive to the needs of the developers. Rather than help them, SCE basically left the third-party developers to figure out the system on their own. Many found the PS2 to be as hard to design for as the infamous Sega Saturn. Oddworld Inhabitants eventually ceased their development for the PS2 and switched to the Xbox.

Many third-party publishers also complained about lower-than-expected sales for their PS2-compatible games. While Electronic Arts said that its sales were within the goals that it had set, it also admitted that those sales came in on the low end of the goals. Much of this was due to SCE's late 2000 announcement of a severe chip shortage that dramatically curtailed the manufacturing of new consoles. This unexpected loss of one million consoles sidelined many third-party companies, who had only found out about the shortage a day earlier than the general public. By that time, it was too late to decrease the number of software discs that they had ordered. In one case, a publisher had produced twice as many copies of a game title than there were PS2 consoles available.

And if making the developers and publishers upset wasn't enough, SCE also went after retailers. There were reports from several, including Babbage's and GameStop, that SCE had threatened them with lower console allocations if their stores didn't remove Xbox marketing material. This threatened reduction was in addition to the reductions already made because of the console shortage.

Despite all of the complaints, the individual companies could do little about it. For most of the year, SCE's PS2 was the only game in town.

Bleem!

Although all of the PlayStation games could be played on the PS2, one company had intended to make them play on the Dreamcast as well.

Bleem!, which had released an emulator that allowed PlayStation games to play on

PCs, finally released their Bleempak, which they had announced at the 2000 E³. The plan had been for Bleem! to release four separate Bleempaks, each capable of playing hundreds of PlayStation games on the Dreamcast. However, after fighting a long, expensive legal battle against SCE, the company decided that the only way it could recoup its losses was by releasing Bleemcasts for only the most popular PlayStation games. Each Bleemcast would retail for $6 and consist of a GD that loaded the emulation software into the Dreamcast. Once loaded, the gamer could then place the PlayStation disc into the Dreamcast and load the game.

Bleemcast

Three Bleemcasts were released in all: *Gran Turismo 2, Metal Gear Solid* and *Tekken 3.* Graphically, the games when played on the Dreamcast were superior to when they were played through the PlayStation. Unfortunately, the legal problems with SCE, combined with the death of the Dreamcast, was just too much for Bleem!. Despite rave reviews, Bleem! closed its doors for good in November 2001.

Bleem! was not alone in closing up shop in 2001. In June, Midway, one of the oldest videogame companies in existence, shut down its arcade division, due to an "ongoing declining demand in the coin-operated arcade videogame market." Midway had been formed in 1978 as the videogame division of the pinball powerhouse Bally, and its first effort was the imported *Space Invaders*, one of the most popular videogame games of all time. Arcade sales leading up to 2001 were so low that the company expected that eliminating the coin-operated business would only result in the reduction of less than 60 employees, which revealed how scaled-down the division had already become.

Bankruptcies

On April 6, the Indrema Corporation closed its doors as well. The company had planned to be the David that was going to take on the Goliaths of the industry. The specs for the proposed console were impressive. Only Microsoft's Xbox, which wouldn't be released until the end of the year, would be more powerful, albeit slightly. And while the Indrema could do double duty as a DVD player like the Xbox and PS2, the console would have also functioned as a Digital Video Recorder similar to the TiVo. But the main selling feature of the Indrema was its open-source, Linux-based operating system, which gave its users the freedom to design their own games without having to pay licensing fees to the manufacturers.

The dream of John Gildred, founder of the Indrema Corporation, was to create a powerful system that avoided direct competition with the powerhouses of SCE and Microsoft by allowing the game players to become the game developers. And although Gildred claimed that nearly 200 games had been in development for the Indrema, potential investors couldn't share Gildred's dream. They assumed that the Indrema would have to compete with SCE and Microsoft no matter what their approach might be. In the end, the Indrema Corporation had to declare bankruptcy, for the simple reason that it couldn't secure the funding that it needed.

Companies weren't only shutting down in the United States. In Japan, SNK, the company that had produced the Neo•Geo consoles, also filed for bankruptcy. This hadn't been quite so unexpected, since Aruze, its parent company, had no interest in the videogame market and had closed all of its overseas subsidiaries in 2000. SNK of Japan closed for good on October 22. Ironically, Aruze had purchased SNK for its intellectual properties, but in the end, the rights to those same properties were put up for auction.

On August 1, Eikichi Kawasaki, the founder of SNK, started a new videogame company called *Playmore*. When SNK's properties went up for auction, Playmore successfully bid on them.

Meanwhile, many of the employees from the old SNK had started their own game-design company called *Brezzasoft*. Playmore soon turned around and purchased Brezzasoft, which was then renamed *SNK Neo•Geo Corporation*. With nearly the same employees, and the same intellectual properties, Playmore continued where SNK had left off. The company resumed designing games for the arcade and home markets, with one difference: No plans were conceived for a console of its own.[15]

Edited Games In A New World

Any discussion about the year 2001 could not be complete without the inclusion of the events that occurred on September 11, which began with armed terrorists high-jacking four planes and ended with a catastrophe beyond anyone's imagination. Unlike the school shootings that had occurred in prior years, the terror attacks of 9-11 could not be mistakenly attributed to videogames. But the videogame industry, like the rest of the civilized world, was profoundly impacted.

Command & Conquer - Red Alert 2

Microsoft Flight Simulator 2000

In the days that followed the attacks, game publishers went through their catalogs and removed anything that might be considered even mildly offensive. Electronic Arts immediately recalled all copies of its PC game *Command and Conquer: Red Alert 2*, because its box's inside gatefold cover displayed a rendering of the World Trade Center exploding. Microsoft recalled its *Flight Simulator 2000* from stores, because it allowed players to fly passenger jets into the World Trade Center. In addition, the company offered a patch to remove the Twin Towers altogether, for those who already owned the game. Microsoft had been set to release *Flight Simulator 2002*, but the game was put on hold temporarily so that the images of the World Trade Center could be removed. It was eventually released on October 19.

Sega of America postponed *Propeller Arena*, a game that it had planned to release on September 19. The game's cover art featured two planes flying over a highly-populated city. Although the company announced that it would change the cover art, the declining popularity of the Dreamcast forced the company to cancel the game altogether.

Activision had released *Spider-Man 2: Enter Electro* for the PlayStation on August 26. These copies were quickly pulled from store shelves following the attacks, because the final battle of the game took place at the tops of the Twin Towers. A redesigned version with a new ending was sent to stores on October 17.

Konami had scheduled *Metal Gear Solid 2: Sons of Liberty* to be released on November 13. But the game required extensive changes, because it had originally shown the Statue of Liberty falling onto the lower half of Manhattan. Konami managed to make the changes and still release the game on time.

One game that had been mildly tweaked to make sure it wasn't deemed offensive in light of the attacks was Rockstar's *Grand Theft Auto III*. The game was eventually released for the PS2 on October 22, but many people still found it highly offensive for other reasons.

Rockstar Grand Theft Auto III

The game was the third installment in a series that had originally been released for PCs and the PlayStation in Europe in 1997 and in North America in 1998. All of the games had the same theme. Players assumed the role of a thug who could roam the city at will on a killing spree. Vehicles could be carjacked and pedestrians could be run down to gather points. Even the police could be killed while players tried to evade them. The original *Grand Theft Auto* had been one of the first violent games to be released for the PlayStation.

The first two releases in the series featured top-down graphics, wherein players looked down upon the city as if it were a map. Although there was a lot of violence, it was displayed at a distance and was somewhat removed, since none of the characters had any particular physical identities. This changed in *Grand Theft Auto III*, which abandoned the top-down display in favor of a first-person, 3D approach.

Playing *Grand Theft Auto III* was like starring as the lead character in a Martin Scorsese movie. The game took place in the fictional Liberty City, which was loosely based on New York City. The player assumed the role of a criminal who went on assignments for the mob, robbed cars, ran over pedestrians, hired prostitutes and evaded the police. Players could also kill the police and the hookers, and anyone else who got in their way. And while these were features that had been included in the previous *Grand Theft Auto* games, the 3D first-person display in *Grand Theft Auto III* made them appear real. While naming it the best game of 2001, the website *GameSpy* also called *Grand Theft Auto III* the "Most Offensive Game of the Year" and referred to it as a "thug simulator." However, despite its content, the game was also innovative with its open-ended game play, which ensured accolades from *GameSpot*, *IGN*, *GamePro* and *Electronic Gaming Monthly*.

The game unsurprisingly received an "M" rating from the ESRB. And while Walmart didn't ban selling the game in its stores, it did require its cashiers to check the identifications of customers, to ensure that they were indeed over 17.

Despite the controversies over it, or perhaps because of them, *Grand Theft Auto III* became the best-selling game of the year in the United States, with nearly two million copies sold between October and the end of December.

3D-Rendered Games

Grand Theft Auto III was not the only high-profile 3D game for the PS2 to come out in 2001. *Final Fantasy X*, the first game in that series to feature 3D renderings and voice actors, sold over 1.4 million copies within four days of its July 19 Japanese release. The game therefore broke the record for the fastest-selling role-playing console game in history. It also became the first PS2 game to eventually sell over two million copies. Overall, most reviewers rated the game as almost perfect. *Game Informer's* Andy Reiner wrote, "*Final Fantasy X* is a breakthrough release, a visionary tale, and a masterpiece for the ages." The magazine rated it 9.75 out of 10.

The excellent ratings and sales for *Final Fantasy X* were good news for SCE, which had invested ¥14.9 billion ($124 million) in Square, the developer of the *Final Fantasy* series. While this gave SCE an 18% stake in the company, it didn't guarantee that Square's games would be available exclusively for SCE's consoles. In the meantime, though, *Final Fantasy X* could only be played on the PS2.

But it wasn't as if Xbox owners were clamoring for *Final Fantasy X*, since the Xbox had its own exclusive 3D game. *Halo: Combat Evolved*, or *Halo* as it was commonly called, had been one of the launch titles for Microsoft's console. Since its release, *Halo* has been referred to as one of the best and most important games of all time by several videogame magazines. And it became one of the main reasons why people bought Xboxes.

Microsoft Halo

Halo was a first-person, science-fiction shooter. While this in itself was not unique, *Halo* set a new standard in first-person shooters. In all previous games of the type, the shooter had to holster one weapon before another, such as a grenade or a knife, could be used. This was a carry-over from old computer text-adventure games such as *Zork*. But *Halo* allowed characters to hold their weapons while they used their hands for other purposes. And they needed all the help they could get to deal with the enemies. *Halo* featured one of the most complex artificial intelligences ever programmed into a game to date. The A.I. varied depending upon the four levels of difficulty. In the most difficult level, enemies behaved exactly as real humans would in similar situations.

While the game was not set up for online play because Microsoft didn't yet have an active network, gamers could link up to four Xboxes together, which allowed up to 16 people to play at one time. However, each Xbox needed to be connected to a separate TV. Two players could play cooperatively on a single Xbox console, but no more than that.

Atari's New Owners

Games like *Grand Theft Auto III* and *Halo* represented a new generation of videogames, one in which the boundaries were unlimited and the graphics were nearly perfect. But the release of these games didn't mean that gamers no longer wanted to play the simpler ones that had withstood the passage of time. Infogrames believed that these older games could hold their own against new technology.

On January 29, Infogrames completed its $100 million purchase of Hasbro Interactive, which was quickly renamed *Infogrames Interactive*. On June 28, the 29th anniversary of the founding of Atari, the new subsidiary released its first product, *Atari Anniversary Edition*, for the Dreamcast and PC. The compilation included twelve classic Atari arcade games, including *Asteroids, Missile Command* and *Pong*. The package was eventually released for the PlayStation in November, which was curious, since the PS2, Xbox and GameCube were all available by that time. Infogrames wasn't willing to gamble on whether or not gamers would shell out $50 just to play old games on their new consoles.

Namco, on the other hand, believed that people would play the old classic games on the next generation systems. On December 4, the company released *Namco Museum* for the PS2 in North America only. This anthology disc was the latest version of a collection that Namco had released for most of the major consoles since the PlayStation. It featured old Namco arcade classics, including *Pac-Man, Ms. Pac-Man* and *Pole Position*.[16]

Meanwhile, a toy company called Toymax also believed that there was new life in the old games. On October 28, the company released its *Activision TV Games Video Game System*. This $20 device looked like a standard console controller, but instead of plugging into a console, it plugged directly into a TV and was ready to play. It was thus referred to as a *plug-and-play* device, although the term originally referred to a computer's ability to automatically configure itself when new items were added to it.

Built into the controller, which required 4 AA batteries, were ten classic Activision games that had been released for the Atari VCS, including *Pitfall!* and *River Raid*. The games, while not emulated from the original code, closely resembled the original ones for the VCS. However, all the games were restricted to one-player, even though most of the originals had allowed for two-player competition.

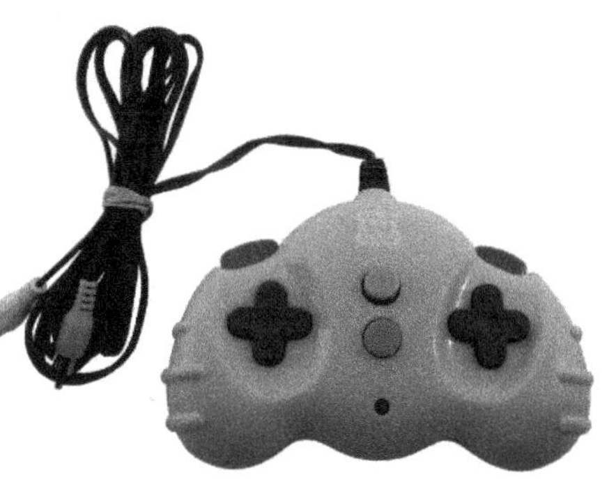

Toymax
Activision TV Games Video Game System

Magazine Births and Deaths

With the release of the Xbox came a new magazine dedicated to that console. Debuting on November 6 in the United States, the *Official Xbox Magazine* was published by Imagine Media, the same company that produced *Next Generation* and the unofficial *PSM*. In the United Kingdom, the magazine was published by Imagine Media's parent company, Future Publishing, which also published *Edge* and the *Official UK PlayStation Magazine*. As an "official" magazine, the *Official Xbox Magazine* was bundled with a game disc that contained game demos, previews, and game trailers.

But while the birth of a new console brought a new magazine, the death of one likewise caused the demise of another. With Sega's decision to discontinue the Dreamcast, the magazines that supported it came to an end as well. The American edition of the *Official Dreamcast Magazine* ceased with the March/April edition after only twelve issues. The British version lasted a bit longer. Its final edition, its 21st, had a cover date of September/October 2001.

By the end of 2001, the world at large was not the same as it had been when the year began. And the same could be said for the videogaming world. Sega, once a major player, was no longer a contender. In its place, for the first time in a decade, was an American console. And the games themselves had grown up. Instead of navigating an innocent, dot-munching creature within the confines of the four corners of the TV screen, players could now navigate real cars through cities with much less restrictive borders, as they ran over virtual people. Videogames were no longer for kids only, although many people outside of the industry failed to realize that.

CHAPTER THIRTY
2002

For Nintendo, the year began with the retirement of Nintendo of America's founder, Minoru Arakawa. Arakawa, the son-in-law of Nintendo's president, Hiroshi Yamauchi, had decided that the time was right to retire, as the U.S. videogaming industry was "extremely strong, and NOA's position within the industry has never been better." Yamauchi's role was filled by Tatsumi Kimishima, the former CFO of the Pokémon Company.

Hiroshi Yamauchi himself retired at the end of May, after 53 years with the company. It had basically been Yamauchi who had transformed Nintendo from a manufacturer of playing-cards to a leader in the videogame industry. He was replaced by Satoru Iwata, who had been a software developer before joining Nintendo two years earlier. Iwata announced changes almost immediately. Unlike the old Nintendo, where Yamauchi basically had the last word on all decisions, Iwata formed a six-man management committee, which he would oversee, to perform the same responsibilities. After a month of settling into his new position, Iwata spoke about the future of videogaming as he saw it. He was not in favor of hardware manufacturers coming out with new and more powerful consoles every few years. He was convinced that quality software was the answer. Iwata was also a proponent of online gaming, but he felt that the majority of gamers were not yet ready for it. Because of this, Nintendo would not focus on it, as its top priority was to create great games. However, he wasn't going to restrict third-party companies from developing GameCube games that could be played online, as long as Nintendo wasn't expected to administer a network. He even encouraged them to develop online games for the GameCube and announced that Nintendo would not demand royalties for any online games that were released for its system.

Consoles Online

On May 13, Nintendo announced that its modems would become available in the fall. Nintendo of Japan released the dial-up Modem Adapter on September 12 and the high-speed Broadband Adapter on October 3. Both adapters retailed for ¥3,800 ($31). Nintendo of America released both adapters on October 29, each with a retail price of $34.95. The adapters plugged into the GameCube through a connector at the console's underside. Sega shipped *Phantasy Star Online Episodes I & II*, which incorporated either adapter for online play, on the same day that the Modem Adapters were released in their respective countries. To play online, the gamer had to subscribe to Sega's service, which cost $9 a month on top of the game's $40 purchase price. The game could also be played in an offline mode, which didn't cost the gamer anything extra.

Nintendo wasn't alone with its online plans. SCE announced in February that it had teamed up with several Japanese Internet Service Providers (ISP). In April, they launched the *PlayStation BB*, a network that served several purposes. The basic network cost approximately ¥1,500 ($11) per month, which varied depending upon the ISP used. It offered movies, music, web browsing, e-mail and even financial information to its subscribers. For an additional one-time fee of ¥18,000 ($135), subscribers could download fully playable games to their hard drives. Hard drives that were sold before the network went live came with an *HDD Utility Disc*, which simply formatted the hard drive and set up folders in which compatible games could save their data. In preparation for the network, newer drives were sold with a *PlayStation Broadband Navigator* disc. In addition to formatting the hard drive as its predecessor had done, the *PlayStation Broadband Navigator* also included a web browser and several tools that aided users in downloading files from the Internet, ripping music from audio CDs, and transferring digital photos from external devices. The *PlayStation Broadband Navigator* also created directories on the hard drive where files could be stored, and from where bootable games could be launched.

While most of the online games that were released didn't cost players any additional fees over what they paid for their subscriptions, a few RPGs did. *Final Fantasy XI*, which came out in Japan on May 16, cost ¥1,280 ($10) per month to play, in addition to the ¥7,800 ($58) needed to purchase the disc.

North American PS2s could finally connect online beginning on August 27, but the system was vastly different from the Japanese one. The hard drive was not yet available but SCE officials claimed that it wouldn't be needed for the online experience, although it was still promised to be released eventually. In addition, the required $40 Network Adapter supported both broadband and dial-up methods. A configuration disc accompanied the adapter to help users connect to several ISPs, including Earthlink and AT&T, but SCE stressed that any ISP could be used.

In North America, unlike as in Japan where each ISP had its own price plan to connect to SCE's network, no additional fees were imposed upon users beyond the regular monthly rate to their ISPs. SCE president Kaz Hirai warned, however, that this pricing model would probably change in the future, and hinted that fees might be imposed as people began downloading music and movies. SCE, like Nintendo, didn't even charge the third-party developers any fees or royalties for the PS2 online games that they created. On the other hand, SCE didn't host third-party games, either. Each publisher was responsible for its own server that the games played on.

SCE released a handful of online games concurrently with the launch of the North American network. Most supported dial-up, the lone exception being *SOCOM: U.S. Navy SEALs*. This game came packed with a headset microphone that allowed gamers to communicate with others who were also playing online.

On August 1, Sega of America opened its SegaNet servers to free play. The problem was that not too many people were interested in using it anymore. The newest game that Americans could play on it was *NHL 2K2*, which Sega of America had released on February 14.[1] In Japan, Sega of Japan and its licensees, continued to release official games but they weren't compatible with the American console. Sega of America had planned to shut down SegaNet for good at the end of the year. However, as a courtesy to its customers who stuck with *Phantasy Star Online*, the company decided to keep it available an additional six months.[2]

Microsoft used E^3 to announce its own online service, *Xbox Live*, which formally launched on November 15, the first anniversary of the Xbox's release. Unlike SCE's free, open network, where individual publishers controlled their own properties, Xbox Live was a closed system. Everything was housed on Microsoft's servers, regardless of the publisher. And access to the network was by subscription only. A would-be subscriber first needed a broadband service from any ISP he chose. Next, he had to purchase a $49.95 *Xbox Live Starter Kit*, which contained a one-year subscription to the service and an *Xbox Voice Communicator*, a headset that inserted into a

Microsoft Xbox Live Starter Kit

slot in the Xbox controller. This was similar to the headset that came with SCE's *SOCOM: U.S. Navy SEALs*, but it also had the ability to alter the user's voice to prevent identification by other online players, and was designed to work with all Xbox Live games.

Something else designed to work with all Xbox Live games was a User ID that the subscriber created. Since all games were hosted by Microsoft, only one ID and password combination was needed to access the network from any game. The ID was stored in the particular Xbox console that the account had been set up from. If someone wanted to access Xbox Live from a different Xbox, he could save his ID onto a removable memory unit, which was then used on the second Xbox.

Once IDs were set up, users could see if any of their friends were online. If so, they could "chat" with them by using an Instant Message-like interface, and they could invite others to enter into an online game. Gamers only needed the particular game's disc in their Xbox's DVD drives in order to play.

Xbox In Japan

Microsoft launched Xbox Live worldwide on the same day. But before this could happen, it had to release the Xbox outside North America. A PAL version of the Xbox came out in Europe on March 14, not long after its Japanese counterpart's release on February 22.

Microsoft Xbox Controller S

The Japanese Xbox was the same as the one that had been released in North America in 2001, except that it came with smaller controllers. Microsoft had reasoned that a smaller controller was needed for the smaller hands of the Japanese population. However, once gamers elsewhere learned about these smaller controllers, they complained to Microsoft to release them everywhere else. Microsoft agreed and released the $40 *Controller S* on April 30. By the end of the year, it replaced the original controller as the one that was packaged with the Xbox, although Microsoft continued to market it as an optional accessory.

As he had done in the United States three months earlier, Bill Gates was on hand to sell the first Japanese Xbox. Unfortunately, the Japanese launch wasn't as successful as Microsoft had hoped it would be. Although lines of customers stood outside major stores for several hours, Microsoft only sold 123,000 Japanese consoles during its first week, even though 250,000 units had been available. This was far less than the 175,000 GameCubes and 680,000 PS2s that had been sold during the same time period following their Japanese launches.

Microsoft had a hard enough time trying to introduce an American console in Japan; it didn't help that a large number of the consoles actually scratched the DVDs that were in them. Microsoft claimed that this wasn't a problem, since the discs would still work. In addition, at ¥34,800 ($263), the Xbox cost more than both the GameCube (¥25,000 [$211]) and PS2 (¥29,800 [$251]). On the software side, only two Xbox titles made it onto Japan's list of the top twenty games during the month of March. Surprisingly, the top-selling Xbox game in America, *Halo*, was not even included among the console's Japanese launch titles.

But the Xbox wasn't suffering just in Japan. Within six weeks of its European release, the price of the console was reduced 1/3 to €299 ($265). When it debuted in Great Britain on May 3, the Xbox was priced at £129 ($183).

In March, SCE lowered the royalty rate that it charged developers to produce PS2 games, from $2.25 to $1.50. It continued with more price cuts on May 14, when it lowered the price of the PS2 to $199 and the PSone to $49. Microsoft responded the very next day by announcing its own price decreases. The American price was lowered to $199, while in Japan, it dropped to ¥24,800 ($199). On May 21, Nintendo reduced the price of the American GameCube to $150.

These price decreases helped. By June, sales of the Xbox increased 131% around the world, and Microsoft met its lower-end goal of moving 4 million consoles by the end of that month. With the Xbox safely meeting its sales expectations, Microsoft began talking about its follow-up. Microsoft CEO Steve Ballmer told a group of Japanese reporters that he expected the second-generation Xbox to be released in 2006. Although he didn't reveal details about the console, Ballmer had made it clear that the *Xbox 2* would not be the rumored *HomeStation,* whose existence had been circulating in the media for several months following a September 2001 article about it in *PC Format* magazine. The HomeStation was to be a multimedia device that used Xbox technology and boasted a larger hard drive with DVR functionality. As the rumor made its rounds, it even advanced to include an upgrade kit that would turn the current Xbox into a HomeStation. Microsoft vehemently denied any existence of the HomeStation.

PS2: Beyond Gaming

SCE wasn't resting on its laurels. It announced in April that it had joined with IBM and Toshiba to develop a new chip, codenamed *Cell,* which would be the heart of its new PlayStation 3 (PS3). Japan's *Financial Times* reported that the new console, which would arrive in 2005, would retail for less than $400 and be backward-compatible with all PlayStation and PS2 games. Meanwhile, SCE was looking at ways that the new chip could be used beyond the PS3. The belief was that the chip could be used in multiple home appliances, and possibly in an entertainment hub, much like the rumored HomeStation. It was a goal that SCE had wanted to accomplish with the PS2 but never achieved.

Although the PS2 didn't become the multimedia device that SCE had anticipated, the company did manage to turn it into a game-development studio. In April, the company began selling a kit through its website to Japanese users that effectively turned the console into a computer that ran under the Linux operating system. The $200 kit consisted of a keyboard, mouse, network adapter, hard drive and computer monitor connector, as well as software. The kits were available to American users beginning in May, and marked the first time that the PS2 hard drive was available outside of Japan. However, the hard drives that were shipped with the Linux kit were not compatible with any PS2 games.

The Linux kit included all of the code libraries that were included with official PS2 development kits. Once Linux was installed on the PS2, would-be developers had access to most of the PS2's architecture, including the Emotion Engine. While PS2-quality games could actually be developed, they could only play on PS2 consoles that had Linux installed. And while games developed with the Linux kit could not be sold via CDs or DVDs, developers could sell their creations through a PS2 Linux website.

In August, Japanese PS2 owners also had the opportunity to turn their consoles into virtual reality devices. The *PUD-J5A* was a ¥59,800 ($500) virtual reality headset based on SCE's Glasstron technology. SCE had marketed various Glasstron headsets since 1997, each consisting of dual-LCD screens and two stereo headphones. Since each Glasstron headset was in fact its own video monitor, any videogame console could direct its video and audio output to it, and gamers could enjoy their games while being isolated from the rest of the world. However, these weren't true virtual reality headsets, since the image on the screen could not adjust when the player moved his head.

SCE PS2 PUD-J5A Virtual Reality Headset

This changed with the PUD-J5A, because it also had a motion-tracking sensor. This meant that if a gamer wearing the headset turned to his left, the image on the screen would change to reflect the new perspective. The PUD-J5A had been designed to work with the PS2. All video and audio output from the PS2 was routed through a USB connection to a special control box that also connected to the headset. Only six games were released that had been specifically designed to work with the headset, including Taito's *Energy Airforce*, a flying simulator. The PUD-J5A was never released in the United States, even though the earlier Glasstron headsets had been.

By the end of the year, SCE announced that it had shipped 50 million PS2 consoles worldwide, roughly doubling the amount of PS2s that had been sold when the year had begun, which had been approximately the same number as the combined total of GameCubes and Xboxes that had been shipped.

Portable Competition

Not too far behind the PS2 in total consoles shipped was the GBA, with 30 million units sold. In February, Nintendo had unexpectedly lowered the price of the handheld to $79 worldwide. Although the device had been doing well in Japan and North America, European sales were poor and Nintendo had originally planned to only lower its price there. But the company realized that since the GBAs were not region-specific, people from around the world might have opted to purchase a lesser-priced GBA from Europe, rather than from their own country. This in turn, would have caused lower-than-expected sales figures in those countries. Nintendo avoided this potential problem by lowering the price across the board.

The poor performance in Europe was puzzling, especially since the device didn't have any competition. That appeared to be changing, as the South Korean company, Game Park, was determined to get its GP32 handheld console worldwide. Game Park made a deal with Infogrames, in which one million units would be sold in North America under the Atari name and would be supported by software from Atari, and Eidos, the developer of *Tomb Raider*. In preparation for this, Game Park displayed the GP32 at E^3 in May, along with a prototype called the *GPI*, which combined the functions of a videogame console, a PDA and a cell phone. Game Park also intended to branch into online gaming, and showed an RF module that would offer wireless capabilities for the GP32. In August, the company announced that it would finally be distributing the GP32 in Europe, with shipments beginning in Great Britain right before Christmas.

Game Park's plans to be a contender against the GBA were certainly ambitious. However, the South Korean government, the very same force that was responsible for the GP32 in the first place, did something that might as well have been a death knell for the fledgling handheld. As of January 1, Japanese goods were once again permitted to be imported into South Korea. In response, a tidal wave of Japanese consoles, including the GBA, legally entered the country for the first time.

Despite the new competition domestically, Game Park released a new console. Cosmetically, the *GP32 FLU* was the same as the original GP32. The difference was that it featured a front-lit screen, something that even the GBA did not have. Unfortunately, the South Korean gaming press practically ignored Game Park's new release in favor of the GBA that consumers were clamoring after.

The GP32 was not the only handheld device that was replaced by a new model. On July 12, Bandai released a new version of its Wonderswan handheld console. The ¥7,500 ($63) *SwanCrystal* featured an enhanced screen display, and was completely compatible with software for the two previous versions. Although Bandai promised software support from top developers such as Square, SCE and Sega, releases for the new console were few and far between. Although the SwanCrystal would linger on store shelves, it would eventually be remembered as Bandai's videogame-console swansong, an unimpressive end for a company that had been involved in videogames since the early '80s, when it imported Intellivisions and Vectrexes into Japan.

Bandai Swan Crystal

As monochrome handheld devices began getting replaced with color models, a new monochrome handheld device appeared that was aimed towards children aged four years and older. The $50 *Pixter* from Fisher-Price featured a large LCD touch-sensitive screen, upon which children could draw using an attached stylus. The device had several built-in activities, such as connect-the-dots and free-style drawing. Although Fisher-Price dubbed the Pixter as a "Creativity System," games and additional activities could be added by purchasing optional software cartridges that plugged into the top of the unit, making this the first programmable console created strictly for young kids since Sega's Pico, which had been discontinued in North America in early 1998.[3]

Not long after the introduction of the Pixter, Fisher-Price released a newer version of the handheld device. The $62 *Pixter Plus,* featured twenty times more memory than the Pixter and had several new features, including the ability to add sound effects and text to the on-screen art that the child created. The child's work was also password-protected,

Fisher-Price Pixter

Fisher-Price Pixter Plus

and the screen itself was protected with a screen saver. The unit also came with a lamp that plugged into a USB-like slot located above the screen.

GBA: From Music To Manhole

The GBA also had some cool accessories that the other portable systems couldn't match. One was the SongPro, which turned the GBA into a portable MP3 player. After a lengthy two-year delay, due to a licensing entanglement with Nintendo, a fully licensed version finally became available through SongPro's website, beginning in September.

The $99 device looked like a standard Game Boy cartridge that could be inserted into either the Game Boy Color or GBA. Users could save up to ten hours worth of music as MP3 files on an SD card that was inserted into the SongPro. Songs could be listened through headphones that plugged into the SongPro, rather than the GBA console.

Users could also store a propriety file format called SongPro Audio (SPA), which could be freely downloaded from the company's website. These files contained visuals such as album covers, song lyrics, and even ads, that could be viewed on the GBA screen.

Another unique item for the GBA was the $40 *e-Reader*, which went on sale in North America on September 16. Like the model that had been released in Japan in 2001, the American e-Reader could be used to load bonus features into specific GBA games. However, additional capabilities were added to the American e-Reader. In addition to having twice as much RAM as the Japanese model, it also contained flash memory, which its predecessor lacked and which gave it the ability to save information. The North American e-Reader also had a built-in NES emulator, and special game cards with classic NES games encoded on them were introduced. Depending upon the size of a particular game, code could be spread out onto as many as nine cards. After all of the code for a given game was swiped into the GBA, the game was then playable on the GBA in the same form as it had appeared on the NES. Free with the e-Reader was a *Manhole-e* card, which contained the code of the liked-named game that had originally appeared as a handheld Game & Watch. Nintendo had planned to release all of the Game & Watch titles onto e-Reader cards, but never followed through.

Finally, the American e-Reader had a link-cable connection, which had not been available on the Japanese one. When the Japanese e-Reader was inserted into the GBA, it blocked the link-cable port that was built into the console, rendering it useless. The American e-Reader contained a male connector that actually plugged into the GBA's link-cable port where the e-Reader was inserted. The top of the e-Reader had its own such port, so when a cable was inserted into the e-Reader, the information passed through it to the GBA.

The inclusion of the link-cable port with the e-Reader was necessary, because when Nintendo of America released the e-Reader, it also had introduced a GameCube game that utilized e-Reader.

Animal Crossing was the American version of *Animal Forest*, which had been released in Japan a year earlier. The American game had several enhancements over the Japanese one, including the incorporation of the e-Reader. Players could purchase packages of cards that provided additional items and features for the game. *Animal Crossing* also introduced a password feature, so players could trade items via e-mail, phone or even written notes. Finally, the hidden Famicom minigames were replaced with NES games.

Nintendo displayed a camera for the GBA at E[3]. Similar to the Game Boy Camera, the *GameEye* could be used to take digital color images, which could then be printed on a proprietary printer that was not shown at the exhibition. Also shown was a game called *Stage Debut*. The premise of this game was that the player took a picture of his face with the GameEye, and then sent the image to a Nintendo character in the game. Sporting the player's face, the character then went on stage and performed, responding to the player's input. Following E[3], the camera and game were never seen again.

WaveBird

While the GBA could be used as a controller for certain GameCube games, Nintendo of America released an entirely new controller for the console on June 10. The *WaveBird* looked almost like a standard controller, except that it was wireless. Instead of having an attached cord that plugged into a controller port, a receiver for the WaveBird plugged into the port. And unlike Nintendo's prior wireless release, the NES Satellite, which used infrared signals, the WaveBird used RF radio signals to communicate with its receiver. The up-side of this was that the controller did not have to be in a direct line of sight with the receiver in order to work accurately. Each WaveBird and matching receiver could be set to one of 16 channels, so up to four WaveBirds could be used at the same time.

Nintendo Wavebird

Functionally, the only difference between the WaveBird and the standard GameCube controller was that the WaveBird lacked a rumble feature. Because the controller required two AA batteries to operate, the rumble feature had been purposely omitted to conserve power.

Nintendo of America bundled the WaveBird controller with the receiver for $34.95 in the United States. When Nintendo of Japan released the WaveBird on December 5, it sold the controller and the receiver for ¥4,500 ($36).

Atari 10-In-One

Another type of controller was sold exclusively through Avon, the catalogue makeup company. The *Atari 10-in-1 TV Games* system looked almost exactly like an old-style Atari 2600 joystick. However, the controller had a compartment beneath it, where four AA batteries were inserted, and a composite video and audio cable that extended from it. This was because the controller was a self-contained game console that had ten original 2600 games built into it.

The $20 plug-and-play controller, which was manufactured by a toy company called Jakks Pacific, was very similar to the Activision TV Games Video Game System that Toymax had released a year earlier. Toymax had planned to release the Atari controller as well, but Jakks Pacific purchased Toymax during the year and rebranded all of its products under its own brand name.

Jakks Pacific Atari 10-in-1 TV Games

The controller contained ten games, including *Asteroids, Missile Command* and *Centipede*. Oddly, the controller also featured *Pong, Breakout* and *Circus Atari*, games that had all originally used the paddle controller rather than the joystick. All of the games had been rewritten, rather than emulated, so there were some slight cosmetic differences between the games and the originals that they had been based on.

Final Fantasy

In January, for the first time, the four-millionth copy of a PS2 game was sold. The game was *Final Fantasy X* from Square. GameCube owners wished that they could play it on their consoles, and after an early March announcement from Nintendo, there was hope that they would one day be able to.

Nintendo revealed at that time that it and the *Final Fantasy* developer, Square, had come to terms, and the third-party developer would once again produce games for Nintendo's consoles after a lapse of more than six years. In spite of statements made by Nintendo's former president, Hiroshi Yamauchi, claiming that Square would never develop Nintendo-compatible games again, it was Yamauchi himself who had been responsible for Square's return. Square's Nintendo development would happen in a new Square subsidiary called Game Developers Studio (GDS), which would be partially funded by *Fund Q*, a program that Yamauchi had set up to aid small third-party companies develop games that employed the GameCube-GBA link. GDS initially employed Akitoshi Kawazu, who had worked on the original *Final Fantasy* games, to set up the division.

SCE, which owned 18% of Square, was not too pleased with the deal, especially when it came to rumors about the online-only *Final Fantasy* being ported to the GameCube. However, such a deal wasn't likely to happen. For one, the game required a hard drive so vast amounts of data could be saved, and Nintendo had no plans to release a hard drive. In fact, Square had initially intended to release an Xbox version of the game, but decided against it because it had deemed the Xbox's 8GB hard drive too small.

Final Fantasy XI was released in Japan for the PS2 on May 16. Surprisingly, three weeks later, only 70,000 copies of the ¥7,800 ($61) game had been purchased, instead of the 200,000-300,000 copies that had been expected. Nintendo's president, Satoru Iwata, blamed it on the fact that most potential gamers simply didn't have the ability to get online. There was some truth in that statement, since the PS2 hard drive and network adapter combination, which were required for online gaming, hadn't been selling as rapidly as SCE would have preferred. Still, Square's president, Yoichi Wada, responded that online games had a different market scale than traditional games, and the two shouldn't be compared. Despite the different attitudes towards online gaming between Nintendo and Square, the new affiliation between the two companies stood firm.

The less-than-stellar reception (in traditional terms) to *Final Fantasy XI* didn't help Square's bottom line, which had been trying to recoup from a 2001 *Final Fantasy* movie that had bombed at the box office. On November 26, Square announced that the company would merge with Enix, another producer of role-playing games. The hope was that the two medium-sized companies could form one large company that could better compete against the American giants like Activision and Electronic Arts.

Other software companies were changing hands as well. Shiny Entertainment, which had been formed by David Perry in 1993 and had successfully released *Earthworm Jim* for the Genesis, had obtained the rights to produce a series of games based on the movie, *The Matrix*. Infogrames purchased the third-party developer for $47 million, with the sole intention of obtaining the *Matrix* games and its development team.

Another company that changed hands was the British developer, Rare, which had developed such groundbreaking games for the N64 as *Donkey Kong Country* and *GoldenEye 007*. Nintendo had owned 49% of Rare, but after Microsoft purchased the other 51% of the company from its founders on September 24, Nintendo sold all of its shares to Microsoft outright. Although development for the GameCube ceased immediately, Rare retained the right to continue developing games for the GBA, since Microsoft didn't have its own handheld console that the GBA could compete against.

Rare had seven games in development for the GBA at the time. While Nintendo would handle the publishing of three of those games, *Donkey Kong Country* and its two sequels, the company was under no obligation to publish the four other games, *It's Mr. Pants*, *Banjo-Kazooie: Grunty's Revenge*, *Banjo Pilot* and *Sabre Wulf*. And although Microsoft allowed its new subsidiary to develop games for a competing system, it was by no means going to publish them.

Microsoft had found itself in a similar situation in June when it developed its own properties, *Oddworld: Munch's Oddysee* and *Monster Truck Madness 2.0*, to play on the GBA. Rather than publish these games for the GBA, Microsoft signed a deal with THQ to publish them.[4]

Controversial Gaming

One third-party vendor, Acclaim, managed to raise controversy with several stunts that it pulled throughout the year. The first occurred in late February, when it released *Shadow Man: 2econd Coming* for the PS2. The game dealt with death, so Acclaim offered to "rent space" on British tombstones so it could place advertising for the game on them. An Acclaim spokesman noted that while many people would find this offensive, others "might see it as a good way of procuring a subsidy to burial costs, to give their loved one a good send-off". The company finally recanted and called it an early April Fool's joke.

The next stunt occurred at the end of August, when Acclaim released *Turok: Evolution* for all three game systems. This time, the company offered a $10,000 savings bond to the first baby born on September 1 that was named *Turok* by parents who had registered on the company's website in advance.

When Acclaim released the European edition of *Burnout 2: Point of Impact* for the PS2 on October 11, it promised that it would pay the fine for any aggressive driver in England who received a speeding ticket on that date. The offer was eventually rescinded after the British government accused Acclaim of encouraging unsafe driving.

Finally, in November, Acclaim released *BMX XXX*, a follow-up to *Dave Mirra Freestyle BMX*, a bicycle motocross game that Acclaim had released in 2000. Although the original had been a serious game in which players assumed the roles of Dave Mirra and other BMX athletes, the 2002 sequel took a different turn. While it was in development, Acclaim's executives discovered that the new game really didn't introduce anything new that would make it stand apart from the original. Since the game was actually pretty bad, they decided to change its focus in order to salvage the time and money that they had sunk into it. They figured that if they added raw humor and sexual innuendos to the game, then people would run out and buy it, no matter how bad it might be. When it was revealed that the game would feature topless women, it garnered more free publicity than it would have received if Acclaim had paid for marketing.

Acclaim BMX XXX

However, there was a price to pay for the gratuitous nudity. Because of it, several retailers, including Walmart and Toys "R" Us, decided not to carry the game. SCE refused to allow the game to be published for the PS2 unless the nudity was removed. Acclaim agreed to censor the nudity from the PS2 edition, but kept the adult humor and situations intact. The game was not sold in Japan, and all three versions had to be censored before they could be released in Australia. When Dave Mirra learned what the game had become, he successfully sued Acclaim to remove his name from the title.

The game did receive a lot of free publicity, just like Acclaim had predicted, but unfortunately, the publicity was all bad, just like the basic game -- which wound up selling less than 100,000 copies worldwide.

Another release that garnered much publicity was Rockstar's *Grand Theft Auto: Vice City*, the fourth installment in the *Grand Theft Auto* series. This game, which was released in the fall for the PS2 and Xbox, was similar to 2001's *Grand Theft Auto III*, with action taking place in Vice City, i.e. Miami, in 1986. Much of the background locale, which included neon lights and beaches, was based on the movie *Scarface* and the TV series *Miami Vice*. In addition to vehicles that were available in *Grand Theft Auto III*, players also had access to helicopters and motorcycles. And players could buy businesses such as strip clubs and car dealerships to generate income. While the game was as violent as its predecessor, its release was met with little protest, and no calls went out tone it down, except in Australia. When it was released in that country in 2003, the ability to pick up a prostitute had to be removed in order for the game to receive an MA15+ rating.

While Australia appeared to be going after games that contained racy adult content, Greece passed a law in early September that appeared to ban the use and ownership of all videogames. This was the result of a government scandal that involved illegal slot machines found in Greek arcades. When the government attempted to outlaw these machines, it created a law that blanketed all forms of arcade devices, including videogames. And a literal interpretation of the law included home gaming consoles. Violators were subject to a fine of up to €75,000 ($73,575) and a jail sentence of up to one year. Within a week of the law's passing, a judge declared it unconstitutional.

Meanwhile, on April 19, a U.S. District Judge ruled to preserve a 2000 law in St. Louis that required children under 17 to have parental consent before they could purchase violent or sexually explicit video games or play these types of games in arcades. The IDSA challenged this law on the grounds that even children had First Amendment rights to access these games. After reviewing four different videogames, Judge Stephen Limbaugh found "no conveyance of ideas, expression, or anything else that could possibly amount to speech." He ruled that videogames had more in common with board games and sports than they did with motion pictures, and thereby were not protected by freedom-of-speech laws.

Ironically, one month earlier, another U.S. District Judge had argued that videogames indeed were protected by freedom-of-speech laws. On March 5, Judge Lewis Babcock dismissed a lawsuit against eleven videogame companies including SCE, Activision and id Software. The suit had blamed them for the shootings at Columbine High School in 1999. Babcock ruled that there was no way anyone in these companies could have foreseen the violence that their products may have inadvertently perpetrated. In his ruling, Babcock rejected an argument by the plaintiffs that videogames should not be protected by First Amendment laws that granted their creators the freedom of speech.

Whether the industry had the right or not to portray violence and gratuitous sex once again became an issue after the NIMF, a watchdog group for the movie and videogame industry, released its seventh annual report card at the end of March. For the first time, the group rated the overall videogame industry with an "F", due to heightened violence in the games, and the continuing failure by both parents and retailers to keep violent games out of the hands of minors. Acclaim's *BMX XXX* led the group's top ten games for kids to avoid, followed by Rockstar's *Grand Theft Auto: Vice City*. The report even blasted the ESRB for being lax with its ratings. The ESRB responded by promising to review its rating system in 2003.

Game Designer Get-Togethers

The people responsible for the games that the NIMF had blasted met on February

28 in Las Vegas for the *D.I.C.E. (Design, Innovate, Communicate, Entertain) Summit*, a new, annual, two-day conference sponsored by the Academy of Interactive Arts & Sciences that emphasized the business and production side of the gaming industry. The Academy also used D.I.C.E. to unveil its annual International Achievement Awards.

Comparisons were immediately made between D.I.C.E. and the annual GDC which was held the following month. GDC was a larger event that was attended by tens of thousands of people involved in the industry, including programmers, producers, designers and artists. D.I.C.E., on the other hand, was lower key and attracted videogame executives and other people who were significant to the business sides of organizations.

D.I.C.E. and the GDC were both closed to the general public. Meanwhile, in 2002, the conference that *was* open to the public, the Tokyo Game Show, went from a biannual schedule to an annual one. The spring show was eliminated. The remaining fall show attracted such a large number of exhibitors that it rivaled E^3. However, in 2002, the Tokyo Game Show had competition when the *Games Convention* opened in Leipzig, Germany. And like the Tokyo Game Show, the Games Convention allowed the general public to attend.

But the existence of public game shows didn't lessen the importance of the trade-only conferences. On March 22, the software company Valve used GDC to introduce its new method of game distribution, which it called *Steam*. After experiencing major disruptions when it attempted to release updates for its online games, the company began building a platform that would update its games automatically. Steam was the result. It was initially used to make the distribution of online computer-game patches seamless. Valve beta-tested Steam through September, 2003, and during that period, anyone who wanted to install its online computer game *Counter-Strike 1.6* had to use Steam for the installation.

Steam wasn't the only alternative that gamers had to purchasing games from retail stores. A new type of distribution service called *GameFly* began on September 8. Modeled after Netflix, GameFly used a business model where subscribers paid a set amount each month for the service. Based on the amount they paid, they were entitled to rent one to four games at one time each month. After they completed a game, they could send it back to GameFly and rent another from the company's library of over 6000 titles. GameFly initially offered games the current consoles, the PS2, Xbox and GameCube but a few months after it was established, the service began offering games for the GBA as well.

Videogames In The Media

Thanks to the continuous growth in the videogame industry, British publisher, Highbury Entertainment, introduced *Games*™, a new multi-format magazine. *Games*™ was targeted towards adults, like its main competitor, *Edge*, and featured dozens of reviews each month, along with developer interviews and profiles of specific companies and games. Unlike *Edge*, *Games*™ also featured a monthly section that discussed videogame history.

Although videogame magazines were flourishing in Great Britain, the opposite was true in the United States where Imagine Media was forced to cut costs. It also changed its name to *Future Network USA* to better reflect its relationship with its British corporate parent, Future Publishing.

Games™

But most American videogamers thought of

Imagine Media as the publisher of *Next Generation* magazine. They were shocked when the magazine was suddenly canceled after its January issue was published. According to Imagine Media's president, Jonathan Simpson-Bint, at one time *Next Generation* had been read by the "top 20 percent of consumers who have 80 percent of the influence." Ironically, as the next generation of consoles, which included the PS2 and Xbox, had appeared, readership in the magazine had begun to fall. In addition, as publishers scrambled to develop games for these new systems, their marketing money that had been allocated to *Next Generation* disappeared. "*Next Generation* appears to have been a magazine of its time," said Simpson-Bint, "and that time now seems to have passed." Surprisingly, that problem didn't appear to affect *Next Generation*'s corporate sibling, *Edge* magazine.

One event that may have accelerated the cancelation of *Next Generation* was the departure of its long-time editor-in-chief, Tom Russo, whose name appeared at the top of the magazine's masthead for the final time in the next-to-last issue (December 2001). Although his final editorial didn't state why he was leaving the magazine, the reason quickly became apparent.

Russo had left Imagine Media to become the Games Editorial Director at *G4*, a new cable channel created by Comcast to compete directly with TechTV. However, while TechTV was geared towards computer enthusiasts, G4 had more videogame-related programming that was aimed at "MTV's demographics". The channel's name, G4, stood for "Games: PC, consoles, handheld and wireless," and the channel catered to "Gamers: casual, hardcore, developers and the curious."

The network launched on April 24, but was only available in households that subscribed to Comcast. Meanwhile, Comcast dropped TechTV from its lineup when it started G4. Among the shows that appeared on G4 were *Portal*, which was about multiplayer online games, *Pulse*, which was a news show about the videogame industry, and *Icons*, a weekly series that discussed the people, companies and even the history of videogames.

History On Display

The history of videogames was also the topic of a new exhibit at the Barbican, a performing arts center in London. *Game On* celebrated the history and culture of videogames and computers from *Spacewar* on the PDP-1 through the GameCube. The exhibit displayed over 125 playable games and included both arcade machines and consoles. In the four months that the exhibit ran, from May 16 through September 15, it garnered over 55,000 visitors.

A museum of a different sort was the *American Classic Arcade Museum,* located inside *Funspot* in Laconia, New Hampshire. Funspot was a family entertainment center that had been established in 1952 by Bob Lawton. In addition to a bowling alley, bingo and miniature golf, the center also featured dozens of classic arcade games that it had accumulated over the years. In September 1998, Gary Vincent, who managed the arcade section of the center, recognized that there were fewer and fewer places where people could actually go and play the classic games that had jumpstarted the arcade videogame industry. He proposed an idea to Lawton for the need to acquire as many of the classic machines as possible to preserve their history. They agreed and the American Classic Arcade Museum was born with Vincent as its curator. In January 2002, the museum incorporated as a non-profit organization, and this allowed people to donate machines to the museum as a tax-write-off, which further increased the museum's inventory. Before long Funspot claimed that it was the largest arcade in the world[5].

While the past was on display, the future of the videogame industry was anybody's guess. Microsoft and SCE had made it clear that their plans were to incorporate online gaming with machines that performed a variety of functions. Nintendo of Japan head Iwata Satoru had made it clear that online gaming wasn't a priority for him, but he didn't see a future in producing newer and more powerful consoles. At the end of October, Peter MacDougall, Nintendo of America's vice-president of sales and marketing, told a packed audience his company's plans. He said that Nintendo was in the software business to stay. And they were in the handheld business to stay. And finally, that they were in the home-console business to stay. And then he told them that Nintendo was already working on the technology that would succeed the GBA and the GameCube.

For Nintendo, the year had begun with a major change in its leadership. The company's millions of fans around the world were happy to hear that the year was ending with "business as usual."

CHAPTER THIRTY-ONE
2003

In 1998, SCE had sold 21.6 million original PlayStation consoles. At the time, that amount had been the most consoles ever sold in one year by a single company. However, that had been the apex of the PlayStation's sales, as they declined each year afterwards.

SCE broke that record in 2002, when it sold 22.52 million PS2s. But as with its previous achievement, the sales peak was followed by a swift decline. SCE only sold 20.1 million PS2 consoles in 2003, not a shabby achievement by any means, and the third highest number of yearly consoles sold to date.

Still, SCE was experiencing problems, especially outside of Japan. Many potential online customers were frustrated because of a shortage of available network adapters. Those who did own the adapters were exasperated as well, because the long-awaited hard drive still wasn't available. And without a hard drive, they couldn't experience *Final Fantasy XI*. SCE finally revealed that the game and the hard drive had been pushed back to a 2004 release.

Logitech PS2 Headset

Other online gamers were dissatisfied, because the headset that came with *SOCOM: U.S. Navy SEALs* could only be used for that game, while the Xbox had a headset that could be used with all of its online games. This problem was settled in September when SCE began selling a Logitech-built headset separately for $30, followed in November by a slew of online games that supported it, including *The Lord of the Rings: The Return of the King* and *FIFA Football 2004*.

In late April, SCE and Toshiba held a joint press conference, during which they announced that they were preparing to build factories to manufacture their new Cell chip, which would be the main processor of the PS3. But they didn't reveal any timeline for a release date for a new console at all.

Although the PS3 was definitely in SCE's future, the company still released new versions of the PS2. One new model featured an improved DVD player that supported progressive scan and could read DVD-R and DVD-RW discs, along with a built-in infrared receiver for the DVD remote that was located above the "eject" button. This replaced the need for a separate IR receiver that plugged into a controller port.

The PSX

Another new console, which had been announced on May 28, looked nothing like the PS2 systems that had preceded it. In fact, it wasn't even called a PS2, even though it was PS2-compatible.

The *PSX* was more akin to the rumored Microsoft HomeStation, which had never appeared, just as Microsoft had said it wouldn't. The PSX looked like a large, silver laserdisc player. But while it couldn't play 12-inch discs, it could play CDs and DVDs, as well as PlayStation and PS2 games, thanks to its Emotion Engine processor. The PSX was fully set up for online gaming with a built-in broadband Internet adapter, and a hard drive that could store either 160GB or 250GB of data, depending upon the model.

The 250GB model could record up to 325 hours of video.

Ken Kutaragi said that the "X" in the console's name meant that it was a "crossover of games and electronics." Besides the features that it shared with the PS2, the PSX contained a TV tuner and a fully functional DVR.

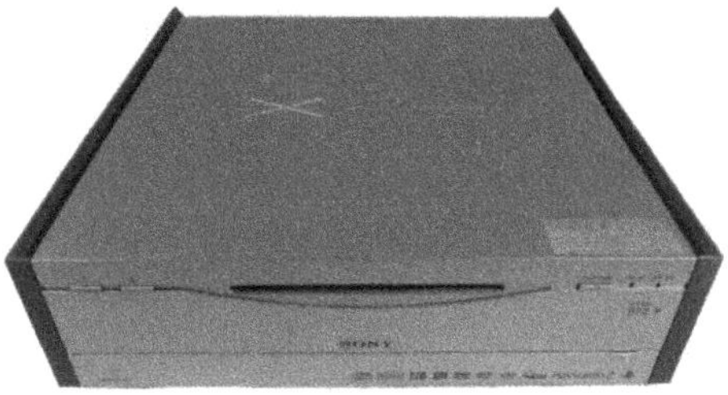

Sony PSX

The PSX was released in Japan on December 13, where it retailed for ¥98,000 ($907) for the 250GB model, and ¥79,800 ($739) for the 160GB model. Sony planned to release it in North America and Europe in March, 2004. Although these prices made the PSX one of the most costly videogame consoles ever produced, Sony pointed out that its targeted user wasn't the average gamer. In addition, the PSX was distributed by Sony itself, and not by SCE, which marketed the Sony-branded game consoles. It was no secret that SCE was the most profitable of all of Sony's consumer divisions, and the others, at the time of the PSX's initial announcement, had just suffered their largest decrease in profits in nearly eight years. Sony didn't view the PSX as a game machine and planned to market it as a multifunction set-top box that would appeal to mature, higher-income users. During the first week of its availability, which was also the week before Christmas, Japanese consumers purchased 100,000 units.

While the PSX technically wasn't a PS2, it was compatible with all of the peripherals that had been released for the gaming console, with one exception. The PS2 multitap allowed up to four players to play using their own controllers, even though there were only two controller ports in the console. The multitap plugged into both controller ports. The only reason it couldn't work with the PSX was because the PSX had its controller ports in the rear of the console, and they were spread too far apart for the multitap to plug into both of them.

The EyeToy

On July 3, SCEE released a new PS2 accessory that would have worked on the PSX if it had been available in Europe, because it plugged into the USB port instead of the controller port. By itself, the *EyeToy* was simply a small webcam that sat above the television. When a gamer faced the TV, his image appeared on the screen. However, when used with its accompanying software, *EyeToy: Play*, the EyeToy represented a new and fun way to play videogames. For the first time since Broderbund had released its U-Force controller for the NES in 1989, an actual handheld controller wasn't needed to play.

SCE EyeToy

EyeToy: Play was a collection of twelve minigames that were deviously simple, and yet outrageously fun. In one of the games, *Keep Ups*, a ball appeared on the screen. The object of the game was for the player to keep the ball in the air by maneuvering his body so his onscreen image came between the ball and bottom of the screen. The software detected if the ball made contact with the player, and if it did, depending upon its angle, it would bounce back up again. In *Wishi Washi*, the player assumed the role of a window washer. The screen displayed a series of dirty windows, and the player had to clean the windows by waving his open palm in front of the camera.

The EyeToy was an immediate success. Because SCEE sold over one million of them between July and October, its manufacturer had to increase production by an additional 50,000 units a month. The EyeToy's appeal continued after it was released in North America on November 4, bundled with *EyeToy: Play*. Ten days later, SCEE released *EyeToy: Groove*, the first dance-type game that didn't require any type of mat. In this game, players had to hit targets on the sides of the screen by moving their arms to the beat of the music. As a bonus, *EyeToy: Groove* also included a built-in calorie counter that estimated the number of calories that were burned while dancing.[1]

Musical Controllers

Also big in Japan were the rhythm games like *Beatmania* and *Dance Dance Revolution*. In 2001, Namco introduced a new series of arcade games called *Taiko no Tatsujin*,[2] which utilized drum controllers. In these games, symbols moved across the screen as a song played in the background. Blue symbols meant that the player had to hit the drum on the side, while red ones indicated that the player should hit the top of the drum. The sizes of the symbols also indicated whether the drum should be hit with one hand or two. Successful hits advanced a meter, and if the meter passed a certain point by the end of the song, the player moved on to the next level.

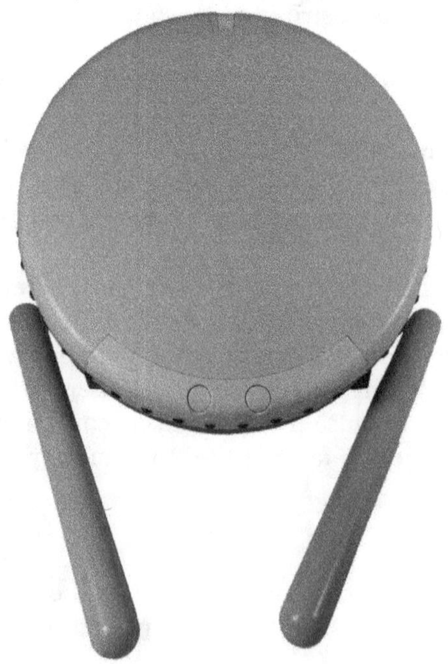

Namco Taiko no Tatsujin

Nintendo Donkey Konga Drums controller

Nintendo Donkey Konga

The arcade games were never released outside of Japan, and Namco released a home version called *Taiko no Tatsujin: Tatakon de Dodon ga Don* for the PS2 in Japan on October 24, 2002. The home version came with a small plastic drum called a *Tatacon*, which was similar in function to the larger drum on the arcade unit.

Throughout 2003, Namco released three more PS2 versions of the game in Japan.[3] The structures of the individual games were basically the same, with only a few minor modifications, and different song lineups between them. The third game of 2003, *Taiko no Tatsujin: Waku Waku anime Matsuri*, was released in Japan on December 18, 2003. But by that time, the PS2 was no longer the only console that a *Taiko no Tatsujin*-like game could be played upon. Six days earlier, on December 12, Nintendo of Japan had released *Donkey Konga* for the GameCube.[4] The game was packaged with a pair of *DK Bongos*, which resembled a pair of small bongo drums. These bongo controllers were slightly different than the single drum that accompanied the home versions of *Taiko no Tatsujin*, but they served the same purpose. *Donkey Konga* had been designed by the same team at Namco that had developed *Taiko no Tatsujin*, and although it wasn't officially a home version of *Taiko no Tatsujin*, it was basically the same game with Donkey Kong and other Nintendo characters thrown in. As in *Taiko no Tatsujin*, different symbols moved across the screen in beat with the music that played in the background. The symbols represented whether the left, right, or both bongos needed to be hit.

Karaoke

Not everybody was interested in playing faux instruments to play rhythm games. Some were content with just singing along to a soundtrack. Konami came to the aid of these people with a new game called *Karaoke Revolution*, which followed the same scrolling format as Konami's other rhythm games.

Unlike its previous rhythm games, Konami planned for *Karaoke Revolution* to be exclusive to the home market. Because Konami wanted to release the game in the United States, it contracted an American company to develop it. Harmonix Music Systems had been founded in 1995 by two MIT students who had interests in programming and music. They had developed two prior music-themed games for the PS2, *FreQuency* and its 2003 sequel, *Amplitude*.

Konami first released *Karaoke Revolution* for the PS2 in Japan on September 25. The song lyrics scrolled up the screen in this ¥3,980 ($36) game. The screen also displayed the appropriate pitches in which the song needed to be sung, along with an indicator of the actual pitch sung. Players could choose from 30 songs to sing along with and the game consisted of several modes. In "Revolution" mode, a player had to sing through a series of stages without making any errors. A simple "Karaoke" mode simply assigned a score for a person's singing, and that score could be uploaded to an online leaderboard.

Naturally, a microphone was needed to play *Karaoke Revolution*, and Konami released a ¥5,800 ($51) USB headset-style microphone that was similar to the headset that came with SCE's *SOCOM: U.S. Navy SEALs*.[5]

The microphone was packaged with the game when Konami released *Karaoke Revolution* in the United States on November 5. Retailing for $30, the American version was a bargain over its Japanese counterpart. The layout of the game was basically the same as the Japanese version, but the modes were slightly different. "Arcade" mode let the player choose several songs that he liked. "Showtime" randomly selected the songs for the player to sing, and started the player off in a house setting. As the player sang successfully, he progressed toward a stadium performance.

Microsoft released a similar product on December 1. The *Xbox Music Mixer* turned the Xbox into a karaoke machine without the need of an expensive peripheral like the one that Sega of Japan had released for the Dreamcast. Bundled with a microphone that plugged into the Xbox controller, the $40 package allowed users to transfer songs from a CD to the Xbox's hard drive. Once there, the vocals could be stripped away from the music. Unfortunately, it also removed much of the music. On top of that, there was a slight delay from when a person sang into the mike to when it played back through the TV. This might not have been so problematical, since the vocals could barely be heard through the TV, even with the volume at its highest setting.

While budding rock superstars favored the PS2's *Karaoke Revolution*, online gamers rallied towards the Xbox in droves. Xbox Live was the most successful of the online gaming services, with more than five million games played on

Microsoft Xbox Music Maker

Microsoft NFL Fever 2004

Microsoft Xbox Wireless Adapter

it during just its inaugural week of operation. On August 28, Microsoft launched *XSN Sports*, a division that would design sports games that could be played on Xbox Live. On that same day the first XSN-designed game, *NFL Fever 2004*, was released. XSN games representing golf, tennis, basketball and several other sports were released during the months that followed.

On October 5, Microsoft upped the ante for its Xbox Live service by releasing the first wireless network adapter for any console. The $140 adapter allowed the gamer to have his or her Xbox in a different room than the Internet router without needing to drill holes in the walls to run connecting Ethernet cable.

But after Microsoft launched the online service in Japan on January 16, it had a hard time trying to find an audience there. Only 370,000 Xbox consoles had been sold in Japan during its first year, compared to the one million GameCubes that Nintendo had sold during the same period.

The Xbox did better in Europe, where it outsold the GameCube by a small margin. In late January, Microsoft created a new corporate vice-president position to oversee the retail and product operations in Japan and Europe, and gave it to Peter Moore, who had resigned from his position as president of Sega of America just a few days earlier.

Microsoft reduced the price of the Xbox again around the world. In April, Europe experienced the first of these price cuts when the console's cost was reduced 20% to €199 ($214), matching that of the GameCube. In Great Britain, the price also fell 20% to £129 ($202). The United States received its price reduction in mid-May, when it dropped $20 to $180, the same as the PS2. However, Nintendo of America struck a mighty blow in September, when it reduced the price of the GameCube to an unbelievable $99. Then in November, Microsoft lowered the price of the Xbox by 30% in Japan where, at ¥16,800 ($155), it became the least expensive Xbox anywhere in the world. The price reduction in Japan had been spurred by SCE's own price-cut one week earlier, when it lowered the price of the PS2 to ¥19,800 ($180).

Game Boy Player

The $99 price for the GameCube moved the consoles out of stores, which was something that Nintendo desperately needed to do. Although the GBA was performing very well, Nintendo had only sold 890,000 GameCube consoles during the first half of its fiscal year, when the company posted its first loss in 40 years. Nintendo even stopped production of the GameCube in January, and many speculated that Nintendo wanted to clear it from store shelves so a new console could replace it in 2004. In July, Nintendo president, Satoru Iwata, announced that the company was indeed "preparing a new product that will give a fresh surprise to consumers," but he didn't elaborate. And in an announcement earlier in the year, he had already said that a new console wouldn't appear until 2005. Nintendo dispelled the rumors that the GameCube would be soon replaced by a new console when it resumed the console's production in November, in order to make adequate supplies available for the upcoming holiday season.

Since the GBA was selling so well and the GameCube wasn't, it wasn't totally unexpected for Nintendo to turn the GameCube into a GBA.

The *Game Boy Player* was essentially a GBA console without a screen or control buttons. It plugged into the hi-speed port at the underside of the GameCube. Once it was connected and a Game Boy cartridge was inserted into the slot in its front, the game was channeled through the GameCube and displayed on the TV that the GameCube was connected to. Game Boy games naturally displayed in monochrome, but Game Boy Color and GBA games appeared in full color. Players could use the standard GameCube controllers to play, or they could connect a GBA to the GameCube and use it as the main controller. In addition, the Game Boy Player could be linked to other GBAs, just as if it were a GBA itself.

Nintendo Game Boy Player

The Game Boy Player was released in Japan on March 3 and sold for ¥5,000 ($41). Nintendo of Japan also released a Game Boy Player specifically for the Panasonic Q, since the bottom of the Q was constructed slightly differently from the GameCube. Nintendo of America released the Game Boy Player on June 24 in North America, where it retailed at $50.

Even the e-Reader could be used with the Game Boy Player, although it was impractical in most cases. While the NES e-Reader games worked perfectly on the big screen when channeled through the GameCube, the GameCube games that used the e-Reader to add additional bonuses, such as *Animal Crossing*, couldn't be used with the Game Boy Player, because the games required the simultaneous use of the GBA and the GameCube to add bonuses through the e-Reader.

Meanwhile, Nintendo continued to support the e-Reader. On June 26, Nintendo of Japan released a ¥4,800 ($40) e-Reader +, which was the same as the American e-Reader and featured the pass-through link ports. On the following day, the company released a new edition of *Animal Forest* that was modeled after the American *Animal Crossing* and was compatible with the e-Reader +.

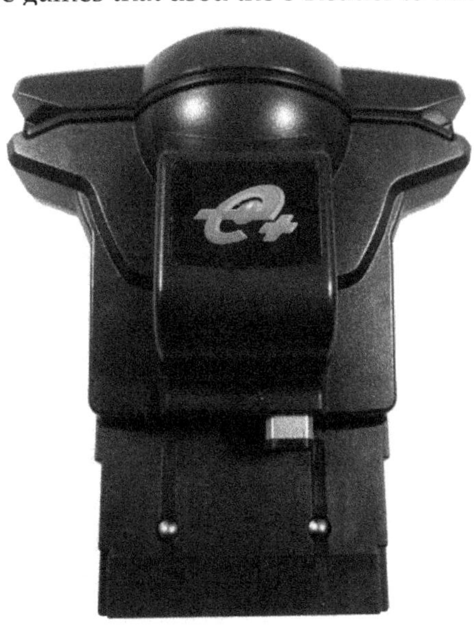

Nintendo e-Reader+

Game Boy Advance SP

One of the advantages of using the Game Boy Player to play GBA games on a conventional TV was that games could be played in a totally dark room, a feat that couldn't be done on the unlit GBA. However, on February 14, two weeks before the release of the Game Boy Player, Nintendo of Japan released a new Game Boy model that did feature a light.

The ¥12,500 ($104) *Game Boy Advance SP* (*GBA SP*[6]) was completely redesigned. Like the original Game Boys, the GBA SP stood vertically, although cartridges were inserted into a slot at the bottom of the unit, rather than the top. However, when the device was not in use, the top half, where the screen was located, could flip down and cover the bottom half, where the controls were.

Nintendo Game Boy Advance SP

The screen on the GBA SP was the same size as the one on the GBA, but it seemed bigger, because the width of the device was just slightly wider than the screen itself. But what made the screen special was that it included a frontlight that could be switched on or off. When the $99 GBA SP was released in the United States on March 23, it became the first-ever Game Boy in America that offered an illuminated screen.

The GBA SP was also the first Game Boy that did not use standard batteries. The device had a rechargeable lithium battery that was installed at the factory and allowed for ten hours of game play with the screen light on, and eighteen hours with it off. The unit came with a charger that could bring the battery to full capacity in three hours. Nintendo also removed the standard headphone jack from the GBA SP. Gamers who wanted to use headphones while playing had two options. They could purchase headphones that had been designed specifically for the GBA SP, or they could purchase a $4.25 adapter from Nintendo's website that standard headphones could plug into. However, in either case, headphones couldn't be used while the unit was charging, because they shared the same port as the charger.

The GBA SP did not replace the GBA, and Nintendo continued to sell the two-year-old handheld for $20 less than the GBA SP. However, it was obvious which model consumers preferred. During the nine-month period ending on December 31, of the 15 million GBA consoles that Nintendo sold around the world, 13 million of them were GBA SPs.

As with all of its consoles, Nintendo had designed the GBA SP to strictly play games. So it took a third-party vendor to turn the handheld device into a movie viewer.

AM3 Advance Movie Adapter

AM3 released the ¥3,200 ($30) *Advance Movie Adapter* in November in Japan. The Advance Movie Adapter was a cartridge that plugged into the GBA and accepted SmartMedia cards that stored up to 24 minutes of video. This video could then be viewed on the GBA's screen, and the GBA's control buttons were used to fast-forward or rewind the video. Three episodes of a popular Japanese cartoon called *Detective Boy Conan* were available on the day that the Advance Movie Adapter was released. Each episode was stored on its own SmartMedia card, which retailed for ¥2,380 ($22). AM3 promised additional movies that could be purchased from stores or downloaded, as well as a possible North American launch, in 2004.

Another type of GBA adapter came out only in Japan on July 18. The *GBA Infrared Adapter* filled a hole that had been left when Nintendo made the transition from the Game Boy Color, which supported infrared communications, to the GBA, which didn't. However, few games supported the feature, which was why Nintendo hadn't included it in the GBA in the first place. Oddly, the GBA Infrared Adapter couldn't even be used with the infrared Game Boy Color games when they were played in the GBA. It only supported one game: *Cyberdrive Zoids* from Tomy, a Japanese toy company. The GBA Infrared Adapter was packaged with the game and its only purpose was to send infrared commands to Tomy's *Zoids*, a collection of plastic model animals that had been around since 1982. Some Zoids contained motors that powered moveable features, and players could use their GBAs to send the commands to make these specific Zoids move.

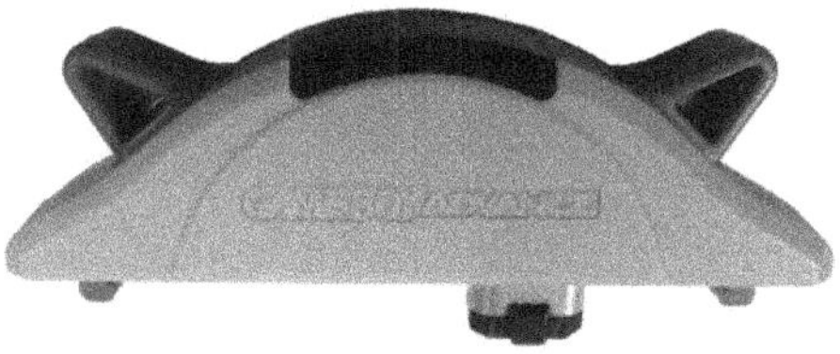

Nintendo Game Boy Infrared Adapter

Tomy Cyberdrive Zoid

PlayStation Portable

It was expected that the GBA SP would be another hit in Nintendo's stable of handheld successes that no other manufacturer could penetrate. But that wasn't from a lack of trying. When SCE attempted to take a stab at it, everybody paid attention.

Ken Kutaragi, CEO of SCE and the "Father of the PlayStation," announced his new "baby" at SCE's pre-E³ conference on May 13. Most people in attendance had expected to hear something about the forthcoming PS3. Instead, Kutaragi spoke about the *PSP (PlayStation Portable)*, which he referred to as "The Walkman of the 21st Century."

The new handheld would feature a 4.5-inch, backlit, LCD widescreen. It would also have built-in stereo speakers and a standard headphone jack. And the device might even double as a cell phone.

Software would be housed on a new medium called the *UMD (Universal Media Disc)*, which was a disc half the size of a DVD, but capable of storing 1.8GB of data. The discs themselves would be housed in caddies to prevent damage.

Kutaragi did not specify either a price or a release date for the new device. In fact, a prototype wasn't even shown. But Kutaragi did offer that the PSP would be launched sometime in 2004, in honor of the PlayStation's tenth anniversary.

Additional information concerning the PSP wasn't disclosed until July 29, during the *PlayStation Meeting*, an infrequent event that SCE used when it needed to reveal something new. At this particular meeting, Kutaragi revealed that

SCE PSP UMD

2003

the PSP, which was now being targeted for a holiday 2004 release, would use a MIPS R4000 processor that was similar to the one in the PlayStation, although it would run about ten times faster at 333 MHz. The processor had two central cores. One would be used for games while the other, which included 2Mb of RAM, would be used to play movies and music.

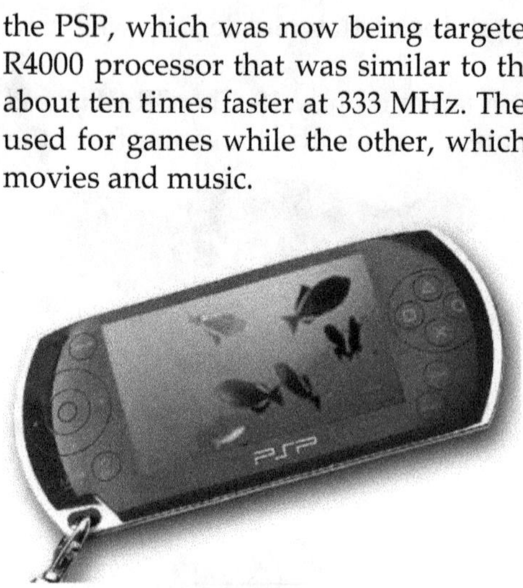

SCE PSP Prototype

Kutaragi also announced that the PSP would feature wireless LAN capability built into the device. SCE had originally planned for this to be optional, but changed its plans at the requests of developers. The PSP would be able to connect to a PS2 either through USB or infrared technology.

Kutaragi also used the PlayStation Meeting to reiterate that a PSP prototype would be revealed at E^3 in spring, 2004. But on November 1, the company held a closed corporate-strategy meeting in New York, and a prototype was revealed to its attendees. Within hours of the meeting, photos of the anticipated handheld began appearing on the Internet. The photo that was leaked to the world showed a device with a sleek horizontal design and a large wide screen in the center. Directional control buttons were on the left side of the unit and the familiar PlayStation control buttons were on the right. Surprisingly, all of the buttons were recessed within the unit. Gamers anxiously awaited its release, and many believed that it would be the handheld that would finally usurp the Game Boy.

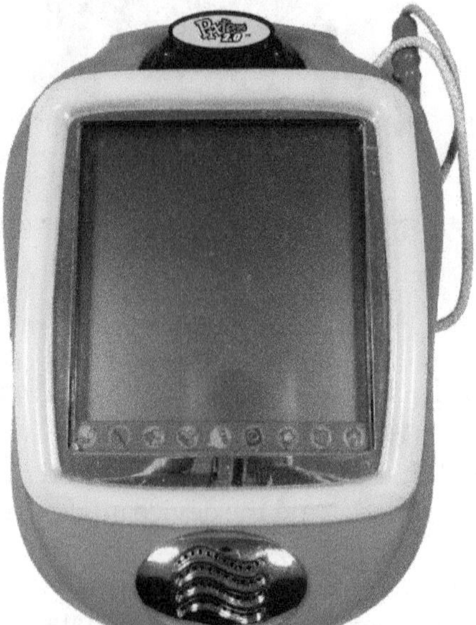

Fisher-Price Pixter 2.0

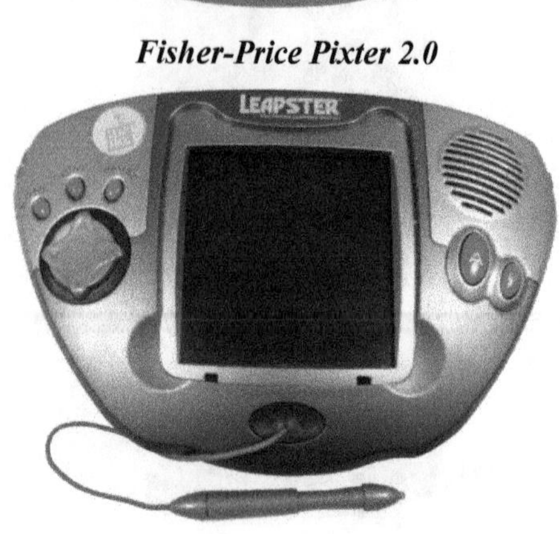

Leapfrog Leapster

Educational Handhelds

While the upcoming PSP seemed to get all the attention, three handhelds were released in 2003 that were totally ignored, if even known, by anyone over the age of ten. One was from Fisher-Price, which introduced a new version of its Pixter handheld unit. The *Pixter 2.0,* which was released early in the year, built upon the Pixter Plus, as it also had a port for the screen lamp. However, the port was relocated to the side of the device. In its place above the screen was a "signal dome" that was used to send messages and drawings wirelessly from one Pixter 2.0 to another. In order for them to communicate together, the two Pixter 2.0 devices had to be within five feet of each other and in a direct line.

The other new handheld for young children that was released during the year was the *Leapster Learning Game System* from LeapFrog Enterprises, a company that developed electronic educational toys. Leapfrog had been started in 1995 by Michael Wood and Robert Lally after Wood, an attorney who helped entrepreneurs fund their products, couldn't find anything that could help his three-year-old son read adequately. In 1997, Tom Kalinske, a former president of Sega of America, joined LeapFrog as Vice Chairman. Two years later, the company launched the *LeapPad,* an interactive children's book much like Sega's Pico, although it didn't connect to a television. It was a hit, and LeapFrog duly became one of history's fastest-growing toy companies.

The Leapster, which launched in late 2003, was the company's first handheld unit, and it looked much like an oversized GBA. The $80 device had a game pad and control buttons, and accepted cartridges that were roughly the size and shape of GBA cartridges. In addition, a stylus, similar to the one that accompanied Tiger Electronics' game.com, was attached to the unit via a short tether. At approximately four inches, the LCD screen on the Leapster was larger than the one on the GBA, but the graphics that it displayed were much inferior. And despite the fact that the Leapster resembled a handheld game console, all of its software was interactive and educational.

All of the software for the Leapster had been designed by LeapFrog, as the company refused to work with third-party publishers. This resulted in a very limited software library that was available for the device.

PDAs and Phones

While the Leapster was clearly targeted towards young children, two other handhelds were released that had been aimed strictly at adults.

Byron Connell and Peng Lim, two former vice-presidents at Palm, a manufacturer of PDAs (Personal Digital Assistants), believed that consumers wanted a PDA that was also a videogame console. They founded a new company called *Tapwave* to create and distribute such a device. The result was the *Zodiac,* which debuted at E³ in May and was released via the company's website in October.

Tapwave Zodiac

The Zodiac was basically a Palm Pilot turned on its side, with a large 4.5-inch, backlit screen, and the addition of 3D graphics processing power and an analog joystick. Like the Leapster, the device came with a stylus, which made entering information into the PDA a breeze. And because the Zodiac used Palm's operating system, it was able to run nearly 19,000 applications that had already been developed for the Palm Pilot. Games that were available for purchase were stored on small SD-type cards and sold for around $30 each. Launch titles included *Spy Hunter* and *Tony Hawk's Pro Skater*. The Zodiac delivered PlayStation-quality graphics and had a built-in rumble feature. It also incorporated blue-tooth technology that accommodated up to eight local players at one time. And like Game Park's GP32, the Zodiac could play emulated games, but without the registration fuss required by the Korean handheld.

But the Zodiac also came with an adult-sized price. Tapwave offered two models that only differed by the amount of internal memory that they contained. A 32Mb unit retailed for $300, while a 128Mb unit sold for $399.

Nokia N-Gage

The other handheld that had been designed for adults was released on October 7, around the same time as the Zodiac. The *N-Gage* from Nokia, a leading manufacturer of cell phones, was actually a handheld videogame console (or a "gamedeck," as Nokia preferred to call it) that could also be used as a phone. While the N-Gage could play Java games like other cell phones, its unique, innovative feature was that it could also play games that were stored on tiny MultiMedia cards. Well-known developers such as Activision, Sega and Taito supported the device, and launch titles included *Sonic N*, *Tomb Raider* and *Bust-a-Move*.

Graphically, games that played on the N-Gage exceeded those on the GBA. Games like *Tomb Raider* and *Tony Hawk's Pro Skater* were almost perfect ports of the PlayStation originals. The screen itself was backlit, which was superior to the front-lit illumination found on the GBA SP.

The N-Gage sounded like a novel idea for a community of gamers who were frequently carrying both a cell phone and a handheld gaming device. In addition, the N-Gage could play MP3 files and also could act as an FM radio.

Unfortunately, the system also had several factors against it right off the bat. The first negative point was its retail price, which was $299, approximately the same price as the Zodiac. Although cell phones were notoriously expensive, they were also usually subsidized by a wireless carrier when a service contract was signed. But the N-Gage was basically sold in gaming stores like GameStop. In fact, it wasn't even compatible with Verizon Wireless' network, which was the largest in the United States, or with any of the services that were available in Japan. The device did miserably on its launch day, with only 5,000 units sold in the United States. The numbers were even more dismal in Great Britain, where only 500 N-Gages were purchased. Within its first two weeks of availability, the GBA SP outsold the N-Gage by 100 to 1. By that time, the game stores that were selling the N-Gage began offering $100 rebates on its purchase.

Another thing about the N-Gage that was absolutely frustrating was the myriad of buttons found on its face. Although the N-Gage was basically the same horizontal shape as the GBA, it had an astounding twenty buttons that gamers had to contend with, along with a 4-way directional pad. It was true that many of the buttons were used by the phone for dialing and texting purposes, but they still made the system appear complicated.

One of the biggest complaints against the N-Gage was how to switch games. New games could be purchased on MultiMedia cards for around $30 each. However, it seemed like the user needed an advanced degree in engineering in order to change the cards. First, the device's plastic cover had to be removed. Once that was done, the battery compartment had to be removed to access the game slot. The battery compartment and plastic cover then had to be replaced after the old game card was removed and the new one was inserted. It was an annoying process that could have been avoided.

Finally, few people wanted to use the N-Gage as a phone because of its weird configuration of speaker and microphone placement. Rather than their being located on the face of the device, where the user could hold the phone with the screen flat against his ear, Nokia chose to place them on the N-Gage's side. This made the device difficult to hold when it was used as a phone, and uncomfortable to use, since only the edge of the unit rested against the ear.

As if Nokia didn't have enough worries, the company confirmed in November that its N-Gage games had been hacked and were available for download from several websites. To make matters worse, not only could these downloaded games play on N-Gages, but they could also play on other Nokia devices. Surprisingly, Nokia reps weren't really too concerned about this latest development. According to one Nokia spokesman, the company had somewhat expected it to happen, because it was a "relatively common occurrence in the gaming industry."

But Nokia was concerned about the complaints that it received concerning the N-Gage's design. In November, sources within the company unofficially announced that it would begin selling a redesigned version of the N-Gage during the following summer.

The N-Gage offered two types of competitive gaming. Two people in the same room could play against each other on individual N-Gages by using a local Bluetooth standard.

But multiplayer games were accomplished through the phone's cellular network, utilizing SNAP (Sega's Network Application Package) technology, which Nokia had purchased from Sega in August. Nokia kept the acronym, but its meaning was changed to "Scalable Network Application Package."

Mergers

Sega's sale of SNAP to Nokia represented one of the final hardware transactions that Sega made, and occurred shortly after Sega had finally shut down its SegaNet network at the end of June. Ironically, during this time that Sega was truly only a software developer, it was awaiting a planned October merger with Sammy, Japan's largest manufacturer of Pachinko and slot machines. The deal had been announced on February 13, following a year when Sega's sales expectations had been cut by half. Sammy, meanwhile, had been using Dreamcast technology in its Pachinko machines and was seeking a way to get closer to the videogaming industry.

As Sega waited for the October merger, several rumors spread that said Sega had planned to merge with other companies including Namco, Electronic Arts and Microsoft. Only the Namco deal contained any inkling of truth, since Sega had sought a merger with Namco long before the deal with Sammy had been announced. However, by year's end, none of these mergers had occurred. The Sammy deal died because both companies couldn't agree to the terms of the merger, and both disputed the value of the other company's assets.

Although the merger didn't proceed, Sammy purchased 39 million shares of Sega in December for ¥45.33 billion ($422 million), which gave it a majority stake in the company.

Had Sega actually merged with Sammy, it wouldn't have been the only merger that took place during the year. On April 1, Square and Enix completed their merger and the new company was called *Square Enix*. And Infogrames did some name-changing of its own. As of May 7, its U.S. subsidiary was officially renamed *Atari, Inc.*, while its European subsidiary was called *Atari Europe*. Finally, the videogame company that it had purchased from Hasbro was given the official name *Atari Interactive*. For the first time in five years, the *Atari* name once again referred to a company and not just a brand.

And while Infogrames had changed a brand name into a company, Mad Catz, a manufacturer of peripherals and accessories, purchased a brand name. In late January, the company purchased the GameShark name and website from InterAct for $5 million. InterAct had sold only the name because its game-cheating device, which had used that name, had been licensed from Datel, which sold its own version of the device in Great Britain under the Action Replay name. Datel decided not to renew InterAct's contract because it opened an American office in June, 2002 with the intention of selling the Action Replay in North America itself. Following the purchase, Mad Catz used the GameShark name on game-saving devices.

Back To Court

But name-changes and mergers weren't the only legalities that occurred during the year. The 3DO Company filed Chapter XI bankruptcy protection on May 28. As a software developer, it had sat on its laurels and hadn't kept up with the latest next-generation systems. To raise cash, the company held a mammoth fire sale of its intellectual properties. Among the companies that bought a piece of the 3DO pie were Ubisoft, Microsoft and Crave. Even 3DO's founder, Trip Hawkins, spent $200,000 and took home several game titles.

Courts were also used to settle the controversy of whether videogames were protected under the First Amendment. In March, the state of Washington passed a law that prohibited minors from purchasing any game that depicted violence against police officers. While obvious games like *Grand Theft Auto III* were affected by this law, even the sale of games like Atari's new *Enter the Matrix* which carried a "Teen" rating, was illegal under the new law. The game rating was inconsequential as far as the law was concerned. And the retail clerk who sold the game, not the retailer, could be fined $500 for the action. The law was scheduled to take effect on July 27.

The ESA declared the law unconstitutional. On June 3, a coalition representing the videogame industry and led by the ESA[7] filed a complaint against the state. Coincidently, shortly after the complaint was filed in Washington, the 8th US Circuit Court of Appeals reversed the decision of the 2002 St. Louis case, in which Judge Limbaugh had ruled in favor of a ban that restricted minors from accessing violent games. The court ruled that the ban in itself was unconstitutional, and in the same decision, ruled that videogames were indeed covered under the First Amendment. However, this ruling only affected the St. Louis ban, and not the Washington one, which would have to wait until 2004 before the courts took another look at it.

BMX athlete Dave Mirra used the courts in February to file a $21-million lawsuit against Acclaim. Mirra was originally supposed to have appeared in the adult-only *BMX XXX*, but he lobbied to keep his image out after Acclaim decided to put nude women into it. However, the company continued to use Mirra's name and image in ads that promoted the game. The suit was eventually settled without any money changing hands, and Mirra's contract with Acclaim was renegotiated to last through 2011. Meanwhile, Acclaim's net revenue for the first quarter of fiscal year 2003 was 22% lower than from the same period a year earlier. To reduce its expenses, Acclaim closed a Salt Lake City development studio, reduced its staff company-wide and discontinued several titles that were under development.

Whereas *BMX XXX* was a poor game that Acclaim had spiced with sexual situations in order to sell copies, *Kakuto Chojin* was a poor game that Microsoft released in 2002 and did nothing to embellish. *Kakuto Chojin* had been Microsoft's first 3D fighter for the Xbox. It had originally been intended as a demo that showed off the Xbox's graphic capabilities, but someone within Microsoft made the unwise decision to release it as an official game. While critics were wowed by the graphics, they were repulsed by its shallow game play.

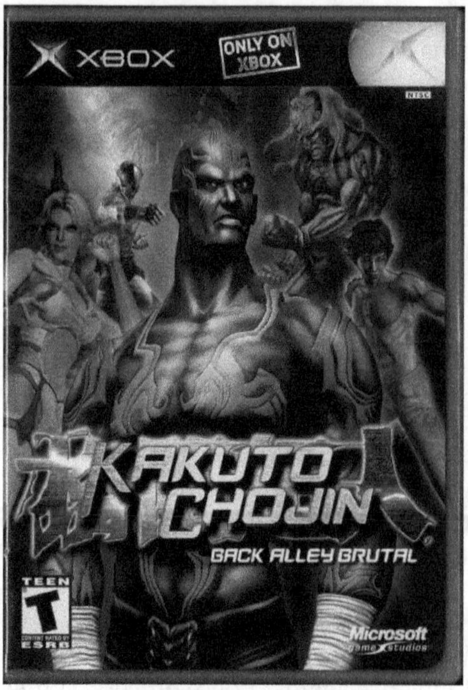

Microsoft Kakuto Chojin

Microsoft removed the game from store shelves in early February, but it wasn't because of the game's lack of sales. It was done because mixed in with the game's background music was an inappropriate verse from the *Quran*, the sacred text of Islam. Microsoft initially planned to reissue the game without the verse, but realized that there was no point in doing so, since its sales had been so poor.

Nvidia Issues

At approximately the same time that Microsoft was discontinuing *Kakuto Chojin*, it was beginning to mend fences with Nvidia, the company that supplied the graphics processing unit for the Xbox. The friction had begun in April, 2002, when Nvidia complained that it lost money on every custom chip that it sold to Microsoft. Nvidia claimed that the price it charged was based on the total number of required chips that Microsoft had forecasted, and which Nvidia allegedly produced. Unfortunately, Microsoft's projections were inflated, and the company didn't sell as many Xboxes as it had hoped it would. This resulted in Nvidia's production of 1.25 million more chips than Microsoft actually purchased. Nvidia wanted to charge Microsoft slightly more for the chips that it actually did buy to compensate for the $13 million that it didn't receive. Microsoft wanted Nvidia to produce only the amount of chips that it actually requested and to reduce the amount that it paid per chip, because it claimed that it was already losing money on every Xbox that it sold.

Nvidia took Microsoft to arbitration, which lasted several months. The two companies finally settled their dispute on February 6. When the arbitration panel sided with Nvidia, and agreed that Microsoft had to pay the price for the number of chips that it had forecasted but had not actually purchased. Following the settlement, both companies agreed to work together to find ways to make the Xbox more profitable. Unlike Sony, whose most profitable product was the PS2, Microsoft's entire entertainment division, which included the Xbox, had a second-quarter operating loss of $348 million.

But this period of goodwill between Nvidia and Microsoft did not last long. On August 14, competing chip maker ATI revealed that it had won a contract from Microsoft to design the graphics chips for the Xbox 2. ATI was already designing the chips for the GameCube, and its contract with Nintendo was much more favorable than the one that Microsoft had with Nvidia. Although ATI designed the chips for Nintendo, Nintendo was directly responsible for manufacturing them, and then paid ATI a royalty for every GameCube console and piece of software that it sold.

The Phantom Phantom

Nvidia wasn't left out in the cold in supplying chips for a new console. On January 20, a Florida-based company called Infinium Labs had announced that it would release a new console by the end of the year, which would use Nvidia's chips. Bu most journalists were skeptical, especially when Infinium Labs didn't return their calls or emails, and the mailing address listed for the company was actually found to be inside of a Mailboxes, Etc. outlet.

The *Phantom,* as the promised console was called, was only going to play games that were already loaded on its hard drive when the console was purchased, or were downloaded from Infinium's servers, either permanently for a one-time fee, or "rented" on a pay-per-play basis for a lower amount. The console itself was planned to be in the $400 range.

Infinium Labs Phantom

Tim Roberts, the CEO of Infinium Labs, announced that the Phantom would be publicly displayed at the *Ultimate Gamers Expo,* a new convention for videogame consumers that had been announced at the end of 2002 and was to be held at the Los Angeles Convention Center between August 15 and August 17. However, one month before it was to take place, the show was abruptly canceled. The Phantom's skeptics merely took this in stride. But to their surprise, Infinium Labs launched a website on August 18 that showcased the console and revealed its specifications, which included a 3.0GHz processor with 512Mb DDR RAM, a Nvidia graphics card, and a wireless controller, keyboard and mouse. By then, the suggested retail price of the console had dropped to $300, with a subscription fee set at $9.95 per month.

By year's end, when the console was originally supposed to be available, nobody outside of Infinium Labs had actually seen it, and the release date was pushed back to early 2004. Infinium Labs also announced that the console would not be available from retailers upon its release. Instead, it would only be available directly through DSL and cable providers, or from Infinium Labs' website. But while the company insisted that it was in discussions with 250 developers, much of the gaming industry remained skeptical of the Phantom's eventual release.

Nintendo iQue

The Phantom wasn't the only console that exclusively used downloaded software. On November 17, Nintendo, in a joint venture with a Chinese company called iQue, released a system called the *iQue Player* only in China. Software for the iQue Player could only be downloaded from the Internet.

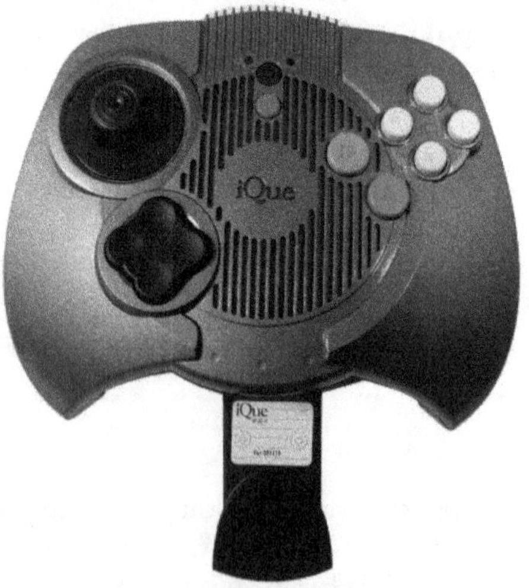

Nintendo iQue Player

The ¥598 ($72) iQue Player looked like a controller that hooked up directly to a television and played N64 games. However, the device did not have games built directly into it like the Jakks Pacific systems. In an attempt to combat piracy, the games were stored on a flash card that was unique to each individual system.

Each system was sold with its own flash card that contained a copy of *Dr. Mario 64*, along with demos for several games, including *The Legend of Zelda: Ocarina of Time*, *Super Mario 64* and *Star Fox 64*. Since only one flash card could work on the particular unit that it came with, games had to be purchased from the Internet for ¥48 ($6), downloaded to a PC, and then transferred to the individual flash card. The catch was that since the flash card only contained 250 blocks of memory, usually only one complete game could reside on it at a time. So in order to play a new game, the previous one had to be overwritten. Fortunately, the flash card retained the history of which games had been bought, so any previously purchased game could be downloaded again without any additional payment required. In all, fourteen games, all being Chinese translations of readily available N64 titles, were released.[8]

Jakks Pacific Activision TV Game

Plug-And-Plays

Early in the year, Jakks Pacific began releasing its *Atari 10-in-1 TV Games* plug-and-play device in retail outlets, under its own brand name on a nationwide basis. Previously, the unit had been sold exclusively through Avon. At the end of the year, in time for the holiday system, Jakks Pacific rereleased its Activision system. While it contained the same games that were in the original unit that had been released by Toymax in 2001, the unit itself was now a handheld joystick controller topped with a round ball for easy grasping. Along with the Activision unit, Jakks Pacific introduced the *Namco TV Games* system, which contained the arcade versions of *Pac-Man*, *Dig Dug*, *Galaxian*, *Rally-X* and *Bosconian*. The device featured the same joystick controller as the Activision one, although the base was much larger, to somewhat resemble an arcade cabinet.

Techno Source, a three-year-old toy and game company, signed a licensing deal with Keith Robinson, a former Intellivision programmer and the current owner of the Intellivision library, to manufacturer a plug-and-play device that featured Intellivision games. The result was released in August. The *25 Intellivision Video Game System* featured 25 games and retailed for $25. A similar device with only ten games was released at the same time.

Jakks Pacific Namco TV Game

25 Intellivision Video Game System

As with the previous plug-and-play devices, the Intellivision games were rewritten and didn't use the actual code from the original Intellivision games. And although Robinson and his team of Blue Sky Rangers were consulted on the ports, the resulting games weren't as close to the originals as many retro gamers would have liked. Mattel had always touted that the graphics and sound of its games were superior to those on the Atari 2600. But most of the games on the Intellivision device didn't duplicate the correct sound, and many of them lacked sound altogether. And the device lacked two-player support, so many of the games had to be retooled for single-player play only. Also, because the games lacked the original controller, with its disc pad and multitude of buttons and game-specific overlays, many had to be reconfigured to accept instructions from a D-pad and analog stick that looked like they were modeled after the ones on the N64 controller.

Still, many people liked the idea of playing old favorites like *Astrosmash* and *Space Armada*. In the end, more copies of the Intellivision plug-and-play had been sold by Techno Source than the number of original Intellivision consoles that had been sold during the console's lifespan.

Console Retirement

On September 25, just two months before Nintendo released the iQue Player, Nintendo of Japan quietly discontinued manufacturing the Famicom, the company's first programmable console, and the Super Famicom. Although Nintendo of America had discontinued the NES in 1995, the market for the Famicom as a low-end gaming machine remained in Japan. At the time of its retirement, the Famicom had been in constant production for just about 20 years, making it the world's longest-running videogame console.

The retirement of the Famicom and Super Famicom removed two consoles from a marketplace that was already very crowded, with several manufacturers vying after the consumers' dollars. Beginning on February 9, Nintendo of America offered one of the following titles free with the purchase of a $150 GameCube: *Metroid Prime, Star Fox Adventures, Mario Party 4* or *Resident Evil*. On the same day, the price of a bundled pack that included a GameCube console, a copy of *Super Mario Sunshine* and a memory card, dropped $30 to $160. Finally, the retail prices of *Luigi's Mansion, Super Smash Bros. Melee* and several other GameCube titles were each reduced from $49.95 to $29.95. According to George Harrison, Nintendo of America's senior vice president of marketing and corporate communications, "For less than $150, players will find a world of quality only available with Nintendo."

Microsoft and SCEA didn't respond immediately to this latest attack from Nintendo. However, at a pre-E^3 press conference on May 13, SCEA fired its shots by announcing that its retailers would be reducing the price of their existing PS2 stock to $179, in order to clear out their inventories. The company then released its new $199 PS2 model with the built-in infrared receiver in June. This price also included the network adapter that SCEA had been selling for $40. Microsoft quickly responded by lowering the price of the Xbox to $179 and keeping it there. SCE matched that price in Japan on November 13, when it lowered the price of the PS2 to ¥19,800 ($180).

Nintendo of Japan initiated a different program to reward its customers (and to ensure that they continued to purchase Nintendo products) On October 31, the company set up *Club Nintendo.* Customers who bought Nintendo hardware or Nintendo-published software, could register a special activation number that was included with the product. They would earn points for each product purchased. After they accumulated enough points, they could cash them in for a number of Nintendo products including downloadable games and exclusive games and controllers.[9]

As 2003 came to an end, people looked forward to what the following year would bring. Although Microsoft and SCE were leaking information about their forthcoming Xbox 2 and PS3, neither company had ever mentioned that its new system would be available in 2004. But there were other videogames products that had been announced. SCE had assured that its new handheld PSP would take on the GBA and that Americans would finally be able to purchase the long-awaited hard drive for their PS2s. Infinium Labs promised that ita Phantom console would finally make an appearance, and perhaps be available for sale altogether. And Microsoft announced that *Halo 2* would finally arrive! It appeared that most of the companies, with the exception of Nintendo, were anxious to reveal what the following year had in store. Only time would tell.

CHAPTER THIRTY-TWO
2004

SCE had teased the public with glimpses of the PSP, its forthcoming handheld, throughout much of 2003. Surprisingly, this constant promotion didn't continue into 2004. But while the promise of a new handheld was thrown to the public, it didn't come from SCE. Instead, it came from Nintendo, which began leaking information about a new handheld that would come out on the heels of the GBA SP. These rumors came directly out of left field, because most people had been expecting a new console from Nintendo, not a handheld.

Initially, all Nintendo disclosed about the device was that it would unofficially be called the Nintendo DS and that it would feature two 3-inch, backlit, LCD screens. A soccer game was presented as an example of how the dual screens might be used. While one screen might display an overview shot of the soccer field, the other might display a close-up of the action.

Nintendo didn't provide any pricing for the device, but revealed that it would be available by the end of the year and that it wouldn't compete with the GBA or GBA SP, which were still selling briskly. In fact, during the GBA SP's first anniversary on the market in late March, Nintendo proudly announced that it had sold 6.5 million of the handheld consoles in North America alone. This was a new sales record for any gaming console in the history of the industry. Nintendo didn't state whether or not the DS would be compatible with the earlier Game Boy software.

The Nintendo DS

Prior to E^3 in mid-May, more about the DS had been revealed, including the look of the console itself. Like the GBA SP, the device was hinged so the top folded over the bottom when it wasn't in use. And like the GBA, the configuration of the console was horizontal instead of vertical. Each half of the console, the upper and the lower, featured one of the 3-inch LCD screens. The bottom half also featured a D-pad to the left of its screen, and control buttons on the right. The device looked very much like the Multi Screen Game & Watches.

The DS made its first appearance at E^3. Although each of its two screens had its own processor, the two ran in tandem with each other. The screens could display information individually, or they could form one larger screen, if that was required by the software. In addition, the bottom screen would also be a touchscreen that would respond to a stylus that would be packaged with the unit. The top screen would not react to the stylus.

The displayed DS also had two cartridge slots. One accepted *Nintendo Game Cards* that resembled small SD cards and could store up to one gigabit of data. The other slot accepted GBA cartridges. The dual screens only worked with the DS-specific software, and the display for the GBA games only appeared on one screen. However, the player could select which screen the game would appear on. Also compatible between the DS and GBA SP was the power cord needed to charge the batteries, which were estimated to last around ten hours. And because the DS used standard headphones, the headphones could be

Nintendo DS Game Card

used while the device was charging.[1]

The DS would have built-in wireless and messaging capabilities. A proprietary connection would allow up to 16 consoles within a radius of about 100 feet to be linked together. And for greater distances, Wi-Fi would take over. Multiplayer games would be accomplished in one of two ways. In some cases, only one game card would be needed and other local DS devices (within 65 feet) could download the needed device from the console that had the Game Card. In other cases, each console would require its own Game Card.

The DS would also have a built-in microphone, which Nintendo said would be used in voice-recognition games like the GameCube's *Hey You, Pikachu!*. It would also be used so people could chat online with other players. The DS on display at E[3] also featured a port that Nintendo didn't discuss, but which industry analysts speculated would be used to connect a headset to the DS. This port was next to a standard headphone jack. But gamers wouldn't need headphones to hear the sounds from the console in full stereo, since the DS had two speakers that played in stereo as well.

Nintendo DS

Online preorders for the DS were only accepted on November 3 in North America, where the price was $150, and in Japan, where it retailed for ¥15,000 ($146). The preorders were only for one day, because all of the online stores outsold their allotments, which had totaled three million units. Nintendo had only planned to have one million handhelds available when the DS launched, so it had to increase its production so enough units would be available for sale in stores, in addition to the number that had already been preordered.

The DS became available on November 21 in North America, marking the first time that Nintendo launched a new product in a country other than Japan. This was done so the new handheld would be available on Black Friday, the day after Thanksgiving, which was customarily the busiest shopping day of the year in the United States. During its first week Nintendo sold 500,000 units, which were packaged with a demo copy of *Metroid Prime Hunters*, and included a built-in application called *PicToChat*, which showed off the wireless capabilities of the DS. Gamers could chat with other DS owners by writing messages on the lower screen with the stylus, and receiving responses on the upper screen.[2] Eleven games were also available within one month of the launch, including *Super Mario 64 DS*.

The DS was released in Japan two weeks later on December 2, along with twelve launch titles. Nintendo of Japan sold 500,000 consoles within four days of its release.

Majesco Advances

Although the DS was backward-compatible with the GBA software, it couldn't accept cartridges from the original Game Boy or Game Boy Color. In fact, the DS wasn't officially a Game Boy. It was a new, completely different handheld that just happened to play GBA games. And while the DS could double as a GBA player, it couldn't play many GBA games to their fullest potential. Multiplayer GBA games, which required the use of the link cable, could not be played on the DS, since the new console lacked a port that the cable could plug into.

On January 29, before the release of the DS, Nintendo of Japan released *Pocket Monsters FireRed* and *Pocket Monsters LeafGreen* for the GBA. These were basically remakes of the original *Pocket Monsters Red* and *Pocket Monsters Green* games, enhanced to take advantage of the GBA's newer technology and graphics. One of the improvements was the ability for multiplay with a wireless adapter, rather than a link cable. To this end, the two ¥4,800 ($45) games were each packaged with a *GBA Wireless Adapter*, a peripheral that plugged into the external extension connector of the GBA. While these *Pocket Monsters* games could be linked with the wired link cable, the cable only allowed two players to connect at one time. The GBA Wireless Adapter allowed up to 39 players could connect in a single game. But since the GBA Wireless Adapters only had a range of about ten feet, those 39 people would have had to be packed pretty close together to take full advantage of the device.

Nintendo GBA Wireless Adapter

In Japan, the Wireless Adapter was only packaged with *Pocket Monsters FireRed* and *Pocket Monsters LeafGreen*. It could not be purchased separately. When the Adapter was released in the United States on September 7, while it was packaged with *Pokémon FireRed* and *Pokémon LeafGreen*, it could also be purchased alone from Nintendo of America's online store for $20. But no matter where the GBA Wireless Adapter was bought from, it couldn't be used as a replacement for the link cable, since it could only be used with games that were specifically designed to utilize it. This problem was resolved on October 7, when Majesco released its *Wireless Link*, a $10 wireless peripheral that completely replaced the link cable. As long as each GBA had its own attached Wireless Link, and all of the participants were in close proximity to one another, games that allowed up to four players could be played wirelessly. But although the Wireless Link replaced the link cable, it couldn't replace the GBA Wireless Adapter.

Majesco Wireless Link

Although the GBA could never replicate the DS's uniquely dual screen, it was given the ability for texting thanks to Majesco. In October, the company released its *Wireless Messenger*, a $30 peripheral that plugged into the GBA's external extension connector. Although it looked very much like Majesco's Wireless Link, it served a very different purpose. Once it was inserted into

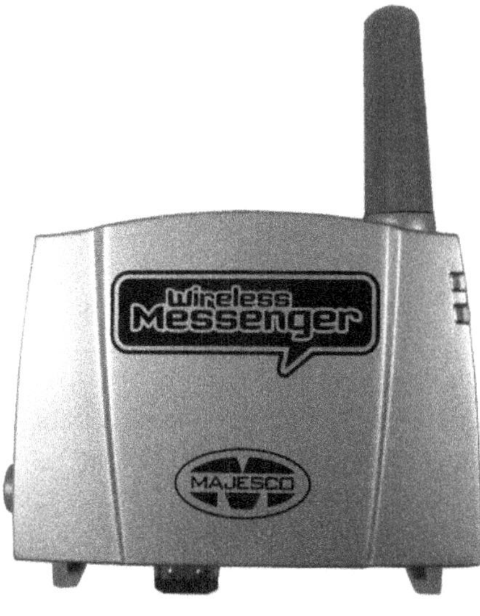

Majesco Wireless Messenger

the GBA, up to four users could send and receive text messages or chat in real time with anyone who also had the device within a three-mile radius. An on-screen virtual keyboard allowed users to draft messages by pointing and clicking with their cursors.

One of the downsides of this device was that it didn't draw power from the GBA itself. It had its own internal battery that could work for one week before it needed to be recharged. But the battery could only be recharged using a GBA AC adapter. This was fine for GBA SP owners, since that device came with its own AC adapter. However, GBA owners had to purchase an adapter, because the GBA used standard batteries and the adapter was optional.

Majesco GBA Video

The wireless devices weren't the only new items that Majesco delivered during the year. On May 1, the company introduced its *GBA Video* line, software that played live-action and animated video on the GBA. This differed from AM3's Advance Movie Adapter, because an adapter wasn't required. Each standard $20 GBA cartridge contained up to 45 minutes of full-motion video.[3] Although the quality of the videos was subpar when compared to a DVD or even broadcast versions of the same show, they were targeted towards young children who wouldn't notice the degradation.

Although the videos could be played on any handheld device that accepted GBA cartridges, they were restricted from playing on a standard television via the Game Boy Player. This was because the individual copyright holders of the various videos didn't want the GBA Videos competing with their counterparts that were already available on DVD.

The format was licensed by Nintendo to play on the GBA, and Majesco offered to license its proprietary technology to any company that wanted it. By year's end, the only company besides Majesco that offered the GBA Videos was Nintendo itself, which released episodes of the *Pokémon* TV series. However, Majesco managed to acquire lucrative videos from Nickelodeon, the Cartoon Network and the Disney Channel.

Meanwhile, AM3 abandoned its plans to export its Advance Movie Adapter outside of Japan. Instead, the company focused on providing the ability to download movie content to flash memory cards that could play on the GBA. During the summer, AM3 placed twenty *Advance Gasha-Pon* vending machines around Tokyo. These machines had one slot that accepted ¥100 (92¢) coins, and another was provided for a blank 32MB flash memory card that sold separately for ¥1,980 ($18). Beginning on August 1, customers could download one of eight cartoons that were stored in the machine onto their blank flash cards for ¥300 ($3).

Among the available cartoons were the first four episodes of the *Pokémon* cartoon, with the second four being made available on September 1. AM3's goal was to have the service available nationwide on October 1, with 3,000 vending machines in place by the end of the year. The long-range vision of the company was to have 10,000 machines installed by the summer of 2005 and to be able to provide additional services, such as downloadable comics, photos, maps and music that could all be played back or viewed on a GBA.

Game Boy's Competition

Nintendo's DS wasn't the only new handheld device that was released during the year. In mid-2004, South Korea-based Game Park released the *GP32 BLU*, which had a backlit screen. Other than the improved screen, the new model was the same as the prior two GP32s, and software was compatible among the three models. With the GP32 BLU, Game Park expanded its horizons and finally released a product outside of South Korea, as it became available in several European countries, including Great Britain.

Game Park GP32 BLU

Because the GP32 BLU was an open-source device, developers could program anything that could potentially play on it, including a GBA emulator. Nintendo had foreseen something like this happening so it had taken legal means to prevent GBA games from playing on devices that it didn't oversee. In January, Nintendo was granted a patent for "software implementation of a handheld videogame hardware platform," which, in theory, prevented other companies from creating software that would emulate Nintendo's games on such devices as PDAs and cell phones. Almost immediately, a Canadian company called Crimson Five was hit with a cease-and-desist notice, because it had been developing a GBA emulator for the Tapwave Zodiac.

Meanwhile, the Zodiac continued to receive accolades from the gaming press. It also achieved retail distribution in the United States when Comp-USA began selling it on June 24. And in mid-November, the console launched in Great Britain, Singapore and South Korea. Additional features were announced for the device in December. First, Tapwave issued word that a Wi-Fi SD card with an "enhanced mail application and web browser" would be available. And then Audible announced that the device would support audio books.

It seemed as if the Zodiac had everything, except people buying it. The fact that Tapwave marketed the Zodiac as a handheld gaming console that doubled as a PDA was inconsequential to most gamers, who had limited cash at their disposal. They weren't willing to spend it on an unproven console when they could use it for the forthcoming PSP or the DS. And die-hard gamers who were willing to give the Zodiac a chance, waited for more third-party developers to sign on. Although Activision, Sega, Atari and Midway all supported the console, the absence of other big publishers, such as Electronic Arts and Konami, was very noticeable. Many developers that supported the Sony and Nintendo consoles didn't feel that they needed to support a fledgling system that might or might not become profitable in the long run. Many developers simply wanted to take a wait-and-see approach. But, of course, this created a *Catch-22* situation. No matter how good a system was, it wasn't going to sell if there wasn't enough software available for it. And developers weren't going to develop for it until it proved that it could sell.

The Zodiac also had to contend with the Nokia N-Gage, another hybrid handheld game console, even though the latter hadn't received glowing raves from the gaming press. It hadn't received praise from software publishers either. John Riccitiello, the COO of Electronic Arts, told Reuters that he "knew [the N-Gage] was a dog" the moment he picked it up for the first time. After GameStop stopped selling the phone in its stores, Nokia executives admitted that the N-Gage wasn't doing as well as they had hoped. Although Nokia said that 600,000 units had been shipped to retailers, the company couldn't predict how many of that number actually were purchased by consumers. Nokia's CEO, Jorma Ollila, hoped that consumers would give the N-Gage another chance and wait at least until November for the device to prove itself.

Nokia N-Gage QD

As it turned out, Ollila had inside information that explained why he believed the public's attitude towards the N-Gage would change. On April 14, Nokia announced the *N-Gage QD* (the "QD" didn't stand for anything). Nokia apparently had listened to the complaints and addressed many of the problems that had confronted users of the original N-Gage. The new unit was 20 percent smaller, which made it easier to hold, and the speaker and microphone were moved to the face of the unit, so it could be pressed against a user's ear comfortably. And the card slot was repositioned to the outside of the unit, so game cards could easily be switched without the need to remove the batteries. And the need to actually replace the batteries would be less frequent, because the battery life was extended.

Some features from the old N-Gage were removed such as USB connectivity and the FM tuner. Nokia also didn't include the software that would allow the N-Gage QD to play MP3 files, although that feature was available for download from a third-party vendor.

The original N-Gage also had tri-band capabilities, which meant that it could operate on three GSM frequencies around the world. This feature was also removed from the N-Gage QD, and individual models could only work in either Europe and Asia or North America. In May, Nokia began shipping the European model, and followed in July with deliveries of the N-Gage QD to North America.

Less features on the device meant that its manufacturing costs were greatly reduced, with the savings passed on to consumers. The price for the U.S. N-Gage QD was $179, more than $100 less than the original N-Gage. And Cingular offered a service whereby consumers could buy an N-Gage QD with a prepaid service plan for only $99.

The release of the N-Gage QD was a good move on Nokia's part. By listening to the complaints and acting upon them, the company was able to bounce back with a device that consumers actually wanted. The company announced on September 1 that it had shipped over one million units of both versions of the N-Gage since the device's introduction less than a year earlier, with 400,000 of that number being N-Gage QDs.

Interestingly enough, Nintendo's DS was not yet available when Nokia shipped its millionth N-Gage, so that was less competition that the mobile phone company had to contend with. And it appeared that it wouldn't be competing with the PSP for a while. SCE had announced early in the year that its much-anticipated handheld console was going to be delayed outside of Japan until spring, 2005. An SCE spokesperson said the company wanted to wait until there was a "reasonable amount of software titles available at launch," although the definition of "reasonable number" was never revealed. The Japanese PSP was still targeted to be released before the end of the year.

The PSP made its official world premiere at E^3. The recessed control buttons that had been shown in the leaked photos were gone and were replaced by a layout that was very similar to the one on the PS2's controller. SCE's CEO, Kaz Hirai, stressed that the PSP wasn't going to merely be a handheld gaming console. He hinted that it would perform a host of other functions, including playing MP3s, web browsing and PDA functions. In addition, the PSP would be able to play movies, and the units on display at E^3 played a short clip from *Spider-Man 2*. And just like games, movies would be sold on the small UMDs that could store slightly more than two hours of video. The quality of the movies would be comparable to DVDs, unlike the lower-quality videos that Majesco offered for the GBA.

The PSP was again shown to the public at the Tokyo Game Show in late September, but two questions remained unanswered about the device. SCE still hadn't announced how much the new device would cost, and there was concern about the battery life, which SCE said would last between two and ten hours, depending upon the application. This worried gamers, because they felt two hours wasn't long enough, especially when the DS had been touted to last six to ten hours.

SCE finally revealed the answers to these questions on October 27, when it announced that the PSP would go on sale in Japan on December 12. The price would be ¥19,800 ($189), a surprising amount since most analysts had expected it to be in the $300 price range. Ken Kutaragi denied that the PSP's price was set at under $200 in order to compete with Nintendo's under-$150 DS. He said that since many of the PSP's parts had been manufactured by Sony itself, the savings were being passed on to consumers. Kutaragi also said that many factors came into play that affected the battery's life, but if a game was played with the screen brightness set to the maximum, the volume set to medium and played through headphones, and the wireless LAN turned off, then the batteries could be expected to last six to eight hours.

Kutaragi also stated that the PSP, like all of Nintendo's handheld consoles, would be region-free. Therefore, a console purchased in Japan would play games released in the United States. This also meant that a lot of Americans would be planning to import Japanese PSPs when the device went on sale. However, SCE was only producing 200,000 units in time for the launch, and it was believed that that number wouldn't satisfy the expected Japanese demand, let alone a probable demand from the rest of the world. An additional 200,000 units were promised to be available in early January.

SCE PSP-1000

Thousands of people lined up to purchase the PSP when it became available on December 12. The PSP was sold in two configurations. The base set, which retailed at the fore-mentioned ¥19,800, included the console, an AC adapter and a battery pack. A ¥24,800 ($236) "Value Pack" included the base set as well as headphones and a case that were also separately. Also included in the "Value Pack" was a Memory Stick Duo, which was actually a flash memory card that was roughly the size of a standard SD card. As expected, all 200,000 units sold out immediately, including 30,000 that had been ordered from outside of Japan. SCE changed its original plans and said that it would release 100,000 additional units every week throughout the remainder of the year, totaling a half-million consoles in all, the same number of DS consoles that Nintendo had made available for its launch.

Gametrac

The release of the PSP meant that two of the three major console manufacturers were also in the handheld business. Microsoft had no plans to enter the fray. However, it did become indirectly involved with a new handheld that had been shown at its CES booth in January. The device on display was the *Gametrac,* a handheld unit from Gametrac Europe, which was the European division of a Jacksonville, Florida-based company called Tiger Telematics, Inc. Microsoft displayed it because it used Microsoft's *Windows CE.Net* operating system.[4]

The Gametrac was targeted towards the teen market, and like many of the other handheld consoles that had been introduced during the year, it had the ability to play movies, music and games, including multiplayer games via Bluetooth, and receive & send text messages. But the Gametrac also had a built-in high resolution camera that separated it from the other handhelds. Yet the Gametrac's most unique aspect was that it also featured GPS technology, which could be used so parents could locate their children easily, or friends who each owned a Gametrac could find one another in large crowds. And exciting new games were being developed that would take advantage of the GPS technology. The *Gametrac* name represented the two main functions of the device: gaming and tracking.

One final aspect of the Gametrac had nothing to do with gaming. Gametrac Europe had partnered with a company called NetLight to wirelessly deliver advertising to Gametrac consoles. Gametrac Europe promoted it by explaining that a restaurant could transmit *SmartAds* to all Gametrac users within a certain distance at a certain time. As Gametrac Europe saw it, this was a win-win situation for Gametrac owners. Not only would they be saving money by taking advantage of the specials that were transmitted to them, but the ads themselves subsidized the cost of the console. However, even with the subsidized costs, the Gametrac was set to retail at £220 ($403) when it launched in Great Britain on October 29.

In late March, Gametrac Europe was sued by UK-based In2Games, which had owned the *Gametrak* name since 2000. In2Games was planning to release a new type of controller later in the year that it planned to call *Gametrak.*

Just before the Gametrac handheld console was scheduled to be displayed at E^3 in May, Gametrac Europe changed the names of both the company and the console to *Gizmondo.* As the newly named Gizmondo Europe explained, the console was "so much more than a gaming device and a GPS. Gizmondo represents the variety of features and the worldwide format that is [sic] captured under the shell of this little multi-entertainer. It's hard to describe the device in traditional words."

Tiger Gizmondo

In September, a Tiger Telematics spokesperson stated that the Gizmondo was on target to be released in Great Britain in October, followed by the rest of Europe, Australia and North America throughout 2005. The company even planned to open a retail store on London's Carnaby Street. However, after the October 29 date, neither the store nor the console was anywhere to be seen. Company officials next promised a November launch, but when that passed, the company finally conceded that the Gizmondo wouldn't be released until 2005.

Unconventional Controllers

The Gametrak controller that In2Games had developed won the top award for "Most Innovative Product" at the Games Convention held in Leipzig, Germany at the end of August. It offered precise and intuitive control for 3D games, and allowed for movement in all directions: forward/backward, left/right and up/down. Because the device was mechanical and used a system of cables, it could perform these functions without any time delay or processor overhead.

The Gametrak was released for the PS2 in Europe on October 22, bundled with a game called *Dark Wind,* which allowed players to box against on-screen opponents. Players wore fingerless gloves that were attached to the Gametrak controller, and every motion that their hands made could be viewed on the TV screen. In2Games had more ambitious ideas and formally announced the controller by stating that by using Gametrak, gamers could "physically punch opponents using boxing gloves" and that "sports games will allow users to pick up and play using real golf clubs or tennis rackets."

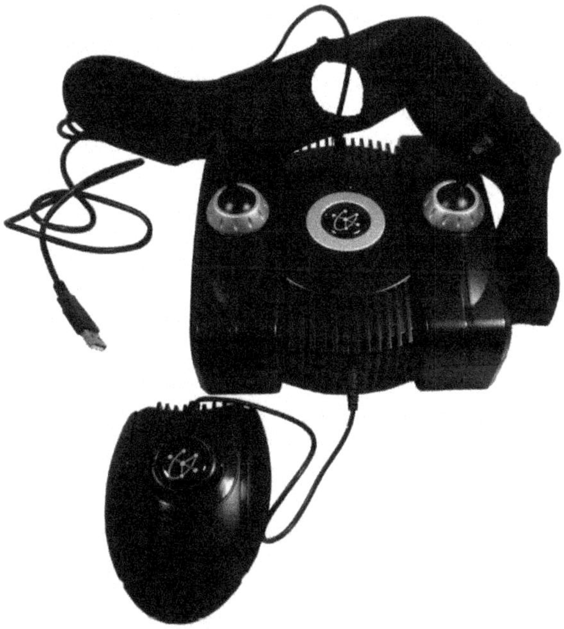

In2Games Gametrak

SCE PS2 Dark Wind

Controllers that looked like actual sports objects were nothing new. Sports Sciences had pioneered the concept in 1994 when it released baseball-bat and golf-club controllers for the SNES and Genesis. But even before In2Games could release the Gametrak controller, a new console came out that used these kinds of controllers exclusively.

The *XaviX Port* was created by SSD Company Limited (SSD), which had started in Japan in 1995 by a group of veteran videogaming engineers, many of whom had been part of Nintendo's original Famicom design team. The console was first shown at the CES in January, and in August it was released in Japan and the United States, where it carried an $80 retail price. Three games, each selling for $50, were initially available. Each game came with its own unique controller. *XaviX Baseball* was packaged with a baseball and bat, *XaviX Tennis* came with two tennis rackets, and *XaviX Bowling* was sold with a

SSD XaviX Port

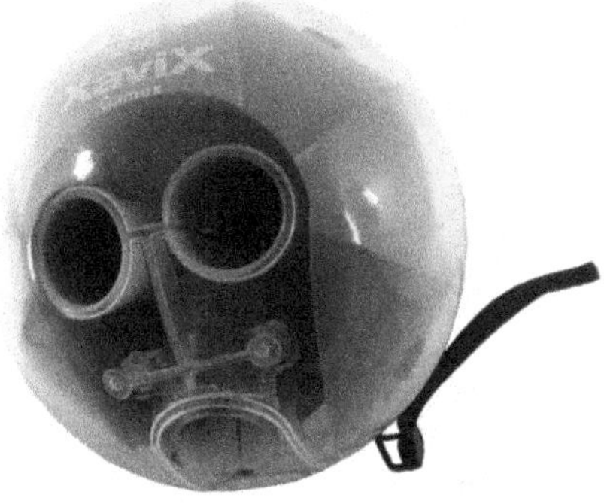

SSD XaviX Bowling Controller

bowling ball.

And while the controllers were indeed distinctive, the mechanics of the system were even more so. The wireless controllers were not connected to the console, which used optical sensors and infrared to detect the player's movements and in turn respond to the speed and direction of the player's motions.

Unlike the other consoles on the market, games for the XaviX were stored on cartridges, and each one contained its own proprietary XaviX multiprocessor. The advantage of this was that as new games were developed, they could benefit from having more sophisticated processors without the console itself requiring upgrades. This was a technique that hadn't been used since 1979, when Milton Bradley used it in the Microvision. The chips in the first three XaviX cartridges used 8-bit 6502 multiprocessors, which were the same processors that had been used in the Nintendo Famicom. And the results were evident. Critics were less than impressed with the system's graphics and sound capabilities, which they compared to the SNES and Genesis.

Despite the lesser quality graphics and sound, the critics praised the innovative controls of the XaviX. Unfortunately, this wasn't enough for the console to compete easily with the major consoles. For one, neither SSD nor the XaviX had any name recognition, especially since the console was completely devoid of a marketing campaign. And the few stores that carried it, mostly stores that didn't carry other videogame consoles, usually treated it as a novelty item.

Logitech, the company that had made the headsets for Konami that were used in *Karaoke Revolution*, announced on February 4, that it had released a new conventional microphone that could be used with that game. The $20 *USB Microphone for PlayStation 2* had a classic long-stemmed look and resembled the microphone that Microsoft had bundled with its *Xbox Music Maker*. Logitech had worked closely with Konami to create a microphone that accurately duplicated the karaoke experience and even included a 15-foot cable so that singers could move freely.

Logitech USB Microphone

SCE SingStar Microphones

On May 21, SCEE released a title for the PS2 that used controllers that looked like microphones. But that was because the controllers actually were microphones! *SingStar*[5] was a karaoke-like game for one or two people. The microphones were used so players could sing along with a music video that displayed the lyrics and the required pitch. The system analyzed each singer's pitch and compared it to the original version. It then awarded points to the singers based on how close they came to the real thing.

Subscription Gaming

With the entry of several new consoles that were not expected to compete against the major three, people wondered about the fate of the one console that had been touted as a definite contender.

In January, Infinium Labs went through a changing of the guard, and Kevin Bachus, formally of Microsoft and one of the four people who had conceived the Xbox, stepped in as President. In May, Bachus formally unveiled a working model of the Phantom at E^3. He announced that the system would be available on November 18, but he stressed that the company was selling a gaming-on-demand subscription service, rather than a console. Customers would be able to get a free console after they signed up for a two-year subscription that would cost them $30 a month.

Each month, a subscriber would be offered a set number of games that he would be able to download to the Phantom's 40GB hard drive. Additional titles would also be available for additional fees, much in the same way as the cable industry offered Movies on Demand. Bachus noted that only PC games would be available for play on the Phantom, but he was certain that this would appeal to consumers.

Infinium Labs was not the only company that thought that a console that only played PC games would be successful. A similar console had been shown earlier in the year at CES. The *ApeXtreme* (Apex Extreme) had been a joint project between consumer electronics manufacturer Apex Digital, and VIA Technologies, a developer of silicon chips. However, instead of using downloaded games, the ApeXtreme played off-the-shelf PC games. The console could accept CDs or DVDs and automatically install the games, since it had more than 2,000 installation scripts built in. Two models were expected to be launched in the spring, one retailing for $299 and the other for $399.

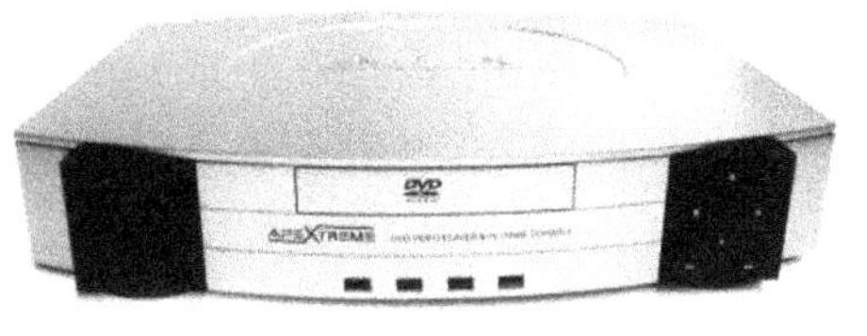

ApeXtreme

Unfortunately, neither of the two consoles was ever released. In the end, Apex decided to scrap the ApeXtreme, despite the fact that the console had been won a "*Best of CES*" award. Although people liked the idea that the system would be able to automatically install any game that had previously been released, it was unlikely that it would work with newer games that used scripts that weren't in the machine, and that would have made the ApeXtreme obsolete pretty quickly. And then there was the belief that if PC gamers wanted to play games on a console, they would simply buy a console.

In September, Infinium Labs announced that the Phantom was once again going to be delayed, this time until 2005. The company claimed that its "marketing and retail partners" had complained that the November 18 release date didn't favor their products, since the targeted consumer base for the Phantom would be purchasing gifts for other people, rather than themselves.

Another setback for the company occurred in late November, when it announced that it needed an additional $11.5 million in funding in order to manufacture and sell 10,000 consoles. After this latest holdup, most analysts agreed that in the end, the Phantom would be just as its name implied.

A New Nintendo Console?

Even if the Phantom did manage to get released, analysts wondered how it could successfully compete with the trio of consoles with brand-name recognition. As was the case with SSD and its XaviX, the Infinium Labs name meant nothing to gamers. And even a well-respected company with a well-known name and respected past didn't guarantee success in the marketplace.

Such was the case with Nintendo. Its GameCube was in third place in sales following the PS2 and Xbox. Although sales spikes had occurred whenever Nintendo lowered its price, the console could never shake the negative criticism that it constantly received for either appearing "toy-ish" or for lacking features such as DVD playback and major online support.

A few noteworthy games were released during the year for the system. *The Legend of Zelda: Four Swords Adventures*, which allowed the GBA to be used as a controller, came out during the first half of the year in both North America and Japan. This was the last GameCube game that Nintendo released that used the GBA as a controller, even though it had been a major feature that the company had touted a year earlier. However, as Nintendo forged ahead with its DS release, support for the GBA and the GameCube were no longer in the forefront. In late September, Nintendo of America released its final GameCube game that used alternative controllers, *Donkey Konga* with its unique bongo drum controllers.

Throughout the year, Nintendo had been dropping hints regarding a new console that would supersede the GameCube. Early in the year, without going into details, a Nintendo spokesperson promised that the company intended to show their new console at the 2005 E^3. At the 2004 E^3, Satoru Iwata, the company's CEO, had admitted that Nintendo was indeed working on a new console that, in his words, "would create a gaming revolution." Indeed, the codename for the new console was *Revolution*. Iwata later explained that new consoles had to do more than simply improve on the prior systems. They had to offer new play experiences as well. They had to present "something no other machine has offered before."

Xbox 2?

Microsoft was just as closed-mouthed about its new console. At the CES in January, all Microsoft Chairman Bill Gates would state about the Xbox 2 was that like Sony, they weren't going to reveal their hand. In February, M-Systems, a manufacturer of flash-memory devices, announced that it had signed a contract with Microsoft wherein it would provide high-capacity, removable storage devices for future Microsoft consoles. This led to speculation as to whether Microsoft was going to forego the little-used hard drive for its next console and replace it with a flash storage device.

Despite the hype that the Xbox had passed the GameCube in sales, the fact was that Microsoft lost money on every console that it sold. While this wasn't unusual in the industry, the Xbox didn't have a stable of must-have games from which it could make back its money. And it didn't help the company's bottom-line when it reduced the price of each unit from $179 to $149 on March 30. Although Microsoft had a gross income of $530 million for the first three months of 2003, the Xbox division ran $209 million in the red during that time. However, sales were rising, 30% higher than during the same period a year earlier. And since corporate Microsoft had $56 billion available in reserves, the company was prepared to lose even more money as it anticipated higher returns in the long run.

On the other hand, Microsoft's online service, Xbox Live, was doing very well. However, on the same day that Microsoft announced the Xbox price cut, it also said it was cancelling its entire forthcoming 2004 line of online games from XSN Sports, due to "quality issues." According to XSN Sports studio manager, Kevin Browne, the division would take a year off to "close the quality gap that [they had] in respect to the EA Sports and ESPN sports titles [from Sega]." On May 4, Microsoft released the final game that featured the XSN logo, *RalliSport Challenge 2*. This was the only game in the 2004 XSN Sports line that was actually released because it had been the only title developed by an independent studio and not XSN Sports.

On May 11, it was announced that Electronic Arts signed with Microsoft to develop online games for Xbox Live, with the first title, *NCAA Football 2005*, arriving on July 15. Naturally with Electronic Arts on board providing hit sports games for Xbox Live, there was no reason to keep XSN Sports open any longer. So on August 20, Microsoft announced the expected news that it was shutting down XSN Sports and laying off 76 employees. A studio in Utah that was responsible for the company's snowboarding and golf titles wasn't affected by the closure but but was instead sold to 2K Games in October.[6]

Microsoft Rallisport Challenge 2

On November 4, Microsoft opened *Xbox Live Arcade*. This was a digital distribution service that allowed gamers to purchase and download games to the console's hard drive. After users signed up for the service through Xbox Live, they received a startup disc in the mail that included a playable copy of *Ms. Pac-Man*. Six downloadable titles were available initially including *Namco Vantage*, a three-game collection that included the classic games *Dig Dug*, *Pole Position* and *Galaga*. By the end of the year twelve titles were available, retailing for between $5 and $15 each.

Microsoft put a lot of effort into Xbox Live. The service launched in Taiwan, Hong Kong and Singapore in April, and within six months, it was used by 12% of the Xbox owners in those regions. Microsoft announced on July 15 that the service had reached one million subscribers worldwide.

Microsoft Xbox Live Arcade

A New PS2

The success of Xbox Live didn't escape the attention of SCE. During the summer, SCE head Kaz Hirai announced that the company was leaning towards creating a central online hub for all PS2 owners, where only one login and password would be required. This was the same model that Microsoft had been using since Xbox Live began. But SCE's service would also borrow features from popular online computer games like *Half-Life* in which users could sell custom virtual properties to other online users. No date was set regarding when these new features would be available.

What did finally become available for the PS2 was the North American hard-disk drive (HDD). Released on March 23, the $100 peripheral was sold with *Final Fantasy XI* loaded on to it. *Final Fantasy XI* could not be played without the HDD, so it made good business sense to bundle the two together. And at the time of the HDD's release, *Final Fantasy XI* was the only game available that could even use the HDD. This changed a week later on March 31, when Capcom released *Resident Evil Outbreak*. Although this online game could be played without the HDD, the game installed 1GB of data onto the hard drive to reduce its loading time. The only other HDD-compatible game that came out during the year was *The Urbz: Sims in the City*, which Electronic Arts released on November 9. As with *Resident Evil Outbreak*, loading times were greatly reduced if the game detected the HDD. In addition, game data could be saved directly to the hard drive.

Despite the anticipation for it, the future of the HDD looked bleak. Without any elaboration, Kaz Hirai stated during his keynote speech at E^3 in May that SCE's engineers were seeking a non-HDD solution for the PS2. Following Microsoft's price decrease for the Xbox, SCE followed suit and reduced the price of the PS2 from $179 to a matching $149. However, while the lowered price resulted in a 216% increase in PS2 sales, HDD sales didn't increase in proportional numbers. The final death knell for the HDD came on November 3, when SCE released a new version of the PS2.

The new PS2 was significantly smaller than the original, but the size wasn't the only thing different between them.[7] The new PS2 featured a top-loading DVD player, instead of the front-loading mechanical drawer. The new PS2 also supported online gaming and had a built-in network adapter, but it didn't support the HDD. Since it had a smaller size, there was no bin that the HDD could be inserted into. Because of this, the new PS2 slim was not 100% compatible with the original, since *Final Fantasy XI* couldn't be played on it.

New SCE PS2

Although the new PS2 contained fewer parts and was therefore less expensive to manufacture, its retail price was set at $149, the same as the former unit. SCE began phasing out the original PS2 the moment the new one became available.

Meanwhile, the price of Sony's PSX, the PS2-DVR hybrid, was lowered in an effort to kick-start interest in it. Despite getting off to a great start at the end of 2003, sales for the unit began staggering after the holidays. Sony halted production of the unit in April, but resumed it again in July when the console was reintroduced with additional features at nearly half the price of the original. Plans to export the PSX outside of Japan were pushed back to 2005; Sony stated that it needed to add additional unnamed features that were specifically geared to American and European consumers.

Before Sony halted production of the PSX, rumors persisted that the features in the PSX would also appear in the PS3. However, as the PSX failed to connect with Japan consumers, those rumors came to a halt. In addition, while SCE raved about its new cell processor that could perform one trillion floating-point calculations per second, engineers within the company were unsure if the cell was capable of performing all of those calculations *and* recording television programs at the same time.

In early January, the Japanese newspaper *Asahi Shimbun* reported that the PS3 would use Sony's new high-density *Blu-ray* DVD format as its software media. Dual-layer Blu-ray discs could store up to 50GB of data, or approximately 12 times the amount that could be stored on a standard DVD. The blue laser itself could read much more information at one time than the standard red lasers that were common. And with this combination of high storage and high access, high-definition games and movies would be possible.

At the annual PlayStation Meeting in July, SCE president Ken Kutaragi shocked everybody, including his own engineers, when he announced that a working PS3 prototype would be up and running at E^3 in the spring of 2005. Most people didn't expect the PS3 to make its debut until 2006. By the end of 2004, Kutaragi also announced that the PS3 would be backward-compatible with both the original PlayStation and the PS2. Other features of the PS3 were still up for speculation. It was a sure bet that the console would have a built-in online adapter, especially since the new, slim PS2 had been released with one. Whether the PS3 would include a hard drive was another story, considering the lack of support that the PS2 HDD had received and its omission from the new PS2. A price for the unit was never revealed either, leading analysts to guess that it could retail at anywhere between $300 and $500.

Law Breakers

As the world waited for the new consoles, two of the most highly anticipated games of the year were released within two weeks of each another. *Grand Theft Auto: San Andreas*, the latest installment in the *Grand Theft Auto* franchise, came out for the PS2 on October 26 in North America and a few days later in Europe and Australia. It followed the same basic play as the two previous games in the series. However, the area that characters could explore was much larger than ever before. The fictional state of San Andreas was modeled after southern California and Nevada, and included three large cities. The game received much acclaim, and many critics declared that it was one of the best games for the PS2. *IGN* and *GameSpot* both awarded it their coveted PS2 Game of the Year award, while Spike TV, during its own annual awards, named it the best game of the year for any system. The game accounted for 54% of all software sales during the 2004 fourth quarter, and by the end of the year, it passed the $300-million mark in sales.

Halo 2 was released for the Xbox on November 9 in North America and two days later in Japan and Europe. In North America, Microsoft sold 2.4 million copies of the $50 game on its launch date, grossing $125 million. This set the record for the most revenue of any entertainment product, including blockbuster movies, during a 24-hour period. And with a total of 3.3 million copies sold during its first month, *Halo 2* became the top-selling videogame for any system during that period. *Halo 2* also accounted for much of the success of Xbox Live, as many people signed on to the service to see previews of the game before it was released, and to partake in multiplayer games after its release.

But some people couldn't wait until the actual release dates for these games. In mid-October, in separate cases, copies of both games were leaked over the Internet. While the perpetrators of these piracies weren't caught, one game pirate in the United States wasn't as fortunate. In February, Sean Michael Breen, who had been distributing illegal software since the 1990s, pleaded guilty to several counts of copyright infringement and mail fraud. In addition to having to pay back close to $700,000 in restitution, he was also sentenced to 50 months in prison, followed by three years of supervised release. Breen, and nearly forty others, had pretended to be game reviewers in order to obtain advance copies of the games.

Other cases regarding copyright infringement occurred in Europe. In December 2003, an Italian court had issued search-and-seizure warrants to companies that purchased PS2 consoles that had been modified with chips that permitted unauthorized uses of the console. The court sided with these companies in January, on the grounds that the "modified chips are not primarily intended to circumvent copyright-protection measures." In this case, the court found that the modified chips were not used so the console could play bootleg games. Instead, they had been used so gamers could play legally imported games and create back-up copies of games.

While Italian laws let consumers to back-up copyrighted material for their own personal use, British law did not permit this. In July, a British court ruled against David Ball for selling modified chips that would allow consumers to circumvent the PS2's copyright protection. So even though the chips could be used to play legally imported copies of games, Ball was found guilty, because the chips allowed gamers to play illegally backed-up games and pirated games.

In the United States, the debate continued over whether the right to play videogames was covered under the First Amendment. Like several other states, Washington had a law that banned consumers under the age of 18 from buying games that displayed violence against police officers. Retailers faced a $500 fine for breaking the law. The state believed that the violence against police officers in games transformed into violence in real life, and that such games should fall under the state's obscenity law. Judge Robert Lasnik argued that there wasn't any proof to substantiate the argument that fictional violence resulted in real-life violence. On July 21, Judge Lasnik declared Washington's law banning violent games unconstitutional under the First Amendment.

But a game didn't have to be violent in order to be banned. On August 31, Gathering, a Texas-based publisher that was owned by Take-Two Interactive, released *The Guy Game* for the PS2 and the Xbox. Basically, this was a party game for one or more players. In the single-player mode, the player was presented with a trivia question and four responses. If the correct answer was selected, the player was awarded points and then shown a full-motion video of a "hottie," a college girl in a bikini on Spring Break, being asked the same question. The player had to then decide whether the girl would provide the same answer to the question as he had. If the girl answered different, she removed her bikini top and revealed her breasts. However, whether the player could see them depended upon a Flash-O-Meter. At level 1, its initial setting, the *Guy Game* logo covered the girl's exposed breasts, so the player couldn't actually see them. At level 2, her breasts were pixilated. They were completely exposed when the Flash-O-Meter was set to level 3. The level on the Flash-O-Meter advanced when the player correctly predicted how the girl would answer the question.

Gathering The Guy Game

Gathering made no pretensions about *The Guy Game* simply being a lewd party game on the level of Acclaim's *BMX XXX*. The game might have fallen completely into obscurity if one of the sixty girls shown in the game hadn't come forward in December and admitted that she had only been 17 years old when her topless scenes had been recorded. This disclosure pushed the harmless game into the realm of illegal child pornography, and it was quickly ordered off the market.

The Guy Game wasn't the only game from a Take-Two Interactive subsidiary to be banned. *Manhunt*, a game released by Rockstar for the PS2 in 2003, became controversial for the way players had to execute their enemies. There were three levels of executions, each one bloodier than the one before it. On July 28, a British 17-year-old who was obsessed with the game killed a 14-year old friend. Although the courts placed the blame solely on the killer, citing the motive as a drug-related robbery, several British retailers voluntarily stopped selling the game. It was banned by law in other countries. On February 3, in Ontario, Canada, *Manhunt* became the first videogame ever to be restricted to adults. Australia initially classified the game so that it could only be purchased by individuals aged 15 years and older. After the British killing, the Australian Classification Board refused to rate *Manhunt* altogether, and on September 28 it became banned in that country.

Despite the complaints about it, *BMX XXX* had never been ordered off the market. However, it did begin a downhill spiral of poor games with equally poor sales for Acclaim, which eventually shut down on August 27 after 17 years in business. When the company filed for Chapter 7 bankruptcy four days later, it was revealed that although Acclaim had nearly $50 million in assets, it also had $100 million in debts.

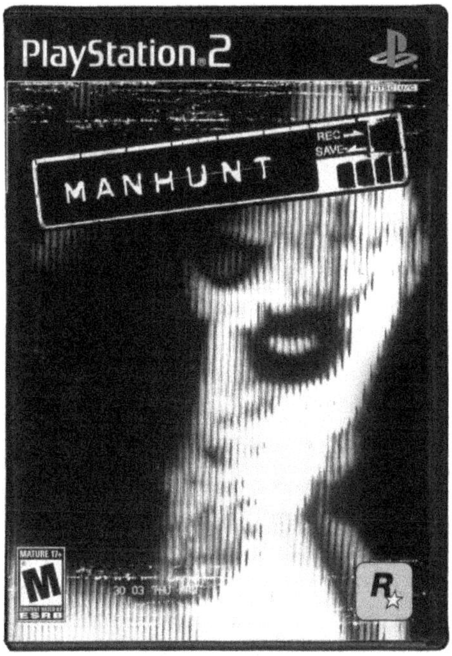

Rockstar Manhunt

Sega almost ended as a business in 2003, when it agreed to merge with Sammy. After the merger did not go through, Sammy purchased a majority of Sega stock. Instead of the former taking over the latter, a holding company, *Sega Sammy Holdings*, was established on October 1. Afterwards, the two companies retained their separate corporate identifies, with the only difference being that Sega's arcade division assumed all of Sammy's arcade enterprises, with the exception of Sammy's core Pachinko/Pachislot business, which accounted for up to 80% of the new company's total revenue. Sega's consumer division continued to develop and publish games for a variety of systems.

Before the holding company was established, Sega of Japan had one bittersweet release. *Puyo Puyo Fever* was a puzzle game that was released for a multitude of consoles in several regions around the world. In North America, Sega of America published only a GameCube version while Atlus published one for the DS. Sega Europe published it for the GameCube, PS2 and Xbox while THQ released a European GBA version. In Japan, Sega of Japan was the sole publisher of the game for all of the major consoles, with the PS2 edition coming out first on February 4. Twenty days later, on February 24, Sega of Japan released *Puyo Puyo Fever* for the Dreamcast. It marked Sega's final act as a first-party publisher. All the games that it published afterwards would be for other companies' consoles.

Sega Puyo Puyo Fever

Children's Consoles

Some console manufacturers didn't have to worry about negative press generated by violent or vulgar games that were produced for their systems. These were the companies that made educational videogame consoles for young children. Several such systems were released during the year.

LeapFrog released a new version of its popular Leapster. The *Leapster L-Max* was essentially the same as the Leapster, but it had an additional feature that allowed it to be connected to a television set. Thus, games could be played on either the small or large screen.

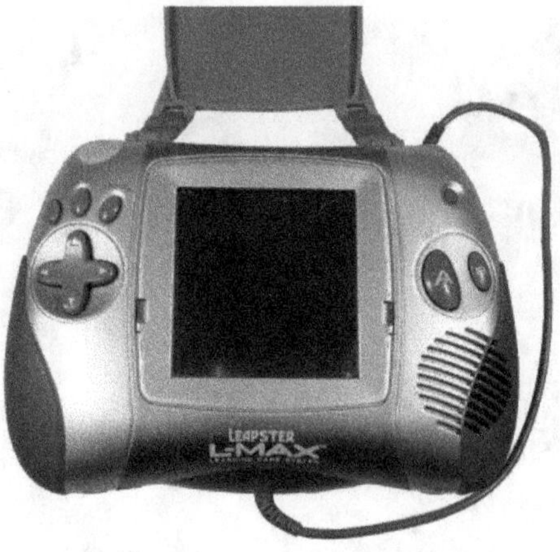

LeapFrog Leapster L-Max

VTech, which in 1983 had released the Variety, a little-known handheld, decided to enter the lucrative educational market. In 2004, it released the *V.Smile,* a console for children between the ages of 3 and 9 that connected directly to a TV. Its appearance slightly resembled an N64 and it accepted software stored on cartridges that VTech called *Smartridges*.

The controller for the V.Smile was laid out horizontally, with two circular parts, joined to resemble a sideways 8. One side contained a large, multidirectional analog joystick, while the opposite side had a large button in its center and four colored, jewel-like buttons above it. Below these were three additional buttons: a *"Learning Zone"* button that would instantly bring the player to a minigame, an exit button and a help button. The entire base could be rotated to make the controller easily used by both right- and left-handed children. The console could accept two controllers, although only one was packaged with the unit. A plastic blue cover at the top of the unit opened up and revealed a storage area for cartridges.

VTech V.Smile

VTech V.Smile Controller

The graphics of the V.Smile games were sprite-based (two-dimensional), and therefore weren't anywhere near as advanced as those that could be found on the popular consoles. But the intended audience of young children wouldn't be turned off by such a display.

VTech also released a handheld version of its V.Smile console that competed directly against LeapFrog's Leapster. The $90 *V.Smile Pocket* could play all of the software designed for the V.Smile console on a 3.5 inch built-in LCD screen. The handheld unit also emulated features found on the V.Smile console right down to its four colorful jewel-like buttons. The pocket unit also allowed for its controls to be swapped so they could be used easily by both right- and left-handed players. The V.Smile Pocket featured a blue ENTER button on one side and a blue controller pad on the other. When a switch on the underside of the unit was toggled, the blue button would flip into the unit and an orange pad appeared in its place. On the opposite side the blue pad flipped to reveal an orange ENTER button. Finally, like the Leapster L-Max, the V.Smile Pocket could connect directly to a television so games could be played on the TV. Despite this, the V.Smile Pocket wasn't a complete replacement for the V.Smile console as it didn't have the capabilities to add a second controller. Due to this, only one-player games could be played on the handheld

VTech V.Smile Pocket

unit.

The third new kid's system was Fisher-Price's $85 *Pixter Color*. This device was slightly wider than the previous versions of the handheld and featured a screen that displayed 128 different colors. Pixter Color cartridges couldn't be used in the older monochrome Pixters, but the monochrome cartridges could be inserted into the Pixter Color with the help of an adapter cartridge. However, the images from these cartridges would display in black and white on the Pixter Color. The latter did not have a port for the lamp to plug into, but it did have a headphone plug. One of the cartridges that was available for the Pixter Color was a digital camera. Kids could take and save up to ten photos, which they could then alter with the drawing tools that were built into the device.

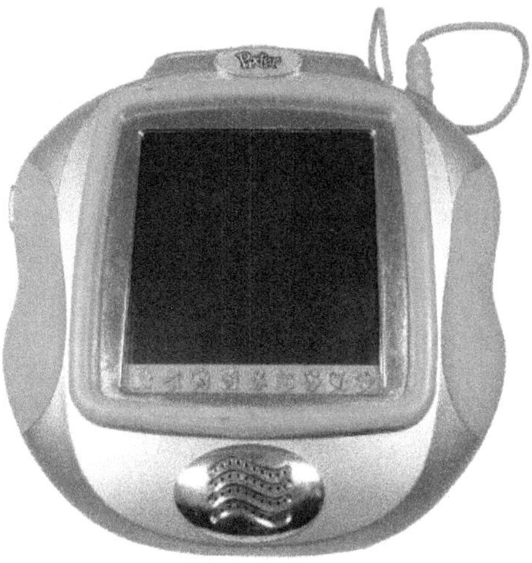

Fisher-Price Pixter Color

Fisher-Price also introduced *Pocket Pixters*. This was a line of $14 mini-Pixter units that were small enough to fit in a pocket. Each unit was self-contained and didn't accept cartridges. Despite their small size, each unit hosted a myriad of activities including "freestyle drawing" in which kids drew pictures from scratch, and "scene starters", where the picture has already been started and kids could add to it. The Pocket Pixter also contained a game, which varied by the unit.

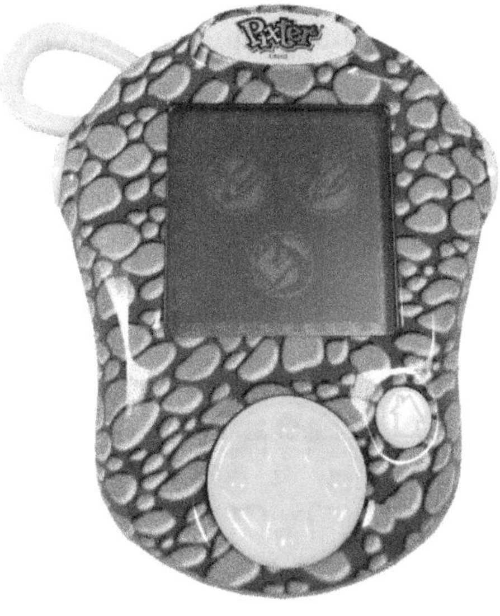

Fisher-Price Pocket Pixter

Retro Gaming Systems

The simple graphic of the educational systems were reminiscent of the earlier consoles from the '90s. But simpler graphics from consoles from the '80s were beginning to make a resurgence. Atari, which hadn't had its name grace a console since the Jaguar, had been discontinued in 1996, released a new type of console in time for the holiday season. The *Atari Flashback* was actually a standalone

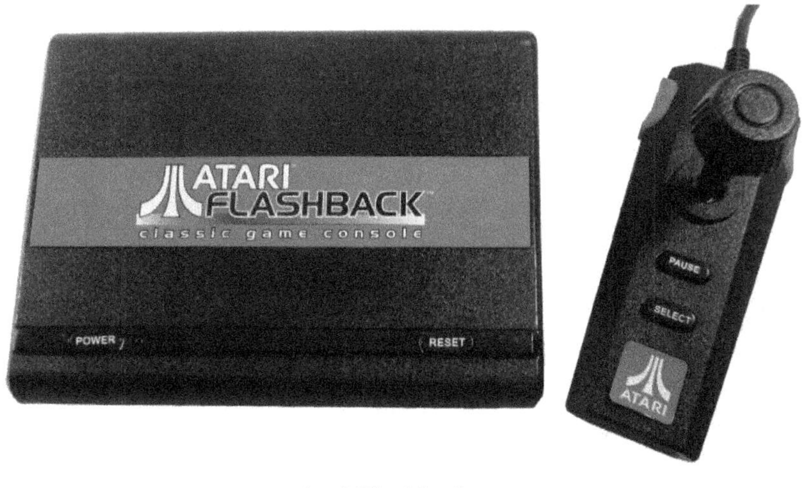

Atari Flashback

system that plugged directly into a TV using standard video cables. Similar to the Atari 10-in-1 TV Games from Jakks Pacific, the $45 Atari Flashback had 20 games built in that had originally been designed for the Atari 2600 and 7800 systems, including *Saboteur*, a 2600 game that had never been officially released. The Atari Flashback itself was styled somewhat after the 7800 console and came with two controllers that resembled the 7800's Proline controllers.

The Atari Flashback had been designed by Curt Vendel, who was the founder and curator of an online website called the *Atari Museum*, which archived Atari's history from its beginning through the Tramiel era. With his knowledge of Atari, Vendel had been hired as a consultant by Hasbro Interactive to provide documentation and expertise for the numerous Atari anthologies that had been released for the various gaming consoles and computers over the years. After Infogrames purchased Hasbro Interactive, the company continued to use Vendel as a consultant with its licensing issues, particularly with the Jakks Pacific plug-and-play devices.

For months, Vendel, an engineer by trade, had unsuccessfully tried to convince Atari to produce its own plug-and-play device. The company finally agreed to do one after a surprise impromptu presentation by Vendel. In July, after five weeks of design and technical discussions, Atari awarded a contract to Vendel's company, Legacy Engineering, to design the Atari Flashback and reprogram 20 games for it in only ten weeks, so it would be ready for sale in time for the holiday buying season. In order to meet this deadline, the system had to be based on an "NES on a chip," and its games had to be ported from the originals. The results were games with varying degrees of quality, from poor to fair. Although the general public was satisfied with the end result, many die-hard Atari fans were not.

Jakks Pacific Atari Paddle TV Games

They weren't happy with the Atari games that Jakks Pacific released with its plug-and-play controllers either, including a new one that came out in the summer. The latest addition to the TV Games plug-and-play series featured Atari 2600 games that used the paddle controller. The *Atari Paddle TV Games* system looked like two 2600 paddle controllers and plugged directly into the video input of a standard television set. Jakks Pacific also released a follow-up to its 2003 anthology, *Namco TV Games*. The new *Namco TV Games Ms. Pac-Man Collection* contained arcade versions of five more Namco games, including *Ms. Pac-Man* and *Pole Position*.

But Jakks Pacific wasn't the only company that was releasing controllers with built-in retro games. Majesco introduced its *TV Arcade* series of plug-and-play joystick devices using licensed titles from Konami. One, *Konami Collector's Series*, was an anthology of six Konami games, including *Frogger*, *Time Pilot* and *Gyruss*, in ports that had originally appeared on the NES. The arcade version of *Frogger* received the star treatment in

Jakks Pacific Ms. Pac-Man Collection

Majesco Konami Collector's Series - Frogger

Majesco's *Frogger* plug-and-play device. However, that was the only game included on the unit, even though it retailed for the same $20 as the *Konami Collector's Series*.

Old games from the '80s weren't the only ones getting the plug-and-play treatment. Some consoles from the '90s were rereleased as well. Radica, a company that made plug-and-play fishing games, released a number of plug-and-play consoles under the *Arcade Legends* label, which featured several Sega Genesis/Mega Drive games. The debut unit, which was simply called *Sega Genesis*,[8] was a $30 plug-and-play unit that had six built-in games including *Sonic the Hedgehog* and *Golden Axe*. The device itself resembled a Genesis/Mega Drive controller. Instead of plugging directly into the TV, it was attached to a secondary unit in which the batteries were kept. This unit looked like a mini Genesis/Mega Drive console. A video line ran from this to the television.

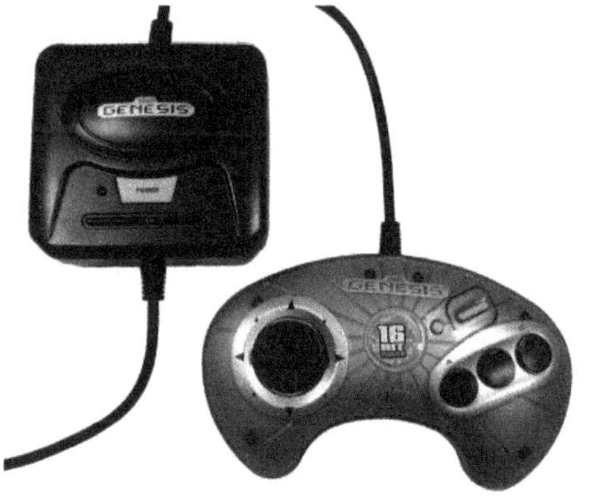

Radica Arcade Legends

Unlike other plug-and-play systems where the games had been rewritten for the new hardware, the Sega Genesis system used the original code. The only problem with this was that two of the games, *Golden Axe* and *Dr. Robotnik's Mean Bean Machine*, offered two-player variations. Unfortunately, these could not be played since the device was for one player only and there was no way to connect a second controller.

Radica's next plug-and-play unit, *Sega Genesis Volume 2*, included additional one-player Genesis games such as *Sonic the Hedgehog 2* and *Columns*. The console itself looked exactly like the original Sega Genesis plug-and-play unit. Radica also introduced a two-player system to its Arcade Legends series. *Street Fighter II* consisted of two games, *Street Fighter II: Special Champion Edition* and *Ghouls'n Ghosts*. In order for two players to compete simultaneously this unit consisted of two Genesis controllers that were both connected to the separate Genesis console battery compartment.

Radica also introduced two additional non-Sega-related plug-and-play devices to its Arcade Legends series. *Space Invaders* contained several Taito games, including *Space*

Radica Tetris

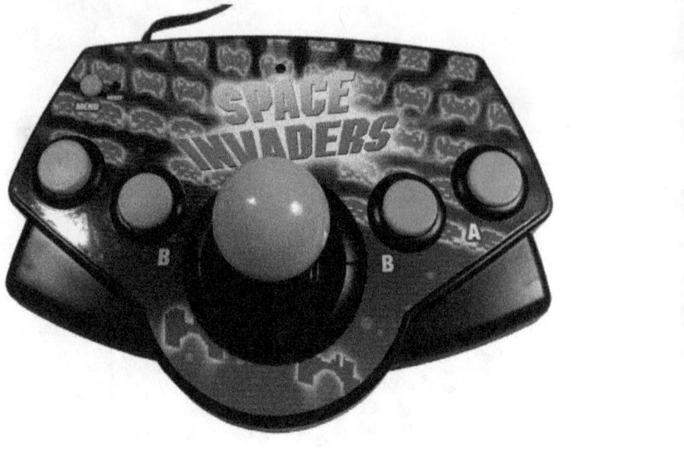

Radica Space Invaders

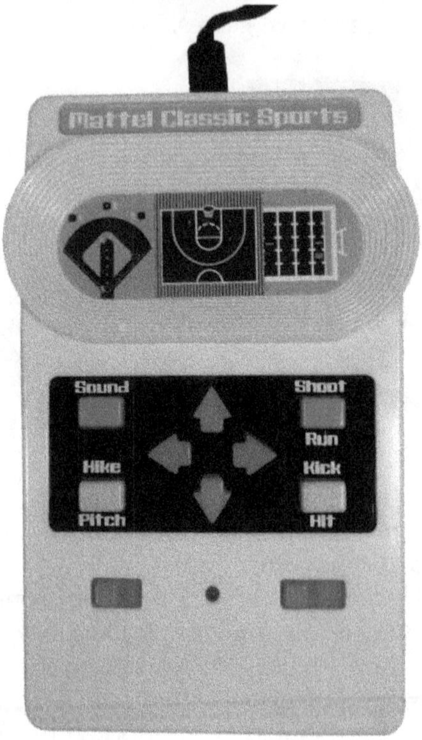

Mattel Classic Sports

Invaders, *Qix* and *Phoenix*. The $25 unit had the feel of the top of an arcade machine, with a large joystick in its center and two bright orange buttons on each side. The other entry in the series was *Tetris*, which consisted of two hand controllers that looked like the blocks that fell in the game.

Mattel released a plug-and-play device that resembled the company's old groundbreaking electronic-sports handhelds that had been released in 1977 and rereleased in 2000. *Classic Sports* looked almost like the original handheld device, but it included composite video cables that plugged directly into a TV. In place of the screen where the action took place were images of a baseball, basketball and football game, the three games that were built in. These games actually played through the TV, on which the players were represented as red blocks, to simulate the red LEDs that had been used on the original handhelds.

Even computer games got the plug-and-play treatment. In late 2004, a company called Mammoth Toys released a joystick controller called the *C64 Direct-to-TV (C64DTV)*. The device, which had been designed by Jerri Ellsworth, a self-taught computer chip designer, contained 30 games that had originally been available for play on Commodore 64 computers. Tulip Computers, the company that had purchased the Commodore name in 1997, had nothing to do with the device, with the exception of licensing the rights to the Commodore name. QVC purchased 250,000 units upon its release and sold 70,000 of them on the first day that they were offered.

In addition to the Atari Flashback, Atari released an anthology of 2600 and arcade games that could be played on the PS2 or the Xbox. *Atari Anthology* went on sale on November 16 and featured 85 games.

Retro collections had been released for modern systems since 1996, when *Arcade's Greatest Hits* was released for a number of consoles and *Arcade Classics* was released for the Game Gear and Genesis. Over the years, several fanzines (fan magazines), including Chris Cavanaugh's *Classic Gamer Magazine*, and Joe Santulli's *Digital Press*, covered older classic games within their pages. Meanwhile, a few of the prozines (professional magazines), such as *Game Informer* and *Games™*, included sections about classic games in the back of each issue. In January, a magazine was launched that was totally dedicated to classic videogames. The magazine, *Retro Gamer*, was put out by a British company, Live Publishing. Issued quarterly, each edition was printed on slick, full-color, high-quality paper. The magazine profiled retro games and current remakes of retro titles, as well as the people and the companies that had roles in videogame and computer-gaming history. Each magazine was accompanied by a CD that contained remakes of popular retro games.

C64 Direct-to-TV

Ironically, as interest in retro games increased, the only magazine that had survived since the original retro era, ran out of lives. *C&VG*, which had been the first videogame-related magazine when it came out in November 1981, two weeks before the influential *Electronic Games*, finally reached the end of the line. The magazine had been purchased by Future Publishing, the publisher of *Edge*, who ceased publishing the print edition with the October edition. From that that time on, the magazine existed only as a website.

The fanzines that had supported the retro movement long before it became popular were magazines that were written and produced by ordinary people, usually teens, who expected little in compensation from their works. As the Internet became more popular, many of these novice writers and publishers moved their publications online, where fan sites took the place that the fanzines once occupied. One such site was *loonygames.com* which, in August 1998, had been started by Jason Bergman as "a site with no news page, no previews and reviews without scores."

From its inception, the site contained a webcomic called *Penny Arcade*, which focused on videogames and their culture. The comic, written by Jerry Holkins and illustrated by Mike Krahulik, became an instant success and eventually had a fan base of over three million.

In 2004, the pair behind *Penny Arcade* decided to start a two-day festival dedicated solely to videogaming. The result was *PAX* (Penny Arcade Expo), which was held in Bellevue, Washington on August 28 and 29. The festival attracted 4,500 attendees and featured an opening keynote address, multiple gaming discussions, exhibitors comprised of both small independent stores & large game publishers and even music concerts inspired by game culture. The festival was a complete success, and plans began to make it an annual event.

One thing that the fans who attended PAX couldn't wait for was a new gaming console after several years without one. As 2004 came to a close, their wait would soon be over.

CHAPTER THIRTY-THREE
2005

The popularity of the plug-and-play devices that connected directly with television sets was soaring. Jakks Pacific, which had released dozens of the devices that had both licensed and original titles built into them, was the undisputed leader of the plug-and-play systems. In March, the company released its first wireless plug-and-play controller.

The *Ms. Pac-Man Wireless TV Games* controller did not plug directly into the TV. Instead, it was sold with a base that plugged into a TV. The controller and base could receive and send signals with each other for a distance of up to 25 feet. The controller, which featured the same games that were built into Jakks Pacific's original *Ms. Pac-Man* controller, also had two additional games, *New Rally-X* and *Bosconian.*

Jakks Pacific
Ms. Pac-Man Wireless TV Games

The new controller also corrected some minor problems that had troubled users of the original unit. One was the awkward use of the joystick in *Pole Position*. Many people instinctively believed that the joystick needed to be pressed to the left or right in order to steer the car. In actuality, the joystick had to be twisted. This was made very clear to users of the new wireless unit. Also, a four-way notch plate was set into the new controller to allow for more precise control in *Ms. Pac-Man*.

Jakks Pacific released a third version of the *Ms. Pac-Man* controller in the fall. This newest model was very similar to the original model, as it wasn't wireless and it didn't include the *New Rally-X* and *Bosconian* games. But it did have a new feature called a *Gamekey*. A Gamekey, which was sold separately for $10, was basically a ROM cartridge that plugged into specific Jakks Pacific plug-and-play devices and added additional games that weren't built into the base unit. Although Jakks Pacific introduced several devices that featured Gamekey slots, Gamekeys made for one device couldn't be used in another. Thus, a Gamekey that was available for Jakks Pacific's *Spider-Man* controller couldn't be used with the *Namco TV Games Ms. Pac-Man Collection*. Gamekeys also had the added ability to store high scores.

Jakks Pacific Gamekey

Jakks Pacific offered two Gamekeys for the newly released *Namco TV Games Ms. Pac-Man Collection*. One featured *Dig Dug* and *New Rally-X*, and the other included *Pac-Man*, *Rally-X* and *Bosconian*.

The Gamekey concept wasn't successful[1] but the Gamekey's failure didn't prevent other companies from releasing programmable plug-and-play devices, even though they may not have marketed them as such.

Atari released the *Atari Flashback 2* on July 24. Similar to the Atari Flashback that had been

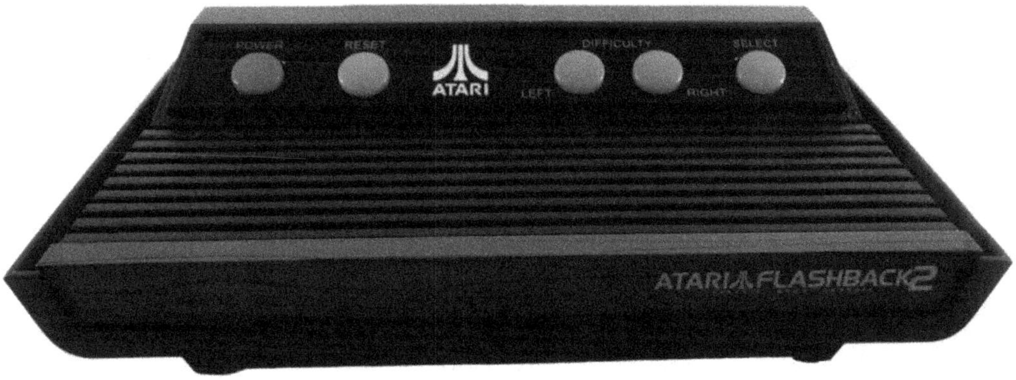

Atari Flashback 2

released a year earlier, the Atari Flashback 2 had 40 built-in games, including several hacks and prototypes, and even two of Activision's best-known games, *Pitfall!* and *River Raid*. Like the original, the Atari Flashback 2 had been designed by Curt Vendel, who had sought to create a unit that could be enjoyed by Atari devotees as well as general consumers.

The console itself resembled an original wood-grained Atari VCS, although it was on a much smaller scale and the game-select switches were replaced by large round buttons. The two joystick controllers that came with the unit looked like smaller versions of the original VCS controllers. But the system was also completely compatible with the original VCS controllers. This was essential, since the Atari Flashback 2 had several paddle games built-in but didn't come with a paddle controller.

The Atari Flashback 2 had been built around a single chip that Vendel had designed, which reproduced the circuitry of the original VCS. The results were games that looked and played exactly as they did on the original VCS. And if anyone actually wanted to play the original games, that could be done as well, although a little preparation needed to be completed first.

Although Atari didn't publicize it, the Atari Flashback 2 could be modified to accept actual VCS cartridges. Vendel published a step-by-step guide on his website, which showed how to open the unit and install a cartridge port. Of course, if it was done wrong, it would nullify the console's warranty. But since the Atari Flashback 2 only retailed for $30, many Atari die-hards were willing to try it.

With Intellivision and 2600 plug-and-play devices available, it was only a matter time before Coleco aficionados yearned for a ColecoVision plug-and-play unit. And it appeared as if they would get their wish, as the Coleco brand-name had been revived. River West Brands, a company that bought old unused brand-names, had purchased the Coleco name in 2002. They then licensed the Coleco brand-name to Techno Source, the company that had released the Intellivision plug-and-play devices in 2003. Techno Source released several handheld and plug-and-play devices under the Coleco name, but they weren't what old-time Coleco players were waiting for.

One plug-and-play unit, the *Coleco Video Game System*, featured six built-in, one-player sports games, including baseball and basketball. Oddly, none of the games on the plug-and-play unit resembled anything that the original Coleco had ever sold. This was because River West Brands only owned the rights to the Coleco

Techno Source Coleco Video Game System

Techno Source
Coleco Head-To-Head Video Game System

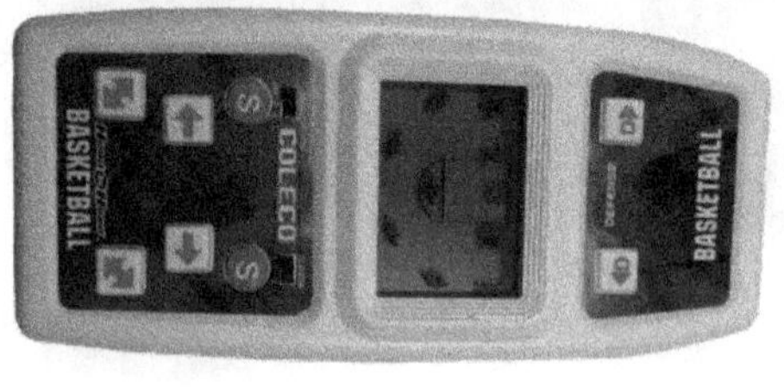

Techno Source Coleco Head-To-Head

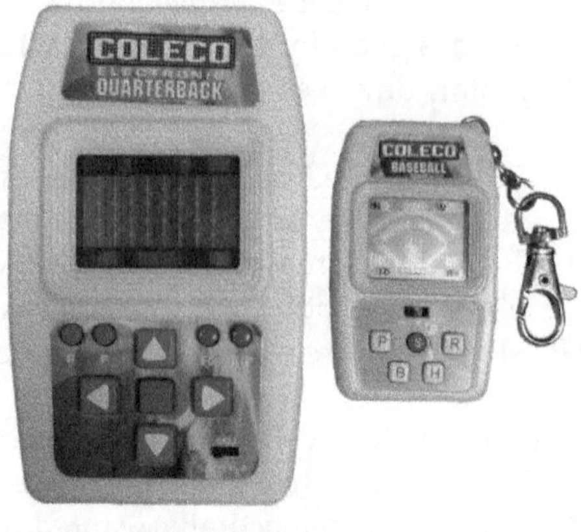

Techno Source Coleco Electronic Sports

name. Hasbro owned all of the non-licensed games that had been released by the original Coleco. Despite this, River West Brands' founder, Paul Earle Jr., hinted that his company was working on a new version of the ColecoVision.

Techno Source also marketed a second plug-and-play set that had twelve games. They were built into two identical units that were daisy-chained together to allow for two-player competition. The two devices were packaged together and called *Head-to-Head* after Coleco's old line of Head-to-Head handheld units, even though they didn't follow the distinctive style of the original Head-to-Head units, which had controls for both players on opposite sides of one unit.

But Techno Source did also revive the original Head-to-Head line of sports handhelds that did have their controls on opposite ends, with a single screen in the center. But while the hardware somewhat resembled the original 1977 Head-to-Head units, the games themselves were not the same at all. One main difference was that the LEDs that had been so memorable in the original games were replaced by LCDs. Techno Source also released the Head-to-Head sports games individually under the Coleco brand name as single-player handhelds with only one set of controls apiece. Two models of each sport were released, one in a standard-sized handheld format and the other as a miniature unit with an attached keychain.

Meanwhile Radica released several more plug-and-play Genesis/Mega Drive units to its Arcade Legends series. *Super Sonic Gold* was very similar to the previous Sega Genesis/Mega Drive collections as it contained four games housed in a Genesis/Mega Drive-type controller. However, three of the games, *Sonic the Hedgehog*, *Sonic the Hedgehog 2* and *Dr. Robotnik's Mean Bean Machine*, had already appeared on the two earlier consoles. Only *Sonic Spinball* was new to any of the Radica plug-and-play collections. An additional unit was sold only in the United Kingdom. *Sensible Soccer Plus* was a collection of three games, including *Sensible Soccer*. As this was a collection of two-player games, the console consisted of two Mega Drive controllers that linked together to a Mega Drive battery compartment, similar to Radica's *Street Fighter II*.

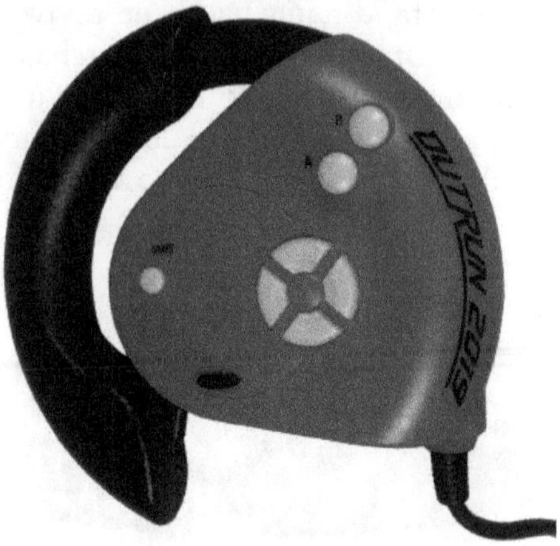

Radica Outrun 2019

The two remaining Radica consoles that were released during the year were completely different from those that preceded them. *Outrun 2019* was a single game that was housed in a controller that resembled a steering wheel. Finally, *Menacer* was a collection of six games that had originally accompanied the Menacer bazooka-like peripheral that Sega had released for the Genesis/Mega Drive in 1992. The controller itself was a light gun that resembled a pistol. Unlike Radica's previous Sega Genesis/Mega Drive plug-and-plays, the batteries were inserted directly into the controller, which plugged directly into the TV's video input.

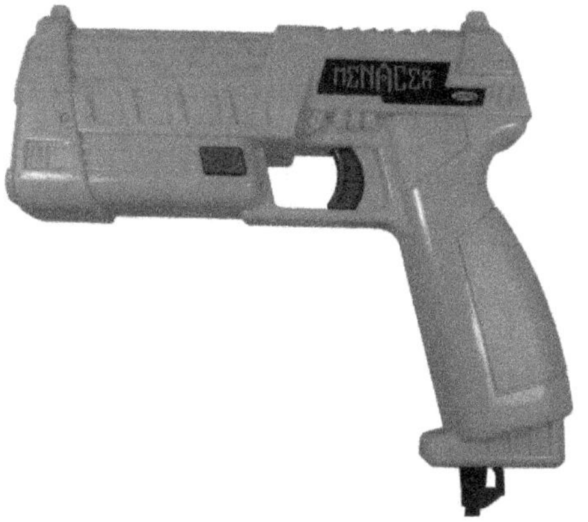

Radica Menacer

Famiclones

Interest in retrogaming wasn't limited just to the built-in games on the plug-and-play units. In 2003, the 20-year patent that had protected Nintendo's Famicom had expired. This led to a glut of *Famiclones*, inexpensive consoles that could legally play Famicom games without the blessing of Nintendo. Although Famiclones had been around before 2003, the producers of those units could have been prosecuted for patent infringement if they had been caught. After 2003, manufacturers of Famiclones no longer had to fear prosecution in Japan.

In 2005, many of the patents that protected the North American NES expired as well, which left the New World vulnerable to the infiltration of low-cost, faux NES consoles. And infiltrate they did. Yobo, a company that had released a Famiclone called *Neo Fami* in Japan, introduced one of the first "legal" Famiclones to North America. The *FC Game Console* cost only about $15, and for that amount, gamers got a system that could play nearly every NES game. In addition, the unit came with an adapter that enabled Famicom cartridges to be played as well. Two controllers were also included, but they didn't look like the original NES controllers. Instead of being rectangular, they were shaped more rounded and sort of resembled SNES controllers. And while the controllers featured D-pads, they weren't the crosshair D-pads that had appeared on nearly every Nintendo console. This was because Nintendo still held a patent on those. The FC Game Console, which was much smaller than an original NES, was available in several colors, but the most popular model was one that was white and red and sort of resembled an original Famicom.

Yobo FC Game Console

Also available for purchase was the *Retro Entertainment System* from a company called Retro-Bit. The console itself looked almost exactly like the one from Yobo, which meant that both companies bought them from the same Chinese manufacturer. The controllers that came with the Retro Entertainment System were rectangular, but they didn't look much like the NES's original controllers either. However, the FC Game Console and the Retro Entertainment System both accepted the original NES's controllers.

A third console came out in September. Messiah's *Generation NEX* cost $60, which was more expensive than the other Famiclones. But the console looked nicer, resembling a somewhat flattened NES. It came with two wired controllers that had the same coloring as the original NES controllers, but like the controllers that came with the FC Game Console, they were rounded and looked more like SNES controllers. Messiah also offered optional wireless controllers.[2]

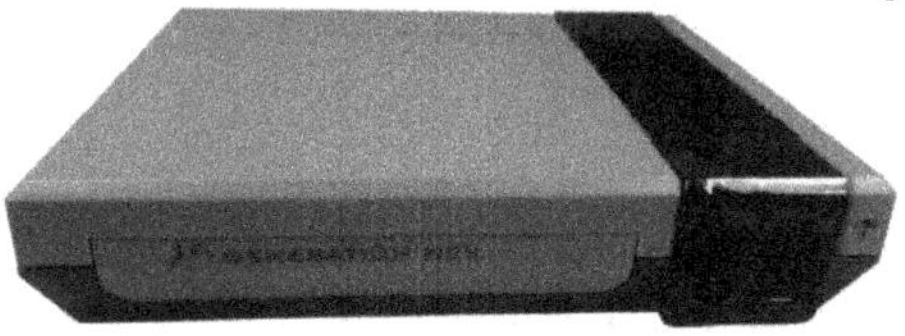

Messiah Generation NEX

The Final Game Boy

The low-cost handheld units that had been released by companies like Jakks Pacific, Techno Source and Radica were niche items that weren't meant to compete against Nintendo's overwhelmingly popular Game Boy or DS.

Although it was still selling steadily, support for the GBA SP began to decline as developers concentrated on the DS and SCE's new PSP. However, even as the attention of software publishers went elsewhere, Nintendo still supported the Game Boy, or so they made it appear.

Nintendo Play-Yan

Nintendo Game Boy Micro

On February 21, Nintendo of Japan began offering through its website the *Play-Yan*, a ¥5,000 ($47) cartridge that played MP3 audio and MPEG-4 video through either the GBA SP or the DS. Although the unit could also work with the GBA, it wasn't recommended, because it required too much power from the console. SD cards that contained the media files were inserted into the Play-Yan, which looked like a black, oversized GBA cartridge. The cartridge could also store thirteen mini-games that could be downloaded from Nintendo of Japan's website.

Nintendo discontinued the Play-Yan on September 11. Two days later, Nintendo of Japan offered a new, smaller unit, the *Play-Yan Micro*, which went along with a new version of the Game Boy that was released the same day. Roughly the shape and size of an NES controller, the *Game Boy Micro* was the smallest incarnation of the Game Boy. Despite its name, the system could only play GBA games. And yet, it was incompatible with the GBA's link cables and wireless adapters. Nintendo had to release new peripherals like the Play-Yan Micro that would work with it, such as the Play-Yan Micro. The e-Reader and GameCube-Game Boy Advance cable were also incompatible with the Game Boy Micro, but Nintendo didn't offer alternative versions for them. Surprisingly, the Game Boy Micro did have a standard headphone jack port.

Retailing at ¥12,000 ($108), the Game Boy Micro cost about the same as the GBA SP: a risky proposition on Nintendo's part, considering that the GBA SP could play all of the Game Boy and Game Boy Color games. But the Game Boy Micro also featured a tiny, backlit screen that was even sharper and brighter than the one on the DS. And the user had five levels of brightness to choose from.

Nintendo GBA SP - brighter

The front of the unit was protected by faceplates. Three different-styled faceplates were bundled with the unit, and additional ones could be purchased. The target customers for the device were kids between 11 and 15 years old.

Nintendo of America released the $100 Game Boy Micro on September 19 in the United States. Until that day, that had been the price of the front-lit GBA SP, which the company then lowered to $80. But Nintendo of America quietly also released an enhanced version of the GBA SP which, like the Game Boy Micro, sported a brighter backlit screen. Where the front-lit GBA SP had a button that was used to turn the light on or off, the new GBA SP had a button that allowed the user to choose between two levels of brightness.

The new GBA SP was not released in Japan.[3] In America, retailers sold both models concurrently for the same $80, until the supplies of the original front-lit GBA SP ran out. Although the two units had different model numbers, the only way that consumers could easily tell them apart was from the front of the new model's box, where the words "Now with a BRIGHTER backlit screen!" were clearly displayed.

The DS Takes Off

Despite the release of the new and improved GBA SP, people still bought the DS. Nintendo sold more than 3 million DS handhelds worldwide during its first six months of availability. Unfortunately, even as developers worked on new software for it, many analysts weren't impressed with the games that were already available. That would change during the second quarter of the year, as software began being released that took advantage of the device's unique features, such as its touchpad, microphone and wireless capabilities.

Nintendogs,[4] which launched in Japan on April 21, and in North America on August 22, took advantage of all of these features. Basically an update of the *Tamagotchi* theme, *Nintendogs* allowed gamers to own and take care of virtual dogs. The touchscreen was used for tasks such as training or walking the dog. The microphone allowed players to create voice commands that the pet could understand and hopefully obey. Finally, the wireless capabilities of the DS allowed dog owners to connect with other *Nintendogs* owners so their dogs could play together. The caveat was that both players had to be on the same local wireless connection.

Nintendo Nintendogs

Nintendogs was a success. Shortly after its Japanese release, the Japanese magazine *Famitsu* reviewed the game and gave it a perfect score: 40 out of 40. Only four other games had ever been awarded such a score in the magazine's 20-year history. The game's release caused sales of the DS to increase 4.2 times over the prior week.

Although *Nintendogs* took advantage of the DS's wireless capabilities, it wasn't an integral part of the gameplay. Since Nintendo executives had publicly announced several times that online play wasn't at the forefront of their priorities, many analysts were led to believe that the online inclusion on *Nintendogs* was just a token effort. Nintendo proved them wrong on November 14 in the United States and on December 8 in Japan, when it launched the *Nintendo Wi-Fi Connection*. This was a free network that Nintendo established for use with a new line games that could be played online. The first game for the DS that used it was released the same day that the network launched. *Mario Kart DS* was a first-person racing game wherein players raced go-karts, using the personas of up

nintendo Wi-Fi connection

Ninteno Wi-Fi Connection Logo

to twelve Nintendo characters. While there were one-player games included, players could compete in real time against up to five other gamers around the world via the Nintendo Wi-Fi Connection.

Mario Kart DS and the Nintendo Wi-Fi Connection were huge successes. After their first week out, 112,000 people had purchased the game, and 52,000 of them had used the Nintendo Wi-Fi Connection to compete in multiplayer games. Within two weeks, two more games were released for the DS that took advantage of the Nintendo Wi-Fi Connection, Activision's *Tony Hawk's American Sk8land*[5] and Nintendo's *Animal Crossing: Wild World,* were released. All games that supported the Nintendo Wi-Fi Connection sported a large blue logo on the face of their packaging.

Although the DS required a wireless connection, not everybody who owned the device had access to one. And since Nintendo didn't offer an Ethernet cable port for the DS, those without wireless access couldn't enjoy the DS's multiplayer games. So in order for people with wired Internet connections to have access to Wi-Fi, Nintendo sold the *Nintendo Wi-Fi USB Connector* from its website. This device, which looked like a standard thumb drive, plugged into an Internet-connected computer's USB port and in effect turned the computer into a Wi-Fi hotspot that provided a Wi-Fi signal to the DS. And for those who didn't have an Internet connection at all, Nintendo of America inked a deal with McDonalds to provide free wireless hotspots at 7,000 of its restaurants around the United States.

Nintendo Wi-Fi USB Connector

Because the DS employed SD-type Game Cards for its software instead of cartridges, it was believed that games that included novelty features could no longer be developed. These were features that relied upon additional hardware that was usually built into the cartridge, such as the accelerometer in *Kirby's Tilt 'n' Tumble or the* vibration feedback that had been introduced in *Pokémon Pinball.* This belief was deemed unfounded as developers figured out ways to get around the DS's apparent limitations. On October 24, Nintendo of America released *Metroid Prime Pinball,* a game that employed a rumble feature. Since the Game Cards were too small to include the rumble technology, the game's developers turned to the unused GBA cartridge slot of the console. They then created a rumble pack that was housed in a GBA-shaped cartridge, which was bundled with the game and plugged into this slot.

Nintendo DS Rumble Pak

PSP In America

The DS's new popularity wasn't due solely to the quality of the new games that were being released for it. On August 22, just in time for the American launch of *Nintendogs,* Nintendo of America reduced the price of the handheld by $20 to $130. This put the cost of the DS at roughly half of SCE's new PSP, which had been released in North America on March 24. Retailing at $250, the American PSP came with all of the accessories that had been included in the Japanese "Value Pack," plus an additional preview UMD and a cleaning cloth. On top of that, the first million units that were sold in the United States included a free *Spider-Man 2* movie on UMD.

Within 48 hours of its North American release, SCEA announced that over 500,000 PSP units had been sold, a vast improvement over its launch in Japan, where it took SCEJ over three weeks to reach that goal. However, sales slowed down dramatically after that second day, and by the end of the first week, SCEA reported that only an additional

103,000 units had been sold.

SCE had earlier promised that one million units would be sold in North America by March 31. However, in order to have that many devices on hand, SCE needed to divert units that had been allotted to Europe. This forced SCEE to postpone its European PSP launch, which had also been planned for March 24, to September 1. And to make sure that the systems being allocated to North America didn't wind up in Europe, SCE announced that it would take legal action against any company that imported the device into Europe. The company followed through with its threats, and small European stores that had imported the PSP were faced with £1,000 ($1,752) fines.

SCEA did not sell out of the million PSPs as it had expected. While potential customers were happy with the PSP's large screen and near-PS2 graphics, many people weren't compelled to run out and buy one because they felt that most of the launch titles were mainly non-unique console ports.

In May, it was discovered that hackers found a way to copy games from a UMD onto a Memory Stick Duo, which could then be loaded into the PSP. This was only a problem for SCE as far as the original PSPs sold in Japan were concerned, as the firmware in subsequent units required that all programs that ran off the Memory Stick Duo had to be authorized and signed by SCE. But the original firmware didn't include this requirement. Although SCE issued an upgrade to its firmware[6] to fix this problem, there was no way for SCE to monitor whether users actually followed through and installed the upgrade, especially those who intended to run illegal software from their Memory Stick Duos. However, as newer games were released, they required the updated firmware in order to run.

Updated firmware often meant new features. On July 27, SCEJ began offering Version 2.0 of its firmware, which installed an official Sony web browser onto the PSP. Other new features gave users the abilities to share photos wirelessly and to use their photos as wallpaper. American users were able to upgrade to this version beginning on August 24.

Although SCE was quick to provide downloadable firmware upgrades from the Internet, it was slow in providing other media through that distribution method. The company had initially wanted to challenge Apple and its online iTunes store by delivering digital music, movies and games to the PSP, but SCE never managed to initiate such a service.

Surprisingly, the market for movies on the UMD format was higher than had been anticipated. Two UMD movies, *Resident Evil: Apocalypse* and *House of Flying Daggers*, each sold over 100,000 copies by the end of May, less than two months after they had been released. By contrast, *Air Force One*, the first DVD to sell 100,000 copies, took almost a year to hit this landmark figure.

Still, nobody was going to buy an expensive handheld gaming device based on the movies that played on it. The bottom line was that people wanted good, original games. Nintendo had proven this when the DS only really caught on after newer original games like *Nintendogs* were released. SCE hoped that the same would happen for the PSP.

The first two must-have games for the PSP came out in the fall. Although they were both sequels of established console games, both were completely new games in their own right. The first was *Grand Theft Auto: Liberty City Stories*, which was released on October 24. Set in the same city as *Grand Theft Auto III*, the action took place in 1998, three years earlier than in the former game.

The other game, *SOCOM: U.S. Navy SEALs Fireteam Bravo*, was released two weeks later, on November 8. The game used the PSP's wireless capabilities to allow up to 16 players at one time through a network connection. The game came out one month after SCE released *SOCOM 3: U.S. Navy SEALs* for the PS2. The outcome of one game affected the play on the other, after data was transferred between the PSP and the PS2.

SCE PSP Headset

SCE Talkman

The addition of an optional $20 PSP headset and microphone gave players of *SOCOM: U.S. Navy SEALs Fireteam Bravo* the ability to chat with other players during online play. But a microphone wasn't limited just to chatting during gaming sessions. On November 17, SCEJ introduced a different type of microphone that plugged into the top of the PSP. The USB microphone was bundled with *Talkman,* an application that turned the PSP into a language translator. The combination allowed the user to speak a Japanese, English, Korean or Mandarin Chinese word or phrase into the microphone and the system would verbally repeat it back in another of the four languages provided.[7]

European Handhelds

Although people may have been unhappy with the initial launch titles available for the PSP, they at least had a number of games to choose from. That wasn't the case for people who bought the £229 ($440) Gizmondo from Tiger Telematics, which was released on March 19 in Great Britain. Although Tiger Telematics had announced that 89 games would be available by the end of the year, only two, *Trailblazer* and a puzzle compilation called *Fathammer Classics Pack,* were actually available for the launch. But Gizmondo games weren't the only things for the handheld that were scarce. The few retailers that stocked the system carried it in such low quantities that it was all but impossible to find. Most sales were made directly through Tiger Telematics, either through the company's website or its own retail store on London's Regent Street. Tiger Telematics chairman Carl Freer said that the Regent Street store had exceeded the company's expectations. In fact, he claimed the store did so well that Tiger Telematics intended to open more retail stores in capital cities around the world within a year, beginning with one at Times Square in New York City. Still, despite the fact that Tiger Telematics executives had bragged that they would sell 4,400 units within an hour of its launch, in reality they only sold 1,000.

Tiger Telematics released a second version of the Gizmondo in April. The new model sold for £129 ($247) and was supposedly equipped with the "Smart Adds" feature, wherein users would receive up to three ads each day. In actuality, the "Smart Adds" feature was never enabled, so although people purchased a less expensive unit that was supposedly subsidized by ads, they never received any ads.

The Gizmondo was released in the United States on October 22, but there weren't any company stores to sell them. Instead, the device was sold exclusively from shopping mall kiosks, where they retailed with the "Smart Adds" enabled for $229 and disabled for $400. Eight games were also for sale, all of which had already been released in Great Britain, where 14 games were available by that time.

Nokia N-Gage QD Silver Edition

On September 1, the same day that the PSP came out in Europe, Nokia released a new version of its N-Gage QD only in Europe, the Middle East and Africa. The *N-Gage QD Silver Edition* was exactly the same as the N-Gage QD, with some minor cosmetic changes and a body that was silver. According to Jukka Hosio, Nokia's Director of Global Sales, this was "one of the season's most fashionable colors." The release of the device was Nokia's response to requests from both consumers and the trade to provide an N-Gage QD variant.

This "new" release from Nokia was the only way for the cell-phone maker to extend the life of the device that pretty much wasn't going anywhere. Nokia had to fend off rumors throughout the year of the N-Gage's demise, especially after it issued a 4th quarter 2004 report that indicated that only 1.3 million of the devices had been sold worldwide, a far cry from the 6-9 million units that the company had predicted would have sold by that time.

By November, Nokia could no longer deny the inevitable, and the company announced the discontinuation of the N-Gage hardware. However, Nokia wasn't giving up on the N-Gage as a gaming platform, and announced that beginning in 2007, the N-Gage operating system would be built into Nokia's Series 60 line of cell phones.

But the N-Gage QD wasn't the only handheld device that failed during the year. It came as no surprise on July 25 when Tapwave announced via its website that it was immediately discontinuing the Zodiac. Despite the raves from critics regarding the combination gaming/PDA device, the public had never embraced it and only 200,000 units had been sold during a two-year period. The reality was that few people were interested in a PDA that played games, and at $299, the low-end Zodiac cost $50 more than the PSP. There was no possible way that Tapwave could compete with the likes of Nintendo and Sony.

Korean Confusion

Game Park was one company that wasn't worried about the Japanese competition. However, when its engineers began to design a follow-up to the GP32 series, there was disagreement between them about the direction that the new handheld should take. One camp wanted to create a 3D device similar to the PSP that would also play downloaded and homebrew software. But the majority of Game Park's engineers wanted a 2D device that they viewed as the logical evolution of the GP32. After the two groups couldn't reach a consensus, the latter faction left Game Park and created a new company that it called *Game Park Holdings*.

Once they were on their own, the engineers at Game Park Holdings designed a new handheld device with hobbyists in mind. They employed a Linux-based, open-architecture operating system, which meant that anyone could create applications that ran on the device without any licensing required. And in addition to playing games, their new creation could play MP3 audio files, MPEG-4 video files and view photos. In addition to being able to save files on SD cards, the device contained 64MB of internal flash memory, half which could be used for personal storage. The result was the $150 *GP2X* that was released on November 10 only in South Korea.

Meanwhile, the engineers who remained at Game Park went on to design the handheld console that had been their original idea. The company announced on August 17 that it would release its new device, the *XGP* (Extreme Game Player), in March 2006. In some ways, the $300 XGP resembled the GP2X, as it also had a Linux operating system, SD card storage and 64MB of internal memory. But the XGP would also have

Game Park Holdings GPX2

a larger, sharper 4-inch screen, and wireless capabilities.

In addition to the base model, Game Park announced two other XGP models. The $150 *XGP Mini,* which was similar to the Game Boy Micro, was a smaller version of the XGP that featured 32MB of internal memory and a 2.2-inch screen. The third announced model was the $75 *XGP Kids,* which was much closer in style to the GP32 rather than the XGP, and was targeted towards children.

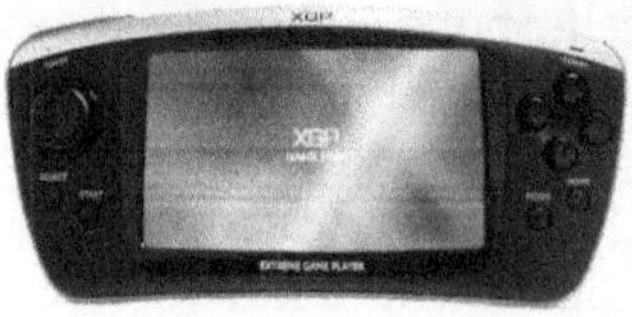

Game Park Holdings XGP

Game Park Holdings XGP Mini

Game Park Holdings XGP Kids

Kids' Controllers

Although Game Park had announced a handheld system for kids, it was Fisher-Price that actually released one with its latest incarnation of its Pixter. The $90 *Pixter Multi-Media* took over where the Pixter Color had left off. It was compatible with all Pixter Color cartridges,[8] and could also play the older black and white Pixter cartridges with a cartridge adapter that accompanied it. The device did not have a slot for the Pixter lamp, but one was not needed since the Pixter Multi-Media featured a backlit screen. It also featured conventional gaming system controls such as a D-pad and A and B buttons.

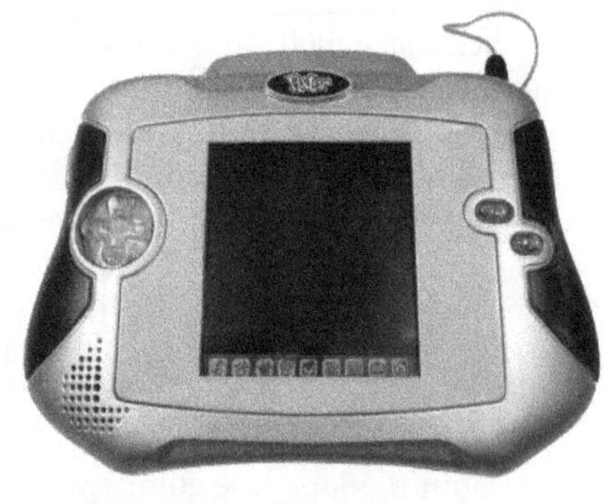

Fisher-Price Pixter Multi-Media

The system's name derived from the fact that it could also play 20-minute videos. Special cartridges, similar to Majesco's GBA Video line, plugged into the device. These cartridges could not be inserted into earlier versions of the Pixter.

On September 8, Warren Buckleitner of *The New York Times* wrote that the Pixter was better than its competing educational consoles in terms of creativity. However, he added that as a gaming device, "the Pixter's spongy controls can leave your thumb sore after just one round of the *Tetris*-like sorting game." He also recommended that parents purchase a portable DVD player for their kids, rather than the Pixter Multi-Media, to view videos. People who were shopping for an educational console apparently agreed, as the Pixter Multi-Media was the last console in the series that Fisher-Price released.

LeapFrog Leapster - new

The Pixter Multi-Media resembled LeapFrog's Leapster L-Max, with a similar color scheme and design. Leapfrog decided to redesign its original Leapster to match the design the Leapster L-Max as well. A new version was released which used the same body as the Leapster L-Max, with the only difference being that there was an area beneath the screen where the stylus could rest when it wasn't being used. LeapFrog also introduced a new color scheme. The main color for the new Leapster was green.[9] Basically the only difference between the new Leapster and the Leapster L-Max was that it didn't have the composite video output that allowed it to be connected to a television.

Instead, LeapFrog released a new model of Leapster that needed a television. The $67 *Leapster TV* was a circular unit that resembled a turtle. In the center of this it sat a large, roundish, removable controller that featured all of the buttons found on the handheld Leapster. The controller also included a touchpad that was protected by a plastic green cover, and a stylus. One slight difference in the controls between the handheld and console models was that the Leapster TV had a large yellow joystick in place of the D-pad that was found on the handheld Leapster.

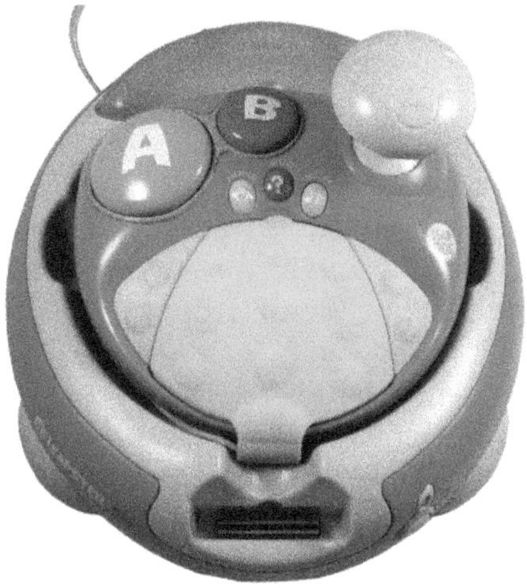

LeapFrog Leapster TV

The first educational programmable console, Sega's Pico, had failed in the United States and was discontinued in 1998.[10] However, in Japan, the Pico thrived. After Sega dropped out of the console business in 2001, its sister company, Sega Toys, took over the distribution of the Pico in Japan and continued to sell it there until August 5, 2005, when it replaced it with a newer console called the *Advanced Pico Beena*. The Beena had improved features over the Pico, such as allowing children to play without the need of a TV and the ability to save games on an SD card.

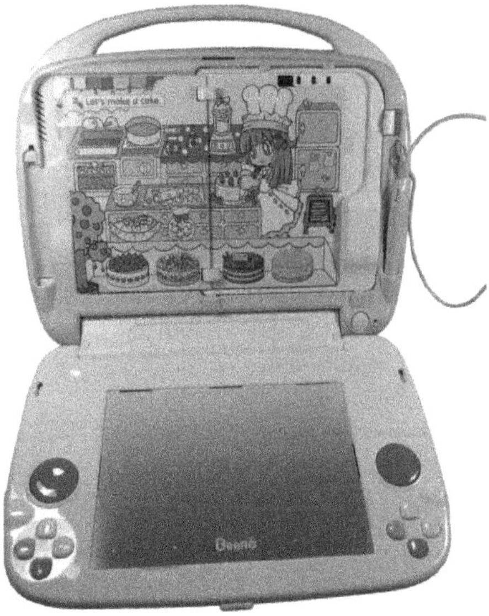

Sega Toys Beena

The Game Wave

The educational consoles were basically unknown to most gamers under the age of ten. But console anonymity wasn't limited just to the educational kids' consoles.

In October, ZAPiT Games of Mississauga, Canada released the *Game Wave*, a family-oriented videogame console that wasn't intended to compete with Nintendo, Sony or Microsoft. The $100 Game Wave was actually a DVD player with a few extra features, and its game controllers were basically television remote controllers.

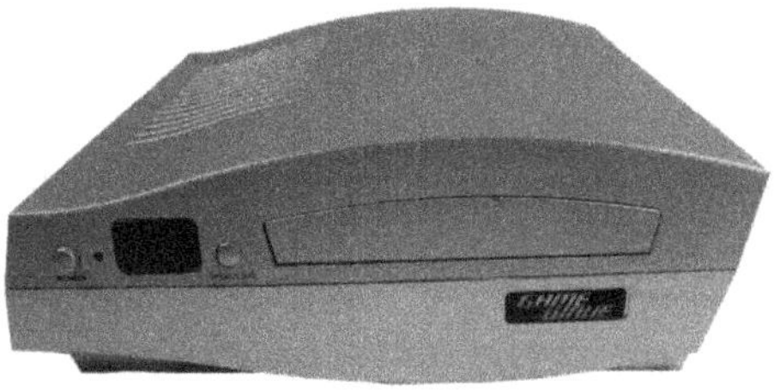

ZapiT Games Game Wave

Games were available on DVD from four genres: trivia, number, word and puzzle games. Although some games allowed up to six people to play at the same time, the majority of the games allowed for four-way play. The console was bundled with four controllers, and additional controllers could be purchased separately. These controllers were color-coded to distinguish them from one another. While every controller could operate the system's DVD player, each individual controller could only manage a similarly colored on-screen player.

Like the kid-oriented consoles from LeapFrog and VTech, the Game Wave wasn't carried in gaming stores like GameStop. Although some Toys "R" Us localities carried the console, the main suppliers, oddly, were religious stores throughout North America.

Another console that wasn't carried in traditional videogame stores, or anywhere else for that matter, was Infinium Labs' Phantom. When the January launch date had arrived, the console was indeed a phantom and the launch was postponed until March. But the new date also passed without any sign of the console. And the Phantom, which had won the "Best Hardware at Show" award at E^3 in 2004, was nowhere to be seen at the 2005 show in June. Meanwhile, Infinium Labs itself was going through changes. The founder, Tim Roberts, resigned from his CEO position and was replaced in August by Kevin Bachus, who had been serving as the company's president. Bachus affirmed that the console would still be released, but didn't specify a new release date, as the company needed to raise $11.5 million.

By this time, the media and gamers alike were tired hearing about the delays of the Phantom, which they had never expected to be a serious contender anyway. But the Phantom's absence from E^3 was barely noticed, since most attendees were more interested in the new consoles that Nintendo, SCE and Microsoft were finally showing to the world.

Xbox 360

Even before E^3, Microsoft had made sure that its new console was in the public's mind. In mid-April, the company announced the system's official name, *Xbox 360*. The name had come as a surprise, since most people had expected it to be called Xbox 2. However, the console's design team felt that "Xbox 2" would be too similar to "PS2, or "PS3", which was the expectant name of SCE's new console. Also, Microsoft wanted people to believe that the videogame industry revolved around the player and not the console. Xbox 360 represented a full circle, with the gamer in the center.

MTV Presents:
The Next Generation Xbox Revealed

Microsoft felt that the first appearance of the Xbox 360 was much too big an event to happen at E^3, a show attended "only" by 70,000 videogame industry insiders. Instead, Microsoft chose to present the console to the world via a televised presentation. On May 12, one week before E^3, MTV aired *MTV Presents: The Next Generation Xbox Revealed*, a half-hour, prime-time special hosted by Elijah Wood. Although the new console made its debut five minutes into the show, most of the broadcast had little to do with the Xbox 360. The rest of the show was dedicated to a distorted history of videogames, two performances by the rock group, The Killers, and one segment in which viewers got to see the cast of another MTV show, *Pimp My Ride*, customize an original Xbox.

Two minutes of the show were spent on a visit to Microsoft's Xbox headquarters, where members of the Xbox 360 design team showed alternative console designs and explained how faceplates could be changed to customize the new console. A designer also pointed out the console's "Ring of Light," but made no attempt to explain its purpose. What the show didn't reveal were the important things that gamers really wanted to know, such as the console's release date and price.

Much of that was announced four days later at E^3, during a Microsoft conference held by Robbie Bach, Senior Vice-President of Microsoft's Home and Entertainment Division, and two Corporate Vice-Presidents, J. Allard and Peter Moore. They told the assembled crowd that the Xbox 360 would be backward-compatible with the "top-selling Xbox games," but the meaning of this was unclear.

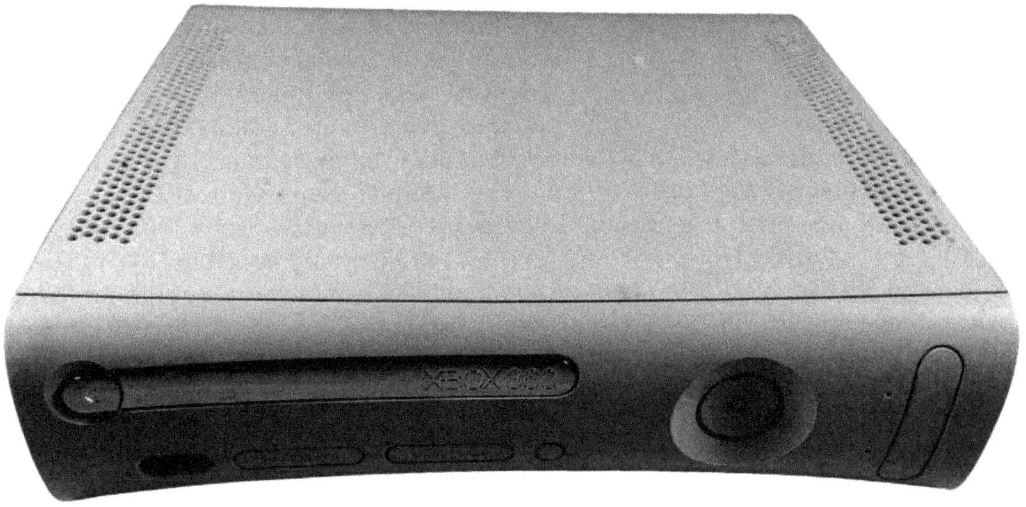

Microsoft Xbox 360

They also said that the Xbox 360 would be released during the 2005 holiday season. Although no specific date was mentioned, they confirmed that the console would be released in North America, Europe and Japan before the year ended.

The console itself was sleek and smaller than the original. Like the PS2, the Xbox 360 could stand vertically or horizontally. The front of the console was simple and included a DVD tray, a power button surrounded by the Ring of Light that had been alluded to during the MTV broadcast, two memory-card slots and two hidden USB ports. Missing from the console were controller ports, because the system could recognize up to four wireless controllers. The controllers themselves were smaller and lighter than the Xbox Controller S, even when batteries were installed. And if gamers wanted to conserve batteries, wired controllers could be plugged via the USB ports. The *Ring of Light* was a circle on the face of the console that was divided into four lighted quadrants. When a controller was activated, one of the quadrants lit up to let the player know which position he was playing in multiplayer games. And since the lights weren't limited to just green, other uses for the Ring of Light were possible, such as being able to monitor the health of each player in a game.

In the center of each controller was an Xbox Guide button, which served several purposes. It had four lights surrounding it, and like a smaller version of the Ring of Light, it notified contestants in split-screen multiplayer games of which part of the screen their characters were in. Pressing this button paused whatever was on the screen and provided the user with an on-screen console menu that allowed him to easily navigate to other Xbox 360 features. Pressing the button a second time resumed the game or movie that had been paused. Finally, the button could also be used to turn either the controller or the console on and off.

One of the features that the Xbox 360 controllers could access was the DVD player. Unlike with the original Xbox, a separate remote controller wasn't required, although one would be available.

All games developed for the Xbox 360 were required to display at a minimum of 720p resolution on high-definition, wide-screen TVs. But they also had to display perfectly on standard non-HD television sets. Microsoft also required that all games offered a minimum of 5.1 multi-channel sound so the audio would be as spectacular as the video.

Xbox Live was also to be enhanced for the new console. Users would no longer need to have credit cards in order to sign on. The new Xbox Live would offer two tiers of service. The silver tier would be absolutely free. Users would be able to access the silver

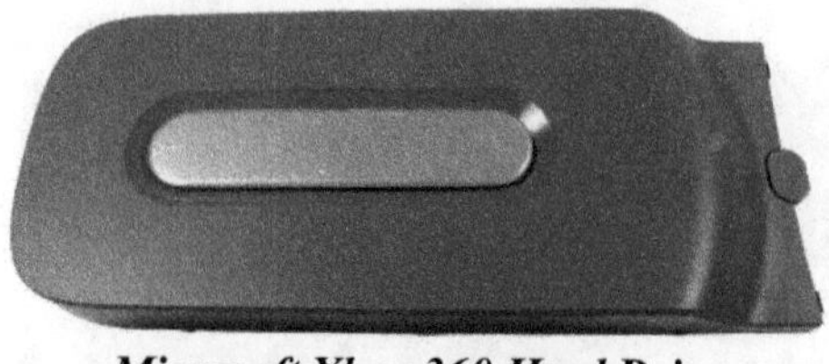

Microsoft Xbox 360 Hard Drive

service the moment they turned on their Xbox 360s for the first time. Online gaming, however, would only be available in the gold tier, which would be subscription-based. Regardless of the tier, once people were on Xbox Live, they would find it easier to navigate than it was on the Xbox.

The internals of the Xbox 360 were just as amazing as what was on the outside. Like its predecessor, the Xbox 360 would ship with a 20GB hard drive. However, the Xbox 360's drive would be removable, making it portable and upgradable. Overall, the system had 512Mb of memory, or eight times that of the original Xbox. Its CPU consisted of three symmetrical cores that ran at 3.2GHz each, and the graphics processor was a 500MHz custom-designed chip. All this added up to a console that was faster and more powerful than any other system on the market.

PlayStation 3

On May 16, the same day as the Microsoft E^3 presentation, SCE showed off a prototype of its new console, officially called the *PlayStation 3 (PS3),* at the Sony Picture Studios. Although the processing power between the two consoles was almost the same, the PS3 took the lead in GigaFLOPs, the number of floating-point operations that could be processed. While the Xbox 360 weighed in at 115 GigaFLOPs, the PS3 practically doubled that number with 218 GigaFLOPs. This additional power would give the PS3 the capability of more advanced physics, more sophisticated artificial intelligence, and larger environments.

Like the Xbox 360, the PS3 would embrace high definition. However, software would be sold on Blu-ray discs, which could each store almost 50GB of data, or the same as ten DVDs. The PS3 would also play Blu-ray movies in high definition. This was especially notable, because any kind of Blu-ray player was not yet available for sale.

And like the Xbox 360, the PS3 would come with a detachable hard drive, but the size of the drive wasn't mentioned at the presentation. In addition, the prototype console had slots that would accept SD cards and flash memory, as well as six USB ports, four of which were on the front of the unit. Although the system would employ up to seven wireless Bluetooth controllers, these four USB ports could be used to charge them, or to insert wired controllers. The prototype controller that was shown had an odd boomerang shape, but SCE didn't go into detail about its functionality.

SCE also announced that the PS3 and the PSP would unite through a Wi-Fi connection. But whether this meant that the two consoles would simply share data or the PSP could be used as a controller for the PS3 in the same fashion that the GBA could be used as a controller for the GameCube, was unclear. Since both units also had USB ports, it was probable that data could be shared via a wired connection. And the PS3 would also support the Memory Stick Duo, so it was conceivable that it could also be used to share data between the two units.

The prototype console also had two HDMI[11] outputs. SCE explained that this would permit two high-def televisions to be connected simultaneously, to give the viewer one 32:9 aspect ratio across both screens, or to use a second screen to provide additional information, similar to the approach that Nintendo used with the DS.

The PS3 would also be backward-compatible with both PS2 and PlayStation software. But like Microsoft, which had been less than forthcoming concerning the Xbox 360's backward-compatibility, SCE didn't reveal how it planned to incorporate this.

The Nintendo Revolution

Nintendo also promised backward-compatibility in its Revolution, the new console that it unveiled in prototype form at its E^3 conference on May 17. Although the system would use standard 5-inch discs as its software media, it would also be able to read the smaller 3-inch GameCube discs. And while the system would employ wireless controllers, it would also have ports that the older GameCube controllers could plug into. Nintendo also announced that the new console would include 512MB of flash memory and would embrace online gaming. While the prototype unit had an Ethernet port for people with Broadband service, Nintendo was focusing on Wi-Fi. And as a commitment to this, Nintendo announced that it would be starting the *Nintendo Wi-Fi Connection* in partnership with *GameSpy*, which operated a network of gaming websites. Online games that Nintendo produced would be available for free play on the network, but third-party publishers would have the option to charge fees for their games.

In addition to being able to play GameCube games, the Revolution would also be capable of playing older Nintendo-branded games, from the NES to the N64. However, the original cartridges from the various consoles would not run on the Revolution. These games would be available for download from the *Nintendo Wi-Fi Connection* for an undisclosed cost. Nintendo president Satoru Iwata said that Nintendo was working with other companies to make their older third-party games available as well.

The Revolution's video resolution would not be high-def. Nintendo didn't want to incur higher costs to either developers or consumers by adding HD, and promised that the graphics would still look great.

The prototype that was shown at E^3 was simplicity itself. Looking like a small cereal box that stood on its side, the Revolution showed no ports at all. Software discs were inserted into a slot, instead being placed on a drawer. An SD card slot was hidden behind a door on the console's face, while the GameCube controller ports were hidden behind a door on the console's top.

Nintendo wasn't ready to reveal too much about the Revolution at E^3. Speculation about its controller ranged from a handheld touchscreen to something based on gyroscopes. All Iwata would say was that the system would be innovative and that its interface "would allow for some brand-new forms of game playing."

More Console Details

On June 9, Ken Kutaragi revealed that the Ethernet functionality that had been built into the prototype PS3 that was shown at E^3 wouldn't be available on the production model. The reason cited was that SCE felt that it was an unneeded expense, since most broadband users owned their own wireless routers anyway. His news wasn't taken with much interest. But Kutaragi created a stir when he said that although the PS3 would have a 2.5-inch port to accommodate a hard drive, the drive itself would be sold separately. SCE management had come to the conclusion that no matter what size drive they included with the console, users would always complain that it wasn't enough, and would purchase a larger one anyhow. Meanwhile, SCE was considering varying-sized drives, such as 80GB or 120GB, that would be available separately. But the public decided that any size hard drive included with the console would be better than no drive at all. A *GamePro* poll revealed that when 2,137 participants were given four choices of what they would do if the PS3 didn't include a hard drive, the most popular response was that they'd go with the Xbox 360, which would include one.

The necessity of the Xbox 360's hard drive came up a few days later, when the issue of the console being backward-compatible with the "top-selling Xbox games" was addressed. It appeared that the Xbox 360's custom graphics chipset that had been developed by ATI was not compatible with the games that ran on the Xbox, which had used a Nvidia graphics chipset. Microsoft's initial plan had been to recompile the top-selling Xbox games and then pre-install the new executable code on the Xbox 360's hard drive and later, as more

Xbox games were recompiled, they would be made available to the Xbox 360 through Xbox Live.

On June 16, it was disclosed that Microsoft, in order to provide backward-compatibility to the Xbox 360, had licensed Nvidia's technology so that the earlier Xbox graphics chipset could be emulated in one of the three cores of the Xbox 360's CPU. However, even after this had been done, it was found that many games remained unplayable on the Xbox 360. Additional patches, or emulation profiles, would be needed for these games. Microsoft planned to have as many of these emulation profiles as possible available on the Xbox 360's hard drive when the system became available. Afterwards, the company would continue to create more emulation profiles and distribute them over Xbox Live.

Microsoft finally announced the price of the Xbox 360 on August 17. The system would retail for $400 and would include a console with a 20GB hard drive, one wireless controller, one HD A/V cable, a faceplate, a headset and, for a limited time, a remote controller that could be used for DVD or CD playback.[12] The set would also ship with a three-month trial Gold membership to Xbox Live that would give users access to online gaming. The system would also include an Ethernet cable, so that the console could be connected to a router. Despite Microsoft's original claim, the Xbox 360 wouldn't be completely wireless straight out of the box, since it lacked a wireless network adapter. Although the original Xbox's wireless network adapter would work on the Xbox 360, Microsoft chose not to include it in the package.

To everyone's surprise, Microsoft also announced a second, less expensive configuration that it intended to sell. The *Core Edition* would cost $300 and would include the console, a faceplate, a standard A/V cable and a wired controller. A hard drive would *not* be part of the package. The Core Edition would also come with an Xbox Live Silver membership that would provide the user with accessibility only to the free content on Xbox Live.

Gamers questioned the Core Edition. The only way they would be able to save games without a hard drive would be with a $40 Memory Card. And there was also the issue that the hard drive would be required to play Xbox games on the Xbox 360. The sole reason that Microsoft released the Core Edition was so that they could deliver a gaming console for under $300. Analysts wondered if this was a good tactic. They feared that most recreational gamers would choose the less expensive package and thereby forego the hard drive. And if that was the case, developers would be hesitant to develop games that took advantage of the hard drive, because only a minority of gamers would own it. The PS2 had already established such a precedent.

The final piece of the Xbox 360 puzzle was delivered in Japan on September 14, the day before the Tokyo Game Show began. Microsoft used that backdrop to finally announce the system's official release dates. Both packages would be available in North America on November 22 and in Europe on December 2. On December 10, only the Core Package would be released in Japan, and it would retail for ¥37,900 ($315).

Revolutionary Controllers

Nintendo also used the Tokyo Game Show to its advantage. On September 16, Satoru Iwata unveiled a working prototype of the Revolution's new interface. As suspected, it was a controller that was totally unlike any Nintendo controller that had preceded it.

The Revolution's controller resembled a television remote, long and thin. Iwata explained that this was intentional, as "there are people who would never touch a [game controller], but would pick up a TV remote." Held vertically, its face featured a D-pad at the top, directly above a large "A" button. Near the bottom were smaller "A" and "B" buttons and on its underside was another large "B" button. In order to make objects on the screen move, the controller merely had to be waved in front of the TV like a wand.

The controller didn't work alone. It interacted with a sensor bar, which plugged into the console and sat either above or below the television. This allowed for virtual-like play. If a game called for the player to wield a sword, then as the player waved the controller, the sword on the screen followed the same moves. In a boxing game, the hand and arm of the on-screen character would behave in the same manner as the person holding the controller.

Design for this new controller had actually begun under the supervision of Shigeru Miyamoto as Nintendo released the GameCube in 2001. The concern then was that game controllers, with their myriad buttons and pads that performed different functions, were becoming too complicated. Nintendo sought a controller that was easy and understandable the first time it was used.

Of course, this new controller wouldn't be sufficient for all types of games. By design, the analog stick that had been included on N64 and GameCube controllers was not included. In its place, Nintendo introduced the *Nunchuck,* an attachment that plugged into the bottom of the main controller and which did have an analog stick, as well as two Z-triggers. Once the Nunchuck was connected to the nameless main controller, players had all of the buttons and triggers that were required to play most games.

The reason the main controller had two sets of "A" and "B" buttons was so that it could easily be used with NES and SNES games that could be downloaded. When used horizontally, the controller's D-pad and two smaller "A" and "B" buttons effectively mimicked the control scheme of the original NES/Famicom controllers.

Blu-ray

Now that all of the major players had revealed their next-generation consoles, it appeared that the PS3 had more to offer. By selecting Blu-ray as its media, SCE gambled that people would purchase the PS3 to play games and to watch high-def movies that would be available on the new format.

Blu-ray, which was developed by Sony, got its name from the type of laser that read the encoded discs. Existing DVD players, including the DVD-9 that was used in the Xbox 360, employed a red laser. Blue lasers had shorter wavelengths than their red counterparts, which meant that the time needed to read information from a disc was faster. Blue lasers were also approximately two and a half times smaller in diameter than red lasers, allowing them to read more precise data from a disc. This in turn allowed more information to be stored on a disc. A Blu-ray disc could hold up to 50GB of data.

Toshiba created a competing blue laser DVD, *HD-DVD,* which had the capacity to store 30GB of data. Both were scheduled to be released during 2006. Manufacturers and movie studios alike quickly took sides about which format they would adopt. Microsoft signed up with the HD-DVD camp in September, but by then, it was too late to incorporate a HD-DVD player into the Xbox 360 without holding up the console's release date. After Bill Gates stated that Microsoft might adapt HD-DVD players in later releases of the Xbox 360, Yoshiro Maruyama, chief of Xbox operations in Japan, quickly told a Japanese magazine that if what Gates had said was true, the HD-DVD drive would only be used to play back high-def movies. Games would not be stored on HD-DVD discs.

Many people feared to adopt either format, because they worried that a format war would cause one to become extinct, like what had happened to Sony's Betamax videotape format, which fell to JVC's rival VHS during the early eighties. As far as gaming was concerned, it really didn't matter which format was used, since an Xbox 360 game wouldn't play on a PS3 even if they both used the same type of disc. But if a company focused on all home entertainment, as Sony did, then it did matter. SCE would be taking a huge gamble by employing the Blu-ray player in the PS3. If the format didn't take off, eventually people wouldn't be able to purchase new Blu-ray movies to view on their machines, and after some time, they would eventually discard it in favor of a system that could play new movies.

Microsoft Setbacks

As promised, Microsoft released the Xbox 360 in North America at 12:01 on the morning of November 22. Lines had formed at stores, with some people waiting nearly 30 hours to claim units. People began forming a line outside a Wilkes-Barre, Pennsylvania Walmart at around 4 PM on November 21, and began getting restless seven hours later. Police were summoned after the crowd began pushing and shoving. A Walmart manager finally came out and handed out 48 vouchers, which allowed each holder to return at midnight to purchase an Xbox 360. But some people weren't content with standing in line. Soon after an Electronics Boutique in Stafford, Virginia opened at midnight, a man robbed the store of two Xbox 360 consoles at gunpoint. He was caught soon afterwards. Many stores reported running out of the Premium sets very quickly, which forced customers to resort to purchasing Core Editions just so they could get the console. And in more than one case, it was reported that store employees actually hoarded consoles in front of waiting customers.

But many people who had managed to snag Xbox 360s went home only to find that their troubles were just beginning as a high number of the consoles were found to be defective. There were many complaints of systems that wouldn't boot, and many that did crashed during games. Some complaints concerned defective hard drives that in some cases scratched the discs beyond repair. Microsoft investigated the complaints, but didn't deem the number of problems serious enough to warrant a recall. The company said that the failure rate was a "very, very small fraction" of the total number of consoles sold. It was later estimated to be at 3% or less of the 325,902 Xbox 360 consoles that had been sold during the first five days of its release.

The occasional console encountered severe overheating of the power supply and CPU, which affected heat-sensitive chips and caused the console to freeze. A Chicago resident, Robert Byers, filed a lawsuit against Microsoft over this problem on December 2. He contended that Microsoft had released a "defectively designed" console in order to beat Sony and Nintendo with the first next-generation console and to get it out in time for Christmas.

Many people also blamed console shortages on this problem. They believed that in Microsoft's zest to get the consoles out to the public as soon as possible, a substantial number of them simply hadn't been manufactured in time. Apparently, the release date also came too early for many of the game publishers. Although eighteen games were available for the launch, some of the games had been rushed to market before they were fully completed, just so they could be available in time for the launch.

Call of Duty 2

One game that had been completed in time for the Xbox 360 launch was Activision's *Call of Duty 2*. This game was the most popular of all the launch titles, and had gone home with 77% (250,000) of all of the Xbox 360 consoles sold within the first five days of the launch. The game took place during World War II, and players assumed the on-screen persona of either a Russian, British or American soldier from a first-person perspective. Xbox Live provided a multiplay experience, in which up to eight gamers could team up. *Call of Duty 2* was well-

Activision Call of Duty 2

received by gamers, and critics praised its graphics and sound as the best that the console offered. *GamePro* awarded it five stars.

Call of Duty 2 was not offered in Japan when the Xbox launched there on December 10. Only seven titles were available, with the most being successful being *Ridge Racer 6*, which sold 29,891 copies. However, Microsoft only sold 41,817 Xbox 360 consoles in Japan within two days after its launch. Japanese consumers simply weren't as interested in the Xbox 360 as they had been with the earlier Japanese consoles released in their country.

Japanese gamers hadn't really been that much interested in the original Xbox as well. Shortly following the Xbox 360's Japanese release, the original console was discontinued only in Japan.

One American game that had been for sale for some time in Japan was *Grand Theft Auto III*, as Capcom had been distributing it there for the PS2 since September, 2003. On June 7, Kanagawa prefecture, a region south of Tokyo, began banning the sale of the game to minors, making it the first game in Japan to be designated as "a harmful publication." The governor of Kanagawa, Shigefumi Matsuzawa, announced that the action was taken because the game's setting was "very similar to real society, and its level of violence and cruelty is extremely high." And since games, unlike movies, were interactive, they allowed users to act as the game's main character, which created an illusion of reality. After the law went into practice, stores within Kanagawa prefecture had to display the game away from all of the other games, and anyone who sold it to someone under 18 faced a fine of up to ¥300,000 ($2,776).

Restrictive Gaming Laws

As in the preceding years, several American states tried to install similar restrictions as Kanagawa prefecture. On March 5, Arkansas Senator Shawn Womack introduced a bill that required all M-rated games sold within his state to be displayed on store shelves that were at least five feet above the ground. Offenders would receive a $500 fine from the Arkansas Department of Health.

March also brought a federal bill from three Washington state representatives, Mary Lou Dickerson, Jim McCune and Jim McDermot, that correlated violent videogames with violent crimes. They held videogame manufacturers, publishers and retailers responsible if it could be proven that a minor committed a violent crime after playing an M-rated game that they had created, distributed or sold. The bill didn't pass.

A "Safe Games" bill was signed into law by Illinois Governor Rob Blagojevich on July 25, which banned "the distribution, sale, rental and availability of violent and sexually explicit video games to minors," and carried a $1,000 fine to violators. The ESA, VSD and Illinois Retail Merchants Association quickly filed a lawsuit challenging the bill, which was set to become law on January 1, 2006. Judge Matthew F. Kennelly declared on December 2 that the bill was unconstitutional, because it restricted free speech.

A similar bill was signed in California on October 7 by Governor Arnold Schwarzenegger, who had had no problems acting in violent movies. One point of Bill 1179 prohibited the sale of violent videogames to minors, with a penalty of a $1,000 fine. The bill, which had been written by California Senator Leland Yee, stated that "even minors who do not commit acts of violence suffer psychological harm from prolonged exposure to violent video games." On December 21, just before the bill would become law on January 1, 2006, U.S. District Judge Ronald Whyte ruled it unconstitutional because it restricted minors' rights to information.

When drafting their anti-violence bills, the states used the ESRB ratings as their guides. Any game that had been rated "M" (Mature) or "AO" (Adults Only) was to be kept out of the hands of minors. On March 2, the ESRB created a new rating category. "E10+" fell between "E" (Everyone) and "T" (Teen) and applied to **everyone aged 10**

and older. Games that were assigned an "E10+" **could** contain "more cartoon, fantasy or mild violence, mild language and/or minimal suggestive themes." Despite that there were now six different rating categories, one more than was used in the movie industry, on November 29 the National Institute On Media and the Family (NIMF) released its annual *Mediawise Video Game Report Card*, which criticized the rating system. The report cited a dearth of games rated "AO" and the failure of retailers to comply with the ratings. The report deemed the rating system "beyond repair."

The United States National Parent Teacher Association immediately issued a press release denouncing the report, which it claimed included erroneous statements about the PTA. It also stated that it didn't agree with the report's negative comments concerning the ESRB or the rating system. The ESRB also had something to say about the report. On December 6, it assigned a failing grade of "F" to NIMF for the report, which it called seriously flawed.

The NIMF's report claimed that there had been a scarcity of "AO" ratings. This was somewhat true. While several PC games had received the dreaded rating, it had never been assigned to a console game. That changed midway through the year, when the rating was assigned to a game that had actually been released with an "M" rating nine months earlier.

Grand Theft Auto: San Andreas had been released for the PS2 on October 26, 2004 and for the Xbox and PCs on June 7. All three versions had been assigned an "M" rating. At one point in the game, there was a scene wherein the player's character, Carl "C.J." Johnson, was invited into his girlfriend's house for coffee. If Carl accepted, the player would then stand outside of the house and listen to the couple having sex inside.

In July, it was discovered that the PC version contained the disabled code of a minigame that brought the player into the house to control Carl's movements while the couple had sex. A mod was released that allowed players to unlock this hidden code. When news of the explicit scene was announced, *Grand Theft Auto: San Andreas'* publisher, Rockstar, quickly denied any involvement with the code. The company claimed that it was the mod that installed the scene into the game, and that the code wouldn't be found in the PS2 or Xbox editions. However, it wasn't long before it was discovered that the disabled code was indeed in the console editions of the game as well. Once this information became public, politicians, including New York Senator Hillary Clinton, once again began decrying the lack of scrutiny in the videogame industry. On July 8, under this pressure, the ESRB decided to reexamine *Grand Theft Auto: San Andreas*. They quickly faulted Rockstar for not taking the *Hot Coffee* code, which it became known as, into account when it had originally applied for a rating. Then on July 20, the ESRB changed its rating of the game to "AO." Many stores that had policies that forbade them from selling "Adult Only" material, including Walmart and Target, removed the game completely. After Rockstar went ahead and removed the Hot Coffee code from all of the game's versions, the ESRB reinstated it "M" rating in the fall.[13]

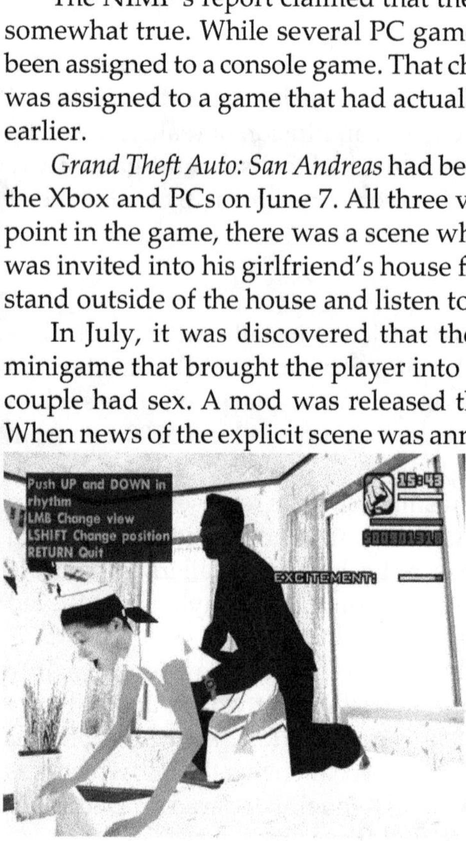

Hot Coffee

Despite its notoriety (or perhaps because of it), *Grand Theft Auto: San Andreas* garnered a myriad of "Best Game" awards, including Spike TV's 2004 videogame award for "Best Soundtrack."

RedOctane Hit and Misses

The game that won the 2005 "Best Soundtrack" award from Spike TV was as different from *Grand Theft Auto: San Andreas* as any game could possibly be. In *Guitar Hero*, gamers used guitar controllers to play in time with musical notes that scrolled down the screen. It was very similar to *GuitarFreaks*, the arcade rhythm game that Konami had released in 1999. And although several home versions of *GuitarFreaks* had been released for the PlayStation and PS2, none of them ever appeared outside of Japan.

RedOctane Guitar Hero

Guitar Hero was developed by Harmonix, a company which had already developed several music-themed games for the PS2, including *FreQuency*, *Amplitude* and Konami's *Karaoke Revolution*.

RedOctane was a company that had marketed music-based gaming peripherals such as dance pads. It had also produced the hardware for Konami's *GuitarFreaks*. In 2004, its management decided that they wanted to bring *GuitarFreaks* to the United States. The company hired Harmonix in late 2004 to develop the software, and the result was *Guitar Hero*, which came out in North America on November 8. The game was sold with a RedOctane-designed, mock Gibson SG guitar that featured five fret buttons (*GuitarFreak*'s guitar only had three).

RedOctane Guitar Hero Guitar

The game featured a career mode, which let beginning guitar players start off with easier games and advance as they got better. It also included a short tutorial to quickly teach the basic game play.

It turned out that people liked pretending that they were guitarists. *Guitar Hero* gave people who had never picked up a guitar in their lives the opportunity to act out aspirations of being rock stars.

Guitar Hero got its big break on November 25, when RedOctane signed a deal with MTV Games, in which the cable network would feature *Guitar Hero* on MTV's shows and websites. Once it was prominently shown on the network, the popularity for the game soared and it became a hit, frequently selling out in game stores and becoming hard to find in time for the holidays. When announcing the partnership between his company and MTV Games, RedOctane CEO Kai Huang referred to *Guitar Hero* and said, "For the first time, rock music is not in the background, but instead, it IS the game!"

But *Guitar Hero* was not the first game that RedOctane released for the PS2 that had been based on a Konami Bemani hit. On June 17, it had released *In the Groove*, the console version of an arcade game that had been released by Roxor Games on August 30, 2004. A sequel, *In the Groove 2*, was released to arcades on June 18, one day after RedOctane's home edition appeared. But as *Guitar Hero* was similar to *GuitarFreaks*, *In the Groove* was very similar to *Dance Dance Revolution*. The games were so much alike that Konami took

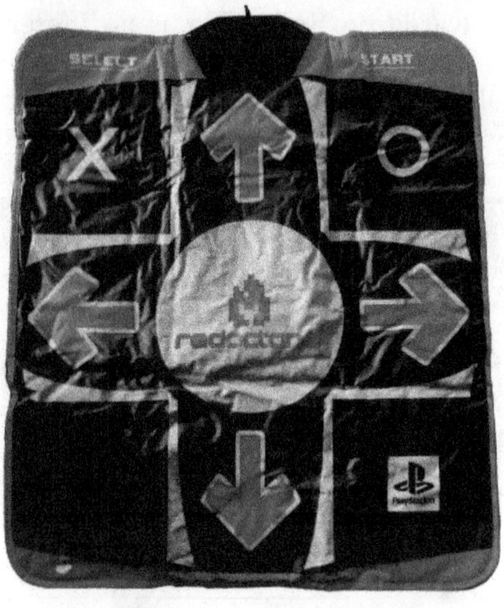

RedOctane In The Groove

Nintendo Dance Dance Revolution Mario Mix Pad

Roxor Games to court on May 9 for several patent infringements. On July 1, Konami amended its lawsuit to include RedOctane because of the home version.[14]

An official version of *Dance Dance Revolution* was released for the GameCube in North America on October 24. *Dance Dance Revolution Mario Mix*[15] marked the first time that a version of *Dance Dance Revolution* becmame available for a Nintendo console outside of Japan. And this wasn't strictly another rehash of *Dance Dance Revolution*. While the gameplay was similar to prior versions, it also featured a new *Mush Mode*, which had in addition to the arrows that told the dancer which square to step on, several items that also fell that the dancer had to contend with. Some items had to be stomped while others had to be avoided. *Dance Dance Revolution* enthusiasts had to option turn this mode off.

The game was bundled with a game pad that was reminiscent to the NES Power Pad and Bandai's *Family Trainer* pad for the Famicom. Several minigames were included with *Dance Dance Revolution Mario Mix* that used the pad for non-*Dance Dance Revolution* exercises.

Music From Screen To Stage

Unlike previous versions of *Dance Dance Revolution Dance* games, which used popular songs that had been licensed by Konami, or songs that had been written by Konami artists that sounded like popular music, *Dance Dance Revolution Mario Mix* mostly used songs that had been written for various Nintendo games, such as *Donkey Kong* and *Super Mario Bros.*

Video game music had been around ever since Al Alcorn figured out how to create the sound of a ball hitting a paddle in *Pong*. Like the graphics it accompanied, videogame music was originally very simple, but as technology improved, so did the music. As games made the transition from being designed and programmed by a single person to large, integrated teams, a music composer was added to the mix. Few composers outside of the videogame industry had achieved the notoriety of their film counterparts, such as John Williams or James Horner. However, within the industry, names like Nobuo Uematsu and Koji Kondo were well-known.

Another well-known composer was Tommy Tallarico, who began composing videogame music in 1991. In 2002, he conceived a videogame concert to showcase famous videogame music performed by a local philharmonic orchestra. Tallarico partnered with another composer, Jack Wall, and for the next three years, he began gathering performance rights from the various gaming companies. When *Video Games Live* opened at the Hollywood Bowl on July 6, Tallarico took the stage, guitar in hand, in front of an audience of more than 11,000 people and backed by 72 musicians from the Los Angeles Philharmonic, as well as a 40-person choir.

FOCUS ON TOMMY TALLARICO

In 1989, 21-year-old Tommy Tallarico left his parents' home in Springfield, MA and moved to Los Angeles to pursue a career in the music industry. Unfortunately, his pursuit ended with him broke and living under a pier. Deciding to take any work that was available, Tallarico found a job through a newspaper ad selling keyboards. Tallarico decided to wear a TurboGrafx-16 shirt for his first day of work. As fate would have it, a producer for a new software company, Virgin Mastertronic, just happened to walk into the store. When he saw Tallarico's shirt he offered Tallarico a job as a game tester for his company, which Tallarico immediately took. Once hired, Tallarico continuously bothered the company's vice president into allowing him work on the music for their games. He was finally given the opportunity to create music (in his spare time for free) for *Prince of Persia* for the Game Boy, which he was already producing and testing. Soon afterwards Tallarico's days as a tester were behind him as Virgin Mastertronic promoted him to create music for them full time.

In 1994, Tallarico founded *Tommy Tallarico Studios*, which today is the multimedia industry's largest audio production house. In 1997, he began hosting, writing and co-producing for a new show called *The Electric Playground*, a daily show that covered videogames and other forms of pop culture. This show has aired continuously since the beginning on several cable networks including Discovery and G4. On July 2012, the name of the show was changed to *EP Daily*.

In 2008, Tallarico was recognized by the *Guinness Book of World Records* scoring the most commercially released games. He has created the music to some of the best-known games over the years including *Earthworm Jim*, *Metroid Prime* and *Tony Hawk's Pro Skater*. Several important websites have deemed his music for *Advent Rising* as "one of the greatest musical scores of all time." He currently has over 300 game titles to his credit and has won more than 50 industry awards, including a Lifetime Achievement Award that he received at the Game Developers Conference in 2012.

In addition to *Video Games Live*, which has put on more than 250 performances on five continents, Tallarico is also the founder of the *Game Audio Network Guild*, a non-profit that educates and heightens the awareness of audio for the interactive world.

Tallarico is also a first-cousin of Steven Tyler, lead singer of the rock group, Aerosmith. In 2002 Tallarico's music was used as the opening song for the group's "Girls of Summer" world tour.

In addition to hearing the orchestral renditions of music from a variety of games, including *Halo, Warcraft* and *Tomb Raider,* and even a medley of classic tunes that included *Pong* and *Donkey Kong,* the audience was shown clips from various videogames on large monitors and treated to a laser-light show.

Video Games Live was a success, and the show's promoter, Clear Channel, made plans to bring it on the road. A summer 2005 North American Tour was quickly announced and dates were set up, beginning with Atlanta on August 13 and ending in Irvine, California on September 11. Clear Channel soon found that their lead and marketing time wasn't long enough to get the word out adequately, so the itinerary was scrapped. New tour dates were announced on September 13, with the tour now scheduled to begin on October 29 in Seattle and terminate in San Antonio on December 3. The Seattle concert took place, along with one in Vancouver on the following night, but the rest of the tour was canceled. Fans who had purchased tickets in advance had to manually request refunds and lost any convenience charges that they had paid. Clear Channel had canceled the tour because "ticket sales were slow and did not reflect the great interest expected." After this fiasco, Tallarico and Wall vowed never to cancel another show again, and decided to do all of the planning and promoting themselves. Once Clear Channel was out of the picture, they focused on 2006.

Game Company Stores

As videogame composers became more known, other people in the industry were also beginning to get recognized. Following the format of Hollywood's historic Walk of Fame, Sony's Metreon mall in San Francisco began its own *Walk of Game* to honor videogaming's achievers and characters. Throughout October 2004, gamers around the world were able to vote for their favorites through either paper ballots or an online site. The top four games or characters, and top two Lifetime Achievers, were inducted into the Walk of Game in a special ceremony at the site on March 8. In 2005, the *Lifetime Achiever* awards went to Nolan Bushnell, who attended the ceremony, and Shigeru Miyamoto, who did not. The characters **Mario, Sonic the Hedgehog** and Link all won honors along with the game *Halo*. All honorees were then awarded with their own customized steel stars, which were etched into two-square-foot tiles on the Metreon's floor. The voting process was repeated throughout October 2005 for the 2006 inductees.

One of the businesses inside the Metreon was the PlayStation Store, which was owned by Sony and only sold PlayStation-related products such as consoles, games and accessories. However, one PS2-related item that was not available at the store was the PSX, since it was only released in Japan. Although Sony had constantly promised that the PSX would eventually be available outside of Japan, that still hadn't occurred by the time 2005 began. The ultimate decision finally came on February 24, when Sony announced once and for all that it was ceasing production of the PSX.

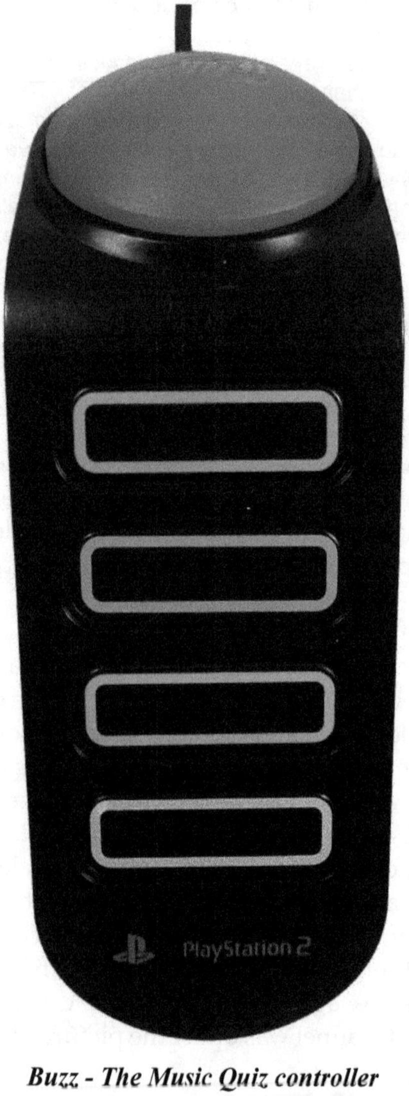

Buzz - The Music Quiz controller

Another Sony product that was not offered at the PlayStation Store was *Buzz!: The Music Quiz*. This was a game for the PS2 that was distributed only in Europe by SCEE. *Buzz!: The Music Quiz*, as its name applied, was a trivia game in which an online emcee named *Buzz* asked contestants questions referring to over 1000 music clips that were included with the game. The contestants consisted of up to four players who used specially-designed controllers that were bundled with the game. Each controller, which plugged into one of the PS2's USB ports, consisted of a large red button and four smaller color coded buttons. To respond to a question, the player had to be the first to hit the red button of his respective controller. Afterwards, he had to select one of the color coded buttons which corresponded to the multiple choice answers on the screen. *Buzz!: The Music Quiz* also offered a solo player mode where a player had to answer a question correctly in the quickest possible time.

When Sony opened the PlayStation Store in 1999, it was the only company-owned store in the United States dedicated to a videogame console. That unique distinction ended on May 14, when Nintendo opened a similar type of store in New York City. *Nintendo World* was located in Rockefeller Center, in the space previously occupied by the Pokémon Center. Pokémon-related products were relegated to their own section within the store. Other sections were dedicated to Nintendo's current consoles, as well as Nintendo-specific clothing and plush toys. Although Shigeru Miyamoto hadn't visited the Metreon in March for the Walk of Game ceremonies, he did visit Nintendo World on September 25, to honor the 20th anniversary of the NES/Famicom version of *Super Mario Bros.* and to promote *Nintendogs* for the DS.

The PlayStation store and Nintendo World were both one-of-a-kind stores that only sold products for their respective systems. But most games and consoles were sold in chain stores, the market leader being GameStop. On April 18, the company got even bigger after it announced that it planned to merge with EB Games, a decision that was approved by shareholders and regulatory agencies on October 10. After the deal closed, GameStop commanded 25% of the retail market, and although EB Games was legally owned by GameStop, its individual stores wouldn't adopt the GameStop name until February 1, 2006.[16]

Despite its huge market share, GameStop did have competition in the form of rentals through mail-order distributors such as GameFly, or downloads from online services such as Xbox Live. A new company launched on October 17 that was a combination of both. *GameTap* was a service from TBS through which subscribers paid $10 a month to play an unlimited number of games on their PCs. Instead of being downloaded onto the computer's hard drive, the games were streamed through GameTap's website, so there was no way the user could save and copy them. The service was hardly a nuisance to modern gamers, as it only offered retro console, PC and arcade games. GameTap began with approximately 300 titles from systems such as the Atari 2600, Intellivision, Genesis and Dreamcast, along with classic arcade games from Midway, Namco, Sega and Taito.

Ironically, several of the companies that had licensed their older classic titles to GameTap were having problems in the present. Atari, which had no hit games during the year, recorded a $32 million loss for the fiscal year ending June 30. To keep the company afloat, Atari turned to its parent, Infogrames, which provided the financial backing that Atari needed to make it through the lean times.

Taito did not have to report a loss, but its overall profit of over ¥1.7 billion ($15 million) had fallen ¥1.8 billion ($16 million) from the year before. Taito's president, Yasuo Nishigaki, attributed the rising cost of playing arcade games as a major factor in the decline of the company's profits.

Namco was also in the black, but was concerned about its shrinking revenue as it paid more to develop games that sold for less. It announced on May 2 that it would merge with Bandai, a company long involved in home gaming, to create a company that would be only second to Sega Sammy Holdings in size and revenue. The new company, Namco Bandai Holdings, became official on September 29.

Despite the grumbling of the game publishers, the year 2005 was actually a record year for gaming. Although sales throughout the year had been pretty dismal, they picked up during the last two weeks before Christmas. By the end of the year, U.S. retailers had sold $10.5 billion worth of hardware, software and accessories.

Not so surprisingly, sales of portable devices exceeded those of consoles. But while the PSP and DS did well, the combined sales for these devices were still much less than that of the GBA, which proved that it still had life in it.

Even with the release of the Xbox 360, the console market didn't perform as well as the portable, although SCE did announce on November 29 that it had shipped its 100 millionth PS2. Now the company looked forward to the release of its PS3 in 2006, a year that Nintendo promised would be revolutionary.

CHAPTER THIRTY-FOUR
2006

The year began, as always, with the annual Consumer Electronics Show (CES) in Las Vegas. But ever since E³ began in 1995, CES had held gradually less relevance for the videogame industry. Even though Nintendo planned to release a new console later in the year, it didn't attend the 2006 CES at all. Sony, which had its hands in many types of consumer electronics, focused mostly on those products and only displayed a mock-up of the forthcoming PS3, along with some pertinent game trailers. The PSP was awarded more exposure, but not really to promote any of its gaming functions. Since 2004, Sony had marketed its *LocationFree* player, a device that could stream live TV broadcasts to computers and its own wireless tablet. Sony used CES to announce that a software upgrade would be available that would permit consumers to use a LocationFree player to stream TV shows to their PSPs.

Microsoft, whose Xbox 360 had been available for less than two months, did have a booth at the show. Bill Gates used the event to announce that an external HD-DVD drive would be coming out for the console.

Although Microsoft had the only next-gen system available for sale, the lone American console manufacturer was having problems with it in the marketplace, specifically in Japan, where the console suffered a poor launch. During its first two days of availability, Microsoft sold only 62,135 consoles. This was less than half of the 123,334 original Xboxes that had been sold in Japan within three days of that console's launch. Many blamed the poor showing on the lack of available quality software. One highly awaited game, *Dead or Alive 4*, simply hadn't been ready in time for the console's release. Things changed a little in March, when the Xbox 360 launched in Australia. Although only 30,000 consoles were sold there during the first week, it was still that country's fastest-selling launch in history.

If Microsoft had made any errors in launching the Xbox 360, it had plenty of time to make up for it, since the PS3 wasn't scheduled to be released until spring. And according to some reports, that time frame was going to change. In February, the analyst firm Merrill Lynch issued a report which speculated that the PS3 would be delayed for at least a year, and when it was finally available, it would sell for at least $800. Merrill Lynch reported that the cause of the high price was the fact that two of its components, the Blu-ray drive and IBM's Cell chip, would cost $350 and $230 respectively. SCE ignored the price allegation and refuted the delay claim by stating that the PS3 was still on target for a spring release.

That changed a month later, when SCE's Ken Kutaragi announced that the console would be released simultaneously around the world in November. The reason given for this delay was because SCE was waiting for a consortium of eight companies to finalize specifications of an advanced copy protection, specifications that were supposed to have been completed in 2005. Production of the console's Blu-ray player couldn't begin until these specifications were set. SCE's plan was to begin production in June, allowing for 2 million units to be on hand in time for the worldwide release with an additional 6 million consoles available by March, 2007. SCE hoped to avoid the shortages that had befallen Microsoft during the Xbox 360 launch, including the one that had occurred because Microsoft had offered two Xbox 360 packages, one with a hard drive and one without. All PS3s were going to be packaged with a 60GB hard drive as standard equipment.

SCE also announced the *PlayStation Network*, Sony's version of Xbox Live. This would be fully accessible from the moment the PS3 was removed from its box. In addition to including a free Internet browser that could open several websites concurrently, the PlayStation Network would feature a virtual marketplace, the *PlayStation Store*, which would offer free, unlimited online gaming. And for a fee, gamers would be able to download older PlayStation and PS2 games from SCE's catalog, which they could store on the hard drive. But this wouldn't be the only way people could play the older games on their PS3s, as the console would be backwards-compatible with both the PS2 and the original PlayStation games.

What SCE did not discuss were the controllers that the PS3 would use. Since 2002, SCE had been involved in a lawsuit with Immersion Corporation for the use of its DualShock controllers, which invalidated patents owned by Immersion.[1] SCE lost a jury trial in September, 2004 and was ordered to pay Immersion $82 million in damages. SCE appealed in March 2003, but was not successful, adding another $9 million to the amount that it owed Immersion. When SCE's Phil Harrison was asked if the lawsuit would have any effect on the PS3 controller's design, he replied that the new controller would be "revealed at E^3."

The Wii

Like SCE, Nintendo preferred to use E^3 as the springboard for its new console, the Revolution, and issued limited information about the system prior to that. The company announced early in 2006 that the Revolution would indeed be released before the year ended. And Nintendo representatives had made it clear that since the company concentrated on playability and not sheer muscle, the console would not be as powerful as the Xbox 360. They had also revealed that while games would be distributed on 12-centimeter proprietary DVDs, which could each store 4.7GB of data, the Revolution would also be able to play the GameCube's 8-centimeter discs without any emulation required. And unlike the GameCube, the Revolution would also be able to play standard DVDs.

The Revolution would have Wi-Fi built in. Gamers would use it to access Nintendo's *Virtual Console*, from where they could purchase and download games from past Nintendo systems, as well as selected Sega Genesis and NEC TurboGrafx-16 games.

On April 27, Nintendo announced that its revolutionary new console was no longer going to be called the Revolution. The new moniker would be the *Wii*, which was pronounced like the English word "we" and was a word that could be remembered by people all around the world, no matter what language they spoke. It meant that the new console was for everybody. Nintendo explained that the word was spelled with "*ii*" to symbolize both the console's innovative new controller and "the image of people gathering to play." But Rob Saunders, the PR manager for Nintendo UK, added a different slant about the console's new name. According to Saunders, the unusual name set Nintendo apart from its competitors by offering something new, whereas the names of the consoles

Nintendo Wii

from SCE and Microsoft were merely "beefed-up versions of what they already offered."

Nintendo also announced that the Wii's controller would officially be called the *Wii Remote*. The controller would communicate with the console via wireless Bluetooth technology, which was different from the radio frequency (RF) technology that Nintendo had used in its previous wireless controller, the Gamecube's WaveBird.[2] But what really made the Wii Remote different from prior controllers was its ability to sense motion. It had a built-in accelerometer that could detect movement on three axes (length, width and depth). This data was sent wirelessly to a separate sensor bar, which was placed near the television screen. The sensor bar then sent the information to the Wii console via an attached cable.

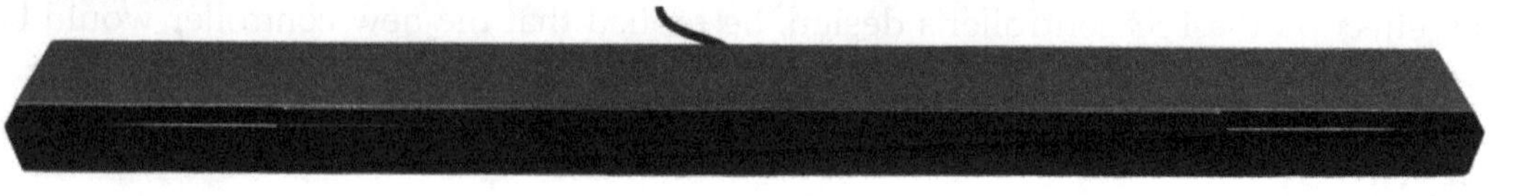

Nintendo Wii Sensor Bar

At E[3] in May, Nintendo opened its pre-show press conference with its legendary designer, Shigeru Miyamoto, dressed in a tuxedo and leading a virtual orchestra using a Wii Remote as a baton. But just as the gathered crowd became somewhat accustomed to the new, revolutionary controller, Nintendo announced that a *second* Wii controller would also be available. Although the *Nunchuck* adapter would provide standard features, such as an analog stick, to the Wii Remote, neither could be used to play the array of classic Nintendo games from the Virtual Console adequately.[3] For this reason, the company

Nintendo Wii Remote

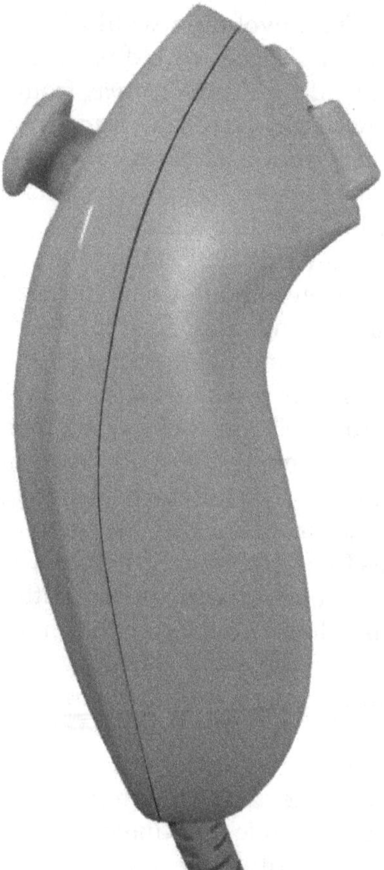

Nintendo Nunchuck

planned to release an optional standard controller that would be used exclusively for the Virtual Console games, and not for any new Wii games.

Nintendo also announced *WiiConnect24*, a feature that would keep the Wii connected to the Internet, even when the unit was turned off, so Nintendo could send system updates at any time to any registered console. But Nintendo also said that the service could be used for gaming purposes, such as allowing gamers to visit another player's *Animal Crossing* town, even when the Wii that hosted the town on was turned off.

Nintendo didn't use E^3 to announce the release date or pricing of the Wii. The company waited until September 6 to reveal that the system would be released in the Americas on November 19 (two days after the PS3's launch), in Japan on December 2 and in Europe on December 8. The console, which would cost $249 in the United States, would include the Wii Remote and Nunchuck, which would also be available for purchase separately for $40 and $20 respectively. Also bundled with the console, with the exception of the Japanese and South Korean versions, would be *Wii Sports*, a collection of games that spotlighted the console's features. Contrary to earlier claims, the Wii would not be able to play standard DVDs, as Nintendo had axed that feature to reduce costs.

Nintendo Wii Sports - Tennis

Nintendo also disclosed specific information about the Virtual Console. Sixty downloadable games would be available before the end of the year. They would cost between $4 and $10 apiece, and would be purchased with Wii points. These points would be available for sale online and would also be awarded to people who registered consoles or purchased games from stores.

2006

When the Wii was turned on, a number of "channels" would appear on the screen. Weather and news channels would deliver content from the Internet. A photo channel would allow users to upload photographs from SD cards to use in slideshows and a shopping channel would be where people could download games to the Virtual Console. There would also be a Nintendo channel, which would provide Nintendo-specific news, and a disc channel where players would go if they had inserted Wii or GameCube discs. And for people who wanted to surf the Internet, there would be an Internet channel that opened an Opera Internet browser[4] when selected.

Finally, there would be a *Mii* Channel. Miis were on-screen characters whose features, including the shapes of their heads, lips, hairstyles, eyes, eyebrows, ears, facial hair and glasses, could be customized. With a little ingenuity, it would be possible for people to create Miis that somewhat resembled themselves. The Miis could then be used as avatars or even as characters in games. In *Wii Sports*, the player's onscreen character was his personal Mii.

The Wii required a wireless signal in order to connect to any of the external channels and

Nintendo Mii

Nintendo Wii LAN Adapter

Nintendo Wii Classic Controller

the Nintendo Wi-Fi Connection.[5] However, those who were wired to the Internet weren't totally out of luck. Although it wasn't publicized by Nintendo, the console's Operations Manual indicated that Internet users on wired networks could use a *Wii LAN Adapter* "when available."

The Wii Lan Adapter came out in Japan on December 30 and cost ¥2,800 ($24).[6] The small device consisted of a plastic box with an Ethernet cable port and a USB plug. To use it, an Ethernet cable needed to be run from the router to the Wii Lan Adapter, which then plugged into one of the USB ports on the back of the Wii console.

Upon the Wii's launch on November 19, Nintendo also released the optional controller that had been promised back in April. The $20 *Wii Classic Controller* was similar in appearance to the SNES controller, and included a D-pad, two analog sticks, and several buttons. The Wii Classic Controller plugged into an expansion port at the bottom of the Wii Remote.[7] Although it was specifically intended to be used to play Virtual Console games, it could also be used with several new Wii games. However, it couldn't be used to play GameCube games.

SCE's Press Announcement

As promised, SCE held a pre-E³ press conference on May 8, two days before the start of the exhibition. Kaz Hirai, head of SCEA, used it to announce that the PS3 was scheduled to be released on November 11 in Japan and on November 17 in the United States. Hirai also said that the PS3 would be launched in Europe in November as well, marking the first time that SCE released a console in all three major markets almost simultaneously.

Hirai also spoke about the PS3's controller, which would feature motion sensors. This meant that games could be controlled by waving the controller in a fashion somewhat similar to the Wii Remote. The PS3's controller wouldn't have a vibration feature, which according to SCE, would interfere with "information detected by the sensor." SCE's ongoing battle with Immersion was not mentioned at all.

Contrary to the earlier announcement that said the PS3 would only be offered in one configuration, Hirai told the assembled audience that the PS3 would actually be released in two flavors. The basic unit would include a 20GB hard drive and would retail for $499. The high-end unit would sell for $599 and would come with a 60GB hard drive. It would also include one HDMI output that would be needed for high-definition televisions, a built-in Wi-Fi adapter and ports for memory sticks, SD cards and flash drives. Naturally, this meant that the high-end inclusions would be absent from the lower-priced model, although according to Phil Harrison, these would be available for sale separately at a later date. While many people were understandably concerned about the high prices of both configurations, SCE pointed out that those prices were actually bargains when compared to how much stand-alone Blu-ray players would cost.[8]

New Xbox 360 Options

At Microsoft's E³ press conference, Bill Gates used his first-ever E³ appearance to tell a gathered audience that by the time either Sony or Nintendo released its new console, Microsoft would have had a strong head-start, with 10 million Xbox 360s sold and more than 160 titles available on the market.

Gates also announced *Live Anywhere*, a new initiative that would permit gamers on any platform that had a Microsoft-based operating system the ability to access Xbox Live, so they could compete against each other in online games. According to Gates, Live Anywhere would be available in 2007.

Microsoft used E^3 to show the Xbox 360's HD-DVD drive and a camera called *Xbox Live Vision*. Both were scheduled to be released in the United States in time for Christmas.

But Microsoft's biggest news at E^3 was that *Halo 3* was in development and would be released sometime in 2007.

While the Xbox 360 seemed to have an advantage over Nintendo and SCE's new consoles, it was struggling against SCE's current system, the PS2.

On April 20, SCEA lowered the retail price of the PS2 by $20 to $130, making it less expensive than Microsoft's original Xbox, which still sold for $150. Ever since the Xbox 360 was released in September 2005, the PS2 outsold it most months. And outside North America, the Xbox 360's sales were hindered because the console was constantly in short supply. But in Japan, where plenty of consoles were available, interest in it was just plain low. In April, the Xbox 360 won its first battle when it outsold the PS2 by 90,000 units. But that bright spot for Microsoft quickly turned-around when SCEA lowered the PS2's price.

The Xbox 360 also trailed behind the original Xbox in sales. By October, only 6 million of the next-generation consoles had been sold worldwide. The Xbox had sold 9 million consoles during the same time period following its release.

Microsoft managed to release some upgrades to make the Xbox 360 more on par with the PS3's highly touted high-definition capabilities. On October 31, a software update addressed over 84 issues and included the ability for the console to provide 1080p resolution to TVs that could support it. The problem, as Sony purists pointed out, was that the Xbox 360 console didn't have an HDMI output port, so true high-definition 1080p resolution could not be achieved. The reality of this, however, was that most people would probably never notice the difference.

As promised, Microsoft released the two new peripherals that it displayed at E^3. The *Xbox Live Vision* camera came out on September 19 in North America, with the other territories receiving it within the following two months. The $35 camera was similar to SCE's EyeToy, and several games used this feature to create images of the player's face within the game. But, as its name implied, the camera was especially designed to be used with an Xbox Live gold subscription so people could video chat or record and send video messages. It also let them personalize their Xbox Live gamer tags with photos.

Microsoft Xbox Live Vision camera

Microsoft released its external HD-DVD player on November 7. At $199, it was an excellent buy, considering that stand-alone HD-DVD players cost much more.[9] Unfortunately, the only people who needed one were those who wanted to watch HD-DVDs, which couldn't play on the Xbox 360's internal drive.

But the HD-DVD drive wouldn't provide the only way for Xbox 360 owners to watch

Microsoft Xbox 360 HD-DVD Player

high-definition movies from their consoles. On November 6, Microsoft announced that it had signed deals with several entertainment companies, including CBS, Paramount Pictures and Warner Bros., to deliver high-def movies and TV programming to the console through Xbox Live, marking the first time that such content could be downloaded to a game console. In all, more than 1,000 hours of content were available through the *Video Marketplace* beginning on November 22.

Launching the PS3

As November approached, SCE's executives became nervous about whether or not they would have enough consoles to fill the large demand that they expected. SCEE officials in Great Britain discussed whether consumers should pay a hefty £150 ($283) deposit or the standard £5 ($9.50) if they wanted to preorder a PS3. They played around with charging a low deposit and not guaranteeing enough consoles available at launch, vs. charging a high deposit and making sure that the console would be on hand. But SCEE's greatest concern was to keep the console out of the hands of black marketers, who would sell them on eBay at exorbitant prices if SCEE couldn't keep up with the demand.

On September 6, SCEE's worry about not having enough consoles available for November's launch became moot. Ken Kutaragi announced on that day that the PS3's European launch would be delayed until March, 2007 to prevent shortages in Japan and the United States. Apparently Sony, which built the components for the new Blu-ray player, had run behind schedule in manufacturing a key laser diode for the unit, which jeopardized the number of available players. On September 30, Sony ceased distributing the diode to third-party Blu-ray manufacturers in order to ensure an ample amount would be available for the PS3.

But even with Europe out of the picture, SCE reduced the number of actual PS3 consoles that would be obtainable at launch. Only 100,000 units would be on hand in Japan

SCE PlayStation 3 (PS3)

for its November 11 debut, and 400,000 for the American release. But despite the fact that the initial number of consoles for sale was cut in half, SCE still went by its original claim that six million units would be available worldwide by March, 2007. Still, it was hard to believe what SCE said, since the company changed its numbers again on October 30 when it announced that only 80,000 consoles would be initially available in Japan at the outset.

But all the news regarding the PS3 wasn't gloomy. During his keynote speech at the Tokyo Game Show at the end of September, Kutaragi announced that the 20GB lower-end PS3s would indeed include HDMI outputs, just like the higher-priced ones. In addition, SCEJ would lower the price of those consoles from ¥60,000 ($515) to ¥49,980 ($429). This price decrease only applied to the 20GB consoles sold in Japan, and the $499 amount would remain in the United States.

All of the PS3 configurations came with a *Sixaxis* controller. This controller closely resembled the PS2's DualShock 2 but also had the ability to sense motion on three plains: up and down, left and right, and forward and backward.

SCE Sixaxis Controller

The Sixaxis was also SCE's first wireless controller. The controller communicated with the console via Bluetooth, but it lacked the ability to automatically find a free Bluetooth address. In ordered to be used wirelessly, it first had to be set up with the console via a wired connection and the Bluetooth address had to be manually selected. The PS3 could handle up to seven controllers at a time and a combination of four numbered LEDs were used to inform which controller belonged to which player.

One difference between prior Japanese launches and this one was that the PS3 could not be pre-ordered due to expected shortage of consoles. In some places, long lines began forming days before November 10. Much of the crowd was made up of poor Chinese nationals who had been hired by Japanese businessmen to score as many consoles as possible so they could offer them on eBay at inflated prices. This also resulted in low software sales, since only the hardware was being purchased for sale on the auction site. The crowd grew uneasy as time passed, resulting in a lot of pushing and shoving. Many stores began distributing their allotment of consoles well before the actual 7:00 AM launch. In fact, most stores were already sold out before 7:00 AM!

In order to keep the Japanese PS3 in Japan, SCEE once again restricted British retailers from importing the device, just as it had done during the PSP's Japanese launch. eBay banned listing PS3s on its British site until February, 2007.

eBay also created new rules in anticipation of the PS3's November 17 North American release. It would only allow sellers with at least 50 prior listings to auction new PS3s. This was to prevent anyone from purchasing a console at retail and then setting up an eBay account with the sole purpose of dumping the console. Despite this safeguard, 14,675 PS3s, with an average price of $1,186, were available on eBay.

The people who stood in lines for hours for the American PS3 faced risks. At 3 AM, twenty people in a line at a Putnam, Connecticut Walmart were accosted by two thugs demanding money. One man was shot and sustained non-fatal injuries after he refused to give up his cash. Police were also summoned to a Henrico, Virginia Target to calm down an unruly crowd of 350 people who were in line at a store that only had eight consoles for sale. The management of a Boston Best Buy had a smarter approach to distributing its allotment of 140 consoles. Its employees handed out vouchers to the first 140 people who showed up and then stopped anyone else from joining the line.

Although SCEA had promised that 400,000 consoles would be available for the American launch, many analysts believed that the actual number was between 150,000 and 200,000. GameStop announced that it probably wouldn't be able to fill all of its preorders right away. And as had been the case with the Xbox 360, some people who did manage to get a PS3 had to settle for a 20GB model, even though they wanted the 60GB one. While SCEA wouldn't provide an exact number of how many consoles had been immediately available, it did say in a statement that it had been pleased with the launch and would focus on getting as many new consoles onto American store shelves in time for the holidays as possible.

Wii Launch

Two days after the PS3 was released, the American Wii launch went off much more smoothly, with no apparent violence reported. In most cases, customers lined up at stores on the morning the consoles became available, although the Toys "R" Us in Times Square opened at midnight to sell the very first Wii. There were enough consoles on hand to ensure that none of the more than 1,000 people who stood in line went home without one. Many of those first Wiis that were bought did wind up on eBay, but the $500 average asking price was much lower than what people had been asking for the PS3.

Console Problems

Although the PS3 wasn't available in large numbers, most of them at least worked. SCE reported a failure rate of less than 1%, an amount that wasn't challenged. Microsoft, on the other hand, placed the failure rate of new Xbox 360s at the industry standard of approximately 3-5%, but many people felt that the actual number was much higher. In addition to an increasingly large number of consoles that were overheating, more and more owners began experiencing the "red ring of death," when three of the LEDs surrounding the power switch flashed red instead of the normal green. This indicated that a general hardware error had occurred. Some people reported that they had exchanged defective machines for new ones, only to have their replacement machines suffer the same problem within hours of being turned on.

When Microsoft had released the Xbox 360 in 2005, it only offered a 90-day warranty with the system, far below the electronic-industry standard of one year. As many of the Xbox 360's defects began appearing after the 90-day warranty period expired, customers had to pay Microsoft to repair the problem. On top of that, they also had to pay to ship their consoles to Microsoft and back.

As negative complaints came in, Microsoft evaluated its warranty policy and, on December 22, announced that it was changing it. From that day on, every Xbox 360 console would carry a 1-year warranty from the date of purchase. The period was also retroactive, and the warranty period of consoles purchased before that date would automatically be extended to one year from the date of purchase. In addition, people who paid to have their consoles repaired by Microsoft were eligible to get the charges reimbursed, including any shipping fees that they had incurred.

Although it was a Band-Aid for good customer relations, the extended warranty didn't solve all of Microsoft's headaches. For one, the warranty was only extended in the United States. Customers in other countries had to continue to get the problem fixed with their own money.

Another problem that Xbox 360 owners had encountered, particularly after October 31, was the tendency for games to lock up. It was believed that an automatic update to the console's operating system caused the freezing problem, and the hope was that Microsoft would find and fix it in a future update. But that ran contrary to another problem with Microsoft, as the company seemed to be ignorant that so many consoles were having problems.

Nintendo also received consumer complaints, but they had nothing to do with the quality of the Wii. Instead, the concern was that people were playing Wii games too zealously. During their constant bodily movements, they were occasionally letting go of their Wii Remotes, sending them flying. Sometimes, the remotes landed harmlessly, but in other cases, they caused property damage by going through TV screens, and even bodily damage by hitting people. Although the Wii Remote had an optional strap protruding from its bottom, some players didn't wrap the strap around their wrists in their zeal to get into a game.

Nintendo, for its part, tried to educate gamers in the proper way to use the controllers. In early December, the company sent emails to registered Wii owners that explained how to correctly use the Wii Remote. In addition, each game that used the Wii Remote displayed a warning message at the beginning, to remind the player how to correctly hold the controller. However, even gamers who properly used the Wii Remotes with the straps around their wrists wound up with runaway controllers. In too many cases, the straps themselves were defective and came apart from the Wii Remotes while in use. Nintendo acknowledged the problem and began using a stronger strap. It also sent up to four of the new straps free to any registered Wii owner who requested them.

By the end of November, all three consoles were available in the United States. Unsurprisingly, with a short supply and high retail price, only 197,000 PS3s were sold. The Wii did much better with 476,000 consoles sold. The one-year-old Xbox 360, which had been available through all of November, did only slightly better with 511,000 consoles sold throughout the month. Microsoft may have won the next-gen battle for November, but it certainly didn't win the war. SCE announced that its six-year-old PS2 had outsold all of the newer consoles, with a total of 664,000 units sold during November.

Mattel Hyperscan

Two other consoles were released during the year in addition to the Wii and PS3. One was from Mattel, which in October began selling its first videogame console since the Intellivision. The $70 *HyperScan* was targeted towards boys aged 8-12 and incorporated two popular pastimes: videogaming and trading-card games like *Pokémon* and *Magic: The Gathering*.

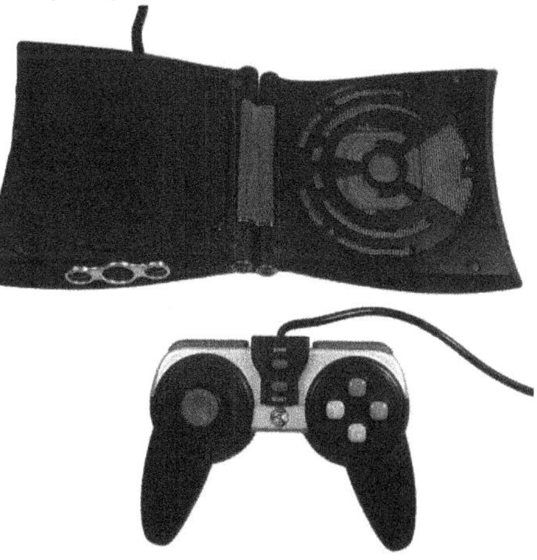

Mattel Hyperscan

The HyperScan console flipped open, much like the Nintendo DS. A CD drive that had to be manually opened and closed took up one side of the console and a scanner was built into the other.

HyperScan games came on CDs and each were packaged with six game cards, all imbedded with an RFID (radio frequency identification) chip. The cards represented characters or modifications and could be traded among players. Additional booster packs, each containing six more cards, could be purchased for $10. Data about the character or modification was stored on the RFID chip.

HyperScan titles were essentially battle games, like those that had been predominantly found on the Neo•Geo. However, in order to battle as a specific character, the player first had to have that character's card in his hand. Information about the character, which was stored on the card's RFID chip, would be scanned into the console by swiping the card over the scanner. Modification cards in the player's deck could be used to enhance the qualities of the character. And if the character won a battle, those enhancements could be downloaded onto the chip in the character's card for use in another game.

The controller, which resembled the original PlayStation's, was unresponsive and cheaply made. The time it took for a game to load from a CD was long, and it had to be done for each new battle. The public response to the HyperScan was unenthusiastic.[10]

V.Flash

The other new console was from VTech, the manufacturer of educational game consoles for kids. The *V.Flash* combined educational games with 3D graphics and was aimed at children aged 6-10. Unlike the software for the previous VTech consoles, V.Flash games only came on CDs. To prevent youngsters from scratching the discs, the CDs were housed in caddies, similar to the PSP's UMD. Standard music CDs could play in the system as well. However, in order to use one, parents had to first place the CD into a second, empty caddy that was bundled with the unit. Once the CD was in place, kids could insert the music CD into the V.Flash and listen to it. The system was not backward-compatible with the V.Smile, which VTech continued to sell. But the controller that came with the V.Flash

VTech V.Flash

VTechV.Flash CD Caddy

did feature the same colorful jewel-like buttons that were found on the V.Smile.

The V.Flash supplied an education niche for children who were getting too old for the V.Smile. And as if to make sure they had all age groups covered, VTech also released a console for children who were too young for the V.Smile.

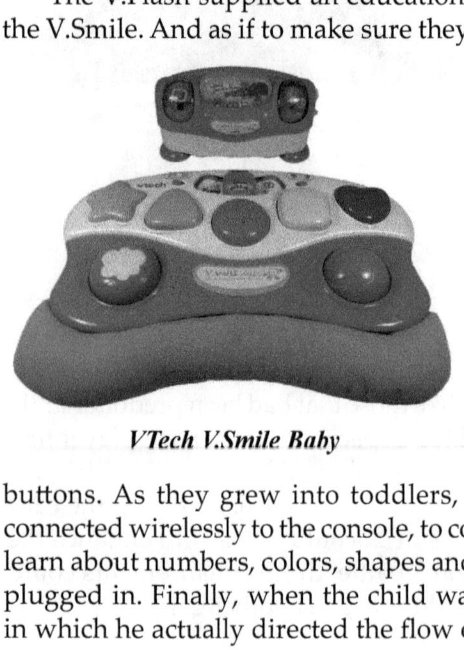

VTech V.Smile Baby

The *V.Smile Baby* was aimed towards kids between nine months and three years old. It consisted of two pieces. One was the console, which accepted game cartridges and connected to the TV. The other was an *Activity Panel*, which looked like a standard infant playboard and consisted of large buttons and rollers.

VTech designed the V.Smile Baby to grow with the child. Infants could only play with the Activity Panel and listen to different electronic sounds that were generated by pressing the buttons. As they grew into toddlers, they could then use the Activity Panel which connected wirelessly to the console, to communicate with the television. Young kids could learn about numbers, colors, shapes and animals depending upon the cartridge that was plugged in. Finally, when the child was old enough, he could play educational games in which he actually directed the flow of the game. Once the child was at ease with this type of edutainment, he was ready to advance to the V.Smile.

Doomed Consoles

Although several new consoles had been released throughout the year, others weren't as fortunate. Gizmondo Europe and its parent company Tiger Telematics filed for bankruptcy in February and its ill-fated Gizmondo was discontinued, with less than 25,000 consoles having been sold worldwide.[11]

Infinium Labs, which had been promising the release of its Phantom console for years, did not enter bankruptcy court, but it did run into major problems. In 2005, the company had hired a stock promoter to inform thousands of investors that the Phantom would be successfully released that year, causing the company's stock to rise quickly. The company's CEO, Tim Roberts, then sold 1.3 million of his personal shares at the inflated price. When it was discovered that the stock promoter's claims to the investors had not been true, the SEC ordered Roberts to pay back all of the profits that he had made from the sale of his stock. Although Infinium Labs' other executives weren't part of this scheme, the company's reputation, which hadn't been stellar to begin with, suffered greatly. Infinium Labs announced in February that the Phantom console was going to be delayed indefinitely, "pending further funding." Then in August, the company quietly removed the console from the "Products" page of its website, thereby sealing the fate of the Phantom once and for all.

Another console that was removed from the marketplace was Sega's Dreamcast. Although the console had actually been discontinued in 2001, Sega of Japan had continued to sell refurbished units through its online store, Sega Direct. And even though Sega itself no longer developed new games for the system, third-party vendors still continued to release new Dreamcast games in Japan.

PSP Developments

As the PS2 continued to thrive, on March 23 SCE quietly laid to rest the PSone, the current incarnation of the original PlayStation. With 103 million units sold, the PlayStation trailed only behind the PS2 in total number of consoles sold. While many lamented the end of this groundbreaking machine, SCE was quick to point out that the PS3, like the PS2 before it, was completely backward-compatible with all PlayStation games. The company also announced a PlayStation emulator for the PSP. However, while the emulator would give the PSP the ability to play original PlayStation games, those games would have to be purchased and downloaded from the PlayStation Network, in the same manner that Nintendo offered its early games through the Virtual Console. This meant that even if someone owned a game that played on the original console, it would have to be purchased again to play on the PSP.

The PSP was compatible with the PS3. After the two systems were wirelessly synched to each other, photos, music and movies could be shared from either unit to the other. Unfortunately, this feature didn't extend to games, which couldn't be shared.

Meanwhile, the future of watching movies on the PSP appeared to be grim, as sales for movies in the UMD format slowed down considerably early in the year. There were several reasons for this. People who already owned a movie on DVD didn't want to have to buy it again on UMD just so they could watch it on their PSPs. Likewise, people didn't want to purchase movies that could play only on the PSP and not on their TVs. In addition, although the UMDs cost about the same as DVDs, they didn't include any of the bonuses that were usually packed onto DVDs. Sony began selling some of its pre-recorded movies in dual packs that, for under $30, included both the DVD and UMD versions of the same movie. But Sony was alone in this endeavor. Warner Bros. canceled six UMD titles that it had planned to release, while Sony and Paramount planned to limit their UMD releases to teen comedies, since *Napoleon Dynamite* had been the highest-selling UMD to date. Walmart announced in late March the possibility of removing UMDs from its shelves, and in early July, Target actually discontinued carrying the format altogether.

SCE Chotto Shot

Although the appeal of the PSP as a movie player seemed to wane, SCE introduced new peripherals that added new uses for the handheld device. A camera that plugged into the USB port of the PSP was released in Japan on November 6. The ¥5,000 ($42) *Chotto Shot* was a 1.3 megapixel camera that could take photographs and record up to 15 seconds of video. Although the Chotto Shot had been developed by SCE Studios London, which had also developed the EyeToy camera for the PS2, none of the EyeToy-type software was available for the PSP. Instead, the device was packaged with a UMD that contained a photo-editing application.[12]

SCE PSP GPS

On December 7, SCEJ released a ¥6,000 ($52) GPS unit for the PSP. This small device, which was about an inch wide, plugged into the same USB port that the Chotto Shot used. A diverse array of software supported the device. In Konami's *Metal Gear Solid: Portable Ops*, the GPS was used to find people near the player's actual, real-life locality, in order to recruit them as soldiers in the game. Sega's *Homestar Portable* was an astronomy program that informed the user where he was and what constellations could be seen above him. Finally, a developer called Edia planned *Navigation Soft*, a standard navigation program that made the PSP similar to the dedicated GPS devices that were becoming popular from Magellan and Garmin.

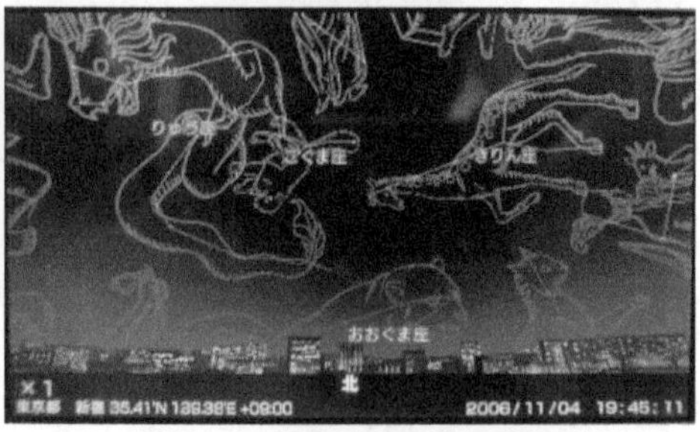

Sega Homestar Portable

Nintendo's Wi-Fi Connection

As SCE continued to release peripherals and software that extended the capabilities of the PSP, Nintendo kept marketing its DS strictly as a handheld gaming console. Sales of the DS were going through the roof. By the end of January, after the portable had spent only thirteen months on the market, Nintendo had sold 5 million in Japan, which made it the fastest selling console in that country's history. In all, over 14 million had been sold worldwide by the end of 2005. In March, SCE tried to keep the PSP somewhat competitive and reduced the price of its device by $50 to $199.

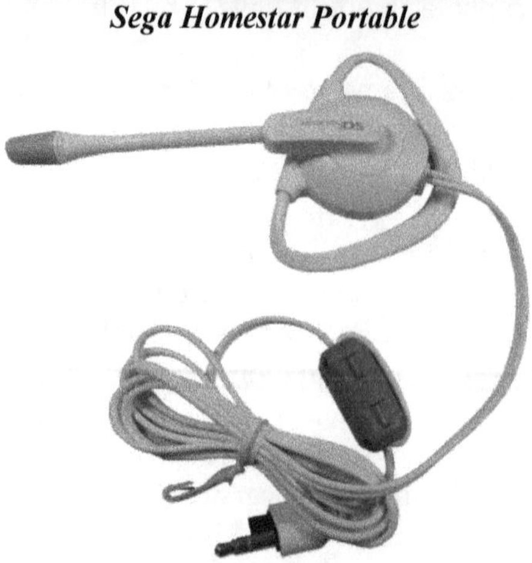

Nintendo DS Headset

The popularity of the wireless DS also led to the success of Nintendo's Wi-Fi Connection, its free online service. On the morning of March 7, a Japanese player became the one millionth member of the service when he signed up to play *Animal Crossing: Wild World*. This milestone occurred only four months after Nintendo had first established the service. By comparison, it had taken Microsoft nineteen months before the one millionth person signed onto its subscription-based Xbox Live.

The Wi-Fi Connection's user base received a boost two weeks later, when Nintendo of America released *Metroid Prime Hunters* for the DS. This first-person space combat game allowed up to four players from around the world to compete via the Wi-Fi Connection. It also allowed gamers to voice chat with one another before and after matches using the DS's built-in microphone. Nintendo of Japan released two more DS games that supported voice chat on September 28, *Pokémon Pearl* and *Pokémon Diamond*.[13] These were the first Pokémon titles for the DS. In conjunction with the release of these games, Nintendo of Japan released a DS headset that fit over one ear, with a microphone that protruded from it. The headset plugged into the DS's earphone jack and could be used with any game that had a voice feature, such as *Nintendogs*, and not just the ones that allowed voice chatting over the Wi-Fi Connection.

DS Download Station

Nintendo also offered a new way to send game demos to DS owners. The *DS Download Station* was set up in retail outlets in Japan, Europe and North America. Gamers could walk up to the DS Download Station with their personal DS units and use the console's menu to get to *DS Download Play*, which was normally used to set up multiplayer games. Once within range of the DS Download Station, the gamer was presented with a menu that listed several demo games. The gamer could then select one of the demo games, which would then automatically load into the DS's memory, where it would stay until the unit was turned off or replaced by another demo game.

Nintendo DS Download Station

In Japan, the DS Download Stations consisted of three PCs that were hooked up to the Internet, which the gamer could easily access from inside the store. However, in North America and Europe, where most stores did not have Internet connections, a different method was conceived. In these territories the DS Download Station consisted of a small white box. Locked inside the box and out of sight of the customers, was a standard DS device with a special DS Download Station Game Card inserted into it. Besides containing several demo games, the Game Card also acted as a server that could send data out to up to fifteen DS units at the same time. When Nintendo decided to offer a new group of demo games, it would simply send a new Game Card volume to stores.[14]

DS Lite

So what does a company do when it has a hot product that everybody seems to want? In Nintendo's case, it released a new model to supersede it. The *DS Lite*, which was announced on January 26, was fully compatible with the original, but its overall dimensions were reduced by two-thirds and its weight was 20% lighter. The new DS Lite also sported the same brighter backlit screen that had been introduced on the newer GBA SP that had been released in the United States in September, 2005. Battery life was also

Nintendo DS Lite

improved. A three-hour charge provided approximately 17 hours of play on the DS Lite, whereas the original DS could only be played for about ten hours after an hour's charge.

The ¥16,800 ($145) DS Lite went on sale in Japan on March 2. Nintendo of Japan had 550,000 units available, but the demand was much greater. This encouraged some distributors to raise their retail prices to as much as ¥23,300 ($201). The device sold out soon after it was launched. It was estimated that 15% of all the DS Lite sales went to unemployed Chinese nationals who had been hired by Japanese businessmen to stand in long lines to buy consoles that could be resold quickly online at hefty profits, just as they had done during the PS3's launch. DS Lite consoles wound up selling for as high as ¥40,000 ($345) each on Japanese auction sites.

Americans could get the DS Lite for $130 each when Nintendo of America released it on June 11. The company sold 136,500 units within two days. Although the frenzy of the Japanese launch didn't carry over to America, lines had still formed on the morning of the device's launch, especially at the Nintendo World store in New York where the first 100 DS Lite customers were each treated to a free copy of *Brain Age*[15] and a DS Lite carrying case.

The DS Lite was a success, but it was still deemed a gaming device, as opposed to the PSP, which SCE continued to push as a multi-functional device. This changed on July 24, when Nintendo of Japan released a product that pushed the DS into a realm beyond gaming.

The product was a web browser provided by Opera, the same company that would supply the browser for the Wii. Unlike the PSP browser, which was freely available through a download, the *Nintendo DS Browser* was sold on a standard Game Card that retailed for ¥3,800 ($33). It was also packaged with a *Memory Expansion Pak* that plugged into the DS's GBA slot and provided an additional 8MB of RAM for the browser to use for cache storage. Two different *DS Memory Expansion Paks* were available. One looked like a standard GBA cartridge and could be used with either the DS or the DS Lite, although it protruded from the bottom of the latter. The other was much more compact and sat flush within the DS Lite. It couldn't be used with the original DS at all.

Nintendo DS Browser

Nintendo Memory Expansion Paks

Making Use of the GBA Slot

As the DS Memory Expansion Pak showed, the GBA slot on the DS and DS Lite wasn't limited only to GBA games. Several peripherals became available that also utilized it. On November 22 Sega of Japan released a DS game called *Oshare Majo: Love And Berry*. This was a game that was well known to most Japanese girls between the ages of 6 and 12 since Sega of Japan had released an arcade version of it in department stores and play areas in October, 2004.[16] This was a rhythm and dance game in which players selected to either be Love or Berry, two 14-year-old female characters. Players "danced" by pressing a button to the beat of a tambourine. The amount of time the player had to dance was determined by the amount of "Dress Up" power she had. Dress Up power was calculated by how fashionable the character was. Girls dressed up their characters by scanning cards that they collected. These cards featured barcodes that contained information regarding clothes, footwear, hair styles or accessories. Players received one card for every ¥100 ($1) that they deposited into the arcade machine.

Sega Love and Berry card reader

The home version of the game used the cards that were dispersed from its arcade counterpart, along with ten cards that were included with the game. These cards could be scanned into the DS using a bundled card reader that plugged into the console's GBA slot.

Nintendo also used the GBA slot for practical reasons. On December 4, Nintendo of Japan released *Sekai no Gohan: Shaberu! DS Oryōri Navi*, which turned the DS into an electronic cookbook that featured 245 dishes.[17] Three days later, on December 7, the company introduced an accessory that made the software easier to use. The ¥1,200 ($13) *Nintendo DS Magnetic Stand* was a plastic piece that plugged into the DS through the GBA

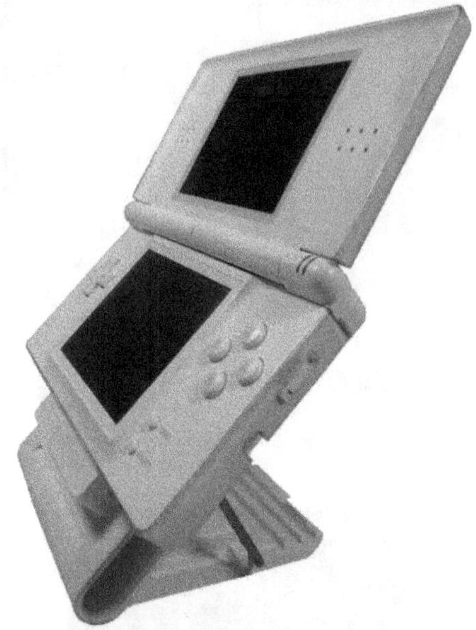

Nintendo DS Magnetic Stand

Nintendo MP3 Player

Visteon Dockable Entertainment

slot. While the stand had two metal legs that allowed the DS to sit on a table top, it also had a magnet within it, so the DS could be attached to a metal surface such as a refrigerator, allowing people to use the cooking software without having to hold the DS.[18]

On December 8, Nintendo of Europe released a peripheral that plugged into the GBA slot that also had nothing to do with games. The *Nintendo MP3 Player* was, as its name implied, a device that allowed music, in the form of MP3 files, to be played through the DS, while song titles and other information appeared on the screen. Despite its name, it also played MP4 video files. In actuality, the €30 ($40) Nintendo MP3 Player was really nothing more than a rebranded Play-Yan Micro that had been available in Japan for more than a year.

In addition to the DS and DS Lite, the Nintendo MP3 Player could also be used with the GBA. Originally, the DS family was supposed to be separate from the GameBoy family, and the two consoles were supposed to coexist in the marketplace. However, sales for the backward-compatible DS caused a considerable decrease in GBA sales. In May, Nintendo president Satoru Iwata commented that due to the overall success of the DS, Nintendo had no plans to extend the life of the Game Boy franchise and would not be introducing a new model that would eventually succeed the GBA.

Ironically, Nintendo announced that it would be discontinuing the GBA just four months after a new device that played GBA cartridges was shown at the winter CES. The *Dockable Entertainment* from Visteon, a manufacturer of auto parts, was basically a portable DVD player that could be mounted from the ceiling of a car's interior to provide video entertainment for kids sitting in the back seat. But unlike other car DVD players, the Dockable Entertainment also featured a Nintendo-licensed GBA slot that allowed kids to play GBA games in lieu of watching DVDs.

The Dockable Entertainment was released on July 28 and was sold only through car dealerships, where it could be installed into new and pre-owned vehicles. The $1,299 unit was bundled with a pair of wireless remote controls, one to operate the DVD player and the other for playing GBA games. Wireless headphones also accompanied the Dockable Entertainment and these could be worn when only one person was using the system, as so as not to disturb others sitting in the car. Otherwise, the sound could be filtered through a specific frequency on the vehicle's radio.[19]

Handhelds with Built-In Games

Coincidentally, when Visteon was introducing its high-end, game-playing, portable DVD player in January, Coby Electronics, a manufacturer of low-end electronics, was releasing a $120 portable DVD player that could also play games. In this case they were twelve licensed Sega Master System games that were built-into the unit.

The Coby *TF-DVD 500* was shaped like a square with rounded corners, and its overall dimensions were slightly larger than a DVD itself. Unlike other portable DVD players on the market that included clamshell lids that opened to reveal screens, the Coby unit had a 3.5-inch LCD screen built into its face. With the device's DVD "Stop" and "Play" control buttons doubling as the Sega Master System's A and B buttons, the unit itself was the controller.

Coby TF-DVD 500

By year's end, the Coby TF-DVD 500 was joined by another handheld device that also included built-in Sega Master System games, as well as several Game Gear titles. The compact device, which was only 5 inches wide and featured a 2.4-inch LCD screen, was called the *Coleco Handheld Electronic 20 in 1 Games*, a very descriptive name since it indeed included 20 built-in games. The $50 unit was commonly called the *Coleco Sonic*.

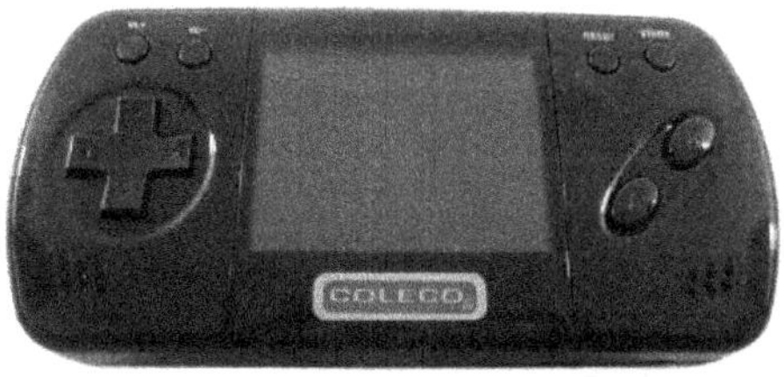

Coleco Handheld Electronic 20 in 1 Games

While the *Coleco Handheld Electronic 20 in 1 Games* may have been a cause for celebration for Sega fans, it was definitely a letdown for ColecoVision enthusiasts, who had been hoping for a new version of the classic console, which had been hinted about a year earlier. But what was promising was that its release meant that the Coleco name wasn't simply a brand name that was licensed to whoever wanted it, as had been the case with the handheld Coleco units that had been released by Techno Source in 2005. River West Brands had created a subsidiary called Coleco Holdings with the specific purpose of releasing new products under the Coleco banner. In addition to the *Coleco Handheld Electronic 20 in 1 Games*, Coleco Holdings released several plug and play devices including *Virtual Ping Pong* and *Virtual Kick Boxing* along with some dedicated handhelds units such as *Word Games* and *Casino Games*.

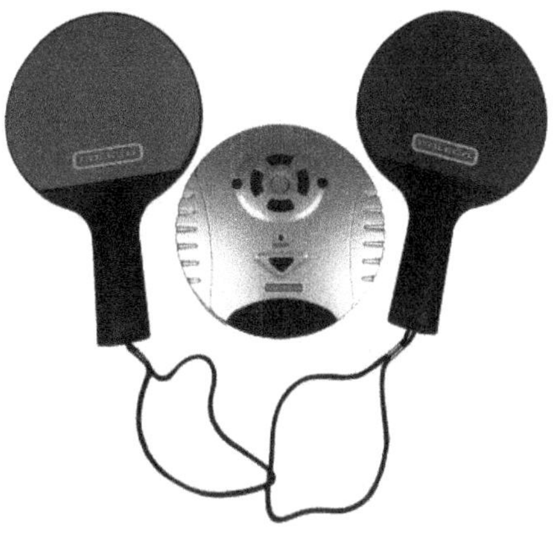
Coleco Virtual Ping-Pong

The *Coleco Handheld Electronic 20 in 1 Games* was only released in the United States (and only at Target), at least under the Coleco brand name. The unit also appeared on Continental Europe where it was called the *Pocket Gear*, and in Canada and Great Britain where it was called the *PlayPal Portable*.

Plug-and-Plays

PlayPal Plug and Play

AtGames POGA

VG Pocket Caplet

VG Pocket Tablet

PlayPal was a brand name of a Canadian company called Kobian Canada Inc. In addition to the PlayPal Portable, Kobian Canada also released a stand-alone unit called the *PlayPal Plug and Play*. While the PlayPal Portable was bundled with a composite video cable and could be played through a television, this wasn't mandatory, since it was a self-contained handheld unit that featured its own 2.4" screen. The PlayPal Plug and Play, on the other hand, required a television set in order to be played. The unit featured 20 built-in games, but twelve of them overlapped the titles that were built-into the PlayPal Portable. And although only two of those twenty games featured Sonic the Hedgehog, the blue unit resembled Sonic's head. Instead of a D-pad, which was on PlayPal Portable and the Coby DVD player, the PlayPal Plug and Play featured a small joystick in the shape of a gloved fist rising out from Sonic's eye.

Coleco Holdings and Kobian Canada both sub-licensed its Sega games from AtGames, a Taiwanese company that had been founded in 2001, under license from Sega. AtGames also released the *POGA*, its own plug-and-play unit, which had 30 built-in Sega Master System and Game Gear games. The *POGA* looked like a game controller although it didn't resemble any controller from a Sega-manufactured console. In fact, a "C" button was included even though the button wasn't even used by any of the games built-into the device.

At roughly the same time that the Coleco Handheld Electronic 20 in 1 Games came out in the United States, a company called Performance Designed Products (PDP) released a handheld device that closely resembled the one from Coleco Holdings. The $40 *VG Pocket Caplet* had the same dimensions as the Coleco Handheld Electronic 20 in 1 Games, but at 2.5 inches, its LCD screen was slightly larger.

The system featured 50 games, and the majority of them were non-licensed clones of retro arcade and console titles, which made it no different from the dozens of other cheap, non-branded plug-and-play devices that were beginning to appear. However, what set the Caplet apart from the rest was that it actually did feature three licensed titles: Taito's *Space Invaders* and *Bust-a-Move*, and Data East's *BurgerTime*.

PDP also released a separate handheld unit called the *VG Pocket Tablet*. This $30 unit was round and only had 25 built-in games that played on a 2-inch screen. Like the Caplet titles, the majority of the games were clones. However, there was one licensed title in the collection, Konami's *Frogger*.

The plug-and-play compilations, especially the ones from Jakks Pacific, were extremely popular in the United States, which had a large base of people who were nostalgic for the old games. Japan didn't have such a target audience so the demand for such compilations just never took off. The first plug-and-play collection of retro games that appeared in Japan was the *Mega Drive Play TV* that had been distributed by Sega Toys in 2004. But this was simply the same unit as Radica's Arcade Legends. And although it was manufactured in Japan by Sega Toys, it had actually been designed in the United States by Radica. It wasn't even localized for the Japanese market as all of the games and instructions were in English.

The first true Japanese-designed plug-and-play devices were released in 2006 by Bandai.[20] The *Let's! TV Play Classic* series consisted of two units featuring Namco games and two with games from Taito with each of the four devices following the same theme. Each featured two classic games, such as *Xevious* and *Mappy*, which were found on the *Namco Nostalgia 1* device, and two modern remixes of the same games. The Namco remixes used mechanics that were similar to the classic titles that they complemented, but the game play was completely different. The Taito remixes shared the same game play as their classic counterparts, but the characters differed.

Although each of the four ¥3,500 ($30) *Let's! TV Play Classic* releases had to be attached to TVs in order to play, they weren't packaged with their own composite video cables. A separate combination AV/power cable that could be used by all four units had to be purchased separately for ¥1,599 ($14).

Bandai Let's! TV Play

People who wanted to play old Sega games weren't limited to the plug-and-play units that had been licensed from AtGames. On November 16, Sega released the *Sega Genesis Collection* for both the PS2 and PSP.[21] This compilation consisted of 28 games that had originally been available for the Genesis. It also featured historical facts about the games, as well as box art and cheat codes. These codes came in handy, because gamers had to obtain specific scores on certain games to unlock more than thirty-five minutes of interviews with Sega of Japan personnel.

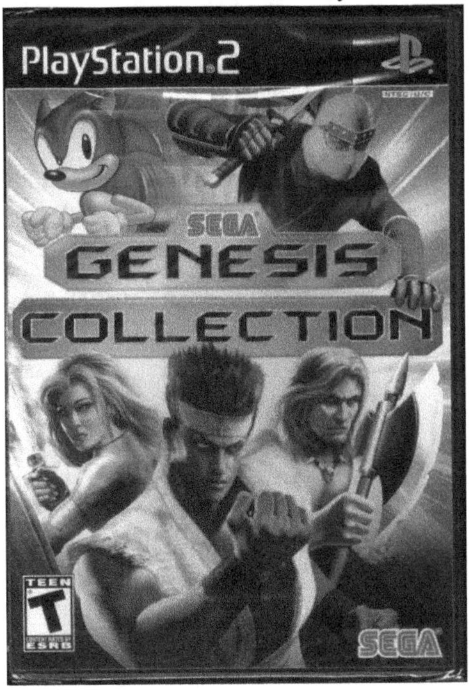

Sega Genesis Collection

In addition to the Genesis games that were readily available, the collection also included older Sega arcade games from the early '80s. Like the interviews, these games had to be unlocked before they could be played. The five bonus arcade games on the PS2 compilation, which included *Zaxxon* and *Tac/Scan*, were different from the bonus games for the PSP, which featured *Super Zaxxon* and *Congo Bongo*.

American Rhythm Games

Following the successful release of *Guitar Hero* in November 2005, Konami saw that Americans were interested in such games and finally went ahead and released *Beatmania* in North America. The game was released for the PS2 on March 28, 2006, and was bundled with a Konami controller, which differed considerably from the ASCII controller that was sold with the Japanese version of *Beatmania*. For one, the new Konami controller featured seven buttons, instead of the five that were on the ASCII model. This was to accommodate the game play that was based on *Beatmania IIDX*, which used seven buttons and had been available in Japanese arcades since 1999. Also, the turntable was much more responsive, which had been a major complaint about the ASCII controller. Finally, the shape was different. Instead of rectangular, the Konami controller was more rectangular and the turntable could detach from the keyboard and be placed on either side of it to give right- and left-handed players an even shot at the game.

Konami also released the new *Beatmania IIDX* controller in Japan but its shape was slightly different. While the turntable end of the American controller had a rounded edge,

Konami Beatmania Controller

Konami Beatmania IIDX Controller

the Japanese one had a straight edge.

As Konami was establishing its rhythm games in North America, the company that introduced home rhythm games to North America was going through changes. In May, RedOctane, the company that published *Guitar Hero*, was purchased by Activision for $100 million. Activision received a mighty return on its investment by the end of the year, thanks to *Guitar Hero II*, which it released for the PS2 on November 7. *Guitar Hero II* followed the same basic play as the original game, with a few changes, such as the introduction of three-note chords that scored additional points. Of course, the 64 songs in the game were different. And while *Guitar Hero II* could be purchased with or without a guitar peripheral, the one that was bundled with the game was a cherry-red version of the Gibson SG guitar peripheral which had been packaged with the original game. *Guitar Hero II* was a complete success. And even though it was released in November, the 1.3 million copies that were sold made it the fifth top-selling videogame of the year. In just two months, *Guitar Hero II* grossed $200 million.

On the same day that it released *Guitar Hero II*, Activision also released *Call of Duty 3*, a multiplayer World War II first-person shooter. This game sold 1.1 million copies by the end of the year, but unlike *Guitar Hero II*, which was only released for the PS2, versions of *Call of Duty 3* were introduced for all three next-gen consoles, as well as the PS2 and the original Xbox. Although the game that played on the latter two systems allowed up to 16 players to compete in multiplayer combat, the versions for the Xbox 360 and PS3 let up to 24 people compete simultaneously. The Wii version didn't allow for multiplayer competition.

Gears of War

Microsoft released a third-person shooter[22] for the Xbox 360, on the very same day that Activision released *Call of Duty 3*. Like *Call of Duty 3*, *Gears of War* had a military theme, although it took place on another planet. On the day that it came out, *Gears of War* became the most-played game on Xbox Live, surpassing *Halo 2*, which had held that title since November, 2004. *Gears of War* also became the fastest-selling game of the year, with 1 million copies sold worldwide in only the first three weeks that it was available.

Gears of War

Although *Gears of War* had been rated "M" by the ESRB, it was never considered controversial, as most of the mature-rated games from another company, Rockstar, had been. And so, when Rockstar announced that it would be releasing a new game called *Bully*, there was no doubt that controversy would follow.[23] Even without seeing the game, several advocacy groups complained that it glamorized school bullying. By the time *Bully* was released for the PS2 on October 17, the ESRB had assigned to it a "Teen" rating, which meant that it was suitable for teenagers. The rating organizations from many other countries followed likewise. But that didn't stop the complaints. After the advocacy groups saw that the game wasn't as violent as they had thought it would be, they complained that it promoted bisexuality since its' main character, who was a male, kissed both girls and boys.

First Amendment Rules

Teen access to violent videogames continued to be a major concern in several states. In Michigan, a law that had passed in September 2005 to ban the sale of violent videogames to minors was supposed to have gone into effect on December 1 of that year. But the Entertainment Software Association (ESA), Video Software Dealers Association (VSDA) and Michigan Retailers Association all filed a suit against the state, on the grounds that the law was unconstitutionally vague and limited First Amendment rights. In November 2005, U.S. District Judge George Steeh issued a preliminary injunction that put the law on hold. The judge eventually agreed with the plaintiffs and made the injunction permanent on April 4, 2006.

Two months later, on June 2, Minnesota passed its own law that banned minors from purchasing violent videogames. This one was a bit different than the laws that had passed in other states, because it didn't punish the retailers for selling adult-themed games to minors. Instead, the minors themselves would be fined $25 for attempting to buy or rent such material. Retailers would only be required to post signs that would inform the minors about the fines. The ESA immediately went into action when the bill passed to prevent it from becoming law on August 1. The result was the same as in Michigan. On July 31, U.S. District Judge James M. Rosenbaum ruled that the law would have violated the First Amendment, and that the state couldn't prove that mature games caused any harm.

Planned laws in Illinois and Louisiana suffered the same fate. In the Illinois case, District Judge Matthew F. Kennelly had declared such a law unconstitutional on December 2, 2005, but the state appealed. The appeal was heard by the Seventh Circuit of the U.S. Court of Appeals, which agreed with the District Court and, on November 28, 2006, declared the law to be unconstitutional. On the very next day, Judge James Brady ruled that the similar Louisiana bill, which had been signed into law on June 15, was unconstitutional as well.

Such laws were not unique to the United States. In Germany, the Unterhaltungssoftware Selbstkontrolle (USK), Germany's equivalent of the ESRB, refused to rate two Xbox 360 games, Capcom's *Dead Rising* and Microsoft's *Gears of War*, due to their excessive violence. While this didn't connote that either game was banned in Germany, it did mean that the games had to be stocked under the counter and not made available to minors. However, since Microsoft had a policy not to release unrated Xbox 360 games in Germany, the two games were not made available in that country.

Changes To E^3

In addition to helping eradicate anti-gaming laws, the ESA also ran E^3, the industry's showcase for new products. And following the 2006 show in May, the ESA decided that massive changes needed to be made.

The 2006 trade-only E^3 had been attended by 60,000 visitors, a reduction of over 13% from the 2005 show, which had attracted a record number of attendees. The show had gotten too big, and this was detrimental to E^3's original purpose of showcasing the industry's new products to retailers and the media. The show had taken on a carnival-like atmosphere and became so noisy that it was almost impossible for publishers and vendors to actually conduct any meaningful business. And it didn't help that there was a multitude of people in attendance who had no business being there. Although E^3 was only open to people in the industry, it seemed that anyone who had a game-related website could obtain a press pass, which led to the attendance of thousands of quasi-press representatives who had no other purpose for being there, other than to play new games for hours on end and to secure swag (promotional giveaways) that they would list on eBay within minutes of receiving it.

On July 31, the ESA announced that at the request of the exhibitors, E^3 would be scaled down considerably. Details for the 2007 show were announced on October 13 by Doug Lowenstein, president of the ESA. According to Lowenstein, the name of the show would be changed to the E^3 Media Festival and it would be held in Los Angeles, although not at the Convention Center, where it had been held continuously every year since 1999. And it wouldn't even be a convention with booths. Instead, exhibitors would set up inside rooms at designated hotels, where they could meet with clients in a more subdued atmosphere.

Another notable change that would be put into effect would be the amount of people who could attend. While the show would still be closed to the public, people who were legitimately in the industry would be able to attend by invitation only. The exhibiters themselves would decide who would be included on the invitation list, which would be limited to approximately 5,000 people.

Although E^3, which dealt with the future of gaming, would be closed to most people, one exhibit that showcased the history of gaming was open to all. Sony's Walk of Game awarded two more people with Lifetime Achievement Awards, to join the prior year's two recipients. The induction ceremony took place on March 16 at the Metreon in San Francisco. The 2006 honors went to Sid Meier and John Carmack, both of whom were computer-gaming luminaries, not console gaming.

The ceremonies marked the second year that the event took place. But it also turned out to be the final time. Shortly after the ceremony, Sony sold the Metreon to the Westfield Group, a leading developer of shopping malls that had no interest in videogame history. When October arrived, the time when the 2007 nominations should have been announced, there was no mention of them.

Ralph Baer & President George W. Bush

Ralph Baer, who had invented the Odyssey, the first videogame console, was never nominated for a Walk of Game Lifetime Achievement Award. But on February 13, he received a much bigger prize. On that day, he was awarded a National Medal of Technology from President George W. Bush at the White House. Baer had been honored for his "groundbreaking and pioneering creation, development and commercialization of interactive video games." Ever since the inception of the National Medal of Technology in 1985, Baer was the only person who had ever been bestowed the honor for work associated with videogames.

By year's end, the three major next-gen consoles had all been released in North America and Japan. The Xbox 360, which had been available for over a year, had failed to be competitive in Japan. And the PS3 was not yet available in Europe. Only the Wii was available in all markets. Now the companies had to focus on quality software.

CHAPTER THIRTY-FIVE
2007

Even though both SCE and Nintendo had managed to get their new consoles into stores in North America and Japan before the end of 2006, the challenge that they faced in 2007 was to make sure a system was available to everyone who wanted to purchase one. While SCE's PS3 shortages stemmed from manufacturing setbacks associated with the Blu-ray drive, Nintendo found itself in a predicament that most companies would want; its Wii was so popular that demand simply outpaced the supply. Nintendo had state prior to the Wii's November 2006 launch that six million consoles would be available by the end of March, 2007. After running their factories at full capacity to manufacture the Wiis in numbers far higher than the company had ever committed to any of its previous consoles, Nintendo met their goal, but it wasn't enough. There was speculation about what actually caused the shortage. In late March, GameStop's COO, Dan DeMatteo, told investors that he believed that Nintendo had intentionally caused the shortage because it had already met its projected sales numbers for the fiscal year. DeMatteo believed that the Wii supply would increase after April 1, when Nintendo's new fiscal year began.

That apparently wasn't the case, because Wii consoles were still scarce after April 1. Perrin Kaplan, Nintendo of America's VP of marketing and corporate affairs, announced on April 11 that the demand for the Wii was so high that the shortages might last for some time.

"Some time" turned out to be the entire year, as demand consistently stayed ahead of the vast number of consoles that Nintendo could supply. Nintendo of America's president, Reggie Fils-Aimé, announced in early October that the company wouldn't be able to deliver enough consoles to meet the demand until early in 2008, thereby missing the lucrative holiday season altogether.

Europe aside, PS3s were finally available at the beginning of the year, although their actual availability had been disputed by SCEA president Jack Tretton during an interview with *EGM*. Tretton had claimed, "If you can find a PS3 anywhere in North America that's been on shelves for more than five minutes, I'll give you $1,200 for it." The remark was quickly refuted by the magazine, which had called 18 stores and found that half of them had PS3s in stock, some with as many as 20 consoles apiece. Tretton's response to this was that these figures were proof that the PS3 sales were "outstanding," since half of the stores called didn't have ample numbers of PS3s available.

Meanwhile in Japan, Wiis were outselling PS3s by a ratio of 2:1. But even though the PS3 was trailing behind the Wii in sales, SCE executives didn't complain about its marketability. Despite its high price and low availability, the PS3 became SCE's fastest-selling console to date, as two million consoles had been sold worldwide within two months of its launch.

PS3s In Europe

The PS3s were finally released in Europe on March 23. SCE opted not to release the 20GB model, since the 60GB model outsold it in all of the areas where both models were available. SCEE announced that if there was a demand for it, the less-expensive 20GB model might be available later in the year, most likely in the summer. Meanwhile, the 60GB model was available and it wasn't cheap. Although Americans had grumbled about the PS3's $599 retail price in the United States, that had actually been a bargain when compared to the console's costs in Europe after exchange rates were figured in. The PS3s that were sold on the Continent retailed at €599 ($797) each, and the price for the British consoles was set at £425 ($834)! And the consoles that were offered in Europe weren't even the same as the ones that had been available in Japan and North America.

The 60GB consoles that were sold in Europe[1] lacked the Emotion Engine chip that gave the PS3 the ability to play PS2 discs without any software emulation. The European consoles used software to make them backward-compatible in a way that was similar to the Xbox 360, which had made people, especially those who lacked a hard drive, very unhappy. SCEE announced at the end of February that the PS3's firmware would constantly be updated through the PlayStation Network to emulate more and more PS2 games. And a list of compatible PS2 games would be posted on a European PlayStation website, although it wouldn't be publicly available until the PS3's official European release on March 23. SCEE officials expected that list would include over 1,000 titles.

SCE decided to exclude the Emotion Engine in favor of software emulation for financial reasons. It was estimated that the company lost $241 on every console sold, so efforts to lower costs were a high priority. Since each Emotion Chip cost approximately $27 to manufacture, and the software emulation cost only $5 per machine, the savings were considerable.

Many analysts pondered how the lack of the chip would affect the European sales. A backward-compatible PS3 was attractive to PS2 owners who already owned PS2 discs, especially since the PS3 didn't offer a vast software library right off the bat. These people would be able to play their old games while waiting for new PS3 titles to become available. But SCE wasn't particularly concerned with backward-compatibility at all, and only included it to appease its consumers. The company was more interested in supplying state-of-the-art games that were specifically designed to play on the PS3.

On the eve of the European launch, it appeared that the analysts who had predicted that the PS3 sales would be poor were correct. To prevent the crimes that had occurred during the Wii launch three months earlier, the police wouldn't allow long lines outside stores overnight. Most stores, such as HMV, decided not to open at midnight and planned to begin selling the PS3 when they opened in the morning. But the Virgin Megastore on Oxford Street kept to its original plans for a midnight launch and invited people to line up inside the store. By 11 PM, just over 100 people took advantage of Virgin's offer to line up inside. More people wandered in during the final hour, just in time for some unannounced festivities. First, one person in line was selected randomly to receive a free PS3 console. Next, it was announced that the first 150 people who purchased PS3s would each get a free copy of *Resistance: Fall of Man*. Finally, at 11:40 PM, it was announced that Sony was giving away a £2,000 ($3,925) 46" HDTV television to each of the first 125 people who bought a PS3, which pretty much included everybody in line.

As it turned out, the analysts who had predicted poor initial European PS3 sales had been wrong. SCEE sold 600,000 PS3s within two days of its European launch. And even though only 165,000 of the 200,000 PS3s that were available for sale in Great Britain actually sold during those two days, the PS3 still wound up being the fastest-selling home console in that country.[2] This didn't make everybody happy. It was reported that 20,000 pre-orders had been canceled during the days leading up to the launch, presumably by people who had expected to have consoles to put on eBay in the event of a shortage.

On April 11, if there was any hope that SCE would release the 20GB PS3 outside of Japan and the United States, it faded when SCEA announced that it would cease marketing the less-expensive console altogether. Even though it had been popular with people who basically wanted inexpensive Blu-ray players and really didn't care about gaming, the 60GB model outsold it by a factor of 9:1, according to SCEA. Meanwhile, SCEJ continued to offer the 20GB model without any immediate plans to discontinue it.

Xbox 360 and PS3 Face Off

SCEA's announcement about phasing out the 20GB PS3 came approximately two weeks after Microsoft announced a new configuration in its Xbox 360 lineup, the *Xbox 360 Elite* system, which became available in the United States on April 29. The new $480 system came in a black case with a black controller, and included an HDMI port and cable and a 120GB hard drive. Surprisingly, the new console wasn't bundled with the HD-DVD drive, because Microsoft felt that the format "was not proven." By this time, movies on Blu-ray were outselling those on HD-DVD. During the first quarter of the year, Blu-rays already accounted for 70% of all pre-recorded high-definition movie sales.

The battle was on! SCEA announced at E³ on July 9 that it would reduce the price of the 60GB PS3 by $100 to $499, the same price as the recently discontinued 20GB console. A new $599 80GB PS3 would be available in August. Then the 60GB consoles would be discontinued, once their inventories had been extinguished. The new 80GB PS3s would not use the Emotion Engine chip. Instead, they would be able to play PS2 titles using software emulation, just like the consoles that were available in Europe. The 80GB console would also come with a free copy of *Motorstorm*, a racing game that had already sold over one million copies. It had become the top-selling PS3 game in Japan when it was released in December, 2006. But the Japanese version hadn't allowed for online play. This was rectified with the release of the game in the United States on March 6 (and three weeks later in Europe), as it allowed up to twelve players to compete against each other online.[3]

On August 6, less than a month after SCEA announced its price decreases, Microsoft followed suit and said that the retail price of all three Xbox 360 configurations would be reduced, beginning on August 8. The Core system, the one without the hard drive, dropped $20 to $280. The newest configuration, the Elite, which had only been available for a few months, was reduced $30 to $450. But the biggest cut, $50, went to the Pro system, which was lowered to $350. And as if to irritate those customers who had purchased the Elite system because of its HDMI output, the less-expensive Pro system began including an HDMI output as well. Microsoft also lowered the price on the optional HD-DVD drive by $20 and, as an incentive, offered five free HD-DVD discs if the unit was purchased by September 1.

Microsoft's price cuts weren't limited to the United States. The company announced similar price reductions in Europe, where the Core edition was lowered €20 ($28) to €280 ($382) and the Pro system went down €50 ($68) to €350 ($477.50).

But Microsoft didn't stop there. On October 22, the company discontinued the Core edition altogether and introduced the *Xbox 360 Arcade*, which was basically the same thing. However, for the same $280, the Xbox 360 Arcade console also included an HDMI output. The system also came with five popular downloadable Xbox Live Arcade games, including *Pac-Man Championship Edition*, and a 250MB memory card to store them on. Microsoft advertised the system as family-friendly and pitted it against the Wii, which was only $30 less and didn't feature high-def output.

As it turned out, SCE wasn't finished releasing new PS3 consoles to compete against the Xbox 360. Between October and November, the company released a new 40GB console in all regions of the world. In North America it retailed for $399, just $50 more than the newly priced 20GB Xbox 360 Core system.

The 40GB PS3 included less features than the models that were already available. Two of the four USB ports were removed, along with the only available memory-card port. Finally, PS2 backward-compatibility was completely removed. Not only could the 40GB model not play PS2 games through the hardware, but support of emulation was also removed. SCE felt by that time that there were enough available PS3 games to keep people occupied without having to go back to PS2 games.

Although the new 40GB PS3 had been intended to compete directly against the Xbox 360, it was the Wii that Microsoft was more concerned about. When the Xbox 360 Arcade was released, the overall Xbox 360, in all of its configurations, led the pack in sales among the three systems, mostly because of the Wii shortages in the marketplace. However, that changed in early September, when the Wii passed the Xbox 360 in sales worldwide.

Microsoft's Appeasement

But the Wii's lead was temporary, as the Xbox 360 made a comeback by the end of September and, in fact, outsold the Wii that month.[4] This was because *Halo 3* was released around the world during a three-day period beginning on September 25. In the United States, the game set a record for the highest grossing entertainment product within 24 hours of its release by grossing $170 million in that time period, breaking the previous record that had been set by *Halo 2* in 2004. By the end of November, *Halo 3* was the best-selling videogame of the year in the United States.

Halo 3's release was one of the most anticipated gaming events of the year, and Microsoft used it to its advantage. During the week ending February 24, the company released *Crackdown*, a *Grand Theft Auto*-type game that was set in an open world. *Crackdown* had originally been planned for the original Xbox, and development had begun in 2002. When the Xbox 360 hardware became available to developers in 2004, a decision was made for the game to be playable on the new console instead. The game went through a testing phase in late 2006 where it failed to challenge its players' reactions or maintain their interest. But after the years of development, Microsoft wasn't willing to abandon the game, so it decided to package it with a bonus that would definitely attract attention. That bonus turned out to be the downloading key to a multiplayer beta version of *Halo 3*. And even though *Crackdown* had nothing to do with *Halo 3*, the *Crackdown* disc was required to download the beta *Halo 3* from Xbox Live. And even after *Halo 3* was downloaded, a copy of *Crackdown* was still needed to launch the game. This had been done to prevent people from renting or borrowing a copy of *Crackdown* just so they could download *Halo 3*. On the strength of the *Halo 3* beta, *Crackdown* became the top-selling Xbox 360 game in February, with sales exceeding 42,700 copies.

Microsoft Crackdown

Microsoft announced on April 10 that the *Halo 3* beta period for the *Crackdown* purchasers would begin at 5:00 AM PST on May 16 and would last through June 6. The *Halo 3* beta was the most highly anticipated downloadable content for the Xbox 360 since its introduction, and thousands of people took off from work and school just so they could participate. But when the appointed hour and day arrived, the *Halo 3* beta couldn't be downloaded.

Microsoft issued a *Crackdown* patch fourteen hours later. But the *Crackdown* code hadn't been the problem. And there had been nothing wrong with the *Halo 3* code, either, since members of the press who had access to it for over a week were able to download it without a problem. But they hadn't needed the *Crackdown* disc to get at it. Microsoft finally admitted that the problem had been with Xbox Live, but the fastest and easiest way that they could fix it was by releasing the *Crackdown* patch. Once the patch was in place, the select thousands of gamers who owned the *Crackdown* disc happily downloaded the game. And to maintain positive relations with its users, Microsoft extended the beta period of *Halo 3* by four days.

Good customer service was important to Microsoft in light of the spate of defective consoles that continued to plague it. Microsoft reported that thanks to the warranty change in December, 2006, its Xbox division had lost $1.9 billion during the fiscal year that ended on June 30. But even after Microsoft spent billions to reimburse customers for the repair and shipping of their malfunctioning consoles, the defects continued.

By the summer, the number of consoles that experienced failures increased. A rumor that spread around the industry placed the defective rate at around 33%, a number that Microsoft neither confirmed nor denied. However, the company finally stopped touting that its failure rate was well within the industry standard of 3-5%.[5] But Microsoft couldn't even pin down the root of the trouble and claimed that each defective console suffered from a unique problem.

Microsoft announced on July 5 that it would extend the Xbox 360's warranty worldwide to three years from the date that the consoles were purchased. The cost to ship a defective unit to be repaired would also be included in the warranty, and anyone who had already paid to get his or her Xbox 360 serviced would be reimbursed. However, this extension only applied to consoles that suffered from the "red ring of death."[6]

Scratched discs were not covered under Microsoft's new warranty plan. On July 9, Microsoft was hit with a $5 million class-action lawsuit from a Florida man who claimed that the optical drive in his Xbox 360 had left "destructive scratches" on his discs, and that Microsoft had refused to fully reimburse him for them.[7]

Microsoft had always contended that it wasn't unusual for a small number of discs to get scratched, and the company warned that the console should never be moved while the optical drive was operating, or even while a disc merely sat idly in the drive. But Kassa, a Dutch consumer-advocacy TV show, didn't agree with Microsoft. Kassa concluded after extensive testing that the problem was caused by a particular TSST (Toshiba Samsung Storage Technology)[8] optical disc drive that Microsoft had used. These drives were missing parts that stabilized the discs and prevented their lenses from contacting the discs. Kassa reported that the problem was mainly found in Xbox 360 consoles that had been manufactured in December 2006. Microsoft, which hadn't taken part in the testing and naturally didn't agree with Kassa's findings, did issue a statement that invited people who faced the problems that Kassa had found to contact the company about how to proceed. Microsoft had a long-standing policy to replace defective, out-of-warranty discs that it published for $20 each.

Overheating was another problem that many Xbox 360 consoles were experiencing. While this didn't particularly destroy the Xbox 360, it did cause the system to lock up, thereby prematurely ending a game that was in play. It was believed that the chips used in the Xbox 360 caused the overheating problem, and Microsoft looked into using smaller chips and processors.

And Microsoft was experiencing problems other than the overheated consoles -- such as the case of the overloaded server.

Xbox Live players had been able to accumulate *Gamerscores* by completing specific challenges or "achievements" within games or by winning matches against online opponents. However, the Gamerscores weren't really good for anything except bragging rights. In theory, the more Gamerscores that a player had, the more respect he could get from his gaming peers.

On February 12, in conjunction with Old Spice, Microsoft initiated *Xbox Rewards*, a program that rewarded frequent American Xbox Live gamers with prizes that ranged from T-shirts to free Xbox 360 games. All they had to do to earn the prizes was register on the Xbox Rewards website and amass 1,500 Gamerscores within a two-month period, ending on April 12. At the beginning of the promotion Microsoft divided users into three tiers according to their annual Xbox Live Gamerscores. The highest tier, which included players who had annual Gamerscores of 10,000 or more, offered the best prizes, such as a free copy of *Fusion Frenzy 2*, a $50 game. In all, Microsoft planned to award $500,000 in prizes.

Unfortunately, the promotion didn't kick off smoothly. The official website from where people had to register didn't launch at midnight as expected, leaving thousands of people waiting around until 8 PM EST when it finally became available. But at that time, so many people attempted to register at once that the website couldn't accommodate everyone and crashed from the load. It took almost a day to get the site up back up and running. Microsoft extended the challenge to April 15, so people would still have a full two months to accumulate their 1,500 Gamerscores. However, if it took them the full two months to do this, they most likely wouldn't receive the prize they wanted. In theory, five million people, the entire subscription base of Xbox Live, were eligible for prizes. But most of the better prizes, including the copy of *Fusion Frenzy 2*, were only limited to 2,500 pieces, and they were given to those who achieved their target scores on a first-come first-serve basis.

Microsoft suffered another setback at the end of the year. Beginning on December 22, Xbox Live began experiencing problems with paid subscribers not being able to sign on, and others being unexpectedly shut out. The outage continued through the end of the year, and Microsoft attributed it to a high rate of volume of people trying to get onto the network at the same time. Larry Hryb, the director of programming for Xbox Live, announced that one of the reasons the problem took so long to fix was because a lot of integral Microsoft personnel had taken off the week of Christmas. This was not an endearing excuse for the millions who were shut out during the outage.

Microsoft didn't just offer free games because of screw-ups. On November 15 Xbox Live celebrated its fifth anniversary and in honor of this event, Microsoft gave away free downloads for *Carcassonne*, a game that had been released less than five months earlier. The game was free to anyone who downloaded it on either November 15 or November 16. Microsoft also recognized its inaugural members who had been with the service since its inception with 500 free Microsoft Points (which were worth approximately $6.25).

Despite the bumps along the way, Xbox Live was still the premier gaming network, and Microsoft intended to keep it that way by adding new services. On May 7, the company integrated Xbox Live with *Windows Live Messenger*, its instant-messaging client that had been around since 1999 for *Windows*. This gave anybody who used a *Windows*-based device the ability to have an online chat with another user. And to make it easier for Xbox 360 owners to use the service, Microsoft released a $30 *Chatpad*, a small QWERTY-style keyboard that latched onto the Xbox 360 controller.

Microsoft Chatpad

Wii Fit

Instead of having peripherals that connected to its controllers, Nintendo had peripheral that its controllers connected to. The *Wii Zapper*, named after the memorable NES light gun, was a plastic shell in which both the Wii Remote and the Nunchuck were inserted. Once both controllers were in place, with the Wii Remote on one end and the Nunchuck on the other, the Wii Zapper resembled a rifle and was used in target games. The peripheral was released in Japan on October 25 bundled with a Sega game called *Ghost Squad*. Nintendo of Japan also offered the Wii Zapper without a game from its online store. Nintendo of America released the Wii Zapper on November 15, packaged with a game called *Link's Crossbow Training*, a game that had been based on *The Legend of Zelda: Twilight Princess*, which had been released for the Wii a year earlier.

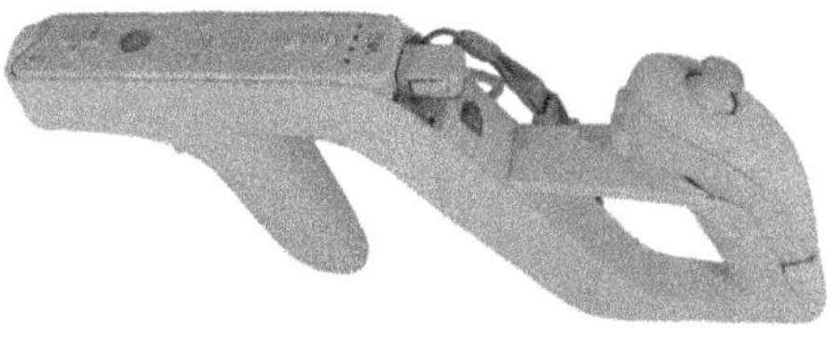

Nintendo Wii Zapper

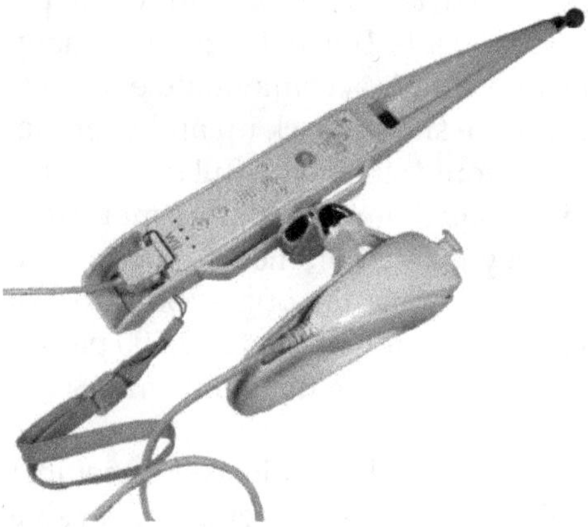

Aksys Hooked! Real Motion Fishing controller

A pair of fishing games was released for the Wii in 2007. *Fishing Master* arrived in Japan on March 31 and in North America on September 18. This was a game where one to four players used their Wii Remotes and Nunchuck controllers as fishing rods to take part in a fishing competition to catch the most fish. *Bass Fishing Wii: Rokumaru Densetsu* from Arc System Works followed in Japan on September 27. This was more of a fishing simulation than a game and up to four virtual fishermen could fish in 6 different locations using four different casting methods. Like *Fishing Master*, *Bass Fishing Wii: Rokumaru Densetsu* used the combination of the Wii Remote and Nunchuck to simulate a fishing rod. The game came to North America on October 30, where the name was changed to *Hooked! Real Motion Fishing.*

The American version of the game was bundled with a *Wii Fishing Rod Controller*. As with the Wii Zapper, the Wii Remote slid into the controller, which looked like a real fishing rod. But the controller also incorporated the Nunchuck, which acted as a rotating reel, to make the simulation even more realistic. Unfortunately, it didn't help. Jonathan Marx wrote in a review for a website called *Cheat Code Central*, "the poor graphics, terrible music, limited content, and the nearly useless Wi-Fi multiplayer make this another Wii fishing title with almost nothing rewarding to offer." *IGN* was less kind and in its review described the game as *painful*. The reviewer stated that he put the Rod Controller aside after just trying it once. But even without the controller, he found the game to be "barely playable."

Nintendo also issued an accessory for the Wii Remote that helped solve the problem of controllers that were flying out of their users' hands. The *Wii Remote Jacket* was a clear silicone sleeve that wrapped around the Wii Remote and served two purposes. It gave the player a better grip on the remote. And it provided a cushion in case the remote did escape from the player's hand. Nintendo began bundling the jackets with the Wii Remotes on October 15. The company also provided up to four free jackets to each Wii owner who requested them through Nintendo's website.

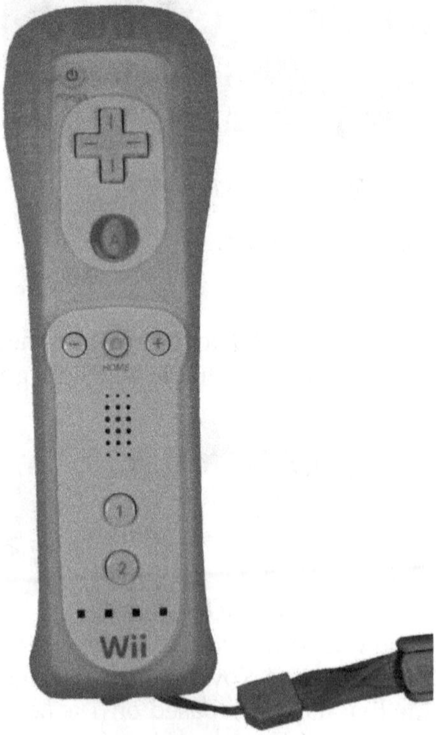

Nintendo Wii Remote Jacket

Nintendo of Japan introduced another Wii

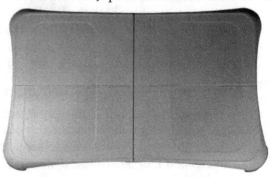

Nintendo Wii Balance Board

peripheral on December 1. The *Wii Balance Board* was a plastic unit that sat on the floor in front of the TV screen. It loosely resembled the Joyboard that Amiga had released for the Atari VCS in 1983. But unlike the Joyboard, which was merely a controller that replaced the joystick, the Wii Balance Board was much more advanced and could measure a person's center of gravity and weight, all of which were sent to the Wii console via Bluetooth technology.

The Wii Balance Board was bundled with *Wii Fit*, a collection of minigames that helped the user set up an exercise regime. Despite the cute graphics featuring Mii characters, *Wii Fit* and the Wii Balance Board introduced the Wii as much more than just a gaming console. The minigames ranged from yoga exercises to balancing to jogging. It could also measure a person's Body-Mass Index and keep track of it over time. Whether *Wii Fit* and the Wii Balance Board actually replaced conventional exercising techniques was up for debate, but enough people believed in it that Nintendo of Japan sold 250,000 units of the ¥8,300 ($74) bundle during its first week of availability.

Nintendo Wii Fit

Augmented Reality

Unlike the Wii, the PS3 didn't have a controller that could track a player's position. However, it did have a camera, the EyeToy, which could place the gamer's image into a game. But the EyeToy had been designed for the PS2, and PS3 software that utilized the peripheral was not available. SCE rectified this by releasing the *PlayStation Eye*, an updated and much more sophisticated version of the EyeToy exclusively for the PS3.

The camera on the PlayStation Eye could capture standard video at four times the resolution and twice the frame-rate of the EyeToy. Its sensitivity to light was also doubled and could produce good-quality video just from the light provided by a television screen.

SCE PlayStation Eye

The PlayStation Eye launched in North America first on October 23 with Japan, Europe and Australia receiving it by October 26. The device was part of a $60 bundle that also included a game called *The Eye of Judgment*, a camera stand, a deck of 30 cards and a mat with a 3x3 grid to place the cards on.

The Eye of Judgment was a turn-based card game for one or two players, in which the object was to occupy five positions on the mat using a combination of character and environment cards. The game was similar to prior card games like *Yu-Gi-Oh*! and Pokémon in which characters "dueled" and the more powerful creature won. While both of these card games were also playable in videogame form, the two formats were never co-joined into one game. In *The Eye of Judgment*, the characters on the cards came alive on the screen. Using the PlayStation Eye that was mounted on the supplied stand, the game mat and all other aspects of reality (such as a player's hands) were visible

SCE PS3 Eye of Judgement

on the TV screen. But *augmented* to this view were the computer-generated characters, which appeared to exist in the real world; at least on the screen.

The Eye of Judgment was the first practical use of *Augmented Reality* in home videogaming. Unlike Virtual Reality, in which the player was immersed within a completely computer-generated environment, Augmented Reality added computer-generated objects to the real world.

New PS3 Controllers

On November 19, a few weeks after the release of the PlayStation Eye, SCEJ released a brand-new version of the standard PS3 controller in Japan. The new *DualShock 3* looked very much like the Sixaxis controller that it replaced except that it was 40% heavier. This was because the new controller also included a rumble feature.

SCE DualShock 3

A controller with a rumble feature had been expected for the PS3 since March 1, when SCE and Immersion, the company behind the rumble technology, announced that they had ended their legal dispute. They then began a business agreement so that Immersion's rumble technology could be incorporated into future PlayStation products. At that time, the two companies had been ambiguous about which specific PlayStation product would use the feature, but since the existing Sixaxis controller didn't have that feature, most people assumed that that was where the force-feedback technology would be heading. And although SCE had once used the excuse that the rumble feature couldn't be included in the Sixaxis controller because of its motion-detection feature, the new DualShock 3 had no trouble incorporating both features.

When the new controller was released, only one game was available that used the rumble feature. This was *Ratchet & Clank Future: Tools of Destruction*, which had been released in Japan on the same day as the controller. Oddly, the game was also released around the world with the rumble feature intact, even though the DualShock 3 wasn't scheduled to appear outside of Japan until 2008. Several games that had already been released, including *Motorstorm*, which was packaged with the 80GB PS3, were issued patches to add compatibility with the DualShock 3 to them. And a general update was made available for the PS3 console that added rumble support to PS2 games.

A controller of a different sort was released for the Xbox 360 on April 3, when Activision issued *Guitar Hero II* for that console in the United States. The *Gibson X-Plorer* guitar controller, which was different from the Gibson SG guitar that had been packaged with the PS2 version of the game, marked the first time a guitar controller was available for a console other than the PS2. The game itself included ten additional songs that had not appeared on the PS2 version, and more songs could be purchased and downloaded from the Xbox Live Marketplace.

A third game in the *Guitar Hero* series appeared on July 24. *Guitar Hero Encore: Rocks the '80s* was released only for the PS2 and didn't come with a guitar controller. The game was very similar to *Guitar Hero II*, and many referred to it as an expansion pack rather than a game in its own right. Critics panned it and said it wasn't worth its $50 price, especially since it contained less songs than either of the prior two titles in the series. Like the *Guitar Hero* titles before it, *Guitar Hero Encore: Rocks the '80s* had been developed by Harmonix. But in September, 2006, just as Activision purchased *Guitar Hero*'s publisher, RedOctane, MTV bought Harmonix for $175 million. Many believed that *Guitar Hero Encore: Rocks the '80s* had been released only to fulfill a contractual obligation between Harmonix and RedOctane.

On October 28, Activision published *Guitar Hero III: Legends of Rock* for all four major consoles, including the PS2. The game was distributed by RedOctane. With Harmonix no longer in the picture, Activision had another company that it owned, Neversoft, do the actual development.[9] The game followed the same format that had been so successful in the earlier editions and introduced a new online multiplay feature.[10] Bundled with the game were wireless Gibson Les Paul guitars. However, the way the guitar communicated with the console differed among the consoles. The Xbox 360 version communicated directly with the console. In the Wii version, the Wii Remote was inserted into the guitar controller frame, and the guitar used the Wii Remote to communicate to the Wii. Because the PS2 did not have native wireless capabilities, it required the use of a dongle, a receiver that plugged into the USB port of the console. However, while the PS3 did have Bluetooth capabilities, they were somewhat limited to the console's Sixaxis controllers. In order for the guitar controller to communicate with the PS3, developer RedOctane used the same technology that it had done with the PS2, and provided a receiver dongle that plugged into the PS3's USB port.

By year's end, *Guitar Hero III: Legends of Rock*, in all of its formats, was the top-selling game of the year.[11]

Rock Band

Guitar Hero III: Legends of Rock was the first installment in the series *Guitar Hero*, which Harmonix didn't have a hand in. But in its place, Harmonix developed a game in which the guitar was only one of the instruments.

Rock Band, which was released by MTV and Electronic Arts for the PS3 and Xbox 360[12] in North America on November 20, was the natural next step in the evolution of *Guitar Hero*. The $170 package included a Fender Stratocaster guitar controller, a drum controller that featured four pads and used real drumsticks, and a microphone. The guitar that came in the package was very similar to the ones that were issued with the *Guitar Hero* games, and any *Guitar Hero* guitar could be used in *Rock Band*. On the other hand, the Fender Stratocaster guitar that was bundled with *Rock Band* couldn't be used in *Guitar Hero II* or *Guitar Hero III: Legends of Rock*. An optional second bass guitar could be added.

In solo *Rock Band* games, players could use the guitar and play the notes that scrolled down the screen in *Guitar Hero* fashion. But *Rock Band* also allowed would-be rock stars to play solo with the drums as well. Or they could use the microphone to sing in Karaoke-like contests.

But the real fun in *Rock Band* began when 2-4 players performed together as a band. In "Band World Tour" mode, the band had to play at 41 different locations within 17 different cities around the world. A band started small, playing at local venues, and as it improved, it unlocked additional equipment, money and fans that would help it become a superstar.[13]

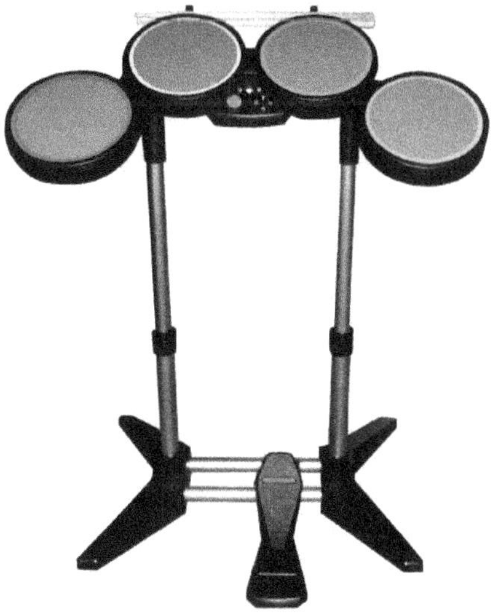

MTV Games Rock Band drums

MTV heavily promoted the game for months before its actual release, including showcasing it at the MTV Video Music Awards on September 9, 2007. The advance promotion worked, and the game was in such demand when it came out that Electronic Arts announced that it couldn't produce enough of them to meet the demand throughout their fiscal year.

Trivia Games

Musical instruments weren't the only type of alternative controllers that were available to gamers. Microsoft and SCE both released controllers that were used to answer multiple-choice questions. Both were bundled with trivia games, a market that ZapIt had tried to enter with its Game Wave, but failed.

SCEA released its trivia game, *Buzz!*, in North America on October 30. The *Buzz!* controllers that SCEA bundled were slightly different from the ones that had been available in Europe. The European controllers had four thin black buttons, each outlined with a different color. The new American controllers featured four buttons that were slightly more pronounced and each one was a different color.[14]

SCE Buzz Controllers

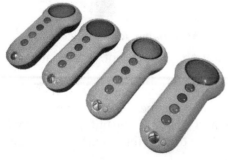

Microsoft Big Button Pads

Microsoft's *Scene It? Lights, Camera, Action,* was released for the Xbox 360 on November 6, one week after the American release of *Buzz!*. It was the console version of a game that had been available on DVD for several years. The object was for at least two players to watch movie clips, and then for one of them to be the first to respond correctly to questions about the clip that they had watched.

The original DVD game on which the Xbox 360 version was based was a board game similar to *Trivial Pursuit,* and all of the questions had to be verbally answered by the contestants. The Xbox 360 edition consisted of multiple-choice questions that were answered by using the controllers. Gamers could use the standard Xbox 360 controllers, with the A, B, X and Y buttons each corresponding to a separate multiple-choice selection on the screen. Or they could use the four custom wireless *Big Button Pads* that were bundled with the game. Like the *Buzz!* controllers, each pad featured a large "buzzer" button and four smaller buttons that corresponded with the answers on the screen.

V.Smile Expands

The trivia games from SCE and Microsoft had been rated "T" and "E" respectively by the ESRB, and both games represented wholesome, non-contentious fun that could be enjoyed by all members of the family. Unfortunately, not all games for those systems could be deemed that way. VTech, on the other hand, continued to produce only clean, educational games for its VTech V.Smile.

VTech released two peripherals for the V.Smile, which perpetuated its idea of educational fun. One was the *V.Smile Smart Keyboard,* which was a full-size computer keyboard. It didn't turn the V.Smile into a computer, but it taught young children how to use one through a series of games. One play mode, Computer Zone, used a "pseudo-Internet" to teach children how to browse the Internet, search for information and how to write responses to simulated emails called *V-Mails*.

The other peripheral that VTech released was the V.*Smile Smartbook*. This turned the V.Smile into an electronic book that was similar to the Pico and Beena from Sega. However, while the Sega units used "books" that doubled as the game cartridges, the V.Smile Smartbook used *smartbooks* that worked in tandem with specific game smartridges.

Both of the VTech add-ons plugged into the V.Smile's left controller port and replaced the standard controller. Meanwhile, VTech introduced a new joystick controller that had a writing pad in place of the prior large button, and an attached stylus to aid children in spelling and letter recognition. This controller was included with a new model of the V.Smile console that also featured a built-in microphone so children could take part in sing-along games. Although all new educational games were developed so they would play on either model of the V.Smile, portions of the games that incorporated either the writing pad or the microphone were disabled when they played on the original V.Smile.

Although VTech had originally designed the V.Smile Pocket to be completely compatible with the V.Smile console, the new products for the V.Smile, the V.Smile Smart Keyboard and the V.Smile Smartbook, were not. And the new features that were incorporated into the new V.Smile model such as the writing pad and the microphone, could not be used with the V.Smile Pocket. The games could that used these features could be played on the handheld unit, but the portions of the games that used the writing pad and microphone were disabled on the V.Smile Pocket, which didn't have those features. However, VTech did release a new slightly slimmer version of the V.Smile Pocket that featured a small, built-in microphone.

VTech V.Smart Smart Keyboard

VTech V.Smart Smartbook

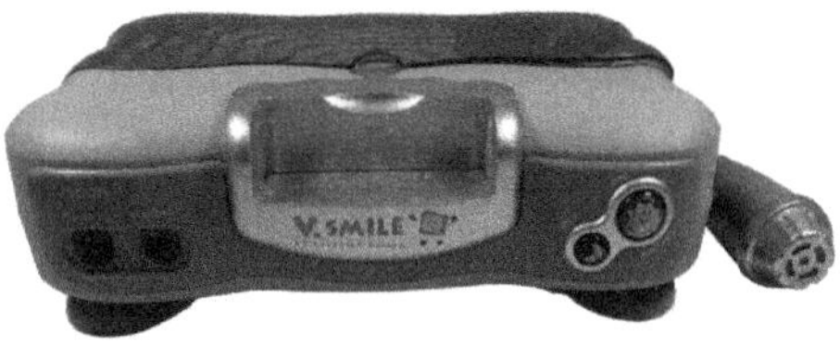

VTech V.Smile '2'

VTech V.Smart '2' controller

VTech V.Smile '2' Pocket

Manhunt 2

The VTech and LeapFrog systems were the only ones that guaranteed that children wouldn't be exposed to violent videogames. And while Nintendo tried to portray a wholesome image with family-oriented games, there were still games released for its systems that carried "M" ratings that were recommended for players seventeen and over. But on the whole, "M" rated games for Nintendo's consoles were pretty rare, especially when compared to the fare that SCE and Microsoft produced.

Sometimes it was unavoidable to purchase an "M" rated game. *Crackdown*, Microsoft's game that had become a best-seller in the United States because it included the *Halo 3* beta download, couldn't even be released in Germany, because the USK refused to rate it due to its violence, making it the third Xbox 360 title in less than a year to suffer this fate. Germany was the exception, however. There was no backlash in the United States over *Crackdown*, even though it had been assigned an "M" rating from the ESRB.

But not all violent games managed to escape controversy, especially ones from Rockstar. Its latest controversial title was *Manhunt 2*, the sequel to *Manhunt*, the violent game that had been banned in several countries in 2003. The controversy began when Rockstar first announced in February that the game would come out for the PS2, PSP and, surprisingly, the Wii, which many people thought was exclusively for family-friendly games. Nintendo defended the game and advised concerned parents to apply PIN settings to prevent their children from playing it. But the real brouhaha began the day before the game's scheduled release, when the ESRB slapped an "AO" rating on it because of its extreme violence. SCE and Nintendo both refused to allow the game to be published for their systems with this notorious rating.

Rockstar cleaned *Manhunt 2* and resubmitted it to the ESRB, which re-rated it with an "M." The game was released in North America on October 29. However, Target still refused to carry it, even with the "M" rating. The game encountered the same problems in Great Britain, where David Cooke, the head of the country's rating body, the British Board of Film Classification (BBFC), announced that even with the changes that Rockstar had instilled, *Manhunt 2* was still banned from being sold in his country, making it only the second game in the history of Great Britain to hold that distinction.[15]

Rockstar also ran into problems after the "M"-rated version of *Manhunt 2* hit the streets. Hackers were able to access the code of the PS and PSP versions, and saw that the violent episodes that had caused the original "AO" rating were still embedded, even though they couldn't be accessed by the player. This was reminiscent of the Hot Coffee scandal that Rockstar had faced with *Grand Theft Auto: San Andreas*. Despite this revelation, the ESRB stuck with its new rating, since Rockstar had disclosed that the code in question had not been removed when the game had been resubmitted for rating.

Sony Slims Down

At the end of 2007, the Wii was the top selling console in the United States, with 6.29 million consoles sold. The Xbox 360 followed, with 4.62 million in sales. Surprisingly, third place was held by the PS2, which continued to enjoy new releases such as *Guitar Hero II, Guitar Hero III: Legends of Rock* and *Madden NFL '08*, all of which were among the top-ten-selling games of the year.

Since the slim PS2 had first been released in 2004, SCE had quietly made minor revisions to it several times. A revision issued on July 5 reduced the console's weight by 10.6oz to 21.2 oz, through a reduction of internal parts. Even the weight of the AC adapter was reduced by 3.5oz to 8.8oz.

In October, the British trade magazine MVC announced that a new "compact" PS2 would be released in the United States in early 2008 and would retail at $99, $30 less than the console currently sold for. The "new" console actually was released on November 22 in Japan, where it sold for ¥16,000 ($147.50), the same price as the PS2 that it replaced. As it turned out, the "newly redesigned" PS2 looked pretty much like its predecessor on the outside. However, internally, the design architecture of the new system was completely changed.

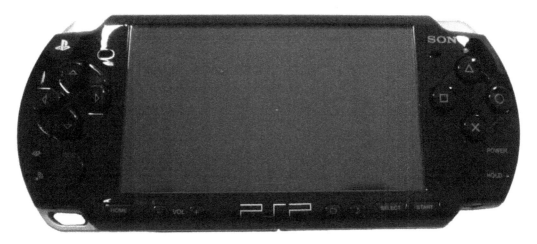

SCE PSP-2000

One noticeable difference was that the power cord no longer needed a power brick, a transformer that acted as an intermediary between the wall plug and the console, which converted incoming AC voltage into safe DC voltage. The new design moved the transformer inside the console. While this raised the weight of the console to 25oz, the overall weight of the PS2 was actually 5oz less than the prior model because of the absence of the power brick.

The PS2 wasn't SCE's only console that received a facelift. On September 10, the company released a new version of the PSP that was 33% lighter and 19% thinner than its predecessor. Other changes included a new UMD drive that helped speed up game-loading times, which had been the object of constant complaints by gamers, especially when the PSP was compared with the DS. The loading time was also improved because the device's RAM had been doubled to 64MB.

In order to make the PSP slimmer, the battery had to be slimmed down as well, reducing its capacity by 1/3. However, SCE's designers managed to make the new battery more efficient, so that it could power the new PSP for about as long as the larger battery powered the older model. There were also two ways to recharge the battery. One way was by connecting the unit to a wall outlet, which was the only way the battery on the previous model could be recharged. But the device also had a USB slot, which allowed the PSP to recharge by being connected to a computer. And thanks to a new video output port, the new PSP could also be connected to a television, on which its games or movies could be viewed.

The new PSP was not given a new name to differentiate it from the older one. Instead, it was referred to by its model number, PSP-2000, whereas the original unit had a model number of PSP-1000. The price of the PSP-2000 was $170, the same as the old one. That price had been established on April 3, when SCEA lowered the PSP's price by $30. That had been done at the request of retailers who had threatened to quit selling PSPs unless SCEA did something to jumpstart the device's sagging sales, which in late 2006 had been down 72% from the same period the year before.

SCE PSP-S310 TV Tuner

The price cuts came to Europe on May 4, when the cost dropped from €200 ($272) to €170 ($231).[16] In addition to the price cut, Europe also received a new peripheral for the PSP. The €50 ($67) *Go!Cam*, which was released on May 25, was the exact same PSP-300 camera that had been released in Japan in 2006 as the Chotto

Nintendo DS Terebi

Nintendo DS Kao Training

Shot. However, unlike the Japanese model, the Go!Cam wasn't packaged with editing software, although SCEE did offer the software for free as a download.

The PSP cameras had been released in Japan, Europe and even Australia. But on September 20 a different type of PSP peripheral was only issued in Japan, and only for the new slimmer PSP-2000s that launched the same day. The ¥6,980 ($61) *PSP-S310* was a tuner that allowed broadcast TV to be displayed on the PSP. Like the Go!Cam camera, the PSP-S310 plugged into the USB slot at the top of the PSP. But unlike the camera, which could work on PSPs from regions such as North America where the camera wasn't available, the PSP-S310 could only be used in Japan. This was because the unit was a 1seg[17] digital tuner that was limited to the Japanese airwaves.

Prior to the release of the PSP-S310, only two heldheld units[18] had official TV-tuner peripherals available for them, and both had been released in 1991. Apparently, handheld TV tuners were released in pairs, because another such device came out exactly two months after the PSP-S310. On November 20, Nintendo of Japan released the *DS Terebi* for the DS and DS Lite. The ¥6,800 ($62) unit plugged directly into the card slot of the DS and also featured a built-in game, *Fire,* which had been one of the four original *Game & Watch* titles. Like the PSP-S310, the DS Terebi was a 1seg tuner and therefore wasn't released, nor could it be used, outside of Japan.

DS Camera

Japanese DS owners could also purchase a camera that plugged into the GBA slot of their consoles. The camera was bundled with a game called *Facening de Hyōjō Yutaka ni Inshō Up: Otona no DS Kao Training,* which was released on August 7. This game employed "Facening," a process to improve facial features by using facial exercises. The camera was used to take an image of a player's face and then the program guided the player through 15 different guided exercises that affected six different facial areas; eyes, cheeks, nose, mouth, jaw and neck. The ¥4,800 ($41) package also included a stand that the handheld could rest on, leaving the player's hands to perform the exercises.[19]

Two DS games were also released in Japan that used the GBA slot to plug in special controllers. The first, released on August 1, was *Slide Adventure: Mag Kid*. In this game, the player controlled a magnet that had to move around a room in order to collect parts of a toy robot. The game employed a unique manner in which to make the magnet move. A *Slide Controller* that plugged into the GBA slot was packaged with the game. Once the controller was plugged in, the DS console sat above it. The bottom of the controller was similar to the bottom of an optical computer mouse. While it sat atop the slide controller, the DS console was in effect, a mouse, and sliding it around a flat surface caused the on-screen magnet to move around. If the DS was pushed forward, the magnet moved upwards. *Slide Adventure: Mag Kid* was the only game that employed the slide controller and the game was never released outside of Japan.

Nintendo Slide Adventure: Mag Kid

Taito released *Arkanoid DS* in Japan on December 4. This was the latest incarnation of *Arkanoid*, a *Breakout*-like game that had first appeared in arcades in 1986. Although this was the first time *Arkanoid* had appeared on a portable console, *Breakout* and Nintendo's *Breakout*-like *Alleyway* had both appeared on the original Game Boy. In both cases, the paddle at the bottom of the screen was moved horizontally using the D-pad. *Arkanoid DS* was packaged with a *Paddle Controller* that plugged into the DS's GBA slot.[20] The controller featured a dial that controlled the movement of the on-screen paddle.[21]

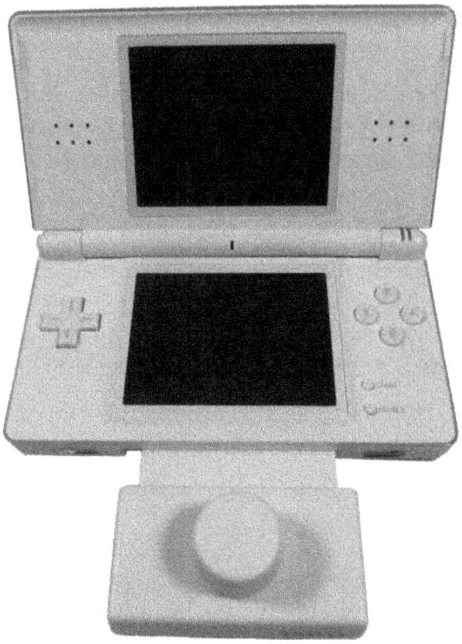

Taito Arkanoid DS Paddle Controller

Although American DS owners were denied the slide controller and paddle controller, they were finally able to use their DS consoles to access the Internet, thanks to the release of the *Nintendo DS Browser*. As had been the case when the browser had been released in Japan and Europe in 2006, it was available with two versions of the 8MB Memory Expansion Pak. The package that contained a Memory Expansion Pak that could only work on the DS Lite was available in stores. The other, which could be used with both the DS and the DS Lite, was only available online through the Nintendo of America website. Both sets sold for $30.

By September 26, the DS had hit the 50-million mark in total sales, which made it the fastest-selling handheld game console of all time. During the week ending November 24, over 653,000 of the consoles were sold in the United States, setting a new sales record for Nintendo of America and breaking a previous record set in 2005, when 600,000 GBAs had been sold in one week. Another record was set in the United Kingdom the following week, when 191,000 DS consoles were sold, breaking a prior record set by the PSP in 2005. The DS was also the top-selling handheld console of the year, with Nintendo selling 8.5 million units, more than double the 3.8 million PSPs that SCE had sold.

Apple iPhone Debuts

On October 30, the South Korean company Game Park Holdings released a new version of its GP2X handheld console. Instead of the small joystick controller that was found on the original GP2X, the new $170 *GP2X F200* had a four-button D-pad in its place. The new unit also came with four pre-loaded games and a metal stylus, which was used for the F200's most major enhancement, a touchscreen.

Game Park Holdings GP2X F200

The touchscreen would be an important component in the future of handheld gaming. Although few realized it at the time, handheld gaming had changed on June 29 when Apple released the *iPhone*, which Apple CEO Steve Jobs introduced as a "widescreen iPod with touch controls," a "revolutionary mobile phone," and a "breakthrough Internet communicator." Games hadn't been part of Jobs' original iPhone description because they weren't a major feature of the device. Still, like the cell phones that Apple hoped it would replace, the iPhone could play simple games that weren't as sophisticated as those designed for the DS and PSP.

And this was something that other companies were trying to improve upon: the successful marriage between cell phones and handheld gaming. It had been attempted before, when Nokia introduced its N-Gage in 2003. But the N-Gage had too many design flaws that prevented it from taking off. Now Nokia was going to try again. The company planned to release the N-Gage technology as software in its dedicated cell phones. Multi-player games could be downloaded from the N-Gage website and played on the phones that had the software built in. The first such phone was the *N81*, which Nokia released on August 29. Although Nokia billed the new N-Gage software as games that could be played on any Nokia phone, the N81 actually included two buttons that were dedicated to games. Unfortunately, there was nothing special about the N81 that made people run out and buy it, especially since Nokia wouldn't launch the new N-Gage service until 2008.

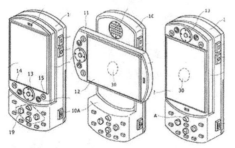

Sony Ericsson, the mobile-phone division of Sony, was also looking into a device that bridged cell phones and handheld videogame consoles. On May 31, the company filed a patent for a phone device that had a swivel screen which, when rotated, displayed a button configuration that was very similar to the one on the PSP. Sony executives were very quiet about the patent, and SCEE CEO David Reeves even flatly denied any knowledge of such a device being in the works.

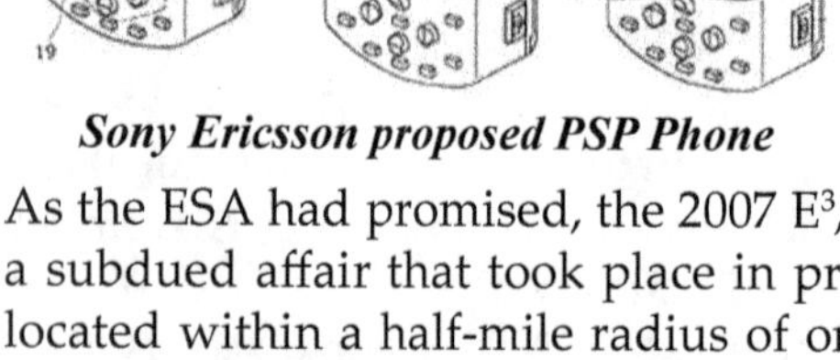

Sony Ericsson proposed PSP Phone

E³ Media & Business Summit

Representatives of the videogame industry gathered between July 11 and July 13 at an airplane hangar in Santa Monica, California. As the ESA had promised, the 2007 E³, now called the *E³ Media & Business Summit*, was a subdued affair that took place in private suites in a handful of Santa Monica hotels located within a half-mile radius of one another. Microsoft actually held its annual E³ press conference at Santa Monica High School.[22]

The Barker Hangar,[23] which was located approximately five miles from the cluster of hotels at Santa Monica Airport, served as the event's main floor, where publishers displayed their products on small, low-key tables that replaced the massive booths that had defined the prior E³ shows. TV monitors sat on the tables and discretely played the games that the publishers were trying to pitch, with the names of the games printed on small placards that sat beneath the monitors. But the real action took place back at the hotels, since the temperature inside the hangar was extremely high, the result of the hot July sun beating down on it.

The E³ Media & Business Summit had been attended by around 10,000 people, a far cry from the more than 60,000 people who had gone to the 2006 show. As if to fill the void left by the absence of the massive E³, *E for All* (Entertainment for All) was held at E³'s former home, the Los Angeles Convention Center, for four days beginning on October 18. The show was organized by IDG World Expo, a corporate cousin to Infotainment World, which had co-founded E³ in 1995. Unlike the industry-only E³, *E for All* was open to the public. Two other public videogame expositions, the Leipzig Games Convention and the Tokyo Game Show, regularly attracted over 150,000 attendees each year. *E for All* didn't do as well. Only 18,000 people paid the $50 to $90 admission. And if these people had been expecting an E³ that was open to the public, they were surely disappointed. While E³ had taken up all of the space in three halls and several lobbies of the Los Angeles Convention Center, *E for All* only utilized 75% of the South Hall. And many of the larger publishers, including Microsoft, SCE and Activision, simply didn't attend.

Activision Merges

Activision had more important things to attend to. On December 2, Vivendi, a French media company whose roots dated back to 1853, announced that it planned to purchase a majority interest in Activision for $18.9 billion, which would make it the largest deal ever in videogame history. Vivendi already owned Blizzard Entertainment, the company behind *World of Warcraft*, an online multiplayer role-playing game that claimed over 9 million subscribers. It was believed that once the merger took place, the new company would be the largest third-party software company in the world. In 2007, Vivendi and Activision had a combined gross revenue of $3.9 billion. Electronic Arts, which currently held the title as the largest company, had revenues of $3.8 million.

Even without a merger, Activision did officially pass Electronic Arts as the top-performing third-party software company in the United States. Much of Activision's success was attributed to its *Guitar Hero* franchise. Both *Guitar Hero II* and *Guitar Hero III: Legends of Rock* were among the top ten best-selling games of the year. The company's *Call of Duty 4: Modern Warfare* was also in the top ten.

The company responsible for the top game of the year, *Halo 3*, also went through changes. On October 5, a Bungie spokesman broke the news that his company, which had been a wholly owned subsidiary of Microsoft since 2000, planned to split from its parent and become independent once again, with Microsoft retaining a small minority stake in Bungie. Microsoft would maintain complete ownership of the *Halo* franchise and would have first right of refusal to publish any future Bungie products.

Magazines Change Hands

Videogame magazines were changing ownership as well. *Nintendo Power*, which Nintendo of America had been publishing since August 1988, was the longest continuously published English-language videogame magazine in print.[24] In 2007, Nintendo of America ceased publication of the magazine and, beginning with the December issue, handed the reins over to Future US, which also published the *Official Xbox Magazine*. Future US also published the independent *PSM* magazine, which it ceased publishing with the December issue. In its place, Future US began publishing *PlayStation: The Official Magazine*, which was sanctioned by SCE. For the first time, one publisher was responsible for producing the official magazines for all of the major console companies.

While it was still called Imagine Media,[25], Future US had also published the *Official Dreamcast Magazine*, which folded with the April 2001 issue when Sega had discontinued the Dreamcast. And while the Dreamcast was pretty much dead after that in most of the world, its popularity still continued in Japan, where Sega had continued to sell refurbished Dreamcast consoles from its Sega Direct website until 2006.

Although Sega of Japan had released its final game for the Dreamcast in 2004, new third-party titles licensed by Sega continued to be released in Japan. That finally came to an end in 2007. Sega of Japan announced on January 18 that it would cease production of its proprietary GD-ROM discs as of February 1. Two Dreamcast titles were produced by their developers before the GD-ROM production was terminated. *Trigger Heart Exelica* was released by Warashi on February 22 and *Karous* was released by Milestone, Inc. on March 8, making it the Dreamcast's final official release. Although the game wasn't sold outside of Japan, the British magazine *Edge* still reviewed it, giving it a 6/10 rating and citing it as "a fair swansong for the machine famous for cell-shaded beauty, niche appeal and passionate, inventive ideas."

Mario Meets Sonic

Sega released a Wii game on November 6 that received much more exposure. *Mario & Sonic at the Olympic Games* marked the first pairing of the iconic characters from Nintendo and Sega in a game together. The two companies had worked together previously in 2001, when they had jointly produced *F-Zero GX*, and plans had been negotiated then to eventually put Mario and Sonic in a game together. After Sega was awarded the license to produce a videogame for the Beijing 2008 Olympics, an event that promoted sportsmanship and trust, it was determined that this was the perfect background against in which to bring the two characters together.

The game was developed by Sega, which also published it in all regions of the world except Japan, where it was released by Nintendo of Japan. The game consisted of 24 Olympic events that pitted a host of Nintendo and Sega characters against one another.

Mario & Sonic at the Olympic Games was a success and was named the game of the year

Mario & Sonic At The Olympic Games

at the Leipzig Games Convention. It was Great Britain's top-selling game in December and ranked #10 in the United States. But while there obviously couldn't be any content in the game that decisively asserted say which character was better, other sales seemed to point towards Mario. Within days of the release of *Mario & Sonic at the Olympic Games*, Nintendo released *Super Mario Galaxy* for the Wii. In the same time period that *Mario & Sonic at the Olympic Games* sold 612,000 units in the United States, *Super Mario Galaxy* sold 1.4 million, making it the #2 game in December,[26] and the #5 game of the year. Another Mario title, *Mario Party 8*, which had been released in North America on May 29, was the #10 game of the year.

Mario also appeared in a hit documentary that came out on August 17. *The King of Kong* followed videogame record holder Steve Wiebe as he attempted to break the world record for *Donkey Kong*, which had been held by *Time* magazine's Gamer of the Century, Billy Mitchell. Much of the film was shot at Funspot in Laconia, New Hampshire, the home of the American Classic Arcade Museum. The movie also featured legendary Twin Galaxies gaming referee, Walter Day, and turned him into a cult hero. *Variety* named the film its #4 movie of the year, while *Film Threat* put it at #3, right after *No Country for Old Men*, which won that year's Oscar for best picture.

The King of Kong brought new interest to classic gaming at a time when the videogame industry was enjoying its best year ever. According to the NPD Group, a company that tracks sales from over 900 retailers, more games had been sold in the United States in 2007 than ever before, with retail sales nearing $18 billion.

And of course, what everybody involved in the industry wondered was whether or not this period of prosperity would continue through 2008.

CHAPTER THIRTY-SIX
2008

When 2008 began, Microsoft found itself in the same position where it had been one year earlier, trying to regain its customer satisfaction. This was in the wake of the massive outage that Xbox Live had experienced during the Christmas holiday. Xbox Live general manager Marc Whitten sent out a brief email to Xbox Live subscribers on January 4, apologizing for the downtime and thanking them for their loyalty. The service had experienced a record number of new subscribers over the Christmas holiday. In addition, on January 3, Xbox Live had the highest number of users ever to be concurrently online. In reward for these accomplishments (and not as compensation for the outage), Xbox Live would offer a free game download that would be named at a later time.

Microsoft announced on January 18 that the free downloadable would be *Undertow,* an underwater racing game from Chair Entertainment that had originally been released on November 21, 2007. Xbox Live subscribers would be able to download the $10 game for free between January 23 and January 27.

But even this free game didn't ensure Microsoft's customer satisfaction. During an interview with *8bitjoystick.com,* an anonymous Xbox 360 hardware designer claimed that failure rates on new Xbox 360 consoles were at around 10%. He also reported that Microsoft had been aware of the design flaws from the beginning, and had done nothing to correct them in its haste to get the Xbox 360 out to retailers before the PS3.

Although the Xbox 360 had outsold the PS3 in North America during every month of 2007, the first two months of 2008 showed a reverse trend, with the PS3 slightly outselling the Xbox 360. According to Microsoft, it had misjudged the demand and couldn't supply enough consoles until the end of February.

Through October, sales between the Xbox 360 and PS3 ran neck and neck. Then Microsoft released *Gears of War 2* on November 7 and all bets were off. The game sold more than two million copies during its first weekend. One million people played the game on Xbox Live, which set a new record for the number of players online simultaneously. Although the game had only been available for less than two months, it made the #7 spot on the top-ten best-selling games of the year, joining three other Xbox 360 titles. Only one PS3 title, *Grand Theft Auto IV,* appeared on the list, and it appeared three positions lower than its Xbox 360 counterpart.

The competition between the Xbox 360 and the PS3 was non-existent in Japan, the PS3's native country. One reason for this was that the Xbox 360 was an American console and the software developed for it reflected American tastes, which in many cases differed greatly from what Japanese gamers wanted.

On August 7, Namco-Bandai released *Tales of Vesperia* in Japan.[1] This was the tenth game in a very popular Japanese series called *Tales,* which had begun in 1995 with *Tales of Phantasia* for the Super Famicom. The response to the release of the new game was overwhelming, and 140,000 copies were sold during its first two weeks. Because Namco-Bandai only released the game for the Xbox 360, die-hard *Tales* fans who didn't own the Microsoft console went out and bought an Xbox 360, resulting in a shortage of the consoles in Japan throughout the rest of August. It was the first time that Microsoft had seen such sales in Japan. Unfortunately, once the demand for the game subsided, sales for the Xbox 360 in Japan reverted back to its pre-August numbers, with Microsoft reclaiming third place in the three-console race.

Price Wars

But Microsoft was making ground. On March 10, the company had lowered the price of the European Xbox 360 by €80 ($123). At €200 ($307), the Arcade model was the lowest-priced videogame console in Europe and its sales immediately doubled.

Xbox 360 prices were slashed in the rest of the world as well. In North America, Microsoft cut the price of its 20GB console from $350 to $300 on July 13. However, this price was only good while supplies of the 20GB model remained in stock. On August 1, Microsoft actually discontinued the 20GB model and replaced it with a 60GB edition that retailed for $350. But even that price turned out to be temporary, as Microsoft knocked off $50 from all of its configurations on September 5, bringing the price of the new 60GB model down to $300. Similar price reductions were put into effect on September 11 in Japan.

The result of these price decreases brought the price of the Xbox 360 Arcade, the model without a hard drive, down to $200 in North America and ¥19,800 ($186) in Japan, making it the lowest-priced next-gen console.

But Microsoft had the highest-priced console as well. SCEA had introduced its own price cuts in July, shortly after the one that Microsoft had issued on its 20GB console. SCEA discontinued its $400 40GB PS3 and then dropped the price of the 80GB model by $100 to $400, making it $50 *less* than the 120GB Xbox 360 Elite. But this 80GB PS3, like the 40GB console that it replaced, was stripped down. It only had two USB ports, no memory card functionality and no PS2 backward-compatibility through either hardware or emulation.

It became like a pricing see-saw. Microsoft introduced more price cuts on September 5. The Xbox 360 Elite was reduced to $400, the same as SCE's 80GB system. The 60GB Xbox 360 dropped $50 to $300. And the Xbox 360 Arcade fell $70 to $200.

On October 31, SCE introduced a 160GB PS3 console in Europe and North America, where it retailed for $500. Other than the hard drive that had twice as much capacity, the 160GB system was the same as the 80GB PS3 that had come out in July.

Microsoft didn't offer an Xbox 360 configuration to match the newest PS3 powerhouse. Instead, it released a $99 *Xbox Live Starter Pack*, which consisted of a 60GB hard drive, a wired headset, an Ethernet cable and a three-month subscription to Xbox Live. This was targeted towards Xbox 360 Arcade owners who wanted to upgrade to the Xbox 360 Core system without having to purchase a brand-new system.

The storage space that the hard drive provided was needed for a mandatory firmware upgrade that Microsoft issued on November 19. Prior updates resided in the system's internal memory, but this latest one required either a 256MB memory card or a hard drive. The update included the ability to install a game from a disc in the console's disc tray directly onto the hard drive to decrease the game's loading time. And when a game began, another new feature informed the player if any of his friends were playing the same game online. Xbox Live also provided information about the game that was in the disc tray.

The update also installed the *New Xbox Experience (NXE)*, which completely changed Xbox Live's dashboard. Navigation was made easier and players were represented by colorful avatars that were much more realistic than their Mii counterparts on the Wii. The avatars could be created in a new *Friends* channel that made it easy for people to find their online friends and activities. *Live Party* was a section of the Friends channel that let up to eight users share photos and chat by voice or text.

Microsoft New Xbox Experience

Avatars also became central features of the PlayStation Network on December 11, when SCE made available a virtual world called *PlayStation Home*. In the forms of their avatars, users could socialize and play games with up to 49 online friends. The service was free to all registered PlayStation Network users. SCE made money when users purchased virtual goods with real money and by selling advertising space within the online world.

SCE also released new accessories to enhance the online experience. On October 14, a *Wireless Bluetooth Headset* and charging cradle was packaged with *SOCOM: U.S. Navy SEALs Confrontation*. The headset, which hooked over either ear, was capable for high-quality voice chats,[2] and the TV screen displayed its volume and battery levels, along with charging and connection statuses. This was followed in December with the release of the $50 *PlayStation 3 Wireless Keypad*. The QWERTY-style keyboard was very similar to Microsoft's Chatpad and latched onto the PS3 controller.

Meanwhile, Nintendo only had one model of the Wii available and it still retailed at its $249 launch price. That amount wasn't expected to drop anytime soon, especially since there was still a shortage of the console in North America. And the shortage wasn't expected to change, although the reason for it was up for speculation. It was widely believed that Nintendo simply wasn't shipping enough consoles to North America, due to the economic conditions in the United States. The dollar had been better when Nintendo had first formulated the console's pricing. However, since then, the dollar had tanked and Nintendo wasn't earning as much per unit in the United States as it did elsewhere in the world. The fact that there was a Wii shortage only in North America seemed to enforce that assumption.

SCE PS3 Keyboard

SCE PS3 Wireless Bluetooth Headset

The down economy was also blamed for shortages that followed the North American release of *Wii Fit*. Nintendo of America had announced in February that it would launch *Wii Fit* bundled with the Wii Balance Board on May 19. It did come out on that date, but only in very limited numbers at the Nintendo Store in New York. The $90 package sold out in less than five hours.

Exercise Software

Wii Fit was released elsewhere in North America two days later on May 21, but again in short supply. Nintendo only shipped 500,000 *Wii Fit* packages to North America, whereas four million had been sent to Europe. But some European countries, such as Great Britain, also experienced shortages.

Another reason for these shortages was that Nintendo hadn't fully foreseen the demand for the Wii Balance Board. No peripheral had ever been in such demand before, and Nintendo wasn't prepared for it. Perhaps it should have been, because the Wii Balance Board was an innovative device that received much good press. *Time* magazine named it one of the ten top gadgets of the year. By the end of the year, Nintendo of America managed to sell over 4½ million *Wii Fit* bundles, making it the #3 game of the year.

Applications for health-conscious individuals weren't limited to the Wii and its Balance Board. On June 20, Ubisoft released *My Weight Loss Coach* in Europe (and in North America four days later) for the DS. This $40 program was for people who were struggling to reduce their weight. The program presented a regimen for people to follow to get to a target weight. One of those regimens was walking, and the game came with a pedometer that the person used to measure his footsteps. The pedometer plugged into the GBA slot of the DS. Unfortunately, the one problem with the program was that the DS had no way to measure a person's actual weight, like the Wii could through the Wii Balance Board. So while the pedometer could measure the steps that a person walked, the person's actual weight had to be entered manually, which unfortunately couldn't correspond with "accurately."

Ubisoft My Weight Loss Coach Pedometer

My Weight Loss Coach was not sold in Japan, but Japanese DS owners were offered their own weight-loss game on November 1, when Nintendo of Japan released *Aruite Wakaru Seikatsu Rhythm DS.* This ¥5,800 ($59) package came with two pedometers, which Nintendo called "Activity Meters." Each game could monitor up to four people, but each Activity Meter was limited to only one person, so additional Meters had to be purchased if more than two people wanted to use the program. Unlike the pedometer from *My Weight Loss Coach,* which had to be clipped to a belt or pocket and frequently fell off, the Activity Meter could be safely stored in a person's pocket while he walked. Afterwards, data from the Activity Meter was sent to the DS via an infrared signal.

Nintendo Aruite Wakaru Seikatsu Rhythm DS Pedometer

A different type of exercise game came to the Wii when Namco-Bandai released *Family Trainer: Athletic World* in Japan on May 29.[3] Like *Wii Fit, Family Trainer: Athletic World* consisted of a series of minigames that were designed to get gamers exercising without even realizing it.

The game was named after the *Family Trainer* bundle that Bandai had released for the Famicom in 1986. That bundle had included a game called *Athletic World* and a Family Trainer mat, which Nintendo purchased and released for the NES as the Power Pad. For the Wii version, Namco-

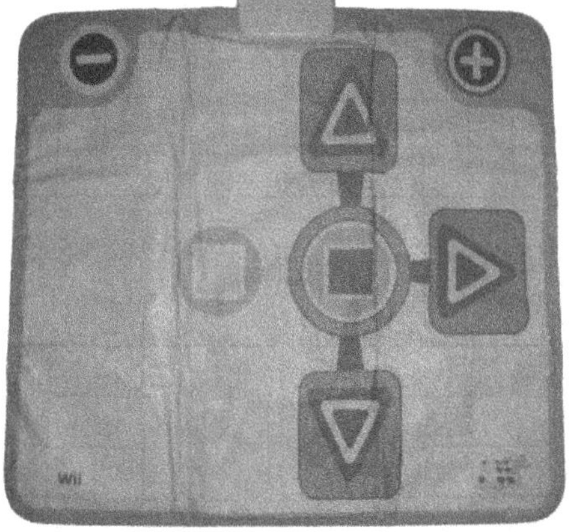

Namco-Bandai Family Trainer Mat

2008

Bandai used a similar two-sided mat that was used in conjunction with the Wii Remote.

Peripherals

Additional games bundled with peripherals were released by Nintendo. *Mario Kart Wii* launched in North America on April 27, approximately two weeks after it came out in Japan and Europe. The game was packaged with the *Wii Wheel* accessory, a plastic steering-wheel. After a Wii Remote was placed in the Wii Wheel, the peripheral could be used to "steer" one of the on-screen cars.

Nintendo Wii Wheel

Nintendo
Super Famicom Classic Controller

Nintendo Wii Speak

Although *Mario Kart Wii* was the sixth game in the *Mario Kart* series, which had begun with the release of *Super Mario Kart* for the Super Famicom in 1992, it was by far the most successful. At year's end, it was the #2 top-selling game of 2008[4] with five million units sold in North America.

Meanwhile more and more Super Famicom games were becoming available for play on the Wii through the Virtual Console.[5] Since the Wii Remote could not be used for Super Famicom games, people who wanted to play those titles had to use the Wii Classic Controller. In April, Nintendo of Japan issued a special version of the Wii Classic Controller, but only to platinum members of the Japanese Club Nintendo.[6] The *Wii Super Famicom Classic Controller* was an exact reproduction of the original Super Famicom controller with the one exception: it plugged into the Wii Remote, rather than the console itself.

Nintendo released a third game-and-peripheral bundle in November in North America and Japan. The *Wii Speak* was a microphone that plugged into the console via the USB port and was designed to sit near the television, along with the sensor bar. The purpose of the Wii Speak microphone was to enhance online play by allowing more than one person in a given room to speak into the microphone at a time. But the Wii Speak was more than a simple microphone. Since it had to be positioned near the television's speaker, it was designed to only pick up the voices in the room and not the gaming sounds coming from the TV.

The Wii Speak was bundled with *Animal Crossing: City Folk*, which was released in the United States, Canada and Japan beginning on November 16. The bundle was released in Europe on December 5, the same day that Nintendo launched a new Wii Speak Channel. This channel was only available to people who owned a Wii Speak microphone, and had to be unlocked before it could be downloaded to the console from the Wii Shop Channel. The 16-digit codes required to unlock it were only included with the Wii Speak. Once the Wii Speak Channel was set up, users could join one of four rooms and be able to chat with other people, who were represented by

Mii characters.

The Wii Speak Channel wasn't the only new feature that users could download from the Wii Shop Channel. On March 25, Nintendo of Japan introduced *WiiWare*.[7] This was a sister service to the Virtual Console, which allowed the development and download of brand-new games, instead of previously released ones. WiiWare was meant to compete with Microsoft's Xbox Live Arcade and SCE's PlayStation Store, which both featured the development of inexpensive, independent games. A WiiWare development kit only cost $2,000, and the one requirement that Nintendo placed on developers was that their games had to be licensed by Nintendo.

Nintendo of Japan launched *WiiWare* with nine titles. The least expensive game, *Okiraku Ping Pong*, cost 500 Wii Points or ¥500 ($5), while the most expensive, *Final Fantasy Crystal Chronicles: My Life as a King*, was only 1,500 Wii Points, or ¥1,500 ($15).

Nintendo Wi-Fi Network Adapter

A wireless connection was an integral component to connecting the Wii with the Internet. Nintendo had previously released two units to aid people who only had wired connections for Wii use. One was the Wii LAN Adapter that plugged into the Wii's USB port and connected it to an Ethernet line. The other was the Nintendo Wi-Fi USB Connector, which sent wireless signals from a personal computer to the Wii. On November 15, 2007, Nintendo had announced that the Nintendo Wi-Fi USB Connector was its best-selling accessory, and then suddenly removed it from sale shortly afterwards without any explanation.[8] Nintendo of Japan released its replacement on September 18. The *Nintendo Wi-Fi Network Adapter* was a stand-alone box that basically could be used as a wireless LAN router for the Wii, DS and any other devices that required a wireless connection. It was only available for sale in Japan, where it retailed for ¥5,800 ($55).

Nintendo Wi-Fi Pay & Play logo

Nintendo introduced a new feature to its Nintendo Wi-Fi Connection, which it called *Pay & Play*. As its name implied, Pay & Play was a service that users paid to receive additional downloadable content to games that they already owned. Pay & Play initiated in Japan on April 1, and the WiiWare title *Final Fantasy Crystal Chronicles: My Life as a King* was the first game to incorporate it, allowing users to purchase a range of additional content including new costumes and new quests.[9] The first physical game that allowed Pay & Play content was Sega's *Samba de Amigo* for the Wii, which was released in North America on September 23. Physical Pay & Play games could be distinguished by a red Nintendo

Wi-Fi Connection logo that was displayed on the front of the packaging.

Receiving TV Broadcasts

On April 9, Wii owners in Great Britain were given the ability to stream content from the BBC using a service called *iPlayer*. The service could be found under the Wii's Internet Channel and allowed users free access to most of the BBC's playlists from the prior seven days. Once someone started viewing something, he had seven days to complete it before the content became inaccessible. British PS3 owners were given access to the service on December 2. Soon afterwards, 6% of all iPlayer traffic went through the PS3.[10] Microsoft and the BBC negotiated to have the iPlayer available through Xbox Live, but Microsoft only wanted to provide it to Xbox Live Gold subscribers, due to the company's policy of not providing any free content to standard Xbox Live users. However, the BBC required that the service should be completely free and available to everyone. Thus, the service wasn't available on the Xbox 360.[11]

Every Xbox Live subscriber around the world did have access to downloadable movies and TV programs through the Video Marketplace. However, the content that could be downloaded from it wasn't free, and Xbox Live members paid for it with Microsoft Points. On July 15, SCE launched a similar service in the United States that provided movie and TV shows through the PlayStation Network.

On November 19, Netflix was added to Xbox Live as part of the New Xbox Experience upgrade. The service was only available to Xbox Live Gold subscribers, and only those who also had a Netflix Unlimited subscription could use it.

The Netflix service provided through Xbox Live differed in one respect from Netflix Unlimited accounts available elsewhere. Movies from Columbia Pictures, which was a subsidiary of Sony, were not available through the Xbox Live Netflix service. And if anyone wanted to use his Xbox 360 console to watch a Columbia Pictures movie in high definition, he was out of luck as well, since high-def movies from Columbia Pictures were only available on Sony's Blu-ray format.

However, beginning in May, all home high-definition movies would only be available on Blu-ray. Warner Bros., the only major studio that still produced home videos in the HD-DVD format, had announced on January 4 that it would begin releasing its high-def home videos only on Blu-ray. Best Buy, Circuit City and Walmart immediately announced that they would discontinue selling HD-DVD discs, while Netflix and Blockbuster announced that they would cease renting them. Toshiba followed with a February 19 announcement that it would cease manufacturing HD-DVD players. A few days later, on February 23, Microsoft had no alternative but to discontinue production of its external HD-DVD drive for the Xbox 360. It then reduced the price of all the remaining $200 HD-DVD players to $50.

PlayTV

As Microsoft quit selling a device that permitted high-definition movies to be played through the Xbox 360, SCEE introduced one that would allow over-the-air broadcast television to be played through the PS3. The *PlayTV* was a dual-television tuner that connected the PS3 to an external television antenna. Once connected, the PlayTV and its accompanying software allowed television broadcasts to stream into the PS3 console, on which it could simply play back the broadcast on the TV screen. However, the PlayTV also turned the PS3 into a DVR (Digital Video Recorder), so TV programs could be saved on the console's hard drive and viewed at later times. Programs

SCE PlayTV

could also be scheduled in advance to record at certain hours and dates. In addition, live viewing could be paused, rewound and resumed at will.

PlayTV could only be used in countries that employed the European DVB-T standard of digital broadcasting. The unit was first released in Great Britain on September 19, where it sold for £70 ($128). This was followed by a staggered release schedule in the rest of Europe throughout the remainder of the year.

Although PlayTV was limited to regions that used the DVB-T standard, the *Remote Play* feature of the PS3 allowed it to be accessed from anywhere in the world. When Remote Play was activated, a person could use his PSP with a wireless Internet connection to sync with his PS3 to watch live or recorded video and schedule recordings.

Talkman

If the person from Great Britain used his PSP to watch his British TV shows in a few foreign countries, such as France or Italy, he might also have used it to converse with the citizens of the country he was visiting, with the help of the PSP language translator software, *Talkman*. *Talkman* had been available in Europe, China and Japan since 2005. On August 7, it finally came to the United States.

The *Talkman* that was released in the United States was different from the versions that had previously come out elsewhere in the world. *Talkman Travel*, as it was called, was only available as a download from the online PlayStation Store. It was offered in three "flavors," each spotlighting a different city, Tokyo, Paris and Rome, and each selling for $6.

SCEA promoted *Talkman Travel* as an "interactive pocket tour guide" and included photos, maps and lists of places to sight-see, eat at or shop at when visiting one of the three supported foreign cities. But it also included commonly used phrases. The user could search through the software's database for a particular English phrase and the PSP would say it back in the language of the selected city with the correct pronunciation.

Unlike its predecessors, *Talkman Travel* didn't require a microphone. All of the phrases were programmed into the software. Whereas the original versions of *Talkman* allowed users to say a particular phrase into the microphone and have the software do its best to translate it, *Talkman Travel* required users to sift through a list of English phrases and select the one that they wanted translated.

Although *Talkman Travel* didn't require a microphone, a new PSP application that was issued in January did.

Skype

SCE announced at CES in early January that it would be issuing new PSP firmware later in the month that would include the popular *Skype* program, which would allow users to make video phone calls over the Internet using their PSPs. Phone calls to any other Skype account would be free and phone calls made from a PSP to a mobile or landline phone would be charged at a low rate. The firmware was planned to be issued in Japan on January 24 and in Europe and North America a week later.

Due to memory constraints on the original PSP, the Skype feature could only work on the newer, slim PSP-2000, which coincidentally was the only model supported by the *Talkman* microphone. SCEJ had planned to sell these *Talkman* microphones separately, but on the day before the Japanese launch, SCEJ announced that it had to postpone the firmware update because its *Talkman* microphones didn't meet Skype's specifications. This didn't stop SCE from issuing the firmware update in Europe and North America on schedule, and people in those countries were able to use their existing microphones if they had one. The *Talkman* microphone had never been released in North America. A headset that included speakers and a microphone was available, but it needed a separate

SCE PSP Headset with Remote Control

Nokia N-Gage Service

remote control unit in order for the microphone to function. Oddly, the remote-control was not available for sale by itself, but it was packaged with a set of ear buds, which didn't include a microphone.[12] So for people to use Skype on their PSPs, they had to purchase both the headsets and the ear buds. But there was one esthetic problem with this setup. The headset was black, while the remote control was white.

SCEA finally alleviated this problem on May 8 with the release of a $30 package that contained the headset and a black remote control. Prominent on the package was a logo that stated "Skype certified."

The firmware upgrade that included Skype was finally issued in Japan on March 18. SCEJ scrapped its plans to issue the *Talkman* microphones separately and eventually released the "Skype certified" headset on June 18 for ¥3,800 ($35).

Phones and Fun

With Skype installed, the PSP became the second handheld videogame console that could also be used as a phone. The first had been the ill-fated Nokia N-Gage. After the N-Gage failed, Nokia harnessed the N-Gage technology into software that could be downloaded to its various cell phones. Beginning February 4, Nokia piloted the N-Gage service to owners of its N81 phone.[13] After these people downloaded and installed the N-Gage application onto their phones, they could then download demos of several games, including *Hooked On: Creatures of the Deep* and *System Rush: Evolution*. And if they liked the games that they demoed, they could purchase them.

The pilot program ended on March 27. All demos that had been downloaded remained playable until the official launch of the service on April 7. At that time, Nokia expanded the service to its N95 phones and offered six games that could be downloaded, demoed and purchased for $9-$16 each. By the end of the year, 28 games were available.

Nokia's goal was to make the cell phone a viable gaming platform. If it succeeded, the company would be in a good position to be the dominant player. Nokia had sold nearly 440 million cell phones (40% of the entire cell-phone market), more than the combined number of Wii, Xbox 360 and PS3 consoles that had been sold.

But gamers didn't take mobile games seriously. The quality of cell-phone games was nowhere near that of the games on handheld consoles. In addition, the cell phones weren't designed to make gaming handy. Buttons that were designed to do other things were usually used as controls.

Apple had similar plans as Nokia, and wanted to make its iPhone the *de facto* device for mobile gaming. Unlike traditional cell phones, the iPhone didn't have standard buttons that had to be jerry-rigged as controllers. But it did have a highly responsive touchscreen, which meant that virtual controls could be designed anywhere on the screen.

Downloadable Content

On July 10, Apple launched an online *App Store*, from where apps (applications) could be downloaded to the iPhone. Within three days, more than ten million downloads were purchased, an astonishing number since only approximately six million iPhones were in circulation at that point. Of the 800 available apps, approximately 160 were games. By the end of the year, the number of available games had risen to 1,800. Anyone with the know-how could write an app and sell it through the App Store, as long as Apple approved it and was paid a small licensing fee. The owner of the app could then set its price and this was usually very nominal, or even free if it contained advertisements. The quality of the games varied from poor to excellent.

AM3 DSVision

The ability to download content on the fly was a major attraction and something that neither the PSP nor the DS was capable of doing. However, AM3, the company that had produced the Advance Movie Adapter for the GBA in 2003, introduced *DSvision*, a Japanese service that let people download movies, books and Manga and play them back on their DS. The content actually had to be downloaded to a PC and then transferred to the DS. This was done using a ¥3,980 ($37) kit that was released on June 26. This kit consisted of a USB flash drive, a DS card and a 512MB micro SD card that inserted into the flash drive and the DS card. The flash drive and its installed micro SD card was plugged into the USB slot of a PC, and content was downloaded from a DSvision website and saved to it. The micro SD card was then removed from the flash drive and inserted into the DS card. Once the DS card was plugged into the DS, the content on the micro SD card could be viewed. The site from where the content was downloaded wasn't available until a week after the kit was released, but AM3 promised that at least 300 titles would be available from the DSvision website when the service launched. However, only 31 titles were on hand when the service actually did go live in August. Over the next few weeks, additional content was added, and in August, *Pokémon* movies were added.

With DSvision, users could download content to their computers and then transfer it to their DS consoles. The same technique was required to download PSP content from the PlayStation Store. It first had to be downloaded to a PS3, from where it was then transferred to the PSP either wirelessly or by copying it to a memory stick. Beginning on October 15, with the release of a firmware upgrade,[14] applications could be downloaded directly to the PSP from the PlayStation Store.

New Handhelds

The new firmware was included in the *PSP-3000*, a new PSP model that SCE launched a day earlier,[15] just a little over a year after the prior model, the PSP-2000, had been issued.

Dimension-wise, the PSP-3000 was exactly the same size and weight as its predecessor. What was different was a built-in microphone, which would have been handy when *Talkman* had launched in North America earlier in the year. The PSP-3000 also featured a brighter screen with improved color reproduction, which cut down the sun's glare when used outside. It also added a half-pixel response time that decreased motion blur.

On November 1, approximately two weeks after SCE released the PSP-3000, Nintendo of Japan did likewise with the DS. The ¥18,900 ($192) *DSi* looked very much like the DS

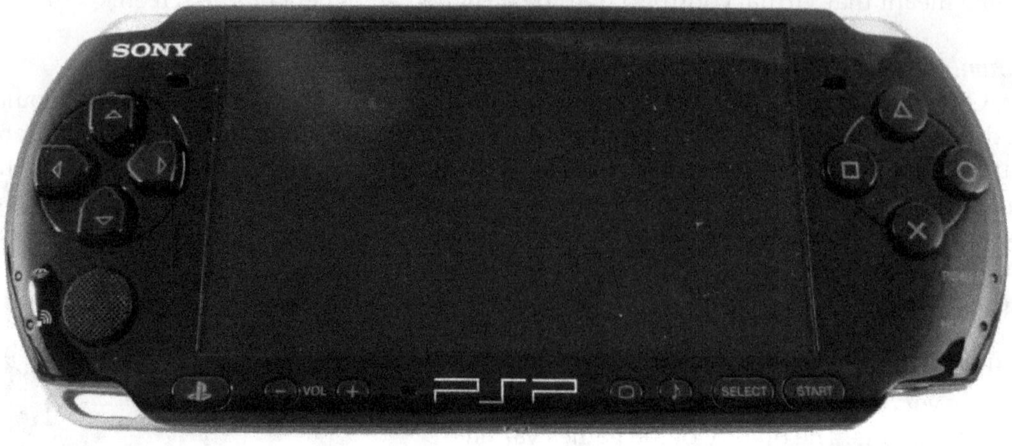

SCE PSP-3000

Nintendo DSi

Lite and was compatible with most DS games. However, it was not compatible with GBA games, since it lacked a GBA slot. In addition, any DS game that required the GBA slot for a peripheral, such as *Slide: Adventure Mag Kid*, could not be played on the DSi.

Although the DSi was just slightly larger than the DS Lite, it weighed .2 oz less. The two 3.25-inch screens on the DSi were 17% larger than the ones on the DS Lite. But under the hood, the DSi was much more powerful, with a processor that ran at 133 Mhz, nearly twice the speed of the one in the DS Lite. And the DSi included 16MB of internal memory, four times that of the DS Lite's.

The DSi also had 256MB of flash memory that was used for storage. Nintendo, like SCE, had been influenced by Apple's App Store and set up the online *DSi Shop* from where *DSiWare*, games and other programs, could be downloaded. The programs were then stored in the DSi's flash memory. And if 256MB wasn't enough room to store the downloaded games, the DSi featured an SD card slot. High-capacity SD (SDHC) cards could store up to an additional 32GB of data.

One program that could be downloaded from the DSi Shop was the *Nintendo DSi Browser*. Unlike the browser for the DS and DS Lite, which had to be purchased, the browser for the DSi was free.

One noticeable feature that set the DSi apart from the DS Lite was its pair of VGA cameras, one between the two screens that pointed towards the user, and the other on the outside of the console that faced away from the user. Unfortunately, there wasn't any practical use for the photos that were taken by these cameras. The only way they could be copied from the DSi was by first saving them to an SD card. But while the photos were stored in the device, they could be used for amusement, such as doodling on or altering the images.

Like SCE and Nintendo, LeapFrog released a handheld console to succeed its current model. The $70 *Leapster 2*, which was designed for children aged 4-8, was launched in early July. It was slightly smaller than its predecessor, the 2005 Leapster, which made it easier for young children to hold. Besides having all of the features of the Leapster,[16] it also had the ability to play games downloaded from the Internet. LeapFrog set up a website called *Leapster Connect* that was accessible via a home computer. New games could be downloaded to the computer and then transferred to the Leapster 2 via a USB cable. The downloaded games were part of the *LeapFrog Learning Path* program, which allowed parents to log onto their own computers and monitor their children's progress in learning about various subjects and concepts. Unfortunately, the LeapFrog Learning Path wasn't yet available when the Leapster 2 was released, and parents had to wait several months before it became operational. Once games were available to download, they could only be saved on an SD card that was available optionally.[17]

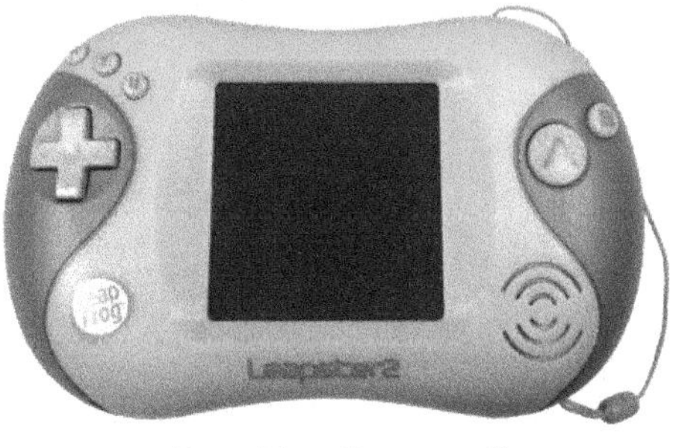

LeapFrog Leapster 2

On August 22, shortly after the Leapster 2 was released, LeapFrog also introduced a new handheld console that was geared towards 6-10 year-olds. The $90 *Didj* was not compatible with the Leapster products, so games that ran on the Leapster would not run on it. Nine games were released with the system, including an educational version of *Sonic the Hedgehog* that taught spelling. Like the Leapster 2, the Didj also had a USB connection to a home computer, which parents could use to customize game content and maximize their children's learning in particular areas through the LeapFrog Connect application.

LeapFrog Didj

VTech released a new handheld console that also connected to the Internet via a PC. The $70 *V.Smile Cyber Pocket* was the latest incarnation in the V.Smile Pocket series and featured the writing pad that had been introduced on the new V.Smile consoles that had been released in 2007. This writing pad,

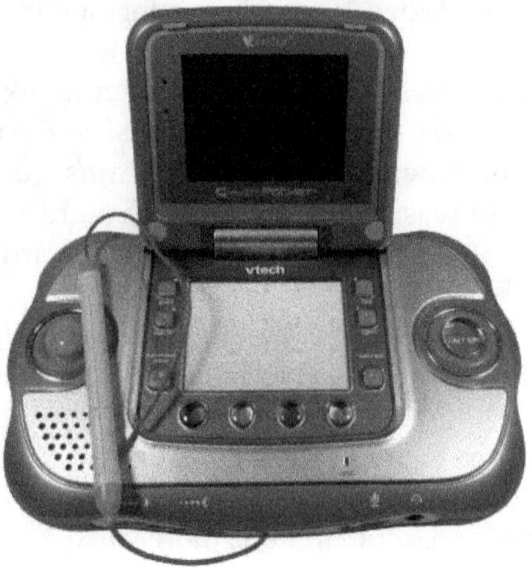

VTech V.Smile Cyber Pocket

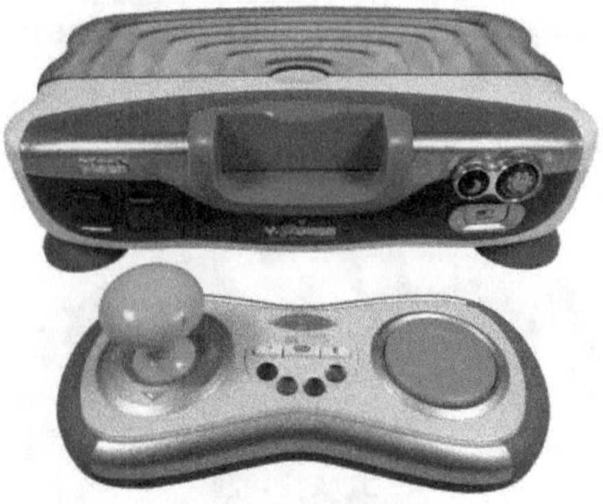

VTech V-Motion

VTech V.Link

with its attached stylus, was located in the center of the console, where the screen had appeared on the earlier V.Smile Pockets. The screen was above it on a hinged flap that closed and covered the writing pad.

In addition to the writing pad, the V.Smile Cyber Pocket included all of the features that were already incorporated on the V.Smile Pocket. The included the reversible joystick and "Enter" button, microphone, jewel-like color buttons and ability to hook up to a television. The V.Smile Cyber Pocket was compatible with software for all other V.Smile consoles.[18]

One of those consoles that the V.Smile Cyber Pocket was compatible with was the *V-Motion*, a new educational console that was VTech's answer to the Wii. The $70 V-Motion used a wireless controller that responded to body movements. However, while the Wii actually got players to work out in some games, all that was required of V-Motion games was to tilt the controller in a certain way. As with other V.Smile products, all Smartridges from prior consoles would play on the V-Motion, although they required a wired controller. V-Motion games could also play on the other V.Smile consoles, but in those cases, the motion feature was disabled.

The V.Smile Cyber Pocket and the V-Motion both connected to *V.Link*, which was VTech's version of LeapFrog's LeapFrog Connect. This was a system that parents could use to track their children's progress. A special flash drive was bundled with each of the consoles and plugged into them via a USB port. Once high scores were saved on the flash drive, it was unplugged from the console and inserted into a PC. The PC was then used to connect to the Internet where the high scores were uploaded from the flash drive to a VTech website. If the scores were high enough, kids could earn gold coins that unlocked online bonus games.

AtGames Galore

The V-Motion wasn't the only new console that used Wii-like wireless controllers. AtGames, the company that had licensed Sega's catalog of Master System and Genesis/Mega Drive games, released two consoles that also seemed to have borrowed from Nintendo's technology. The *Arcade Motion* was a blue console that was in the shape of Sonic the Hedgehog's head. The unit was packaged with a pair of wireless, elongated controllers that somewhat resembled the shape of the Wii Remote. The Arcade Motion had seven built-in sports games including tennis and boxing, which required players to use their bodies along with the controllers. The console also had 15 built-in Genesis/Mega Drive games and 25 generic arcade games that didn't employ motion sensing and used the wireless controllers as standard controllers. Additional games could be added by downloading them onto an SD card, which could then be inserted into the console.

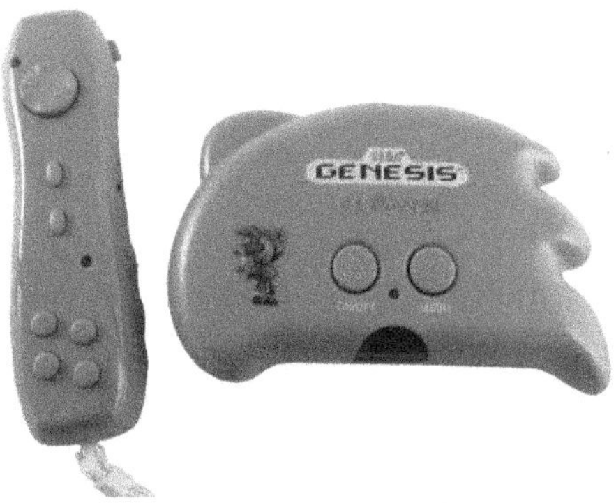

AtGames Arcade Motion

AtGames' *Arcade Motion Classic* was similar to the Arcade Classic and also contained 40 built-in games, including 20 Sega games. This unit used the same motion controllers as the Arcade Motion, although they were white, instead of blue. The unit was also bundled with plastic sports accessories, including a baseball bat, golf club, tennis racket and ping-pong paddles, which attached to the end of the controller. Although they didn't add any additional functionality to the controllers, they were designed to make the player feel more like he was actually playing the actual sport.

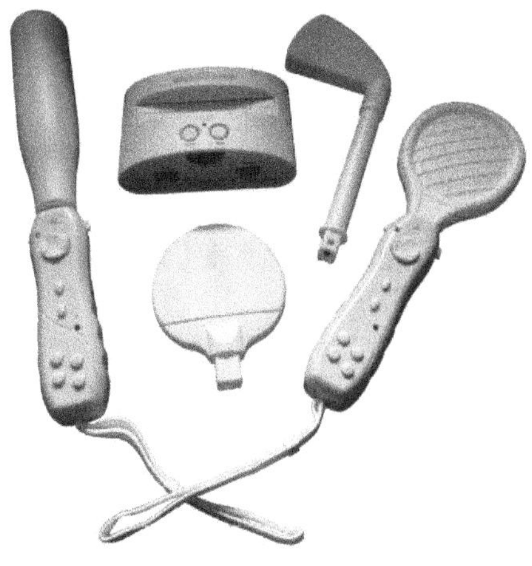

AtGames Arcade Motion Classic

The Arcade Motion Classic console differed from the Arcade Motion, as it resembled a small, white Genesis/Mega Drive console, complete with a cartridge slot. The unit accepted actual Genesis or Mega Drive cartridges, depending upon the country that it was purchased in. However, it didn't have a slot that could accept SD cards. This wasn't a major handicap because AtGames sold the *Firecore Passport*, which was basically a cartridge that had its own SD card slot. When the Firecore Passport cartridge with an inserted SD card was plugged into the console, the games on the SD card could be accessed and played through the Arcade Motion Classic.

AtGames also introduced several motionless consoles that the Firecore Passport could be used with. The *Arcade Classic* was basically the same console as the Arcade Motion Classic; however it was black like the original Genesis/

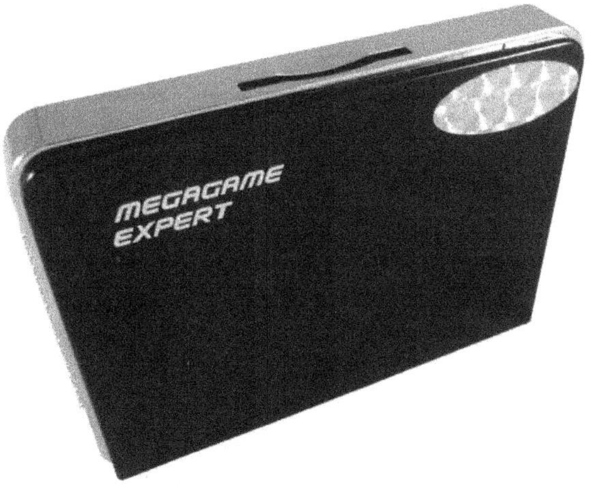

Firecore AtGames Passport

AtGames Arcade Classic

Mega Drive. AtGames actually released two versions of the Arcade Classic and both were packaged with controllers that looked like the original Genesis/Mega Drive controllers. One version came with two wired controllers that plugged into the controller ports in the front of the console. The other accepted the wired controllers, but it was packaged with non-motion-detecting wireless controllers. The Arcade Classic had 20 built-in Genesis/Mega Drive games, but only eight of them, including *Columns* and *Sonic Spinball*, overlapped the 15 Sega games that were built into the Arcade Motion and Arcade Motion Classic systems.

Many of the games that had been included on the fore-mentioned AtGames consoles also found their ways to the *Arcade Master*, a table-top plug-and-play system that had a large built-in joystick and six controller buttons. This unit featured 26 built-in Genesis/Mega Drive games, and additional games could be added via an SD card that could be inserted directly into the unit.

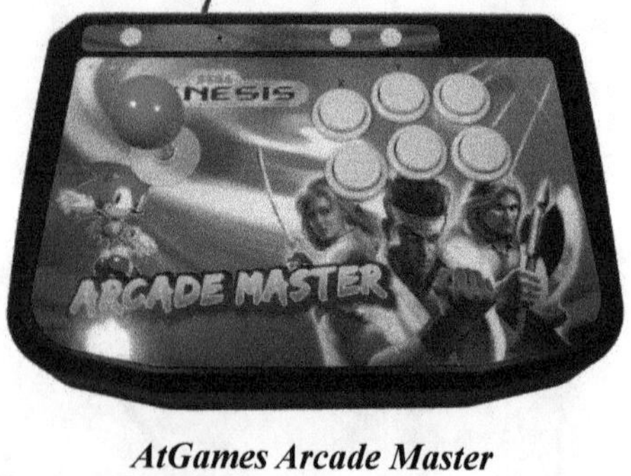

AtGames Arcade Master

Finally, AtGames released a pair of handheld consoles. The *Arcade Gamer Portable* featured a D-Pad, two control buttons and 30 built-in 8-bit Sega Master System and Game Gear games. The *Arcade Portable* looked very much like the Arcade Gamer Portable, but it featured *three* controller buttons and included 20 built-in 16-bit Genesis/Mega Drive games.[19] Neither system featured an SD card slot, so they were limited to the built-in titles.

AtGames Arcade Gamer Portable

AtGames Arcade Portable

Music Games en Masse

In addition to the educational videogame consoles that VTech and LeapFrog marketed, both companies also manufactured electronic toys including guitars and drum sets. These allowed toddlers to mimic what their older brethren were doing on the gaming consoles, as interest in rhythm games such as *Guitar Hero* and *Rock Band* continued.

Guitar Hero went portable on June 22 when Activision released *Guitar Hero: On Tour* for the DS and DS Lite. Instead of a guitar controller, *Guitar Hero: On Tour* was packaged with a *Guitar Grip* that plugged into the DS's GBA cartridge port.[20] This Guitar Grip had four color-coded fret buttons that coincided with the descending colored notes on the screen.[21]

The DS had to be held vertically like a book with the upper screen on the left. This screen displayed the descending notes. The touchscreen on the right displayed a guitar, and the player had to strum the instrument's strings using a special stylus that looked like a guitar pick.

Activision released a second *Guitar Hero* game for the DS on November 16. *Guitar Hero: On Tour Decades* was basically the same as *Guitar Hero: On Tour*, but it displayed different graphics and songs. Each of the handheld versions of the game included less than 30 songs, a far cry from the approximate 70 titles that came with their console

Activision Guitar Hero Guitar Grip

Guitar Hero - On Tour

counterparts. But *Guitar Hero: On Tour Decades* introduced a "*Share the Music*" feature during two-player competition. When one competitor used the original *Guitar Hero: On Tour* and the other used *Guitar Hero: On Tour Decades,* songs from both games could be used during the competition.

Beginning on June 27, Activision released *Guitar Hero: Aerosmith.* The game did not introduce any new features and played virtually the same as *Guitar Hero III: Legends of Rock.* However, it featured the members and songs of the rock group Aerosmith and included a few locked video interviews. *Guitar Hero: Aerosmith* only included 31 songs, and additional songs could not be purchased and downloaded. Because the game was essentially the same as *Guitar Hero III: Legends of Rock,* which came with 73 songs and cost approximately the same amount, *Guitar Hero: Aerosmith* primarily attracted only Aerosmith fans.

Guitar Hero: Aerosmith marked the first time that a rhythm game focused on a single group, but it wouldn't be the last. On November 2, MTV released the second of its *Track Packs,*[22] an expansion set that contained new songs that weren't previously available for *Rock Band.*[23] *AC/DC Live: Rock Band Track Pack* featured all 18 songs from an August 17, 1991 AC/DC concert that had been available only on video since 1992.[24]

The race was on between MTV and Activision to sign lucrative, exclusive contracts with famous bands for their respective music games. MTV and Harmonix, the company that had developed *Rock Band,* scored a major triumph on October 30 when they announced that they had signed a contract with Apple Corps, Ltd. to produce a videogame based on The Beatles' music. Alex Rigopoulos, the co-founder of Harmonix, said that the game wouldn't simply be another *Rock Band* that showcased The Beatles' music. He said that the game, which would come out in 2009, would be a "full, new music game built from the ground up."

Meanwhile, MTV did release another *Rock Band. Rock Band 2* came out for the Xbox 360 on September 14, with versions for the three other main consoles arriving over the following three months. The game was similar to its predecessor, with a few new features thrown in. The instrument controllers were slightly improved, but all controllers from either set were interchangeable. *Rock Band 2* featured 84 new songs and one of them, *Shackler's Revenge,* was the first brand-new Guns N' Roses single released in over ten years. In addition to the songs included on the game disc, an additional 20 songs were available as a free download.[25] Although songs that people had downloaded to the original *Rock Band* were immediately available in *Rock Band 2,* the songs that came with the original game weren't. Players could export 55 of the *Rock Band* titles to *Rock Band 2* for a small fee.

To complete the effect of being a live band on stage, Performance Designed Products (PDP) released a $100 *Rock Band Stage Kit* on November 11.[26] This two-piece kit provided smoke effects, a strobe light and a high-powered multi-colored LED light effect to

Rock Band Stage Kit

Guitar Hero World Tour Drums

performances.

This wasn't just a smoke generator that sensed the sounds around it, PDP) had worked with Harmonix to include cues into its music tracks that would program the Rock Band Stage Kit to respond to the cues in perfect time with the music and control the lighting to actually be in sync with the lights displayed on the screen.

On October 26, before the Wii and PS2 editions of *Rock Band 2* were released, owners of those consoles were able to purchase a different band videogame. On that date, Activision released *Guitar Hero: World Tour* in North America for all four major consoles. This game followed the same format as the prior *Guitar Hero* games and added *Rock Band*-style drums and vocals. The instrument controllers that were packed with the PS3 and Xbox 360 versions of the game were even compatible with *Rock Band*.

There was a new feature in *Guitar Hero: World Tour* that had not appeared in either version of *Rock Band*. "Music Studio" allowed players to create their own original songs that could contain up to five tracks (bass, drums, rhythm guitar, lead guitar and keyboard) and could play for up to three minutes. Completed songs could then be uploaded to the *GH Tunes* service,[27] where other players could download and rate them. There were some restrictions. The songs couldn't include vocals, and any songs that violated existing copyrights would be removed from GH Tunes.

Although many critics found the instrument controllers that came with *Guitar Hero: World Tour* to be superior to the ones that came with *Rock Band 2*, the general consensus was that *Rock Band 2* was a better game. Still, between *Rock Band 2*'s staggered release over a three-month period and the fact that the *Guitar Hero* name was better recognized, *Guitar Hero: World Tour* outsold *Rock Band 2* by more than double. By year's end, 3.4 million copies of *Guitar Hero: World Tour* had been sold in North America, compared to the 1.4 million copies of *Rock Band 2*. Although most critics preferred *Rock Band 2* over *Guitar Hero: World Tour*, the disparities between the two were minimal and both games were recommended.

Meanwhile on July 10, the company that had invented the rhythm genre of games in 1997, Konami, filed a lawsuit against Harmonix, claiming that *Rock Band* had violated its patents in relation to "simulated musical instruments, a music-game system and a 'musical-rhythm matching game'." Konami sought financial restitution and an order preventing *Rock Band* from being sold with the music instrument controllers that were in contention.[28]

Konami had paired its *GuitarFreaks* with its *DrumMania* in Japanese arcades to create the first band game. Now Konami was going directly against the *Guitar Hero* and *Rock Band* franchises in North America. On October 15 the company released *Rock Revolution* for the PS3 and Xbox 360.[29]

Unfortunately, the innovation that Konami had used for its earlier games was completely absent from *Rock Revolution*, which was basically a poor imitation of *Rock Band*. Even the critics agreed that its quality didn't come anywhere near either of its competitors. IGN succinctly reported that "there is no reason for *Rock Revolution* to exist." Consumers apparently agreed. During October, Activision had sold 534,000 copies of *Guitar Hero: World Tour* in only six days. Konami took 18 days to sell less than 3,000 copies of *Rock Revolution*.

Konami Rock Revolution Drums

The game was criticized in all areas. It only featured 41 tracks, much less than its competitors, and most of those songs were cover versions. *Rock Band 2* and *Guitar Hero: World Tour* had used tracks by the original artists.

A bundled package of *Rock Revolution* only included a drum set, which real-life drummers found difficult to work with. *Games*™ magazine called it the "worst music controller ever conceived" with "no intuitive way to use them effectively," since the six pads were small and bunched together. The guitar controllers weren't treated so harshly, since there weren't any. Players were expected to use guitars from competing games. And the game didn't come with a microphone, either, but one wasn't needed, since Konami didn't include vocals in the mix.[30] Apparently, Konami didn't want the game to compete with its own *Karaoke Revolution* series.

Despite Konami's resistance to compete with itself in the karaoke market, it did face competition. In its defense, *Karaoke Revolution* was the only karaoke game that was published by a third-party company, and it was the only one available for all of the major consoles; SCE's *SingStar* series was only available for PlayStations. But just as the band-oriented games began coming out with special editions that focused on specific bands, SCE followed suit with *SingStar ABBA*, which was released between mid-November and early December in Europe, Australia and North America.

Microsoft jumped into the karaoke market on November 18 when it released *Lips* in North America. The game was packaged with two wireless microphones, which set it apart from the other karaoke games on the market. These microphones also had built-in motion sensors that caused lights on the microphones to flash on and off with the music. *Lips* came with its own song library, and additional songs could easily be added by connecting a device that stored them, such as an iPod, to the Xbox 360 via the USB port.

Karaoke became available on the Wii on December 18 when Hudson Soft released *Karaoke Joysound Wii* in Japan. This package came with a USB microphone and 70 songs. New songs could be downloaded for additional fees from *Joysound*, a Japanese karaoke service provider.

Microsoft Lips

Tracking Videogame Sales

In 2007, *Guitar Hero II* and *Guitar Hero III: Legends of Rock* had both made the list of the top

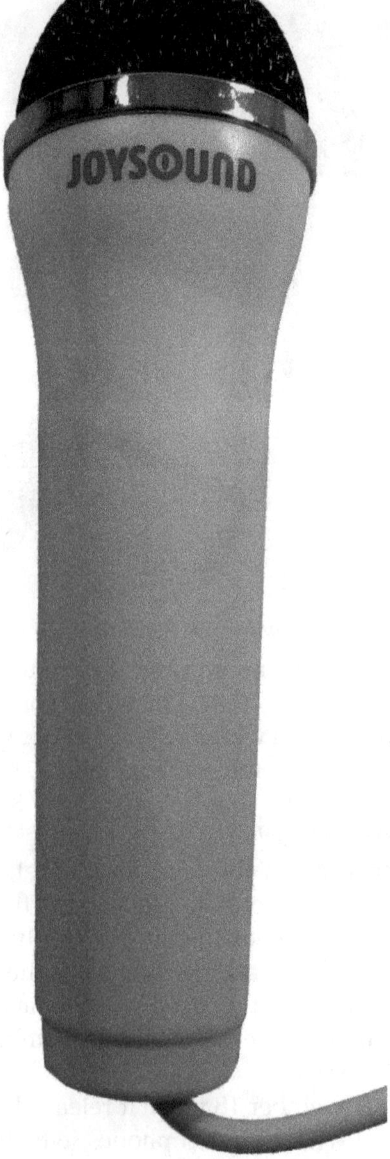
Nintendo Karaoke Joysound

ten best-selling games of the year. However, in both cases, these applied only to the PS2 editions of the games. The NPD Group, the company that tracked sales in North America, treated each edition of a title as a separate sales entity. Thus, although *Guitar Hero III: Legends of Rock* had been the top-selling game of 2007 in total number of sales, only the PS2 version made the top-ten list, because NPD counted them separately.

Guitar Hero: World Tour was the top-selling game of 2008 when all versions of a game were taken into account. However, because NPD counted each console version separately, no version of the game appeared on a list of the top-ten best-selling games of the year at all. On the other hand, one title earned two positions on the top-ten list. Rockstar's latest release, *Grand Theft Auto IV*, made the #5 position with its Xbox 360 edition and #8 with its PS3 version.

Both editions of *Grand Theft Auto IV* were released worldwide on April 29[31] and broke several *Guinness Book* records. Rockstar sold 3.6 million copies of the game in its first 24 hours and grossed $310 million, breaking the $170 million record that *Halo 3* had established in 2007.

The release of *Grand Theft Auto IV* brought the usual complaints that had plagued previous installments of the franchise. Initially, Australia and New Zealand would only allow an edited version of the game to be released, but when the game actually came out, it was the full version that had been issued everywhere else. However, two violent incidents were attributed to the game. The first occurred on June 27 in New Hyde Park, NY when six teenagers went on a crime spree of mugging, assault, vandalism and attempted carjacking. When they were caught, they said that they had been inspired by the actions in *Grand Theft Auto IV*.

Things were worse in Bangkok, Thailand. On August 4, an 18-year-old student wanted to see if it was as easy to rob a real taxi as it was in the game. Unfortunately, the student killed the cab driver while attempting to steal the vehicle. This crime led to the banning of further sales of *Grand Theft Auto IV*, and all *Grand Theft Auto* titles, in that country.

While *Grand Theft Auto IV* managed to stay on store shelves in most places, a game exclusive to the PS3 was recalled immediately.

LittleBigPlanet had first been announced at the GDC in March, 2007. The game offered three modes: playing, creating and sharing. The *Play* mode was a platform game in which the goal was to reach the end of each level while collecting keys that could unlock mini-levels. The *Create* mode allowed players to edit their characters as well as the levels that they were trying to get through. In addition, by using the Level Editor, players could create brand-new levels of varying complexity. Finally, the *Share* mode allowed players to upload the levels that they created or modified to the PlayStation Network, where other players could use it.

LittleBigPlanet was one of the most highly anticipated games of the year, and SCEA offered bonus gifts to people who pre-ordered it. The game was scheduled to be released in North America on October 21, and it began shipping to retailers a few days earlier. Some online retailers immediately began shipping the game to people who had pre-ordered them.

After one of the people who received a pre-ordered game played it, he noticed that the lyrics to one of the songs in the game contained two passages from the Koran, and he mentioned this in a forum on the PlayStation Network. Although nobody actually complained about the lyrics, which were believed to be in Somali, SCE decided on October 17 to recall all of the games that had already been shipped to retailers and customers worldwide, in order to remove what it interpreted as volatile content. SCE actually released the game with the lyrics removed on October 27.

New Companies From Old

In 2008, two of the oldest videogame companies were back in the news. On March 6, Infogrames, the majority stockholder of Atari, Inc., offered to purchase all of the remaining public shares of Atari, Inc. for $11 million. Atari, Inc. agreed to this on April 30. The deal closed on October 8 when Atari, Inc. became a wholly owned subsidiary of Infogrames. As part of the deal, the Atari, Inc. brand would thereafter only be used for the publishing end of games, and not the development.

As Atari, Inc. shrunk to a fraction of what it had once been, Activision, the industry's original third-party developer publisher, grew even larger. On July 9, Vivendi purchased 52% of Activision in a deal valued at $18.9 billion. A new holding company, *Activision Blizzard*, was established, and the former Activision and Blizzard became individual subsidiaries of that company.

The corporate headquarters for Activision Blizzard was located in Santa Monica, CA, where one year earlier, the poorly received E^3 Media & Business Summit had been held. Activision Blizzard elected not to attend the 2008 show, which began on July 15. Aware of the unpopularity of the 2007 show, the ESA moved it back to the Los Angeles Convention Center, but relegated it to only one hall. It was once again a subdued affair, with only 5,000 people in attendance, half the number that had showed up for the 2007 show. While the exhibiting companies were allowed to have booths instead of tables, the booths from all of the companies had to be the same size.

With the failure of the second E^3 Media & Business Summit, the ESA announced on October 22 that the original E^3 format would return in 2009. Admission would not be by invitation only, but would still be restricted to people who were associated with the industry.

The 2009 E^3 would be administered by IDG World Expo, the same company that was in charge of the public E for All. The show had been scheduled to return in 2008 on the weekend of August 28, but as it turned out, that was the same weekend that the annual PAX was scheduled to run in Seattle. IDG World Expo announced on February 11 that it was rescheduling E for All for the weekend of October 3, but didn't acknowledge PAX, which had 37,000 attendees in 2007, as the cause for the date change. Instead, it mentioned that the change was made so that E for All would coincide with *GreenXchange*, an environmental event that IDG was also setting up to take place on the same weekend at the Los Angeles Convention Center.

By the end of August, it appeared that few videogame companies were planning on attending E for All. The only major companies to sign up were Microsoft and Electronic Arts. In the end, the attendance for E for All was lower than it had been the year before.

Only 15,000 people showed up, compared to the record-breaking 58,000 people who had attended PAX. And Leipzig, the major convention that was open to the public in Germany at the end of August, had 203,000 registered attendees. On October 24, IDG officially announced that there would not be a 2009 E for All.

As 2008 came to a close, the sales figures for the consoles were the same as the year before in North America. The Wii, with more than 10 million units, outsold the second-place Xbox 360 by more than double. The PS3 trailed behind the Xbox 360, with approximately one million consoles separating them. The fourth-place console was now the PS2, with about 2½ million units sold. In the handheld market, the DS still outshone the PSP by more than double, with nearly 10 million units sold, but it had relinquished its position as the number-one videogame console to the Wii.

In the United States, videogame revenue hit a record $22 billion. In addition, 2008 was the fourth consecutive year in which overall earnings surpassed those of the previous year. But this news was bittersweet. With sales of its consoles continuing to trail in the marketplace, third-place SCE experienced losses that extended to its corporate parent, Sony. The company announced on December 9 that it would terminate 16,000 jobs around the world and close 10% of its factories, in order to save $1.1 billion by the end of its next financial year in March 2010. Sony executives didn't announce which Sony divisions would take most of the hits, but with fourth-quarter sales of SCE's consoles down from the same period in 2007 it was safe to assume that changes needed to occur with the new year.

CHAPTER THIRTY-SEVEN
2009

Although 2008 had been a record year for the videogame industry, the new year kicked in on a sour note. On January 7, Ziff-Davis Media announced that it would cease publishing its long-running *Electronic Gaming Monthly* magazine with the January 2009 edition, which was already on the stands.[1] Ziff-Davis stated that because demand for print was declining for advertisers and readers alike, it made no economic sense for the company to continue producing the magazine. However, Ziff-Davis also sold its network of videogame websites, including its flagship site *1UP*, to the Hearst Corporation's UGO Entertainment. The reality was that Ziff-Davis wanted to get out of the gaming business, so it could concentrate on its sites that were based around its *PC Mag* brand.

Ziff-Davis may have seen the writing on the videogame industry's wall. For instance, SCE's fortunes certainly didn't improve with the new year. Its corporate parent Sony posted a net loss of ¥98.9 billion ($1 billion) at the end of its fiscal year on March 31, marking its first reported loss since 1995. Despite this bad news, SCE had some cause for optimism. It had suffered from an operating loss of ¥58.5 billion ($612 million), but that loss was an improvement from the year before, when it had lost ¥124.5 billion ($1.3 billion). SCE had been suffering from falling revenues worldwide since September, 2008, and SCE's CFO, Nobuyuki Oneda, blamed it on a sudden deterioration of the economy. During that period, the company's sales fell by 1/3 to ¥393.8 billion ($4.36 billion) and its operating profits fell 97% to ¥400 million ($4.42 million).

Surprisingly, sales for the PSP and PS3 had been up slightly from the prior year. But the nine-year-old PS2 saw a significant drop. The 7.91 million units that had been sold around the world represented a 58% decrease from the year before. SCE attempted to turn the tide on the struggling PS2 on April 1 by reducing its price from $129 to $99. Retailers had hoped to see a reduction in the PS3's price as well, but that wasn't going to happen anytime soon.

January had been good for Nintendo and Microsoft. Wii, DS and Xbox 360 sales were all higher in January 2009 than they had been during the same period a year earlier. Microsoft also experienced first-quarter Xbox 360 sales that exceeded those from the same period one year earlier. Nintendo did better in January and February, but its fortunes suddenly changed in March as both the Wii and the DS sold 100,000 less units than they had in March 2008. The decrease in Wii sales was attributed to the fact that no killer software had been released for the system that month. In March 2008, Nintendo of America had issued *Super Smash Bros. Brawl*, which had gone on to become one of the top five games of the year. Similarly, *Resident Evil 5* came out for both the Xbox 360 and the PS3 in March, 2009, which had led to additional sales of those consoles.

The DS's lowered sales may be attributed to gamers simply waiting for something better. While perhaps not "better," the new DSi was released worldwide outside of Japan on April 5. In the United States, where the new handheld console sold for $170, the Nintendo World store in New York and the GameStop at Universal CityWalk in Los Angeles stayed open on the eve of the release and began selling the unit at midnight. Nintendo of America moved 435,000 of the handheld units during its first two days, nearly double the number of DS Lites that had been sold during the same time frame following its debut.

The *DSi LL*, an oversized version of the DSi,[2] was released in Japan on November 21. The new ¥20,000 ($225) unit was an inch wider than the regular DSi and featured two 4.5-inch screens, which were one inch larger than the ones on the DSi. The screens also had wider viewing angles that allowed spectators to easily watch the action that took place

Nintendo DSi LL

Game Park Holdings GP2X Wiz

on them. The original DSi remained available and cost ¥1,100 ($13) less. The two units worked the same, but the DSi LL came with two styluses. A short one was 92mm long, slightly longer than the one that came with the DSi. The other was larger and fatter and measured at 129mm in length. The new unit was also bundled with three built-in DSiWare titles. According to Nintendo, the DSi LL was targeted more towards people who used handheld devices for accessing the Internet, which was sometimes difficult to do when using the small screens of the DSi or smart phones.

Since its inception, the DS in all of its forms dominated the handheld market. In February, South Korean president Lee Myung-bak remarked that his country needed to develop a game console like a DS. By coincidence, the South Korean company Game Park Holdings did release a new handheld console on May 12. The $180 *GP2X Wiz* was the successor to Game Park Holdings' GP2X F200 that had come out in 2007, and it was the first console from either Game Park or Game Park Holdings that was released outside of South Korea. The GP2X Wiz did have some similarities with the DS, such as a built-in microphone, a touchscreen and unlike the GP2X F200, it had a stylus that could be stored within the unit. But where Nintendo's device was only to be used with games that had been licensed by Nintendo, Game Park Holdings used an open-source approach and invited anyone to write his own homebrew programs either in the console's native language or in Adobe *Flash*.

The GP2X Wiz had not been designed to compete with the DS. It was popular with hackers and gamers who liked the idea that most classic games could be emulated on it. Emulation was also popular on the PSP, although it wasn't a feature that was supported by SCE.[3]

PSP Go

But SCE was constantly looking for new features for the PSP, which could never come near the DS in sales. On May 20, CNET reported that SCE was seeking to add music downloads to the PlayStation Store, particularly for the PSP.

As it turned out, downloading did become a major feature of the PSP, and not only for music downloads. On October 1, SCE released a new PSP in North America and Europe.[4] The *PSP Go* did not replace the year-old PSP-3000, but it wasn't compatible with it, either. Unlike all the programmable handhelds that preceded it, software for the PSP Go could only be downloaded, in this case from the PlayStation Store. Since the unit didn't have a UMD drive, it didn't even look like the other PSPs. With a width of 3.8 inches, it was .5 inches slimmer than the prior models. Its screen, which was the same size as on the other PSPs, dominated the unit's face. The portion holding the screen slid upwards to reveal the standard PlayStation controller buttons beneath it.

The PSP Go lacked the USB port and video output slot that had been built into the two PSP models that preceded it. Instead, it had a multi-use connector port that several other types of cables could plug into. One cable that used this port was bundled with the

SCE PSP Go

PSP Go. The opposite end was a standard USB plug that could be used to charge the PSP Go's battery or to transfer data from a PSP, PS3 or PC.

Retailing at $250, the PSP Go appeared to offer less than the PSP-3000, and yet it cost nearly $80 more. Even more astounding was the fact that the new handheld PSP Go cost only $50 less than the PS3, which included a Blu-ray player. On the other hand, the PSP Go featured 16GB of memory for internal storage (the PSP-3000 only had 64MB) and Bluetooth compatibility. While SCEE offered three free downloads from a list of 17 titles to PSP owners who bought the PSP Go, North American PSP owners weren't given such incentives to purchase the new handheld. This was due to "legal and technical reasons," according to John Koller, SCEA's Director of Hardware Marketing. However, Koller did promise that as long as the PSP was a viable product, titles would always be available as downloads and on UMD.[5] Unfortunately, not all games could run on the PSP Go. Those that utilized the Go!Cam camera couldn't run on the new system because it lacked a USB slot, which the camera needed to plug into.

The real question was whether or not the PSP Go was even feasible at all. One Dutch retailer refused to carry it partly because of its high price. But the fact that only downloadable games could run on it prevented the store from profiting from any software sales. A British retailer declared that the "PSP Go [was] a No-Go" but still decided to carry it, even though he had no intention of promoting it. In the United States, NPD, the company that tracked sales, lumped PSP Go sales into the same category as the PSP-3000. In October, the two consoles sold 174,500 units combined. That was less than the sole number of PSP-3000s that had sold in September.

Zeebo

Even though the PSP Go was a hard sell because it could only play downloadable

Zeebo

games, one company felt that such a console was just the perfect fit for emerging markets such as Brazil and China, where rampant software piracy dissuaded the major hardware manufacturers from selling their products. A downloadable game that didn't physically exist outside of its console couldn't be readily copied. With this in mind, San Diego-based Zeebo, Inc.[6] released the *Zeebo* in limited quantities in Rio De Janeiro, Brazil on June 1 with a retail price of R$499,00 ($256.50). The wireless system came with three built-in games, including *FIFA 09*,[7] and three additional games could be downloaded for free.[8] Over 20 more games from well-known software publishers such as Activision and Namco could be purchased and downloaded from an online store using *Z-Credits*, a virtual currency.

Zeebo, Inc. lowered the price of the Zeebo in September to R$399,00 ($220.50) and then again in November to R$299,00 ($174). It remained at that price in December when the system was finally released nationwide. The Zeebo was released in Mexico on November 4, where it sold for 2,499 pesos ($188). The Mexican console came with five built-in games, and an additional six games, all in Spanish, were available to purchase.[9]

Motion Controllers

Although the PSP Go launched in October, it actually debuted in early June at E³. After an absence of two years while the poorly received E³ Media & Business Summit was held in its place, E³ returned in its original form with over 41,000 attendees and 216 exhibitors.

Some of the biggest news items from the show were about peripherals that weren't even going to be released during 2009. Heavily influenced by the success of the Wii, both Microsoft and SCE offered their own motion controllers for their respective consoles.

SCE showed off the *PlayStation Motion Controller* at its pre-E³ press conference. This device, which the press referred to as a wand, resembled a microphone with a vertical base that had several buttons and a small white orb atop it that changed colors depending upon the game. The PlayStation Motion Controller was similar to the Wii Remote, as it was held in the player's hand and its movement affected what happened on the screen. However, while the coordinates of the Wii Remote were read by the sensor bar, the PlayStation Motion Controller worked with the already available PlayStation Eye. The camera not only tracked the PlayStation Motion Controller, but it also put the player's image on the screen, and the software displayed the controller as anything the game required it to be, such as a sword. SCE expected to release the new controller during the spring of 2010.

Although it was easy to believe that the popular Wii Remote inspired the PlayStation Motion Controller, that wasn't exactly the case. Preliminary work on the controller had actually begun in 1999. But at that time, the inertial sensors required by the device to detect motion were too expensive to make it commercially feasible. SCEE proceeded to work on a hands-free device, which was released as the EyeToy in 2003. By 2008, the Wii was a success, and the cost of the inertial sensors had fallen considerably. This led SCEE to resume development of its own motion-sensitive controller.

Microsoft used its pre-E³ press conference to divulge information about its own motion controller, which it called by its code name, *Project Natal*.[10] While the Wii used a motion controller that worked with a motion sensor, and the PS3 would use a motion controller that worked with a camera, Project Natal, which was expected to be released in time for

Christmas, 2010, was a motion sensor with a built-in camera.

The Project Natal device looked like a wide, oversized web-cam. It sat on a plastic base and could be positioned either above or below the television screen, just like the Wii motion sensor. In the center of the unit was an infrared sensor that registered the depth, width and height of the objects in front of it. The device also had an RGB camera that could recognize up to six faces and a microphone that could not only detect different voices, but also detected variances in the voices that it recognized.

Microsoft demonstrated Project Natal with two games. *Ricochet* was a mini-game that had been developed specifically to show off the capabilities of the device. This was a simple game that was similar to one that was already available on *Wii Fit,* in which players had to rebound balls that came at them. In the Wii version, players used the Wii Remote to smack virtual soccer balls back to a goal. But on the Xbox 360, their bodies were the controllers and they had to use their arms and legs to hit or kick the balls back.

Another demo allowed people to play the driving game *Burnout Paradise* without any controllers. Gamers merely had to put their hands in a steering position to control their on-screen vehicles. They also used their feet to press virtual gas and brake pedals.

Additional Alternative Controllers

Nintendo, which already had a popular motion-sensitive controller and therefore didn't need to spend time making similar introductions, showed a new peripheral during its pre-E^3 press conference. One end of the *Wii Vitality Sensor* connected to the Wii Remote and the other snapped onto a person's finger to "gain information relating to his inner world in order to achieve greater relaxation." The problem was that no one mentioned what kind of applications would use the Wii Vitality Sensor or when it would be available.[11]

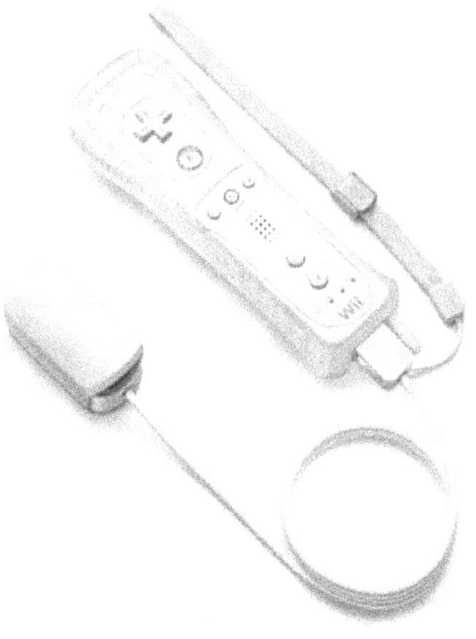

Nintendo Wii Vitality Sensor

Nintendo did release the *Wii MotionPlus* on June 8. Nintendo had previewed this new $20 peripheral one year earlier at the 2008 E^3 Media & Business Summit. The *Wii MotionPlus* plugged into the expansion port at the bottom of the Wii Remote and provided the latter with a greater degree of accuracy than could be obtained without it. However, it could only be used in games that were specifically designed to take advantage of the Wii MotionPlus. Only three such games were available when the device was released,[12] and in all three cases, its use was optional, since the games could be played without the Wii MotionPlus attached to the Wii Remote. The first game that required the Wii MotionPlus was *Wii Sports Resort.* It came out on July 26 in North America and was bundled with the Wii MotionPlus.

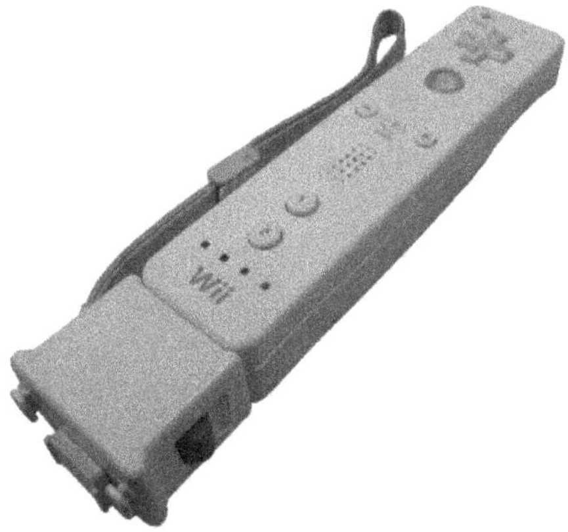

Nintendo Wii Motion Plus

The Wii MotionPlus peripheral extended the length of the Wii Remote by an additional 1.5 inches. Since it plugged into the Wii Remote's expansion port, it too featured an expansion port

2009

Nintendo Wii Classic Controller Pro

that the Nunchuck controller could plug into.

Another peripheral that plugged into the Wii Remote's expansion port was the Wii Classic Controller, which had been released as part of the Wii's 2006 launch. In August, Nintendo of Japan released a new ¥2,000 ($21) *Wii Classic Controller Pro,*[13] which was basically an update of the Wii Classic Controller. Like the original, it too could only be used for Virtual Console games and a limited number of Wii titles.

This controller was slightly bigger than its predecessor and had grips that extended from beneath it for better stability. Whereas the original resembled a Super Famicom controller, the new one looked like one for the GameCube. The cord that plugged into the Wii Remote's expansion port extended from the top of the controller, instead of the bottom as it had been on the Wii Classic Controller. And the slot on the Wii Classic Controller that had been originally planned with an added clip for attachment to the Wii Remote was removed from the new controller.

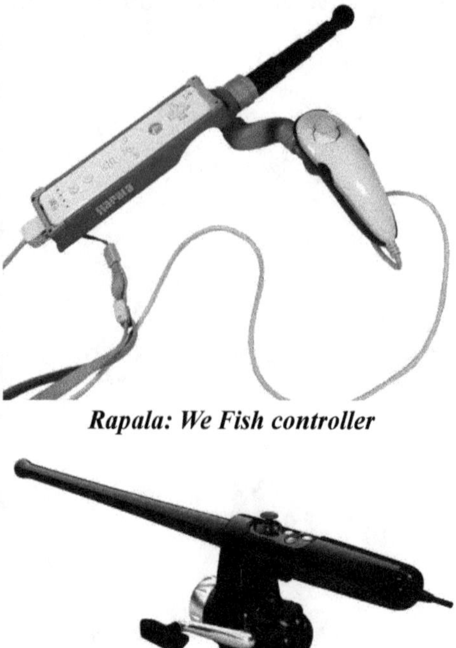

***Rapala: We Fish* controller**

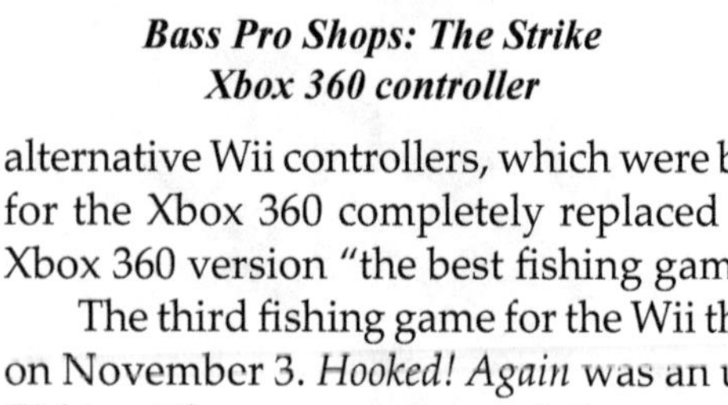

***Bass Pro Shops: The Strike* Xbox 360 controller**

Unfortunately, games that used these alternative peripheral controllers didn't necessarily enhance a poor game as people learned in 2007 with the release of *Hooked! Real Motion Fishing*. In 2009, three new fishing games were released for the Wii that came with their own alternative controllers. In the case of the first, *Rapala: We Fish,* which arrived on September 29, the controls ruined the gaming experience. Although *Gamezone* liked the gameplay, it found that "controlling your boat as well as fishing is done using the Wii Remote's motion sensors; the boat controls are especially cumbersome as the boat will get stuck when trying to turn around. As *We Fish* relies on being quick and turning in your fish as fast as possible, the controls will factor in to a lot of your losses." The fishing rod peripheral that accompanied the game didn't aid in the situation.

Bass Pro Shops: The Strike was released on October 6, one week after *Rapala: We Fish*. In addition to it coming out for the Wii, a version was also released for the Xbox 360. Unlike the alternative Wii controllers, which were built around the Wii Remote. The fishing controller for the Xbox 360 completely replaced the Xbox 360 controller. *GamePro* found the $80 Xbox 360 version "the best fishing game out there."[14]

The third fishing game for the Wii that came with a fishing rod controller was released on November 3. *Hooked! Again* was an update to the poorly received *Hooked! Real Motion Fishing*. The game supported the new *Wii MotionPlus,* which forced a design change to the fishing rod controller since it needed to be extended to contain the Wii Remote with an attached *Wii MotionPlus*

The multitude of fishing games that were released, were specifically targeted towards people who enjoyed to fish. Another type of outdoors sports that involved trapping and killing animals was hunting and it too was represented in videogames. While any game that consisted of a player searching and shooting on-screen characters could be deemed as a hunting game, the hunting genre represented games where the object was to bag animals for sport. The first such game, *Cabela's Big Game Hunter*, was released for Windows computers in 1998. A PS2 version of the game was released in 2002, marking the first time that such a hunting game was available on a home videogame console. Activision continued to release a new version of the game every few years and when the 2010 edition was released for the Wii on September 29, it made history again. Even though rifle controllers had been around since Magnavox released one for the Odyssey in 1972, the first rifle controller bundled with a hunting game didn't occur until Activision packaged one with *Cabela's Big Game Hunter 2010*.

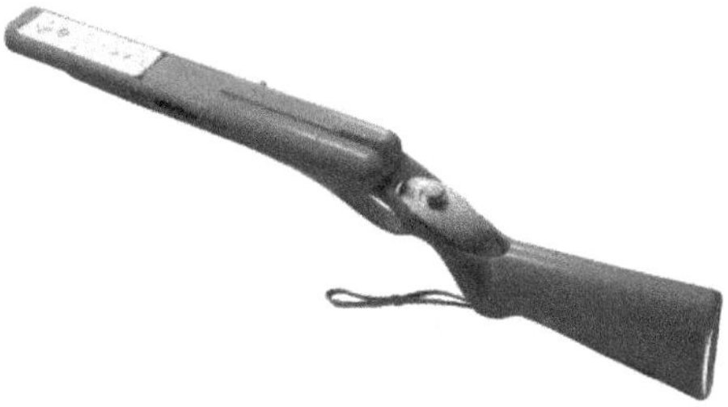

Cabela's Big Game Hunter 2010 Top Shot Rifle

A different type of alternative controller was released for the Wii a week later on November 10 in the PAL territories, including Europe and Australia. *Baby and Me*, from 505 Games, was a *Tamagotchi*-like game that allowed little girls to care for a baby from birth through its first birthday. The game was sold with a pouch that held a Wii Remote that could then be tied around a doll. The game would then allow the child to take care of the doll, which would respond with giggles, gurgling or cries through the Wii Remote's speaker. In addition, the Wii Balance Board could be used to rock the doll to sleep, burp the doll or teach the baby doll to walk.

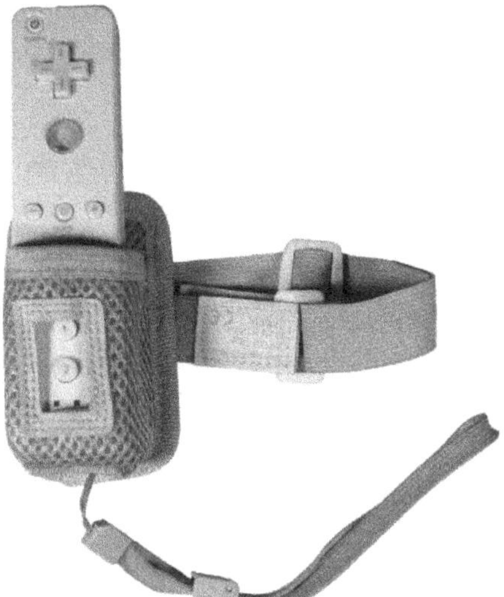

505 Games Baby & Me

A special deluxe edition of the game was sold only in Australia and New Zealand. This version was packaged with an actual doll with a slot in its back that the Wii Remote could be inserted directly into. This in effect turned the doll into a controller.

Because *Baby and Me* was only released for the Wii, PS3 owners in Europe and Australia couldn't take care of virtual babies. But they were able to care for virtual pets after *EyePet* was released on October 23. Unlike the virtual pets that preceded it, the EyePet, a combination of a puppy, monkey and kitten, resided in the real world, which was captured on the screen using the PlayStation Eye. Using augmented reality technology, *EyePet* presented gamers on the screen along with the creature that they could play and care for. They could "pet" the animal by flexing their fingers in the air, which displayed on the screen as if they were actually touching it.

Another game that employed augmented reality was released for the European PSP on November 13. *Invizimals* was a Pokémon-type game in which players had to search and capture hidden creatures. However, whereas Pokémon resided in a computer-generated world, the Invizimals lived in the real world, but were invisible to the naked eye. Bundled with the game was a new camera. The PSP-450 camera

SCE PSP-450 Camera

was wider than its predecessor, the PSP-300, which was also known as the Go!Cam. The resolution of both cameras was the same, although the PSP-450 didn't feature the SXGA (1280x960) mode that had been available on the PSP-300. The PSP-450 also required the latest PSP operating system, version 6, which had been available since September 10.

The Beatles And Other Rock Bands

Another game that had been developed solely for the PSP was *Rock Band Unplugged* from MTV and Electronic Arts. *Rock Band Unplugged*, which launched on June 9, was the first version of *Rock Band* to appear on a handheld console. It took the standard *Guitar Hero*-like formula, in which the player had to press one of the standard PSP buttons in time with the notes that fell down the screen. But in *Rock Band* fashion, several instruments had to be used. The player, while monitoring the falling notes, also had to anticipate which instruments should be used (lead guitar, bass guitar, drums and vocals) and switch instruments by pressing the unit's shoulder buttons. Unlike the console version of *Rock Band*, *Rock Band Unplugged* was only for one player. However, it did allow players to create their own bands and take them on tour.

Two band games arrived for consoles in September. Activision's *Guitar Hero 5*, which came out in North America on September 1, was similar to the earlier *Guitar Hero: World Tour* with a few enhancements. Among them was a redesigned menu that made navigating very easy. Another new feature gave multiple band members the ability to play the same instruments, whereas in *Guitar Hero: World Tour*, each player was required to have a different instrument. The changes were well received by consumers, and *Guitar Hero 5* enjoyed one of the best launches in the history of the *Guitar Hero* franchise.

The Beatles: Rock Band was released a week later on September 9, the same day that a highly touted box set of remastered Beatles CDs came out. Despite Harmonix co-founder Alex Rigopoulos' assurance that the game wouldn't be just another *Rock Band* featuring the Beatles, that's basically what the finished product turned out to be. But there were a few differences. Gameplay was slightly altered. The "Career" mode from previous *Rock Band* games that players had used to guide their bands from creation to stardom was substituted by a "Story" mode that allowed players to perform through a lengthy history of the Beatles, from their early days at the Cavern Club to their final live concert atop the Apple building in 1969. *The Beatles: Rock Band* also added two additional vocals, which allowed up to three players to harmonize. A final change was the elimination of the drum fills and whammy-bar effects that had allowed players to creatively jam at the end of a song. This had been done to preserve the songs just as the Beatles had recorded them.

The Beatles: Rock Band featured 45 songs, less than other *Rock Band* installments. Additional songs from three Beatles albums became available for downloading. However, none of the songs that were playable on this set could be used with other *Rock Band* games.

The Beatles: Rock Band was one of the most expensive videogames ever released. The game software alone cost $60 and it was compatible with the instruments that worked on the other *Rock Band* sets.[15] A "Special Value" set that contained standard *Rock Band* guitars and drums retailed for $160. Finally, there was a $250 limited "Premium" set that included *Rock Band 2* drums with a Beatles kick-drum head branded with the Ludwig name, a facsimile Höfner bass-guitar controller that was a replica of the guitar used by Paul McCartney,[16] and a microphone stand. Despite the high price, the game sold relatively well. Within a week of its launch, sales of all three configurations did better than MTV had forecasted, and 25% of its initial inventory had already been sold.

Although *The Beatles: Rock Band* sold in respectable numbers, it didn't do as well as either of its two predecessors. One reason was that it was band-centric, and hardcore Beatles fans, many of whom were already in their sixties, weren't exactly in the demographic that was interested in videogames. Another small contingent of buyers consisted of Beatles collectors, who purchased the game because of the previously unreleased excerpts of studio conversation that were included along with the main songs. However, the high cost of the different configurations was also a factor. But there was one reason that few seemed to want to acknowledge, and that was the simple fact that there simply was a glut of rhythm games on the market. And two more were released on November 11: MTV's *Lego Rock Band* and Activision's *Band Hero*. Although seven new *Guitar Hero* and *Rock Band* titles were released in 2009,[17] gross sales of rhythm games dropped to $875 million during the year, approximately half of what had been earned in 2008, which had been the peak for rhythm-game sales.

Be The DJ

Also included in those sales figures was a new type of rhythm game that Activision launched on October 27. *DJ Hero* allowed players to act as club DJs. The controller was a turntable that had three different-colored buttons built into its grooves. Attached to the table was a section that featured a cross-fader slider and an incremental encoder knob. This section could be removed and reversed, so left- or right-handed players wouldn't be handicapped by the control layout.

Although *DJ Hero* never made NPD's list of the top ten selling games of any month, Activision issued a press release that stated that NPD had named the game as the highest-grossing new IP (Intellectual Property) of the year. However, the press release did not cite any sales figures and it was questionable whether *DJ Hero* was even a new IP at all. Activision CEO Bobby Kotick stated, "*DJ Hero* has transformed music gaming by marrying an innovative turntable controller

Activision DJ Hero

The game play was similar to *Guitar Hero.* The buttons on the turntable had to be pressed in sync with the symbols that fell down the screen along three separate colored record grooves, each corresponding to one of the buttons on the turntable. Sometimes a continuous stream shifted to the left or right to identify that a different track in the mix was playing. To keep up, the player had to slide the cross-fader to either the left or right as displayed by the on-screen stream.

Two players could compete in one game with two separate turntables. Two players could also play together with one acting as the DJ who used the turntable, while the other acted as a guitarist and used a *Guitar Hero* guitar controller. The split screen showed the *DJ Hero* playfield on one side and a *Guitar Hero*-type playfield on the other.

DJ Hero was praised by most journalists and critics from both inside and outside of the videogame industry. *Time* named it the third-best videogame of the year, while *USA Today* called it the best music game of the year. But despite these acclaims, *DJ Hero* was not a financial success. When the game had first been announced, Doug Creutz, an analyst with Cowan and Company, had predicted that Activision would sell 2.5 million copies by the end of the year. However, after a survey with retailers one week prior to the release showed a lack of pre-orders, Creutz lowered his expectations to 1.6 million. But even that number was too optimistic. Following *DJ Hero*'s actual release, only a combined total of 122,000 units were sold in October for the four consoles that it could play on.[18] Several reasons were blamed for the failure of the much-hyped game, none withstanding the high price of the unit. Another reason cited was that too many people simply didn't even know what a DJ did or what a turntable was. Unlike *Guitar Hero,* which vicariously fulfilled the common fantasy of becoming an adept guitar player, few videogamers had aspirations to become professional DJs.

and exhilarating game-play with the biggest artists and incredible music from around the world." But the turntable wasn't as innovative as Kotick wanted people to believe. Konami, the company that had invented rhythm games, had released a turntable controller for its *Beatmania* game in 1998. And in late 2008, around the same time that *DJ Hero* was announced, Genius Products announced that it was producing a DJ game called *Scratch: The Ultimate DJ*, which was being developed by 7 Studios. The game was planned to be released in the fall of 2009 and would include its own turntable controller, the "Scratch Deck," which would be built by Numark Industries, a manufacturer of professional DJ equipment.[19]

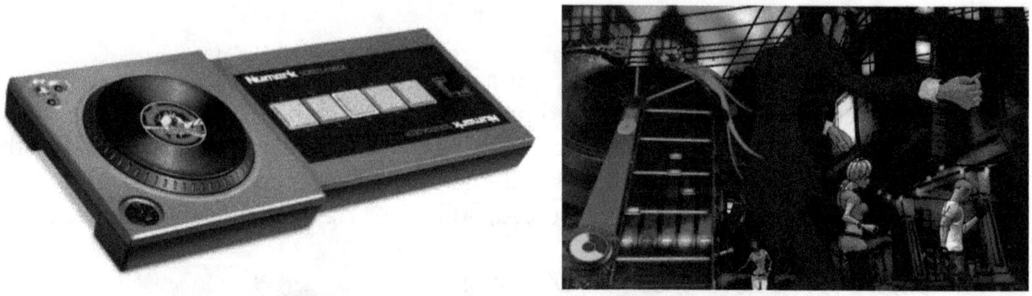

Genius Products Scratch - The Ultimate DJ

In early January, Genius began receiving requests from several game publishers, including Activision, to purchase the rights to *Scratch: The Ultimate DJ*. When Genius refused to sell, Activision went ahead and purchased 7 Studios, the company that was under contract with Genius to develop the game. On April 15, Genius filed a lawsuit against Activision and 7 Studios, claiming that the two companies had conspired to keep *Scratch: The Ultimate DJ* from getting into stores before *DJ Hero* by withholding "work product," which included source code and the turntable controller.

Activision was allowed to continue working on *DJ Hero*, but 7 Studios was ordered to turn all of the source code over to Genius immediately.[20] Genius announced in August that it had hired Bedlam Games to complete the development of *Scratch: The Ultimate DJ*, which would be released for the Xbox 360 and PS3 in early 2010, nearly six months after the release of *DJ Hero*.[21]

Good and Bad Activision Games

Activision released another game with a deluxe controller on November 17 in North America, and this one had been designed with teens in mind. *Tony Hawk: Ride* was the latest in a series of Tony Hawk-branded skateboard games, and was the first to feature its own skateboard controller. The $120 game was available for all three major systems. The Wii skateboard differed from previous alternative Wii controllers, because it didn't need to house the Wii Remote. Like the PS3 version, the Wii model was sold with a dongle that plugged into the Wii's USB port and received the infrared signal sent by the skateboard controller.

Activision Tony Hawk Ride Skateboard controller

The skateboard controller was only four inches smaller than an actual skateboard. However, it featured two built-in accelerometers and infrared sensors on all of its sides to register the player's hands and feet and to send this information to the console. Unfortunately, all of these sensors did a poor job of registering the player's movements. *Tony Hawk: Ride* was the 12th game in the Tony Hawk series, which had been steadily declining in sales since its introduction in 1999. The skateboard controller was supposed to provide a more realistic experience and regenerate the series. Instead, it was widely criticized by the press as the worst one yet.[22]

Activision Tony Hawk Ride dongle

Activision had better luck with a game it released a week earlier that didn't require a special controller. *Call of Duty: Modern Warfare 2*, a sequel to *Call of Duty 4: Modern Warfare*, was released on November 10. By the end of that day, it had earned $310 million in the United States and Great Britain, a new launch record in the videogaming industry. In the United States alone, 4.7 million copies were sold that first day, earning it another record.[23]

Activision Call of Duty - Modern Warfare 2 No Russian

The game caused controversy around the world because of its "No Russian" third level. In this optional mission, the player is part of a group of armed Russian terrorists marauding through a Russian airport terminal and shooting everybody in sight. Never before has such a large-scale killing of innocent civilians ever been presented in a game. Japanese and German versions of the game were modified so that the game ended if the player "killed" a civilian. In Great Britain, it became the first in the Call of Duty series to receive an 18 rating from the BBFC, that country's equivalent to the ESRB. The Australian Classification Board initially gave the game an MA15+ rating but was pressured to change that to an R18+ once word of the mission became widespread. An R18+ would have prevented the game from being sold in Australia. In the end the Australian Classification Board said that it did not have the authority to change an existing rating.

The Xbox 360 version of *Call of Duty: Modern Warfare 2* wound up being North America's number-one game of the year in sales. The PS3 version was the number-eight game of the year and the only PS3 title that made the top ten. The only other Xbox 360 title that made the top ten was *Halo 3 ODST*, which came in at number nine. The remaining spots were all dominated by Nintendo titles. The tenth-place title, *Pokémon Platinum Version*, was for the DS and the six remaining top ten positions were held by Wii titles. The fourth highest-selling game was *Wii Fit*, which continued to dominate sales even though it had been available since early 2008. On October 4, Nintendo of America released *Wii Fit Plus*. This title contained all of the exercises that had been found on the original *Wii Fit*, and added 15 new balance and aerobics exercises to the mix, along with an easier-to-use menu interface.

Keeping In Shape With Nintendo

Another Wii game that got people moving was *Just Dance*, which Ubisoft initially released in North America on November 17. As its title declared, this was a game in which the only thing up to four players had to do was dance. Unlike dancers in Konami's popular *Dance Dance Revolution*, the ones dancing to *Just Dance* didn't have to be concerned with onscreen prompts that directed them to which square they had to step on. All they had to do was imitate the moves of their onscreen avatars while holding their Wii Remotes. Many critics complained that the game (if it could be deemed a game) was shallow, since it didn't present any challenges. There were no buttons to press, no songs to unlock and no progress to be achieved. And while the 32 songs on the track list represented a wide array of musical genres, additional tunes could not be downloaded. Despite this, the game sold well. Just during the two months that it was available in 2009, *Just Dance* became Ubisoft's fastest-selling Wii title.[24]

Ubisoft Wii Motion Tracking Camera

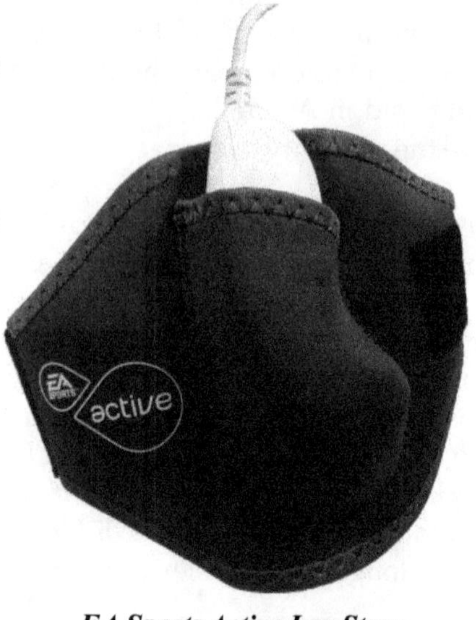

EA Sports Active Leg Strap

While dancing could be considered as a form of exercise, the purpose of *Just Dance* wasn't to keep players fit. However, on November 24, one week after the release of *Just Dance*, Ubisoft released *Your Shape*, which as its name implied, was intended to keep its users in shape. Users worked with an onscreen workout buddy. In North America this buddy was actress/model Jenny McCarthy.[25] Unfortunately, all the program provided were a series of aerobic exercises targeted towards females. Most people found the program repetitive and dull. A *Gamespot* review even went as far as to call the exercises so "bland that they give aerobicizing wannabes an excuse to drift back to their couches". But not all aspects of *Your Shape* was criticized. One part was even praised. The game was bundled with a USB motion-tracking camera that looked similar to SCE's EyeToy. The camera scanned the user's entire body and then allowed the user to select a part of their body that they wanted to focus on.

Your Shape was compared with Nintendo's *Wii Fit* and Electronic Arts' *EA Sports Active: Personal Trainer*, which had been released in May. This product was praised by most gaming journalists and was basically everything that *Your Shape* wasn't. It wasn't tailored just towards females and it wasn't repetitive. Workouts could be customized and users could choose from daily 20-minute workout regimens or a 30-day Challenge mode. Activities were varied and included such exercises as boxing, inline skating, aerobic dancing, hitting and throwing a baseball, swinging a tennis racquet and shooting a basketball. While some activities could use the Wii Balance Board, it wasn't required. However, the Wii Remote was used along with the Nunchuck, which needed to be enclosed in a special pouch that strapped around the user's leg in order to keep track of his lower body movements.

Electronic Arts sold over 600,000 units worldwide in a period of two weeks, making it their best-selling Wiigame to date. The program was so popular that Electronic Arts released an expansion pack called *EA Sports Active: More Workouts* on November 17, one week before the release of Ubisoft's *Your Shape*.

Health-conscious DS owners also had access to a personal train when Nintendo released *Aruite Wakaru Seikatsu Rhythm DS* outside of Japan. The game was released on

May 25 in North America, where it was called *Personal Trainer: Walking*. It arrived in PAL countries on June 5, where it was called *Walk with Me*!

Personal Trainer: Walking (and its PAL equivalent) had one advantage over the similar *My Weight Loss Coach* that had been released in the same regions in 2008. The pedometer that came with the former game had to be inserted into the DS's GBA slot, which meant that it couldn't be used with the DSi, since that model lacked the GBA slot. Because *Personal Trainer: Walking* interacted with the handheld console via an infrared signal, it could be used with all DS models, including the new DSi.

Nintendo of Japan released two more DS games that were packaged with pedometers on September 12, but these games were not designed for the health-conscious. *Pocket Monsters HeartGold* and *Pocket Monsters SoulSilver* were updated versions of *Pocket Monsters Gold* and *Pocket Monsters Silver*, which had been released in Japan for the Game Boy Color in 1999. Each of the ¥4,800 ($53) games was packaged with a "Pokéwalker," a pedometer that was not unlike the Activity Meter that came with *Personal Trainer: Walking*. The Pokéwalker was round with a flat underside and resembled a Pokéball. It had an LCD screen in its center and three buttons to access menus and commands. Its features were somewhat similar to those on the Pokémon Pikachu 2 GS handheld unit that Nintendo had released in 2000.

Nintendo Pokéwalker

Players could send any Pocket Monster into the Pokéwalker via an infrared connection. When the player physically walked with the Pokéwalker, the Pocket Monster that was loaded into it gained Experience Points, which cumulatively raised the Pocket Monster's level. Each Pocket Monster also earned one Watt for every 20 steps taken. These Watts could then be traded for a "Poké Radar" that helped it find other Pocket Monsters to battle or a "Dowsing Machine" that helped find items to use. Items that were found could be sent to the DS via the infrared connection.

Two individual Pokéwalkers could be linked via the infrared connection so that the Pocket Monsters inside them could play together. After playing, each Pocket Monster would receive an item that could be loaded into the main game in the DS.

Price Reductions

Although Wii software dominated the charts,[26] the console itself was no longer doing so well. For the first time in 20 years, Nintendo's overall profits declined, and the company had to readjust its forecast for its fiscal year that ended in March, 2010. The company had originally predicted profits of $3.3 billion, but after six months of Wii sales declining to half of what they had been the year before, Nintendo cut its forecasted profit to $2.53 billion. To help boost sales, Nintendo of America lowered the price of the Wii console from $250 to $200 on September 27. This was the same price that Microsoft's Xbox 360 cost without a hard drive.

The Nintendo price cut followed reductions from both Microsoft and SCE. Microsoft had dropped the price of the 60GB Xbox 360 Pro system by $50 to $250 on August 28, the same day it announced that that configuration was being phased out. The company also dropped the price of the 120GB Elite system by $100 to $300,[27] and that was to match price reductions that had been imposed by SCE nine days earlier on August 19.

On that date, SCE had dropped the price of its 80GB consoles to $300 and the 160GB consoles to $400. SCE's price cuts were only temporary and limited to the existing store stock, because the company was discontinuing the consoles. On September 1, SCE released a new $300 120GB PS3.[28] This new model was much smaller than the previous models, and although it officially was still called the PS3, it was referred to as the *PS3 Slim*. The new system was 32% smaller and 36% lighter, and used 34% less energy than the original model. The public responded favorably towards the PS3 Slim, and during September (and only September), it outsold both the Wii and Xbox 360 individually.

SCE PS3 Slim

Some companies released new, inexpensive versions of their consoles without any fanfare. Although VTech and LeapFrog continued to sell their popular handheld consoles, the new models in the stores contained less features than the ones that had preceded them.

The new versions of VTech's V.Smile Pocket and V.Smile Cyber Pocket had several features

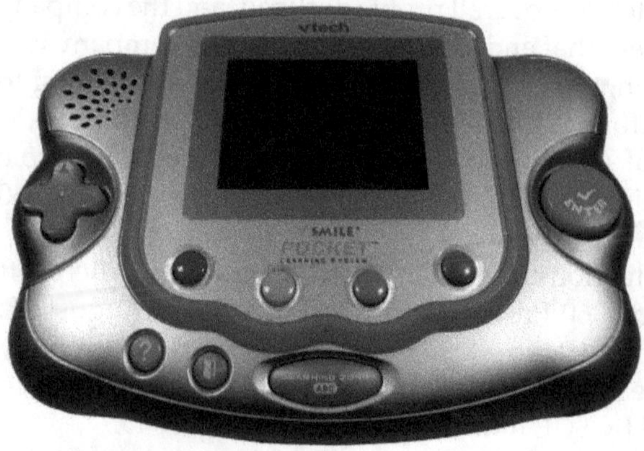

VTech V.Smile Pocket - new version

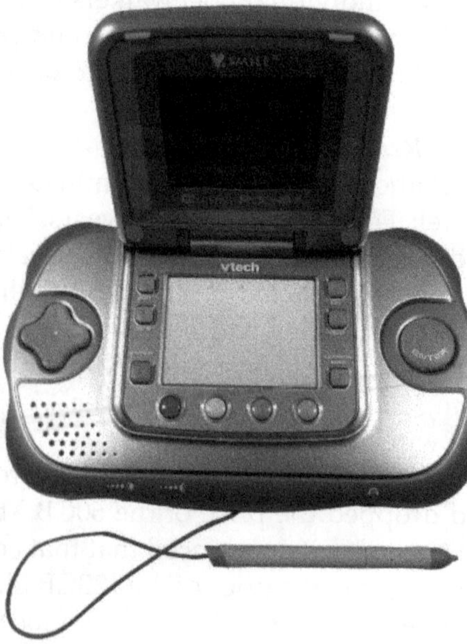

VTech V.Smile Cyber Pocket - new version

eliminated. Among them was the ability to hook the consoles up to televisions. Also missing was the microphone that had once been on the faces of the individual consoles. The jewel-like color buttons were replaced by cheap, colored buttons that no longer resembled jewels. The joystick and Enter buttons were no longer reversible. And finally, the joystick itself was replaced with a cross-styled D-pad. The D-pad was on the left side of the console and the Enter button was on the right.

The change that LeapFrog made to the Leapster 2 was less apparent. On older models, an SD card to save games could be added and replaced by the user. The new Leapster 2s that were released in 2009 had built-in SD cards, which couldn't be accessed or removed by the user at all.

All Games By AtGames

AtGames, the company that managed to repackage Sega's 8- and 16-bit games in seemingly endless ways, introduced a new handheld, which it called the *Arcade Ultimate.* This was nearly the same console that AtGames had released in 2008 as the Arcade Portable, with a few changes in the game lineup. Although the two handhelds looked remarkably alike there were a few differences between the two. The Arcade Ultimate included an SD card slot so additional games could be added. It also had six control buttons whereas the Arcade Portable only had three. But these extra buttons weren't necessarily needed. In lieu of them the Arcade Ultimate could also accept the external wireless controllers that were used with the Arcade Classic console.

AtGames Arcade Ultimate

Hyperkin and Retro-Bit, two of the companies that had made names for themselves selling Famiclones, also released products that had been manufactured by AtGames. Both companies released handheld devices that were very similar to AtGames' own Arcade Ultimate. Hyperkin's *Genmobile* and Retro-Bit's *Retrogen* even had the same 20 games that came with the Arcade Ultimate built-into them. However, just like the Famiclones, the Genmobile and Retrogen also had cartridge slots and could accept both Genesis *and* Mega Drive cartridges.

Hyperkin and Retro-Bit also released consoles that were manufactured by AtGames. Retro-Bit's Arcade Classic looked very much like AtGames's console of the same name with the one exception that it came with wired controllers instead of wireless ones. Hyperkin's *Gencore* was packaged with the same wired Genesis-styled controllers but the console itself, which was blue and shaped like Sonic the Hedgehog's head, looked very much like AtGames' Arcade Motion with the addition of a cartridge slot.

Online Features

While AtGames may have lured consumers to its products with low prices and a large selection of built-in games, Microsoft, SCE and Nintendo had to find other reasons to get people to buy their consoles. Important considerations were the number of games that were available and the amount of features that the console offered. Beginning on November 17, Xbox Live Gold members aged 18 and over gained access to Facebook and Twitter via their Xbox 360s. American and British Xbox Live Gold members also had access to *Last.fm*, a music-streaming service.

Throughout much of 2009, the Xbox 360 was also the only console that offered Netflix. That changed in November, when the streaming movie service became accessible on the PS3 as well. However, in order to use it, potential viewers first had to order a Blu-ray disc directly from Netflix. This disc had to always be present in the console's Blu-ray drawer in order for Netflix to be used. But while PS3 owners needed this disc to use the service, it was freely available to them if they already had Netflix subscriptions. Netflix subscribers who owned Xbox 360s could only use the service if they purchased Xbox Live Gold memberships.

Netflix wasn't available for the Wii, but Wii owners living in Japan had their own service from which they could download videos. *Wii no Ma* launched on May 1 and provided family-oriented content that had been produced exclusively for Nintendo. The videos could also be downloaded to a DSi and stored on SD cards. Plans were made to bring the *Wii no Ma* service worldwide.[29]

In 1968, Margaret Woodbury Strong, a Rochester, New York-based collector of toys and dolls, founded a museum based around her huge collection. This eventually evolved into the *Strong Museum of Play*, a museum dedicated to the history, preservation and education of all types on toys.[30] In 2009, the museum expanded with the formation of the *International Center for the History of Electronic Games* (ICHEG), a subset of the museum that was devoted to electronic games, which included videogames, computer games, arcade games, handheld games, and pinball machines. For the first time, videogames were given a permanent place inside a major museum.

Despite having the least amount of downloadable features, the Wii was still the best-selling console, with more than 9.5 million sold in North America during the year. That was more than the total number of Xbox 360 and PS3 sales combined. But Wii sales had actually fallen 5.5% in North America during 2009, while they had risen for the Xbox 360 and PS3. PS3 sales actually rose 22% in North America from the previous year (although PS2 sales decreased by 28%).[31]

Although these numbers reflected the state of affairs in North America, worldwide numbers seemed to follow the same pattern. All in all, the total number of units sold actually decreased by about 1.5% from 2008. Sales, which included both hardware and software, fell by 7%. That wasn't totally unexpected, since 2008 had been the best year the industry ever had, but most people had expected for the growth to continue. However, there was optimism that this decline was just a temporary pause.

With *Call of Duty: Modern Warfare 2* becoming the fastest-selling game of all time in November, and with overall North American sales in December being the best that NPD had ever recorded, there was hope that 2010 would be better.

CHAPTER THIRTY-EIGHT
2010

Coming off the worst year that the videogame industry had endured in some time, there were high hopes and expectations that 2010 would be an improvement. However, some analysts expected the decline to continue. They appeared to be correct as January sales continued in the same downward spiral as the months that preceded it. Unfortunately, the trend was worse than some analysts had anticipated. Software sales in January totaled $597.9 million, 12% lower than from January 2009. Michael Pachter, an analyst with Wedbush Morgan, had only forecasted a 4% plunge. Console revenue was even lower. The $353.7 million in hardware sales constituted a 21% decrease from the year before.

Of the top ten games based on quantity sold in the United States in January, only three were brand-new titles that had been released during that month, and they were all for the Xbox 360.[1] The lone non-new Xbox 360 title that made the list was the record-breaking *Call of Duty: Modern Warfare 2*. And the PS3 version of that game was the only PS3 title that made the list altogether. The remaining five games were all for the Wii. Not one game for a portable system made January's Top Ten.

The Wii and DS continued to outsell the competition, although their sales numbers fell dramatically from the prior year. January sales for the Wii were down 31%, while the DS, in all of its combinations, suffered a 17% decrease. Xbox 360 sales were up 7.7% and sales for the PS3, which still trailed the Xbox 360, increased by 36%!

The worst-performing console was the PS2, which continued to sell after nearly ten years on the market. But only 41,700 of them had sold in the United States during January, a 59% decrease from January, 2009. Yet despite these numbers, SCE didn't indicate that it planned to discontinue producing or supporting the most successful console in the history of the industry.

Meanwhile, Microsoft had other plans for its original Xbox console. Although it had ceased production of the Xbox in late 2006, the company continued to support the machine. This was about to end. Microsoft announced in early March that it was discontinuing out-of-warranty service for the console. And any original console still under warranty that needed repairs would be upgraded to a reconditioned Xbox 360 Pro. But owners of original Xbox consoles that were in good condition were also about to receive the shaft. On April 15, Microsoft discontinued the ability to access Xbox Live through an original Xbox console. This also eliminated downloadable Xbox games that could be played on the Xbox 360. According to Larry Hryb, Microsoft's Director of Xbox Programming, this was done so Xbox Live could continue to "evolve and fully harness the power of the Xbox 360" without being constricted to the limitations of the Xbox. Ironically, a new Xbox Live feature debuted on March 24 that was an entry into gaming's past, not its future.

Microsoft's *Game Room* was a virtual retro-videogame arcade that was accessed through Xbox Live. Its front end could be freely downloaded from Xbox Live's Marketplace. After it was installed, it displayed a three-story arcade with four different rooms on each floor. Microsoft released two free downloadable Game Packs, each consisting of fifteen emulated Atari 2600, Intellivision and classic Atari and Konami arcade games. Once downloaded, the games appeared in arcade cabinets and were assigned to different rooms, such as the Konami or Intellivision room. Afterwards, the gamer could move the cabinets

Microsoft Game Room

to any room in the arcade. Each game could be demoed once for free. Afterwards, gamers had to pay 240 Microsoft Points ($3) per title for unlimited play.

Microsoft promised to release additional Game Packs weekly. However, by the end of the year, only eleven more Packs became available, with the final one coming out on December 22. Like the first two, all of the new Game Packs contained arcade and 2600 games from Atari, Intellivision games from Intellivision Productions Inc. and arcade games from Konami. The new sets also included Activision games for the Atari 2600.

Wii Netflix Streaming Disc

The Xbox Live Game Room was Microsoft's answer to Nintendo's Virtual Console. And on April 12, Wii owners gained accessibility to Netflix, which was already available for the Xbox 360 and PS3. Unfortunately, content accessed through the Wii's Netflix could not be viewed in high definition. And like its PS3 counterpart, the Wii version required a special disc to access the service. But this requirement ended on October 18, when the Netflix application became freely downloadable through the Wii Shop Channel. And on the following day, a downloadable version became available to PS3 owners through the PlayStation Network.

Wii and PS3 users didn't have to pay for anything other than a Netflix account in order to use the service because, unlike Microsoft, Nintendo and SCE didn't require their users to pay to use their networks. However, this changed for PS3 users on June 29, when SCEA launched a new premium service called *PlayStation Plus*. For $50 a year, PlayStation Plus offered subscribers features that were not available to non-paying users of the PlayStation Network, which continued unchanged. Such features included the ability for game demos and updates to automatically download to the PS3. Subscribers could also download free games that they could access as long as they maintained their PlayStation Plus subscriptions. They could also download games that they could try out for free for one hour, after which they could purchase them at a discount. American PlayStation Plus subscribers could also freely download *Qore,* a monthly, interactive online magazine that had been offered via a subscription basis since its introduction in June, 2008.

With Microsoft and SCE now offering fee-based areas on their respective online networks, Nintendo also looked into the viability of adding some kind of premium portion to its online service. However, by the end of 2010, Nintendo's online services remained completely free.

Cloud Gaming

The Internet was increasingly becoming a major component to gaming. It was essential for online gaming, where people could compete against or alongside players in other parts of the world. On March 2, NPD announced the results of a market-research study that it had initiated, entitled "Online Gaming 2010." According to the study, 54% of all gamers participated in online gaming, a slight decrease from 2009. However, while console gamers favored the Xbox 360 for online gaming and 48% of all Xbox 360 owners used it for that purpose, 85% of all online gamers used PCs.

But, of course, gamers didn't use the Internet strictly for online-play games. More and more were using it to purchase their gaming. During 2010, 28% of all game sales were completed through digital deliveries, an increase of 8% from 2009. However, since these totals included subscriptions, full games, add-on content, mobile apps and games played through social networks such as Facebook, it was difficult to gauge exactly how digital downloads competed with physical media purchases. Although NPD didn't count downloaded games as part of its monthly sales review, it did track their progress.[2] The number of apps downloaded to iPhones, iPads and Android-based smart phones far exceeded the number of games purchased on physical media. However, in terms of revenue, the physical games far exceeded the downloaded ones, which were usually offered for free or at very little cost and were totally devoid of any packaging or distribution charges.

Physical media still dominated the console gaming world. During 2010, 483 million games grossing over $21 billion were purchased for the Wii, Xbox 360 and PS3. In comparison, only 39 million games, costing $311 million, were downloaded to the same three consoles.

The numbers were different in the computer gaming world. During the first six months of the year, 11.2 million PC games were purchased through digital download channels, as opposed to the 8.2 million physical units that were purchased during the same period. PC owners also had more places they could download games from as opposed to console owners, who could only download their games from the networks provided by their consoles' manufacturers. Among the companies that offered digital downloads to PCs (and sometimes Macs) were Steam, Impulse, GOG.com and Direct2Drive.

Downloadable games were also offered for handhelds and smart phones, and while Apple had a profitable business with its iTunes, other companies weren't as fortunate. Nokia shut down its N-Gage service on October 31 due to the lack of consumer interest. Apparently, only die-hard gamers had embraced it. Although Nokia continued to offer games for its phones through its *Ovi Store*, which was its version of iTunes, games specifically designed for the N-Gage platform were discontinued.

One problem with downloadable games was the amount of time it took to download them. Depending upon the size of the game and speed of the Internet connection, some games could take a very long time before they were ready to be played. This problem was eliminated with *Cloud Gaming* or *Gaming on Demand*, in which the game resided on a server and compressed data was streamed to the player's PC or console as the game was being played.[3] Unlike downloadable games, streamed games could not be saved to a hard drive. Two companies offering cloud gaming emerged with completely different business plans. *Gaikai*, which had been co-founded by game industry veteran David Perry, took the approach of using its technology in the presentation of demos and trailers. A gamer could select a title from a company's website (or an online game review) and the game could then be played directly from the host site. At the end of the trial, the gamer could then elect to purchase the game from the host, while Gaikai received a portion of the revenue for its technology.[4]

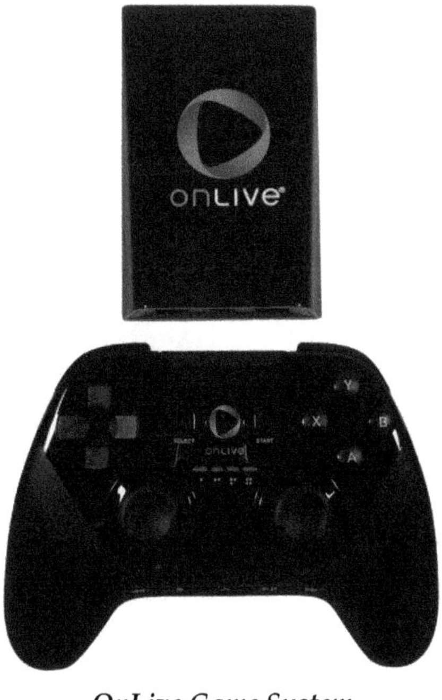

OnLive Game System

The other company that embraced cloud gaming was OnLive, which had been started by Steve Perlman, who had previously developed WebTV and Apple's QuickTime. OnLive, unlike Gaikai, used a business model that streamed complete games directly to the customer's PC or Mac.

The service launched on June 17, and people

who signed up for it were charged a $15-per-month subscription fee.[5] As subscribers, they could purchase games, which meant they could play them as long as they remained subscribers and OnLive remained in business. They could also "rent" a game for less than the purchase price, and this gave them access to that game for a few days. Subscribers could also try out any game that OnLive offered for free for 30 minutes, after which they had to either purchase or rent the game in order to access it.

Unlike Gaikai's service, OnLive required that users first download a 1MB file to their computers before it could be used. This meant that computers that had download restrictions set by their administrators couldn't access the games that OnLive offered. On the other hand, unlike Gaikai, OnLive wasn't restricted to just computers.

On December 2, OnLive released its $99 *OnLive Game System*, which consisted of a console, a controller and one free game valued at up to $50. The *OnLive Microconsole*, which was the size of a small, portable hard drive, connected to a high-def TV via an HDMI cable. However, the console could only connect to the Internet via a broadband hookup, which meant that an Ethernet cable was needed to connect the console to a router. Although broadband connections were faster, Wi-Fi connections were becoming more common. The OnLive Microconsole's controller was wireless and resembled an Xbox 360 controller with the addition of five media buttons on its front. These buttons were used to control streaming game trailers by allowing viewers to fast-forward, rewind or pause the trailer in the same manner that one could control a movie that was being viewed from a disc.

PlayStation Phone

Since the OnLive Game System was released at the end of the year, it wasn't possible to determine if a console that could only play games from the Internet was successful or not. The only other console that could only play downloaded games was SCE's handheld PSP Go, which had never been fully embraced by consumers. In order to boost sales, SCEE began selling the unit with ten free downloadable games beginning in June. SCEA offered three free games. Despite this promotion, neither division saw a major increase in PSP Go sales. In October, SCEA dropped the price of the PSP Go by $50 to $200, but that too failed to attract many more customers. At about that time, rumors began circulating that SCE was already showing off a new version of the PSP to its publishing partners. In addition, this new handheld, if it did indeed exist, would double as a smart phone, thanks to a partnership between SCE and its corporate cousin, Sony Ericsson, a manufacturer of mobile phones. On March 4, Sony Ericsson had announced that it was indeed coming out with a device code-named *PlayStation Phone*, but it didn't elaborate exactly what that would be.

Meanwhile, SCE continued to support its existing PSP. In Japan, PSP owners were given the ability to watch television shows from their PSPs. However, in order to do this, they also needed a PS3 and a peripheral called the *torne*, which was released in Japan on March 18. The ¥9,980 ($110) torne was a small DVR unit that connected to the PS3 via USB and was very similar to the PlayTV that had been released for the European PS3 in 2008. Like the PlayTV, the torne saved TV broadcasts, which could then be watched on a PSP that was connected to the PS3 via the Remote Play feature. However, in addition to this, the broadcasts could be saved to a memory stick, something that the PlayTV couldn't do. And once they were on a memory stick, they could be transferred directly to the

SCE torne

PSP, thus eliminating the Wi-Fi connection that was required with the PlayTV.

Since the torne was restricted to Japan, North American PSP owners couldn't watch TV broadcasts on their handheld units. However, on October 12, a PSP camera was finally released in North America. This was the PSP-450, the same camera that had been released in late 2009 in the rest of the world. The camera was bundled with *Invizimals,* which was also released in North America for the first time. It was also bundled with the PSP version of *EyePet* that came out on November 2.

Handhelds For Limited Users

While only rumors came from the Sony camp regarding a possible new handheld device, Panasonic, which had been out of the videogame business since the 3DO console had been laid to rest in 2003, revealed in October its plans to release a new handheld console in mid-2011. The *Jungle* would have a clam-shell design like the DS. When open, the upper portion of the clam would reveal a high-def screen, while a full QWERTY keyboard, along with a touchpad and two D-pads, would be found on the lower portion. The main focus of the Jungle would be online gaming.

Panasonic Jungle

Ironically, a new handheld that also featured a QWERTY keyboard was actually released in July. However, it had been designed for kids 3-8 years old. The *MobiGo* was the latest educational console from VTech. On the surface, the $60 unit resembled VTech's 2009 rerelease of the V.Smile Pocket, with a screen in the center surrounded by a D-pad on the left and an "Enter" button on the right. But that's where the similarity ended, as the MobiGo was not compatible with any of the V.Smile software. The MobiGo also had a touchscreen that did not need a stylus. And when the bottom of the screen was pressed down, it flipped forward to reveal the keyboard beneath it, similar to the way the PSP Go had its controls hidden beneath the screen.

VTech MobiGo

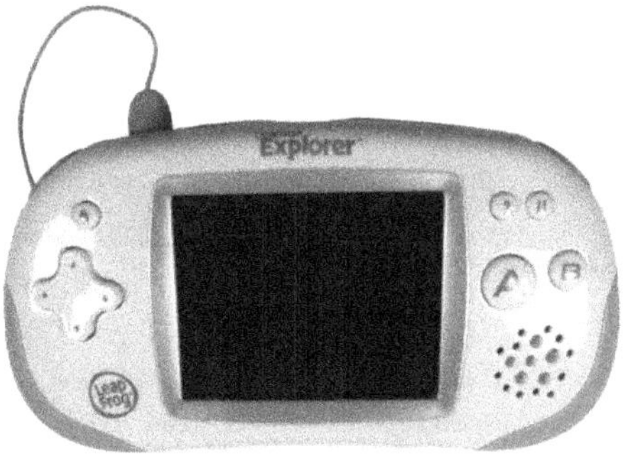

LeapFrog Leapster Explorer

Coincidentally, at about the same time that the MobiGo was released, LeapFrog introduced its latest handhold console for kids 4-9 years old. Although it looked pretty much like the Leapster 2 that it followed, the $70 *Leapster Explorer* was not compatible with the software from the previous Leapster models, although it could play cartridges designed for the Didj. Software could be added to the device in two ways. One was by purchasing cartridges, which cost approximately $25 each. And the other was by downloading applications, called *Leaplets,* to a home computer and then transferring them to the Leapster Explorer through a supplied USB cable. Leaplets cost between $7.50 and $15 each, and in addition to educational games, they included e-books and videos. Beginning in October, kids who owned Leapster Explorers were given the opportunity to make their own videos. At that time, LeapFrog released a $25 camera that could be used to take photos and videos, which could then be edited on the device and uploaded to LeapFrog's website, from where they could be shared.

Like the Didj, the Leapster Explorer utilized an ARM9 processor and a Linux operating system. While that meant nothing to the kids who used the system, hackers recognized it as an inexpensive console that they could easily write software for. The low cost was even more apparent on August 16, when Game Park Holdings released its latest open-source handheld console. The new *Caanoo* also utilized an ARM9 processor with a Linux operating system, but it cost $150 and it wasn't as easily available as the Leapster Explorer.

Game Park Holdings Caanoo

The Caanoo was the successor to Game Park Holdings' GP2X Wiz, which had been released only one year earlier. The new console featured a larger screen,[6] a tilt sensor, vibration feedback and an analog stick. The Caanoo also had the ability to play networked games with the addition of an optional Wi-Fi USB dongle that Game Park Holdings offered in October.[7]

The three new handheld consoles that were released during the year, the MobiGo, Leapster Explorer and Caanoo, were all targeted towards specific audiences. However, most people wanting non-phone handheld consoles continued to purchase a member of Nintendo's DS family. By March 31, the end of Nintendo's fiscal year, the company had sold 128.9 million units to date, making the DS the top-selling handheld console of all time. Included in that number was the $190 *DSi XL*, the American version of the DSi LL, which Nintendo of America had released two days earlier, and which had been on European shelves for only three weeks.

On March 23, five days before Nintendo of America released the DSi XL, Nintendo of Japan announced a new handheld console that would succeed the DS brand. The announcement simply stated that Nintendo would launch the *3DS* during the fiscal year ending in March, 2011 and that it would play three-dimensional games without the need of special glasses. More details would follow during E^3 in June.

As promised, the 3DS was unveiled at E^3 in June. It looked very similar to the DSi, with an additional camera lens on its shell, so it could take three-dimensional photos.[8] Above the D-pad was a *Slide Pad*, an analog stick that allowed 360-degree input. Internally, the 3DS had motion sensors and gyroscopes, although games that demonstrated their functions weren't shown.

To the right of the upper screen was a sliding tab that permitted users to adjust the degree of three-dimensional graphics displayed on the screen. At the lowest setting, games were displayed in 2D, just like on a DSi. At its highest setting, the 3D display was so real that *GamesRadar* compared looking at the screen with looking out a window. The gaming website called the 3DS "the most impressive piece of kit that [they've] seen in 20 years of gaming." Most reviewers agreed.

Nintendo of Japan waited until September 29 before it finally announced that the official Japanese release date of the 3DS would be February 26, 2011. Nothing was mentioned about when the new device would be available in the rest of the world.

The timing of Nintendo of Japan's surprise announcement introducing the 3DS may have jeopardized DSi XL's sales in North America, since many potential customers may have deemed it technologically inferior to the new console and decided to wait until the new one became available. On the other hand, the release of the DSi in late 2008 and early 2009 didn't dampen sales for the DS or DS Lite. In fact, it was during this time, at the height of the DS's popularity, that two new products were released that utilized the

DS's GBA cartridge port. On April 13, Valcon Games released *Easy Piano*, a title that had been available in Europe since December, 2009, in North America. *Easy Piano* was a music tutorial that allowed users to play popular songs such as *Material Girl*, simply by pressing the stylus against the appropriate piano keys on the screen. Or they could physically press keys on a real 13-key keyboard that plugged into the GBA cartridge port.

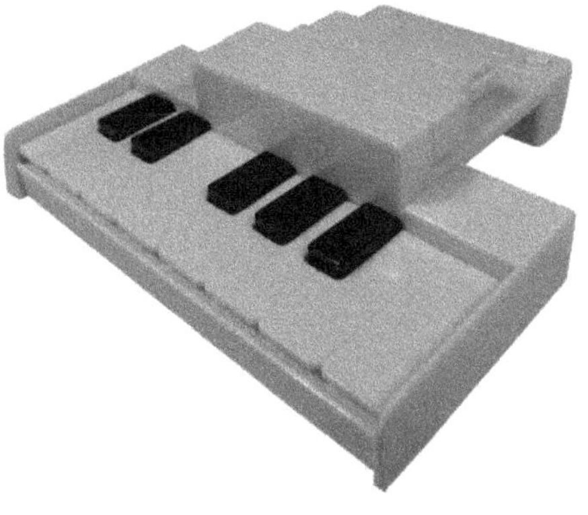

Valcon Games Easy Piano

Two weeks after the American release of *Easy Piano*, a 147-year-old pharmaceutical company decided to release a product that would turn the DS into a medical device. On April 26, Bayer, best-known for discovering aspirin, introduced the *Didget*, a glucose monitoring device that was targeted towards children with diabetes. And although it could be used as a stand-alone monitoring device, the $75 Didget was designed to work with the DS. The unit was packaged with a DS game called *Knock 'Em Downs: World's Fair*. Kids who monitored their glucose levels regularly would be awarded with points. The Didget could then be connected to the DS through the GBA cartridge slot and those points could then be used to unlock new game levels.

Bayer Didget

A different type of health monitor was released on November 16 Electronic Arts issued *EA Sports Active 2*, for all three major consoles.[9] This $100 program provided an on-screen, customizable personal trainer to guide the user in up to 70 (depending on the console) exercises. And unlike previous exercise programs, *EA Sports Active 2* monitored the user's progress and sent the information online where it could be tracked by the user, or shared with other people. The program was packaged with a heart rate monitor that wrapped around the player's arm to measure intensity. But the inclusion of the heart monitor was the only thing that the versions for the three consoles had in common. The PS3 and Wii versions also came with tracking monitors that were wrapped around the user's leg. And the PS3 edition came with a second tracking monitor that wrapper around the user's arm, a function that was accomplished by the Wii Remote in the Wii version.[10] Signals were received from these monitors by a receiver that looked like a flash drive, which plugged into the PS3 and Wii's USB port. The Xbox 360 version only came with the heart monitor and its information, along with the user's body movement, was monitored by the Kinect.

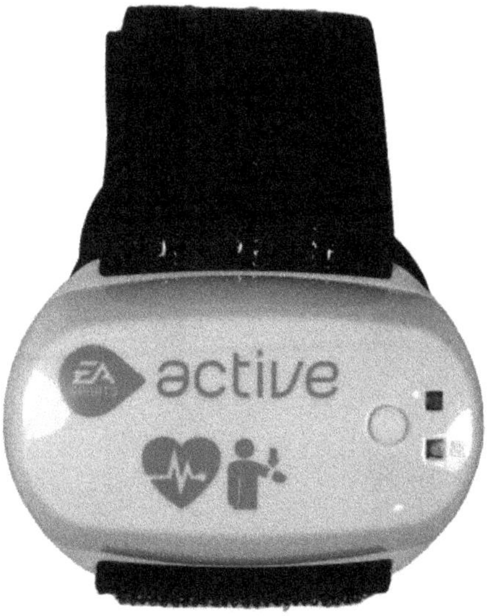

EA Sports Active Heart Monitor

2010

uDraw

One thing that differentiated Nintendo's handheld consoles from the Wii was the need of a stylus for input. By its very nature, the Wii had no use for a stylus, since the user couldn't very well draw on a television screen. But that changed in North America on November 14, when software publisher THQ released a peripheral that allowed players to nearly do that very thing. The $70 *uDraw Game Tablet* let players draw pictures with an attached stylus. The tablet was packaged with *uDraw Studio,* which provided editing tools and displayed the drawings on the screen. And while drawings couldn't be printed from the tablet, they could be saved to an SD card so print-outs could later be made from a computer. Unfortunately, there was no way to transfer the drawing from the SD card back to the tablet for editing.

THQ UDraw Game Tablet

The uDraw was wireless and communicated with the Wii through the Wii Remote, which sat in a compartment on the left side of the tablet.[11] The tablet was also a controller in its own right. Tilting the uDraw while playing specifically-designed uDraw games could alter the game play, thanks to built-in accelerometers that worked with the Wii Remote.

In addition to *uDraw Studio,* which was bundled with the uDraw, THQ only had two additional uDraw titles available at the time of the device's release. *Dood's Big Adventure* was a quest that consisted of 60 minigames in which drawing and coloring played a major role in getting the player to the end. *Pictionary*[12] was a video version of the board game, in which players drew their clues directly on the uDraw.

Despite having only two available titles, THQ sold 1.2 million uDraws in only six weeks. Since the company had initially anticipated sales of only one million units by March, 2011, it had to ramp up its production to meet a new projected demand of 1.7 million units by May, 2011.

Another specialty Wii controller was released by Majesco in North America on November 5 and in the rest of the world within the following month. *Babysitting Mama* was a simulation similar to *Baby and Me,* which had been released in Europe and Australia in 2009. The $50 bundle came with the game software and a plush baby doll that had a compartment in its back where the Wii Remote, with an attached Nunchuck, tucked into it. *Babysitting Mama* consisted of more than 40 minigames that represented mundane tasks such as feeding a baby or rocking it to sleep. The tasks were accomplished by correctly moving the doll or by using the Nunchuck properly as per the onscreen instructions. Although the game didn't sell in the same numbers that THQ had enjoyed with the uDraw, it, along with *Zumba Fitness,* did well enough to help Majesco recover

Majesco Babysitting Mama

from a $2.1 million loss that it suffered at the end of its fiscal year on October 31, due to a 20% decrease in revenue.

Other alternative controllers continued to be released. Two more fishing controllers were released for the Wii. One was bundled with *Kevin VanDam's Big Bass Challenge* from Zoo Games, which came out on November 23. The other arrived two months earlier on September 28. In addition to the rod controller for the Wii, Activision also released *Rapala Pro Bass Fishing* for the Xbox 360 and PS3.[13] The fishing rod controllers that were bundled with these two editions were, for the first time, wireless.

Kinecting the PS Move

The uDraw Game Tablet and *Babysitting Mama* doll controllers, like all alternative Wii controllers with the exception of the Tony Hawk skateboard controller, operated with a Wii Remote inside of them. However, these peripherals could not incorporate the extra sensitivity provided by the Wii MotionPlus since the expansion device added 1½ inches to the length of the Wii Remote, rendering it too long to fit inside the peripherals. Nintendo rectified this problem on October 28 when it released the *Wii Remote Plus* in Australia, with the rest of the world receiving it during the following two weeks. The Wii Remote Plus was a standard-sized Wii Remote with the components of the Wii MotionPlus built-into it. This opened the way for developers to design new alternative controllers that took advantage of the Wii MotionPlus feature.

By the time the Wii Remote Plus was released, the Wii was no longer the only console that used motion controllers. SCE released its new PlayStation motion controller first. At the Game Developers Conference on March 10, the name of the new controler was officially revealed to be the *PlayStation Move.* SCE also disclosed that an additional controller, similar to Nintendo's Nunchuck, would be available. This controller was originally called the PlayStation Move *sub-controller,* but in April, SCE announced that its official name would be the *PlayStation Move Navigation Controller.*

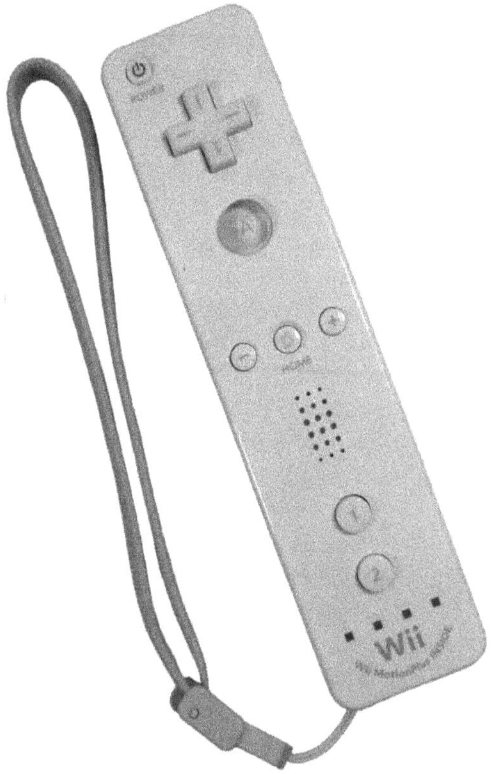

Nintendo Wii Remote Plus

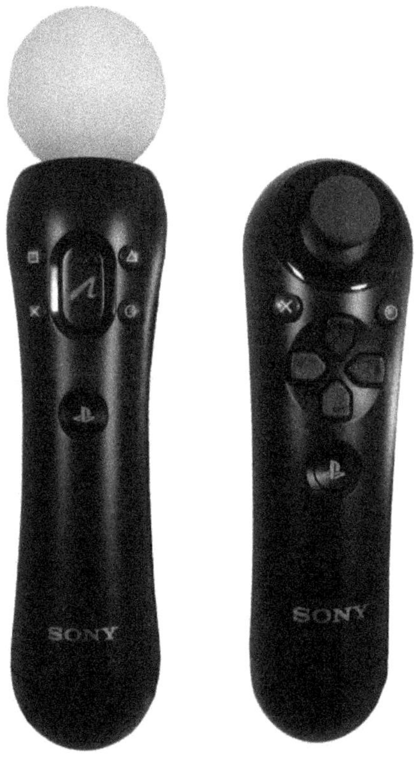

SCE PlayStation Move

SCE first released the PlayStation Move in continental Europe on September 15 and in Australia, Great Britain and North America during the following two days.[14] In the United States, the PlayStation Move retailed for $50, while the Navigation Controller sold for $30. Both required the already available $40 PlayStation Eye camera in order to work. SCE issued patches for several PS3 games, including *High Velocity Bowling*, so they would be compatible with the PlayStation Move. Other games, such as *EyePet*,[15] were rereleased to include Move functionality. Upon the Move's launch, SCE also released several games, including *Sports Champions*, SCE's answer to *Wii Sports*, which exclusively used the PlayStation Move controller. Curiously, none of the launch titles made use of the Navigation Controller.

The PlayStation Move was acclaimed by most reviewers in the industry. The only fault that many found was not in the hardware itself, but in the poor choice of games that were available with its launch. Still, the PlayStation Move sold very well. Over one million units were sold in North America, with 1.5 million in Europe during its first month.

Microsoft showed off its motion controller at E3, where it announced that the unit would not be called Project Natal. Instead, the official name of the device was the *Kinect* (a combination of "kinetic" and "connect"). But referring to the Kinect as a controller was a misnomer. The Wii Remote and PlayStation Move were controllers. Players had to hold them and they had to be detected by the system. With the Kinect, Microsoft eliminated the concept of a physical controller from the game play, as gamers didn't have to hold anything in their hands. In effect, their bodies were the controllers that the Xbox 360 detected.

Microsoft Kinect

The Kinect could actually distinguish between four different gamers and recognize up to twenty distinct joints for each of them. while ignoring anyone else who might get in the way. The device also accepted voice commands. And human interaction wasn't restricted only to games. Users could access the console's dashboard menus strictly by speaking the name of the menu that they wanted to access or by waving their hands. Although some applications, such as Netflix, weren't yet accessible through the Kinect, Microsoft expected all of them to be within a short time.

In order to connect the Kinect to the Xbox 360 console, a *Kinect Sensor Power Supply* was required. This consisted of two separate cables that joined together and plugged into the Kinect. The end of one of the cables plugged into a USB slot on the back of the console and the end of the other plugged into an electrical outlet to supply power to the Kinect. However, at E3, Microsoft introduced a new Xbox 360 console that included an auxiliary port for the Kinect to plug into. This port was not only used to exchange data between the Kinect and the console, but also supplied power to the Kinect from the console. The secondary cable that plugged into an electrical outlet was no longer required.

This new *Xbox 360 S* was released on June 19[16] and sold for $300. The unit was 18% lighter and 12% smaller than its predecessor, and included such features as a 250 GB hard drive,[17] built-in Wi-Fi and five USB ports. Microsoft also claimed that the new console had safeguards to better prevent it from overheating, which was believed to have caused the dreaded "red ring of death" on so many previous models. And just to be on the safe side, the company even removed the red LEDs from the power button altogether. If a failure did occur, it would be displayed in green.

Microsoft released the Kinect in North America on November 4 and in the rest of the world during the following two weeks. In North America, the Kinect retailed for $150, a price that many thought was high, especially when compared to the $50 that the PlayStation Move went for. However, as Microsoft pointed out, although the PlayStation Move only cost a third of the Kinect, gamers also had to purchase the navigation controller

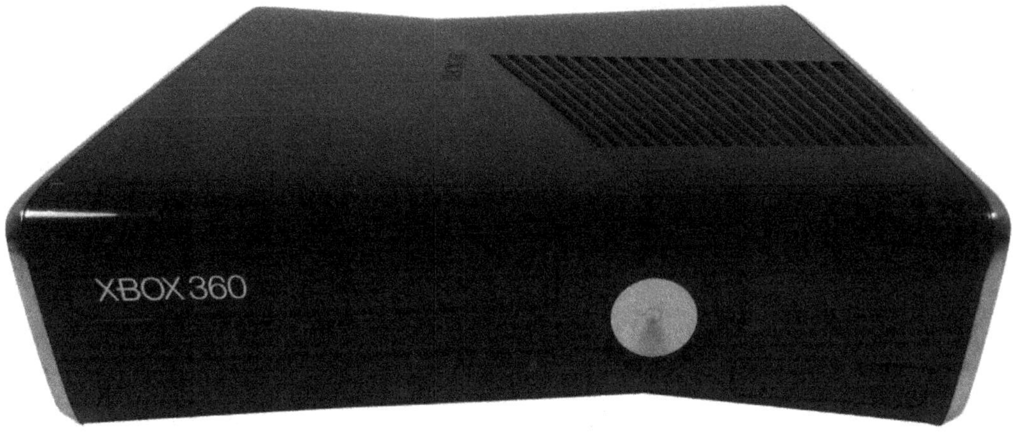

Microsoft Xbox 360 S

and the PlayStation Eye, which brought the final cost to $150. And while SCE offered bundles that made its motion controllers slightly less expensive, gamers still had to buy extra PlayStation Move and navigation controllers if they wanted additional players to participate. Kinect owners didn't have to buy anything extra to allow up to four players to partake.

By the end of the year, Microsoft sold more than seven million Kinects, earning the company a Guinness World Record for the "fastest selling consumer electronics device." During December, more than half of the Xbox 360 consoles sold were bundled with Kinects.

And bundled with every Kinect was *Kinect Adventures!*, a collection of five multiplayer adventure and sports minigames that demonstrated the Kinect's features. Many reviewers complained that while the minigames adequately demonstrated the capabilities of the Kinect, on the whole they were shallow. GamesRadar said that *Kinect Adventures!* wouldn't have succeeded if it had been sold at retail, "but as a day-one pack-in, it serves as an entertaining tutorial for your new toy." As a pack-in, the game benefited from the Kinect sales and wound up being the #7 game of the year in sales.[18] Ironically, the game that held the top position was *Wii Sports*, the game that was bundled with the Wii.

Microsoft Kinect Adventures!

Besides *Kinect Adventures!*, eleven other games were released on the Kinect's launch day. All were sold in purple cases that differentiated them from the non-Kinect Xbox 360 games that came in green cases. These included *Kinect Joy Ride*, a racing simulation, *Kinect Sports*, a collection of sports games, and *Kinectimals*, a virtual-animal game similar to SCE's *EyePet*.

Dance Games Take Off

Two of the Kinect launch titles were dancing games. One was from Konami, the company that had created the dancing genre with *Dance Dance Revolution*. In its new *Dance Evolution*,[19] dancers had to react to four kinds of prompts that appeared on the screen. "Steps" required the dancer to step in time. "Poses" were silhouettes that the dancer had to imitate. "Streams" were lines that traveled around the screen and which the dancer had to follow with her hands. Finally, "Ripples" were circles that appeared on the screen, and which the dancer had to stab. Ultimately, *Dance Evolution* came off simply as a Kinect

Konami Dance Evolution

version of *Dance Dance Revolution,* a game that, despite its name, was basically one of following cues, and in which actual dancing was basically just a byproduct.

Had *Dance Evolution* been the only dance-genre game that was released for the Kinect, it might have been received more favorably. Unfortunately for Konami, it came out the same day as *Dance Central,* which was the top-rated game (83%) of all the Kinect launch titles. In fact, according to *GameRankings.com,* a site that displayed a game's average rating as culled from dozens of reviews, *Dance Central* was the only Kinect launch title that even scored higher than 76%.

Dance Central, designed by Harmonix and distributed by MTV Games, was all about the dancing. Unlike Konami's game, where players had to react to on-screen prompts, here they had to follow the avatar's dance moves precisely in order to score points. The game had several degrees of difficulty, but they only differed in how forgiving the computer was for incorrect moves. And unlike Ubisoft's *Just Dance,* where each dancer had to hold a Wii Remote, dancers in *Dance Central* didn't have to hold anything.

Although *Dance Central* only allowed one dancer at a time, it also featured a competition mode that let two dancers alternatively compete for the highest score, but they had to take turns. The game came with 32 songs, and an additional nine could be downloaded from Xbox Live.

Ironically, Konami released a new version of *Dance Dance Revolution* for the Wii and PS3 on November 16.[20] Both games included features that permitted the use of their respective consoles' motion controllers, but neither game analyzed the dancer's body moves as did *Just Dance* or *Dance Central.* Instead, the modes that utilized the motion controllers used them in conjunction with a dance pad, not instead of. The screen displayed prompts that told the dancer when to wave the motion controllers. The Wii version also used the Wii Balance Board in some modes.

Sales for *Dance Dance Revolution* for either system weren't anywhere near those of the competing dance programs. MTV sold nearly 1.4 million copies of *Dance Central* in just nine weeks. Ubisoft's *Just Dance* had only sold 705,000 units in seven weeks during its first year in 2009. But the game took off in 2010, and Ubisoft sold an additional 4.5 million copies during the year,[21] making it the highest-selling third-party game for the Wii. This success naturally led to a sequel, and Ubisoft released *Just Dance 2* on October 12. This game was much better received by the press and earned a *GameRankings.com* rating of 77%, as opposed to the original, which had only scored a 48%. The game came with 47 songs, and an additional 25 could be downloaded from the Wii Shop. By the end of the year, with sales of 4.8 million copies, *Just Dance 2* outsold *Dance Central.*

SingStar

Just as Konami had started the dance genre with *Dance Dance Revolution,* it had also kick-started the karaoke genre with *Karaoke Revolution.* Nine home versions of that game were released in North America between 2003 and 2009 for the PS3, Xbox 360 and Wii. On September 5, Konami released a new karaoke game in North America. *Def Jam Rapstar* was basically a rap version of *Karaoke Revolution.*[22] Rappers were judged based on their lyrics, timing and pitch. And in the PS3 and Xbox 360 versions, performances could be recorded via the PlayStation Eye or Xbox Live Vision[23] and uploaded to the *Def Jam Rapstar* website, where others could see the performance and vote on them.[24] Reviews for the game varied, but the bottom line was that it would appeal strictly to fans of hip-hop and few others.

A second karaoke game exclusively for the PS3 came out in early November that combined elements of SCE's popular *SingStar* series with Ubisoft's *Just Dance*. Released only in North America and Europe, *SingStar Dance* was similar to *Just Dance*, in which one or two players followed the dance moves of the on-screen avatars by waving their PlayStation Move controllers. However, *SingStar Dance* was also part of SCE's popular *SingStar* karaoke series, and all 30 songs included on the disc could be used for either dancing or karaoke. However, this wasn't enough to redeem the title in reviewers' eyes, and the game only scored a *GameRankings.com* score of 65%.

A companion game to *SingStar Dance* scored slightly higher, ranking at 71%. SCEE released *SingStar Guitar* only in Europe on October 15. This was a karaoke game that was similar to all of the *SingStar* titles that had preceded it. But in addition to one or two singers belting out songs into microphones, the game added a feature that allowed one or two additional players to play a *Guitar Hero*-type game with the same songs. SCEE didn't supply guitar controllers, but nearly any guitar controller that was compatible with *Guitar Hero* or *Rock Band* would work.

SingStar Guitar was just one of the surprisingly several *Guitar Hero*-type games that were released during the year. The *Guitar Hero* series had reached its peak with 2007's *Guitar Hero III: Legends of Rock*, which sold nearly 14 million units. The following year's *Guitar Hero: World Tour* only sold 8 million units and sales for 2009's *Guitar Hero 5* didn't even hit 4 million. MTV's *Rock Band* franchise didn't do much better, as sales of each new *Rock Band* set were markedly lower than the one that preceded it. This downward trend continued with the June 8 release of *Green Day: Rock Band*,[25] a band-centric game similar to *The Beatles: Rock Band*. While Green Day fans rejoiced, everyone else apparently yawned at it. MTV sold only 63,000 copies of the game during June, the lowest sales performance of any *Rock Band* title.

Real Guitars

Activision released yet another incarnation of *Guitar Hero* on September 24 in Europe and four days later in North America. Realizing that sales were declining with every new release, Activision attempted to revitalize the genre by returning to *Guitar Hero*'s roots, as it tried to appease everyone and include every musical genre imaginable. To this end, *Guitar Hero: Warriors of Rock* focused on heavy metal and placed more emphasis on the guitar play, although it retained the drums and vocals.

The game received decent reviews, but sales were below expectations. Only 86,000 units were sold during its first week in North America, and the game earned less than $1 million by year's end. Although the game appealed to its core audience of heavy-metal rockers, it was no longer an innovative novelty that everyone had to own. To most people, it was just another *Guitar Hero*, which they had seen *ad nauseam*. After releasing four different console versions of *Guitar Hero* in 2009 for an increasingly disinterested audience, Activision only put out the one in 2010. Yet despite the poor performance by *DJ Hero* in 2009, the company still released a sequel to it on October 19. *DJ Hero 2* was available without a controller for $60 and bundled with the original *DJ Hero* turntable controller for $100, which was a much more reasonable price than the bundled *DJ Hero* had cost a year earlier.

Minor enhancements were made to the original game, which made *DJ Hero 2* more playable, and it earned more praise from reviewers. But despite the great reviews, the game failed to sell well. The combined gross sales of *Guitar Hero: Warriors of Rock* and *DJ Hero 2* were less than $1 million, which was much lower than the collective sales of *Guitar Hero 5* and *DJ Hero* in 2009.

On October 19, the same day that Activision released *DJ Hero 2*, Seven45 Studios

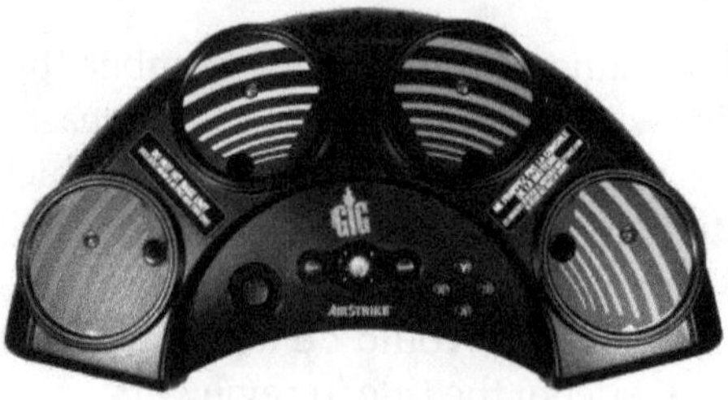

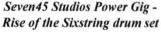

Seven45 Studios Power Gig - Rise of the Sixstring drum set

released its first (and only) videogame for the Xbox 360 and PS3. *Power Gig: Rise of the SixString* was built on the premise that titles like *Guitar Hero* and *Rock Band* were merely games packaged with toy guitars that didn't actually teach users how to play the instruments they were simulating. First Act, a manufacturer of musical instruments, decided to change that model and create a music/rhythm game that was bundled with an authentic guitar. In 2007, it set up Seven45 Studios to develop and publish videogames, and the result was *Power Gig.* The game was bundled with a real six-stringed guitar. The problem was that the strings weren't really used in the execution of the game. Like all other guitar controllers, the *Power Gig* guitar featured five colored bars on its fret area, and those were used to play along with the accompanying game. Occasionally, a "power chord" could be initiated that required the use of one string, whereas such chords actually require multiple strings on real guitars. And while the guitar could technically be used by people who wanted to learn how to play, at $180, it certainly wasn't worth buying in lieu of an actual guitar.

An accompanying drum kit dumbfounded critics even more than the guitar. It didn't look like a drum kit, and it detected hits very poorly. The website *Giant Bomb* named *Power Gig* the worst game of the year.

Even if Seven45 Studios had delivered and made *Power Gig* an excellent game with quality equipment, it still would have had a hard time competing with *Rock Band 3,* MTV's latest foray into the music/rhythm business.

Rock Band 3 was released on October 26, exactly one week after *Power Gig.* The game allowed for three-part vocal harmonies, which had previously only been available on the band-centric *Rock Band* sets. In April, peripheral-maker Mad Catz became the official manufacturer of *Rock Band* controllers, and the company introduced a new set of cymbals to complement the existing drum sets. A new 25-key (two-octave) keyboard controller was also introduced.[26] The *Rock Band 3 Wireless Keyboard* featured a handle on one side and could be used flat on a table or stand, or worn like a guitar. It was also MIDI-compatible,[27] which allowed it to be used as a real piano keyboard outside of *Rock Band* 3. Harmonix had to adapt its current catalog of songs to be compatible with the new vocal and keyboard features. However, by doing this, downloadable content was restricted only to *Rock Band 3,* as it contained features that were not compatible with the earlier versions.

MTV Rock Band 3

Mad Catz Rock Band 3 Piano Controller

Previously, in all versions of *Rock Band,* as in *Guitar Hero,* the guitar player had to press one of five colored fret buttons as each on-screen note scrolled down one of five color-corresponding columns. Knowledge of music notation was not necessary, since players didn't have to distinguish one musical note from another. Seven45 Studios had tried to improve on this with *Power Gig,* which featured a "real" guitar that had six strings, but it still used the same basic premise of five different colored fret buttons.

Rock Band 3 changed this with a new "Pro" mode, which brought into the game a new realm of reality. "Pro" mode was for people who wanted to play the actual notes in the song. Players in "Pro" mode could choose several levels ranging from "Easy" to "Difficult," which varied the number of notes that had to be hit during a given session. And there was also a "Training" level that actually taught people how to play musical instruments.

In order to play in "Pro" mode, only "Pro" instruments could be used. These included former *Rock Band* drum sets, as long as at least one of the new cymbals was attached, and the new keyboard controller. Although guitar controllers from previous *Rock Band* sets could be used in *Rock Band 3*'s "Basic" mode, they couldn't be used in "Pro" mode. Instead, Mad Catz introduced two new "Pro" guitar controllers that could be used.

Mad Catz launched the $150 Fender Mustang Pro guitar on *Rock Band 3*'s release day. Although it wasn't an actual guitar, it looked closer to the real thing than the plastic guitar controllers that had come before it. Instead of five or ten fret buttons, the Mustang Pro had 102, arranged in 17 rows (frets), each with six buttons (strings). And instead of a strum bar that had appeared on the previous guitar controllers, the Mustang Pro featured six real strings on its base for actual strumming. Rather than having notes traveling down five colored columns as in the "Basic" mode and earlier *Rock Band* games, the screens in "Pro Guitar" games had the numbers 1-17, which represented the 17 frets, scrolling down any of six columns, each representing a different string. This let players know exactly which fret buttons needed to be pressed and which strings needed to be strummed. And to make sure that people watched the screen instead of looking at the guitar, the screen also displayed the numbers of the fret buttons that they pressed, so they would be aware of their mistakes and learn from them. The Mustang Pro was backward-compatible, which allowed people to use it in "Basic" mode, or with early *Rock Band* games by merely using the top five frets, which were color-coded. And since the Mustang Pro was MIDI-compatible, it could also be used as an actual electric guitar outside of the game.

Mad Catz Rock Band 3 Fender Mustang

But even though Mad Catz' Fender Mustang Pro looked almost like the real guitar from Fender, it wasn't. On November 2, Harmonix announced that a new $280 guitar controller would be available on March 1, 2011, with preordering to begin on January 1, 2011. Then Best Buy announced on December 7 that it would begin taking preorders for the guitar on December 15, which it would sell exclusively through March, 2011. The *Squier Stratocaster* would be manufactured by Fender, the guitar company that had built the genuine guitar that the controller was modeled after. It would be a full-sized six-string guitar with 22 frets that would sense the player's fingers on the strings. The Squier Stratocaster would be capable of doubling as a controller in the "Pro Guitar" or "Pro Bass" modes, and as a real electric guitar outside of *Rock Band 3*.

The controllers manufactured by Mad Catz, as well as prior *Rock Band* controllers, were all console-specific. This meant that a specific Wii-compatible guitar controller could only be played with the Wii versions of *Rock Band*, and only a PS3-compatible guitar would play on the PS3 versions. This would not be the case with the Squier Stratocaster. Only

Mad Catz Rock Band Midi Adapter

one model would be available, and it would be able to be used with all three flavors of *Rock Band 3*.

In order for the Squier Stratocaster to be used with any of the *Rock Band 3* editions, an adapter would be needed. Mad Catz released a $40 *Rock Band MIDI Adapter* for each of the three consoles on December 26, well in advance of the forthcoming Squier Stratocaster guitar controller. The adapter also allowed for the use of authentic MIDI keyboards and cymbals in the Pro Mode of *Rock Band 3*, instead of the new controllers from Mad Catz. However, with the exception of the Squier Stratocaster, other MIDI-compatible guitars could not be used in *Rock Band 3*.

Everything about *Rock Band 3*, including the new peripherals and the track list, was praised by the critics. Griffen McElroy of *Joystiq* wrote that *Rock Band 3* was "the greatest rhythm game ever made." *Edge*, *Eurogamer* and *G4* all awarded it perfect scores in their reviews. And yet despite the acclaim, *Rock Band 3* was not a hit.

The Decline of Instrument Controllers

When *Guitar Hero: Warriors of Rock* was released in Great Britain at the end of September, it entered the charts at #6 and declined rapidly through the following weeks. Analysts believed that its poor showing was due to people waiting for *Rock Band 3*. By its fourth week it was at #27, right behind *Rock Band 3*, which had entered the charts at #26. It never went any higher.

It looked as if it was the end of the rhythm-game genre, or at least the instrument-based part of it, since the dance games were doing very well. After earning $1.8 billion in sales in 2008, which then dropped to $870 million in 2009, the instrument-based genre didn't even break $400 million in 2010. But although sales of its new games were in decline, Harmonix had found another way to produce income.

The ability to add additional music to *Rock Band* was beneficial not only to consumers who could build upon the tracks included with the games, but also to the companies that were involved in the production of the games. Game developers and publishers all received pieces of the money pie that was generated from the sale of downloadable songs. And while music rhythm-genre games were experiencing a downturn, sales of additional downloadable songs were higher than ever. Over 60 million songs had been downloaded just for the *Rock Band* franchise, as well as millions more for the games in the *Guitar Hero* series. But there were also costs involved in obtaining rights to the songs, and big-name artists could command high royalties for the inclusion of their songs.

On March 4, Harmonix set up the *Rock Band Network*, a service that allowed independent bands or individuals to produce their own songs that could then be purchased and downloaded by *Rock Band* users. This in turn fattened Harmonix's downloadable *Rock Band* catalog very inexpensively. Copyright holders of songs from the Rock Band Network only netted 30% of each song's selling price,[28] which could be priced from $1 to $3.

There were only a few requirements concerning who could add a song to the Rock Band Network. The content creator had to live in the United States and had to first purchase a $100 license to Microsoft's XNA Creator's Club. He also had to own a modified version of *Reaper*, which was an inexpensive digital audio editor that could run on both PC and MAC computers. Each song normally took 20-40 hours to convert into a format that *Rock Band* could recognize. Once the songs were ready and uploaded, other members of the

XNA Creator's Club reviewed them to make sure that they didn't violate any copyrights or contain profanity. Once songs were approved, they could immediately be purchased exclusively by Xbox 360 owners in the United States, Canada and Europe for a period of 30 days. After that time, selected tracks became available to PS3 and Wii owners in the same regions. The PS3 service began on April 22 and the Wii followed on September 7.[29]

Despite the revenue that Harmonix brought in from its downloadable content, the company lost $316 million during the year through September 30. On November 11, its parent company Viacom announced its intention to sell Harmonix, which it classified as a "discontinued business." On December 23, it was announced that Harmonix was sold to Harmonix-SBE Holdings, a holding company set up by investment firm Columbus Nova. Viacom had sold Harmonix for only *fifty* dollars, with Harmonix-SBE Holdings assuming a debt of $100 million. Viacom also received a $50 million tax write-off for unloading Harmonix.

Between January and October, revenue from music rhythm games totaled less than $250 million. That was way down from the same period two years earlier, when the returns had equaled $1.6 billion. But although the genre was indeed crumbling, it didn't signal an end to the videogame industry as a whole. At the end of the year, the top ten software titles had collectively sold an astounding 92 million units around the world. And of those ten games, half of them were carry-overs from the prior year, with *Wii Sports* leading the pack for the fourth year in a row. Strangely, only three publishers had games in the top ten, and six of these games were from Nintendo (with five of the titles being for the Wii and the sixth for the DS[30]). Microsoft occupied the seventh and eighth-placed slots with *Kinect Adventures!* and *Halo: Reach*, a prologue to the *Halo* trilogy. And Activision occupied two positions, fourth and fifth, with one title, *Call of Duty: Black Ops*.

Activision released *Call of Duty: Black Ops* on November 9 for all three consoles and the DS. It was Activision's first *Call of Duty* game since the record-breaking *Call of Duty: Modern Warfare 2* one year earlier. Within 24 hours of its release, *Call of Duty: Black Ops* broke the record set by its predecessor. It shattered another record four days later, when it earned $650 million in worldwide sales, a $100 million increase over *Call of Duty: Modern Warfare 2's* five-day sales.

Despite the success of *Call of Duty: Modern Warfare 2*, overall software sales were down for the year. In North America, they totaled $9.4 billion, a 6% decrease from the year before. North American console sales totaled $6.3 billion, 13% below 2009's total. Only sales for the Xbox 360 increased from the prior year. In fact, in December alone, Microsoft claimed that it had sold 1.9 million consoles, making it a record month for the Xbox 360.

The year 2010 marked a milestone for Nintendo of America as the company sold its 47 millionth DS during the year. That made the handheld console America's best-selling videogame system of all time.[31]

But the year 2010 also marked the second year in a row when overall sales were lower than the year before. This was the first time that this had occurred since the revitalization of the videogame industry in 1985.

That was one record that the industry could do without.

CHAPTER THIRTY-NINE
2011

The year 2011 began poorly, pretty much like the one it followed. In the United States, software sales for January totaled $576 million, a decline of 5% from the year before. Consoles did even worst as retail sales dropped 8% to $324 million.[1] Wii sales fell an astounding 31% from the prior year while the PS3 suffered a minor setback with a 4% decrease. The only console that improved over the previous January was the Xbox 360, which saw an increase of 14% with 381,000 units sold. This was the second month in a row that Microsoft saw its sales improve. By the end of 2011 the company had sold 7.7 million Xbox 360s, making it the top-selling videogame system in the United States, outselling its competitors every month except for June when the Wii outsold it by a paltry 3,000 units.

Although the PS3 never took the number one spot in the United States, the 2.6 million consoles that SCEA sold during the year only trailed the second-place Wii by approximately 100,000 units. But it was a different story worldwide. When 2011 came to an end the PS3 was the top-selling console of the year.[2]

PlayStation Network Goes Dark

SCE was able to achieve these sales figures even as it went through a crisis where its customers couldn't access the PlayStation Network for 24 days. Sometime between April 17 and April 19, the PlayStation Network was the target of an "external intrusion," resulting in the theft of the personal information of around 77 million accounts, making it the largest data security breach in history. Although no one claimed responsibility for the breach, SCE accused the group Anonymous, an international group of activists that were known to hack many high-profile websites. Although Anonymous denied having any role in the PlayStation Network breach, it did concede that it was possible that one or more of its many members could have been involved independently.

SCE shut down the PlayStation Network on April 20, in order "to verify the smooth and secure operation of [its] network services going forward." Unfortunately, gamers had no access to online games and music while the PlayStation Network was unavailable. Oddly, some PS3 games from Capcom couldn't even be played offline. This was because the copy protection that Capcom used required an active connection with the PlayStation Network even though the games themselves didn't.

Initially, SCE had no idea how long the network would be down. On April 26 the company announced that it would have the network back up within a week. However, the PlayStation Network didn't actually become fully operational again until May 14. After the PlayStation Network resumed service, SCE provided a free month to its PlayStation Plus service for all PlayStation Network members. Additionally, all PlayStation Network members were offered two free downloadable PS3 or PSP games from a list of four or five games that varied by region.

One PS3 game that had an online component that not been affected by the breach was *Portal 2*, a puzzle game from Valve that had been released on April 19. Just the fact that *Portal 2* was even available on the PS3 was something that hadn't been expected prior to 2010's E³. In 2007, Valve had released *The Orange Box*, a compilation of several of its games. Electronic Arts had developed a PS3 version but the result was riddled with bugs, which Valve president Gabe Newell publicly blamed on the console. So it was a surprise when Newell had used E³ to announce that *Portal 2* would be coming out on the PS3, which he called "the most open platform of all the current generation consoles."

In reality, Valve had an ulterior motive for working with the PS3. Valve ran *Steam*, an online service that was used to distribute games and updates from a variety of PC game publishers. Valve wanted to get Steam onto home consoles. Unfortunately, its console of choice, the Xbox 360, couldn't support Steam due to Xbox Live's rules governing how patches and new content could be delivered to the console.[3] When it was released, the PS3 version of *Portal 2* was the first console game that supported Steam. And since this was a network outside of the PlayStation Network, it hadn't been affected by the security breach.

World-wide sales for the PS3 dropped during the two months following the breach and the console lagged slightly behind the Wii. After the PS3 regained the number-one position in July, Jack Tretton, president and CEO of SCEA, made an unexpected announcement. During his August 11 keynote address at Gamescom, a trade-only videogame show similar to E³ that was held annually in Cologne, Germany,[4] Tretton revealed that the retail price for the PS3 would be decreased globally, effective at that moment. In North America this amounted to a $50 reduction as the 160GB model fell to $250 and the 320GB version was reduced to $300.

Accessories For The Senses

The PS3 price decrease occurred shortly before SCE offered a new set of headphones for the console. The *Wireless Stereo Headset*, which came out on September 6, marked the first time that SCE marketed a PS3-compatible headphone that sat over both ears, unlike 2008's Wireless Bluetooth Headset that hung over one ear. And unlike SCE's prior headset that could only receive chat information, the new headset received all game sounds, which were reproduced in simulated 7.1 surround sound.

SCE PS3 Wireless Stereo Headset

Although third-party over-the-head headsets were available for the PS3, they were generally expensive and very difficult to connect to the console. This was because the PS3 didn't have a standard jack that the headphones could simply plug into. The $100 *Wireless Stereo Headset* simply attached to the PS3 through a USB wireless adapter.

Ears weren't the only sense organs that were rewarded with a PS3 accessory. Eyes received a treat on November 13 when SCE released the *PlayStation 3D Display*, a 24-inch 1080p monitor that included an innovative new feature called *SimulView*.[5] Normally in multiplayer games, the display is split in two, with each of the two players having their own half of the screen. SimulView gave each of the players the entire screen to themselves. This could only happen when a game that supported the feature was played and when

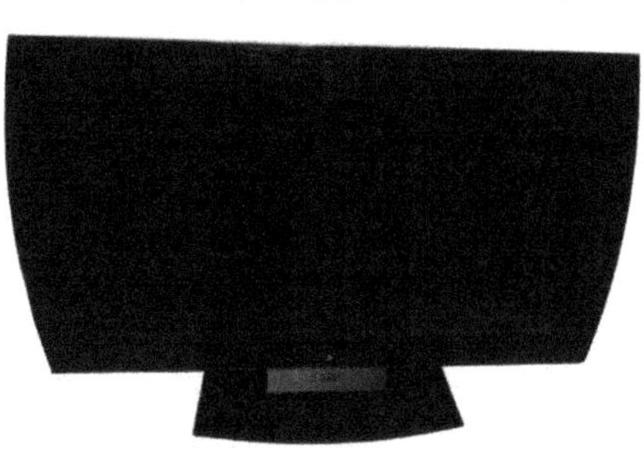

SCE PlayStation 3D Display

SCE PlayStation 3D Glasses

each player wore his own pair of 3D glasses.[6] Four such games were available when the PlayStation 3D Display launched, and one of them, *MotorStorm Apocalypse* was included in a $500 bundle that also included one set of 3D glasses.

PlayStation Vita

Meanwhile, SCE was gearing up to launch a new handheld device that it had officially announced on January 27. Code-named *Next Generation Portable* (*NGP*), the new device looked pretty much like the existing PSP. However, under the hood it featured an ARM Cortex-A9 processor that provided power comparable to the PS3. The NGP would be the successor to the PSP, and not merely the latest version of the latter. While the NGP would technically be backward-compatible to the PSP, it would only be able to play downloaded PSP games. Since the NGP would not include a UMD drive, PSP games that were available on UMDs naturally would have no way to be loaded into the new device. NGP software would also be available on memory cards similar to the media used by Nintendo for the DS. But like the PSP, the NGP would be able to connect to the PS3. Photos, music and videos stored on the PS3 would be available through the NGP. And gamers would even be able to use the NGP as a controller with a secondary screen on some PS3 games. However, this was a feature that would be determined by individual game developers and wouldn't be available for all of them. But SCE did issue a new PS3 operating system on November 30 which included the NGP in many of the PS3's functions including Remote Play, which would give NGP users the ability to remotely access their PS3 content. Remote Play was a feature that was already available to PSP users although very few games actually supported it.

SCE PlayStation Vita

SCEJ launched the NGP in Japan on December 17.[7] However, by that time it was no longer called by that name. SCE had revealed at E^3 on June 6 that the official name of the new handheld console would be the *PlayStation Vita* (or *PS Vita*).[8] And in September at the Tokyo Game Show, it was revealed that the handheld would be region-free.

The PS Vita featured two analog sticks, a 5-inch touchscreen, a touchpad on its rear side, a D-pad, left and right shoulder buttons, a front and rear camera, GPS technology, a motion sensor, a gyroscope and an accelerometer. Two versions of the PS Vita were released. One included both 3G and Wi-Fi capabilities and sold for ¥29,980 ($386). The other, a less-expensive model that only used Wi-Fi, was available for ¥24,980 ($322).

The PS Vita launched with 22 games. Twenty of them were available in both physical and digital forms while the remaining two, *AR Combat DigiQ: Tomodachi Sensha-tai* and *Toro's Friend Network* could only be downloaded from the PlayStation Network. The physical software that was distributed on SD-like cards retailed at an average of about ¥5,930 ($76) each. Downloaded games, on the other hand, had an average price of ¥4,690 ($60). Games that could be downloaded included those specifically designed for the PS Vita, along with PSP and PC Engine games. However, the downloaded games needed to be stored on memory cards and SCE used a proprietary card that was much more expensive than a standard SD card. Four memory cards were available ranging from a ¥2,200 ($28) 4GB model to a 32GB card that sold for ¥9,500 ($122).[9]

SCEJ had initially manufactured 500,000 units for the PS Vita's December 17 launch. However, in order to be sure that the system was readily available to people who hadn't preordered, the company built an additional 200,000 units. This turned out to be unnecessary. In all, SCEJ sold approximately 325,000 PS Vitas during its first week. But sales dropped an amazing 78% to only 71,500 units during its second week, which was also the week before Christmas.

PlayStation Certified Smart Phones

While the PS Vita was not a new version of the PSP, it also wasn't the revered PlayStation Phone that had been expected to appear in 2011. But even though SCE didn't release a PlayStation Phone, it did announce a new framework called *PlayStation Suite* that would provide PlayStation games to smart phones and tablets that used Google's Android operating system. The first app that would be available on *PlayStation Suite* would be an emulator for the original PlayStation. One clever feature built into the framework provided a virtual game pad that would appear on the screen if such a pad wasn't built into the hardware. And to make sure that the hardware manufacturers adhered to SCE's rules, the device had to be *PlayStation Certified* in order for the apps to be installed. One of the first devices to be PlayStation Certified had been the PS Vita, although it wasn't a smart phone and didn't have an Android operating system.

The first PlayStation Certified smart phone was formally introduced on February 13 at the Mobile World Congress 2011 in Barcelona, Spain. The *Xperia Play*, which was manufactured by SCE's corporate cousin, Sony Ericsson, was the closest device to the fabled PlayStation Phone that the world would see. When the phone was held vertically it looked like most other smart phones in the Xperia line and featured a large vertical touchscreen and four Android-function buttons below it. However, when the phone was held horizontally, the screen could be pushed forward to reveal a control panel beneath it, much like the PSP Go. The control panel included four directional buttons, a touchpad and the four PlayStation-specific buttons. The $199 Xperia Play was scheduled to arrive in the United States on May 26 exclusively through Verizon Wireless.[10]

Despite the similarities in appearance between the Xperia Play and the PSP Go, the two units were two totally different products. The Xperia Play was primarily a smart phone from Sony Ericsson that could play games downloaded from either the PlayStation Suite or the Android Market, while the PSP Go was an authentic member of SCE's PSP line that played games downloaded from the PlayStation Network's PlayStation Store. And while the Xperia Play was just beginning its production life, the PSP Go was coming to an end. SCE announced on April 19 that it would be discontinuing the PSP Go so that it could better concentrate on the forthcoming PS Vita. The company planned to continue supporting the device with firmware updates and repairs but no new units would be manufactured.

Sony Ericsson Xperia Play

Although SCE had claimed to drop the PSP Go in favor of the PS Vita, most people thought that the PSP Go was being discontinued because of poor sales. But in fairness, SCE never publicly revealed sales statistics for the PSP Go. Sales totals for all PSP models had always been lumped together. And the PSP Go apparently wasn't doing poorly in all regions. SCEA announced on April 21 that it would continue to manufacture and distribute the PSP Go in North America.

Although they lost the PSP Go, Europe and other PAL regions learned in mid-August that they would receive a new handheld console that wouldn't be available anywhere else. During its opening keynote address at Gamescom, SCE revealed the upcoming PSP-E1000, a €99 ($137), no-frills version of the PSP-3000, which SCEE released on October 26. This lower-priced model was absent several features found on the PSP-3000 including Wi-Fi, which eliminated gamers from playing multiplayer games over the Internet. Also missing was video output, a microphone and stereo speakers. And unlike the previous PSP models, the rechargeable battery was built-in and therefore could not be replaced by the user if it failed.[11] On the positive side, the new console featured an improved screen and a UMD drive that loaded games slightly faster than its predecessor.

SCEE PSP-E1000

3DS Features

SCE had revealed the existence of the PS Vita in late January for only one reason. For six months the gaming industry had been gearing up for the arrival of Nintendo's new handheld, the 3DS. By revealing its cards, SCE divulged that it also had a new console on 39 the horizon, which did not feature 3D graphics but was more powerful than what Nintendo was about to offer. And although the announcement of the PS Vita didn't alter Nintendo's handheld plans, it did directly affect the fate of another previously-announced console. On March 1, Panasonic cancelled its unreleased Jungle, citing "changes in the market."

Nintendo 3DS

Nintendo 3DS Charging Cradle

Still, the hype that preceded the 3DS made it one of the most anticipated consoles ever. In addition to the 3D graphics,[12] the 3DS had several new features that made it much more than an expensive DSi with extras. The unit featured a new analog stick called the "Circle Pad", which was positioned above the D-pad. Nintendo also introduced two new internal features that extended the unit's portability using Wi-Fi. However, in order to use these features, the 3DS had to be powered on at all times. But the 3DS constantly consumed some battery power even when it was in "Sleep" mode. Fortunately, Nintendo made it easier than ever for 3DS users to recharge their units. Included with every 3DS was a charging cradle that plugged into a wall outlet. The 3DS had to merely be placed on the cradle to recharge.

SpotPass allowed the 3DS to automatically connect to the Internet from nearby wireless LAN access points. *StreetPass* had the 3DS automatically search for and communicate with other nearby 3DS systems. In order to use SpotPass and StreetPass effectively, users had to walk around with their 3DS consoles. But Nintendo added another feature to the 3DS that rewarded them when they did. A built-in pedometer measured users' footsteps and rewarded them with *Play Coins,* a feature that Nintendo had successfully employed for the DSi when it bundled the Pokéwalker pedometer with *Pokémon HeartGold Version* and *Pokémon SoulSilver Version.* One Play Coin was earned for every 100 steps walked with a maximum of ten per day. The coins collected on the 3DS could be used to purchase content for some games.

The 3DS also had a pair of built-in augmented reality (AR) titles, games in which the screen displayed computer graphics over a real backdrop. One of them, *AR Games,* was a collection of minigames that spotlighted the AR capabilities of the system. While only three of the minigames could be initially played, clearing them unlocked additional games, which could then be purchased using up to three Play Coins.

The other AR game built-into the 3DS was *Face Raiders,* a first-person game where players had to shoot down a marauding group of enemies that were made up of actual faces taken with the 3DS cameras. And since the game took place in the "real world", people in the background were subject to have photos of their faces added to the invading pack. This game also highlighted the system's internal gyroscope as players targeted the invaders by moving their 3DS consoles in all directions. The system also had an internal accelerometer, however it wasn't used in any of the built-in games.[13]

The 3DS debuted on February 26 in Japan where it retailed for ¥25,000 ($306). Nearly all of the 400,000 units that had been allocated for the launch were sold out that day, although many stores had sold out their allotted consoles a month earlier when the 3DS became available for pre-ordering. Although there are no accurate numbers detailing how many of the Japanese units were ordered from outside Japan, the recipients of those units were shocked to learn about a change in Nintendo's handheld policies when the 3DS was released in their own countries.

Ever since the original Game Boy had been released in 1989, handheld game consoles, no matter where they were purchased, could accept software from anywhere in the world.[14] But the 3DS was the first handheld that was completely regional-locked across the board. 3DS software released in one region would not play on hardware from another region. This only applied to 3DS software, however. Any 3DS could still play all DS software from around the world with the exception of a few DSi-exclusive titles. Nintendo cited two reasons for doing this. One was so the software could have built-in parental controls that complied with game ratings that differed from region to region. The other was so Nintendo could supply system and content updates only to specific territories.

The 3DS launched in Europe on March 25 and two days later in North America, where it sold for $250, Nintendo's most expensive portable console ever. Nintendo of America held an official launch party at Best Buy's Union Square store in New York City. The hundreds of people who lined up outside the store were given 3D glasses, which they ceremoniously threw in the air at the stroke of midnight to symbolize the birth of 3D gaming without the need of glasses.

After its debut at E^3 in 2010, the 3DS had been one of the most eagerly awaited consoles. Reviewers had nothing but good things to say about it. And the hoopla paid off for Nintendo as the 3DS became Nintendo of America's fastest selling handheld upon its launch. The company sold over 400,000 units by the end of its first week, and similar results were enjoyed by Nintendo divisions around the world wherever the 3DS was released.

The 3DS Underperforms

But the love affair for the 3DS didn't last long. While the new handheld got off to a great start in Japan at the end of February, on March 11 a devastating earthquake and tsunami slowed domestic sales dramatically. Fortunately no Nintendo employees had been injured or killed and the company's Kyoto headquarters did not suffer any damage. But although North America and Europe didn't undergo any catastrophes, 3DS sales began tumbling in those regions within the second week of the console's availability. Michael Pachter, an analyst with Wedbush Morgan, said that in order to increase sales, Nintendo needed to lower the price of the 3DS or to release better games for it. Only three of the initial fifteen North American launch titles were from Nintendo itself and none of them featured any of Nintendo's core characters such Mario, Zelda or Pokémon. Reviewers complained that many of the launch titles were simple and not challenging for seasoned gamers while others simply didn't showcase the 3D-effect well enough. At $40 a game, consumers expected more. Apparently the media expected more as well and attacked the new system. *The Sun*, a British tabloid, reported in a number of articles that the 3DS hurt its users' eyes and Nintendo that had been been besieged with complaints. Nintendo naturally denied these allegations but too many of *The Sun*'s five million daily readers believed it and kept away from the device.

Only one launch title, Capcom's *Super Street Fighter IV 3D Edition,* received rave reviews for taking full advantage of the features that the 3DS offered, including online play, good-looking 3D graphics, use of the touchscreen, StreetPass and Play Coins. The game *wound up being the top-selling software for the 3DS during the week of its North American launch with nearly 71,000 copies sold. By that time the game had already been available in Japan for six weeks. Globally, the game sold nearly 218,000 units and was the second best-selling 3DS title. The top-selling game for the system, with nearly 300,000 units sold, was Nintendogs + cats.* However, this was a combined total for three separate games: *Nintendogs + cats: French Bulldog & New Friends, Nintendogs + cats: Golden Retriever & New Friends* and *Nintendogs + cats: Toy Poodle & New Friends.*[15]

By this time, the four top-selling 3DS games[16] collectively sold only a total of 756,325 units worldwide. In comparison, the top-selling DS games, *Pokémon Black* and *Pokémon White Version,* together had sold over 4 million units during their initial six weeks, and that was only in Japan. On March 6, three weeks before the launch of the 3DS, these games were released for the DSi in North America where they jointly sold 1.08 million copies, a new launch-day record for Nintendo. But while these games could play on the 3DS, that wasn't a sufficient enough reason for people to run out and purchase a 3DS when a DSi cost $100 less. And the fact that these highly-awaited games came out two weeks before the 3DS didn't help 3DS sales either.

Following the 3DS's launch, twelve games were released for it in North America between April 10 and June 14 by third-party publishers. None of them did very well. But the 3DS's lack of must-have software wasn't the only problem that plagued the console. Some of the features that had been announced for the console simply were not ready in time for its launch. The Nintendo eShop, an online store, wouldn't be ready until May, and until it was available, many of the promised features such as an Internet browser, Netflix, unique games, trailers and demos, and the 3DS Virtual Console with its selection of Game Boy, Game Boy Color, TurboGrafx-16 and Game Gear titles, could not be downloaded to the 3DS. In early May, Nintendo pushed back the date of the arrival of the Nintendo eShop and 3DS Internet browser again, this time to June 6 in North America and June 7 in the PAL regions and Japan. But the long-awaited Netflix that was supposed to be accessible from the Nintendo eShop still wasn't available at that time.[17]

Then, during the last two weeks of June, Nintendo released its first 3DS game that featured some of its core characters. *The Legend of Zelda: Ocarina of Time 3D* became the top-selling game in each region on the day it was released. The game topped the million mark in sales within ten weeks of its launch, the first 3DS game to reach that plateau.

Despite *The Legend of Zelda: Ocarina of Time 3D* and the availability of the downloadable content, the 3DS still failed to sell in numbers that Nintendo had been accustomed to with all of its prior handheld consoles. On July 28, the company announced that it had operated at a ¥37,712 ($484) million loss during its April-June quarter. It also announced that Nintendo of America had only sold 830,000 3DS units during the three months that it had been available, an unbelievably low number for a Nintendo handheld device.

Nintendo found itself in a *Catch-22* predicament with the 3DS. One reason it wasn't selling well was because people weren't thrilled with its existing selection of games. But on the other hand, many publishers including Sega and Konami, postponed the release of games because of its low sales. Capcom terminated the release of its planned *Mega Man Legends* altogether.

The 3DS Turn-Around

In an attempt to turn sales around, Nintendo announced that it would lower the price of the 3DS beginning on August 12. In North America the price would drop from $250 to $170. In Japan the decrease would be even more drastic, with the unit falling to ¥15,000 ($196) from ¥25,000 ($327). Nintendo president Satoru Iwata admitted that while Nintendo regularly lowered prices on its consoles to increase sales, it never before had to make such a move for a system that was less than six months old.[18] And since Nintendo didn't want to disenchant its customers who had purchased the unit at the original price, it offered them 20 free downloads from the Nintendo eShop beginning on September 1. Ten of those games would be from a selection of NES titles that wouldn't be available to the general public until sometime in 2012, which would include *Super Mario Bros. and Donkey Kong Jr.* In addition, Nintendo also offered ten free downloadable GBA games to the early 3DS adoptees and these would be exclusive games that would never be available to the general public.

Between August 1 and August 11, the day before the new price went into effect, Nintendo of America sold 50,000 3DS consoles. The company then went on to sell 185,000 more units between August 12 and the end of that month. Similar sales increases occurred in other regions such as Japan and Europe. By the end of the year Nintendo had sold 13.25 million 3DS consoles around the world. This beat the 9 million DS consoles that Nintendo sold, and marked the first time that the DS had been outsold by another handheld console.

On November 3, Nintendo of Japan released a 3DS game that, if it had been a launch title, would have probably helped make the 3DS successful from its initial release. *Super Mario 3D Land,* which was released in North America on November 13 and in Europe five days later, was an updated version of *Super Mario Bros.* The game included two-dimensional side-scrolling from the earlier *Super Mario Bros.* games, as well as the three-dimensional open-world feature that had been introduced to the series with 1996's *Super Mario 64.* And by using the 3DS's autostereoscopic technology, depth perception was added, although it wasn't required to play the game. Nintendo also used the 3DS's autostereoscopic technology to make hidden objects easier to find when the feature was turned on. The game also used other fundtions of the 3DS including the gyroscope and the Street Pass to aid in the game.

During the week it was released, *Super Mario 3D Land* was the top-selling 3DS game, as well as the number-one handheld game. By the end of the year it was the #6 videogame in sales, with more than 4.5 million units sold.

Although SCE's PS Vita, which arrived in Japan in mid-December, was no match for the 3DS in sales, it had one feature that Nintendo designers had apparently liked even since SCE first revealed its new handheld in January. But at that time it was too late to make any design changes to the 3DS, which was already in production and awaiting its Japanese release only a month later. The feature was a second analog stick, which

Nintendo Expansion Slide Pro

was located to the right of the PS Vita's screen. The 3DS only had one analog stick, the circle pad, on its left side. And so, without releasing a new version of the 3DS, Nintendo's designers figured a way to add a second analog stick to the handheld console.

On December 10, one week before the Japanese launch of the PS Vita, Nintendo of Japan introduced the ¥1,500 ($19) *Expansion Slide Pad,* a new accessory that added a second circle pad along with two shoulder trigger buttons that complemented the already present shoulder buttons. These two new triggers and circle pad couldn't be employed by existing games, only in specific new games, including Capcom's *Monster Hunter Tri G,* with which the Expansion Slide Pad was bundled.

The Wii Downturn

Nintendo had no problems with the DS handing its lucrative top sales position over to the 3DS. But the DS wasn't the only Nintendo console that conceded first place in sales. For the first time since its release in 2006, the Wii wasn't the top-selling console of the year. Globally, the PS3 led with 14.6 million units sold while the Xbox 360 trailed slightly behind at 13.8 million. The Wii came in third with 11.5 million units.

The decline of the Wii was not so unexpected. Although it was the newest of the three consoles, it was the only one that did not output high-definition video. That was okay
39 when it had the lowest price and was the only kid on the block with a motion controller. But once the Kinect and PlayStation Move were introduced and released, the Wii's edge began to crumble.

On April 25, Nintendo announced that a high-def successor to the Wii was coming and that it would be shown at E^3 in June, even though it wouldn't actually be available until sometime in 2012. But before then, Nintendo lowered the price of the Wii on May 15. In the United States this amounted to a $50 decrease that brought the price of the console down to $150. And *Mario Kart* was bundled with the console along with a steering wheel peripheral.

The new console that Nintendo displayed at E^3 was called the *Wii U,* which Reggie Fils-Aimé, president of Nintendo of America, explained was a continuation of the wordplay that had started with the Wii. While "wii" stood for "we," a word that meant inclusive and social, the "U" signified "you".

Physically, the Wii U resembled a Wii that sat horizontally, rather than vertically. But while Nintendo confirmed that the console would feature hi-res video, the company was more interested in showcasing the console's controller, which looked like a large handheld device with a 6.2-inch touchscreen in its center. In fact, at ten inches wide and five inches from top to bottom, this controller was only slightly bigger than a Sega Game Gear.[19] And in addition to the screen, the device had two circle pads, a D-pad, four shoulder buttons, four control buttons, stereo speakers, a camera and a microphone. Internally it also had features found in the 3DS such as a gyroscope and an accelerometer. And it even had rumble functionality, which wasn't in the 3DS. But despite the controller's similarities to a portable handheld console, Nintendo stressed that it wasn't a handheld device at all. For one, it couldn't work independently. It had to be in range of the Wii U console in order to operate correctly.

But games could be played on the controller as if it was a handheld device. Or, a game

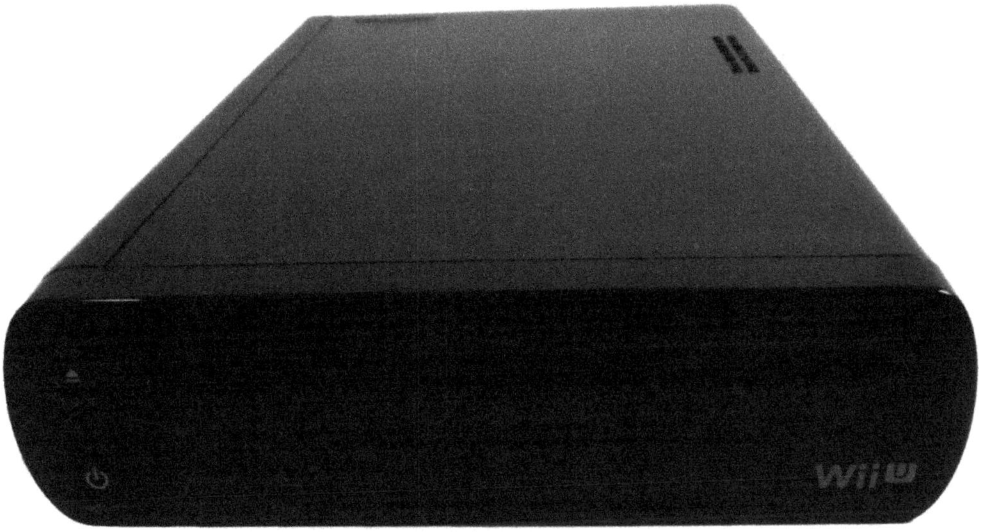

Nintendo Wii U

could be played first through a television, and then switched to the controller if someone else wanted to use the TV. Its screen could also be used as an accessory to what was on the screen, much like the 3DS with its two independent screens. Finally, the controller could be used strictly as a Wii Remote. For example, in a game where enemies flung boulders at the player, the player could move the controller around in the air like a shield to deflect the on-screen boulders.

The Wii U would be completely compatible with all Wii software and peripherals, such as the Wii Balance Board. And up to four Wii Remotes could be used with the Wii U. However, only one Wii U controller would be available for the console. But this still meant that up to five players could participate at one time.

On October 23, Nintendo released the *Wii Family Edition* in North America.[20] This was a bundle that included a Wii console, a Wii Remote Plus and Nunchuk, and two games, *Wii Sports* and *Wii Party*. The set retailed for the same $150 that the Wii had already been selling at. But the Wii console that came in the Wii Family Edition was not backward-compatible with the GameCube since it didn't have ports for the GameCube controller or memory cards. The console was also different cosmetically. Labels were applied to it sideways because the new Wii was meant to sit horizontally, while the original had stood vertically. The new Wii looked pretty much like the Wii U that was shown at E³.

Nintendo Wii Family Edition

THQ's Gamble

When the Wii U was introduced at E³, executives at THQ wondered about the implications it would have on their uDraw Game Tablet, which they had released for the Wii in 2010. After all, the Wii U controller somewhat resembled the uDraw, and with its touchscreen, it could theoretically perform the same functions. As it turned out, the Wii U would be the last of THQ's problems.

Despite the unexpected success of the uDraw, THQ only introduced four new titles for the device[21] and they were released during a span that ranged from April 12 to November 1. Despite the sales appeal of the uDraw, no other publisher supported it with software.

THQ uDraw (Xbox 360 & PS3)

Still, THQ hoped lightning would strike more than once. On November 15, just about one year to the day since the uDraw had launched, THQ introduced uDraws for the Xbox 360 and PS3. These $80 units differed from the previous Wii model in several ways. For one, they were black whereas the Wii model had been white. And they were controllers in themselves. Both featured a D-pad on the left and four console-specific buttons on the right. There were also reset and select buttons near the top, next to a storage area for the attached stylus. And since they didn't require that an existing controller be placed in them, the screen was centered, unlike the Wii model that had its screen to the right of where the Wii Remote sat.

THQ also released a new uDraw for the Wii. But the only difference between it and the original was that it was black instead of white. Like the Xbox 360 and PS3 models, the new Wii uDraw was packaged with *uDraw Studio: Instant Artist*, an updated version of the software that had been packaged with the original uDraw.

The magic that THQ had achieved with the original Wii uDraw wasn't replicated. Right from the start, the company realized that the new tablets weren't selling well. On December 7, less than a month after they were released, THQ announced lower-than-expected earnings for the quarter and the new uDraws were to blame. No reason for the lack of interest in the uDraws were given but it didn't help that only three software titles were available for the PS3 and Xbox 360 uDraws, the packed-in *uDraw Studio: Instant Artist*, *Pictionary: Ultimate Edition*, an updated version of the original Wii *uDraw Pictionary*, and one new game for all three systems, *Marvel Super Hero Squad: Comic Combat*. The five titles that had previously been released for the Wii uDraw never came out in PS3 or Xbox 360 uDraws editions.[22]

THQ estimated that it lost nearly $100 million due to the failure of the uDraw. Fourteen million units languished unsold in warehouses, while an additional million were sold at discounted prices. As a result, THQ reported a net loss of $56 million for the quarter. By December 12 the company laid off 30 members of its uDraw design team, which effectively discontinued the uDraw for good.[23]

Ironically, on December 6, one day before THQ reported its dismal earnings, Ubisoft released its $60 *Drawsome*! tablet only for the Wii. The white unit looked very similar to the original uDraw, complete with a compartment on the left side to hold the Wii Remote. The drawing surface itself was 8.5 inches wide, 2.5 inches wider than the one on the uDraw. And the stylus was not tethered to the tablet, although it actually communicated with the tablet wirelessly. The Drawsome! was packaged with *Drawsome! Artist*, which allowed users to draw pictures to display on the screen, and *Drawsome! Sketch*, which was the Drawsome! equivalent of the uDraw's *Dood's Big Adventure*. No other titles were available for it. Despite their similarities, software for the Drawsome! was not compatible with the uDraw.

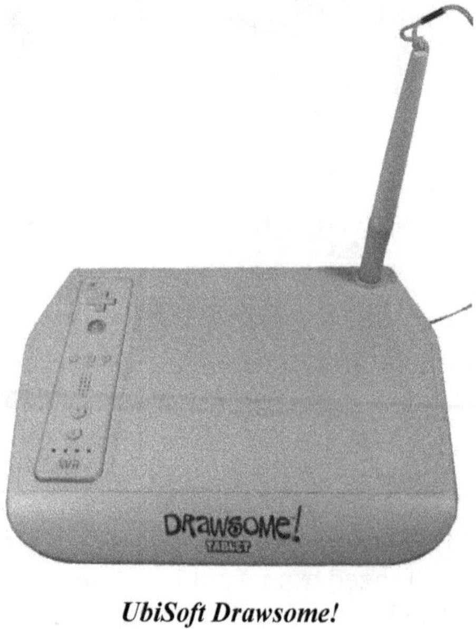

UbiSoft Drawsome!

Guitar Zeroes

THQ's uDraw wasn't the only peripheral that

went from riches to rags in the period of just one year. Microsoft and SCE had similar occurrences although the end-result wasn't as drastic. Both companies initially experienced higher than expected sales, only to see those sales plummet in less than a year. Microsoft had sold 8 million Kinects in the first 60 days following its November, 2010 release, a feat that had garnered it a Guinness world record. But during the eight months between March and November 2011, only 2 million additional Kinects were sold. The PlayStation Move had a similar sales history, although it wasn't as successful as the Kinect had been following its introduction. Despite this, the general consensus among developers was that motion controllers were not a fad and would be around for a long time.

But other peripherals and the games they were used for apparently were fads, and although they were around for several years and made a lot of money, they finally came to an end. Such was the fate of the music-rhythm games like *Guitar Hero* and *Rock Band*. At least one *Guitar Hero* title had been released each year since its introduction in 2005. The series' peak was the 2007 title *Guitar Hero III: Legends of Rock*, which in total sold nearly 15.6 million units. But the most recent title, 2010's *Guitar Hero: Warriors of Rock*, only sold 1.3 million units, the worst performance of any *Guitar Hero*-branded title.

On February 9, Activision announced that it was shutting down its *Guitar Hero* division. The company blamed the shutdown on the decline of the music-themed genre[24] along with the high cost for licensing the music and producing the games. The time and money spent to produce a *Guitar Hero* game wasn't worth Activision Blizzard's while, especially since it was already making a ton of money from its *Call of Duty* and *Warcraft* franchises.

Activision had planned a sequel to *Guitar Hero: Warriors of Rock*, but it was scrapped when the company decided exit from the music-genre business. Also scrapped was a title in development called *Sing Hero*, which was to be a karaoke-type game.

Ironically, Viacom disbanded MTV Games one week earlier, on February 2. MTV Games had been created for the sole purpose of distributing *Rock Band*. And since Viacom unloaded *Rock Band*'s developer, Harmonix, in late 2010, there was nothing for MTV Games to distribute. Harmonix, however, continued to support *Rock Band 3* by continuously adding new titles to the Rock Band Network. And as promised, the authentic $280 Fender *Rock Band 3* Squier Stratocaster guitar was officially released on March 1. But whether people were able to find one was a different matter. In the United States, the instrument was sold exclusively through Best Buy and everyone who had preordered the guitar from Best Buy beginning on December 15, received one. But finding one at the retail level after March 1 became pretty sketchy as not every Best Buy store even carried the guitar. The quest to get one outside of the United States, was even more difficult since they weren't even released until May. And at that point people had to search for independent stores that carried the guitar since few large stores, including Canadian Best Buys didn't stock it. And the window for people to find and purchase the Squier Stratocaster was very narrow. On June 9, Fender inconspicuously announced that they were no longer producing the guitar. The announcement was so discreet that Harmonix didn't even officially know this until June 20.

Fender Squier Stratocaster

Mad Catz continued to support *Rock Band 3* with its array of Pro controllers including the Mustang Pro guitar and the keyboard controller. But with MTV out of the picture, nobody was publishing the game any longer. Meanwhile, Mad Catz was looking beyond merely being a manufacturer of peripherals. On June 2, the company formed a game development branch called ThunderHawk Studios with the intention to develop multiplayer, online flight simulation games, which would naturally play better using the company's flight simulation controllers. The company's long-term goal, according to Mad Catz president, Darren Richardson, was to expand its participation in developing, publishing and distributing games. On July 8, Mad Catz signed an agreement with Microsoft, which made it a licensed publisher of Xbox 360 games and the company planned to release its first title, *War Wings: Hell Catz*, sometime in 2012. And while the game would be sold by itself, it would also be available bundled with a Mad Catz Pacific AV8R flight stick controller.[25]

But flight simulation controllers weren't the only peripherals that Mad Catz manufactured that could be bundled with software. The problem that Mad Catz encountered with its *Rock Band 3* peripherals was that the software was no longer being produced. Since Mad Catz was now an official licensee for the Xbox 360 it was able to negotiate with Harmonix and emerge as the new publisher and distributor for the Xbox 360 version of *Rock Band 3*, which became Mad Catz' first software title when it re-launched the game on November 23.

Mad Catz packaged the game in three separate bundles, each containing a guitar controller and five free downloadable tracks by the Red Hot Chili Peppers. A $70 bundle included a Fender Stratocaster guitar controller while an $80 package included a Fender Precision Bass guitar.[26] Finally, for people who wanted to learn how to play the guitar, the $150 package was bundled with the Fender Mustang Pro guitar controller.

By the time the $150 *Rock Band 3* package was released, it already had competition. This came in the form of Ubisoft's *Rocksmith*, a new music-rhythm title that was released for the Xbox 360 and PS3 in North America on October 18. Unlike the previous games in the genre, the main purpose of *Rocksmith* was to teach people how to play the guitar. To this end, the $80 software was compatible with most standard electric guitars, not specialty-made guitars like Fender's Squier Stratocaster for *Rock Band 3*. One end of a "Hercules" adapter that was packaged with the software connected to the output jack of the guitar, and the other end plugged into the USB port of the console. And for people who didn't own a guitar, a $200 package that included a real Gibson Epiphone Les Paul Junior guitar was available.

UbiSoft Rocksmith

The basic game play in *Rocksmith* was similar to the music-rhythm games that preceded it with notes traveling down a visual representation of the guitar's fretboard. While this play allowed the player to go on a *journey* from novice to professional through rehearsals and performances, the game also featured *guitarcades*, a number of mini-games that emphasized certain guitar playing concepts. These were presented in the form of classic videogames. For example, in *Super Ducks* players had to "shoot" on-screen ducks by plucking a corresponding string at the correct fret.

Activision Tops The Charts

In February, one reason that Activision had cited for the cancelation of the *Guitar Hero* series was because the payback that it received in the declining music rhythm market wasn't worth the time and money spent developing it, especially when Activision had other top-selling gaming franchises. *Call of Duty* was one such franchise. In 2010, *Call of Duty: Black Ops* had sold more than 19 million units, making it the top-selling title of the year. On November 8, Activision released the latest game in the series, *Call of Duty: Modern Warfare 3*, which became another monster hit for the company. In the United States and Great Britain alone the game sold 6.5 million copies and grossed $400 million during its first 24 hours, making it the biggest launch of all time for any type of entertainment product, breaking the record set by *Call of Duty: Black Ops* just one year earlier. On November 24 it grossed over $1 billion, which earned it the record of being the fastest entertainment product to gross $1 billion and breaking the January, 2010 record set by the movie *Avatar*, which took 17 days to top the $1 billion mark.

By year's end, *Call of Duty: Modern Warfare 3* had sold more than 23 million units in just eight weeks. By itself, the Xbox 360 version sold 12.5 million units, making it the top-selling game of the year globally.[27]

Skylanders

Activision wasn't only selling top-selling videogames. Between October 13 and October 16, Activision began releasing *Skylanders* toys in Australia, Europe and North America. When they were introduced at Toy Fair in February, CNN predicted that they would be among the "hottest toys for 2011.

The Skylanders were a series of over 30 character figurines that could be purchased for $8 apiece. The story behind these characters was they had originally existed in a videogame world called *Skylands*, where they kept the peace. However, an evil oppressor named Kaos tried to take over Skylands by turning the Skylanders into three-inch figurines and teleporting them outside the videogame into the real world. The object of the game was to get them back into the videogame to thwart Kaos and save Skylands.

Activision Skylanders - Spyro's Adventure

Skylands existed in a game called *Skylanders: Spyro's Adventure*, which was part of a $70 bundle that also included three Skylanders figurines and a *Portal of Power*, a device that communicated wirelessly with a Wii, PS3 or 3DS.[28]

The human player was assigned the role of a Portal Master, whose job was to return the earth-bound Skylanders back to Skylands and to accompany them on a journey to collect elements needed to save the world. This was done by placing a figurine atop the Portal of Power, which instantly transported that character into the game where it was controlled by the player. A special chip inside the figurine kept track of the figurine's stats and objects gathered along the journey. Two figurines could be inserted into a game at one time for two-player games, where the players could work combatively or cooperativly to save the world.

Skylanders: Spyro's Adventure took the *Pokémon* concept to a new level. Where *Pokémon* required players to "collect" virtual creatures in order to successfully complete the game, *Skylanders: Spyro's Adventure* required players to collect physical characters by purchasing additional figurines of varying skills in order to achieve the highest score. And to make

Activision Wappy Dog

this quest even more difficult, some figurines were available exclusively at certain stores such as Toys 'R' Us and Walmart.

On November 8 Activision took another virtual theme and combined it with a physical element. *Wappy Dog* was a physical version of pet simulation games such *Tamagotchi* and *Nintendogs*. The $50 package consisted of a game for the DS, and a robot toy puppy. As in previous virtual pet games, players had to feed, groom and take care of their pets through the DS software. The robot dog connected to the DS wirelessly and responded to the commands that were set through the console.

A Final Verdict

By the time the "M"-rated *Call of Duty: Modern Warfare 3* came out, there was no longer any question about who could purchase the game in the United States. In 2005, California, like many other states before it, passed laws prohibiting the sale of violent videogames to minors. In 2006, a lower court prevented the laws from takng effect. California appealed this ruling and on February 9, 2009, a U.S. Appeals Court sided against the state and ruled that the laws violated free speech. California quickly appealed the verdict all the
39 way to the U.S. Supreme Court, which looked at the evidence on November 2, 2010. It announced its decision on June 27, 2011. By a 7-2 vote, the Court called California's 2005 law an unconstitutional violation of free-speech rights. This case was finally settled in California, and a federal precedent had been set against any other state that dared to enact similar laws.

The one problem with any of the laws that banned minors from purchasing or renting violent videogames was how to enforce them. In most cases, the responsibility was placed on the retailer, who was supposed to check the purchaser's ID. But what would happen in the case where human intervention was not required? This scenario became a reality on April 28 when Redbox, a company that offered inexpensive DVD rentals through its thousands of kiosks that were set up in grocery and convenience stores nationwide, announced that it would add videogames rentals through its kiosks as well. This followed a successful test in selected markets that began in August, 2009. In the nearly two years that followed, Redbox rented more than one million games from 5,000 kiosks. Beginning on June 17, the addition of videogames became permanent and Redbox began supplying all of it's 21,000 kiosks with videogames for the three major consoles at $2-a-day rentals.

More Of The Same From AtGames

One console that the Redbox didn't offer software for was Atari's venerable 2600, especially since Atari Games had discontinued it twenty years earlier. But interest in the console and its games still persisted, especially after a copy of an obscure 2600 game from 1983 called *Air Raid* from an equally obscure company called Men-A-Vision made national news when it had sold for a staggering $31,600 through an online auction site on April 10, 2010. Suddenly, people were scouring their closets and attics in search for their old 2600 collections. What made this copy of *Air Raid* so expensive was that it came with a box, which collectors hadn't even known existed. *Air Raid* made the news again on October 22 when a loose copy of the game (no box), sold for $3,575.

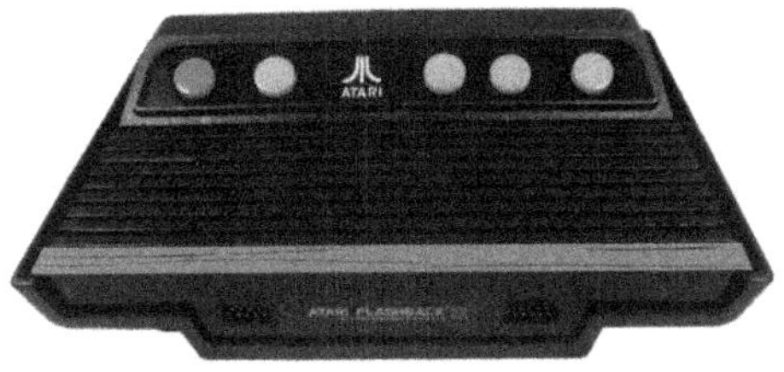

AtGames Flashback 3

In September, one month before the sale of the *Air Raid* cartridge, a new version of the standalone Atari Flashback was released. Unlike the prior Atari Flashback consoles, which had been manufactured by Atari, Inc., the $60 *Atari Flashback 3* was built under license from Atari by AtGames, the Taiwanese company that had released *en masse* inexpensive consoles with built-in Sega games. Externally, the Atari Flashback 3 resembled the Atari Flashback 2.[29] Internally, the 60 built-in games were emulated since the console did not feature Curt Vendel's customized chip. In addition, AtGames didn't include the ability to modify the console so a cartridge port could be added.

AtGames Arcade Blast

AtGames also released some more new systems that had built-in 16-bit Sega games. One was the *Arcade Blast*, a plug-and-play that hooked directly up to a television and looked like an old Genesis controller. The Arcade Blast featured 12 games that had already been included on several earlier AtGames consoles.

AtGames also reissued its Arcade Motion console that it had originally released in 2008. Like the originial, the *Arcade Motion Dual* looked liked Sonic's head and was packed with Wii-type motion controllers. In addition to the 15 games Sega 16-bit games and 25 generic games that had been built into the original, the Arcade Motion Dual featured an additional five Sega games that had already appeared on other AtGames consoles, and 50 generic games, bringing the grand total of games to 70. But the new console lacked an SD card slot that had been on the original, so additional games could not be added to the unit.

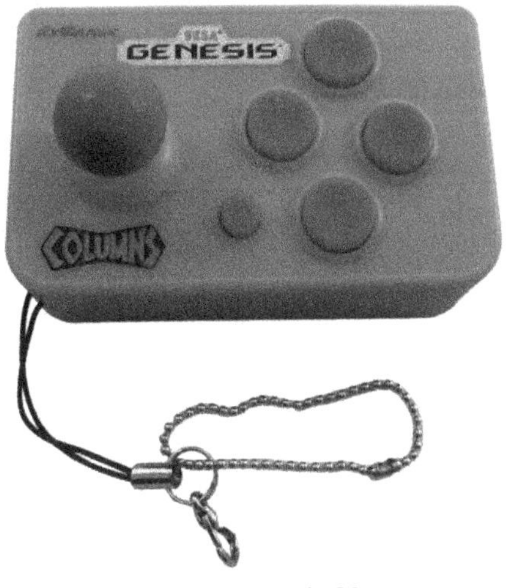

AtGames Arcade Nano

AtGames also released seven other plug-and-play units under the *Arcade Nano* series. Each device in this series was a different color and included five different built-in Genesis/Mega Drive games and five generic games. The units themselves looked like miniature versions of the Arcade Master, with dimensions that measured only 2.5 inches wide and 1.5 inches long. Each Arcade Nano console had four control buttons and a tiny joystick and was powered by only one AAA battery.

The AtGames systems only played retro games that were built-into them. Therefore, the oldest available system that played brand-new games was the PS2. The ten-year old console still had strong sales in Eastern Europe, Southeast Asia, the Middle East and South America. SCE announced on January 31 that it had sold a record 150 million PS2 consoles since it had been introduced in March, 2000,[30] making it the first console to achieve this milestone. A staggering 1.52 billion DVDs representing 10,828 titles had been released for the console during that time. By the end of the year, Nintendo also broke the 150 million sales barrier with its DS, which had debuted five years later than the PS2. But the DS number also included the different DS variations such as the DS Lite, DSi and DSi XL.

Despite these achievements, overall videogame sales for physical goods fell again during 2011. This marked the fifth straight year that Japan's sales totals were lower than the year before. In the United States, where sales dipped 8% to $17 billion, it marked the third straight year of sales declines. Two reasons blamed for this drop was the lack of new hardware, with the current consoles reaching the end of their life cycle and a rise in digital sales.

But the trend to move towards digital didn't only affect gaming sales. Print magazines were also suffering as more and more readers turned to the Internet to get their timely information. And less readers meant lower circulations, which in turn led to reduced ad revenue. One casualty of this was *GamePro* magazine, which had been in print since May, 1989. The magazine announced in its October issue that it was switching from a monthly schedule to a quarterly one beginning with the following issue. But that only hastened the end. *GamePro Quarterly*, as the new updated magazine was called, arrived on newsstands in early November. Unfortunately, on November 30, the magazine announced that as of December 5, the magazine would cease publishing. The website would also be shuttered that same day and would be incorporated into *PC World*'s site,[31] which was also owned by *GamePro*'s parent, IDG Communications.

GamePro - Final Issue

GamePro had been in print continuously for 22 years and 7 months, and had the second longest run of all general English-language videogame magazines. The only one that lasted longer was Great Britain's *C&VG*, which had been the world's first videogame magazine when it came out in November, 1981. It's print reign lasted 22 years and 11 months. But at the end of 2011, the longest videogame-related magazine was Future's company-specific *Nintendo Power*, which by that time was in print 23 years and 4 months.

But that was about to change as well.

CHAPTER FORTY
2012

The decline of gaming sales continued into the new year. In the United States, overall sales, which included consoles, software and accessories, fell 32% in January 2012 from January 2011's figures. This was much larger than the 15% drop that analysts from companies such as Wedbush Securities and Sterne Agee had predicted. Consoles suffered the worst decline. Although $200 million had been spent on consoles in January, this was 38% lower than the console sales in January 2011.

Globally, the best-selling console overall in January was the PS3, with 1.2 million units sold. In North America, the top-selling console was the Xbox 360. The 3DS earned the second-place position in the North American and worldwide charts.

The 3DS Rebounds

On February 20, just six days before the Japanese 3DS's first anniversary, Nintendo of Japan announced that it had sold five million 3DS consoles to date. This was the shortest amount of time that any console took to reach that milestone and it beat the previous record holder, the DS, by two months.

As if to commemorate this achievement, Nintendo released its Expansion Slide Pad outside of Japan. It was called the *Circle Pad Pro* when it was released in Europe on January 27 and in North America on February 7. These dates correlated with the release of Capcom's *Resident Evil: Revelations,* a game that utilized the second circle pad and additional trigger buttons. In Europe, the game was bundled with the Circle Pad Pro and was distributed by Capcom. Nintendo of America, however, chose to sell the $20 peripheral without the game. And in many cases, people who bought *Resident Evil: Revelations* couldn't even find the Circle Pad Pro, since the only store that carried it was GameStop, which had exclusive rights to sell it. But while GameStop was the only independent retailer that could sell the Circle Pad Pro through the Internet, it had to share online sales with Nintendo of America, which also offered it through its own online store.

Another new game that could use the Circle Pad Pro was Nintendo's *Kid Icarus: Uprising,* a sequel to *Kid Icarus,* a game that had originally been released for the Famicom Disc System in 1986. *Kid Icarus: Uprising,* which was supposed to be a 3DS launch title, was finally released in Japan on March 22, and a day later in North America and Europe. The game was sold with a few extras, such as six augmented reality cards that allowed 3D battles to take place. The game also came with a 3DS stand that the console could sit upon so the player didn't have to hold it for extended periods as he played.

Nintendo 3DS Stand

Kid Icarus: Uprising utilized the Circle Pad Pro only to add a second circle pad so "lefties" wouldn't have a disadvantage when competing with right-handed players. However, the Circle Pad Pro wasn't required for left-handed players, because they could also reconfigure the console's four control buttons on the right side of the unit to perform the same functions. Initially, the inclusion of a second circle pad may have seemed like a good idea to Nintendo's designers at a time when it was too late to incorporate it into the 3DS. But by the time Nintendo released the *Circle Pad Pro* outside

Nintendo 3DS XL

of Japan, a second circle pad no longer seemed so imperative. Only a dozen or so games actually used the second circle pad, and the prospect of the release of any more games that supported it didn't appear too promising.

The fate of the second circle pad was sealed when Nintendo released a new version of the 3DS on July 28. The *3DS XL*, which came out in Europe and Japan,[1] was an oversized version of the 3DS, just as the DSi XL[2] had been a larger version of the DSi. The new console featured screens that were 90% larger than those on the 3DS, but they retained their original resolution. Battery life was also slightly extended. The new 3DS XL only featured one single circle pad, just like the 3DS.

In order to keep the retail price of the 3DS XL affordable,[3] Nintendo eliminated some items that had been packaged with the 3DS. Instead of bundling the 3DS XL with the power adapter and charging cradle, Nintendo offered the adapter separately, or bundled with the charging cradle.[4]

Nintendo of America released the 3DS XL in North America on August 25 and decided to include the power adapter with the $200 unit, as it had done with the 3DS. A charging cradle for the 3DS XL was excluded, but Nintendo of America offered one for sale from its online store for $19.

Although interest in the second circle pad seemed to be on the wane, on November 15 Nintendo of Japan still went ahead and released an *Expansion Slide Pad LL* for the 3DS LL. This ¥1,500 ($19) unit worked for the 3DS LL in the same fashion that the original Expansion Slide Pad worked with the 3DS. The peripheral acted as a cradle that the handheld console sat in, and provided the second circle pad and two additional shoulder buttons to the 3DS LL.

Nintendo Network

On January 26, Nintendo of Japan launched a new online service called the *Nintendo Network*. This was Nintendo's attempt to create a total inclusive network that would be similar in scope to the PlayStation Network and Xbox Live. The network was controlled by Nintendo itself and warehoused on Nintendo's own servers and connected a variety of services, including the ability to download entire games. The Nintendo Network was completely different from the Nintendo Wi-Fi Connection, which according to Nintendo's president, Satoru Iwata, "had been created as a way for developers to experiment with their own network infrastructures and concepts." Nintendo, in fact, had little to do with the Nintendo Wi-Fi Connection, which was actually administered by GameSpy, who also owned the servers that housed the service.

Bundled PS Vitas

Sales for the 3DS continued to soar. Unfortunately, the same wasn't true for SCE's PS Vita. Since its Japanese debut in late December, 2011, its sales plummeted more and more with each passing week until they reached their lowest point during the week of February 13, when SCEJ sold only 12,309 units.[5]

It was amid this backdrop that SCE launched the PS Vita in North America. Although the official PS Vita launch date was set for February 22 in all territories outside of Japan, SCEA compiled "First Edition" bundles that were available on February 15, one week earlier. These bundles consisted of a limited-edition carrying case, a 4GB memory card and *Little Deviants*, a brand-new title that consisted of 30 mini-games that showcased many of the PS Vita's features. The $350 bundle that was available in the United States also included a PS Vita console that featured 3G and Wi-Fi, while a C$300 Canadian bundle came with a console that only had Wi-Fi capabilities.

Both console configurations were available on February 22 when the PS Vita was officially released globally. In the United States, the Wi-Fi-only model sold for $200, while the PS Vita that supported both Wi-Fi and 3G cost $50 more. The global launch began well and SCE announced at the end of February that it had sold 1.2 million PS Vitas worldwide. The company confirmed a month later that it had sold an additional 600,000 units, which brought its total up to 1.8 million, and made the PS Vita the second best-selling handheld (after the 3DS).

But for some unknown reason, sales suddenly dropped in half in April and the PS Vita never really recovered afterwards. In May, with only 172,000 units sold around the world, the PS Vita came in dead last among the handhelds. It came back to second place in June, but the difference in sales between it and the DS, which was the worst-selling handheld that month, was less than 22,000 units. By the end of the year, with more than 3.5 million units sold, the PS Vita came in third place among the four handhelds, outselling the eight-year-old DS by nearly 662,000 units. But unfortunately for SCE, it couldn't compete with SCE's own seven-year-old PSP, which outsold the PS Vita by over 545,000 units. In the end the PS Vita only captured 9.4% of all handheld sales.

The proportion was a bit different in the United States. While the PS Vita still came in third among the four handheld consoles, it commanded 16.9% of the market. However, this was at the expense of the PSP, which came in last place every month of the year.[6] But the PS Vita didn't come close to the 3DS's sales. SCEA had its best month in December, when it sold nearly 250,000 PS Vitas, but it still trailed far behind the 1.2 million 3DSs that Nintendo of America had sold.

2012

SCE had hoped to remedy that. On June 4, it announced several "cross-platform" methods to make the PS Vita more attractive to consumers, especially those who owned PS3 consoles. One such initiative was *Cross Buy*, in which PS3 versions of SCE games were packaged with codes that allowed consumers to download free copies of the PS Vita versions. The first game to offer this was *PlayStation All-Stars Battle Royale*, which was released on November 21.[7] Cross-Buy allowed consumers to purchase two versions of the game for the price of one.

SCE Cross-Buy

Once someone had both versions of *PlayStation All-Stars Battle Royale* available on his PS3 and PS Vita consoles, he could take advantage of other "Cross" features. One was *Cross-Play*, which allowed gamers to compete with one another among different gaming platforms. So while three gamers could battle each other in *PlayStation All-Stars Battle Royale* on the PS3, a fourth player could also be part of the game while playing it on the PS Vita.

Cross-Save allowed players to save games on their PS3s and then continue them at later times on the PS Vita. A game played on the PS Vita could be saved and resumed on the PS3 as well.

The final "Cross" initiative, the *Cross-Controller*, was first featured in *LittleBigPlanet 2*, even though that game had been available since January, 2011, a year and a half before SCE even had announced the "Cross" features. This was accomplished through a downloadable upgrade that SCE issued on December 19.[8]

Cross-Controller basically turned the PS Vita into an additional PS3 controller. This offered new gaming experiences on the PS3, because the games that embraced the Cross-Controller could also incorporate the PS Vita's special features that weren't found on the standard controller, such as its touchscreen, touchpad and cameras. Other Cross-Controller purposes allowed the TV screen to show a major portion of the game while the PS Vita's screen displayed ancillary information, similar to what the 3DS achieved through its dual screens. But the Cross-Controller didn't just assign the role of PS3 controller to the PS Vita. It also permitted the PS Vita to act as a PS3 monitor through a wireless connection. This allowed the gamer to switch his game from a TV set to the PS Vita instantly, specifically when someone else wanted to use the television.

Xbox SmartGlass

Microsoft, which didn't have a handheld console that could serve as a second screen for the Xbox 360, came up with an alternative method of doing the very same thing. On October 26, the company released an Xbox 360 application called *Xbox SmartGlass,* which was compatible with all sorts of devices, including tablets and smartphones that employed iOS or Android operating systems. Once SmartGlass was loaded onto these devices, they could be used a secondary screens for games playing on the Xbox 360, in the same manner that SCE paired the PS Vita with the PS3. It also let the mobile device act as an additional controller for the Xbox 360.

But SmartGlass didn't just connect mobile devices with the Xbox 360. It also provided supplementary content to TV programs that were watched using the Xbox 360 console as a tuner. While a particular show might be viewed on the TV, a second screen on a mobile device could offer information about the show. SmartGlass would also bring Microsoft's *Internet Explorer* to the Xbox 360, which would allow people to surf the Internet on their TV sets. And so users could easily navigate the browser that was displayed on the screen, SmartGlass could also turn their mobile devices into computer mice.

Wii U GamePad

Microsoft released SmartGlass on October 26, nearly five months after first announcing

Nintendo Wii U GamePad

it at E³ in June. Many people quickly compared it to Airplay, Apple's method that enabled a player to start a game on his iPad or iPhone and then switch it over to his television through Apple TV. But comparisons to Nintendo's forthcoming system, the Wii U, were also inevitable, since one of the main features of the new console was the ability to seamlessly transfer games from the television to the *Wii U GamePad*, a handheld controller device that was to be packaged with the unit.

Looking much like THQ's original uDraw for the Wii, the Wii U GamePad had features that were found on standard Nintendo controllers, such as a D-pad, a set of control buttons and even a pair of circle pads. In fact, the Wii U GamePad contained additional features that were found on the 3DS, including a front-facing camera, stereo speakers, a gyroscope and an accelerometer. In the center of the unit was a 6.2" touchscreen that could be manipulated with fingers or an included stylus. In fact, the only thing that restricted the Wii U GamePad from qualifying as a handheld unit in its own right was the minor detail that it could only be used in tandem with the Wii U console. This didn't mean that Wii U games were restricted to the main TV. Most games allowed gamers to play using either the television or the Wii U GamePad screen. But many games also used both screens, as the screen on the Wii U GamePad was used to supplement what was displayed on the television.

Nintendo released two configurations of the Wii U in North America on November 18.[9] The $300 "basic" set consisted of a white console with 8GB of internal flash storage and a white Wii U GamePad. A $350 "premium" set included a black console with 32GB of internal flash storage,[10] a black Wii U GamePad, the charging cradle that hadn't been included with the 3DS XL, a stand similar to the one for the 3DS that was packaged with *Kid Icarus: Uprising* (which the Wii U GamePad could sit upon), Wii sensor bars and *Nintendo Land*, a collection of mini-games that highlighted the features of the Wii U and the Wii U GamePad. Oddly, the Japanese premium set included neither the Wii sensor bars nor *Nintendo Land* or any other software. Instead, those who purchased the Japanese premium set were promised access to a beta edition of *Dragon Quest X*[11] when it became available.[12]

The Wii U GamePad was not the only controller that was available for the Wii U, although it was the only one that was packaged with the console. Wii Remotes could also be used with the console, but they had to be purchased separately. Nintendo also released a $50 *Wii U Pro Controller,* a wireless controller that looked very much like the Wii Classic Controller Pro, which Nintendo had originally released so Virtual Console games could be played on the Wii.

Nintendo Wii U Pro Controller

The Wii U Pro Controller, which could last up to eight hours on a single charge,[13] featured all of the same buttons as the Wii U GamePad, including the two circle pads, the D-pad and the usual set of control buttons and shoulder buttons. Conspicuously missing was the screen in the center, so naturally Wii U games that required the screen couldn't be played with the Wii U Pro Controller. On the other hand, original Wii games, which could be played on the Wii U, couldn't be used with the Wii U Pro Controller. This even applied to Wii games that could be used with the Wii Classic Controller Pro.

A different type of 'controller' was also released with the Wii U's launch. The $30 *Wii U Microphone* was a Nintendo-branded dynamic microphone that could be used with any Wii U game that supported microphones. Nintendo even had its own such game

Nintendo Wii U Microphone

available for the launch. *Sing Party* was a karaoke-type party game where one person assumed the role of the performer. The performer used the Wii U GamePad in one hand to view song lyrics, which allowed him to walk among the other players without having to keep looking at the TV screen. In his other hand he held the Wii U Microphone, which he sang into. Meanwhile, the other players watched the screen, which also displayed the lyrics that they could sing along to, as they mimicked the dance moves of the on-screen dancer. The only problem with this setup was that the Wii U Microphone plugged into the Wii U's USB port, so the performer was able to stray from the console only as far as the length of the cord.

The Wii U Microphone was released as a stand-alone product for only one reason. *Sing Party* itself was bundled with the microphone, and since the game only supported one microphone at a time, there wasn't any reason that owners of the game need to go out and purchase another microphone. As it turned out, the only reason Nintendo offered the microphone separately was so people who purchased a downloadable copy of the game would be able to get one.[14]

Nintendo of America sold out of its initial allotment of 400,000 Wii U consoles during its first week of availability. By the end of the year over 933,000 units had been sold. Unfortunately, this number wasn't extraordinary at all, especially for a new console from Nintendo. The company sold almost 954,000 original Wiis during November and December, which included the two weeks before the Wii U was released. But SCEA sold over 1.4 million PS3 consoles during the same time period and Microsoft blew both companies away by clearing 3.3 million Xbox 360 consoles.

The Wii U did slightly better outside of North America. During December, which was basically the only month that the console was really available, Nintendo sold 1.26 million systems. Only the PS3, with 2.85 million units sold, did better. Outside of North America, the Wii U outsold the Xbox 360 by 20,000 units and the original Wii by 500,000 units.

Wii Mini

Despite the introduction of the Wii U, which was backward-compatible with the Wii, Nintendo was by no means phasing out the original Wii console. In fact, on December 7, it unexpectedly released a redesigned model of the console exclusively in Canada. The black-with-red-trim *Wii Mini* was a bare-bones version of the Wii. It came packaged with one red Wii Remote Plus, a red Nunchuck controller and a sensor bar. It didn't include a game. This was one step that Nintendo took to keep the price of the Wii Mini at the C$100 mark.

Nintendo also kept the price low by removing the motorized assembly in the disc drive that automatically sucked in and spit out discs. A pop-up lid was added to the console, requiring that discs be inserted and removed manually, similar to Sega's 1993 redesigned Sega CD 2. But because of another price-reducing move, Canadians who owned the Wii Mini had to physically handle a lot more discs than their Wii-owning counterparts. This was because Wii Mini games could only be loaded from discs, albeit a selection of more than 1,400 Wii titles were available.[15]

The reason for this was because the console didn't support ethernet or Wi-Fi and therefore couldn't connect to the Internet. And although the console did have a USB

Nintendo Wii Mini

port that Nintendo's Wii LAN Adapter could plug into, the adapter couldn't work with the Wii Mini. Thus, WiiWare and Virtual Console games could not be played, since they could not be downloaded. And original Wii games that had been downloaded and saved onto SD cards couldn't be played either, because the Wii Mini lacked an SD card slot. But games weren't the only type of software that owners of the Canadian console missed out on. Streaming services such as Netflix were also unavailable on the Wii Mini.[16]

Nintendo felt that there was justification for removing the online capabilities from the Wii Mini. According to Matt Ryan, the communications manager of Nintendo of Canada, the Wii Mini was directed towards "gamers who have not bought a Wii yet, and gamers who have a Wii and want a second one for the cottage, or the chalet, or whatever, who actually don't need the online functionality." One reason why Canada may have been designated to sell the console was that its Internet standards were among the lowest of any OECD[17] country, which resulted in higher costs and slower speeds. Online games were more expensive to play in Canada than in other industrialized countries. Whether the Wii Mini would be available elsewhere besides Canada was a mystery, since Nintendo was mum on the matter.[18]

PS3 Super Slim

The removal of the disc drive-door wasn't exclusive to the Wii. The PS3 suffered the same fate when SCEA released its third reconfiguration of the console on September 25. Like the Wii Mini, the *PS3 Super Slim*[19] required that discs be inserted and removed manually. Since the dimensions of the Wii Mini were only slightly larger than a disc itself, it featured a lid that had to be manually opened and closed. The PS3 Super Slim, on the other hand, was 11.4 inches wide (which made it 20% smaller than its predecessor, the PS3 Slim). The disc drive was located on the right side of the console and was protected

SCE PS3 Super Slim

by a cover that slid horizontally.

Another Leap Forward

The Wii U wasn't the only new console that was released during 2012 that was backward-compatible with a previous model. In August LeapFrog released the $70 *Leapster GS*, which replaced the Leapster Explorer. The new Leapster GS was compatible with all Leapster Explorer programs and apps, but featured like a built-in camera, videorecorder, a microphone, a larger screen, a faster processor and 2GB of memory compared to the 512MB in the earlier model. Another new feature to the Leapster line was the inclusion of a motion detector, which allowed children to play games by tilting and turning the device. All these extra features were included in a unit that was slightly slimmer and lighter than its predecessor.

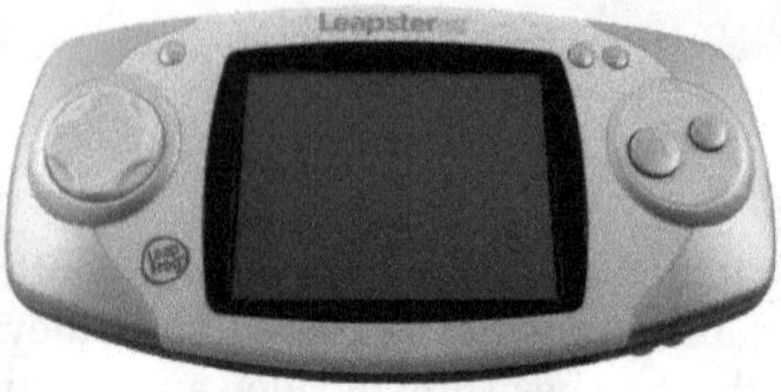

LeapFrog Leapster GS

More Sega and Atari AtGames

One thing that didn't change with the Leapster GS was its simple graphics and low resolution. The graphics were similar to those on the consoles from the 1990s such as the SNES and Genesis. But consoles that played games with simple grpahics were still being released. On November 13, AtGames, which had released the Atari Flashback 3 in 2011, came out with an even newer version, the *Atari Flashback 4*. Externally, the two units looked exactly the same and even shared a $60 retail price. But the Atari Flashback 4 had 75 built-in games, 15 more than its predecessor. And included in this lineup was a third-party title, *Polaris* from Tigervision. But what also set the Atari Flashback 4 apart from the Atari Flashback 3 was the inclusion of wireless joystick controllers. And while original Atari 2600 paddle controllers could be used with the Atari Flashback 4, AtGames also sold brand-new paddle controllers for the console, marking the first time in over 20 years that such controllers were available. Unfortunately, the controllers were the only original 2600 components that could work with the Atari Flashback 4. The new

AtGames Flashback 4

console didn't let users install a cartridge port like they could on the Atari Flashback 2.

This wasn't an issue with another retro console that AtGames also released on November 13. The $60 *Classic Game Console* was a reissue of the wireless Arcade Classic unit that AtGames had released in 2008. Its wireless controllers automatically turned on when the console was powered up, which made them different from the Atari Flashback 4's wireless controllers, which had their own power switches. Like the original Arcade Classic, the Classic Game Console accepted original Genesis/Mega Drive cartridges. It differed from the original version in only one respect. Whereas the 2008 model had 20 built-in Sega 16-bit games and 20 generic games, the new one featured 80 games, of which 40 were from Sega. However, 37 of these 40 Sega titles had already appeared on previous AtGames consoles.

But the remaining three titles, *Ecco II: The Tides of Time*, *Golden Axe II* and *Streets of Rage 3*, weren't unique from all other AtGames consoles either. On the same day that AtGames released the Atari Flashback 4 and the Classic Game Console, it also offered a $60 handheld called the *Arcade Ultimate Portable*. Basically, this was the same unit as the Arcade Ultimate that AtGames had released in 2009. However, in addition to the 20 games that had been built-into the earlier unit, the Arcade Ultimate Portable also featured an additional 17 Sega 16-bit games that had previously appeared on other AtGames consoles, including the three "new" titles that were on the Classic Game Console. But the Arcade Ultimate Portable also featured three Sega titles that had never appeared on any AtGames console before, *Mega Man: The Wily Wars*, *Street Fighter II* and *Super Street Fighter II*. Rounding out the collection were the same 40 generic games that were on the Classic Game Console, bringing the total to 80. Additional games stored on an SD card could also be played.

AtGames Arcade Ultimate Portable

Neo•Geo X

AtGames wasn't the only company that released a retro console. Tommo, an American company that had been established in 1989 as a wholesaler of imported videogames, and went on to become a publisher of games for several Nintendo and SCE systems, introduced its first console on December 18. The $200 *Neo•Geo X* was a handheld unit that was pre-loaded with 20 classic Neo•Geo games, including *Metal Slug* and *Fatal Fury*. The unit itself resembled an iPhone with a black face and silver metal borders. However, it was held horizontally and had an analog joypad, four controller buttons and a 4.3" LCD screen. Games could also be channeled directly to a TV though a composite A/V output. The unit also had an SD card slot so additional games could be added.[20] The unit was not compatible with software for the Neo•Geo Pocket or Neo•Geo Pocket Color.

Tommo NeoGeo X

The unit came with a docking station that resembled an original Neo•Geo AES console. This docking station featured composite video and HDMI video outputs so games could be played on the TV while the unit was charging. And since players didn't have access to the Neo•Geo X's built-in controls while it was docked, the unit was supplied with an external controller that looked and behaved exactly like an original Neo•Geo AES controller. However, since it connected to the docking station via two USB ports, the Neo•Geo X controller wasn't compatible with the original Neo•Geo AES, nor could the original controllers work with the Neo•Geo X docking station.

Retro Peripheral

One retro console that wasn't rereleased from AtGames or Tommo was the ColecoVision.[21] However, ever since Kevin Horton released *Kevtris*, the first homebrew game for the ColecoVision, in 1996, More than 100 homebrew games had been released for the original system, which kept it alive for many retro gamers. In December, one of the publishers of homebrew ColecoVision games, OpCode Games, released the first homebrew peripheral, the *Super Game Module*, which was based on the original Expansion Module #3 that Coleco had planned to release for the ColecoVision in 1983.[22]

Opcode Games ColecoVision Super Game Module

The new $90 Super Game Module performed the same function as the planned original. It plugged into the ColecoVision's expansion port and increased the console's main memory from 1KB to 32KB, in addition to doubling the system's sound capacity. The increased power would allow for new games that consisted of up to 1MB of code. But there were some differences in the modules themselves. The new games for the original module were to be stored on wafers, which were actually small, high-speed cassette tapes. The wafers would be inserted into a small wafer drive on the left side of the module. The front of the module was to feature an additional expansion port, so other peripherals, such as Expansion Module #1, the driving controller, could be used along with new enhanced games. The new Super Game Module was much smaller than the original. It plugged into the expansion port but didn't have its own port built-in. And games for it came in standard sized cartridges that plugged into the ColecoVision's cartridge slot.

Game Gadget

The Neo•Geo X was manufactured by Tommo under license from SNK. Tommo also distributed the system in North America. In Europe, the console was distributed by Blaze Europe, a major distributor of videogame accessories and software. Blaze also represented AtGames and was responsible for the European distribution of the Atari Flashback 3 and several of the Sega consoles.[23]

Blaze liked how AtGames used new consoles to recycle retro games and decided to create an "iPod" for retro games, for which customers could purchase and download games from an iTunes-like online storefront. Since Blaze was a distributor and not a manufacturer, it licensed and rebranded the Dingoo A320, an open-sourced device from Hong Kong that had sold in the millions since its debut in 2009. The result was the *Game Gadget*, which, according to Blaze, was a handheld device that was "capable of playing potentially over 100,000 classic titles across multiple platforms from the early years of gaming to more recent times." Prior to the Game Gadget's release, Mark Garrett, who was responsible for securing game licenses for Blaze, claimed that the company was communicating with "all the major publishers." However, he couldn't directly state who these publishers were, because of non-disclosure agreements in their contracts.

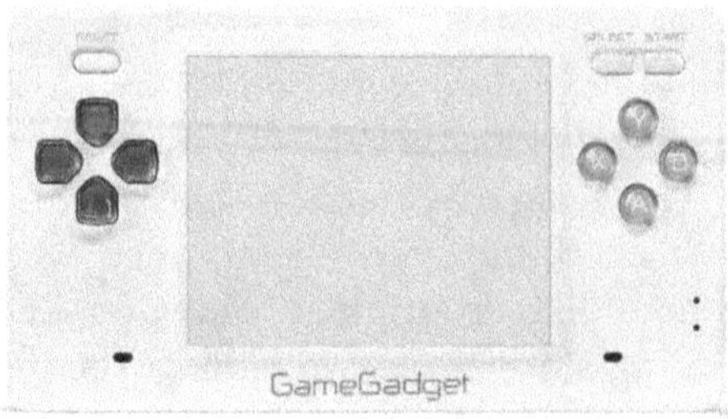

Blaze Game Gadget

Blaze released the £100 ($157) Game Gadget

exclusively in Great Britain on April 6. The unit itself resembled the lower portion of the original Nintendo DS, with a 3.5" LCD screen in the center, four directional buttons on the left side and four controller buttons on the right. Unfortunately, the unit was troubled right from the start. First of all, it couldn't be used directly out of the box. It first had to be activated, a procedure done by downloading free software from Blaze's website.[24] However, this software wasn't available until several weeks after the Game Gadget's launch. But once people could register and use their new handhelds, they discovered a bug in the hardware. Apparently, this device couldn't work properly unless a set of headphones was plugged into it first. To quickly alleviate this problem, Blaze began bundling its stock of Game Gadgets with headphones until a new bug-free replacement became available.

Another oddity of the console was its lack of a physical volume control. To change the volume, one first had to go to an on-screen menu and then navigate through several options before arriving at a volume option. The volume could then be changed through the software. However, since a game could not be played while the volume was being changed, it was difficult to figure out an optimum setting without trial and error.

People discovered another problem when they were ready to download games to their Game Gadgets. The tens of thousands of retro games that were supposed to be available were nowhere to be found. In fact, the only retro games that Blaze offered for sale from its online store were approximately 30 16-bit Sega games that retailed for approximately £3 ($4.76) each. Unfortunately, these were the same Sega games that AtGames had been circulating through its consoles for years! A few shareware titles were also available, but they were nothing that would make anyone want to run out and purchase a Game Gadget.

However, according to Blaze, people were running out and buying Game Gadgets. In fact, Blaze said that there was such a "phenomenal demand" for the device that the company was able to reduce its production costs "well ahead of schedule." And it was because of this that Blaze reduced the price of the Game Gadget to £60 ($97). And they even refunded £40 ($65) to everyone who had bought the unit at its original price.

By the end of June, customer service for the Game Gadget was handed over to Xploder, a company that marketed game-cheating hardware. The reason for the handoff was that because Blaze was a distributor, it didn't have experience with the general public. But Xploder's customer service was less than satisfactory. Forum boards, which were the main source of news for Game Gadget owners, had rude administrators. By mid-summer, Blaze resumed dealing directly with its customers but had no new news to offer. And then the company went silent and didn't offer anything to its customers or to the media. This blackout remained until the end of October, when Blaze relaunched the Game Gadget. However, it was no longer the "iPod of retro-gaming." Now they marketed the Game Gadget as "a slicker version of the Dingoo, but at half the price."

With Blaze's new business model for the Game Gadget, the device could still play thousands of games. However, there was no longer going to be any central online store to purchase them from. But since it used the same open-source Linux operating system as the Dingoo, users could install emulators that could play a multitude of retro games. However, the legality of those games would be in question. The Game Gadget could not access the nearly 800,000 applications from Apple's App Store, as they played only on Apple's own proprietary hardware.

Google's Android Operating System

Google also had its own mobile operating system called Android, which had been available since 2008. Like Linux, Android was open-source, which allowed mobile-phone manufacturers to use it, and even modify it, freely. By May, 2012, Android was installed on more mobile devices than any other operating system and app developers were quick to realize this. On March 6, Google merged its Android Market and Google Music storefronts into one larger hub called *Google Play*, where over 450,000 apps were available to download.

Because of its incompatible operating system, the Game Gadget couldn't play Android games. But other manufacturers began to realize that they could produce handheld devices that used the Android operating system. And then they could be marketed as gaming consoles.

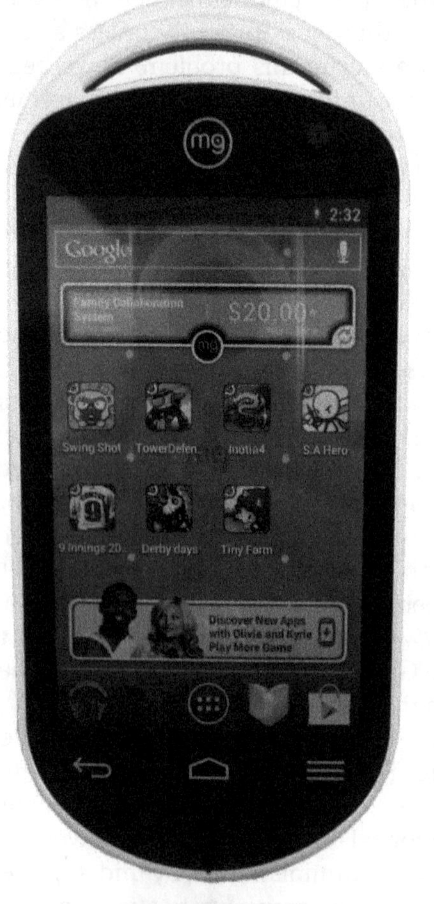

PlayMG MG

JXD V5200

JXD S7300

One of the first such devices arrived in November. This was the *MG*, a $150 unit targeted towards kids from a company called PlayMG. This egg-shaped unit was 5.8″ by 2.6″ and featured a 4″ screen. Because the MG was equipped with Android 4.0, it had access to the wide range of apps on Google Play. However, in order for children to download apps, a debit account from SpendSmart, a service that provided prepaid debit cards specifically for kids, was required. This service then kept track of how much money remained in the account and what the money was used for, although it didn't give parents the ability to preapprove the purchases that their children made.

The MG was quickly joined by another Android-powered handheld device. The *JXD V5200* was from a Chinese manufacturer called JXD and it wasn't geared towards children. JXD itself had come to the attention of retro-gamers in 2007, when it had released the *JXD 301*, a handheld device similar to Game Park's GP32 that could play 8-bit emulated games. JXD followed this in 2009 with the JXD 1000, a handheld that physically resembled SCE's PSP. JXD continuously upgraded its consoles, and in 2012, it released the JXD V5200, which physically resembled the JXD 1000 but was also built around an Android operating system, allowing it to play games downloaded from Google Play.

JXD introduced its first tablet at the end of 2012. The *JXD S7300* was basically an oversized JXD V5200 and looked very much like Nintendo's Wii U GamePad, with a 7″ screen in the center, a joystick on each side of the screen that resembled the Wii U GamePad's circle pads, a D-pad below the left joystick, four controller buttons below the right joystick and four shoulder buttons. All of these buttons mimicked with more precision the virtual buttons that enabled the games to be played on touch screens.

The JXD S7300 was revealed very late in the year and was therefore not actually available for sale in 2012.[25] But it wasn't the only tablet-like game console that was introduced. In January, a startup company called Wikipad, Inc. unveiled its first products at CES. The *Wikipad* was a tablet with an 8" screen, 8GB memory and an Android operating system. But unlike other tablets on the market, the Wikipad had been built specifically for gaming. Wikipad, Inc. even designed a special U-shaped controller that would be included with the tablet. The left stem of the "U" held a D-pad and thumb-pad and the right side had control buttons and a second thumb-pad. Shoulder buttons were built into the upper edge of the controller. The tablet itself slid into the center of the controller, connecting via a USB port. Once joined, the Wikipad became a handheld game device that was capable of downloading and playing Android-based games. And while most Android games downloaded from Google Play utilized the touchscreen, they were all completely playable on the Wikipad. In addition, new games were in development that incorporated the physical control buttons. Wikipad, Inc. showed a 2D version and a 3D version of the Wikipad. at CES and announced that it planned to release the new device in October at a retail price of $250.

Wikipad

Wikipad, Inc. announced in May that it was teaming up with Gaikai, David Perry's game-streaming company, making the Wikipad the first tablet that would use the service.[26] Less than two months later on July 2, SCE purchased Gaikai for $380 million, with plans to create a cloud-based service that would provide PlayStation games to new SCE consoles and Sony televisions. SCE's purchase of Gaikai didn't affect Gaikai's partnership with Wikipad, Inc.

Another SCE feature that was announced for the Wikipad was *PlayStation Mobile*, which was planned to launch on October 3. PlayStation Mobile had previously been known as PlayStation Suite and was the software framework that had been created to provide downloadable SCE content to the PS Vita and PlayStation-Certified Android devices. The Wikipad was to be PlayStation Certified.

More specifications about the Wikipad were announced at the beginning of September. By that time, the tablet was sporting a 10.1" display, 16GB internal storage and a retail price set at $499. It also had a rear-facing, built-in, 8-megapixel camera and a 2-megapixel camera in the front. Wikipad, Inc. also announced that the 3D version that had been shown at CES would not be available when the unit began shipping on October 31. GameStop began taking preorders for the 2D model on September 7.

The Wikipad wasn't released on the promised date. Instead, Wikipad, Inc. issued a press release that stated that the launch would be delayed, due to a "last-minute opportunity to enhance the Wikipad bundle, as well as a minor refinement needed to ensure our first customers are completely satisfied with the Wikipad." Wikipad, Inc. didn't specify what these enhancements were, but they pushed back the release of the Wikipad into 2013.

Not all of the tablet gaming consoles that were introduced in 2012 were held over for a 2013 release, at least not outside of North America. Archos, a French manufacturer of low-cost electronic devices, announced at the end of August its own Android-based game console tablet that would sell for less than £130 ($206). The *Archos GamePad* had a 7" screen and 8GB internal storage. Like the JXD S7300, it had two analog sticks and a multitude of control, directional and shoulder buttons that took the place of the virtual controllers that were built into

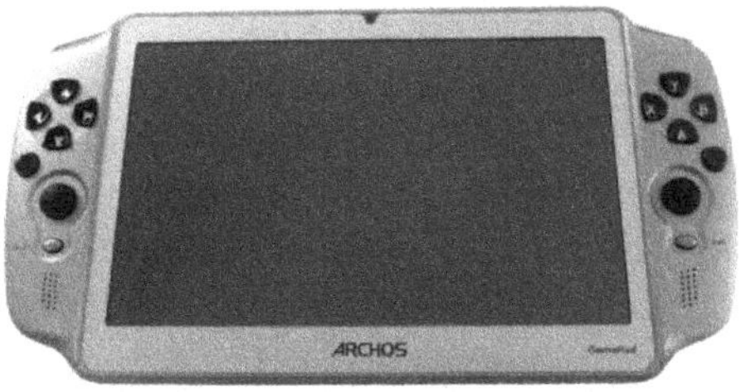

Archos GamePad

Android-based games, although those games could also be played the way they were designed, using the tablet's touchscreen.

The Archos GamePad was released in Europe on December 6, where it retailed for €150 ($195). This made it the first of the gaming tablets to actually become available.[27] Unfortunately, the reception for the device was less than spectacular. Among the complaints that were posted in online reviews from sites such as *Eurogamer.Net*, was the low quality plastic used in the device's casing and the absence of a D-pad in favor of four distinct directional buttons that made diagonal movement difficult. Archos raved about an included mapping tool that would convert the touchscreen-based controls of Android games to work with the hardware controls, but the tool rarely worked correctly. But the Archos Gamepad also suffered from lag that might be permissible in a tablet, but shouldn't be apparent in a device designed for gaming. And then there was one final problem uncovered about the Archos GamePad. It couldn't hold a charge for long. After beginning with a fully charged battery, the device would need to be recharged after less than two hours of heavy duty game play.

The Ouya

Since Android-based gaming devices were coming out in both handheld and tablet versions, it was only natural for them to be built-into consoles as well. One such console was announced on July 3. The *Ouya*, from a company called Ouya, Inc., would employ an Android 4.1 operating system and would carry a $99 retail price. However, unlike the other Android-based devices that depended upon Google Play to obtain inexpensive games, the Ouya would have its own online storefront that would feature games written specifically for the device just like the PS3, Xbox 360 and Wii. This was something akin to the business model that Zeebo, Inc. had employed for its failed Zeebo console. However, one difference was that Ouya, Inc. required that every game that was developed for the console had to feature some kind of free aspect to it. It didn't matter if developers generated revenue by requiring gamers to pay to advance to new levels, or to pay to buy items to use in a game. As long as a user could play some part of the game for free, it could be developed for the Ouya.

The Ouya attracted the attention of a number of big-name developers, including Namco Bandai and Square Enix, who announced that a port of the DS version of *Final Fantasy III* would be available as an Ouya launch title. But game creation wouldn't be restricted to commercial developers. Anybody could design software for the Ouya. One of the apps built into the console would be a Software Development Kit (SDK) that would enable anybody to create a game and then publish it through Ouya's online store. And no developers, no matter how big or small they might be, would be required to pay Ouya, Inc. any licensing fees, retail fees or publishing fees for the right to sell their games.

Ouya, Inc. needed to raise capital so they could make the Ouya a reality. A Kickstarter[28] campaign began on July 10 so the company could raise $950,000 by August 10. By the time that date arrived, Ouya, Inc. had raised over $8.5 million from over 63,000 backers, which made it the second-highest funded project in Kickstarter's brief history. Everyone who pledged at least $99 was awarded his own Ouya console when it became available.

The success of the Kickstarter campaign guaranteed that the Ouya would be released in March, 2013: the month that Ouya, Inc. had originally promised. However, development kits, which had been offered through Kickstarter to anyone who pledged at least $700, began shipping on December 28. The development model was housed in a clear plastic shell that let developers see the components inside, and shipped with a pair of clear controllers. However, aside from this, these early development models differed little from the production consoles that would ship in 2013, since in theory, all Ouya consoles could be used for development.

Another Android-based gaming console was introduced on December 12. The team behind the *eSfere* wanted to create a console that would allow for all apps that were available on Google Play to be downloaded and played on a large-screen television. They also wanted to retain the original game-play by providing a controller that featured a touchpad instead of buttons and D-pads. However, with the realization that some gamers actually preferred controllers over touchpads, a set of silicone controls, including joysticks, buttons and D-pads, would be provided that the gamer could place anywhere on the touchpad to use instead.

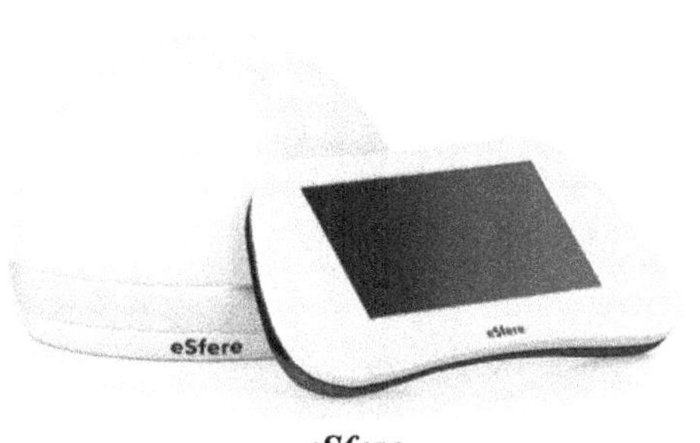

eSfere

eSfere Control buttons

The eSfere would feature the same Nvidia Tegra 3 graphics processor as the Ouya, but would contain twice as much RAM and flash storage. However, the eSfere's designers believed that the console should be attractive as well as functional so the console would be offered in several colors. But the icing on the cake was that three matching flower vases would also be available.

eSfere Entertainment, the company behind the eSfere, began a 41-day crowd-funding campaign on *Indiegogo*, an alternative to Kickstarter. Although the company eventually planned to sell the eSfere for $125, backers could claim a unit by only pledging a minimum of $99 through Indiegogo. eSfere Entertainment's goal was to raise $390,000 by January 21, 2013.

Dismal Sales

The ever-growing popularity of gaming tablets and smartphones coincided with the decline of console gaming. When Nintendo announced its earnings in May for its fiscal year that ended on March 31, it reported a loss for the first time since it had begun reporting its earnings in 1981. After netting ¥77.6 billion ($937 million) the year before, Nintendo's latest earnings fell short by ¥43.2 billion ($522 million). The company's console sales had fallen considerably short of its projections. Nintendo had expected to sell 13 million Wiis, but the actual number sold was only 9.8 million. And the 3DS, which had been gaining steam since its dismal launch, fell short of Nintendo's projected 16 million consoles sold by 2.5 million units.

Sony's 2011 fiscal year ended on March 31 as well, and it ended just as bleakly as Nintendo's. Although Sony's Consumer Products & Services division, which included SCE, had sales of ¥3.13 trillion ($38.2 billion), this amount was actually down 18.5% from the prior year. Sony partially blamed the division's shortcomings on SCE and blamed this drop on the price reduction of the PS3. The lower sales for the PS2 were allegedly "due to platform migration." SCE's misfortunes continued into the first quarter of the 2012 fiscal year, when it reported in August that its sales for the PSP and PS3 had dropped 14.5% from the first quarter of the 2011 fiscal year. Although SCE suffered losses of ¥3.5 billion ($43 million), that number would have been even higher if it hadn't been offset by the sale of 12 million PS Vitas, since that handheld hadn't been available during most of 2011.

Microsoft's financial news was just as dismal. Its Electronic and Devices (E&D) division announced that it had experienced a $229 million loss during its fiscal 2012 third quarter, which had followed a $210 million second-quarter profit. Although Microsoft's E&D division was also the home to Windows Phone and Skype, it was the Xbox 360 that caused the loss. The company only sold 1.4 million Xbox 360 consoles during the quarter, a 48% drop from the same period a year earlier. But Microsoft had hopes in the console arena. Despite its soft sales, the Xbox 360 was the top-selling console in the United States for the 15th month in a row. And because Xbox Live was profitable, the overall losses for the E&D division were lower than they might have been. And it wasn't as if the E&D division's parent was suffering. Microsoft's $17.4 billion revenue had exceeded its own expectations.

New Consoles

Despite the losses incurred by the manufacturers, the industry was gearing up for the next generation of consoles. Nintendo was the first out of the gate with its Wii U. And although neither SCE nor Microsoft had new consoles available during 2012, they were hard at work developing them.

In early April that SCE released a development kit that had consisted merely of a graphics card. A second development kit released in the fall was formally called *Orbis*.[29] It consisted of a modified PC that had up to 16GB RAM and featured an AMD processing unit and an HD graphics card. Two additional upgraded development kits were planned to be issued in 2013 and the completed console was expected to hit store shelves in time for the 2013 holiday season.

Although SCE wasn't spilling any specifics about the new console, information did leak from people who were using the development kits. And some of these details weren't popular with consumers. One in particular was that the new SCE console wouldn't be compatible with software designed for the PS3. And if another rumor was true, not only would PS3 owners have to immediately obtain software when they purchased the new console, but they would be forced to purchase *new* games for it. The rumor, which SCE would not confirm, was that the new console would be unable to play used games. This story arose from the fact that SCE had filed a patent for technology that would force people to register every game disc with the machine on which it would be played. If a disc had already been registered with another machine, as a second-hand game would have been, then it wouldn't be able to play on the newer machine. But unforeseen problems would arise if SCE decided to institute this procedure. For example, what would happen when a gamer's console broke and had to be replaced? Would he have to replace the game as well? And what would occur in situations in which a gamer owned more than one console? Would he have to buy multiple copies of one game just so he could play it in different rooms of his own home?

Michael Pachter, an analyst with Wedbush Securities, couldn't see the advantage in this. While he felt that it was true that some software publishers, such as Activision and Electronic Arts, might "slightly benefit" from this move because they would no longer lose revenue from games that were purchased once and then rented over and over again, it would probably be a disaster for SCE in the long run. Pachter believed that game stores like GameStop, which made most of their money from used games, would simply refuse to carry SCE's new console, causing its sales to suffer. But, Pachter pointed out, GameStop only had the upper hand if SCE "unilaterally" didn't accept used games. Unfortunately, rumors out of the Microsoft camp implied that they were considering this as well for the new console that they were working on.

Microsoft had also begun sending development kits out for its next-generation system during the summer, and while the media referred to the new system as the *Xbox 720*, the official name for the development kit was *Durango*. Microsoft, like SCE, didn't publicly announce what features would be available on the new system, but aspects about it were leaked from various sources anyway. Apparently, the new system would incorporate a newly designed Kinect, downloadable and streaming game access, coordination with tablets and smart phones either through SmartGlass or another technology, and integration with 3D glasses that Microsoft was developing under the codename *Fortaleza*.

As far as Microsoft was publicly concerned, the existence of the Fortaleza 3D glasses was strictly a rumor, and didn't publicly comment about it. But if these 3D glasses actually existed, then they were going to go against real competition. In June, a start-up company called Oculus VR revealed its forthcoming project at E³. The *Oculus Rift* was an inexpensive, virtual reality, head-mounted display, designed especially for gaming. It would feature immersive stereoscopic 3D rendering, a wide field of view (110° diagonally and 90° horizontally), a high-resolution display (1280 x 800) and ultra-low latency head tracking (six degrees). The unit would initially be specifically designed to work with PCs, but the goal was to eventually make it compatible with gaming consoles as well.

Although Oculus VR was already funded to produce Oculus Rift prototypes, it wanted to get them into the hands of developers, so on August 1, it started a Kickstarter campaign to raise $250,000. Each backer who invested only $300 would receive a working Oculus Rift prototype unit, access to a downloadable software-development kit, and a copy of the PC version of *Doom 3 BFG Edition*. Within 36 hours of starting the campaign, $1 million was pledged for the development kits. By the end of the campaign, Oculus VR had raised over $2.4 million.[30]

Virtual Books and Guides

The world that the Oculus Rift immersed players into via virtual reality was completely computer-generated. Another way that players could feel like they were part of a game was through augmented reality, wherein the computer-generated world became part of the real physical world. SCE had used the technology before with *The Eye of Judgment* and *EyePet*. Now it was going after it in a bigger way.

SCE introduced *Wonderbook* at E³. This was a PS3 peripheral that looked like a physical book. However, instead of words and pictures, Wonderbook featured augmented-reality cards, which allowed the "stories" in the book to come to life with the assistance of the PlayStation Eye.

In November, SCE released Wonderbook in North America and Europe. The device was packaged with *Book of Spells*, which wasn't really a game. It was modeled after the *Book of Spells* that appeared in the *Harry Potter* series, and SCE had worked with Harry Potter's creator, J.K. Rowling, to develop it. Players acted as wizards and used their PlayStation Moves as magic wands to control objects on the screen. These objects also appeared in 3D off-screen.

SCE planned additional software for the Wonderbook, including another Harry Potter-themed book.[31] Although many critics argued that *Book of Spells* wasn't really a game, the reviews for it were mostly positive. After all, SCE and Microsoft were trying to elevate their consoles into all-purpose home entertainment units, instead of merely being videogame consoles. Nintendo remained the only console manufacturer that had no problem calling its products videogames. But even Nintendo's consoles had been used with Nintendo's blessing[32] over the years for non-gaming purposes.

And that trend continued into the present. In 2012, Nintendo partnered with the Louvre

SCE Wonderbook

2012

museum in Paris to develop an application for the 3DS that provided a walking tour for guests of the institution. The finished product, which had been designed in part by Shigeru Miyamoto, was released on April 11, and was only available in customized 3DS units[33] that could be rented at the museum itself.

The *Nintendo 3DS Guide: Louvre* was basically a guided tour of the Louvre. The 3DS's upper screen presented an interactive map of the museum that the guest could follow. Over 400 works of art were captured in photos, and each was displayed on the screen as the person reached the physical piece of art. The bottom screen displayed informative instructions, while an audio track told the guest about each work of art as it was approached. Guests could also search for particular works of art, and the 3DS would provide directions to get them to the displays and let them know how long the walk would take.[34]

Nintendo 3DS Guide - Louvre

As the Louvre used videogame technology to aid people in art appreciation, the Smithsonian American Art Museum in Washington D.C. was exhibiting videogames. The *Art of Video Games,* which ran at the museum from mid-March through the end of September before going on the road, showcased 80 games with screenshots and video footage. Some of these games had been selected in 2011 by the public through a special website that was active for two months. Over 119,000 people cast more than 3.7 million votes during that time.

The exhibit was divided into five historical eras, displaying photos and videos of games from the 1970s through to the present. Five games, including *Pac-Man* and *Super Mario Bros.,* were also available to play. And video interviews with key industry trendsetters, including Nolan Bushnell, David Perry and Tommy Tallarico, were available for viewing. Approximately 680,000 people visited the exhibit during its six-month run in Washington.

Wreck-It Ralph

People also flocked to movie theaters to see a videogame-related feature film that opened on November 2. *Wreck-It Ralph* was an animated movie from Walt Disney that told the story of the title character, a villain in a fictional arcade game called *Fix-It Felix, Jr.* Each night after the arcade closed, the characters from all of the machines were able to leave their collective videogame worlds and socialize in the real world. However, because Wreck-It Ralph was the game's villain, he was ostracized by the general population. In a quest to get others to like him, Wreck-It Ralph entered a different fictitious game, *Hero's Duty,* where he hoped to earn a medal and be celebrated by the community. However, since he didn't return to the *Fix-It Felix, Jr.* game, that machine was deemed as malfunctioning and an arcade attendant unplugged it, causing its characters to find themselves homeless. So the title character of *Fix-It Felix, Jr.* went on a quest to find Wreck-It Ralph and return him to the game in which he belonged.

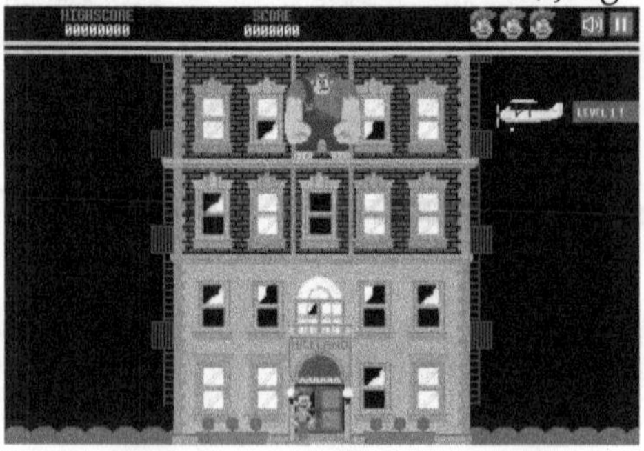

Wreck It Ralph

Gamers loved the film, especially since it featured "cameos" of many beloved characters from modern and classic arcade games, including *Pac-Man, Q*Bert, Frogger* and even *Pong*! And although it wasn't officially confirmed by Disney, the arcade owner was purportedly modeled after legendary videogame scorekeeper, Walter Day.

But *Wreck-It Ralph* apparently appealed to non-gamers as well. It wound up the 14th-highest-grossing movie of the year.

More Closings

Wreck-It Ralph primarily appealed to retro gamers because of the classic game-character cameos. But retro games were making news in other ways as well. In fact, one particular game from 1982 made headlines. The game was *Air Raid*, the extremely rare game for the Atari 2600 that had been released in very limited quantities by a nondescript third-party company called Men-A-Vision. *Air Raid* was so rare that only a handful was known to exist, and it wasn't until 2011 that a boxed copy of the game was actually discovered. That copy sold for an unbelievable $31,600. But as it turned out, it wasn't the only boxed copy that still existed. In 2012, the first complete copy of the game, one that included a box and an instruction manual, turned up. This one was also offered through an online auction, and on October 24, it sold for a record-breaking $33,433.30.

But not all news concerning retro games was good. Hudson Soft, which had been in business since 1973, and had been one of Nintendo's earliest licensees, closed its doors as an independent company on March 1. But this was something that had been expected since August 2001, when Hudson Soft had sought new funding after its main bank failed. Konami had come to its rescue at that time by purchasing 5.6 million shares of the company, making it Hudson Soft's largest shareholder. Konami purchased an additional three million shares in 2005, and became Hudson Soft's majority stockholder, as it owned more than 50% of the shares. And then on April 1, 2011, Hudson Soft became a wholly owned subsidiary of Konami. It continued as a Konami brand for nearly a year, until Konami finally merged it into its Konami Digital Entertainment group in 2012 and retired the Hudson Soft name for good.

Unfortunately, Hudson Soft wasn't the only long-running recognizable name to disappear. Future US announced in August that it would cease publication of *Nintendo Power*, which by that time was the longest continuously-run, English-language videogame publication of all time, having been published on a regular schedule for over 24 years without missing a beat.[35]

***Nintendo Power* Final**

Nintendo Power had debuted as a bi-monthly magazine in the summer of 1988 with a July/August cover date. It had replaced the game company's *Nintendo Fun Club News*, which had been a free giveaway to registered NES owners. As an in-house Nintendo publication, *Nintendo Power* didn't contain any outside advertising. It also didn't mention any unlicensed games that played on Nintendo consoles. But it was good to its subscribers, and over the years, provided free gifts, including games, such as the NES game *Dragon Warrior*, which was sent to subscribers in 1990, around the same time that the magazine went monthly.

In 2007, Nintendo had handed over the responsibility of publishing *Nintendo Power* to Future US. However, five years later, when it was time to renew Future US's contract, Nintendo opted against it. Future US decided not to pursue a new contract and cited that Nintendo had been "difficult to work with," and had no interest in taking part in the digital ingenuities that the publisher deemed necessary for the magazine's survival. Since Nintendo itself didn't want to resume control of the magazine, the final issue of *Nintendo Power* hit newsstands on December 11, with a cover that was nostalgic of the magazine's first, a scene out of *Super Mario Bros. 2* with Mario jumping over a toadstool with his enemy, Wart, on his heels.

The demise of *Nintendo Power* might have been a signal that Nintendo was no longer relevant. Combined sales for the Wii and Wii U were less than either of the Xbox 360 and PS3.[36] This trend was also reflected in software sales, in which games that played on Nintendo consoles h istorically dominated. Since at least 2005, games for Nintendo consoles had conquered each year's top-ten best-selling list compiled by *VGChartz.com*. This changed slightly in 2011, when only half of the top-ten games of the year were for Nintendo systems. But at the end of 2012, this number had dropped to only three.[37]

But the list of the top-ten best games only told one side of the story. What it didn't tell was that these ten games accounted for 46% of sales during December, compared to 36% from the year before. And since sales themselves were down 22% from the prior year, it was the non-high-profile games that were taking the hit. Thanks to competition from digital services and rentals, only the higher-profile physical games were actually making money. So in order to stem this downward trend, publishers simply began to release fewer titles. And those that were released were safer titles, as far as the publishers were concerned. Fourteen of the top sixteen games of the year had sequence numbers in their titles, including *Call of Duty: Black Ops II*, which took the top two positions.[38] Of the remaining two, thirteenth-place *Super Mario 3D Land* for the 3DS was also part of a profitable series. The lone unique title, and the only game in the global top ten that was a holdover from 2011, was the Xbox 360 game *Kinect Adventures!*, which with 4.5 million units sold, ranked as the eighth top-selling game of the year.

Other games that made up the top-sixteen list were *FIFA Soccer 13* for the PS3 (5.58 million units), *Just Dance 4* for the Wii (4.47 million units) and *Mario Kart 7* for the 3DS (3.38 million).

Software sales weren't the only category that was down. Hardware sales were down as well, 27% from 2011! As the year came to a close, people wondered where the future of console was heading. As consoles like the Ouya began inching towards Android operating systems and downloadable software, all eyes were focused on what SCE and Microsoft had in development.

CHAPTER FORTY-ONE
2013

The year 2013 had been expected to be a revolutionary one in the annals of videogame history. This was to be the year that microconsoles,[1] driven by Google's Android operating system, would outsell traditional, software-driven consoles. These new low-priced microconsoles would offer inexpensive, downloadable games that would play on standard television sets and would cost much less than games available for standard gaming consoles.

Leading the pack into this new era was the Ouya, the $99 microconsole that had been partially funded through a 2012 Kickstarter campaign. During the waning days of 2012, 1,200 developers who had paid at least $699 for development systems actually received their units. And an online developer's kit became accessible to them on December 21, 2012.

The Kickstarter campaign had mentioned that the consumer Ouya microconsoles would be delivered sometime in March, 2013. So when the first sunrise appeared in the new year, those 1,200 developers spent their time trying to figure out how to create the games that would have to be available a mere two months later.

However, on the second day of the year, there was an announcement that the Ouya would already have competition. On that day, a company called PlayJam launched its own Kickstarter campaign to raise $100,000 for the *GameStick*, which was dubbed "The Most Portable TV Games Console Ever Created." The word *portable* in the tagline was slightly confusing, because it usually inferred that the device was a handheld unit that could be played anywhere. This was not the case with the GameStick, which still required a television set. What PlayJam meant was that it would be easy to transport the GameStick from one location to another, as it was not a large, clunky console. In fact, the word *console* was also something of a misnomer. If ever the term *microconsole* was appropriate, it was here.

GameStick with controller

In both size and appearance, the GameStick looked exactly like a flash drive with a male HDMI connector at one end. All that was required to hook the GameStick to a TV set was to plug the GameStick into the HDMI port of the television. The GameStick was so small that it could be stored inside its own controller when not in use.

Although the GameStick would be Android-based, it would only be able to play games that would be developed specifically for it, and which would be purchased and downloaded exclusively from PlayJam's own online storefront. As was the case with the Ouya, Android games that could be downloaded from Google Play wouldn't work on the GameStick.

The retail price for the GameStick was $79, $20 less than the Ouya, and the first 250 people who backed the device on Kickstarter only had to pledge $69 for each unit. These 250 microconsoles were claimed very quickly, along with many more soon afterwards, as PlayJam's $100,000 goal was reached from over 1,000 backers within 30 hours after the Kickstarter campaign began. On January 9, with three weeks still remaining in the month-long campaign, PlayJam announced additional features when new monetary milestones were met. The GameStick would be offered in two colors after $320k was reached, and in four colors after $450K was pledged. And if the fundraiser raised $560K, a MicroSD slot would be added to every GameStick, increasing the microconsole's total storage capacity by 32GB to 40GB. By the end of the month-long campaign, PlayJam had elicited nearly $700K.

Less than a week after the world learned about the GameStick, Nvidia, the company that supplied the Tegra 3 GPU processor that would be used in the Ouya and eSfere, used CES to announce its own Android-gaming system. *Project Shield* would be a portable gaming device that would be built around Nvidia's newly announced Tegra 4 chip, which would be six times as powerful as the Tegra 3.

Project Shield looked very much like a standard game controller for the Xbox 360 or PS3. It had two analog sticks, a D-pad, four control buttons and four shoulder buttons. However, much like the DS family of handheld consoles, Project Shield had a clamshell-style, 5" multi-touchscreen that flipped over onto the body of the console when not in use.

Games played on the handheld console could also be ported to a standard television, which made Project Shield competitive with the eSfere. Additionally, online games that could be streamed to PCs could be channeled over Wi-Fi to the Project Shield console from the PC.

Unlike the Ouya and GameStick, Project Shield could play games downloaded from Google Play. In addition, games could be downloaded from *TegraZone,* Nvidia's own online storefront, which presented games specifically optimized for devices that used Nvidia's Tegra GPU. TegraZone didn't actually host any games, but merely acted as a bookmark. Games that were selected from TegraZone were actually downloaded from Google Play.

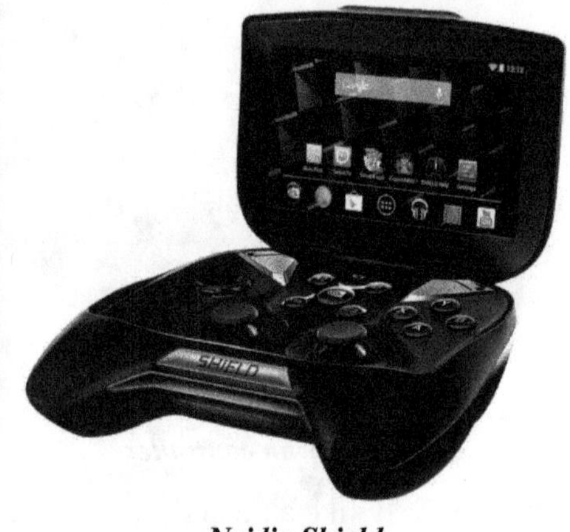

Nvidia Shield

In May, Nvidia dropped the word "Project" and officially called its new console the *Shield.* The company also announced that the Shield would begin shipping in June and would carry a $350 retail price. *Gamesindustry International,* a website that covered the global videogames industry, quickly pointed out that this was the same price as the Wii U when it had launched, and $50 more than SCE's PS Vita. Those two consoles were still struggling to find audiences.

The Shield's ability to play games downloaded from Google Play made it similar to the eSfere, which had been going through its crowdfunding campaign at the time that Nvidia introduced its new console. The fact that the eSfere could play games from Google Play was its major selling point over the Ouya. But whether or not this enhanced the desirability of the console was not really known. When the eSfere's crowdfunding campaign came to an end on January 21, it hadn't come close to reaching its goal. Only 18 people had pledged a total of $2,404 to support the eSfere, a far cry from the $390,000 that eSfere Entertainment had sought.

After the eSfere died, another company still found the idea of a microconsole that could download games from Google Play and play them on standard television sets appealing. On June 6, peripheral-manufacturer Mad Catz announced *Project Mojo* to its investors. This was an Android-based microconsole that was part of the company's new *GameSmart* line, which consisted of mobile gaming accessories for smartphones and tablets. By the time that Mad Catz introduced the new microconsole to the world five days later at E[3], its name had been shortened simply to *MOJO.*

As with the failed eSfere, games would not be specifically developed for the MOJO. Instead, it would run games and other apps downloaded directly from Google Play. But the MOJO wasn't simply an eSfere with Mad Catz's name plate on it. For one, Mad Catz didn't bother to add a touchpad to the MOJO's controller, which had the same features that were found on the OnLive Game System. In addition to a D-pad, two analog sticks and a set of control buttons, the controller also featured media buttons that would give users the capability to fast forward, rewind, play and pause any video content that might be running on the console.

The MOJO would be packaged with a "travel" clip that would connect to the controller. Once this was attached, an Android smart phone or 7" tablet could snap in and effectively turn the controller into a handheld game console. Once a smart device was attached, the MOJO controller would closely resemble Nvidia's Shield, which was the console that the MOJO was directly compared with, since both featured Nvidia's new Tegra 4 GPU. But a complete comparison couldn't be made, because Mad Catz hadn't disclosed the MOJO's retail price. Industry analysts believed that Mad Catz had a better product, but only if they could release the MOJO, which would launch sometime in 2013, at a price point that would be substantially lower than the Shield's $350.

The Gamepop

Basically, there were two types of Android-based gaming platforms. The inexpensive models like the Ouya and the GameStick required software that was developed specifically for those individual consoles. In most cases, these were ports of existing games that could easily be modified. However, games that people may have already paid for that resided on their Android-smartphones had to be repurchased (if they were available), to play on these microconsoles.

The other type of Android gaming console was the one that allowed games to be downloaded directly from Google Play. So as long as a Google Play account was used, games already purchased for other devices could be freely downloaded to these machines, which included the Nvidia Shield and the Mad Catz MOJO. However, there was a tradeoff. While the software was inexpensive, the hardware was not.

Bluestacks, a company that had developed software that allowed Apple's iOS mobile apps to run on personal computers, announced a third type of microconsole on May 9. In addition to running Android apps like all of the other new microconsoles, the *Gamepop* would also run iOS apps without using any of Apple's own code. Bluestacks also wanted to become the Netflix of console gaming, and charge each customer a $6.99 subscription fee for a month's worth of unlimited gaming. The Netflix analogy wasn't actually correct, because that service allowed customers to watch unlimited streaming videos of whatever they wanted. Instead, the Gamepop would come preloaded with 500 of the most popular games from Google Play. Bluestacks planned to offer its microconsole, and a standard controller, free to anyone who signed up and subscribed during May and June, even though the service wasn't planned to start until the end of the year. And while the controller would be shipped with the microconsole, it wouldn't be required for game play. Standard smartphones could also be used as controllers.

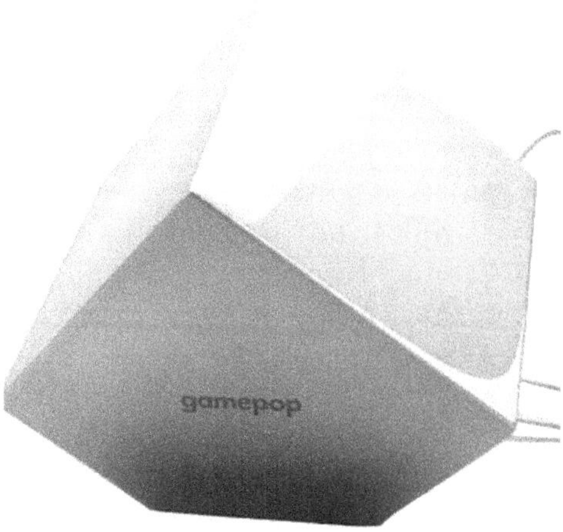

Bluestacks Gamepop

Bluestacks Gamepop Mini

At the end of June, Bluestacks announced another new microconsole, the *Gamepop Mini*, which was roughly the size of a pack of chewing gum. Once this microconsole was available, it would be the one that Bluestacks would offer free with a subscription, while the original Gamepop would cost $129. But Bluestacks wasn't specific about exactly what the difference was between the two microconsoles, besides their sizes. It only stated that the Gamepop was more powerful than the Gamepop Mini and that "there *may* also be more peripherals available for the Gamepop."

Android Consoles Hit The Street

By the time Bluestacks showed the original Gamepop to the public at E^3, the Ouya, the first of the new Android-based microconsoles, was already in the hands of consumers. Actually, the new system had begun shipping to its 50,000 Kickstarter backers on March 28.[2] While reviews of the microconsole were generally favorable, many critics panned the controller, which they found to be much lower in quality than those for the Xbox 360 and PS3. To many users, it seemed very cheaply made. It also had a serious design flaw that disrupted game play. The controller was powered by two AA batteries that were stored in two separate compartments. Two faceplates on the top of the controller had to be removed to access these compartments. The faceplate on the right side contained four cut-out holes for the control buttons to fit through, and sometimes, a control button became stuck under the faceplate. Many gamers got around this problem by using a different controller atogether. Since the Ouya's controller used Bluetooth to communicate with the console, any Bluetooth controller, including the PS3's, could be used with the Ouya.

Ouya with controller

As the Kickstarter backers began receiving their systems, they discovered that an astonishing 104 games were immediately available for downloading. This was the largest number of games that had ever been available during any console launch. And as Ouya, Inc. required, all of them could be tried for free. Unfortunately, Ouya, Inc. had never imposed any conditions on how developers could get gamers to purchase games. In some games, payment was required to advance to new levels, while in others, payments had to be made after a certain number of lives had been lost. Vendors didn't have to alert players in advance about how or when a payment would be necessary and consumers weren't told in advance how much a game would actually cost if they chose to pay. It was only at the point during the game at which they had to agree to pay that they learned how much they would actually owe.

The Ouya was scheduled to launch in retail stores on June 4, even though all of the Kickstarter backers had not yet received their systems. That date was pushed back, but not so all of the backers could receive their systems before the retail customers. It was to ensure the stores that they would have adequate stock on hand to fulfill their preorders. The Ouya officially launched in retail stores, including Amazon, Best Buy, Target, GameStop and the UK's GAME, on June 25. But this wasn't the only snub to Kickstarter backers who still hadn't received their consoles. The retail editions were shipped with controllers that contained enlarged control button cut-outs, so the buttons couldn't get stuck.

Amazon temporarily sold out of the Ouya within hours of its availability. But despite this immense interest in the system, the overall impression of the microconsole was not good. People still felt that the controller was cheaply made. And now, Ouya features that had sounded good a year earlier appeared to turn popular opinion against the microconsole. While many praised it for having an open architecture so anyone could develop games, the fact that games had to be written specifically for the system no longer sounded so appealing. Even though close to 200 games were available in time for the retail launch, that number was trifling when compared to the thousands that were available through Google Play for the many Android-based handheld consoles that came out throughout the year.

The first such device to leave the gate in the United States was the Archos GamePad, which was released in March through online retailers. It had already come out in Europe in December, 2012, and reviewers there were not impressed by it. The American response to the $179 device was basically the same. *Consumer Reports* called it a "good idea with so-so results" and *Engadget* recommended that consumers "pass on it."

Many of the people who panned the Archos GamePad suggested that consumers wait instead for the Wikipad from Wikipad, Inc. This hybrid tablet/handheld, which had originally been supposed to come out in late 2012, had finally launched on June 11 during E^3. The version of the Wikipad that was released featured a 7" screen, instead of the 10.1 inches that had been previously shown. The unit sold for $250, which was the original price that Wikipad, Inc. had stated it would cost.

Consumer Tablet Reports magazine gave the Wikipad a 4.5 star rating and placed it in its "best buy" category. But that was the problem with the Wikipad. Although Wikipad, Inc. had attempted to create an Android-based handheld device that would appeal to gamers, the bottomline was that the Wikipad was really a tablet. And although it contained Nvidia's Tegra 3 processor that was capable of playing most of the Android games that could be downloaded from Google Play, Nvidia had already introduced the Tegra 4, which rendered the Wikipad obsolete for die-hard gamers. And unlike *Consumer Tablet Reports*, which reviewed the Wikipad as a tablet, technology website IGN reviewed it as a handheld console, and its verdict of the device was that it was a "mostly failed attempt at turning an Android tablet into a gaming handheld."

Nvidia had planned to release its own Android-based handheld, the Shield, with its brand-new, lightning-fast Tegra 4 processer, on June 27. Unfortunately, this date had to be rescheduled at the 11th hour, due to an undisclosed third-party "mechanical" issue. After Nvidia officially released the Shield on July 31, critics quickly scrambled to find something that they could complain about. But while most journalists praised the Shield's quality, they determined that the $300 price of the unit was too high to make it a contender against the traditional handheld consoles from Nintendo and SCE. And while people had faulted the $99 Ouya for *only* having approximately 200 games available at launch, even though that was a number that was unheard-of for a new console, the complaint about the Shield was that the collective quality of the thousands of games that were available from Google Play wasn't high enough to justify spending $300 on a console to play them.

Not all new handhelds that were being offered were Android-based. A new Kickstarter campaign that launched on January 8 was for the *Zero*, a "retrogaming" handheld "built for gamers, by gamers." The Linux-based, open-sourced system was from a company called Games Console Worldwide, which had been founded by Justin Barwick, a former Internet retailer of prior Linux-based systems such as the Dingoo A320 and the Caanoo from Game Park Holdings. Barwick had believed that the new Android-based consoles that were proliferating were merely "walled gardens, designed solely for consumption." He decided to use his connections within the Linux community to design and build a handheld that the user completely controlled. He referred to it as a retrogaming device because Linux emulators were available for nearly every videogame console and PC that

GCW Zero

came out before 2000.

The Kickstarter campaign aimed to raise $135,000, and all supporters who pledged at least $135 would receive a unit when they became available. By the time the campaign ended on January 28, Barwick had raised $238,498! He began shipping the units to backers on July 25.

The Zero received mixed reviews, many of which complained that a lot of the features on the system, including an FM radio and HDMI output didn't work on the device, although GCW promised that they would be included in future updates. However, the main consensus was that the console, with its 3.5 inch low-resolution screen, was adequate as a device that could be used to play old games with a variety of available emulators, which had been Barwick's plan all along.

The PlayStation 4

Despite the conceived move to the Android-based systems, traditional consoles weren't down and out yet. In February, the "rumor" that SCE was working on a successor to the PS3 was officially revealed to be true, and everyone knew that once SCE made this disclosure, Microsoft wouldn't be too far behind.

SCE officially announced its new console at the PlayStation Meeting, which was held in New York and streamed around the world on February 20. As expected, the name of the new console would be the *PlayStation 4 (PS4)* and it would be released in time for the holidays. A price wasn't disclosed at the time.

SCE's president, Andrew House, said that the PS4 would provide "experiences that surpass gamers' wildest expectations." The console's architecture abandoned the PS3's Cell in favor of one that would be more PC-like and easier for developers to work with. The console would contain a state-of-the-art AMD Radeon GPU that could also be used for general-purpose computing and would ease some of the work done by the console's AMD X86 CPU, freeing it for more complicated computations. The GPU would be capable of processing 1.84 teraFlops,[3] ten times more powerful than the PS3, and hence the world's most powerful game console.

The console would come with 8GB of RAM, which would aid the processing units. Much of this memory would be used to accelerate software load times, so players could power up their systems and quickly resume games where they had left off. Similarly, gamers who wanted to quickly jump into downloaded games wouldn't have to wait until the downloads completed before they could start playing. Games could even be downloaded while the console was off. And in addition to downloaded games, people would be able to play streaming games, thanks to the Gaikai technology that SCE had purchased in 2012. According to David Perry, Gaikai's CEO, gamers would be able to sample any game that they streamed from Gaikai. If they didn't like the game, they wouldn't have to pay for it.

SCE designed the PS4 to emphasize social gameplay. Gaikai would notify users whenever one of their friends bought a game from its service. The console would also enable its users to watch games that were being played by their friends. A player could also hit a new *SHARE* button on the controller that would allow him to sift through the previous 15 minutes of a game and let him select a screenshot or video clip, which he could then share through social media.

Although an actual PS4 wasn't shown at the PlayStation Meeting, the console's new *DualShock 4* controller was on display. A PS4 console could accommodate up to four of the wireless controllers simultaneously. The new controllers were somewhat similar in appearance to the PS3's DualShock 3,[4] and incorporated several new features,

SCE DualShock 4

SCE PlayStation Camera

including the SHARE button and a touchpad that was modeled after the one on the PS Vita. The controller also featured a new color display bar. Each of the four controllers that were configured to a console would have its own unique color, which developers could incorporate into their games.

The colors could also be used in tandem with a new, optional camera that SCE planned to release along with the PS4. This *PlayStation Camera* would be able to sense players' locations by the colored lights of their controllers. It would have more similarities with Microsoft's Kinect than with SCE's prior cameras, the EyeToy and the PlayStation Eye. The new horizontally-shaped unit would be equipped with two lenses and would be able to distinguish one player from another when one was directly in front of the other. It also improved upon the PlayStation Eye's ability to detect the motion of the PlayStation Move, as well as new Move functionality that was built into the DualShock 4 controllers.

The PS3's PlayStation Move controller was not modified and was completely compatible with the PS4. But the Move was the only PS3 item that was compatible with the PS4, including games. SCE had made it clear that the PS4 would not play PS3 software at all, not even games that were downloaded from the PlayStation Network. The PS4 would also be incompatible with the earlier PS2 and original PlayStation games, at least initially.[5] Finally, the console wouldn't even be able to play back standard music CDs.

The Durango: Restrictions Central

Although Microsoft hadn't officially confirmed the existence of a new console by the time SCE announced the PS4, rumors persisted. Information about Microsoft's development hardware, the Durango, leaked to the press two weeks before SCE introduced the PS4. According to *Edge* magazine, Microsoft's new console would require a constant Internet connection and games would need activation codes. This coupling suggested that any new game that had been purchased on disc had to be registered before it could be played. It was further implied that this action was required so games could not be resold. Once an activation code was registered and tied to one machine, it could not be used on another. The implications of this were horrendous. Not only would it crush the used-game market, which most stand-alone stores -- including GameStop -- depended upon for much of their revenue, but it even meant that someone who legitimately owned a game couldn't even take it to a friend's house to play. Or even worse, a household with multiple consoles was limited to playing the game only on the console that it was registered from. This was the same type of rumor that was leaked in 2012 about the PS4, a rumor that hadn't been confirmed or denied by SCE.

Additional information regarding the Durango was leaked to the press in mid-March. This time, it stated that all consoles would be equipped with hard drives that would have enough capacity to "hold a large number of games." It went on to say that all games had to be installed to the hard drive before they could be played. The games couldn't be accessed directly from the optical discs that they came on. This source also confirmed that the console had to be connected to the Internet and powered on at all times.

Another leaked rumor concerned the Kinect for the new console. Apparently, a patent filed by Microsoft stated that the Kinect would be able to count how many people were in a room, which caused many people to have concerns about potential privacy violations. Germany's Commissioner of Federal Data Protection, Peter Schaar, expressed fears that the console and Kinect would quietly gather voice and other data, and was concerned about what Microsoft might want with such information. Meanwhile in Australia, the Kinect met all of the requirements needed to be defined as a genuine surveillance device.

Microsoft's New Consoles

Microsoft took its time to respond to SCE's PlayStation Meeting in February, as well as the questions that were mounting about the Durango. The company finally revealed its intentions at a press conference on May 21, when Don Mattrick, head of Microsoft's Interactive Entertainment Business division, introduced "the ultimate all-in-one home entertainment system."

Mattrick went on and summarized the console as "the one with the power to create experiences that look and feel like nothing else. The one that makes your TV more intelligent. The one system for a new generation." And that was the simple premise behind the name of the new machine. Microsoft didn't call it the Xbox 720, or even by its code name Durango. Instead, Microsoft gave its new third-generation Xbox the name *Xbox One*, signifying that this was the *one* console that people needed to go to for a myriad of functions.

Of course, this name was potentially confusing, since many people thought of the original Xbox as Xbox One, much in the same way that SCE had called its revamped, original PlayStation the PSone. But Microsoft was not concerned. Jeff Henshaw, a Microsoft program manager, felt that there might be some initial confusion, but that people would quickly realize that the original Xbox and the new Xbox One were worlds apart, and they would quickly become accustomed to the moniker of the new machine.

Microsoft had a fully working Xbox One console to show off. It really wasn't much different from the PS4 that SCE had not yet shown.[6] Both would come with Blu-ray players, 8GB RAM, 8 Core[7] processors, 500GB hard drives and AMD GPUs, although the one in the Xbox One would only process at 1.31 teraFlops. Like the PS4, the Xbox One offered the ability for online gamers to chat among one another while playing, and the ability to begin playing downloadable games while they were still loading. Both systems also featured DVRs that allowed players to record their game footage and share it with their friends. However, Microsoft required a yearly $60 subscription to Xbox Live Gold in order to use this feature, while all PS4 users could use it freely. The Xbox Live Gold subscription was required for other features as well. While streaming services such as Netflix and Hulu Plus would be available to all PS4 users who had subscriptions to them, they would only be available to the Xbox One users who had Xbox Live Gold subscriptions. But Xbox One owners who did have the gold subscription would be able to seamlessly switch between

Microsoft Xbox One

these services and games, because Microsoft's console was the only one that offered an HDMI-in port, so all video was channeled through the console before getting to the TV.

The controller for the Xbox One didn't appear to be too different from the one for the Xbox 360, which many people had ranked as the best overall console controller. However, Microsoft had 105 people work over two years to improve the controller, and in the end, the company claimed that there were approximately 40 differences between the new controller and its predecessor, and that so many of the features had been altered that the Xbox 360 controllers couldn't be used with the new Xbox One. Two features that Microsoft had toyed with were a touchpad and speakers, but unlike SCE, Microsoft had decided against employing them on the new controller. Instead, improvements were made to the D-pad, analog sticks and triggers, all of which had small rumble motors inside them. These acted in concert with the rumble feature that was part of the controller itself and which gave players new sensations in both their palms and fingertips.

The *Kinect 2.0* for the Xbox One was an updated version of the one that was already out for the Xbox 360. It provided greater accuracy with three times the fidelity, and had a 60% wider field of vision that could detect users up to three feet from the sensor, which was three feet farther from the far end of where the original Kinect was capable of sensing. It could also detect information from players, including their heart rates, wrist rotations, facial expressions and the positions and orientations of 25 of their individual joints. And unlike the original Kinect, it would also work well in small rooms and in rooms with low lighting.

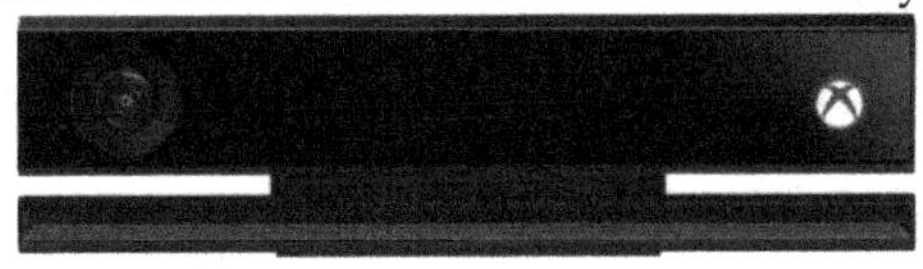

Microsoft Kinect 2

Microsoft confirmed the rumor that the Kinect 2.0 needed to be connected to the console in order for the Xbox One to work. The company also confirmed that the Kinect 2.0 always had to be on. This would allow developers to include voice and gesture commands into their games, with the knowledge that every Xbox One user would be able to use them. Users would even be able to turn on their consoles just by speaking a command to the ever-listening Kinect 2.0.

It was also true that the Xbox One would require an Internet connection. However, it wouldn't always have to be connected, which meant that if a user lost his Internet connection for any reason, he wouldn't be restricted from playing games offline. However, Microsoft was vague about whether or not there was a limit to how much time a user could be offline before having to connect to the Internet again. According to Phil Harrison, Microsoft's Vice-President, the system would have to be connected to the Internet at least once a day in order to operate properly. But he couldn't state what would happen if that once-a-day rule wasn't complied with.

Finally, Microsoft confirmed what Xbox 360 gamers didn't want to hear: the fact that the Xbox One would not be backward-compatible with software from either of the two previous Xbox consoles. This didn't come as too much of a surprise, since backward-compatibility wasn't one of Microsoft's major concerns when they had designed the Xbox 360, either.[8] But once this news became official, the remaining question about software remained unanswered. Would users still be able to purchase used software for the Xbox One? Microsoft was elusive with its answer to this one.

As had been rumored, the Xbox One would require a one-time activation code for every game added to the console. Once a game was loaded onto the console's hard drive, the physical disc was no longer needed for that console. In fact, the disc could then be used to load the game onto multiple Xbox One consoles. However, no matter what console the game was loaded on, it could only be played if that console had been logged onto by the profile holder who had originally registered the game. If any other profile was used, Microsoft would require that the game be registered from the new profile through Xbox

Live, which would necessitate payment for the game before it could be played.

As far as used games were concerned, people would be able to purchase them and load them onto their hardware. However, Microsoft would require each game to be registered, and the price of admission would be whatever the going rate of that game might be at the time. So it wouldn't matter whether someone purchased a new or used version of a given game; the overall price would be about the same for the two.

Gamers weren't the only people who didn't want to hear Microsoft' announcements. On May 22, the company delivered news that infuriated independent developers as well. Since 2008, Microsoft had invited independent developers of games that had limited appeal to publish their games through Xbox Live. This gave the developers the opportunity to offer their games inexpensively to a worldwide audience. Microsoft required that any such game included an eight-minute trial period, so users could experience the game without having to buy it first. At the end of the trial period, the user would be informed that he would have to buy the game to continue playing. Games cost between $1 and $5, depending upon their size. Microsoft's plan with the independent developers was so successful that SCE, Nintendo and even Ouya, Inc. adopted similar programs for their hardware.

Unfortunately, Microsoft was changing the rules for independent developers where the Xbox One was concerned. They would no longer be able to publish their games independently. Instead, Microsoft was requiring them to sign publishing deals with either Microsoft itself, or an established third-party publisher, who would then publish the games for them.

Finally, on June 6, Microsoft officially confirmed that the Xbox One would indeed have to be connected to the Internet at least once a day, even if all of the games were to be played offline. And if an account was being accessed from a console that it hadn't been originally registered from, it was required to connect to the Internet every hour, or else the offline gaming would be suspended until the connection was made. Microsoft went on to explain that this frequent Internet connection was only required when games were played. It didn't need to be done to watch movies from a disc or live television.

Microsoft also clarified its unpopular Xbox One policy regarding used games. There would be no restrictions on buying and selling used games published by Microsoft. These games would be able to be transferred to new machines for no cost, as long they were bought and sold by retailers that were signed with Microsoft. However, third-party publishers could make their own rules on whether they would allow used copies of their games to be resold, or if they wanted to charge a licensee fee for any transfer, at a rate that would be entirely up to them.

Gamers would also be allowed to give away their physical discs, but only to people who had been on their "Friends" lists for more than 30 days. And each disc could only be given away once. Unfortunately, games could not initially be loaned or rented, but Microsoft was looking into a way to make that happen.

Microsoft held its next press conference five days later, in Los Angeles at 9:30 in the morning, on the day before the start of E^3. The company showcased the games that it would be releasing, with the most newsworthy being *Halo* for the Xbox One. Microsoft also said a little about how SmartGlass would interact with the Xbox One. The application, which would be natively built into the new console, would allow gamers to receive hints about the games that they were playing on their iPads, iPhones or Windows tablets.

Microsoft used the E^3 press conference to announce that the Xbox One would be available in November and would sell for $499. But the company also surprised the assembled crowd by announcing that a brand new console, the *Xbox 360 E*, was being launched that very day. Internally, the Xbox 360 E was virtually comparable to the current Xbox 360 S, but externally it looked like it could be the Xbox One's younger sibling. The

Microsoft Xbox 360 E

new Xbox 360 was slightly smaller than its predecessor, and ran quieter and cooler. While the two consoles shared the same retail price, $299, the Xbox 360 E contained less features. For example, Microsoft had removed a dedicated optical audio-out that had been on the earlier models, along with a multi-AV port that left only a jack for a 1/8" AV cable. Also one USB port was removed with four remaining. Although these missing features were ones that most people never used anyway, it still irked others that Microsoft was charging the same price but offering less.

But at this price, the Xbox 360 E did include something that the Xbox One wouldn't: a headset. Although a headset that would plug directly into the Xbox One controllers would be available for the Xbox One, it would have to be purchased separately. If users decided not to purchase the headset, they would still be able to chat online through the microphone built into the Kinect 2.0, which would be bundled with the Xbox One. Headsets that worked with the Xbox 360 would not be compatible with the Xbox One, due to a proprietary connection to the controller.

Sony Fires Back

SCE held its E^3 press conference later the same day and publicly showed the actual PS4 console for the first time. It was slightly smaller than the PS3 Slim, and a bit smaller than the Xbox One. The unit looked like two all-black rectangular units stacked one atop the other, with a small indented area between them. The two halves were slightly offset and angled, absent the curves that had been so apparent on all of the PS3 iterations. In the front of the unit, within the indented area, was a slot for Blu-ray discs on the left and two USB ports on the right. The DualShock 4 controllers could be charged by plugging them into the USB slots, even while the console was turned off.

Because Microsoft had "gone first," SCE had the benefit of trumping its competitor on several fronts, including the price. Retailing at $399, the PS4 would cost $100 less than the Xbox One.[9] But Jack Tretton, SCE's president, also chose to tell the assembled audience about the requirements and restrictions that the PS4 wasn't burdened with, rather than focusing on its particular strengths. It wouldn't require users to connect with the Internet at least once every 24 hours while playing single-player games offline. And SCE wasn't

SCE PlayStation 4

placing any restrictions upon the resale or purchase of used games. Finally, a game only had to be purchased once, regardless of how many different consoles it was going to play on.

SCE did require that most games designed to play on the PS4 also had to be able to play on the PS Vita, through the Remote Play feature. The only exceptions to this requirement were PS4 games that were designed to use the peripherals, such as the PlayStation Move and the PlayStation Camera, which could not be used with the PS Vita.

The *coup de grace* to the Xbox One was dealt the following day, June 11, when Shuhei Yoshida, president of SCE Worldwide Studios,[10] confirmed via Twitter that the PS4, unlike the Xbox One, would be region-free.

On June 12, Microsoft's Don Mattrick responded to Tretton's dig regarding that people playing games offline on the PS4 didn't need to check onto the Internet every day. He stated that Microsoft already had a product available for people who'd rather play games offline all the time, and it was called the Xbox 360. However, Microsoft announced a week later, on June 19, that in response to an outpouring of complaints from consumers and journalists alike, it was lifting its offline-gaming restriction that required the Xbox One to connect to the Internet at least once a day. Don Mattrick said that after a one-time system setup, the Xbox One would never again have to be connected online if the user only wanted to play offline, disc-based games. He also mentioned that there wouldn't be any restrictions on buying and selling used games, regardless of the publisher. In addition, like the PS4, the Xbox One would not be regionally locked. Gamers would be able to purchase physical software from anywhere in the world that would play on any machine.

On July 24, Microsoft reversed another of its unpopular Xbox One policies. It did away with the requirement that independent developers had to sign with Microsoft or a third-party publisher in order for their games to be published and distributed. Microsoft's latest mantra was that "every person can be a creator. That every Xbox One can be used for development." In that regard, the $500 consumer Xbox One, like the $100 Ouya, would double as a debugging console. Debugging consoles usually cost much more than the consumer models, so this came as welcome news to the developers.

Microsoft reversed yet another detested Xbox One policy on August 12, when it announced that the Kinect 2.0 wouldn't need to be connected to the Xbox One for the console to function correctly. And although the Kinect 2.0 was no longer required, it was still going to be packaged with the console. Bundled alongside it would be a headset, reversing yet another statement from Microsoft.

With all of the restrictions out of the way, the Xbox One was more similar to the PS4. Now the two consoles could be compared on equal footing as the days towards their launch approached. While it was true that the Xbox One did cost $100 more than the PS4, consumers were urged to remember that the Xbox One came with the Kinect 2.0. Since SCE offered the similar PlayStation Camera as a $59 option for the PS4 to anyone who wanted a complete package, there was only a $41 difference between the two consoles. But for people who weren't interested in a motion controller, Microsoft was making them pay $100 for a peripheral that wasn't required and which they probably wouldn't want to use.[11]

Nintendo 2DS

While Microsoft went through a summer of flip-flopping to keep up with SCE, Nintendo was silent. Since the Wii U had launched in November, 2012, sales of the console had been pretty lackluster. The Wii U's poor sales led several publishers to walk away from it. In May, Electronic Arts confirmed that it would not port its popular titles to the Wii U, since the console's sales figures didn't equate to a number that EA required for its games to be financially viable. Frank Gibeau, an executive with EA, later stated that it would be more than happy to develop games for the Wii U if Nintendo could sell more units. But it was a vicious circle. Third-party publishers were staying away from the Wii U, because there weren't enough units sold to support their games. And there weren't enough consoles sold because consumers weren't finding enough quality games to make it worth their while to purchase.

But Nintendo deserved much of the blame for the Wii U's poor performance. Following Nintendo's release of *New Super Mario Bros. U* and *Nintendo Land* during the Wii U launch, there had been a scarcity of new first-party Wii U titles, the ones that people always ran out to purchase. Nintendo hoped to turn the tide and used E^3 to show off new titles that featured its beloved characters *en masse*. Such titles included *The Legend of Zelda: The Wind Waker HD*, *Super Mario 3D World* and *Mario Kart 8*.

One other highly anticipated game that had been shown at E^3 was a title that had originally been announced at E^3 two years earlier on June 7, 2011. At that time, Nintendo had told the assembled crowd that *Super Smash Bros.*, a hugely popular series that had been around since the N64 and had sold over 10 million copies, would be coming out for both the 3DS and the newly announced Wii U. Little else was told about the game, although Nintendo president Satoru Iwata confirmed that the two versions of the game would somehow link with each other. Since *Super Smash Bros.* had been one of the first Nintendo-branded games announced for the Wii U, it had been assumed that it would have been one of the launch titles. Nintendo had used the 2012 E^3 to confirm that the new *Super Smash Bros.* was indeed in development and Masahiro Sakurai, the developer of the previous *Super Smash Bros. Brawl* for the Wii, was working with Namco Bandai on the game. This led to speculation that Namco characters such as *Pac-Man* and *Dig Dug* might appear in the new game. Release dates were not specified.

One year later at the 2013 E^3, attendees got to see trailers of the forthcoming game. They also learned that Capcom's Mega Man would be included as one of the characters. But as far as a release date, all they learned was that the Wii U edition wouldn't appear until the fourth quarter of 2014.

The 3DS version of *Super Smash Bros.* would arrive one quarter sooner. But unlike the Wii U, which needed such a high-profile game to increase its dismal sales, the 3DS, in both of its configurations, was doing just fine, and in fact was leading in sales among all of the consoles.[12]

Nintendo announced a new version of the 3DS on August 28. It included all of the features of the 3DS, with the exception of the ability to display games in what appeared to be three-dimensional. Appropriately, Nintendo called this new two-dimensional version the *2DS*. According to Nintendo of America president Reggie Fils-Aimé, the 2DS was an "entry-level handheld system" that was geared towards children younger than seven, while the 3DS was recommended for children seven and older.

But there were other differences between the 2DS and 3DS besides how the games were displayed. To keep costs low, only one monaural speaker was built into the 2DS, although full-stereo sound could be heard if headphones were used. The biggest change was in the unit's appearance. The 2DS did not employ the clamshell design that Nintendo had used for all of its DS devices. The new one-piece design, which completely eliminated any chance of young kids breaking the halves apart, was basically the same size as a completely open 3DS laid flat on its back. The single design lowered production costs for Nintendo, since it didn't require that two independent pieces needed to be joined together. Costs were reduced even further, because the 2DS only required one screen. However, the plastic face on the front of the 2DS gave the appearance that there were two separate, distinct screens.

Nintendo 2DS

The Atari Flashback 64

In September, as the world anxiously awaited the release of the new consoles from Microsoft and SCE, AtGames quietly released two more plug-and-play consoles. However, unlike the earlier systems that always offered more than the console that they superseded, these new plug-and-play consoles offered less.

The first was the *Atari Flashback 64*, which swayed from the previous systems in the Atari Flashback series in that the number in the title represented the number of games on the console, and not the numerical order in which it was released. The Atari Flashback 64 had 64 built-in games, whereas 2012's Atari Flashback 4 had featured 75 games. And the reduction in titles meant that this unit didn't have any new games that weren't on prior Atari Flashbacks. The unit also came with wired joysticks, whereas the Atari Flashback

AtGames Atari Flashback 64

4 had shipped with wireless controllers.

The other non-new console that AtGames released was another version of the Sega Genesis that it had already released in 2012. However, unlike the Classic Game Console from a year earlier that included 80 games, the new model only featured 60 games.

Archos Tries Again

On October 9, Archos tried its hand again at a handheld console. After its Archos GamePad had been berated by the press for several reasons, the company actually heeded some of the comments and went back to the drawing board. The result was the €180 ($243) *Archos GamePad 2*, which was released in Europe. This device was more suitable for gaming than its predecessor, as it featured a sharper screen, a quad-core ARM Cortex-A9 processor and 2GB of RAM. It also had a much improved battery life. But not all changes were necessarily better. Archos also improved the game-mapping function so the controls worked much better with games that had been designed for touchscreens. However, in order to map a game, the game had to be running, which made the process very cumbersome. Despite the improvements over the original Archos Gamepad, the Archos GamePad 2 still wasn't accepted by most reviewers. *Engadget*'s conclusion was to "pass on it."

Archos GamePad 2

American consumers never had the chance to pass on the Archos GamePad 2. Although Archos had announced that a $200 unit would be released in the United States during the fourth quarter, that launch never actually took place.

New PS Vitas

But Americans didn't really miss the Archos Gamepad 2, as Nintendo released the 2DS three days later on October 12 in Europe and Australia along with North America, where it sold for $129, $40 less than the 3DS. The 2DS launched the same day that Nintendo released its latest two highly-awaited Pokémon titles, *Pokémon X* and *Pokémon Y*. Ironically, these were the first Pokémon games that invoked full 3D polygonal graphics, a feature that would be lost on the 2DS. When the 2DS was released in South Korea on December 7, it was bundled with a digital copy of either *Pokémon X* or *Pokémon Y*, depending upon the console's color.

The 2DS was not sold in Japan, which made it the first Nintendo console not to be sold in that country. However, on October 10, two days before the 2DS launched, a new version of the PS Vita was released only in Japan, following price decreases on the original PS Vita that had taken place there months earlier. On February 18, SCEJ had dropped the prices of both of its PS Vitas, the Wi-Fi model, which had retailed for ¥24,980 ($270), and the higher priced 3G/Wi-Fi model that had been selling for ¥29,980 ($325). These amounts had remained unchanged since the device's launch in December, 2011. Both models were reduced to ¥19,980 ($216).[13]

The new ¥18,980 ($193) *PS Vita Slim* cost even less than its price-reduced predecessor, while still maintaining all of its features.[14] It was 20% thinner and 15% lighter, included 1GB of RAM (up from 512MB) and offered an additional hour of battery life. The PS Vita Slim also featured an LCD touchscreen in place of the OLED (Organic Light-Emitting Diode) touchscreen that had been on the original PS Vita. According to SCE, the new screen presented "better contrast and more natural-looking colors than the current OLED display." And while the screen produced better looking colors, the console itself was available in six designer colors, including yellow, blue and pink.

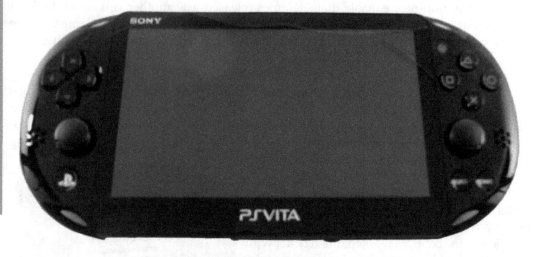

SCE Vita Slim

The PS Vita Slim was successful upon its launch. SCEJ sold 60,166 units during its initial week, compared to the 3,538 original PS Vitas that had been sold in Japan during the previous week. However, despite this achievement, SCE didn't indicate if the PS Vita Slim might be sold outside of Japan.[15]

SCE released another version of the PS Vita exclusively in Japan a month later on November 14, again without indicating as to whether or not it would ever be available anywhere else.[16] Actually, the ¥9,954 ($100) *PS Vita TV* was essentially a hybrid between a standard console and a handheld. It was the approximate size of a PS Vita, but it didn't feature any controls such as analog sticks, D-pads, buttons or even a built-in screen. But the PS Vita TV, which did include an HDMI-out port and slots for PS Vita game and memory cards, was in fact a PS Vita that channeled its output to a standard television set. The unit worked with a standard wireless DualShock 3 controller,[17] and if the user didn't own one, it could be purchased bundled with the PS Vita TV for ¥14,994 ($150).

SCE PS Vita TV

The PS Vita TV was compatible with most PS Vita games, including digital PS Vita, PSP, original PlayStation and even PC Engine games downloaded from the PlayStation Network. However, any game that required the touchscreen, touchpad, microphone or camera couldn't be used since these features weren't included on the PS Vita TV. And when the PS4 became available, its Remote Play feature could be used to stream games from a PS4 in one room to a PS Vita TV in another, allowing the PS4 games to be played on a television that was in a different location than the console.[18]

Before the PS Vita TV was actually released, SCEJ promoted it heavily along with the Namco Bandai game *God Eater 2*, which would be released the very same day for both the PS Vita and the PSP. The PS Vita version of *God Eater 2* wound up being the top-selling Japanese game of the week, beating out other new games, including *Call of Duty: Ghosts* for the PS3. Along with the 266,000 physical copies of the PS Vita version of the game that SCEJ sold during its first week, the company also sold 42,172 PS Vita TVs and 46,350 PS Vitas.

In November, SCEJ began offering a free downloadable app that basically turned the PS Vita into a PocketStation, the memory unit that had only been released in Japan between 1999 and 2002 for the original PlayStation. Although 42 mini-games were available, each one could only be obtained if the player owned the corresponding PlayStation game that accessed it.[19] SCE didn't announce any plans to release the PocketStation app outside of Japan.

PS4 Against The GameStick

On November 15, the day after SCE released the PS Vita TV in Japan, it launched the PS4 in North America, making it the first PlayStation that didn't come out in Japan first.[20] Within 24 hours of its availability, SCEA had sold over one million of the new consoles, a far cry from the 82,000 PS3 consoles that had been sold during its first day. Microsoft responded to the successful launch by tweeting "Congratulations on your launch, Sony" on its official Xbox Twitter account. In Great Britain, where the PS4 became available for purchase on November 29, SCEE sold more than 250,000 units within its first 48 hours, making it that country's fastest-selling console ever. SCE claimed on December 3 that more than 2.1 million consoles had been sold around the world.

The PS4 wasn't the only console that came out on November 15. On that very same day, PlayJam released its Android-based GameStick at GameStop and through Amazon.[21] Originally, the GameStick had been scheduled to come out in March. However, the high demand for it through its Kickstarter campaign, as well as production issues, forced several changes in its launch schedule. Kickstarter backers actually received their microconsoles in late August, but PlayJam had to keep juggling the release day for the retail units. After a November 8 launch couldn't be met, PlayJam finally settled on the following week, although it knew full well that that the GameStick would be pitted directly against the PS4. But PlayJam didn't want to delay the GameStick's launch any longer.

But it really didn't matter when they released the GameStick, because as sales of the previous Android microconsoles had shown, there wasn't any way that the GameStick was going to seriously compete with the PS4, Xbox One or even the Wii U. The best PlayJam could hope to do was beat the Ouya at its own game, but even that didn't appear to be realistic, considering all of the press that the Ouya had received.

The Xbox One Launch

On November 22, exactly one week after its own release date, the PS4's real competition, the Xbox One, launched in North America, Brazil, Australia and parts of Europe.[22] Although Microsoft held several launch events around the world that were streamed live via Spike TV, Xbox.com and Xbox Live, its launch headquarters was centered in New York at the Best Buy Theater in Times Square, where, after midnight, the first 1,000 purchasers of either an Xbox One console or game was invited to a live performance by Macklemore and Ryan Lewis. In addition, all 22 launch titles were available for play, so people could try them all out before they bought them.

Microsoft announced that it had sold one million consoles within 24 hours of the launch, making the Xbox One the company's fastest-selling console ever. SCE followed Microsoft's lead and tweeted on its PlayStation Twitter account, "Congrats, @Xbox @ Microsoft! #NextGeneration #GreatnessAwaits." One week later, Microsoft dominated American sales during Black Friday (the day after Thanksgiving) by capturing 60% of the console market with sales for both the Xbox One and the Xbox 360. SCE only captured 30% of the market with combined PS3 and PS4 sales. However, some analysts contended that it wasn't an even match, because of a shortage of PS4 consoles and the fact that Walmart
 had discounted the Xbox 360 to only $99, the same price as the Ouya microconsole.

Mad Catz MOJO

Meanwhile, a much more expensive microconsole hit store shelves on December 10, when Mad Catz released its Android-based *MOJO* in North America and Great Britain. The MOJO boasted Nvidia's new Tegra 4 processor, which made it much faster than its two direct competitors, the Ouya and GameStick. But unlike those two microconsoles, the MOJO didn't require games that were specifically modified or written for it. The MOJO played the games from Google Play and utilized a standard Android user interface to access them. However, the MOJO wasn't compatible with all of the games that were available for smart phones. Any game that required a touchpad, which was not a feature on the MOJO, could not be downloaded to the microconsole. While many of the games that required touchpads simply didn't appear when the MOJO accessed the Google Play menu, the ones that were listed were accompanied by a message that read, "Your device is not compatible with this version."

Mad Catz MOJO

The MOJO's controller was the best of the microconsole controllers. This was to be expected, since Mad Catz manufactured gaming controllers. The wireless *CTRLR*, as it was called, could actually be used with any console that supported Bluetooth. It even had a built-in clamp, so Android smart phones could attach to it and in effect act as handheld consoles.

Most critics raved about the MOJO and reported that it was the best microconsole available. Unfortunately, nobody believed it was worth its high retail price. The MOJO sold for $250, making it more expensive than the Xbox 360 or PS3, which already had large software libraries and used games that could be purchased for about the same prices as the games on Google Play.[23]

While the MOJO represented a footnote in videogame history, it was not a console that was meant to seriously go up against those from SCE and Microsoft. But the competition between the PS4 and the Xbox One was up and running. Analysts predicted that the PS4 would be the victor by the end of the year, taking into account the fact that it cost $100 less. Although both companies sold over one million consoles during their respective launches, it should be noted that the Xbox One launched in 13 countries, while the PS4 was initially released only in the United States and Canada.

Nintendo Stays Alive With Software

The Wii U wasn't part of this console competition. SCE and Microsoft each sold more new consoles in two days than Nintendo had done in a year. During the second quarter of the year, which ended on June 30, Nintendo only sold 323,688 Wii U consoles, just slightly more than half of its first-quarter sales. The seven-year-old Wii had outsold the Wii U by over 150,000 units during this same period. But June was the final month that the Wii actually outsold the Wii U. In July, Nintendo sold nearly 40,000 more Wii U consoles than Wiis.[24]

Sales for the Wii U really began improving on September 20, when Nintendo lowered the price of the Wii U deluxe set by $50 to $300. This was done in conjunction with the digital release of *The Legend of Zelda: The Wind Waker HD*[25] in North America. The company also offered a limited-edition $300 Wii U bundle that, along with a black console and GamePad controller adorned with gold lettering, included a gold crest and symbols from the game, a code to download a digital copy of a book that told the history of *The Legend of Zelda* series, and a code that enabled the user to download a copy of *The Legend of Zelda: The Wind Waker HD* from the Nintendo eShop. Nintendo saw a 200% increase in Wii U sales following the price cut and the release of the game.

Physical copies of *The Legend of Zelda: The Wind Waker HD* came out on September 26, initially in Japan, where Nintendo of Japan sold over 30,000 copies within a week. Physical releases followed in North America and Europe on October 4, which led to a 685% increase of Wii U sales in Great Britain! By the end of the year, Nintendo had sold 786,505 physical copies of the game around the world.[26]

Although *The Legend of Zelda: The Wind Waker HD* led to a resurgence of the Wii U, it wasn't the console's best-selling game of the year. That title went to *New Super Mario Bros. U*, which had been one of the system's launch titles. Nintendo had sold 2.2 million copies of the game in 2013. However, that number was minute when compared to the top-selling games of other systems. When the year ended, *New Super Mario Bros. U* was only ranked 17th in the global top-selling games of the year. In fact, only six Wii U titles even made the top 100.[27]

However, the Wii U did have more software in the top 100 than either of its two main competitors, the PS4 or the Xbox One. The PS4 had five titles in the top 100, with the highest charting position being 35. The Xbox One only had three games in the top 100, and its best-selling title ranked at 45. *Call of Duty: Ghosts* was the best-selling game for both consoles.

One of the Wii U titles that entered the European charts on December 13 was *Wii U Fit*,[28] an update to the exercise title that Nintendo had released for the Wii. As in *Wii Fit*, the Wii Balance Board was used in many of the exercises. In addition, the Wii U GamePad

Nintendo Wii U Fit Meter

could also be used for new types of activities, or simply could be used in place of a television set.

Another piece of hardware that worked specifically with *Wii U Fit* was the *Fit Meter*, which was similar to the Pokéwalker. However, the Fit Meter did more than just count steps. It also measured calories burned and changes in elevation. Then with the touch of a button, this data could be synced with the Wii U GamePad. *Wii U Fit* could then present detailed graphs that showed all of the activity.

Grand Theft Auto V

The majority of the games ranked in the top 100 were for the older generation of consoles, the PS3 and Xbox 360, which still sold in extraordinary numbers. While Nintendo sold 2.2 million Wii U consoles during 2013, that total was only a drop in the bucket when compared to the 6.5 million Xbox 360 consoles and 8.7 million PS3s that had been sold around the world throughout the year. The top two positions in the top 100 were held by the PS3 and Xbox 360 versions of *Grand Theft Auto V*, which combined, sold more than 29 million units.[29] This number was achieved in the 3½ months following the September 17 release of the game. By September 20, the game had passed $1 billion in sales, making it the fastest selling entertainment product in history. A digital version was released for the PS3 on October 7 and broke the record for the top selling PS3 game in the PlayStation Store. This feat was duplicated for the Xbox 360 when the digital version became available on Xbox Live on October 18. Altogether, *Grand Theft Auto V* broke seven *Guinness Book* records.

In terms of game-play, *Grand Theft Auto V* departed somewhat from the previous games in the series, as the player could choose from three lead protagonists instead of just one. Some missions required players to switch between all three characters as the game progressed. Critics loved the game. *Metacritic* and *GameRankings* both gave it such high ratings that it became one of the highest rated games on either site. In addition to the selection of protagonists, they also loved the open world that was featured in the game. Los Santos was a near-perfect rendering of Los Angeles, and gamers could explore every facet of it.

Grand Theft Auto V was an experience that could only be enjoyed by one person, and it didn't have an online component. However, beginning on October 1, two weeks after *Grand Theft Auto V* launched, purchasers were given the opportunity to access *Grand Theft Auto Online*, a game that contained all of the features of *Grand Theft Auto V* and allowed up to 16 people to team up or compete in *Grand Theft Auto*-style missions. Like the single-player games, *Grand Theft Auto Online* was set in the fictional city of Los Santos, which was located in the state of San Andreas. But Rockstar's plan was to keep adding to the setting until one day, there wouldn't be any limitations, and the entire world would be the backdrop of the game.

Grand Theft Auto Online faced some hurdles when it went live on October 1. Many players had trouble connecting to the game online, while others had the game freeze on them after they already began playing. Rockstar issued a patch on October 5, but problems continued as many players discovered that their online characters and properties were disappearing. Rockstar issued another patch on October 10 and then offered a "stimulus package" totaling $500,000 in gaming currency (GTA$) to all players who had sampled *Grand Theft Auto Online* anytime during the month of October. While the critical reviews for *Grand Theft Auto Online* were less than promising during its first few weeks, they turned around by the end of the month, when most of the game's bugs had been eradicated. On October 7, *IGN*'s Keza MacDonald had warned, "The game is not fully functional [and] does not make for a stress-free experience." By October 22, she reported that the game still wasn't up to its potential, but she said it in a different way. "*GTA Online* is good, then – properly great, even, when everything comes together – but not as good as I suspect it's one day going to be."

Toys-To-Life

Although no other single game could come close to *Grand Theft Auto V*'s extraordinary 3-day $1 billion gross, Activision announced in early February that its line of *Skylanders* Toys-to-Life games had grossed over $1 billion worldwide. This total was achieved through the sales of *Skylanders: Spyro's Adventure* and its 32 figurines, along with a new game, *Skylanders: Giants*, which had debuted in October, 2012, along with eight new figurines.

In October 2013, Activision's coffers overflowed again when it released the third entry in the series, *Skylanders: Swap Force*. This game introduced 16 new figurines, but each of these had upper and lower halves that were connected with a magnet. Each half contained its own unique microchip, and the halves could be separated from one figurine and then adjoined to others, providing a total of 256 unique combinations. But because the original Portal of Power that had been supplied with the Starter Packs of *Skylanders: Spyro's Adventure* and *Skylanders: Giants* could only receive information from the lower halves of the new figurines, a new Portal of Power that could also read data from the upper halves was supplied with the Starter Pack of the new game.

But by the time *Skylanders: Swap Force* was released in October, it was no longer the only example of Toys-to-Life available.

Nintendo of Japan entered the Toys-to-Life arena on April 24, when it released *Pokémon Scramble U*, a downloadable game for the Wii U. The game was basically a battle between Pokémon in order to collect all 649 creatures. Throughout the battles, players were awarded with coins that they could use to power up certain Pokémon characters. However, the only way to power up a Pokémon once the coins had been collected, was to purchase its physical version.

Nintendo of Japan released 18 figurines that cost ¥200 ($2) apiece. Data from the figurines was read into the game through an NFC (Near-Field Communication) square that was built into the lower left corner of the Wii U GamePad,[30] which had been unused until the release of this game.

Nintendo Pokemon Figurine

Unlike as in *Skylanders*, the Pokémon figurines weren't required to play the game, and only enhanced the game play. When Nintendo of America released the game as *Pokémon Rumble U* in the United States on August 29, it offered the figurines on a limited basis in selected GameStop stores. Meanwhile, the figurines weren't available at all in Canada.[31]

On August 18, Disney Interactive introduced its own Toys-to-Life series, which it called *Disney Infinity*. Unlike Nintendo's Toys-to-Life attempt, Disney Infinity was very similar to *Skylanders*. It consisted of a line of figurines that came to life in the videogame when they were placed on an *Infinity Base*, which was bundled with each

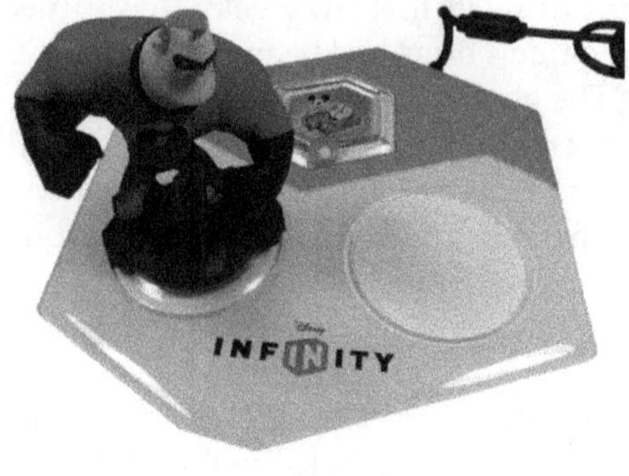

Disney Infinity

$60 Starter Pack. The latter also included three figurines and a game disc. The Infinity Base differed slightly from *Skylanders'* Portal of Power, as it allowed the placement of a hexagonal *world disc* along with two figurines. The world discs were used to unlock different Play Sets that could be purchased separately.

The Disney Infinity figurines were based on Disney characters, and the Starter Set came with figurines from three Disney and Pixar movies: *Pirates of the Caribbean, The Incredibles* and *Monsters University*. A world disc for each of these movies was also included. Additional Play Sets for other movies, including *Cars* and *Toy Story*, were available separately. However, figurines from a particular movie could only be used in that movie's Play Set.

Disney Infinity offered two modes of game play. *Play Set* mode provided unique playing experiences for up to two players, and were unlocked through the world discs. *Toy Box* mode was an open-world environment in which any figurine from any Play Set could venture. The figurines could bring tools into the Toy Box world that they had collected in the Play Set world, and the players could use them to create their own games.

THQ Closes Shop

Grand Theft Auto in both its console and online forms was an undisputed success for Rockstar. But not every software company had such a successful year. One such company was THQ, which couldn't even succeed at its own bankruptcy.

The company had declared bankruptcy on December 19, 2012, and the plan was that it would be sold to Clearlake Capital Group, a private equity firm, for $60 million, with the hope that THQ could continue to function in its entirety. Unfortunately, the sale was not approved by the bankruptcy court, because the majority of creditors believed that THQ's individual properties, which included design studios and game franchises, would be more valuable if they were sold off piecemeal. And so an auction was held on January 22. Among the bidders were Sega, which for a total of $26.2 million, acquired THQ's Vancouver design studio Relic, along with a new PC game, *Company of Heroes 2*, which THQ had planned to release in March. Ubisoft scored THQ's largest design studio, THQ Montreal, for $2.5 million. And for $3.3 million, Ubisoft also purchased a title, *South Park: The Stick of Truth.*[32] Even Take-Two, the parent company of Rockstar, got something out of the auction. For $10.9 million, its 2K Games subsidiary acquired *Evolve*, a game that had been deemed as one of the most attractive of THQ's properties. In the end, the creditors had been right and the auction brought in $73 million, more than they would have received if THQ had been sold whole. And after 23 years, THQ was no more.[33]

But THQ wasn't the oldest game developer to shut its doors during 2013. In April, LucasArts, the developer of *Star Wars* games and other titles, shut down after nearly 31 years in business. And unlike THQ's financial woes, the closing of LucasArts had nothing to do with bankruptcies.

The company, which had originally been called Lucasfilm Games, had been formed in May, 1982 by George Lucas to be the videogame-development arm of his company, Lucasfilm. Lucasfilm Games was renamed LucasArts during a reorganization in 1990. In October 2012, the Walt Disney Company purchased Lucasfilm and acquired LucasArts as part of the deal. Unfortunately, since Disney already had a game-development group, it didn't feel the need to keep LucasArts in operation. The division was shut down on April 3 and its projects were either assigned internally to Disney Interactive, or licensed out to independent developers.

At roughly the same time that Disney was shutting down LucasArts, Harmonix, the company that created *Guitar Hero* and *Rock Band*, was putting to bed its five year tradition of releasing new downloadable content for the *Rock Band* series. For 275 consecutive weeks the company released over 4,000 songs, even after Mad Catz took over the development and distribution of *Rock Band 3* in 2011. The reason behind this closure was so Harmonix could transition its staff who were responsible for the downloads on to other projects that weren't immediately specified.[34] Harmonix downloaded its final song, Don McLean's *American Pie*, on April 2.

NPD reported that retail software sales in 2013 amounted to $8.17 billion in the United States. This figure, which included $1.83 billion in used-game sales, was down 2% from 2012's totals. Meanwhile, Superdata reported that digital sales in the United States, including revenue from full game downloads, add-on content, subscriptions, mobile games and social-network games, totaled $11.7 billion, a number that was 10% higher than what had been generated from digital downloading in 2012. Yet while digital sales appeared to be on the rise, interest in the Android-based consoles wasn't anywhere near as had been anticipated. Although hardware sales in 2013 had risen 5% from the year before and hit a three-year high, this had been due to the extraordinary interest in the PS4 and Xbox One.

Despite prophesies of doom that interest in console-based games was waning, it remained as strong as ever at the conclusion of 2013.

CHAPTER 42
2014

The year 2013 would be a tough act to follow, as a record number of new consoles had been released. Despite the plethora of Android devices that had appeared on the scene, standard videogame consoles still ruled as far as sales were concerned. The November, 2013 launches of the PS4 and Xbox One had been the two most successful console launches in gaming history.

The Android-Explosion Aftermath

The new Android-based microconsoles didn't sell anywhere near as well as had been expected. The Ouya, which had done so well during its Kickstarter campaign, had faltered terribly. Although the company released a new $129 console on January 31 with 16GB of storage, which was twice as much as the original model contained, Ouya soon knew that it had to change its focus. In early March, it announced *Ouya Everywhere*, its plan to become a software company that would distribute Android games that could be embedded directly into TVs and set-top boxes, as well as other Android-based consoles, specifically Mad Catz' MOJO. After this announcement, *Forbes* declared the Ouya console to be basically dead. This seemed to be confirmed a month later, when it was revealed that sales for *Towerfall*, the system's top-selling exclusive game, had only numbered 7,000. And to make matters worse, the game was no longer exclusive to the Ouya. *Towerfall* had been released for the PS4 on March 11.

A few days after Ouya announced its focus towards software, Bluestacks, which had never even gotten its Gamepop out the door, announced a similar strategy. It planned to supply game content to cable companies, which they could then bundle with their other services. Although their business model had changed, Bluestacks still insisted that the monthly fee to consumers would remain at $6.99.

Bluestacks also changed the appearance of its console. Unlike the two models that it introduced in 2013, the new console would be about the size of the Gamepop Mini and would plug directly into the HDMI input of a television. Bluestacks also revealed

Bluestacks Gamepop Console

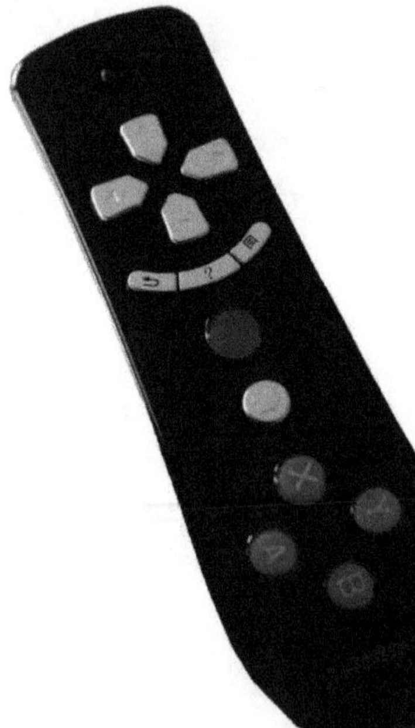

Bluestacks Gamepop Controller

its controller for the first time. It looked like a traditional television remote control, but it featured a D-pad as well as four control buttons. The remote operated in one of two ways, depending upon the game that was being played. If held vertically, it operated like a wand, similar to the Wii Remote. On-screen objects could be moved simply by waving the wand. When held horizontally, the controller could act like a standard controller with the D-pad and control buttons, or as a steering wheel in racing games.

FOCUS ON NEW ANDROID MICROCONSOLES

Two new Android-based microconsoles were released in 2014 but these were all-purpose devices that could also play games. The *Fire TV* from Amazon was released on April 2. This $100 unit resembled a 4.5" black square. The unit was sold with a standard remote control that could be used for media control and included a button and microphone that could be used for audio searches. This remote could also be used to play the Android games that were available. However, for the best gaming experiences, Amazon offered a $40 Bluetooth *Fire Game Controller* that was configured like an Xbox 360 controller.

With so many companies releasing microconsoles that employed the Android operating system, it was only a matter of time for Google to get on board with its own unit. The $80 *Nexus* Player, which was developed by Google and Asus, was released on November 3. The console differed from Amazon's Fire TV as it was round instead of square, but it also came with a similar remote that was used to access media and play casual games (any Android smart phone with Google Play services could also provide the same functions as the remote). And as with Amazon's device, a $39 optional gamepad was also available.

LeapFrog LeapTV

The Gamepop wasn't the only new console that came with a multifunctional controller based on the Wii Remote. LeapFrog, the manufacturer of educational gaming systems for kids, released a new console on October 21 that also embraced the technology. The $150 *LeapTV* was a console targeted towards children aged 3-8. It employed motion technology that tracked not just the controller, as Nintendo's Wii did, but also the player's body, as did Microsoft's consoles that were paired with a Kinect camera.

The LeapTV came with an oddly shaped round controller that had two handles and could be used in two ways. The handles could rotate, so they could either be end-to-end or side-by-side. When in the latter position, i.e. *Classic Mode*, it could be used like a standard controller, complete with a thumbstick and a pair of A/B buttons. When the controller's handles were rotated away from each other in *Pointer Mode*, it could be used as a sword or baseball bat that would be recognized by the console, just like a Wii Remote. The LeapTV detected motion from both the controller and the player via a Kinect-like camera that could be mounted above the TV.

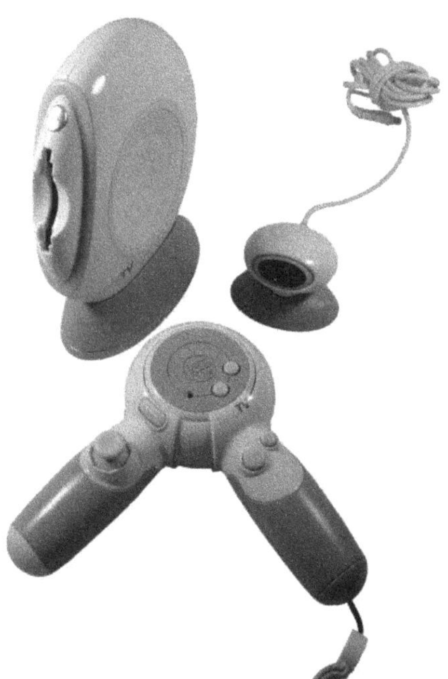

LeapFrog LeapTV

LeapFrog had eight game cartridges available at the time of the console's launch, which made the LeapTV the only game console that still utilized cartridges. However, by year's end, nearly 100 digital games were available that could simply be downloaded directly into the console's 16GB of flash memory. Game cartridges retailed at $30, while the downloadable content from the *LeapConnect* app store could be purchased for between $5 and $15.

Motionless Detection

While Bluestacks and LeapFrog were heralding their new fancy controllers that mimicked the motion detection of the Wii Remote, the traditional console manufacturers were slowly moving away from motion detection. Although the Wii U could use the Wii Remotes for Wii motion games, few new Wii U games became available that utilized them.

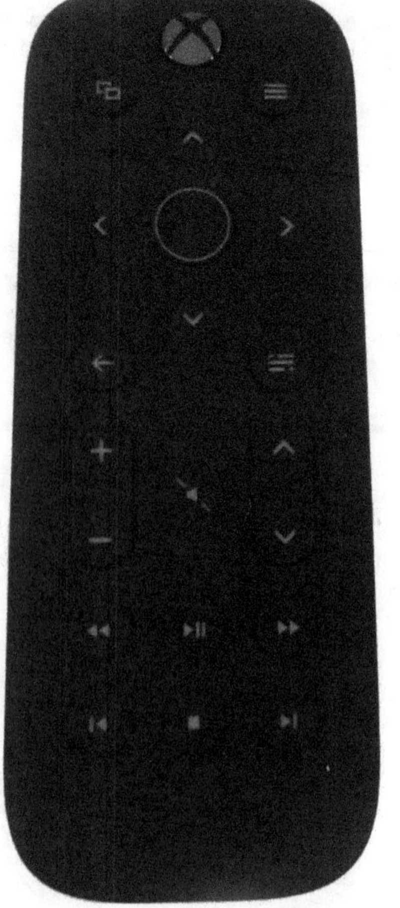

Microsoft Xbox One Media Remote

Microsoft was determined to make the Xbox One the entertainment hub of people's living rooms, and the Kinect was an integral part of this set-up, since people could just speak voice commands to their Xbox One to turn on the television or change the channel. But many people were not comfortable with vocally commanding the operation of their televisions, and even when they did, the Kinect sometimes had trouble responding, leading to an infuriating experience just to change a channel.

On March 4, Microsoft released a new remote that wouldn't replace the Kinect, but would make it easier to operate. As its name implied, the $24.99 *Xbox One Media Remote* allowed users to adjust the way they watched media with the Xbox One, and which had nothing to do with gaming in any way. The remote could be used to perform simple tasks, such as raising the volume, which previously could only be accomplished by saying "Xbox, Volume Up" over and over again until the desired volume was reached.[1]

But even though the Xbox One Media Remote made the Kinect more manageable, the bottom line was that people didn't want to spend the additional $100 that the Xbox One cost over the PS4. The price difference covered a peripheral that many really didn't want to use. With the PS4 outselling the Xbox One by 7-5, Microsoft had no choice but to give in to the Kinect detractors. On June 9, Microsoft finally offered the Xbox One without the Kinect and with a $400 price that matched the PS4.

While most consumers and developers were happy with this decision, there were a few developers who were not. Among them was Harmonix, the developer of music games. Harmonix was developing a new game called *Fantasia: Music Evolved*, which was to be exclusive to the Xbox One. And the Kinect was the sole reason for this exclusivity. According to Jonathan Mintz, the lead designer of the game, "We really want players to feel like they are physically shaping music and using it to transform worlds. The Kinect is the best tool for allowing us to realize that vision right now." However, with the Kinect not being included with every Xbox One, people who didn't own the device would be less likely to purchase the game. Although the game garnered good reviews upon its release in late October, sales were poor.[2]

Virtual Reality

SCE continued to sell the PlayStation Move, even though less games that used the peripheral had been released in 2014 than during the prior year. But this didn't mean SCE was through with motion games. In fact, on March 18, SCE introduced a new project that was designed to work nicely with the PlayStation Move when it was finally released.

Project Morpheus[3] was a Virtual Reality headset that would work with the PS4 and the PS Vita that had been in development for over three years. SCE had always planned on having some type of head-mounted VR technology. When the PlayStation Move was being developed, it was designed to work with a VR headset, even though one wasn't yet even in the planning stage.

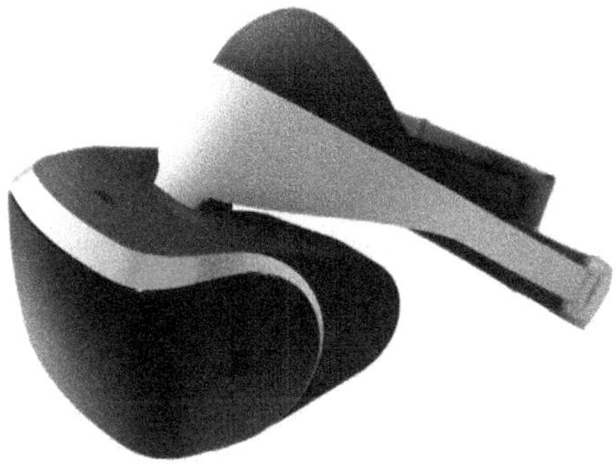

SCE Project Morpheus

Video headsets weren't new to Sony. In 1997, the company had released the Glasstron, which was basically a headset with two half-inch LCD screens that gave the impression of watching a 52-inch television from 6.5 feet away. But the Glasstron couldn't even be considered rudimentary virtual reality, since what the person saw on the two screens didn't change when he moved his head. In 2002, SCEJ introduced a new version of the Glasstron, the PUD-J5A, which did allow for head tracking and was compatible with the PS2. Unfortunately, its ¥59,800 ($500) price and limited number of games kept most gamers away. The device was quietly discontinued. During the following year, SCE found a new way to get people immersed into their games when it released the EyeToy. Project Morpheus, the company's latest attempt to get players to feel they were part of the game, was shown at several gaming shows, including the GDC and E[3]. However, despite the press that Project Morpheus was getting, SCE was in no rush to release it.

But Project Morpheus wasn't the only VR helmet that was being shown. Developers had been working on virtual reality for almost as long as there had been videogames, and no one had ever come close to perfecting an affordable system that could be enjoyed at home. The technology was always just a little bit out of reach, but it was getting closer every day. By 2014, it seemed closer than ever to getting home virtual reality into the marketplace. And several companies were striving to get there first.

Oculus VR had been working on its Oculus Rift headset since 2012, and on March 25, it was announced that the company had been purchased by Facebook for $2 billion in cash and $1.6 billion in Facebook stock. The common belief was that the Oculus Rift would either be a gaming console in itself, or a peripheral for an existing system. Oculus VR dispelled both notions when it announced that the Oculus Rift would need to be connected to a PC running Microsoft Windows. Regardless of which platform the Oculus Rift was connected to, there would also need to be a way for people to interact with that platform. On June 24, it was announced that Oculus VR had purchased Carbon Design, a Seattle-based, award-winning firm that had designed the original Kinect for Microsoft along with the Xbox 360 controller.

Controller Adapters

According to several online polls, many people considered the Xbox 360 controller to have been the best controller of all time. Unfortunately, a lot of people didn't share that opinion with its replacement for the Xbox One. Or more to the point, they weren't happy with the way the included headset plugged into the controller.

The headset plugged into an expansion port that was located on the Xbox 360

Microsoft Xbox One Controller Port & Headset Connector

Microsoft Xbox One Stereo Headset Adapter

controller. The expansion port was proprietary and not all prior headsets, even including those from Microsoft for the Xbox 360, could be used with it. This was in contrast with the PS4 controller, which had a standard, built-in 3.5mm port that allowed any compatible headset to be used.

The Xbox One headset's cord terminated in a small, plastic, triangular unit. This unit featured buttons that allowed the user to adjust the headset's volume and a mute button to turn the microphone on or off. It also included a USB plug that was bordered by two small, plastic rods. These plugged into a corresponding expansion port in the controller that consisted of a USB port that was between two small holes.

In order for Xbox One users to use alternative headsets, Microsoft released the *Xbox One Stereo Headset Adapter* in March. This $24.99 device was exactly the same as the plastic triangular unit that was at the end of the Xbox One headset, and it plugged directly into the expansion port on the Xbox One controller. Instead of having a cord that attached to the headset, however, it had a 3.5mm port.[4]

Whereas Microsoft released an adapter that plugged into a controller, Nintendo released an adapter that controllers plugged into. This happened when Nintendo of America finally released one of its most anticipated games for the Wii U on November 21.[5] *Super Smash Bros. for Wii U* was the fifth installment of the *Super Smash Bros.* series.[6] Although the game was playable on the Wii U using all of the controllers available for that system, many players preferred to play it with the GameCube controller. When *Super Smash Bros. Brawl* had been released for the Wii, it had been easy to attach the old GameCube controller, since the original Wii was compatible with the GameCube software and controllers. That was no longer the case with the Wii U. So in order to appease the thousands of fans who wanted to play the new game with their old GameCube controllers, Nintendo released the $20 *GameCube Controller Adapter*, a small plastic box that plugged into the Wii U and featured four GameCube controller ports on one side. Two of these adapters could be plugged into the Wii U, so up to eight players could partake in a game. The GameCube controller was so popular that Nintendo released a special *Super Smash Bros.* version, so gamers who didn't own the original GameCube controller could still play on the Wii U with the popular controller. Sadly, the adapter and GameCube controller could only work with *Super Smash Bros. for Wii U* and no other Wii U game.

Nintendo Super Smash Bros Controller

Nintendo Super Smash Bros. Wii U Adapter

Super Smash Bros. for Wii U became the fastest selling Wii U game in the United States, with 490,000 copies sold during its first three days. By the end of the year, that number rose to over 1.3 million. Unfortunately, Nintendo underestimated how many people might want to play it using their GameCube controllers. The adapters sold out soon after their release, and Nintendo couldn't issue any information concerning when they would again become available.[7]

Nintendo Amiibo

Even harder to obtain than the GameCube Controller Adapter by itself was a special $100 bundle that included the *Super Smash Bros. for Wii U* game, GameCube controller and GameCube Controller Adapter. This bundle was only available in North America, although a separate bundle that only contained the game and adapter was available around the world.

Another bundle, available only in Europe, included a *Super Smash Bros. for Wii U* game and a Mario *Amiibo* figurine. Amiibo were Nintendo's answer to *Skylanders* and *Disney Infinity*: small plastic characters that used NFC to transfer their data into a compatible Wii U videogame. Unlike the NFC figurines that Nintendo had released in 2013, the Amiibo had substantial roles in the games that they were compatible with.

The November 21 release of twelve Amiibo corresponded with the North American release of *Super Smash Bros. for Wii U*. Each of the $12.99 figurines, including Donkey Kong and Pikachu, was a character in the game, and when utilized, they activated a computer-controlled version of themselves into the game. The player could then choose to team up with the computer-controlled character or compete against it. As games progressed, the character learned how to react to the player's moves, and this could be saved back into the figurine to be used at a later time, or perhaps even in a different game. Many of the figurines, including Mario and Princess Peach, could also be used with *Mario Kart 8*, a game that had been released in late May. Although a November 14 downloadable update added Amiibo support, data could only be read into the game from the supported Amiibo. Information could not be saved back to the Amiibo.[8]

Nintendo Amiibo

Nintendo released six more Amiibo on December 14. By then, it was apparent that of the eighteen Amiibo that had been released, some were harder to find than others. A week earlier, Nintendo had confirmed with *Wired* that it was indeed deliberately not replenishing some of the figurines after their initial shipments, due to "shelf-space constraints." While popular characters such as Mario and Link would always be available, others would only be around on a limited basis. The problem with discontinuing figurines was that the functionality of those characters would be unavailable to most players. In late December, Shigeru Miyamoto said that Nintendo was looking into this problem. One possible solution was that the functionality could become available in the form of inexpensive cards.

Amiibo were hot! At year's end, Best Buy announced that Amiibo sales had tied those of *Disney Infinity* and had surpassed *Skylanders*. Nintendo sold over 1.3 million copies of *Super Smash Bros. for Wii U* by the end of the year, and nearly the same number of Amiibo figurines had been sold during the same period. Meanwhile, third-party companies decided to jump on the Amiibo bandwagon. Bandai-Namco announced that it would include Amiibo support in its 3DS game *One Piece: Super Grand Battle! X*, which had been released in Japan on November 13. A downloadable upgrade would be issued sometime during the winter, and this would allow Nintendo costumes to be unlocked with certain Amiibo figurines.[9]

New Nintendo 3DS

Another 3DS game that supported Amiibo **was** *Super Smash Bros. for Nintendo 3DS*, which had been released in Japan on September 13 and on October 3 in North America and Europe, several weeks before the Amiibo were released. The only problem was that the 3DS itself didn't support the Amiibo technology. Unlike the Wii U, which had an NFC square embedded in the lower left corner of the Wii U GamePad, the 3DS had no such thing. But Nintendo was prepared and on October 11, the company released two new consoles in Japan: the *New Nintendo 3DS* and *New Nintendo 3DS LL.*

The two handheld consoles were upgraded versions of the 3DS systems that were already available. The ¥16,000 ($148) New Nintendo 3DS was slightly thicker and a bit heavier than the 3DS that it replaced, while the ¥18,800 ($174) New Nintendo 3DS LL was slightly thinner and a little lighter than the original 3DS LL. The smaller model also featured a display screen that was slightly larger than its predecessor. It also featured multi-colored control buttons that were reminiscent of the Super Famicom controller.[10] Above these buttons was an additional analog *C-stick* that, along with two new triggers labeled ZR and ZL along the top edge between the L and R shoulder pads, eliminated the need for the Expansion Slide Pad. To make room for the new triggers, the cartridge port was relocated to the bottom edge of the unit. A different card slot was removed altogether.

New Nintendo 3DS & New Nintendo 3DS LL

The original 3DS had a slot on its bottom side where an SD card could be inserted for additional storage. The SD card was replaced with a MicroSD card in the New Nintendo 3DS. However, the slot that this card had to be inserted into was relocated to the battery compartment. And to access it required the removal of the console's back panel.

There were additional enhancements inside the systems. The new consoles rectified one of the major complaints of the originals: the displayed 3D effect was too narrow, and unless the person looked at the screen from just the correct angle, it became very difficult to look at. This led many people to just turn the 3D option off (or buy a 2DS). The New Nintendo 3DS corrected this problem with a new head-tracking camera and infrared sensor, which were located above the main screen.

Also new to the consoles was a faster processor than the one found in the original 3DS. Nintendo didn't publicize which type of processor it used, so there was no way to tell how much faster it was compared to the original. However, Nintendo announced that it was developing a New Nintendo 3DS version of the Wii game *Xenoblade Chronicles* that would take advantage of the added processing power. And while the New Nintendo 3DS consoles could play all games that had been released for the original 3DS, *Xenoblade Chronicles* would only be able to play on the new consoles.

The final major improvement made by the new consoles was the inclusion of NFC technology, which would thus support the new Amiibo. In order to communicate with the console, the Amiibo would be placed directly atop the bottom screen. Unfortunately, the New Nintendo 3DS consoles weren't released in Japan until October 11, nearly a month after the Japanese release of *Super Smash Bros. for Nintendo 3DS*, the first 3DS game that supported Amiibo. But that didn't really matter, since the Amiibo figurines themselves weren't even available until November 21, when they were launched along with *Super Smash Bros. for Wii U*.

November 21 was also the date that Nintendo released the New Nintendo 3DS consoles in Australia. However, these were the only two territories where the consoles were available during 2014. This meant that gamers outside of these two countries would not be able to retrieve and save Amiibo information for any Amiibo-compatible 3DS game. But even in Japan and Australia, gamers would be forced to purchase the new 3DS consoles if they wanted access to their Amiibo from their handheld. Fortunately, Nintendo had a solution in store for this problem. The company announced that an external adapter would be available that would provide the RFC capability to the original 3DS consoles.

Flashbacks Galore

Americans couldn't purchase the New Nintendo 3DS, which was an updated version of an older console. However, on October 1, three other classic videogame consoles were revived in modern forms when AtGames introduced three new $40 entries into its Flashback series. The first was the *Atari Flashback 5*. Externally, this console looked no different than the previous Atari Flashback 4, but internally it housed 92 built-in games, 17 more than the prior model. Five of those games were homebrews that had been distributed in cartridge form by Good Deal Games, a New York-based online retailer of games for retro systems. The remaining "new" twelve games were M-Network titles that were under license from Intellivision Productions. These joined Tigervision's *Polaris* as the console's only third-party titles.

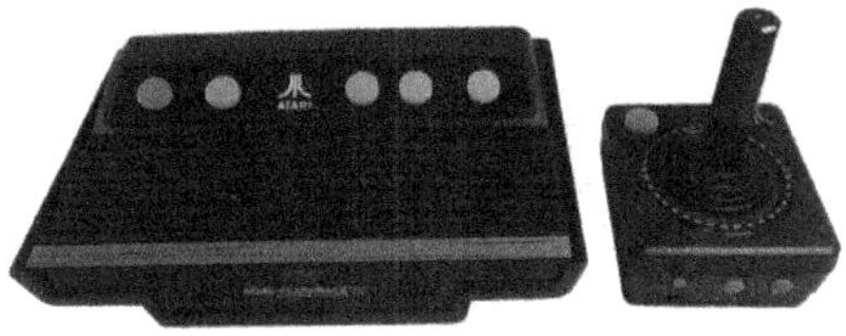

AtGames Atari Flashback 5

But AtGames wasn't content with just acquiring the games that Mattel Electronics had released for the Atari 2600. The company also licensed the original Intellivision titles that the M-Network games were based upon. And 60 of those games were built-into a new system called *Intellivision Flashback*.

Just as the Atari Flashbacks resembled smaller versions of the original console, the Intellivision Flashback looked like a tiny copy of the original Intellivision. Although the shape of the unit was more akin to the Intellivision II, since it was a square instead of a rectangle, AtGames got the basic look of the system correct. The only major difference was that the original Intellivision had a built-in area to store its two

AtGames Intellivision Flashback

controllers and the Intellivision Flashback didn't.

The controllers themselves were near-perfect replicas of the original Intellivision controllers. These controllers plugged into the front of the console, unlike the original Intellivision, which had hard-wired controllers. The controllers also supported the original Intellivision overlays, and a set of overlays for ten games was bundled with the unit.[11]

Unlike the Atari Flashback 5, which included 13 third-party games, the Intellivision Flashback didn't have any. However, among the 60 built-in games were six never-before-released original titles. Three games that had required the Intellivoice were also included, and the Intellivision Flashback was able to reproduce all of the voices without the need for the speech module.

The games themselves bore the names that Intellivision Productions, and not Mattel Electronics, had used. All licensed trademarks were removed. Thus, the game that had originally been called *Advanced Dungeons & Dragons* in cartridge form carried the name *Crown of Kings* on the Intellivision Flashback.

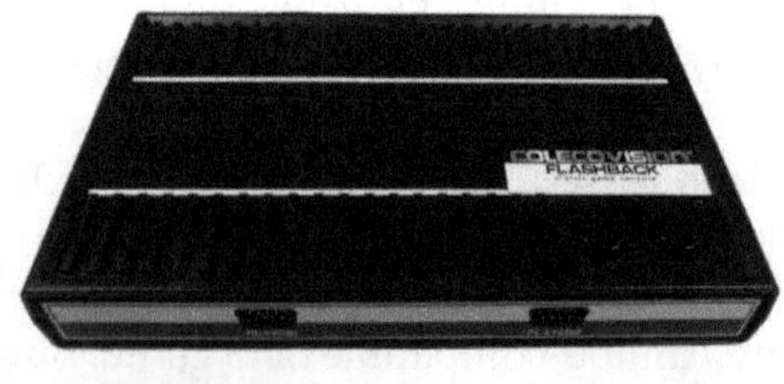

AtGames ColecoVision Flashback

ColecoVision Controllers

Whereas the Intellivision Flashback didn't include any games from third-party publishers, the third new unit from AtGames featured games from more than a dozen third-party publishers. While the *ColecoVision Flashback* did include some titles that had originally been published by Coleco, the majority of the 60 games in the collection came from Epyx, Imagic, Sunrise Software and even Atari, to name a few.

Like the other Flashbacks, the ColecoVision Flashback resembled a smaller version of the console that it was based on and it lacked the cartridge slot and Expansion Module Interface that were found on the original. And like the Intellivision Flashback, the controllers could not be stored within the console itself. In fact, the physical dimensions of the ColecoVision Flashback were the same as the Intellivision Flashback's, and the Reset and Power buttons and controller ports were in the exact same spots on both systems. Externally, the only differences between the two were their appearances, as each one mimicked the original console that it was based on.

The ColecoVision Flashback controllers resembled the originals, but they weren't quite right. Unlike the Intellivision Flashback controllers, which were exact replicas, the ColecoVision Flashback controllers were off a bit. They were slightly smaller. And because the controllers were smaller, the original overlays could not be used. The keypad was also different. The original controller had white numeric keys with black print, and black * and # keys with white print. All of the buttons on the new controller were black with white print.

PlayStation Now

Although Project Morpheus was still a few years in the future, a new project that SCE had announced at CES on January 7 came to fruition. *PlayStation Now* was born from SCE's $380 million acquisition of Gaikai in 2012. What it promised was to allow gamers access to a large online library of PS3 games that could be streamed to their PS3, PS4 or

PS Vita, or even to many Sony Bravia televisions and Blu-ray players. SCE even said that the service would also be available on non-Sony televisions, such as smart TVs built by Samsung.

Games could be rented for three months, one month, one week or even only four hours, and the price varied depending upon the amount of rental time. Early users of the system complained that most of the games were too expensive, as a three-month rental could cost as high as $50, much more than if a used version of the same game were to be purchased in a store.[12] SCE claimed that it would look into subscription rates, which would in effect turn PlayStation Now into a videogame equivalent of Netflix. However, subscription rates weren't available by the end of the year and games continued to be rented.

Although PlayStation Now wasn't officially available in 2014, it did go through beta trials throughout the year. An open North American beta period began for PS4 owners on July 31, for PS3 owners on September 18, and for PS Vita owners on October 14. On that same date, SCEA released the $100 PS Vita TV in North America, where it was called the *PlayStation TV*. PlayStation Now also supported the PlayStation TV, and North American beta trials for that product began on the day it was released.

Electronic Arts pitched a different type of subscription gaming service to both SCE and Microsoft. SCE wasn't interested, since it had its own service and didn't feel that the EA subscription fees ($5 per month or $30 per year) were good values for its customers. However, Microsoft was interested in what EA had to offer, and *EA Access* for the Xbox One launched on August 11.

The two subscription services weren't quite the same. PlayStation Now provided streaming games, which were all stored and processed on an external server. EA Access was a downloading service where an unlimited number of select EA games could be downloaded to and stored on an Xbox One console. If the player didn't renew his subscription, the downloaded games remained stored on his console, although they could not be accessed. In addition, games that were rented and downloaded could later be purchased at a discount.

Nintendo Wi-Fi Connection Terminates

On May 20, the Nintendo Wi-Fi Connection, which provided online support to DS and Wii consoles, was permanently shut down. Fortunately, this didn't leave DS and Wii games unplayable, since the Nintendo Wi-Fi Connection mainly supported them by providing free, unlocked, downloadable content. Wii U and 3DS games were totally unaffected by the shutdown, since their online capabilities were serviced by the Nintendo Network, which Nintendo had introduced in 2012.

The demise of the Nintendo Wi-Fi Connection was due to the shutdown of servers that had been owned by GameSpy. In fact, Nintendo wasn't the only publisher that had been affected by this shutdown, nor were the DS and Wii the only consoles. By some estimates, nearly 800 publishers and developers were affected, including Electronic Arts, Ubisoft and Capcom. The problem began in August, 2012, when GameSpy, which had been owned by IGN since 2004, was sold to Glu Mobile, a mobile-game publisher. By the end of the year, Glu Mobile began shutting down servers for many older games without informing their publishers. As publishers requested that Glu Mobile turn the servers back on, Glu Mobile responded that they would do so only if the publishers paid fees that were much higher than what they had been paying. And because access to these servers was basically written into the games themselves, the publishers couldn't simply move them to other servers without spending tens of thousands of dollars for redevelopment.

In preparation of the inevitable day when Glu Mobile would finally shut down the GameSpy servers altogether, some companies, such as Activision and Rockstar, sought alternative methods to keep the online components of their games active. Nintendo simply decide to walk away from its games that relied upon the GameSpy servers, as the cost would have been too prohibitive to support hundreds of games, many of which weren't even being played any longer.

Alamogordo Revisited

Two events occurred during the year that brought the history of videogames to the forefront of mainstream media.

The first began on April 26, when a film crew descended upon the Alamogordo, New Mexico landfill where Atari had buried thousands of cartridges in 1983. Over the years, the story of the mass burial had taken on legend-like proportions. Many believed that Atari had buried millions of unsold 2600 *E.T.* cartridges, the game that had allegedly single-handedly caused the infamous videogame crash of 1983. Others believed that it was inconceivable for Atari to bury cartridges when they could have simply gotten rid of them by discounting them. Even Howard Scott Warshaw, the designer of *E.T.*, had thought that the burial story was a myth.

In 2013, Fuel Industries, a Canadian entertainment company, received exclusive access to the site. Their objective was to excavate the landfill and see what they turned up, with the intention of producing a documentary of the event. They then proposed the idea

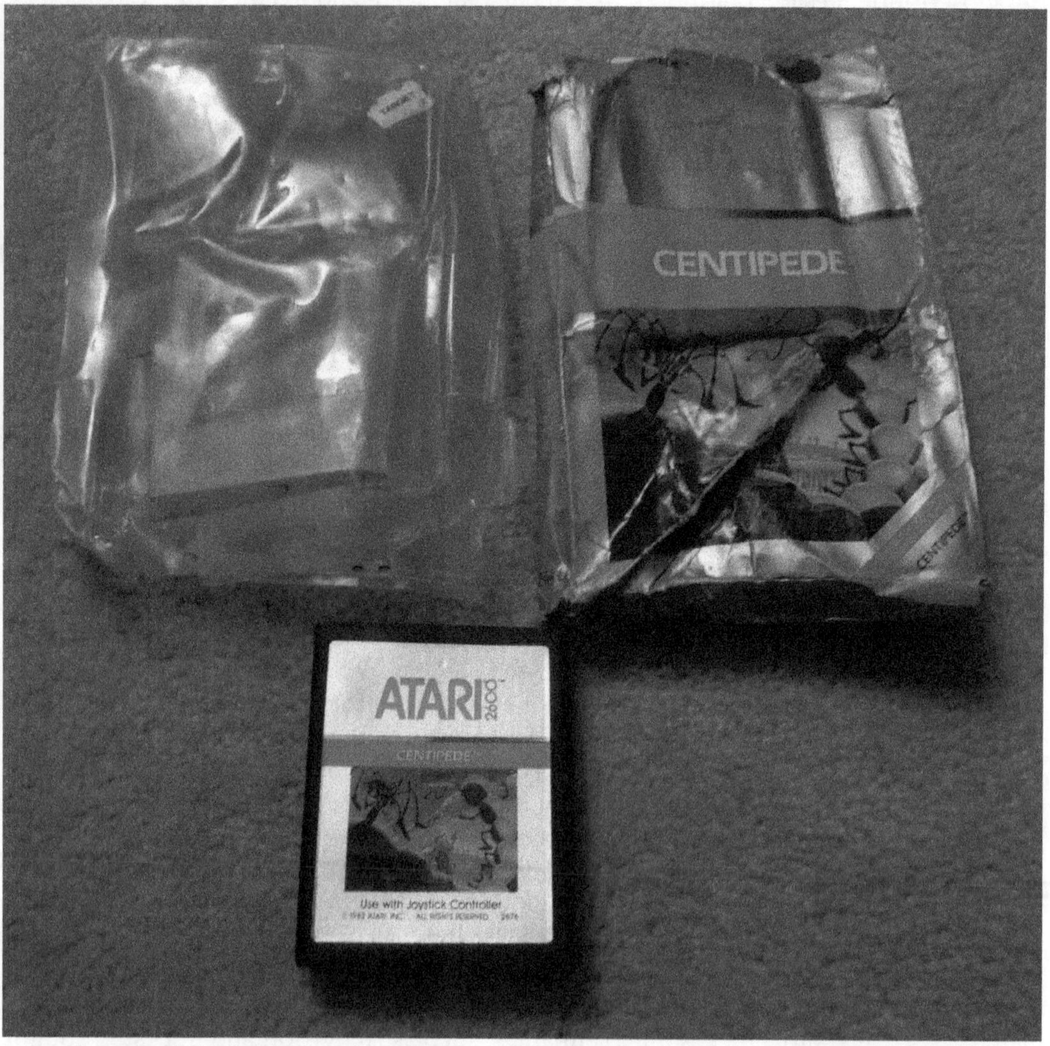

Excavated Centipede Cartridge Still Operable After Being Buried More Than 30 Years

to Xbox Entertainment Studios, a studio that Microsoft had created in 2012 to produce content for Xbox Live. Xbox Entertainment Studios immediately joined the $50,000 project as co-producer.

The dig was not carried out in vain. Cartridges and other objects were actually unearthed, and the first cartridge that was discovered was an *E.T.* in reasonably good condition. But *E.T.* wasn't the only game that was dug up during the five weeks of grueling excavation in the hot New Mexico desert. Thirty-one individual titles were recovered, including *Defender* and *Galaxian* for the Atari 2600 and *Qix* for the Atari 5200. Even 2600 joysticks and *Star Raiders* keypad controllers were found. All in all, of the estimated 70,000 cartridges that had originally been buried, over 1,300 cartridges were recovered, and surprisingly, many were still in playable condition, despite Atari's original statement that only defective games had been discarded.[13] Because the remaining cartridges were deeper in the landfill and much more difficult to recover, the excavation was simply refilled without any plans to retrieve them.

All of the items unearthed were technically owned by the city of Alamogordo, and the documentary producers received a percentage of the haul. The city promised that many of the cartridges would be donated to museums around the world so they could be put on display. On November 5, the city offered nearly one hundred cartridges on eBay, with bids beginning at between $50 and $100. In total, over $37,000 had been bid for the individual items in the group by the time the auction ended on November 13. A second group of cartridges was then offered through eBay on November 26.[14] The documentary about the dig, *Atari: Game Over*, began airing on Xbox Live on November 20.[15]

Death of a Legend

Videogame history returned to the forefront of the mainstream media in a somber way on December 6, when Ralph Baer, the man who had first conceived of interactive television, passed away in his New Hampshire home at the age of 92. Although he held the title as the "Father of the Videogame Console," Baer had done more than invent the videogame. Included among his many other consumer inventions were talking greeting cards for Hallmark, recordable talking books for Golden Books and the *Bike Max* (the first talking bicycle speedometer and odometer) for Milton Bradley, which had also produced Baer's *Simon*, one of the most successful electronic toys of all time, which was still being sold 36 years after it had first been introduced. But his contribution to the videogame industry was his true love, and he worked hard to preserve his legacy.

In 2006, Baer had donated the original Brown Box, along with several other prototypes, to the Smithsonian Institution, which cataloged everything but didn't put any of it on display, much to Baer's irritation. Finally, in 2014, as Baer's health slowly deteriorated, the Smithsonian Institution finally decided to place his Manchester, NH lab on display. It had been Baer's fervent wish to see the exhibit, but unfortunately, he died before it could happen.

PlayStation Experience

Ironically, on the very day that Ralph Baer passed away, as much of the gaming world was reflecting on the industry's past, thousands of people assembled at The Venetian in Las Vegas for the first annual *PlayStation Experience*. This was a mammoth two-day event that was not unlike E^3, although it was open to the public, who paid $50 for a one-day pass or $90 for both days. It focused solely on SCE's consoles and the games that played on them. PlayStation Experience featured keynote speeches and discussion panels, along with demos and plenty of hands-on play of new games. And since it had been scheduled three weeks before Christmas, it offered people a chance to see why they should purchase a PS4 or PS Vita for the holidays.

Magazines – New and Old

One of the exhibits shown at PlayStation Experience was a lineup of each one of SCE's consoles from the original PlayStation to the PS4, including the PSP and PS Vita. This was to showcase the 20th anniversary of the release of the PlayStation in Japan on December 3, 1994.

Retro Magazine

Ironically, a new magazine with a similar theme, showcasing the games of the past while providing information about the games of the present, had launched nearly a year earlier.

Retro was the brainchild of Mike Kennedy, who in March 2008 had founded *Game Gavel*, an online videogame auction site that provided an alternative to eBay. The idea of *Retro* was to fill a gap that began to widen as more and more print magazines were folding in the United States. While the magazine covered videogames from all eras, Kennedy's idea was to assemble many well-known writers from classic videogaming magazines, such as *EGM*, to produce a high-quality print magazine (although digital and online versions would also be available) that would be aimed towards sophisticated gaming fans of all ages. Funding for the magazine was obtained through a Kickstarter campaign in 2013, and although many people scoffed at the idea of a new print magazine in a digital age, by the end of the campaign, 2,345 backers had pledged nearly $76,000, which proved that there was a definite interest in such a magazine. Although the magazine targeted a December 2013 release, the first issue wasn't actually available until January, 2014. By the end of the year, Kennedy claimed that *Retro*'s circulation was 40,000 readers from 35 different countries.

Retro thrived despite the contemporary thought that print magazines could not survive, and it joined the only other highly circulated American videogame magazine, *Game Informer*.

Things were a bit different in Great Britain, where print magazines seemed to flourish. Between Imagine's *Games™* and *Retro Gamer*, and Future's *Edge* and *Gamesmaster*, the videogaming industry was well represented. But that wasn't to say that magazines in the United Kingdom stayed in print forever. On June 14, *The Guardian* revealed that UK consumer magazines had lost almost one million print sales during the first half of the year, a trend that had been occurring for more than a decade. Indeed, the print edition of *C&VG*, the world's first magazine dedicated to videogames, had continued on as a website ever since Future pulled the plug on its print edition in late 2004. But on May 15, the company announced that it planned to shut down the UK-specific *C&VG* website, due to several quarters of poor financial results. It planned to concentrate on *GamesRadar*, a website that also had a following in the United States. In June, Future had a change of heart and announced that it would keep the *C&VG* brand alive, at least until the end of the year. But in November, Future revamped the *GamesRadar* site and renamed it *GamesRadar+* to reflect its new television, film and science-fiction sections, which had previously appeared on other Future–owned sites. In December, it was announced that the *C&VG* content would be moving to GamesRadar+ as well, and the original *C&VG* site would be permanently shut down.[16]

Year-End Totals

The consolidation of multiple videogame-related websites occurred at a time when less consoles were being sold. Although nearly 46 million consoles had been sold worldwide during 2014, that number was approximately three million less than the number sold in 2013, when the PS4 and Xbox One had been available for less than two months. In fact, the year 2014 marked the sixth year in a row in which the total number of consoles sold was less than that of the prior year. And the total amount spent on videogame hardware and software in Japan was at its lowest point since 1990.

The PS4 was the top-selling console of the year, with 14.4 million units sold around the world. It was the number-one console in North America, where 4.8 million consoles had been sold; and in Europe, where 5.9 million systems had been purchased. That number was higher in Europe, because the Xbox One did much poorer outside North America. Although the Xbox One was the second top-selling console in North America, where 4.3 million systems had been sold, elsewhere in the world the PS4 was followed by the 3DS. In Japan, less than 46,000 Xbox Ones were sold, but that was in a country where consoles didn't do so well overall. SCEJ sold less than a million PS4s, fewer than the 1.1 million PS Vitas that were sold during the same time period. The 3DS, with 3.1 million units sold, was the top-selling system in Japan.

As far as software was concerned, Nintendo ruled the roost in Japan. All of the titles in the top ten were from Nintendo, with eight for the 3DS and the remaining two for the Wii U. The top-selling game was *Youkai Watch 2 Ganso*, a role-playing game that was not released outside of Japan. Number two in Japanese sales was the combined total of *Pocket Monsters Omega Ruby* and *Pocket Monsters Alpha Sapphire*, which basically held the top position everywhere else in the world. Globally, the pair of games sold 7.3 million units. But that top position might have been in contention, since it was held by two games. The worldwide number-two spot was occupied by Activision's *Call of Duty: Advanced Warfare* for the PS4. This sequel sold 5.6 million copies. However, when the total units sold for all four of the game's formats were tallied, that number was over 16 million.[17]

But the amount sold was even higher than what was reported. This was because the NPD Group, the company that tracked the sales statistics, only reported the performance of physical media. While NPD reported that sales of games on physical media had dropped 17% during the first 11 months of 2014, Superdata, a company that tracked digital sales, claimed a rise of 12% in such sales between July, 2013 and July, 2014.

Between 2009 and 2013, game software sales on physical media dropped from 80% to 53%. In 2014, the bottom fell out, and for the first time, digital sales outnumbered physical sales 52% to 48%.

The game was changing. While this statistic was not good for retailers such as GameStop, it was good news for the videogame publishers, who could release more titles without having to worry about costs for packaging, manufacturing and physical distribution.

A new era in videogames was just beginning.

CHAPTER FORTY-THREE
2015

In 2014, digital game sales had surpassed those of physical games for the first time, with a majority of sales attributed to mobile gaming, which had also seen its share of growth throughout the years. Unfortunately, while the mobile-gaming industry had grown in 2014 from the year before, the percentage of the growth was substantially lower than it had been in prior years. In 2013, there was a 61% growth over 2012's sales. In 2014, that percentage had dropped to only 30%. Some questioned whether or not the bottom had fallen from the mobile gaming industry as smart phones were giving way to smart TVs.

Android TVs and Microconsoles

A smart TV was basically a television that could do much more than provide media for viewing. While some televisions were being manufactured with the necessary software embedded into them, more and more television sets were turned into smart televisions by the addition of set-top boxes. Televisions and set-top boxes that used the Android operating system were dubbed *Android TVs*. Several Android TV boxes were released during the year.

The first, Razer's $80 *Forge TV*, was released on May 5. Razer, a manufacturer of computer gaming peripherals, promised console-quality game-play and also released the *Serval*, a $60 Bluetooth controller. Games could be streamed from PCs and downloaded from either Google Play or *Cortex*, Razer's online storefront, which offered over 1,000 applications, the largest library of Android content available for the Forge TV. Razer had acquired this content by purchasing Ouya on June 12. The Ouya console was immediately discontinued and its technical team was assigned to the Forge TV group.

Razer Forge TV

Many independent Ouya developers voiced their concern that money that Ouya owed them would not be paid. Razer, in an effort to stay on good terms with the developers, offered to pay whatever Ouya owed them, as long as they signed a new contract with Razer. The new contract was basically the same as the old one, except that apps wouldn't be exclusive to the Forge TV, but would be available to all microconsoles that ran under the Android operating system.

Nvidia released its $200 *SHIELD Android TV* on May 28. Originally called the *SHIELD Console*, the SHIELD Android TV, Nvidia's third Android-based device, followed its original handheld Shield, which arrived in 2013; and a *Shield Tablet* that was released in 2014. Like the less expensive Forge TV, the SHIELD Android TV could stream PC games. However, these streaming games came from the cloud, and not a nearby computer.

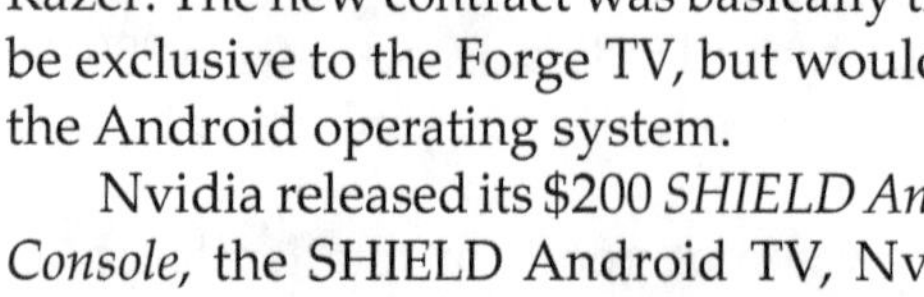

Nvidia SHIELD Console

China

Two additional Android-based microconsoles were announced early in the year by Chinese manufacturers. These were not Android TVs, as they were only designed to play games, and followed the model set by GameStick. They could play any game available from Google Play, as well as additional games through the online storefronts set up by the manufacturers.

The *OBox* (online box) was from Snail, which had been one of China's first online game developers when it was founded in 2000. The OBox was announced at CES in January and displayed at E^3 in June. The machine was designed for hardcore gamers, and Snail planned to offer it in several configurations, which included two different processors, two different HDMI setups, and four different hard drives of various capacities, ranging from 500GB to 4 terabytes. Snail didn't reveal a retail price, nor could it pinpoint a release date, although the console was scheduled to be released in China first.[1]

Snail Games Obox

Although the OBox seemed somewhat suspicious because of its name, which was too similar to Microsoft's Xbox, the other new Android console out of China appeared to be a complete rip-off of an existing gaming console. The *Ouye* was announced in August on a Chinese crowd-funding site, which declared a goal of $15,000. The unit closely resembled a PS4 and included a controller that looked very much like the one supplied with the Xbox One. The company behind the Ouye claimed that it had spent six months working on a unique design of the console. But despite its very high-tech appearance, the Ouye was only going to sell for $70 and would only feature 2GB of RAM and 16GB of flash storage.

OUYE

Even by Chinese standards, the Ouye was a blatant rip-off, and Chinese consumers accused the company behind it of stealing ideas from others. Chinese websites said that the Ouye "tarnished China's image to foreigners." Due to this unprecedented backlash, the crowdfunding campaign was canceled and the Ouye was put to rest.

The fact that the Chinese were blaming the Ouye for tarnishing its image was laughable, since China had a reputation for counterfeit games and low quality assurance. In 2014, China's videogame industry claimed to be the world's biggest in number of consumers. But the industry consisted mainly of imported PC and mobile games that had been modified for the local market.

While the PC- and mobile-gaming industry flourished in China, the console market was non-existent. The only way Chinese residents could purchase a PS4 or Xbox One was through the black market. Since 2000, the sales of foreign-made videogame consoles were deemed illegal by China's Ministry of Culture, which feared that they would have "adverse effects" on China's youth. However, that law was rescinded in 2014, and this paved the way for foreign consoles to become available in July. But this didn't mean that Nintendo, SCE and Microsoft would make a major killing in China. Although it was estimated that there were 515 million gamers in China, only 9 million were interested in playing games on consoles; and these gamers couldn't even purchase the most popular titles. Even though the consoles were permissible, software that featured political content or realistic violence remained illegal, thereby preventing games such as *Halo* and *Grand Theft Auto* from entering the country. But there was another reason why sales remained low for the foreign consoles. An imported PS4 retailed for about $460 in China, a country where most everyone earned less than $645 a month.

Console Fever

Despite the lackluster performance in China, the console-gaming industry was business as usual everywhere else in the world. In the United States, Microsoft had temporarily lowered the price of its Xbox One by $50 over the 2014 Christmas holidays, thus enjoying a substantial increase in sales, which ultimately exceeded ten million. These beat Nintendo's Wii U sales by two million, even though the latter console had been available a year longer.

Microsoft was so pleased with this that the offer was repeated in mid-January, and an Xbox One could be purchased without a bundled Kinect for $349. This promotion was also successful, and at the end of January, Microsoft proudly announced that the number of Xbox Ones sold around the world had increased to over 11 million.

Despite that number, Xbox One sales still lagged behind those of SCE's PS4. Following an extremely successful holiday season in 2014 that saw over 4 million units sold, SCE had entered 2015 with over 18 million consoles in consumer hands. That number continued to climb, and by the beginning of March, SCE was happy to report that over 20 million PS4s had been sold in 123 countries.

PlayStation Now Subscriptions

Many PS4 owners were happy with a promise that SCE had made in 2014 concerning subscriptions to its PlayStation Now streaming service. The service went live in North America on January 13, and offered subscriptions, as opposed to rentals, which beta users had felt was too expensive. The subscriptions, which offered unlimited access to more than 100 PS3 games, were priced at $19.99 per month, or $44.99 quarterly. In May, SCE extended the service to PS3 owners, along with select Sony Blu-ray players and televisions. As of June 10 the latter included select Samsung smart TVs.

As PlayStation Now was being unfurled, the other game-streaming service, OnLive, announced on April 2 that it was shutting down as of April 30. Its 140 patents were purchased by SCE.

Nintendo News

Nintendo's outlook at the beginning of the year wasn't as rosy as that of Microsoft and SCE. With only 9.2 million Wii U consoles sold since its late 2012 debut, many people expected Nintendo to discontinue the product.[2] Nintendo president Satoru Iwata insisted in late January that the "Wii U [wasn't] over yet." However, analyst Michael Pachter of Wedbush Securities claimed in a February interview with *Game Informer* that Nintendo was in denial about the Wii U's poor sales. Pachter blamed this on Nintendo's determination to make a profit on the console rather than just the software, challenging the business model that had been in place since Atari released the VCS in 1977. Pachter reasoned that the Xbox One only cost $50 more than the Wii U and offered much more, including a large third-party library. If Nintendo were willing to forego its profit on the console, he argued, it would be able to sell the Wii U for much less than the Xbox One and attract many more buyers.

Nintendo's fiscal year ended on March 31, at which time the company released its earnings for that year. These showed that the Wii U had failed to meet sales expectations.[3] Fortunately for Nintendo, it didn't have to depend solely upon the Wii U to stay in business. It still owned the handheld market with the 3DS, and although mobile-gaming sales were dipping into the handheld's bottom-line, Nintendo had some comfort in knowing that there was little danger of the 3DS falling to the only other handheld videogame console, SCE's PS Vita.

Worldwide 3DS sales had topped 50 million units by the end of 2014. This sales surge was partially attributed to the release of the New Nintendo 3DS models that had been released in Japan and Australia during the fourth quarter of the year. On February 13, Nintendo released the New Nintendo 3DS LL in Europe and in North America, where it was called the *New Nintendo 3DS XL*. The regular-sized handheld, the *New Nintendo 3DS*, was not released in North America. This was a decision made by Nintendo of America. A vague reason for this was explained to *Kotaku* in mid-January: "We think New Nintendo 3DS XL makes the most sense for our market. Nintendo makes different systems at different price points for a whole range of consumers, and New Nintendo 3DS XL simply expands those choices even further."

The New Nintendo 3DS had a more powerful CPU than the original model. While games tended to load faster on the new machine, there wasn't any software available that had been especially designed to take advantage of the extra power. That changed in April, when Nintendo released *Xenoblade* for the New Nintendo 3DS only.[4] This was a port of a Wii game that had originally been planned for the 3DS rather than the Wii U, because Nintendo felt that modern gamers would want to play it on the go. However, a true port couldn't be made for the 3DS, because the processing power of the Wii was greater than that of the 3DS; but a port for the New Nintendo 3DS was possible. The game's packaging had a large red arrow that made it clear that it would only run on that platform.

Only For New Nintendo 3DS

Toys-to-Life

Nintendo released the New Nintendo 3DS mainly for compatibility with its Amiibo figurines, which previously only worked with the Wii U. The New Nintendo 3DS had an NFC reader/writer located beneath the bottom screen. However, Nintendo wasn't forcing Amiibo fans to purchase the New Nintendo 3DS if they wanted to get the most out of their figurines. The company released a $20 *NFC Reader/Writer* for the original 3DS on July 30 in Japan, on September 25 in North America and on October 2 everywhere else.[5]

With the success of Amiibo, Nintendo was naturally criticized for copying *Skylanders* and *Disney Infinity*. In March, Satoru Iwata told *Time* magazine that Amiibo brought "something new to the table" rather than merely copying the prior toys-to-life figurines. Iwata felt that Amiibo could do things for Nintendo's games that couldn't be

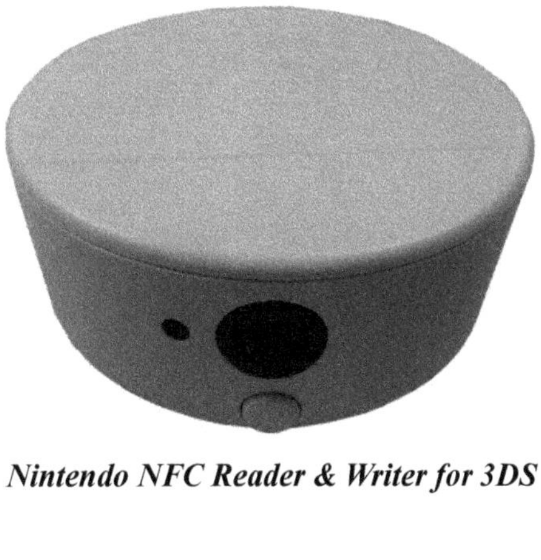

Nintendo NFC Reader & Writer for 3DS

Lego Dimensions

done anywhere else.

But each of the toys-to-life games were unique in their own ways. And the field was getting larger when Warner Bros. released its own version, *Lego Dimensions*, at the end of September in North America, Europe and Australia. *Lego Dimensions* was the latest in a long line of Lego-themed games that had been available on videogame consoles since *Lego Racers* came out for the N64 and PlayStation in late 1999.[6]

Lego Dimensions differed from the other toys-to-life games, as the player had to build the NFC reader/writer out of Lego blocks, which came with the set. Instead of being figurines, the characters, which were based on different Warner Bros. franchises, were also built from Lego blocks. The $100 starter pack came with Batman, Gandalf from *The Lord of the Rings*, and Wyldstyle from *The Lego Movie*. And although they came from different backgrounds, all characters in *Lego Dimensions* could be used in all games, and each offered unique skills and powers. Of course, this also meant that other characters could be purchased separately, in order to unlock different parts of the game.

In 2014, *Disney Infinity* had been the best-selling of the toys-to-life series. Despite this, Disney Interactive announced in April that it was laying-off dozens of employees from its *Disney Infinity* studios. A spokesman for Disney Interactive claimed that this was done to "create efficiencies and streamline [their] operations." Despite these major layoffs, Disney Interactive released *Disney Infinity 3.0*[7] in late August in North America and Europe. This game centered around the *Star Wars* franchise, which Disney had acquired in 2012 as part of its purchase of Lucasfilm.[8] Reviews for *Disney Infinity 3.0* were mostly excellent, with many saying it was the best of the series. IGN called it the "most polished, cohesive, and enjoyable one to date."

One problem that Nintendo faced with its Amiibo was that some of the figurines became very difficult to find, in some cases because they were sold only at certain retailers. In North America, Toys 'R' Us, Best Buy, GameStop, Target, Walmart and *Amazon.com* all had their own exclusive figurines. Another problem was that many Amiibo were only available for limited durations. Some figurines were discontinued to make room on store shelves for new ones. People had complained that if they couldn't get a particular Amiibo, they would lose the specific game functionality that it provided. On February 17, Satoru Iwata verified that Nintendo would issue Amiibo cards as a way to provide the functionality lost from discontinued figurines. To start, individual Amiibo cards that supported a newly released 3DS game called *Animal Crossing: Happy Home Designer* became available on July 30 with the release of the game in Japan. Over 312,000 packs were sold in four days. Unfortunately, these weren't the Amiibo cards that would replace discontinued figurines.

Animal Crossing Amiibo Card

In fact, Nintendo wouldn't produce Amiibo figurines to be used with *Animal Crossing: Happy Home Designer*. Only the Amiibo cards could be used with the game. It was unclear if these were the Amiibo cards that Satoru Iwata had referred about since Amiibo cards that replaced previously-released Amiibo figurines were never actually released.

The Amiibo cards, like the figurines, each contained an NFC chip that worked with the NFC reader/writer on the Wii U GamePad and both sizes of the New Nintendo 3DS. Nintendo had been mum about whether or not the regular New Nintendo 3DS would be released in North America, so it wasn't quite so unexpected when the smaller handheld console his American store shelves on September 25. However, it was only available as part of a bundle that included two cover plates, an Amiibo card, a download code for *Animal Crossing: Happy Home Designer* and a special *Animal Crossing*-themed console. There was still no way to purchase a non-themed regular version of the console.

One plan that Nintendo had for the 3DS was to port popular smartphone games to it, as opposed to developing games for smartphones. The first such game was *Puzzles & Dragons Z*, which had been released in Japan in December, 2013. Within six months of its release, Nintendo of Japan had shipped over 1.5 million copies.

Puzzles & Dragons Z was the 3DS version of *Puzzles & Dragons*, which had come out for iOS and Android smartphones during 2012. The elder game was a product of GungHo Online Entertainment. The player had to match three identical orbs within a grid. Each match would award him a monster that would attack enemy monsters. The type of monster awarded depended upon the particular orb that had been matched, as well as the number of orbs included in the match. The game was free to download, but players could spend money in the game for various reasons. And spend they did. By April, 2013, *Puzzles & Dragons* was the world's #1 grossing app, and by early 2014, it became the first mobile game to earn over $1 billion.

Nintendo of Japan released a second version of the game on April 29. *Puzzles & Dragons: Super Mario Bros. Edition* was basically the same game as *Puzzles & Dragons Z*, except that it used familiar Nintendo characters instead of the monsters featured in the original game. Both of the new games were finally released outside of Japan in a single package in May.

Puzzle & Dragons

Although Nintendo president Satoru Iwata had stated that Nintendo wouldn't enter the mobile market, the company announced on March 17 that it had formed a partnership with DeNA, a Japanese provider of mobile and online services, including games. Together, the two companies would create new, original games that used Nintendo's characters and were strictly for the mobile market. Although the first product of the Nintendo/DeNA partnership wouldn't be available for a year, Nintendo did release its first smartphone app in August.

Pokémon Shuffle became freely available for iOS and Android devices in Japan on August 24, with availability in the rest of the world occurring a week later. In the game, players fought against Pokémon by matching three or more identical Pokémon in a row.

Pokemon Shuffle Mobile

Although *Pokémon Shuffle* was Nintendo's first game for a smart device, it wasn't an original game, which was what Nintendo and DeNA had set out to release. Instead, *Pokémon Shuffle* was a port of a 3DS game that Nintendo had released as a free digital download in February. The game followed a model set by other smartphone apps, such as *Candy Crush Saga,*[9] which was free to play, but in which players could purchase additional lives or other content with real money.

Although Nintendo seemed on its way to becoming an app developer, Satoru Iwata had made it clear in March that the company wouldn't abandon the console market in favor of the new mobile games. On the contrary, Iwata disclosed that Nintendo was working on a new console with a "brand-new concept." This new console was codenamed *NX*, but Iwata was unwilling to reveal more than that.

In June, a Japanese business website called *Nikkei* reported a rumor that the NX would be Android-based. Nintendo would therefore have quick access to people who were already developing for the Android platform. Nintendo quickly responded by denying the rumor.

Although Iwata claimed that Nintendo would not discontinue the Wii U, it did end something else. The company announced On January 20 that Club Nintendo would be history as of June 30 in North America and on September 30 in Europe and Japan. Consumers would lose any remaining coins that they might have after that date. In order to help them cash in their coins, Nintendo added several new downloadable games and rewards during the remaining months of the service. Nintendo's reason for shutting down Club Nintendo was that it planned to institute a new loyalty program. This new program, *My Nintendo*, was announced in October. *My Nintendo* would award players with points for purchases made on all Nintendo consoles and mobile software.

Xbox One Updates

Since the NX was a complete mystery, no one knew whether or not it would be backward-compatible with prior Nintendo consoles. Microsoft, on the other hand, began equipping Xbox One consoles with the ability to play select Xbox 360 games. An Xbox 360 emulator was included as part of a July 7 system update, but this emulator could only recognize Xbox 360 games that were repackaged "in an Xbox One format." When someone who owned a digital version of the original Xbox 360 wanted to play the game on his Xbox One, the repackaged version would automatically download to his console the first time he tried to play it. When someone with a physical copy of the Xbox 360 game wanted to play, that disc had to be inserted into the Xbox One. The first time the disc was inserted, the console would automatically download the game "in the Xbox One format" to the console's hard drive. However, the game could only be played as long as the disc was in the machine. And even though the digital version of the game then resided on the hard drive, the physical copy still had to be inserted into the machine in order to play the game.

Microsoft had more than 100 Xbox 360 games available for the Xbox One when the update became available in July. More were planned, although any game that supported the Kinect -- or any other peripherals that plugged into the Xbox 360's USB ports -- would not be offered.

The November 12 system update brought a new interface to the Xbox One called the *New Xbox One Experience*. At its core was Microsoft's latest operating system for PCs, *Windows 10*, which had gone into general release on July 29. This new update allowed for cross-platform gaming between the Xbox One and other *Windows 10* devices, including computers and tablets. For the first time, gamers were able to stream selected games from the console to the computer, and even play certain Xbox One games from the computer.

One feature that had been removed with the installation of the New Xbox One Experience was the ability to use hand gestures to navigate the Xbox One dashboard via the Kinect. Although this had been one of the least-used features of the console, it provided another reason for some to believe that Microsoft was planning to withdraw the Kinect. However, the ability to navigate the Xbox One dashboard with voice commands, which were also channeled through the Kinect, remained in place. According to Aaron Greenberg, the Xbox Head of Games Marketing, Microsoft was going to continue supporting the peripheral. Meanwhile, as per user requests, Microsoft began looking into the feasibility of adding keyboard and mouse controls to Xbox One games.

Although the Xbox 360 peripherals that required the USB port could not be used on the Xbox One, Microsoft made it easier for gamers to use headsets that required standard 3.5mm jacks. The original Xbox One controller did not include such a jack. In 2014, Microsoft had tried to appease those who wanted to use their Xbox 360 headsets by devising the Xbox One Stereo Headset Adapter, which plugged into the Xbox One controller and included the required 3.5mm jack. But on June 16, Microsoft negated the need for the adapter when it released a new controller that had such a jack, along with an expansion port.[10]

Microsoft Xbox One controller with 3.5mm jack

2015

The new Xbox One controller, like those that preceded it, had been designed for all gamers. However, as eSports[11] became more popular and lucrative,[12] professional game players desired a high-quality controller. Microsoft came to their aid and released the *Xbox One Elite Wireless Controller* on October 27. This was made from stainless-steel components, which distinguished it from the standard controllers that were constructed entirely from plastic. It was designed ergonomically and was highly customizable. The base of the D-pad was magnetic, so players could switch between standard cross-shaped D-pads and circular ones. The two analog sticks could be alternated between small and large sizes, and could feature either concave or convex tops. But all of this quality wasn't available cheaply. The Xbox One Elite Wireless Controller retailed for $150.

Three weeks after the new controller came out, Microsoft released a peripheral that could be used with it, along with any other Xbox One controller. The $35 *Xbox One Chatpad* plugged into the expansion port of the controller and featured hard, plastic, backlit keys that included default shortcuts for taking a screenshot or recording a game.

Xbox One Elite Wireless Controller

For older Xbox One controllers that didn't have 3.5mm jacks, the Xbox One Chatpad

Microsoft Xbox One Chatpad

could double as an Xbox One Stereo Headset Adapter, which meant that it had its own built-in headphone jack. Ironically, the Xbox One Chatpad could work with Xbox 360 headsets that required such jacks, but it couldn't work with the newer Xbox One headsets, which required expansion ports because the Xbox One Chatpad plugged into the only expansion port. To compensate for this, Microsoft bundled a free 3.5mm headset with the Xbox One Chatpad.

Virtual Reality

On June 12, Microsoft announced that another product would be bundled with the Xbox One controller. This product was the Oculus Rift, the virtual reality headset that had been in development since 2012. Although the Oculus Rift would not work directly with the Xbox One, Xbox One games could be streamed to it using PCs running *Windows 10*. However, these games would not appear in true virtual reality through the Oculus Rift.

Oculus announced on May 6 that the Oculus Rift would finally be available during the first quarter of 2016, with preorders commencing on January 6, 2016. Although the company had previously insisted that the unit would cost between $300 and $400, it now revealed that the cost of the unit, along with a PC computer that could handle it, would be approximately $1,500. In a May 6 article, *The Verge* reported that a PC with the specifications that the Oculus Rift required could be purchased for less than $1,000, revealing a much more expensive price for the headset than Oculus implied.

There was speculation that the Oculus Rift someday be capable of direct use with the Xbox One someday. But according to Nate Mitchell, the Vice President of Product at Oculus, the company had been so busy focusing on *Windows 10* that no one looked into the possibility of bringing the headset to a console. However, neither company ruled out the possibility.

Samsung Gear VR

A form of virtual reality headset that Oculus had a hand in was released on November 27. The $100 *Gear VR* was manufactured by Samsung and worked with several of its Android smartphones. The phone attached to the front of the headset and its screen was used for viewing.

While Microsoft didn't have a VR headset at the ready,[13] SCE was moving ahead with its Project Morpheus. On March 3, during the GDC, Shuhei Yoshida, president of SCE Worldwide Studios, announced that the device would be launched sometime during the first half of 2016. Several of the developers under the SCE Worldwide Studios umbrella were working on games for the headset, and one in particular, London Studio, announced in October that it had created over 100 prototype games. By that time, the unit had been officially renamed *PlayStation VR (PSVR)*. It was also confirmed that the unit would be priced approximately the same as the PS4 itself. Andrew House, CEO of SCE, confirmed to Bloomberg in September that the PSVR would cost at least $300, and most likely around $400. But at that price, it would be more expensive than a PS4 console, especially since SCE was lowering the price of its console around the world. The price decrease began in Japan on September 15, when the cost fell ¥5,000 ($42) to ¥34,980 ($292). SCEA lowered the price of its PS4 on October 8, dropping it $50 to $349.

The price decrease chiefly stemmed from the release of a new PS4 model, CUH-1200, which came out during the summer. The console's exterior was changed from a glossy finish to matte, and mechanical buttons replaced touch-sensitive ones. Internally, the new console featured a smaller motherboard and a power supply that had a lower voltage output and weighed nearly 3 ounces less than the one in the prior model. This resulted in a product that was quieter and more energy-efficient.

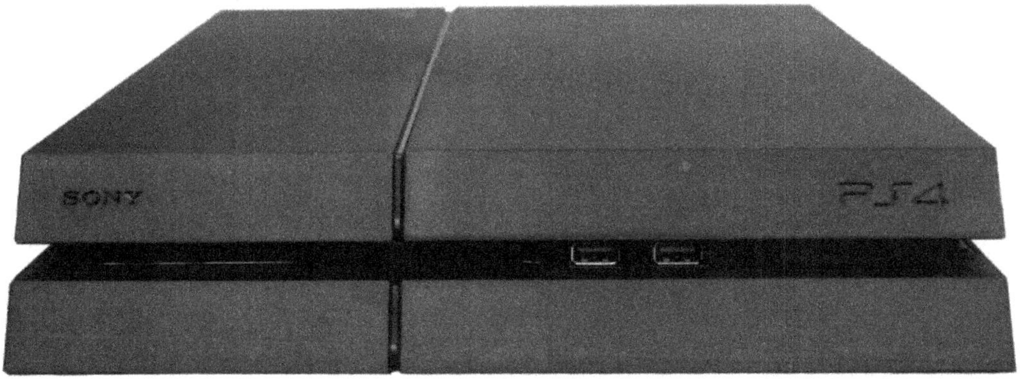

SCE PS4-CUH-1200

By October, the PS4 exceeded SCE's sales expectations and retained the distinction of being the company's fastest selling console. SCE had sold over 25 million PS4s around the world within two years of the console's launch, and it was well ahead of its competitors. Phil Spencer, who led Microsoft's Xbox division, even admitted at Geekwire Summit 2015 in October that he doubted if the Xbox One could ever catch up with the PS4. However, the Xbox One was selling better than its predecessor. After two years, the combination of PS4/Xbox One sales was 40% higher than the PS3/Xbox 360 combination during the same two-year period.

PS Vita's Underperformance

Unfortunately, SCE's other console, the PS Vita, was doing the complete opposite. The company devoted little space for it at E^3, and many speculated that this meant the end of SCE's handheld unit. Although Shuhei Yoshida didn't confirm that the PS Vita was being put out to pasture, he did say in a September statement that a successor to the device was unlikely, since smartphones were "currently dominating the portable-gaming scene." A few weeks later, on October 23, Masayasu Ito, SCE's Senior Vice-President, announced that SCE would no longer develop games for the PS Vita. However, this didn't mean that the company was giving up on the unit. Ito explained that third-party developers were working hard to create excellent games for it, and that this left SCE with the resources to concentrate on the PS4. However, this was contradicted a week later, when Jim Ryan, the head of SCEE, stated that the company was still developing content for the PS Vita. He then covered for Ito by saying that what Ito had actually meant was that SCE wasn't producing any AAA games for the handheld unit.[14]

While the PS Vita received a minute amount of display space at E^3, its non-portable sibling, the PlayStation TV, wasn't displayed at all. Since its North American launch in October, 2014, the device had failed to make an impact among gamers, even after many retailers dropped its price from the suggested \$100 to as low as \$40. In an interview with *Game Informer*, Shuhei Yoshida said that the unit "didn't capture the consumers' imagination" and that it was "a hard concept to explain." Yoshida explained that if the company referred to it as a "video-streaming device", there were other devices on the market that did video streaming much better and in higher definition. Yoshida felt that it wasn't easy to say that the PlayStation TV unit could do one specific thing "extremely good," but that it was a good value at its original price.

Even after the strict price reductions, however, the device failed to sell in numbers that made SCE comfortable. By the end of the year, the company was selling it through its own online store for $20, a price that Best Buy matched. But by that time, it was a fire sale. SCE officially terminated the PlayStation TV device in North America and Europe at the end of the year.[15]

Nintendo Woes

Nintendo continued a downward trend throughout 2015. Although the 3DS was outselling the PS Vita, after four years on the market, its sales numbers nowhere resembled the figures that the DS had shown during the same period.[16] Meanwhile, the Wii U was selling poorly and a much anticipated game for it, *The Legend of Zelda: Breath of the Wild,* had not been shown at E^3, The new NX console wasn't expected to be released until sometime in 2016. All this resulted in the company's stagnant stock prices, which had essentially remained flat since around 2011. The stock did rise but it driven by the Nintendo's mobile news, not its consoles.

But Nintendo's woes went beyond its games. The members and fans of the videogaming industry were shocked to learn that on July 11, the company's president, Satoru Iwata, had succumbed at the age of 55 to complications arising from a tumor in his bile duct. Tatsumi Kimishima, a former CEO of Nintendo of America, was selected to replace Iwata as head of Nintendo on September 14, possibly in the interest of Nintendo's survival. While Iwata had referred to himself as a "creative in a suit," Kimishima came from a business background, and this was something that Nintendo desperately needed at that time. At the end of September, which was midway through the company's fiscal year, its financial reports were lower than expected. But while profits were down,[17] revenue had increased by 19.1%. Kimishima expected this to improve during the second half of the fiscal year, which would end in March, 2016. He was also optimistic about the company's future. He anticipated that within three years, Nintendo's profits would exceed what the company had made during the heyday of the Wii. He attributed this new growth to the mobile games that would be coming out in 2016.

Sequel Mania

One thing was certain: Nintendo was no longer dominating the list of top-ten games. At the end of 2015, the company only had one game on the list, and surprisingly, it was for the Wii U and not the 3DS. Released at the end of May, it was called *Splatoon*. In this underwater game, players assumed the roles of Inklings, humanoids that could turn into squid. As humans, they could shoot their own colored ink, and as squid, they could only swim through their own colored ink. The object of the game was to color the most territory. The game could be played solo, against another person, or in an online match that consisted of two four-man teams. Upon its release, the game was praised for its new take on the first-person shooter genre. At year's end, the game had made it to the tenth position of the top ten games sold in the U.S., and the seventh position of the global list.

But it was a traditional shooter that dominated the top position on both lists. Activision's *Call of Duty: Black Ops 3* for the PS4 had sold 10.74 million copies worldwide in just 9 weeks, whereas *Splatoon* had sold 4 million copies in 32 weeks. The Xbox One version of *Call of Duty: Black Ops 3* sold an additional 6 million copies in the same time frame, and earned its way into the 4th position of the global top ten.[18]

Call of Duty: Black Ops 3 was not the only sequel that made the top ten. In fact, Nintendo's *Splatoon* was the only original game on the list. Like *Call of Duty: Black Ops 3*, Bethesda Softworks' *Fallout 4* occupied two spots on the top-ten lists, one for the PS4 and the other, slightly lower position for the Xbox One. *Halo 5 (Guardians)* was on the list exclusively for the Xbox One, while the PS4 version of *Star Wars: Battlefront*[19] made the

#3 position on both the U.S. and global lists.[20]

Battle of the Bands

Oddly, two highly touted sequels to *Rock Band* and *Guitar Hero,* which were both released in October, failed to make the lists altogether.

Harmonix had originally announced *Rock Band 4* in February, one month after it released the first new downloadable content for *Rock Band 3* in nearly three years. Mad Catz announced in April that it would be co-publishing the game and providing the wireless guitar controllers. Harmonix required that the game would be completely compatible with all of the controllers that had been used in the previous *Rock Band* games. This wasn't a simple request, since the console technology had changed drastically. Mad Catz succeeded in the end, however, and most older peripherals were compatible, as long as they were from the same console family. This meant that the Fender Stratocaster guitar from the PS2 version of *Rock Band 2* could be played with *Rock Band 4* for the PS4, but not with the Xbox version of the game.

Getting the Xbox 360 controllers to work with the Xbox One was another obstacle. The wireless Xbox 360 controllers used native wireless capabilities, which were quite different in the Xbox One, rendering the Xbox 360 music controllers useless. To correct this, Mad Catz developed a *Legacy Adapter,* which converted the Xbox 360 signals into something that the Xbox One, into which the adapter was plugged, could understand. The Legacy Adapter was only packaged with Xbox One versions of the game that weren't bundled with controllers, and it added $20 to the price over the PS4 version. The Legacy Adapter only worked with the wireless controllers None of the wired controllers that worked with the previous versions of *Rock Band* for the Xbox 360, including all drum kits, would work with *Rock Band 4*. Since there wasn't going to be a Wii U version of *Rock Band 4,* none of the Wii instruments were compatible at all.

Mad Catz Legacy Adapter

Despite its compatibility with the older instrument controllers, the new *Rock Band* wasn't quite the same as its predecessor. Harmonix dropped support for the Fender Mustang Pro guitar and the Wireless Keyboard.

Harmonix also made sure that all songs that had been available for the earlier games would work with the new version. This was a major accomplishment, as Harmonix had to seek out and establish new licensing deals with many of the artists and music publishers. Harmonix also had to make sure that any content that had been downloaded for the earlier games would work on the new one.[21]

The game-play was mainly unchanged for *Rock Band 4*. However, a new solo freestyle mode was added, and this allowed guitarists to improvise during their solo parts, without being penalized for straying from the songs' defined notes and chords. But some features were removed, including the practice mode and online multiplayer capability.[22]

While Harmonix was preparing the release of its first *Rock Band* game in five years, Activision was readying its own music rhythm game after five years. *Guitar Hero Live* was announced in April, two months after Harmonix announced *Rock Band 4*. But this wasn't a case of "keeping up with the Joneses." Activision had been interested in reinventing the franchise as early as 2011. A *Guitar Hero 7* had been in development, but this was considered a "disaster" and eventually canceled. In 2012, the job of reviving the game was given to FreeStyleGames, the Activision-owned studio that had developed the pair of *DJ Hero* games. The studio was given free reign over what to develop, but they were also instructed to innovate rather than continue with what had been done before.

Unlike *Rock Band 4*, which was completely compatible with all instruments from the prior *Rock Bands* (including some *Guitar Hero* instruments that could also work with *Rock Band*), *Guitar Hero Live* was a complete reboot from the earlier games, and none of the previous instruments could be used with it. After experimenting with a game that wouldn't use a controller at all, FreeStyleGames settled on a guitar controller that was different from the original *Guitar Hero* controller. A sixth button was added and the layout was divided into two rows containing three frets apiece.

Activision Guitar Hero Live

Activision Guitar Hero Live GHTV

The game itself was somewhat similar to the original, but was displayed from the viewpoint of the lead guitarist looking out at an audience, which was made up of real people, since full-motion video had been used. This audience responded to the guitarist's performance. As the performer became more popular, the audience became larger. This "Live Mode" consisted of ten bands, and the player got to perform three sets with each. However, he had to perform correctly to unlock each set and move on to the following band.

Songs that had been downloaded from earlier versions of *Guitar Hero* could not be used with the new rendition, either. In fact, *Guitar Hero Live* did not even have an option to download new songs. While the game disc included 42 songs that could be used in
43 Live Mode, additional songs could be obtained through a new feature called "GHTV Mode," which Activision billed as the "first 24-hour playable music-video network." Gamers could play along with the songs that were being streamed, or for a small price, they could request songs that weren't part of the regular rotation.

Aspiring guitarists playing along in the GHTV mode also had the opportunity to play online against up to ten other guitarists from around the world, who were playing at the same time. Although players could not see the other guitarists perform, a real-time scoreboard registered how each of the players was doing.

Online performances were not available in the Live Mode or in *Rock Band 4*. Something else not found in the game was the ability to play on consoles other than the PS4 and Xbox One. In addition to these two, *Guitar Hero Live* was also available for the Wii U, PS3, Xbox 360 and even iPhones and certain Android smartphones.

But the two music games did have one thing in common. Both failed to meet their sales expectations, depending on who was doing the reporting. Harmonix claimed that *Rock Band 4* had met all of its sales outlooks by the end of the year. But Mad Catz, which published and distributed the title, and which had sunk a lot of money into the development, manufacture and distribution of the guitar controllers, felt differently. Despite the fact that Mad Catz saw a sales increase by 114%, which had been attributed to *Rock Band 4*, the actual sales total was far less than what the company had expected, and resulted in thousands of unsold guitar controllers sitting in warehouses.[23] As far as the failure of *Guitar Hero Live* was concerned, Activision admitted "lower than expected performance."

Nobody could pinpoint the exact reason why the two music games failed, but there were several theories. Chief among them was the idea that people simply didn't want to pay a lot of money for expensive controllers. But compatibility seemed to be an issue for both franchises. People who had invested in downloadable songs and controllers from earlier installments in the *Guitar Hero* series were unhappy with *Guitar Hero Live's* inability to use them. And *Rock Band 4's* ability to use earlier controllers kept many people from spending money on the new controllers that Mad Catz ultimately had to stockpile. Also, European PS4 owners were having problems accessing the songs that they owned, and this led many others to think twice before purchasing the game.

The Retro Video Games System Fiasco

Rock Band 4 and *Guitar Hero Live* represented a gaming genre that had been around since 1999, with the introduction of Konami's *GuitarFreaks*. The developers of these two gaming franchises weren't currently targeting an audience that was nostalgic for the earlier games. Instead, they had hoped to win over new gamers that had never been exposed to the earlier games.

Meanwhile, there was an audience that wanted the older, retro games. This was evident in the release each year of retro consoles such as AtGames' Flashback. In October, AtGames released its latest console, the Atari *Flashback 6*, which featured 100 built-in games. And people were even more interested in classic games especially after it was reported in mainstream news outlets in January that bidding for a near-mint, sealed copy of Bandai's *Stadium Events* for the NES on eBay had surpassed the $100,000 mark.[24] However, most of the high bids had been false and the game actually sold for $35,100.

With sales of physical games falling as more and more people purchased and downloaded digital games, retailer GameStop sought new ways to generate profits. On April 25, approximately 250 GameStop stores in New York City and Birmingham, Alabama, began a pilot program in which they accepted used retro games and consoles as trade-ins, including the NES, SNES, Genesis, the original PlayStation, N64 and Dreamcast. The pilot program was a success, and the company forecasted that it would need approximately two months to amass enough inventory to begin selling the old games and consoles in its stores.

But old games weren't the only software that was available for the classic consoles. In many cases, new homebrew games were also being developed. And since people were definitely buying new "old" games for classic systems, perhaps they'd also be interested in buying new "old" games for a new console. This was exactly what Mike Kennedy, the publisher of *Retro* magazine, had in mind when he conceived the *Retro Video Games System (Retro VGS)*. Kennedy believed that people would purchase an inexpensive console that played new 8- and 16-bit games that were stored on cartridges. According to Kennedy, his envisioned solid-state flash RAM cartridges would be less expensive, and hold more data, than the cartridges of the past.

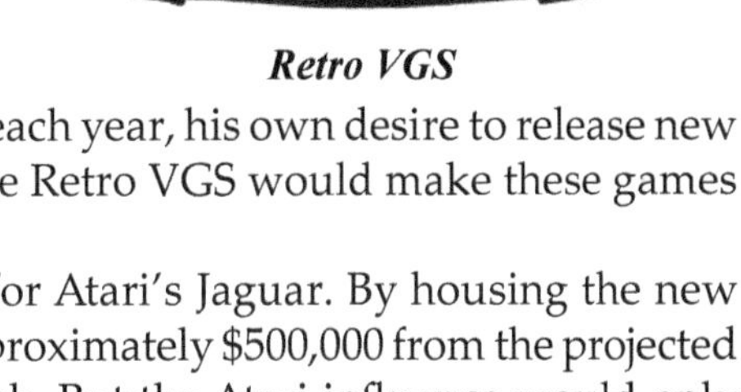

Retro VGS

Many people were thrilled with the prospect of a new console that played games on cartridges. Keith Robinson of Intellivision Productions welcomed the console; with the number of Intellivision consoles still in operation dwindling each year, his own desire to release new games on cartridges was unrealistic. However, the Retro VGS would make these games possible again.

Kennedy had purchased the original molds for Atari's Jaguar. By housing the new system in a Jaguar shell, he was able to subtract approximately $500,000 from the projected cost of designing a new console body from scratch. But the Atari influence would only apply to the console exterior and the cartridge shells. The architecture on the inside would be new. The controller would also be new, and would connect to the console via a USB port. But there would also be two 9-pin "retro" controller ports that would allow the gamer to use original Atari 2600 or Sega Genesis controllers.

Kennedy said in April that he wanted to keep the unit inexpensively priced at $150. A Kickstarter campaign was planned for later in the year, to raise money for the console's manufacture. Throughout the year, online forums, especially those on *AtariAge*, were abuzz with speculations on the console from skeptics and devotees alike. In early September, shortly before the campaign was set to launch, a decision was made to pull it from Kickstarter and use Indiegogo instead. The reason for the change was believed to be Kickstarter's requirement of a working prototype, and such a trial version of the Retro VGS did not exist. This was flatly denied by those involved with the project. The goal of the Indiegogo campaign was to raise $1.95 million. The price of the console was doubled to $300 for the first 500 units sold, with the remainder starting at $350.[25] The campaign went live on September 19 and was planned to span 40 days, with delivery of the unit scheduled for November, 2016.

The fact that there wasn't a prototype and a high price that rivaled those of current generation consoles, such as the PS4 and Xbox One, gave many prospective backers a wait-and-see attitude. Others were simply skeptical about Kennedy's ability to deliver the Retro VGS, and voiced their opinions in forums and podcasts and on YouTube. In the end, the naysayers won out. Kennedy pulled the plug on the Indiegogo campaign on September 29, only ten days after it began. By that time, he had raised $81,000, only 4% of his goal. John Carlsen, the hardware engineer, quit the Retro VGS team[26] on September 30. Soon afterwards, Kennedy blamed the fiasco on Carlsen, whom he said had driven up the price of the hardware and led it to failure. Meanwhile, Kennedy vowed that the Retro VGS was not dead, and that a new Kickstarter campaign would begin by the end of the year.

On December 17, before the Kickstarter campaign was launched, it was announced that the name of Kennedy's company had been changed to Retro VGS, Inc., and that it had aligned with Coleco Holdings to launch a new console, the Coleco *Chameleon*. This wasn't just a rebranded Retro VGS, as the 9-pin retro controller ports had been replaced with additional USB ports. Kennedy once again hinted at a $150 price, but the Kickstarter campaign was now being pushed to the end of February, 2016, as Kennedy first wanted to exhibit the Chameleon at the New York Toy Fair in early February.

History Revisited

While one Kickstarter campaign was put on hold, another, which had succeeded four years earlier, was finally coming to fruition. On July 3, 2011, Joe Santulli, John Hardie and Sean Kelly, the organizers of the popular Classic Gaming Expo, began a Kickstarter campaign to fund the *Videogame History Museum*, which would open at an undisclosed time and would "house the world's most comprehensive videogame archive in the Silicon Valley area of California." The 60-day campaign sought to raise $30,000, which was exceeded by over $20,000 when it ended on September 1, 2011. Some of that money was used in February, 2012 to open a small room at the D.I.C.E. Summit in Las Vegas, where rare memorabilia and games were displayed. One of the room's visitors was Randy Pitchford, the CEO and co-founder of Gearbox Software. As it turned out, he had been interested in opening his own videogame museum.

Thanks to Pitchford's contacts, the city government of Frisco, Texas (to which Gearbox would soon relocate) approved a $1.2 million *National Videogame Museum* in September, 2014. Construction of the museum took place throughout 2015, with the hope of opening by the end of the year. Unfortunately, the date was unrealistic and the museum's grand opening had to be pushed into 2016.

One of the artifacts on display in the National Videogame Museum that people would have to wait to see was a replica of Ralph Baer's Brown Box, the prototype of the Magnavox

Odyssey, the world's first videogame console. After donating the original Brown Box to the Smithsonian Institution in 2006, Baer had made several dozen reproduction units, so other museums around the world could each have them on display.

Ralph Baer's Lab at the Smithsonian

On July 1, the original Brown Box was finally exhibited for the public at the Smithsonian's National Museum of American History in Washington, D.C.[27] The prototype was put on display behind glass, along with Baer's actual workbench, books and equipment from his home lab in Manchester, NH.[28]

Pixels

A different type of "history" came out on July 24. *Pixels* was a live-action movie, which featured dozens of videogame characters from the '80s as enemies. The premise of the movie was that a videotape that featured videogame footage was sent into space in a time capsule in 1982. Aliens get hold of the footage and attack earth with a pixelated version of a ship from *Galaga*. The aliens then challenge Earth in real versions of videogames and if the aliens win, they will attack Earth. Like *Wreck-It Ralph*, *Pixels* featured a variety of videogame characters from *Pac-Man*, *Q*Bert*, *Centipede*, *Donkey Kong* and even *Arkanoid*. However, the movie was not as successful as *Wreck-It Ralph*. While videogame fans loved the movie, most critics panned it.

As the videogame industry's past became more and more accessible, and certainly easier for people to see and experience up close and personally, its future was murkier than ever.

CHAPTER FORTY-FOUR
2016

The first videogame-related news of the year occurred on January 6 at the annual CES in Las Vegas. After years of speculation and delays, Oculus finally announced a release price and date for its long-awaited Oculus Rift virtual reality headset. On that day, the company began accepting preorders for the unit, which would begin shipping on March 28. The Oculus Rift would cost $599 and would come with the VR headset that slipped over the head and connected to the PC; an Oculus Sensor, which would track the player's head movements; and a wireless Xbox One controller. The company also announced that an Oculus Remote would be included in the introductory package, but was very vague about the device's purpose. The company merely described it as a "new input device we designed to make it simple and intuitive to navigate VR experiences." Oculus was also vague concerning the future of the Oculus Remote, saying only that it was available "for now." The introductory package would also ship with two games, *EVE: Valkyrie* and *Lucky's Tale*.

While many people were shocked at the $599 price, especially since the company had been saying for years that the price would be in the $300-$400 range, many went ahead and preordered a set. The initial batch of headsets sold out within a half-hour. A second batch of headsets was expected to ship in April, around the same time that the units would start appearing in retail stores, although Oculus would not disclose which stores would carry the unit.

People who thought the price of the Oculus Rift was high may have changed their opinion on February 29, when Valve Corporation began taking pre-orders for the Rift's first serious competition, the *HTC Vive*. The suggested retail price for the *HTC Vive* was $799, and it was planned to be released on April 5.[1] Like the Oculus Rift, the HTC Vive was designed to interact with high-end PCs.

Because of the two VR helmets' dependencies on expensive PCs, the Oculus Rift and HTC Vive were expected to appeal to die-hard gamers and not to the general public, who would have to wait for the first VR headset designed to work with an existing gaming console. On March 15, two weeks after Valve[2] announced the release date for the *HTC Vive*, SCE used the Game Developers Conference to announce its specifics for the PlayStation VR (PSVR), which would be available on October 13.

The PSVR would only cost $399 and would work on all existing PS4 consoles. The headset would be packaged with a pair of stereo headphones and the cables to connect the unit to the console. However, it would not come with a $60 PlayStation Camera, which would be required to play any PSVR game, or Move controllers, which would be needed by some of the virtual reality games.[3]

The purchase of a PlayStation Camera reduced the difference in price between the PSVR and the Oculus Rift to $140. However, to compare the two headsets by price was unfair, because the two certainly were not equal in quality. SCE never claimed that the PSVR was a high-end VR headset like the Oculus Rift. And even if people thought that the $200 difference between the Oculus Rift and the PS4 was negligible, the Rift still required a high-end computer that cost about $1,000 dollars.[4]

The Rift would include two 1080 x 1200-pixel OLED displays, whereas the resolution of the PSVR would be lower, at 960 x 1080 pixels. And the Oculus Rift would run with a rate of 90 frames per second (fps), which most developers felt was the minimum frame rate for a comfortable VR experience. The PSVR would only run at 60 fps. When Oculus tested its headset with the lower frame rate, testers were able to perceive some flickers and were prone to motion sickness. SCE didn't plan to raise the frame rate on the headset, because the PS4 console wouldn't be able to handle it.

However, on March 18, during GDC, *Kotaku* had published a story from undisclosed sources that revealed that SCE was going to release a new PS4 model that would feature increased graphical power and games that were capable of running at 4K resolution.[5] A new graphics processing unit would be included in the machine that would allow it to support the higher-resolution games, as well as add processing power to better play the PSVR games. Although SCE declined to talk publicly about this new console, dubbed the "PS4.5," the company apparently showed it to developers at the GDC.

In April, SCE combined with Sony Network Entertainment to become Sony Interactive Entertainment (SIE). Andrew House, who had been CEO of SCE before the merge, retained the position.

On June 10, three days before the start of E^3, House admitted to the *Financial Times* about the existence of the PS4.5, which by then was called by its second working title, the *PS4 Neo*. House confirmed what *Kotaku* had revealed nearly two months earlier and said, "The Neo) is intended to sit alongside and complement the standard PS4. We will be selling both [versions] through the life cycle." House did not provide any more details about the PS4 Neo, other than to say that it would not be shown at E^3. Indeed, SIE's 6 PM press conference on June 13 concentrated mostly on the price and release date of the PSVR, details that had already been disclosed at GDC in March.

New From Microsoft

Microsoft held its E^3 press conference earlier that same day, using its time to introduce two new consoles, one of which appeared to be similar to the PS4 Neo. This console was code-named *Project Scorpio* and wasn't scheduled to be released until the end of 2017. This model, which Microsoft called the "most powerful console ever," would feature 6 teraflops of processing power (compared to 1.31 teraflops on the Xbox One). It would run 4K games natively and support High Dynamic Range (HDR) lighting[6] and high-end virtual reality, although Microsoft wasn't planning a VR headset. Aaron Greenberg, Xbox's head of games marketing, called Project Scorpio the "beginning of the end of traditional console life cycles for Microsoft." Greenberg also stated that there wouldn't be any games exclusive to Project Scorpio. Any game that took full advantage of the console's capabilities would also have to play on an older Xbox One in a limited fashion.[7]

The other console that Microsoft introduced was the *Xbox One S*. This console, whose software was fully compatible with the current Xbox One, would be white and feature a sleek new design. It would also be 40% smaller than the current model and would, in fact, be the smallest and most compact Xbox console ever offered. It would support 4K video resolution from Blu-ray, and several streaming services such as Netflix and Amazon. In addition, older Xbox One 1080p games could be up-scaled to 4K. The Xbox One S was scheduled to be released in several configurations in August, with preorders commencing the day of the E^3 press conference.

Microsoft actually introduced *three* consoles at the press conference that would play Xbox One games. The third was a PC with the *Windows 10* operating system. With *Xbox Play Anywhere*, gamers could download Xbox One games either from the Windows Store or the Xbox Games Store, and they would play directly on the PC. Previously, Xbox One games needed to be streamed from an Xbox One console in order to play on a PC with *Windows 10*. *Xbox Play Anywhere* was scheduled to launch in September.

Microsoft did introduce something at the E^3 press conference that was available right away. The *Xbox Design Lab* gave users the ability to customize the colors on their own Xbox One controllers, which were only available from the online Microsoft store. From the Xbox Design Lab website, users could select from several different colors to apply to several different parts of the controller, including the body, bumpers and triggers,

Xbox Design Lab controller

D-pad, thumbstick and back. In addition, several different styles could be selected for the controller buttons. In all, Microsoft claimed that there were more than 8 million color combinations to choose from. The unique controller sold for $79.99, and for an additional $9.99, the controller could be personally laser-engraved.

Nintendo Steals the Show

Like Microsoft and SIE, Nintendo did not display a new console at E³, although it too had one in the pipeline. The NX had been mentioned in March, 2015, but Nintendo revealed nothing about it during the remainder of the year. Finally, at an investor's meeting, the company mentioned that the unit would be released in March, 2017. The *Los Angeles Times* reported this news on April 27, with a headline that declared, "Nintendo dates its successor to the Wii U, the NX." Although it was known that the Wii U was doing poorly in the marketplace, no one at Nintendo ever said that the NX would replace it. Indeed, on the same day that the *Los Angeles Times* printed its story, *Geek.com* published a story with the headline, "Nintendo NX launches March 2017, won't simply replace Wii U and 3DS," echoing the words that Nintendo CEO Tatsumi Kimishima had stated at the meeting. He confirmed this during a May, 2016 interview with Japanese newspaper *Asahi Shimbun*, but added that the NX would "slow Wii U sales" when more information about it was revealed.

44

That information was not revealed at E³. Instead, Nintendo used the massive trade show to finally show one of its most anxiously awaited titles, *The Legend of Zelda: Breath of the Wild*. Originally designed for the Wii U, the game would be released in March 2017 for the NX as well as the Wii U. It was the most talked-about game at E³, and attendees stood in lines for hours in order to play it. *GameSpot* called it "the most interesting and exciting game Nintendo has made in years."

The Legend of Zelda: Breath of the Wild

By announcing that *The Legend of Zelda: Breath of the Wild* would be available for the NX, Nintendo gave people a reason to purchase the new console without actually having to see it. At a shareholders' meeting that followed the exhibition, Shigeru Miyamoto explained that Nintendo couldn't yet tip its hand on what the NX was, because the company's competitors might copy ideas from it if it were shown off too soon. However, whether it was part of Nintendo's plan or not, information about what the NX was quickly began to surface.

On July 27, *Eurogamer* published an article from a "number of *well-placed* sources" that stated that the NX would be a portable, handheld console with detachable controllers. The controllers could then be attached to a docking unit, which could be connected to a TV or monitor, so games could be played on a big screen just as with a standard console. However, the unit would not be backward-compatible with the Wii U. Instead of optical discs, it would employ game cards similar to those used by the 3DS, even though it would not be compatible with that system's, either.[8] Sources also said that the NX would be powered by a new operating system, and not by Android as had been previously reported. When asked by *Eurogamer* to confirm the new rumors, Nintendo merely repeated that the only official information about the NX was its March, 2017 release. However, *NintendoLife* backed up *Eurogamer*'s story on August 16, when it published information about a Nintendo handheld patent that had been recently updated to include detachable D-pads.

While Nintendo was remaining mum about its forthcoming console, a different, non-Nintendo platform could suddenly run Nintendo games. On March 17, Nintendo of Japan and DeNA released their first original application for iOS and Android devices. *Miitomo*, however, wasn't exactly a game. It was a social-networking app that allowed friends to communicate with one another through questions and answers. The user's onscreen personas were Miis that were created through the app.[9]

Miitomo

Miitomo was extremely popular. After three days, it became the most downloaded free app in Japan. But people weren't using it strictly for social media. They were also earning *Miitomo Coins* by making purchases within the app. The coins could be used to buy new clothes for the Mii. And with a daily change of clothes, players could earn *Miitomo Platinum Points*, which could then be exchanged for items on *My Nintendo*, Nintendo's successor to Club Nintendo. My Nintendo had been launched in Japan on the same day that *Miitomo* was released.[10]

Miitomo downloads started strong. The app boasted over one million users within three days of its Japanese launch. That number tripled within 24 hours, following its launch around the world on March 31. By the end of April, the app had over 10 million users. However, by the time May arrived, the numbers began to turn around, and only about 25% of those 10 million were still using the app regularly.

Pokémon Go

Nintendo's next app would ultimately have the same result, but it would initially be something that everybody talked about.

Pokémon Go, which was released on July 6 in the United States, Australia and New Zealand,[11] utilized augmented reality technology to cast animated Pokémon characters into the real world. Players became real-life Pokémon hunters as they used their smartphones to capture these Pokémon, which they could "see" imposed on the screens of their devices.

Pokémon Go, which had originally been conceived by Tsunekazu Ishihara, the president of The Pokémon Company, and Satoru Iwata, the late CEO of Nintendo, began as *Pokémon Challenge*, an April Fool's gag through *Google Maps*. The gag was so well-received that they decided to create a complete, fully playable version. As it turned out, Ishihara was a fan of *Ingress*, a mobile game that had been developed and released in late 2014 by Niantic, Inc.[12] *Ingress* combined augmented reality with a GPS to create a map of the surrounding area that displayed the locations of objects that players needed for the game. Ishihara felt that the background of *Ingress* was perfect for his game, so Niantic was contracted to create *Pokémon Go*, based upon *Ingress*.

The game began in *Map Mode*, where a map displayed the player's immediate location. If there were any nearby, the map would also show the location of *PokéStops*, which were used by players to obtain needed supplies such as berries, potions and Pokéballs. Large tower-like structures might also appear, and these were the locations of gyms, which were used for team battles.[13] And if there were any nearby, the map would also disclose the location of Pokémon, which had to be captured.[14]

Once a player found himself in the vicinity of a Pokémon, he could switch to *Camera Mode*, which would show the actual creature augmented into the real world. By swiping the Pokéball at the bottom of the screen in the direction of the Pokémon, the monster could be "captured" and added to the player's Pokédex. There were 151 Pokémon to be captured in all, and some were easier to obtain than others.[15] In fact, four could only be found on specific continents, which meant that capturing them all required a lot of traveling. Still, it wasn't impossible, and on August 4, it was revealed that Nick Johnson of Brooklyn, NY had become the first person to capture all 142 Pokémon that were available in the United States. Fortunately, Marriott and Expedia sponsored his trips to Paris, Hong Kong and Australia, where he was able to complete his set.

Pokémon Go Map Mode

Pokémon Go Camera Mode

On August 8, *Pokémon Go* achieved over 100 million downloads through Google Play alone. Two days later, it was awarded five *Guinness World Records*, including one for being the most downloaded mobile game within its first month. It became the fastest game to reach the #1 downloaded-app spot on both Google Play and the App Store. The gaming and mainstream press marveled at the game's phenomenal success.

Unfortunately, not all of the press was good, since the game was burdened with problems right from the beginning. For example, on the day of its American launch, the servers became so overloaded that many people couldn't gain access, and some who did experienced freezing or crashing. The CEO of Niantic, John Hanke, apologized by saying that they "weren't provisioned for what happened." This wasn't restricted to the U.S., and similar problems occurred around the world whenever the game was launched.

But the worst publicity wasn't caused by glitches in the system. Rather, it was caused by the success of the app. Some people were concentrating so intently on the game that they didn't pay attention to their surroundings. They fell into holes or wandered into the paths of oncoming cars. One teenager in Guatemala was ambushed was killed while playing the game. In Japan, a woman crossing a street was killed when a car, driven by a man playing the game, rammed into her. Even the locations of the Pokéspots and gyms caused problems, as they appeared in sensitive areas such as the Korean Demilitarized Zone and the United States Holocaust Memorial Museum. Another PokéSpot was found on an Indonesian military base, causing a major incident when a player tried to illegally access it.

Nintendo had planned to sell a device at the end of July that would have avoided many of the calamities caused by people looking at their screens instead of where they were going. However, the release of the $35 *Pokémon Go Plus* was delayed until September 16, to be absolutely sure that the game properly worked with it. The Pokémon Go Plus was a small device that could be pinned to a player's shirt or attached to a wrist band and worn like a watch, and it communicated with the mobile device that was playing *Pokémon Go* via Bluetooth. Once the device was paired with the game, the phone could be put away. The Pokémon Go Plus alerted the player through pulsing vibrations and blinking colored lights that a Pokémon or PokéStop was in the vicinity. Once the player was upon it, all he had to do was press a button on the Pokémon Go Plus in order to capture the creature or receive goods from the shop.

Pokémon Go Plus

The Pokémon Go Plus sold out the day it was released, showing that there was still major interest in *Pokémon Go*. The number of possible consumers for the device had been in question, because participation in the game had peaked on July 15. By the time the Pokémon Go Plus was released, the game had lost 79% of its players. However, this still left approximately 21 million active players who were keenly committed to the game and who were probably interested in the Pokémon Go Plus.

Nintendo's stock dropped dramatically around the same time that the public began leaving the game, but there wasn't any relationship between the two events. The stock had risen by 10% upon the initial launch of *Pokémon Go* and didn't stop there. Within a week of the launch, the company's shares had risen by 50%, with trading of Nintendo shares amounting to 25% of all trades on the Tokyo Stock Exchange. By July 22, Nintendo's net worth had risen by ¥1.8 trillion ($17.6 billion). However, the stock dropped abruptly on July 25, when it was revealed that Nintendo had nothing to do with *Pokémon Go*, and that whatever it earned was through the 32% of The Pokémon Company that it owned. This had hardly been top-secret news; nevertheless, Nintendo's value fell 17% or approximately $6.4 billion, the highest drop that the company had experienced since 1990. However, even after the decline of *Pokémon Go*, the game continued to be one of the top-earning mobile games.

Despite Nintendo's non-involvement in *Pokémon Go*, many investors stuck with the company because it was involved in other mobile games that were expected to be released before the end of the year, including games based on *Animal Crossing* and *Fire Emblem*. Both had the potential to make a lot of money if they were done right.

Super Mario Run

The first actual mobile game to emerge from Nintendo's partnership with DeNA was released worldwide for iOS devices on December 15.[16] *Super Mario Run* was a mobile version of *Super Mario Bros.* Just as in the original console game, the on-screen Mario had to avoid enemies, jump over obstacles and collect coins. The player controlled Mario's jumps by tapping the device's screen. The longer the screen was touched, the higher Mario jumped. No other input was required by the player.

Super Mario Run

The game broke iOS records by scoring more than 50 million downloads during its initial week. Before its release, Nintendo's stock prices had risen to the levels that it had enjoyed during the peak of *Pokémon Go*. Investors liked the fact that Nintendo owned all of *Super Mario Run* instead of just a percentage, so the company would take in 100% of the game's revenue. But the gravy train that investors expected to keep rolling came to a halt five days after *Super Mario Run*'s release, when Nintendo's shares dropped by 11%.[17] This was caused by bad publicity from the users themselves.

Like many mobile games, *Super Mario Run* was free to download and try out. However, after the third level, players had to pay a one-time fee of $10 to continue. Many felt that this was an astronomical amount to pay for a mobile game when others generally cost only a few dollars, and some were even free because of built-in ads. Other games, such as the acclaimed *Candy Crush Saga*, used a *freemium* model that gave players the option to purchase low-cost items that could help them continue in the game.[18] However, players weren't forced to buy these options and could continue without them. So even though the game was widely loved, many were infuriated by the fact that Nintendo was charging them so much to continue. They complained about this in the only way they could--by giving the game bad reviews on *iTunes*. Before long, there were 50,000 reviews of the game on *iTunes*, approximately half of which sported one star out of five, simply because the reviewers were upset about Nintendo's pricing. The average rating of 2.5 dissuaded many people from trying the game out, and completely scared investors, who hadn't expected such a response. By the end of the year, out of 78 million downloads, only 5% of the trial users had gone on to pay for the complete game.[19]

New Nintendo Consoles

Super Mario Run wasn't the only Nintendo product that consumers were complaining about at the end of the year.

On October 20, the company finally revealed information about its secretive NX console, and most of the rumors that *Eurogamer* had reported in July proved to be true. The system would be called the *Switch*, which was appropriate, because it was a hybrid system that switched between a console and a handheld. The Switch resembled a 7-inch tablet with wireless controllers, called *Joy-Cons*, which slid into each end of the unit. The unit could be played like a handheld with the Joy-Cons attached, or it could sit on its own and the gamer could play with the unattached Joy-Cons in his hands. In that event, the system could also be inserted into a "Switch Dock," which connected to a television, and then a game could be played uninterrupted on a TV, just as with a standard console. For this television play, the unit would be packed with an accessory called the *Grip* that the Joy-Cons could be attached to, and which was held like a standard controller. It would be debatable whether the Switch could be considered a console or a handheld, but for game media, it would follow the lead of Nintendo's handheld:[20] Like the 3DS, the Switch would utilize game cards instead of discs.

Nintendo Switch inside Switch Dock with Joy-Con controllers in front attached to the Grip

Tatsumi Kimishima's vague statement in May, in which he'd said that the new console would "slow Wii U sales," now made sense. In the eyes of many, the Switch was what the Wii U should have been: a console that could double as a handheld. The Wii U was such a device, albeit in a very limited capacity. Unfortunately, not all games supported the separate Wii U Gamepad, and those that did still had to be near the console in order to work.

Nintendo Switch with Joy-Cons attached

However, revealing what the Switch was didn't slow Wii U sales as Kimishima had predicted, because sales for the Wii U were already very slow. By the end of the year, Nintendo had sold less than 14 million units worldwide, making the Wii U the company's worst-selling console. Its second worst, the GameCube, had sold almost 23 million units. The Wii U numbers weren't bound wasn't bound to change in the new year. Nintendo had announced that it wouldn't be manufacturing or shipping any more Wii Us after the current fiscal year, which ended on March 31, 2017. By the end of 2016, store shelves whad already been emptied of the unwanted console.[21]

Historically, the weeks leading up to Christmas are the most profitable for retailers and manufacturers alike. With the Switch not yet available and the Wii U practically dead in the water, Nintendo was still prepared for the holidays with a new console that it had announced in July. The *NES Classic Edition* was a plug-and-play version of the original NES, but on a much smaller scale. While looking exactly like an NES to the smallest detail, the unit could literally fit in the palm of someone's hand. The console did not accept the original NES cartridges, or in fact any cartridges at all, but it had 30 classic NES titles built in. The unit had an HDMI output to TV and included a controller that looked like the original, but could also plug into the Wii Remote and be used with the Virtual Console on the Wii and Wii U. A second controller was available for purchase separately. Nintendo stressed that the NES Classic could not connect to the Internet, and that games from the Virtual Console could not be downloaded onto it.

Nintendo also released the small NES plug-and-play in Europe, where it was called the *Nintendo Classic Mini*. It was also called the *Nintendo Classic Mini* in Japan, but that version of the console resembled a handheld version of the Famicom. It was packaged with two controllers, whereas the NES models only came with one.

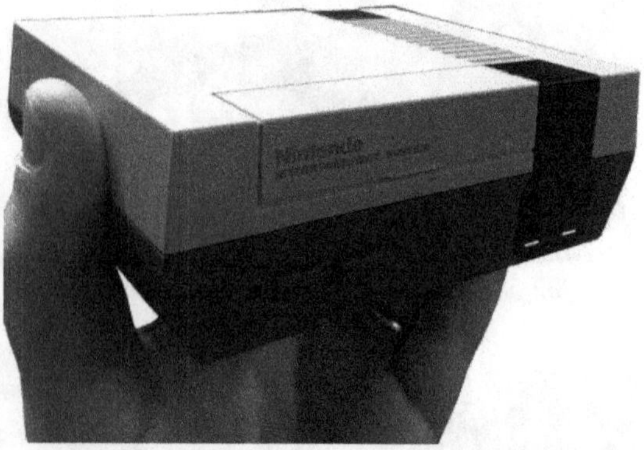

Nintendo NES Classic Edition

Nintendo Classic Mini

The $60 NES Classic was released during the second week of November. In general, those who purchased it were very happy with it, with the one exception that the controller cable was too short and players had to sit directly in front of their TVs to play. That problem was quickly solved by third-party vendors, who began selling extension cables. However, this problem hadn't been experienced by most people who wanted NES Classics because they hadn't been able to find any; the units sold out almost as quickly as they had been made available.

This seemed to be a problem every time Nintendo released new hardware: limited supply and huge demand. It had last besieged the company two months earlier, during the release of the *Pokémon Go Plus*. However, the absent NES Classics affected many more people than the *Pokémon Go Plus*, especially considering that the shortage of this perfect Christmas present occurred close to the holidays. And as with so many console launches, the NES Classic began appearing on eBay at prices zeroing in on the $200 mark. Although Nintendo promised a "steady flow of additional systems through the holiday shopping season and into the new year," these shipments were few and far between. It just became a matter of being in the right place at the right time. Some people complained that they had attempted to purchase the units online from sources such as Amazon and Best Buy as soon as they'd become available, only to receive a message that they were sold out before the ordering process was even completed. As the holidays grew closer and the units were nowhere to be found, more and more people gave in to the scalpers.[22]

Portable Plug-And-Plays

While the NES Classic, might have been the most desirable, it was not the only new plug-and-play that came out near Christmas. On October 4, AtGames continued its yearly tradition of releasing a new Atari Flashback. The latest edition, the *Flashback 7*, was identical to its predecessor, except that it included one additional game, bringing the total to 101. The new game was *Frogger*, although it was neither the Parker Brothers nor the Starpath version that had been released for the original VCS in the early eighties. This new version was a faithful translation the original arcade game.[23] The Flashback 7 was sold with two wireless joystick controllers, although a deluxe edition with two hard-wired controllers was released a month later.

AtGames also offered a new MegaDrive/Genesis console featuring 80 games. As in the previous Sega consoles that AtGames had produced, half of the contents were original Sega games, while the other half were generic titles, trite games that had never been part of the Sega catalog. Unlike the NES Classic, neither the Atari nor Sega unit from AtGames had an HDMI output to a modern television. However, the Sega console did accept the original game cartridges.

AtGames also released a new edition of its Arcade Ultimate Portable, the Sega Genesis unit that had built-in games and also accepted additional games that were stored on an SD card. Like the AtGames console, the Arcade Ultimate Portable contained 40 legitimate games and 40 generics. The company also offered, for the first time ever, a portable unit that played Atari VCS games. The *Atari Flashback Portable* looked exactly like the Arcade Ultimate Portable, except that 60 Atari VCS games were built in. And unlike the console members of the Atari Flashback series, the Atari Flashback Portable allowed for adding more games via an SD card. Atari VCS fans had been hoping for a portable version of the console ever since the release of the first Flashback in 2004. Now they finally got their wish.

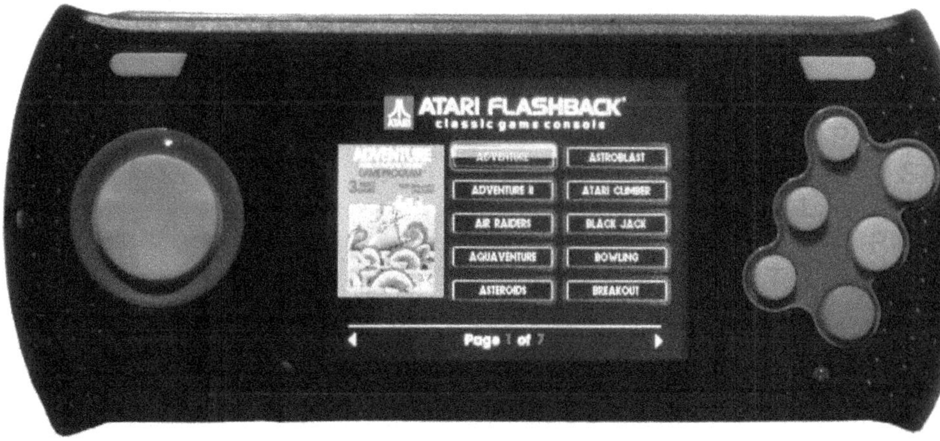

AtGames Atari Flashback Portable

People who wanted to try out VCS games weren't limited to the new Flashback units. Atari and AtGames made the games available for the PS4 and Xbox One as well. Two sets, *Atari Flashback Classics Volume 1* and *Atari Flashback Classics Volume 2*, were released on October 12 for both consoles. Each $20 volume featured 50 games, with the majority from the VCS and a handful being arcade ports.

New Consoles and Features

By the time the *Atari Flashback Classics* were released, some consumers were able to play them on brand-new consoles. On August 2, Microsoft had released a $399 "special edition" of its Xbox One S, which contained 2 TB of storage. Two "standard" models followed on August 23, a 500 GB model that sold for $299, and a 1 TB model that retailed

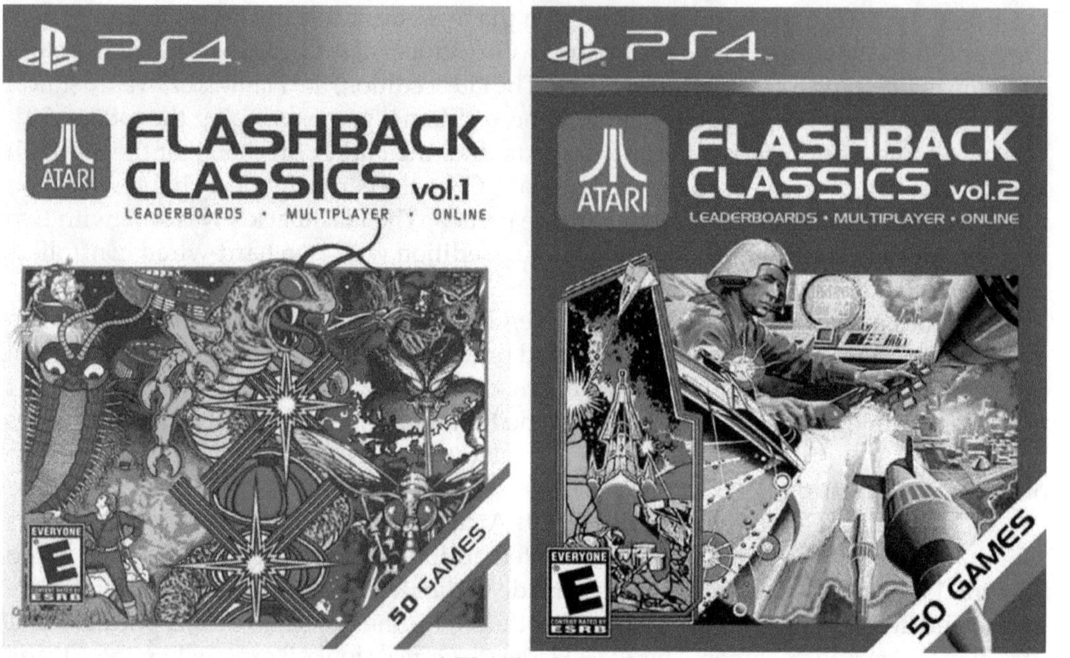

Atari Flashback Classics

at $349. As promised earlier in the year, the consoles were much smaller than the Xbox One and were capable of playing 4K videos from either their 4K Ultra HD Blu-ray players or Netflix streams. While 4K games could not be played, HDR games were supported. The only problem was that there weren't any HDR games available at the time of the Xbox One S's release.[24 25] Despite its smaller size (or perhaps because of it), the new console did not require an external power supply as had its predecessor, which had used a power supply that was the size of a brick.

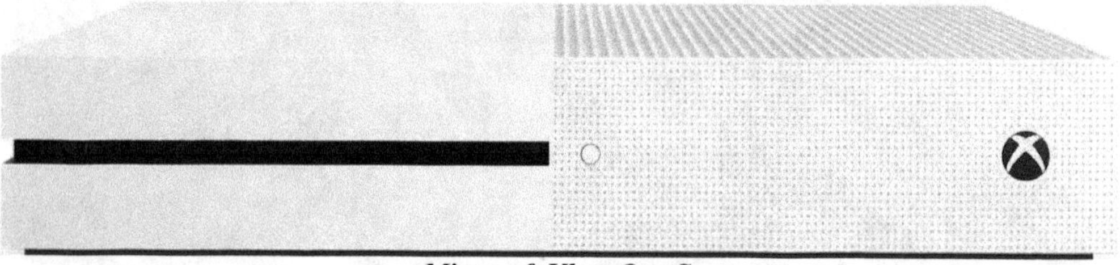

Microsoft Xbox One S

One thing that didn't come with the Xbox One S was the nearly forgotten Kinect. In fact, the peripheral that Microsoft had wanted to be constantly joined to the original Xbox One could not even connect directly to the Xbox One S. For those who still intended to use their Kinects with their new consoles, Microsoft made available a $40 adapter that could be used to attach a Kinect to either an Xbox One S or a PC.

The controller that came with the Xbox One S was slightly smaller than the one that was packaged with the Xbox One. The controller was white[26] to match the console, and its plastic was textured on the bottom to provide an improved feel. The D-pad was more responsive and it supported Bluetooth, which made the controller easier to pair up to a computer without the need of an adapter. This was especially important for people who wanted to download Xbox One games directly to their PCs. And they were able to do so shortly after the debut of the Xbox One S consoles. On September 12, Microsoft officially launched *Xbox Play Anywhere*, the service that permitted digital games to be played not only on an Xbox One, but also directly on a *Windows 10* PC without the need to stream them from the console. The console and PC both required special updates to enable the activation of Xbox Play Anywhere. The console update occurred on July 30, and the PC one happened a few days later, on August 2.[27]

The press loved the Xbox One S, with many writing that it should have been the console that Microsoft originally released. However, they cautioned their readers about buying them. They wrote that there was no reason for an original Xbox One owner to purchase one. But if the new console was desired as a replacement, the reader was advised to wait for the release of Project Scorpio, whenever that might be. However, they encouraged people who were buying their first Xbox One console to go and purchase them.

On September 7, SIE unveiled its rivals to the Xbox One S and Project Scorpio. A new, smaller version of the PS4, dubbed the *PS4 Slim,* was released on September 15. Like the Xbox One S, the new PS4 was 40% smaller than the console that it replaced, and it shipped with a slightly updated DualShock 4 controller. Other than that, it was basically the same as the prior PS4, right down to the price. Like the model that had been introduced in 2015, the new PS4 retailed at $300 and came with a 500 GB hard drive.

SIE PS4 Slim

The critics weren't as enthusiastic about the PS4 Slim as they had been about the Xbox One S. However, they provided the same advice. The PS4 Slim was good for people looking to buy PS4s for the first time, but PS4 owners didn't need to go out and replace them. If they were dead set about replacing them, they should wait for the PS4 Neo. And the wait for the PS4 Neo would be a lot shorter than the wait for Project Scorpio.

At its September 7 meeting, SIE announced that the official name of the PS4 Neo would be the *PS4 Pro.* Details about the new console were also revealed. It was scheduled for a November 10 release, with a $400 price tag. The console would have a graphics-processing

SIE PS4 Pro

speed of 4.2 teraflops, which was more than twice the speed of what the PS4 Slim offered and slightly less than what Project Scorpio was rumored to provide. And unlike Project Scorpio and even the Xbox One S, the PS4 Pro would not include a 4K Ultra HD Blu-ray player. This meant that the console could not support 4K movies from physical sources. It was, however, capable of playing back 4K movies streamed from Netflix and YouTube. Games were another story. The same games that had been designed for the PS4 could be used with the PS4 Pro, and special hardware and rendering techniques would upgrade them to 4K. SIE's excuse for not including the high-def Blu-ray player was that the PS4 Pro was a game machine, first and foremost. For the first time in many years, SIE was promoting its product as a gaming console, and not a general entertainment machine.

The PS4 Pro also supported HDR right out of the box, but HDR wasn't limited strictly to that console. On September 13, SIE issued an update to the firmware of the PS4 and PS4 Slim that provided HDR support. At that time, however, there weren't any games yet available that supported HDR. SIE was using the same approach as Microsoft: All games had to be playable on all formats of the PS4. However, games could be enhanced to maximize the new features on the PS4 Pro, as long as they were still playable on the PS4 and PS4 Slim. SIE didn't want people to have to repurchase games that they already owned just to get copies that had the 4K or HDR enhancements. So, when the PS4 Pro was released, patches for several games were also sent out to include the enhancements. SIE didn't require that games be enhanced, leaving that decision to the individual developers and publishers, which could issue patches to enhance just the resolution, just the high dynamic range or both.

Within three weeks of its release, SIE claimed that sales for the PS4 Pro were much higher than the company had anticipated. And it looked like first-time PS4 buyers were selecting the PS4 Pro over the PS4 Slim. One thing that was not known was whether another PlayStation platform that SIE released on October 13 was contributing to those PS4 Pro sales

This other platform was the $400 PlayStation VR (PSVR), which SIE referred to as a console, and not an expensive peripheral. Upon its release, there was trepidation over whether the unit would succeed or not. The Oculus Rift and HTC Vive had both had hearty launches early in the year. But due to their success, they sold out quickly, and this led to a long period during which they were simply unavailable, causing consumer interest to greatly subside. Since Oculus and HTC wouldn't disclose their sales figures, a research firm called SuperData Research estimated that 243,000 Oculus Rift units and 420,000 HTC Vive headsets had been sold by the end of the year. SIE's goal was to sell 1 million PSVRs within six months; but because Andrew House, the head of SIE, was conservative about how many units should be initially manufactured, SIE ran into the same shortage problems as Oculus and HTC.[28]

Naturally, comparisons were made between the PSVR and its two more-expensive PC adversaries. While people found the quality of the graphics to be better on the Oculus Rift and the HTC Vive, they also felt that the PSVR was the lightest and most comfortable. One thing that made the PSVR light was that it didn't have built-in headphones. Instead, it included an audio jack, so players could plug in their own headphones, or use the set of earbuds that was included with the unit. The PSVR headset was also incapable of its own tracking, so it required the PlayStation Camera to assist in this feature. Additionally, the PSVR was designed so a player who wore glasses could also use the headset with ease.

The PSVR completely immersed people into the games. The DualShock 4 controllers that they held in their hands were simulated on their headset screen, so they could actually see what their in-game counterparts were holding. Some games required PlayStation Move controllers, and they too were simulated on the screen. But the resolution of the world that the gamers were immersed in was less than astounding, and those who were expecting graphics that equaled what the PS4 output to traditional displays may have been disappointed. While SIE was pushing the envelope with 4K games on its upcoming PS4 Pro, the standard PS4 delivered games in 1080p resolution. However, the PSVR only displayed them in 720p resolution.[29] And HDR, the latest new acronym in the console handbook, was non-existent. This lack of HDR caused problems for people who owned HDR-compliant televisions. This was because the PSVR was packaged with a *PSVR Processor Unit*, which was placed between the PS4 and the display devices. It was basically a splitter through which the video sent from the console was passed along to the TV and the VR headset. The only problem was that unlike the consoles themselves, the PSVR Processor Unit didn't support HDR. This was not a problem for people who didn't have HDR-compliant TVs. But it was a big deal for those who did. While it didn't matter that the headset could not receive an HDR signal, the fact that the TV couldn't either eliminated any reason to own an HDR-supported television in the first place. The only way these people could take advantage of the HDR enhancement, which was something that SIE was pushing by making it available for all of its PS4 consoles, was by disconnecting the PSVR Processor Unit and having the console send the signal directly to the television. Of course, the PSVR Processor Unit would have to be connected again when the gamer wanted to play virtual reality games.

In North America, 32 games that could use the PSVR were released on the same day that it launched, either in physical form or as digital downloads. Games that could be played on the PSVR came in three formats, and the packaging of the physical games easily let the consumer know which was which. First there were games that could only be played with the PSVR, and these were each designated as a "PLAYSTATION VR GAME" on the front of the packaging, beneath the PS4 logo. Then there were some titles that could be played on a TV in standard 2D, but featured a "VR mode". When this was activated, the game was played using the PSVR, and it took on a whole new dimension. Games with a VR mode were specified via the text "PLAYSTATION VR MODE INCLUDED" beneath the PS4 logo. While many of the games that included the VR mode used it as a way to introduce people to virtual reality, one of the launch titles, *Rez Infinite*, was actually a fully blown VR game that could also be played on a TV. However, this update to the game, which had come out for the PS2 and Dreamcast in 2001, really shone in VR. Tetsuya Mizuguchi, the game's producer, said that his original vision of the game was to "let players have the ability to look up, down and behind them, but the technology of 2001 prevented that." Indeed, *Polygon* called *Rez Infinite* "one of the first masterpieces of VR."

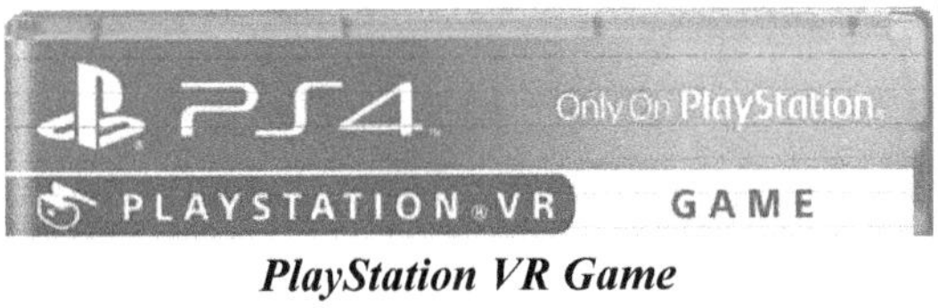

PlayStation VR Game

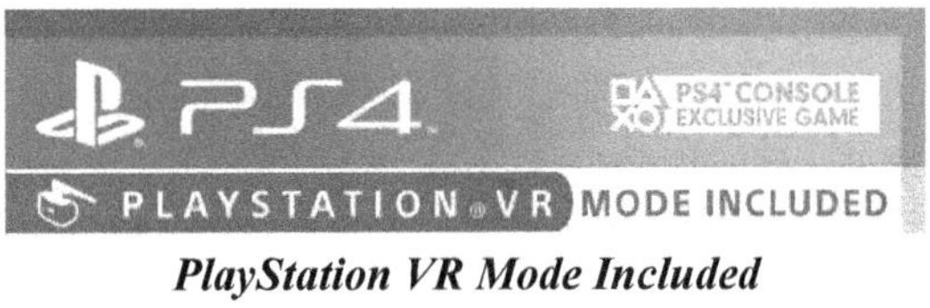

PlayStation VR Mode Included

The third type of game that could be played using the VR headset was a standard PS4 game. The PSVR included a "Cinematic Mode", in which anything that could be displayed on the TV screen, including a Blu-ray or Netflix movie, could display through the VR headset. This would give the viewer the impression that he was watching the display on a very large screen that was right in front of him.[30] However, as the size of the displayed image increased, the gaps between the pixels would increase as well, causing the display to be more distorted than normal.[31]

One misconception about virtual reality was that it cut people off from the rest of the world. While that might have been somewhat true, since the player wasn't aware of his actual surroundings while in a virtual world, he was still connected to the world. The PSVR included a feature called the "PSVR Social Screen." This displayed everything that the player viewed through his VR glasses on the television that the PS4 was connected to, in full high resolution. Not only could others view what the PSVR player was seeing, but they could play against him if the game had been written for more than one player. And someone didn't even have to be in the same room to compete with the virtual reality player. If it was an online game, then the player in the VR headset could play against anyone on the planet, even another person playing in virtual reality. One of the launch titles, *EVE: Valkyrie*, took this even one step further. It had originally been released for the Windows PC in March as an Oculus Rift launch title, but its developers, CCP Games, said later that the original plan was that the game could be played online between all three VR platforms. The release of the PSVR version achieved this goal. CCP Games then went the final mile by releasing the game for the HTC Vive on November 17.

History In Person

Although the PSVR represented the first commercial virtual reality add-on for an existing videogame console, it was not the first virtual reality device created by a videogame company. Both Sega and Atari had attempted years earlier to release such products. Unfortunately, for various reasons, neither Sega's VR headset nor Atari's Jaguar VR had made it beyond the prototype stage.

These VR prototypes have fallen into private hands and are occasionally shown to the public. Some places where people showed off their exclusive, rare consoles and games were at videogame conventions, such as *Classic Gaming Expo*, which had a room set aside for its popular *Videogame History Museum*. Eventually, this temporary exhibit, which was also shown at industry events such as E^3 and the GDC, finally transformed into a permanent brick-and-mortar structure. After several years in the planning stage, the *National Videogame Museum* in Frisco, Texas finally opened its doors on April 2.

Although there were other videogame museums in the country, such as the *International Center for the History of Electronic Games (ICHEG)*, they were each part of something else. The ICHEG was part of the Strong Museum, and while it could boast a large collection of videogame artifacts available for research, only a small percentage of its collection was on display for viewing on the museum floor. The National Videogame Museum had 10,400 square feet dedicated to its massive collection of videogame memorabilia on display. Among the features of the museum was the world's largest *Home Pong* console, a wall displaying a time-line of 50 consoles sold in North America, a section devoted to handheld games, another section exhibiting board games that had been inspired by videogames, and an arcade featuring games from the '70s and '80s. Finally, the museum had on display dozens of prototypes, including the Sega Neptune and the Atari Mindlink.

NVM - World's Largest Home Pong Console

NVM - Videogame Inspired Boardgames

Record Breaker

While the National Videogame Museum claimed the world's largest *Home Pong* console, Bandai-Namco revealed its world's largest *Pac-Man* arcade machine in May. The $11,000 machine consisted of two parts. One was a screen that measured 5.6′ x 8.8′ and was made up of thousands of multi-color LEDs. The second was a podium that stood 5¼′ in front of the screen. This podium featured a pair of joysticks, to allow for two-player games. However, in addition to the classic game, in which the players alternated turns in order to try achieving the higher score, it also featured a unique cooperative mode, in which the two players worked together, with each controlling his own Pac-Man around the maze.

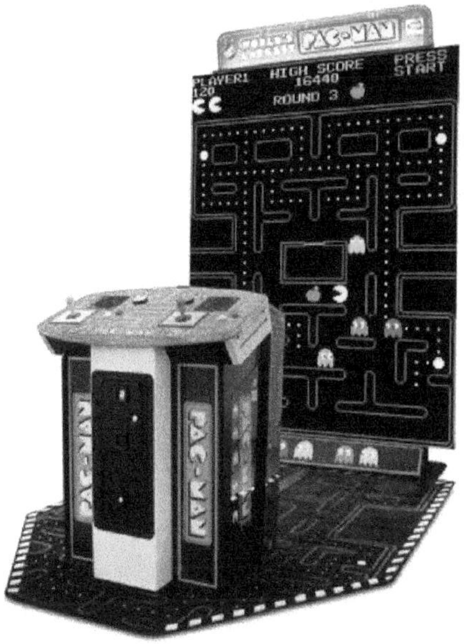

World's Largest Pac-Man

This new version of *Pac-Man* had an added attraction that wasn't available anywhere else. Bandai-Namco called it an interactive billboard. While the game was in the attract mode, the arcade operator could display up to three advertisements on the screen.

Rock Band Recovery

Bandai-Namco figured out how to breathe new life into an old game. Mad Catz was not as fortunate. Its involvement in the rebirth of the *Rock Band* franchise did not help the company at all. Besides the suffering it underwent, due to poor sales of *Rock Band 4*, the money and attention that Mad Catz threw into the game caused other areas of its business to underperform. In February, following the game's disappointing sales, Mad Catz posted a quarterly net loss that was 75% greater than the same quarter's loss in 2014. Even worse, its six-month loss was 157% higher than during the same period in 2014. In monetary terms, Mad Catz went from a $4.7-million-dollar profit in fiscal 2015 to a $11.6-million-dollar loss during fiscal 2016, which ended on March 31.

Prior to the public announcement of this news, three of Mad Catz's top executives resigned from the company. In an attempt to save $5 million a year, the company then laid off 37% of its employees.

Meanwhile, it was business as usual at Harmonix, which had been routinely providing patches for *Rock Band 4*. On March 1, the company announced that it wanted to produce the first-ever version of *Rock Band* for PCs, and started a 35-day crowd-funding campaign on *Fig*, in order to raise $1.5 million dollars.[32] Harmonix also planned to have a new line of instrument controllers available in time for the 2016 holiday season, and the company expected that Mad Catz would create them. Unfortunately, Mad Catz, strapped for cash, couldn't undertake this assignment, especially since it had $8.3 million of *Rock Band 4* inventory remaining in its warehouses.

On March 7, Harmonix terminated its contract with Mad Catz and signed a deal with peripheral manufacturer, Performance Designed Products (PDP), the company that had released the Rock Band Stage Kit in 2008. The termination of the Harmonix contract gave Mad Catz a 120-day wind-down period to sell its remaining inventory. After September 6, it would no longer have the license to do so.

Mad Catz did manage to sell all of the remaining *Rock Band 4* inventory before the end of the wind-down period, but the game didn't bring in as much revenue as the company had expected. On September 16, it announced that it had sold its Saitek division to

Logitech for $13 million. Saitek, which Mad Catz had purchased in 2007 for $30 million, specialized in flight sticks and steering-wheel controllers for simulation games. On November 3, the company announced its fiscal 2017 second-quarter results, and exhibited optimism about its future.[33]

PDP Rock Band Fender Jaguar w/ Rock Band Fender Jaguar Guitar Controller Charger

Rock Band 4's new controllers from PDP were released on October 18, along with a $30 expansion pack called *Rock Band Rivals*, which featured two new modes: a competitive mode called *Rivals* and a story mode called *Rockudrama*. The expansion set could be purchased alone, and the instruments that worked with *Rock Band 4* could be used. Or it could be purchased with the new controllers from PDP. This included a wireless drum kit that responded better than previous models to different strike strengths. The new *Fender Jaguar* guitar controller was also somewhat better than the Fender Stratocaster that Mad Catz had supplied. The controller buttons were redesigned so they didn't accidentally get pressed during game-play. And the neck folded over to make storage of the guitar easier, a first for a *Rock Band* instrument. However, many people may have preferred to keep their fake Fender Jaguars out on display when they weren't being used, so PDP sold a stand for the guitar to sit on, and which could recharge the guitar's batteries at the same time. The $30 *Rock Band Fender Jaguar Guitar Controller Charger* was designed exclusively for that controller. Included with the charger was a battery pack, which replaced the two AA batteries normally required by the guitar. The charger connected to the battery pack, and LED lights in the charger indicated whether the unit was charging or completely charged.

On November 25, PDP released its $30 *Rock Band Wired Legacy Adapter*. This item finally allowed people with the Xbox One version of *Rock Band 4* to use their wired legacy-instrument controllers, which couldn't be used with Mad Catz' Legacy Adapter. The Rock Band Wired Legacy Adapter was designed to work specifically with the Drum Rocker from ION.[34] It also supported the Xbox 360 Rock Band Midi Adapter, so any MIDI drum kits that worked with it could also be used with *Rock Band 4*. Finally, the Rock Band Wired Legacy Adapter supported PDP's own Rock Band Stage Kit.

PDP Rock Band Wired Legacy Adapter

The release of the Rock Band Wired Legacy Adapter was welcome news to people who had spent hundreds of dollars on equipment, only to discover that *Rock Band 4* had made it obsolete. However, not everyone who needed the adapter was happy. It was only available in North America, so anyone outside the continent who owned the wired Xbox 360 controllers appeared to be out of luck. But after December 19, less than a month after the adapter came out, they were joined by Americans, who soon discovered that the adapter was sold out everywhere. This wasn't widely reported by the press, especially since potential customers of the more popular NES Classic Edition were going through the same problem at the same time. But to those who had expected to easily find the adapter, this was of major concern.

A reason for the shortage was finally explained in an email from a PDP customer representative to a consumer who had inquired about the adapter being sold out: "The Rock Band Legacy Adapters will no longer be produced, as they were produced in limited quantity, per our agreement with Harmonix." Unfortunately, this had never been publicized. Many who missed out immediately went to the Harmonix forum sites to complain, and to promise that they would never again purchase another product from Harmonix or PDP.[35]

To Infinity and Be Gone!

Mad Catz was not alone in experiencing poor sales. Even the mega-company Disney was feeling a pinch. On May 10, it reported its second-quarter and six months earnings for fiscal 2016, which had ended on April 2. Although the company's net revenues were higher than they had been for the same period a year earlier, the growth did not meet the company's expectations. And even though they thought that they had a good product in *Disney Infinity*, they were also very concerned about the volatile toys-to-life market. Disney didn't have enough confidence that the market would remain stable. The company announced that it would release two final playsets, *Alice Through the Looking Glass* and *Finding Dory*, and close its doors in June. *Finding Dory*, and the final Disney Infinity figure, Nemo, were released on June 24.

Along with the cancelation of *Disney Infinity*, Disney closed down the studio that had produced it, Avalanche Software, resulting in the loss of 300 jobs. Avalanche Software had been in business since 1995, and Disney had acquired them in 2005. But this was also the last remaining studio that was part of the Disney Interactive Studio umbrella that developed console games. Between 2008 and 2012, the company had lost over $200 million per year and shut down three other studios under its control: Propaganda Games, Black Rock Studio and Junction Point Studios. And these closures all followed the shuttering of LucasArts, soon after Disney had purchased Lucasfilm. The sudden success of Disney Infinity merely postponed Avalanche Software's fate, and once Disney felt that the party was over, it abandoned ship as soon as possible. However, this didn't mean the end of all console games based on Disney properties. Once Disney Interactive Studio and Avalanche Software were shuttered, Disney announced that it would license out its properties for future games.

Avalanche Software wasn't the oldest software company that shut down during 2016. On December 8, Majesco closed its doors after more than 30 years in business. The company that had started by reissuing old games at discount prices, and which later manufactured the Sega Genesis 3, had found success with the Wii, thanks to the *Cooking Mama* series and a string of exercise games using licensed properties such as Jillian Michaels and Zumba. Unfortunately, as the Wii audience disappeared, so did Majesco's profits. In 2013, while the company geared itself to the mobile and digital market, it invested approximately $4 million to purchase Orid Media Limited and Pariplay Limited, two online gambling companies. It was thus able to establish a subsidiary called GMS Entertainment, which was set up to look into "emerging growth opportunities in the social and online casino gaming industry to supplement [the company's] existing business." Majesco also started another subsidiary called Midnight City, which was a publishing label that distributed downloadable content from independent developers.

In early 2014, Majesco announced a 64% drop in revenue and severed its relationship with Zumba, which left it without any forthcoming physical games. Instead, the company planned to concentrate on the digital releases from Midnight City, along with GMS Entertainment-based casino. However, Majesco continued to bleed cash and, in November of 2014, announced that its future was questionable after it had suffered major losses during the quarter that ended on July 31, 2014. The company sold its share of GMS Entertainment to raise much needed cash.

In March, 2015, it was revealed that development for *Gone Home*, a PC game that Midnight City had planned to release for consoles, was canceled because of Majesco's financial problems. In August, 2015, Majesco replaced its CEO and trimmed its workforce down from 16 employees to only 5. It announced at that time that it would only distribute games digitally. Things began to turn around for the company after that. In January 2016, Midnight City released two new games, high-definition versions of *A Boy and His Blob* and *Gone Home*. The latter had been reported as cancelled nearly a year earlier. These would wind up being the final games of Majesco's long history. On December 12, the company suddenly abandoned the videogame business when it merged with PolarityTE, a medical company that developed tissue-regeneration technology.

Shown At the Show

A company whose name had last been seen on a gaming console one year before Majesco was even established was all set to do it again. While the Coleco name had been licensed for several hand-held devices since 2005, the last time it had appeared on a console was in 1985, the ColecoVision's was cancelled. That was alleged to change in 2016, with the release of the Coleco Chameleon, the revamped version of the Retro VGS that had caused much trepidation among retro-gamers in 2015. Although little had been said about the Chameleon, aside from its announcement, Mike Kennedy, whose company, Retro VGS, Inc. was developing the console, assured patrons that the Kickstarter campaign would begin following the console's debut at the New York Toy Fair in February.

As promised, beginning on February 13, a working model of the Coleco Chameleon was shown at the Toy Fair, where it was seen by many people in the toy industry, including buyers from Toys 'R' Us, who had expressed an interest in carrying the $150 console. However, a video of Mike Kennedy displaying the prototype was shown on his Facebook page, and the AtariAge forums became abuzz again. In the video, Kennedy was seen playing a multicart that included several SNES games. It was also noted that he was using an SNES controller. This led to speculation that there was an SNES 2 board hidden inside the Chameleon shell, rather than a unique, original board. One viewer also noticed that the power light on the "prototype" did not light up, even though the unit was obviously on. On February 26, the Kickstarter campaign scheduled to begin on that day was suddenly canceled, as people demanded to see photos showing the inside of the console.

As with the Retro VGS, observers believed that the postponement of the campaign was due to Kickstarter's requirement of a working prototype. In answer to the accusations on AtariAge, the Chameleon team released a photo of a clear-shelled console with a circuit board inside. However, one sharp-eyed viewer actually recognized the "circuit board" as a capture card, which is normally used to record video onto a hard disk. Following this debacle, Coleco issued an ultimatum to Kennedy that if its own independent engineer couldn't verify a working prototype within seven days, it would wash its hands of the Chameleon altogether. Before the end of the seven-day period, Chris Cardillo, a partner with Coleco Holdings, announced that Retro VGS, Inc. had told him that they wouldn't provide a prototype "because it [was] not sufficient to demonstrate at [that] time." Coleco Holdings amicably terminated its agreement with Retro VGS, Inc., and the Retro VGS/

Chameleon saga came to an end once and for all.

Nintendo completely dominated videogame news as the year came to an end. Its mobile games had begun with a bang, but before long, they sputtered. Its first entry in the plug-and-play market was an enormous success by all accounts, except that it couldn't be found anywhere. And the company was only months away from launching a totally new product that it hoped would have as big an impact as the Wii had.

The first VR headset for a console had been released, and now everybody looked ahead to what Microsoft would offer. What was in the pipeline with Project Scorpio and how would that play into SIE's future plans? And if it embraced virtual reality and most expected it would, would its VR system be competitive against SIE's?

Whatever the answers to these questions might have been, one thing was for certain: The videogame industry would continue to make more history.

APPENDIX I
THE TETRIS STORY

In June 1984, Alexey Pajitnov was an artificial-intelligence researcher at the Computer Center in Moscow's Soviet Academy of Sciences. The Academy regularly received new computer hardware that Pajitnov would test by writing simple computer programs to run on them. When the Computer Center received an Electronica 60, a Soviet-made computer that had no graphical capabilities, Pajitnov decided to test it by writing a simple program based on pentominoes, a game that he had enjoyed as a child. Pentominoes were geometric figures that were comprised of five squares, attached at the edges. A total of twelve unique figures could be formed from the five squares.

With help from a colleague named Dmitry Pavlovsky, Pajitnov programmed the game, but instead of using pentominoes, he settled on tetrominoes, which were constructed from only four squares. The result was only seven geometric forms instead of twelve. He called the game *Tetris,* which was combined from the names of two games that Pajitnov loved to play: tetrominoes and *tennis*.

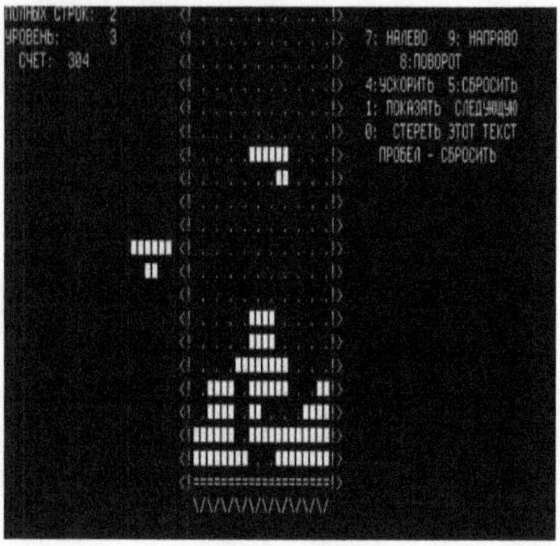

Original Tetris

After they had a working game running on the Electronica 60, 16-year old Vadim Gerasimov ported it to an IBM PC. By July, 1986, the PC version had been smuggled into Hungary, where it was next converted for the Apple II and Commodore 64 computers.

Robert Stein, the founder of a European company called Andromeda Software, encountered *Tetris* while he was in Hungary. Realizing the commercial potential of the game, he quickly went to the Hungary Institute of Technology seeking the rights to market the game in the West. They directed Stein to the Computer Center of the Soviet Academy of Sciences. Stein traveled to Moscow, where he met with Pajitnov and offered to purchase the rights to the game. Pajitnov expressed interest in Stein's offer and Stein returned home to Great Britain, believing that the two of them had made a deal. Based upon this belief that he was going to obtain the rights to the game, Stein had begun shopping it as soon as he returned to England. Mirrorsoft, a British software company,[1] agreed to purchase the European rights to the game, while its American subsidiary, Spectrum Holobyte, bought the American and Japanese rights. Stein promised to sell both companies all of the rights to *Tetris* with the exception of arcade and handheld versions.

Because he lived in a Communist country, Pajitnov could not personally profit from his game. However, he was allowed to assign his rights to his employer, the Academy of Sciences, which could then license the game for him. He agreed to this and granted the Academy of Sciences the rights to *Tetris,* for ten years.

On November 5, 1986, Stein offered the Soviets a 75% royalty of whatever he received for *Tetris,* along with a $10,000 advance. The Academy of Sciences responded on November 11 that these terms were agreeable, but they noted that their deal was for IBM-compatible versions of *Tetris* only. Non-IBM versions would be considered at a future time. In December, Stein received a telex inviting him to Moscow. He made the trip and met with Pajitnov and several other people from the Academy of Sciences, but in the end, he returned home without a signed contract.

Several months passed without anything happening. Stein began panicking. Mirrorsoft was pressuring him for a signed contract because they were planning to release PC-compatible versions of *Tetris*. In April, 1987, he finally revealed to the Soviets that he had licensed the PC-compatible *Tetris* rights to Mirrorsoft and Spectrum Holobyte, and he stressed to the Soviets that he really needed a signed contract from them. In June, 1987, Stein couldn't put off Mirrorsoft any longer, and he finally signed a contract that licensed the PC-compatible rights to Mirrorsoft and Spectrum Holobyte. In spite of the Soviet silence, Stein's contract with Mirrorsoft and Spectrum Holobyte specified that he was indeed the rightful owner of the game's copyright and was free to grant the license. He sent a copy of this contract to the Soviet Union, but still did not receive a response. In December 1987, after several more months without a response, Stein once again sent a letter to the Academy of Sciences, in which he pleaded for them to confirm his rights to *Tetris*. At the very least, he requested from them a simple letter that declared that they approved the contract he had signed with Mirrorsoft and Spectrum Holobyte.

At this time in Moscow, Pajitnov was completing a new project that he believed could be sold as educational software. He met with Alexander Alexinko, a director with Elorg (Elektronorgtechnica), a newly created government organization intended for the import and export of computer hardware and software. When Pajitnov mentioned all of the problems he was having licensing *Tetris*, Alexinko informed him that because the Academy of Sciences was an academic institution, it was restricted from taking part in any commerce. Alexinko told Pajitnov that from then on, he and Elorg would be handling the negotiations for *Tetris*.

People in the West got their first look at *Tetris* when Spectrum Holobyte displayed it at CES on January 7, 1988. One person who was completely enamored by the game was Henk Rogers, who had founded a Japanese software-publishing company called Bullet-Proof Software. Even before *Tetris* was released, he knew he wanted the rights to publish the game in Japan, and he met with representatives from Spectrum Holobyte, who apparently owned the game's Japanese rights. The companies struck two separate deals, one for the computer-game rights and the other for the home videogame rights.

Mirrorsoft Tetris

Mirrorsoft and Spectrum Holobyte both released *Tetris* for IBM-compatible computers in their respective countries on January 27, 1988. Although everyone who had seen the game believed that it would be successful, no one had anticipated that it would become a global phenomenon that would even be noticed by the mainstream media. Upon watching a story about *Tetris* on television, Elorg's Alexinko learned that Robert Stein had sublicensed a game that he never had any rights to in the first place. Elorg contacted Stein in February 1988 to inform him that it was taking over the negotiations, and whatever deal he might have made with Pajitnov and the Academy of Sciences was not valid. Stein quickly responded by threatening Elorg that he would make the Soviets look very bad to the international community if they stopped a commercial deal. But that could be avoided by working out a deal that would be politically and economically beneficial to both of them. Elorg decided to go with the latter.

Stein flew to Moscow and met with Alexinko on February 24, 1988. They discussed a written contract that would include the stipulation that Elorg had to approve any version of *Tetris* that might be developed in the West.

The contract between Stein and Elorg was finally signed in May, 1988. While it gave Stein the exclusive right to market *Tetris* for any home computer, it specifically forbade him any rights to arcade, console and handheld versions, and any other media "that weren't even dreamt up yet." Versions for all of the popular home computers were quickly released, and *Tetris* soon became the top-selling computer game in England and the United States.

On May 30, Mirrorsoft sub-licensed the arcade and home-console rights for *Tetris* to Atari Games, even though arcade games had never been part of the deal that Stein had negotiated with Mirrorsoft. Atari Games' plan was to release an arcade version of *Tetris* and for its subsidiary, Tengen, to release a Nintendo NES version.

Meanwhile, Henk Rogers shored up his deal with Spectrum Holobyte for the Japanese *Tetris* computer rights, and the two companies agreed to do the same for the console rights two days later. However, after the first contract had been signed, Spectrum Holobyte notified its sister company, Mirrorsoft, about the deal. Mirrorsoft responded and said that Spectrum Holobyte couldn't go through with the home-console sale, because Mirrorsoft had already sold those rights to Atari Games. Unfortunately, there was nothing that Spectrum Holobyte could do about it. Both companies were owned by Robert Maxwell, who was more interested in the British software company, which was run by his son, Kevin Maxwell. Spectrum Holobyte told Mirrorsoft that they at least had to honor the contract that was signed with Henk Rogers' Bullet-Proof Software for the Japanese computer license. Mirrorsoft agreed to this, since it didn't see much value in it. Spectrum Holobyte then told Henk Rogers that he would have to negotiate directly with Atari Games to obtain the Japanese home-console rights for *Tetris*.

While Mirrorsoft and Spectrum Holobyte were selling licenses that they didn't actually own, Robert Stein was trying to secure these rights for himself from the Soviets. Stein met with Alexinko in Paris on July 5 with the intention of securing the coin-op rights for *Tetris*. He guaranteed to pay Elorg $30,000 as an advance against royalties. Naturally, Alexinko was skeptical, especially since his main reason for the meeting was to complain that Elorg hadn't received royalties for any computer sales, even though the game had been on the market for nearly six months.

Following the meeting, Stein and Alexinko telexed back and forth to each other. Stein claimed that he was being pressured and sorely needed a written contract for the coin-op rights by mid-August. Alexinko responded by telling Stein to add a clause to their original contract, stating that a monthly 5% fee would be charged for late royalty payments. Stein agreed to this and once again requested that they finalize the coin-op contract. This was again followed by months of silence from the Soviet side.

On August 16, 1988, as Stein tried to get the permissions for the coin-ops from Alexinko, Henk Rogers went directly to Atari Games to secure the Japanese home-console rights. Atari Games wasn't particularly interested in Japanese rights at all. They had sold the Japanese coin-op rights to Sega, and had no problem striking a similar deal with Rogers for the console rights. Rogers negotiated with Atari Games for two months and in October, 1988, he finally scored a written contract that gave him the right to release *Tetris* on all Japanese consoles, including Nintendo's Famicom. After quickly writing a Famicom version of the game, he produced a videotape that showed his game *Tetris* in play. He then met with Mirrorsoft in London to get their approval. By the time Rogers returned home to Japan, he had received a fax from a Mirrorsoft attorney that gave him permission to produce the game.

Rogers' Bullet-Proof Software released *Tetris* for several Japanese home computers on November 18, 1988. One month later, on December 22, 1988, it released the game for the Famicom, marking the first time that *Tetris* appeared on a home console anywhere. On the splash screen of all of the Japanese releases was a notice that said that the game had been licensed to Robert Stein's company, Andromeda Software, and sub-licensed to Mirrorsoft, Sphere Inc., Tengen and Bullet-Proof Software. The Famicom edition was a huge success and nearly two million copies were sold.

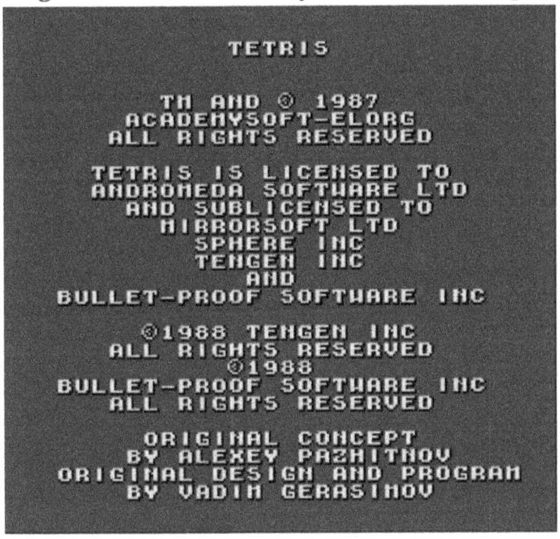
TETRIS
TM AND © 1987
ACADEMYSOFT-ELORG
ALL RIGHTS RESERVED
TETRIS IS LICENSED TO
ANDROMEDA SOFTWARE LTD
AND SUBLICENSED TO
MIRRORSOFT LTD
SPHERE INC
TENGEN INC
AND
BULLET-PROOF SOFTWARE INC
©1988 TENGEN INC
ALL RIGHTS RESERVED
©1988
BULLET-PROOF SOFTWARE INC
ALL RIGHTS RESERVED
ORIGINAL CONCEPT
BY ALEXEY PAZHITNOV
ORIGINAL DESIGN AND PROGRAM
BY VADIM GERASIMOV

Splash screen -BPS with Tengen

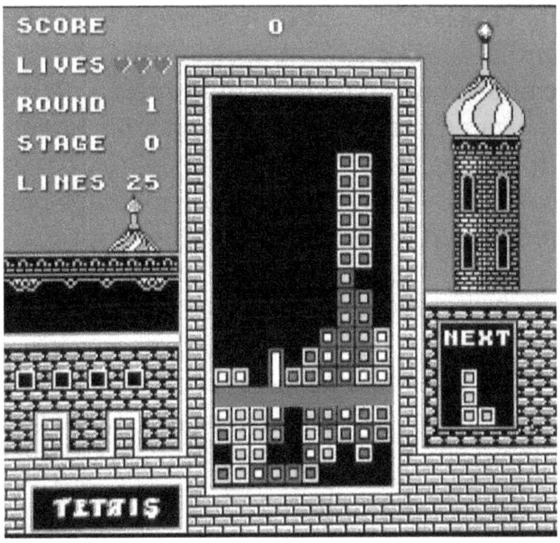
SCORE 0
LIVES
ROUND 1
STAGE 0
LINES 25
NEXT
TETRIS

Famicom Tetris

Henk Rogers had a great relationship with Nintendo[2] and visited the corporate headquarters regularly. On one such visit, he was shown a preview of Nintendo's top-secret Game Boy before it had been announced to the general public. Minoru Arakawa, president of Nintendo of America, told Rogers that the new handheld console would be bundled with *Super Mario Land*. Rogers told him that while a Game Boy that came with *Super Mario Land* would appeal to little boys, if Nintendo wanted to sell the Game Boy to *everyone*, they should include *Tetris* with it instead. Arakawa agreed and asked Rogers to obtain the handheld rights to the game.

Rogers contacted Stein on November 15, 1988 and let him know that he was interested in the *Tetris* handheld rights. Stein responded that he had been in touch with Elorg about those rights, but that the agency hadn't decided what it would do with them. For the next two months, Rogers continued to remind Stein about the handheld *Tetris* rights, but that led nowhere. Rogers finally came to the conclusion that he couldn't depend on Stein to work in his behalf and in February, 1989, he decided to visit Moscow on his own.

In addition to not receiving an answer from Elorg regarding the handheld rights, Stein was also concerned about securing the coin-op rights, especially since an arcade version of *Tetris* had already been released in North America by Atari Games and in Japan by Sega. And even though he had never sold the arcade rights to Mirrorsoft in the beginning, he felt that he would be the fall guy if the company were sued. He decided he would have to take a trip to Moscow to negotiate with Elorg face-to-face.

When Kevin Maxwell, who ran Mirrorsoft, heard that Stein was planning a trip to the Soviet Union for a meeting with Elorg, he realized that Stein might not have owned any *Tetris* rights other than the computer ones. This was a major problem, since Mirrosoft and Spectrum Holobyte had sublicensed the arcade and console rights to Atari Games, Sega and Bullet-Proof Software. Maxwell decided that he too had to travel to the Soviet Union and beat Stein to the meeting with Elorg, so he could obtain the rights that he thought he had licensed but now was unsure about.

As it turned out, all three men, Robert Stein, Kevin Maxwell and Henk Rogers, had arrived in Moscow at the same time.

On February 20, 1989, Rogers sought out Alexey Pajitnov, who led him to Elorg. There, Rogers met with Nikolai Belikov, who had replaced Alexander Alexinko at the bargaining table. Rogers impressed the Soviets with his sincerity, and Belicov asked him to return the following day, when Stein and Kevin Maxwell would also be in the building.

On the following day, February 21, 1989, Belicov met first with Rogers, who was told that the Soviets agreed to award the *Tetris* handheld license to him. Rogers was enthused and in his excitement, he showed Belicov a copy of his Famicom *Tetris*. Belicov became confused when he was confronted with the cartridge, because Elorg had never licensed the game's console rights to anyone. Rogers explained that he had sublicensed the rights from Tengen, a company that Belicov had never heard of. Rogers then recounted how he had flown to England with a videotape of the game in play, which he assumed had been forwarded to the Soviets for their approval. Belicov claimed that had never seen the tape, adding that only the computer rights had been licensed, and that those had been sold to Andromeda. He then showed Rogers the signed contract between Elorg and Stein, which stated that it pertained only to home computer systems.

Although Rogers was shocked when he realized that he had purchased licensing rights from a company that had never owned them in the first place, his primary concern was to maintain the trust he had built with the Soviets in order to retain the handheld rights that he had just secured. Rogers told Belicov that he had been the victim of a lie when he purchased the *Tetris* console rights, and offered to make amends by writing a check to Elorg on the spot for royalties that the 130,000 copies of Famicom *Tetris* had earned. Belicov agreed and then gave Rogers three weeks to decide if he wanted to make an offer for the game's console rights. Although Rogers definitely wanted to make an offer, he worried that Mirrorsoft and Atari Games, both huge companies, would also go after the console rights, and he didn't have the resources to compete with them. Fortunately, he had friends with deep pockets in the industry who could go up against them, and that was Nintendo.

Robert Stein was next summoned to Elorg's offices, where Belikov presented him with an amendment to their original contract, which he was told to sign. Stein was confused, because he was in the Soviet Union to negotiate for the arcade and handheld rights, not to amend his existing contract. But Belikov warned him that negotiations would only continue after he signed the amendment. Stein examined the addendum, which had been backdated to the date when the original contract had originally been signed, May 10, 1988. He concentrated on the part that discussed royalty payments, something that he had been negligent in doing, and the penalties for late and missed payments. What Stein did not notice was the line that amended the original contract's definition of a home computer to "a processor, monitor, disk drive(s), keyboard and operating system."

Stein agreed to the new conditions only if he and Elorg could work out terms to include arcade and handheld licenses. He produced a document that detailed minimum guaranteed sales, advances and royalty percentages. Belikov told him that the handheld rights weren't yet available, but if Stein could come up with a $150,000 advance within six weeks, he could buy the arcade rights.[3] Stein agreed to these terms, so at least the arcade games from Atari Games and Sega were legal. But Tengen still planned to release *Tetris* for the NES.

Belikov's final meeting on February 21, 1989 was with Kevin Maxwell, who was also after the arcade and handheld licenses. Belikov immediately showed Maxwell the Famicom *Tetris* cartridge that Henk Rogers had given him, but the cartridge meant nothing to Maxwell, since he was unaware that his own company had licensed the *Tetris*

APPENDIX I

console rights to Atari Games. After he saw the Mirrorsoft name included in the copyright notice on the cartridge's label, he claimed that the game was a counterfeit cartridge, since Mirrorsoft had never possessed the console rights.

Since Maxwell had traveled to the Soviet Union to bargain for the arcade and handheld - not console - rights, he really didn't take the Famicom cartridge seriously. But since the console rights were being disputed, Maxwell told Belikov that he would make an offer for them after they negotiated for the arcade and handhelds rights and he returned to England. But Belikov told him that they had to clear up the console problem before they could move on to the other licenses. Belikov gave Maxwell a "protocol agreement" that gave Mirrorsoft the right of first refusal to any available *Tetris* licenses that remained, as long as Maxwell made an offer for the console licenses within one week of their meeting. In return, Elorg would gain the rights to publish Maxwell Communications software in the Soviet Union.

Following Belikov's three separate meetings with the three publishers, he sent a letter to Rogers that confirmed that the *Tetris* licenses for consoles, which he defined as computers without keyboards, had not been granted to anyone. Upon Rogers' return to Japan, he called Nintendo of America president Minoru Arakawa, and told him that the console rights to *Tetris* were available and that he controlled the handheld rights, which he had promised to sublicense to Nintendo for its forthcoming Game Boy.

When Henk Rogers returned to the Soviet Union on March 15, 1989, he had been authorized to make an offer for the *Tetris* console rights on behalf of Nintendo. This offer, while never disclosed to the public, was so high that even the Soviet negotiators were surprised. Minoru Arakawa wanted to be sure that no one, especially Mirrorsoft and Atari Games, would exceed the offer.

It turned out not to matter, since Mirrorsoft never submitted a bid and Atari Games wasn't even aware that the rights were up for sale. Rogers summoned Arakawa to Moscow, since a licensing deal appeared to be imminent. Arakawa, accompanied by Nintendo of America CEO Howard Lincoln, arrived in the Soviet Union on March 22, 1989. A contract awarding Nintendo the *Tetris* console rights followed three days later. Belikov then announced that the *Tetris* console rights had been assigned to Nintendo, and that no other company, including Mirrorsoft, Andromeda, or Tengen, was authorized to produce *Tetris* on any home videogame system.

Mirrorsoft's Kevin Maxwell informed his father that Elorg had broken the protocol agreement that he had received from them. Robert Maxwell decided to contact his friend Mikhail Gorbachev, the president of the Soviet Union, to let him know what Elorg had done. Nikolai Belikov wasn't worried. He felt that Nintendo would bring more money to the Soviet Union than anything that Robert Maxwell had done for the country. Maxwell flew to Moscow to meet with Gorbachev, who assured him that he "should no longer worry about the Japanese company."

When Howard Lincoln returned to Moscow on April 13, 1989, he learned that the Soviet government was investigating Elorg and threatening to prosecute those members of Elorg who failed to cooperate. But Belikov stuck to his guns. He felt that his deal with Nintendo had been legal, and he had the papers to prove it. In the end, Gorbachev agreed with him. When confronted with the news that the console rights to *Tetris* were definitely going to "the Japanese company," Robert Maxwell merely shrugged.

Once the Soviets decreed that the console rights belonged to Nintendo, Henk Rogers felt relieved. Nintendo sublicensed the Japanese console rights to Bullet-Proof Software, and all he had to do was produce a new copyright screen and game boxes that declared that the game had been sublicensed from Nintendo and not Mirrorsoft and Tengen. He was safe to continue selling his Famicom copies of *Tetris*.

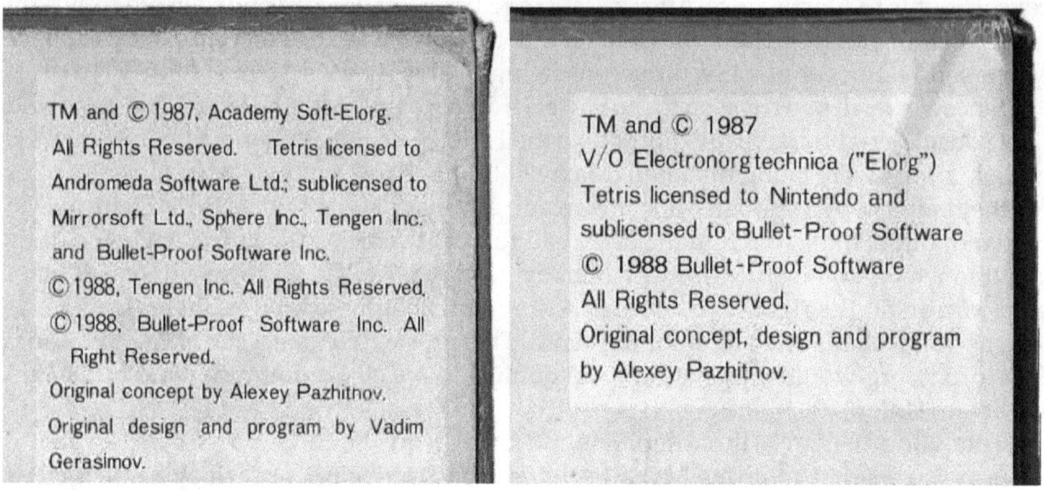
TM and ©1987, Academy Soft-Elorg.
All Rights Reserved. Tetris licensed to
Andromeda Software Ltd.; sublicensed to
Mirrorsoft Ltd., Sphere Inc., Tengen Inc.
and Bullet-Proof Software Inc.
©1988, Tengen Inc. All Rights Reserved.
©1988, Bullet-Proof Software Inc. All
Right Reserved.
Original concept by Alexey Pazhitnov.
Original design and program by Vadim
Gerasimov.
TM and © 1987
V/O Electronorgtechnica ("Elorg")
Tetris licensed to Nintendo and
sublicensed to Bullet-Proof Software
© 1988 Bullet-Proof Software
All Rights Reserved.
Original concept, design and program
by Alexey Pazhitnov.

Label change between Andromeda-licensed (left) and Nintendo-licensed (right) Famicom Tetris.

But in the United States, Atari Games wouldn't let go. While still in Moscow, Lincoln had received a call from Nintendo of America, which had apparently been sued by Tengen. He then began interviewing as many people as possible at Elorg to make sure that all of their paperwork was in order. When he was satisfied, Lincoln returned to the United States and immediately filed a countersuit against Tengen. Upon conducting a background search, he discovered that Tengen had filed trademark-registration applications for *Tetris* in several countries, including the United States, Japan, Canada and Great Britain.

Despite the oncoming court battle, Tengen released its NES version of *Tetris* on May 17, 1989. It was a hit. Even people who already owned versions of *Tetris* on their computers had to have copies of Tengen's version, which offered a unique dual-play mode. The screen displayed two *Tetris* boards instead of one, letting two players compete at the same time. And the graphics, which featured three-dimensional blocks, looked much nicer than those in versions that had preceded it.

But no matter how nice the game looked or played, its days were extremely numbered. A pretrial hearing between Nintendo of America and Tengen began in Federal District Judge Fern Smith's San Francisco courtroom[4] on June 15, 1989.

Hideyuki Nakajima, president of Atari Games, testified that when Tengen had still been a Nintendo licensee, the Japanese company had no problem with awarding them with a "Seal of Approval" to release *Tetris* for the NES. It was only after Tengen began manufacturing games on its own and filed an antitrust suit against Nintendo that the entire conflict over the *Tetris* console rights began. Nakajima believed that the whole squabble that they were going through was really an act of revenge against Atari Games by Howard Lincoln and Minoru Arakawa.

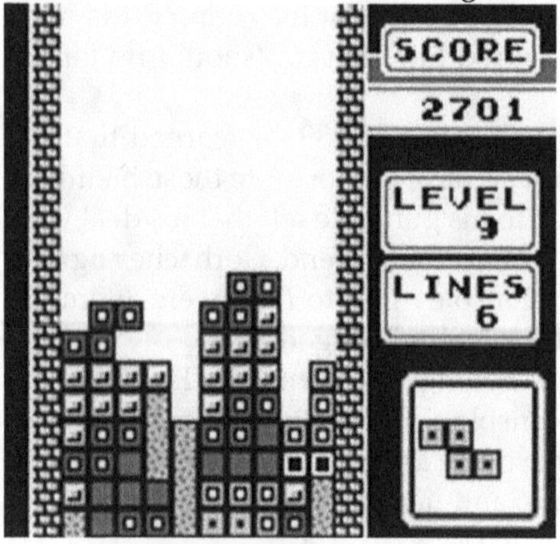

Nintendo Game Boy Tetris

Judge Smith reviewed all of the testimonies and documents and finally came to the conclusion that if the suit would go to trial, Nintendo would most likely win. She ordered Tengen to remove its version of *Tetris*, approximately 150,000 units, from store shelves beginning on June 21, 1989. She canceled the trial altogether on November 13, 1989 when she ruled that Nintendo owned the rights to the game.

Nintendo of America released its handheld

Game Boy on July 31, 1989 and bundled it with *Tetris*. Nintendo of Japan had released the Game Boy a month earlier, and although it hadn't included any packed-in games, *Tetris* was available separately to Japanese consumers. The Japanese and American versions of Game Boy *Tetris* were the same gam that had been developed by Bullet-Proof Software. Nintendo published it under a sublicense from Bullet-Proof Software. Thanks to the inclusion of *Tetris,* Nintendo of America sold millions of Game Boys. Incredibly, nearly half of those Game Boys (46%) were sold to adults.

Nintendo of America finally released its NES version of *Tetris* in November, 1989. Like the Famicom version, the game had been developed by Bullet-Proof Software, but the two were not exact copies of each other. The Nintendo versions lacked the two-person simultaneous play and three-dimensional blocks that had been found on Tengen's version. People who played both copies found Nintendo's edition to be inferior. However, since it was the only version that was legally available for the NES, it sold 8 million copies.

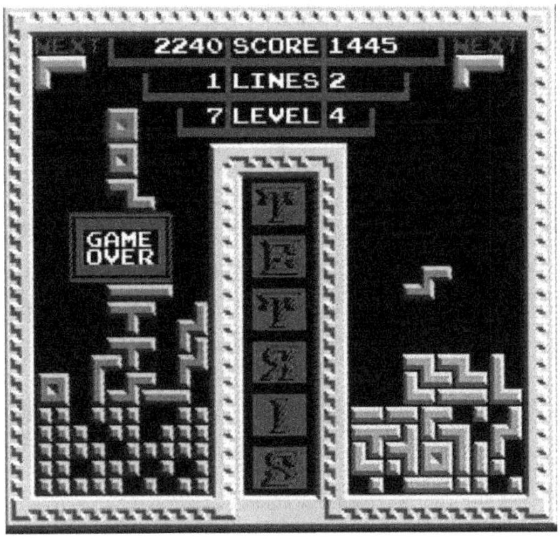

Tengen NES Tetris

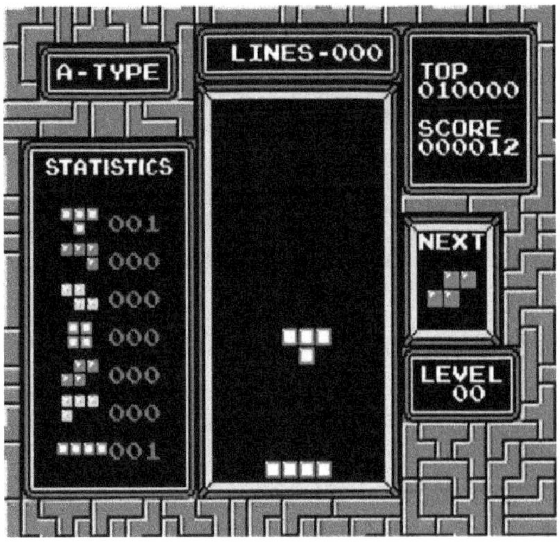

Nintendo NES Tetris

Following Nintendo's victory pertaining to the *Tetris* license, the companies and people that thought they had rights to it were left to pick up the pieces. Atari Games refused to pay Mirrorsoft any royalties that it had earned, which included revenue from Tengen's NES *Tetris* cartridges before they were removed from the market, 17,500 arcade units, and royalties earned from the Japanese Sega coin-ops. In addition, since the sublicense that Atari Games had sold to Henk Rogers was invalid, they received nothing from all of the Famicom *Tetris* cartridges that Bullet-Proof Software had sold. Mirrorsoft in turn did not pay Robert Stein any of the royalties that he was entitled to. Stein then had nothing to give to Elorg, which eventually revoked his license in 1990 for failing to pay them royalties. Spectrum Holobyte was then forced to negotiate directly with Elorg, in order to retain its computer license.[5] In 1992, Elorg also took away Stein's coin-op licenses for failing to pay a percentage of the royalties that, paradoxically, he wasn't receiving.

The person who benefited the least from *Tetris* was its designer, Alexey Pajitnov, since he couldn't profit from his creation under the Communist regime that he lived under. And even after he emigrated to the United States in 1991, he still couldn't profit from his game, since Elorg controlled the rights to it. After the fall of the Soviet Union in the same year, Elorg continued on as a private organization and still reaped from the *Tetris* profits, without sharing any with Pajitnov. That concluded in 1996, when the ten-year period that Pajitnov had originally assigned to the Academy of Sciences finally came to an end. However, Elorg would not relinquish those rights, and claimed that they had been granted in perpetuity. Rather than fight them, Pajitnov sought Henk Rogers' help with the reclamation of his rights to the game. Rogers created a company called Blue Planet Software,[6] which then teamed up with Elorg to create *The Tetris Company*, a company that protected the *Tetris* trademarks by licensing them to companies who had to follow certain guidelines.

In 2005, Rogers bought out Elorg's half of The Tetris Company and then formed a new company called *Tetris Holding*, which assumed ownership of the licenses that Elorg had held. He thus became half-owner of The Tetris Company, as well as Blue Planet Software.

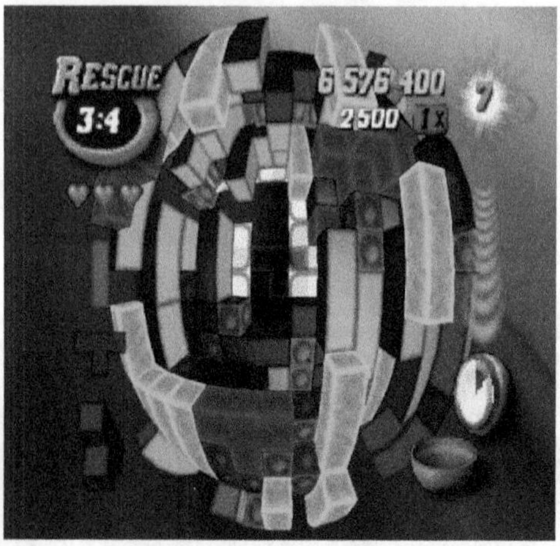

Tetrisphere

Since its initial availability in 1986, the popularity of *Tetris* has never abated. With 143 million physical copies having collectively sold for just about every video game console and computer that has ever been made, *Tetris* is the number-one videogame of all time. And with at least 30 variants such as *Tetrisphere, Tetris Blast, Hatris* and *Welltris, Tetris* has spawned more sequels than any other videogame in history.

In 2012, Tetris Holding announced that more than one billion games of *Tetris* were being played online each month. This was the same year that Apple announced that *Tetris* was one of the top-selling apps of the year. By 2014, more than 425 million paid copies of the game had been downloaded.

And Alexey Pajitnov is finally cashing in on the success of *Tetris*. As part-owner of The Tetris Company, he gets a piece of every dollar earned from those downloads.

APPENDIX II
BY THE NUMBERS

Videogame Consoles

Manufacturer	Platform	Released	Units Sold (in millions)
Sony	PlayStation 2	2000	157.68
Sony	PlayStation	1994	104.25
Nintendo	Wii	2006	100.76
Microsoft	Xbox 360	2005	84
Sony	PlayStation 3	2006	83.8
Nintendo	Famicom/NES	1983	61.91
Nintendo	Super Famicom/SNES	1990	49.10
Sony	PlayStation 4	2013	43.5
Sega	Mega Drive / Genesis	1988	33.75
Nintendo	Nintendo 64	1996	32.93 [
Atari	Atari 2600	1977	27.64
Microsoft	Xbox	2001	24.65
Nintendo	GameCube	2001	21.74
Sega	SG-1000/Master System	1985	10–13
Nintendo	Wii U	2012	13.02
Microsoft	Xbox One	2013	10
NEC	TurboGrafx-16	1987	10
Sega	Saturn	1994	8.82
Sega	Dreamcast	1998	8.20
Sega	Sega CD	1991	6
Atari	Atari 7800	1986	4.30
Nintendo	Color TV Game	1977	3
Mattel	Intellivision	1980	3
Magnavox/Philips	Magnavox Odyssey[2]	1978	2
Coleco	ColecoVision	1982	2
Panasonic	3DO Interactive Multiplayer	1993	2
Coleco	Telstar	1976	1
Atari	Atari 5200	1982	1

Source: vgchartz.com

[1] Includes SG-1000, SG-1000 II, Mark 3, and Sega Master System

[2] Includes PC-Engine, TurboGrafx-16, SuperGrafx, TurboDuo, TurboExpress

[3] Includes Color TV Game 6, Color TV Game 15, Color TV Racing 112 & Color TV Game Block Kuzushi

Handheld Game Consoles

Manufacturer	Platform	Released	Units sold (in millions)
Nintendo	Nintendo DS	2004	154.88
Nintendo	Game Boy & Game Boy Color	1989 & 1998	118.69
Sony	PlayStation Portable (PSP)	2004	82
Nintendo	Game Boy Advance/SP	2001	81.51
Nintendo	Nintendo 3DS	2011	59.79
Sony	PlayStation Vita	2011	13
Sega	Game Gear	1990	10.62
Bandai	Wonderswan	1999	3.5
Nokia	N-Gage	2003	3
SNK	Neo Geo Pocket/ Neo Geo Pocket Color	1998 & 1999	2
NEC	TurboExpress	1990	1.5
Atari	Lynx	1989	1
Sega	Nomad	1995	1

Source: vgchartz.com

APPENDIX III
TOP SELLING GAMES

Title	Year	System	Total (in millions)
Wii Sports	2006	Nintendo Wii	82.69 *
Super Mario Bros.	1985	Nintendo Famicom/NES	40.24
Mario Kart Wii	2008	Nintendo Wii	36.38
Tetris	1989	Nintendo Game Boy/Game Boy Color	35 *
Wii Sports Resort	2009	Nintendo Wii	32.8
Pokemon Red / Green/ Blue	1996	Nintendo Game Boy	31.37
New Super Mario Bros.	2006	Nintendo DS	30.79
Wii Play	2006	Nintendo Wii	28.82
Duck Hunt	1984	Nintendo Famicom / NES	28.31*
New Super Mario Bros. Wii	2009	Nintendo Wii	29.32
Grand Theft Auto: San Andreas	2004	Sony PS2	27.5
Mario Kart DS	2005	Nintendo DS	25.36
Nintendogs	2005	Nintendo SD	24.67
Kinect Adventures!	2010	Microsoft Xbox 360	24 *
Pokemon Gold /Silver	1999	Game Boy Color	23.10
Wii Fit	2007	Nintendo Wii	22.69
Wii Fit Plus	2009	Nintendo Wii	21.51
Grand Theft Auto V	2013	PlayStation 3	21.3
Super Mario World	1990	Nintendo Super Famicom/SNES	20.61
Super Mario Land	1989	Nintendo Game Boy	20.6
Brain Age: Train your Brain in Minutes a Day	2005	Nintendo DS	20.13

Source: vgchartz.com

* Pack-in games

APPENDIX IV
BIBLIOGRAPHY

BOOKS

Baer, Ralph. Videogames: In The Beginning. Springfield, NJ: Rolenta Press. 2005.

Benford, Tom. Welcome To... CD-ROM. New York: MIS: Press. 1993.

Blumenthal, Howard J. The Complete Guide To Electronic Games. New York: New American Library. 1981.

Bruck, Connie. Master of the Game. New York: Simon & Schuster. 1994.

Burnham, Van. Supercade: A Visual History of the Videogame Age 1971-1984. Cambridge, MA:MIT Press. 2001.

Campbell-Kelly, Martin, and William Aspray. Computer: A History of the Information Machine. New York: Basic Books. 1996.

Cohen, Scott. Zap: The Rise And Fall of Atari. New York: McGraw-Hill. 1984.

Collector Value Guide. Pokémon. Middletown, CT: CheckerBee Publishing. 1999.

Consumer Guide. The Complete Book of Video Games. New York: Warner Books. 1977.

Costello, Matthew J. The Greatest Games of All Time. New York: John Wiley & Sons. 1991.

D'Ignazio, Fred. Electronic Games. New York: Franklin Watts. 1982.

DeGeorge, Gail. The Making of a Blockbuster. New York: John Wiley & Sons. 1996.

DeKeles, Jon C.A. Video Game Quest. Northridge CA: DMS. 1990.

Dillon, Roberto. The Golden Age of Video Games. Boca Raton, FL: CRC Press. 2011.

Donovan, Tristan. Replay: The History of Video Games. East Sussex: Yellow Ant. 2010.

Edwards, Benj. "The MIT Dropouts Who Created Ms. Pac-Man: A 35th-Anniversary Oral History." fastcompany.com. Fast Company, Feb. 02, 2017. Web.

Edwards, Benj. "The Untold Story Of The Invention Of The Game Cartridge." fastcompany.com. Fast Company, Jan. 22, 2015. Web.

Feldman, Tony. Multimedia. London. Blueprint. 1994.

Forster, Winnie. The Encyclopedia of Game Machines. Magdalena Gniatczynska. 2005.

Freed, Les. The History of Computers. Emeryville, California: Ziff-Davis Press. 1995.

Goldberg, Harold. All Your Base Are Belong To Us. New York: Three Rivers Press. 2011.

Goldberg, Marty, and Curt Vendel. Atari Inc. – Business Is Fun. Camel, NY: Syzygy Publishing. 2012.

Gorges, Florent. The History of Nintendo 1889-1980. France: Pix 'N Love Publishing. 2010.

Harris, Blake J. Console Wars: Sega, Nintendo, and the Battle That Defined a Generation. New York: It Books. 2014.

Hayses, Michael, and Stuart Dinsey. Games War. London: Bowerdean Publishing. 1995.

Hirschfeld, Tom. How To Master Home Video Games. New York: Bantam. 1982.

Horowitz, Ken. Playing at the Next Level: A History of American Sega Games. Jefferson, NC: McFarland & Company. 2016.

Katz, Arnie, and Bill Kunkel. The Player's Strategy Guide to Atari VCS Home Video Games. New York: Dell. 1982.

Kent, Steven L. The First Quarter. Bothell, Washington: BWD Press. 2000.

Kent, Steven L. The Ultimate History of Video Games. Roseville, CA: Prima Publishing. 2001.

Kohler, Chris. Power-Up: How Japanese Video Games Gave the World an Extra Life. Indianapolis, IN: Brady Games. 2005.

Kubey, Craig. The Winner's Book of Video Games. New York: Warner Books. 1982.

Kurtz, Bill. The Encyclopedia of Arcade Video Games. Atglen, PA: Schiffer Publishing Ltd. 2004.

Kushner, David. Jacked: The Outlaw Story of Grand Theft Auto. Hoboken, NJ: John Wiley & Sons. 2012.

Lavroff, Nicholas. Behind The Scenes At Sega. Rocklin, CA: Prima Publishing. 1994.

Linzmayer, Owen W. Apple Confidential. San Francisco: No Starch Press. 1999.

Lowe Jr, Walter. Playboy's Guide To Rating The Video Games. New York: Playboy Paperbacks. 1982.

Miller, G. Wayne. Toy Wars: The Epic Struggle Between G.I. Joe, Barbie, and the Companies That Make Them. Holbrook, MA. Adams Media. 1998.

Montfort, Nick, and Ian Bogost. Racing The Beam. Cambridge, MA: MIT Press. 2009.

Pettus, Sam. Service Games: The Rise And Fall Of Sega. 2012.

Pimentel, Ken, and Kevin Teixeira. Virtual Reality: Through The New Looking Glass. New York: McGraw-Hill. 1993.

Poole, Steven. Trigger Happy. New York: Arcade Publishing. 2000.

Ryan, Jeff. Super Mario. New York: Portfolio/Penguin. 2011.

Sandler, Corey, and Tom Badgett. Ultimate Sega Game Strategies For The Master and Genesis Systems.

New York: Bantam. 1990.
Sawyer, Ben. The Ultimate Game Developer's Sourcebook. Scottsdale AZ: Coriolis Group Books. 1996.
Sheff, David. Game Over. New York: Random House. 1993.
Sheff, David. Video Games. New York: Random House. 1994.
Steinberg, Scott. Music Games Rock: Rhythm Gaming's Greatest Hits Of All Time. Lilburn GA: P3: Power Play Publishing. 2011
Stern, Sydney Ladensohn, and Ted Schoenhaus. Toyland: The High-Stakes of the Toy Industry. Chicago: Contemporary Books. 1990.
Sullivan, George. Screen Play: The Story of Video Games. New York: Frederick Warne. 1983.
Swisher, Kara. aol.com. New York: Times Business. 1998.
Takahashi, Dean. Opening The Xbox. Roseville, CA: Prima Publishing. 2002.
Uston, Ken. Ken Uston's Guide To Buying and Beating the Home Video Games. New York: Signet. 1982.
Veit, Stan. Stan Veit's History of the Personal Computer: Asheville NC: Worldcomm. 1993.
Watson Jr, Thomas J. Father Son & Co. New York: Bantam Books. 1990.
Wozniak, Steve, with Gina Smith. iWoz. New York: W. W. Norton & Company. 2007.

PERIODICALS

Alexander, Michael: "Video Games: How High Is Up?", *Dealerscope II*, 8/82.
Blanchet, Michael: "Game Room", *Video Review*, 2/83-6/83.
Blumenthal, Howard: "Mattel's Intellivision", *Video*, 8/80.
Brandt, Richard, Neil Gross, and Peter Coy: "Sega!" *Business Week*, 2/21/94.
Butterworth, Brent: "Multimedia: Video's Newest Wave", *Video*, 11/90.
Butterworth, Brent, and Kenneth Korman: "CDs Go Interactive", *Video*, 6/91.
Butterworth, Brent, and Kenneth Korman: "CD-I Test Drive", *Video*, 12/91.
Elmer-Dewitt, Philip: "The Amazing Video Game Boom", *Time*, 9/27/93.
Fagan, Gregory P: "Hunting The Big Game", *Video Review*, 12/88.
Goldberg, Ron: "Interactive Compact Disc: First Look", *Video Review*, 3/92.
Goldberg, Ron: "Round Two", *Video*, 6/92.
Hacker, Randi: "Games", *Video Review*, 8/82.
Hajdu, David: "It's All In The Game: A Complete Guide To The First Generation of VCR Games", *Video Review*, 12/86.
Haleff, Maxine, and Frank Lovcce:"Interactive Discs-Will They Make Movies Obsolete?", *Video Review*, 7/81.
Jacobs, Barry: "From Pong To Porn: Sex Games", *Video Review*, 12/82.
Jacobs, Barry: "Phone Home Video", *Video Review*, 9/83.
Katz, Arnie, and Bill Kunkel: "Video's Guide To Electronic Games", *Video*, 11/82.
Katz, Arnie, and Bill Kunkel: "Computer Games Erupt!", *Video*, 3/84.
Katz, Arnie, and Joyce Worley: "The History of Video Gaming... Part 1: In The Beginning", *ANALOG Computing*, 4/88.
Katz, Arnie, and Joyce Worley: "The History of Video Gaming... Part 2: The Golden Age Dawns", *ANALOG Computing*, 5/88.
Katz, Arnie, and Joyce Worley: "The History of Video Gaming... Part 3: The Golden Age", *ANALOG Computing*, 6/88.
Kesten, Louis: "The New Video Toy Chest", *Video*, 6/87.
Kesten, Lou: "Video Games Bounce Back", *Video*, 12/87.
Kesten, Lou: "Where The Toys Are", *Video*, 12/88.
Kesten, Lou: "Game Wars!", *Video*, 10/89.
Kumin, Daniel: "JVC RG-M10BU X'EYE", *CD Review*, 10/94.
Kunkel, Bill, and Frank Laney Jr (Arnie Katz): "Arcade Alley", *Video*, 4/80-8/84.
Kunkel, Bill, and Frank Laney Jr: "Ten Years of Video Games", *Video*, 12/81.
Kunkel, Bill, and Arnie Katz: "Big Games: Five That Made The Difference", *Video*, 8/84.
Laney Jr, Frank, and Bill Kunkel: "The Space Invaders Saga", *Video*, 6/81.
Levine, Martin: "Games At CES: Separating the Hits From the Misses", *Consumer Electronics*, 12/82.
Levine, Martin: "Changing Games Market: How Much Fun Is Left?", *Consumer Electronics*, 7/83.
Levine, Martin: "Tomorrow's Games Market: More Violence or New Vitality?", *Consumer Electronics*, 9/83.
Lovece, Frank: "Complete Shopper's Guide To All The Latest Video-Game Gear", *Video Review*, 10/82.
Lovece, Frank: "The Honest-To-Goodness History of Home Video Games", *Video Review*, 6/83.
Mannes, George: "CDTV: First Look", *Video Review*, 7/91.
Moore, Myra: "Games Grow Up:, *Video*, 4/91.
Onosko, Tim: "Electronic Delivery", *Video*, 2/84.

Onosko, Timothy: "Let The Games Begin", *Video*, 11/86.
Pappas, Lee H: "Darkness At Noon", *ANALOG Computing*, 6/84.
Pappas, Lee H, and Jon A Bell: "The New Atari: An Interview With Jack Tramiel", *ANALOG Computing*, 1/85.
Prince, Suzan D: "1982 Video Game Plans", *Videoplay*, 11/81.
Skow, John: "Games That Play People", *Time*, 1/18/82.
Stedman, Nancy: "Fields of Dreams", Video, 5/91.
Trost, Mark: "Pac-Mail: Every Player Should Know About Videogame Exchange Clubs", *Video Review*, 11/82.
Trost, Mark: "The Dollars And Sense of Videogames For Rent", *Video Review*, 3/83.
Tzannes, Alexis: "The First Microprocessor Pinball Machine". *Gameroom*, 6/99.
Video Review: "The Great Videogame Shootout", *Video Review*, 12/87.
Wielage, Marc: "Game Room", *Video Review*, 9/82-1/83.
Willcox, James K: "Video Games At Hyperspeed", *Video Review*, 12/91.
Willcox, James K: "Multimedia Playground", *Video*, 8/94.
Wiswell, Phil: "Games", *Video Review*, 5/81-6/82.
Wiswell, Phil: "The Collector's Handbook To Valuable and Rare Videogames", *Video Review*, 2/84.
Worley, Joyce, Arnie Katz, and Bill Kunkel: "Video Games: A Buyer's Guide To The Systems", *ANALOG Computing*, 10/87.
Zahner, Kurt: "Imagine the Boob Tube as a Thinking Machine", *Video Review*, 2-3/93.

APPENDIX IV

The following magazines were used extensively during the creation of this book:
Edge: October 1993 - February 2017.
EGM[2]: July 1994 - July 1998.
Expert Gamer: August 1998 - October 2001.
Electronic Fun With Computers And Games: November 1982 - March 1984.
Computer Fun: April 1984 - May 1984.
Electronic Games: Winter 1982 - April 1985.
Computer Entertainment: May 1985 - August 1985.
Electronic Games: October 1992-July 1995.
Fusion: August 1995-February 1996.
Intelligent Gamer's Fusion: March 1996-May 1996.
Intelligent Gamer: June 1996-January 1997.
Electronic Gaming Monthly: August 1998 - March-April 2013.
Game Buyer: July 1998-October 1998.
Game Informer: Fall 1991 - February 2017.
Game Players: April/May 1989-September 1996.
Gamepro: May 1989 - Winter 2011.
Gamer's Republic: June 1998-March 2001
Games™: December 2002 - February 2017.
Next Generation: January 1995 - January 2002.
Play: January 2002 - February 2010.
Pocket Games: Summer 1999 - June 2006.
Retro Gamer: January 2004 - February 2017.
Ultimate Gamer: July 1995-January 1996.
Ultra Game Players: October 1996-June 1998.
Video Games: August 1982 - Fall 1984.
VideoGames & Computer Entertainment: December 1988 - August 1983.
VideoGames: September 1993-August 1996.
Videogaming Illustrated: August 1982 - December 1983.
Video And Computer Illustrated: January 1984 - March 1984.

WEBSITES OF INTEREST

1Up	`www.1up.com/`
8-Bit Rocket	`www.8bitrocket.com/`
American Classic Arcade Museum	`www.classicarcademuseum.org/`
Armchair Arcade	`www.armchairarcade.com`
AtariAge	`www.atariage.com`
Atari Museum	`atarimuseum.com/`

Chronology of Video Game Systems	www.islandnet.com/~kpolsson/vidgame
Digital Press	www.digitpress.com
Gamasutra	www.gamasutra.com
Gamespot	www.gamespot.com/
Giant Bomb	www.giantbomb.com/
GoodDealGames	www.gooddealgames.com
IGN	www.ign.com/
Intellivision Lives	www.intellivisionlives.com/
National Videogame Museum	nvmusa.org/
Nintendo Wiki	nintendo.wikia.com/wiki/Nintendo_Wiki
Pong Story	www.pong-story.com/
Sega Retro	segaretro.org/
Strong Museum of Play	www.museumofplay.org/
The Golden Age Arcade Historian	allincolorforaquarter.blogspot.co.uk/
They Create Worlds	videogamehistorian.wordpress.com/about/
Video Game Console Library	videogameconsolelibrary.com/
Wikipedia	www.wikipedia.org

ENDNOTES

CHAPTER 1

[1] The annexation of Austria into Nazi Germany.

[2] Rogers Majestic was owned by Philips, a Dutch electronics company. Philips would later purchase Magnavox, the company responsible for marketing the first home videogame console.

[3] Electronic Delay Storage Automatic Calculator

CHAPTER 2

[1] While Rob Geiman and Charles Fibian, the two other representatives from Nutting Associates indicated in the guest book the name of the company that they represented, Bushnell surreptitiously left the field blank. In addition, Geiman's and Fibian's signatures were one line apart while Bushnell's was on a completely different page.

[2] The person at the Secretary of State office who like the word ATARI, was Jerry Brown, a future governor of California.

CHAPTER 3

[1] Prior to starting Service Games, Bromberg ran a different distribution company, *Standard Games*, which provided vending machines and jukeboxes to the west coast. This company was founded in 1934 and was sold in 1945.

[2] In 1966 the Nakamura Manufacturing Company, which would later be called Namco, released a three-player mechanical submarine game also called *Periscope*. This was then licensed to Sega where it was redesigned as a one-player game. Upon the release of the Sega version in the United States in 1968, both versions went on to become international hits.

[3] In 1974, Atari released *Quadrapong*, which was the same game as *Elimination.*

[4] Videogames that were housed in tables were commonly called *cocktail tables*. Although *Elimination* wasn't technically a cocktail table since its curved top prevented drinks from being placed atop it, it is generally considered the first game to appear in a cocktail table.

CHAPTER 4

[1] This tagline would be granted a trademark in 1976.

[2] Discrete components include individual transistors, resistors, diodes and capacitors.

[3] DNA had been established in 1970 by Dave Nutting to create arcade games under contract with Bally. Dave Nutting was the brother of Nutting Associates' Bill Nutting.

[4] The first commercial solid state pinball machine was *The Spirit of '76*, which was released in mid-1975. The table, which had been designed by DNA, had been based on the *Flicker* prototype and licensed to Mirco Games.

[5] Bally's first solid state pinball machine, *Freedom*, was based on the *Flicker* prototype, which had been patented by DNA. Afterwards, Bally began releasing solid state machines of its own design. However, other manufacturers, Gottlieb and Williams, copied the *Flicker* design for their own sold state tables. Bally eventually purchased DNA and assumed its patents, which led to a lawsuit against Gottlieb and Williams in 1980. Bally eventually shut down DNA in 1984.

[6] It was long believed that the game was patterned and named after a 1975 movie called *Death Race 2000*. However, this was not the case at all.

[7] Atari produced a pre-production color version of *Gotcha* in October, 1973, which featured a yellow maze. However, the color version of the game was not officially marketed.

[8] The game was in black and white. The screen had colored overlays over the rows to make them appear differently.

[9] Philips, a Dutch-based electronics company, released the Odyssey 200 in Europe under the Philips label. Philips had purchased Magnavox in 1974.

[10] Tele-Games was short for *Television Games.*

[11] According to *Nihon Keizai Shimbun*, the Odyssey was imported into Japan by a Tokyo-based company called

Jolieb Co. Ltd. However, other sources state that the toy company, Nintendo, imported the console. Nintendo had manufactured the Odyssey light guns for Magnavox so they were made aware of the console well before other companies. Since no Odysseys have ever turned up with Japanese packaging or instructions, it's possible that the console that was sold in Japan was same model that was sold in the United States.

[12] The Electrotennis was packaged with its own separate UHF antenna that could be hooked up to any television.

[13] The TV Fun was also sold at Sears, where it was called *Hockey Jockari.*

[14] Magnavox also released a 19" television that had the components of the Odyssey 300 built into it. Because the console didn't have to be connected to a television with an RF modulator, the picture quality on this television was better. A pair of special hand controllers were packaged with the television, and these allowed players to control the paddles while sitting in front of the television.

[15] Jerry Lawson had been a member of a computer users' group called the *Bay Area Amateur Computer Users' Group*, a monthly gathering of early computer hobbyists that included Steve Jobs, Steve Wozniak and Eugene Jarvis. Lawson was one of only two black members, the other being Ron Jones, who would later form a company called Songpro.

[16] The Central Processing Unit.

CHAPTER 5

[1] Signetics was established in 1961. It was the first company that had been created with the specific purpose to manufacture integrated circuits.

[2] In 1978, Philips followed the Odyssey 2001 with the *Odyssey 2100.* While the two consoles were basically the same externally, the Odyssey 2100 played a total of 24 variants of six games.

[3] *Video Pinball* also included a home version of Atari's popular arcade game, *Breakout.*

[4] Two other arcade games that employed handlebar controllers had also appeared in 1976. Digital Games Incorporated's *Heavy Traffic* and Sega's *Moto-Cross* were both first-person racing games. *Moto-Cross* is most remembered for the vibration from the handlebar controls when a collision with another bike occurred.

[5] The game played Volley, Tennis, and Hockey in one and two-player modes

[6] The 15th game was a one-player target shooting game in which the left paddle was used to fire "shots" at targets on the right side of the screen.

[7] Nintendo released *Wild Gunman* in 1984 as a videogame for its Famicom gaming console.

[8] On a raster monitor the front end of the CRT was typically coated with chemicals called phosphors. An electrode (electron gun) in the back end of the CRT fired electrons that lit up the phosphors. The CRT consisted of horizontal scan lines and the electron gun traversed across each of the lines from top to bottom 30-60 times per second and created an image that consisted of two-dimensional pixels (picture elements).

[9] Fortunately, other companies improved on the vector technology, and more impressive games employing vector graphics were released in 1979.

[10] Following Warner's purchase of Atari, Joe Keenan remained as president and Nolan Bushnell stayed on as Chairman of the Board.

[11] The console was sold at Sears as the *Video Arcade* under the Tele-Games brand label.

[12] Several retailers in the Silicon Valley area where Atari was headquartered began selling the system on September 11.

[13] The VCS included only 128 bytes of RAM (Random-Access Memory). While a program could contain up to 4,096 (4k) bytes of code, only 128 bytes could be loaded into the VCS at a time to be processed.

CHAPTER 6

[1] All waves started from the same row and at the same speed from the fifth level on.

[2] The displayed score rolled back to 0 after 9,999

[3] That revenue came to a halt when the pro football season ended at the end of January, 1979. The appeal for *Space Invaders* continued.

[4] The Atari game *Breakout* exemplifies how analog and digital controllers differ. Both types could be used to operate the paddle at the bottom of the screen. Turning an analog dial would cause the on-screen paddle to move

left or right. And the speed of the paddle could vary depending upon how fast or slow the dial was rotated. The same paddle could be operated by pressing a digital joystick to the left or right. Pressing it to the left would turn on a certain circuit, which in turn would move the paddle to the left. Pressing the stick to the right would shut off the first circuit and turn on a second, which would tell the paddle to move to the right. However, while the player would have control of the paddle's direction, there would be no way to alter the speed that the paddle moved.

[5] Only 37 games were actually produced. Some games that had been proposed had to be scrapped because the VC4000 wasn't technologically advanced enough able to play them. *Rodeo*, for example, which should have been game #35, had to be abandoned because the console simply couldn't display long lassos that were needed in the game.

[6] The Videopac G7000 was distributed under several brand names in Europe besides Philips. In addition, in 1979 Philips released the *C52* in France. This was essentially a Videopac G7000 with a localized French keyboard. Philips also distributed the console in Canada where it retained the Odyssey^2 name.

[7] Power was turned on and off by inserting or removing the main power supply.

[8] Atari would later rename the game to *A Game of Concentration.*

[9] A roulette wheel was displayed on the same box as the chess piece, but a roulette game was never designed for the VCS.

[10] The three new keyboard Videocarts were *Casino Poker*, *Space Odyssey* and *Pro-Football.* They didn't follow the standard numbering scheme of the regular Videocarts and were numbered K-1, K-2 and K-3. The cartridges themselves were also black instead of yellow.

CHAPTER 7

[1] In an interview with the website *Classic Consoles Center*, Hans-Heinz Bieling, the designer of several VC4000 games, said that Philips licensed the general concept of the system to both Radofin and Interton.

[2] Raskin's computer would be released in January, 1984. It would be called the *Macintosh.*

[3] In October, Nintendo released an arcade game called *Sheriff*, which featured cabinet artwork by Miyamoto. The game featured a hero cowboy who had to shoot down sixteen rouge cowboys while avoiding their own gunfire, in order to save a beautiful woman from their clutches. In 1980, Exidy would license the game and release it in the United States where it would be called *Bandido.* This would be the first Nintendo game to be distributed in the United States.

[4] The terms *cartridge* and *cassette* were interchangeable. Bandai specifically referred to its plug-in software as cassettes.

[5] The Intellivision actually used GI's AY-3-8914, which was a variant of the AY-3-8910.

[6] Oddly, the *Space Invaders* Videocart displayed a 1977 copyright date, one year before Taito actually released the game in arcades.

[7] The 20 Videocarts were numbered 1-18 and 20-21. Number 19, *Checkers*, wouldn't be released until 1980. Zircon also offered Videocart #51, a demo cartridge, for the same $20 price.

[8] The bottom of a brochure that Zircon distributed for Christmas 1982 referred to the Channel F as the "Fairchild Video Entertainment Computer."

CHAPTER 8

[1] Atari also planned to release a handheld version of *Space Invaders*, featuring a 32x32 pixel LCD screen and a dial controller. A similar *Super Breakout* handheld unit was also developed. Atari's marketing department put an end to those projects, fearing that their sales would interfere with the VCS versions of those games.

[2] While Robinett's *Adventure* is commonly regarded as the first game to feature an Easter egg, the first appearance of an Easter egg actually preceded *Adventure* by almost five years. Michael Glass, a developer for Fairchild, programmed his name into a Channel F demo cart in 1976. The name would appear if the 1, 3 and 4 buttons were pressed at the same time at the conclusion of the demo.

[3] Steven Wright's soccer game would make history again in 1981 when its name was changed to *Pele's Soccer*, marking the first celebrity endorsement of a videogame. Pelé was a professional soccer player who played for the New York Cosmos, a team that, like Atari, was owned by Warner Communications.

CHAPTER 9

[1] The Remote Control VCS was also known as the Atari *2700*, due to its model number being CX-2700.

[2] After *Ms. Pac-Man* was released and became very successful, Midway began licensing the *Ms. Pac-Man* characters without paying a royalty to GCC. GCC took Midway to court in 1983 and they eventually settled with three-way agreement between GCC, Midway and Namco. However, in 2000, Namco of America released a combination arcade machine that featured *Ms. Pac-Man* and *Galaga*, without consulting GCC. When the original members of GCC contacted Namco of America regarding this, they were confronted by executives who had never even heard of them. Namco of America and GCC soon entered into arbitration that lasted five years, the two companies finally reached a confidential agreement.

CHAPTER 10

[1] Arcade games did become three-dimensional with the July release of Sega's *SubRoc-3D*, a first person shooter where the object was to shoot approaching enemies below and above water. Players looked through a periscope, which provided different images to each eye. Ironically, Coleco licensed the game from Sega and in 1983 released a 2D ColecoVision version of the game which it simply called *SubRoc*.

[2] Ironically, Expansion Module #2 plugged into the controller port and not the "Expansion Module Interface" slot.

[3] Atari revised the 5200 console in 1983 by limiting it to only two controller ports and having it use a conventional power supply and RF switch.

[4] The Philips Videopac version of this game released in Europe was simply called *Munchkin*. The *K.C.* in the Odyssey[2] title was an inside joke and referred to Kenneth C. Menkin, the president of Philips Consumer Electronics, the division of North American Philips, which Odyssey fell under.

[5] Games by Apollo folded in early 1983

CHAPTER 11

[1] The computer upgrade was never released. However, GCE did release two peripherals for the Vectrex. One was the *3D Imager*, which plugged into the second controller slot and allowed people to play 3D games. The other was a light pen that permitted users to draw pictures, compose music, or animate their own cartoons directly on the screen.

[2] Only two games, *Bump'n'Jump* and *Masters of the Universe: The Power of He-Man*, were ultimately released without the M-Network designation.

[3] Amiga also announced a Power-Stick with a keypad that would be compatible with the ColecoVision and Intellivision. This controller was never released.

[4] Joystick controllers for the Atari VCS could also be used with the Atari 400 and 800 and Commodore VIC-20 computers.

[5] Zircon later added an actual red firing button to the side of Video Command.

[6] In March, 1984, Texas Instruments decided it couldn't compete in the home computer market and discontinued the TI-99/4A. The MBX died along with the computer.

[7] In 1974, due to complicated business reasons, Gulf & Western created an American company called Sega Enterprises, Inc., which became a subsidiary of Paramount Pictures, which was also owned by Gulf & Western. The Japanese business, Sega Enterprises, Ltd., in effect became a subsidiary under the new American Sega Enterprises, Inc.

[8] In 1979, Sega of America merged with Gremlin Industries, an arcade videogame company. The merged company was called *Sega Electronics, Inc.*

[9] Sega Enterprises,Inc.. released a handful of console and computer games in 1984. However, these home translations of arcade games that had been licensed from Bally.

[10] In later years, CMOS memory would be used in game cartridges to retain high scores or levels achieved, but the Master Module was the first example of its use in a cartridge.

[11] Romox would eventually shut down for good in 1985.

[12] Prior to releasing its own handheld console, Palmtex was a North American distributor of Nintendo's Game & Watch series.

[13] Coleco actually licensed *Dragon's Lair* for $2 million, which fueled speculation that the company would release a laserdisc module for both the ColecoVision and Adam.

[14] Kassar was actually fired from Atari because the company lost millions of dollars under his watch. The company reported it to the press as a resignation.

[15] The "SC" in the product name stood for "Sega Computer."

[16] Sega's goal with the SC-3000 was to establish a computer standard and thus allowed other companies to clone the machine. The only such machine to become available was the *Othello Multivision* from Tsukuda Original.

[17] Sega had planned to release an *SC-5000* computer along with the SC-3000. The SC-5000 was to be more powerful than the SC-3000 and would have had a keyboard with fully-sculptured keys.

[18] The "SG" in the product name stood for "Sega Game."

[19] Sega sold 160,000 SG-1000 consoles during its first year on the market.

[20] Although the graphics from the Famicom were first rate, the console could only connect to a standard television set via an RF modulator, which greatly curtailed the overall picture quality. Shortly after the release of the Famicom, Sharp Corporation introduced its *My Computer TV C1* to the Japanese market. This unit was a television with a built-in Famicom that displayed beautiful images without any outside interference. The picture was so clear that Japanese magazines used the C1 to take game screenshots that they then published. The C1 was sold in two sizes. A 19" model cost ¥145,000 ($627) and a 14" sold for ¥93,000 ($402). A later model called the *Sharp Nintendo Television*, was sold in North America in 1989.

[21] In 1982, Jay Miner, one of the original designers of the Atari 800, approached the management at Atari with an idea for a new game machine that would employ a 16-bit Motorola 68000 processor. After Atari showed little interest in the machine, Miner left Atari and joined Zimast, a company that manufactured chips for pacemakers. Shortly afterwards a group of Texas investors approached Larry Kaplan of Activision, to invest $7 million in a new videogame company that would use hardware based around a customized 68000 chip. Kaplan called Miner and invited him to join the company, which was called *Hi-Toro*. Kaplan planned for him and Activision to develop software for the system while Miner would design the hardware and Zimast would manufacture the chips. After Miner, joined, Kaplan suddenly changed his mind and left, leaving Miner as the chief engineer and forcing him to resign from Zimast. A group of designers, which included Miner's Atari-colleague, Joe Decuir, was assembled, and they spent the following two years creating the hardware and operating system for the game machine that was code-named "Lorraine". During this time someone realized that there was a Japanese lawnmower company called Toro, so the name of the company was changed to *Amiga*, which was the Spanish word for a female friend.

CHAPTER 12

[1] The SG-1000 II control pad featured a round D-pad as opposed to the cross-shaped one on the Famicom control pad.

[2] Hayao Nakayama had become the chairman of Sega after David Rosen retired in 1982.

[3] Gulf & Western finally shut down Sega Enterprises, Inc. at the end of the year. It started a new company called *Ages* (Sega spelt backwards) to deal with any remaining issues regarding intellectual properties.

[4] In 1985, Warner Communications sold controlling interest (60%) of Atari Games to Namco America for $10 million. Unfortunately, this led to friction between the head of Namco, Masaya Nakamura, and Hide Nakajima, who ran Namco America. Nakamura viewed Atari Games as a competitor and didn't like sharing its ownership with Warner Communications. In 1986, Namco sold 20% of its interest in Atari Games to Nakajima and his employees. With no majority shareholder (Namco and Warner each controlled 40%), Atari Games became autonomous with Nakajima at the helm.

[5] Tramiel purposely did not include an "i" in the spelling of his new company because he wanted people to pronounce it correctly, since his own last name was commonly mispronounced. The "i" in his last name was actually silent.

[6] The computer that Atari released in 1985 used a Motorola 68000 microprocessor. Although the 68000 was commonly believed to have a 16-bit architecture, it actually was a 32-bit microprocessor with a 16-bit external data bus. For this reason Atari called its new line of computers the *Atari ST*, with "ST" being an acronym for "**S**ixteen/**T**hirty-two."

[7] Originally, the Halcyon was designed around an RCA CED videodisc player, which provided random access. Unfortunately, RCA cancelled the CED shortly before the Halcyon's completion. The Halcyon had to be quickly redesigned to use a higher-cost laserdisc player although they only allowed thirty minutes of viewing on each side of the laserdisc.

[8] Each game consisted of a laserdisc and a 16K cartridge. The disc contained the audio and video of the game while the cartridge included the game's vocabulary for speech recognition and any logic that was required to play.

[9] Few people purchased the Halcyon following its January, 1985 commercial release. RDI Video Systems went bankrupt and closed down before 1985 ended. Only the two initial games were ever released.

CHAPTER 13

[1] The Court reached a verdict in Magnavox's favor on March 17, 1986. Activision filed an appeal on the following day.

[2] Since the Famicom was selling well in Japan, Nintendo simply sold the robot controller as a peripheral called the *Famicom Robot*. It was released on July 26, three months before ROB infiltrated American toy stores.

[3] 128K Sega My Cards were planned but never released.

[4] The superior audio was available through a peripheral called the *FM Sound Unit*. However, this optional ¥6,800 ($56) peripheral wouldn't be released until 1987 and it only improved the audio in certain games. The video was improved through the inclusion of an A/V output that could be used instead of the standard RF output that was also provided.

[5] The company had already reaffirmed a presence in North America for its arcade games. During the year, the Sega Enterprises, Ltd. opened up a North American headquarters for its arcade division and called it *Sega Enterprises, Inc.* (sometimes referred as *Sega Enterprises, Inc. (USA)*

[6] By the 1990's most arcade games utilized the JAMMA standard..

CHAPTER 14

[1] Surprisingly, while Nintendo awarded licenses to prospective publishers, it didn't want to pay any more royalties for a patent that had been licensed from Magnavox. Magnavox had filed a patent infringement suit against Nintendo because it felt that the NES light gun infringed upon Ralph Baer's precision target shooting patent. Nintendo then turned around and *sued* Magnavox claiming that Magnavox and Sanders had deceived the Patent Office when it had applied for its '507 patent) for one on-screen symbol making contact with another on-screen symbol. Although the '507 patent had been contested many times, the suits always resulted in Magnavox's favor. Nintendo tried to prove that Baer hadn't invented the routine and even brought in Willy Higinbotham, whose named had never been associated with videogames before, to testify. Judge Leonard Sand decided that Higinbotham's *Tennis for Two*, which displayed on an oscilloscope, was not a forerunner to Baer's patent. The suit finally ended in 1991 when Nintendo paid Magnavox $10 million to settle all differences and cover previously unpaid royalties. Baer claimed that Nintendo "got off cheap."

[2] The Famicom Disc System could not be used to save *Family BASIC* data since both needed to use the Famicom's cartridge slot.

[3] Sega of America was initially set up at the same location as Sega Enterprises, Inc., however there was no daily interaction between the employees of the two companies.

[4] In 1999, Curt Vendel, curator of the online Atari Museum, was provided with the original source code for the High Score cartridge from Gary Rubio, the original designer. From this Vendel was able to build, and sell, working copies of the High Score cartridge for use with the 7800.

[5] In 1988, Telegames, a company that had been selling brand-new copies of games for older systems since 1986, licensed the Dina 2-in-1 from Bit Corporation to sell in the United States. Telegames changed the name of the console to the *Telegames Personal Arcade*, and sold it through its website for $40. On its packaging, the Telegames Personal Arcade advertised that it was compatible "with over 100 hundred ColecoVision cartridges," but didn't mention that it was also compatible with the Sega SG-1000. This was because the console was aimed at American consumers, who had no idea what the SG-1000 was. Still, the Telegames Personal Arcade was shipped with two cartridge ports, and no mention of what the second one was used for.

CHAPTER 15

[1] In addition to Japan, the Video Challenger was also available in Great Britain, Brazil and Canada.

[2] Beginning in 1987, Data East also manufactured pinball machines including several innovative ones. *Laser War* was the first pinball machine to feature stereo sound and *Checkpoint* was the first to use a dox-matrix display. Data East Pinball remained in business until 1994, when the company was sold to Sega.

[3] On February 26, Bandai released a third title for the Japanese *Family Trainer*. *Aerobics Studio* combined the board game *Twister* with music. The player had to imitate the moves of an on-screen aerobics teachers and try to last without making any errors throughout the length of a song. Although the game would be released in the United States in 1989 as *Dance Aerobics*, it was not a big hit. However it sowed the seeds for a genre that would be popular a decade later.

[4] A second cassette containing additional songs was released on February 18, 1988.

[5] ASCII, the company that manufactured the NES Advantage for Nintendo, did sell versions of the controller for the Famicom under its own name.

[6] This is not the same Sega Europe, Ltd. that was established in 1984. That company was renamed Sega ATP Europe, Ltd., and operated as a subsidiary of Sega Operations UK, Ltd., which itself was a subsidiary of the newer Sega Europe, Ltd. Sega ATP Europe, Ltd. eventually became its own independent company, West End Amusements, Ltd.

[7] Following Sony's backstab by Nintendo, Sega of America head, Tom Kalinske, came up with an idea for a joint Sega/Sony console. Kalinske took this idea to Japan where Sony executives were keen on the idea. However, when it was proposed to Sega, its president, Hayao Nakayama, rejected it immediately.

[8] The largest game ever released for the Neo•Geo was *The King of Fighters 2003*, which held 716MB. It came out in 2003.

[9] Warner Communications had merged with Time Inc. in January, 1990, creating the world's largest media corporation, *Time Warner Inc.*

[10] Nintendo released its 16-bit console in Europe in spring, 1992. The console was identical in appearance to the Japanese Super Famicom, but it was called the Super NES.

[11] While the official launch date for the SNES was September 9, many retailers began selling it as early as August 23.

[12] Datel actually had been in business much longer than Codemasters. The company began in 1980 selling computer peripherals. In 1983, it sold the first Action Replay devices for Commodore 64 and Amiga computers.

[13] Sega of America licensed the Master Gear Converter and released it under its own name during the first quarter of 1992.

[14] A home edition of *Time Traveler* was released by Digital Leisure in 2001, but the innovative holographic visuals were necessarily removed.

[15] *Game Informer*, which would eventually become one of the most successful American videogame magazines, began in August, 1991 as a 6-page bi-monthly catalog of items for sale at Funcoland, a retailer of used videogames.

CHAPTER 16

[1] This type of joystick would reappear again in 1996 and would commonly be called a "thumbstick."

[2] Years later, as other console manufacturers released devices for multiplayer use, *multitap* became a generic term for such items.

[3] Games could only be saved if there was instructions in the code that implemented it.

[4] Japan began applying taxes to all consumer products in mid-1989. At that time NEC began packaging the *PC Engine CD-ROM²* along with the Interface Unit.

[5] In 1989 Sharp introduced its CZ-830 computer, which was a computer with a built-in PC Engine.

[6] Damages in the lawsuit were handed down in 1990. The amount was so large it contributed to Mediagenic's bankruptcy in 1991.

CHAPTER 17

[1] The two companies eventually settled out of court in 1994.

[2] See Appendix 1: "The *Tetris* Story" for more information.

[3] Tengen contended that the NES was a computer, and that it had the right to release *Tetris* for computers. However, its licensing contract defined computers as devices that hooked up to monitors. The judge sided with Nintendo, because the NES, like the Famicom, could only hook up to a standard TV using an RF modulator. Ironically, during the same year, Sharp released the *Famicom Titler*, which was essentially a Famicom that connected to computer monitors using RCA-type video jacks. The ¥43,000 ($299) unit also allowed input from video cameras. Using a built-in keyboard, users could add sub-titles to the games or videos that were in play, and vocals could be added via an attached microphone.

[4] This was done to protect licensing agreements with third-party companies. In many cases, one software company might have held the American rights to a game, while a separate company could have held the Japanese rights. If an American gamer could import the Japanese cartridge, then the American licensee would have lost income from that sale. Meanwhile, Mega Drives could accept Genesis cartridges.

[5] The console was also released in Europe where it was simply called the TurboGrafx.

[6] NEC America also released a *TurboBooster Plus*, which was the equivalent of the PC Engine's Backup Booster. The TurboBooster Plus unit had composite video output in addition to the ability to save games. A TurboGrafx-16 version of the Backup Booster II was never released.

[7] "*Tennokoe 2*" means "The Voice of Heaven 2". The name was a nod to Hudson Soft's 1987 Famicom RPG, *Momotarō Densetsu*. The password system in that game was called *Tennokoe*.

[8] Hudson Soft began supporting the Tennokoe 2 in some of its games, even before the unit itself was available.

[9] The SuperGrafx was compatible with the PC Engine CD-ROM^2 only with the addition of a special adaptor, the *RAU-30*, which wouldn't be released until April 20, 1990. This ¥6,900 ($44) unit consisted of two connected pieces. One plugged into the Interface Unit on the side where the PC Engine normally plugged into. The corresponding piece plugged into the CD port of the SuperGrafx console.

[10] Because of its shape, none of the backup devices from NEC and Hudson Soft could be used with the Shuttle. Instead, it released a unit called the *Backup Unit*, which was basically a Backup Booster II that was shaped differently to fit in the Shuttle.

[11] Konix inevitably ran out of money in 1990. With no one to bail them out, Konix was forced to declare bankruptcy, and the Multi-System died along with the company. However, in March, 1992, a new British company, MSU (**M**ulti-**S**ystem **UK**), was formed by people who had been involved in the development of the Konix Multi-System, with the sole intention of getting that unit to market. Their updated version of the machine would incorporate a 32-bit processor that would run at 30Mhz and be exclusively CD-based. The company planned to sell 150,000 units in early 1994 in England and the rest of Europe. No decision had been made at the time whether or not the machine would be available in the United States. As time moved on and the prospects of releasing the system dimmed, the company changed its focus from marketing the Multi-System directly to licensing the system's chipset to other manufacturers. A Taiwanese company, TCX licensed it and in 1994 actually released a system called the *Multi-System II*. Unfortunately, this system looked nothing at all like the Konix Multi-System and was basically a multimedia console that disappeared not long after it was released in Asia.

[12] Hasbro took the #1 spot from Mattel during the mid-eighties.

[13] Another reason given to the cancellation of the Control-Vision was due to the death of Hasbro CEO Stephen Hassenfeld on June 25. Hassenfeld had been a major proponent of the Control-Vision. His brother, Alan Hassenfeld, who took his place as CEO, was not a fan of the project.

CHAPTER 18

[1] Approximately twice as many copies more *Super Mario Bros.* cartridges were distributed than *Super Mario Bros. 3*, but *Super Mario Bros.* had been included with the NES.

[2] Diversifying to NES games wasn't enough to keep INTV in business. The company filed for bankruptcy protection in late 1990 and permanently shut its doors in 1991. INTV's remaining inventory was then sold by mail order through Telegames and by special order through Radio Shack's in-store catalog.

[3] Amstrad discontinued the GX4000 in mid-1991 after selling only 15,000 units. The console was never released outside of Europe.

[4] The Card Catcher could be used with the Sega Master System II, although it had never been released in North America.

[5] Sega didn't have a European headquarters as it did in North America. The systems were imported into individual European countries by different local importers. Following the success of the European Sega Master System II, Sega opened Sega Europe in 1991. Still, Europe was too big for even Sega Europe to cover adequately, so licensing agreements were still made with several importers to cover countries including Greece, Portugal and Sweden.

[6] SNK eventually released four games for the Super Famicom beginning in 1993.

[7] The Neo•Geo MVS was released in the United States on August 22, 1990.

[8] The TurboGrafx-16 could only display 512 simultaneous colors.

[9] The TurboExpress actually retailed for $300 when it was released in the United States.

CHAPTER 19

[1] NEC also tried to sell the PC Engine Duo as a portable machine. On the same day that the PC Engine Duo was released, NEC also began shipping the *Duo Monitor*, a ¥79,800 ($592), a 4-inch color LCD monitor. To complete the illusion that the PC Engine Duo was a portable system NEC also released a battery pack and charger for it. Although the *Duo Monitor* had the PC Engine Duo logo on it, it could in fact accept video from any system that

had composite A/V output.

[2] The only PC Engine console that could not plug into the Super CD-ROM² was the Shuttle.

[3] The adapter needed to connect the LT to the Super CD-ROM² wouldn't be available until March, 1992. Despite its reliance on an adapter to connect to the Super CD-ROM², the LT could plug directly into the Interface Unit to connect with the original PC Engine CD-ROM².

[4] In 1993, Amstrad released the *Mega PC* in Europe and Australia. The Mega PC was an IBM-compatible computer that had a built-in Sega Mega Drive.

[5] Mastertronic had acquired the British distribution rights to the Sega Master System in Great Britain in 1987, and had successfully pitted it against the NES in that country. Virgin Games purchased Mastertronic in 1988 and became Virgin Mastertronic.

[6] This is not the same Sega Europe, Ltd. that was established in 1984. That company was renamed Sega ATP Europe, Ltd., and operated as a subsidiary of Sega Operations UK, Ltd., which itself was a subsidiary of the newer Sega Europe, Ltd. Sega ATP Europe, Ltd. eventually became its own independent company, West End Amusements, Ltd.

[7] Following Sony's backstab by Nintendo, Sega of America head, Tom Kalinske, came up with an idea for a joint Sega/Sony console. Kalinske took this idea to Japan where Sony executives were keen on the idea. However, when it was proposed to Sega, its president, Hayao Nakayama, rejected it immediately.

[8] The largest game ever released for the Neo•Geo was *The King of Fighters 2003*, which held 716MB. It came out in 2003.

[9] Warner Communications had merged with Time Inc. in January, 1990, creating the world's largest media corporation, *Time Warner Inc.*

[10] Nintendo released its 16-bit console in Europe in spring, 1992. The console was identical in appearance to the Japanese Super Famicom, but it was called the Super NES.

[11] While the official launch date for the SNES was September 9, many retailers began selling it as early as August 23.

[12] Datel actually had been in business much longer than Codemasters. The company began in 1980 selling computer peripherals. In 1983, it sold the first Action Replay devices for Commodore 64 and Amiga computers.

[13] Sega of America licensed the Master Gear Converter and released it under its own name during the first quarter of 1992.

[14] A home edition of *Time Traveler* was released by Digital Leisure in 2001, but the innovative holographic visuals were necessarily removed.

[15] *Game Informer*, which would eventually become one of the most successful American videogame magazines, began in August, 1991 as a 6-page bi-monthly catalog of items for sale at Funcoland, a retailer of used videogames.

CHAPTER 20

[1] *Shining Force CD*, a game that was released in 1994, required the use of the Backup RAM cartridge to unlock a hidden level.

[2] A fifth CD-ROM console was announced by Taito, the Japanese arcade company that had been responsible for *Space Invaders*. The *WOWOW*, named after a Japanese television station, was to be used to play home versions of Taito's arcade games. In addition to playing CD-ROM games, the console would have also been capable of downloading games from satellite transmissions. Although a prototype of the WOWOW was displayed, the console was never released.

[3] Electronic Arts originally reversed-engineered the Genesis so they could produce games that could play on the Genesis and not have to pay Sega an $8 per cartridge licensing fee. After they succeeded they went to Sega and offered to pay $2 per cartridge or else they would distribute their games and Sega would receive nothing. Sega agreed to EA's terms.

[4] The TurboDuo would be the only all-in-one (capable of playing both CDs and cartridges/cards in one unit) videogame console released in the United States.

[5] The Tandy VIS was a commercial failure. Tandy stopped all development of the system on January 10, 1993, after losing between $50 and $75 million from the system. The company soon began selling the system for $399 under its Memorex brand name through direct catalog sales but that also failed to generate significant sales. Tandy finally liquidated its inventory of VIS players to Tiger Direct, which sold the systems for $40. Following the failure of the VIS, Tandy exited the personal computer business, which it had helped pioneer.

[6] In 1993, Sega would team up with AT&T to create a similar online gaming platform, frightening away most of Baton's investors. Although Baton had sold a $300,000 order in advance, the loss of the investors left Rupp without the funds that he needed to manufacturer the modems, forcing him to shut down the company.

[7] The *Maxivision 30* was downgraded to 15 games upon its release and was called the *Maxivision 15-in-1*.

[8] In November, 2009, *Game Informer* named its "Top 200 Games of all Time". *A Link to the Past* ranked number 12. *Sonic the Hedgehog 2* ranked number 97 on that same list.

[9] *Barcode World* was the only Famicom game that connected to the Barcode Battler II. However, between 1993 and 1995, seven such games were released for the Super Famicom. An intermediary device called the *Barcode Battler II Interface* connected to the Barcode Battler II and to the Super Famicom through its right controller port.

[10] In 1993, Namcot released its second, and final game for the Barcode Boy, called *Monster Maker: Barcode Saga*. In 1998, a Japanese company called TAM released its own barcode reader for the Game Boy Color, which also plugged into the expansion port with a link cable. However, this unit didn't sit over the console's cartridge slot and therefore had to dangle from it when it was being used. *Barcode Taisen Bardigun* was the only game that TAM released for this barcode reader.

CHAPTER 21

[1] Although the Amiga CD^{32} sold well in Europe, it didn't sell well enough to make up for the lost sales in the United States. Commodore declared bankruptcy in April 1994.

[2] Ironically, Nintendo only released five games that used the Super FX chip, and the only one that even came out in 1993 had already been available by the time Nintendo of America showcased its new releases at the summer CES. This game was *Star Fox*, which was released in Japan on February 21 and in North America on March 23. On June 3, the game was released in Europe where it was called *Starwing*.

[3] The advantage of the 12-inch LD-ROM was expanded storage. A standard CD-ROM could only store 540 megabytes of data. In addition to the 540 megabytes that was dedicated to full bandwidth audio, the LD-ROM also had room 108,000 full bandwidth still photos or 60 minutes of moving video.

[4] The PAC released in Japan could not play games from TurboGrafx-16 TurboChips, and the version released in the United States could not play games from PC Engine HuCards. However, $CD\text{-}ROM^2$ discs from either system were compatible with one another.

[5] The Jaguar's North American release schedule was almost as Atari had announced at its prior press conference. However, the Jaguar wasn't released in Europe until June 27, 1994. It was released in Japan on November 21, 1994.

[6] Nintendo of Japan had its own system that it installed in Japanese hotels. The *Super Famicom Box* was similar to the Neo•Geo Deck, whereas hotel guests could play five minutes of a game for a preset amount. The Super Famicom Box had slots for two game cartridges. However, these were not standard Super Famicom cartridges. Instead, they were large cartridges that were nearly the size of those used with the Neo•Geo AES, and each one contained two games. This allowed hotel guests to choose from up to four games.

[7] 3DO also instituted a rating system for games that played on its consoles. The rating system was voluntary and decided by a game's publisher.

[8] The code was: ABACABB

CHAPTER 22

[1] The ESRB officially opened on September 1.

[2] Only three games were ever branded with the Deep Water label. One was *Eternal Champions: Challenge From The Dark Side*, which came out in 1994 for the Mega CD and Sega CD and one was *Duke Nukem 3D*, which was released for the Sega Saturn in 1997. Some copies of the Genesis game *X-Perts* also featured the Deep Water sticker on the rear of the packaging but this was only to cover an erroneous note that the cartridge featured a battery back-up for game-saving.

[3] On January 21, Nintendo of Japan released *Fire Emblem: Mystery of the Emblem* for the Super Famicom. This was the system's first game that used a 24-megabit cartridge.

[4] When *Killer Instinct* was released in arcades on October 28 by Midway and Nintendo, it was discovered that it wasn't based on the Project Reality hardware as promised, although it did use the same MIPS R4300i microprocessor. The release of *Killer Instinct* did make history, however. It was the first arcade game that utilized an internal hard drive, which allowed it to store more detailed graphics.

[5] The Voice/Data Communicator was cancelled altogether in 1995.

[6] Two additional games were released that could utilize the Jaglink and both came out after the Jaguar was discontinued in 1996. *Aircars* was released by ICD Inc. in 1997 and 4Play/ScatoLOGIC Inc. released *Battlesphere* in 2000. Since both games were released in very limited quantities, multiplayer competition would have been difficult since both players would each have had to own a copy of the game.

[7] CPS stood for **C**apcom **P**ower **S**ystem.

[8] The CPS Changer was not a hit and Capcom only supported it for two years, with only eleven games being released in that time. The CPS technology did reach American shores, but only in arcades.

[9] Capcom also released the *Power Stick Fighter MD*, which was a version of the Power Stick Fighter that could be used with the Sega Mega Drive without an adapter.

[10] Turbo Zone Direct finally shut down in January 2008, after supporting the Turbo community for close to 14 years.

[11] The internal card could also be installed on PC-compatible computers to let them play PC-FX software.

[12] Fujitsu supported the systems until around 1999, and then completely abandoned the console gaming market.

[13] A PAL version was released in 1995 in Europe, where it was called the *Multi-Mega*.

[14] The actual name of the 32X differed within the region that it was distributed. In North America its official name was the *Genesis 32X*. In Japan it was called the *Super 32X*. And in Europe and Australia it went by *Mega Drive 32X*.

[15] The shapes on the buttons were a pink square, a green triangle, a red circle and a blue 'X'.

[16] The *Yonezawa* portion of the name would be removed in April, 1998, after which the company was called *Sega Toys*.

[17] See Chapter 4.

[18] Nintendo appealed the verdict and in 1996 the U.S. Court of Appeals overturned the district court's ruling.

[19] *Donkey Kong Country* would eventually become the best-selling SNES title ever, generating over $420 million in sales.

[20] Eager to form a partnership to bring it to consumers, Reflection showed it to several companies that turned it down, including Sega, Hasbro and Mattel. After Gunpei Yokoi saw a demonstration of it, he figured that it was an innovative product that other companies couldn't duplicate, so he was responsible for getting Nintendo to sign an exclusive agreement with Reflection.

[21] *Sonic the Hedgehog 3* was released in PAL regions on February 24 and in Japan on May 27.

[22] Unfortunately, the cost of the New Leaf technology was too expensive to make the system economically feasible. Blockbuster severed its ties with IBM in February, 1995.

[23] *Double Dragon* was the lowest grossing videogame-inspired movie until the July 21, 2007 debut of *Postal*, which only drew in $147,000.

[24] In 2008, *Time* magazine included all three movies, *Super Mario Brothers*, *Double Dragon* and *Street Fighter*, in its list of the top ten worst videogame-inspired movies.

[25] *Street Fighter*'s $99 million box-office gross was passed in August 18, 1995 with the release of *Mortal Kombat*, which raked in $122 million and only cost $18 million. That was surpassed in June 2001, by the $115 million *Lara Croft: Tomb Raider*, which earned $275 million. That remained the highest-grossing videogame-related movie until the May, 2010 release of the computer-game-inspired *Prince of Persia: The Sands of Time*, which earned $336 million at the box-office.

[26] Capcom actually developed a home videogame in conjunction with the movie that featured live-action scenes from the film. *Street Fighter: The Movie* was released in August, 1995 by Capcom in Japan and by Acclaim everywhere else. In June of 1995, Capcom also released an unrelated arcade game that was also called *Street Fighter: The Movie*. The arcade version had been developed by Incredible Technologies.

CHAPTER 23

[1] It was believed that the console cost Sega $380 to build, so retailers didn't make any profit from the hardware that they sold.

[2] Video CDs, or VCDs, which were introduced in 1993, could contain 73 minutes of analog video and digital audio. The quality of the picture was similar to video from a VHS tape. VCDs became popular in Asia, an area where VHS players were not yet commonly available due to their high price. Special cards that could be inserted into the back of a Saturn and allow it to play VCDs became available in Japan and Europe.

[3] Hitachi also produced an add-on karaoke unit that sat under any Saturn console. It was released on April 1 along with the HiSaturn.

[4] Only approximately 2,000 Game Navi HiSaturns and 1,000 LCD screens were ever shipped.

[5] The sticker fad began in June when *Print Club* machines, which printed stickers, were installed in arcades. These machines were the idea of 30-year-old Sasaki Miho, who thought it would be neat to print a small sticker with her image on it. A male band called SMAP, which was popular with teenage girls, began offering stickers of themselves through the Print Club machines to fans of their TV show. Other television shows began doing similar things and pretty soon the stickers from the Print Club machines were the most popular thing in Japan among Japanese pre-teen and teenage girls. By the end of 1996, even adults were into them and 10,000 Print Machines were in operation in Japan. That number rose to 25,000 by the spring of 1998.

[6] Critics praised the game, which would eventually sell over four million copies and would appear on many *Greatest Videogames of All Time* lists.

[7] Nintendo of Japan continued to sell its smaller, redesigned Famicom, and would continue to do so until 2003, even though no new 8-bit software would ever be released for it again.

[8] Even after a $100 price decrease, which brought the price of the unit down to $80, Sega of America couldn't convince gamers to buy the Nomad. The company eventually discontinued the device in 1999, after reducing the price again to a mere $50. The unit was never released in Japan or Europe, and marked Sega's departure from the handheld gaming scene.

[9] Sega quietly discontinued the 32X in early 1996. The last official game for the system was *Spider-Man: Web of Fire*, which was released on January 25, 1996.

[10] The Tiger deal also did not include the *Wonderbook*, an electronic book that Sega had developed with a company called RKS. The Wonderbook was supposed to come out during 1995 but was never released.

[11] Nintendo of America was also the victim of a potential theft at the winter CES. Shawn J. Freeman of Arizona was arrested at the show for attempting to steal a preproduction copy of Nintendo's *Star Fox 2*. Freeman, who was eventually charged with Felony Grand Larceny, had allegedly planned to pirate the game.

[12] A summer CES was held in 1996 in Orlando but the number of companies that exhibited was minimal. In 1997, a summer CES show was scheduled to be held in Atlanta in conjunction with the spring Comdex computer show. After only two dozen exhibitors signed up, the CES part of the show was cancelled. Afterwards, there would no longer be a summer CES.

[13] Although Datel already had a Pro Action Replay for the Saturn that was only available through mail order, it would be replaced by the GameShark in January 1996, when the new unit was scheduled to be released.

[14] The term "homebrew" was coined by Ed Federmeyer, who had been inspired by a computer users' group called the *Bay Area Amateur Computer Users' Group*, a monthly gathering of early computer hobbyists, including Steve Jobs, Steve Wozniak and Eugene Jarvis. The group had been commonly called the *Homebrew Computer Club*.

The first homebrew program came out in 1993 and had had been written by a hobbyist named Harry Dodgson. His *7800/2600 Monitor Cartridge* allowed Atari 7800 owners to develop 2600 and 7800 games without the need of a 7800 development system. Federmeyer had heard about the *7800/2600 Monitor Cartridge* but was unable to purchase one. However, an article by Dodgson inspired him to write his own 2600 application. The result was *SoundX*, a sound generator that displayed the sound capabilities of the 2600. The application was released on cartridge by Randy Crihfield of Hozer Video Games in 1994. After *SoundX* experienced strong sales, Crihfield encouraged Federmeyer to write a game for the 2600 and the result was *Edtris 2600*.

CHAPTER 24

[1] The Saturn featured a small amount of internal memory for saving games that was powered by a lithium battery.

[2] The original *Pilotwings* had been a launch title for the SNES.

[3] The PlayStation was the first console that was regionally-locked through software. Earlier Japanese consoles, such as Nintendo's Famicom and the Sega Master System, used cartridges that would not fit in consoles sold in other countries.

[4] The game was renamed to Clayfighter 63 1/3 and released for the North American N64 on October 23, 1997.

[5] The Pippin console would eventually be discontinued altogether in 1997.

[6] A gray Shuttle Mouse had actually been released on November 22, 1994 in Japan where it retailed for ¥3,000 ($31). A newer white one that also sold for ¥3,000 ($27) came out on July 5, 1996.

[7] Although the Saturn had a replaceable lithium battery, this was just used to power the memory used for game saves and the console's internal clock.

[8] *King of Fighters '95* was released in Europe in July, 1997 and retailed for £39.99 ($68). It never came out in North America.

[9] The 1MB Extended RAM Cartridge was pretty much made obsolete on November 27, 1997 when Sega of Japan released a new 4MB version, which retailed at the same ¥5,800 ($46) as the original.

[10] The game was *Ultraman: Hikari no Kyojin Densetsu*, which was released by Bandai on December 20.

[11] Keith Feinstein, the man behind Videotopia, went on to create other major travelling museum exhibits including *Be The Dinosaur* and *Be The Astronaut.*

[12] Although Capcom would release a Saturn version of *Resident Evil* during the summer of 1997, the damage was already done.

[13] *Final Fantasy VII* was released for the Japanese PlayStation on January 31, 1997 and in North America on September 7, 1997.

[14] *Parappa the Rapper* was released in Japan on December 6. By the end of 1997, it would be the 7th top-selling console game in Japan.

[15] The Game Boy Pocket did not have an LED power indicator like the original Game Boy had. A new version was released on April 28, 1997, which included the power indicator.

CHAPTER 25

[1] In Japan the budget series was called "The Best" while in Europe and Australia it was known as "Essentials."

[2] The Net Yaroze console was black instead of gray to distinguish it from a standard PlayStation console.

[3] Waka Manufacturing returned on July 30, 1998 with *Saturn Music School 2*, which also was packaged with a MIDI Interface Box. A set containing an actual keyboard was not offered.

[4] In all, only five NetLink-compatible games were released.

[5] MGA added *Space Invaders* to both the *Classic Game Collection* and *Keychain Game* series in 1998. Over the following years, the company would rotate and rerelease these same games in different forms. In 1999, MGA introduced the *Color FX* series, in which the games had color backgrounds. The units were similar to Nintendo's *Panorama Game & Watch* series, in which the player viewed the actual screen through a mirror that was set within the device. Three games were released in a larger unit and five games were released in a smaller keychain unit with an attached keychain. These were followed in 2000 with the *Color FX2* series, in which the screens had color backgrounds and the mirror was no longer required. The dimensions of the individual handheld units were roughly the same as the original Game Boy's. Finally, in 2005, MGA released five games in a new *Classic Arcade* series. The LCD screens were once again monochrome, but the devices resembled the arcade cabinets of the original games.

[6] In 1998, Tiger changed the name of the keychain series to *Extreme Chain Games* and introduced four additional games, including *Frogger* and *Millipede*.The units also featured a longer, coiled keychain.

[7] The Nintendo Power service had no relationship with the American magazine of the same name.

[8] Nintendo of Japan planned to extend the Nintendo Power service to the Game Boy on November 1, 1999. However, a major September, 1999 earthquake in Taiwan, the country where the RAM cartridges were manufactured, made it difficult for a reliable supply of cartridges to be available. Nintendo of Japan eventually released the ¥2,500 ($23) Game Boy RAM cartridge on March 1, 2000.

[9] The Nintendo Power service partly ended on August 31, 2001, when Lawson stopped selling blank cartridges and downloadable games. Beginning on the following day, Nintendo of Japan allowed customers to send their RAM cartridges directly to them and they replaced the games. The service ended for good in February, 2007.

[10] The Glove was also similar to Anaphase Unlimited's Game Glove, which had never been released. An inventor named Adam N. Ullman had worked on both devices.

[11] A Saturn Glove was never released.

[12] *HipHopMania*, a variation of *Beatmania*, arrived in American arcades in early 1998. Unfortunately it couldn't match the success that *Beatmania* enjoyed in Japan.

CHAPTER 26

[1] The biosensor was also available separately, although it wasn't used in any other game.

[2] It didn't. SETA only released five games for the N64. *Tetris 64*, which followed *Morita Shogi 64* was the fifth and final game that the company released for the console. The company eventually shut down on January 23, 2009 after 23 years in business.

[3] SmartMedia cards were developed by Toshiba and released in 1995 to compete against computer floppy disks. They were slightly larger than SD cards, which were introduced in 1999.

[4] *Mario Party* would be released in North America on February 8, 1999 and in Europe a month later.

[5] The Expansion Pak was released in Japan in June, 1999. Although several dozen games would eventually support the Expansion Pak, only three, *Donkey Kong 64*, *The Legend of Zelda: Majora's Mask* and *Perfect Dark*, would require it.

[6] Bandai released a similar unit, the *Handy Sonar*, for its WonderSwan handheld unit on May 22, 1999.

[7] Although the Sega-branded Dreamcast VGA Box wasn't released outside of Japan, many third-party companies released their own versions that were.

[8] Tiger Electronics actually advertised that the game.com Pocket Pro had a backlit screen, when in reality, the screen was frontlit.

[9] In order to avoid any confusion that might arise between two companies owning the Atari name, Williams renamed its Atari Games division to Midway Games West in January 2000.

[10] The plaintiffs were the Video Software Dealers Association.

[11] Beginning in December 2008, Konami began marketing its own *Beatmania* controller in Japan, which it called the *DJ Station Pro*. Besides featuring a turntable that was more responsive than the one on the ASCII controller, the DJ Station Pro also included sliding stereo headphone volume controls.

[12] The SETA Aleck 64 system was used between 1998 and 2003. In all that time only ten games were released for it.

CHAPTER 27

[1] The player didn't actually start with lives. He started as a rabbit and degenerated into a turtle if struck once. From a turtle he degenerated into a worm. If struck as a worm, the game ended. The player evolved to the next higher life form when he successfully reached the end of the level. A rabbit evolved into a princess.

[7] Atlus released additional *Pokeler* packages in 2000, which included new accessories to the PocketStation. Among the sets were *Sno Pokeler*, which came with a snow board and snow goggles, and *Pokeler DX Pink*, which turned the PocketStation into a female robot.

[3] Sega of Japan initially included a 33.6k modem adapter with its Dreamcast. This was later upgraded to a 56k modem.

[4] On July 15, Sega of Japan did offer the Ethernet connector. The ¥6,470 ($60) *Dreamcast LAN Adapter* transferred data at a maximum of 10 megabits per second. While this was much faster than the modems that were shipped with the Dreamcast, it couldn't be used for online gaming. The only software that it was compatible with was the *Dream Passport 2* web browser that it was bundled with.

[5] One of the original code names for the console was *DirectX Box*, which referred to Microsoft's collection of Application Programming Interfaces (APIs) called *Direct X*. This was eventually shortened to Xbox.

[6] RandNet was short for the term "Recruit and Nintendo network".

[7] Because of the limited numbers of 64DD users, the RandNet service did not have enough subscribers to support it, and Nintendo of Japan shut it down in 2001.

[8] In all, there would be four *Mario Artist* titles. Talent Studio, Communication Kit and Polygon Studio would all be released in 2000.

[9] The *Sharkwire* was actually released nationwide on January 1, 2000.

[10] SNK was the only publisher that released software that utilized the *Neo•Geo Pocket/Dreamcast Setsuzoku Cable*.

[11] *Sonic the Hedgehog Pocket Adventure* was released in Japan on May 25, 2000.

[12] Tiger discontinued the system, which only had nineteen games available for it, in 2000.

[13] Although 57 individual Pokémon creatures were offered, there were actually 59 individual toys to collect since three different Pikachus were available.

[14] The Pokémon slogan was "Gotta catch 'em all."

[15] Sega of America would release *Seaman* on August 9, 2000.

[16] *Seaman* was the only Japanese Dreamcast game that used the Dreamcast Microphone.

[17] Sega released *Sega Bass Fishing* for the Nintendo Wii in 2008 but did not design a special controller for it. The original Dreamcast version was released for Microsoft's Xbox 360 as part of a Dreamcast collection in 2011.

[18] The law did not pass in 1999. Quebec tried to revive it in 2009.

[19] By 2009 Stern Pinball's sales tripled and there was a resurgence in pinball. In 2011 a new company, *Jersey Jack Pinball*, began business. Its first table, *The Wizard of Oz*, which was released in April 2013, was the first pinball machine to be built in the United States since 2001 by a company other than Stern Pinball.

[20] *Shenmue* was released in North America and Europe in November, 2000.

CHAPTER 28

[1] SCEJ eventually followed suit and replaced the original console with the new one on December 8.

[2] The PSone was released in the United States on September 19 with little fanfare.

[3] Global A released a similar game, *The Maestro Music II* for the Japanese PS2 on August 2, 2001. SCEJ also released a game for the PS2 where the player acted as an orchestra conductor. *Bravo Music*, which came out on January 17, 2002, could be played using either the PS2 controller or an optional baton peripheral. This game appeared in the United States from Eidos as *Mad Maestro*! on March 12, 2002 and a week later in Europe but the baton peripheral was not available.

[4] The first game released in North America to offer the Picture Paradise technology, was *Monster Rancher 3*, which came out on September 24, 2001.

[5] Even though SCE supplied 100,000 units every week, the PS2 remained virtually sold out until March, 2001.

[6] Sega also released *Shakka to Tambourine!* in Japanese arcades. This game was very similar to *Samba de Amigo*, but used tambourines instead of maracas. A home version of the game was released exclusively in Japan on September 9, 2002, and only for the PS2. The home version was called *MiniMoni Shakka to Tambourine! Dapyon!* due to a licensing tie-in with a Japanese pop group called *MiniMoni*.

[7] Multiplayer is defined as more than two players.

[8]Sega Europe also used *ChuChu Rocket!* to demonstrate the Dreamcast's online abilities. In Europe it was released on June 9 and was offered for free in a manner similar to *Sega Swirl*'s distribution. More than 25,000 subscribers to Sega Europe's online gaming network, Dreamarena, received the game for free. It was also included on *Dreamkey 1.5*, Sega Europe's web browser that was packaged with the console.

[9] i-mode was a cellular technology that provided access to the Internet from mobile phones. It was introduced in Japan in early 1999. i-mode phones were basically the first smart phones to offer web browsing.

[10] The new technology wouldn't come to North America until *Kirby's Tilt 'n' Tumble* was released in April, 2001,

[11] Jones and Fairchild's Jerry Lawson, were the sole black members of the Homebrew Computer Club.

[12] Both WonderSwans needed a WonderWave in order to transfer data.

[13] Bandai also released a WonderBorg that was PC-compatible. This version was imported to the United States in 2001 by Tiger Electronics.

[14] The game was also sold in a premium edition which included a pink *Sakura Taisen*-branded Game Boy Color console.

[15] There were three other titles in the *Mario Artist* that were canceled as well: *Game Maker*, *Graphical Message Maker* and *Video Jockey Maker*.

CHAPTER 29

[1] While the Majesco Game Gear often gets criticized for not being compatible with the TV Tuner, in reality most Sega Game Gears were not compatible with it either. The TV Tuner will only work with the first batch of Game Gears that Sega released in 1990. After that, a change was made to the Game Gear that rendered the TV Tuners as useless.

[2] The PC Card was a credit card-sized device that housed the wireless components.

[3] This would only work with the PSone console and not the original PlayStation.

[4] The remote control worked in conjunction with a small infrared receiver that plugged into any controller port.

This receiver not only received and sent signals between the console and the remote, but it also unlocked the DVD capabilities of the Xbox.

[5] Several years later, entertainment website IGN would call the Xbox controller the second worst controller ever designed, with Atari's Jaguar taking the top prize. IGN was owned by Imagine Media, the publisher of *Next Generation* magazine. When originally founded in 1996, the website was called the *Imagine Games Network.*

[6] Sega had published *Sonic Jam* for the game.com in 1997 and *Sonic the Hedgehog Pocket Adventure* for the Neo•Geo Pocket Color in 1999.

[7] In 2002, the Dreamcast version of *Rez* was released in Europe, while the PS2 version came out in North America,

[8] A rail shooter is a game where the player-controlled object moves along a predetermined path, which the player cannot alter generally.

[9] Two days before *Rez* was released in Japan, SCEA released a different type of musical game. *FreQuency* was also "on rails" but players had to press the appropriate controller buttons as they passed over musical notes. The game was developed by Harmonix Music Systems and would become the basis for the *Guitar Hero* and *Rock Band* series.

[10] The Trance Vibrator was only released in Japan.

[11] *Napoleon, Top Gear GT Championship, Play Novel: Silent Hill* and *Monster Guardians.*

[12] Nintendo of Japan released two more games that used the Mobile Adapter in 2002. *Mail de Cute* for the GBA came out on February 14, 2002 and *Hello Kitty no Happy House* for the Game Boy Color came out on March 2, 2002. The mobile service was finally put to rest on December 14, 2002.

[13] When *Pocket Monsters Crystal Version* was converted into English for its 2001 North American release, the program code that utilized the mobile link was retained, but the game was unable to access the Internet. Likewise, the Pokémon Communications Center where most of the mobile activity took place was replaced with the original Pokémon Center. Since the code was still active but inaccessible, only gamers who used a cheating device such as a GameShark were able to obtain the GS Ball.

[14] The Dreamcast version of the game was simply called *Sonic Adventure 2.*

[15] Playmore acquired the SNK name from Aruze in 2003 and on July 7, 2003, the company changed its name to SNK Playmore.

[16] Namco would release *Namco Museum* for the Xbox and GameCube in 2002.

CHAPTER 30

[1] *NHL 2K2* was the last official game released for the American Dreamcast, although homebrewers would continue to produce Dreamcast titles for several years afterwards.

[2] SegaNet was shuttered for good on June 30, 2003.

[3] The Pico continued to flourish in Japan, where it was distributed by Sega Toys.

[4] Rare and Microsoft signed a similar deal with THQ, which gave the latter company the rights to publish the four stray Rare games for the GBA.

[5] This claim was certified by the *Guinness Book of World Records* in 2008.

CHAPTER 31

[1] *Eyetoy: Groove* was released in North America on April 20, 2004, two months after the EyeToy debuted in Japan. Surprisingly, the device never caught on in Japan as it did elsewhere in the world.

[2] Taiko is a form of Japanese drum.

[3] The game was released in North America under the name *Taiko Drum Master* on October 26, 2004.

[4] *Donkey Konga* was released in North America on September 27, 2004.

[5] Konami's headset could also used in a PS2 game called *Operator's Side*, which SCEJ released in Japan on January 30. This game was the first-ever to use only the microphone as a controller. Consumers had the option to purchase the game bundled with a Logitech USB headset or without the headset, if they already owned one that could plug into the console's USB slot. On March 2, 2004, Konami released the game in North America, where it was renamed *Lifeline. Lifeline* was not bundled with a USB headset.

[6] The SP stood for *special.*

[7] On July 16, the ESA renamed itself as the Interactive Digital Software Association (IDSA)

[8] All of Nintendo's handheld consoles beginning with the GBA were released in China under the iQue brand name. These systems were no different from their counterparts released elsewhere in the world. In 2013, iQue bcame a wholly-owned subsidiary of Nintendo.

[9] Nintendo of Europe was the first Nintendo subsidiary to start a loyalty program. The European club, which was called *Nintendo VIP 24:7*, launched on May 3, 2002, the same that that the GameCube was released in Europe. Nintendo of Europe changed the name of its club to Club Nintendo on December 8, 2006, the day the Wii launched in Europe. Nintendo of America began its own Club Nintendo on October 2, 2008.

CHAPTER 32

[1] The GBA SP headphones plugged into the same port as the battery charger.

[2] On November 16, one week before the DS came out, Sega released *Feel The Magic XY♥XX*, a series of minigames that highlighted the touchscreen and microphone features of the DS. It was released as *Kimi no Tame Nara Shineru* in Japan on December 2, the same day that the DS was released in that country. Finally, it came out in Europe, where it went by its working title, *Project Rub*, on March 11, 2005, which was the DS's launch date in that region.

[3] The GBA Video cartridges were white to distinguish them from the standard black GBA cartridges.

[4] The Gametrac was powered by the same ARM9 processor as the DS.

[5] *SingStar* was the first of 34 games in the series that would be produced by SCEE for Sony consoles through 2011. The games usually varied simply by the songs that were included. The series became available in the United States in 2007 with the third title, *SingStar Pop.*

[6] 2K Games closed the Utah studio in late April, 2006.

[7] SCE continued to call the new console by the PS2 name although the press and public commonly referred to it as the *PS2 Slim.*

[8] The unit was called the *Sega Mega Drive* outside of North America. In Japan, it was distributed by Sega Toys instead of Radica.

CHAPTER 33

[1] Jakks Pacific discontinued the Gamekeys in 2006.

[2] Over the years, additional Famiclones were released. In 2009, both Yobo and Retro-Bit introduced consoles that could accept SNES/Super Famicom cartridges along with the NES and Famicom cartridges. Hyperkin also entered the fray in 2009 with the *Retron 1*, which was also reminiscent of Yobo's FC Game Console. By 2014, Hyperkin was the leading manufacturer of alternative consoles and its *Retron 5* could accept cartridges from nine different systems, including the Genesis, Mega Drive, Game Boy and GBA.

[3] The new GBA SP was released in very limited numbers in Europe in 2006.

[4] Three versions of *Nintendogs* were initially released: one featuring Dachshunds, one with Labradors, and a third with Chihuahuas.

[5] *Tony Hawk's American Sk8land* was not released in Japan.

[6] PSP firmware could be upgraded in one of three ways:

- downloading it from the Internet directly into the PSP
- downloading it to a home computer and then transferring it to the PSP via a USB connection
- loading it from a game UMD that contained newer firmware than the one already installed on the device

[7] *Talkman* was released in Europe in May, 2006. In June 2006, SCEJ released *Talkman Euro*, a version released in Japan that translated French, Spanish, German, Italian and Japanese.

[8] The Pixter Color digital camera could not be used with the Pixter Multi-Media.

[9] A pink version of the new Leapster was also released.

[10] Majesco briefly distributed the Pico in North America in 1999.

[11] High-Definition Multimedia Interface - a cable used to transfer uncompressed video data and digital audio data from a a source device to a monitor or digital audio player.

[12] The $400 Xbox 360 system would unofficially be referred to as either the Pro or Premium edition.

[13] *Grand Theft Auto: San Andreas* would go on to become the top-selling PS2 game of all time with 27.5 million

copies sold as of April, 2017.

[14] The case ended on October 18, 2006 when Konami purchased the intellectual rights to the game as part of its settlement. A planned *In the Groove 3* was never released to arcades while a home version of *In the Groove 2* was also scrapped. The arcade and home version of the games that had already been released were not recalled.

[15] The game was called *Dance Dance Revolution with Mario* in Japan where it was released on July 14.

[16] Stores in several countries including Canada and Australia, retained the EB Games name.

CHAPTER 34

[1] Immersion had also sued Microsoft, but Microsoft quickly settled and licensed Immersion's technology.

[2] The Wii accepted the WaveBird and other GameCube controllers, but this was only for playing GameCube games. However, some Wii games, including *Super Smash Bros. Brawl,* were also designed to use the GameCube controllers.

[3] When the Wii Remote was held sideways, it could be used to play Famicom/NES games, however, it couldn't be used for Super Famicom/SNES or N64 games.

[4] The browser first needed to be purchased using Wii points.

[5] The first Wii game that was compatible with the Nintendo Wi-Fi Connection was *Pokémon Battle Revolution,* which was released in Japan on December 14. It didn't come out in North America until June 25, 2007, and Europe on December 7, 2007.

[6] The Wii Lan Adapter was released in the United States in January, 2007. However, the $25 unit was only available through Nintendo's website.

[7] The underside of the Wii Classic Controller featured a slot that could be opened by pressing a button at the top center of the controller. The official purpose of this slot was to insert a clip that would attach the controller to the Wii Remote. Nintendo decided not to release the clip, which left the slot without any purpose.

[8] Samsung shipped the BD-P1000, the first consumer Blu-ray player, on June 25, and it retailed for $1,000. Ironically, as SCE attempted to make the $600 PS3 look like a good buy because of its inexpensive Blu-ray player, Jamie McDonald, a vice president with Sony Europe, made it sound as if Blu-ray players were irrelevant. During an interview McDonald predicted that within five years, most content would be downloaded to videogame consoles, rather than stored on optical discs, rendering the Blu-ray player unnecessary.

[9] Toshiba released the first two commercial HD-DVD players in the United States on April 18, 2006. They were priced at $499 and $799.

[10] Only five games were released for the HyperScan. Mattel discontinued the system at the end of 2007.

[11] In 2008, *GamePro* magazine named the Gizmondo the worst console of all time.

[12] The Chotto Shot camera was also referred to by its model number: PSP-300.

[13] *Pokémon Pearl* and *Pokémon Diamond* would be released in North America on April 22, 2007.

[14] Nintendo issued 19 volumes of DS Download Station Game Cards in all.

[15] *Brain Age* was released on April 16 in North America under the Nintendo label. On June 5, Nintendo launched a new brand called *Touch! Generations*, that included Wii and DS games that were designed to appeal to a broader audience than traditional videogamers. Subsequent copies of *Brain Age* that came out after June 5 were released under the Touch! Generations label.

[16] *Love and Berry: Dress Up and Dance!*, an English version of the arcade game, was released outside of Japan in 2006.

[17] Prior to the December 4 release of *Sekai no Gohan: Shaberu! DS Oryōri Navi* by Nintendo of Japan, the program was released around the world under different titles. In Europe and Australia, where it was released on June 20 and July 3 respectively, it was called *Cooking Guide: Can't Decide What to Eat?* The North American version was called *Personal Trainer: Cooking* when it was released on November 24 and was part of Nintendo's *Personal Trainer* series.

[18] Although the cooking software was released around the world, the *DS Magnetic Stand* was only released in Japan.

[19] By the time that Visteon began selling the Dockable Entertainment, the GBA was quickly reaching the end of its lifespan. Nintendo ceased marketing the GBA in Japan in 2006, in Europe in 2007, and finally in North America in 2008. The website *technologytell.com* speculated that Visteon chose not to update its licensing agreement with Nintendo to make the device compatible with the DS because its use of dual screens and touchscreen technology

would have been impractical, since the screen would have been out of the physical reach of the players using it.

[20] Although the packaging of the *Let's! TV Play Classic* series said they had been released by Bandai, in actuality that company really no longer existed. In 2005, Namco and Bandai had merged to become Namco-Bandai Holdings. On March 31, 2006, the holding company started a new division, Namco-Bandai Games, which was comprised of the videogame development divisions from both Bandai and Namco.

[21] The *Sega Mega Drive Collection* was released in Europe and Australia in February, 2007. The collection was never released in Japan.

[22] In a first-person game, the player views the on-screen world from the perspective of the character. In a third-person game, the on-screen character can be seen, but shooting usually takes place from an over-the-shoulder angle.

[23] While controversy seemed to follow every game that Rockstar released, on May 23, the company released a game for the Xbox 360 that included its name in the title, just so people would know that it was capable of publishing non-violent games as well. *Rockstar Games Presents Table Tennis* was one of the only titles from the company that had been assigned an "Everyone" rating from the ESRB.

CHAPTER 35

[1] These consoles were sold in PAL regions, which also included Australia and the Middle East.

[2] SCEE had sold 185,000 PSPs within two days of that system's launch, which made it the over-all fastest-selling system in Great Britain.

[3] An update issued on June 20 provided the Japanese version of *Motorstorm* with online play.

[4] Microsoft sold 528,000 Xbox 360 consoles in September, compared to the 501,000 Wiis that Nintendo sold.

[5] In comparison, SCEE claimed that the failure rate on the PS3 was "around .02%".

[6] The term "bricked" Xbox 360 console became popular. A "bricked" console was generally one that had been damaged beyond simple repair, which rendered it about as useful as a brick.

[7] A Federal Court in Seattle denied certification of the class-action suit on October 5, 2009.

[8] TSST, a manufacturer of optical drives, was a joint venture between Samsung and Toshiba.

[9] Neversoft only developed the PS3 and Xbox 360 versions of the game. The Wii version was developed by Vicarious Visions and Budcat Creations developed the PS2 version.

[10] The online multiplay feature was not available on the PS2 version of the game.

[11] Activision announced in early 2009 that *Guitar Hero III: Legends of Rock* had become the first game to ever generate $1 billion in sales.

[12] A PS2 edition was released on December 17 but a Wii version was delayed until January, 2008.

[13] The PS3 and Xbox 360 versions of *Rock Band* also offered an online option so band members didn't have to be at the same location.

[14] SCEE would switch to these new *Buzz!* controllers as well.

[15] The first game to be banned in Great Britain was *Carmageddon*, a violent, driving computer game that came out in 1997. After ten months of appeals, the BBFC eventually allowed the game to be sold in the country.

[16] In Great Britain the price was reduced from £150 ($299) to £130 ($259).

[17] ISDB-T, the Japanese standard for high-definition television, consists of 50 channels with each channel divided into 13 segments. Twelve of the segments are allocated for high-definition receivers, and the one remaining segment (1seg) is used for narrowband receivers such as cell phones.

[18] The Sega Game Gear and the NEC TurboExpress.

[19] This game came out on August 23, 2010 in Europe where it was called *Face Training*. Since it was released for the Nintendo DSi, which had a built-in camera, the package did not include a camera, However, a stand was part of the package.

[20] This wasn't the first time a paddle controller was packaged with *Arkanoid*. The Famicom and NES versions also came with paddle controllers.

[21] The version of *Arkanoid DS* that was released in North America on August 1, 2008, did not utilize the paddle controller.

[22] Ironically, Santa Monica High School and the Los Angeles Convention Center, which had previously housed

E³, were both located on Pico Boulevard, although 14 miles separated them.

[23] The historic Barker Hangar is billed as one of Southern California's premier venues for charity, corporate and private events.

[24] The longest, continuously published videogame magazine in any language is held by the Japanese magazine, *Famitsu*, which began publication on June 6, 1986 under the name, *Famicom Tsūshin.*

[25] Future US had been called Imagine Media until 2002.

[26] #1 was *Call of Duty 4: Modern Warfare*

CHAPTER 36

[1] The game was released in North America on August 26.

[2] Game sounds were not broadcasted to the *Wireless Bluetooth Headset.*

[3] The game was released on August 9 in Europe where it was called *Family Trainer*. The North American version was called *Active Life: Outdoor Challenge* when it came out on September 9.

[4] As of 2013, *Mario Kart Wii* was the best-selling racing game of all time.

[5] *Super Mario Kart* would be added to the Virtual Console in 2009.

[6] The *Wii Super Famicom Classic Controller* was offered as the *Wii Super SNES Classic Controller* to European and Australian Club Nintendo members in 2010.

[7] WiiWare launched in North America on May 12 and in the PAL regions on May 20.

[8] Buffalo Technology, the manufacturer of the Nintendo Wi-Fi USB Connector, had lost a lawsuit that prevented it from dealing with any products that adhered to U.S. 802.11a/g standards. The Nintendo Wi-Fi USB Connector was one such product.

[9] Users who purchased *Final Fantasy Crystal Chronicles: My Life as a King* before April 1 had to download an update in order to access the Pay & Play content.

[10] iPlay was available on a wide number of platforms including cable and satellite TV and Windows and Mac computers.

[11] iPlayer became available on the Xbox 360 on March 12, 2012.

[12] The ear bud and remote control were also packaged with the original PSP when it was first released. However, the combination was not included with subsequent PSP-1000 bundles and was never packaged with the PSP-2000.

[13] Nokia called the pilot program "First Access".

[14] Version 5.0

[15] The PSP-3000 shipped on October 14 as part of a $200 *Ratchet & Clank: Size Matters* bundle in North America. It was formally released on December 15 without the bundle and sold for $170.

[16] The composite video output added to the Leapster L-Max was not included on the Leapster 2.

[17] Initially, the SD card for the Leapster 2 had to be purchased separately, and LeapFrog offered two free games that could be downloaded and added to the card. Beginning in the summer of 2009, LeapFrog included an inaccessible SD card inside the Leapster 2, and offered one free game.

[18] The peripherals that plugged into the V.Smile controller ports, such as the V.Smile Smart Keyboard, could not be used with the V.Smile Cyber Pocket.

[19] Three of the twenty built-in games hadn't been included on any other AtGames console.

[20] *Guitar Hero: On Tour* could not play on the DSi when it became available because the DSi didn't have the GBA cartridge port needed for the Guitar Grip accessory.

[21] This was not the first time that a rhythm-game that utilized a peripheral was available on a handheld unit. In 2000, Konami released *Dance Dance Revolution GB* in Japan for the Game Boy Color. The game came with a plastic pad that clipped over the front of the Game Boy Color and featured four directional buttons arranged in a cross-hair fashion. Instead of placing their feet in the appropriate places on a dance pad, gamers had to press the correct buttons as directed by the onscreen prompts.

[22] These were called *Song Packs* in Europe.

[23] The first Track Pack was an exception. *Rock Band Track Pack Vol. 1* was released on July 15 for the Wii and

PS2 and contained songs that had been previously available for download only for the PS3 and Xbox 360 versions of *Rock Band.*

[24] The video, entitled *Live At Donington*, had most recently been released on Blu-ray in 2007.

[25] *Rock Band 2* for the Wii supported downloaded content, which the original *Rock Band* didn't. However, downloaded content wasn't available to the Wii until January 13, 2009.

[26] The Rock Band Stage Kit was only available for the Xbox 360 version of the game.

[27] The PS2 version did not support the GH Tunes service.

[28] Harmonix sued Konami over patent violations in 2009. Both suits were dropped on September 15, 2010. Details regarding the settlement were not disclosed.

[29] It was released for the Wii on November 11.

[30] The DS version of *Rock Revolution* did include vocals.

[31] The Japanese edition of *Grand Theft Auto IV* was released on October 30.

CHAPTER 37

[1] In May, *EGM*'s founder, Steve Harris, purchased the rights to the magazine. On December 21, he announced that he would resume publishing the magazine with the April, 2010 issue, which became available in March, 2010.

[2] The DSi LL had originally been conceived in 2007 as a larger version of the DS Lite. However, Nintendo president Satoru Iwata put it on hold due to the DS Lite's overwhelming popularity.

[3] The GP2X Wiz was not the only handheld that supported open-source software development. The *Dingoo A320* was released by a Hong Kong-based company called Dingoo in February, 2009. Another, the Pandora, was manufactured by a group of GP2X distributors and users and was released on May 21, 2010.

[4] The new PSP was released in Japan on November 1.

[5] Koller was wrong about this. On October 1, SCE began selling *PlayStation Minis*, small games that were under 100MB that could be developed quickly and cheaply. Most PlayStation Mini games cost less than $3.50 apiece. They were initially available for the PSP (and PSP Go), but a December 8 update to the PS3's operating system included the ability to play them on a PS3. PlayStation Minis were only available via downloading.

[6] Zeebo, Inc. began in 2007 as Tectoy of America, a division of Tectoy, a Brazilian electronics company. Tectoy was known for distributing Sega consoles and software in Brazil.

[7] This game was called *FIFA Soccer 09* in North America. All games for the Brazilian Zeebo were in Portuguese.

[8] The free downloadable games were specifically *Prey Evil, Zeebo Extreme Rolimã* and *Zeebo Extreme Jetboard.*

[9] After consoles were released in Russia and India in 2010, the Zeebo was discontinued on September 30, 2011.

[10] The word "natal" meant "of or relating to birth." Project Natal symbolized the rebirth of the way people played videogames.

[11] The Wii Vitality Sensor was not released in 2009. Nintendo of America president Reggie Fils-Aimé said that more details concerning the peripheral would be announced at E[3] in 2010, but that never happened. At the 2011 E[3], Shigeru Miyamoto said that the device had trouble performing 100% of the time, but that Nintendo still hoped to release it someday. That hope was extinguished on July 5, 2013 when Satoru Iwata announced that the Wii Vitality Sensor wouldn't work with 10% of its testers and was therefore being cancelled.

[12] The three games were *Virtua Tennis 2009* from Sega and *Grand Slam Tennis* & *Tiger Woods PGA Tour 10* from EA Sports.

[13] The Wii Classic Controller Pro was released in Europe in November and in North America in April, 2010.

[14] In May, 2011, The World Fishing Network placed *Bass Pro Shops: The Strike* at the top of its list of the Top 10 Best Fishing Games of All Time. The Xbox 360 rod controller was preferred over the Wii model.

[15] Some *Guitar Hero* guitars also worked with *The Beatles: Rock Band.*

[16] Rickenbacker 325 and Gretsch Duo Jet guitar controllers could also be purchased separately.

[17] Activision also released *Guitar Hero: Metallica* in late March and *Guitar Hero: Van Halen* in December.

[18] The Xbox 360 version sold the most units: 62,000. The PS2 version sold the least: 3,000 units.

[19] SCEE released *DJ: Decks & FX* for the PS2 in September, 2004. This game did not come with a DJ table

peripheral. Instead, the DJ used an on-screen deck to mix songs that were included with the game.

[20] In October, Activision laid-off 30 employees from 7 Studios, half of its total staff, with the intention of making the development company focus on music-based games. Activision shut the company down completely in February, 2011.

[21] Bedlam Games closed its doors in August, 2011, and no other studio was hired to complete *Scratch: The Ultimate DJ*. As of April, 2017, the game has not been released.

[22] The website *GameTrailers* named *Tony Hawk: Ride* the most disappointing game of the year, while *GamesRadar* called it the worst game of 2009.

[23] A $150 "Prestige Edition" of *Call of Duty: Modern Warfare 2* came with a real, working set of night-vision goggles, although it wasn't used in the game.

[24] Ubisoft had released 42 titles for the Wii through the end of 2009.

[25] The version of the game that was released in PAL regions featured a workout buddy who wasn't modeled after anybody.

[26] The remaining games that had made the top-ten list were *New Super Mario Bros. Wii*, a new title that had been released in November, *Mario Kart Wii* and *Wii Play*.

[27] Microsoft also packaged a standard AV cable with the repriced system in place of the HDMI cable that came with the former set.

[28] A 250GB model that retailed for $350 was released on November 3.

[29] Nintendo ended the service on April 30, 2012 without it ever leaving Japan.

[30] In 2010, the museum became known simply as *The Strong*.

[31] There was a greater disparity in handheld sales. Nintendo sold over 11 million DS units, an increase of 13%. However, PSP sales fell by an alarming 35% to 1.3 million.

CHAPTER 38

[1] The three games were *Mass Effect 2*, *Army of Two: The 40th Day* and *Darksiders*.

[2] A new company, *Superdata*, had been established in 2009 to track the sale of downloadable games, as well as provide statistics on popular online gaming including MMOs, mobile and social games.

[3] The term "cloud" is basically referring to a series of servers at a remote location.

[4] Gaikai entered a public Beta testing phase in November and officially launched on February 27, 2011.

[5] The subscription fee was eliminated on October 4.

[6] The Caanoo had a 3.5 inch screen compared to the 2.8 inch screen on the GP2X Wiz.

[7] The Caanoo would be Game Park Holdings' final console. After the console failed to catch on in the marketplace, the company canceled the console in September, 2011 and turned its attention to developing software. The company closed its doors completely in April, 2012.

[8] Like the DSi, the 3DS had one camera lens on the inside of the unit above the screen, which could only take two-dimensional photos.

[9] The PS3 version was released on November 18.

[10] Electronic Arts released another program on November 16 only for the Wii. *EA Sports Active NFL Training Camp*, was similar to *EA Sports Active 2* but it simulated an NFL training camp and included over 70 drills and challenges that were designed to improve strength, power and conditioning, reaction skills, agility and first step quickness. The program tracked the body with a wireless motion tracker that wrapped around the player's leg and a heart monitor that wrapped around their arm.

[11] Non-uDraw games and Wii system menus could not be accessed with the Wii Remote while the controller was inside the compartment.

[12] A videogame version of *Pictionary* had previously been released by LJN in 1990 for the NES. In that version, the player had to "draw" objects on the TV screen using the NES controller, via an onscreen cursor.

[13] Activision also released versions of the game for the PS2, DS and PSP.

[14] A Japanese release didn't occur until October 21.

[15] A non-PlayStation Move version of *EyePet* had already been available in Japan and Europe. *EyePet: Move Edition* was first released in North America on September 5 and later released in Europe and Japan.

[16] Microsoft discontinued the Xbox 360 Elite and Xbox 360 Arcade models on that same date. Remaining stock of the Xbox 360 Elite was reduced to $250, and remaining Xbox 360 Arcades were thereafter sold for $150. On August 3, Microsoft replaced the Arcade model, which did not include a hard drive, with a $200 Xbox 360 S that included a 4 GB hard drive.

[17] This was the highest-capacity hard drive available for an Xbox 360 to date. SCE trumped it on July 29, when it released a 360 GB PS3 Slim for ¥34,980 ($387) in Japan, and elsewhere in the world in mid-September.

[18] By 2013, Microsoft sold enough Kinect units to make *Kinect Adventures!* the #1 Xbox 360 title in sales.

[19] In North America the game was *Dance Masters*.

[20] Four prior versions of *Dance Dance Revolution* had been released for the Wii since 2007, but this was the first edition to use the game's original title. This was also the first time the game had been publishered for the PS3.

[21] In January and February alone, 1.3 million copies of *Just Dance* were sold.

[22] In October, 2004, Eidos released *Get On Da Mic* for the PS2. This was the first and only hip-hop karaoke videogame prior to the release of *Def Jam Rapstar*. It was a commercial failure.

[23] Kinect support was added by the end of the year.

[24] The site was shut down on October 5, 2011.

[25] *Green Day: Rock Band* was revealed to the public on March 26 at *Pax East* in Boston. This was a PAX convention held on the east coast for the first time, and was attended by over 52,000 people. In order to differentiate between the two shows, the name of the original Washington PAX event was changed to *PAX Prime*.

[26] The Rock Band 3 Wireless Keyboard controller marked only the third time that such a controller had been available in North America, the first being the Music Keyboard component for Mattel Electronics' Entertainment Computer System in 1983, and the second being 1990's *Miracle Piano Teaching System*. The Rock Band 3 Wireless Keyboard was not released in Japan where, in 2000, Konami had exclusively released a keyboard controller for the PS2 for its game, *Keyboardmania*.

[27] MIDI (Musical Instrument Digital Interface) is a technical standard that allows certain electronic objects, such as musical instruments and computers to communicate with each other.

[28] In contrast, Apple paid developers of apps sold through the iTunes App Store 70% of each app's selling price.

[29] Rock Band Network support for the Wii ended on January 18, 2011, due to limited demand from owners of that console.

[30] The only new title from Nintendo that made the top-ten list was *Super Mario Galaxy 2* for the Wii, which had been released globally between May 23 and June 30. It was #10 on the chart. The ninth-position titles, *Pokémon HeartGold Version* and *Pokémon SoulSilver Version*, had come out in Japan in 2009. They were released, along with bundled Pokewalker pedometers, in the rest of the world in March.

[31] Includes the DS, DS Lite, DSi and DSi XL.

CHAPTER 39

[1] Accessories, fueled by Kinect and PlayStation Move sales, increased by 6% to $235 million. However, the total gross of all videogame products dropped 4% to $1.14 billion.

[2] SCE sold 14.6 million PS3s worldwide. It was followed by the Xbox 360 with 13.8 million units and the Wii with 11.5 million.

[3] Valve did release an Xbox 360 version of *Portal 2*. Despite the absence of Steam, the Xbox 360 version outsold the PS3 version.

[4] The first Gamescom was held in August 2009.

[5] The PlayStation 3D Display was not the first monitor that Sony released that supported a PlayStation. In 2010 Sony had released a 22-inch 720p Bravia television in Great Britain that featured a built-in PS2 system and sold for £199 ($311).

[6] The 3D glasses retailed for $70 each.

[7] SCE planned to release the new handheld outside of Japan in early 2012.

[8] *Vita* is Latin for "life."

[9] A standard 32GB SD card retailed for about ¥3,878 ($50).

[10] Unfortunately, SCE did not roll out the PlayStation Suite by the time the PlayStation Certified devices were available to the public. Xperia Play owners could play *Crash Bandicoot*, which was installed in the device, or games that they purchased from Google or Verizon Wireless. In June, 2012, SCE announced that it was renaming the PlayStation Suite to *PlayStation Mobile*, which it officially launched on October 3, 2012.

[11] The PSP Go also had a built-in battery.

[12] The PS3 supported 3D since a 2010 update and Microsoft added 3D functionality to the Xbox 360 with a December 22 update. In both cases, games that supported 3D functionality had to be viewed on 3D monitors while players wore special glasses.

[13] One of the first games to use of the accelerometer was Ubisoft's *Asphalt 3D*, which was one of the 3DS launch titles in North America, Europe and Australia. Unfortunately, the accelerometer went against the 3D effect in a sense that the player's head would have to be completely still in order to observe the 3D effect.

[14] There were some minor exceptions. While all PSPs could play UMD games purchased anywhere in the world, UMD movies could only play on PSPs from the same region. Most DSi games could play on all DSi (and DS) systems. However, DSi-exclusive games, those that used specific features of the DSi such as the camera and were not backward-compatible, were limited only to the hardware from the same region. Only four of those games had been released.

[15] The three *Nintendogs + cats* games were all launch titles for the 3DS. These were updated versions of the highly-rated *Nintendogs* which had gone on to become the second most successful game for the DS (*New Super Mario Bros*. was number one) with worldwide-sales of over 24 million units.

[16] *Super Street Fighter IV 3D Edition, Nintendogs + cats*, *Pilotwings Resort* and *Lego Star Wars III: The Clone Wars*.

[17] Netflix finally went live on the 3DS on July 14.

[18] This wasn't entirely true. Nintendo of Europe had lowered the price of the Nintendo 64 two months after its release although that was in response to price reductions from its competitors.

[19] The Game Gear was 8.5 inches wide and four inches from top to bottom.

[20] The Wii Family Edition was released in Europe on November 3.

[21] The four uDraw titles were *SpongeBob SquigglePants, Kung Fu Panda 2, The Penguins of Madagascar: Dr. Blowhole Returns – Again*! and *Disney Princess: Enchanting Storybooks*.

[22] Although THQ released versions of *Kung Fu Panda 2* and *The Penguins of Madagascar: Dr. Blowhole Returns – Again*! for the PS3 and Xbox 360 on the same day that the Wii uDraw versions debuted, they were not compatible with the uDraw.

[23] THQ never recovered from this. The company, which had been established in 1989, declared bankruptcy on December 19, 2012 and its properties were auctioned off in 2013.

[24] Ironically, many critics blamed Activision for the decline of the music-themed genre because it oversaturated the market with too many new versions of *Guitar Hero*.

[25] *War Wings: Hell Catz* was renamed *Damage Inc. Pacific Squadron WWII* and was released for the Xbox 360 and the PS3.

[26] The Fender Stratocaster and Precision Bass guitar controllers had originally been released by Mad Catz for *Rock Band 2*.

[27] *Call of Duty: Modern Warfare 3* for the PS3, with over 10 million units sold, was the second top-selling game of the year.

[28] The Portal of Power connected to the Xbox 360 by plugging directly to the console's USB port. This Portal of Power could not be used with the other consoles.

[29] The Atari Flashback 3 also lacked a B/W setting, which had been included on the Atari Flashback 2. In addition, the joysticks plugged into the front of the Atari Flashback 3, not in the rear as they had done on the Atari Flashback 2 and the original 2600.

[30] This number represented the amount of consoles that SCE shipped to stores, not the actual number that was purchased by consumers.

[31] *PC World*'s website had a page dedicated to videogaming and they called this page *GamePro*. The *GamePro* name was removed in 2012. Note that this only occurred in North America. Several other websites owned by IDG, including those in Latin America and the United Kingdom, still use the *GamePro* name.

CHAPTER 40

[1] The console was called the 3DS LL in Japan.

[2] The DSi XL was called the DSi LL in Japan.

[3] The 3DS XL sold for ¥18,900 ($241) in Japan and €180 ($222) in Europe.

[4] In Japan, the power adapter cost ¥1,500 ($19). The charging cradle cost an additional ¥1,200 ($15).

[5] PS Vita sales were even lower than sales for the PSP, which totaled 14,824 units the same week.

[6] Although the PS Vita debuted in the middle of February, it still outsold the PSP that month by nearly 200,000 units.

[7] *PlayStation All-Stars Battle Royale* was SCE's answer to Nintendo's *Super Smash Bros.*, a fighting game in which up to four players battled each other in the guise of characters from several SCE games, including *PaRappa the Rapper* and *Devil May Cry*. Twenty characters were supplied with the game, and four additional characters could be purchased online and downloaded.

[8] The ability to add cross-controller functionally to the game cost $5 and had to be downloaded as a patch to both the PS3 and the Vita. The new functionally could only be used with new levels that were included in the download, and not with the preexisting levels that came with the original game.

[9] Nintendo released the Wii U in Europe and Australia on November 30 and in Japan on December 8.

[10] The memory of both Wii U consoles could be expanded by an additional 32GB using SD/SDHC cards or up to 3TB with the addition of an external USB hard drive.

[11] *Dragon Quest X* was the latest in a series of wildly popular Massively Multiplayer Online Role-Playing Games (MMORPG) from Square Enix that were only available in Japan.

[12] The beta version of *Dragon Quest X* became available in early March, 2013. The game was released on March 30, 2013.

[13] PS3 and Xbox 360 controllers needed to be charged every 10-20 hours.

[14] As it turned out, *Sing Party* was the only game released by Nintendo that used the Wii U Microphone.

[15] The Wii Mini was neither backward-compatible with the GameCube nor forward-compatible with the Wii U.

[16] In addition, downloadable game fixes or patches could not be incorporated through the Wii Mini. This was a major concern, considering that two weeks after Nintendo released *The Legend of Zelda: Skyward Sword* in November 2011, a game-breaking bug was discovered. This bug was eventually eradicated with the creation of the *Zelda Data Restoration Channel*, which was made available through the Wii Shop Channel, which of course could only be accessed via an online connection.

[17] The Organization for Economic Co-operation and Development (OECD) is an international, economic organization made up of 34 countries to stimulate economic progress and world trade.

[18] The Wii Mini was eventually released without fanfare in the United Kingdom on March 22, 2013 and in the United States on November 17, 2013.

[19] A $270, 250GB model was initially released, followed by a $300, 500GB model on October 30. Japan received both models on October 4. Europe received the 500GB model on September 28 and a 12GB unit on September 25. The 12GB unit was eventually released on August 18, 2013 in North America, where it retailed for $200.

[20] Additional games for the Neo•Geo X weren't actually available until June 2013, when five game cards were released. Each game card retailed for $25 and included three games.

[21] AtGames did release a ColecoVision Flashback unit in 2014.

[22] In 2010, Curt Vendel of Legacy Engineering took preorders for his *7800 Expansion Module*, which basically did the same thing for the Atari 7800 that the Super Game Module did for the ColecoVision. Despite an original release window of January, 2013, the 7800 Expansion Module has still not been released as of April, 2017.

[23] AtGames handled the European distribution of the Atari Flashback 4 itself.

[24] This software had to be downloaded to a PC and then transferred to the Game Gadget via a USB connection.

[25] The JXD S7300 was released in January, 2013.

[26] Tablets weren't the only hardware outside of traditional computers that Gaikai was being installed onto. LG Technologies announced at CES in January that Gaikai would be built-into its new television sets.

[27] According to Archos, the Archos GamePad would be available in North America in February 2013.

[28] *Kickstarter* is a crowdfunding website that began on August 28, 2009. Projects are presented online and the public has the opportunity to fund the projects within a given time period. If the requested amount is pledged in full within that time period, then the project is funded and those who pledged must pay the amount that they promised. If the project doesn't get fully funded within the allotted time, then the people who pledged don't have to pay anything and project doesn't get funded.

[29] *Orbis* was a Latin word that meant circle or ring. This was not something that meant anything to anybody. But when the name was paired with another SCE product with a Latin name, the Vita, the combination stood for "the circle of life." How that phrase played into SCE's grand scheme was anybody's guess.

[30] Oculus Rift prototype units began shipping to Kickstarter backers in March, 2013.

[31] Three Wonderbook titles were released in 2013. *Diggs Nightcrawler* came out in Europe in May and in North America in November. *Walking with Dinosaurs* and *Book of Potions* were both released in November in Europe and North America. Meanwhile, Wonderbook launched in Japan with *Book of Spells* on November 7, 2013.

[32] In 1991, Nintendo had allowed its licensee GameTek to release several cartridges that turned the original Game Boy into a language translator or a personal organizer.

[33] The unit was only "customized" in the sense that its game card was screwed directly in, which prevented removal.

[34] Nintendo released the *Nintendo 3DS Guide: Louvre* as a downloadable application in late 2013. Copies could be purchased in any of seven different languages, and in North America, the package retailed for $19.99. Nintendo also offered a physical copy of *Nintendo 3DS Guide: Louvre* exclusively at the Louvre gift shops. This was the only 3DS title that wasn't hampered by regional lockouts and would work on any 3DS, no matter which country it was purchased in.

[35] This record was broken by *Game Informer* with its November, 2015 issue.

[36] Nintendo's two handheld devices did, however, outsell the two handhelds from SCE.

[37] The three were: *Just Dance 4* for the Wii, *Pokémon Black Version 2* and *Pokémon White Version 2* jointly for the DS, and *New Super Mario Bros. 2* for the 3DS.

[38] The Xbox 360 version held the top position with 10.4 million units sold, while the PS3 version was #2 with 8.7 million units sold.

CHAPTER 41

[1] The term *microconsole* began as the name of the console that OnLive had released in 2010. However, after the Ouya was introduced, the term expanded to include all Android-based consoles.

[2] Even before the first Ouya shipped, Julie Uhrman , the CEO of Ouya, Inc., spoke about releasing a new model every year to take advantage of faster and cheaper processors that would be available.

[3] *FLOPS* stands for "FLoating point Operations Per Second". The PS4 would be capable of performing 1.84 trillion operations per second.

[4] The DualShock 3 controller would not work with the PS4. The DualShock 4 controller would work with the PS3, but not optimally, and would require a microUSB connection.

[5] David Perry said that after the PS4 launched , there was a possibility that Gaikai might provide cloud-based emulation, which would let the older games play on the new system.

[6] Like SCE, Microsoft didn't announce a release date or a price for its new console.

[7] Cores are independent central processing units. A multi-processor can run multiple instructions simultaneously.

[8] Don Mattrick told the *Wall Street Journal*, "If you're backwards compatible, you're really backwards." He went on to say that since only 5% of customers play games from older systems, it wasn't worth it for Microsoft to make that feature possible.

[9] SCE also announced that additional DualShock 4 controllers would sell for $59, and the new PlayStation Camera, which wasn't included with the console, would also retail for $59.

[10] SCE Worldwide Studios was a group of game development companies that were owned by SCE, that had been formed on September 14, 2005.

[11] Microsoft reversed that policy as well on June 9, 2014, when it began shipping $399 Xbox One consoles without the Kinect 2.0 peripheral.

[12] On March 22, Nintendo of Europe began selling its *Circle Pad Pro XL* for the 3DS XL exclusively through its online store. This was followed by Nintendo of America on April 19. The Circle Pad Pro XL was the same unit as the Expansion Slide Pad LL that Nintendo of Japan had begun selling in November, 2012. It was essentially a larger Circle Pad Pro, which was already available for the 3DS from GameStop and Nintendo's website. Unfortunately, only six games supported the Circle Pad Pro and Circle Pad Pro XL, so it wasn't expected to be a major seller.

[13] In late August, SCE followed suit with similar price cuts in Europe and North America, where the price of the PS Vita dropped from its original $250 to $200 for either of the models. SCE also dropped the price of its proprietary memory cards, which cost much more than the standard SD memory cards that could be used in Nintendo's handheld devices.

[14] The PS Vita Slim was only available in a Wi-Fi model.

[15] The PS Vita Slim was eventually released in Europe on February 7, 2014. In North America it came out on May 6, 2014 as part of a $200 bundle that contained the console, an 8GB memory card, and a voucher to download a copy of Gearbox Software's *Borderlands 2*. Finally, the console was released in Australia on June 6, 2014. The PS Vita Slim consoles were only available in black outside of Japan.

[16] The PS Vita TV was eventually released in Hong Kong, Indonesia, Malaysia, Singapore, South Korea, Thailand and the Philippines on January 16, 2014. SCE announced on June 9, 2014 that it would be available in North America, Europe and Australia during the third quarter of 2014.

[17] The PS Vita TV could also use DualShock 4 controllers following a firmware update on March 25, 2014.

[18] The Remote Play ability to stream games from a PS4 to a PS Vita TV would be enabled following an April 30, 2014 PS4 firmware update.

[19] The player needed to own the downloaded PS Vita version of the PlayStation game, not the original disc.

[20] The PS4 was eventually released in Japan on February 22, 2014.

[21] The GameStick was released in Great Britain on December 20 and carried by GAME, a British videogame chain.

[22] All other countries wouldn't receive their Xbox Ones until September, 2014.

[23] Mad Catz lowered the price of the MOJO to $200 on March 6, 2014.

[24] Nintendo quietly shut down production of the Wii on October 21, but continued to sell it until stock ran out. Following a minor surge for the 2013 holiday season, the number of Wiis that were sold declined each month. Between January and May 2014, Nintendo only sold a total of 248,621 Wiis. This was over 100,000 less than it had sold solely in December, 2013 (384,295).

[25] This game was a remake of *The Legend of Zelda: The Wind Waker*, which had been available for the GameCube.

[26] An additional 363,495 digital copies of the game were sold.

[27] Two of the games that made the top 100, *New Super Luigi U* and *The Legend of Zelda: The Wind Waker HD*, were initially released as downloadable content. Those sales were not included in the tallies that made up the top 100.

[28] A downloadable demo version of *Wii U Fit* was offered for on November 1. Physical copies weren't released in North America until January 10, 2014 and on February 1, 2014 in Japan.

[29] The PS3 version of *Grand Theft Auto V* sold over 16 million units, while the Xbox 360 version sold 13 million units.

[30] NFC was the same technology that the Skylanders' Portal of Power used to read data from its figurines.

[31] Nintendo of Europe released *Pokémon Rumble U* on August 15 and made its figurines readily available.

[32] Ubisoft released *South Park: The Stick of Truth* in March, 2014 to overwhelmingly positive reviews.

[33] Nordic Games acquired THQ's trademarks on June 12, 2014. The company had also purchased THQ's *Darksiders* franchise, for which it planned to release new games under the THQ label.

[34] In September, 2014, Harmonix closed down its Rock Band Network, and cited the same reasons that it was changing its focus to new projects.

CHAPTER 42

[1] Less than one month after Microsoft released the Xbox One Media Remote, the company changed its focus on the direction that the Xbox One was heading. On March 31, Phil Spencer, a 25-year veteran with Microsoft, was appointed head of the company's Xbox division. After reviewing the product, Spencer admitted that Microsoft had "made poor choices" on how it handled the Xbox One during the preceding twelve months. He then made the decision that the Xbox One would be about "games first".

[2] *Fantasia: Music Evolved* only sold 38,000 units during the ten weeks that it was available in North America. Half of those sales occurred during the final two weeks of the year. However, whether these low sales could be attributed to the fact that the Kinect wasn't standard with the Xbox One would only be speculation.

[3] The headset was officially named the *PlayStation VR* on September 15, 2015.

[4] The *Xbox One Stereo Headset Adapter* only provided chat audio to the headset. In order to receive *game* audio, additional optical cables were needed to connect the adapter to the Xbox One's optical audio output port, or directly to the television's audio output port. Not all Xbox 360 headsets would work with the *Xbox One Stereo Headset Adapter*. Early versions of the Xbox 360 Headset were incompatible, as well as all versions of the Xbox 360 Wireless Headset.

[5] The North American release of *Super Smash Bros. for Wii U* preceded the Japanese release by two weeks.

[6] The previous installments were 1999's *Super Smash Bros.* for the N64; 2001's *Super Smash Bros. Melee* for the GameCube; and 2008's *Super Smash Bros. Brawl* for the Wii. Officially, *Super Smash Bros. for Nintendo 3DS*, which was released in North America on October 3 and two weeks earlier in Japan, was the fourth installment.

[7] The adapters became available in limited supplies throughout the first half of 2015. However, in most cases, retailers sold out of them very quickly. People who wanted the adapters either had to wait and hope that they could locate an adapter from a legitimate retailer, purchase an inexpensive third-party adapter, or buy one off of eBay at a marked-up price.

[8] *Mario Party 10* was released in March, 2015, and could read data from all previously released Amiibo. Several Amiibo, including Mario and Princess Peach, could also save data from the game. And while certain Amiibo could save data from multiple games, each figurine could only save information from one game at a time.

[9] The upgrade was issued in February, 2015.

[10] The button colors were Y = Green, X = Blue, A = Red, and B = Yellow. In the center of each button was the button's letter printed in white. The buttons were gray on the New Nintendo 3DS LL, but the letter printed on each button matched the color of the corresponding button on the smaller console.

[11] A complete set of overlays for all of the games that were built-in the Intellivision Flashback could be purchased from Intellivision Productions for a nominal fee.

[12] Rental prices were actually set by the individual game publishers and not SCE.

[13] The contents of the dump had actually turned out to be surplus inventory from Atari's El Paso, Texas warehouse.

[14] Cartridges were auctioned on eBay in four rounds, with the final round beginning in late June, 2015.

[15] The documentary aired despite the fact that its co-producer, Xbox Entertainment Studios, had closed its doors three weeks earlier on October 29.

[16] The *C&VG* site was shut down on February 26, 2015, along with the online sites of *Edge* and *Gamesmaster*.

[17] PS4 = 5,637,175, Xbox One = 3,858,968, PS3 = 3,521,743, Xbox 360 = 3,443,751

CHAPTER 43

[1] Snail also revealed the *W3D*, which was a conventional smartphone that included two analog sticks and four control buttons.

[2] Nintendo of Japan did cease manufacturing the white 8GB model in June, but it added a white 32GB model in its place.

[3] Nintendo had forecast 3.6 million unit sales. The actual number was 3.38 million.

[4] The game was called *Xenoblade Chronicles 3D* outside of Japan.

[5] The NFC Reader/Writer could also be used with the 3DS XL and the 2DS.

[6] *Lego Island*, which came out for PCs in 1997. was the first Lego-themed videogame.

[7] Disney had released *Disney Infinity: Marvel Super Heroes* in September, 2014. This set was unofficially called *Disney Infinity 2.0.*

[8] *Disney Infinity 3.0* wasn't limited to *Star Wars*. Figurines from several Disney franchises, including *Frozen*, *Finding Dory* and *The Jungle Book*, were also released.

[9] *Candy Crush Saga* was developed by King Digital Entertainment. In February, 2016, King was acquired by Activision Blizzard for $5.9 billion.

[10] The new controller was included in a $399 bundle that included an Xbox One console with one terabyte (1TB) of storage. The existing model with 500GB of storage was reduced to $349.

[11] eSports was the term used for organized, competitive videogaming tournaments, especially among professional gamers.

[12] In October, Activision announced the formation of a new eSports division, led by Steve Bornstein, a former CEO of ESPN and the NFL Network.

[13] At E^3, Microsoft showed off *HoloLens*, a headset that could project holographic images using augmented reality technology.

[14] AAA is a classification term used for high-quality games with the highest development budgets.

[15] SCE announced in February, 2016 that the PS Vita TV was discontinued in Asia as well.

[16] The DS, which included all versions of the unit, had more than 84 million units shipped by the end of its fourth year. In comparison, the 3DS only sold 50 million units during the same length of time.

[17] Nintendo's profits had fallen from ¥14.3 billion ($118 million) to ¥11.45 billion ($95 million).

[18] The Xbox One version of *Call of Duty: Black Ops 3* held the #2 position in the American top ten.

[19] *Star Wars: Battlefront* is considered a *reboot* of a previous game with the same name. This means that there is no continuity between the previous games and this one, as there would be in a sequel.

[20] Rounding out the American top ten were two sports games, *NBA 2K16* for the PS4, and *Madden NFL 16*, which held positions for both the Xbox One and PS4. The global top ten was rounded out with three PS4 games: *Grand Theft Auto V*, which was the only carry-over on the list from 2014, *Uncharted: The Nathan Drake Collection*, and *FIFA 16*.

[21] In theory, people would be able to use the downloaded songs that they paid for in earlier versions of *Rock Band*. In reality, however, each song had to be downloaded again into the new console. And the songs could only be downloaded one at a time, not in batches. Meanwhile, only about half of the total number of downloadable tracks were available for the European PS4. The problem was that SCEE had different technical requirements for downloadable content than SCEA or Microsoft.

[22] Harmonix announced that it would include a synchronous online function in an expansion pack called *Rock Band Rivals*, which was scheduled to be released in the fall of 2016.

[23] After announcing its 2015 end-of-year figures in February, 2016, three of Mad Catz' top executives resigned from the company, which had laid off 37% of its employees. In mid-2016, Harmonix replaced Mad Catz with Performance Designed Products (PDP). This was the company that had released the Rock Band Stage Kit in 2008. Mad Catz never rececovered and on March 30, 2017 filed for Chapter 7 bankruptcy, which meant the company shut down and began to sell off its assets.

[24] *Stadium Events* had been recalled by Bandai in 1988 after Nintendo licensed Bandai's *Family Fun Fitness* mat and rebranded it as the *Power Pad*. The game was renamed *World Class Track Meet* when it was rereleased by Nintendo. Only 2,000 copies of *Stadium Events* were manufactured and only 200 were sold, making it one of the rarest and most collectible videogame cartridges around.

[25] Each console would come with a controller and a game, *Jason Hunter and the Caverns of Death*, which was publicized as a new "retro-styled" game. It would be a product of CollectorVision, a Quebec-based company that began in 2008 and became one of the top companies dedicated to creating new games for old systems.

[26] The third member of the team was software engineer, Steve Woita.

[27] The Museum also possessed an original *Pong* arcade machine that had been donated by Nolan Bushnell.

[28] A second lab, from Baer's Florida condo, was put on display at the Strong Museum of Play in Rochester, NY on June 9, 2016.

CHAPTER 44

[1] Retailers such as Amazon sold the HTC Vive for a hundred dollars less than the suggested price.

[2] The HTC Vive was co-developed by HTC, a Chinese electronics company, and Valve.

[3] SCE announced on March 18 that it would offer a $500 bundle that would include the camera and two Move controllers along with the headset.

[4] According to SCE, 36 million PS4 consoles had been sold to date, and all were capable of playing virtual reality

games with the PSVR. Although there was no estimate of the number of high-end computers in use that could handle the Oculus Rift or the HTC Vive, most experts agreed that the number couldn't come close to that of the PS4s.

[5] 4K resolution is approximately four times the pixel size of 1080p, the current display standard for games. In 2016, as 4K Ultra High Definition monitors and televisions became more affordable, the console manufacturers scrambled to ensure that their systems were compatible. As it turned out, both the Xbox One and PS4 already supported the new standard, somewhat. Both systems could output data in 4K resolution, but only for personal contents, such as photos and videos -- not for games.

[6] HDR expanded the visual range of on-screen colors and contrasts. However, a monitor or television that supported the technology had to be used.

[7] This was, however, later retracted by Shannon Loftis, Microsoft's general manager of game publishing, who stated that exclusivity would be up to the individual game developers.

[8] Nintendo initially wanted to create a system that would only accept digital downloads, but later decided against it.

[9] *Miitomo* was similar to an earlier DS game called *Tomodachi Collection*, which had been released solely in Japan in 2009. Many of the developers who had worked on *Tomodachi Collection* were also involved with *Miitomo.*

[10]*Miitomo* and *My Nintendo* were launched outside of Japan in sixteen Western countries, including the United States and the United Kingdom, on March 31.

[11] The rest of the world received *Pokémon Go* between mid-July and early August.

[12] Niantic was an independent developer that was founded in 2010 as part of Google.

[13] A player could only enter a gym if he had reached Level 5 in the game and joined a team.

[14] The locations of PokéStops were determined by the locations of portals in Niantic's previous game, *Ingress.*

[15] Six of the 151 were originally thought to be unattainable, so a perfect set meant capturing 145 Pokémon. On July 24, Niantic's CEO, John Hanke, said at the San Diego Comic-Con, "There are some rare ones that haven't shown up yet that will be showing up." This presumably referred to the missing six Pokémon.

[16] An Android version was released worldwide on March 22, 2017.

[17] Nintendo wasn't alone in the fallout. DeNA's stock fell by 14% during the same period.

[18] One of the most successful freemium games, *Clash of Clans*, grossed nearly $1 billion throughout the year.

[19] Nintendo's next mobile game, *Fire Emblem Heroes*, which was released on February 2, 2017, followed the freemium model.

[20] Nintendo officially stated that the Switch was a "home gaming system first and foremost."

[21] The Wii U was officially discontinued on January 31, 2017.

[22] Nintendo continued to issue sporadic, limited releases of the NES Classic well into April, 2017. Suddenly on April 13, Nintendo of America unexpectedly announced that it was discontinuing the console immediately. This caused the selling price of the unit on eBay to rise sharply. The only reason given by Nintendo was that the unit was "never meant to be a 'long-term product'" and that the "production of it was always meant to be limited." Speculation of the cancelation presumed that Nintendo wanted to concentrate on Switch production, and that the company would be releasing an SNES Classic at the end of 2017. Nintendo confirmed neither of these rumors. Within days of the Nintendo of America announcement, Nintendo of Europe and Nintendo of Japan made similar announcements regarding their respective versions of the console. Nintendo disclosed that 2.3 million consoles had been sold worldwide during the six months of availability.

[23] The Flashback 7 version of *Frogger* did not include the familiar *Frogger* background music, because Konami had never owned the rights to it.

[24] The first Xbox One game that supported HDR was *NBA 2K17*, which was released on September 20.

[25] Another potential problem was that the HDR standard that Microsoft selected was HDR10, which was a relatively new standard that wasn't yet found on many television sets.

[26] Microsoft called the color *Robot White.*

[27] Xbox Play Anywhere didn't just permit Xbox One games to play on a PC. It also allowed for cross-console play. A game played on the console could be continued on a PC and *vice versa.*

[28] SIE eventually met its initial sales goal. It had sold 915,000 PSVRs by February 19, 2017.

[29] The PS4 Pro would be able to increase the PSVR's resolution to 1080p. However, not all games could achieve this resolution, even when played on the PS4 Pro. Only PS4 Pro-supported PSVR titles could improve the resolution,

frame rates and textures, and provide clearer text.

[30] Users could choose from three sizes for their virtual screens in Cinematic Mode: large resolution simulated a 226-inch screen, medium simulated a 163-inch display, and the small setting simulated a 117 inch TV.

[31] This is known as the *screen door effect.*

[32] The campaign ended on April 5 after raising only 52% of its goal.

[33] Mad Catz filed for Chapter 7 bankruptcy on March 30, 2017.

[34] The Drum Rocker was a professional, high-quality, $300 drum kit manufactured by Ion Audio for the PS3 and Xbox 360 versions of *Rock Band* and *Rock Band 2*. In 2008, it was named the Best Peripheral/Hardware at the Game Critics Awards.

[35] PDP again offered the Rock Band Wired Legacy Adapter in mid-April, 2017 through its website. However, only 150 were available and they sold out within two hours. Afterwards, PDP received sporadic shipments until May 10.

APPENDIX 1

[1] Mirrorsoft was owned by Robert Maxwell, who also owned several publishing companies around the world.

[2] Rogers' relationship with Nintendo went back to 1985, after Rogers read an article that stated that Nintendo's president, Hiroshi Yamauchi, was a fan of the board game, *Go*. Coincidentally, Rogers had just received a version of *Go* that could be played on the Commodore 64. Rogers decided that the game could be easily converted for the Famicom, since the Commodore 64 and the Famicom shared the same 6502 processor. He then sent Yamauchi a fax about the game and Yamauchi invited Rogers for an immediate meeting at Nintendo's headquarters. Although Yamauchi would not grant top PC gaming companies such as Square and Enix to publish Famicom games, he advanced Rogers $300,000 to create the game. Rogers then found the British programmer who had designed the Commodore 64 version of *Go* and convinced him to move to Japan to work on the Famicom version.

When the game was completed, Rogers brought it to Yamauchi to try. Yamauchi easily beat the game and said it wasn't strong enough for Nintendo to publish. Rogers than asked if he could publish it himself adding that he would pay Yamauchi ¥100 ($0.63) for every copy he sold. Yamauchi agreed.

Thus began a long friendship that Rogers shared with Yamauchi until Yamauchi's death in 2013. After Bullet-Proof Software published its *Go* game *Igo Kyuroban Taikyoku* for the Famicom Disc System in 1986, Rogers visited with Yamauchi regularly. He always scheduled late appointments so the two could play *Go* afterwards

[3] Stein signed a contract for the *Tetris* arcade rights on February 24, 1989.

[4] Judge Smith was also the presiding judge over Nintendo of America's antitrust and breach-of-contract lawsuit against Atari Games.

[5] Robert Maxwell's business empire, including Mirrorsoft, went bankrupt in 1991 following his mysterious death. An investment company purchased Maxwell's interests in Spectrum Holobyte, and this allowed the latter company to stay afloat.

[6] Blue Planet Software shared the same initials as Rogers' other company, Bullet-Proof Software.

INDEX

INDEX

INDEX

INDEX

INDEX

INDEX

INDEX

INDEX

INDEX

INDEX

INDEX

INDEX

INDEX

INDEX

INDEX

INDEX

INDEX

INDEX

INDEX

INDEX

INDEX

INDEX

INDEX

INDEX

INDEX

ILLUSTRATION INDEX

ILLUSTRATION INDEX

ABOUT THE AUTHOR

Leonard Herman, *The Game Scholar,* is regarded as one of the earliest videogame historians. The first edition of *Phoenix: The Fall & Rise of Home Videogames,* which was published in 1994, is considered to be the first serious and comprehensive book about the history of videogames. Mr. Herman became hooked on videogames after he played *Pong* at a local bowling alley in 1972. He became interested in home videogames when he purchased his Atari VCS in May, 1979. Mr. Herman, who is an award-winning lyricist, has written articles for *Videogaming & Computer Illustrated, Games Magazine, Electronic Gaming Monthly, The Official U.S. PlayStation Magazine, Pocket Games, Classic Gamer Magazine, Edge, Game Informer, Classic Gamer Magazine, Manci Games, Gamespot.com* and *Video Game Trader,* a magazine that he also edited. He has also contributed articles to several videogame-related books, including *Supercade, The Video Game Explosion* and *The Encyclopedia of Video Games.*

Mr. Herman has also written the book *ABC To the VCS (A Directory of Software for the Atari 2600),* a compendium of game summaries. He has also written and designed user's manuals for the following Atari VCS games: *Cracked, Save the Whales, Pick-Up, Rush Hour, Looping, The Entity* and *Lasercade,* as well as the user's guide to *Ralph Baer's Pinball!* for the Odyssey^2.

In 1994, Mr. Herman founded Rolenta Press, a publisher of videogame books, whose catalogue included *Videogames: In the Beginning,* by Ralph H. Baer, the inventor of the videogame console, and *Confessions of the Game Doctor* by Bill Kunkel, the world's first videogame journalist. In 2008, *Game Informer* magazine rated *Confessions of the Game Doctor* #5 on its list of the top ten videogame books of all time. *Phoenix* came in at #2.

Mr. Herman has served as an advisor for *Videotopia, Classic Gaming Expo* and the *National Videogame Museum.* He has appeared in several episodes of G4's *Icons* and in the documentary, *The King of Arcades.*

In 2003, Mr. Herman received a *Classic Gaming Expo Achievement Award* in recognition for his accomplishments in documenting game history.

Mr. Herman resides in New Jersey with his wife Tamar and his sons Ronnie and Gregory.

Printed in the USA
CPSIA information can be obtained
at www.ICGtesting.com
LVHW012025121023
760591LV00082B/539

9 780964 384804